COLLINS
POCKET
GERMAN
DICTIONARY

GERMAN ▶ ENGLISH   ENGLISH ▶ GERMAN

HarperCollins*Publishers*

second edition/zweite Auflage 1996

© HarperCollins Publishers 1996
© William Collins Sons & Co. Ltd. 1990
latest reprint 1997

HarperCollins Publishers
P.O. Box, Glasgow G4 0NB, Great Britain
ISBN 0 00 470397-9

Veronika Calderwood-Schnorr • Ute Nicol • Peter Terrell
Helga Holtkamp • Horst Kopleck • John Whitlam

contributors to second edition/Mitarbeiter der 2. Auflage
Bob Grossmith • Horst Kopleck

editorial staff/Manuskriptbearbeitung
Joyce Littlejohn • Elspeth Anderson

series editor/Gesamtleitung
Lorna Sinclair Knight

Typeset by Morton Word Processing Ltd, Scarborough

*Printed and bound in Great Britain by Caledonian International
Book Manufacturing Ltd, Glasgow, G64*

INTRODUCTION

We are delighted you have decided to buy the Collins Pocket German Dictionary and hope you will enjoy and benefit from using it at home, at school, on holiday or at work.

The innovative use of colour guides you quickly and efficiently to the word you want, and the comprehensive wordlist provides a wealth of modern and idiomatic phrases not normally found in a dictionary this size.

In addition, the supplement provides you with guidance on using the dictionary, along with entertaining ways of improving your dictionary skills.

We hope that you will enjoy using it and that it will significantly enhance your language studies.

ZUM GEBRAUCH IHRES COLLINS TASCHENWÖRTERBUCHS

Das Wörterbuch enthält eine Fülle von Informationen, die mit Hilfe von unterschiedlichen Schriften und Schriftgrößen, Symbolen, Abkürzungen und Klammern vermittelt werden. Die dabei verwendeten Regeln und Symbole werden in den folgenden Abschnitten erklärt.

Stichwörter

Die Wörter, die Sie im Wörterbuch nachschlagen — „Stichwörter" — sind alphabetisch geordnet. Sie sind rot gedruckt, damit man sie schnell erkennt. Die beiden Stichwörter oben auf jeder Seite geben das erste und letzte Wort an, das auf der betreffenden Seite behandelt wird.

Informationen zur Verwendung oder zur Form bestimmter Stichwörter stehen in Klammern hinter der Lautschrift. Sie erscheinen meist in abgekürzter Form und sind kursiv gedruckt (z.B. *(fam)*, *(COMM)*).

Wo es angebracht ist, werden mit dem Stichwort verwandte Wörter im selben Artikel behandelt (z.B. accept, acceptance). Sie sind wie das Stichwort fett, aber etwas kleiner gedruckt.
Häufig verwendete Ausdrücke, in denen das Stichwort vorkommt (z.B. **to be cold**), sind in einer anderen Schrift halbfett gedruckt.

Lautschrift

Die Lautschrift für jedes Stichwort (zur Angabe seiner Aussprache), steht in eckigen Klammern direkt hinter dem Stichwort (z.B. Quark [kvark]; knead [niːd]). Die Symbole der Lautschrift sind auf Seite xii erklärt.

Übersetzungen

Die Übersetzungen des Stichworts sind normal gedruckt. Wenn es mehr als eine Bedeutung oder Verwendung des Stichworts gibt, sind diese durch ein Semikolon voneinander getrennt. Vor den Übersetzungen stehen oft andere, kursiv gedruckte Wörter in Klammern. Sie geben an, in welchem Zusammenhang das Stichwort erscheinen könnte (z.B. rough *(voice)* oder *(weather)*), oder sie sind Synonyme (z.B. rough *(violent)*).

Schlüsselwörter

Besonders behandelt werden bestimmte deutsche und englische Wörter, die man als „Schlüsselwörter" der jeweiligen Sprache betrachten kann. Diese Wörter kommen beispielsweise sehr häufig vor oder werden unterschiedlich verwendet (z.B. sein, auch; get, that). Mit Hilfe von Rauten und Ziffern können Sie die verschiedenen Wortarten und Verwendungen unterscheiden. Weitere nützliche Hinweise finden Sie kursiv und in Klammern in der jeweiligen Sprache des Benutzers.

Grammatische Informationen

Wortarten stehen in abgekürzter Form kursiv gedruckt hinter der Aussprache des Stichworts (z.B. *vt, adv, conj*).

Die unregelmäßigen Formen englischer Substantive und Verben stehen in Klammern vor der Wortart (z.B. **man** (*pl* men) *n*, **give** (*pt* gave, *pp* given) *vt*).

USING YOUR COLLINS POCKET DICTIONARY

A wealth of information is presented in the dictionary, using various typefaces, sizes of type, symbols, abbreviations and brackets. The conventions and symbols used are explained in the following sections.

Headwords

The words you look up in a dictionary — "headwords" — are listed alphabetically. They are printed in **red type** for rapid identification. The two headwords appearing at the top of each page indicate the first and last word dealt with on the page in question.

Information about the usage or form of certain headwords is given in brackets after the phonetic spelling. This usually appears in abbreviated form and in italics (e.g. (*umg*), (*COMM*)).

Where appropriate, words related to headwords are grouped in the same entry (**Glück, glücken**) in a slightly smaller bold type than the headword.

Common expressions in which the headword appears are shown in a different bold roman type (e.g. **Glück haben**).

Phonetic spellings

The phonetic spelling of each headword (indicating its pronunciation) is given in square brackets immediately after the headword (e.g. **Quark** [kvark]). A list of these symbols is given on page xii.

Meanings

Headword translations are given in ordinary type and, where more than one meaning or usage exists, these are separated by a semi-colon. You will often find other words in italics in brackets before the translations. These offer suggested contexts in which the headword might appear (e.g. **eng** (*Kleidung*) or (*Freundschaft*)) or provide synonyms (e.g. **eng** (*fig: Horizont*)).

"Key" words

Special status is given to certain German and English words which are considered as "key" words in each language. They may, for example, occur very frequently or have several types of usage (e.g. **sein, auch; get, that**). A combination of lozenges and numbers helps you to distinguish different parts of speech and different meanings. Further helpful information is provided in brackets and in italics in the relevant language for the user.

Grammatical information

Parts of speech are given in abbreviated form in italics after the phonetic spellings of headwords (e.g. *vt, av, konj*).

Genders of German nouns are indicated as follows: *m* for a masculine and *f* for a feminine and *nt* for a neuter noun. The genitive and plural forms of regular nouns are shown on the table on page xi. Nouns which do not follow these rules have the genitive and plural in brackets immediately preceding the gender (e.g. **Spaß**, (-es, ⁼e), *m*).

Adjectives are normally shown in their basic form (e.g. **groß** *adj*), but where they are only used attributively (i.e. before a noun) feminine and neuter endings follow in brackets (**hohe (r, s)** *adj attrib*).

ABKÜRZUNGEN

ABBREVIATIONS

Abkürzung	abk, abbr	abbreviation
Akkusativ	acc	accusative
Adjektiv	adj	adjective
Adverb	adv	adverb
Landwirtschaft	AGR	agriculture
Akkusativ	akk	accusative
Anatomie	ANAT	anatomy
Architektur	ARCHIT	architecture
Astrologie	ASTROL	astrology
Astronomie	ASTRON	astronomy
attributiv	attrib	attributive
Kraftfahrzeuge	AUT	automobiles
Hilfsverb	aux	auxiliary
Luftfahrt	AVIAT	aviation
besonders	bes	especially
Biologie	BIOL	biology
Botanik	BOT	botany
britisch	BRIT	British
Chemie	CHEM	chemistry
Film	CINE	cinema
Handel	COMM	commerce
Komparativ	compar	comparative
Computer	COMPUT	computing
Konjunktion	conj	conjunction
Kochen und Backen	COOK	cooking
zusammengesetztes Wort	cpd	compound
Dativ	dat	dative
bestimmter Artikel	def art	definite article
Diminutiv	dimin	diminutive
kirchlich	ECCL	ecclesiastical
Eisenbahn	EISENB	railways
Elektrizität	ELEK, ELEC	electricity
besonders	esp	especially
und so weiter	etc	et cetera
etwas	etw	something
Euphemismus, Hüllwort	euph	euphemism
Interjektion, Ausruf	excl	exclamation
Femininum	f	feminine
übertragen	fig	figurative
Finanzwesen	FIN	finance
nicht getrennt gebraucht	fus	(phrasal verb) inseparable
Genitiv	gen	genitive
Geographie	GEOG	geography
Geologie	GEOL	geology
Grammatik	GRAM	grammar

Geschichte	HIST	history
unpersönlich	impers	impersonal
unbestimmter Artikel	indef art	indefinite article
umgangssprächlich (! vulgär)	inf(!)	informal (! particularly offensive)
Infinitiv, Grundform	infin	infinitive
nicht getrennt gebraucht	insep	inseparable
unveränderlich	inv	invariable
unregelmäßig	irreg	irregular
jemand	jd	somebody
jemandem	jdm	(to) somebody
jemanden	jdn	somebody
jemandes	jds	somebody's
Rechtswesen	JUR	law
Kochen und Backen	KOCH	cooking
Komparativ	kompar	comparative
Konjunktion	konj	conjunction
Sprachwissenschaft	LING	linguistics
Literatur	LITER	of literature
Maskulinum	m	masculine
Mathematik	MATH	mathematics
Medizin	MED	medicine
Meteorologie	MET	meteorology
militärisch	MIL	military
Bergbau	MIN	mining
Musik	MUS	music
Substantiv, Hauptwort	n	noun
nautisch, Seefahrt	NAUT	nautical, naval
Nominativ	nom	nominative
Neutrum	nt	neuter
Zahlwort	num	numeral
Objekt	obj	object
oder	od	or
sich	o.s.	oneself
Parlament	PARL	parliament
abschätzig	pej	pejorative
Photographie	PHOT	photography
Physik	PHYS	physics
Plural	pl	plural
Politik	POL	politics
Präfix, Vorsilbe	pp	prefix
Präposition	präp, prep	preposition
Typographie	PRINT	printing
Pronomen, Fürwort	pron	pronoun
Psychologie	PSYCH	psychology
1. Vergangenheit, Imperfekt	pt	past tense
Radio	RAD	radio
Eisenbahn	RAIL	railways
Religion	REL	religion

jemand(-en, -em)	sb	someone, somebody
Schulwesen	SCH	school
Naturwissenschaft	SCI	science
Singular, Einzahl	sg	singular
etwas	sth	something
Konjunktiv	sub	subjunctive
Subjekt	subj	(grammatical) subject
Superlativ	superl	superlative
Technik	TECH	technology
Nachrichtentechnik	TEL	telecommunications
Theater	THEAT	theatre
Fernsehen	TV	television
Typographie	TYP	printing
umgangssprachlich (! vulgär)	umg(!)	informal (! particularly offensive)
Hochschulwesen	UNIV	university
unpersönlich	unpers	impersonal
unregelmäßig	unreg	irregular
(nord)amerikanisch	US	(North) America
gewöhnlich	usu	usually
Verb	vb	verb
intransitives Verb	vi	intransitive verb
reflexives Verb	vr	reflexive verb
transitives Verb	vt	transitive verb
Zoologie	ZOOL	zoology
zusammengesetztes Wort	zW	compound
zwischen zwei Sprechern	—	change of speaker
ungefähre Entsprechung	≈	cultural equivalent
eingetragenes Warenzeichen	®	registered trademark

Warenzeichen

Wörter, die unseres Wissens eingetragene
Warenzeichen darstellen, sind als solche
gekennzeichnet. Es ist jedoch zu
beachten, daß weder das Vorhandensein
noch das Fehlen derartiger
Kennzeichnungen die Rechstlage
hinsichtlich eingetragener Warenzeichen
berührt.

Note on trademarks

Words which we have reason to believe
constitute trademarks have been
designated as such. However, neither
the presence nor the absence of such
designation should be regarded as
affecting the legal status of any
trademark.

REGULAR GERMAN NOUN ENDINGS

nom		gen	pl
-ant	*m*	-anten	-anten
-anz	*f*	-anz	-anzen
-ar	*m*	-ar(e)s	-are
-chen	*nt*	-chens	-chen
-e	*f*	-	-n
-ei	*f*	-ei	-eien
-elle	*f*	-elle	-ellen
-ent	*m*	-enten	-enten
-enz	*f*	-enz	-enzen
-ette	*f*	-ette	-etten
-eur	*m*	-eurs	-eure
-euse	*f*	-euse	-eusen
-heit	*f*	-heit	-heiten
-ie	*f*	-ie	-ien
-ik	*f*	-ik	-iken
-in	*f*	-in	-innen
-ine	*f*	-ine	-inen
-ion	*f*	-ion	-ionen
-ist	*m*	-isten	-isten
-ium	*nt*	-iums	-ien
-ius	*m*	-ius	-iusse
-ive	*f*	-ive	-iven
-keit	*f*	-keit	-keiten
-lein	*nt*	-leins	-lein
-ling	*m*	-lings	-linge
-ment	*nt*	-ments	-mente
-mus	*m*	-mus	-men
-schaft	*f*	-schaft	-schaften
-tät	*f*	-tät	-täten
-tor	*m*	-tors	-toren
-ung	*f*	-ung	-ungen
-ur	*f*	-ur	-uren

PHONETIC SYMBOLS / LAUTSCHRIFT

[ː] *length mark/Längezeichen* ['] *stress mark/Betonung*
['] *glottal stop/Knacklaut*

all vowel sounds are approximate only
alle Vokallaute sind nur ungefähre Entsprechungen

lie	[aɪ]	weit	day	[eɪ]	
now	[aʊ]	Haut	girl	[ɜː]	
above	[ə]	bitte	board	[ɔː]	
green	[iː]	viel	root	[uː]	Hut
pity	[ɪ]	Bischof	come	[ʌ]	Butler
rot	[ɒ,ɔ]	Post	salon	[ɔ̃]	Champignon
full	[ʊ]	Pult	avant	[ɑ̃]	Ensemble
			(garde)		
bet	[b]	Ball	fair	[ɛə]	mehr
dim	[d]	dann	beer	[ɪə]	Bier
face	[f]	Faß	toy	[ɔɪ]	Heu
go	[g]	Gast	pure	[ʊə]	
hit	[h]	Herr	wine	[w]	
you	[j]	ja	thin	[θ]	
cat	[k]	kalt	this	[əʊ]	
lick	[l]	Last			
must	[m]	Mast	Hast	[a]	mash
nut	[n]	Nuß	Ensemble	[ã]	avant
bang	[ŋ]	lang			(garde)
pepper	[p]	Pakt	Metall	[e]	meths
sit	[s]	rasse	häßlich	[ɛ]	
shame	[ʃ]	Schal	Cousin	[ɛ̃]	
tell	[t]	Tal	vital	[i]	
vine	[v]	was	Moral	[o]	
loch	[x]	Bach	Champignon	[õ]	salon
zero	[z]	Hase	ökonomisch	[ø]	
leisure	[ʒ]	Genie	gönnen	[œ]	
			Heu	[ɔY]	toy
bat	[æ]		kulant	[u]	
farm	[ɑː]	Bahn	physisch	[y]	
set	[e]	Kette	Müll	[Y]	
			ich	[ç]	

[*] r can be pronounced before a vowel; Bindungs-R

NUMMER

NUMBERS

ein(s)	1	one
zwei	2	two
drei	3	three
vier	4	four
fünf	5	five
sechs	6	six
sieben	7	seven
acht	8	eight
neun	9	nine
zehn	10	ten
elf	11	eleven
zwölf	12	twelve
dreizehn	13	thirteen
vierzehn	14	fourteen
fünfzehn	15	fifteen
sechzehn	16	sixteen
siebzehn	17	seventeen
achtzehn	18	eighteen
neunzehn	19	nineteen
zwanzig	20	twenty
einundzwanzig	21	twenty-one
zweiundzwanzig	22	twenty-two
dreißig	30	thirty
vierzig	40	forty
fünfzig	50	fifty
sechzig	60	sixty
siebzig	70	seventy
achtzig	80	eighty
neunzig	90	ninety
hundert	100	a hundred
hunderteins	101	a hundred and one
zweihundert	200	two hundred
zweihunderteins	201	two hundred and one
dreihundert	300	three hundred
dreihunderteins	301	three hundred and one
tausend	1000	a thousand
tausend(und)eins	1001	a thousand and one
fünftausend	5000	five thousand
eine Million	1000000	a million

erste(r,s)	1.	first	1st
zweite(r,s)	2.	second	2nd
dritte(r,s)	3.	third	3rd
vierte(r,s)	4.	fourth	4th

fünfte(r,s)	5.	fifth	5th
sechste(r,s)	6.	sixth	6th
siebte(r,s)	7.	seventh	7th
achte(r,s)	8.	eighth	8th
neunte(r,s)	9.	ninth	9th
zehnte(r,s)	10.	tenth	10th
elfte(r,s)	11.	eleventh	11th
zwölfte(r,s)	12.	twelfth	12th
dreizehnte(r,s)	13.	thirteenth	13th
vierzehnte(r,s)	14.	fourteenth	14th
fünfzehnte(r,s)	15.	fifteenth	15th
sechzehnte(r,s)	16.	sixteenth	16th
siebzehnte(r,s)	17.	seventeenth	17th
achtzehnte(r,s)	18.	eighteenth	18th
neunzehnte(r,s)	19.	nineteenth	19th
zwanzigste(r,s)	20.	twentieth	20th
einundzwanzigste(r,s)	21.	twenty-first	21st
dreißigste(r,s)	30.	thirtieth	30th
hundertste(r,s)	100.	hundredth	100th
hunderterste(r,s)	101.	hundred-and-first	101st
tausendste(r,s)	1000.	thousandth	1000th

Brüche usw.

Fractions etc.

ein Halb	$\frac{1}{2}$	a half	
ein Drittel	$\frac{1}{3}$	a third	
ein Viertel	$\frac{1}{4}$	a quarter	
ein Fünftel	$\frac{1}{2}$	a fifth	
null Komma fünf	0,5	(nought) point five	0.5
drei Komma vier	3,4	three point four	3.4
sechs Komma acht neun	6,89	six point eight nine	6.89
zehn Prozent	10%	ten per cent	
hundert Prozent	100%	a hundred per cent	

Beispiele

Examples

er wohnt in Nummer 10

he lives at number 10

es steht in Kapitel 7

it's in chapter 7

auf Seite 7

on page 7

er wohnt im 7. Stock

he lives on the 7th floor

er wurde 7.

he came in 7th

im Maßstab eins zu zwanzigtausend

scale one to twenty thousand

UHRZEIT

THE TIME

wieviel Uhr ist es?, wie spät ist es?

what time is it?

es ist ...

it's ...

Mitternacht, zwölf Uhr nachts	midnight, twelve p.m.
ein Uhr (morgens *or* früh)	one o'clock (in the morning), one (a.m.)
fünf nach eins, ein Uhr fünf	five past one
zehn nach eins, ein Uhr zehn	ten past one
Viertel nach eins, ein Uhr fünfzehn	a quarter past one, one fifteen
fünf vor halb zwei, ein Uhr fünfundzwanzig	twenty-five past one, one twenty-five
halb zwei, ein Uhr dreißig	half past one, one thirty
fünf nach halb zwei, ein Uhr fünfunddreißig	twenty-five to two, one thirty-five
zwanzig vor zwei, ein Uhr vierzig	twenty to two, one forty
Viertel vor zwei, ein Uhr fünfundvierzig	a quarter to two, one forty-five
zehn vor zwei, ein Uhr fünfzig	ten to two, one fifty
zwölf Uhr (mittags), Mittag	twelve o'clock, midday, noon
halb eins (mittags *or* nachmittags), zwölf Uhr dreißig	half past twelve, twelve thirty (p.m.)
zwei Uhr (nachmittags)	two o'clock (in the afternoon), two (p.m.)
halb acht (abends)	half past seven (in the evening), seven thirty (p.m.)

um wieviel Uhr?

at what time?

um Mitternacht	at midnight
um sieben Uhr	at seven o'clock
in zwanzig Minuten	in twenty minutes
vor fünfzehn Minuten	fifteen minutes ago

DEUTSCH - ENGLISCH
GERMAN - ENGLISH

A a

Aal [aːl] (-(e)s, -e) *m* eel

Aas [aːs] (-es, -e *od* **Äser**) *nt* carrion;
~geier *m* vulture

ab [ap] *präp +dat* from; **Kinder ab 12
Jahren** children from the age of 12; **ab
morgen** from tomorrow; **ab sofort** as of
now
♦ *adv* **1** off; **links ab** to the left; **der
Knopf ist ab** the button has come off; **ab
nach Hause!** off you go home
2 (*zeitlich*): **von da ab** from then on; **von
heute ab** from today, as of today
3 (*auf Fahrplänen*): **München ab 12.20**
leaving Munich 12.20
4: **ab und zu** *od* **an** now and then *od*
again

Abänderung ['ap'ɛndəruŋ] *f* alteration

Abbau ['apbau] (-(e)s) *m* (+*gen*)
dismantling; (*Verminderung*) reduction
(in); (*Verfall*) decline (in); (*MIN*) mining;
quarrying; (*CHEM*) decomposition; **a~en** *vt*
to dismantle; (*MIN*) to mine; to quarry;
(*verringern*) to reduce; (*CHEM*) to break
down

abbeißen ['apbaisən] (*unreg*) *vt* to bite
off

abbekommen ['apbəkɔmən] (*unreg*) *vt*
(*Deckel, Schraube, Band*) to loosen; **etwas
~** (*beschädigt werden*) to get damaged;
(: *Person*) to get injured

abbestellen ['apbəʃtɛlən] *vt* to cancel

abbezahlen ['apbətsaːlən] *vt* to pay off

abbiegen ['apbiːgən] (*unreg*) *vi* to turn
off; (*Straße*) to bend ♦ *vt* to bend;
(*verhindern*) to ward off

abbilden ['apbıldən] *vt* to portray

Abbildung *f* illustration

abblenden ['apblɛndən] *vt, vi* (*AUT*) to dip

(*BRIT*), to dim (*US*)

Abblendlicht *nt* dipped (*BRIT*) *od* dimmed
(*US*) headlights *pl*

abbrechen ['apbrɛçən] (*unreg*) *vt, vi* to
break off; (*Gebäude*) to pull down; (*Zelt*)
to take down; (*aufhören*) to stop; (*COMPUT*)
to abort

abbrennen ['apbrɛnən] (*unreg*) *vt* to
burn off; (*Feuerwerk*) to let off ♦ *vi* (*aux
sein*) to burn down

abbringen ['apbrıŋən] (*unreg*) *vt*: **jdn
von etw ~** to dissuade sb from sth; **jdn
vom Weg ~** to divert sb

abbröckeln ['apbrœkəln] *vt, vi* to
crumble off *od* away

Abbruch ['apbrux] *m* (*von Verhandlungen
etc*) breaking off; (*von Haus*) demolition;
jdm/etw ~ tun to harm sb/sth; **a~reif**
adj only fit for demolition

abbrühen ['apbryːən] *vt* to scald;
abgebrüht (*umg*) hard-boiled

abbuchen ['apbuːxən] *vt* to debit

abbürsten ['apbyrstən] *vt* to brush off

abdanken ['apdaŋkən] *vi* to resign;
(*König*) to abdicate

Abdankung *f* resignation; abdication

abdecken ['apdɛkən] *vt* to uncover;
(*Tisch*) to clear; (*Loch*) to cover

abdichten ['apdıçtən] *vt* to seal; (*NAUT*) to
caulk

abdrehen ['apdreːən] *vt* (*Gas*) to turn off;
(*Licht*) to switch off; (*Film*) to shoot ♦ *vi*
(*Schiff*) to change course

Abdruck ['apdruk] *m* (*Nachdrucken*)
reprinting; (*Gedrucktes*) reprint; (*Gips~,
Wachs~*) impression; (*Finger~*) print;
a~en *vt* to print, to publish

abdrücken ['apdrykən] *vt* (*Waffe*) to fire;
(*Person*) to hug, to squeeze

Abend ['aːbənt] (-s, -e) *m* evening; **guten
~** good evening; **zu ~ essen** to have

dinner *od* supper; **a~** *adv*: **heute a~** this evening; **~brot** *nt* supper; **~essen** *nt* supper; **~kasse** *f* box office; **~kleid** *nt* evening dress; **~kurs** *m* evening classes *pl*; **~land** *nt* (*Europa*) West; **a~lich** *adj* evening; **~mahl** *nt* Holy Communion; **~rot** *nt* sunset; **a~s** *adv* in the evening

Abenteuer ['a:bəntɔʏər] (**-s, -**) *nt* adventure; **a~lich** *adj* adventurous

Abenteurer (**-s, -**) *m* adventurer; **~in** *f* adventuress

aber ['a:bər] *konj* but; (*jedoch*) however ♦ *adv*: **tausend und ~ tausend** thousands upon thousands; **das ist ~ schön** that's really nice; **nun ist ~ Schluß!** now that's enough!; **vielen Dank — ~ bitte!** thanks a lot — you're welcome; **A~glaube** *m* superstition; **~gläubisch** *adj* superstitious

aberkennen ['ap'ɛrkɛnən] (*unreg*) *vt* (*JUR*): **jdm etw ~** to deprive sb of sth, to take sth (away) from sb

abermals ['a:bərma:ls] *adv* once again

Abf. *abk* (= *Abfahrt*) dep.

abfahren ['apfa:rən] (*unreg*) *vi* to leave, to depart ♦ *vt* to take *od* cart away; (*Strecke*) to drive; (*Reifen*) to wear; (*Fahrkarte*) to use

Abfahrt ['apfa:rt] *f* departure; (*SKI*) descent; (*Piste*) run; **~slauf** *m* (*SKI*) descent, run down; **~szeit** *f* departure time

Abfall ['apfal] *m* waste; (*von Speisen etc*) rubbish (*BRIT*), garbage (*US*); (*Neigung*) slope; (*Verschlechterung*) decline; **~eimer** *m* rubbish bin (*BRIT*), garbage can (*US*); **a~en** (*unreg*) *vi* (*auch fig*) to fall *od* drop off; (*POL, vom Glauben*) to break away; (*sich neigen*) to fall *od* drop away

abfällig ['apfɛlɪç] *adj* disparaging, deprecatory

abfangen ['apfaŋən] (*unreg*) *vt* to intercept; (*Person*) to catch; (*unter Kontrolle bringen*) to check

abfärben ['apfɛrbən] *vi* to lose its colour; (*Wäsche*) to run; (*fig*) to rub off

abfassen ['apfasən] *vt* to write, to draft

abfertigen ['apfɛrtɪgən] *vt* to prepare for dispatch, to process; (*an der Grenze*) to

clear; (*Kundschaft*) to attend to

abfeuern ['apfɔʏərn] *vt* to fire

abfinden ['apfɪndən] (*unreg*) *vt* to pay off ♦ *vr* to come to terms; **sich mit jdm ~/ nicht ~** to put up with/not get on with sb

Abfindung *f* (*von Gläubigern*) payment; (*Geld*) sum in settlement

abflauen ['apflauən] *vi* (*Wind, Erregung*) to die away, to subside; (*Nachfrage, Geschäft*) to fall *od* drop off

abfliegen ['apfli:gən] (*unreg*) *vi* (*Flugzeug*) to take off; (*Passagier auch*) to fly ♦ *vt* (*Gebiet*) to fly over

abfließen ['apfli:sən] (*unreg*) *vi* to drain away

Abflug ['apflu:k] *m* departure; (*Start*) take-off; **~zeit** *f* departure time

Abfluß ['apflʊs] *m* draining away; (*Öffnung*) outlet

Abflußrohr *nt* drain pipe; (*von sanitären Anlagen auch*) waste pipe

abfragen ['apfra:gən] *vt* (*bes SCH*) to test orally (on)

Abfuhr ['apfu:r] (**-, -en**) *f* removal; (*fig*) snub, rebuff

abführen ['apfy:rən] *vt* to lead away; (*Gelder, Steuern*) to pay ♦ *vi* (*MED*) to have a laxative effect

Abführmittel ['apfy:rmɪtəl] *nt* laxative, purgative

abfüllen ['apfʏlən] *vt* to draw off; (*in Flaschen*) to bottle

Abgabe ['apga:bə] *f* handing in; (*von Ball*) pass; (*Steuer*) tax; (*eines Amtes*) giving up; (*einer Erklärung*) giving

Abgang ['apgaŋ] *m* (*von Schule*) leaving; (*THEAT*) exit; (*MED: Ausscheiden*) passing; (: *Fehlgeburt*) miscarriage; (*Abfahrt*) departure; (*der Post, von Waren*) dispatch

Abgas ['apga:s] *nt* waste gas; (*AUT*) exhaust

abgeben ['apge:bən] (*unreg*) *vt* (*Gegenstand*) to hand *od* give in; (*Ball*) to pass; (*Wärme*) to give off; (*Amt*) to hand over; (*Schuß*) to fire; (*Erklärung, Urteil*) to give; (*darstellen, sein*) to make ♦ *vr*: **sich mit jdm/etw ~** to associate with sb/bother with sth; **jdm etw ~** (*überlassen*) to let sb have sth

abgebrüht ['apgəbry:t] (*umg*) *adj*
(*skrupellos*) hard-boiled
abgehen ['apge:ən] (*unreg*) *vi* to go
away, to leave; (*THEAT*) to exit; (*Baby*) to
be aborted; (*Knopf etc*) to come off;
(*abgezogen werden*) to be taken off;
(*Straße*) to branch off ♦ *vt* (*Strecke*) to go
od walk along; **etw geht jdm ab** (*fehlt*) sb
lacks sth
abgelegen ['apgəle:gən] *adj* remote
abgemacht ['apgəmaxt] *adj* fixed; **~!**
done!
abgeneigt ['apgənaikt] *adj* disinclined
Abgeordnete(r) ['apgə'ɔrdnətə(r)] *mf*
member of parliament; elected
representative
abgeschlossen ['apgəʃlɔsən] *adj attrib*
(*Wohnung*) self-contained
abgeschmackt ['apgəʃmakt] *adj*
tasteless
abgesehen ['apgəze:ən] *adj*: **es auf
jdn/etw ~ haben** to be after sb/sth; **~
von ...** apart from ...
abgespannt ['apgəʃpant] *adj* tired out
abgestanden ['apgəʃtandən] *adj* stale;
(*Bier auch*) flat
abgestorben ['apgəʃtɔrbən] *adj* numb;
(*BIOL, MED*) dead
abgetragen ['apgətra:gən] *adj* shabby,
worn out
abgewinnen ['apgəvinən] (*unreg*) *vt*:
einer Sache etw/Geschmack ~ to get
sth/pleasure from sth
abgewöhnen ['apgəvø:nən] *vt*: **jdm/
sich etw ~** to cure sb of sth/give sth up
abgleiten ['apglaitən] (*unreg*) *vi* to slip,
slide
abgöttisch ['apgœtiʃ] *adj*: **~ lieben** to
idolize
abgrenzen ['apgrɛntsən] *vt* (*auch fig*) to
mark off; to fence off
Abgrund ['apgrʊnt] *m* (*auch fig*) abyss
abhacken ['aphakən] *vt* to chop off
abhaken ['apha:kən] *vt* (*auf Papier*) to
tick off
abhalten ['aphaltən] (*unreg*) *vt*
(*Versammlung*) to hold; **jdn von etw ~**
(*fernhalten*) to keep sb away from sth;
(*hindern*) to keep sb from sth

abhanden [ap'handən] *adj*: **~ kommen**
to get lost
Abhandlung ['aphandlʊŋ] *f* treatise,
discourse
Abhang ['aphaŋ] *m* slope
abhängen ['aphɛŋən] *vt* (*Bild*) to take
down; (*Anhänger*) to uncouple; (*Verfolger*)
to shake off ♦ *vi* (*unreg: Fleisch*) to hang;
von jdm/etw ~ to depend on sb/sth
abhängig ['aphɛŋɪç] *adj*: **~ (von)**
dependent (on); **A~keit** *f*: **A~keit (von)**
dependence (on)
abhärten ['aphɛrtən] *vt, vr* to toughen
(o.s.) up; **sich gegen etw ~** to inure o.s.
to sth
abhauen ['aphaʊən] (*unreg*) *vt* to cut off;
(*Baum*) to cut down ♦ *vi* (*umg*) to clear
off *od* out
abheben ['aphe:bən] (*unreg*) *vt* to lift
(up); (*Karten*) to cut; (*Masche*) to slip;
(*Geld*) to withdraw, to take out ♦ *vi*
(*Flugzeug*) to take off; (*Rakete*) to lift off;
(*KARTEN*) to cut ♦ *vr* to stand out
abheften ['aphɛftən] *vt* (*Rechnungen etc*)
to file away
abhetzen ['aphɛtsən] *vr* to wear *od* tire
o.s. out
Abhilfe ['aphilfə] *f* remedy; **~ schaffen** to
put things right
abholen ['apho:lən] *vt* (*Gegenstand*) to
fetch, to collect; (*Person*) to call for; (*am
Bahnhof etc*) to pick up, to meet
abholzen ['aphɔltsən] *vt* (*Wald*) to clear
abhorchen ['aphɔrçən] *vt* (*MED*) to listen
to a patient's chest
abhören ['aphø:rən] *vt* (*Vokabeln*) to test;
(*Telefongespräch*) to tap; (*Tonband etc*) to
listen to
Abhörgerät *nt* bug
Abitur [abi'tu:r] (**-s, -e**) *nt* German
school-leaving examination; **~i'ent(in)**
m(f) candidate for school-leaving
certificate
Abk. *abk* (= *Abkürzung*) abbr.
abkapseln ['apkapsəln] *vr* to shut *od* cut
o.s. off
abkaufen ['apkaʊfən] *vt*: **jdm etw ~**
(*auch fig*) to buy sth from sb
abkehren ['apke:rən] *vt* (*Blick*) to avert,

to turn away ♦ *vr* to turn away

abklingen ['apklıŋən] (*unreg*) *vi* to die away; (*Radio*) to fade out

abknöpfen ['apknœpfən] *vt* to unbutton; **jdm etw ~** (*umg*) to get sth off sb

abkochen ['apkɔxən] *vt* to boil

abkommen ['apkɔmən] (*unreg*) *vi* to get away; **A~ (-s, -)** *nt* agreement; **von der Straße/von einem Plan ~** to leave the road/give up a plan

abkömmlich ['apkœmlıç] *adj* available, free

abkratzen ['apkratsən] *vt* to scrape off ♦ *vi* (*umg*) to kick the bucket

abkühlen ['apky:lən] *vt* to cool down ♦ *vr* (*Mensch*) to cool down *od* off; (*Wetter*) to get cool; (*Zuneigung*) to cool

abkürzen ['apkʏrtsən] *vt* to shorten; (*Wort auch*) to abbreviate; **den Weg ~** to take a short cut

Abkürzung *f* (*Wort*) abbreviation; (*Weg*) short cut

abladen ['apla:dən] (*unreg*) *vt* to unload

Ablage ['apla:gə] *f* (*für Akten*) tray; (*für Kleider*) cloakroom

ablassen ['aplasən] (*unreg*) *vt* (*Wasser, Dampf*) to let off; (*vom Preis*) to knock off ♦ *vi*: **von etw ~** to give sth up, to abandon sth

Ablauf ['aplauf] *m* (*Abfluß*) drain; (*von Ereignissen*) course; (*einer Frist, Zeit*) expiry (*BRIT*), expiration (*US*); **a~en** (*unreg*) *vi* (*abfließen*) to drain away; (*Ereignisse*) to happen; (*Frist, Zeit, Paß*) to expire ♦ *vt* (*Sohlen*) to wear (down *od* out)

ablegen ['aple:gən] *vt* to put *od* lay down; (*Kleider*) to take off; (*Gewohnheit*) to get rid of; (*Prüfung*) to take, to sit; (*Zeugnis*) to give

Ableger (-s, -) *m* layer; (*fig*) branch, offshoot

ablehnen ['aple:nən] *vt* to reject; (*Einladung*) to decline, to refuse ♦ *vi* to decline, to refuse

ablehnend *adj* (*Haltung, Antwort*) negative; (*Geste*) disapproving; **ein ~er Bescheid** a rejection

Ablehnung *f* rejection; refusal

ableiten ['aplaıtən] *vt* (*Wasser*) to divert; (*deduzieren*) to deduce; (*Wort*) to derive

Ableitung *f* diversion; deduction; derivation; (*Wort*) derivative

ablenken ['aplɛŋkən] *vt* to turn away, to deflect; (*zerstreuen*) to distract ♦ *vi* to change the subject

Ablenkung *f* distraction

ablesen ['aple:zən] (*unreg*) *vt* to read out; (*Meßgeräte*) to read

abliefern ['apli:fərn] *vt* to deliver; **etw bei jdm/einer Dienststelle ~** to hand sth over to sb/in at an office

Ablieferung *f* delivery

abliegen ['apli:gən] (*unreg*) *vi* to be some distance away; (*fig*) to be far removed

ablösen ['aplø:zən] *vt* (*abtrennen*) to take off, to remove; (*in Amt*) to take over from; (*Wache*) to relieve

Ablösung *f* removal; relieving

abmachen ['apmaxən] *vt* to take off; (*vereinbaren*) to agree

Abmachung *f* agreement

abmagern ['apma:gərn] *vi* to get thinner

Abmagerungskur *f* diet; **eine ~ machen** to go on a diet

Abmarsch ['apmarʃ] *m* departure

abmelden ['apmɛldən] *vt* (*Zeitungen*) to cancel; (*Auto*) to take off the road ♦ *vr* to give notice of one's departure; (*im Hotel*) to check out; **jdn bei der Polizei ~** to register sb's departure with the police

abmessen ['apmɛsən] (*unreg*) *vt* to measure

Abmessung *f* measurement

abmontieren ['apmɔnti:rən] *vt* to take off

abmühen ['apmy:ən] *vr* to wear o.s. out

Abnahme ['apna:mə] *f* (+*gen*) removal; (*COMM*) buying; (*Verringerung*) decrease (in)

abnehmen ['apne:mən] (*unreg*) *vt* to take off, to remove; (*Führerschein*) to take away; (*Prüfung*) to hold; (*Maschen*) to decrease ♦ *vi* to decrease; (*schlanker werden*) to lose weight; **(jdm) etw ~** (*Geld*) to get sth (out of sb); (*kaufen, umg: glauben*) to buy sth (from sb); **jdm Arbeit ~** to take work off sb's shoulders

Abnehmer (-s, -) *m* purchaser, customer

Abneigung ['apnaɪɡʊŋ] *f* aversion, dislike

abnorm [ap'nɔrm] *adj* abnormal

abnutzen ['apnʊtsən] *vt* to wear out

Abnutzung *f* wear (and tear)

Abonnement [abɔn(ə)'mãː] (-s, -s) *nt* subscription

Abonnent(in) [abɔ'nɛnt(ɪn)] *m(f)* subscriber

abonnieren [abɔ'niːrən] *vt* to subscribe to

Abordnung ['apˈɔrdnʊŋ] *f* delegation

abpacken ['appakən] *vt* to pack

abpassen ['appasən] *vt* (*Person, Gelegenheit*) to wait for; (*in Größe: Stoff etc*) to adjust

abpfeifen ['appfaɪfən] (*unreg*) *vt, vi* (*SPORT*): **(das Spiel)** ~ to blow the whistle (for the end of the game)

Abpfiff ['appfɪf] *m* final whistle

abplagen ['applaːɡən] *vr* to wear o.s. out

abprallen ['appralən] *vi* to bounce off; to ricochet

abputzen ['apputsən] *vt* to clean

abraten ['apraːtən] (*unreg*) *vi*: **jdm von etw** ~ to advise sb against sth, to warn sb against sth

abräumen ['aprɔʏmən] *vt* to clear up *od* away

abreagieren ['apreagiːrən] *vt*: **seinen Zorn (an jdm/etw)** ~ to work one's anger off (on sb/sth) ♦ *vr* to calm down

abrechnen ['apreçnən] *vt* to deduct, to take off ♦ *vi* to settle up; (*fig*) to get even

Abrechnung *f* settlement; (*Rechnung*) bill

Abrede ['apreːdə] *f*: **etw in** ~ **stellen** to deny *od* dispute sth

abregen ['apreːɡən] (*umg*) *vr* to calm *od* cool down

Abreise ['apraɪzə] *nf* departure; **a~n** *vi* to leave, to set off

abreißen ['apraɪsən] (*unreg*) *vt* (*Haus*) to tear down; (*Blatt*) to tear off

abrichten ['apʁɪçtən] *vt* to train

abriegeln ['apriːɡəln] *vt* (*Tür*) to bolt; (*Straße, Gebiet*) to seal off

Abriß ['apʁɪs] (-sses, -sse) *m* (*Übersicht*) outline

Abruf ['apruːf] *m*: **auf** ~ on call; **a~en** (*unreg*) *vt* (*Mensch*) to call away; (*COMM: Ware*) to request delivery of

abrunden ['aprʊndən] *vt* to round off

abrüsten ['apryst ən] *vi* to disarm

Abrüstung *f* disarmament

abrutschen ['aprʊtʃən] *vi* to slip; (*AVIAT*) to sideslip

Abs. *abk* (= *Absender*) sender; from

Absage ['apzaːɡə] *f* refusal; **a~n** *vt* to cancel, to call off; (*Einladung*) to turn down ♦ *vi* to cry off; (*ablehnen*) to decline

absägen ['apzɛːɡən] *vt* to saw off

absahnen ['apzaːnən] *vt* to skim

Absatz ['apzats] *m* (*COMM*) sales *pl*; (*Bodensatz*) deposit; (*neuer Abschnitt*) paragraph; (*Treppen~*) landing; (*Schuh~*) heel; ~**gebiet** *nt* (*COMM*) market

abschaben ['apʃaːbən] *vt* to scrape off; (*Möhren*) to scrape

abschaffen ['apʃafən] *vt* to abolish, to do away with

Abschaffung *f* abolition

abschalten ['apʃaltən] *vt, vi* (*auch umg*) to switch off

abschätzen ['apʃɛtsən] *vt* to estimate; (*Lage*) to assess; (*Person*) to size up

abschätzig ['apʃɛtsɪç] *adj* disparaging, derogatory

Abschaum ['apʃaʊm] (-(e)s) *m* scum

Abscheu ['apʃɔʏ] (-(e)s) *m* loathing, repugnance; **a~erregend** *adj* repulsive, loathsome; **a~lich** [ap'ʃɔʏlɪç] *adj* abominable

abschicken ['apʃɪkən] *vt* to send off

abschieben ['apʃiːbən] (*unreg*) *vt* to push away; (*Person*) to pack off; (: *POL*) to deport

Abschied ['apʃiːt] (-(e)s, -e) *m* parting; (*von Armee*) discharge; **(von jdm)** ~ **nehmen** to say goodbye (to sb), to take one's leave (of sb); **seinen** ~ **nehmen** (*MIL*) to apply for discharge; ~**sbrief** *m* farewell letter; ~**sfeier** *f* farewell party

abschießen ['apʃiːsən] (*unreg*) *vt* (*Flugzeug*) to shoot down; (*Geschoß*) to fire; (*umg: Minister*) to get rid of

abschirmen ['apʃɪrmən] *vt* to screen

abschlagen ['apʃlaːgən] (*unreg*) *vt* (*abhacken, COMM*) to knock off; (*ablehnen*) to refuse; (*MIL*) to repel

abschlägig ['apʃlɛːgɪç] *adj* negative

Abschlagszahlung *f* interim payment

abschleifen ['apʃlaɪfən] (*unreg*) *vt* to grind down; (*Rost*) to polish off ♦ *vr* to wear off

Abschlepp- ['apʃlɛp] *zW:* **~dienst** *m* (*AUT*) breakdown service (*BRIT*), towing company (*US*); **a~en** *vt* to (take in) tow; **~seil** *nt* towrope

abschließen ['apʃliːsən] (*unreg*) *vt* (*Tür*) to lock; (*beenden*) to conclude, to finish; (*Vertrag, Handel*) to conclude ♦ *vr* (*sich isolieren*) to cut o.s. off; **~d** *adj* concluding

Abschluß ['apʃlʊs] *m* (*Beendigung*) close, conclusion; (*COMM: Bilanz*) balancing; (*von Vertrag, Handel*) conclusion; **zum ~** in conclusion; **~feier** *f* (*SCH*) end-of-term party; **~prüfung** *f* final exam

abschmieren ['apʃmiːrən] *vt* (*AUT*) to grease, to lubricate

abschneiden ['apʃnaɪdən] (*unreg*) *vt* to cut off ♦ *vi* to do, to come off

Abschnitt ['apʃnɪt] *m* section; (*MIL*) sector; (*Kontroll~*) counterfoil; (*MATH*) segment; (*Zeit~*) period

abschöpfen ['apʃœpfən] *vt* to skim off

abschrauben ['apʃraʊbən] *vt* to unscrew

abschrecken ['apʃrɛkən] *vt* to deter, to put off; (*mit kaltem Wasser*) to plunge in cold water; **~d** *adj* deterrent; **~des Beispiel** warning

abschreiben ['apʃraɪbən] (*unreg*) *vt* to copy; (*verlorengeben*) to write off; (*COMM*) to deduct

Abschrift ['apʃrɪft] *f* copy

Abschuß ['apʃʊs] *m* (*eines Geschützes*) firing; (*Herunterschießen*) shooting down; (*Tötung*) shooting

abschüssig ['apʃʏsɪç] *adj* steep

abschütteln ['apʃʏtəln] *vt* to shake off

abschwächen ['apʃvɛçən] *vt* to lessen; (*Behauptung, Kritik*) to tone down ♦ *vr* to lessen

Abschweifung ['apʃvaɪfʊŋ] *f* digression

abschwellen ['apʃvɛlən] (*unreg*) *vi*

(*Geschwulst*) to go down; (*Lärm*) to die down

abschwören ['apʃvøːrən] *vi* (+*dat*) to renounce

absehbar *adj* foreseeable; **in ~er Zeit** in the foreseeable future; **das Ende ist ~** the end is in sight

absehen ['apzeːən] (*unreg*) *vt* (*Ende, Folgen*) to foresee ♦ *vi:* **von etw ~** to refrain from sth; (*nicht berücksichtigen*) to leave sth out of consideration

abseilen ['apzaɪlən] *vr* (*Bergsteiger*) to abseil (down)

abseits ['apzaɪts] *adv* out of the way ♦ *präp* +*gen* away from; **A~** *nt* (*SPORT*) offside

Absend- ['apzɛnd] *zW:* **a~en** (*unreg*) *vt* to send off, to dispatch; **~er (-s, -)** *m* sender

absetzen ['apzɛtsən] *vt* (*niederstellen, aussteigen lassen*) to put down; (*abnehmen*) to take off; (*COMM: verkaufen*) to sell; (*FIN: abziehen*) to deduct; (*entlassen*) to dismiss; (*König*) to depose; (*streichen*) to drop; (*hervorheben*) to pick out ♦ *vr* (*sich entfernen*) to clear off; (*sich ablagern*) to be deposited

Absetzung *f* (*FIN: Abzug*) deduction; (*Entlassung*) dismissal; (*von König*) deposing; (*Streichung*) dropping

absichern ['apzɪçərn] *vt* to make safe; (*schützen*) to safeguard ♦ *vr* to protect o.s.

Absicht ['apzɪçt] *f* intention; **mit ~** on purpose; **a~lich** *adj* intentional, deliberate

absinken ['apzɪŋkən] (*unreg*) *vi* to sink; (*Temperatur, Geschwindigkeit*) to decrease

absitzen ['apzɪtsən] (*unreg*) *vi* to dismount ♦ *vt* (*Strafe*) to serve

absolut [apzoˈluːt] *adj* absolute; **A~ismus** [-ˈtɪsmʊs] *m* absolutism

absolvieren [apzɔlˈviːrən] *vt* (*SCH*) to complete

absonder- ['apzɔndər] *zW:* **~lich** *adj* odd, strange; **~n** *vt* to separate; (*ausscheiden*) to give off, to secrete ♦ *vr* to cut o.s. off; **A~ung** *f* separation; (*MED*) secretion

abspalten ['apʃpaltən] *vt* to split off

abspannen ['apʃpanən] *vt* (*Pferde*) to

unhitch; (*Wagen*) to uncouple
abspeisen ['apʃpaɪzən] *vt* (*fig*) to fob off
abspenstig ['apʃpɛnstɪç] *adj*: (**jdm**) ~
machen to lure away (from sb)
absperren ['apʃpɛrən] *vt* to block *od*
close off; (*Tür*) to lock
Absperrung *f* (*Vorgang*) blocking *od*
closing off; (*Sperre*) barricade
abspielen ['apʃpiːlən] *vt* (*Platte,
Tonband*) to play; (*SPORT: Ball*) to pass
♦ *vr* to happen
absplittern ['apʃplɪtərn] *vt* to chip off
Absprache ['apʃpraːxə] *f* arrangement
absprechen ['apʃprɛçən] (*unreg*) *vt*
(*vereinbaren*) to arrange; **jdm etw** ~ to
deny sb sth
abspringen ['apʃprɪŋən] (*unreg*) *vi* to
jump down/off; (*Farbe, Lack*) to flake off;
(*AVIAT*) to bale out; (*sich distanzieren*) to
back out
Absprung ['apʃprʊŋ] *m* jump
abspülen ['apʃpyːlən] *vt* to rinse;
(*Geschirr*) to wash up
abstammen ['apʃtamən] *vi* to be
descended; (*Wort*) to be derived
Abstammung *f* descent; derivation
Abstand ['apʃtant] *m* distance; (*zeitlich*)
interval; **davon** ~ **nehmen, etw zu tun**
to refrain from doing sth; ~ **halten** (*AUT*)
to keep one's distance; **mit** ~ **der beste**
by far the best
abstatten ['apʃtatən] *vt* (*Dank*) to give;
(*Besuch*) to pay
abstauben ['apʃtaʊbən] *vt, vi* to dust;
(*umg: stehlen*) to pinch; (*: schnorren*) to
scrounge
Abstecher ['apʃtɛçər] (**-s, -**) *m* detour
abstehen ['apʃteːən] (*unreg*) *vi* (*Ohren,
Haare*) to stick out; (*entfernt sein*) to
stand away
absteigen ['apʃtaɪgən] (*unreg*) *vi* (*vom
Rad etc*) to get off, to dismount; **in einem
Gasthof** ~ to put up at an inn; (**in die
zweite Liga**) ~ to be relegated (to the
second division)
abstellen ['apʃtɛlən] *vt* (*niederstellen*) to
put down; (*entfernt stellen*) to pull out;
(*hinstellen: Auto*) to park; (*ausschalten*) to
turn *od* switch off; (*Mißstand, Unsitte*) to

stop; (*ausrichten*): ~ **auf** +*akk* to gear to
Abstellgleis *nt* siding
Abstellkammer *f* boxroom
Abstellraum *m* storage room
abstempeln ['apʃtɛmpəln] *vt* to stamp
absterben ['apʃtɛrbən] (*unreg*) *vi* to die;
(*Körperteil*) to go numb
Abstieg ['apʃtiːk] (**-(e)s, -e**) *m* descent;
(*SPORT*) relegation; (*fig*) decline
abstimmen ['apʃtɪmən] *vi* to vote ♦ *vt*: ~
(**auf** +*akk*) (*Instrument*) to tune (to);
(*Interessen*) to match (with); (*Termine,
Ziele*) to fit in (with) ♦ *vr* to agree
Abstimmung *f* vote
Abstinenz [apsti'nɛnts] *f* abstinence;
teetotalism; ~**ler(in)** (**-s, -**) *m(f)* teetotaller
abstoßen ['apʃtoːsən] (*unreg*) *vt* to push
off *od* away; (*verkaufen*) to unload;
(*anekeln*) to repel, to repulse; ~**d** *adj*
repulsive
abstrakt [ap'strakt] *adj* abstract ♦ *adv*
abstractly, in the abstract
abstreiten ['apʃtraɪtən] (*unreg*) *vt* to
deny
Abstrich ['apʃtrɪç] *m* (*Abzug*) cut; (*MED*)
smear; ~**e machen** to lower one's sights
abstufen ['apʃtuːfən] *vt* (*Hang*) to
terrace; (*Farben*) to shade; (*Gehälter*) to
grade
abstumpfen ['apʃtʊmpfən] *vt* (*auch fig*)
to dull, to blunt ♦ *vi* to become dulled
Absturz ['apʃtʊrts] *m* fall; (*AVIAT*) crash
abstürzen ['apʃtyrtsən] *vi* to fall; (*AVIAT*)
to crash
absuchen ['apzuːxən] *vt* to scour, to
search
absurd [ap'zʊrt] *adj* absurd
Abszeß [aps'tsɛs] (**-sses, -sse**) *m* abscess
Abt [apt] (**-(e)s, ⁔e**) *m* abbot
Abt. *abk* (= *Abteilung*) dept.
abtasten ['aptastən] *vt* to feel, to probe
abtauen ['aptaʊən] *vt, vi* to thaw
Abtei [ap'taɪ] (**-, -en**) *f* abbey
Abteil [ap'taɪl] (**-(e)s, -e**) *nt* compartment;
'**a~en** *vt* to divide up; (*abtrennen*) to
divide off; ~**ung** *f* (*in Firma, Kaufhaus*)
department; (*in Krankenhaus*) section;
(*MIL*) unit
abtippen ['aptɪpən] *vt* (*Text*) to type up

abtransportieren ['aptranspɔrtiːrən] *vt* to take away, to remove

abtreiben ['aptraɪbən] (*unreg*) *vt* (*Boot, Flugzeug*) to drive off course; (*Kind*) to abort ♦ *vi* to be driven off course; to abort

Abtreibung *f* abortion

abtrennen ['aptrɛnən] *vt* (*lostrennen*) to detach; (*entfernen*) to take off; (*abteilen*) to separate off

abtreten ['aptreːtən] (*unreg*) *vt* to wear out; (*überlassen*) to hand over, to cede ♦ *vi* to go off; (*zurücktreten*) to step down

Abtritt ['aptrɪt] *m* resignation

abtrocknen ['aptrɔknən] *vt, vi* to dry

abtun ['aptuːn] (*unreg*) *vt* to take off; (*Gewohnheit*) to give up; (*fig*) to dismiss

abwägen ['apvɛːgən] (*unreg*) *vt* to weigh up

abwälzen ['apvɛltsən] *vt* (*Schuld, Verantwortung*): ~ **(auf** +*akk***)** to shift (onto)

abwandeln ['apvandəln] *vt* to adapt

abwandern ['apvandərn] *vi* to move away; (*FIN*) to be transferred

abwarten ['apvartən] *vt* to wait for ♦ *vi* to wait

abwärts ['apvɛrts] *adv* down

Abwasch ['apvaʃ] **(-(e)s)** *m* washing-up; **a~en** (*unreg*) *vt* (*Schmutz*) to wash off; (*Geschirr*) to wash (up)

Abwasser ['apvasər] **(-s, -wässer)** *nt* sewage

abwechseln ['apvɛksəln] *vi, vr* to alternate; (*Personen*) to take turns; **~d** *adj* alternate

Abwechslung *f* change

abwegig ['apveːgɪç] *adj* wrong

Abwehr ['apveːr] **(-)** *f* defence; (*Schutz*) protection; (~*dienst*) counterintelligence (service); **a~en** *vt* to ward off; (*Ball*) to stop

abweichen ['apvaɪçən] (*unreg*) *vi* to deviate; (*Meinung*) to differ

abweisen ['apvaɪzən] (*unreg*) *vt* to turn away; (*Antrag*) to turn down; **~d** *adj* (*Haltung*) cold

abwenden ['apvɛndən] (*unreg*) *vt* to avert ♦ *vr* to turn away

abwerfen ['apvɛrfən] (*unreg*) *vt* to throw off; (*Profit*) to yield; (*aus Flugzeug*) to drop; (*Spielkarte*) to discard

abwerten ['apveːrtən] *vt* (*FIN*) to devalue

abwertend *adj* (*Worte, Sinn*) pejorative

abwesend ['apveːzənt] *adj* absent

Abwesenheit ['apveːzənhaɪt] *f* absence

abwickeln ['apvɪkəln] *vt* to unwind; (*Geschäft*) to wind up

abwimmeln ['apvɪməln] (*umg*) *vt* (*Menschen*) to get shot of

abwischen ['apvɪʃən] *vt* to wipe off *od* away; (*putzen*) to wipe

Abwurf ['apvʊrf] *m* throwing off; (*von Bomben etc*) dropping; (*von Reiter, SPORT*) throw

abwürgen ['apvʏrgən] (*umg*) *vt* to scotch; (*Motor*) to stall

abzahlen ['aptsaːlən] *vt* to pay off

abzählen ['aptsɛːlən] *vt, vi* to count (up)

Abzahlung *f* repayment; **auf ~ kaufen** to buy on hire purchase

abzapfen ['aptsapfən] *vt* to draw off; **jdm Blut ~** to take blood from sb

abzäunen ['aptsɔʏnən] *vt* to fence off

Abzeichen ['aptsaɪçən] *nt* badge; (*Orden*) decoration

abzeichnen ['aptsaɪçnən] *vt* to draw, to copy; (*Dokument*) to initial ♦ *vr* to stand out; (*fig: bevorstehen*) to loom

Abziehbild *nt* transfer

abziehen ['aptsiːən] (*unreg*) *vt* to take off; (*Tier*) to skin; (*Bett*) to strip; (*Truppen*) to withdraw; (*subtrahieren*) to take away, to subtract; (*kopieren*) to run off ♦ *vi* to go away; (*Truppen*) to withdraw

abzielen ['aptsiːlən] *vi*: ~ **auf** +*akk* to be aimed at

Abzug ['aptsuːk] *m* departure; (*von Truppen*) withdrawal; (*Kopie*) copy; (*Subtraktion*) subtraction; (*Betrag*) deduction; (*Rauch~*) flue; (*von Waffen*) trigger

abzüglich ['aptsyːklɪç] *präp* +*gen* less

abzweigen ['aptsvaɪgən] *vi* to branch off ♦ *vt* to set aside

Abzweigung *f* junction

ach [ax] *excl* oh; ~ **ja!** (oh) yes; ~ **so!** I

see; **mit A~ und Krach** by the skin of one's teeth

Achse ['aksə] *f* axis; (*AUT*) axle

Achsel ['aksəl] (-, -n) *f* shoulder; **~höhle** *f* armpit

acht [axt] *num* eight; **~ Tage** a week; **A~**[1] (-, -en) *f* eight; (*beim Eislaufen etc*) figure (of) eight

Acht[2] (-, -en) *f*: **sich in ~ nehmen (vor** +*dat*) to be careful (of), to watch out (for); **etw außer ~ lassen** to disregard sth; **a~bar** *adj* worthy

achte(r, s) ['axtə(r, s)] *adj* eighth; **A~l** *num* eighth

achten ['axtən] *vt* to respect ♦ *vi*: **~ (auf** +*akk*) to pay attention (to); **~, daß ...** to be careful that ...

ächten ['ɛçtən] *vt* to outlaw, to ban

Achterbahn ['axtər-] *f* roller coaster

Achterdeck *nt* (*NAUT*) afterdeck

acht- *zW*: **~fach** *adj* eightfold; **~geben** (*unreg*) *vi*: **~geben (auf** +*akk*) to pay attention (to); **~hundert** *num* eight hundred; **~los** *adj* careless; **~mal** *adv* eight times; **~sam** *adj* attentive

Achtung ['axtuŋ] *f* attention, (*Ehrfurcht*) respect ♦ *excl* look out!; (*MIL*) attention!; **alle ~!** good for you/him *etc*

achtzehn *num* eighteen

achtzig *num* eighty

ächzen ['ɛçtsən] *vi* to groan

Acker ['akər] (-s, ⁿ) *m* field; **~bau** *m* agriculture; **a~n** *vt, vi* to plough; (*umg*) to slog away

ADAC [a:de:'a:tse:] *abk* (= *Allgemeiner Deutscher Automobil-Club*) ≈ AA, RAC

addieren [a'di:rən] *vt* to add (up)

Addition [aditsi'o:n] *f* addition

ade [a'de:] *excl* bye!

Adel ['a:dəl] (-s) *m* nobility; **a~ig** *adj* noble

adeln *vt* to raise to the peerage

Ader ['a:dər] (-, -n) *f* vein

Adjektiv ['atjɛkti:f] (-s, -e) *nt* adjective

Adler ['a:dlər] (-s, -) *m* eagle

adlig *adj* noble

Admiral [atmi'ra:l] (-s, -e) *m* admiral

Adopt- *zW*: **a~ieren** [adɔp'ti:rən] *vt* to adopt; **~ion** [adɔptsi'o:n] *f* adoption;

~iveltern [adɔp'ti:f-] *pl* adoptive parents; **~ivkind** *nt* adopted child

Adreßbuch *nt* directory; (*privat*) address book

Adress- *zW*: **~e** [a'drɛsə] *f* address; **a~ieren** [adrɛ'si:rən] *vt*: **~ieren (an** +*akk*) to address (to)

Adria ['a:dria] (-) *f* Adriatic

Advent [at'vɛnt] (-(e)s, -e) *m* Advent; **~skalender** *m* Advent calendar; **~skranz** *m* Advent wreath

Adverb [at'vɛrp] *nt* adverb

aero- [aero] *präfix* aero-

Aerobic [ae'rɔbɪk] *nt* aerobics *sg*

Affäre [a'fɛ:rə] *f* affair

Affe ['afə] (-n, -n) *m* monkey

affektiert [afɛk'ti:rt] *adj* affected

Affen- *zW*: **a~artig** *adj* like a monkey; **mit a~artiger Geschwindigkeit** like a flash; **~hitze** (*umg*) *f* incredible heat; **~schande** (*umg*) *f* crying shame

affig ['afɪç] *adj* affected

Afrika ['a:frika] (-s) *nt* Africa; **~ner(in)** [-'ka:nər(ɪn)] (-s, -) *m(f)* African; **a~nisch** *adj* African

After ['aftər] (-s, -) *m* anus

AG [a:'ge:] *abk* (= *Aktiengesellschaft*) ≈ Ltd. (*BRIT*); ≈ Inc. (*US*)

Agent [a'gɛnt] *m* agent; **~ur** *f* agency

Aggregat [agre'ga:t] (-(e)s, -e) *nt* aggregate; (*TECH*) unit

Aggress- *zW*: **~ion** [agrɛsi'o:n] *f* aggression; **a~iv** [agre'si:f] *adj* aggressive; **~ivität** [agresivi'tɛ:t] *f* aggressiveness

Agrarpolitik [a'gra:r-] *f* agricultural policy

Ägypt- [ɛ'gypt] *zW*: **~en** (-s) *nt* Egypt; **~er(in)** (-s, -) *m(f)* Egyptian; **ä~isch** *adj* Egyptian

ah [a:] *excl* ah

aha [a'ha:] *excl* aha

ähneln ['ɛ:nəln] *vi* +*dat* to be like, to resemble ♦ *vr* to be alike *od* similar

ahnen ['a:nən] *vt* to suspect; (*Tod, Gefahr*) to have a presentiment of

ähnlich ['ɛ:nlıç] *adj* (+*dat*) similar (to); **Ä~keit** *f* similarity

Ahnung ['a:nuŋ] *f* idea, suspicion;

presentiment; **a~slos** *adj* unsuspecting
Ahorn ['a:hɔrn] (-s, -e) *m* maple
Ähre ['ɛ:rə] *f* ear
Aids [e:dz] *nt* AIDS *sg*
Akademie [akade'mi:] *f* academy
Akademiker(in) [aka'de:mikər(ın)] (-s, -) *m(f)* university graduate
akademisch *adj* academic
akklimatisieren [aklimati'zi:rən] *vr* to become acclimatized
Akkord [a'kɔrt] (-(e)s, -e) *m* (*MUS*) chord; **im ~ arbeiten** to do piecework
Akkordeon [a'kɔrdeɔn] (-s, -s) *nt* accordion
Akkusativ ['akuzati:f] (-s, -e) *m* accusative
Akne ['aknə] *f* acne
Akrobat(in) [akro'ba:t(ın)] (-en, -en) *m(f)* acrobat
Akt [akt] (-(e)s, -e) *m* act; (*KUNST*) nude
Akte ['aktə] *f* file; **~nkoffer** *m* attaché case; **a~nkundig** *adj* on the files; **~nschrank** *m* filing cabinet; **~ntasche** *f* briefcase
Aktie ['aktsiə] *f* share
Aktien- *zW:* **~gesellschaft** *f* joint-stock company; **~index** (-(e)s, -e *od* -**indices**) *m* share index; **~kurs** *m* share price
Aktion [aktsi'o:n] *f* campaign; (*Polizei~, Such~*) action; **~är** [-'nɛ:r] (-s, -e) *m* shareholder
aktiv [ak'ti:f] *adj* active; (*MIL*) regular; **~ieren** [-'vi:rən] *vt* to activate; **A~i'tät** *f* activity
Aktualität [aktuali'tɛ:t] *f* topicality; (*einer Mode*) up-to-dateness
aktuell [aktu'ɛl] *adj* topical; up-to-date
Akupunktur [akupuŋk'tu:r] *f* acupuncture
Akustik [a'kustik] *f* acoustics *pl*
akut [a'ku:t] *adj* acute
Akzent [ak'tsɛnt] *m* accent; (*Betonung*) stress
akzeptieren [aktsep'ti:rən] *vt* to accept
Alarm [a'larm] (-(e)s, -e) *m* alarm; **~anlage** *f* alarm system; **a~bereit** *adj* standing by; **~bereitschaft** *f* stand-by; **a~ieren** [-'mi:rən] *vt* to alarm
Alban- [al'ba:n] *zW:* **~er(in)** [al'ba:nər(ın)] (-s, -) *m(f)* (*GEOG*) Albanian; **~ien** (-s) *nt* Albania; **a~isch** *adj* Albanian

albern ['albərn] *adj* silly
Album ['albʊm] (-s, **Alben**) *nt* album
Alge ['algə] *f* algae
Algebra ['algebra] (-) *f* algebra
Alger- [al'ge:r] *zW:* **~ien** (-s) *nt* Algeria; **~ier(in)** (-s, -) *m(f)* Algerian; **a~isch** *adj* Algerian
alias ['a:lias] *adv* alias
Alibi ['a:libi] (-s, -s) *nt* alibi
Alimente [ali'mɛntə] *pl* alimony *sg*
Alkohol ['alkoho:l] (-s, -e) *m* alcohol; **a~frei** *adj* non-alcoholic; **~iker(in)** [alko'ho:likər(ın)] (-s, -) *m(f)* alcoholic; **a~isch** *adj* alcoholic; **~verbot** *nt* ban on alcohol
All [al] (-s) *nt* universe; **a~'abendlich** *adj* every evening; **'a~bekannt** *adj* universally known

alle(r, s) ['alə(r, s)] *adj* **1** (*sämtliche*) all; **wir alle** all of us; **alle Kinder waren da** all the children were there; **alle Kinder mögen ...** all children like ...; **alle beide** both of us/them; **sie kamen alle** they all came; **alles Gute** all the best; **alles in allem** all in all
2 (*mit Zeit- oder Maßangaben*) every; **alle vier Jahre** every four years; **alle fünf Meter** every five metres
♦ *pron* everything; **alles was er sagt** everything he says, all that he says
♦ *adv* (*zu Ende, aufgebraucht*) finished; **die Milch ist alle** the milk's all gone, there's no milk left; **etw alle machen** to finish sth up

Allee [a'le:] *f* avenue
allein [a'lain] *adv* alone; (*ohne Hilfe*) on one's own, by oneself ♦ *konj* but, only; **nicht ~** (*nicht nur*) not only; **A~erziehende(r)** *mf* single parent; **A~gang** *m:* **im A~gang** on one's own; **~stehend** *adj* single
allemal [alə'ma:l] *adv* (*jedesmal*) always; (*ohne weiteres*) with no bother; **ein für ~** once and for all
allenfalls ['alənfals] *adv* at all events; (*höchstens*) at most

aller- ['alər] *zW:* **~beste(r, s)** *adj* very best; **~dings** *adv* (*zwar*) admittedly; (*gewiß*) certainly

Allergie [aler'gi:] *f* allergy; **all'ergisch** *adj* allergic

aller- *zW:* **~hand** (*umg*) *adj inv* all sorts of; **das ist doch ~hand!** that's a bit much; (*lobend*) good show!; **A~'heiligen** *nt* All Saints' Day; **~höchstens** *adv* at the very most; **~lei** *adj inv* all sorts of; **~letzte(r, s)** *adj* very last; **~seits** *adv* on all sides; **prost ~seits!** cheers everyone!

Allerwelts- *in zW* (*Durchschnitts-*) common; (*nichtssagend*) commonplace

alles *pron* everything; **~ in allem** all in all; **~ Gute!** all the best!

Alleskleber (**-s, -**) *m* multi-purpose glue

allgemein ['algə'maɪn] *adj* general; **im ~en** in general; **~gültig** *adj* generally accepted

Allgemeinwissen *nt* general knowledge

Alliierte(r) [ali'ɪrtə(r)] *m* ally

all- *zW:* **~jährlich** *adj* annual; **~mählich** *adj* gradual; **A~tag** *m* everyday life; **~täglich** *adj, adv* daily; (*gewöhnlich*) commonplace; **~tags** *adv* on weekdays; **~'wissend** *adj* omniscient; **~zu** *adv* all too; **~zuoft** *adv* all too often; **~zuviel** *adv* too much

Allzweck- ['altsvɛk-] *in zW* multi-purpose

Alm [alm] (**-, -en**) *f* alpine pasture

Almosen ['almo:zən] (**-s, -**) *nt* alms *pl*

Alpen ['alpən] *pl* Alps

Alphabet [alfa'be:t] (**-(e)s, -e**) *nt* alphabet; **a~isch** *adj* alphabetical

Alptraum ['alptraum] *m* nightmare

SCHLÜSSELWORT

als [als] *konj* **1** (*zeitlich*) when; (*gleichzeitig*) as; **damals, als ...** (in the days) when ...; **gerade, als ...** just as ...
2 (*in der Eigenschaft*) than; **als Antwort** as an answer; **als Kind** as a child
3 (*bei Vergleichen*) than; **ich kam später als er** I came later than he (did) *od* later than him; **lieber ... als ...** rather ... than ...; **nichts als Ärger** nothing but trouble
4: als ob/wenn as if

also ['alzo:] *konj* so; (*folglich*) therefore; **~ gut** *od* **schön!** okay then; **~, so was!** well really!; **na ~!** there you are then!

Alt [alt] (**-s, -e**) *m* (*MUS*) alto

alt *adj* old; **alles beim ~en lassen** to leave everything as it was

Altar [al'ta:r] (**-(e)s, -äre**) *m* altar

Altbau *m* old building

altbekannt *adj* long-known

Alteisen *nt* scrap iron

Alten(wohn)heim *nt* old people's home

Alter ['altər] (**-s, -**) *nt* age; (*hohes*) old age; **im ~ von** at the age of; **a~n** *vi* to grow old, to age

Alternativ- [altɛrna'ti:f] *in zW* alternative; **~e** *f* alternative; **~medizin** *f* alternative medicine

Alters- *zW:* **~grenze** *f* age limit; **~heim** *nt* old people's home; **~rente** *f* old age pension; **a~schwach** *adj* (*Mensch*) frail; **~versorgung** *f* old age pension

Altertum *nt* antiquity

alt- *zW:* **A~glas** *nt* glass for recycling; **A~glascontainer** *m* bottle bank; **~klug** *adj* precocious; **~modisch** *adj* old-fashioned; **A~papier** *nt* waste paper

Alufolie ['a:lufo:liə] *f* aluminium foil

Aluminium [alu'mi:nium] (**-s**) *nt* aluminium, aluminum (*US*); **~folie** *f* tinfoil

Alzheimer-Krankheit ['æltshaɪmər-] *f* Alzheimer's (disease)

am [am] = **an dem**; **~ Schlafen** (*umg*) sleeping; **~ 15. März** on March 15th; **~ besten/schönsten** best/most beautiful

Amateur [ama'tø:r] *m* amateur

Amboß ['ambɔs] (**-sses, -sse**) *m* anvil

ambulant [ambu'lant] *adj* outpatient

Ambulanz [ambu'lants] *f* outpatients *sg*

Ameise ['a:maɪzə] *f* ant

Ameisenhaufen *m* ant hill

Amerika [a'me:rika] (**-s**) *nt* America; **~ner(in)** [-'ka:nər(ɪn)] (**-s, -**) *m(f)* American; **a~nisch** [-'ka:nɪʃ] *adj* American

Amnestie [amnɛs'ti:] *f* amnesty

Ampel ['ampəl] (-, -n) f traffic lights pl
amputieren [ampu'tiːrən] vt to amputate
Amsel ['amzəl] (-, -n) f blackbird
Amt [amt] (-(e)s, ¨er) nt office; (Pflicht) duty; (TEL) exchange; a~**ieren** [am'tiːrən] vi to hold office; a~**lich** adj official
Amts- zW: ~**richter** m district judge; ~**stunden** pl office hours; ~**zeit** f period of office
amüsant [amy'zant] adj amusing
amüsieren [amy'ziːrən] vt to amuse ♦ vr to enjoy o.s.

SCHLÜSSELWORT

an [an] präp +dat 1 (räumlich: wo?) at; (auf, bei) on; (nahe bei) near; **an diesem Ort** at this place; **an der Wand** on the wall; **zu nahe an etw** too near to sth; **unten am Fluß** down by the river; **Köln liegt am Rhein** Cologne is on the Rhine
2 (zeitlich: wann?) on; **an diesem Tag** on this day; **an Ostern** at Easter
3: **arm an Fett** low in fat; **an etw sterben** to die of sth; **an (und für) sich** actually
♦ präp +akk 1 (räumlich: wohin?) to; **er ging ans Fenster** he went (over) to the window; **etw an die Wand hängen/ schreiben** to hang/write sth on the wall
2 (zeitlich: woran?): **an etw denken** to think of sth
3 (gerichtet an) to; **ein Gruß/eine Frage an dich** greetings/a question to you
♦ adv 1 (ungefähr) about; **an die hundert** about a hundred
2 (auf Fahrplänen): **Frankfurt an 18.30** arriving Frankfurt 18.30
3 (ab): **von dort/heute an** from there/ today onwards
4 (angeschaltet, angezogen) on; **das Licht ist an** the light is on; **ohne etwas an** with nothing on; siehe auch **am**

analog [ana'loːk] adj analogous; A~**ie** [-'giː] f analogy
Analyse [ana'lyːzə] f analysis
analysieren [analy'ziːrən] vt to analyse
Ananas ['ananas] (-, - od -se) f pineapple
Anarchie [anar'çiː] f anarchy

Anatomie [anato'miː] f anatomy
anbahnen ['anbaːnən] vt, vr to open up
Anbau ['anbau] m (AGR) cultivation; (Gebäude) extension; a~**en** vt (AGR) to cultivate; (Gebäudeteil) to build on
anbehalten ['anbəhaltən] (unreg) vt to keep on
anbei [an'baɪ] adv enclosed
anbeißen ['anbaɪsən] (unreg) vt to bite into ♦ vi to bite; (fig) to swallow the bait; **zum A~** (umg) good enough to eat
anbelangen ['anbəlaŋən] vt to concern; **was mich anbelangt** as far as I am concerned
anbeten ['anbeːtən] vt to worship
Anbetracht ['anbətraxt] m: **in ~** +gen in view of
anbiedern ['anbiːdərn] vr: **sich ~ (bei)** to make up (to)
anbieten ['anbiːtən] (unreg) vt to offer ♦ vr to volunteer
anbinden ['anbɪndən] (unreg) vt to tie up; **kurz angebunden** (fig) curt
Anblick ['anblɪk] m sight; a~**en** vt to look at
anbrechen ['anbrɛçən] (unreg) vt to start; (Vorräte) to break into ♦ vi to start; (Tag) to break; (Nacht) to fall
anbrennen ['anbrɛnən] (unreg) vi to catch fire; (KOCH) to burn
anbringen ['anbrɪŋən] (unreg) vt to bring; (Ware) to sell; (festmachen) to fasten
Anbruch ['anbrux] m beginning; **~ des Tages/der Nacht** dawn/nightfall
anbrüllen ['anbrylən] vt to roar at
Andacht ['andaxt] (-, -en) f devotion; (Gottesdienst) prayers pl
andächtig ['andɛçtɪç] adj devout
andauern ['andauərn] vi to last, to go on; ~**d** adj continual
Anden ['andən] pl Andes
Andenken ['andɛŋkən] (-s, -) nt memory; souvenir
andere(r, s) ['andərə(r, s)] adj other; (verschieden) different; **ein ~s Mal** another time; **kein ~r** nobody else; **von etw ~m sprechen** to talk about something else; ~**rseits** adv on the other

hand

andermal *adv*: **ein ~** some other time

ändern ['ɛndərn] *vt* to alter, to change
♦ *vr* to change

andernfalls ['andərnfals] *adv* otherwise

anders ['andərs] *adv*: **~ (als)** differently
(from); **wer ~?** who else?; **jd/irgendwo ~**
sb/somewhere else; **~ aussehen/klingen**
to look/sound different; **~artig** *adj*
different; **~herum** *adv* the other way
round; **~wo** *adv* somewhere else;
~woher *adv* from somewhere else

anderthalb ['andərt'halp] *adj* one and a
half

Änderung ['ɛndəruŋ] *f* alteration, change

anderweitig ['andər'vaitıç] *adj* other
♦ *adv* otherwise; (*anderswo*) elsewhere

andeuten ['andɔytən] *vt* to indicate;
(*Wink geben*) to hint at

Andeutung *f* indication; hint

Andrang ['andraŋ] *m* crush

andrehen ['andre:ən] *vt* to turn *od*
switch on; **jdm etw ~** (*umg*) to unload sth
onto sb

androhen ['andro:ən] *vt*: **jdm etw ~** to
threaten sb with sth

aneignen ['an'aıgnən] *vt*: **sich** *dat* **etw ~**
to acquire sth; (*widerrechtlich*) to
appropriate sth

aneinander [an'aı'nandər] *adv* at/on/to
etc one another *od* each other; **~geraten**
(*unreg*) *vi* to clash

Anekdote [anɛk'do:tə] *f* anecdote

anekeln ['an'e:kəln] *vt* to disgust

Anemone [ane'mo:nə] *f* anemone

anerkannt ['an'ɛrkant] *adj* recognized,
acknowledged

anerkennen ['an'ɛrkɛnən] (*unreg*) *vt* to
recognize, to acknowledge; (*würdigen*) to
appreciate; **~d** *adj* appreciative

Anerkennung *f* recognition,
acknowledgement; appreciation

anfachen ['anfaxən] *vt* to fan into flame;
(*fig*) to kindle

anfahren ['anfa:rən] (*unreg*) *vt* to deliver;
(*fahren gegen*) to hit; (*Hafen*) to put into;
(*fig*) to bawl out ♦ *vi* to drive up;
(*losfahren*) to drive off

Anfahrt ['anfa:rt] *f* (*Anfahrtsweg*,

Anfahrtszeit) departure

Anfall ['anfal] *m* (*MED*) attack; **a~en**
(*unreg*) *vt* to attack; (*fig*) to overcome ♦ *vi*
(*Arbeit*) to come up; (*Produkt*) to be
obtained

anfällig ['anfɛlıç] *adj* delicate; **~ für etw**
prone to sth

Anfang ['anfaŋ] (**-(e)s, -fänge**) *m*
beginning, start; **von ~ an** right from the
beginning; **zu ~** at the beginning; **~ Mai**
at the beginning of May; **a~en** (*unreg*) *vt*,
vi to begin, to start; (*machen*) to do

Anfänger(in) ['anfɛŋər(ın)] (**-s, -**) *m(f)*
beginner

anfänglich ['anfɛŋlıç] *adj* initial

anfangs *adv* at first; **A~buchstabe** *m*
initial *od* first letter

anfassen ['anfasən] *vt* to handle;
(*berühren*) to touch ♦ *vi* to lend a hand
♦ *vr* to feel

anfechten ['anfɛçtən] (*unreg*) *vt* to
dispute; (*beunruhigen*) to trouble

anfertigen ['anfɛrtıgən] *vt* to make

anfeuern ['anfɔyərn] *vt* (*fig*) to spur on

anflehen ['anfle:ən] *vt* to implore

anfliegen ['anfli:gən] (*unreg*) *vt* to fly to

Anflug ['anflu:k] *m* (*AVIAT*) approach;
(*Spur*) trace

anfordern ['anfɔrdərn] *vt* to demand;
(*COMM*) to requisition

Anforderung *f* (*+gen*) demand (for)

Anfrage ['anfra:gə] *f* inquiry; **a~n** *vi* to
inquire

anfreunden ['anfrɔyndən] *vr* to make
friends

anfügen ['anfy:gən] *vt* to add; (*beifügen*)
to enclose

anfühlen ['anfy:lən] *vt*, *vr* to feel

anführen ['anfy:rən] *vt* to lead; (*zitieren*)
to quote; (*umg: betrügen*) to lead up the
garden path

Anführer *m* leader

Anführung *f* leadership; (*Zitat*)
quotation; **~szeichen** *pl* quotation
marks, inverted commas

Angabe ['anga:bə] *f* statement; (*TECH*)
specification; (*umg: Prahlerei*) boasting;
(*SPORT*) service

angeben ['ange:bən] (*unreg*) *vt* to give;

(*anzeigen*) to inform on; (*bestimmen*) to set ♦ *vi* (*umg*) to boast; (*SPORT*) to serve

Angeber (-s, -; *umg*) *m* show-off; **Angebe'rei** (*umg*) *f* showing off

angeblich ['ange:plɪç] *adj* alleged

angeboren ['angəbo:rən] *adj* inborn, innate

Angebot ['angəbo:t] *nt* offer; ~ **(an** +*dat*) (*COMM*) supply (of)

angebracht ['angəbraxt] *adj* appropriate, in order

angegriffen ['angəgrɪfən] *adj* exhausted

angeheitert ['angəhaɪtərt] *adj* tipsy

angehen ['ange:ən] (*unreg*) *vt* to concern; (*angreifen*) to attack; (*bitten*): **jdn** ~ **(um)** to approach sb (for) ♦ *vi* (*Feuer*) to light; (*umg*: *beginnen*) to begin; **~d** *adj* prospective

Angehörige(r) *mf* relative

Angeklagte(r) ['angəkla:ktə(r)] *mf* accused

Angel ['aŋəl] (-, -n) *f* fishing rod; (*Tür~*) hinge

Angelegenheit ['angəle:gənhaɪt] *f* affair, matter

Angel- *zW*: **~haken** *m* fish hook; **a~n** *vt* to catch ♦ *vi* to fish; **~n** (-s) *nt* angling, fishing; **~rute** *f* fishing rod

angemessen ['angəmɛsən] *adj* appropriate, suitable

angenehm ['angəne:m] *adj* pleasant; **~!** (*bei Vorstellung*) pleased to meet you

angeregt ['angəre:kt] *adj* animated, lively

angesehen ['angəze:ən] *adj* respected

angesichts ['angəzɪçts] *präp* +*gen* in view of, considering

angespannt ['angəʃpant] *adj* (*Aufmerksamkeit*) close; (*Arbeit*) hard

Angestellte(r) ['angəʃtɛltə(r)] *mf* employee

angestrengt ['angəʃtrɛŋt] *adv* as hard as one can

angetan ['angəta:n] *adj*: **von jdm/etw ~ sein** to be impressed by sb/sth; **es jdm ~ haben** to appeal to sb

angetrunken ['angətrʊŋkən] *adj* tipsy

angewiesen ['angəvi:zən] *adj*: **auf jdn/ etw ~ sein** to be dependent on sb/sth

angewöhnen ['angəvø:nən] *vt*: **jdm/ sich etw ~** to get sb/become accustomed to sth

Angewohnheit ['angəvo:nhaɪt] *f* habit

angleichen ['anglaɪçən] (*unreg*) *vt, vr* to adjust

angreifen ['angraɪfən] (*unreg*) *vt* to attack; (*anfassen*) to touch; (*Arbeit*) to tackle; (*beschädigen*) to damage

Angreifer (-s, -) *m* attacker

Angriff ['angrɪf] *m* attack; **etw in ~ nehmen** to make a start on sth

Angst [aŋst] (-, ᵉe) *f* fear: **jdm ist a~** sb is afraid *od* scared; ~ **haben (vor** +*dat*) to be afraid *od* scared (of); ~ **haben um jdn/etw** to be worried about sb/sth; **jdm a~ machen** to scare sb; **~hase** (*umg*) *m* chicken, scaredy-cat

ängst- ['ɛŋst] *zW*: **~igen** *vt* to frighten ♦ *vr*: **sich ~igen (vor** +*dat* od **um)** to worry (o.s.) (about); **~lich** *adj* nervous; (*besorgt*) worried; **Ä~lichkeit** *f* nervousness

anhaben ['anha:bən] (*unreg*) *vt* to have on; **er kann mir nichts ~** he can't hurt me

anhalt- ['anhalt] *zW*: **~en** (*unreg*) *vt* to stop ♦ *vi* (*andauern*) to persist; (*jdm*) **etw ~en** to hold sth up (against sb); **jdn zur Arbeit/Höflichkeit ~en** to make sb work/be polite; **~end** *adj* persistent; **A~er** (-s, -) *m* hitch-hiker; **per A~er fahren** to hitch-hike; **A~spunkt** *m* clue

anhand [an'hant] *präp* +*gen* with

Anhang ['anhaŋ] *m* appendix; (*Leute*) family; supporters *pl*

anhäng- ['anhɛŋ] *zW*: **~en** (*unreg*) *vt* to hang up; (*Wagen*) to couple up; (*Zusatz*) to add (on); **A~er** (-s, -) *m* supporter; (*AUT*) trailer; (*am Koffer*) tag; (*Schmuck*) pendant; **A~erschaft** *f* supporters *pl*; **~lich** *adj* devoted; **A~lichkeit** *f* devotion; **A~sel** (-s, -) *nt* appendage

Anhäufung ['anhɔyfʊŋ] *f* accumulation

anheben ['anhe:bən] (*unreg*) *vt* to lift up; (*Preise*) to raise

anheizen ['anhaɪtsən] *vt* (*Stimmung*) to lift; (*Moral*) to boost

Anhieb ['anhi:b] *m*: **auf ~** at the very first go; (*kurz entschlossen*) on the spur of the moment

Anhöhe ['anhø:ə] *f* hill

anhören ['anhø:rən] *vt* to listen to; (*anmerken*) to hear ♦ *vr* to sound

animieren [ani'mi:rən] *vt* to encourage, to urge on

Anis [a'ni:s] (**-es, -e**) *m* aniseed

Ank. *abk* (= *Ankunft*) arr.

Ankauf ['ankaʊf] *m* (*von Wertpapieren, Devisen, Waren*) purchase

ankaufen ['ankaʊfən] *vt* to buy .

Anker ['aŋkər] (**-s, -**) *m* anchor; **vor ~ gehen** to drop anchor; **a~n** *vt, vi* to anchor

Anklage ['ankla:gə] *f* accusation; (*JUR*) charge; **~bank** *f* dock; **a~n** *vt* to accuse; **jdn (eines Verbrechens) a~n** (*JUR*) to charge sb (with a crime)

Ankläger ['anklɛ:gər] *m* accuser

Anklang ['anklaŋ] *m*: **bei jdm ~ finden** to meet with sb's approval

Ankleidekabine *f* changing cubicle

ankleiden ['anklaɪdən] *vt, vr* to dress

anklopfen ['anklɔpfən] *vi* to knock

anknüpfen ['anknʏpfən] *vt* to fasten *od* tie on; (*fig*) to start ♦ *vi* (*anschließen*): **~ an** +*akk* to refer to

ankommen ['ankɔmən] (*unreg*) *vi* to arrive; (*näherkommen*) to approach; (*Anklang finden*): **bei jdm (gut) ~** to go down well with sb; **es kommt darauf an** it depends; (*wichtig sein*) that (is what) matters; **es darauf ~ lassen** to let things take their course; **gegen jdn/etw ~** to cope with sb/sth; **bei jdm schlecht ~** to go down badly with sb

ankreuzen ['ankrɔʏtsən] *vt* to mark with a cross; (*hervorheben*) to highlight

ankündigen ['ankʏndɪgən] *vt* to announce

Ankündigung *f* announcement

Ankunft ['ankʊnft] (**-, -künfte**) *f* arrival; **~szeit** *f* time of arrival

ankurbeln ['ankʊrbəln] *vt* (*AUT*) to crank; (*fig*) to boost

Anlage ['anla:gə] *f* disposition; (*Begabung*) talent; (*Park*) gardens *pl*; (*Beilage*) enclosure; (*TECH*) plant; (*FIN*) investment; (*Entwurf*) layout

Anlaß ['anlas] (**-sses, -lässe**) *m*: **~ (zu)** cause (for); (*Ereignis*) occasion; **aus ~** +*gen* on the occasion of; **~ zu etw geben** to give rise to sth; **etw zum ~ nehmen** to take the opportunity of sth

anlassen (*unreg*) *vt* to leave on; (*Motor*) to start ♦ *vr* (*umg*) to start off

Anlasser (**-s, -**) *m* (*AUT*) starter

anläßlich ['anlɛslɪç] *präp* +*gen* on the occasion of

Anlauf ['anlaʊf] *m* run-up; **a~en** (*unreg*) *vi* to begin; (*neuer Film*) to show; (*SPORT*) to run up; (*Fenster*) to mist up; (*Metall*) to tarnish ♦ *vt* to call at; **rot a~en** to blush; **angelaufen kommen** to come running up

anlegen ['anle:gən] *vt* to put; (*anziehen*) to put on; (*gestalten*) to lay out; (*Geld*) to invest ♦ *vi* to dock; **etw an etw** *akk* **~** to put sth against *od* on sth; **ein Gewehr ~ (auf** +*akk*) to aim a weapon (at); **es auf etw** *akk* **~** to be out for sth/to do sth; **sich mit jdm ~** (*umg*) to quarrel with sb

Anlegestelle *f* landing place

anlehnen ['anle:nən] *vt* to lean; (*Tür*) to leave ajar; **(sich) an etw** *akk* **~** to lean on/against sth

Anleihe ['anlaɪə] *f* (*FINANZ*) loan

anleiten ['anlaɪtən] *vt* to instruct

Anleitung *f* instructions *pl*

anlernen ['anlɛrnən] *vt* to teach, to instruct

anliegen ['anli:gən] (*unreg*) *vi* (*Kleidung*) to cling; **A~ (-s, -)** *nt* matter; (*Wunsch*) wish; **~d** *adj* adjacent; (*beigefügt*) enclosed

Anlieger (**-s, -**) *m* resident; **„~ frei"** "residents only"

anmachen ['anmaxən] *vt* to attach; (*Elektrisches*) to put on; (*Zigarette*) to light; (*Salat*) to dress

anmaßen ['anma:sən] *vt*: **sich** *dat* **etw ~** (*Recht*) to lay claim to sth; **~d** *adj* arrogant

Anmaßung *f* presumption

anmelden ['anmɛldən] *vt* to announce ♦ *vr* (*sich ankündigen*) to make an appointment; (*polizeilich, für Kurs etc*) to register

Anmeldung *f* announcement; appointment; registration

anmerken ['anmɛrkən] *vt* to observe; (*anstreichen*) to mark; **sich** *dat* **nichts ~ lassen** to not give anything away

Anmerkung *f* note

Anmut ['anmuːt] (-) *f* grace; **a~en** *vt* to give a feeling; **a~ig** *adj* charming

annähen ['annɛːən] *vt* to sew on

annähern ['annɛːərn] *vr* to get closer; **~d** *adj* approximate

Annäherung *f* approach; **~sversuch** *m* advances *pl*

Annahme ['annaːmə] *f* acceptance; (*Vermutung*) assumption

annehm- ['annɛːm] *zW:* **~bar** *adj* acceptable; **~en** (*unreg*) *vt* to accept; (*Namen*) to take; (*Kind*) to adopt; (*vermuten*) to suppose, to assume ♦ *vr* (*+gen*) to take care (of); **A~lichkeit** *f* comfort

Annonce [a'nõːsə] *f* advertisement

annoncieren [anõ'siːrən] *vt, vi* to advertise

annullieren [anʊ'liːrən] *vt* to annul

Anode [a'noːdə] *f* anode

anonym [ano'nyːm] *adj* anonymous

Anorak ['anorak] (-s, -s) *m* anorak

anordnen ['an'ɔrdnən] *vt* to arrange; (*befehlen*) to order

Anordnung *f* arrangement; order

anorganisch ['an'ɔrgaːnɪʃ] *adj* inorganic

anpacken ['anpakən] *vt* to grasp; (*fig*) to tackle; **mit ~** to lend a hand

anpassen ['anpasən] *vt:* (*jdm*) **~** to fit (on sb); (*fig*) to adapt ♦ *vr* to adapt

anpassungsfähig *adj* adaptable

Anpfiff ['anpfɪf] *m* (*SPORT*) (starting) whistle; kick-off; (*umg*) rocket

anprallen ['anpralən] *vi:* **~ (gegen** *od* **an** *+akk*) to collide (with)

anprangern ['anpraŋərn] *vt* to denounce

anpreisen ['anpraɪzən] (*unreg*) *vt* to extol

Anprobe ['anproːbə] *f* trying on

anprobieren ['anprobiːrən] *vt* to try on

anrechnen ['anrɛçnən] *vt* to charge; (*fig*) to count; **jdm etw hoch ~** to value sb's

sth greatly

Anrecht ['anrɛçt] *nt:* **~ (auf** *+akk***)** right (to)

Anrede ['anreːdə] *f* form of address; **a~n** *vt* to address; (*belästigen*) to accost

anregen ['anreːgən] *vt* to stimulate; **angeregte Unterhaltung** lively discussion; **~d** *adj* stimulating

Anregung *f* stimulation; (*Vorschlag*) suggestion

anreichern ['anraɪçərn] *vt* to enrich

Anreise ['anraɪzə] *f* journey; **a~n** *vi* to arrive

Anreiz ['anraɪts] *m* incentive

anrichten ['anrɪçtə] *f* sideboard; **a~n** *vt* to serve up; **Unheil a~n** to make mischief

anrüchig ['anryçɪç] *adj* dubious

anrücken ['anrʏkən] *vi* to approach; (*MIL*) to advance

Anruf ['anruːf] *m* call; **a~en** (*unreg*) *vt* to call out to; (*bitten*) to call on; (*TEL*) to ring up, to phone, to call

ans [ans] = **an das**

Ansage ['anzaːgə] *f* announcement; **a~n** *vt* to announce ♦ *vr* to say one will come; **~r(in)** (-s, -) *m(f)* announcer

ansammeln ['anzaməln] *vt* (*Reichtümer*) to amass ♦ *vr* (*Menschen*) to gather, to assemble ♦ (*Wasser*) to collect

Ansammlung *f* collection; (*Leute*) crowd

ansässig ['anzɛsɪç] *adj* resident

Ansatz ['anzats] *m* start; (*Haar~*) hairline; (*Hals~*) base; (*Verlängerungsstück*) extension; (*Veranschlagung*) estimate; **~punkt** *m* starting point

anschaffen ['anʃafən] *vt* to buy, to purchase

Anschaffung *f* purchase

anschalten ['anʃaltən] *vt* to switch on

anschau- ['anʃaʊ] *zW:* **~en** *vt* to look at; **~lich** *adj* illustrative; **A~ung** *f* (*Meinung*) view; **aus eigener A~ung** from one's own experience

Anschein ['anʃaɪn] *m* appearance; **allem ~ nach** to all appearances; **den ~ haben** to seem, to appear; **a~end** *adj* apparent

Anschlag ['anʃlaːk] *m* notice; (*Attentat*) attack; (*COMM*) estimate; (*auf Klavier*) touch; (*Schreibmaschine*) character; **a~en**

['anʃlaːgən] (*unreg*) *vt* to put up; (*beschädigen*) to chip; (*Akkord*) to strike; (*Kosten*) to estimate ♦ *vi* to hit; (*wirken*) to have an effect; (*Glocke*) to ring; (*Hund*) to bark; **an etw** *akk* **a~en** to hit against sth

anschließen ['anʃliːsən] (*unreg*) *vt* to connect up; (*Sender*) to link up ♦ *vi*: **an etw** *akk* ~ to adjoin sth; (*zeitlich*) to follow sth ♦ *vr*: **sich jdm/etw** ~ to join sb/sth; (*beipflichten*) to agree with sb/sth; **sich an etw** *akk* ~ to adjoin sth; **~d** *adj* adjacent; (*zeitlich*) subsequent ♦ *adv* afterwards

Anschluß ['anʃlus] *m* (*ELEK, EISENB*) connection; (*von Wasser etc*) supply; **im** ~ **an** +*akk* following; ~ **finden** to make friends

anschmiegsam ['anʃmiːkzaːm] *adj* affectionate

anschnallen ['anʃnalən] *vt* to buckle on ♦ *vr* to fasten one's seat belt

anschneiden ['anʃnaɪdən] (*unreg*) *vt* to cut into; (*Thema*) to introduce

anschreiben ['anʃraɪbən] (*unreg*) *vt* to write (up); (*COMM*) to charge up; (*benachrichtigen*) to write to

anschreien ['anʃraɪən] (*unreg*) *vt* to shout at

Anschrift ['anʃrɪft] *f* address

Anschuldigung ['anʃuldɪguŋ] *f* accusation

anschwellen ['anʃvɛlən] (*unreg*) *vi* to swell (up)

anschwindeln ['anʃvɪndəln] *vt* to lie to

ansehen ['anzeːən] (*unreg*) *vt* to look at; **jdm etw** ~ to see sth (from sb's face); **jdn/etw als etw** ~ to look on sb/sth as sth; ~ **für** to consider; **A**~ (-*s*) *nt* respect; (*Ruf*) reputation

ansehnlich ['anzeːnlɪç] *adj* fine-looking; (*beträchtlich*) considerable

ansetzen ['anzɛtsən] *vt* (*festlegen*) to fix; (*entwickeln*) to develop; (*Fett*) to put on; (*Blätter*) to grow; (*zubereiten*) to prepare ♦ *vi* (*anfangen*) to start, to begin; (*Entwicklung*) to set in; (*dick werden*) to put on weight ♦ *vr* (*Rost etc*) to start to develop; ~ **an** +*akk* (*anfügen*) to fix on to;

(*anlegen, an Mund etc*) to put to

Ansicht ['anzɪçt] *f* (*Anblick*) sight; (*Meinung*) view, opinion; **zur** ~ on approval; **meiner** ~ **nach** in my opinion; ~**skarte** *f* picture postcard; ~**ssache** *f* matter of opinion

anspannen ['anʃpanən] *vt* to harness; (*Muskel*) to strain

Anspannung *f* strain

anspielen ['anʃpiːlən] *vi* (*SPORT*) to start play; **auf etw** *akk* ~ to refer *od* allude to sth

Anspielung *f*: ~ (**auf** +*akk*) reference (to), allusion (to)

Ansporn ['anʃpɔrn] (-(*e*)*s*) *m* incentive

Ansprache ['anʃpraːxə] *f* address

ansprechen ['anʃprɛçən] (*unreg*) *vt* to speak to; (*bitten, gefallen*) to appeal to ♦ *vi*: (**auf etw** *akk*) ~ to react (to sth); **jdn auf etw** *akk* (**hin**) ~ to ask sb about sth; ~**d** *adj* attractive

anspringen ['anʃprɪŋən] (*unreg*) *vi* (*AUT*) to start ♦ *vt* to jump at

Anspruch ['anʃprux] *m* (*Recht*): ~ (**auf** +*akk*) claim (to); **hohe Ansprüche stellen/haben** to demand/expect a lot; **jdn/etw in** ~ **nehmen** to occupy sb/take up sth; **a~slos** *adj* undemanding; **a~svoll** *adj* demanding

anstacheln ['anʃtaxəln] *vt* to spur on

Anstalt ['anʃtalt] (-, -*en*) *f* institution; ~**en machen, etw zu tun** to prepare to do sth

Anstand ['anʃtant] *m* decency

anständig ['anʃtɛndɪç] *adj* decent; (*umg*) proper; (*groß*) considerable

anstandslos *adv* without any ado

anstarren ['anʃtarən] *vt* to stare at

anstatt [an'ʃtat] *präp* +*gen* instead of ♦ *konj*: ~ **etw zu tun** instead of doing sth

Ansteck- ['anʃtɛk] *zW*: **a~en** *vt* to pin on; (*MED*) to infect; (*Pfeife*) to light; (*Haus*) to set fire to ♦ *vr*: **ich habe mich bei ihm angesteckt** I caught it from him ♦ *vi* (*fig*) to be infectious; **a~end** *adj* infectious; ~**ung** *f* infection

anstehen ['anʃteːən] (*unreg*) *vi* to queue (up) (*BRIT*), to line up (*US*)

ansteigen ['anʃtaɪgən] *vt* (*Straße*) to

climb; (*Gelände, Temperatur, Preise*) to rise

anstelle [an'ʃtɛlə] *präp +gen* in place of; **~n** ['an-] *vt* (*einschalten*) to turn on; (*Arbeit geben*) to employ; (*machen*) to do ♦ *vr* to queue (up) (*BRIT*), to line up (*US*); (*umg*) to act

Anstellung *f* employment; (*Posten*) post, position

Anstieg ['anʃtiːk] (**-(e)s, -e**) *m* (*+gen*) climb; (*fig: von Preisen etc*) increase (in)

anstiften ['anʃtɪftən] *vt* (*Unglück*) to cause; **jdn zu etw ~** to put sb up to sth

Anstifter (**-s, -**) *m* instigator

anstimmen ['anʃtɪmən] *vt* (*Lied*) to strike up with; (*Geschrei*) to set up

Anstoß ['anʃtoːs] *m* impetus; (*Ärgernis*) offence; (*SPORT*) kick-off; **der erste ~** the initiative; **~ nehmen an** +*dat* to take offence at; **a~en** (*unreg*) *vt* to bump; (*mit Fuß*) to kick ♦ *vi* to knock, to bump; (*mit der Zunge*) to lisp; (*mit Gläsern*): **a~en (auf** +*akk*) to drink (to), to drink a toast (to)

anstößig ['anʃtøːsɪç] *adj* offensive, indecent

anstreichen ['anʃtraiçən] (*unreg*) *vt* to paint

Anstreicher (**-s, -**) *m* painter

anstrengen ['anʃtrɛŋən] *vt* to strain; (*JUR*) to bring ♦ *vr* to make an effort; **~d** *adj* tiring

Anstrengung *f* effort

Anstrich ['anʃtrɪç] *m* coat of paint

Ansturm ['anʃtʊrm] *m* rush; (*MIL*) attack

Antarktis [ant'ʔarktɪs] (**-**) *f* Antarctic

antasten ['antastən] *vt* to touch; (*Recht*) to infringe upon; (*Ehre*) to question

Anteil ['antail] (**-s, -e**) *m* share; (*Mitgefühl*) sympathy; **~ nehmen (an** +*dat*) to share (in); (*sich interessieren*) to take an interest (in); **~nahme** (**-**) *f* sympathy

Antenne [an'tɛnə] *f* aerial

Anti- ['anti] *in zW* anti; **~alko'holiker** *m* teetotaller; **a~autori'tär** *adj* anti-authoritarian; **~biotikum** [antibi'oːtikʊm] (**-s, -ka**) *nt* antibiotic

antik [an'tiːk] *adj* antique; **A~e** *f*

(*Zeitalter*) ancient world; (*Kunstgegenstand*) antique

Antilope [anti'loːpə] *f* antelope

Antiquariat [antikvari'aːt] (**-(e)s, -e**) *nt* secondhand bookshop

Antiquitäten [antikvi'tɛːtən] *pl* antiques; **~händler** *m* antique dealer

antiseptisch [-'zɛptɪʃ] *adj* antiseptic

Antrag ['antraːk] (**-(e)s, -träge**) *m* proposal; (*PARL*) motion; (*Gesuch*) application

antreffen ['antrɛfən] (*unreg*) *vt* to meet

antreiben ['antraibən] (*unreg*) *vt* to drive on; (*Motor*) to drive; (*anschwemmen*) to wash up ♦ *vi* to be washed up

antreten ['antreːtən] (*unreg*) *vt* (*Amt*) to take up; (*Erbschaft*) to come into; (*Beweis*) to offer; (*Reise*) to start, to begin ♦ *vi* (*MIL*) to fall in; (*SPORT*) to line up; **gegen jdn ~** to play/fight (against) sb

Antrieb ['antriːp] *m* (*auch fig*) drive; **aus eigenem ~** of one's own accord

antrinken ['antrɪŋkən] (*unreg*) *vt* (*Flasche, Glas*) to start to drink from; **sich** *dat* **Mut/einen Rausch ~** to give o.s. Dutch courage/get drunk; **angetrunken sein** to be tipsy

Antritt ['antrɪt] *m* beginning, commencement; (*eines Amts*) taking up

antun ['antuːn] (*unreg*) *vt*: **jdm etw ~** to do sth to sb; **sich** *dat* **Zwang ~** to force o.s.; **sich** *dat* **etwas ~** to (try to) take one's own life

Antwort ['antvɔrt] (**-, -en**) *f* answer, reply; **a~en** *vi* to answer, to reply

anvertrauen ['anfertrauən] *vt*: **jdm etw ~** to entrust sb with sth; **sich jdm ~** to confide in sb

anwachsen ['anvaksən] (*unreg*) *vi* to grow; (*Pflanze*) to take root

Anwalt ['anvalt] (**-(e)s, -wälte**) *m* solicitor; lawyer; (*fig*) champion

Anwältin ['anvɛltɪn] *f siehe* **Anwalt**

Anwärter ['anvɛrtər] *m* candidate

anweisen ['anvaizən] (*unreg*) *vt* to instruct; (*zuteilen*) to assign

Anweisung *f* instruction; (*COMM*) remittance; (*Post~, Zahlungs~*) money order

anwend- ['anvɛnd] *zW*: **~bar** ['anvɛnt-] *adj* practicable, applicable; **~en** (*unreg*) *vt* to use, to employ; (*Gesetz, Regel*) to apply; **A~ung** *f* use; application

anwesend ['anveːzənt] *adj* present; **die A~en** those present

Anwesenheit *f* presence

anwidern ['anviːdərn] *vt* to disgust

Anwohner(in) ['anvoːnər(ın)] (**-s, -**) *m(f)* neighbour

Anzahl ['antsaːl] *f*: **~** (**an** +*dat*) number (of); **a~en** *vt* to pay on account; **~ung** *f* deposit, payment on account

Anzeichen ['antsaıçən] *nt* sign, indication

Anzeige ['antsaıgə] *f* (*Zeitungs~*) announcement; (*Werbung*) advertisement; (*bei Polizei*) report; **~ erstatten gegen jdn** to report sb (to the police); **a~n** *vt* (*zu erkennen geben*) to show; (*bekanntgeben*) to announce; (*bei Polizei*) to report

anziehen ['antsiːən] (*unreg*) *vt* to attract; (*Kleidung*) to put on; (*Mensch*) to dress; (*Seil*) to pull tight; (*Schraube*) to tighten; (*Knie*) to draw up; (*Feuchtigkeit*) to absorb ♦ *vr* to get dressed; **~d** *adj* attractive

Anziehung *f* (*Reiz*) attraction; **~skraft** *f* power of attraction; (*PHYS*) force of gravitation

Anzug ['antsuːk] *m* suit; (*Herankommen*): **im ~ sein** to be approaching

anzüglich ['antsyːklıç] *adj* personal; (*anstößig*) offensive; **A~keit** *f* offensiveness; (*Bemerkung*) personal remark

anzünden ['antsyndən] *vt* to light

Anzünder *m* lighter

anzweifeln ['antsvaıfəln] *vt* to doubt

apathisch [a'paːtıʃ] *adj* apathetic

Apfel ['apfəl] (**-s, ⁿ**) *m* apple; **~saft** *m* apple juice; **~sine** [-'ziːnə] *f* orange

Apostel [a'pɔstəl] (**-s, -**) *m* apostle

Apotheke [apo'teːkə] *f* chemist's (shop), drugstore (*US*); **~r(in)** (**-s, -**) *m(f)* chemist, druggist (*US*)

Apparat [apa'raːt] (**-(e)s, -e**) *m* piece of apparatus; camera; telephone; (*RADIO, TV*) set; **am ~!** speaking!; **~ur** [-'tuːr] *f* apparatus

Appartement [apartə'mãː] (**-s, -s**) *nt* flat

appellieren [apɛ'liːrən] *vi*: **~** (**an** +*akk*) to appeal (to)

Appetit [ape'tiːt] (**-(e)s, -e**) *m* appetite; **guten ~** enjoy your meal; **a~lich** *adj* appetizing; **~losigkeit** *f* lack of appetite

Applaus [ap'laus] (**-es, -e**) *m* applause

Aprikose [apri'koːzə] *f* apricot

April [a'prıl] (**-(s), -e**) *m* April

Aquarell [akva'rɛl] (**-s, -e**) *nt* watercolour

Aquarium [a'kvaːriom] *nt* aquarium

Äquator [ɛ'kvaːtɔr] (**-s**) *m* equator

Arab- ['arab] *zW*: **~er(in)** (**-s, -**) *m(f)* Arab; **~ien** [a'raːbiən] *nt* Arabia; **a~isch** [a'raːbıʃ] *adj* Arabian

Arbeit ['arbaıt] (**-, -en**) *f* work *no art*; (*Stelle*) job; (*Erzeugnis*) piece of work; (*wissenschaftliche*) dissertation; (*Klassen~*) test; **das war eine ~** that was a hard job; **a~en** *vi* to work ♦ *vt* to work, to make; **~er(in)** (**-s, -**) *m(f)* worker; (*ungelernt*) labourer; **~erschaft** *f* workers *pl*, labour force; **~geber** (**-s, -**) *m* employer; **~nehmer** (**-s, -**) *m* employee

Arbeits- *in zW* labour; **arbeitsam** *adj* industrious; **~amt** *nt* employment exchange; **~erlaubnis** *f* work permit; **a~fähig** *adj* fit for work, able-bodied; **~gang** *m* operation; **~kräfte** *pl* (*Mitarbeiter*) workforce; **a~los** *adj* unemployed, out-of-work; **~lose(r)** *f(m)* unemployed person; **~losigkeit** *f* unemployment; **~markt** *m* job market; **~platz** *m* job; place of work; (*Großraumbüro*) workstation; **a~scheu** *adj* work-shy; **~tag** *m* work(ing) day; **a~unfähig** *adj* unfit for work; **~zeit** *f* working hours *pl*

Archäologe [arçɛo'loːgə] (**-n, -n**) *m* archaeologist

Architekt(in) [arçi'tɛkt(ın)] (**-en, -en**) *m(f)* architect; **~ur** [-'tuːr] *f* architecture

Archiv [ar'çiːf] (**-s, -e**) *nt* archive

arg [ark] *adj* bad, awful ♦ *adv* awfully, very

Argentin- [argen'tiːn] *zW*: **~ien** (**-s**) *nt* Argentina, the Argentine; **~ier(in)** (**-s, -**) *m(f)* Argentinian; **a~isch** *adj* Argentinian

Ärger ['ɛrɡər] (-s) *m* (*Wut*) anger; (*Unannehmlichkeit*) trouble; **ä~lich** *adj* (*zornig*) angry; (*lästig*) annoying, aggravating; **ä~n** *vt* to annoy ♦ *vr* to get annoyed

arg- *zW:* **~listig** *adj* cunning, insidious; **~los** *adj* guileless, innocent

Argument [arɡu'mɛnt] *nt* argument

argwöhnisch *adj* suspicious

Arie ['aːriə] *f* aria

Aristokrat [aristo'kraːt] (-en, -en) *m* aristocrat; **~ie** [-'tiː] *f* aristocracy

Arktis ['arktɪs] (-) *f* Arctic

Arm [arm] (-(e)s, -e) *m* arm; (*Fluß~*) branch

arm *adj* poor

Armatur [arma'tuːr] *f* (*ELEK*) armature; **~enbrett** *nt* instrument panel; (*AUT*) dashboard

Armband *nt* bracelet; **~uhr** *f* (wrist) watch

Arme(r) *mf* poor man(woman); **die ~n** the poor

Armee [ar'meː] *f* army

Ärmel ['ɛrməl] (-s, -) *m* sleeve; **etw aus dem ~ schütteln** (*fig*) to produce sth just like that; **~kanal** *m* English Channel

ärmlich ['ɛrmlɪç] *adj* poor

armselig *adj* wretched, miserable

Armut ['armuːt] (-) *f* poverty

Aroma [a'roːma] (-s, Aromen) *nt* aroma; **~therapie** *f* aromatherapy; **a~tisch** [aro'maːtɪʃ] *adj* aromatic

arrangieren [arã'ʒiːrən] *vt* to arrange ♦ *vr* to come to an arrangement

Arrest [a'rɛst] (-(e)s, -e) *m* detention

arrogant [aro'ɡant] *adj* arrogant

Arsch [arʃ] (-es, ᴇ *m* arse (*BRIT!*), ass (*US!*)

Art [aːrt] (-, -en) *f* (*Weise*) way; (*Sorte*) kind, sort; (*BIOL*) species; **eine ~ (von) Frucht** a kind of fruit; **Häuser aller ~** houses of all kinds; **es ist nicht seine ~, das zu tun** it's not like him to do that; **ich mache das auf meine ~** I do that my (own) way

Arterie [ar'teːriə] *f* artery; **~nverkalkung** *f* arteriosclerosis

artig ['aːrtɪç] *adj* good, well-behaved

Artikel [ar'tiːkəl] (-s, -) *m* article

Artillerie [artɪlə'riː] *f* artillery

Artischocke [arti'ʃɔkə] *f* artichoke

Arznei [aːrts'naɪ] *f* medicine; **~mittel** *nt* medicine, medicament

Arzt [aːrtst] (-es, ᴇ) *m* doctor

Ärztin ['ɛːrtstɪn] *f* doctor

ärztlich ['ɛːrtstlɪç] *adj* medical

As [as] (-ses, -se) *nt* ace

Asche ['aʃə] *f* (-, -n) ash, cinder; **~nbahn** *f* cinder track; **~nbecher** *m* ashtray; **~rmittwoch** *m* Ash Wednesday

Äser ['ɛːzər] *pl von* **Aas**

Asi- [a'ziː] *zW:* **~en** (-s) *nt* Asia; **~at(in)** [azi'aːt(ɪn)] (-en, -en) *m(f)* Asian; **a~atisch** [-'aːtɪʃ] *adj* Asian

asozial ['azotsiaːl] *adj* antisocial; (*Familien*) asocial

Aspekt [as'pɛkt] (-(e)s, -e) *m* aspect

Asphalt [as'falt] (-(e)s, -e) *m* asphalt; **a~ieren** [-'tiːrən] *vt* to asphalt

aß *etc* [aːs] *vb siehe* **essen**

Asse ['asə] *pl von* **As**

Assistent(in) [asɪs'tɛnt(ɪn)] *m(f)* assistant

Assoziation [asotsiatsi'oːn] *f* association

Ast [ast] (-(e)s, ᴇ) *m* bough, branch

ästhetisch [ɛs'teːtɪʃ] *adj* aesthetic

Asthma ['astma] (-s) *nt* asthma; **~tiker(in)** [ast'maːtikər(ɪn)] (-s, -) *m(f)* asthmatic

Astro- [astro] *zW:* **~'loge** (-n, -n) *m* astrologer; **~lo'gie** *f* astrology; **~'naut** (-en, -en) *m* astronaut; **~'nom** (-en, -en) *m* astronomer; **~no'mie** *f* astronomy

Asyl [a'zyːl] (-s, -e) *nt* asylum; (*Heim*) home; (*Obdachlosen~*) shelter

Atelier [atəli'eː] (-s, -s) *nt* studio

Atem ['aːtəm] (-s) *m* breath; **den ~ anhalten** to hold one's breath; **außer ~** out of breath; **a~beraubend** *adj* breathtaking; **a~los** *adj* breathless; **~pause** *f* breather; **~zug** *m* breath

Atheismus [ate'ɪsmus] *m* atheism

Atheist *m* atheist; **a~isch** *adj* atheistic

Athen [a'teːn] (-s) *nt* Athens

Äther ['ɛːtər] (-s, -) *m* ether

Äthiopien [ɛti'oːpiən] (-s) *nt* Ethiopia

Athlet [at'leːt] (-en, -en) *m* athlete

Atlantik (-s) *m* Atlantic (Ocean)
atlantisch *adj* Atlantic
Atlas ['atlas] (- *od* -ses, -se *od* **Atlanten**) *m* atlas
atmen ['a:tmən] *vt, vi* to breathe
Atmosphäre [atmo'sfɛːrə] *f* atmosphere
atmosphärisch *adj* atmospheric
Atmung ['a:tmʊŋ] *f* respiration
Atom [a'to:m] (-s, -e) *nt* atom; **a~ar** [ato'ma:r] *adj* atomic; **~bombe** *f* atom bomb; **~energie** *f* atomic *od* nuclear energy; **~kern** *m* atomic nucleus; **~kraftwerk** *nt* nuclear power station; **~krieg** *m* nuclear *od* atomic war; **~müll** *m* atomic waste; **~strom** *m* (electricity generated by) nuclear power; **~versuch** *m* atomic test; **~waffen** *pl* atomic weapons; **a~waffenfrei** *adj* nuclear-free; **~zeitalter** *nt* atomic age
Attentat ['atənta:t] (-(e)s, -e) *nt*: ~ (**auf** +*akk*) (attempted) assassination (of)
Attentäter ['atəntɛːtər] *m* (would-be) assassin
Attest [a'tɛst] (-(e)s, -e) *nt* certificate
Attraktion [atraktsi'o:n] *f* (*Tourismus, Zirkus*) attraction
attraktiv [atrak'ti:f] *adj* attractive
Attrappe [a'trapə] *f* dummy
Attribut [atri'bu:t] (-(e)s, -e) *nt* (*GRAM*) attribute
ätzen ['ɛtsən] *vi* to be caustic
ätzend *adj* (*Säure*) corrosive; (*fig: Spott*) cutting
au [aʊ] *excl* ouch!; ~ **ja!** oh yes!

───── SCHLÜSSELWORT ─────

auch [aʊx] *adv* 1 (*ebenfalls*) also, too, as well; **das ist auch schön** that's nice too *od* as well; **er kommt - ich auch** he's coming - so am I, me too; **auch nicht** not ... either; **ich auch nicht** nor I, me neither; **oder auch** or; **auch das noch!** not that as well!
2 (*selbst, sogar*) even; **auch wenn das Wetter schlecht ist** even if the weather is bad; **ohne auch nur zu fragen** without even asking
3 (*wirklich*) really; **du siehst müde aus - bin ich auch** you look tired - (so) I am;

so sieht es auch aus it looks like it too
4 (*auch immer*): **wer auch** whoever; **was auch** whatever; **wie dem auch sei** be that as it may; **wie sehr er sich auch bemühte** however much he tried

───── SCHLÜSSELWORT ─────

auf [aʊf] *präp* +*dat* (*wo?*) on; **auf dem Tisch** on the table; **auf der Reise** on the way; **auf der Post/dem Fest** at the post office/party; **auf der Straße** on the road; **auf dem Land/der ganzen Welt** in the country/the whole world
♦ *präp* +*akk* (*wohin?*) on(to); **auf den Tisch** on(to) the table; **auf die Post gehen** to go to the post office; **auf das Land** into the country; **etw auf einen Zettel schreiben** to write sth on a piece of paper
2: **auf deutsch** in German; **auf Lebenszeit** for my/his lifetime; **bis auf ihn** except for him; **auf einmal** at once; **auf seinen Vorschlag (hin)** at his suggestion
♦ *adv* 1 (*offen*) open; **das Fenster ist auf** the window is open
2 (*hinauf*) up; **auf und ab** up and down; **auf und davon** up and away; **auf!** (*los!*) come on!
3 (*aufgestanden*) up; **ist er schon auf?** is he up yet?
♦ *konj*: **auf daß** (so) that

aufatmen ['aʊf'a:tmən] *vi* to heave a sigh of relief
aufbahren ['aʊfba:rən] *vt* to lay out
Aufbau ['aʊfbaʊ] *m* (*Bauen*) building, construction; (*Struktur*) structure; (*aufgebautes Teil*) superstructure; **a~en** *vt* to erect, to build (up); (*Existenz*) to make; (*gestalten*) to construct; **a~en (auf** +*dat*) (*gründen*) to found *od* base (on)
aufbauschen ['aʊfbaʊʃən] *vt* to puff out; (*fig*) to exaggerate
aufbekommen ['aʊfbəkɔmən] (*unreg*) *vt* (*öffnen*) to get open; (*Hausaufgaben*) to be given
aufbessern ['aʊfbɛsərn] *vt* (*Gehalt*) to

increase

aufbewahren ['aʊfbəvaːrən] *vt* to keep; (*Gepäck*) to put in the left-luggage office (*BRIT*) *od* baggage check (*US*)

Aufbewahrung *f* (safe)keeping; (*Gepäck~*) left-luggage office (*BRIT*), baggage check (*US*)

aufbieten ['aʊfbiːtən] (*unreg*) *vt* (*Kraft*) to summon (up); (*Armee, Polizei*) to mobilize; (*Brautpaar*) to publish the banns of

aufblasen ['aʊfblaːzən] (*unreg*) *vt* to blow up, to inflate ♦ *vr* (*umg*) to become big-headed

aufbleiben ['aʊfblaɪbən] (*unreg*) *vi* (*Laden*) to remain open; (*Person*) to stay up

aufblenden ['aʊfblɛndən] *vt* (*Scheinwerfer*) to switch on full beam ♦ *vi* (*Fahrer*) to have the lights on full beam; (*AUT: Scheinwerfer*) to be on full beam

aufblicken ['aʊfblɪkən] *vi* to look up; ~ **zu** to look up at; (*fig*) to look up to

aufblühen ['aʊfblyːən] *vi* to blossom, to flourish

aufbrauchen ['aʊfbraʊxən] *vt* to use up

aufbrausen ['aʊfbraʊzən] *vi* (*fig*) to flare up; **~d** *adj* hot-tempered

aufbrechen ['aʊfbrɛçən] (*unreg*) *vt* to break *od* prise (*BRIT*) open ♦ *vi* to burst open; (*gehen*) to start, to set off

aufbringen ['aʊfbrɪŋən] (*unreg*) *vt* (*öffnen*) to open; (*in Mode*) to bring into fashion; (*beschaffen*) to procure; (*FIN*) to raise; (*ärgern*) to irritate; **Verständnis für etw ~** to be able to understand sth

Aufbruch ['aʊfbrʊx] *m* departure

aufbrühen ['aʊfbryːən] *vt* (*Tee*) to make

aufbürden ['aʊfbʏrdən] *vt*: **jdm etw ~** to burden sb with sth

aufdecken ['aʊfdɛkən] *vt* to uncover

aufdrängen ['aʊfdrɛŋən] *vt*: **jdm etw ~** to force sth on sb ♦ *vr* (*Mensch*): **sich jdm ~** to intrude on sb

aufdrehen ['aʊfdreːən] *vt* (*Wasserhahn etc*) to turn on; (*Ventil*) to open up

aufdringlich ['aʊfdrɪŋlɪç] *adj* pushy

aufeinander [aʊf'aɪˈnandər] *adv* on top of each other; (*schießen*) at each other;

(*vertrauen*) each other; **~folgen** *vi* to follow one another; **~folgend** *adj* consecutive; **~prallen** *vi* to hit one another

Aufenthalt ['aʊf'ɛnthalt] *m* stay; (*Verzögerung*) delay; (*EISENB: Halten*) stop; (*Ort*) haunt

Aufenthaltserlaubnis *f* residence permit

auferlegen ['aʊf'ɛrleːgən] *vt*: (*jdm*) ~ to impose (upon sb)

Auferstehung ['aʊf'ɛrʃteːʊŋ] *f* resurrection

aufessen ['aʊf'ɛsən] (*unreg*) *vt* to eat up

auffahr- ['aʊffaːr] *zW*: **~en** (*unreg*) *vi* (*herankommen*) to draw up; (*hochfahren*) to jump up; (*wütend werden*) to flare up; (*in den Himmel*) to ascend ♦ *vt* (*Kanonen, Geschütz*) to bring up; **~en auf** +*akk* (*Auto*) to run *od* crash into; **~end** *adj* hot-tempered; **A~t** *f* (*Hausauffahrt*) drive; (*Autobahnauffahrt*) slip road (*BRIT*), (*freeway*) entrance (*US*); **A~unfall** *m* pile-up

auffallen ['aʊffalən] (*unreg*) *vi* to be noticeable; **jdm ~** to strike sb; **~d** *adj* striking

auffällig ['aʊffɛlɪç] *adj* conspicuous, striking

auffangen ['aʊffaŋən] (*unreg*) *vt* to catch; (*Funkspruch*) to intercept; (*Preise*) to peg

auffassen ['aʊffasən] *vt* to understand, to comprehend; (*auslegen*) to see, to view

Auffassung *f* (*Meinung*) opinion; (*Auslegung*) view, concept; (*auch: Auffassungsgabe*) grasp

auffindbar ['aʊffɪntbaːr] *adj* to be found

auffordern ['aʊffɔrdərn] *vt* (*befehlen*) to call upon, to order; (*bitten*) to ask

Aufforderung *f* (*Befehl*) order; (*Einladung*) invitation

auffrischen ['aʊffrɪʃən] *vt* to freshen up; (*Kenntnisse*) to brush up; (*Erinnerungen*) to reawaken ♦ *vi* (*Wind*) to freshen

aufführen ['aʊffyːrən] *vt* (*THEAT*) to perform; (*in einem Verzeichnis*) to list, to specify ♦ *vr* (*sich benehmen*) to behave

Aufführung *f* (*THEAT*) performance; (*Liste*) specification

Aufgabe ['aʊfgaːbə] *f* task; (*SCH*) exercise; (*Haus~*) homework; (*Verzicht*) giving up; (*von Gepäck*) registration; (*von Post*) posting; (*von Inserat*) insertion

Aufgang ['aʊfgaŋ] *m* ascent; (*Sonnen~*) rise; (*Treppe*) staircase

aufgeben ['aʊfgeːbən] (*unreg*) *vt* (*verzichten*) to give up; (*Paket*) to send, to post; (*Gepäck*) to register; (*Bestellung*) to give; (*Inserat*) to insert; (*Rätsel, Problem*) to set ♦ *vi* to give up

Aufgebot ['aʊfgəboːt] *nt* supply; (*Ehe~*) banns *pl*

aufgedunsen ['aʊfgədʊnzən] *adj* swollen, puffed up

aufgehen ['aʊfgeːən] (*unreg*) *vi* (*Sonne, Teig*) to rise; (*sich öffnen*) to open; (*klarwerden*) to become clear; (*MATH*) to come out exactly; ~ **(in** +*dat*) (*sich widmen*) to be absorbed (in); **in Rauch/ Flammen** ~ to go up in smoke/flames

aufgelegt ['aʊfgəleːkt] *adj*: **gut/schlecht** ~ **sein** to be in a good/bad mood; **zu etw** ~ **sein** to be in the mood for sth

aufgeregt ['aʊfgəreːkt] *adj* excited

aufgeschlossen ['aʊfgəʃlɔsən] *adj* open, open-minded

aufgeweckt ['aʊfgəvɛkt] *adj* bright, intelligent

aufgießen ['aʊfgiːsən] (*unreg*) *vt* (*Wasser*) to pour over; (*Tee*) to infuse

aufgreifen ['aʊfgraɪfən] (*unreg*) *vt* (*Thema*) to take up; (*Verdächtige*) to pick up, to seize

aufgrund [aʊf'grʊnt] *präp* +*gen* on the basis of; (*wegen*) because of

aufhaben ['aʊfhaːbən] (*unreg*) *vt* to have on; (*Arbeit*) to have to do

aufhalsen ['aʊfhalzən] (*umg*) *vt*: **jdm etw** ~ to saddle *od* lumber sb with sth

aufhalten ['aʊfhaltən] (*unreg*) *vt* (*Person*) to detain; (*Entwicklung*) to check; (*Tür, Hand*) to hold open; (*Augen*) to keep open ♦ *vr* (*wohnen*) to live; (*bleiben*) to stay; **sich mit etw** ~ to waste time over sth

aufhängen ['aʊfhɛŋən] (*unreg*) *vt* (*Wäsche*) to hang up; (*Menschen*) to hang ♦ *vr* to hang o.s.

Aufhänger (**-s, -**) *m* (*am Mantel*) loop; (*fig*) peg

aufheben ['aʊfheːbən] (*unreg*) *vt* (*hochheben*) to raise, to lift; (*Sitzung*) to wind up; (*Urteil*) to annul; (*Gesetz*) to repeal, to abolish; (*aufbewahren*) to keep ♦ *vr* to cancel itself out; **bei jdm gut aufgehoben sein** to be well looked after at sb's; **viel A~(s) machen (von)** to make a fuss (about)

aufheitern ['aʊfhaɪtərn] *vt, vr* (*Himmel, Miene*) to brighten; (*Mensch*) to cheer up

aufhellen ['aʊfhɛlən] *vt, vr* to clear up; (*Farbe, Haare*) to lighten

aufhetzen ['aʊfhɛtsən] *vt* to stir up

aufholen ['aʊfhoːlən] *vt* to make up ♦ *vi* to catch up

aufhorchen ['aʊfhɔrçən] *vi* to prick up one's ears

aufhören ['aʊfhøːrən] *vi* to stop; ~, **etw zu tun** to stop doing sth

aufklappen ['aʊfklapən] *vt* to open

aufklären ['aʊfklɛːrən] *vt* (*Geheimnis etc*) to clear up; (*Person*) to enlighten; (*sexuell*) to tell the facts of life to; (*MIL*) to reconnoitre ♦ *vr* to clear up

Aufklärung *f* (*von Geheimnis*) clearing up; (*Unterrichtung, Zeitalter*) enlightenment; (*sexuell*) sex education; (*MIL, AVIAT*) reconnaissance

aufkleben ['aʊfkleːbən] *vt* to stick on

Aufkleber (**-s, -**) *m* sticker

aufknöpfen ['aʊfknœpfən] *vt* to unbutton

aufkommen ['aʊfkɔmən] (*unreg*) *vi* (*Wind*) to come up; (*Zweifel, Gefühl*) to arise; (*Mode*) to start; **für jdn/etw** ~ to be liable *od* responsible for sb/sth

aufladen ['aʊflaːdən] (*unreg*) *vt* to load

Auflage ['aʊflaːgə] *f* (*Zeitung*) circulation; (*Buch*) edition; (*Bedingung*) condition; **jdm etw zur** ~ **machen** to make sth a condition for sb

auflassen ['aʊflasən] (*unreg*) *vt* (*offen*) to leave open; (*aufgesetzt*) to leave on

auflauern ['aʊflaʊərn] *vi*: **jdm** ~ to lie in wait for sb

Auflauf ['aʊflaʊf] *m* (*KOCH*) pudding; (*Menschen~*) crowd

aufleben ['aʊfleːbən] *vi* (*Mensch, Gespräch*) to liven up; (*Interesse*) to revive

auflegen ['aʊfleːgən] *vt* to put on; (*Telefon*) to hang up; (*TYP*) to print
auflehnen ['aʊfleːnən] *vt* to lean on ♦ *vr* to rebel
Auflehnung *f* rebellion
auflesen ['aʊfleːzən] (*unreg*) *vt* to pick up
aufleuchten ['aʊflɔʏçtən] *vi* to light up
auflockern ['aʊflɔkərn] *vt* to loosen; (*fig: Eintönigkeit etc*) to liven up
auflösen ['aʊfløːzən] *vt* to dissolve; (*Haare etc*) to loosen; (*Mißverständnis*) to sort out ♦ *vr* to dissolve; to come undone; to be resolved; **(in Tränen) aufgelöst sein** to be in tears
Auflösung *f* dissolving; (*fig*) solution
aufmachen ['aʊfmaxən] *vt* to open; (*Kleidung*) to undo; (*zurechtmachen*) to do up ♦ *vr* to set out
Aufmachung *f* (*Kleidung*) outfit, get-up; (*Gestaltung*) format
aufmerksam ['aʊfmɛrkzaːm] *adj* attentive; **jdn auf etw** *akk* **~ machen** to point sth out to sb; **A~keit** *f* attention, attentiveness
aufmuntern ['aʊfmʊntərn] *vt* (*ermutigen*) to encourage; (*erheitern*) to cheer up
Aufnahme ['aʊfnaːmə] *f* (*Beginn*) beginning; (*in Verein etc*) admission; (*in Liste etc*) inclusion; (*Notieren*) taking down; (*PHOT*) shot; (*auf Tonband etc*) recording; **a~fähig** *adj* receptive; **~prüfung** *f* entrance test
aufnehmen ['aʊfneːmən] (*unreg*) *vt* to receive; (*hochheben*) to pick up; (*beginnen*) to take up; (*in Verein etc*) to admit; (*in Liste etc*) to include; (*fassen*) to hold; (*notieren*) to take down; (*fotografieren*) to photograph; (*auf Tonband, Platte*) to record; (*FIN: leihen*) to take out; **es mit jdm ~ können** to be able to compete with sb
aufopfern ['aʊf'ɔpfərn] *vt*, *vr* to sacrifice; **~d** *adj* selfless
aufpassen ['aʊfpasən] *vi* (*aufmerksam sein*) to pay attention; **auf jdn/etw ~** to look after *od* watch sb/sth; **aufgepaßt!** look out!
Aufprall ['aʊfpral] (**-s, -e**) *m* impact;

a~en *vi* to hit, to strike
Aufpreis ['aʊfpraɪs] *m* extra charge
aufpumpen ['aʊfpʊmpən] *vt* to pump up
aufräumen ['aʊfrɔʏmən] *vt*, *vi* (*Dinge*) to clear away; (*Zimmer*) to tidy up
aufrecht ['aʊfrɛçt] *adj* (*auch fig*) upright; **~erhalten** (*unreg*) *vt* to maintain
aufreg- ['aʊfreːg] *zW*: **~en** *vt* to excite ♦ *vr* to get excited; **~end** *adj* exciting; **A~ung** *f* excitement
aufreibend ['aʊfraɪbənt] *adj* strenuous
aufreißen ['aʊfraɪsən] (*unreg*) *vt* (*Umschlag*) to tear open; (*Augen*) to open wide; (*Tür*) to throw open; (*Straße*) to take up
aufreizen ['aʊfraɪtsən] *vt* to incite, to stir up; **~d** *adj* exciting, stimulating
aufrichten ['aʊfrɪçtən] *vt* to put up, to erect; (*moralisch*) to console ♦ *vr* to rise; (*moralisch*): **sich ~ (an** +*dat*) to take heart (from)
aufrichtig ['aʊfrɪçtɪç] *adj* sincere, honest; **A~keit** *f* sincerity
aufrücken ['aʊfrʏkən] *vi* to move up; (*beruflich*) to be promoted
Aufruf ['aʊfruːf] *m* summons; (*zur Hilfe*) call; (*des Namens*) calling out; **a~en** (*unreg*) *vt* (*Namen*) to call out; (*auffordern*): **jdn a~en (zu)** to call upon sb (for)
Aufruhr ['aʊfruːr] (**-(e)s, -e**) *m* uprising, revolt
aufrührerisch ['aʊfryːrərɪʃ] *adj* rebellious
aufrunden ['aʊfrʊndən] *vt* (*Summe*) to round up
Aufrüstung ['aʊfrʏstʊŋ] *f* rearmament
aufrütteln ['aʊfrʏtəln] *vt* (*auch fig*) to shake up
aufs [aʊfs] = **auf das**
aufsagen ['aʊfzaːgən] *vt* (*Gedicht*) to recite
aufsammeln ['aʊfzaməln] *vt* to gather up
aufsässig ['aʊfzɛsɪç] *adj* rebellious
Aufsatz ['aʊfzats] *m* (*Geschriebenes*) essay; (*auf Schrank etc*) top
aufsaugen ['aʊfzaʊgən] (*unreg*) *vt* to soak up

aufschauen ['aʊfʃaʊən] *vi* to look up
aufscheuchen ['aʊfʃɔyçən] *vt* to scare *od* frighten away
aufschieben ['aʊfʃiːbən] (*unreg*) *vt* to push open; (*verzögern*) to put off, to postpone
Aufschlag ['aʊfʃlaːk] *m* (*Ärmel~*) cuff; (*Jacken~*) lapel; (*Hosen~*) turn-up; (*Aufprall*) impact; (*Preis~*) surcharge; (*Tennis*) service; **a~en** [-gən] (*unreg*) *vt* (*öffnen*) to open; (*verwunden*) to cut; (*hochschlagen*) to turn up; (*aufbauen: Zelt, Lager*) to pitch, to erect; (*Wohnsitz*) to take up ♦ *vi* (*aufprallen*) to hit; (*teurer werden*) to go up; (*Tennis*) to serve
aufschließen ['aʊfʃliːsən] (*unreg*) *vt* to open up, to unlock ♦ *vi* (*aufrücken*) to close up
Aufschluß ['aʊfʃlʊs] *m* information; **a~reich** *adj* informative, illuminating
aufschnappen ['aʊfʃnapən] *vt* (*umg*) to pick up ♦ *vi* to fly open
aufschneiden ['aʊfʃnaɪdən] (*unreg*) *vt* to cut open; (*Brot*) to cut up; (*MED: Geschwür*) to lance ♦ *vi* to brag
Aufschneider (**-s, -**) *m* boaster, braggart
Aufschnitt ['aʊfʃnɪt] *m* (slices of) cold meat
aufschrauben ['aʊfʃraʊbən] *vt* (*fest~*) to screw on; (*lösen*) to unscrew
aufschrecken ['aʊfʃrɛkən] *vt* to startle ♦ *vi* (*unreg*) to start up
aufschreiben ['aʊfʃraɪbən] (*unreg*) *vt* to write down
aufschreien ['aʊfʃraɪən] (*unreg*) *vi* to cry out
Aufschrift ['aʊfʃrɪft] *f* (*Inschrift*) inscription; (*auf Etikett*) label
Aufschub ['aʊfʃuːp] (**-(e)s, -schübe**) *m* delay, postponement
Aufschwung ['aʊfʃvʊŋ] *m* (*Elan*) boost; (*wirtschaftlich*) upturn, boom; (*SPORT*) circle
Aufsehen ['aʊfzeːən] (**-s**) *nt* sensation, stir
aufsehen (*unreg*) *vi* to look up; **~ zu** to look up at; (*fig*) to look up to
aufsehenerregend *adj* sensational
Aufseher(in) (**-s, -**) *m(f)* guard; (*im*

Betrieb) supervisor; (*Museums~*) attendant; (*Park~*) keeper
aufsein ['aʊfzaɪn] (*unreg; umg*) *vi* (*Tür, Geschäft etc*) to be open; (*Mensch*) to be up
aufsetzen ['aʊfzɛtsən] *vt* to put on; (*Flugzeug*) to put down; (*Dokument*) to draw up ♦ *vr* to sit up(right) ♦ *vi* (*Flugzeug*) to touch down
Aufsicht ['aʊfzɪçt] *f* supervision; **die ~ haben** to be in charge
aufsitzen ['aʊfzɪtsən] (*unreg*) *vi* (*aufrecht hinsitzen*) to sit up; (*aufs Pferd, Motorrad*) to mount, to get on; (*Schiff*) to run aground; **jdm ~** (*umg*) to be taken in by sb
aufsparen ['aʊfʃpaːrən] *vt* to save (up)
aufsperren ['aʊfʃpɛrən] *vt* to unlock; (*Mund*) to open wide
aufspielen ['aʊfʃpiːlən] *vr* to show off
aufspießen ['aʊfʃpiːsən] *vt* to spear
aufspringen ['aʊfʃprɪŋən] (*unreg*) *vi* (*hochspringen*) to jump up; (*sich öffnen*) to spring open; (*Hände, Lippen*) to become chapped; **auf etw** *akk* **~** to jump onto sth
aufspüren ['aʊfʃpyːrən] *vt* to track down, to trace
aufstacheln ['aʊfʃtaxəln] *vt* to incite
Aufstand ['aʊfʃtant] *m* insurrection, rebellion
aufständisch ['aʊfʃtɛndɪʃ] *adj* rebellious, mutinous
aufstecken ['aʊfʃtɛkən] *vt* to stick on, to pin up; (*umg*) to give up
aufstehen ['aʊfʃteːən] (*unreg*) *vi* to get up; (*Tür*) to be open
aufsteigen ['aʊfʃtaɪgən] (*unreg*) *vi* (*hochsteigen*) to climb; (*Rauch*) to rise; **auf etw** *akk* **~** to get onto sth
aufstellen ['aʊfʃtɛlən] *vt* (*aufrecht stellen*) to put up; (*aufreihen*) to line up; (*nominieren*) to nominate; (*formulieren: Programm etc*) to draw up; (*leisten: Rekord*) to set up
Aufstellung *f* (*SPORT*) line-up; (*Liste*) list
Aufstieg ['aʊfʃtiːk] (**-(e)s, -e**) *m* (*auf Berg*) ascent; (*Fortschritt*) rise; (*beruflich, SPORT*) promotion
aufstoßen ['aʊfʃtoːsən] (*unreg*) *vt* to

push open ♦ *vi* to belch
aufstützen ['aʊfʃtʏtsən] *vt* (*Körperteil*) to prop, to lean; (*Person*) to prop up ♦ *vr*: **sich auf etw** *akk* ~ to lean on sth
aufsuchen ['aʊfzuːxən] *vt* (*besuchen*) to visit; (*konsultieren*) to consult
Auftakt ['aʊftakt] *m* (MUS) upbeat; (*fig*) prelude
auftanken ['aʊftaŋkən] *vi* to get petrol (BRIT) *od* gas (US) ♦ *vt* to refuel
auftauchen ['aʊftaʊxən] *vi* to appear; (*aus Wasser etc*) to emerge; (*U-Boot*) to surface; (*Zweifel*) to arise
auftauen ['aʊftaʊən] *vt* to thaw ♦ *vi* to thaw; (*fig*) to relax
aufteilen ['aʊftaɪlən] *vt* to divide up; (*Raum*) to partition
Aufteilung *f* division; partition
Auftrag ['aʊftraːk] **(-(e)s, -träge)** *m* order; (*Anweisung*) commission; (*Aufgabe*) mission; **im ~ von** on behalf of; **a~en** [-gən] (*unreg*) *vt* (*Essen*) to serve; (*Farbe*) to put on; (*Kleidung*) to wear out; **jdm etw a~en** to tell sb sth; **dick a~en** (*fig*) to exaggerate; **~geber (-s, -)** *m* (COMM) purchaser, customer
auftreiben ['aʊftraɪbən] (*unreg*) *vt* (*umg: beschaffen*) to get
auftreten ['aʊftreːtən] (*unreg*) *vt* to kick open ♦ *vi* to appear; (*mit Füßen*) to tread; (*sich verhalten*) to behave; **A~ (-s)** *nt* (*Vorkommen*) appearance; (*Benehmen*) behaviour
Auftrieb ['aʊftriːp] *m* (PHYS) buoyancy, lift; (*fig*) impetus
Auftritt ['aʊftrɪt] *m* (*des Schauspielers*) entrance; (*Szene: auch fig*) scene
auftun ['aʊftuːn] (*unreg*) *vt* to open ♦ *vr* to open up
aufwachen ['aʊfvaxən] *vi* to wake up
aufwachsen ['aʊfvaksən] (*unreg*) *vi* to grow up
Aufwand ['aʊfvant] **(-(e)s)** *m* expenditure; (*Kosten auch*) expense; (*Luxus*) show
aufwärmen ['aʊfvɛrmən] *vt* to warm up; (*alte Geschichten*) to rake up
aufwärts ['aʊfvɛrts] *adv* upwards; **A~entwicklung** *f* upward trend

Aufwasch *m* washing-up
aufwecken ['aʊfvɛkən] *vt* to wake up, to waken up
aufweisen ['aʊfvaɪzən] (*unreg*) *vt* to show
aufwenden ['aʊfvɛndən] (*unreg*) *vt* to expend; (*Geld*) to spend; (*Sorgfalt*) to devote
aufwendig *adj* costly
aufwerfen ['aʊfvɛrfən] (*unreg*) *vt* (*Fenster etc*) to throw open; (*Probleme*) to throw up, to raise
aufwerten ['aʊfveːrtən] *vt* (FIN) to revalue; (*fig*) to raise in value
aufwickeln ['aʊfvɪkəln] *vt* (*aufrollen*) to roll up; (*umg: Haar*) to put in curlers
aufwiegen ['aʊfviːgən] (*unreg*) *vt* to make up for
Aufwind ['aʊfvɪnt] *m* up-current
aufwirbeln ['aʊfvɪrbəln] *vt* to whirl up; **Staub** ~ (*fig*) to create a stir
aufwischen ['aʊfvɪʃən] *vt* to wipe up
aufzählen ['aʊftsɛːlən] *vt* to list
aufzeichnen ['aʊftsaɪçnən] *vt* to sketch; (*schriftlich*) to jot down; (*auf Band*) to record
Aufzeichnung *f* (*schriftlich*) note; (*Tonband~*) recording; (*Film~*) record
aufzeigen ['aʊftsaɪgən] *vt* to show, to demonstrate
aufziehen ['aʊftsiːən] (*unreg*) *vt* (*hochziehen*) to raise, to draw up; (*öffnen*) to pull open; (*Uhr*) to wind; (*umg: necken*) to tease; (*großziehen: Kinder*) to raise, to bring up; (*Tiere*) to rear
Aufzug ['aʊftsuːk] *m* (*Fahrstuhl*) lift, elevator; (*Aufmarsch*) procession, parade; (*Kleidung*) get-up; (THEAT) act
aufzwingen ['aʊftsvɪŋən] (*unreg*) *vt*: **jdm etw** ~ to force sth upon sb
Augapfel *m* eyeball; (*fig*) apple of one's eye
Auge ['aʊgə] **(-s, -n)** *nt* eye; (*Fett~*) globule of fat; **unter vier ~n** in private
Augen- *zW*: **~blick** *m* moment; **im ~blick** at the moment; **a~blicklich** *adj* (*sofort*) instantaneous; (*gegenwärtig*) present; **~braue** *f* eyebrow; **~weide** *f* sight for sore eyes; **~zeuge** *m* eye

witness
August [aʊ'gʊst] (-(e)s *od* -, -e) *m* August
Auktion [aʊktsi'o:n] *f* auction
Aula ['aʊla] (-, **Aulen** *od* -s) *f* assembly
hall

SCHLÜSSELWORT
---

aus [aʊs] *präp +dat* 1 (*räumlich*) out of;
(*von ... her*) from; **er ist aus Berlin** he's
from Berlin; **aus dem Fenster** out of the
window
2 (*gemacht/hergestellt aus*) made of; **ein
Herz aus Stein** a heart of stone
3 (*auf Ursache deutend*) out of; **aus
Mitleid** out of sympathy; **aus Erfahrung**
from experience; **aus Spaß** for fun
4: **aus ihr~wird nie etwas** she'll never
get anywhere
♦ *adv* 1 (*zu Ende*) finished, over; **aus und
vorbei** over and done with
2 (*ausgeschaltet, ausgezogen*) out;
(*Aufschrift an Geräten*) off; **Licht aus!**
lights out!
3 (*in Verbindung mit von*): **von Rom aus**
from Rome; **vom Fenster aus** out of the
window; **von sich aus** (*selbständig*) of
one's own accord; **von ihm aus** as far as
he's concerned

ausarbeiten ['aʊsʔarbaɪtən] *vt* to work
out
ausarten ['aʊsʔartən] *vi* to degenerate;
(*Kind*) to become overexcited
ausatmen ['aʊsʔa:tmən] *vi* to breathe out
ausbaden ['aʊsba:dən] (*umg*) *vt*: **etw ~
müssen** to carry the can for sth
Ausbau ['aʊsbaʊ] *m* extension,
expansion; removal; **a~en** *vt* to extend, to
expand; (*herausnehmen*) to take out, to
remove; **a~fähig** *adj* (*fig*) worth
developing
ausbessern ['aʊsbɛsərn] *vt* to mend, to
repair
ausbeulen ['aʊsbɔʏlən] *vt* to beat out
Ausbeute ['aʊsbɔʏtə] *f* yield; (*Fische*)
catch; **a~n** *vt* to exploit; (*MIN*) to work
ausbild- ['aʊsbɪld-] *zW*: **~en** *vt* to
educate; (*Lehrling, Soldat*) to instruct, to
train; (*Fähigkeiten*) to develop;

(*Geschmack*) to cultivate; **A~er (-s, -)** *m*
instructor; **A~ung** *f* education; training,
instruction; development; cultivation
ausbleiben ['aʊsblaɪbən] (*unreg*) *vi*
(*Personen*) to stay away, not to come;
(*Ereignisse*) to fail to happen, not to
happen
Ausblick ['aʊsblɪk] *m* (*auch fig*) prospect
(*lit, fig*), outlook, view
ausbrechen ['aʊsbrɛçən] (*unreg*) *vi* to
break out ♦ *vt* to break off; **in Tränen/
Gelächter ~** to burst into tears/out
laughing
ausbreiten ['aʊsbraɪtən] *vt* to spread
(out); (*Arme*) to stretch out ♦ *vr* to
spread; **sich über ein Thema ~** to
expand *od* enlarge on a topic
ausbrennen ['aʊsbrɛnən] (*unreg*) *vt* to
scorch; (*Wunde*) to cauterize ♦ *vi* to burn
out
Ausbruch ['aʊsbrʊx] *m* outbreak; (*von
Vulkan*) eruption; (*Gefühls~*) outburst;
(*von Gefangenen*) escape
ausbrüten ['aʊsbry:tən] *vt* (*auch fig*) to
hatch
Ausdauer ['aʊsdaʊər] *f* perseverance,
stamina; **a~nd** *adj* persevering
ausdehnen ['aʊsde:nən] *vt, vr* (*räumlich*)
to expand; (*zeitlich, auch Gummi*) to
stretch; (*Nebel, fig: Macht*) to extend
ausdenken ['aʊsdɛŋkən] (*unreg*) *vt*: **sich
dat etw ~** to think sth up
Ausdruck ['aʊsdrʊk] *m* expression,
phrase; (*Kundgabe, Gesichts~*) expression;
(*COMPUT*) print-out, hard copy; **a~en** *vt*
(*COMPUT*) to print out
ausdrücken ['aʊsdrʏkən] *vt* (*auch vr:
formulieren, zeigen*) to express; (*Zigarette*)
to put out; (*Zitrone*) to squeeze
ausdrücklich *adj* express, explicit
ausdrucks- *zW*: **~los** *adj* expressionless,
blank; **~voll** *adj* expressive; **A~weise** *f*
mode of expression
auseinander [aʊsʔaɪ'nandər] *adv*
(*getrennt*) apart; **~ schreiben** *vt* to write as
separate words; **~bringen** (*unreg*) *vt* to
separate; **~fallen** (*unreg*) *vi* to fall apart;
~gehen (*unreg*) *vi* (*Menschen*) to
separate; (*Meinungen*) to differ;

(*Gegenstand*) to fall apart; (*umg: dick werden*) to put on weight; **~halten** (*unreg*) *vt* to tell apart; **~nehmen** (*unreg*) *vt* to take to pieces, to dismantle; **~setzen** *vt* (*erklären*) to set forth, to explain ♦ *vr* (*sich verständigen*) to come to terms, to settle; (*sich befassen*) to concern o.s.; **A~setzung** *f* argument

ausfahren ['aʊsfaːrən] (*unreg*) *vt* (*spazierfahren: im Auto*) to take for a drive; (*: im Kinderwagen*) to take for a walk; (*liefern*) to deliver

Ausfahrt ['aʊsfaːrt] *f* (*des Zuges etc*) leaving, departure; (*Autobahn~*) exit; (*Garagen~ etc*) exit, way out; (*Spazierfahrt*) drive, excursion

Ausfall ['aʊsfal] *m* loss; (*Nichtstattfinden*) cancellation; (*MIL*) sortie; (*Fechten*) lunge; (*radioaktiv*) fall-out; **a~en** (*unreg*) *vi* (*Zähne, Haare*) to fall *od* come out; (*nicht stattfinden*) to be cancelled; (*wegbleiben*) to be omitted; (*Person*) to drop out; (*Lohn*) to be stopped; (*nicht funktionieren*) to break down; (*Resultat haben*) to turn out; **~straße** *f* arterial road

ausfertigen ['aʊsfɛrtɪɡən] *vt* (*förmlich: Urkunde, Paß*) to draw up; (*Rechnung*) to make out

Ausfertigung ['aʊsfɛrtɪɡʊŋ] *f* drawing up; making out; (*Exemplar*) copy

ausfindig ['aʊsfɪndɪç] *adj*: **~ machen** to discover

ausfließen ['aʊsfliːsən] (*unreg*) *vt* (*herausfließen*): **~ (aus)** to flow out (of); (*auslaufen: Öl etc*): **~ (aus)** to leak (out of)

Ausflucht ['aʊsflʊxt] (*-, -flüchte*) *f* excuse

Ausflug ['aʊsfluːk] *m* excursion, outing

Ausflügler ['aʊsflyːklər] (*-s, -*) *m* tripper

Ausfluß ['aʊsflʊs] *m* outlet; (*MED*) discharge

ausfragen ['aʊsfraːɡən] *vt* to interrogate, to question

ausfressen ['aʊsfrɛsən] (*unreg*) *vt* to eat up; (*aushöhlen*) to corrode; (*umg: anstellen*) to be up to

Ausfuhr ['aʊsfuːr] (*-, -en*) *f* export, exportation ♦ *in zW* export

ausführ- ['aʊsfyːr] *zW*: **~en** *vt*

(*verwirklichen*) to carry out; (*Person*) to take out; (*Hund*) to take for a walk; (*COMM*) to export; (*erklären*) to give details of; **~lich** *adj* detailed ♦ *adv* in detail; **A~lichkeit** *f* detail; **A~ung** *f* execution, performance; (*Durchführung*) completion; (*Herstellungsart*) version; (*Erklärung*) explanation

ausfüllen ['aʊsfʏlən] *vt* to fill up; (*Fragebogen etc*) to fill in; (*Beruf*) to be fulfilling for

Ausgabe ['aʊsɡaːbə] *f* (*Geld*) expenditure, outlay; (*Aushändigung*) giving out; (*Gepäck~*) left-luggage office; (*Buch*) edition; (*Nummer*) issue; (*COMPUT*) output

Ausgang ['aʊsɡaŋ] *m* way out, exit; (*Ende*) end; (*Ausgangspunkt*) starting point; (*Ergebnis*) result; (*Ausgehtag*) free time, time off; **kein ~** no exit

Ausgangspunkt *m* starting point

Ausgangssperre *f* curfew

ausgeben ['aʊsɡeːbən] (*unreg*) *vt* (*Geld*) to spend; (*austeilen*) to issue, to distribute ♦ *vr*: **sich für etw/jdn ~** to pass o.s. off as sth/sb

ausgebucht ['aʊsɡəbuːxt] *adj* (*Vorstellung, Flug, Maschine*) fully booked

ausgedient ['aʊsɡədiːnt] *adj* (*Soldat*) discharged; (*verbraucht*) no longer in use; **~ haben** to have done good service

ausgefallen ['aʊsɡəfalən] *adj* (*ungewöhnlich*) exceptional

ausgeglichen ['aʊsɡəɡlɪçən] *adj* (well-) balanced; **A~heit** *f* balance; (*von Mensch*) even-temperedness

ausgehen ['aʊsɡeːən] (*unreg*) *vi* to go out; (*zu Ende gehen*) to come to an end; (*Benzin*) to run out; (*Haare, Zähne*) to fall *od* come out; (*Feuer, Ofen, Licht*) to go out; (*Strom*) to go off; (*Resultat haben*) to turn out; **mir ging das Benzin aus** I ran out of petrol (*BRIT*) *od* gas (*US*); **auf etw** *akk* **~** to aim at sth; **von etw ~** (*wegführen*) to lead away from sth; (*herrühren*) to come from sth; (*zugrunde legen*) to proceed from sth; **wir können davon ~, daß ...** we can take as our starting point that ...; **leer ~** to get nothing; **schlecht ~** to turn out badly

Ausgehverbot *nt* curfew

ausgelassen ['aʊsɡəlasən] *adj* boisterous, high-spirited

ausgelastet ['aʊsɡəlastət] *adj* fully occupied

ausgelernt ['aʊsɡəlɛrnt] *adj* trained, qualified

ausgemacht ['aʊsɡəmaxt] *adj* settled; (*umg: Dummkopf etc*) out-and-out, downright; **es war eine ~e Sache, daß ...** it was a foregone conclusion that ...

ausgenommen ['aʊsɡənɔmən] *präp* +*gen* except ♦ *konj* except; **Anwesende sind ~** present company excepted

ausgeprägt ['aʊsɡəprɛ:kt] *adj* distinct

ausgerechnet ['aʊsɡərɛçnət] *adv* just, precisely; **~ du/heute** you of all people/ today of all days

ausgeschlossen ['aʊsɡəʃlɔsən] *adj* (*unmöglich*) impossible, out of the question

ausgeschnitten ['aʊsɡəʃnɪtən] *adj* (*Kleid*) low-necked

ausgesprochen ['aʊsɡəʃprɔxən] *adj* (*Faulheit, Lüge etc*) out-and-out; (*unverkennbar*) marked ♦ *adv* decidedly

ausgezeichnet ['aʊsɡətsaɪçnət] *adj* excellent

ausgiebig ['aʊsɡi:bɪç] *adj* (*Gebrauch*) thorough, good; (*Essen*) generous, lavish; **~ schlafen** to have a good sleep

Ausgleich ['aʊsɡlaɪç] **(-(e)s, -e)** *m* balance; (*Vermittlung*) reconciliation; (*SPORT*) equalization; **zum ~ einer Sache** *gen* in order to offset sth; **a~en** (*unreg*) *vt* to balance (out); to reconcile; (*Höhe*) to even up ♦ *vi* (*SPORT*) to equalize

ausgraben ['aʊsɡra:bən] (*unreg*) *vt* to dig up; (*Leichen*) to exhume; (*fig*) to unearth

Ausgrabung *f* excavation; (*Ausgraben auch*) digging up

Ausguß ['aʊsɡʊs] *m* (*Spüle*) sink; (*Abfluß*) outlet; (*Tülle*) spout

aushalten ['aʊshaltən] (*unreg*) *vt* to bear, to stand; (*Geliebte*) to keep ♦ *vi* to hold out; **das ist nicht zum A~** that is unbearable

aushandeln ['aʊshandəln] *vt* to negotiate

aushändigen ['aʊshɛndɪɡən] *vt*: **jdm etw ~** to hand sth over to sb

Aushang ['aʊshaŋ] *m* notice

aushängen ['aʊshɛŋən] (*unreg*) *vt* (*Meldung*) to put up; (*Fenster*) to take off its hinges ♦ *vi* to be displayed ♦ *vr* to hang out

ausharren ['aʊsharən] *vi* to hold out

ausheben ['aʊshe:bən] (*unreg*) *vt* (*Erde*) to lift out; (*Grube*) to hollow out; (*Tür*) to take off its hinges; (*Diebesnest*) to clear out; (*MIL*) to enlist

aushecken ['aʊshɛkən] (*umg*) *vt* to cook up

aushelfen ['aʊshɛlfən] (*unreg*) *vi*: **jdm ~** to help sb out

Aushilfe ['aʊshɪlfə] *f* help, assistance; (*Person*) (temporary) worker

Aushilfskraft *f* temporary worker

aushilfsweise *adv* temporarily, as a stopgap

ausholen ['aʊsho:lən] *vi* to swing one's arm back; (*zur Ohrfeige*) to raise one's hand; (*beim Gehen*) to take long strides; **weit ~** (*fig*) to be expansive

aushorchen ['aʊshɔrçən] *vt* to sound out, to pump

aushungern ['aʊshʊŋərn] *vt* to starve out

auskennen ['aʊskɛnən] (*unreg*) *vr* to know a lot; (*an einem Ort*) to know one's way about; (*in Fragen etc*) to be knowledgeable

Ausklang ['aʊsklaŋ] *m* end

auskleiden ['aʊsklaɪdən] *vr* to undress ♦ *vt* (*Wand*) to line

ausklingen ['aʊsklɪŋən] (*unreg*) *vi* (*Ton, Lied*) to die away; (*Fest*) to peter out

ausklopfen ['aʊsklɔpfən] *vt* (*Teppich*) to beat; (*Pfeife*) to knock out

auskochen ['aʊskɔxən] *vt* to boil; (*MED*) to sterilize; **ausgekocht** (*fig*) out-and-out

Auskommen ['aʊskɔmən] **(-s)** *nt*: **sein ~ haben** to have a regular income; **a~** (*unreg*) *vi*: **mit jdm a~** to get on with sb; **mit etw a~** to get by with sth

auskosten ['aʊskɔstən] *vt* to enjoy to the full

auskundschaften ['aʊskʊntʃaftən] *vt* to

spy out; (*Gebiet*) to reconnoitre

Auskunft ['aʊskʊnft] (-, **-künfte**) *f*
information; (*nähere*) details *pl*,
particulars *pl*; (*Stelle*) information office;
(*TEL*) directory inquiries *sg*

auslachen ['aʊslaxən] *vt* to laugh at, to
mock

ausladen ['aʊslaːdən] (*unreg*) *vt* to
unload; (*umg: Gäste*) to cancel an
invitation to

Auslage ['aʊslaːgə] *f* shop window
(display); **~n** *pl* (*Ausgabe*) outlay *sg*

Ausland ['aʊslant] *nt* foreign countries
pl; **im ~** abroad; **ins ~** abroad

Ausländer(in) ['aʊslɛndər(ɪn)] (-s, -) *m(f)*
foreigner

ausländisch *adj* foreign

Auslandsgespräch *nt* international call

Auslandsreise *f* trip abroad

auslassen ['aʊslasən] (*unreg*) *vt* to leave
out; (*Wort etc auch*) to omit; (*Fett*) to melt;
(*Kleidungsstück*) to let out ♦ *vr*: **sich über
etw** *akk* **~** to speak one's mind about sth;
seine Wut *etc* **an jdm ~** to vent one's
rage *etc* on sb

Auslassung *f* omission

Auslauf ['aʊslaʊf] *m* (*für Tiere*) run;
(*Ausfluß*) outflow, outlet; **a~en** (*unreg*) *vi*
to run out; (*Behälter*) to leak; (*NAUT*) to
put out (to sea); (*langsam aufhören*) to
run down

Ausläufer ['aʊslɔʏfər] *m* (*von Gebirge*)
spur; (*Pflanze*) runner; (*MET: von Hoch*)
ridge; (: *von Tief*) trough

ausleeren ['aʊsleːrən] *vt* to empty

auslegen ['aʊsleːgən] *vt* (*Waren*) to lay
out; (*Köder*) to put down; (*Geld*) to lend;
(*bedecken*) to cover; (*Text etc*) to interpret

Auslegung *f* interpretation

ausleiern ['aʊslaɪərn] *vi* (*Gummi*) to wear
out

Ausleihe ['aʊslaɪə] *f* issuing; (*Stelle*) issue
desk; **a~n** (*unreg*) *vt* (*verleihen*) to lend;
sich *dat* **etw a~n** to borrow sth

Auslese ['aʊsleːzə] *f* selection; (*Elite*)
elite; (*Wein*) choice wine; **a~n** (*unreg*) *vt*
to select; (*umg: zu Ende lesen*) to finish

ausliefern ['aʊsliːfərn] *vt* to deliver (up),
to hand over; (*COMM*) to deliver; **jdm/etw**

ausgeliefert sein to be at the mercy of
sb/sth

auslöschen ['aʊslœʃən] *vt* to extinguish;
(*fig*) to wipe out, to obliterate

auslosen ['aʊsloːzən] *vt* to draw lots for

auslösen ['aʊsløːzən] *vt* (*Explosion,
Schuß*) to set off; (*hervorrufen*) to cause,
to produce; (*Gefangene*) to ransom;
(*Pfand*) to redeem

Auslöser (-s, -) *m* (*PHOT*) release

ausmachen ['aʊsmaxən] *vt* (*Licht, Radio*)
to turn off; (*Feuer*) to put out; (*entdecken*)
to make out; (*vereinbaren*) to agree;
(*beilegen*) to settle; (*Anteil darstellen,
betragen*) to represent; (*bedeuten*) to
matter; **macht es Ihnen etwas aus,
wenn ...?** would you mind if ...?

ausmalen ['aʊsmaːlən] *vt* to paint; (*fig*)
to describe; **sich** *dat* **etw ~** to imagine
sth

Ausmaß ['aʊsmaːs] *nt* dimension; (*fig
auch*) scale

ausmessen ['aʊsmɛsən] (*unreg*) *vt* to
measure

Ausnahme ['aʊsnaːmə] *f* exception; **~fall**
m exceptional case; **~zustand** *m* state of
emergency

ausnahmslos *adv* without exception

ausnahmsweise *adv* by way of
exception, for once

ausnehmen ['aʊsneːmən] (*unreg*) *vt* to
take out, to remove; (*Tier*) to gut; (*Nest*)
to rob; (*umg: Geld abnehmen*) to clean
out; (*ausschließen*) to make an exception
of ♦ *vr* to look, to appear; **~d** *adj*
exceptional

ausnützen ['aʊsnʏtsən] *vt* (*Zeit,
Gelegenheit*) to use, to turn to good
account; (*Einfluß*) to use; (*Mensch,
Gutmütigkeit*) to exploit

auspacken ['aʊspakən] *vt* to unpack

auspfeifen ['aʊspfaɪfən] (*unreg*) *vt* to
hiss/boo at

ausplaudern ['aʊsplaʊdərn] *vt*
(*Geheimnis*) to blab

ausprobieren ['aʊsprobiːrən] *vt* to try
(out)

Auspuff ['aʊspʊf] (-(e)s, -e) *m* (*TECH*)
exhaust; **~rohr** *nt* exhaust (pipe); **~topf**

m (*AUT*) silencer

ausradieren ['aʊsradiːrən] *vt* to erase, to rub out; (*fig*) to annihilate

ausrangieren ['aʊsrãʒiːrən] (*umg*) *vt* to chuck out

ausrauben ['aʊsraʊbən] *vt* to rob

ausräumen ['aʊsrɔʏmən] *vt* (*Dinge*) to clear away; (*Schrank, Zimmer*) to empty; (*Bedenken*) to dispel

ausrechnen ['aʊsrɛçnən] *vt* to calculate, to reckon

Ausrede ['aʊsreːdə] *f* excuse; **a~n** *vi* to have one's say ♦ *vt*: **jdm etw a~n** to talk sb out of sth

ausreichen ['aʊsraɪçən] *vi* to suffice, to be enough; **~d** *adj* sufficient, adequate; (*SCH*) adequate

Ausreise ['aʊsraɪzə] *f* departure; **bei der ~** when leaving the country; **~erlaubnis** *f* exit visa; **a~n** *vi* to leave the country

ausreißen ['aʊsraɪsən] (*unreg*) *vt* to tear *od* pull out ♦ *vi* (*Riß bekommen*) to tear; (*umg*) to make off, to scram

ausrenken ['aʊsrɛŋkən] *vt* to dislocate

ausrichten ['aʊsrɪçtən] *vt* (*Botschaft*) to deliver; (*Gruß*) to pass on; (*Hochzeit etc*) to arrange; (*in gerade Linie bringen*) to get in a straight line; (*angleichen*) to bring into line; (*TYP*) to justify; **ich werde es ihm ~** I'll tell him; **etwas/nichts bei jdm ~** to get somewhere/nowhere with sb

ausrotten ['aʊsrɔtən] *vt* to stamp out, to exterminate

ausrücken ['aʊsrʏkən] *vi* (*MIL*) to move off; (*Feuerwehr, Polizei*) to be called out; (*umg: weglaufen*) to run away

Ausruf ['aʊsruːf] *m* (*Schrei*) cry, exclamation; (*Bekanntmachung*) proclamation; **a~en** (*unreg*) *vt* to cry out, to exclaim; to call out; **~ezeichen** *nt* exclamation mark

ausruhen ['aʊsruːən] *vt, vr* to rest

ausrüsten ['aʊsrʏstən] *vt* to equip, to fit out

Ausrüstung *f* equipment

ausrutschen ['aʊsrʊtʃən] *vi* to slip

Aussage ['aʊszaːgə] *f* (*JUR*) statement; **a~n** *vt* to say, to state ♦ *vi* (*JUR*) to give evidence

ausschalten ['aʊsʃaltən] *vt* to switch off; (*fig*) to eliminate

Ausschank ['aʊsʃaŋk] (-(e)s, -schänke) *m* dispensing, giving out; (*COMM*) selling; (*Theke*) bar

Ausschau ['aʊsʃaʊ] *f*: **~ halten (nach)** to look out (for), to watch (for); **a~en** *vi*: **a~en (nach)** to look out (for), to be on the look-out (for)

ausscheiden ['aʊsʃaɪdən] (*unreg*) *vt* to take out; (*MED*) to secrete ♦ *vi*: **~ (aus)** to leave; (*SPORT*) to be eliminated (from) *od* knocked out (of)

Ausscheidung *f* separation; secretion; elimination; (*aus Amt*) retirement

ausschenken ['aʊsʃɛŋkən] *vt* (*Alkohol, Kaffee*) to pour out; (*COMM*) to sell

ausschildern ['aʊsʃɪldərn] *vt* to signpost

ausschimpfen ['aʊsʃɪmpfən] *vt* to scold, to tell off

ausschlafen ['aʊsʃlaːfən] (*unreg*) *vi, vr* to have a good sleep ♦ *vt* to sleep off; **ich bin nicht ausgeschlafen** I didn't have *od* get enough sleep

Ausschlag ['aʊsʃlaːk] *m* (*MED*) rash; (*Pendel~*) swing; (*Nadel~*) deflection; **den ~ geben** (*fig*) to tip the balance; **a~en** [-gən] (*unreg*) *vt* to knock out; (*auskleiden*) to deck out; (*verweigern*) to decline ♦ *vi* (*Pferd*) to kick out; (*BOT*) to sprout; **a~gebend** *adj* decisive

ausschließen ['aʊsʃliːsən] (*unreg*) *vt* to shut *od* lock out; (*fig*) to exclude

ausschließlich *adj* exclusive ♦ *adv* exclusively ♦ *präp +gen* exclusive of, excluding

Ausschluß ['aʊsʃlʊs] *m* exclusion

ausschmücken ['aʊsʃmʏkən] *vt* to decorate; (*fig*) to embellish

ausschneiden ['aʊsʃnaɪdən] (*unreg*) *vt* to cut out; (*Büsche*) to trim

Ausschnitt ['aʊsʃnɪt] *m* (*Teil*) section; (*von Kleid*) neckline; (*Zeitungs~*) cutting; (*aus Film etc*) excerpt

ausschreiben ['aʊsʃraɪbən] (*unreg*) *vt* (*ganz schreiben*) to write out (in full); (*ausstellen*) to write (out); (*Stelle, Wettbewerb etc*) to announce, to advertise

Ausschreitung ['aʊsʃraɪtʊŋ] *f* (*gew pl*)

riot

Ausschuß ['aʊsʃʊs] m committee, board; (*Abfall*) waste, scraps pl; (COMM: *auch*: ~*ware*) reject

ausschütten ['aʊsʃʏtən] vt to pour out; (*Eimer*) to empty; (*Geld*) to pay ♦ vr to shake (with laughter)

ausschweifend ['aʊsʃvaɪfənt] adj (*Leben*) dissipated, debauched; (*Phantasie*) extravagant

aussehen ['aʊszeːən] (*unreg*) vi to look; **es sieht nach Regen aus** it looks like rain; **es sieht schlecht aus** things look bad; **A~ (-s)** nt appearance

aussein ['aʊszaɪn] (*unreg, umg*) vi (*zu Ende sein*) to be over; (*nicht zu Hause sein*) to be out; (*nicht brennen*) to be out; (*abgeschaltet sein: Radio, Herd*) to be off

außen ['aʊsən] adv outside; (*nach ~*) outwards; ~ **ist es rot** it's red (on the) outside

Außen- zW: ~**bordmotor** m outboard motor; ~**dienst** m: **im ~dienst sein** to work outside the office; ~**handel** m foreign trade; ~**minister** m foreign minister; ~**ministerium** nt foreign office; ~**politik** f foreign policy; **a~politisch** adj (*Entwicklung, Lage*) foreign; ~**seite** f outside; ~**seiter (-s, -)** m outsider; ~**stehende(r)** mf outsider; ~**welt** f outside world

außer ['aʊsər] präp +dat (*räumlich*) out of; (*abgesehen von*) except ♦ konj (*ausgenommen*) except; ~ **Gefahr** out of danger; ~ **Zweifel** beyond any doubt; ~ **Betrieb** out of order; ~ **Dienst** retired; ~ **Landes** abroad; ~ **sich** dat **sein** to be beside o.s.; ~ **sich** akk **geraten** to go wild; ~ **wenn** unless; ~ **daß** except; ~**dem** konj besides, in addition

äußere(r, s) ['ɔʏsərə(r, s)] adj outer, external

außergewöhnlich adj unusual

außerhalb präp +gen outside ♦ adv outside

äußerlich adj external

äußern vt to utter, to express; (*zeigen*) to show ♦ vr to give one's opinion; (*Krankheit etc*) to show itself

außerordentlich adj extraordinary

außerplanmäßig adj unscheduled

äußerst ['ɔʏsərst] adv extremely, most; ~**e(r, s)** adj utmost; (*räumlich*) farthest; (*Termin*) last possible; (*Preis*) highest

Äußerung f remark, comment

aussetzen ['aʊszɛtsən] vt (*Kind, Tier*) to abandon; (*Boote*) to lower; (*Belohnung*) to offer; (*Urteil, Verfahren*) to postpone ♦ vi (*aufhören*) to stop; (*Pause machen*) to have a break; **jdm/etw ausgesetzt sein** to be exposed to sb/sth; **an jdm/etw etwas ~** to find fault with sb/sth

Aussicht ['aʊszɪçt] f view; (*in Zukunft*) prospect; **etw in ~ haben** to have sth in view

Aussichts- zW: **a~los** adj hopeless; ~**punkt** m viewpoint; **a~reich** adj promising; ~**turm** m observation tower

aussöhnen ['aʊszøːnən] vt to reconcile ♦ vr to reconcile o.s., to become reconciled

aussondern ['aʊszɔndərn] vt to separate, to select

aussortieren ['aʊszɔrtiːrən] vt to sort out

ausspannen ['aʊsʃpanən] vt to spread od stretch out; (*Pferd*) to unharness; (*umg*: *Mädchen*) **(jdm) jdn ~** to steal sb (from sb) ♦ vi to relax

aussperren ['aʊsʃpɛrən] vt to lock out

ausspielen ['aʊsʃpiːlən] vt (*Karte*) to lead; (*Geldprämie*) to offer as a prize ♦ vi (KARTEN) to lead; **jdn gegen jdn ~** to play sb off against sb; **ausgespielt haben** to be finished

Aussprache ['aʊsʃpraːxə] f pronunciation; (*Unterredung*) (frank) discussion

aussprechen ['aʊsʃprɛçən] (*unreg*) vt to pronounce; (*äußern*) to say, to express ♦ vr (*sich äußern*) **sich ~ (über** +akk**)** to speak (about); (*sich anvertrauen*) to unburden o.s. (about od on); (*diskutieren*) to discuss ♦ vi (*zu Ende sprechen*) to finish speaking

Ausspruch ['aʊsʃprʊx] m saying, remark

ausspülen ['aʊsʃpyːlən] vt to wash out; (*Mund*) to rinse

Ausstand ['aʊsʃtant] m strike; **in den ~ treten** to go on strike
ausstatten ['aʊsʃtatən] vt (Zimmer etc) to furnish; (Person) to equip, to kit out
Ausstattung f (Ausstatten) provision; (Kleidung) outfit; (Aussteuer) dowry; (Aufmachung) make-up; (Einrichtung) furnishing
ausstechen ['aʊsʃtɛçən] (unreg) vt (Augen, Rasen, Graben) to dig out; (Kekse) to cut out; (übertreffen) to outshine
ausstehen ['aʊsʃteːən] (unreg) vt to stand, to endure ♦ vi (noch nicht dasein) to be outstanding
aussteigen ['aʊsʃtaɪgən] (unreg) vi to get out, to alight
ausstellen ['aʊsʃtɛlən] vt to exhibit, to display; (umg: ausschalten) to switch off; (Rechnung etc) to make out; (Paß, Zeugnis) to issue
Ausstellung f exhibition; (FIN) drawing up; (einer Rechnung) making out; (eines Passes etc) issuing
aussterben ['aʊsʃtɛrbən] (unreg) vi to die out
Aussteuer ['aʊsʃtɔʏər] f dowry
Ausstieg ['aʊsʃtiːk] (-(e)s, -e) m exit
ausstopfen ['aʊsʃtɔpfən] vt to stuff
ausstoßen ['aʊsʃtoːsən] (unreg) vt (Luft, Rauch) to give off, to emit; (aus Verein etc) to expel, to exclude; (Auge) to poke out
ausstrahlen ['aʊsʃtraːlən] vt, vi to radiate; (RADIO) to broadcast
Ausstrahlung f radiation; (fig) charisma
ausstrecken ['aʊsʃtrɛkən] vt, vr to stretch out
ausstreichen ['aʊsʃtraɪçən] (unreg) vt to cross out; (glätten) to smooth (out)
ausströmen ['aʊsʃtrøːmən] vi (Gas) to pour out, to escape ♦ vt to give off; (fig) to radiate
aussuchen ['aʊszuːxən] vt to select, to pick out
Austausch ['aʊstaʊʃ] m exchange; **a~bar** adj exchangeable; **a~en** vt to exchange, to swap; **~motor** m reconditioned engine
austeilen ['aʊstaɪlən] vt to distribute, to give out

Auster ['aʊstər] (-, -n) f oyster
austoben ['aʊstoːbən] vr (Kind) to run wild; (Erwachsene) to sow one's wild oats
austragen ['aʊstraːgən] (unreg) vt (Post) to deliver; (Streit etc) to decide; (Wettkämpfe) to hold
Australien [aʊsˈtraːliən] (-s) nt Australia
Australier(in) (-s, -) m(f) Australian
australisch adj Australian
austreiben ['aʊstraɪbən] (unreg) vt to drive out, to expel; (Geister) to exorcize
austreten ['aʊstreːtən] (unreg) vi (zur Toilette) to be excused ♦ vt (Feuer) to tread out, to trample; (Schuhe) to wear out; (Treppe) to wear down; **aus etw ~** to leave sth
austrinken ['aʊstrɪŋkən] (unreg) vt (Glas) to drain; (Getränk) to drink up ♦ vi to finish one's drink, to drink up
Austritt ['aʊstrɪt] m emission; (aus Verein, Partei etc) retirement, withdrawal
austrocknen ['aʊstrɔknən] vt, vi to dry up
ausüben ['aʊsʔyːbən] vt (Beruf) to practise, to carry out; (Funktion) to perform; (Einfluß) to exert; **einen Reiz auf jdn ~** to hold an attraction for sb; **eine Wirkung auf jdn ~** to have an effect on sb
Ausverkauf ['aʊsfɛrkaʊf] m sale; **a~en** vt to sell out; (Geschäft) to sell up; **a~t** adj (Karten, Artikel) sold out; (THEAT: Haus) full
Auswahl ['aʊsvaːl] f: **eine ~ (an** +dat**)** a selection (of), a choice (of)
auswählen ['aʊsvɛːlən] vt to select, to choose
Auswander- ['aʊsvandər] zW: **~er** m emigrant; **a~n** vi to emigrate; **~ung** f emigration
auswärtig ['aʊsvɛrtɪç] adj (nicht am/vom Ort) out-of-town; (ausländisch) foreign
auswärts ['aʊsvɛrts] adv outside; (nach außen) outwards; **~ essen** to eat out; **A~spiel** ['aʊsvɛrtsʃpiːl] nt away game
auswechseln ['aʊsvɛksəln] vt to change, to substitute
Ausweg ['aʊsveːk] m way out; **a~los** adj hopeless

ausweichen ['ausvaɪçən] (*unreg*) *vi*: **jdm/etw ~** to move aside *od* make way for sb /sth; (*fig*) to side-step sb/sth; **~d** *adj* evasive

ausweinen ['ausvaɪnən] *vr* to have a (good) cry

Ausweis ['ausvaɪs] (**-es, -e**) *m* identity card; passport; (*Mitglieds~, Bibliotheks~ etc*) card; **a~en** [-zən] (*unreg*) *vt* to expel, to banish ♦ *vr* to prove one's identity; **~papiere** *pl* identity papers; **~ung** *f* expulsion

ausweiten ['ausvaɪtən] *vt* to stretch

auswendig ['ausvɛndɪç] *adv* by heart; **~ lernen** to learn by heart

auswerten ['ausvɛrtən] *vt* to evaluate

Auswertung *f* evaluation, analysis; (*Nutzung*) utilization

auswirken ['ausvɪrkən] *vr* to have an effect

Auswirkung *f* effect

auswischen ['ausvɪʃən] *vt* to wipe out; **jdm eins ~** (*umg*) to put one over on sb

Auswuchs ['ausvuːks] *m* (out)growth; (*fig*) product

auswuchten ['ausvuxtən] *vt* (*AUT*) to balance

auszahlen ['austsaːlən] *vt* (*Lohn, Summe*) to pay out; (*Arbeiter*) to pay off; (*Miterbe*) to buy out ♦ *vr* (*sich lohnen*) to pay

auszählen ['austsɛːlən] *vt* (*Stimmen*) to count; (*BOXEN*) to count out

auszeichnen ['austsaɪçnən] *vt* to honour; (*MIL*) to decorate; (*COMM*) to price ♦ *vr* to distinguish o.s.

Auszeichnung *f* distinction; (*COMM*) pricing; (*Ehrung*) awarding of decoration; (*Ehre*) honour; (*Orden*) decoration; **mit ~** with distinction

ausziehen ['austsiːən] (*unreg*) *vt* (*Kleidung*) to take off; (*Haare, Zähne, Tisch etc*) to pull out; (*nachmalen*) to trace ♦ *vr* to undress ♦ *vi* (*aufbrechen*) to leave; (*aus Wohnung*) to move out

Auszug ['austsuːk] *m* (*aus Wohnung*) removal; (*aus Buch etc*) extract; (*Konto~*) statement; (*Ausmarsch*) departure

Auto ['auto] (**-s, -s**) *nt* (motor-)car; **~ fahren** to drive; **~atlas** *m* road atlas;

~bahn *f* motorway; **~bahndreieck** *nt* motorway junction; **~bahnkreuz** *nt* motorway intersection; **~bus** *m* bus; **~fahrer(in)** *m(f)* motorist, driver; **~fahrt** *f* drive; **a~gen** [-'geːn] *adj* autogenous; **~'gramm** *nt* autograph; **~'mat** *m* (**-en, -en**) *m* machine; **~matik** [auto'maːtɪk] *f* (*AUT*) automatic; **a~'matisch** *adj* automatic; **a~nom** [-'noːm] *adj* autonomous

Autor(in) ['autor, au'toːrɪn, *pl* -'toːrən] (**-s, -en**) *m(f)* author

Auto- *zW*: **~radio** *nt* car radio; **~reifen** *m* car tyre; **~reisezug** *m* motorail train; **~rennen** *nt* motor racing

autoritär [autori'tɛːr] *adj* authoritarian

Autorität *f* authority

Auto- *zW*: **~stopp** *m*: **per ~stopp fahren** to hitch-hike; **~telefon** *nt* car phone; **~unfall** *m* car *od* motor accident; **~verleih** *m* car hire (*BRIT*) *od* rental (*US*); **~wäsche** *f* car wash

Axt [akst] (**-, ⁓e**) *f* axe

B b

Baby ['beːbi] (**-s, -s**) *nt* baby; **~nahrung** *f* baby food; **~sitter** ['beːbizɪtər] (**-s, -**) *m* baby-sitter

Bach [bax] (**-(e)s, ⁓e**) *m* stream, brook

Backbord (**-(e)s, -e**) *nt* (*NAUT*) port

Backe ['bakə] *f* cheek

backen (*unreg*) *vt, vi* to bake

Backenzahn *m* molar

Bäcker ['bɛkər] (**-s, -**) *m* baker; **~ei** *f* bakery; (*~laden*) baker's (shop)

Backform *f* baking tin

Back- *zW*: **~obst** *nt* dried fruit; **~ofen** *m* oven; **~pflaume** *f* prune; **~pulver** *nt* baking powder; **~stein** *m* brick

Bad [baːt] (**-(e)s, ⁓er**) *nt* bath; (*Schwimmen*) bathe; (*Ort*) spa

Bade- ['baːdə] *zW*: **~anstalt** *f* (swimming) baths *pl*; **~anzug** *m* bathing suit; **~hose** *f* bathing *od* swimming trunks *pl*; **~mantel** *m* bath(ing) robe; **~meister** *m* baths attendant; **~mütze** *f* bathing cap; **b~n** *vi* to bathe, to have a bath ♦ *vt* to bath; **~ort** *m* spa; **~tuch** *nt*

bath towel; **~wanne** f bath (tub);
~zimmer nt bathroom

Bagatelle [baga'tɛlə] f trifle

Bagger ['bagər] (-s, -) m excavator; (NAUT)
dredger; **b~n** vt, vi to excavate; to dredge

Bahn [ba:n] (-, -en) f railway, railroad
(US); (Weg) road, way; (Spur) lane;
(Renn~) track; (ASTRON) orbit; (Stoff~)
length; **b~brechend** adj pioneering;
~damm m railway embankment; **b~en**
vt: **sich/jdm einen Weg b~en** to clear a
way/a way for sb; **~fahrt** f railway
journey; **~hof** m station; **auf dem ~hof**
at the station; **~hofshalle** f station
concourse; **~hofsvorsteher** m station-
master; **~linie** f (railway) line; **~steig** m
platform; **~übergang** m level crossing,
grade crossing (US); **~wärter** m
signalman

Bahre ['ba:rə] f stretcher

Bakterien [bak'te:riən] pl bacteria pl

Balance [ba'lã:sə] f balance, equilibrium

balan'cieren vt, vi to balance

bald [balt] adv (zeitlich) soon; (beinahe)
almost; **~ig** ['baldıç] adj early, speedy

Baldrian ['baldria:n] (-s, -e) m valerian

Balkan ['balka:n] (-s) m: **der ~** the
Balkans pl

Balken ['balkən] (-s, -) m beam; (Trag~)
girder; (Stütz~) prop

Balkon [bal'kõ:] (-s, -s od -e) m balcony;
(THEAT) (dress) circle

Ball [bal] (-(e)s, ⸚e) m ball; (Tanz) dance,
ball

Ballast ['balast] (-(e)s, -e) m ballast; (fig)
weight, burden

Ballen ['balən] (-s, -) m bale; (ANAT) ball;
b~ vt (formen) to make into a ball;
(Faust) to clench ♦ vr (Wolken etc) to
build up; (Menschen) to gather

Ballett [ba'lɛt] (-(e)s, -e) nt ballet

Ballkleid nt evening dress

Ballon [ba'lõ:] (-s, -s od -e) m balloon

Ballspiel nt ball game

Ballungsgebiet ['baluŋsgebi:t] nt
conurbation

Baltikum ['baltikʊm] (-s) nt: **das ~** the
Baltic States

Bambus ['bambʊs] (-ses, -se) m bamboo;

~rohr nt bamboo cane

Banane [ba'na:nə] f banana

Band¹ [bant] (-(e)s, ⸚e) m (Buch~) volume

Band² (-(e)s, ⸚er) nt (Stoff~) ribbon, tape;
(Fließ~) production line; (Faß~) hoop;
(Ton~) tape; (ANAT) ligament; **etw auf ~
aufnehmen** to tape sth; **am laufenden ~**
(umg) non-stop

Band³ (-(e)s, -e) nt (Freundschafts~ etc)
bond

Band⁴ [bɛnt] (-, -s) f band, group

band etc vb siehe **binden**

Bandage [ban'da:ʒə] f bandage

banda'gieren vt to bandage

Bande ['bandə] f band; (Straßen~) gang

bändigen ['bɛndıgən] vt (Tier) to tame;
(Trieb, Leidenschaft) to control, to
restrain

Bandit [ban'di:t] (-en, -en) m bandit

Band- zW: **~nudel** f (KOCH: gew pl)
ribbon noodles (pl); **~scheibe** f (ANAT)
disc; **~wurm** m tapeworm

bange ['baŋə] adj scared; (besorgt)
anxious; **jdm wird es ~** sb is becoming
scared; **jdm ~ machen** to scare sb; **~n** vi:
um jdn/etw ~n to be anxious od worried
about sb/sth

Banjo ['banjo, 'bɛndʒo] (-s, -s) nt banjo

Bank¹ [baŋk] (-, ⸚e) f (Sitz~) bench;
(Sand~ etc) (sand)bank, (sand)bar

Bank² (-, -en) f (Geld~) bank

Bankanweisung f banker's order

Bankett [baŋ'kɛt] (-(e)s, -e) nt (Essen)
banquet; (Straßenrand) verge (BRIT),
shoulder (US); **~e** f verge (BRIT), shoulder
(US)

Bankier [baŋki'e:] (-s, -s) m banker

Bank- zW: **~konto** m bank account;
~leitzahl f bank sort code number;
~note f banknote; **~raub** m bank
robbery

Bankrott [baŋ'krɔt] (-(e)s, -e) m
bankruptcy; **~ machen** to go bankrupt;
b~ adj bankrupt

Bann [ban] (-(e)s, -e) m (HIST) ban;
(Kirchen~) excommunication; (fig: Zauber)
spell; **b~en** vt (Geister) to exorcize;
(Gefahr) to avert; (bezaubern) to enchant;
(HIST) to banish

Banner (-s, -) *nt* banner, flag

Bar (-, -s) *f* bar

bar [baːr] *adj* (+*gen*) (*unbedeckt*) bare; (*frei von*) lacking (in); (*offenkundig*) utter, sheer; **~e(s) Geld** cash; **etw (in) ~ bezahlen** to pay sth (in) cash; **etw für ~e Münze nehmen** (*fig*) to take sth at its face value

Bär [bɛːr] (-en, -en) *m* bear

Baracke [baˈrakə] *f* hut

barbarisch [barˈbaːrɪʃ] *adj* barbaric, barbarous

Bar- *zW*: **b~fuß** *adj* barefoot; **~geld** *nt* cash, ready money; **b~geldlos** *adj* non-cash

Barhocker *m* bar stool

Barkauf *m* cash purchase

Barkeeper [ˈbaːrkiːpər] (-s, -) *m* barman, bartender

barmherzig [barmˈhɛrtsɪç] *adj* merciful, compassionate

Barometer [baroˈmeːtər] (-s, -) *nt* barometer

Baron [baˈroːn] (-s, -e) *m* baron; **~in** *f* baroness

Barren [ˈbarən] (-s, -) *m* parallel bars *pl*; (*Gold~*) ingot

Barriere [bariˈɛːrə] *f* barrier

Barrikade [bariˈkaːdə] *f* barricade

Barsch [barʃ] (-(e)s, -e) *m* perch

barsch *adj* brusque, gruff

Barschaft *f* ready money

Barscheck *m* open *od* uncrossed cheque (*BRIT*), open check (*US*)

Bart [baːrt] (-(e)s, ˛e) *m* beard; (*Schlüssel~*) bit

bärtig [ˈbɛːrtɪç] *adj* bearded

Barzahlung *f* cash payment

Base [ˈbaːzə] *f* (*CHEM*) base; (*Kusine*) cousin

Basel [ˈbaːzəl] *nt* Basle

Basen *pl von* **Base; Basis**

BASIC [ˈbeːsik] *nt* (*COMPUT*) BASIC

basieren [baˈziːrən] *vt* to base ♦ *vi* to be based

Basis [ˈbaːzɪs] (-, **Basen**) *f* basis

Baß [bas] (**Basses, Bässe**) *m* bass

Bassin [baˈsɛ̃ː] (-s, -s) *nt* pool

Baßstimme *f* bass voice

Bast [bast] (-(e)s, -e) *m* raffia

basteln *vt* to make ♦ *vi* to do handicrafts

bat *etc* [baːt] *vb siehe* **bitten**

Bataillon [batalˈjoːn] (-s, -e) *nt* battalion

Batik [ˈbaːtik] *f* (*Verfahren*) batik

Batist [baˈtɪst] (-(e)s, -e) *m* batiste

Batterie [batəˈriː] *f* battery

Bau [bau] (-(e)s) *m* (*Bauen*) building, construction; (*Aufbau*) structure; (*Körper~*) frame; (*~stelle*) building site; (*pl Baue*: *Tier~*) hole, burrow; (: *MIN*) working(s); (*pl Bauten*: *Gebäude*) building; **sich im ~ befinden** to be under construction; **~arbeiter** *m* building worker

Bauch [baux] (-(e)s, **Bäuche**) *m* belly; (*ANAT auch*) stomach, abdomen; **~fell** *nt* peritoneum; **b~ig** *adj* bulbous; **~nabel** *m* navel; **~redner** *m* ventriloquist; **~schmerzen** *pl* stomachache; **~tanz** *m* belly dance; belly dancing; **~weh** *nt* stomachache

bauen [ˈbauən] *vt, vi* to build; (*TECH*) to construct; **auf jdn/etw ~** to depend *od* count upon sb/sth

Bauer¹ [ˈbauər] (-n *od* -s, -n) *m* farmer; (*Schach*) pawn

Bauer² (-s, -) *nt od m* (bird-)cage

Bäuerin [ˈbɔyərɪn] *f* farmer; (*Frau des Bauers*) farmer's wife

bäuerlich *adj* rustic

Bauern- *zW*: **~haus** *nt* farmhouse; **~hof** *m* farm(yard)

Bau- *zW*: **b~fällig** *adj* dilapidated; **~gelände** *f* building site; **~genehmigung** *f* building permit; **~herr** *m* purchaser; **~kasten** *m* box of bricks; **~land** *nt* building land; **b~lich** *adj* structural

Baum [baum] (-(e)s, **Bäume**) *m* tree

baumeln [ˈbauməln] *vi* to dangle

bäumen [ˈbɔymən] *vr* to rear (up)

Baum- *zW*: **~schule** *f* nursery; **~stamm** *m* tree trunk; **~stumpf** *m* tree stump; **~wolle** *f* cotton

Bau- *zW*: **~plan** *m* architect's plan; **~platz** *m* building site

bausparen *vi* to save with a building society

Bausparkasse *f* building society
Bausparvertrag *m* building society savings agreement
Bau *zW:* **~stein** *m* building stone, freestone; **~stelle** *f* building site; **~teil** *nt* prefabricated part (of building); **~ten** *pl von* **Bau**; **~weise** *f* (method of) construction; **~werk** *nt* building; **~zaun** *m* hoarding
Bayer(in) ['baɪər(ɪn)] *m(f)* Bavarian
Bayern ['baɪərn] *nt* Bavaria
bayrisch ['baɪrɪʃ] *adj* Bavarian
Bazillus [ba'tsɪlʊs] (-, **Bazillen**) *m* bacillus
beabsichtigen [bə''apzɪçtɪgən] *vt* to intend
beachten [bə''axtən] *vt* to take note of; (*Vorschrift*) to obey; (*Vorfahrt*) to observe
beachtlich *adj* considerable
Beachtung *f* notice, attention, observation
Beamte(r) [bə''amtə(r)] (-n, -n) *m* official; (*Staats~*) civil servant; (*Bank~ etc*) employee
Beamtin *f siehe* **Beamte(r)**
beängstigend [bə''ɛŋstɪgənt] *adj* alarming
beanspruchen [bə''anʃprʊxən] *vt* to claim; (*Zeit, Platz*) to take up, to occupy; **jdn ~** to take up sb's time
beanstanden [bə''anʃtandən] *vt* to complain about, to object to
beantragen [bə''antra:gən] *vt* to apply for, to ask for
beantworten [bə''antvɔrtən] *vt* to answer
Beantwortung *f* (+gen) reply (to)
bearbeiten [bə''arbaɪtən] *vt* to work; (*Material*) to process; (*Thema*) to deal with; (*Land*) to cultivate; (*CHEM*) to treat; (*Buch*) to revise; (*umg: beeinflussen wollen*) to work on
Bearbeitung *f* processing; cultivation; treatment; revision
Beatmung [bə''a:tmʊŋ] *f* respiration
beaufsichtigen [bə''aʊfzɪçtɪgən] *vt* to supervise
Beaufsichtigung *f* supervision
beauftragen [bə''aʊftra:gən] *vt* to

instruct; **jdn mit etw ~** to entrust sb with sth
Beauftragte(r) *mf* (*dekl wie adj*) representative
bebauen [bə'baʊən] *vt* to build on; (*AGR*) to cultivate
beben ['be:bən] *vi* to tremble, to shake; **B~** (-s, -) *nt* earthquake
Becher ['bɛçər] (-s, -) *m* mug; (*ohne Henkel*) tumbler
Becken ['bɛkən] (-s, -) *nt* basin; (*MUS*) cymbal; (*ANAT*) pelvis
bedacht [bə'daxt] *adj* thoughtful, careful; **auf etw** *akk* **~ sein** to be concerned about sth
bedächtig [bə'dɛçtɪç] *adj* (*umsichtig*) thoughtful, reflective; (*langsam*) slow, deliberate
bedanken [bə'daŋkən] *vr:* **sich (bei jdm) ~** to say thank you (to sb)
Bedarf [bə'darf] (-(e)s) *m* need, requirement; (*COMM*) demand; **je nach ~** according to demand; **bei ~** if necessary; **~ an etw** *dat* **haben** to be in need of sth
Bedarfsfall *m* case of need
Bedarfshaltestelle *f* request stop
bedauerlich [bə'daʊərlɪç] *adj* regrettable
bedauern [bə'daʊərn] *vt* to be sorry for; (*bemitleiden*) to pity; **B~** (-s) *nt* regret; **~swert** *adj* (*Zustände*) regrettable; (*Mensch*) pitiable, unfortunate
bedecken [bə'dɛkən] *vt* to cover
bedeckt *adj* covered; (*Himmel*) overcast
bedenken [bə'dɛŋkən] (*unreg*) *vt* to think over, to consider; **B~** (-s, -) *nt* (*Überlegen*) consideration; (*Zweifel*) doubt; (*Skrupel*) scruple
bedenklich *adj* doubtful; (*bedrohlich*) dangerous, risky
Bedenkzeit *f* time to think
bedeuten [bə'dɔʏtən] *vt* to mean; to signify; (*wichtig sein*) to be of importance; **~d** *adj* important; (*beträchtlich*) considerable
bedeutsam *adj* (*wichtig*) significant
Bedeutung *f* meaning; significance; (*Wichtigkeit*) importance; **b~slos** *adj* insignificant, unimportant; **b~svoll** *adj* momentous, significant

bedienen [bə'di:nən] *vt* to serve;
(*Maschine*) to work, to operate ♦ *vr* (*beim
Essen*) to help o.s.; **sich jds/einer Sache
~** to make use of sb/sth
Bedienung *f* service; (*Kellnerin*)
waitress; (*Verkäuferin*) shop assistant;
(*Zuschlag*) service (charge)
bedingen [bə'dɪŋən] *vt* (*verursachen*) to
cause
bedingt *adj* (*Richtigkeit, Tauglichkeit*)
limited; (*Zusage, Annahme*) conditional
Bedingung *f* condition; (*Voraussetzung*)
stipulation; **b~slos** *adj* unconditional
bedrängen [bə'drɛŋən] *vt* to pester, to
harass
bedrohen [bə'dro:ən] *vt* to threaten
Bedrohung *f* threat, menace
bedrücken [bə'drʏkən] *vt* to oppress, to
trouble
bedürf- [bə'dʏrf] *zW:* **~en** (*unreg*) *vi* +*gen*
to need, to require; **B~nis** (**-ses, -se**) *nt*
need; **B~nisanstalt** *f* public convenience,
comfort station (*US*); **~tig** *adj* in need,
poor, needy
beeilen [bə'aɪlən] *vr* to hurry
beeindrucken [bə''aɪndrʊkən] *vt* to
impress, to make an impression on
beeinflussen [bə''aɪnflʊsən] *vt* to
influence
beeinträchtigen [bə''aɪntrɛçtɪɡən] *vt* to
affect adversely; (*Freiheit*) to infringe
upon
beend(ig)en [bə''ɛnd(ɪɡ)ən] *vt* to end, to
finish, to terminate
beengen [bə''ɛŋən] *vt* to cramp; (*fig*) to
hamper, to oppress
beerben [bə''ɛrbən] *vt:* **jdn ~** to inherit
from sb
beerdigen [bə''e:rdɪɡən] *vt* to bury
Beerdigung *f* funeral, burial; **~sinstitut**
nt funeral director's
Beere ['be:rə] *f* berry; (*Trauben~*) grape
Beet [be:t] (**-(e)s, -e**) *nt* bed
befähigen [bə'fɛ:ɪɡən] *vt* to enable
befähigt *adj* (*begabt*) talented; **~ (für)**
(*fähig*) capable (of)
Befähigung *f* capability; (*Begabung*)
talent, aptitude
befahrbar [bə'fa:rba:r] *adj* passable;

(*NAUT*) navigable
befahren [bə'fa:rən] (*unreg*) *vt* to use, to
drive over; (*NAUT*) to navigate ♦ *adj* used
befallen [bə'falən] (*unreg*) *vt* to come
over
befangen [bə'faŋən] *adj* (*schüchtern*) shy,
self-conscious; (*voreingenommen*) biased
befassen [bə'fasən] *vr* to concern o.s.
Befehl [bə'fe:l] (**-(e)s, -e**) *m* command,
order; **b~en** (*unreg*) *vt* to order ♦ *vi* to
give orders; **jdm etw b~en** to order sb to
do sth; **~sverweigerung** *f*
insubordination
befestigen [bə'fɛstɪɡən] *vt* to fasten;
(*stärken*) to strengthen; (*MIL*) to fortify; **~
an** +*dat* to fasten to
Befestigung *f* fastening; strengthening;
(*MIL*) fortification
befeuchten [bə'fɔyçtən] *vt* to damp(en),
to moisten
befinden [bə'fɪndən] (*unreg*) *vr* to be;
(*sich fühlen*) to feel ♦ *vt:* **jdn/etw für** or
als etw ~ to deem sb/sth to be sth ♦ *vi:* **~
(über** +*akk*) to decide (on), to adjudicate
(on); **B~** (**-s**) *nt* health, condition;
(*Meinung*) view, opinion
befolgen [bə'fɔlɡən] *vt* to comply with,
to follow
befördern [bə'fœrdərn] *vt* (*senden*) to
transport, to send; (*beruflich*) to promote
Beförderung *f* transport; promotion
befragen [bə'fra:ɡən] *vt* to question
befreien [bə'fraɪən] *vt* to set free;
(*erlassen*) to exempt
Befreier (**-s, -**) *m* liberator
Befreiung *f* liberation, release; (*Erlassen*)
exemption
befremden [bə'frɛmdən] *vt* to surprise,
to disturb; **B~** (**-s**) *nt* surprise,
astonishment
befreunden [bə'frɔyndən] *vr* to make
friends; (*mit Idee etc*) to acquaint o.s.
befreundet *adj* friendly
befriedigen [bə'fri:dɪɡən] *vt* to satisfy;
~d *adj* satisfactory
Befriedigung *f* satisfaction, gratification
befristet [bə'frɪstət] *adj* limited
befruchten [bə'frʊxtən] *vt* to fertilize;
(*fig*) to stimulate

Befruchtung *f*: **künstliche ~** artificial insemination

Befugnis [bə'fu:knɪs] (-, -se) *f* authorization, powers *pl*

befugt *adj* authorized, entitled

Befund [bə'fʊnt] (-(e)s, -e) *m* findings *pl*; (*MED*) diagnosis

befürchten [bə'fyrçtən] *vt* to fear

Befürchtung *f* fear, apprehension

befürworten [bə'fy:rvɔrtən] *vt* to support, to speak in favour of

Befürworter (-s, -) *m* supporter, advocate

begabt [bə'ga:pt] *adj* gifted

Begabung [bə'ga:bʊŋ] *f* talent, gift

begann *etc* [bə'gan] *vb siehe* **beginnen**

begeben [bə'ge:bən] (*unreg*) *vr* (*gehen*) to betake o.s.; (*geschehen*) to occur; **sich ~ nach** *od* **zu** to proceed to(wards); **B~heit** *f* occurrence

begegnen [bə'ge:gnən] *vi*: **jdm ~** to meet sb; (*behandeln*) to treat sb; **einer Sache** *dat* **~** to meet with sth

Begegnung *f* meeting

begehen [bə'ge:ən] (*unreg*) *vt* (*Straftat*) to commit; (*abschreiten*) to cover; (*Straße etc*) to use, to negotiate; (*Feier*) to celebrate

begehren [bə'ge:rən] *vt* to desire

begehrt *adj* in demand; (*Junggeselle*) eligible

begeistern [bə'gaɪstərn] *vt* to fill with enthusiasm, to inspire ♦ *vr*: **sich für etw ~** to get enthusiastic about sth

begeistert *adj* enthusiastic

Begierde [bə'gi:rdə] *f* desire, passion

begierig [bə'gi:rɪç] *adj* eager, keen

begießen [bə'gi:sən] (*unreg*) *vt* to water; (*mit Alkohol*) to drink to

Beginn [bə'gɪn] (-(e)s) *m* beginning; **zu ~** at the beginning; **b~en** (*unreg*) *vt, vi* to start, to begin

beglaubigen [bə'glaʊbɪgən] *vt* to countersign

Beglaubigung *f* countersignature

begleichen [bə'glaɪçən] (*unreg*) *vt* to settle, to pay

Begleit- [bə'glaɪt] *zW*: **b~en** *vt* to accompany; (*MIL*) to escort; **~er** (-s, -) *m* companion; (*Freund*) escort; (*MUS*)

accompanist; **~schreiben** *nt* covering letter; **~umstände** *pl* concomitant circumstances; **~ung** *f* company; (*MIL*) escort; (*MUS*) accompaniment

beglücken [bə'glʏkən] *vt* to make happy, to delight

beglückwünschen [bə'glʏkvʏnʃən] *vt*: **~ (zu)** to congratulate (on)

begnadigen [bə'gna:dɪgən] *vt* to pardon

Begnadigung *f* pardon, amnesty

begnügen [bə'gny:gən] *vr* to be satisfied, to content o.s.

Begonie [bə'go:niə] *f* begonia

begonnen *etc* [bə'gɔnən] *vb siehe* **beginnen**

begraben [bə'gra:bən] (*unreg*) *vt* to bury

Begräbnis [bə'grɛ:pnɪs] (-ses, -se) *nt* burial, funeral

begreifen [bə'graɪfən] (*unreg*) *vt* to understand, to comprehend

begreiflich [bə'graɪflɪç] *adj* understandable

Begrenztheit [bə'grɛntstshaɪt] *f* limitation, restriction; (*fig*) narrowness

Begriff [bə'grɪf] (-(e)s, -e) *m* concept, idea; **im ~ sein, etw zu tun** to be about to do sth; **schwer von ~** (*umg*) slow, dense; **b~sstutzig** *adj* slow, dense

begründ- [bə'grʏnd] *zW*: **~en** *vt* (*Gründe geben*) to justify; **~et** *adj* well-founded, justified; **B~ung** *f* justification, reason

begrüßen [bə'gry:sən] *vt* to greet, to welcome

Begrüßung *f* greeting, welcome

begünstigen [bə'gʏnstɪgən] *vt* (*Person*) to favour; (*Sache*) to further, to promote

begutachten [bə'gu:t'axtən] *vt* to assess

begütert [bə'gy:tərt] *adj* wealthy, well-to-do

behaart [bə'ha:rt] *adj* hairy

behäbig [bə'hɛ:bɪç] *adj* (*dick*) portly, stout; (*geruhsam*) comfortable

behagen [bə'ha:gən] *vi*: **das behagt ihm nicht** he does not like it; **B~** (-s) *nt* comfort, ease

behaglich [bə'ha:klɪç] *adj* comfortable, cosy; **B~keit** *f* comfort, cosiness

behalten [bə'haltən] (*unreg*) *vt* to keep, to retain; (*im Gedächtnis*) to remember

Behälter [bə'hɛltər] (**-s, -**) *m* container, receptacle

behandeln [bə'handəln] *vt* to treat; (*Thema*) to deal with; (*Maschine*) to handle

Behandlung *f* treatment; (*von Maschine*) handling

beharren [bə'harən] *vi*: **auf etw** *dat* ~ to stick *od* keep to sth

beharrlich [bə'harlıç] *adj* (*ausdauernd*) steadfast, unwavering; (*hartnäckig*) tenacious, dogged; **B~keit** *f* steadfastness; tenacity

behaupten [bə'hauptən] *vt* to claim, to assert, to maintain; (*sein Recht*) to defend ♦ *vr* to assert o.s.

Behauptung *f* claim, assertion

beheben [bə'he:bən] (*unreg*) *vt* to remove

beheizen [bə'haɪtsən] *vt* to heat

behelfen [bə'hɛlfən] (*unreg*) *vr*: **sich mit etw** ~ to make do with sth

behelfsmäßig *adj* improvised, makeshift; (*vorübergehend*) temporary

behelligen [bə'hɛlɪgən] *vt* to trouble, to bother

beherbergen [bə'hɛrbɛrgən] *vt* to put up, to house

beherrschen [bə'hɛrʃən] *vt* (*Volk*) to rule, to govern; (*Situation*) to control; (*Sprache, Gefühle*) to master ♦ *vr* to control o.s.

beherrscht *adj* controlled

Beherrschung *f* rule; control; mastery

beherzigen [bə'hɛrtsɪgən] *vt* to take to heart

beherzt *adj* courageous, brave

behilflich [bə'hɪlflɪç] *adj* helpful; **jdm** ~ **sein (bei)** to help sb (with)

behindern [bə'hɪndərn] *vt* to hinder, to impede

Behinderte(r) *mf* disabled person

Behinderung *f* hindrance; (*Körper~*) handicap

Behörde [bə'hø:rdə] *f* (*auch pl*) authorities *pl*

behördlich [bə'hø:rtlıç] *adj* official

behüten [bə'hy:tən] *vt* to guard; **jdn vor etw** *dat* ~ to preserve sb from sth

behutsam [bə'hu:tza:m] *adj* cautious, careful; **B~keit** *f* caution, carefulness

---

SCHLÜSSELWORT

bei [baɪ] *präp +dat* **1** (*nahe bei*) near; (*zum Aufenthalt*) at, with; (*unter, zwischen*) among; **bei München** near Munich; **bei uns** at our place; **beim Friseur** at the hairdresser's; **bei seinen Eltern wohnen** to live with one's parents; **bei einer Firma arbeiten** to work for a firm; **etw bei sich haben** to have sth on one; **jdn bei sich haben** to have sb with one; **bei Goethe** in Goethe; **beim Militär** in the army

2 (*zeitlich*) at, on; (*während*) during; (*Zustand, Umstand*) in; **bei Nacht** at night; **bei Nebel** in fog; **bei Regen** if it rains; **bei solcher Hitze** in such heat; **bei meiner Ankunft** on my arrival; **bei der Arbeit** when I'm *etc* working; **beim Fahren** while driving

---

beibehalten ['baɪbəhaltən] (*unreg*) *vt* to keep, to retain

beibringen ['baɪbrɪŋən] (*unreg*) *vt* (*Beweis, Zeugen*) to bring forward; (*Gründe*) to adduce; **jdm etw** ~ (*lehren*) to teach sb sth; (*zu verstehen geben*) to make sb understand sth; (*zufügen*) to inflict sth on sb

Beichte ['baɪçtə] *f* confession; **b~n** *vt* to confess ♦ *vi* to go to confession

Beichtstuhl *m* confessional

beide(s) ['baɪdə(s)] *pron, adj* both; **meine ~n Brüder** my two brothers, both my brothers; **die ersten ~n** the first two; **wir ~** we two; **einer von ~n** one of the two; **alles ~s** both (of them)

beider- ['baɪdər] *zW*: **~lei** *adj inv* of both; **~seitig** *adj* mutual, reciprocal; **~seits** *adv* mutually ♦ *präp +gen* on both sides of

beieinander [baɪaɪ'nandər] *adv* together

Beifahrer ['baɪfa:rər] *m* passenger; **~sitz** *m* passenger seat

Beifall ['baɪfal] (**-(e)s**) *m* applause; (*Zustimmung*) approval

beifällig ['baɪfɛlɪç] *adj* approving;

(*Kommentar*) favourable

beifügen ['baɪfyːgən] *vt* to enclose

beige ['beːʒə] *adj* beige, fawn

beigeben ['baɪgeːbən] (*unreg*) *vt* (*zufügen*) to add; (*mitgeben*) to give ♦ *vi* (*nachgeben*) to give in

Beihilfe ['baɪhɪlfə] *f* aid, assistance; (*Studien~*) grant; (*JUR*) aiding and abetting

beikommen ['baɪkɔmən] (*unreg*) *vi* +*dat* to get at; (*einem Problem*) to deal with

Beil [baɪl] (-(e)s, -e) *nt* axe, hatchet

Beilage ['baɪlaːgə] *f* (*Buch~ etc*) supplement; (*KOCH*) vegetables and potatoes *pl*

beiläufig ['baɪlɔyfɪç] *adj* casual, incidental ♦ *adv* casually, by the way

beilegen ['baɪleːgən] *vt* (*hinzufügen*) to enclose, to add; (*beimessen*) to attribute, to ascribe; (*Streit*) to settle

Beileid ['baɪlaɪt] *nt* condolence, sympathy; **herzliches ~** deepest sympathy

beiliegend ['baɪliːgənt] *adj* (*COMM*) enclosed

beim [baɪm] = **bei dem**

beimessen ['baɪmɛsən] (*unreg*) *vt* (+*dat*) to attribute (to), to ascribe (to)

Bein [baɪn] (-(e)s, -e) *nt* leg

beinah(e) ['baɪnaː(ə)] *adv* almost, nearly

Beinbruch *m* fracture of the leg

beinhalten [bə'''ɪnhaltən] *vt* to contain

beipflichten ['baɪpflɪçtən] *vi*: **jdm/etw ~** to agree with sb/sth

beisammen [baɪ'zamən] *adv* together; **B~sein** (-s) *nt* get-together

Beischlaf ['baɪʃlaːf] *m* sexual intercourse

Beisein ['baɪzaɪn] (-s) *nt* presence

beiseite [baɪ'zaɪtə] *adv* to one side, aside; (*stehen*) on one side, aside; **etw ~ legen** (*sparen*) to put sth by; **jdn/etw ~ schaffen** to put sb/get sth out of the way

beisetzen ['baɪzɛtsən] *vt* to bury

Beisetzung *f* funeral

Beisitzer ['baɪzɪtsər] (-s, -) *m* (*bei Prüfung*) assessor

Beispiel ['baɪʃpiːl] (-(e)s, -e) *nt* example; **sich** (*dat*) **an jdm ein ~ nehmen** to take sb as an example; **zum ~** for example; **b~haft** *adj* exemplary; **b~los** *adj*

unprecedented; **b~sweise** *adv* for instance *od* example

beißen ['baɪsən] (*unreg*) *vt*, *vi* to bite; (*stechen: Rauch, Säure*) to burn ♦ *vr* (*Farben*) to clash; **~d** *adj* biting, caustic; (*fig auch*) sarcastic

Beistand ['baɪʃtant] (-(e)s, ⁻e) *m* support, help; (*JUR*) adviser

beistehen ['baɪʃteːən] (*unreg*) *vi*: **jdm ~** to stand by sb

beisteuern ['baɪʃtɔyərn] *vt* to contribute

beistimmen ['baɪʃtɪmən] *vi* +*dat* to agree with

Beitrag ['baɪtraːk] (-(e)s, ⁻e) *m* contribution; (*Zahlung*) fee, subscription; (*Versicherungs~*) premium; **b~en** ['baɪtraːgən] (*unreg*) *vt*, *vi*: **b~en (zu)** to contribute (to); (*mithelfen*) to help (with)

beitreten ['baɪtreːtən] *vi* +*dat* to join

Beitritt ['baɪtrɪt] *m* joining, membership

Beiwagen *m* (*Motorrad~*) sidecar

Beize ['baɪtsə] *f* (*Holz~*) stain; (*KOCH*) marinade

beizeiten [baɪ'tsaɪtən] *adv* in time

bejahen [bə'jaːən] *vt* (*Frage*) to say yes to, to answer in the affirmative; (*gutheißen*) to agree with

bejahrt [bə'jaːrt] *adj* aged, elderly

bekämpfen [bə'kɛmpfən] *vt* (*Gegner*) to fight; (*Seuche*) to combat ♦ *vr* to fight

Bekämpfung *f* fight, struggle

bekannt [bə'kant] *adj* (well-)known; (*nicht fremd*) familiar; **mit jdm ~ sein** to know sb; **jdn mit jdm ~ machen** to introduce sb to sb; **das ist mir ~** I know that; **es/sie kommt mir ~ vor** it/she seems familiar; **B~e(r)** *mf* acquaintance, friend; **B~enkreis** *m* circle of friends; **~geben** (*unreg*) *vt* to announce publicly; **~lich** *adv* as is well known, as you know; **~machen** *vt* to announce; **B~machung** *f* publication; announcement; **B~schaft** *f* acquaintance

bekehren [bə'keːrən] *vt* to convert ♦ *vr* to be *od* become converted

Bekehrung *f* conversion

bekennen [bə'kɛnən] (*unreg*) *vt* to confess; (*Glauben*) to profess; **Farbe ~**

(*umg*) to show where one stands

Bekenntnis [bə'kɛntnɪs] (**-ses, -se**) *nt* admission, confession; (*Religion*) confession, denomination

beklagen [bə'kla:gən] *vt* to deplore, to lament ♦ *vr* to complain; **~swert** *adj* lamentable, pathetic

bekleiden [bə'klaɪdən] *vt* to clothe; (*Amt*) to occupy, to fill

Bekleidung *f* clothing

beklemmen [bə'klɛmən] *vt* to oppress

beklommen [bə'klɔmən] *adj* anxious, uneasy; **B~heit** *f* anxiety, uneasiness

bekommen [bə'kɔmən] (*unreg*) *vt* to get, to receive; (*Kind*) to have; (*Zug*) to catch, to get ♦ *vi*: **jdm ~** to agree with sb

bekömmlich [bə'kœmlɪç] *adj* easily digestible

bekräftigen [bə'krɛftɪgən] *vt* to confirm, to corroborate

bekreuzigen [bə'krɔʏtsɪgən] *vr* to cross o.s.

bekümmern [bə'kʏmərn] *vt* to worry, to trouble

bekunden [bə'kundən] *vt* (*sagen*) to state; (*zeigen*) to show

belächeln [bə'lɛçəln] *vt* to laugh at

beladen [bə'la:dən] (*unreg*) *vt* to load

Belag [bə'la:k] (**-(e)s, ⁼e**) *m* covering, coating; (*Brot~*) spread; (*Zahn~*) tartar; (*auf Zunge*) fur; (*Brems~*) lining

belagern [bə'la:gərn] *vt* to besiege

Belagerung *f* siege

Belang [bə'laŋ] (**-(e)s**) *m* importance; **~e** *pl* (*Interessen*) interests, concerns; **b~los** *adj* trivial, unimportant

belassen [bə'lasən] (*unreg*) *vt* (*in Zustand, Glauben*) to leave; (*in Stellung*) to retain

belasten [bə'lastən] *vt* to burden; (*fig: bedrücken*) to trouble, to worry; (*COMM: Konto*) to debit; (*JUR*) to incriminate ♦ *vr* to weigh o.s. down; (*JUR*) to incriminate o.s.; **~d** *adj* (*JUR*) incriminating

belästigen [bə'lɛstɪgən] *vt* to annoy, to pester

Belästigung *f* annoyance, pestering

Belastung [bə'lastʊŋ] *f* load; (*fig: Sorge etc*) weight; (*COMM*) charge, debit(ing);

(*JUR*) incriminatory evidence

belaufen [bə'laʊfən] (*unreg*) *vr*: **sich ~ auf** +*akk* to amount to

beleben [bə'le:bən] *vt* (*anregen*) to liven up; (*Konjunktur, jds Hoffnungen*) to stimulate ♦ *vr* (*Augen*) to light up; (*Stadt*) to come to life

belebt [bə'le:pt] *adj* (*Straße*) busy

Beleg [bə'le:k] (**-(e)s, -e**) *m* (*COMM*) receipt; (*Beweis*) documentary evidence, proof; (*Beispiel*) example; **b~en** [bə'le:gən] *vt* to cover; (*Kuchen, Brot*) to spread; (*Platz*) to reserve, to book; (*Kurs, Vorlesung*) to register for; (*beweisen*) to verify, to prove; (*MIL: mit Bomben*) to bomb; **~schaft** *f* personnel, staff; **b~t** *adj*: **b~tes Brot** open sandwich

belehren [bə'le:rən] *vt* to instruct, to teach

Belehrung *f* instruction

beleibt [bə'laɪpt] *adj* stout, corpulent

beleidigen [bə'laɪdɪgən] *vt* to insult, to offend

Beleidigung *f* insult; (*JUR*) slander; libel

belesen [bə'le:zən] *adj* well-read

beleuchten [bə'lɔʏçtən] *vt* to light, to illuminate; (*fig*) to throw light on

Beleuchtung *f* lighting, illumination

Belgien ['bɛlgiən] *nt* Belgium; **Belgier(in)** *m(f)* Belgian; **belgisch** *adj* Belgian

belichten [bə'lɪçtən] *vt* to expose

Belichtung *f* exposure; **~smesser** *m* exposure meter

Belieben [bə'li:bən] *nt*: **(ganz) nach ~** (just) as you wish

beliebig [bə'li:bɪç] *adj* any you like ♦ *adv* as you like; **ein ~es Thema** any subject you like *od* want; **~ viel/viele** as much/many as you like

beliebt [bə'li:pt] *adj* popular; **sich bei jdm ~ machen** to make o.s. popular with sb; **B~heit** *f* popularity

beliefern [bə'li:fərn] *vt* to supply

bellen ['bɛlən] *vi* to bark

belohnen [bə'lo:nən] *vt* to reward

Belohnung *f* reward

belügen [bə'ly:gən] (*unreg*) *vt* to lie to, to deceive

belustigen [bə'lʊstɪgən] *vt* to amuse
Belustigung *f* amusement
bemalen [bə'maːlən] *vt* to paint
bemängeln [bə'mɛŋəln] *vt* to criticize
bemerk- [bə'mɛrk] *zW*: **~bar** *adj*
perceptible, noticeable; **sich ~bar**
machen (*Person*) to make *od* get o.s.
noticed; (*Unruhe*) to become noticeable;
~en *vt* (*wahrnehmen*) to notice, to
observe; (*sagen*) to say, to mention;
~enswert *adj* remarkable, noteworthy;
B~ung *f* remark; (*schriftlich auch*)
note
bemitleiden [bə'mɪtlaɪdən] *vt* to pity
bemühen [bə'myːən] *vr* to take trouble
od pains
Bemühung *f* trouble, pains *pl*, effort
benachbart [bə'naxbaːrt] *adj*
neighbouring
benachrichtigen [bə'naːxrɪçtɪgən] *vt* to
inform
Benachrichtigung *f* notification,
information
benachteiligen [bə'naːxtaɪlɪgən] *vt* to
put at a disadvantage; to victimize
benehmen [bə'neːmən] (*unreg*) *vr* to
behave; **B~** (**-s**) *nt* behaviour
beneiden [bə'naɪdən] *vt* to envy; **~swert**
adj enviable
benennen [bə'nɛnən] (*unreg*) *vt* to name
Bengel ['bɛŋəl] (**-s, -**) *m* (little) rascal *od*
rogue
benommen [bə'nɔmən] *adj* dazed
benoten [bə'noːtən] *vt* to mark
benötigen [bə'nøːtɪgən] *vt* to need
benutzen [bə'nʊtsən] *vt* to use
benützen [bə'nʏtsən] *vt* to use
Benutzer (**-s, -**) *m* user
Benutzung *f* utilization, use
Benzin [bɛnt'siːn] (**-s, -e**) *nt* (*AUT*) petrol
(*BRIT*), gas(oline) (*US*); **~kanister** *m* petrol
(*BRIT*) *od* gas (*US*) can; **~tank** *m* petrol
tank (*BRIT*), gas tank (*US*); **~uhr** *f* petrol
(*BRIT*) *od* gas (*US*) gauge
beobachten [bə'oːbaxtən] *vt* to observe;
Beobachter (**-s, -**) *m* observer; (*eines*
Unfalls) witness; (*PRESSE, TV*) correspon-
dent; **Beobachtung** *f* observation
bepacken [bə'pakən] *vt* to load, to pack

bequem [bə'kveːm] *adj* comfortable;
(*Ausrede*) convenient; (*Person*) lazy,
indolent; **~en** *vr*: **sich ~en(, etw zu tun)**
to condescend (to do sth); **B~lichkeit**
[-lɪçkaɪt] *f* convenience, comfort;
(*Faulheit*) laziness, indolence
beraten [bə'raːtən] (*unreg*) *vt* to advise;
(*besprechen*) to discuss, to debate ♦ *vr* to
consult; **gut/schlecht ~ sein** to be well/
ill advised; **sich ~ lassen** to get advice
Berater (**-s, -**) *m* adviser
Beratung *f* advice; (*Besprechung*)
consultation; **~sstelle** *f* advice centre
berauben [bə'raʊbən] *vt* to rob
berechenbar [bə'rɛçənbaːr] *adj*
calculable
berechnen [bə'rɛçnən] *vt* to calculate;
(*COMM: anrechnen*) to charge; **~d** *adj*
(*Mensch*) calculating, scheming
Berechnung *f* calculation; (*COMM*) charge
berechtigen [bə'rɛçtɪgən] *vt* to entitle; to
authorize; (*fig*) to justify
berechtigt [bə'rɛçtɪçt] *adj* justifiable,
justified
Berechtigung *f* authorization; (*fig*)
justification
bereden [bə'reːdən] *vt* (*besprechen*) to
discuss; (*überreden*) to persuade ♦ *vr* to
discuss
Bereich [bə'raɪç] (**-(e)s, -e**) *m* (*Bezirk*)
area; (*PHYS*) range; (*Ressort, Gebiet*) sphere
bereichern [bə'raɪçərn] *vt* to enrich ♦ *vr*
to get rich
bereinigen [bə'raɪnɪgən] *vt* to settle
bereisen [bə'raɪzən] *vt* (*Land*) to travel
through
bereit [bə'raɪt] *adj* ready, prepared; **zu**
etw ~ sein to be ready for sth; **sich ~**
erklären to declare o.s. willing; **~en** *vt*
to prepare, to make ready; (*Kummer,*
Freude) to cause; **~halten** (*unreg*) *vt* to
keep in readiness; **~legen** *vt* to lay out;
~machen *vt, vr* to prepare, to get ready;
~s *adv* already; **B~schaft** *f* readiness;
(*Polizei*) alert; **B~schaftsdienst** *m*
emergency service; **~stehen** (*unreg*) *vi*
(*Person*) to be prepared; (*Ding*) to be
ready; **~stellen** *vt* (*Kisten, Pakete etc*) to
put ready; (*Geld etc*) to make available;

(*Truppen, Maschinen*) to put at the ready; **~willig** *adj* willing, ready; **B~willigkeit** *f* willingness, readiness

bereuen [bə'rɔʏən] *vt* to regret

Berg [bɛrk] (**-(e)s, -e**) *m* mountain; hill; **b~ab** *adv* downhill; **~arbeiter** *m* miner; **b~auf** *adv* uphill; **~bahn** *f* mountain railway; **~bau** *m* mining

bergen ['bɛrgən] (*unreg*) *vt* (*retten*) to rescue; (*Ladung*) to salvage; (*enthalten*) to contain

Berg- *zW*: **~führer** *m* mountain guide; **~gipfel** *m* peak, summit; **b~ig** ['bɛrgɪç] *adj* mountainous; hilly; **~kamm** *m* ridge, crest; **~kette** *f* mountain range; **~mann** (*pl* **Bergleute**) *m* miner; **~rettungsdienst** *m* mountain rescue team; **~rutsch** *m* landslide; **~steigen** *nt* mountaineering; **~steiger(in)** (**-s, -**) *m(f)* mountaineer, climber

Bergung ['bɛrguŋ] *f* (*von Menschen*) rescue; (*von Material*) recovery; (*NAUT*) salvage

Bergwacht *f* mountain rescue service

Bergwerk *nt* mine

Bericht [bə'rɪçt] (**-(e)s, -e**) *m* report, account; **b~en** *vt, vi* to report; **~erstatter** (**-s, -**) *m* reporter; (newspaper) correspondent

berichtigen [bə'rɪçtɪgən] *vt* to correct

Berichtigung *f* correction

Bernstein ['bɛrnʃtaɪn] *m* amber

bersten ['bɛrstən] (*unreg*) *vi* to burst, to split

berüchtigt [bə'rʏçtɪçt] *adj* notorious, infamous

berücksichtigen [bə'rʏkzɪçtɪgən] *vt* to consider, to bear in mind

Berücksichtigung *f* consideration

Beruf [bə'ruːf] (**-(e)s, -e**) *m* occupation, profession; (*Gewerbe*) trade; **b~en** (*unreg*) *vt*: **b~en zu** to appoint to ♦ *vr*: **sich auf jdn/etw b~en** to refer *od* appeal to sb/sth ♦ *adj* competent, qualified; **b~lich** *adj* professional

Berufs- *zW*: **~ausbildung** *f* job training; **~berater** *m* careers adviser; **~beratung** *f* vocational guidance; **~geheimnis** *nt* professional secret; **~leben** *nt*

professional life; **b~mäßig** [-mɛsɪç] *adj* professional; **~schule** *f* vocational *od* trade school; **~sportler** [-ʃpɔrtlər] *m* professional (sportsman); **b~tätig** *adj* employed; **b~unfähig** *adj* unfit for work; **~verkehr** *m* rush-hour traffic

Berufung *f* vocation, calling; (*Ernennung*) appointment; (*JUR*) appeal; **~ einlegen** to appeal

beruhen [bə'ruːən] *vi*: **auf etw** *dat* **~** to be based on sth; **etw auf sich ~ lassen** to leave sth at that

beruhigen [bə'ruːɪgən] *vt* to calm, to pacify, to soothe ♦ *vr* (*Mensch*) to calm (o.s.) down; (*Situation*) to calm down

Beruhigung *f* soothing; (*der Nerven*) calming; **zu jds ~** (in order) to reassure sb; **~smittel** *nt* sedative

berühmt [bə'ryːmt] *adj* famous; **B~heit** *f* (*Ruf*) fame; (*Mensch*) celebrity

berühren [bə'ryːrən] *vt* to touch; (*gefühlsmäßig bewegen*) to affect; (*flüchtig erwähnen*) to mention, to touch on ♦ *vr* to meet, to touch

Berührung *f* contact

besagen [bə'zaːgən] *vt* to mean

besagt *adj* (*Tag etc*) said

besänftigen [bə'zɛnftɪgən] *vt* to soothe, to calm

Besatz [bə'zats] (**-es, ⁻e**) *m* trimming, edging

Besatzung *f* garrison; (*NAUT, AVIAT*) crew; **~smacht** *f* occupying power

beschädigen [bə'ʃɛːdɪgən] *vt* to damage; **Beschädigung** *f* damage; (*Stelle*) damaged spot

beschaffen [bə'ʃafən] *vt* to get, to acquire ♦ *adj*: **das ist so ~, daß** that is such that; **B~heit** *f* (*von Mensch*) constitution, nature

Beschaffung *f* acquisition

beschäftigen [bə'ʃɛftɪgən] *vt* to occupy; (*beruflich*) to employ ♦ *vr* to occupy *od* concern o.s.

beschäftigt *adj* busy, occupied

Beschäftigung *f* (*Beruf*) employment; (*Tätigkeit*) occupation; (*Befassen*) concern

beschämen [bə'ʃɛːmən] *vt* to put to shame; **~d** *adj* shameful; (*Hilfsbe-*

reitschaft) shaming
beschämt *adj* ashamed
beschatten [bə'ʃatən] *vt* to shade;
(*Verdächtige*) to shadow
Bescheid [bə'ʃait] (**-(e)s, -e**) *m*
information; (*Weisung*) directions *pl*; ~
wissen (über +*akk*) to be well-informed
(about); **ich weiß** ~ I know; **jdm** ~ **geben**
od **sagen** to let sb know
bescheiden [bə'ʃaidən] (*unreg*) *vr* to
content o.s. ♦ *adj* modest; **B~heit** *f*
modesty
bescheinen [bə'ʃainən] (*unreg*) *vt* to
shine on
bescheinigen [bə'ʃainɪgən] *vt* to certify;
(*bestätigen*) to acknowledge
Bescheinigung *f* certificate; (*Quittung*)
receipt
beschenken [bə'ʃɛŋkən] *vt*: **jdn mit etw**
~ to give sb sth as a present
bescheren [bə'ʃeːrən] *vt*: **jdm etw** ~ to
give sb sth as a Christmas present; **jdn** ~
to give Christmas presents to sb
Bescherung *f* giving of Christmas
presents; (*umg*) mess
beschildern [bə'ʃildərn] *vt* to put signs/a
sign on
beschimpfen [bə'ʃɪmpfən] *vt* to abuse
Beschimpfung *f* abuse; insult
Beschlag [bə'ʃlaːk] (**-(e)s, ⁺e**) *m*
(*Metallband*) fitting; (*auf Fenster*)
condensation; (*auf Metall*) tarnish; finish;
(*Hufeisen*) horseshoe; **jdn/etw in** ~
nehmen *od* **mit** ~ **belegen** to monopolize
sb/sth; **b~en** [bə'ʃlaːgən] (*unreg*) *vt* to
cover; (*Pferd*) to shoe ♦ *vi*, *vr* (*Fenster etc*)
to mist over; **b~en sein (in** *od* **auf** +*dat*)
to be well versed (in); **b~nahmen** *vt* to
seize, to confiscate; to requisition; **~nah-**
mung *f* confiscation, sequestration
beschleunigen [bə'ʃlɔynɪgən] *vt* to
accelerate, to speed up ♦ *vi* (*AUT*) to
accelerate
Beschleunigung *f* acceleration
beschließen [bə'ʃliːsən] (*unreg*) *vt* to
decide on; (*beenden*) to end, to close
Beschluß [bə'ʃlus] (**-sses, ⁺sse**) *m*
decision, conclusion; (*Ende*) conclusion,
end

beschmutzen [bə'ʃmutsən] *vt* to dirty,
to soil
beschönigen [bə'ʃøːnɪgən] *vt* to gloss
over
beschränken [bə'ʃrɛŋkən] *vt*, *vr*: **(sich)**
~ **(auf** +*akk*) to limit *od* restrict (o.s.) (to)
beschränk- *zW*: **~t** *adj* confined,
restricted; (*Mensch*) limited, narrow-
minded; **B~ung** *f* limitation
beschreiben [bə'ʃraibən] (*unreg*) *vt* to
describe; (*Papier*) to write on
Beschreibung *f* description
beschriften [bə'ʃrɪftən] *vt* to mark, to
label
Beschriftung *f* lettering
beschuldigen [bə'ʃuldɪgən] *vt* to accuse
Beschuldigung *f* accusation
Beschuß [bə'ʃus] *m*: **jdn/etw unter** ~
nehmen (*MIL*) to open fire on sb/sth
beschützen [bə'ʃʏtsən] *vt*: ~ **(vor** +*dat*)
to protect (from); **Beschützer (-s, -)** *m*
protector
Beschwerde [bə'ʃveːrdə] *f* complaint;
(*Mühe*) hardship; **~n** *pl* (*Leiden*) trouble
beschweren [bə'ʃveːrən] *vt* to weight
down; (*fig*) to burden ♦ *vr* to complain
beschwerlich *adj* tiring, exhausting
beschwichtigen [bə'ʃvɪçtɪgən] *vt* to
soothe, to pacify
beschwindeln [bə'ʃvindəln] *vt*
(*betrügen*) to cheat; (*belügen*) to fib to
beschwingt [bə'ʃvɪŋt] *adj* in high spirits
beschwipst [bə'ʃvɪpst] (*umg*) *adj* tipsy
beschwören [bə'ʃvøːrən] (*unreg*) *vt*
(*Aussage*) to swear to; (*anflehen*) to
implore; (*Geister*) to conjure up
beseitigen [bə'zaitɪgən] *vt* to remove
Beseitigung *f* removal
Besen ['beːzən] (**-s, -**) *m* broom; **~stiel** *m*
broomstick
besessen [bə'zɛsən] *adj* possessed
besetz- [bə'zɛts] *zW*: **~en** *vt* (*Haus,*
Land) to occupy; (*Platz*) to take, to fill;
(*Posten*) to fill; (*Rolle*) to cast; (*mit*
Edelsteinen) to set; **~t** *adj* full; (*TEL*)
engaged, busy; (*Platz*) taken; (*WC*)
engaged; **B~zeichen** *nt* engaged tone;
B~ung *f* occupation; filling; (*von Rolle*)
casting; (*die Schauspieler*) cast

besichtigen [bə'zɪçtɪgən] *vt* to visit, to have a look at

Besichtigung *f* visit

Besied(e)lung [bə'zi:d(ə)lʊŋ] *f* population

besiegen [bə'zi:gən] *vt* to defeat, to overcome

besinnen [bə'zɪnən] (*unreg*) *vr* (*nachdenken*) to think, to reflect; (*erinnern*) to remember; **sich anders ~** to change one's mind

besinnlich *adj* contemplative

Besinnung *f* consciousness; **zur ~ kommen** to recover consciousness; (*fig*) to come to one's senses; **b~slos** *adj* unconscious

Besitz [bə'zɪts] (**-es**) *m* possession; (*Eigentum*) property; **b~en** (*unreg*) *vt* to possess, to own; (*Eigenschaft*) to have; **~er(in)** (**-s, -**) *m(f)* owner, proprietor; **~ergreifung** *f* occupation, seizure

besoffen [bə'zɔfən] (*umg*) *adj* drunk, stoned

besohlen [bə'zo:lən] *vt* to sole

Besoldung [bə'zɔldʊŋ] *f* salary, pay

besondere(r, s) [bə'zɔndərə(r, s)] *adj* special; (*eigen*) particular; (*gesondert*) separate; (*eigentümlich*) peculiar

Besonderheit [bə'zɔndərhaɪt] *f* peculiarity

besonders [bə'zɔndərs] *adv* especially, particularly; (*getrennt*) separately

besonnen [bə'zɔnən] *adj* sensible, level-headed

besorg- [bə'zɔrg] *zW*: **~en** *vt* (*beschaffen*) to acquire; (*kaufen auch*) to purchase; (*erledigen: Geschäfte*) to deal with; (*sich kümmern um*) to take care of; **B~nis** (**-, -se**) *f* anxiety, concern; **~t** [bə'zɔrçt] *adj* anxious, worried; **B~theit** *f* anxiety, worry; **B~ung** *f* acquisition; (*Kauf*) purchase

bespielen [bə'ʃpi:lən] *vt* to record

bespitzeln [bə'ʃpɪtsəln] *vt* to spy on

besprechen [bə'ʃprɛçən] (*unreg*) *vt* to discuss; (*Tonband etc*) to record, to speak onto; (*Buch*) to review ♦ *vr* to discuss, to consult

Besprechung *f* meeting, discussion; (*von Buch*) review

besser ['bɛsər] *adj* better; **~gehen** (*unreg*) *vi unpers*: **es geht ihm ~** he is feeling better; **~n** *vt* to make better, to improve ♦ *vr* to improve; (*Menschen*) to reform; **B~ung** *f* improvement; **gute B~ung!** get well soon!; **B~wisser** (**-s, -**) *m* know-all

Bestand [bə'ʃtant] (**-(e)s, ⁻e**) *m* (*Fortbestehen*) duration, stability; (*Kassen~*) amount, balance; (*Vorrat*) stock; **~ haben, von ~ sein** to last long, to endure

beständig [bə'ʃtɛndɪç] *adj* (*ausdauernd: auch fig*) constant; (*Wetter*) settled; (*Stoffe*) resistant; (*Klagen etc*) continual

Bestandsaufnahme [bə'ʃtantsaufna:mə] *f* stocktaking

Bestandteil *m* part, component; (*Zutat*) ingredient

bestärken [bə'ʃtɛrkən] *vt*: **jdn in etw** *dat* **~** to strengthen *od* confirm sb in sth

bestätigen [bə'ʃtɛ:tɪgən] *vt* to confirm; (*anerkennen, COMM*) to acknowledge

Bestätigung *f* confirmation; acknowledgement

bestatten [bə'ʃtatən] *vt* to bury

Bestattung *f* funeral; **~sinstitut** *nt* funeral director's

bestaunen [bə'ʃtaunən] *vt* to marvel at, gaze at in wonder

beste(r, s) ['bɛstə(r, s)] *adj* best; **so ist es am ~n** it's best that way; **am ~n gehst du gleich** you'd better go at once; **jdn zum ~n haben** to pull sb's leg; **einen Witz etc zum ~n geben** to tell a joke *etc*; **aufs ~** in the best possible way; **zu jds B~n** for the benefit of sb

bestechen [bə'ʃtɛçən] (*unreg*) *vt* to bribe

bestechlich *adj* corruptible

Bestechung *f* bribery, corruption

Besteck [bə'ʃtɛk] (**-(e)s, -e**) *nt* knife, fork and spoon, cutlery; (*MED*) set of instruments

bestehen [bə'ʃte:ən] (*unreg*) *vi* to be; to exist; (*andauern*) to last ♦ *vt* (*Probe, Prüfung*) to pass; (*Kampf*) to win; **~ auf** +*dat* to insist on; **~ aus** to consist of

bestehlen [bə'ʃte:lən] (*unreg*) *vt*: **jdn**

(um etw) ~ to rob sb (of sth)
besteigen [bə'ʃtaɪɡən] (*unreg*) *vt* to climb, to ascend; (*Pferd*) to mount; (*Thron*) to ascend
Bestell- [bə'ʃtɛl] *zW:* ~**buch** *nt* order book; **b~en** *vt* to order; (*kommen lassen*) to arrange to see; (*nominieren*) to name; (*Acker*) to cultivate; (*Grüße, Auftrag*) to pass on; ~**ung** *f* (*COMM*) order; (*Bestellen*) ordering
bestenfalls ['bɛstən'fals] *adv* at best
bestens ['bɛstəns] *adv* very well
besteuern [bə'ʃtɔʏərn] *vt* (*jdn, Waren*) to tax
Bestie ['bɛstiə] *f* (*auch fig*) beast
bestimm- [bə'ʃtɪm] *zW:* ~**en** *vt* (*Regeln*) to lay down; (*Tag, Ort*) to fix; (*beherrschen*) to characterize; (*vorsehen*) to mean; (*ernennen*) to appoint; (*definieren*) to define; (*veranlassen*) to induce; ~**t** *adj* (*entschlossen*) firm; (*gewiß*) certain, definite; (*Artikel*) definite ♦ *adv* (*gewiß*) definitely, for sure; **suchen Sie etwas B~tes?** are you looking for something in particular?; **B~theit** *f* firmness; certainty; **B~ung** *f* (*Verordnung*) regulation; (*Festsetzen*) determining; (*Verwendungszweck*) purpose; (*Schicksal*) fate; (*Definition*) definition
Bestleistung *f* best performance
bestmöglich *adj* best possible
bestrafen [bə'ʃtra:fən] *vt* to punish
Bestrafung *f* punishment
bestrahlen [bə'ʃtra:lən] *vt* to shine on; (*MED*) to treat with X-rays
Bestrahlung *f* (*MED*) X-ray treatment, radiotherapy
Bestreben [bə'ʃtre:bən] (-**s**) *nt* endeavour, effort
bestreichen [bə'ʃtraɪçən] (*unreg*) *vt* (*Brot*) to spread
bestreiten [bə'ʃtraɪtən] (*unreg*) *vt* (*abstreiten*) to dispute; (*finanzieren*) to pay for, to finance
bestreuen [bə'ʃtrɔʏən] *vt* to sprinkle, to dust; (*Straße*) to grit
bestürmen [bə'ʃtʏrmən] *vt* (*mit Fragen, Bitten etc*) to overwhelm, to swamp

bestürzend [bə'ʃtʏrtsənd] *adj* (*Nachrichten*) disturbing
bestürzt [bə'ʃtʏrtst] *adj* dismayed
Bestürzung *f* consternation
Besuch [bə'zu:x] (-(**e**)**s**, -**e**) *m* visit; (*Person*) visitor; **einen** ~ **machen bei jdm** to pay sb a visit *od* call; ~ **haben** to have visitors; **bei jdm auf** *od* **zu** ~ **sein** to be visiting sb; **b~en** *vt* to visit; (*SCH etc*) to attend; **gut b~t** well-attended; ~**er(in)** (-**s**, -) *m(f)* visitor, guest; ~**szeit** *f* visiting hours *pl*
betätigen [bə'lɛ:tɪɡən] *vt* (*bedienen*) to work, to operate ♦ *vr* to involve o.s.; **sich als etw** ~ to work as sth
Betätigung *f* activity; (*beruflich*) occupation; (*TECH*) operation
betäuben [bə'tɔʏbən] *vt* to stun; (*fig: Gewissen*) to still; (*MED*) to anaesthetize
Betäubung *f* (*Narkose*): **örtliche** ~ local anaesthetic
Betäubungsmittel *nt* anaesthetic
Bete ['be:tə] *f*: **rote** ~ beetroot (*BRIT*), beet (*US*)
beteiligen [bə'taɪlɪɡən] *vr*: **sich** ~ **(an** +*dat*) to take part (in), to participate (in), to share (in); (*an Geschäft: finanziell*) to have a share (in); **jdn** ~ **(an** +*dat*) to give sb a share *od* interest (in)
Beteiligte(r) *mf* (*Mitwirkender*) partner; (*finanziell*) shareholder
Beteiligung *f* participation; (*Anteil*) share, interest; (*Besucherzahl*) attendance
beten ['be:tən] *vt, vi* to pray
beteuern [bə'tɔʏərn] *vt* to assert; (*Unschuld*) to protest
Beteuerung *f* assertion; protestation; assurance
Beton [be'tõ:] (-**s**, -**s**) *m* concrete
betonen [bə'to:nən] *vt* to stress
betonieren [beto'ni:rən] *vt* to concrete
Betonung *f* stress, emphasis
betören [bə'tø:rən] *vt* to beguile
betr. *abk* (= *betrifft*) re
Betracht [bə'traxt] *m*: **in** ~ **kommen** to be considered *od* relevant; **etw in** ~ **ziehen** to take sth into consideration; **außer** ~ **bleiben** not to be considered; **b~en** *vt* to look at; (*fig*) to look at, to

consider; **~er(in)** (-s, -) *m(f)* observer

beträchtlich [bə'trɛçtlɪç] *adj* considerable

Betrachtung *f* (*Ansehen*) examination; (*Erwägung*) consideration

Betrag [bə'tra:k] (-(e)s, ⸚e) *m* amount; **b~en** [bə'tra:gən] (*unreg*) *vt* to amount to ♦ *vr* to behave; **~en** (-s) *nt* behaviour

Betreff *m*: **~ Ihr Schreiben vom ...** re your letter of ...

betreffen [bə'trɛfən] (*unreg*) *vt* to concern, to affect; **was mich betrifft** as for me; **~d** *adj* relevant, in question

betreffs [bə'trɛfs] *präp +gen* concerning, regarding; (*COMM*) re

betreiben [bə'traɪbən] (*unreg*) *vt* (*ausüben*) to practise; (*Politik*) to follow; (*Studien*) to pursue; (*vorantreiben*) to push ahead; (*TECH*: *antreiben*) to drive

betreten [bə'tre:tən] (*unreg*) *vt* to enter; (*Bühne etc*) to step onto ♦ *adj* embarrassed; **B~ verboten** keep off/out

Betreuer(in) [bə'trɔʏər(ɪn)] (-s, -) *m(f)* (*einer Person*) minder; (*eines Gebäude, Arbeitsgebiet*) caretaker; (*SPORT*) coach

Betreuung *f* care

Betrieb [bə'tri:p] (-(e)s, -e) *m* (*Firma*) firm, concern; (*Anlage*) plant; (*Tätigkeit*) operation; (*Treiben*) traffic; **außer ~ sein** to be out of order; **in ~ sein** to be in operation

Betriebs- *zW*: **~ausflug** *m* works outing; **b~fähig** *adj* in working order; **~ferien** *pl* company holidays (*BRIT*), company vacation *sg* (*US*); **~klima** *nt* (working) atmosphere; **~kosten** *pl* running costs; **~rat** *m* workers' council; **b~sicher** *adj* safe (to operate); **~störung** *f* breakdown; **~system** *nt* (*COMPUT*) operating system; **~unfall** *m* industrial accident; **~wirtschaft** *f* economics

betrinken [bə'trɪŋkən] (*unreg*) *vr* to get drunk

betroffen [bə'trɔfən] *adj* (*bestürzt*) full of consternation; **von etw ~ werden** *od* **sein** to be affected by sth

betrüben [bə'try:bən] *vt* to grieve

betrübt [bə'try:pt] *adj* sorrowful, grieved

Betrug [bə'tru:k] (-(e)s) *m* deception;

(*JUR*) fraud

betrügen [bə'try:gən] (*unreg*) *vt* to cheat; (*JUR*) to defraud; (*Ehepartner*) to be unfaithful to ♦ *vr* to deceive o.s.

Betrüger (-s, -) *m* cheat, deceiver; **b~isch** *adj* deceitful; (*JUR*) fraudulent

betrunken [bə'trʊŋkən] *adj* drunk

Bett [bɛt] (-(e)s, -en) *nt* bed; **ins** *od* **zu ~ gehen** to go to bed; **~bezug** *m* duvet cover; **~decke** *f* blanket; (*Daunen~*) quilt; (*Überwurf*) bedspread

Bettel- ['bɛtəl] *zW*: **b~arm** *adj* very poor, destitute; **~ei** [bɛtə'laɪ] *f* begging; **b~n** *vi* to beg

bettlägerig ['bɛtlɛ:gərɪç] *adj* bedridden

Bettlaken *nt* sheet

Bettler(in) ['bɛtlər(ɪn)] (-s, -) *m(f)* beggar

Bett- *zW*: **~(t)uch** *nt* sheet; **~vorleger** *m* bedside rug; **~wäsche** *f* bed linen; **~zeug** *nt* bedlinen *pl*

beugen ['bɔʏgən] *vt* to bend; (*GRAM*) to inflect ♦ *vr* (*sich fügen*) to bow

Beule ['bɔʏlə] *f* bump, swelling

beunruhigen [bə'ʊnru:ɪgən] *vt* to disturb, to alarm ♦ *vr* to become worried

Beunruhigung *f* worry, alarm

beurlauben [bə'u:rlaʊbən] *vt* to give leave *od* a holiday to (*BRIT*), to grant vacation time to (*US*)

beurteilen [bə'ʊrtaɪlən] *vt* to judge; (*Buch etc*) to review

Beurteilung *f* judgement; review; (*Note*) mark

Beute ['bɔʏtə] (-) *f* booty, loot

Beutel (-s, -) *m* bag; (*Geld~*) purse; (*Tabak~*) pouch

Bevölkerung [bə'fœlkərʊŋ] *f* population

bevollmächtigen [bə'fɔlmɛçtɪgən] *vt* to authorize

Bevollmächtigte(r) *mf* authorized agent

bevor [bə'fo:r] *konj* before; **~munden** *vt insep* to treat like a child; **~stehen** (*unreg*) *vi*: **(jdm) ~stehen** to be in store (for sb); **~stehend** *adj* imminent, approaching; **~zugen** *vt insep* to prefer

bewachen [bə'vaxən] *vt* to watch, to guard

Bewachung *f* (*Bewachen*) guarding; (*Leute*) guard, watch

bewaffnen [bə'vafnən] *vt* to arm
Bewaffnung *f* (*Vorgang*) arming;
(*Ausrüstung*) armament, arms *pl*
bewahren [bə'va:rən] *vt* to keep; **jdn vor**
jdm/etw ~ to save sb from sth/sth
bewähren [bə'vε:rən] *vr* to prove o.s.;
(*Maschine*) to prove its worth
bewahrheiten [bə'va:rhaɪtən] *vr* to
come true
bewährt *adj* reliable
Bewährung *f* (*JUR*) probation
bewältigen [bə'vεltɪgən] *vt* to overcome;
(*Arbeit*) to finish; (*Portion*) to manage
bewandert [bə'vandərt] *adj* expert,
knowledgeable
bewässern [bə'vεsərn] *vt* to irrigate
Bewässerung *f* irrigation
bewegen [bə've:gən] *vt*, *vr* to move; **jdn**
zu etw ~ to induce sb to do sth; **~d**
touching, moving
Beweg- [bə've:k] *zW*: **~grund** *m* motive;
b~lich *adj* movable, mobile; (*flink*) quick;
b~t *adj* (*Leben*) eventful; (*Meer*) rough;
(*ergriffen*) touched
Bewegung *f* movement, motion; (*innere*)
emotion; (*körperlich*) exercise; **~sfreiheit**
f freedom of movement; (*fig*) freedom of
action; **b~slos** *adj* motionless
Beweis [bə'vaɪs] (**-es**, **-e**) *m* proof;
(*Zeichen*) sign; **b~en** [-zən] (*unreg*) *vt* to
prove; (*zeigen*) to show; **~mittel** *nt*
evidence
Bewerb- [bə'vεrb] *zW*: **b~en** (*unreg*) *vr*
to apply (for); **~er(in)** (**-s**, **-**) *m(f)*
applicant; **~ung** *f* application
bewerkstelligen [bə'vεrkʃtεlɪgən] *vt* to
manage, to accomplish
bewerten [bə'vε:rtən] *vt* to assess
bewilligen [bə'vɪlɪgən] *vt* to grant, to
allow
Bewilligung *f* granting
bewirken [bə'vɪrkən] *vt* to cause, to
bring about
bewirten [bə'vɪrtən] *vt* to feed, to
entertain (to a meal)
bewirtschaften [bə'vɪrtʃaftən] *vt* to
manage
Bewirtung *f* hospitality
bewog *etc* [bə'vo:k] *vb siehe* **bewegen**

bewohn- [bə'vo:n] *zW*: **~bar** *adj*
habitable; **~en** *vt* to inhabit, to live in;
B~er(in) (**-s**, **-**) *m(f)* inhabitant; (*von*
Haus) resident
bewölkt [bə'vœlkt] *adj* cloudy, overcast
Bewölkung *f* clouds *pl*
Bewunder- [bə'vundər] *zW*: **~er** (**-s**, **-**) *m*
admirer; **b~n** *vt* to admire; **b~nswert**
adj admirable, wonderful; **~ung** *f*
admiration
bewußt [bə'vust] *adj* conscious;
(*absichtlich*) deliberate; **sich** *dat* **einer**
Sache *gen* **~ sein** to be aware of sth;
~los *adj* unconscious; **B~losigkeit** *f*
unconsciousness; **B~sein** *nt*
consciousness; **bei B~sein** conscious
bezahlen [bə'tsa:lən] *vt* to pay for
Bezahlung *f* payment
bezaubern [bə'tsaʊbərn] *vt* to charm
bezeichnen [bə'tsaɪçnən] *vt*
(*kennzeichnen*) to mark; (*nennen*) to call;
(*beschreiben*) to describe; (*zeigen*) to show,
to indicate; **~d** *adj*: **~d (für)**
characteristic (of), typical (of)
Bezeichnung *f* (*Zeichen*) mark, sign;
(*Beschreibung*) description
bezeugen [bə'tsɔʏgən] *vt* to testify to
Bezichtigung [bə'tsɪçtɪgʊŋ] *f* accusation
beziehen [bə'tsi:ən] (*unreg*) *vt* (*mit*
Überzug) to cover; (*Bett*) to make; (*Haus,*
Position) to move into; (*Standpunkt*) to
take up; (*erhalten*) to receive; (*Zeitung*) to
subscribe to, to take ♦ *vr* (*Himmel*) to
cloud over; **etw auf jdn/etw ~** to relate
sth to sb/sth; **sich ~ auf** +*akk* to refer to
Beziehung *f* (*Verbindung*) connection;
(*Zusammenhang*) relation; (*Verhältnis*)
relationship; (*Hinsicht*) respect; **~en**
haben (*vorteilhaft*) to have connections
od contacts; **b~sweise** *adv* or; (*genauer*
gesagt auch) that is, or rather
Bezirk [bə'tsɪrk] (**-(e)s**, **-e**) *m* district
Bezug [bə'tsu:k] (**-(e)s**, **ᵉe**) *m* (*Hülle*)
covering; (*COMM*) ordering; (*Gehalt*)
income, salary; (*Beziehung*): **~ (zu)**
relation(ship) (to); **in b~ auf** +*akk* with
reference to; **~ nehmen auf** +*akk* to refer
to
bezüglich [bə'tsy:klɪç] *präp* +*gen*

concerning, referring to ♦ *adj* (*GRAM*) relative; **auf etw** *akk* ~ relating to sth
bezwecken [bə'tsvɛkən] *vt* to aim at
bezweifeln [bə'tsvaɪfəln] *vt* to doubt, to query
BH *m abk von* **Büstenhalter**
Bhf. *abk* (= **Bahnhof**) station
Bibel ['biːbəl] (-, -n) *f* Bible
Biber ['biːbər] (-s, -) *m* beaver
Biblio- [biblio] *zW:* ~**graphie** [-gra'fiː] *f* bibliography; ~**thek** [-'teːk] (-, -en) *f* library; ~**thekar(in)** [-te'kaːr(ɪn)] (-s, -e) *m(f)* librarian
biblisch ['biːblɪʃ] *adj* biblical
bieder ['biːdər] *adj* upright, worthy; (*Kleid etc*) plain
bieg- ['biːg] *zW:* ~**en** (*unreg*) *vt, vr* to bend ♦ *vi* to turn; ~**sam** ['biːk-] *adj* flexible; **B~ung** *f* bend, curve
Biene ['biːnə] *f* bee
Bienenhonig *m* honey
Bienenwachs *nt* beeswax
Bier [biːr] (-(e)s, -e) *nt* beer; ~**deckel** *m* beer mat; ~**krug** *m* beer mug
Biest [biːst] (-s, -er; *umg: pej*) *nt* (*Tier*) beast, creature; (*Mensch*) beast
bieten ['biːtən] (*unreg*) *vt* to offer; (*bei Versteigerung*) to bid ♦ *vr* (*Gelegenheit*): **sich jdm** ~ to present itself to sb; **sich** *dat* **etw** ~ **lassen** to put up with sth
Bikini [bi'kiːni] (-s, -s) *m* bikini
Bilanz [bi'lants] *f* balance; (*fig*) outcome; ~ **ziehen (aus)** to take stock (of)
Bild [bɪlt] (-(e)s, -er) *nt* (*auch fig*) picture; photo; (*Spiegel~*) reflection; ~**bericht** *m* photographic report
bilden ['bɪldən] *vt* to form; (*erziehen*) to educate; (*ausmachen*) to constitute ♦ *vr* to arise; (*erziehen*) to educate o.s.
Bilderbuch *nt* picture book
Bilderrahmen *m* picture frame
Bild- *zW:* ~**fläche** *f* screen; (*fig*) scene; ~**hauer** (-s, -) *m* sculptor; **b~hübsch** *adj* lovely, pretty as a picture; **b~lich** *adj* figurative; pictorial; ~**schirm** *m* television screen; (*COMPUT*) monitor; **b~schön** *adj* lovely; ~**ung** [-dʊŋ] *f* formation; (*Wissen, Benehmen*) education
Billard ['bɪljart] (-s, -e) *nt* billiards *sg*;

~**kugel** *f* billiard ball
billig ['bɪlɪç] *adj* cheap; (*gerecht*) fair, reasonable; ~**en** ['bɪlɪɡən] *vt* to approve of
Binde ['bɪndə] *f* bandage; (*Arm~*) band; (*MED*) sanitary towel; ~**gewebe** *nt* connective tissue; ~**glied** *nt* connecting link; **b~n** (*unreg*) *vt* to bind, to tie; ~**strich** *m* hyphen; ~**wort** *nt* conjunction
Bindfaden ['bɪnt-] *m* string
Bindung *f* bond, tie; (*Ski~*) binding
binnen ['bɪnən] *präp* (+*dat od gen*) within; **B~hafen** *m* river port; **B~handel** *m* internal trade
Binse ['bɪnzə] *f* rush, reed; ~**nwahrheit** *f* truism
Bio- [bio] *in zW* bio-; ~**chemie** *f* biochemistry; ~**graphie** [-gra'fiː] *f* biography; ~**loge** [-'loːɡə] (-n, -n) *m* biologist; ~**logie** [-lo'ɡiː] *f* biology; **b~logisch** [-'loːɡɪʃ] *adj* biological; ~**top** *m od nt* biotope
Birke ['bɪrkə] *f* birch
Birnbaum *m* pear tree
Birne ['bɪrnə] *f* pear; (*ELEK*) (light) bulb

SCHLÜSSELWORT

bis [bɪs] *präp* +*akk, adv* **1** (*zeitlich*) till, until; (*bis spätestens*) by; **Sie haben bis Dienstag Zeit** you have until *od* till Tuesday; **bis Dienstag muß es fertig sein** it must be ready by Tuesday; **bis auf weiteres** until further notice; **bis in die Nacht** into the night; **bis bald/gleich** see you later/soon
2 (*räumlich*) (up) to; **ich fahre bis Köln** I'm going to *od* I'm going as far as Cologne; **bis an unser Grundstück** (right *od* up) to our plot; **bis hierher** this far
3 (*bei Zahlen*) up to; **bis zu** up to
4: **bis auf etw** *akk* (*außer*) except sth; (*einschließlich*) including sth
♦ *konj* **1** (*mit Zahlen*) to; **10 bis 20** 10 to 20
2 (*zeitlich*) till, until; **bis es dunkel wird** till *od* until it gets dark; **von ... bis ...** from ... to ...

Bischof ['bɪʃɔf] (-s, ⁻e) *m* bishop
bischöflich ['bɪʃøːflɪç] *adj* episcopal
bisher [bɪs'heːr] *adv* till now, hitherto;
~**ig** *adj* till now
Biskuit [bɪs'kviːt] (-(e)s, -s *od* -e) *m od nt*
(fatless) sponge
Biß [bɪs] (-sses, -sse) *m* bite
biß *etc vb siehe* **beißen**
bißchen ['bɪsçən] *adj, adv* bit
Bissen ['bɪsən] (-s, -) *m* bite, morsel
bissig ['bɪsɪç] *adj* (*Hund*) snappy;
(*Bemerkung*) cutting, biting
bist [bɪst] *vb siehe* **sein**
bisweilen [bɪs'vaɪlən] *adv* at times,
occasionally
Bit [bɪt] *nt* (*COMPUT*) bit
Bitte ['bɪtə] *f* request; **b~** *excl* please; (*wie
b~?*) (I beg your) pardon?; (*als Antwort
auf Dank*) you're welcome; **darf ich? --
aber b~!** may I? — please do; **b~ schön!**
it was a pleasure; **b~n** (*unreg*) *vt, vi:* **b~n
(um)** to ask (for); **b~nd** *adj* pleading,
imploring
bitter ['bɪtər] *adj* bitter; ~**böse** *adj* very
angry; **B~keit** *f* bitterness; ~**lich** *adj*
bitter
Blähungen ['blɛːʊŋən] *pl* (*MED*) wind *sg*
blamabel [bla'maːbəl] *adj* disgraceful
Blamage [bla'maːʒə] *f* disgrace
blamieren [bla'miːrən] *vr* to make a fool
of o.s., to disgrace o.s. ♦ *vt* to let down, to
disgrace
blank [blaŋk] *adj* bright; (*unbedeckt*) bare;
(*sauber*) clean, polished; (*umg: ohne Geld*)
broke; (*offensichtlich*) blatant
blanko ['blaŋko] *adv* blank; **B~scheck** *m*
blank cheque
Bläschen ['blɛːsçən] *nt* bubble; (*MED*)
(small) blister
Blase ['blaːzə] *f* bubble; (*MED*) blister;
(*ANAT*) bladder; ~**balg** (-(e)s, -bälge) *m*
bellows *pl*; **b~n** (*unreg*) *vt, vi* to blow
Blas- ['blaːs] *zW:* ~**instrument** *nt* wind
instrument; ~**kapelle** *f* brass band
blaß [blas] *adj* pale
Blässe ['blɛsə] (-) *f* paleness, pallor
Blatt [blat] (-(e)s, ⁻er) *nt* leaf; (*von Papier*)
sheet; (*Zeitung*) newspaper; (*KARTEN*) hand
blättern ['blɛtərn] *vi:* **in etw** *dat* ~ to leaf

through sth
Blätterteig *m* flaky *od* puff pastry
blau [blaʊ] *adj* blue; (*umg*) drunk, stoned;
(*KOCH*) boiled; (*Auge*) black; ~**er Fleck**
bruise; **Fahrt ins B~e** mystery tour;
~**äugig** *adj* blue-eyed
Blech [blɛç] (-(e)s, -e) *nt* tin, sheet metal;
(*Back~*) baking tray; ~**büchse** *f* tin, can;
~**dose** *f* tin, can; **b~en** (*umg*) *vt, vi* to
fork out; ~**schaden** *m* (*AUT*) damage to
bodywork
Blei [blaɪ] (-(e)s, -e) *nt* lead
Bleibe ['blaɪbə] *f* roof over one's head;
b~n (*unreg*) *vi* to stay, to remain; **b~nd**
adj (*Erinnerung*) lasting (*Schaden*)
permanent; **b~nlassen** (*unreg*) *vt* to
leave (alone)
bleich [blaɪç] *adj* faded, pale; ~**en** *vt* to
bleach
Blei- *zW:* **b~ern** *adj* leaden; **b~frei** *adj*
(*Benzin*) lead-free; ~**stift** *m* pencil;
~**stiftspitzer** *m* pencil sharpener
Blende ['blɛndə] *f* (*PHOT*) aperture; **b~n** *vt*
to blind, to dazzle; (*fig*) to hoodwink;
b~nd (*umg*) *adj* grand; **b~nd aussehen**
to look smashing
Blick [blɪk] (-(e)s, -e) *m* (*kurz*) glance,
glimpse; (*Anschauen*) look; (*Aussicht*)
view; **b~en** *vi* to look; **sich b~en lassen**
to put in an appearance; ~**fang** *m* eye-
catcher
blieb *etc* [bliːp] *vb siehe* **bleiben**
blind [blɪnt] *adj* blind; (*Glas etc*) dull; ~**er
Passagier** stowaway; **B~darm** *m*
appendix; **B~darmentzündung** *f*
appendicitis; **B~enschrift** ['blɪndən-] *f*
Braille; **B~heit** *f* blindness; ~**lings** *adv*
blindly; **B~schleiche** *f* slow worm
blinken ['blɪŋkən] *vi* to twinkle, to
sparkle; (*Licht*) to flash, to signal; (*AUT*) to
indicate ♦ *vt* to flash, to signal
Blinker (-s, -) *m* (*AUT*) indicator
Blinklicht *nt* (*AUT*) indicator; (*an
Bahnübergangen usw*) flashing light
blinzeln ['blɪntsəln] *vi* to blink, to wink
Blitz [blɪts] (-es, -e) *m* (flash of) lightning;
~**ableiter** *m* lightning conductor; **b~en**
vi (*aufleuchten*) to flash, to sparkle; **es b~t**
(*MET*) there's a flash of lightning; ~**licht**

nt flashlight; **b~schnell** *adj* lightning
♦ *adv* (as) quick as a flash
Block [blɔk] **(-(e)s, =e)** *m* block; (*von Papier*) pad; **~ade** [blɔ'ka:də] *f* blockade; **~flöte** *f* recorder; **b~frei** *adj* (*POL*) unaligned; **b~ieren** [blɔ'ki:rən] *vt* to block ♦ *vi* (*Räder*) to jam; **~schrift** *f* block letters *pl*
blöd [blø:t] *adj* silly, stupid; **~eln** ['blø:dəln] (*umg*) *vi* to act the goat (*fam*), to fool around; **B~sinn** *m* nonsense; **~sinnig** *adj* silly, idiotic
blond [blɔnt] *adj* blond, fair-haired

SCHLÜSSELWORT

bloß [blo:s] *adj* **1** (*unbedeckt*) bare; (*nackt*) naked; **mit der bloßen Hand** with one's bare hand; **mit bloßem Auge** with the naked eye
2 (*alleinig, nur*) mere; **der bloße Gedanke** the very thought; **bloßer Neid** sheer envy
♦ *adv* only, merely; **laß das bloß!** just don't do that!; **wie ist das bloß passiert?** how on earth did that happen?

Blöße ['blø:sə] *f* bareness; nakedness; (*fig*) weakness
bloßlegen *vt* to expose
bloßstellen *vt* to show up
blühen ['bly:ən] *vi* to bloom (*lit*), to be in bloom; (*fig*) to flourish
blühend *adj* (*Pflanze*) blooming; (*Aussehen*) blooming, radiant; (*Handel*) thriving, booming
Blume ['blu:mə] *f* flower; (*von Wein*) bouquet; **~nkohl** *m* cauliflower; **~ntopf** *m* flowerpot; **~nzwiebel** *f* bulb
Bluse ['blu:zə] *f* blouse
Blut [blu:t] **(-(e)s)** *nt* blood; **b~arm** *adj* anaemic; (*fig*) penniless; **b~befleckt** *adj* bloodstained; **~druck** *m* blood pressure
Blüte ['bly:tə] *f* blossom; (*fig*) prime
Blutegel *m* leech
bluten *vi* to bleed
Bluter *m* (*MED*) haemophiliac
Bluterguß *m* haemorrhage; (*auf Haut*) bruise
Blütezeit *f* flowering period; (*fig*) prime

Blut- *zW:* **~gruppe** *f* blood group; **b~ig** *adj* bloody; **b~jung** *adj* very young; **~probe** *f* blood test; **~spender** *m* blood donor; **~transfusion** *f* (*MED*) blood transfusion; **~ung** *f* bleeding, haemorrhage; **~vergiftung** *f* blood poisoning; **~wurst** *f* black pudding
Bö [bø:] **(-, -en)** *f* squall
Bock [bɔk] **(-(e)s, =e)** *m* buck, ram; (*Gestell*) trestle, support; (*SPORT*) buck; **~wurst** *f* type of pork sausage
Boden ['bo:dən] **(-s, =)** *m* ground; (*Fuß~*) floor; (*Meeres~, Faß~*) bottom; (*Speicher*) attic; **b~los** *adj* bottomless; (*umg*) incredible; **~schätze** *pl* mineral resources; **~see** *m*: **der ~see** Lake Constance; **~turnen** *nt* floor exercises *pl*
Böe ['bø:ə] *f* squall
Bogen ['bo:gən] **(-s, -)** *m* (*Biegung*) curve; (*ARCHIT*) arch; (*Waffe, MUS*) bow; (*Papier*) sheet
Bohle ['bo:lə] *f* plank
Bohne ['bo:nə] *f* bean
bohnern *vt* to wax, to polish
Bohnerwachs *nt* floor polish
Bohr- ['bo:r] *zW:* **b~en** *vt* to bore; **~er** **(-s, -)** *m* drill; **~insel** *f* oil rig; **~maschine** *f* drill; **~turm** *m* derrick
Boje ['bo:jə] *f* buoy
Bolivien [bo'li:viən] *nt* Bolivia
Bolzen ['bɔltsən] **(-s, -)** *m* bolt
bombardieren [bɔmbar'di:rən] *vt* to bombard; (*aus der Luft*) to bomb
Bombe ['bɔmbə] *f* bomb
Bombenangriff *m* bombing raid
Bombenerfolg (*umg*) *m* smash hit
Bon [bɔŋ] **(-s, -s)** *m* voucher, chit
Bonbon [bõ'bõ:] **(-s, -s)** *m od nt* sweet
Boot [bo:t] **(-(e)s, -e)** *nt* boat
Bord [bɔrt] **(-(e)s, -e)** *m* (*AVIAT, NAUT*) board ♦ *nt* (*Brett*) shelf; **an ~** on board
Bordell [bɔr'dɛl] **(-s, -e)** *nt* brothel
Bordstein *m* kerb(stone)
borgen ['bɔrgən] *vt* to borrow; **jdm etw ~** to lend sb sth
Borke ['bɔrkə] *f* (*BOT*) bark
borniert [bɔr'ni:rt] *adj* narrow-minded
Börse ['bø:rzə] *f* stock exchange; (*Geld~*) purse; **~nmakler** *m* stockbroker

Borste ['bɔrstə] f bristle
Borte ['bɔrtə] f edging; (*Band*) trimming
bös [bøːs] *adj* = **böse**
bösartig ['bøːs-] *adj* malicious
Böschung ['bœʃʊŋ] f slope; (*Ufer~ etc*) embankment
böse ['bøːzə] *adj* bad, evil; (*zornig*) angry
boshaft ['boːshaft] *adj* malicious, spiteful
Bosheit f malice, spite
Bosnien und Herzegowina ['bɔsniən, hɛrtsə'goːvina] *nt* Bosnia (and) Herzegovina
böswillig ['bøːsvɪlɪç] *adj* malicious
bot *etc* [boːt] *vb siehe* **bieten**
Botanik [bo'taːnɪk] f botany
botanisch [bo'taːnɪʃ] *adj* botanical
Bot- ['boːt] *zW:* ~**e** (**-n, -n**) *m* messenger; ~**schaft** f message, news; (*POL*) embassy; ~**schafter** (**-s, -**) *m* ambassador
Bottich ['bɔtɪç] (**-(e)s, -e**) *m* vat, tub
Bouillon [bu'ljõ:] (**-, -s**) f consommé
Bowle ['boːlə] f punch
Box- [bɔks] *zW:* **b~en** *vi* to box; ~**er** (**-s, -**) *m* boxer; ~**handschuh** *m* boxing glove; ~**kampf** *m* boxing match
boykottieren [bɔykɔ'tiːrən] *vt* to boycott
brach *etc* [braːx] *vb siehe* **brechen**
brachte *etc* ['braxtə] *vb siehe* **bringen**
Branche ['brãːʃə] f line of business; ~**nverzeichnis** *nt* yellow pages *pl*
Brand [brant] (**-(e)s, ⁻e**) *m* fire; (*MED*) gangrene; **b~en** ['brandən] *vi* to surge; (*Meer*) to break; **b~marken** *vt* to brand; (*fig*) to stigmatize; ~**salbe** f ointment for burns; ~**stifter** [-ʃtɪftər] *m* arsonist, fire-raiser; ~**stiftung** f arson; ~**ung** f surf
Branntwein ['brantvaɪn] *m* brandy
Brasilien [bra'ziːliən] *nt* Brazil
Brat- ['braːt] *zW:* ~**apfel** *m* baked apple; **b~en** (*unreg*) *vt* to roast; to fry; ~**en** (**-s, -**) *m* roast, joint; ~**hähnchen** *nt* roast chicken; ~**huhn** *nt* roast chicken; ~**kartoffeln** *pl* fried *od* roast potatoes; ~**pfanne** f frying pan
Bratsche ['braːtʃə] f viola
Bratspieß *m* spit
Bratwurst f grilled/fried sausage
Brauch [braʊx] (**-(e)s, Bräuche**) *m* custom; **b~bar** *adj* usable, serviceable;

(*Person*) capable; **b~en** *vt* (*bedürfen*) to need; (*müssen*) to have to; (*inf: verwenden*) to use
Braue ['braʊə] f brow
brauen *vt* to brew
Braue'rei f brewery
braun [braʊn] *adj* brown; (*von Sonne auch*) tanned
Bräune ['brɔynə] (**-**) f brownness; (*Sonnen~*) tan; **b~n** *vt* to make brown; (*Sonne*) to tan
braungebrannt *adj* tanned
Brause ['braʊzə] f shower bath; (*von Gießkanne*) rose; (*Getränk*) lemonade; **b~n** *vi* to roar; (*auch vr: duschen*) to take a shower
Braut [braʊt] (**-, Bräute**) f bride; (*Verlobte*) fiancée
Bräutigam ['brɔytɪgam] (**-s, -e**) *m* bridegroom; fiancé
Brautpaar *nt* bride and (bride)groom, bridal pair
brav [braːf] *adj* (*artig*) good; (*ehrenhaft*) worthy, honest
bravo ['braːvo] *excl* well done
BRD ['beːʔɛr'deː] (**-**) f *abk* = **Bundesrepublik Deutschland**
Brech- ['brɛç] *zW:* ~**eisen** *nt* crowbar; **b~en** (*unreg*) *vt, vi* to break; (*Licht*) to refract; (*fig: Mensch*) to crush; (*speien*) to vomit; ~**reiz** *m* nausea, retching
Brei [braɪ] (**-(e)s, -e**) *m* (*Masse*) pulp; (*KOCH*) gruel; (*Hafer~*) porridge
breit [braɪt] *adj* wide, broad; **B~e** f width; (*bes bei Maßangaben*) breadth; (*GEOG*) latitude; ~**en** *vt:* **etw über etw** *akk* ~**en** to spread sth over sth; **B~engrad** *m* degree of latitude; ~**machen** *vr* to spread o.s. out; ~**treten** (*unreg; umg*) *vt* to go on about
Brems- ['brɛms] *zW:* ~**belag** *m* brake lining; ~**e** [-zə] f brake; (*ZOOL*) horsefly; **b~en** [-zən] *vi* to brake ♦ *vt* (*Auto*) to brake; (*fig*) to slow down; ~**flüssigkeit** f brake fluid; ~**licht** *nt* brake light; ~**pedal** *nt* brake pedal; ~**spur** f skid mark (*s pl*); ~**weg** *m* braking distance
Brenn- ['brɛn] *zW:* **b~bar** *adj* inflammable; **b~en** (*unreg*) *vi* to burn, to

be on fire; (*Licht, Kerze etc*) to burn ♦ *vt* (*Holz etc*) to burn; (*Ziegel, Ton*) to fire; (*Kaffee*) to roast; **darauf b~en, etw zu tun** to be dying to do sth; **~(n)essel** *f* stinging nettle; **~punkt** *m* (*PHYS*) focal point; (*Mittelpunkt*) focus; **~spiritus** *m* methylated spirits; **~stoff** *m* fuel

brenzlig ['brɛntslɪç] *adj* (*fig*) precarious

Brett [brɛt] (-(e)s, -er) *nt* board, plank; (*Bord*) shelf; (*Spiel~*) board; **~er** *pl* (*SKI*) skis; (*THEAT*) boards; **Schwarze(s) ~** notice board; **~erzaun** *m* wooden fence; **~spiel** *nt* board game

Brezel ['breːtsəl] (-, -n) *f* pretzel

brichst *etc* [brɪçst] *vb siehe* **brechen**

Brief [briːf] (-(e)s, -e) *m* letter; **~freund** *m* penfriend; **~kasten** *m* letterbox; **b~lich** *adj, adv* by letter; **~marke** *f* (postage) stamp; **~öffner** *m* letter opener; **~papier** *nt* notepaper; **~tasche** *f* wallet; **~träger** *m* postman; **~umschlag** *m* envelope; **~waage** *f* letter scales; **~wechsel** *m* correspondence

briet *etc* [briːt] *vb siehe* **braten**

Brikett [briˈkɛt] (-s, -s) *nt* briquette

brillant [brɪlˈjant] *adj* (*fig*) brilliant; **B~** (-en, -en) *m* brilliant, diamond

Brille ['brɪlə] *f* spectacles *pl*; (*Schutz~*) goggles *pl*; (*Toiletten~*) (toilet) seat; **~ngestell** *nt* (spectacle) frames

bringen ['brɪŋən] (*unreg*) *vt* to bring; (*mitnehmen, begleiten*) to take; (*einbringen: Profit*) to bring in; (*veröffentlichen*) to publish; (*THEAT, CINE*) to show; (*RADIO, TV*) to broadcast; (*in einen Zustand versetzen*) to get; (*umg: tun können*) to manage; **jdn dazu ~, etw zu tun** to make sb do sth; **jdn nach Hause ~** to take sb home; **jdn um etw ~** to make sb lose sth; **jdn auf eine Idee ~** to give sb an idea

Brise ['briːzə] *f* breeze

Brit- ['briːt] *zW*: **~e** *m* Briton; **~in** *f* Briton; **b~isch** *adj* British

bröckelig ['brœkəlɪç] *adj* crumbly

Brocken ['brɔkən] (-s, -) *m* piece, bit; (*Fels~*) lump of rock

brodeln ['broːdəln] *vi* to bubble

Brokat [broˈkaːt] (-(e)s, -e) *m* brocade

Brokkoli ['brɔkoli] *pl* (*BOT*) broccoli

Brombeere ['brɔmbeːrə] *f* blackberry, bramble (*BRIT*)

Bronchien ['brɔnçiən] *pl* bronchia(l tubes) *pl*

Bronchitis (-) *f* bronchitis

Bronze ['brõːsə] *f* bronze

Brosche ['brɔʃə] *f* brooch

Broschüre [brɔˈʃyːrə] *f* pamphlet

Brot [broːt] (-(e)s, -e) *nt* bread; (*Laib*) loaf

Brötchen ['brøːtçən] *nt* roll

Bruch [brʊx] (-(e)s, ¨e) *m* breakage; (*zerbrochene Stelle*) break; (*fig*) split, breach; (*MED: Eingeweide~*) rupture, hernia; (*Bein~ etc*) fracture; (*MATH*) fraction

brüchig ['brʏçɪç] *adj* brittle, fragile; (*Haus*) dilapidated

Bruch- *zW*: **~landung** *f* crash landing; **~strich** *m* (*MATH*) line; **~stück** *nt* fragment; **~teil** *m* fraction; **~zahl** [brʊxtsaːl] *f* (*MATH*) fraction

Brücke ['brʏkə] *f* bridge; (*Teppich*) rug

Bruder ['bruːdər] (-s, ¨) *m* brother

brüderlich ['bryːdərlɪç] *adj* brotherly

Brühe ['bryːə] *f* broth, stock; (*pej*) muck

Brühwürfel *m* (*KOCH*) stock cube

brüllen ['brʏlən] *vi* to bellow, to roar

brummen ['brʊmən] *vi* (*Bär, Mensch etc*) to growl; (*Insekt*) to buzz; (*Motoren*) to roar; (*murren*) to grumble ♦ *vt* to growl

brünett [brʏˈnɛt] *adj* brunette, dark-haired

Brunnen ['brʊnən] (-s, -) *m* fountain; (*tief*) well; (*natürlich*) spring

brüsk [brʏsk] *adj* abrupt, brusque

Brust [brʊst] (-, ¨e) *f* breast; (*Männer~*) chest

brüsten ['brʏstən] *vr* to boast

Brust- *zW*: **~fellentzündung** *f* pleurisy; **~kasten** *m* chest; **~schwimmen** *nt* breast-stroke

Brüstung ['brʏstʊŋ] *f* parapet

Brut [bruːt] (-, -en) *f* brood; (*Brüten*) hatching

brutal [bruˈtaːl] *adj* brutal; **B~iˈtät** *f* brutality

brüten ['bryːtən] *vi* (*auch fig*) to brood

Brutkasten *m* incubator

brutto ['bruto] *adv* gross; **B~ein-kommen** *nt* gross salary; **B~gehalt** *nt* gross salary; **B~gewicht** *nt* gross weight; **B~lohn** *m* gross wages *pl*; **B~sozialprodukt** *nt* gross national product

BSE *f* (= *Bovine Spongiforme Enzephalopathie*) BSE

Bube ['bu:bə] (**-n, -n**) *m* (*Schurke*) rogue; (*KARTEN*) jack

Buch [bu:x] (**-(e)s, ⁻er**) *nt* book; (*COMM*) account book; **~binder** *m* bookbinder; **~drucker** *m* printer

Buche *f* beech tree

buchen *vt* to book; (*Betrag*) to enter

Bücher- ['by:çər] *zW*: **~brett** *nt* bookshelf; **~ei** [-'raɪ] *f* library; **~regal** *nt* bookshelves *pl*, bookcase; **~schrank** *m* bookcase

Buch- *zW*: **~fink** *m* chaffinch; **~führung** *f* book-keeping, accounting; **~halter(in)** (**-s, -**) *m(f)* book-keeper; **~handel** *m* book trade; **~händler(in)** *m(f)* bookseller; **~handlung** *f* bookshop

Büchse ['byksə] *f* tin, can; (*Holz~*) box; (*Gewehr*) rifle; **~nfleisch** *nt* tinned meat; **~nmilch** *f* (*KOCH*) evaporated milk, tinned milk; **~nöffner** *m* tin *od* can opener

Buch- *zW*: **~stabe** ['bu:xʃta:bə] (**-ns, -n**) *m* letter (of the alphabet); **b~stabieren** [bu:xʃta'bi:rən] *vt* to spell; **b~stäblich** ['bu:xʃtɛ:plɪç] *adj* literal

Bucht [buxt] (**-, -en**) *f* bay

Buchung ['bu:xʊŋ] *f* booking; (*COMM*) entry

Buckel ['bʊkəl] (**-s, -**) *m* hump

bücken ['bykən] *vr* to bend

Bückling ['byklɪŋ] *m* (*Fisch*) kipper; (*Verbeugung*) bow

Bude ['bu:də] *f* booth, stall; (*umg*) digs *pl* (*BRIT*)

Büfett [by'fe:] (**-s, -s**) *nt* (*Anrichte*) sideboard; (*Geschirrschrank*) dresser; **kaltes ~** cold buffet

Büffel ['byfəl] (**-s, -**) *m* buffalo

Bug [bu:k] (**-(e)s, -e**) *m* (*NAUT*) bow; (*AVIAT*) nose

Bügel ['by:gəl] (**-s, -**) *m* (*Kleider~*) ha..ger; (*Steig~*) stirrup; (*Brillen~*) arm; **~brett** *nt* ironing board; **~eisen** *nt* iron; **~falte** *f* crease; **b~frei** *adj* crease-resistant, noniron; **b~n** *vt, vi* to iron

Bühne ['by:nə] *f* stage; **~nbild** *nt* set, scenery

Buhruf ['bu:ru:f] *m* boo

buk *etc* [bu:k] *vb siehe* **backen**

Bulgarien [bʊl'ga:riən] *nt* Bulgaria

Bullauge *nt* (*NAUT*) porthole

Bull- ['bʊl] *zW*: **~dogge** *f* bulldog; **~dozer** ['bʊldo:zər] (**-s, -**) *m* bulldozer; **~e** (**-n, -n**) *m* bull

Bumerang ['bu:məraŋ] (**-s, -e**) *m* boomerang

Bummel ['bʊməl] (**-s, -**) *m* stroll; (*Schaufenster~*) window-shopping; **~ant** [-'lant] *m* slowcoach; **~ei** [-'laɪ] *f* wandering; dawdling; skiving; **b~n** *vi* to wander, to stroll; (*trödeln*) to dawdle; (*faulenzen*) to skive, to loaf around; **~streik** ['bʊməlʃtraɪk] *m* go-slow

Bund¹ [bʊnt] (**-(e)s, ⁻e**) *m* (*Freundschafts~ etc*) bond; (*Organisation*) union; (*POL*) confederacy; (*Hosen~, Rock~*) waistband

Bund² (**-(e)s, -e**) *nt* bunch; (*Stroh~*) bundle

Bündel ['byndəl] (**-s, -**) *nt* bundle, bale; **b~n** *vt* to bundle

Bundes- ['bʊndəs] *in zW* Federal (*bes West German*); **~bahn** *f* Federal Railways *pl*; **~bürger** *m* West German citizen; **~hauptstadt** *f* Federal capital; **~kanzler** *m* Federal Chancellor; **~land** *nt* Land; **~liga** *f* football league; **~präsident** *m* Federal President; **~rat** *m* upper house of West German Parliament; **~regierung** *f* Federal government; **~republik** *f* Federal Republic (of West Germany); **~staat** *m* Federal state; **~tag** *m* West German Parliament; **~wehr** *f* West German Armed Forces *pl*

bündig ['byndɪç] *adj* (*kurz*) concise

Bündnis ['byntnɪs] (**-ses, -se**) *nt* alliance

Bunker ['bʊŋkər] (**-s, -**) *m* bunker

bunt [bʊnt] *adj* coloured; (*gemischt*) mixed; **jdm wird es zu ~** it's getting too much for sb; **B~stift** *m* coloured pencil, crayon

Burg [bʊrk] (**-, -en**) *f* castle, fort

Bürge ['byrgə] (-n, -n) *m* guarantor; **b~n**
vi: **b~n für** to vouch for

Bürger(in) ['byrgər(ın)] (-s, -) *m(f)* citizen;
member of the middle class; **~krieg** *m*
civil war; **b~lich** *adj* (*Rechte*) civil;
(*Klasse*) middle-class; (*pej*) bourgeois;
~meister *m* mayor; **~recht** *nt* civil
rights *pl*; **~schaft** *f* population, citizens
pl; **~steig** *m* pavement

Bürgschaft *f* surety; **~ leisten** to give
security

Büro [by'ro:] (-s, -s) *nt* office;
~angestellte(r) *mf* office worker;
~klammer *f* paper clip; **~kra'tie** *f*
bureaucracy; **b~'kratisch** *adj*
bureaucratic; **~schluß** *m* office closing
time

Bursch (-en, -en) *m* = Bursche

Bursche ['burʃə] (-n, -n) *m* lad, fellow;
(*Diener*) servant

Bürste ['byrstə] *f* brush; **b~n** *vt* to brush

Bus [bus] (-ses, -se) *m* bus

Busch [buʃ] (-(e)s, ⁻e) *m* bush, shrub

Büschel ['byʃəl] (-s, -) *nt* tuft

buschig *adj* bushy

Busen ['bu:zən] (-s, -) *m* bosom; (*Meer~*)
inlet, bay

Buße ['bu:sə] *f* atonement, penance;
(*Geld*) fine

büßen ['by:sən] *vi* to do penance, to
atone ♦ *vt* to do penance for, to atone for

Bußgeld ['bu:sgɛlt] *nt* fine

Büste ['bystə] *f* bust; **~nhalter** *m* bra

Butter ['butər] (-) *f* butter; **~blume** *f*
buttercup; **~brot** *nt* (piece of) bread and
butter; (*umg*) sandwich; **~brotpapier** *nt*
greaseproof paper; **~dose** *f* butter dish;
b~weich ['butɐvaiç] *adj* soft as butter;
(*fig*, *umg*) soft

b.w. *abk* (= *bitte wenden*) p.t.o.

bzgl. *abk* (= *bezüglich*) re

bzw. *abk* = beziehungsweise

C c

ca. *abk* (= *circa*) approx.

Café [ka'fe:] (-s, -s) *nt* café

Cafeteria [kafete'ri:a] (-, -s) *f* cafeteria

Camcorder (-s, -s) *m* camcorder

Camp- ['kɛmp] *zW*: **c~en** *vi* to camp; **~er**
(-s, -) *m* camper; **~ing** (-s) *nt* camping;
~ingkocher *m* camping stove; **~ingplatz**
m camp(ing) site

CD *f abk* (*disc*) CD; **~-Spieler** *m* CD
(player)

Cellist [tʃɛ'lıst] *m* cellist

Cello ['tʃɛlo] (-s, -s *od* Celli) *nt* cello

Celsius ['tsɛlzius] (-) *nt* Celsius

Chamäleon [ka'mɛ:leɔn] (-s, -s) *nt*
chameleon

Champagner [ʃam'panjər] (-s, -) *m*
champagne

Champignon ['ʃampinjõ] (-s, -s) *m*
button mushroom

Chance ['ʃã:s(ə)] *f* chance, opportunity

Chaos ['ka:ɔs] (-, -) *nt* chaos

chaotisch [ka'o:tıʃ] *adj* chaotic

Charakter [ka'raktər, *pl* karak'te:rə] (-s,
-e) *m* character; **c~fest** *adj* of firm
character, strong; **c~i'sieren** *vt* to
characterize; **c~istisch** [karakte'rıstıʃ]
adj: **c~istisch (für)** characteristic (of),
typical (of); **c~los** *adj* unprincipled;
~losigkeit *f* lack of principle;
~schwäche *f* weakness of character;
~stärke *f* strength of character; **~zug** *m*
characteristic, trait

charmant [ʃar'mant] *adj* charming

Charme [ʃarm] (-s) *m* charm

Charterflug ['(t)ʃa:rtərflu:k] *m* charter
flight

Chauffeur [ʃɔ'føːr] *m* chauffeur

Chauvinist [ʃovi'nıst] *m* chauvinist,
jingoist

Chef [ʃɛf] (-s, -s) *m* head; (*umg*) boss;
~arzt *m* senior consultant; **~in** (*umg*) *f*
boss

Chemie [çe'mi:] (-) *f* chemistry; **~faser** *f*
man-made fibre

Chemikalie [çemi'ka:liə] *f* chemical

Chemiker ['çe:mikər] (-s, -) *m*
(industrial) chemist

chemisch ['çe:mıʃ] *adj* chemical; **~e
Reinigung** dry cleaning

Chicorée [ʃiko're:] (-s) *m od f* chicory

Chiffre ['ʃıfrə] *f* (*Geheimzeichen*) cipher;
(*in Zeitung*) box number

Chile ['çiːle, 'tʃiːle] *nt* Chile
Chin- ['çiːn] *zW*: **~a** *nt* China; **~akohl** *m*
Chinese leaves; **~ese** [-'neːzə] *m* Chinese;
~esin *f* Chinese; **c~esisch** *adj* Chinese
Chirurg [çi'rʊrk] (-en, -en) *m* surgeon;
~ie [-'giː] *f* surgery; **c~isch** *adj* surgical
Chlor [kloːr] (-s) *nt* chlorine; **~o'form** (-s)
nt chloroform
Cholera ['koːlera] (-) *f* cholera
cholerisch [ko'leːrɪʃ] *adj* choleric
Chor [koːr] (-(e)s, ⁻e) *m* choir;
(*Musikstück, THEAT*) chorus; **~al** [ko'raːl]
(-s, -äle) *m* chorale
Choreograph [koreo'graːf] (-en, -en) *m*
choreographer
Christ [krɪst] (-en, -en) *m* Christian;
~baum *m* Christmas tree; **~enheit** *f*
Christendom; **~entum** *nt* Christianity;
~in *f* Christian; **~kind** *nt* ≈ Father
Christmas; (*Jesus*) baby Jesus; **c~lich** *adj*
Christian; **~us** (-) *m* Christ
Chrom [kroːm] (-s) *nt* (*CHEM*) chromium;
chrome
Chron- ['kroːn] *zW*: **~ik** *f* chronicle;
c~isch *adj* chronic; **c~ologisch**
[-o'loːgɪʃ] *adj* chronological
Chrysantheme [kryzan'teːmə] *f*
chrysanthemum
circa ['tsɪrka] *adv* about, approximately
Clown [klaʊn] (-s, -s) *m* clown
Cocktail ['kɔkteːl] (-s, -s) *m* cocktail
Cola ['koːla] (-, -s) *f* Coke ®
Computer [kɔm'pjuːtər] (-s, -) *m*
computer; **~spiel** *nt* computer game
Conférencier [kõferãsi'eː] (-s, -s) *m*
compère
Cord [kɔrt] (-s) *m* cord, corduroy
Couch [kaʊtʃ] (-, -es *od* -en) *f* couch
Coupé [ku'peː] (-s, -s) *nt* (*AUT*) coupé,
sports version
Coupon [ku'põː] (-s, -s) *m* coupon;
(*Stoff~*) length of cloth
Cousin [ku'zɛ̃ː] (-s, -s) *m* cousin; **~e**
[ku'ziːnə] *f* cousin
Creme [krɛːm] (-, -s) *f* cream; (*Schuh~*)
polish; (*Zahn~*) paste; (*KOCH*) mousse;
c~farben *adj* cream(-coloured)
cremig *adj* creamy
Curry ['kœri] (-s) *m od nt* curry powder;

~pulver *nt* curry powder
Cursor ['kœrsər] *m* cursor
Cutter ['katər] (-s, -) *m* (*CINE*) editor

D d

da [daː] *adv* **1** (*örtlich*) there; (*hier*) here;
da draußen out there; **da bin ich** here I
am; **da, wo** where; **ist noch Milch da?** is
there any milk left?
2 (*zeitlich*) then; (*folglich*) so
3: **da haben wir Glück gehabt** we were
lucky there; **da kann man nichts
machen** nothing can be done about it
♦ *konj* (*weil*) as, since

dabehalten (*unreg*) *vt* to keep
dabei [da'baɪ] *adv* (*räumlich*) close to it;
(*noch dazu*) besides; (*zusammen mit*) with
them; (*zeitlich*) during this; (*obwohl doch*)
but, however; **was ist schon ~?** what of
it?; **es ist doch nichts ~, wenn ...** it
doesn't matter if ...; **bleiben wir ~** let's
leave it at that; **es bleibt ~** that's settled;
das Dumme/Schwierige ~ the stupid/
difficult part of it; **er war gerade ~, zu
gehen** he was just leaving; **~sein** (*unreg*)
vi (*anwesend*) to be present; (*beteiligt*) to
be involved; **~stehen** (*unreg*) *vi* to stand
around
Dach [dax] (-(e)s, ⁻er) *nt* roof; **~boden** *m*
attic, loft; **~decker** (-s, -) *m* slater, tiler;
~fenster *nt* skylight; **~luke** *f* skylight;
~pappe *f* roofing felt; **~rinne** *f* gutter
Dachs [daks] (-es, -e) *m* badger
dachte *etc* ['daxtə] *vb siehe* **denken**
Dackel ['dakəl] (-s, -) *m* dachshund
dadurch [da'dʊrç] *adv* (*räumlich*)
through it; (*durch diesen Umstand*)
thereby, in that way; (*deshalb*) because of
that, for that reason ♦ *konj*: **~, daß**
because
dafür [da'fyːr] *adv* for it; (*anstatt*)
instead; **er kann nichts ~** he can't help
it; **er ist bekannt ~** he is well-known for

that; **was bekomme ich ~?** what will I get for it?

dafürkönnen *unreg (vt)*: **er kann nichts dafür** he can't help it

dagegen [da'ge:gǝn] *adv* against it; (*im Vergleich damit*) in comparison with it; (*bei Tausch*) for it/them ♦ *konj* however; **ich habe nichts ~** I don't mind; **ich war ~** I was against it; **~ kann man nichts tun** one can't do anything about it; **~halten** (*unreg*) *vt* (*vergleichen*) to compare with it; (*entgegnen*) to object to it; **~sprechen** (*unreg*) *vi*: **es spricht nichts ~** there's no reason why not

daheim [da'haɪm] *adv* at home; **D~** (**-s**) *nt* home

daher [da'he:r] *adv* (*räumlich*) from there; (*Ursache*) from that ♦ *konj* (*deshalb*) that's why

dahin [da'hɪn] *adv* (*räumlich*) there; (*zeitlich*) then; (*vergangen*) gone; **~'gegen** *konj* on the other hand; **~gehend** *adv* on this matter; **~gestellt** *adv*: **~gestellt bleiben** to remain to be seen; **~gestellt sein lassen** to leave open *od* undecided

dahinten [da'hɪntǝn] *adv* over there

dahinter [da'hɪntǝr] *adv* behind it; **~kommen** (*unreg*) *vi* to get to the bottom of it

Dahlie ['da:liǝ] *f* dahlia

dalli ['dali] (*umg*) *adv* chop chop

damalig ['da:ma:lɪç] *adj* of that time, then

damals ['da:ma:ls] *adv* at that time, then

Damast [da'mast] (**-(e)s, -e**) *m* damask

Dame ['da:mǝ] *f* lady; (*SCHACH, KARTEN*) queen; (*Spiel*) draughts *sg*; **d~nhaft** *adj* ladylike; **~nwahl** *f* ladies' excuse-me

damit [da'mɪt] *adv* with it; (*begründend*) by that ♦ *konj* in order that, in order to; **was meint er ~?** what does he mean by that?; **genug ~!** that's enough!; **~ eilt es nicht** there's no hurry

dämlich ['dɛ:mlɪç] (*umg*) *adj* silly, stupid

Damm [dam] (**-(e)s, ⁻e**) *m* dyke; (*Stau~*) dam; (*Hafen~*) mole; (*Bahn~, Straßen~*) embankment

dämmen ['dɛmǝn] *vt* (*Wasser*) to dam up; (*Schmerzen*) to keep back

dämmer- *zW*: **~ig** *adj* dim, faint; **~n** *vi* (*Tag*) to dawn; (*Abend*) to fall; **D~ung** *f* twilight; (*Morgen~*) dawn; (*Abend~*) dusk

dämonisch [dɛ'mo:nɪʃ] *adj* demoniacal

Dampf [dampf] (**-(e)s, ⁻e**) *m* steam; (*Dunst*) vapour; **d~en** *vi* to steam

dämpfen ['dɛmpfǝn] *vt* (*KOCH*) to steam; (*bügeln*) to iron with a damp cloth; (*fig*) to dampen, to subdue

Dampf- *zW*: **~kochtopf** *m* pressure cooker; **~schiff** *nt* steamship; **~walze** *f* steamroller

danach [da'na:x] *adv* after that; (*zeitlich*) after that, afterwards; (*gemäß*) accordingly; according to which; according to that; **er sieht ~ aus** he looks it

Däne (**-n, -n**) *m* Dane

daneben [da'ne:bǝn] *adv* beside it; (*im Vergleich*) in comparison; **~benehmen** (*unreg*) *vr* to misbehave; **~gehen** (*unreg*) *vi* to miss; (*Plan*) to fail

Dän- ['dɛ:n] *zW*: **~emark** *nt* Denmark; **~in** *f* Dane; **d~isch** *adj* Danish

Dank [daŋk] (**-(e)s**) *m* thanks *pl*; **vielen** *od* **schönen ~** many thanks; **jdm ~ sagen** to thank sb; **d~** *präp* (*+dat od gen*) thanks to; **d~bar** *adj* grateful; (*Aufgabe*) rewarding; **~barkeit** *f* gratitude; **d~e** *excl* thank you, thanks; **d~en** *vi* *+dat* to thank; **d~enswert** *adj* (*Arbeit*) worthwhile; rewarding; (*Bemühung*) kind; **d~sagen** *vi* to express one's thanks

dann [dan] *adv* then; **~ und wann** now and then

daran [da'ran] *adv* on it; (*stoßen*) against it; **es liegt ~, daß ...** the cause of it is that ...; **gut/schlecht ~ sein** to be well-/badly off; **das Beste/Dümmste ~** the best/stupidest thing about it; **ich war nahe ~, zu ...** I was on the point of ...; **er ist ~ gestorben** he died from it *od* of it; **~gehen** (*unreg*) *vi* to start; **~setzen** *vt* to stake; **er hat alles ~gesetzt, von Glasgow wegzukommen** he has done his utmost to get away from Glasgow

darauf [da'raʊf] *adv* (*räumlich*) on it; (*zielgerichtet*) towards it; (*danach*) afterwards; **es kommt ganz ~ an, ob ...**

it depends whether ...; **die Tage** ~ the days following *od* thereafter; **am Tag** ~ the next day; **~folgend** *adj* (*Tag, Jahr*) next, following; **~legen** *vt* to lay *od* put on top

daraus [da'raʊs] *adv* from it; **was ist** ~ **geworden?** what became of it?; ~ **geht hervor, daß** ... this means that ...

Darbietung ['da:rbi:tʊŋ] *f* performance

darf *etc* [darf] *vb siehe* **dürfen**

darin [da'rɪn] *adv* in (there), in it

Dar- ['da:r] *zW:* **d~legen** *vt* to explain, to expound, to set forth; **~legung** *f* explanation; **~leh(e)n** (-s, -) *nt* loan

Darm [darm] (-(e)s, -e) *m* intestine; (*Wurst~*) skin; **~grippe** *f* (*MED*) gastric influenza *od* flu; **~saite** *f* gut string

darstellen ['da:rʃtɛlən] *vt* (*abbilden, bedeuten*) to represent; (*THEAT*) to act; (*beschreiben*) to describe ♦ *vr* to appear to be

Darsteller(in) (-s, -) *m(f)* actor (actress)

Darstellung *f* portrayal, depiction

darüber [da'ry:bər] *adv* (*räumlich*) over it, above it; (*fahren*) over it; (*mehr*) more; (*währenddessen*) meanwhile; (*sprechen, streiten*) about it; ~ **geht nichts** there's nothing like it

darum [da'rʊm] *adv* (*räumlich*) round it ♦ *konj* that's why; **er bittet** ~ he is pleading for it; **es geht** ~, **daß** ... the thing is that ...; **er würde viel ~ geben, wenn** ... he would give a lot to ...; **ich tue es** ~, **weil** ... I am doing it because ...

darunter [da'rʊntər] *adv* (*räumlich*) under it; (*dazwischen*) among them; (*weniger*) less; **ein Stockwerk** ~ one floor below (it); **was verstehen Sie** ~? what do you understand by that?

das [das] *def art* the ♦ *pron* that

Dasein ['da:zaɪn] (-s) *nt* (*Leben*) life; (*Anwesenheit*) presence; (*Bestehen*) existence

dasein (*unreg*) *vi* to be there

daß [das] *konj* that

dasselbe [das'zɛlbə] *art, pron* the same

dastehen ['da:ʃte:ən] (*unreg*) *vi* to stand there

Datei [da:'taɪ] *f* file

Datenbank ['da:tənbaŋk] *f* data base

Datensichtgerät *nt* visual display unit, VDU

Datenverarbeitung *f* data processing

datieren [da'ti:rən] *vt* to date

Dativ ['da:ti:f] (-s, -e) *m* dative (case)

Dattel ['datəl] (-, -n) *f* date

Datum ['da:tʊm] (-s, **Daten**) *nt* date; **Daten** *pl* (*Angaben*) data *pl*

Dauer ['daʊər] (-, -n) *f* duration; (*gewisse Zeitspanne*) length; (*Bestand, Fortbestehen*) permanence; **es war nur kurzer** ~ it didn't last long; **auf die** ~ in the long run; (*auf längere Zeit*) indefinitely; **~auftrag** *m* standing order; **d~haft** *adj* lasting, durable; **~karte** *f* season ticket; **~lauf** *m* jog(ging); **d~n** *vi* to last; **es hat sehr lang ged~t, bis er** ... it took him a long time to ...; **d~nd** *adj* constant; **~welle** *f* perm, permanent wave; **~wurst** *f* German salami; **~zustand** *m* permanent condition

Daumen ['daʊmən] (-s, -) *m* thumb

Daune ['daʊnə] *f* down; **~ndecke** *f* down duvet, down quilt

davon [da'fɔn] *adv* of it; (*räumlich*) away; (*weg von*) from it; (*Grund*) because of it; **das kommt** ~! that's what you get; ~ **abgesehen** apart from that; ~ **sprechen/ wissen** to talk/know of *od* about it; **was habe ich** ~? what's the point?; **~kommen** (*unreg*) *vi* to escape; **~laufen** (*unreg*) *vi* to run away

davor [da'fo:r] *adv* (*räumlich*) in front of it; (*zeitlich*) before (that); ~ **warnen** to warn about it

dazu [da'tsu:] *adv* (*legen, stellen*) by it; (*essen, singen*) with it; **und** ~ **noch** and in addition; **ein Beispiel/seine Gedanken** ~ one example for/his thoughts on this; **wie komme ich denn** ~? why should I?; ~ **fähig sein** to be capable of it; **sich** ~ **äußern** to say something on it; **~gehören** *vi* to belong to it; **~kommen** (*unreg*) *vi* (*Ereignisse*) to happen too; (*an einen Ort*) to come along

dazwischen [da'tsvɪʃən] *adv* in between; (*räumlich auch*) between (them); (*zusammen mit*) among them; **der**

Unterschied ~ the difference between them; **~kommen** (*unreg*) tr (*hineingeraten*) to get caught up in it; **es ist etwas ~gekommen** something cropped up; **~reden** *vi* (*unterbrechen*) to interrupt; (*sich einmischen*) to interfere; **~treten** (*unreg*) *vi* to intervene

Debatte [de'batə] *f* debate

Deck [dɛk] (**-(e)s, -s** *od* **-e**) *nt* deck; **an ~ gehen** to go on deck

Decke *f* cover; (*Bett~*) blanket; (*Tisch~*) tablecloth; (*Zimmer~*) ceiling; **unter einer ~ stecken** to be hand in glove; **~l** (**-s, -**) *m* lid; **d~n** *vt* to cover ♦ *vr* to coincide

Deckung *f* (*Schützen*) covering; (*Schutz*) cover; (*SPORT*) defence; (*Übereinstimmen*) agreement; **d~sgleich** *adj* congruent

Defekt [de'fɛkt] (**-(e)s, -e**) *m* fault, defect; **d~** *adj* faulty

defensiv [defɛn'si:f] *adj* defensive

definieren [defi'ni:rən] *vt* to define

Definition [definitsi'o:n] *f* definition

Defizit ['de:fitsit] (**-s, -e**) *nt* deficit

deftig ['dɛftɪç] *adj* (*Essen*) large; (*Witz*) coarse

Degen ['de:gən] (**-s, -**) *m* sword

degenerieren [degene'ri:rən] *vi* to degenerate

dehnbar ['de:nba:r] *adj* elastic; (*fig: Begriff*) loose

dehnen *vt, vr* to stretch

Deich [daɪç] (**-(e)s, -e**) *m* dyke, dike

Deichsel ['daɪksəl] (**-, -n**) *f* shaft

deichseln (*umg*) *vt* (*fig*) to wangle

dein(e) [daɪn(ə)] *adj* (*D~ in Briefen*) your; **~e(r, s)** *pron* yours; **~er** (*gen von* **du**) *pron* of you; **~erseits** *adv* on your part; **~esgleichen** *pron* people like you; **~etwegen** *adv* (*für dich*) for your sake; (*wegen dir*) on your account; **~etwillen** *adv:* **um ~etwillen = deinetwegen**; **~ige** *pron:* **der/die/das ~ige** yours

dekadent [deka'dɛnt] *adj* decadent

Deklination [deklinatsi'o:n] *f* declension

deklinieren [dekli'ni:rən] *vt* to decline

Dekolleté [dekɔl'te:] (**-s, -s**) *nt* low neckline

Deko- [deko] *zW:* **~rateur** [-ra'tø:r] *m*

window dresser; **~ration** [-ratsi'o:n] *f* decoration; (*in Laden*) window dressing; **d~rativ** [-ra'ti:f] *adj* decorative; **d~rieren** [-'ri:rən] *vt* to decorate; (*Schaufenster*) to dress

Delegation [delegatsi'o:n] *f* delegation

delegieren [dele'gi:rən] *vt:* **~ an** +*akk* (*Aufgaben*) to delegate to

delikat [deli'ka:t] *adj* (*zart, heikel*) delicate; (*köstlich*) delicious

Delikatesse [delika'tɛsə] *f* delicacy; **~n** *pl* (*Feinkost*) delicatessen food; **~ngeschäft** *nt* delicatessen

Delikt [de'lɪkt] (**-(e)s, -e**) *nt* (*JUR*) offence

Delle ['dɛlə] (*umg*) *f* dent

Delphin [dɛl'fi:n] (**-s, -e**) *m* dolphin

dem [de(:)m] *art dat von* **der; das**

Demagoge [dema'go:gə] (**-n, -n**) *m* demagogue

dementieren [demɛn'ti:rən] *vt* to deny

dem- *zW:* **~gemäß** *adv* accordingly; **~nach** *adv* accordingly; **~nächst** *adv* shortly

Demokrat [demo'kra:t] (**-en, -en**) *m* democrat; **~ie** [-'ti:] *f* democracy; **d~isch** *adj* democratic; **d~isieren** [-i'zi:rən] *vt* to democratize

demolieren [demo'li:rən] *vt* to demolish

Demon- [demɔn] *zW:* **~strant(in)** [-'strant(ɪn)] *m(f)* demonstrator; **~stration** [-stratsi'o:n] *f* demonstration; **d~strativ** [-stra'ti:f] *adj* demonstrative; (*Protest*) pointed; **d~strieren** [-'stri:rən] *vt, vi* to demonstrate

Demoskopie [demosko'pi:] *f* public opinion research

Demut ['de:mu:t] (**-**) *f* humility

demütig ['de:my:tɪç] *adj* humble; **~en** ['de:my:tɪgən] *vt* to humiliate; **D~ung** *f* humiliation

demzufolge ['de:mtsu'fɔlgə] *adv* accordingly

den [de(:)n] *art akk von* **der**

denen ['de:nən] *pron* (*dat pl*) **der; die; das**

Denk- ['dɛŋk] *zW:* **d~bar** *adj* conceivable; **~en** (**-s**) *nt* thinking; **d~en** (*unreg*) *vt, vi* to think; **d~faul** *adj* lazy; **~fehler** *m* logical error; **~mal** (**-s, ⁻er**) *nt*

monument; **d~würdig** *adj* memorable;
~zettel *m*: **jdm einen ~zettel verpassen**
to teach sb a lesson

denn [dɛn] *konj* for ♦ *adv* then; (*nach
Komparativ*) than; **warum ~?** why?

dennoch ['dɛnɔx] *konj* nevertheless

Denunziant [denʊntsi'ant] *m* informer

deponieren [depo'ni:rən] *vt* (*COMM*) to
deposit

Depot [de'po:] **(-s, -s)** *nt* warehouse;
(*Bus~*, *EISENB*) depot; (*Bank~*) strongroom,
safe (*US*)

Depression [depresi'o:n] *f* depression

depres'siv *adj* depressive

deprimieren [depri'mi:rən] *vt* to depress

SCHLÜSSELWORT

der [de:r] (*f* **die**, *nt* **das**, *gen* **des**, **der**,
des, *dat* **dem**, **der**, **dem**, *akk* **den**, **der**,
das, *pl* **die**) *def art* the; **der Rhein** the
Rhine; **der Klaus** (*umg*) Klaus; **die Frau**
(*im allgemeinen*) women; **der Tod/das
Leben** death/life; **der Fuß des Berges**
the foot of the hill; **gib es der Frau** give
it to the woman; **er hat sich die Hand
verletzt** he has hurt his hand
 ♦ *relativ pron* (*bei Menschen*) who, that;
(*bei Tieren, Sachen*) which, that; **der
Mann, den ich gesehen habe** the man
who *od* whom *od* that I saw
 ♦ *demonstrativ pron* he/she/it; (*jener,
dieser*) that; (*pl*) those; **der/die war es** it
was him/her; **der mit der Brille** the one
with glasses; **ich will den (da)** I want
that one

---

derart ['de:r'a:rt] *adv* so; (*solcher Art*)
such; **~ig** *adj* such, this sort of

derb [dɛrp] *adj* sturdy; (*Kost*) solid; (*grob*)
coarse

der- *zW*: **~'gleichen** *pron* such; **~'jenige**
pron he; she; it; the one (who); that
(which); **~'maßen** *adv* to such an extent,
so; **~'selbe** *art, pron* the same;
~'weil(en) *adv* in the meantime; **~'zeitig**
adj present, current; (*damalig*) then

des [dɛs] *art gen von* **der**

desertieren [dezɛr'ti:rən] *vi* to desert

desgleichen ['dɛs'glaiçən] *adv* likewise,

also

deshalb ['dɛs'halp] *adv* therefore, that's
why

Desinfektion [dezɪnfɛktsi'o:n] *f*
disinfection; **~smittel** *nt* disinfectant

desinfizieren [dezɪnfi'tsi:rən] *vt* to
disinfect

dessen ['dɛsən] *pron gen von* **der**; **das**;
~'ungeachtet *adv* nevertheless,
regardless

Dessert [dɛ'sɛ:r] **(-s, -s)** *nt* dessert

destillieren [dɛstɪ'li:rən] *vt* to distil

desto ['dɛsto] *adv* all the, so much the; **~
besser** all the better

deswegen ['dɛs've:gən] *konj* therefore,
hence

Detail [de'tai] **(-s, -s)** *nt* detail

Detektiv [detɛk'ti:f] **(-s, -e)** *m* detective

deut- ['dɔyt] *zW*: **~en** *vt* to interpret, to
explain ♦ *vi*: **~en (auf +akk)** to point (to
od at); **~lich** *adj* clear; (*Unterschied*)
distinct; **D~lichkeit** *f* clarity; distinctness

Deutsch [dɔytʃ] *nt* German

deutsch *adj* German; **auf ~** in German;
D~e Demokratische Republik German
Democratic Republic, East Germany; **~es
Beefsteak** ≈ hamburger; **D~e** *f* German;
D~er *m* German; **ich bin D~er** I am
German; **D~land** *nt* Germany

Devise [de'vi:zə] *f* motto, device; **~n** *pl*
(*FIN*) foreign currency, foreign exchange

Dezember [de'tsɛmbər] **(-s, -)** *m*
December

dezent [de'tsɛnt] *adj* discreet

dezimal [detsi'ma:l] *adj* decimal;
D~bruch *m* decimal (fraction);
D~system *nt* decimal system

d.h. *abk* (= *das heißt*) i.e.

Dia ['di:a] **(-s, -s)** *nt* (*PHOT*) slide,
transparency

Diabetes [dia'be:tɛs] **(-, -)** *m* (*MED*)
diabetes

Diagnose [dia'gno:zə] *f* diagnosis

diagonal [diago'na:l] *adj* diagonal; **D~e** *f*
diagonal

Dialekt [dia'lɛkt] **(-(e)s, -e)** *m* dialect;
d~isch *adj* dialectal; (*Logik*) dialectical

Dialog [dia'lo:k] **(-(e)s, -e)** *m* dialogue

Diamant [dia'mant] *m* diamond

Diaprojektor ['diːaprojɛktɔr] *m* slide projector

Diät [diˈɛːt] (-, -en) *f* diet

dich [dɪç] (*akk von* **du**) *pron* you; yourself

dicht [dɪçt] *adj* dense; (*Nebel*) thick; (*Gewebe*) close; (*undurchlässig*) (water)tight; (*fig*) concise ♦ *adv*: ~ **an/bei** close to; **~bevölkert** *adj* densely *od* heavily populated; **D~e** *f* density; thickness; closeness; (water)tightness; (*fig*) conciseness; **~en** *vt* (*dicht machen*) to make watertight; to seal; (*NAUT*) to caulk; (*LITER*) to compose, to write ♦ *vi* to compose, to write; **D~er(in)** (-s, -) *m(f)* poet; (*Autor*) writer; **~erisch** *adj* poetical; **~halten** (*unreg; umg*) *vi* to keep one's mouth shut; **D~ung** *f* (*TECH*) washer; (*AUT*) gasket; (*Gedichte*) poetry; (*Prosa*) (piece of) writing

dick [dɪk] *adj* thick; (*fett*) fat; **durch ~ und dünn** through thick and thin; **D~darm** *m* (*ANAT*) colon; **D~e** *f* thickness; fatness; **~flüssig** *adj* viscous; **D~icht** (-s, -e) *nt* thicket; **D~kopf** *m* mule; **D~milch** *f* soured milk

die [diː] *def art siehe* **der**

Dieb(in) [diːp, 'diːbɪn] (-(e)s, -e) *m(f)* thief; **d~isch** *adj* thieving; (*umg*) immense; **~stahl** (-(e)s, ˈeˑ) *m* theft

Diele ['diːlə] *f* (*Brett*) board; (*Flur*) hall, lobby

dienen ['diːnən] *vi*: (*jdm*) ~ to serve (sb)

Diener (-s, -) *m* servant; **~in** *f* (maid)servant; **~schaft** *f* servants *pl*

Dienst [diːnst] (-(e)s, -e) *m* service; **außer ~** retired; ~ **haben** to be on duty

Dienstag ['diːnstaːk] *m* Tuesday; **d~s** *adv* on Tuesdays

Dienst- *zW*: **~bote** *m* servant; **~geheimnis** *nt* official secret; **~gespräch** *nt* business call; **d~habend** *adj* (*Arzt*) on duty; **~leistung** *f* service; **d~lich** *adj* official; **~mädchen** *nt* (house)maid; **~reise** *f* business trip; **~stelle** *f* office; **~vorschrift** *f* official regulations *pl*; **~weg** *m* official channels *pl*; **~zeit** *f* working hours *pl*; (*MIL*) period of service

dies ['diːs] *pron* (*demonstrativ: sg*) this;

(: *pl*) these; **~bezüglich** *adj* (*Frage*) on this matter; **~e(r, s)** ['diːzə(r, s)] *pron* this (one)

Diesel ['diːzəl] *m* (*Kraftstoff*) diesel

dieselbe [diːˈzɛlbə] *pron, art* the same

Dieselöl ['diːzəlˈøːl] *nt* diesel oil

diesig ['diːzɪç] *adj* drizzly

dies- *zW*: **~jährig** *adj* this year's; **~mal** *adv* this time; **~seits** *präp* +*gen* on this side; **D~seits** (-) *nt* this life

Dietrich ['diːtrɪç] (-s, -e) *m* picklock

diffamieren [dɪfaˈmiːrən] (*pej*) *vt* to defame

differential [dɪfɛrɛntsiˈaːl] *adj* differential; **D~rechnung** *f* differential calculus

Differenz [dɪfəˈrɛnts] (-, -en) *f* (*Unterschied*) difference; **~en** *pl* (*geh: Meinungsverschiedenheit*) difference (of opinion)

differenzieren [dɪfɛrɛnˈtsiːrən] *vt* to make distinctions in; **differenziert** *adj* (*Mensch etc*) complex

digital [digiˈtaːl] *adj* digital

Dikt- [dɪkt] *zW*: **~aphon** [-aˈfoːn] *nt* dictaphone; **~at** [-ˈtaːt] (-(e)s, -e) *nt* dictation; **~ator** [-ˈtaːtɔr] *m* dictator; **d~atorisch** [-aˈtoːrɪʃ] *adj* dictatorial; **~atur** [-aˈtuːr] *f* dictatorship; **d~ieren** [-ˈtiːrən] *vt* to dictate

Dilemma [diˈlɛma] (-s, -s *od* -ta) *nt* dilemma

Dilettant [dilɛˈtant] *m* dilettante, amateur; **d~isch** *adj* amateurish, dilettante

Dimension [dimɛnziˈoːn] *f* dimension

Ding [dɪŋ] (-(e)s, -e) *nt* thing, object; **d~lich** *adj* real, concrete; **~s(bums)** ['dɪŋks(bʊms)] (-; *umg*) *nt* thingummybob

Diphtherie [dɪftəˈriː] *f* diphtheria

Diplom [diˈploːm] (-(e)s, -e) *nt* diploma, certificate; **~at** [-ˈmaːt] (-en, -en) *m* diplomat; **~atie** [-aˈtiː] *f* diplomacy; **d~atisch** [-ˈmaːtɪʃ] *adj* diplomatic; **~ingenieur** *m* qualified engineer

dir [diːr] (*dat von* **du**) *pron* (to) you

direkt [diˈrɛkt] *adj* direct; **D~or** *m* director; (*SCH*) principal, headmaster; **D~übertragung** *f* live broadcast

Dirigent [diri'gɛnt] *m* conductor
dirigieren [diri'giːrən] *vt* to direct; (*MUS*) to conduct
Dirne ['dɪrnə] *f* prostitute
Diskette [dɪs'kɛtə] *f* diskette, floppy disk
Diskont [dɪs'kɔnt] (-s, -e) *m* discount; **~satz** *m* rate of discount
Diskothek [dɪskoˈteːk] (-, -en) *f* disco(theque)
diskret [dɪs'kreːt] *adj* discreet; **D~ion** [dɪskretsi'oːn] *f* discretion
Diskussion [dɪskusi'oːn] *f* discussion; debate; **zur ~ stehen** to be under discussion
diskutieren [dɪsku'tiːrən] *vt, vi* to discuss; to debate
Distanz [dɪs'tants] *f* distance
distan'zieren *vr*: **sich von jdm/etw ~** to distance o.s. from sb/sth
Distel ['dɪstəl] (-, -n) *f* thistle
Disziplin [dɪstsi'pliːn] *f* discipline
Dividende [divi'dɛndə] *f* dividend
dividieren [divi'diːrən] *vt*: **(durch etw) ~** to divide (by sth)
DM [deː'ɛm] *abk* (= *Deutsche Mark*) German Mark
D-Mark ['deːmark] *f* D Mark, German Mark

SCHLÜSSELWORT

doch [dɔx] *adv* 1 (*dennoch*) after all; (*sowieso*) anyway; **er kam doch noch** he came after all; **du weißt es ja doch besser** you know better than I do anyway; **und doch ...** and yet ...
2 (*als bejahende Antwort*) yes I do/it does *etc*; **das ist nicht wahr - doch!** that's not true - yes it is!
3 (*auffordernd*): **komm doch** do come; **laß ihn doch** just leave him; **nicht doch!** oh no!
4: **sie ist doch noch so jung** but she's still so young; **Sie wissen doch, wie das ist** you know how it is(, don't you?); **wenn doch** if only
♦ *konj* (*aber*) but; (*trotzdem*) all the same; **und doch hat er es getan** but still he did it

Docht [dɔxt] (-(e)s, -e) *m* wick
Dock [dɔk] (-s, -s *od* -e) *nt* dock
Dogge ['dɔgə] *f* bulldog
Dogma ['dɔgma] (-s, -men) *nt* dogma; **d~tisch** [-'maːtɪʃ] *adj* dogmatic
Dohle ['doːlə] *f* (*ZOOL*) jackdaw
Doktor ['dɔktor, *pl* -'toːrən] (-s, -en) *m* doctor
Dokument [doku'mɛnt] *nt* document
Dokumentar- [dokumɛn'taːr] *zW*: **~bericht** *m* documentary; **~film** *m* documentary (film); **d~isch** *adj* documentary
Dolch [dɔlç] (-(e)s, -e) *m* dagger
dolmetschen ['dɔlmɛtʃən] *vt, vi* to interpret
Dolmetscher (-s, -) *m* interpreter
Dom [doːm] (-(e)s, -e) *m* cathedral
dominieren [domi'niːrən] *vt* to dominate ♦ *vi* to predominate
Dompfaff ['doːmpfaf] *m* bullfinch
Donau ['doːnau] *f* Danube
Donner ['dɔnər] (-s, -) *m* thunder; **d~n** *vi unpers* to thunder
Donnerstag ['dɔnərstaːk] *m* Thursday
doof [doːf] (*umg*) *adj* daft, stupid
Doppel ['dɔpəl] (-s, -) *nt* duplicate; (*SPORT*) doubles; **~bett** *nt* double bed; **d~deutig** *adj* ambiguous; **~fenster** *nt* double glazing; **~gänger** (-s, -) *m* double; **~punkt** *m* colon; **~stecker** *m* two-way adaptor; **d~t** *adj* double; **in d~ter Ausführung** in duplicate; **~verdiener** *m* person with two incomes; (*pl*: *Paar*) two-income family; **~zentner** *m* 100 kilograms; **~zimmer** *nt* double room
Dorf [dɔrf] (-(e)s, ⁺er) *nt* village; **~bewohner** *m* villager
Dorn¹ [dɔrn] (-(e)s, -en) *m* (*BOT*) thorn
Dorn² (-(e)s, -e) *m* (*Schnallen~*) tongue, pin
dornig *adj* thorny
dörren ['dœrən] *vt* to dry
Dörrobst ['dœr'oːpst] *nt* dried fruit
Dorsch [dɔrʃ] (-(e)s, -e) *m* cod
dort [dɔrt] *adv* there; **~ drüben** over there; **~her** *adv* from there; **~hin** *adv* (to) there; **~ig** *adj* of that place; in that town
Dose ['doːzə] *f* box; (*Blech~*) tin, can

Dosen *pl von* **Dose**; **Dosis**
Dosenöffner *m* tin *od* can opener
Dosis ['do:zɪs] (-, **Dosen**) *f* dose
Dotter ['dɔtər] (-s, -) *m* (egg) yolk
Down-Syndrom [daʊnzyn'dro:m] *nt*
(*MED*) Down's Syndrome
Drache ['draxə] (-n, -n) *m* (*Tier*) dragon
Drachen (-s, -) *m* kite
Draht [dra:t] (-(e)s, ⁺e) *m* wire; **auf ~
sein** to be on the ball; **d~ig** *adj* (*Mann*)
wiry; **~seil** *nt* cable; **~seilbahn** *f* cable
railway, funicular; **~zange** *f* pliers *pl*
Drama ['dra:ma] (-s, **Dramen**) *nt* drama,
play; **~tiker** [-'ma:tikər] (-s, -) *m*
dramatist; **d~tisch** [-'ma:tɪʃ] *adj*
dramatic
dran [dran] (*umg*) *adv*: **jetzt bin ich ~!**
it's my turn now; *siehe* **daran**
Drang [draŋ] (-(e)s, ⁺e) *m* (*Trieb*): **~
(nach)** impulse (for), urge (for), desire
(for); (*Druck*) pressure
drängeln ['drɛŋəln] *vt, vi* to push, to
jostle
drängen ['drɛŋən] *vt* (*schieben*) to push,
to press; (*antreiben*) to urge ♦ *vi* (*eilig
sein*) to be urgent; (*Zeit*) to press; **auf etw**
akk **~** to press for sth
drastisch ['drastɪʃ] *adj* drastic
drauf [drauf] (*umg*) *adv* = **darauf**;
D~gänger (-s, -) *m* daredevil
draußen ['drausən] *adv* outside, out-of-
doors
Dreck [drɛk] (-(e)s) *m* mud, dirt; **d~ig** *adj*
dirty, filthy
Dreh- ['dre:] *zW*: **~arbeiten** *pl* (*CINE*)
shooting *sg*; **~bank** *f* lathe; **~buch** *nt*
(*CINE*) script; **d~en** *vt* to turn, to rotate;
(*Zigaretten*) to roll; (*Film*) to shoot ♦ *vi* to
turn, to rotate ♦ *vr* to turn; (*handeln
von*): **es d~t sich um ...** it's about ...;
~orgel *f* barrel organ; **~tür** *f* revolving
door; **~ung** *f* (*Rotation*) rotation; (*Um~,
Wendung*) turn; **~zahl** *f* rate of
revolutions; **~zahlmesser** *m* rev(olution)
counter
drei [draɪ] *num* three; **D~eck** *nt* triangle;
~eckig *adj* triangular; **~einhalb** *num*
three and a half; **~erlei** *adj inv* of three
kinds; **~fach** *adj* triple, treble ♦ *adv*

three times; **~hundert** *num* three
hundred; **D~'königsfest** *nt* Epiphany;
~mal *adv* three times; **~malig** *adj* three
times
dreinreden ['draɪnre:dən] *vi*: **jdm ~**
(*dazwischenreden*) to interrupt sb; (*sich
einmischen*) to interfere with sb
Dreirad *nt* tricycle
dreißig ['draɪsɪç] *num* thirty
dreist [draɪst] *adj* bold, audacious;
D~igkeit *f* boldness, audacity
drei- *zW*: **~viertel** *num* three-quarters;
D~viertelstunde *f* three-quarters of an
hour; **~zehn** *num* thirteen
dreschen ['drɛʃən] (*unreg*) *vt* (*Getreide*)
to thresh; (*umg: verprügeln*) to beat up
dressieren [drɛ'si:rən] *vt* to train
drillen ['drɪlən] *vt* (*bohren*) to drill, to
bore; (*MIL*) to drill; (*fig*) to train
Drilling *m* triplet
drin [drɪn] (*umg*) *adv* = **darin**
dringen ['drɪŋən] (*unreg*) *vi* (*Wasser,
Licht, Kälte*): **~ (durch/in** +*akk*) to
penetrate (through/into); **auf etw** *akk* **~**
to insist on sth
dringend ['drɪŋənt] *adj* urgent
dringlich ['drɪŋlɪç] *adj* urgent
Dringlichkeit *f* urgency
drinnen ['drɪnən] *adv* inside, indoors
dritte(r, s) ['drɪtə(r, s)] *adj* third; **~ Welt**
Third World; **D~s Reich** Third Reich;
D~l (-s, -) *nt* third; **~ns** *adv* thirdly
droben ['dro:bən] *adv* above, up there
Droge ['dro:gə] *f* drug; **d~nabhängig**
adj addicted to drugs; **~nhändler** *m* drug
pedlar, pusher; **~rie** [dro:gə'ri:] *f*
chemist's shop
Drogist [dro'gɪst] *m* pharmacist, chemist
drohen ['dro:ən] *vi*: **(jdm) ~** to threaten
(sb)
dröhnen ['drø:nən] *vi* (*Motor*) to roar;
(*Stimme, Musik*) to ring, to resound
Drohung ['dro:ʊŋ] *f* threat
drollig ['drɔlɪç] *adj* droll
Drossel ['drɔsəl] (-, -n) *f* thrush
drüben ['dry:bən] *adv* over there, on the
other side
drüber ['dry:bər] (*umg*) *adv* = **darüber**
Druck [drʊk] (-(e)s, -e) *m* (*PHYS, Zwang*)

pressure; (*TYP: Vorgang*) printing;
(: *Produkt*) print; (*fig: Belastung*) burden,
weight; **~buchstabe** *m* block letter
drücken ['drʏkən] *vt* (*Knopf, Hand*) to
press; (*zu eng sein*) to pinch; (*fig: Preise*)
to keep down; (: *belasten*) to oppress, to
weigh down ♦ *vi* to press; to pinch ♦ *vr*:
sich vor etw *dat* ~ to get out of (doing)
sth; **~d** *adj* oppressive
Drucker (-s, -) *m* printer
Drücker (-s, -) *m* button; (*Tür~*) handle;
(*Gewehr~*) trigger
Druck- *zW*: **~e'rei** *f* printing works,
press; **~erschwärze** *f* printer's ink;
~fehler *m* misprint; **~knopf** *m* press
stud, snap fastener; **~sache** *f* printed
matter; **~schrift** *f* block *od* printed letters
pl
drum [drʊm] (*umg*) *adv* = **darum**
drunten ['drʊntən] *adv* below, down
there
Drüse ['dryːzə] *f* gland
Dschungel ['dʒʊŋəl] (-s, -) *m* jungle
du [duː] (*nom*) *pron* (*D~ in Briefen*) you;
D~ sagen = **duzen**
Dübel ['dyːbəl] (-s, -) *m* Rawlplug ®
ducken ['dʊkən] *vt* (*Kopf, Person*) to
duck; (*fig*) to take down a peg or two ♦ *vr*
to duck
Duckmäuser ['dʊkmɔʏzər] (-s, -) *m* yes-
man
Dudelsack ['duːdəlzak] *m* bagpipes *pl*
Duell [du'ɛl] (-s, -e) *nt* duel
Duft [dʊft] (-(e)s, ⁺e) *m* scent, odour;
d~en *vi* to smell, to be fragrant; **d~ig**
adj (*Stoff, Kleid*) delicate, diaphanous
dulden ['dʊldən] *vt* to suffer; (*zulassen*) to
tolerate ♦ *vi* to suffer
duldsam ['dʊltzaːm] *adj* tolerant
dumm [dʊm] *adj* stupid; (*ärgerlich*)
annoying; **der D~e sein** to be the loser;
~erweise *adv* stupidly; **D~heit** *f*
stupidity; (*Tat*) blunder, stupid mistake;
D~kopf *m* blockhead
dumpf [dʊmpf] *adj* (*Ton*) hollow, dull;
(*Luft*) musty; (*Erinnerung, Schmerz*)
vague
Düne ['dyːnə] *f* dune
düngen ['dʏŋən] *vt* to manure

Dünger (-s, -) *m* dung, manure;
(*künstlich*) fertilizer
dunkel ['dʊŋkəl] *adj* dark; (*Stimme*) deep;
(*Ahnung*) vague; (*rätselhaft*) obscure;
(*verdächtig*) dubious, shady; **im ~n**
tappen (*fig*) to grope in the dark
Dunkel- *zW*: **~heit** *f* darkness; (*fig*)
obscurity; **~kammer** *f* (*PHOT*) dark room;
d~n *vi unpers* to grow dark; **~ziffer** *f*
estimated number of unreported cases
dünn [dʏn] *adj* thin; **~flüssig** *adj* watery,
thin
Dunst [dʊnst] (-es, ⁺e) *m* vapour; (*Wetter*)
haze
dünsten ['dʏnstən] *vt* to steam
dunstig ['dʊnstɪç] *adj* vaporous; (*Wetter*)
hazy, misty
Duplikat [dupli'kaːt] (-(e)s, -e) *nt*
duplicate
Dur [duːr] (-, -) *nt* (*MUS*) major

SCHLÜSSELWORT

durch [dʊrç] *präp +akk* **1** (*hindurch*)
through; **durch den Urwald** through the
jungle; **die ganze Welt reisen** to travel
all over the world
2 (*mittels*) through, by (means of);
(*aufgrund*) due to, owing to; **Tod durch
Herzschlag/den Strang** death from a
heart attack/by hanging; **durch die Post**
by post; **durch seine Bemühungen**
through his efforts
♦ *adv* **1** (*hindurch*) through; **die ganze
Nacht durch** all through the night; **den
Sommer durch** during the summer; **8
Uhr durch** past 8 o'clock; **durch und
durch** completely
2 (*durchgebraten etc*): **(gut) durch** well-
done

durch- *zW*: **~arbeiten** *vt, vi* to work
through ♦ *vr* to work one's way through;
~'aus *adv* completely; (*unbedingt*)
definitely; **~aus nicht** absolutely not;
~blättern *vt* to leaf through
Durchblick ['dʊrçblɪk] *m* view; (*fig*)
comprehension; **d~en** *vi* to look through;
(*umg: verstehen*): **(bei etw) d~en** to
understand (sth); **etw d~en lassen** (*fig*) to

hint at sth
durchbrechen ['dʊrçbrɛçən] (*unreg*) *vt, vi* to break; **durch'brechen** (*unreg*) *vt insep* (*Schranken*) to break through; (*Schallmauer*) to break; (*Gewohnheit*) to break free from
durchbrennen ['dʊrçbrɛnən] (*unreg*) *vi* (*Draht, Sicherung*) to burn through; (*umg*) to run away
durchbringen (*unreg*) *vt* (*Kranken*) to pull through; (*unreg; umg: Familie*) to support; (*durchsetzen: Antrag, Kandidat*) to get through; (*vergeuden: Geld*) to get through, to squander
Durchbruch ['dʊrçbrʊx] *m* (*Öffnung*) opening; (*MIL*) breach; (*von Gefühlen etc*) eruption; (*der Zähne*) cutting; (*fig*) breakthrough; **zum ~ kommen** to break through
durch- *zW*: **~dacht** [-'daxt] *adj* well thought-out; **~'denken** (*unreg*) *vt* to think out; **~drehen** *vt* (*Fleisch*) to mince ♦ *vi* (*umg*) to crack up
durcheinander [dʊrçaɪ'nandər] *adv* in a mess, in confusion; (*umg: verwirrt*) confused; **~ trinken** to mix one's drinks; **D~ (-s)** *nt* (*Verwirrung*) confusion; (*Unordnung*) mess; **~bringen** (*unreg*) *vt* to mess up; (*verwirren*) to confuse; **~reden** *vi* to talk at the same time
durch- *zW*: **~fahren** (*unreg*) *vi* (*durch Tunnel usw*) to drive through; (*ohne Unterbrechung*) to drive straight through; (*ohne anzuhalten*): **der Zug fährt bis Hamburg ~** the train runs direct to Hamburg; (*ohne Umsteigen*): **können wir ~fahren?** can we go direct?, can we go non-stop?; **D~fahrt** *f* transit; (*Verkehr*) thoroughfare; **D~fall** *m* (*MED*) diarrhoea; **~fallen** (*unreg*) *vi* to fall through; (*in Prüfung*) to fail; **~finden** (*unreg*) *vr* to find one's way through; **~'forschen** *vt insep* to explore; **~fragen** *vr* to find one's way by asking
durchführ- ['dʊrçfy:r-] *zW*: **~bar** *adj* feasible, practicable; **~en** *vt* to carry out; **D~ung** *f* execution, performance
Durchgang ['dʊrçgaŋ] *m* passage(way); (*bei Produktion, Versuch*) run; (*SPORT*)
round; (*bei Wahl*) ballot; **„~ verboten"** "no thoroughfare"
Durchgangslager *nt* transit camp
Durchgangsverkehr *m* through traffic
durchgefroren ['dʊrçgefro:rən] *adj* (*Mensch*) frozen stiff
durchgehen ['dʊrçge:ən] (*unreg*) *vt* (*behandeln*) to go over ♦ *vi* to go through; (*ausreißen: Pferd*) to break loose; (*Mensch*) to run away; **mein Temperament ging mit mir durch** my temper got the better of me; **jdm etw ~ lassen** to let sb get away with sth; **~d** *adj* (*Zug*) through; (*Öffnungszeiten*) continuous
durch- *zW*: **~greifen** (*unreg*) *vi* to take strong action; **~halten** (*unreg*) *vi* to last out ♦ *vt* to keep up; **~kommen** (*unreg*) *vi* to get through; (*überleben*) to pull through
durch'kreuzen *vt insep* to thwart, to frustrate
durch- *zW*: **~lassen** (*unreg*) *vt* (*Person*) to let through; (*Wasser*) to let in; **~lesen** (*unreg*) *vt* to read through; **~'leuchten** *vt insep* to X-ray; **~machen** *vt* to go through; **die Nacht ~machen** to make a night of it; **D~marsch** *m* march through
Durchmesser (-s, -) *m* diameter
durch- *zW*: **~'nässen** *vt insep* to soak (through); **~nehmen** (*unreg*) *vt* to go over; **~numerieren** *vt* to number consecutively; **~queren** [dʊrç'kve:rən] *vt insep* to cross; **D~reiche** *f* (*serving*) hatch; **D~reise** *f* transit; **auf der D~reise** passing through; (*Güter*) in transit; **~ringen** (*unreg*) *vr* to reach a decision after a long struggle; **~rosten** *vi* to rust through
durchs [dʊrçs] = **durch das**
Durchsage ['dʊrçza:gə] *f* intercom *od* radio announcement
durchschauen ['dʊrçʃauən] *vi* to look *od* see through; (*Person, Lüge*) to see through
durchscheinen ['dʊrçʃaɪnən] (*unreg*) *vi* to shine through; **~d** *adj* translucent
Durchschlag ['dʊrçʃla:k] *m* (*Doppel*) carbon copy; (*Sieb*) strainer; **d~en** ['-gən] (*unreg*) *vt* (*entzweischlagen*) to split (in two); (*sieben*) to sieve ♦ *vi* (*zum Vor-*

schein kommen) to emerge, to come out ♦ *vr* to get by; **d~end** *adj* resounding

durchschneiden ['dʊrçʃnaɪdən] (*unreg*) *vt* to cut through

Durchschnitt ['dʊrçʃnɪt] *m* (*Mittelwert*) average; **über/unter dem ~** above/below average; **im ~** on average; **d~lich** *adj* average ♦ *adv* on average

Durchschnittsgeschwindigkeit *f* average speed

Durchschnittswert *m* average

durch- *zW:* **D~schrift** *f* copy; **~sehen** (*unreg*) *vt* to look through; **~setzen** *vt* to enforce ♦ *vr* (*Erfolg haben*) to succeed; (*sich behaupten*) to get one's way; **seinen Kopf ~setzen** to get one's way; **~'setzen** *vt insep* to mix

Durchsicht ['dʊrçzɪçt] *f* looking through, checking; **d~ig** *adj* transparent

durch- *zW:* **~sprechen** (*unreg*) *vt* to talk over; **~stehen** (*unreg*) *vt* to live through; **~stöbern** (*auch untr*) *vt* (*Kisten*) to rummage through, to rifle through; (*Haus, Wohnung*) to ransack; **~streichen** (*unreg*) *vt* to cross out; **~'suchen** *vt insep* to search; **D~'suchung** *f* search; **~trieben** [-'tri:bən] *adj* cunning, wily; **~'wachsen** *adj* (*Speck*) streaky; (*fig: mittelmäßig*) so-so; **D~wahl** *f* (*TEL*) direct dialling; **~weg** *adv* throughout, completely; **~ziehen** (*unreg*) *vt* (*Faden*) to draw through ♦ *vi* to pass through; **D~zug** *m* (*Luft*) draught; (*von Truppen, Vögeln*) passage

dürfen ['dʏrfən] (*unreg*) *vi* **1** (*Erlaubnis haben*) to be allowed to; **ich darf das** I'm allowed to (do that); **darf ich?** may I?; **darf ich ins Kino?** can *od* may I go to the cinema?; **es darf geraucht werden** you may smoke

2 (*in Verneinungen*): **er darf das nicht** he's not allowed to (do that); **das darf nicht geschehen** that must not happen; **da darf sie sich nicht wundern** that shouldn't surprise her

3 (*in Höflichkeitsformeln*): **darf ich Sie bitten, das zu tun?** may *od* could I ask

you to do that?; **was darf es sein?** what can I do for you?

4 (*können*): **das dürfen Sie mir glauben** you can believe me

5 (*Möglichkeit*): **das dürfte genug sein** that should be enough; **es dürfte Ihnen bekannt sein, daß ...** as you will probably know ...

dürftig ['dʏrftɪç] *adj* (*ärmlich*) needy, poor; (*unzulänglich*) inadequate

dürr [dʏr] *adj* dried-up; (*Land*) arid; (*mager*) skinny; **D~e** *f* aridity; (*Zeit*) drought; (*Magerkeit*) skinniness

Durst [dʊrst] *m* thirst; **~ haben** to be thirsty; **d~ig** *adj* thirsty

Dusche ['dʊʃə] *f* shower; **d~n** *vi, vr* to have a shower

Düse ['dy:zə] *f* nozzle; (*Flugzeug~*) jet

Düsen- *zW:* **~antrieb** *m* jet propulsion; **~flugzeug** *nt* jet (plane); **~jäger** *m* jet fighter

Dussel ['dʊsəl] (-s, -; *umg*) *m* twit

düster ['dy:stər] *adj* dark; (*Gedanken, Zukunft*) gloomy

Dutzend ['dʊtsənt] (-s, -e) *nt* dozen; **d~(e)mal** *adv* a dozen times; **d~weise** *adv* by the dozen

duzen ['du:tsən] *vt*: **(jdn) ~** to use the familiar form of address "du" (to *od* with sb)

Dynamik [dy'na:mɪk] *f* (*PHYS*) dynamics *sg*; (*fig: Schwung*) momentum; (*von Mensch*) dynamism

dynamisch [dy'na:mɪʃ] *adj* (*auch fig*) dynamic

Dynamit [dyna'mi:t] (-s) *nt* dynamite

Dynamo [dy'na:mo] (-s, -s) *m* dynamo

D-Zug ['de:tsu:k] *m* through train

E e

Ebbe ['ɛbə] *f* low tide

eben ['e:bən] *adj* level, flat; (*glatt*) smooth ♦ *adv* just; (*bestätigend*) exactly; **~ deswegen** just because of that; **~bürtig** *adj*: **jdm ~bürtig sein** to be sb's equal; **E~e** *f* plain; (*fig*) level; **~falls** *adv* likewise; ~**so** *adv* just as

Eber ['e:bər] (-s, -) *m* boar; ~**esche** *f* mountain ash, rowan

ebnen ['e:bnən] *vt* to level

Echo ['eço] (-s, -s) *nt* echo

echt [ɛçt] *adj* genuine; (*typisch*) typical; **E~heit** *f* genuineness

Eck- ['ɛk] *zW*: ~**ball** *m* corner (kick); ~**e** *f* corner; (*MATH*) angle; **e~ig** *adj* angular; ~**zahn** *m* eye tooth

ECU [e'ky:] (-, -s) *m* (*FINANZ*) ECU

edel ['e:dəl] *adj* noble; **E~metall** *nt* rare metal; **E~stein** *m* precious stone

EDV [e:de:'fau] (-) *f abk* (= *elektronische Datenverarbeitung*) electronic data processing

Efeu ['e:fɔy] (-s) *m* ivy

Effekt [ɛ'fɛkt] (-s, -e) *m* effect

Effekten [ɛ'fɛktən] *pl* stocks

effektiv [ɛfɛk'ti:f] *adj* effective, actual

EG ['e:'ge:] *f abk* (= *Europäische Gemeinschaft*) EC

egal [e'ga:l] *adj* all the same

Ego- [e:go] *zW*: ~**ismus** [-'ismus] *m* selfishness, egoism; ~**ist** [-'ist] *m* egoist; **e~istisch** *adj* selfish, egoistic

Ehe ['e:ə] *f* marriage

ehe *konj* before

Ehe- *zW*: ~**beratung** *f* marriage guidance (counselling); ~**bruch** *m* adultery; ~**frau** *f* married woman; wife; ~**leute** *pl* married people; **e~lich** *adj* matrimonial; (*Kind*) legitimate

ehemalig *adj* former

ehemals *adv* formerly

Ehemann *m* married man; husband

Ehepaar *nt* married couple

eher ['e:ər] *adv* (*früher*) sooner; (*lieber*) rather, sooner; (*mehr*) more

Ehering *m* wedding ring

Eheschließung *f* marriage ceremony

eheste(r, s) ['e:əstə(r, s)] *adj* (*früheste*) first, earliest; **am ~n** (*liebsten*) soonest; (*meist*) most; (*wahrscheinlichst*) most probably

Ehr- ['e:r] *zW*: **e~bar** *adj* honourable, respectable; ~**e** *f* honour; **e~en** *vt* to honour

Ehren- ['e:rən] *zW*: ~**gast** *m* guest of honour; **e~haft** *adj* honourable; ~**platz** *m* place of honour *od* (*US*) honor; ~**runde** *f* lap of honour; ~**sache** *f* point of honour; **e~voll** *adj* honourable; ~**wort** *nt* word of honour

Ehr- *zW*: ~**furcht** *f* awe, deep respect; **e~fürchtig** *adj* reverent; ~**gefühl** *nt* sense of honour; ~**geiz** *m* ambition; **e~geizig** *adj* ambitious; **e~lich** *adj* honest; ~**lichkeit** *f* honesty; **e~los** *adj* dishonourable; ~**ung** *f* honour(ing); **e~würdig** *adj* venerable

Ei [ai] (-(e)s, -er) *nt* egg

ei *excl* well, well

Eich- *zW*: ~**e** ['aiçə] *f* oak (tree); ~**el** (-, -n) *f* acorn; ~**hörnchen** *nt* squirrel; ~**maß** *nt* standard

Eid [ait] (-(e)s, -e) *m* oath

Eidechse ['aidɛksə] *f* lizard

eidesstattlich *adj*: ~**e Erklärung** affidavit

Eidgenosse *m* Swiss

Eidotter ['aidɔtər] *nt* egg yolk

Eier- *zW*: ~**becher** *m* eggcup; ~**kuchen** *m* omelette; pancake; ~**likör** *m* advocaat; ~**schale** *f* eggshell; ~**stock** *m* ovary; ~**uhr** *f* egg timer

Eifer ['aifər] (-s) *m* zeal, enthusiasm; ~**sucht** *f* jealousy; **e~süchtig** *adj*: **e~süchtig (auf** +*akk*) jealous (of)

eifrig ['aifriç] *adj* zealous, enthusiastic

Eigelb ['aigɛlp] (-(e)s, -) *nt* egg yolk

eigen ['aigən] *adj* own; (*~artig*) peculiar; **mit der/dem ihm ~en ...** with that ... peculiar to him; **sich** *dat* **etw zu ~ machen** to make sth one's own; **E~art** *f* peculiarity; characteristic; ~**artig** *adj* peculiar; **E~bedarf** *m*: **zum E~bedarf** for (one's own) personal use/domestic requirements; **der Vermieter machte E~bedarf geltend** the landlord showed he needed the house/flat for himself; ~**händig** *adj* with one's own hand; **E~heim** *nt* owner-occupied house; **E~heit** *f* peculiarity; ~**mächtig** *adj* high-handed; **E~name** *m* proper name; ~**s** *adv* expressly, on purpose; **E~schaft** *f* quality, property, attribute; **E~schaftswort** *nt* adjective; **E~sinn** *m* obstinacy; **~sinnig** adj obstinate; **~tlich** adj actual, really ♦ adv actually, really; **E~tor** nt own goal; **E~tum** nt property; **E~tümer(in)** (-s, -) m(f) owner, proprietor; **~tümlich** adj peculiar; **E~tümlichkeit** f peculiarity; **E~tumswohnung** f freehold flat

eignen ['aɪɡnən] vr to be suited

Eignung f suitability

Eil- ['aɪl] zW: **~bote** m courier; **~brief** m express letter; **~e** f haste; **es hat keine ~e** there's no hurry; **e~en** vi (Mensch) to hurry; (dringend sein) to be urgent; **e~ends** adv hastily; **~gut** nt express goods pl, fast freight (US); **e~ig** adj hasty, hurried; (dringlich) urgent; **es e~ig haben** to be in a hurry; **~zug** m semi-fast train, limited stop train

Eimer ['aɪmər] (-s, -) m bucket, pail

ein [aɪn] adv: **nicht ~ noch aus wissen** not to know what to do

ein(e) num one ♦ indef art a, an

einander [aɪ'nandər] pron one another, each other

einarbeiten ['aɪnarbaɪtən] vt to train ♦ vr: **sich in etw** akk **~** to familiarize o.s. with sth

einatmen ['aɪnaːtmən] vt, vi to inhale, to breathe in

Einbahnstraße ['aɪnbaːnʃtraːsə] f one-way street

Einband ['aɪnbant] m binding, cover

einbauen ['aɪnbauən] vt to build in; (Motor) to install, to fit

Einbaumöbel pl built-in furniture sg

einbegriffen ['aɪnbəɡrɪfən] adj included

einberufen ['aɪnbəruːfən] (unreg) vt to convene; (MIL) to call up

einbeziehen ['aɪnbətsiːən] (unreg) vt to include

einbiegen ['aɪnbiːɡən] (unreg) vi to turn

einbilden ['aɪnbɪldən] vt: **sich** dat **etw ~** to imagine sth

Einbildung f imagination; (Dünkel) conceit; **~skraft** f imagination

Einblick ['aɪnblɪk] m insight

einbrechen ['aɪnbrɛçən] (unreg) vi (in Haus) to break in; (Nacht) to fall; (Winter) to set in; (durchbrechen) to break; **~ in**
+akk (MIL) to invade

Einbrecher (-s, -) m burglar

einbringen ['aɪnbrɪŋən] (unreg) vt to bring in; (Geld, Vorteil) to yield; (mitbringen) to contribute

Einbruch ['aɪnbrʊx] m (Haus~) break-in, burglary; (Eindringen) invasion; (des Winters) onset; (Durchbrechen) break; (MET) approach; (MIL) penetration; **(bei/vor) ~ der Nacht** at/before nightfall; **e~ssicher** adj burglar-proof

einbürgern ['aɪnbʏrɡərn] vt to naturalize ♦ vr to become adopted

Einbuße ['aɪnbuːsə] f loss, forfeiture

einbüßen ['aɪnbyːsən] vt to lose, to forfeit

einchecken ['aɪntʃɛkən] vt, vi to check in

eincremen ['aɪnkreːmən] vt to put cream on

eindecken ['aɪndɛkən] vr: **sich (mit etw) ~** to lay in stocks (of sth); to stock up (with sth)

eindeutig ['aɪndɔʏtɪç] adj unequivocal

eindringen ['aɪndrɪŋən] (unreg) vi: **~ (in** +akk) to force one's way in(to); (in Haus) to break in(to); (in Land) to invade; (Gas, Wasser) to penetrate; **(auf jdn) ~** (mit Bitten) to pester (sb)

eindringlich adj forcible, urgent

Eindringling m intruder

Eindruck ['aɪndrʊk] m impression

eindrücken ['aɪndrʏkən] vt to press in

eindrucksvoll adj impressive

eine(r, s) pron one; (jemand) someone

eineiig ['aɪn'aɪɪç] adj (Zwillinge) identical

eineinhalb ['aɪn'aɪn'halp] num one and a half

einengen ['aɪn'ɛŋən] vt to confine, to restrict

einer- ['aɪnər] zW: **'E~'lei** (-s) nt sameness; **'~'lei** adj (gleichartig) the same kind of; **es ist mir ~lei** it is all the same to me; **~seits** adv on the one hand

einfach ['aɪnfax] adj simple; (nicht mehrfach) single ♦ adv simply; **E~heit** f simplicity

einfädeln ['aɪnfɛːdəln] vt (Nadel, Faden) to thread; (fig) to contrive

einfahren ['aɪnfaːrən] (*unreg*) *vt* to bring in; (*Barriere*) to knock down; (*Auto*) to run in ♦ *vi* to drive in; (*Zug*) to pull in; (*MIN*) to go down

Einfahrt *f* (*Vorgang*) driving in; pulling in; (*MIN*) descent; (*Ort*) entrance

Einfall ['aɪnfal] *m* (*Idee*) idea, notion; (*Licht~*) incidence; (*MIL*) raid; **e~en** (*unreg*) *vi* (*Licht*) to fall; (*MIL*) to raid; (*einstürzen*) to fall in, to collapse; (*einstimmen*): **(in etw** *akk***) e~en** to join in (with sth); **etw fällt jdm ein** sth occurs to sb; **das fällt mir gar nicht ein** I wouldn't dream of it; **sich** *dat* **etwas e~en lassen** to have a good idea

einfältig ['aɪnfɛltɪç] *adj* simple(-minded)

Einfamilienhaus [aɪnfaˈmiːliənhaʊs] *nt* detached house

einfarbig ['aɪnfarbɪç] *adj* all one colour; (*Stoff etc*) self-coloured

einfetten ['aɪnfɛtən] *vt* to grease

einfließen ['aɪnfliːsən] (*unreg*) *vi* to flow in

einflößen ['aɪnfløːsən] *vt*: **jdm etw ~** to give sb sth; (*fig*) to instil sth in sb

Einfluß ['aɪnflʊs] *m* influence; **~bereich** *m* sphere of influence

einförmig ['aɪnfœrmɪç] *adj* uniform; **E~keit** *f* uniformity

einfrieren ['aɪnfriːrən] (*unreg*) *vi* to freeze (in) ♦ *vt* to freeze

einfügen ['aɪnfyːgən] *vt* to fit in; (*zusätzlich*) to add

Einfuhr ['aɪnfuːr] (*-*) *f* import

einführen ['aɪnfyːrən] *vt* to bring in; (*Mensch, Sitten*) to introduce; (*Ware*) to import

Einführung *f* introduction

Eingabe ['aɪngaːbə] *f* petition; (*COMPUT*) input

Eingang ['aɪngaŋ] *m* entrance; (*COMM: Ankunft*) arrival; (*Erhalt*) receipt; **e~s** *adv* at the outset ♦ *präp* +*gen* at the outset of

eingeben ['aɪngeːbən] (*unreg*) *vt* (*Arznei*) to give; (*Daten etc*) to enter

eingebildet ['aɪngəbɪldət] *adj* imaginary; (*eitel*) conceited

Eingeborene(r) ['aɪngəboːrənə(r)] *mf* native

Eingebung *f* inspiration

eingedenk ['aɪngədɛŋk] *präp* +*gen* bearing in mind

eingefleischt ['aɪngəflaɪʃt] *adj* (*Gewohnheit, Vorurteile*) deep-rooted

eingehen ['aɪngeːən] (*unreg*) *vi* (*Aufnahme finden*) to come in; (*Sendung, Geld*) to be received; (*Tier, Pflanze*) to die; (*Firma*) to fold; (*schrumpfen*) to shrink ♦ *vt* to enter into; (*Wette*) to make; **auf etw** *akk* **~** to go into sth; **auf jdn ~** to respond to sb; **jdm ~** (*verständlich sein*) to be comprehensible to sb; **~d** *adj* exhaustive, thorough

Eingemachte(s) ['aɪngəmaxtə(s)] *nt* preserves *pl*

eingenommen ['aɪngənɔmən] *adj*: **~ (von)** fond (of), partial (to); **~ (gegen)** prejudiced (against)

eingeschrieben ['aɪngəʃriːbən] *adj* registered

eingespielt ['aɪngəʃpiːlt] *adj*: **aufeinander ~ sein** to be in tune with each other

Eingeständnis ['aɪngəʃtɛntnɪs] (**-ses, -se**) *nt* admission, confession

eingestehen ['aɪngəʃteːən] (*unreg*) *vt* to confess

eingestellt ['aɪngəʃtɛlt] *adj*: **auf etw ~ sein** to be prepared for sth

eingetragen ['aɪngətraːgən] *adj* (*COMM*) registered

Eingeweide ['aɪngəvaɪdə] (**-s, -**) *nt* innards *pl*, intestines *pl*

Eingeweihte(r) ['aɪngəvaɪtə(r)] *mf* initiate

eingewöhnen ['aɪngəvøːnən] *vr*: **sich ~ in** +*akk* to settle (down) in

eingleisig ['aɪnglaɪzɪç] *adj* single-track

eingreifen ['aɪngraɪfən] (*unreg*) *vi* to intervene, to interfere; (*Zahnrad*) to mesh

Eingriff ['aɪngrɪf] *m* intervention, interference; (*Operation*) operation

einhaken ['aɪnhaːkən] *vt* to hook in ♦ *vr*: **sich bei jdm ~** to link arms with sb ♦ *vi* (*sich einmischen*) to intervene

Einhalt ['aɪnhalt] *m*: **~ gebieten** +*dat* to put a stop to; **e~en** (*unreg*) *vt* (*Regel*) to keep ♦ *vi* to stop

einhändigen ['aɪnhɛndɪgən] *vt* to hand in

einhängen ['aɪnhɛŋən] *vt* to hang; (*Telefon*) to hang up ♦ *vi* (*TEL*) to hang up; **sich bei jdm ~** to link arms with sb

einheimisch ['aɪnhaɪmɪʃ] *adj* native; **E~e(r)** *mf* local

Einheit ['aɪnhaɪt] *f* unity; (*Maß, MIL*) unit; **e~lich** *adj* uniform; **~spreis** *m* standard price

einholen ['aɪnho:lən] *vt* (*Tau*) to haul in; (*Fahne, Segel*) to lower; (*Vorsprung aufholen*) to catch up with; (*Verspätung*) to make up; (*Rat, Erlaubnis*) to ask ♦ *vi* (*einkaufen*) to shop

Einhorn ['aɪnhɔrn] *nt* unicorn

einhüllen ['aɪnhʏlən] *vt* to wrap up

einhundert ['aɪnhʊndɐt] *num* one hundred, a hundred

einig ['aɪnɪç] *adj* (*vereint*) united; **sich** *dat* **~ sein** to be in agreement; **~ werden** to agree

einige(r, s) ['aɪnɪgə(r, s)] *adj, pron* some ♦ *pl* some; (*mehrere*) several; **~mal** *adv* a few times; **~n** *vt* to unite ♦ *vr*: **sich ~n (auf** +*akk*) to agree (on)

einigermaßen *adv* somewhat; (*leidlich*) reasonably

einig- *zW*: **~gehen** (*unreg*) *vi* to agree; **E~keit** *f* unity; (*Übereinstimmung*) agreement; **E~ung** *f* agreement; (*Vereinigung*) unification

einkalkulieren ['aɪnkalkuli:rən] *vt* to take into account, to allow for

Einkauf ['aɪnkaʊf] *m* purchase; **e~en** *vt* to buy ♦ *vi* to shop; **e~en gehen** to go shopping

Einkaufs- *zW*: **~bummel** *m* shopping spree; **~korb** *m* shopping basket; **~wagen** *m* shopping trolley; **~zentrum** *nt* shopping centre

einklammern ['aɪnklamɐn] *vt* to put in brackets, to bracket

Einklang ['aɪnklaŋ] *m* harmony

einklemmen ['aɪnklɛmən] *vt* to jam

einkochen ['aɪnkɔxən] *vt* to boil down; (*Obst*) to preserve, to bottle

Einkommen ['aɪnkɔmən] **(-s, -)** *nt* income; **~(s)steuer** *f* income tax

Einkünfte ['aɪnkʏnftə] *pl* income *sg*, revenue *sg*

einladen ['aɪnla:dən] (*unreg*) *vt* (*Person*) to invite; (*Gegenstände*) to load; **jdn ins Kino ~** to take sb to the cinema

Einladung *f* invitation

Einlage ['aɪnla:gə] *f* (*Programm~*) interlude; (*Spar~*) deposit; (*Schuh~*) insole; (*Fußstütze*) support; (*Zahn~*) temporary filling; (*KOCH*) noodles *pl*, vegetables *pl etc* in soup

einlagern *vt* to store

Einlaß **(-sses, -lässe)** *m* (*Zutritt*) admission

einlassen ['aɪnlasən] (*unreg*) *vt* to let in; (*einsetzen*) to set in ♦ *vr*: **sich mit jdm/ auf etw** *akk* **~** to get involved with sb/ sth

Einlauf ['aɪnlaʊf] *m* arrival; (*von Pferden*) finish; (*MED*) enema; **e~en** (*unreg*) *vi* to arrive, to come in; (*in Hafen*) to enter; (*SPORT*) to finish; (*Wasser*) to run in; (*Stoff*) to shrink ♦ *vt* (*Schuhe*) to break in ♦ *vr* (*SPORT*) to warm up; (*Motor, Maschine*) to run in; **jdm das Haus e~en** to invade sb's house

einleben ['aɪnle:bən] *vr* to settle down

einlegen ['aɪnle:gən] *vt* (*einfügen: Blatt, Sohle*) to insert; (*KOCH*) to pickle; (*Pause*) to have; (*Protest*) to make; (*Veto*) to use; (*Berufung*) to lodge; (*AUT: Gang*) to engage

einleiten ['aɪnlaɪtən] *vt* to introduce, to start; (*Geburt*) to induce

Einleitung *f* introduction; induction

einleuchten ['aɪnlɔʏçtən] *vi*: **(jdm) ~** to be clear *od* evident (to sb); **~d** *adj* clear

einliefern ['aɪnli:fɐn] *vt*: **~ (in** +*akk*) **to** take (into)

Einliegerwohnung ['aɪnli:gɐvo:nʊŋ] *f* self-contained flat; (*für Eltern, Großeltern*) granny flat

einlösen ['aɪnlø:zən] *vt* (*Scheck*) to cash; (*Schuldschein, Pfand*) to redeem; (*Versprechen*) to keep

einmachen ['aɪnmaxən] *vt* to preserve

einmal ['aɪnma:l] *adv* once; (*erstens*) first; (*zukünftig*) sometime; **nehmen wir ~ an** just let's suppose; **noch ~** once more;

nicht ~ not even; **auf** ~ all at once; **es war** ~ once upon a time there was/were; **E~eins** *nt* multiplication tables *pl*; **~ig** *adj* unique; (*nur einmal erforderlich*) single; (*prima*) fantastic

Einmarsch ['aɪnmarʃ] *m* entry; (*MIL*) invasion; **e~ieren** *vi* to march in

einmischen ['aɪnmɪʃən] *vr*: **sich** ~ (**in** +*akk*) to interfere (with)

einmütig ['aɪnmy:tɪç] *adj* unanimous

Einnahme ['aɪnna:mə] *f* (*von Medizin*) taking; (*MIL*) capture, taking; **~n** *pl* (*Geld*) takings, revenue *sg*; **~quelle** *f* source of income

einnehmen ['aɪnne:mən] (*unreg*) *vt* to take; (*Stellung, Raum*) to take up; ~ **für/gegen** to persuade in favour of/against; **~d** *adj* charming

Einöde ['aɪnʼøːdə] *f* desert, wilderness

einordnen ['aɪnʼɔrdnən] *vt* to arrange, to fit in ♦ *vr* to adapt; (*AUT*) to get into lane

einpacken ['aɪnpakən] *vt* to pack (up)

einparken ['aɪnparkən] *vt* to park

einpendeln ['aɪnpɛndəln] *vr* to even out

einpflanzen ['aɪnpflantsən] *vt* to plant; (*MED*) to implant

einplanen ['aɪnpla:nən] *vt* to plan for

einprägen ['aɪnprɛːɡən] *vt* to impress, to imprint; (*beibringen*): (**jdm**) ~ to impress (on sb); **sich** *dat* **etw** ~ to memorize sth

einrahmen ['aɪnra:mən] *vt* to frame

einräumen ['aɪnrɔymən] *vt* (*ordnend*) to put away; (*überlassen: Platz*) to give up; (*zugestehen*) to admit, to concede

einreden ['aɪnre:dən] *vt*: **jdm/sich etw** ~ to talk sb/o.s. into believing sth

einreiben ['aɪnraɪbən] (*unreg*) *vt* to rub in

einreichen ['aɪnraɪçən] *vt* to hand in; (*Antrag*) to submit

Einreise ['aɪnraɪzə] *f* entry; **~bestimmungen** *pl* entry regulations; **~erlaubnis** *f* entry permit; **~genehmigung** *f* entry permit; **e~n** *vi*: (**in ein Land**) to enter (a country)

einrichten ['aɪnrɪçtən] *vt* (*Haus*) to furnish; (*schaffen*) to establish, to set up; (*arrangieren*) to arrange; (*möglich machen*) to manage ♦ *vr* (*in Haus*) to

furnish one's house; **sich** ~ (**auf** +*akk*) (*sich vorbereiten*) to prepare o.s. (for); (*sich anpassen*) to adapt (to)

Einrichtung *f* (*Wohnungs~*) furnishings *pl*; (*öffentliche Anstalt*) organization; (*Dienste*) service

einrosten ['aɪnrɔstən] *vi* to get rusty

einrücken ['aɪnrykən] *vi* (*MIL: in Land*) to move in

Eins [aɪns] (-, **-en**) *f* one; **e~** *num* one; **es ist mir alles e~** it's all one to me

einsam ['aɪnza:m] *adj* lonely, solitary; **E~keit** *f* loneliness, solitude

einsammeln ['aɪnzaməln] *vt* to collect

Einsatz ['aɪnzats] *m* (*Teil*) inset; (*an Kleid*) insertion; (*Verwendung*) use, employment; (*Spiel~*) stake; (*Risiko*) risk; (*MIL*) operation; (*MUS*) entry; **im** ~ in action; **e~bereit** *adj* ready for action

einschalten ['aɪnʃaltən] *vt* (*einfügen*) to insert; (*Pause*) to make; (*ELEK*) to switch on; (*Anwalt*) to bring in ♦ *vr* (*dazwischentreten*) to intervene

einschärfen ['aɪnʃɛrfən] *vt*: **jdm etw** ~ to impress sth (up)on sb

einschätzen ['aɪnʃɛtsən] *vt* to estimate, to assess ♦ *vr* to rate o.s.

einschenken ['aɪnʃɛŋkən] *vt* to pour out

einschicken ['aɪnʃɪkən] *vt* to send in

einschl. *abk* (= *einschließlich*) incl.

einschlafen ['aɪnʃla:fən] (*unreg*) *vi* to fall asleep, to go to sleep

einschläfernd ['aɪnʃlɛːfərnt] *adj* (*MED*) soporific; (*langweilig*) boring; (*Stimme*) lulling

Einschlag ['aɪnʃla:k] *m* impact; (*fig: Beimischung*) touch, hint; **e~en** [-ɡən] (*unreg*) *vt* to knock in; (*Fenster*) to smash, to break; (*Zähne, Schädel*) to smash in; (*AUT: Räder*) to turn; (*kürzer machen*) to take up; (*Ware*) to pack, to wrap up; (*Weg, Richtung*) to take ♦ *vi* to hit; (*sich einigen*) to agree; (*Anklang finden*) to work, to succeed; **in etw** *akk*/**auf jdn e~en** to hit sth/sb

einschlägig ['aɪnʃlɛːɡɪç] *adj* relevant

einschließen ['aɪnʃliːsən] (*unreg*) *vt* (*Kind*) to lock in; (*Häftling*) to lock up; (*Gegenstand*) to lock away; (*Bergleute*) to cut off; (*umgeben*) to surround; (*MIL*) to encircle; (*fig*) to include, to comprise ♦ *vr* to lock o.s. in

einschließlich *adv* inclusive ♦ *präp* +*gen* inclusive of, including

einschmeicheln ['aɪnʃmaɪçəln] *vr*: **sich ~ (bei)** to ingratiate o.s. (with)

einschnappen ['aɪnʃnapən] *vi* (*Tür*) to click to; (*fig*) to be touchy; **eingeschnappt sein** to be in a huff

einschneidend ['aɪnʃnaɪdənt] *adj* drastic

Einschnitt ['aɪnʃnɪt] *m* cutting; (*MED*) incision; (*Ereignis*) decisive point

einschränken ['aɪnʃrɛŋkən] *vt* to limit, to restrict; (*Kosten*) to cut down, to reduce ♦ *vr* to cut down (on expenditure)

Einschränkung *f* restriction, limitation; reduction; (*von Behauptung*) qualification

Einschreib- ['aɪnʃraɪb] *zW*: **~(e)brief** *m* recorded delivery letter; **e~en** (*unreg*) *vt* to write in; (*Post*) to send recorded delivery ♦ *vr* to register; (*UNIV*) to enrol; **~en** *nt* recorded delivery letter

einschreiten ['aɪnʃraɪtən] (*unreg*) *vi* to step in, to intervene; **~ gegen** to take action against

einschüchtern ['aɪnʃʏçtərn] *vt* to intimidate

einschulen ['aɪnʃuːlən] *vt*: **eingeschult werden** (*Kind*) to start school

einsehen ['aɪnzeːən] (*unreg*) *vt* (*hineinsehen in*) to realize; (*Akten*) to have a look at; (*verstehen*) to see; **E~ (-s)** *nt* understanding; **ein E~ haben** to show understanding

einseitig ['aɪnzaɪtɪç] *adj* one-sided

Einsend- ['aɪnzɛnd] *zW*: **e~en** (*unreg*) *vt* to send in; **~er (-s, -)** *m* sender, contributor; **~ung** *f* sending in

einsetzen ['aɪnzɛtsən] *vt* to put (in); (*in Amt*) to appoint, to install; (*Geld*) to stake; (*verwenden*) to use; (*MIL*) to employ ♦ *vi* (*beginnen*) to set in; (*MUS*) to enter, to come in ♦ *vr* to work hard; **sich für jdn/etw ~** to support sb/sth

Einsicht ['aɪnzɪçt] *f* insight; (*in Akten*) look, inspection; **zu der ~ kommen, daß ...** to come to the conclusion that ...; **e~ig** *adj* (*Mensch*) judicious; **e~slos** *adj*

unreasonable; **e~svoll** *adj* understanding

Einsiedler ['aɪnziːdlər] *m* hermit

einsilbig ['aɪnzɪlbɪç] *adj* (*auch fig*) monosyllabic; (*Mensch*) uncommunicative

einspannen ['aɪnʃpanən] *vt* (*Papier*) to insert; (*Pferde*) to harness; (*umg: Person*) to rope in

Einsparung ['aɪnʃpaːrʊŋ] *f* economy, saving

einsperren ['aɪnʃpɛrən] *vt* to lock up

einspielen ['aɪnʃpiːlən] *vr* (*SPORT*) to warm up ♦ *vt* (*Film: Geld*) to bring in; (*Instrument*) to play in; **sich aufeinander ~** to become attuned to each other; **gut eingespielt** running smoothly

einsprachig ['aɪnʃpraːxɪç] *adj* monolingual

einspringen ['aɪnʃprɪŋən] (*unreg*) *vi* (*aushelfen*) to help out, to step into the breach

Einspruch ['aɪnʃprʊx] *m* protest, objection; **~srecht** *nt* veto

einspurig ['aɪnʃpuːrɪç] *adj* (*EISENB*) single-track; (*AUT*) single-lane

einst [aɪnst] *adv* once; (*zukünftig*) one day, some day

Einstand ['aɪnʃtant] *m* (*TENNIS*) deuce; (*Antritt*) entrance (to office)

einstecken ['aɪnʃtɛkən] *vt* to stick in, to insert; (*Brief*) to post; (*ELEK: Stecker*) to plug in; (*Geld*) to pocket; (*mitnehmen*) to take; (*überlegen sein*) to put in the shade; (*hinnehmen*) to swallow

einstehen ['aɪnʃteːən] (*unreg*) *vi*: **für jdn/etw ~** to guarantee sb/sth; (*verantworten*): **für etw ~** to answer for sth

einsteigen ['aɪnʃtaɪgən] (*unreg*) *vi* to get in *od* on; (*in Schiff*) to go on board; (*sich beteiligen*) to come in; (*hineinklettern*) to climb in

einstellen ['aɪnʃtɛlən] *vt* (*aufhören*) to stop; (*Geräte*) to adjust; (*Kamera etc*) to focus; (*Sender, Radio*) to tune in; (*unterstellen*) to put; (*in Firma*) to employ, to take on ♦ *vi* (*Firma*) to take on staff/workers ♦ *vr* (*anfangen*) to set in; (*kommen*) to arrive; **sich auf jdn ~** to adapt to sb; **sich auf etw** *akk* **~** to prepare o.s. for sth

Einstellung *f* (*Aufhören*) suspension, cessation; adjustment; focusing; (*von Arbeiter etc*) appointment; (*Haltung*) attitude

Einstieg ['aɪnʃtiːk] (-(e)s, -e) *m* entry; (*fig*) approach

einstig ['aɪnstɪç] *adj* former

einstimmig ['aɪnʃtɪmɪç] *adj* unanimous; (*MUS*) for one voice

einstmalig ['aɪnstmaːlɪç] *adj* former

einstmals *adv* once, formerly

einstöckig ['aɪnʃtœkɪç] *adj* two-storeyed

Einsturz ['aɪnʃtʊrts] *m* collapse

einstürzen ['aɪnʃtʏrtsən] *vi* to fall in, to collapse

einstweilen *adv* meanwhile; (*vorläufig*) temporarily, for the time being

einstweilig *adj* temporary

eintägig ['aɪntɛːgɪç] *adj* one-day

eintasten ['aɪntastən] *vt* to key (in)

eintauschen ['aɪntaʊʃən] *vt*: ~ (**gegen** *od* **für**) to exchange (for)

eintausend ['aɪntaʊzənt] *num* one thousand

einteilen ['aɪntaɪlən] *vt* (*in Teile*) to divide (up); (*Menschen*) to assign

einteilig *adj* one-piece

eintönig ['aɪntøːnɪç] *adj* monotonous

Eintopf ['aɪntɔpf] *m* stew; **~gericht** *nt* stew

Eintracht ['aɪntraxt] (-) *f* concord, harmony

einträchtig ['aɪntrɛçtɪç] *adj* harmonious

Eintrag ['aɪntraːk] (-(e)s, ¬e) *m* entry; **amtlicher** ~ entry in the register; **e~en** [-gən] (*unreg*) *vt* (*in Buch*) to enter; (*Profit*) to yield ♦ *vr* to put one's name down; **jdm etw e~en** to bring sb sth

einträglich ['aɪntrɛːklɪç] *adj* profitable

eintreffen ['aɪntrɛfən] (*unreg*) *vi* to happen; (*ankommen*) to arrive

eintreten ['aɪntreːtən] (*unreg*) *vi* to occur; (*sich einsetzen*) to intercede ♦ *vt* (*Tür*) to kick open; ~ **in** +*akk* to enter; (*in Club, Partei*) to join

Eintritt ['aɪntrɪt] *m* (*Betreten*) entrance; (*Anfang*) commencement; (*in Club etc*) joining

Eintritts- *zW*: **~geld** *nt* admission charge; **~karte** *f* (admission) ticket; **~preis** *m* admission charge

einüben ['aɪnʔyːbən] *vt* to practise

Einvernehmen ['aɪnfɛrneːmən] (-s, -) *nt* agreement, harmony

einverstanden ['aɪnfɛrʃtandən] *excl* agreed, okay ♦ *adj*: ~ **sein** to agree, to be agreed

Einverständnis ['aɪnfɛrʃtɛntnɪs] *nt* understanding; (*gleiche Meinung*) agreement

Einwand ['aɪnvant] (-(e)s, ¬e) *m* objection

Einwanderer ['aɪnvandərər] *m* immigrant

einwandern *vi* to immigrate

Einwanderung *f* immigration

einwandfrei *adj* perfect ♦ *adv* absolutely

Einwegflasche ['aɪnveːkflaʃə] *f* no-deposit bottle

Einwegspritze *f* disposable syringe

einweichen ['aɪnvaɪçən] *vt* to soak

einweihen ['aɪnvaɪən] *vt* (*Kirche*) to consecrate; (*Brücke*) to open; (*Gebäude*) to inaugurate; ~ (**in** +*akk*) (*Person*) to initiate (in)

Einweihung *f* consecration; opening; inauguration; initiation

einweisen ['aɪnvaɪzən] (*unreg*) *vt* (*in Amt*) to install; (*in Arbeit*) to introduce; (*in Anstalt*) to send

einwenden ['aɪnvɛndən] (*unreg*) *vt*: **etwas** ~ **gegen** to object to, to oppose

einwerfen ['aɪnvɛrfən] (*unreg*) *vt* to throw in; (*Brief*) to post; (*Geld*) to put in, to insert; (*Fenster*) to smash; (*äußern*) to interpose

einwickeln ['aɪnvɪkəln] *vt* to wrap up; (*fig: umg*) to outsmart

einwilligen ['aɪnvɪlɪgən] *vi*: ~ (**in** +*akk*) to consent (to), to agree (to)

Einwilligung *f* consent

einwirken ['aɪnvɪrkən] *vi*: **auf jdn/etw** ~ to influence sb/sth

Einwohner ['aɪnvoːnər] (-s, -) *m* inhabitant; **~meldeamt** *nt* registration office; **~schaft** *f* population, inhabitants *pl*

Einwurf ['aɪnvʊrf] *m* (*Öffnung*) slot; (*von*

Münze) insertion; *(von Brief)* posting; *(Einwand)* objection; *(SPORT)* throw-in

Einzahl ['aɪntsaːl] *f* singular; **e~en** *vt* to pay in; **~ung** *f* paying in

einzäunen ['aɪntsɔʏnən] *vt* to fence in

Einzel ['aɪntsəl] **(-s, -)** *nt (TENNIS)* singles; **~fahrschein** *m* one-way ticket; **~fall** *m* single instance, individual case; **~handel** *m* retail trade; **~handelspreis** *m* retail price; **~heit** *f* particular, detail; **e~n** *adj* single; *(vereinzelt)* the odd ♦ *adv* singly; **e~n angeben** to specify; **der/die e~ne** the individual; **das e~ne** the particular; **ins e~ne gehen** to go into detail(s); **~teil** *nt* component (part); **~zimmer** *nt* single room

einziehen ['aɪntsiːən] *(unreg) vt* to draw in, to take in; *(Kopf)* to duck; *(Fühler, Antenne, Fahrgestell)* to retract; *(Steuern, Erkundigungen)* to collect; *(MIL)* to draft, to call up; *(aus dem Verkehr ziehen)* to withdraw; *(konfiszieren)* to confiscate ♦ *vi* to move in; *(Friede, Ruhe)* to come; *(Flüssigkeit)* to penetrate

einzig ['aɪntsɪç] *adj* only; *(ohnegleichen)* unique; **das ~e** the only thing; **der/die ~e** the only one; **~artig** *adj* unique

Einzug ['aɪntsuːk] *m* entry, moving in

Eis [aɪs] **(-es, -)** *nt* ice; *(Speise~)* ice cream; **~bahn** *f* ice *od* skating rink; **~bär** *m* polar bear; **~becher** *m* sundae; **~bein** *nt* pig's trotters *pl*; **~berg** *m* iceberg; **~café** *nt* ice-cream parlour *(BRIT)* or parlor *(US)*; **~decke** *f* sheet of ice; **~diele** *f* ice-cream parlour

Eisen ['aɪzən] **(-s, -)** *nt* iron

Eisenbahn *f* railway, railroad *(US)*; **~abteil** *nt* railway compartment; **~er (-s, -)** *m* railwayman, railway employee, railroader *(US)*; **~schaffner** *m* railway guard; **~wagen** *m* railway carriage

Eisenerz *nt* iron ore

eisern ['aɪzərn] *adj* iron; *(Gesundheit)* robust; *(Energie)* unrelenting; *(Reserve)* emergency

Eis- [aɪs] *zW:* **e~frei** *adj* clear of ice; **~hockey** *nt* ice hockey; **e~ig** ['aɪzɪç] *adj* icy; **e~kalt** *adj* icy cold; **~kunstlauf** *m* figure skating; **~laufen** *nt* ice skating;

~pickel *m* ice-axe; **~schießen** *nt* ≈ curling; **~schrank** *m* fridge, ice-box *(US)*; **~würfel** *m* ice cube; **~zapfen** *m* icicle; **~zeit** *f* ice age

eitel ['aɪtəl] *adj* vain; **E~keit** *f* vanity

Eiter ['aɪtər] **(-s)** *m* pus; **e~ig** *adj* suppurating; **e~n** *vi* to suppurate

Eiweiß **(-es, -e)** *nt* white of an egg; *(CHEM)* protein

Ekel¹ ['eːkəl] **(-s)** *m* nausea, disgust

Ekel² **(-s, -)** *nt (umg: Mensch)* nauseating person

ekelerregend *adj* nauseating, disgusting

ekelhaft *adj* nauseating, disgusting

ekelig *adj* nauseating, disgusting

ekeln *vt* to disgust ♦ *vr:* **sich ~ (vor** +*dat)* to loathe, to be disgusted (at); **es ekelt jdn** *od* **jdm** sb is disgusted

eklig *adj* nauseating, disgusting

Ekstase [ɛkˈstaːzə] *f* ecstasy

Ekzem [ɛkˈtseːm] **(-s, -e)** *nt (MED)* eczema

Elan [eˈlãː] **(-s)** *m* elan

elastisch [eˈlastɪʃ] *adj* elastic

Elastizität [elastitsiˈtɛːt] *f* elasticity

Elch [ɛlç] **(-(e)s, -e)** *m* elk

Elefant [eleˈfant] *m* elephant

elegant [eleˈgant] *adj* elegant

Eleganz [eleˈgants] *f* elegance

Elek- [eˈlɛk] *zW:* **~triker** [-trikər] **(-s, -)** *m* electrician; **e~trisch** [-trɪʃ] *adj* electric; **e~trisieren** [-triˈziːrən] *vt (auch fig)* to electrify; *(Mensch)* to give an electric shock to ♦ *vr* to get an electric shock; **~trizität** [-tritsiˈtɛːt] *f* electricity; **~trizitätswerk** *nt* power station; *(Gesellschaft)* electric power company

Elektro- [eˈlɛktro] *zW:* **~de** [-ˈtroːdə] *f* electrode; **~herd** *m* electric cooker; **~n (-s, -en)** *nt* electron; **~nenrechner** [elɛkˈtroːnən-] *m* computer; **~nik** *f* electronics *sg;* **e~nisch** *adj* electronic; **e~nische Post** electronic mail; **e~nischer Briefkasten** electronic mailbox; **~rasierer** *m* electric razor

Elektrotechnik *f* electrical engineering

Element [eleˈmɛnt] **(-s, -e)** *nt* element; *(ELEK)* cell, battery; **e~ar** [-ˈtaːr] *adj* elementary; *(naturhaft)* elemental

Elend ['eːlɛnt] **(-(e)s)** *nt* misery; **e~** *adj*

miserable; **~sviertel** *nt* slum
elf [ɛlf] *num* eleven; **E~** (-, **-en**) *f* (SPORT) eleven
Elfe *f* elf
Elfenbein *nt* ivory
Elfmeter *m* (SPORT) penalty (kick)
Elite [e'li:tə] *f* elite
Elixier [elɪ'ksi:r] (-s, -e) *nt* elixir
Ellbogen *m* elbow
Elle ['ɛlə] *f* ell; (*Maß*) yard
Ellenbogen *m* elbow
Ell(en)bogenfreiheit *f* (*fig*) elbow room
Ellipse [ɛ'lɪpsə] *f* ellipse
Elsaß ['ɛlzas] (- *od* **-sses**) *nt*: **das ~** Alsace
Elster ['ɛlstər] (-, **-n**) *f* magpie
Eltern ['ɛltərn] *pl* parents; **~beirat** *m* (SCH) ≈ PTA (BRIT), parents' council; **~haus** *nt* home; **e~los** *adj* parentless
Email [e'ma:j] (-s, **-s**) *nt* enamel; **e~lieren** [ema'ji:rən] *vt* to enamel
Emanzipation [emantsipatsi'o:n] *f* emancipation
emanzi'pieren *vt* to emancipate
Embryo ['ɛmbryo] (-s, **-s** *od* **Embryonen**) *m* embryo
Emi- *zW*: **~'grant(in)** *m(f)* emigrant; **~gration** [emigratsi'o:n] *f* emigration; **e~'grieren** *vi* to emigrate
Emissionen [emɪsi'o:nən] *pl* emissions
Empfang [ɛm'pfaŋ] (-(e)s, *ə*e) *m* reception; (*Erhalten*) receipt; **in ~ nehmen** to receive; **e~en** (*unreg*) *vt* to receive ♦ *vi* (*schwanger werden*) to conceive
Empfäng- [ɛm'pfɛŋ] *zW*: **~er** (-s, -) *m* receiver; (COMM) addressee, consignee; **e~lich** *adj* receptive, susceptible; **~nis** (-, **-se**) *f* conception; **~nisverhütung** *f* contraception
Empfangs- *zW*: **~bestätigung** *f* acknowledgement; **~dame** *f* receptionist; **~schein** *m* receipt; **~zimmer** *nt* reception room
empfehlen [ɛm'pfe:lən] (*unreg*) *vt* to recommend ♦ *vr* to take one's leave; **~swert** *adj* recommendable
Empfehlung *f* recommendation
empfiehlst *etc* [ɛm'pfi:lst] *vb siehe* **empfehlen**

empfind- [ɛm'pfɪnt] *zW*: **~en** [-dən] (*unreg*) *vt* to feel; **~lich** *adj* sensitive; (*Stelle*) sore; (*reizbar*) touchy; **~sam** *adj* sentimental; **E~ung** [-duŋ] *f* feeling, sentiment
empfohlen *etc* [ɛm'pfo:lən] *vb siehe* **empfehlen**
empor [ɛm'po:r] *adv* up, upwards
empören [ɛm'pø:rən] *vt* to make indignant; to shock ♦ *vr* to become indignant; **~d** *adj* outrageous
Emporkömmling [ɛm'po:rkœmlɪŋ] *m* upstart, parvenu
Empörung *f* indignation
emsig ['ɛmzɪç] *adj* diligent, busy
End- ['ɛnd] *in zW* final; **~e** (-s, **-n**) *nt* end; **am ~e** at the end; (*schließlich*) in the end; **am ~e sein** to be at the end of one's tether; **~e Dezember** at the end of December; **zu ~e sein** to be finished; **e~en** *vi* to end; **e~gültig** ['ɛnt-] *adj* final, definite
Endivie [ɛn'di:viə] *f* endive
End- *zW*: **e~lich** *adj* final; (MATH) finite ♦ *adv* finally; **~lich!** at last!; **komm e~lich!** come on!; **e~los** *adj* endless, infinite; **~spiel** *nt* final(s); **~spurt** *m* (SPORT) final spurt; **~station** *f* terminus; **~ung** *f* ending
Energie [enɛr'gi:] *f* energy; **~bedarf** *m* energy requirement; **e~los** *adj* lacking in energy, weak; **~versorgung** *f* supply of energy; **~wirtschaft** *f* energy industry
energisch [e'nɛrgɪʃ] *adj* energetic
eng [ɛŋ] *adj* narrow; (*Kleidung*) tight; (*fig: Horizont*) narrow, limited; (*Freundschaft, Verhältnis*) close; **~ an etw** *dat* close to sth
Engagement [āgaʒə'mā:] (-s, **-s**) *nt* engagement; (*Verpflichtung*) commitment
engagieren [āga'ʒi:rən] *vt* to engage ♦ *vr* to commit o.s.; **ein engagierter Schriftsteller** a committed writer
Enge ['ɛŋə] *f* (*auch fig*) narrowness; (*Land~*) defile; (*Meer~*) straits *pl*; **jdn in die ~ treiben** to drive sb into a corner
Engel ['ɛŋəl] (-s, -) *m* angel; **e~haft** *adj* angelic
engherzig *adj* petty
England *nt* England

Engländer(in) *m(f)* Englishman(woman)
englisch *adj* English
Engpaß *m* defile, pass; *(fig, Verkehr)* bottleneck
en gros [ã'gro:] *adv* wholesale
engstirnig ['ɛŋʃtɪrnɪç] *adj* narrow-minded
Enkel ['ɛŋkəl] (-s, -) *m* grandson; **~in** *f* granddaughter
Enkelkind *nt* grandchild
enorm [e'nɔrm] *adj* enormous
Ensemble [ã'sãbəl] (-s, -s) *nt* company, ensemble
entbehren [ɛnt'be:rən] *vt* to do without, to dispense with
entbehrlich *adj* superfluous
Entbehrung *f* deprivation
entbinden [ɛnt'bɪndən] *(unreg) vt* (+*gen*) to release (from); *(MED)* to deliver ♦ *vi* to give birth
Entbindung *f* release; *(MED)* confinement; **~sheim** *nt* maternity hospital
entdeck- [ɛnt'dɛk] *zW:* **~en** *vt* to discover; **E~er** (-s, -) *m* discoverer; **E~ung** *f* discovery
Ente ['ɛntə] *f* duck; *(fig)* canard, false report
enteignen [ɛnt''aignən] *vt* to expropriate; *(Besitzer)* to dispossess
enterben [ɛnt''ɛrbən] *vt* to disinherit
entfallen [ɛnt'falən] *(unreg) vi* to drop, to fall; *(wegfallen)* to be dropped; **jdm ~** *(vergessen)* to slip sb's memory; **auf jdn ~** to be allotted to sb
entfalten [ɛnt'faltən] *vt* to unfold; *(Talente)* to develop ♦ *vr* to open; *(Mensch)* to develop one's potential
Entfaltung *f* unfolding; *(von Talenten)* development
entfern- [ɛnt'fɛrn] *zW:* **~en** *vt* to remove; *(hinauswerfen)* to expel ♦ *vr* to go away, to withdraw; **~t** *adj* distant; **weit davon ~t sein, etw zu tun** to be far from doing sth; **E~ung** *f* distance; *(Wegschaffen)* removal; **E~ungsmesser** (-s, -) *m* (PHOT) rangefinder
entfremden [ɛnt'frɛmdən] *vt* to estrange, to alienate
Entfremdung *f* alienation, estrangement

entfrosten [ɛnt'frɔstən] *vt* to defrost
Entfroster (-s, -) *m* (AUT) defroster
entführ- [ɛnt'fy:r] *zW:* **~en** *vt* to carry off, to abduct; to kidnap; **E~er** *m* kidnapper; **E~ung** *f* abduction; kidnapping
entgegen [ɛnt'ge:gən] *präp* +*dat* contrary to, against ♦ *adv* towards; **~bringen** *(unreg) vt* to bring; **jdm etw ~bringen** *(fig)* to show sb sth; **~gehen** *(unreg) vi* +*dat* to go to meet, to go towards; **~gesetzt** *adj* opposite; *(widersprechend)* opposed; **~halten** *(unreg) vt* *(fig)* to object; **E~kommen** *nt* obligingness; **~kommen** *(unreg) vi* +*dat* to approach; to meet; *(fig)* to accommodate; **~kommend** *adj* obliging; **~nehmen** *(unreg) vt* to receive, to accept; **~sehen** *(unreg) vi* +*dat* to await; **~setzen** *vt* to oppose; **~treten** *(unreg) vi* +*dat* to step up to; *(fig)* to oppose, to counter; **~wirken** *vi* +*dat* to counteract
entgegnen [ɛnt'ge:gnən] *vt* to reply, to retort
entgehen [ɛnt'ge:ən] *(unreg) vi* *(fig):* **jdm ~** to escape sb's notice; **sich** *dat* **etw ~ lassen** to miss sth
entgeistert [ɛnt'gaistərt] *adj* thunderstruck
Entgelt [ɛnt'gɛlt] (-(e)s, -e) *nt* compensation, remuneration
entgleisen [ɛnt'glaizən] *vi* (EISENB) to be derailed; *(fig: Person)* to misbehave; **~ lassen** to derail
entgräten [ɛnt'grɛ:tən] *vt* to fillet, to bone
Enthaarungscreme [ɛnt'ha:rʊŋs-] *f* hair-removing cream
enthalten [ɛnt'haltən] *(unreg) vt* to contain ♦ *vr:* **sich (von etw) ~** to abstain (from sth), to refrain (from sth)
enthaltsam [ɛnt'haltza:m] *adj* abstinent, abstemious
enthemmen [ɛnt'hɛmən] *vt:* **jdn ~** to free sb from his inhibitions
enthüllen [ɛnt'hʏlən] *vt* to reveal, to unveil
Enthusiasmus [ɛntuzi'asmʊs] *m* enthusiasm

entkommen [ɛnt'kɔmən] (*unreg*) *vi*: ~
(**aus** *od* +*dat*) to get away (from), to
escape (from)

entkräften [ɛnt'krɛftən] *vt* to weaken, to
exhaust; (*Argument*) to refute

entladen [ɛnt'la:dən] (*unreg*) *vt* to
unload; (*ELEK*) to discharge ♦ *vr* (*ELEK,
Gewehr*) to discharge; (*Ärger etc*) to vent
itself

entlang [ɛnt'laŋ] *adv* along; ~ **dem Fluß,
den Fluß** ~ along the river; **~gehen**
(*unreg*) *vi* to walk along

entlarven [ɛnt'larfən] *vt* to unmask, to
expose

entlassen [ɛnt'lasən] (*unreg*) *vt* to
discharge; (*Arbeiter*) to dismiss

Entlassung *f* discharge; dismissal

entlasten [ɛnt'lastən] *vt* to relieve;
(*Achse*) to relieve the load on;
(*Angeklagten*) to exonerate; (*Konto*) to
clear

Entlastung *f* relief; (*COMM*) crediting

entlegen [ɛnt'le:gən] *adj* remote

entlocken [ɛnt'lɔkən] *vt*: (**jdm etw**) ~ to
elicit (sth from sb)

entmündigen [ɛnt'myndɪgən] *vt* to
certify

entmutigen [ɛnt'mu:tɪgən] *vt* to
discourage

entnehmen [ɛnt'ne:mən] (*unreg*) *vt* +*dat*
to take out of, to take from; (*folgern*) to
infer from

entrahmen [ɛnt'ra:mən] *vt* to skim

entreißen [ɛnt'raɪsən] (*unreg*) *vt*: **jdm
etw** ~ to snatch sth (away) from sb

entrichten [ɛnt'rɪçtən] *vt* to pay

entrosten [ɛnt'rɔstən] *vt* to derust

entrüst- [ɛnt'ryst] *zW*: **~en** *vt* to incense,
to outrage ♦ *vr* to be filled with
indignation; **~et** *adj* indignant, outraged;
E~ung *f* indignation

entrümpeln *vt* to clear out

entschädigen [ɛnt'ʃɛ:dɪgən] *vt* to
compensate

Entschädigung *f* compensation

entschärfen [ɛnt'ʃɛrfən] *vt* to defuse;
(*Kritik*) to tone down

Entscheid [ɛnt'ʃaɪt] (**-(e)s, -e**) *m*
decision; **e~en** [-dən] (*unreg*) *vt, vi, vr* to

decide; **e~end** *adj* decisive; (*Stimme*)
casting; **~ung** *f* decision

entschieden [ɛnt'ʃi:dən] *adj* decided;
(*entschlossen*) resolute; **E~heit** *f* firmness,
determination

entschließen [ɛnt'ʃli:sən] (*unreg*) *vr* to
decide

entschlossen [ɛnt'ʃlɔsən] *adj*
determined, resolute; **E~heit** *f*
determination

Entschluß [ɛnt'ʃlʊs] *m* decision;
e~freudig *adj* decisive; **~kraft** *f*
determination, decisiveness

entschuldigen [ɛnt'ʃʊldɪgən] *vt* to
excuse ♦ *vr* to apologize

Entschuldigung *f* apology; (*Grund*)
excuse; **jdn um** ~ **bitten** to apologize to
sb; **~!** excuse me; (*Verzeihung*) sorry

entsetz- [ɛnt'zɛts] *zW*: **~en** *vt* to horrify;
(*MIL*) to relieve ♦ *vr* to be horrified *od*
appalled; **E~en** (**-s**) *nt* horror, dismay;
~lich *adj* dreadful, appalling; **~t** *adj*
horrified

Entsorgung [ɛnt'zɔrgʊŋ] *f* (*von
Kraftwerken, Chemikalien*) (waste)
disposal

entspannen [ɛnt'ʃpanən] *vt, vr* (*Körper*)
to relax; (*POL: Lage*) to ease

Entspannung *f* relaxation, rest; (*POL*)
détente; **~spolitik** *f* policy of détente

entsprechen [ɛnt'ʃprɛçən] (*unreg*) *vi*
+*dat* to correspond to; (*Anforderungen,
Wünschen*) to meet, to comply with; **~d**
adj appropriate ♦ *adv* accordingly

entspringen [ɛnt'ʃprɪŋən] (*unreg*) *vi*
(+*dat*) to spring (from)

entstehen [ɛnt'ʃte:ən] (*unreg*) *vi*: ~ (**aus**
od **durch**) to arise (from), to result (from)

Entstehung *f* genesis, origin

entstellen [ɛnt'ʃtɛlən] *vt* to disfigure;
(*Wahrheit*) to distort

entstören [ɛnt'ʃtø:rən] *vt* (*RADIO*) to
eliminate interference from; (*AUT*) to
suppress

enttäuschen [ɛnt'tɔʏʃən] *vt* to
disappoint

Enttäuschung *f* disappointment

entwaffnen [ɛnt'vafnən] *vt* (*lit, fig*) to
disarm

entwässern [ɛnt'vɛsərn] *vt* to drain
Entwässerung *f* drainage
entweder ['ɛntveːdər] *konj* either
entwenden [ɛnt'vɛndən] (*unreg*) *vt* to purloin, to steal
entwerfen [ɛnt'vɛrfən] (*unreg*) *vt* (*Zeichnung*) to sketch; (*Modell*) to design; (*Vortrag, Gesetz etc*) to draft
entwerten [ɛnt'veːrtən] *vt* to devalue; (*stempeln*) to cancel
Entwerter (**-s, -**) *m* ticket punching machine
entwickeln [ɛnt'vɪkəln] *vt, vr* (*auch* PHOT) to develop; (*Mut, Energie*) to show (o.s.), to display (o.s.)
Entwicklung [ɛnt'vɪklʊŋ] *f* development; (*PHOT*) developing
Entwicklungs- *zW*: **~hilfe** *f* aid for developing countries; **~jahre** *pl* adolescence *sg*; **~land** *nt* developing country
entwöhnen [ɛnt'vøːnən] *vt* to wean; (*Süchtige*): (**einer Sache** *dat od* **von etw**) **~** to cure (of sth)
Entwöhnung *f* weaning; cure, curing
entwürdigend [ɛnt'vʏrdɪgənt] *adj* degrading
Entwurf [ɛnt'vʊrf] *m* outline, design; (*Vertrags~, Konzept*) draft
entziehen [ɛnt'tsiːən] (*unreg*) *vt* (+*dat*) to withdraw (from), to take away (from); (*Flüssigkeit*) to draw (from), to extract (from) ♦ *vr* (+*dat*) to escape (from); (*jds Kenntnis*) to be outside *od* beyond; (*der Pflicht*) to shirk (from)
Entziehung *f* withdrawal; **~sanstalt** *f* drug addiction/alcoholism treatment centre; **~skur** *f* treatment for drug addiction/alcoholism
entziffern [ɛnt'tsɪfərn] *vt* to decipher; to decode
entzücken [ɛnt'tsʏkən] *vt* to delight; **E~** (**-s**) *nt* delight; **~d** *adj* delightful, charming
entzünden [ɛnt'tsʏndən] *vt* to light, to set light to; (*fig, MED*) to inflame; (*Streit*) to spark off ♦ *vr* (*auch fig*) to catch fire; (*Streit*) to start; (*MED*) to become inflamed
Entzündung *f* (*MED*) inflammation

entzwei [ɛnt'tsvai] *adv* broken; in two; **~brechen** (*unreg*) *vt, vi* to break in two; **~en** *vt* to set at odds ♦ *vr* to fall out; **~gehen** (*unreg*) *vi* to break (in two)
Enzian ['ɛntsiaːn] (**-s, -e**) *m* gentian
Epidemie [epide'miː] *f* epidemic
Epilepsie [epile'psiː] *f* epilepsy
Episode [epi'zoːdə] *f* episode
Epoche [e'pɔxə] *f* epoch; **e~machend** *adj* epoch-making
Epos ['eːpɔs] (**-s, Epen**) *nt* epic (poem)
er [eːr] (*nom*) *pron* he; it
erarbeiten [ɛr'arbaitən] *vt* to work for, to acquire; (*Theorie*) to work out
erbarmen [ɛr'barmən] *vr* (+*gen*) to have pity *od* mercy (on); **E~** (**-s**) *nt* pity
erbärmlich [ɛr'bɛrmlɪç] *adj* wretched, pitiful; **E~keit** *f* wretchedness
erbarmungslos [ɛr'barmʊŋsloːs] *adj* pitiless, merciless
erbau- [ɛr'bau] *zW*: **~en** *vt* to build, to erect; (*fig*) to edify; **E~er** (**-s, -**) *m* builder; **~lich** *adj* edifying
Erbe[1] ['ɛrbə] (**-n, -n**) *m* heir
Erbe[2] *nt* inheritance; (*fig*) heritage
erben *vt* to inherit
erbeuten [ɛr'bɔytən] *vt* to carry off; (*MIL*) to capture
Erb- [ɛrb] *zW*: **~faktor** *m* gene; **~folge** *f* (line of) succession; **~in** *f* heiress
erbittern [ɛr'bɪtərn] *vt* to embitter; (*erzürnen*) to incense
erbittert [ɛr'bɪtərt] *adj* (*Kampf*) fierce, bitter
erblassen [ɛr'blasən] *vi* to (turn) pale
erbleichen [ɛr'blaiçən] (*unreg*) *vi* to (turn) pale
erblich ['ɛrplɪç] *adj* hereditary
erblinden [ɛr'blɪndən] *vi* to go blind
erbosen [ɛr'boːzən] *vt* to anger ♦ *vr* to grow angry
erbrechen [ɛr'brɛçən] (*unreg*) *vt, vr* to vomit
Erbschaft *f* inheritance, legacy
Erbse ['ɛrpsə] *f* pea
Erbstück *nt* heirloom
Erd- ['eːrd] *zW*: **~achse** *f* earth's axis; **~atmosphäre** *f* earth's atmosphere; **~beben** *nt* earthquake; **~beere** *f*

strawberry; **~boden** *m* ground; **~e** *f* earth; **zu ebener ~e** at ground level; **e~en** *vt* (*ELEK*) to earth

erdenklich [ɛr'dɛŋklɪç] *adj* conceivable

Erd- *zW:* **~gas** *nt* natural gas; **~geschoß** *nt* ground floor; **~kunde** *f* geography; **~nuß** *f* peanut; **~öl** *nt* (mineral) oil

erdrosseln [ɛr'drɔsəln] *vt* to strangle, to throttle

erdrücken [ɛr'drʏkən] *vt* to crush

Erdrutsch *m* landslide

Erdteil *m* continent

erdulden [ɛr'dʊldən] *vt* to endure, to suffer

ereifern [ɛr'aifərn] *vr* to get excited

ereignen [ɛr'aignən] *vr* to happen

Ereignis [ɛr'aignɪs] (**-ses, -se**) *nt* event; **e~los** *adj* uneventful; **e~reich** *adj* eventful

ererbt [ɛr'ɛrpt] *adj* (*Haus*) inherited; (*Krankheit*) hereditary

erfahren [ɛr'fa:rən] (*unreg*) *vt* to learn, to find out; (*erleben*) to experience ♦ *adj* experienced

Erfahrung *f* experience; **e~sgemäß** *adv* according to experience

erfassen [ɛr'fasən] *vt* to seize; (*fig: einbeziehen*) to include, to register; (*verstehen*) to grasp

erfind- [ɛr'fɪnd] *zW:* **~en** (*unreg*) *vt* to invent; **E~er** (**-s, -**) *m* inventor; **~erisch** *adj* inventive; **E~ung** *f* invention

Erfolg [ɛr'fɔlk] (**-(e)s, -e**) *m* success; (*Folge*) result; **e~en** [-gən] *vi* to follow; (*sich ergeben*) to result; (*stattfinden*) to take place; (*Zahlung*) to be effected; **e~los** *adj* unsuccessful; **~losigkeit** *f* lack of success; **e~reich** *adj* successful; **e~versprechend** *adj* promising

erforderlich *adj* requisite, necessary

erfordern [ɛr'fɔrdərn] *vt* to require, to demand

erforschen [ɛr'fɔrʃən] *vt* (*Land*) to explore; (*Problem*) to investigate; (*Gewissen*) to search

Erforschung *f* exploration; investigation; searching

erfreuen [ɛr'frɔyən] *vr*: **sich ~ an** +*dat* to enjoy ♦ *vt* to delight; **sich einer Sache**

gen ~ to enjoy sth

erfreulich [ɛr'frɔylɪç] *adj* pleasing, gratifying; **~erweise** *adv* happily, luckily

erfrieren [ɛr'fri:rən] (*unreg*) *vi* to freeze (to death); (*Glieder*) to get frostbitten; (*Pflanzen*) to be killed by frost

erfrischen [ɛr'frɪʃən] *vt* to refresh

Erfrischung *f* refreshment; **~sgetränk** *nt* (liquid) refreshment; **~sraum** *m* snack bar, cafeteria

erfüllen [ɛr'fʏlən] *vt* (*Raum etc*) to fill; (*fig: Bitte etc*) to fulfil ♦ *vr* to come true

ergänzen [ɛr'gɛntsən] *vt* to supplement, to complete ♦ *vr* to complement one another

Ergänzung *f* completion; (*Zusatz*) supplement

ergeben [ɛr'ge:bən] (*unreg*) *vt* to yield, to produce ♦ *vr* to surrender; (*folgen*) to result ♦ *adj* devoted, humble; **sich etw** *dat* ~ (*sich hingeben*) to give o.s. up to sth, to yield to sth; **dem Trunk** ~ addicted to drink

Ergebnis [ɛr'ge:pnɪs] (**-ses, -se**) *nt* result; **e~los** *adj* without result, fruitless

ergehen [ɛr'ge:ən] (*unreg*) *vi* to be issued, to go out ♦ *vi unpers*: **es ergeht ihm gut/schlecht** he's faring ok/badly ♦ *vr*: **sich in etw** *dat* ~ to indulge in sth; **etw über sich ~ lassen** to put up with sth

ergiebig [ɛr'gi:bɪç] *adj* productive

Ergonomie [ɛrgono'mi:] *f* ergonomics

Ergonomik [ɛrgo'no:mɪk] *f* = **Ergonomie**

ergreifen [ɛr'graifən] (*unreg*) *vt* (*auch fig*) to seize; (*Beruf*) to take up; (*Maßnahmen*) to resort to; (*rühren*) to move; **~d** *adj* moving, touching

ergriffen [ɛr'grɪfən] *adj* deeply moved

Erguß [ɛr'gʊs] *m* discharge; (*fig*) outpouring, effusion

erhaben [ɛr'ha:bən] *adj* raised, embossed; (*fig*) exalted, lofty; **über etw** *akk* ~ **sein** to be above sth

erhalten [ɛr'haltən] (*unreg*) *vt* to receive; (*bewahren*) to preserve, to maintain; **gut** ~ in good condition

erhältlich [ɛr'hɛltlɪç] *adj* obtainable,

available

Erhaltung *f* maintenance, preservation

erhärten [ɛrˈhɛrtən] *vt* to harden; (*These*) to substantiate, to corroborate

erheben [ɛrˈheːbən] (*unreg*) *vt* to raise; (*Protest, Forderungen*) to make; (*Fakten*) to ascertain, to establish ♦ *vr* to rise (up); **sich über etw** *akk* ~ to rise above sth

erheblich [ɛrˈheːplɪç] *adj* considerable

erheitern [ɛrˈhaɪtərn] *vt* to amuse, to cheer (up)

Erheiterung *f* exhilaration; **zur allgemeinen** ~ to everybody's amusement

erhitzen [ɛrˈhɪtsən] *vt* to heat ♦ *vr* to heat up; (*fig*) to become heated

erhoffen [ɛrˈhɔfən] *vt* to hope for

erhöhen [ɛrˈhøːən] *vt* to raise; (*verstärken*) to increase

erhol- [ɛrˈhoːl] *zW*: ~**en** *vr* to recover; (*entspannen*) to have a rest; ~**sam** *adj* restful; **E~ung** *f* recovery; relaxation, rest; ~**ungsbedürftig** *adj* in need of a rest, run-down; **E~ungsgebiet** *nt* ≈ holiday area; **E~ungsheim** *nt* convalescent home

erhören [ɛrˈhøːrən] *vt* (*Gebet etc*) to hear; (*Bitte etc*) to yield to

erinnern [ɛrˈʔɪnərn] *vt*: ~ (**an** +*akk*) to remind (of) ♦ *vr*: **sich (an etw** *akk*) ~ to remember (sth)

Erinnerung *f* memory; (*Andenken*) reminder

erkältet [ɛrˈkɛltət] *adj* with a cold; ~ **sein** to have a cold

Erkältung *f* cold

erkennbar *adj* recognizable

erkennen [ɛrˈkɛnən] (*unreg*) *vt* to recognize; (*sehen, verstehen*) to see

erkennt- *zW*: ~**lich** *adj*: **sich** ~**lich zeigen** to show one's appreciation; **E~lichkeit** *f* gratitude; (*Geschenk*) token of one's gratitude; **E~nis** (-, -**se**) *f* knowledge; (*das Erkennen*) recognition; (*Einsicht*) insight; **zur E~nis kommen** to realize

Erkennung *f* recognition

Erkennungszeichen *nt* identification

Erker [ˈɛrkər] (-**s**, -) *m* bay; ~**fenster** *nt*

bay window

erklär- [ɛrˈklɛːr] *zW*: ~**bar** *adj* explicable; ~**en** *vt* to explain; ~**lich** *adj* explicable; (*verständlich*) understandable; **E~ung** *f* explanation; (*Aussage*) declaration

erkranken [ɛrˈkraŋkən] *vi* to fall ill

Erkrankung *f* illness

erkund- [ɛrˈkund] *zW*: ~**en** *vt* to find out, to ascertain; (*bes MIL*) to reconnoitre, to scout; ~**igen** *vr*: **sich** ~**igen (nach)** to inquire (about); **E~igung** *f* inquiry; **E~ung** *f* reconnaissance, scouting

erlahmen [ɛrˈlaːmən] *vi* to tire; (*nachlassen*) to flag, to wane

erlangen [ɛrˈlaŋən] *vt* to attain, to achieve

Erlaß [ɛrˈlas] (-**sses**, -**lässe**) *m* decree; (*Aufhebung*) remission

erlassen (*unreg*) *vt* (*Verfügung*) to issue; (*Gesetz*) to enact; (*Strafe*) to remit; **jdm etw** ~ to release sb from sth

erlauben [ɛrˈlaubən] *vt*: (**jdm etw**) ~ to allow *od* permit (sb (to do) sth) ♦ *vr* to permit o.s., to venture

Erlaubnis [ɛrˈlaupnɪs] (-, -**se**) *f* permission; (*Schriftstück*) permit

erläutern [ɛrˈlɔytərn] *vt* to explain

Erläuterung *f* explanation

Erle [ˈɛrlə] *f* alder

erleben [ɛrˈleːbən] *vt* to experience; (*Zeit*) to live through; (*mit~*) to witness; (*noch mit~*) to live to see

Erlebnis [ɛrˈleːpnɪs] (-**ses**, -**se**) *nt* experience

erledigen [ɛrˈleːdɪgən] *vt* to take care of, to deal with; (*Antrag etc*) to process; (*umg: erschöpfen*) to wear out; (: *ruinieren*) to finish; (: *umbringen*) to do in

erleichtern [ɛrˈlaɪçtərn] *vt* to make easier; (*fig: Last*) to lighten; (*lindern, beruhigen*) to relieve

Erleichterung *f* facilitation; lightening; relief

erleiden [ɛrˈlaɪdən] (*unreg*) *vt* to suffer, to endure

erlernen [ɛrˈlɛrnən] *vt* to learn, to acquire

erlesen [ɛrˈleːzən] *adj* select, choice

erleuchten [ɛr'lɔʏçtən] *vt* to illuminate; *(fig)* to inspire

Erleuchtung *f (Einfall)* inspiration

Erlös [ɛr'løːs] (**-es, -e**) *m* proceeds *pl*

erlösen [ɛr'løːzən] *vt* to redeem, to save

Erlösung *f* release; *(REL)* redemption

ermächtigen [ɛr'mɛçtɪgən] *vt* to authorize, to empower

Ermächtigung *f* authorization; authority

ermahnen [ɛr'maːnən] *vt* to exhort, to admonish

Ermahnung *f* admonition, exhortation

ermäßigen [ɛr'mɛːsɪgən] *vt* to reduce

Ermäßigung *f* reduction

ermessen [ɛr'mɛsən] *(unreg) vt* to estimate, to gauge; **E~** (**-s**) *nt* estimation; discretion; **in jds E~ liegen** to lie within sb's discretion

ermitteln [ɛr'mɪtəln] *vt* to determine; *(Täter)* to trace ♦ *vi*: **gegen jdn ~** to investigate sb

Ermittlung [ɛr'mɪtlʊŋ] *f* determination; *(Polizei~)* investigation

ermöglichen [ɛr'møːklɪçən] *vt (+dat)* to make possible (for)

ermorden [ɛr'mɔrdən] *vt* to murder

Ermordung *f* murder

ermüden [ɛr'myːdən] *vt, vi* to tire; *(TECH)* to fatigue; **~d** *adj* tiring; *(fig)* wearisome

Ermüdung *f* fatigue; **~serscheinung** *f* sign of fatigue

ermutigen [ɛr'muːtɪgən] *vt* to encourage

ernähr- [ɛr'nɛːr] *zW:* **~en** *vt* to feed, to nourish; *(Familie)* to support ♦ *vr* to support o.s., to earn a living; **sich ~en von** to live on; **E~er** (**-s, -**) *m* breadwinner; **E~ung** *f* nourishment; nutrition; *(Unterhalt)* maintenance

ernennen [ɛr'nɛnən] *(unreg) vt* to appoint

Ernennung *f* appointment

erneu- [ɛr'nɔʏ] *zW:* **~ern** *vt* to renew; to restore, to renovate; **E~erung** *f* renewal; restoration; renovation; **~t** *adj* renewed, fresh ♦ *adv* once more

ernst [ɛrnst] *adj* serious; **E~** (**-es**) *m* seriousness; **das ist mein E~** I'm quite serious; **im E~** in earnest; **E~ machen**

mit etw to put sth into practice; **E~fall** *m* emergency; **~gemeint** *adj* meant in earnest, serious; **~haft** *adj* serious; **E~haftigkeit** *f* seriousness; **~lich** *adj* serious

Ernte ['ɛrntə] *f* harvest; **e~n** *vt* to harvest; *(Lob etc)* to earn

ernüchtern [ɛr'nʏçtərn] *vt* to sober up; *(fig)* to bring down to earth

Erober- [ɛr'ʔoːbər] *zW:* **~er** (**-s, -**) *m* conqueror; **e~n** *vt* to conquer; **~ung** *f* conquest

eröffnen [ɛr'ʔœfnən] *vt* to open ♦ *vr* to present itself; **jdm etw ~** to disclose sth to sb

Eröffnung *f* opening

erörtern [ɛr'ʔœrtərn] *vt* to discuss

Erotik [e'roːtɪk] *f* eroticism

erotisch *adj* erotic

erpress- [ɛr'prɛs] *zW:* **~en** *vt (Geld etc)* to extort; *(Mensch)* to blackmail; **E~er** (**-s, -**) *m* blackmailer; **E~ung** *f* extortion; blackmail

erprobt [ɛr'proːpt] *adj (Gerät, Medikamente)* proven, tested

erraten [ɛr'raːtən] *(unreg) vt* to guess

erreg- [ɛr'reːg] *zW:* **~en** *vt* to excite; *(ärgern)* to infuriate; *(hervorrufen)* to arouse, to provoke ♦ *vr* to get excited *od* worked up; **E~er** (**-s, -**) *m* causative agent; **E~ung** *f* excitement

erreichbar *adj* accessible, within reach

erreichen [ɛr'raɪçən] *vt* to reach; *(Zweck)* to achieve; *(Zug)* to catch

errichten [ɛr'rɪçtən] *vt* to erect, to put up; *(gründen)* to establish, to set up

erringen [ɛr'rɪŋən] *(unreg) vt* to gain, to win

erröten [ɛr'røːtən] *vi* to blush, to flush

Errungenschaft [ɛr'rʊŋənʃaft] *f* achievement; *(umg: Anschaffung)* acquisition

Ersatz [ɛr'zats] (**-es**) *m* substitute; replacement; *(Schaden~)* compensation; *(MIL)* reinforcements *pl*; **~dienst** *m (MIL)* alternative service; **~reifen** *m (AUT)* spare tyre; **~teil** *nt* spare (part)

erschaffen [ɛr'ʃafən] *(unreg) vt* to create

erscheinen [ɛr'ʃaɪnən] *(unreg) vi* to

appear

Erscheinung f appearance; (*Geist*) apparition; (*Gegebenheit*) phenomenon; (*Gestalt*) figure

erschießen [ɛrˈʃiːsən] (*unreg*) vt to shoot (dead)

erschlagen [ɛrˈʃlaːgən] (*unreg*) vt to strike dead

erschöpf- [ɛrˈʃœpf] zW: **~en** vt to exhaust; **~end** adj exhaustive, thorough; **E~ung** f exhaustion

erschrecken [ɛrˈʃrɛkən] vt to startle, to frighten ♦ vi to be frightened *od* startled; **~d** adj alarming, frightening

erschrocken [ɛrˈʃrɔkən] adj frightened, startled

erschüttern [ɛrˈʃʏtərn] vt to shake; (*fig*) to move deeply

Erschütterung f shaking; shock

erschweren [ɛrˈʃveːrən] vt to complicate

erschwinglich adj within one's means

ersetzen [ɛrˈzɛtsən] vt to replace; **jdm Unkosten** *etc* **~** to pay sb's expenses *etc*

ersichtlich [ɛrˈzɪçtlɪç] adj evident, obvious

ersparen [ɛrˈʃpaːrən] vt (*Ärger etc*) to spare; (*Geld*) to save

Ersparnis (-, -se) f saving

SCHLÜSSELWORT

erst [eːrst] adv **1** first; **mach erst mal die Arbeit fertig** finish your work first; **wenn du das erst mal hinter dir hast** once you've got that behind you

2 (*nicht früher als, nur*) only; (*nicht bis*) not till; **erst gestern** only yesterday; **erst morgen** not until tomorrow; **erst als** only when, not until; **wir fahren erst später** we're not going until later; **er ist (gerade) erst angekommen** he's only just arrived

3: **wäre er doch erst zurück!** if only he were back!
---

erstatten [ɛrˈʃtatən] vt (*Kosten*) to (re)pay; **Anzeige** *etc* **gegen jdn ~** to report sb; **Bericht ~** to make a report

Erstaufführung [ˈeːrstˈaʊffyːrʊŋ] f first performance

erstaunen [ɛrˈʃtaʊnən] vt to astonish ♦ vi to be astonished; **E~ (-s)** nt astonishment

erstaunlich adj astonishing

erst- [ˈeːrst] zW: **E~ausgabe** f first edition; **~beste(r, s)** adj first that comes along; **~e(r, s)** adj first

erstechen [ɛrˈʃtɛçən] (*unreg*) vt to stab (to death)

erstehen [ɛrˈʃteːən] (*unreg*) vt to buy ♦ vi to (a)rise

erstens [ˈeːrstəns] adv firstly, in the first place

ersticken [ɛrˈʃtɪkən] vt (*auch fig*) to stifle; (*Mensch*) to suffocate, to smother ♦ vi (*Mensch*) to suffocate; (*Feuer*) to be smothered; **in Arbeit ~** to be snowed under with work

erst- zW: **~klassig** adj first-class; **E~kommunion** f first communion; **~malig** adj first; **~mals** adv for the first time

erstrebenswert [ɛrˈʃtreːbənsveːrt] adj desirable, worthwhile

erstrecken [ɛrˈʃtrɛkən] vr to extend, to stretch

ersuchen [ɛrˈzuːxən] vt to request

ertappen [ɛrˈtapən] vt to catch, to detect

erteilen [ɛrˈtailən] vt to give

Ertrag [ɛrˈtraːk] (**-(e)s, ⁻e**) m yield; (*Gewinn*) proceeds pl

ertragen [ɛrˈtraːgən] (*unreg*) vt to bear, to stand

erträglich [ɛrˈtrɛːklɪç] adj tolerable, bearable

ertrinken [ɛrˈtrɪŋkən] (*unreg*) vi to drown; **E~ (-s)** nt drowning

erübrigen [ɛrˈʔyːbrɪgən] vt to spare ♦ vr to be unnecessary

erwachen [ɛrˈvaxən] vi to awake

erwachsen [ɛrˈvaksən] adj grown-up; **E~e(r)** mf adult; **E~enbildung** f adult education

erwägen [ɛrˈvɛːgən] (*unreg*) vt to consider

Erwägung f consideration

erwähn- [ɛrˈvɛːn] zW: **~en** vt to mention; **~enswert** adj worth mentioning; **E~ung** f mention

erwärmen [ɛr'vɛrmən] *vt* to warm, to heat ♦ *vr* to get warm, to warm up; **sich ~ für** to warm to

Erwarten *nt*: **über meinen/unseren** *usw* **~** beyond my/our *etc* expectations; **wider ~** contrary to expectations

erwarten [ɛr'vartən] *vt* to expect; (*warten auf*) to wait for; **etw kaum ~ können** to be hardly able to wait for sth

Erwartung *f* expectation; **e~sgemäß** *adv* as expected; **e~svoll** *adj* expectant

erwecken [ɛr'vɛkən] *vt* to rouse, to awake; **den Anschein ~** to give the impression

Erweis [ɛr'vaıs] (**-es, -e**) *m* proof; **e~en** (*unreg*) *vt* to prove ♦ *vr*: **sich e~en (als)** to prove (to be); **jdm einen Gefallen/ Dienst e~en** to do sb a favour/service

Erwerb [ɛr'vɛrp] (**-(e)s, -e**) *m* acquisition; (*Beruf*) trade; **e~en** [-bən] (*unreg*) *vt* to acquire

erwerbs- *zW*: **~los** *adj* unemployed; **E~quelle** *f* source of income; **~tätig** *adj* (gainfully) employed

erwidern [ɛr'vi:dərn] *vt* to reply; (*vergelten*) to return

erwischen [ɛr'vıʃən] (*umg*) *vt* to catch, to get

erwünscht [ɛr'vynʃt] *adj* desired

erwürgen [ɛr'vyrgən] *vt* to strangle

Erz [e:rts] (**-es, -e**) *nt* ore

erzähl- [ɛr'tsɛ:l] *zW*: **~en** *vt* to tell ♦ *vi*: **sie kann gut ~en** she's a good story-teller; **E~er** (**-s, -**) *m* narrator; **E~ung** *f* story, tale

Erzbischof *m* archbishop

erzeug- [ɛr'tsɔYgl] *zW*: **~en** *vt* to produce; (*Strom*) to generate; **E~nis** (**-ses, -se**) *nt* product, produce; **E~ung** *f* production; generation

erziehen [ɛr'tsi:ən] (*unreg*) *vt* to bring up; (*bilden*) to educate, to train

Erzieher(in) (**-s, -**) *m(f)* (*Berufsbezeichnung*) teacher

Erziehung *f* bringing up; (*Bildung*) education

Erziehungsbeihilfe *f* educational grant

Erziehungsberechtigte(r) *mf* parent; guardian

erzielen [ɛr'tsi:lən] *vt* to achieve, to obtain; (*Tor*) to score

erzwingen [ɛr'tsvıŋən] (*unreg*) *vt* to force, to obtain by force

es [ɛs] (*nom, akk*) *pron* it

Esche ['ɛʃə] *f* ash

Esel ['e:zəl] (**-s, -**) *m* donkey, ass

Eskalation [ɛskalatsi'o:n] *f* escalation

Eskimo ['ɛskimo] (**-s, -s**) *m* eskimo

eßbar ['ɛsba:r] *adj* eatable, edible

Eßbesteck *nt* knife, fork and spoon

Eßecke *f* dining area

essen ['ɛsən] (*unreg*) *vt, vi* to eat; **E~** (**-s, -**) *nt* meal; food

Essig ['ɛsıç] (**-s, -e**) *m* vinegar; **~gurke** *f* gherkin

Eß- ['ɛs] *zW*: **~kastanie** *f* sweet chestnut; **~löffel** *m* tablespoon; **~tisch** *m* dining table; **~waren** *pl* foodstuffs, provisions; **~zimmer** *nt* dining room

etablieren [eta'bli:rən] *vr* to become established; to set up in business

Etage [e'ta:ʒə] *f* floor, storey; **~nbetten** *pl* bunk beds; **~nwohnung** *f* flat

Etappe [e'tapə] *f* stage

Etat [e'ta:] (**-s, -s**) *m* budget

etc *abk* (= *et cetera*) etc

etepetete [e:təpe'te:tə] (*umg*) *adj* fussy

Ethik ['e:tık] *f* ethics *sg*

ethisch ['e:tıʃ] *adj* ethical

Etikett [eti'kɛt] (**-(e)s, -e**) *nt* label; tag; **~e** *f* etiquette, manners *pl*

etliche ['ɛtlıçə] *pron pl* some, quite a few

etliches *pron* a thing or two

Etui [ɛt'vi:] (**-s, -s**) *nt* case

etwa ['ɛtva] *adv* (*ungefähr*) about; (*vielleicht*) perhaps; (*beispielsweise*) for instance; **nicht ~** by no means; **~ig** ['ɛtvaıç] *adj* possible

etwas *pron* something; anything; (*ein wenig*) a little ♦ *adv* a little

euch [ɔYç] *pron* (*akk von ihr*) you; yourselves; (*dat von ihr*) (to) you

euer ['ɔYər] *pron* (*gen von ihr*) of you ♦ *adj* your

Eule ['ɔYlə] *f* owl

eure *adj f siehe* **euer**

eure(r, s) ['ɔYrə(r, s)] *pron* yours; **~rseits** *adv* on your part; **~s** *adj nt siehe*

euer; **~sgleichen** *pron* people like you; **~twegen** *adv (für euch)* for your sakes; *(wegen euch)* on your account; **~twillen** *adv:* **um ~twillen = euretwegen**

eurige ['ɔʏrɪgə] *pron:* **der/die/das ~** yours

Euro- *zW:* **~pa** [ɔʏ'ro:pa] *nt* Europe; **~päer(in)** [ɔʏro'pɛːər(ɪn)] *mf* European; **e~päisch** *adj* European; **~pameister** [ɔʏ'ro:pa-] *m* European champion; **~scheck** *m (FINANZ)* eurocheque

Euter ['ɔʏtər] **(-s, -)** *nt* udder

ev. *abk* = **evangelisch**

evakuieren [evaku'iːrən] *vt* to evacuate

evangelisch [evaŋ'geːlɪʃ] *adj* Protestant

Evangelium [evaŋ'geːliʊm] *nt* gospel

eventuell [evɛntu'ɛl] *adj* possible ♦ *adv* possibly, perhaps

evtl. *abk* = **eventuell**

EWG [eːveː'geː] **(-)** *f abk* (= *Europäische Wirtschaftsgemeinschaft*) EEC, Common Market

ewig ['eːvɪç] *adj* eternal; **E~keit** *f* eternity

exakt [ɛ'ksakt] *adj* exact

Examen [ɛ'ksaːmən] **(-s, -** *od* **Examina)** *nt* examination

Exemplar [ɛksɛm'plaːr] **(-s, -e)** *nt* specimen; *(Buch~)* copy; **e~isch** *adj* exemplary

exerzieren [ɛksɛr'tsiːrən] *vi* to drill

Exil [ɛ'ksiːl] **(-s, -e)** *nt* exile

Existenz [ɛksɪs'tɛnts] *f* existence; *(Unterhalt)* livelihood, living; *(pej: Mensch)* character; **~minimum (-s)** *nt* subsistence level

existieren [ɛksɪs'tiːrən] *vi* to exist

exklusiv [ɛksklu'ziːf] *adj* exclusive; **~e** [-'ziːvə] *adv* exclusive of, not including ♦ *präp +gen* exclusive of, not including

exotisch [ɛ'ksoːtɪʃ] *adj* exotic

Expedition [ɛkspeditsi'oːn] *f* expedition

Experiment [ɛksperi'mɛnt] *nt* experiment; **e~ell** [-'tɛl] *adj* experimental; **e~ieren** [-'tiːrən] *vi* to experiment

Experte [ɛks'pɛrtə] **(-n, -n)** *m* expert, specialist

Expertin *f* expert, specialist

explo- [ɛksplo'] *zW:* **~dieren** [-'diːrən] *vi*

to explode; **E~sion** [-zi'oːn] *f* explosion; **~siv** [-'ziːf] *adj* explosive

Export [ɛks'pɔrt] **(-(e)s, -e)** *m* export; **~eur** [-'tøːr] *m* exporter; **~handel** *m* export trade; **e~ieren** [-'tiːrən] *vt* to export; **~land** *nt* exporting country

Expreßgut [ɛks'prɛs-] *nt* express goods *pl*, express freight

Expreßzug *m* express (train)

extra ['ɛkstra] *adj inv (umg: gesondert)* separate; *(besondere)* extra ♦ *adv (gesondert)* separately; *(speziell)* specially; *(absichtlich)* on purpose; *(vor Adjektiven, zusätzlich)* extra; **E~ (-s, -s)** *nt* extra; **E~-ausgabe** *f* special edition; **E~blatt** *nt* special edition

Extrakt [ɛks'trakt] **(-(e)s, -e)** *m* extract

extravagant [ɛkstrava'gant] *adj* extravagant

extrem [ɛks'treːm] *adj* extreme; **~istisch** [-'mɪstɪʃ] *adj (POL)* extremist; **E~itäten** [-'tɛːtən] *pl* extremities

exzentrisch [ɛks'tsɛntrɪʃ] *adj* eccentric

Exzeß [ɛks'tsɛs] **(-sses, -sse)** *m* excess

F f

Fa. *abk* (= *Firma*) firm; *(in Briefen)* Messrs

Fabel ['faːbəl] **(-, -n)** *f* fable; **f~haft** *adj* fabulous, marvellous

Fabrik [fa'briːk] *f* factory; **~ant** [-'kant] *m (Hersteller)* manufacturer; *(Besitzer)* industrialist; **~arbeiter** *m* factory worker; **~at** [-'kaːt] **(-(e)s, -e)** *nt* manufacture, product; **~gelände** *nt* factory site

Fach [fax] **(-(e)s, ⁻er)** *nt* compartment; *(Sachgebiet)* subject; **ein Mann vom ~** an expert; **~arbeiter** *m* skilled worker; **~arzt** *m* (medical) specialist; **~ausdruck** *m* technical term

Fächer ['fɛçər] **(-s, -)** *m* fan

Fach- *zW:* **~geschäft** *nt* specialist shop; **~hochschule** *f* ≈ technical college; **~kraft** *f* skilled worker, trained employee; **f~kundig** *adj* expert, specialist; **f~lich** *adj* professional; expert;

~mann (*pl* **-leute**) *m* specialist;
f~männisch *adj* professional; **~schule** *f*
technical college; **f~simpeln** *vi* to talk
shop; **~werk** *nt* timber frame
Fackel ['fakəl] (-, **-n**) *f* torch
fad(e) [faːt, 'faːdə] *adj* insipid;
(*langweilig*) dull
Faden ['faːdən] (**-s**, ⁀) *m* thread;
f~scheinig *adj* (*auch fig*) threadbare
fähig ['fɛːɪç] *adj*: ~ (**zu** *od* +*gen*) capable
(of); able (to); **F~keit** *f* ability
fahnden ['faːndən] *vi*: ~ **nach** to search
for
Fahndung *f* search; **~sliste** *f* list of
wanted criminals, wanted list
Fahne ['faːnə] *f* flag, standard; **eine** ~
haben (*umg*) to smell of drink; **~nflucht**
f desertion
Fahrausweis *m* ticket
Fahrbahn *f* carriageway (*BRIT*), roadway
Fähre ['fɛːrə] *f* ferry
fahren ['faːrən] (*unreg*) *vt* to drive; (*Rad*)
to ride; (*befördern*) to drive, to take;
(*Rennen*) to drive in ♦ *vi* (*sich bewegen*) to
go; (*Schiff*) to sail; (*abfahren*) to leave;
mit dem Auto/Zug ~ to go *od* travel by
car/train; **mit der Hand** ~ **über** +*akk* to
pass one's hand over
Fahr- *zW*: **~er(in)** (**-s**, **-**) *m(f)* driver;
~erflucht *f* hit-and-run; **~gast** *m*
passenger; **~geld** *nt* fare; **~karte** *f* ticket;
~kartenausgabe *f* ticket office;
~kartenautomat *m* ticket machine;
~kartenschalter *m* ticket office;
f~lässig *adj* negligent; **f~lässige Tötung**
manslaughter; **~lehrer** *m* driving
instructor; **~plan** *m* timetable;
f~planmäßig *adj* scheduled; **~preis** *m*
fare; **~prüfung** *f* driving test; **~rad** *nt*
bicycle; **~radweg** *m* cycle lane; **~schein**
m ticket; **~scheinentwerter** *m*
(automatic) ticket stamping machine
Fährschiff ['fɛːrʃɪf] *nt* ferry(-boat)
Fahrschule *f* driving school
Fahrstuhl *m* lift (*BRIT*), elevator (*US*)
Fahrt [faːrt] (-, **-en**) *f* journey; (*kurz*) trip;
(*AUT*) drive; (*Geschwindigkeit*) speed; **gute**
~! have a good journey
Fährte ['fɛːrtə] *f* track, trail

Fahrtkosten *pl* travelling expenses
Fahrtrichtung *f* course, direction
Fahrzeug *nt* vehicle; **~brief** *m* log book
fair [fɛːr] *adj* fair
Faktor ['faktɔr] *m* factor
Fakultät [fakul'tɛːt] *f* faculty
Falke ['falkə] (**-n**, **-n**) *m* falcon
Fall [fal] (**-(e)s**, ⁀e) *m* (*Sturz*) fall;
(*Sachverhalt, JUR, GRAM*) case; **auf jeden** ~,
auf alle Fälle in any case; (*bestimmt*)
definitely; **auf keinen** ~! no way!; **~e** *f*
trap; **f~en** (*unreg*) *vi* to fall; **etw f~en**
lassen to drop sth
fällen ['fɛlən] *vt* (*Baum*) to fell; (*Urteil*) to
pass
fallenlassen (*unreg*) *vt* (*Bemerkung*) to
make; (*Plan*) to abandon, to drop
fällig ['fɛlɪç] *adj* due
falls [fals] *adv* in case, if
Fallschirm *m* parachute; **~springer** *m*
parachutist
falsch [falʃ] *adj* false; (*unrichtig*) wrong
fälschen ['fɛlʃən] *vt* to forge
fälsch- *zW*: **~lich** *adj* false; **~licherweise**
adv mistakenly; **F~ung** *f* forgery
Falte ['faltə] *f* (*Knick*) fold, crease;
(*Haut~*) wrinkle; (*Rock~*) pleat; **f~n** *vt* to
fold; (*Stirn*) to wrinkle
faltig *adj* (*Hände, Haut*) wrinkled;
(*zerknittert: Rock*) creased
familiär [famili'ɛːr] *adj* familiar
Familie [fa'miːliə] *f* family
Familien- *zW*: **~betrieb** *m* family
business; **~kreis** *m* family circle;
~mitglied *nt* member of the family;
~name *m* surname; **~stand** *m* marital
status
Fan (**-s**, **-s**) *m* fan
Fanatiker [fa'naːtikər] (**-s**, **-**) *m* fanatic
fanatisch *adj* fanatical
fand *etc* [fant] *vb siehe* **finden**
Fang [faŋ] (**-(e)s**, ⁀e) *m* catch; (*Jagen*)
hunting; (*Kralle*) talon, claw; **f~en**
(*unreg*) *vt* to catch ♦ *vr* to get caught;
(*Flugzeug*) to level out; (*Mensch: nicht
fallen*) to steady o.s.; (*fig*) to compose o.s.;
(*in Leistung*) to get back on form
Farb- ['farb] *zW*: **~abzug** *m* colour print;
~aufnahme *f* colour photograph; **~band**

nt typewriter ribbon; **~dia** *nt* colour slide; **~e** *f* colour; (*zum Malen etc*) paint; (*Stoffarbe*) dye; **f~echt** *adj* colourfast

färben ['fɛrbən] *vt* to colour; (*Stoff, Haar*) to dye

farben- ['farbən-] *zW:* **~blind** *adj* colourblind; **~freudig** *adj* colourful; **~froh** *adj* colourful, gay

Farb- *zW:* **~fernsehen** *nt* colour television; **~film** *m* colour film; **~foto** *nt* colour photograph; **f~ig** *adj* coloured; **~ige(r)** *mf* coloured (person); **~kasten** *m* paintbox; **f~lich** *adj* colour; **f~los** *adj* colourless; **~stift** *m* coloured pencil; **~stoff** *m* dye; **~ton** *m* hue, tone

Färbung ['fɛrbʊŋ] *f* colouring; (*Tendenz*) bias

Farn [farn] (-(e)s, -e) *m* fern; bracken

Fasan [fa'zaːn] (-(e)s, -e(n)) *m* pheasant

Fasching ['faʃɪŋ] (-s, -e *od* -s) *m* carnival

Faschismus [fa'ʃɪsmʊs] *m* fascism

Faschist *m* fascist

Faser ['faːzər] (-, -n) *f* fibre; **f~n** *vi* to fray

Faß [fas] (-sses, **Fässer**) *nt* vat, barrel; (*für Öl*) drum; **Bier vom ~** draught beer

Fassade [fa'saːdə] *f* façade

fassen ['fasən] *vt* (*ergreifen*) to grasp, to take; (*inhaltlich*) to hold; (*Entschluß etc*) to take; (*verstehen*) to understand; (*Ring etc*) to set; (*formulieren*) to formulate, to phrase ♦ *vr* to calm down; **nicht zu ~** unbelievable

Fassung ['fasʊŋ] *f* (*Umrahmung*) mounting; (*Lampen~*) socket; (*Wortlaut*) version; (*Beherrschung*) composure; **jdn aus der ~ bringen** to upset sb; **f~slos** *adj* speechless

fast [fast] *adv* almost, nearly

fasten ['fastən] *vi* to fast; **F~zeit** *f* Lent

Fastnacht *f* Shrove Tuesday; carnival

faszinieren [fastsi'niːrən] *vt* to fascinate

fatal [fa'taːl] *adj* fatal; (*peinlich*) embarrassing

faul [faʊl] *adj* rotten; (*Person*) lazy; (*Ausreden*) lame; **daran ist etwas ~** there's something fishy about it; **~en** *vi* to rot; **~enzen** *vi* to idle; **F~enzer** (-s, -) *m* idler, loafer; **F~heit** *f* laziness; **~ig** *adj*

putrid

Faust ['faʊst] (-, **Fäuste**) *f* fist; **auf eigene ~** off one's own bat; **~handschuh** *m* mitten

Favorit [favo'riːt] (-en, -en) *m* favourite

faxen ['faksən] *vt* to fax; **jdm etw ~** to fax sth to sb

FCKW *m abk* (= *Fluorchlorkohlenwasserstoff*) CFC

FDP [ɛfdeː'peː] (-) *f abk* (= *Freie Demokratische Partei*) Free Democratic Party

Februar ['feːbruaːr] (-(s), -e) *m* February

fechten ['fɛçtən] (*unreg*) *vi* to fence

Feder ['feːdər] (-, -n) *f* feather; (*Schreib~*) pen nib; (*TECH*) spring; **~ball** *m* shuttlecock; **~bett** *nt* continental quilt; **~halter** *m* penholder, pen; **f~leicht** *adj* light as a feather; **f~n** *vi* (*nachgeben*) to be springy; (*sich bewegen*) to bounce ♦ *vt* to spring; **~ung** *f* (*AUT*) suspension

Fee [feː] *f* fairy

Fegefeuer *nt* purgatory

fegen ['feːgən] *vt* to sweep

fehl [feːl] *adj:* **~ am Platz** *od* **Ort** out of place; **~en** *vi* to be wanting *od* missing; (*abwesend sein*) to be absent; **etw ~t jdm** sb lacks sth; **du ~st mir** I miss you; **was ~t ihm?** what's wrong with him?; **F~er** (-s, -) *m* mistake, error; (*Mangel, Schwäche*) fault; **~erfrei** *adj* faultless; without any mistakes; **~erhaft** *adj* incorrect; faulty; **~erlos** *adj* flawless, perfect; **F~geburt** *f* miscarriage; **~gehen** (*unreg*) *vi* to go astray; **F~griff** *m* blunder; **F~konstruktion** *f* badly designed thing; **~schlagen** (*unreg*) *vi* to fail; **F~start** *m* (*SPORT*) false start; **F~zündung** *f* (*AUT*) misfire, backfire

Feier ['faɪər] (-, -n) *f* celebration; **~abend** *m* time to stop work; **~abend machen** to stop, to knock off; **jetzt ist ~abend!** that's enough!; **f~lich** *adj* solemn; **~lichkeit** *f* solemnity; **~lichkeiten** *pl* (*Veranstaltungen*) festivities; **f~n** *vt, vi* to celebrate; **~tag** *m* holiday

feig(e) ['faɪg(ə)] *adj* cowardly

Feige *f* fig

Feigheit *f* cowardice

Feigling *m* coward

Feile [faɪlə] *f* file

feilschen *vi* to haggle

fein [faɪn] *adj* fine; (*vornehm*) refined; (*Gehör etc*) keen; **~!** great!

Feind [faɪnt] (**-(e)s, -e**) *m* enemy; **f~lich** *adj* hostile; **~schaft** *f* enmity; **f~selig** *adj* hostile; **~seligkeit** *f* hostility

Fein- *zW:* **f~fühlig** *adj* sensitive; **~gefühl** *nt* delicacy, tact; **~heit** *f* fineness; refinement; keenness; **~kostgeschäft** *nt* delicatessen (shop); **~schmecker** (**-s, -**) *m* gourmet

Feinwäsche *f* delicate clothing (*when washing*)

Feld [fɛlt] (**-(e)s, -er**) *nt* field; (*SCHACH*) square; (*SPORT*) pitch; **~herr** *m* commander; **~stecher** (**-s, -**) *m* binoculars *pl*; **~weg** *m* path

Feldzug *m* (*fig*) campaign

Felge [ˈfɛlgə] *f* (wheel) rim

Fell [fɛl] (**-(e)s, -e**) *nt* fur; coat; (*von Schaf*) fleece; (*von toten Tieren*) skin

Fels [fɛls] (**-en, -en**) *m* rock; (*Klippe*) cliff

Felsen [ˈfɛlzən] (**-s, -**) *m* = **Fels**; **f~fest** *adj* firm

feminin [femiˈniːn] *adj* feminine; (*pej*) effeminate

Fenster [ˈfɛnstər] (**-s, -**) *nt* window; **~bank** *f* windowsill; **~laden** *m* shutter; **~leder** *nt* chamois (leather); **~platz** *m* window seat; **~scheibe** *f* windowpane

Ferien [ˈfeːriən] *pl* holidays, vacation *sg* (*US*); **~ haben** to be on holiday; **~kurs** *m* holiday course; **~lager** *nt* holiday camp; **~reise** *f* holiday; **~wohnung** *f* holiday apartment

Ferkel [ˈfɛrkəl] (**-s, -**) *nt* piglet

fern [fɛrn] *adj, adv* far-off, distant; **~ von hier** a long way (away) from here; **der F~e Osten** the Far East; **F~amt** *nt* (*TEL*) exchange; **F~bedienung** *f* remote control; **F~e** *f* distance; **~er** *adj* further ♦ *adv* further; (*weiterhin*) in future; **F~gespräch** *nt* trunk call; **F~glas** *nt* binoculars *pl*; **~halten** (*unreg*) *vt, vr* to keep away; **F~licht** *nt* (*AUT*) full beam; **F~meldeamt** *nt* international exchange; **F~rohr** *nt* telescope; **F~ruf** *m* (*förmlich*)

telephone number; **F~schreiben** *nt* telex; **F~sehapparat** *m* television set; **F~sehen** (**-s**) *nt* television; **im F~sehen** on television; **~sehen** (*unreg*) *vi* to watch television; **F~seher** *m* television; **F~sprecher** *m* telephone; **F~sprechzelle** *f* telephone box *od* booth (*US*); **F~steuerung** *f* remote control; **F~straße** *f* ≈ 'A' road (*BRIT*), highway (*US*); **F~verkehr** *m* long-distance traffic

Ferse [ˈfɛrzə] *f* heel

fertig [ˈfɛrtɪç] *adj* (*bereit*) ready; (*beendet*) finished; (*gebrauchs~*) ready-made; **~bringen** (*unreg*) *vt* (*fähig sein*) to be capable of; **F~gericht** *nt* precooked meal; **F~haus** *nt* kit house, prefab; **F~keit** *f* skill; **~machen** *vt* (*beenden*) to finish; (*umg: Person*) to finish; (: *körperlich*) to exhaust; (: *moralisch*) to get down ♦ *vr* to get ready; **~stellen** *vt* to complete

Fessel [ˈfɛsəl] (**-, -n**) *f* fetter; **f~n** *vt* to bind; (*mit Fesseln*) to fetter; (*fig*) to spellbind; **f~nd** *adj* fascinating, captivating

Fest (**-(e)s, -e**) *nt* party; festival; **frohes ~!** Happy Christmas!

fest [fɛst] *adj* firm; (*Nahrung*) solid; (*Gehalt*) regular ♦ *adv* (*schlafen*) soundly; **~e Kosten** fixed cost; **~angestellt** *adj* permanently employed; **~binden** (*unreg*) *vt* to tie, to fasten; **~bleiben** (*unreg*) *vi* to stand firm; **F~essen** *nt* banquet; **~halten** (*unreg*) *vt* to seize, to hold fast; (*Ereignis*) to record ♦ *vr:* **sich ~halten (an** +*dat*) to hold on (to); **~igen** *vt* to strengthen; **F~igkeit** *f* strength; **F~ival** [ˈfɛstɪval] (**-s, -s**) *nt* festival; **F~land** *nt* mainland; **~legen** *vt* to fix ♦ *vr* to commit o.s.; **~lich** *adj* festive; **~liegen** (*unreg*) *vi* (*feststehen: Termin*) to be confirmed, be fixed; **~machen** *vt* to fasten; (*Termin etc*) to fix; **F~nahme** *f* arrest; **~nehmen** (*unreg*) *vt* to arrest; **F~rede** *f* address; **~setzen** *vt* to fix, to settle; **F~spiele** *pl* (*Veranstaltung*) festival *sg*; **~stehen** (*unreg*) *vi* to be certain; **~stellen** *vt* to establish; (*sagen*) to remark; **F~tag** *m* feast day, holiday; **F~ung** *f* fortress; **F~wochen** *pl* festival *sg*

Fett [fɛt] (-(e)s, -e) *nt* fat, grease
fett *adj* fat; (*Essen etc*) greasy; (*TYP*) bold;
~**arm** *adj* low fat; ~**en** *vt* to grease;
F~fleck *m* grease stain; ~**ig** *adj* greasy,
fatty
Fetzen ['fɛtsən] (-s, -) *m* scrap
feucht [fɔʏçt] *adj* damp; (*Luft*) humid;
F~igkeit *f* dampness; humidity
Feuer ['fɔʏər] (-s, -) *nt* fire; (*zum
Rauchen*) a light; (*fig: Schwung*) spirit;
~**alarm** *m* fire alarm; **f~fest** *adj*
fireproof; ~**gefahr** *f* danger of fire;
f~gefährlich *adj* inflammable; ~**leiter** *f*
fire escape ladder; ~**löscher** (-s, -) *m* fire
extinguisher; ~**melder** (-s, -) *m* fire
alarm; **f~n** *vt, vi* (*auch fig*) to fire; ~**stein**
m flint; ~**treppe** *f* fire escape; ~**wehr**
(-, -en) *f* fire brigade; ~**wehrauto** *nt* fire
engine; ~**wehrmann** *m* fireman; ~**werk**
nt fireworks *pl*; ~**zeug** *nt* (cigarette)
lighter
Fichte ['fıçtə] *f* spruce, pine
Fieber ['fi:bər] (-s, -) *nt* fever,
temperature; **f~haft** *adj* feverish;
~**thermometer** *nt* thermometer;
fiebrig *adj* (*Erkältung*) feverish
fiel *etc* [fi:l] *vb siehe* **fallen**
fies [fi:s] (*umg*) *adj* nasty
Figur [fi'gu:r] (-, -en) *f* figure; (*Schach~*)
chessman, chess piece
Filet [fi'le:] (-s, -s) *nt* (*KOCH*) fillet
Filiale [fili'a:lə] *f* (*COMM*) branch
Film [fılm] (-(e)s, -e) *m* film; ~**aufnahme**
f shooting; **f~en** *vt, vi* to film; ~**kamera** *f*
cine-camera
Filter ['fıltər] (-s, -) *m* filter; **f~n** *vt* to
filter; ~**papier** *nt* filter paper; ~**zigarette**
f tipped cigarette
Filz [fılts] (-es, -e) *m* felt; **f~en** *vt* (*umg*)
to frisk ♦ *vi* (*Wolle*) to mat; ~**stift** *m* felt-
tip pen
Finale [fi'na:lə] (-s, -(s)) *nt* finale; (*SPORT*)
final(s)
Finanz [fi'nants] *f* finance; ~**amt** *nt*
Inland Revenue Office; ~**beamte(r)** *m*
revenue officer; **f~iell** [-tsi'ɛl] *adj*
financial; **f~ieren** [-'tsi:rən] *vt* to finance;
f~kräftig *adj* financially strong;
~**minister** *m* Chancellor of the

Exchequer (*BRIT*), Minister of Finance
Find- ['fınd] *zW:* **f~en** (*unreg*) *vt* to find;
(*meinen*) to think ♦ *vr* to be (found); (*sich
fassen*) to compose o.s.; **ich f~e nichts
dabei, wenn ...** I don't see what's wrong
if ...; **das wird sich f~en** things will
work out; ~**er** (-s, -) *m* finder; ~**erlohn** *m*
reward (*for sb who finds sth*); **f~ig** *adj*
resourceful
fing *etc* [fıŋ] *vb siehe* **fangen**
Finger ['fıŋər] (-s, -) *m* finger; ~**abdruck**
m fingerprint; ~**hut** *m* thimble; (*BOT*)
foxglove; ~**nagel** *m* fingernail; ~**spitze** *f*
fingertip
fingiert *adj* made-up, fictitious
Fink [fıŋk] (-en, -en) *m* finch
Finn- [fın] *zW:* ~**e** (-n, -n) *m* Finn; ~**in** *f*
Finn; **f~isch** *adj* Finnish; ~**land** *nt*
Finland
finster ['fınstər] *adj* dark, gloomy;
(*verdächtig*) dubious; (*verdrossen*) grim;
(*Gedanke*) dark; **F~nis** (-) *f* darkness,
gloom
Firma ['fırma] (-, -men) *f* firm
Firmen- ['fırmən] *zW:* ~**inhaber** *m*
owner of firm; ~**schild** *nt* (shop) sign;
~**zeichen** *nt* trademark
Firnis ['fırnıs] (-ses, -se) *m* varnish
Fisch [fıʃ] (-(e)s, -e) *m* fish; ~**e** *pl* (*ASTROL*)
Pisces *sg*; **f~en** *vt, vi* to fish; ~**er** (-s, -) *m*
fisherman; ~**e'rei** *f* fishing, fishery;
~**fang** *m* fishing; ~**geschäft** *nt*
fishmonger's (shop); ~**gräte** *f* fishbone
fit [fıt] *adj* fit
Fitneß ['fıtnɛs] (-, -) *f* (physical) fitness
fix [fıks] *adj* fixed; (*Person*) alert, smart; ~
und fertig finished; (*erschöpft*) done in;
~**ieren** [fı'ksi:rən] *vt* to fix; (*anstarren*) to
stare at
flach [flax] *adj* flat; (*Gefäß*) shallow
Fläche ['flɛçə] *f* area; (*Ober~*) surface
Flachland *nt* lowland
flackern ['flakərn] *vi* to flare, to flicker
Flagge ['flagə] *f* flag
flaggen *vi* to fly a flag
Flamingo [fla'mıŋgo] (-s, -s) *m* (*ZOOL*)
flamingo
flämisch ['flɛ:mıʃ] *adj* (*LING*) Flemish
Flamme ['flamə] *f* flame

Flandern ['flandərn] *nt* Flanders

Flanell [fla'nɛl] (*-s, -e*) *m* flannel

Flanke ['flaŋkə] *f* flank; (*SPORT: Seite*) wing

Flasche ['flaʃə] *f* bottle; (*umg: Versager*) wash-out

Flaschen- *zW:* **~bier** *nt* bottled beer; **~öffner** *m* bottle opener; **~zug** *m* pulley

flatterhaft *adj* flighty, fickle

flattern ['flatərn] *vi* to flutter

flau [flau] *adj* weak, listless; (*Nachfrage*) slack; **jdm ist ~** sb feels queasy

Flaum [flaum] (*-(e)s*) *m* (*Feder*) down; (*Haare*) fluff

flauschig ['flauʃɪç] *adj* fluffy

Flaute ['flautə] *f* calm; (*COMM*) recession

Flechte ['flɛçtə] *f* plait; (*MED*) dry scab; (*BOT*) lichen; **f~n** (*unreg*) *vt* to plait; (*Kranz*) to twine

Fleck [flɛk] (*-(e)s, -e*) *m* spot; (*Schmutz~*) stain; (*Stoff~*) patch; (*Makel*) blemish; **nicht vom ~ kommen** (*auch fig*) not to get any further; **vom ~ weg** straight away

Flecken (*-s, -*) *m* = **Fleck**; **f~los** *adj* spotless; **~mittel** *nt* stain remover; **~wasser** *nt* stain remover

fleckig *adj* spotted; stained

Fledermaus ['fle:dərmaus] *f* bat

Flegel ['fle:gəl] (*-s, -*) *m* (*Mensch*) lout; **f~haft** *adj* loutish, unmannerly; **~jahre** *pl* adolescence *sg*

flehen ['fle:ən] *vi* to implore; **~tlich** *adj* imploring

Fleisch [flaiʃ] (*-(e)s*) *nt* flesh; (*Essen*) meat; **~brühe** *f* beef tea, meat stock; **~er** (*-s, -*) *m* butcher; **~e'rei** *f* butcher's (shop); **f~ig** *adj* fleshy; **f~los** *adj* meatless, vegetarian

Fleiß [flaɪs] (*-es*) *m* diligence, industry; **f~ig** *adj* diligent, industrious

fletschen ['flɛtʃən] *vt* (*Zähne*) to show

flexibel [flɛ'ksi:bəl] *adj* flexible

Flicken ['flɪkən] (*-s, -*) *m* patch; **f~** *vt* to mend

Flieder ['fli:dər] (*-s, -*) *m* lilac

Fliege ['fli:gə] *f* fly; (*Kleidung*) bow tie; **f~n** (*unreg*) *vt, vi* to fly; **auf jdn/etw f~n** (*umg*) to be mad about sb/sth; **~npilz** *m*

toadstool; **~r** (*-s, -*) *m* flier, airman

fliehen ['fli:ən] (*unreg*) *vi* to flee

Fliese ['fli:zə] *f* tile

Fließ- ['fli:s] *zW:* **~band** *nt* production *od* assembly line; **f~en** (*unreg*) *vi* to flow; **f~end** *adj* flowing; (*Rede, Deutsch*) fluent; (*Übergänge*) smooth

flimmern ['flɪmərn] *vi* to glimmer

flink [flɪŋk] *adj* nimble, lively

Flinte ['flɪntə] *f* rifle; shotgun

Flitterwochen *pl* honeymoon *sg*

flitzen ['flɪtsən] *vi* to flit

Flocke ['flɔkə] *f* flake

flog *etc* [flo:k] *vb siehe* **fliegen**

Floh [flo:] (*-(e)s, ⁓e*) *m* flea; **~markt** *m* flea market

florieren [flo'ri:rən] *vi* to flourish

Floskel ['flɔskəl] (*-, -n*) *f* set phrase

Floß [flo:s] (*-es, ⁓e*) *nt* raft, float

floß *etc vb siehe* **fließen**

Flosse ['flɔsə] *f* fin

Flöte ['flø:tə] *f* flute; (*Block~*) recorder

Flötist(in) [flø'tɪst(ɪn)] *m(f)* flautist

flott [flɔt] *adj* lively; (*elegant*) smart; (*NAUT*) afloat; **F~e** *f* fleet, navy

Fluch [flu:x] (*-(e)s, ⁓e*) *m* curse; **f~en** *vi* to curse, to swear

Flucht [fluxt] (*-, -en*) *f* flight; (*Fenster~*) row; (*Zimmer~*) suite; **f~artig** *adj* hasty

flücht- ['flʏçt] *zW:* **~en** *vi, vr* to flee, to escape; **~ig** *adj* fugitive; (*vergänglich*) transitory; (*oberflächlich*) superficial; (*eilig*) fleeting; **F~igkeitsfehler** *m* careless slip; **F~ling** *m* fugitive, refugee

Flug [flu:k] (*-(e)s, ⁓e*) *m* flight; **im ~** airborne, in flight; **~blatt** *nt* pamphlet

Flügel ['fly:gəl] (*-s, -*) *m* wing; (*MUS*) grand piano

Fluggast *m* airline passenger

flügge ['flʏgə] *adj* (fully-)fledged

Flug- *zW:* **~gesellschaft** *f* airline (company); **~hafen** *m* airport; **~lärm** *m* aircraft noise; **~linie** *f* airline; **~plan** *m* flight schedule; **~platz** *m* airport; (*klein*) airfield; **~reise** *f* flight; **~verkehr** *m* air traffic; **~zeug** *nt* (aero)plane, airplane (*US*); **~zeugentführung** *f* hijacking of a plane; **~zeughalle** *f* hangar; **~zeugträger** *m* aircraft carrier

Flunder ['flʊndər] (-, -n) *f* flounder
flunkern ['flʊŋkərn] *vi* to fib, to tell stories
Fluor ['flu:ɔr] (-s) *nt* fluorine
Flur [flu:r] (-(e)s, -e) *m* hall; (*Treppen~*) staircase
Fluß [flʊs] (-sses, ˙sse) *m* river; (*Fließen*) flow; **im ~ sein** (*fig*) to be in a state of flux
flüssig ['flʏsɪç] *adj* liquid; **F~keit** *f* liquid; (*Zustand*) liquidity; **~machen** *vt* (*Geld*) to make available
flüstern ['flʏstərn] *vt, vi* to whisper
Flut [flu:t] (-, -en) *f* (*auch fig*) flood; (*Gezeiten*) high tide; **f~en** *vi* to flood; **~licht** *nt* floodlight
Fohlen ['fo:lən] (-s, -) *nt* foal
Föhn [fø:n] (-(e)s, -e) *m* (*warmer Fallwind*) föhn
Föhre ['fø:rə] *f* Scots pine
Folge ['fɔlgə] *f* series, sequence; (*Fortsetzung*) instalment; (*Auswirkung*) result; **in rascher ~** in quick succession; **etw zur ~ haben** to result in sth; **~n haben** to have consequences; **einer Sache** *dat* **~ leisten** to comply with sth; **f~n** *vi* +*dat* to follow; (*gehorchen*) to obey; **jdm f~n können** (*fig*) to follow *od* understand sb; **f~nd** *adj* following; **f~ndermaßen** *adv* as follows, in the following way; **f~rn** *vi*: **f~rn (aus)** to conclude (from); **~rung** *f* conclusion
folglich *adv* consequently
folgsam *adj* obedient
Folie ['fo:liə] *f* foil
Folklore ['fɔlklo:r] *f* folklore
Folter ['fɔltər] (-, -n) *f* torture; (*Gerät*) rack; **f~n** *vt* to torture
Fön [fø:n] (-(e)s, -e; ®) *m* hair-dryer
Fondue [fõ'dy:] (-s, -s *od* -, -s) *nt od f* (*KOCH*) fondue
fönen *vt* to (blow) dry
Fönfrisur *f* blow-dry hairstyle
Fontäne [fɔn'tɛ:nə] *f* fountain
Förder- ['fœrdər] *zW*: **~band** *nt* conveyor belt; **~korb** *m* pit cage; **f~lich** *adj* beneficial
fordern ['fɔrdərn] *vt* to demand
fördern ['fœrdərn] *vt* to promote;

(*unterstützen*) to help; (*Kohle*) to extract
Forderung ['fɔrdəruŋ] *f* demand
Förderung *f* promotion; help; extraction
Forelle [fo'rɛlə] *f* trout
Form [fɔrm] (-, -en) *f* shape; (*Gestaltung*) form; (*Guß~*) mould; (*Back~*) baking tin; **in ~ sein** to be in good form *od* shape; **in ~ von** in the shape of
Formali'tät *f* formality
Format [fɔr'ma:t] (-(e)s, -e) *nt* format; (*fig*) distinction
formbar *adj* malleable
Formel (-, -n) *f* formula
formell [fɔr'mɛl] *adj* formal
formen *vt* to form, to shape
Formfehler *m* faux-pas, gaffe; (*JUR*) irregularity
formieren [-'mi:rən] *vt* to form ♦ *vr* to form up
förmlich ['fœrmlɪç] *adj* formal; (*umg*) real; **F~keit** *f* formality
formlos *adj* shapeless; (*Benehmen etc*) informal
Formu'lar (-s, -e) *nt* form
formu'lieren *vt* to formulate
forsch [fɔrʃ] *adj* energetic, vigorous
forschen *vi*: **~ (nach)** to search (for); (*wissenschaftlich*) to (do) research; **~d** *adj* searching
Forscher (-s, -) *m* research scientist; (*Natur~*) explorer
Forschung ['fɔrʃuŋ] *f* research
Forst [fɔrst] (-(e)s, -e) *m* forest
Förster ['fœrstər] (-s, -) *m* forester; (*für Wild*) gamekeeper
fort [fɔrt] *adv* away; (*verschwunden*) gone; (*vorwärts*) on; **und so ~** and so on; **in einem ~** on and on; **~bestehen** (*unreg*) *vi* to survive; **~bewegen** *vt, vr* to move away; **~bilden** *vr* to continue one's education; **~bleiben** (*unreg*) *vi* to stay away; **F~dauer** *f* continuance; **~fahren** (*unreg*) *vi* to depart; (*fortsetzen*) to go on, to continue; **~führen** *vt* to continue, to carry on; **~gehen** (*unreg*) *vi* to go away; **~geschritten** (*fig*) advanced; **~müssen** (*unreg*) *vi* to have to go; **~pflanzen** *vr* to reproduce; **F~pflanzung** *f* reproduction
fortschaffen *vt* to remove

fortschreiten (*unreg*) *vi* to advance
Fortschritt ['fɔrtʃrɪt] *m* advance; **~e machen** to make progress; **f~lich** *adj* progressive
fort- *zW*: **~setzen** *vt* to continue; **F~setzung** *f* continuation; (*folgender Teil*) instalment; **F~setzung folgt** to be continued; **~während** *adj* incessant, continual
Foto ['fo:to] (**-s, -s**) *nt* photo(graph); **~apparat** *m* camera; **~'graf** *m* photographer; **~gra'fie** *f* photography; (*Bild*) photograph; **f~gra'fieren** *vt* to photograph ♦ *vi* to take photographs; **~kopie** *f* photocopy
Fr. *abk* (= *Frau*) Mrs, Ms
Fracht [fraxt] (**-, -en**) *f* freight; (*NAUT*) cargo; (*Preis*) carriage; **~ zahlt Empfänger** (*COMM*) carriage forward; **~er** (**-s, -**) *m* freighter, cargo boat; **~gut** *nt* freight
Frack [frak] (**-(e)s, ⁻e**) *m* tails *pl*
Frage ['fra:gə] (**-, -n**) *f* question; **etw in ~ stellen** to question sth; **jdm eine ~ stellen** to ask sb a question, to put a question to sb; **nicht in ~ kommen** to be out of the question; **~bogen** *m* questionnaire; **f~n** *vt, vi* to ask; **~zeichen** *nt* question mark
fraglich *adj* questionable, doubtful
fraglos *adv* unquestionably
Fragment [fra'gmɛnt] *nt* fragment
fragwürdig ['fra:kvʏrdɪç] *adj* questionable, dubious
Fraktion [fraktsi'o:n] *f* parliamentary party
frankieren [fraŋ'ki:rən] *vt* to stamp, to frank
franko ['fraŋko] *adv* post-paid; carriage paid
Frankreich ['fraŋkraɪç] (**-s**) *nt* France
Franse ['franzə] *f* fringe
Franzose [fran'tso:zə] *m* Frenchman
Französin [fran'tsø:zɪn] *f* Frenchwoman
französisch *adj* French
fraß *etc* [fras] *vb siehe* **fressen**
Fratze ['fratsə] *f* grimace
Frau [fraʊ] (**-, -en**) *f* woman; (*Ehe~*) wife; (*Anrede*) Mrs, Ms; **~ Doktor** Doctor;

~enarzt *m* gynaecologist;
~enbewegung *f* feminist movement;
~enzimmer *nt* female, broad (*US*)
Fräulein ['frɔʏlaɪn] *nt* young lady;
(*Anrede*) Miss, Ms
fraulich ['fraʊlɪç] *adj* womanly
frech [frɛç] *adj* cheeky, impudent; **F~heit** *f* cheek, impudence
frei [fraɪ] *adj* free; (*Stelle, Sitzplatz*) free, vacant; (*Mitarbeiter*) freelance; (*unbekleidet*) bare; **sich** *dat* **einen Tag ~ nehmen** to take a day off; **von etw ~ sein** to be free of sth; **im F~en** in the open air; **~ sprechen** to talk without notes; **~ Haus** (*COMM*) carriage paid; **~er Wettbewerb** fair/open competition; **F~-bad** *nt* open-air swimming pool; **~-bekommen** (*unreg*) *vt*: **jdn ~bekommen** to get sb freed; **einen Tag ~bekommen** to get a day off; **~gebig** *adj* generous; **~halten** (*unreg*) *vt* to keep free; **~händig** *adv* (*fahren*) with no hands; **F~heit** *f* freedom; **~heitlich** *adj* liberal; **F~heits-strafe** *f* prison sentence; **F~karte** *f* free ticket; **~lassen** (*unreg*) *vt* to (set) free; **~legen** *vt* to expose; **~lich** *adv* certainly, admittedly; **ja ~lich** yes of course; **F~lichtbühne** *f* open-air theatre; **F~lichtmuseum** *nt* open-air museum; **~machen** *vt* (*Post*) to frank ♦ *vr* to arrange to be free; (*entkleiden*) to undress; **Tage ~machen** to take days off; **~sprechen** (*unreg*) *vt*: **~sprechen (von)** to acquit (of); **F~spruch** *m* acquittal; **~stehen** (*unreg*) *vi*: **es steht dir ~, das zu tun** you're free to do that ♦ *vt* (*leerstehen: Wohnung, Haus*) to lie/stand empty; **~stellen** *vt*: **jdm etw ~stellen** to leave sth (up) to sb; **F~stoß** *m* free kick
Freitag *m* Friday; **f~s** *adv* on Fridays
frei- *zW*: **~willig** *adj* voluntary; **F~zeit** *f* spare *od* free time; **F~zeitzentrum** *nt* leisure centre; **~zügig** *adj* liberal, broad-minded; (*mit Geld*) generous
fremd [frɛmt] *adj* (*unvertraut*) strange; (*ausländisch*) foreign; (*nicht eigen*) someone else's; **etw ist jdm ~** sth is foreign to sb; **~artig** *adj* strange; **F~enführer** ['frɛmdən-] *m* (tourist) guide;

F~enverkehr *m* tourism; F~enzimmer *nt* guest room; F~körper *m* foreign body; ~ländisch *adj* foreign; F~sprache *f* foreign language; F~wort *nt* foreign *od* loan word

Frequenz [fre'kvɛnts] *f* (*RAD*) frequency

fressen ['frɛsən] (*unreg*) *vt, vi* to eat

Freude ['frɔydə] *f* joy, delight

freudig *adj* joyful, happy

freuen ['frɔyən] *vt unpers* to make happy *od* pleased ♦ *vr* to be glad *od* happy; freut mich! pleased to meet you; sich auf etw *akk* ~ to look forward to sth; sich über etw *akk* ~ to be pleased about sth

Freund [frɔynt] (-(e)s, -e) *m* friend; boyfriend; ~in [-dɪn] *f* friend; girlfriend; f~lich *adj* kind, friendly; f~licherweise *adv* kindly; ~lichkeit *f* friendliness, kindness; ~schaft *f* friendship; f~schaftlich *adj* friendly

Frieden ['fri:dən] (-s, -) *m* peace; im ~ in peacetime

Friedens- *zW:* ~schluß *m* peace agreement; ~vertrag *m* peace treaty; ~zeit *f* peacetime

fried- ['fri:t] *zW:* ~fertig *adj* peaceable; F~hof *m* cemetery; ~lich *adj* peaceful

frieren ['fri:rən] (*unreg*) *vt, vi* to freeze; ich friere, es friert mich I'm freezing, I'm cold

Friesland ['fri:z-] *nt* Friesland

frigid(e) [fri'gi:t, fri'gi:də] *adj* frigid

Frikadelle [frika'dɛlə] *f* rissole

Frikassee [frika'se:] (-s, -s) *nt* (*KOCH*) fricassee

frisch [frɪʃ] *adj* fresh; (*lebhaft*) lively; ~ gestrichen! wet paint!; sich ~ machen to freshen (o.s.) up; F~e *f* freshness; liveliness

Friseur [fri'zø:r] *m* hairdresser

Friseuse [fri'zø:zə] *f* hairdresser

frisieren [fri'zi:rən] *vt* to do (one's hair); (*fig: Abrechnung*) to fiddle, to doctor ♦ *vr* to do one's hair

Frisiersalon *m* hairdressing salon

frißt *etc* [frɪst] *vb siehe* fressen

Frist (-, -en) *f* period; (*Termin*) deadline; f~gerecht *adj* within the stipulated time

od period; f~los *adj* (*Entlassung*) instant

Frisur [fri'zu:r] *f* hairdo, hairstyle

frivol [fri'vo:l] *adj* frivolous

froh [fro:] *adj* happy, cheerful; ich bin ~, daß ... I'm glad that ...

fröhlich ['frø:lɪç] *adj* merry, happy; F~keit *f* merriness, gaiety

fromm [frɔm] *adj* pious, good; (*Wunsch*) idle

Frömmigkeit ['frœmɪçkaɪt] *f* piety

Fronleichnam [fro:n'laɪçna:m] (-(e)s) *m* Corpus Christi

Front [frɔnt] (-, -en) *f* front; f~al [frɔn'ta:l] *adj* frontal

fror *etc* [fro:r] *vb siehe* frieren

Frosch [frɔʃ] (-(e)s, ⁻e) *m* frog; (*Feuerwerk*) squib; ~mann *m* frogman; ~schenkel *m* frog's leg

Frost [frɔst] (-(e)s, ⁻e) *m* frost; ~beule *f* chilblain

frösteln ['frœstəln] *vi* to shiver

frostig *adj* frosty

Frostschutzmittel *nt* anti-freeze

Frottee [frɔ'te:] (-(s), -s) *nt od m* towelling

Frottier(hand)tuch [frɔ'ti:r(hant)tu:x] *nt* towel

Frucht [fruxt] (-, ⁻e) *f* (*auch fig*) fruit; (*Getreide*) corn; f~bar *adj* fruitful, fertile; ~barkeit *f* fertility; f~ig *adj* (*Geschmack*) fruity; f~los *adj* fruitless; ~saft *m* fruit juice

früh [fry:] *adj, adv* early; heute ~ this morning; F~aufsteher (-s, -) *m* early riser; F~e *f* early morning; ~er *adj* earlier; (*ehemalig*) former ♦ *adv* formerly; ~er war das anders that used to be different; ~estens *adv* at the earliest; F~jahr *nt* spring; F~ling *m* spring; ~reif *adj* precocious; F~stück *nt* breakfast; ~stücken *vi* to (have) breakfast; F~stücksbüfett *nt* breakfast buffet; ~zeitig *adj* early; (*pej*) untimely

frustrieren [frus'tri:rən] *vt* to frustrate

Fuchs [fuks] (-es, ⁻e) *m* fox

fuchsen (*umg*) *vt* to rile, to annoy

fuchsteufelswild *adj* hopping mad

fuchteln ['fuxtəln] *vi* to gesticulate wildly

Fuge ['fu:gə] *f* joint; (*MUS*) fugue

fügen ['fy:gən] *vt* to place, to join ♦ *vr*: **sich ~ (in** +*akk*) to be obedient (to); (*anpassen*) to adapt oneself (to) ♦ *vr* (*unpers*) to happen

fügsam ['fy:kza:m] *adj* obedient

fühl- *zW*: **~bar** *adj* perceptible, noticeable; **~en** *vt*, *vi*, *vr* to feel; **F~er (-s, -)** *m* feeler

fuhr *etc* [fu:r] *vb siehe* **fahren**

führen ['fy:rən] *vt* to lead; (*Geschäft*) to run; (*Name*) to bear; (*Buch*) to keep ♦ *vi* to lead ♦ *vr* to behave

Führer ['fy:rər] **(-s, -)** *m* leader; (*Fremden~*) guide; **~schein** *m* driving licence

Führung ['fy:ruŋ] *f* leadership; (*eines Unternehmens*) management; (*MIL*) command; (*Benehmen*) conduct; (*Museums~*) conducted tour; **~szeugnis** *nt* certificate of good conduct

Fülle ['fylə] *f* wealth, abundance; **f~n** *vt* to fill; (*KOCH*) to stuff ♦ *vr* to fill (up)

Füllen (-s, -) *nt* foal

Füller (-s, -) *m* fountain pen

Füllfederhalter *m* fountain pen

Füllung *f* filling; (*Holz~*) panel

fummeln ['fuməln] (*umg*) *vi* to fumble

Fund [funt] **(-(e)s, -e)** *m* find

Fundament [-da'mɛnt] *nt* foundation; **fundamen'tal** *adj* fundamental

Fundbüro *nt* lost property office, lost and found (*US*)

Fundgrube *f* (*fig*) treasure trove

fundiert [fun'di:rt] *adj* sound

fünf [fynf] *num* five; **~hundert** *num* five hundred; **F~kampf** *m* pentathlon; **~te(r, s)** *adj* fifth; **F~tel (-s, -)** *nt* fifth; **~zehn** *num* fifteen; **~zig** *num* fifty

Funk [fuŋk] **(-s)** *m* radio, wireless; **~e (-ns, -n)** *m* (*auch fig*) spark; **f~eln** *vi* to sparkle; **~en (-s, e)** *m* (*auch fig*) spark; **f~en** *vi* (*durch Funk*) to signal, to radio; (*umg: richtig funktionieren*) to work ♦ *vt* (*Funken sprühen*) to shower with sparks; **endlich hat es bei ihm gef~t** (*umg*) the penny has finally dropped, he's finally got it; **~er (-s, -)** *m* radio operator; **~gerät** *nt* radio set; **~rufempfänger** *m* pager, paging device; **~streife** *f* police radio

patrol; **~telefon** *nt* cellphone

Funktion [fuŋktsi'o:n] *f* function; **f~ieren** [-'ni:rən] *vi* to work, to function

für [fy:r] *präp* +*akk* for; **was ~** what kind *od* sort of; **das F~ und Wider** the pros and cons *pl*; **Schritt ~ Schritt** step by step; **F~bitte** *f* intercession

Furche ['furçə] *f* furrow

Furcht [furçt] **(-)** *f* fear; **f~bar** *adj* terrible, frightful

fürchten ['fyrçtən] *vt* to be afraid of, to fear ♦ *vr*: **sich ~ (vor** +*dat*) to be afraid (of)

fürchterlich *adj* awful

furchtlos *adj* fearless

furchtsam *adj* timid

füreinander [fy:r'ai'nandər] *adv* for each other

Furnier [fur'ni:r] **(-s, -e)** *nt* veneer

fürs [fy:rs] = **für das**

Fürsorge ['fy:rzɔrgə] *f* care; (*Sozial~*) welfare; **~r(in) (-s, -)** *m(f)* welfare worker; **~unterstützung** *f* social security, welfare benefit (*US*); **fürsorglich** *adj* attentive, caring

Fürsprache *f* recommendation; (*um Gnade*) intercession

Fürsprecher *m* advocate

Fürst [fyrst] **(-en, -en)** *m* prince; **~entum** *nt* principality; **~in** *f* princess; **f~lich** *adj* princely

Furunkel [fu'ruŋkəl] **(-s, -)** *nt od m* (*MED*) boil

Fuß [fu:s] **(-es, ⁺e)** *m* foot; (*von Glas, Säule etc*) base; (*von Möbel*) leg; **zu ~** on foot; **~ball** *m* football; **~ballplatz** *m* football pitch; **~ballspiel** *nt* football match; **~ballspieler** *m* footballer; **~boden** *m* floor; **~bremse** *f* (*AUT*) footbrake; **~ende** *nt* foot; **~gänger(in) (-s, -)** *m(f)* pedestrian; **~gängerzone** *f* pedestrian precinct; **~nagel** *m* toenail; **~note** *f* footnote; **~spur** *f* footprint; **~tritt** *m* kick; (*Spur*) footstep; **~weg** *m* footpath

Futter ['futər] **(-s, -)** *nt* fodder, feed; (*Stoff*) lining; **~al [-'ra:l] (-s, -e)** *nt* case

füttern ['fytərn] *vt* to feed; (*Kleidung*) to line

Futur [fu'tu:r] (-s, -e) *nt* future

G g

g *abk* = **Gramm**

gab *etc* [ga:p] *vb siehe* **geben**

Gabe ['ga:bə] *f* gift

Gabel ['ga:bəl] (-, -n) *f* fork; **~ung** *f* fork

gackern ['gakərn] *vi* to cackle

gaffen ['gafən] *vi* to gape

Gage ['ga:ʒə] *f* fee; salary

gähnen ['gɛ:nən] *vi* to yawn

Galerie [galə'ri:] *f* gallery

Galgen ['galgən] (-s, -) *m* gallows *sg*; **~frist** *f* respite; **~humor** *m* macabre humour

Galle ['galə] *f* gall; (*Organ*) gall-bladder; **~nstein** *m* gallstone

Galopp [ga'lɔp] (-s, -s *od* -e) *m* gallop; **g~ieren** [-'pi:rən] *vi* to gallop

Gamasche [ga'maʃə] *f* gaiter; (*kurz*) spat

gammeln ['gaməln] (*umg*) *vi* to bum around

Gammler(in) (-s, -; *pej*) *m(f)* layabout, loafer (*inf*)

Gang [gaŋ] (-(e)s, ̈e) *m* walk; (*Boten~*) errand; (*~art*) gait; (*Abschnitt eines Vorgangs*) operation; (*Essens~, Ablauf*) course; (*Flur etc*) corridor; (*Durch~*) passage; (*TECH*) gear; **in ~ bringen** to start up; (*fig*) to get off the ground; **in ~ sein** to be in operation; (*fig*) to be under way

gang *adj*: **~ und gäbe** usual, normal

gängig ['gɛŋɪç] *adj* common, current; (*Ware*) in demand, selling well

Ganove [ga'no:və] (-n, -n; *umg*) *m* crook

Gans [gans] (-, ̈e) *f* goose

Gänse- ['gɛnzə] *zW*: **~blümchen** *nt* daisy; **~füßchen** (*umg*) *pl* (*Anführungszeichen*) inverted commas; **~haut** *f* goose pimples *pl*; **~marsch** *m*: **im ~marsch** in single file; **~rich** (-s, -e) *m* gander

ganz [gants] *adj* whole; (*vollständig*) complete ♦ *adv* quite; (*völlig*) completely; **~ Europa** all Europe; **sein ~es Geld** all his money; **~ und gar nicht** not at all; **es**

sieht **~ so aus** it really looks like it; **aufs G~e gehen** to go for the lot

gänzlich ['gɛntslɪç] *adj* complete, entire ♦ *adv* completely, entirely

Ganztagsschule *f* all-day school

gar [ga:r] *adj* cooked, done ♦ *adv* quite; **~ nicht/nichts/keiner** not/nothing/nobody at all; **~ nicht schlecht** not bad at all

Garage [ga'ra:ʒə] *f* garage

Garantie [garan'ti:] *f* guarantee; **g~ren** *vt* to guarantee; **er kommt g~rt** he's guaranteed to come

Garbe ['garbə] *f* sheaf; (*MIL*) burst of fire

Garde *f* guard

Garderobe [gardə'ro:bə] *f* wardrobe; (*Abgabe*) cloakroom; **~nfrau** *f* cloakroom attendant

Gardine [gar'di:nə] *f* curtain

garen ['ga:rən] *vt, vi* to cook

gären ['gɛ:rən] (*unreg*) *vi* to ferment

Garn [garn] (-(e)s, -e) *nt* thread; yarn (*auch fig*)

Garnele [gar'ne:lə] *f* shrimp, prawn

garnieren [gar'ni:rən] *vt* to decorate; (*Speisen, fig*) to garnish

Garnison [garni'zo:n] (-, -en) *f* garrison

Garnitur [garni'tu:r] *f* (*Satz*) set; (*Unterwäsche*) set of (matching) underwear; **erste ~** (*fig*) top rank; **zweite ~** second rate

garstig ['garstɪç] *adj* nasty, horrid

Garten ['gartən] (-s, ̈) *m* garden; **~arbeit** *f* gardening; **~gerät** *nt* gardening tool; **~lokal** *nt* beer garden; **~schere** *f* pruning shears *pl*; **~tür** *f* garden gate

Gärtner(in) ['gɛrtnər(ɪn)] (-s, -) *m(f)* gardener; **~ei** [-'raɪ] *f* nursery; (*Gemüse~*) market garden (*BRIT*), truck farm (*US*)

Gärung ['gɛ:rʊŋ] *f* fermentation

Gas [ga:s] (-es, -e) *nt* gas; **~ geben** (*AUT*) to accelerate, to step on the gas; **~hahn** *m* gas tap; **~herd** *m* gas cooker; **~kocher** *m* gas cooker; **~leitung** *f* gas pipe; **~pedal** *nt* accelerator, gas pedal

Gasse ['gasə] *f* lane, alley

Gast [gast] (-es, ̈e) *m* guest; (*in Lokal*) patron; **bei jdm zu ~ sein** to be sb's guest; **~arbeiter(in)** *m(f)* foreign worker

Gästebuch ['gɛstəbu:x] *nt* visitors' book,

guest book

Gast- *zW:* **g~freundlich** *adj* hospitable; **~geber** (-s, -) *m* host; **~geberin** *f* hostess; **~haus** *nt* hotel, inn; **~hof** *m* hotel, inn; **g~ieren** [-'tiːrən] *vi (THEAT)* to (appear as a) guest; **g~lich** *adj* hospitable; **~rolle** *f* guest role; **~spiel** *nt (THEAT)* guest performance; **~stätte** *f* restaurant; pub; **~wirt** *m* innkeeper; **~wirtschaft** *f* hotel, inn; **~zimmer** *nt* (guest) room

Gaswerk *nt* gasworks *sg*

Gaszähler *m* gas meter

Gatte ['gatə] (-n, -n) *m* husband, spouse

Gatter ['gatər] (-s, -) *nt* railing, grating; *(Eingang)* gate

Gattin *f* wife, spouse

Gattung ['gatʊŋ] *f* genus; kind

Gaudi ['gaʊdi] *(umg; SÜDD, ÖSTERR) nt od f* fun

Gaul [gaʊl] (-(e)s, Gäule) *m* horse; nag

Gaumen ['gaʊmən] (-s, -) *m* palate

Gauner ['gaʊnər] (-s, -) *m* rogue; **~ei** [-'raɪ] *f* swindle

Gaze ['gaːzə] *f* gauze

geb. *abk* = **geboren**

Gebäck [gə'bɛk] (-(e)s, -e) *nt* pastry

gebacken [gə'bakən] *adj* baked; *(gebraten)* fried

Gebälk [gə'bɛlk] (-(e)s) *nt* timberwork

Gebärde [gə'bɛːrdə] *f* gesture; **g~n** *vr* to behave

gebären [gə'bɛːrən] *(unreg) vt* to give birth to, to bear

Gebärmutter *f* uterus, womb

Gebäude [gə'bɔʏdə] (-s, -) *nt* building; **~komplex** *m* (building) complex

Gebell [gə'bɛl] (-(e)s) *nt* barking

geben ['geːbən] *(unreg) vt, vi* to give; *(Karten)* to deal ♦ *vb unpers:* **es gibt** there is/are; there will be ♦ *vr (sich verhalten)* to behave, to act; *(aufhören)* to abate; **jdm etw ~** to give sb sth *od* sth to sb; **ein Wort gab das andere** one angry word led to another; **was gibt's?** what's up?; **was gibt es im Kino?** what's on at the cinema?; **sich geschlagen ~** to admit defeat; **das wird sich schon ~** that'll soon sort itself out

Gebet [gə'beːt] (-(e)s, -e) *nt* prayer

gebeten *vb siehe* **bitten**

Gebiet [gə'biːt] (-(e)s, -e) *nt* area; *(Hoheits~)* territory; *(fig)* field; **g~en** *(unreg)* vt to command, to demand; **g~erisch** *adj* imperious

Gebilde [gə'bɪldə] (-s, ~) *nt* object

gebildet *adj* cultured, educated

Gebirge [gə'bɪrgə] (-s, -) *nt* mountain chain

Gebiß [gə'bɪs] (-sses, -sse) *nt* teeth *pl*; *(künstlich)* dentures *pl*

gebissen *vb siehe* **beißen**

geblieben [gə'bliːbən] *vb siehe* **bleiben**

geblümt [gə'blyːmt] *adj (Kleid, Stoff, Tapete)* floral

geboren [gə'boːrən] *adj* born; *(Frau)* née

geborgen [gə'bɔrgən] *adj* secure, safe

Gebot [gə'boːt] (-(e)s, -e) *nt* command; *(REL)* commandment; *(bei Auktion)* bid

geboten *vb siehe* **bieten**

Gebr. *abk* (= *Gebrüder*) Bros.

gebracht [gə'braxt] *vb siehe* **bringen**

gebraten [gə'braːtən] *adj* fried

Gebräu [gə'brɔʏ] (-(e)s, -e) *nt* concoction

Gebrauch [gə'braʊx] (-(e)s, Gebräuche) *m* use; *(Sitte)* custom; **g~en** *vt* to use

gebräuchlich [gə'brɔʏçlɪç] *adj* usual, customary

Gebrauchs- *zW:* **~anweisung** *f* directions *pl* for use; **g~fertig** *adj* ready for use; **~gegenstand** *m* commodity

gebraucht [gə'braʊxt] *adj* used; **G~wagen** *m* secondhand *od* used car

gebrechlich [gə'brɛçlɪç] *adj* frail

gebrochen [gə'brɔxən] *adj* broken

Gebrüder [gə'bryːdər] *pl* brothers

Gebrüll [gə'brʏl] (-(e)s) *nt* roaring

Gebühr [gə'byːr] (-, -en) *f* charge, fee; **nach ~** fittingly; **über ~** unduly; **g~en** *vi:* **jdm g~en** to be sb's due *od* due to sb ♦ *vr* to be fitting; **g~end** *adj* fitting, appropriate ♦ *adv* fittingly, appropriately

Gebühren- *zW:* **~einheit** *f (TEL)* unit; **~erlaß** *m* remission of fees; **~ermäßigung** *f* reduction of fees; **g~frei** *adj* free of charge; **g~pflichtig** *adj* subject to a charge

gebunden [gə'bʊndən] *vb siehe* **binden**

Geburt [gəˈbuːrt] (-, -en) *f* birth
Geburtenkontrolle *f* birth control
Geburtenreglung *f* birth control
gebürtig [gəˈbʏrtɪç] *adj* born in, native of; **~e Schweizerin** native of Switzerland
Geburts- *zW:* **~anzeige** *f* birth notice; **~datum** *nt* date of birth; **~jahr** *nt* year of birth; **~ort** *m* birthplace; **~tag** *m* birthday; **~urkunde** *f* birth certificate
Gebüsch [gəˈbʏʃ] (-(e)s, -e) *nt* bushes *pl*
gedacht [gəˈdaxt] *vb siehe* **denken**
Gedächtnis [gəˈdɛçtnɪs] (-ses, -se) *nt* memory; **~feier** *f* commemoration
Gedanke [gəˈdaŋkə] (-ns, -n) *m* thought; **sich über etw** *akk* **~n machen** to think about sth
Gedanken- *zW:* **~austausch** *m* exchange of ideas; **g~los** *adj* thoughtless; **~strich** *m* dash; **~übertragung** *f* thought transference, telepathy
Gedeck [gəˈdɛk] (-(e)s, -e) *nt* cover(ing); (*Speisenfolge*) menu; **ein ~ auflegen** to lay a place
gedeihen [gəˈdaɪən] (*unreg*) *vi* to thrive, to prosper
Gedenken [gəˈdɛŋkən] *nt:* **zum ~ an jdn** in memory of sb; **g~** (*unreg*) *vi* +*gen* (*sich erinnern*) to remember; (*beabsichtigen*) to intend
Gedenk- *zW:* **~feier** *f* commemoration; **~minute** *f* minute's silence; **~tag** *m* remembrance day
Gedicht [gəˈdɪçt] (-(e)s, -e) *nt* poem
gediegen [gəˈdiːgən] *adj* (good) quality; (*Mensch*) reliable, honest
Gedränge [gəˈdrɛŋə] (-s) *nt* crush, crowd; **ins ~ kommen** (*fig*) to get into difficulties
gedrängt *adj* compressed; **~ voll** packed
gedrückt [gəˈdrʊkt] *adj* (*deprimiert*) low, depressed
gedrungen [gəˈdrʊŋən] *adj* thickset, stocky
Geduld [gəˈdʊlt] *f* patience; **g~en** [gəˈdʊldən] *vr* to be patient; **g~ig** *adj* patient, forbearing; **~sprobe** *f* trial of (one's) patience
gedurft [gəˈdʊrft] *vb siehe* **dürfen**
geehrt [gəˈeːrt] *adj:* **Sehr ~e Frau X!**

Dear Mrs X
geeignet [gəˈaɪgnət] *adj* suitable
Gefahr [gəˈfaːr] (-, -en) *f* danger; **~ laufen, etw zu tun** to run the risk of doing sth; **auf eigene ~** at one's own risk
gefährden [gəˈfɛːrdən] *vt* to endanger
Gefahrenquelle *f* source of danger
Gefahrenzulage *f* danger money
gefährlich [gəˈfɛːrlɪç] *adj* dangerous
Gefährte [gəˈfɛːrtə] (-n, -n) *m* companion; (*Lebenspartner*) partner
Gefährtin [gəˈfɛːrtɪn] *f* (female) companion; (*Lebenspartner*) (female) partner
Gefälle [gəˈfɛlə] (-s, -) *nt* gradient, incline
Gefallen¹ [gəˈfalən] (-s, -) *m* favour
Gefallen² (-s) *nt* pleasure; **an etw** *dat* **Gefallen finden** to derive pleasure from sth
gefallen *pp von* **fallen** ♦ *vi:* **jdm ~** to please sb; **er/es gefällt mir** I like him/it; **das gefällt mir an ihm** that's one thing I like about him; **sich** *dat* **etw ~ lassen** to put up with sth
gefällig [gəˈfɛlɪç] *adj* (*hilfsbereit*) obliging; (*erfreulich*) pleasant; **G~keit** *f* favour; helpfulness; **etw aus G~keit tun** to do sth out of the goodness of one's heart
gefälligst *adv* kindly
gefangen [gəˈfaŋən] *adj* captured; (*fig*) captivated; **G~e(r)** *mf* prisoner, captive; **~halten** (*unreg*) *vt* to keep prisoner; **G~nahme** *f* capture; **~nehmen** (*unreg*) *vt* to take prisoner; **G~schaft** *f* captivity
Gefängnis [gəˈfɛŋnɪs] (-ses, -se) *nt* prison; **~strafe** *f* prison sentence; **~wärter** *m* prison warder; **~zelle** *f* prison cell
Gefäß [gəˈfɛːs] (-es, -e) *nt* vessel (*auch ANAT*), container
gefaßt [gəˈfast] *adj* composed, calm; **auf etw** *akk* **~ sein** to be prepared *od* ready for sth
Gefecht [gəˈfɛçt] (-(e)s, -e) *nt* fight; (*MIL*) engagement
Gefieder [gəˈfiːdər] (-s, -) *nt* plumage, feathers *pl*
gefleckt [gəˈflɛkt] *adj* spotted, mottled
geflogen [gəˈfloːgən] *vb siehe* **fliegen**

geflossen [gə'flɔsən] *vb siehe* **fließen**
Geflügel [gə'fly:gəl] (-s) *nt* poultry
Gefolge [gə'fɔlgə] (-s, -) *nt* retinue
Gefolgschaft *f* following
gefragt [gə'fra:kt] *adj* in demand
gefräßig [gə'frɛ:sɪç] *adj* voracious
Gefreite(r) [gə'fraɪtə(r)] *m* lance corporal; (*NAUT*) able seaman; (*AVIAT*) aircraftman
gefrieren [gə'fri:rən] (*unreg*) *vi* to freeze
Gefrier- *zW:* **~fach** *nt* icebox; **~fleisch** *nt* frozen meat; **g~getrocknet** [-gətrɔknət] *adj* freeze-dried; **~punkt** *m* freezing point; **~schutzmittel** *nt* antifreeze; **~truhe** *f* deep-freeze
gefroren [gə'fro:rən] *vb siehe* **frieren**
Gefühl [gə'fy:l] (-(e)s, -e) *nt* feeling; **etw im ~ haben** to have a feel for sth; **g~los** *adj* unfeeling
gefühls- *zW:* **~betont** *adj* emotional; **G~duselei** [-du:zə'laɪ] *f* over-sentimentality; **~mäßig** *adj* instinctive
gefüllt [gə'fʏlt] *adj* (*KOCH*) stuffed
gefunden [gə'fʊndən] *vb siehe* **finden**
gegangen [gə'gaŋən] *vb siehe* **gehen**
gegeben [gə'ge:bən] *vb siehe* **geben**
♦ *adj* given; **zu ~er Zeit** in good time
gegebenenfalls [gə'ge:bənənfals] *adv* if need be

SCHLÜSSELWORT

gegen ['ge:gən] *präp +akk* **1** against; **nichts gegen jdn haben** to have nothing against sb; **X gegen Y** (*SPORT, JUR*) X versus Y; **ein Mittel gegen Schnupfen** something for colds
2 (*in Richtung auf*) towards; **gegen Osten** to(wards) the east; **gegen Abend** towards evening; **gegen einen Baum fahren** to drive into a tree
3 (*ungefähr*) round about; **gegen 3 Uhr** around 3 o'clock
4 (*gegenüber*) towards; (*ungefähr*) around; **gerecht gegen alle** fair to all
5 (*im Austausch für*) for; **gegen bar** for cash; **gegen Quittung** against a receipt
6 (*verglichen mit*) compared with

Gegenangriff *m* counter-attack

Gegenbeweis *m* counter-evidence
Gegend ['ge:gənt] (-, -en) *f* area, district
Gegen- *zW:* **g~ei'nander** *adv* against one another; **~fahrbahn** *f* oncoming carriageway; **~frage** *f* counter-question; **~gewicht** *nt* counterbalance; **~gift** *nt* antidote; **~leistung** *f* service in return; **~mittel** *nt* antidote, cure; **~satz** *m* contrast; **~sätze überbrücken** to overcome differences; **g~sätzlich** *adj* contrary, opposite; (*widersprüchlich*) contradictory; **~seite** *f* opposite side, reciprocal; **sich g~seitig helfen** to help each other; **~spieler** *m* opponent; **~stand** *m* object; **~stimme** *f* vote against; **~stoß** *m* counterblow; **~stück** *nt* counterpart; **~teil** *nt* opposite; **im ~teil** on the contrary; **g~teilig** *adj* opposite, contrary
gegenüber [ge:gən''y:bər] *präp +dat* opposite; (*zu*) to(wards); (*angesichts*) in the face of ♦ *adv* opposite; **G~** (-s, -) *nt* person opposite; **~liegen** (*unreg*) *vr* to face each other; **~stehen** (*unreg*) *vr* to be opposed (to each other); **~stellen** *vt* to confront; (*fig*) to contrast; **G~stellung** *f* confrontation; (*fig*) contrast; **~treten** (*unreg*) *vi +dat* to face
Gegen- *zW:* **~verkehr** *m* oncoming traffic; **~vorschlag** *m* counterproposal; **~wart** *f* present; **g~wärtig** *adj* present ♦ *adv* at present; **das ist mir nicht mehr g~wärtig** that has slipped my mind; **~wert** *m* equivalent; **~wind** *m* headwind; **g~zeichnen** *vt, vi* to countersign
gegessen [gə'gɛsən] *vb siehe* **essen**
Gegner ['ge:gnər] (-s, -) *m* opponent; **g~isch** *adj* opposing; **~schaft** *f* opposition
gegr. *abk* (= *gegründet*) est.
gegrillt [gə'grɪlt] *adj* grilled
Gehackte(s) [gə'haktə(s)] *nt* mince(d meat)
Gehalt¹ [gə'halt] (-(e)s, -e) *m* content
Gehalt² (-(e)s, ¨er) *nt* salary
Gehalts- *zW:* **~empfänger** *m* salary earner; **~erhöhung** *f* salary increase; **~zulage** *f* salary increment
gehaltvoll *adj* (*nahrhaft*) nutritious

gehässig [gəˈhɛsɪç] *adj* spiteful, nasty
Gehäuse [gəˈhɔyzə] (-s, -) *nt* case; casing; (*von Apfel etc*) core
Gehege [gəˈheːgə] (-s, -) *nt* reserve; (*im Zoo*) enclosure
geheim [gəˈhaɪm] *adj* secret; **G~dienst** *m* secret service, intelligence service; **~halten** (*unreg*) *vt* to keep secret; **G~nis** (-ses, -se) *nt* secret; mystery; **~nisvoll** *adj* mysterious; **G~nummer** *f* (*TEL*) secret number; **G~polizei** *f* secret police
gehemmt [gəˈhɛmt] *adj* inhibited, self-conscious
gehen [ˈgeːən] (*unreg*) *vt, vi* to go; (*zu Fuß ~*) to walk ♦ *vb unpers*: **wie geht es (dir)?** how are you *od* things?; ~ **nach** (*Fenster*) to face; **mir/ihm geht es gut** I'm/he's (doing) fine; **geht das?** is that possible?; **geht's noch?** can you manage?; **es geht** not too bad, O.K.; **das geht nicht** that's not on; **es geht um etw** sth is concerned, it's about sth
gehenlassen (*unreg*) *vr* (*unbeherrscht sein*) to lose control (of o.s.) ♦ *vt* to let/leave alone; **laß mich gehen!** leave me alone!
geheuer [gəˈhɔyər] *adj*: **nicht ~** eerie; (*fragwürdig*) dubious
Gehilfe [gəˈhɪlfə] (-n, -n) *m* assistant
Gehilfin *f* assistant
Gehirn [gəˈhɪrn] (-(e)s, -e) *nt* brain; **~erschütterung** *f* concussion; **~wäsche** *f* brainwashing
gehoben [gəˈhoːbən] *pp of* **heben** ♦ *adj* (*Position*) elevated; high
geholfen [gəˈhɔlfən] *vb siehe* **helfen**
Gehör [gəˈhøːr] (-(e)s) *nt* hearing; **musikalisches ~** ear; ~ **finden** to gain a hearing; **jdm ~ schenken** to give sb a hearing
gehorchen [gəˈhɔrçən] *vi* +*dat* to obey
gehören [gəˈhøːrən] *vi* to belong ♦ *vr unpers* to be right *od* proper
gehörig *adj* proper; ~ **zu** *od* +*dat* belonging to; part of
gehorsam [gəˈhoːrzaːm] *adj* obedient; **G~** (-s) *m* obedience
Gehsteig [ˈgeːʃtaɪk] *m* pavement, sidewalk (*US*)

Gehweg [ˈgeːveːk] *m* pavement, sidewalk (*US*)
Geier [ˈgaɪər] (-s, -) *m* vulture
Geige [ˈgaɪgə] *f* violin
Geiger (-s, -) *m* violinist
Geigerzähler *m* geiger counter
geil [gaɪl] *adj* randy (*BRIT*), horny (*US*)
Geisel [ˈgaɪzəl] (-, -n) *f* hostage
Geist [gaɪst] (-(e)s, -er) *m* spirit; (*Gespenst*) ghost; (*Verstand*) mind
geisterhaft *adj* ghostly
Geistes- *zW*: **g~abwesend** *adj* absent-minded; **~blitz** *m* brainwave; **~gegenwart** *f* presence of mind; **g~krank** *adj* mentally ill; **~kranke(r)** *mf* mentally ill person; **~krankheit** *f* mental illness; **~wissenschaften** *pl* the arts; **~zustand** *m* state of mind
geist- *zW*: **~ig** *adj* intellectual; mental; (*Getränke*) alcoholic; **~ig behindert** mentally handicapped; **~lich** *adj* spiritual, religious; clerical; **G~liche(r)** *m* clergyman; **G~lichkeit** *f* clergy; **~los** *adj* uninspired, dull; **~reich** *adj* clever; witty; **~voll** *adj* intellectual; (*weise*) wise
Geiz [gaɪts] (-es) *m* miserliness, meanness; **g~en** *vi* to be miserly; **~hals** *m* miser; **g~ig** *adj* miserly, mean; **~kragen** *m* miser
gekannt [gəˈkant] *vb siehe* **kennen**
geknickt [gəˈknɪkt] *adj* (*fig*) dejected
gekonnt [gəˈkɔnt] *adj* skilful ♦ *vb siehe* **können**
Gekritzel [gəˈkrɪtsəl] (-s) *nt* scrawl, scribble
gekünstelt [gəˈkʏnstəlt] *adj* artificial, affected
Gel [geːl] (-s, -e) *nt* gel
Gelächter [gəˈlɛçtər] (-s, -) *nt* laughter
geladen [geˈlaːdən] *adj* loaded; (*ELEK*) live; (*fig*) furious
Gelage [gəˈlaːgə] (-s, -) *nt* banquet
gelähmt [gəˈlɛːmt] *adj* paralysed
Gelände [gəˈlɛndə] (-s, -) *nt* land, terrain; (*von Fabrik, Sport~*) grounds *pl*; (*Bau~*) site; **~lauf** *m* cross-country race
Geländer [gəˈlɛndər] (-s, -) *nt* railing; (*Treppen~*) banister(s)
gelangen [gəˈlaŋən] *vi*: ~ (**an** +*akk od*

zu) to reach; (*erwerben*) to attain; **in jds Besitz** +*akk* ~ to come into sb's possession

gelangweilt [gə'laŋvaɪlt] *adj* bored

gelassen [gə'lasən] *adj* calm, composed; **G~heit** *f* calmness, composure

Gelatine [ʒɛla'tiːnə] *f* gelatine

geläufig [gə'lɔyfɪç] *adj* (*üblich*) common; **das ist mir nicht** ~ I'm not familiar with that

gelaunt [gə'laʊnt] *adj*: **schlecht/gut** ~ in a bad/good mood; **wie ist er** ~? what sort of mood is he in?

gelb [gɛlp] *adj* yellow; (*Ampellicht*) amber; **~lich** *adj* yellowish; **G~sucht** *f* jaundice

Geld [gɛlt] (-(e)s, -er) *nt* money; **etw zu** ~ **machen** to sell sth off; **~anlage** *f* investment; **~automat** *m* cash dispenser; **~beutel** *m* purse; **~börse** *f* purse; **~geber** (-s, -) *m* financial backer; **g~gierig** *adj* avaricious; **~schein** *m* banknote; **~schrank** *m* safe, strongbox; **~strafe** *f* fine; **~stück** *nt* coin; **~wechsel** *m* exchange (of money)

Gelee [ʒe'leː] (-s, -s) *nt od m* jelly

gelegen [gə'leːgən] *adj* situated; (*passend*) convenient, opportune ♦ *vb siehe* **liegen**; **etw kommt jdm** ~ sth is convenient for sb

Gelegenheit [gə'leːgənhaɪt] *f* opportunity; (*Anlaß*) occasion; **bei jeder** ~ at every opportunity; **~sarbeit** *f* casual work; **~skauf** *m* bargain

gelegentlich [gə'leːgəntlɪç] *adj* occasional ♦ *adv* occasionally; (*bei Gelegenheit*) some time (or other) ♦ *präp* +*gen* on the occasion of

gelehrt [gə'leːrt] *adj* learned; **G~e(r)** *mf* scholar; **G~heit** *f* scholarliness

Geleise [gə'laɪzə] (-s, -) *nt* = **Gleis**

Geleit [gə'laɪt] (-(e)s, -e) *nt* escort; **g~en** *vt* to escort

Gelenk [gə'lɛŋk] (-(e)s, -e) *nt* joint; **g~ig** *adj* supple

gelernt [gə'lɛrnt] *adj* skilled

Geliebte(r) [gə'liːptə(r)] *mf* sweetheart, beloved

geliehen [gə'liːən] *vb siehe* **leihen**

gelind(e) [gə'lɪnt, gə'lɪndə] *adj* mild, light; (*fig: Wut*) fierce; **gelinde gesagt** to put it mildly

gelingen [gə'lɪŋən] (*unreg*) *vi* to succeed; **es ist mir gelungen, etw zu tun** I succeeded in doing sth

gell [gɛl] *excl* isn't it?; aren't you? *etc*

geloben [gə'loːbən] *vt, vi* to vow, to swear

gelten ['gɛltən] (*unreg*) *vt* (*wert sein*) to be worth ♦ *vi* (*gültig sein*) to be valid; (*erlaubt sein*) to be allowed ♦ *vb unpers*: **es gilt, etw zu tun** it is necessary to do sth; **jdm viel/wenig** ~ to mean a lot/not to mean much to sb; **was gilt die Wette?** what do you bet?; **jdm** ~ (*gemünzt sein auf*) to be meant for *od* aimed at sb; **etw** ~ **lassen** to accept sth; **als** *od* **für** ~ to be considered to be sth; **jdm** *od* **für jdn** ~ (*betreffen*) to apply to *od* for sb; **~d** *adj* prevailing; **etw ~d machen** to assert sth; **sich ~d machen** to make itself/o.s. felt

Geltung ['gɛltʊŋ] *f*: ~ **haben** to have validity; **sich/etw** *dat* ~ **verschaffen** to establish one's position/the position of sth; **etw zur** ~ **bringen** to show sth to its best advantage; **zur** ~ **kommen** to be seen/heard *etc* to its best advantage

Geltungsbedürfnis *nt* desire for admiration

Gelübde [gə'lypdə] (-s, -) *nt* vow

gelungen [gə'lʊŋən] *adj* successful

gemächlich [gə'mɛːçlɪç] *adj* leisurely

Gemahl [gə'maːl] (-(e)s, -e) *m* husband; **~in** *f* wife

Gemälde [gə'mɛːldə] (-s, -) *nt* picture, painting

gemäß [gə'mɛːs] *präp* +*dat* in accordance with ♦ *adj* (+*dat*) appropriate (to)

gemäßigt *adj* moderate; (*Klima*) temperate

gemein [gə'maɪn] *adj* common; (*niederträchtig*) mean; **etw** ~ **haben (mit)** to have sth in common (with)

Gemeinde [gə'maɪndə] *f* district, community; (*Pfarr~*) parish; (*Kirchen~*) congregation; **~steuer** *f* local rates *pl*;

~verwaltung f local administration;
~wahl f local election
Gemein- zW: **g~gefährlich** adj
dangerous to the public; **~heit** f
commonness; mean thing to do/to say;
~platz m commonplace, platitude;
g~sam adj joint, common (auch MATH)
♦ adv together, jointly; **g~same Sache
mit jdm machen** to be in cahoots with
sb; **etw g~sam haben** to have sth in
common; **~samkeit** f community, having
in common; **~schaft** f community; **in
~schaft mit** jointly od together with;
g~schaftlich adj = **gemeinsam**;
~schaftsarbeit f teamwork; team effort;
~sinn m public spirit
Gemenge [gə'mɛŋə] (-s, -) nt mixture;
(Hand~) scuffle
gemessen [gə'mɛsən] adj measured
Gemetzel [gə'mɛtsəl] (-s, -) nt slaughter,
carnage, butchery
Gemisch [gə'mɪʃ] (-es, -e) nt mixture;
g~t adj mixed
gemocht [gə'mɔxt] vb siehe **mögen**
Gemse ['gɛmzə] f chamois
Gemüse [gə'my:zə] (-s, -) nt vegetables
pl; **~garten** m vegetable garden;
~händler m greengrocer
gemußt [gə'mʊst] vb siehe **müssen**
gemustert [gə'mʊstərt] adj patterned
Gemüt [gə'my:t] (-(e)s, -er) nt
disposition, nature; person; **sich** dat **etw
zu ~e führen** (umg) to indulge in sth; **die
~er erregen** to arouse strong feelings;
g~lich adj comfortable, cosy; (Person)
good-natured; **~lichkeit** f
comfortableness, cosiness; amiability
Gemüts- zW: **~mensch** m sentimental
person; **~ruhe** f composure; **~zustand** m
state of mind
gemütvoll adj warm, tender
Gen [ge:n] (-s, -e) nt gene
genannt [gə'nant] vb siehe **nennen**
genau [gə'nau] adj exact, precise ♦ adv
exactly, precisely; **etw ~ nehmen** to take
sth seriously; **~genommen** adv strictly
speaking; **G~igkeit** f exactness, accuracy;

~so adv just the same; **~so gut** just as
good
genehm [gə'ne:m] adj agreeable,
acceptable; **~igen** vt to approve, to
authorize; **sich** dat **etw ~igen** to indulge
in sth; **G~igung** f approval,
authorization; (Schriftstück) permit
General [gene'ra:l] (-s, -e od ⁼e) m
general; **~direktor** m director general;
~konsulat nt consulate general; **~probe**
f dress rehearsal; **~streik** m general
strike; **g~überholen** vt to overhaul
thoroughly; **~versammlung** f general
meeting
Generation [generatsi'o:n] f generation
Generator [gene'ra:tɔr] m generator,
dynamo
generell [genə'rɛl] adj general
genesen [gə'ne:zən] (unreg) vi to
convalesce, to recover
Genesung f recovery, convalescence
genetisch [ge'ne:tɪʃ] adj genetic
Genf [genf] nt (GEOG) Geneva; **der ~er
See** Lake Geneva
genial [geni'a:l] adj brilliant
Genick [gə'nɪk] (-(e)s, -e) nt (back of the)
neck
Genie [ʒe'ni:] (-s, -s) nt genius
genieren [ʒe'ni:rən] vt to bother ♦ vr to
feel awkward od self-conscious; **geniert
es Sie, wenn ...?** do you mind if ...?
genießbar adj edible; drinkable
genießen [gə'ni:sən] (unreg) vt to enjoy;
to eat; to drink
Genießer (-s, -) m epicure; pleasure
lover; **g~isch** adj appreciative ♦ adv with
relish
genommen [gə'nɔmən] vb siehe **nehmen**
Genosse [gə'nɔsə] (-n, -n) m (bes POL)
comrade, companion; **~nschaft** f
cooperative (association)
Genossin f (bes POL) comrade,
companion
Gentechnik ['ge:ntɛçnɪk] f genetic
engineering
genug [gə'nu:k] adv enough
Genüge [gə'ny:gə] f: **jdm/etw ~ tun** od
leisten to satisfy sb/sth; **g~n** vi (+dat) to
be enough (for); **g~nd** adj sufficient

genügsam [gə'nyːkzaːm] *adj* modest, easily satisfied; **G~keit** *f* undemandingness

Genugtuung [gə'nuːktuːʊŋ] *f* satisfaction

Genuß [gə'nʊs] (**-sses, ⁻sse**) *m* pleasure; (*Zusichnehmen*) consumption; **in den ~ von etw kommen** to receive the benefit of sth

genüßlich [gə'nʏslɪç] *adv* with relish

Genußmittel *pl* (semi-)luxury items

geöffnet [gə'œfnət] *adj* open

Geograph [geo'graːf] (**-en, -en**) *m* geographer; **Geogra'phie** *f* geography; **g~isch** *adj* geographical

Geologe [geo'loːgə] (**-n, -n**) *m* geologist; **Geolo'gie** *f* geology

Geometrie [geome'triː] *f* geometry

Gepäck [gə'pɛk] (**-(e)s**) *nt* luggage, baggage; **~abfertigung** *f* luggage office; **~annahme** *f* luggage office; **~aufbewahrung** *f* left-luggage office (*BRIT*), baggage check (*US*); **~aufgabe** *f* luggage office; **~ausgabe** *f* luggage office; **~netz** *nt* luggage-rack; **~träger** *m* porter; (*Fahrrad*) carrier; **~wagen** *m* luggage van (*BRIT*), baggage car (*US*)

gepflegt [gə'pfleːkt] *adj* well-groomed; (*Park etc*) well looked after

Gerade *f* straight line; **g~'aus** *adv* straight ahead; **g~'heraus** *adv* straight out, bluntly; **g~stehen** (*unreg*) *vi:* **für jdn/etw g~stehen** to be answerable for sb('s actions)/sth; **g~wegs** *adv* direct, straight; **g~zu** *adv* (*beinahe*) virtually, almost

---
SCHLÜSSELWORT
---

gerade [gə'raːdə] *adj* straight; (*aufrecht*) upright; **eine gerade Zahl** an even number
♦ *adv* **1** (*genau*) just, exactly; (*speziell*) especially; **gerade deshalb** that's just *od* exactly why; **das ist es ja gerade!** that's just it!; **gerade du** you especially; **warum gerade ich?** why me (of all people)?; **jetzt gerade nicht!** not now!; **gerade neben** right next to
2 (*eben, soeben*) just; **er wollte gerade**

aufstehen he was just about to get up; **gerade erst** only just; **gerade noch** (only) just

gerannt [gə'rant] *vb siehe* **rennen**

Gerät [gə'rɛːt] (**-(e)s, -e**) *nt* device; (*Werkzeug*) tool; (*SPORT*) apparatus; (*Zubehör*) equipment *no pl*

geraten [gə'raːtən] (*unreg*) *vi* (*gedeihen*) to thrive; (*gelingen*): (**jdm**) **~** to turn out well (for sb); **gut/schlecht ~** to turn out well/badly; **an jdn ~** to come across sb; **in etw** *akk* **~** to get into sth; **in Angst ~** to get frightened; **nach jdm ~** to take after sb

Geratewohl [gəraːtə'voːl] *nt:* **aufs ~** on the off chance; (*bei Wahl*) at random

geräuchert [gə'rɔʏçərt] *adj* smoked

geräumig [gə'rɔʏmɪç] *adj* roomy

Geräusch [gə'rɔʏʃ] (**-(e)s, -e**) *nt* sound, noise; **g~los** *adj* silent

gerben ['gɛrbən] *vt* to tan

gerecht [gə'rɛçt] *adj* just, fair; **jdm/etw ~ werden** to do justice to sb/sth; **G~igkeit** *f* justice, fairness

Gerede [gə'reːdə] (**-s**) *nt* talk, gossip

geregelt [gə'reːgəlt] *adj* (*Arbeit*) steady, regular; (*Mahlzeiten*) regular, set

gereizt [gə'raɪtst] *adj* irritable; **G~heit** *f* irritation

Gericht [gə'rɪçt] (**-(e)s, -e**) *nt* court; (*Essen*) dish; **mit jdm ins ~ gehen** (*fig*) to judge sb harshly; **das Jüngste ~** the Last Judgement; **g~lich** *adj* judicial, legal ♦ *adv* judicially, legally

Gerichts- *zW:* **~barkeit** *f* jurisdiction; **~hof** *m* court (of law); **~kosten** *pl* (legal) costs; **~saal** *m* courtroom; **~verfahren** *nt* legal proceedings *pl*; **~verhandlung** *f* trial; **~vollzieher** *m* bailiff

gerieben [gə'riːbən] *adj* grated; (*umg: schlau*) smart, wily ♦ *vb siehe* **reiben**

gering [gə'rɪŋ] *adj* slight, small; (*niedrig*) low; (*Zeit*) short; **~fügig** *adj* slight, trivial; **~schätzig** *adj* disparaging

geringste(r, s) *adj* slightest, least; **~nfalls** *adv* at the very least

gerinnen [gə'rɪnən] (*unreg*) *vi* to congeal; (*Blut*) to clot; (*Milch*) to curdle

Gerippe [gəˈrɪpə] (-s, -) *nt* skeleton
gerissen [gəˈrɪsən] *adj* wily, smart
geritten [gəˈrɪtən] *vb siehe* **reiten**
gern(e) [ˈgɛrn(ə)] *adv* willingly, gladly;
~**(e) haben**, ~**(e) mögen** to like; **etwas**
~**(e) tun** to like doing something; **ich**
möchte ~**(e) ...** I'd like ...; **ja,** ~**(e)** yes,
please; yes, I'd like to; ~**(e) geschehen**
it's a pleasure
gerochen [gəˈrɔxən] *vb siehe* **riechen**
Geröll [gəˈrœl] (-(e)s, -e) *nt* scree
Gerste [ˈgɛrstə] *f* barley; ~**nkorn** *nt* (*im*
Auge) stye
Geruch [gəˈrux] (-(e)s, ⸚e) *m* smell, odour;
g~los *adj* odourless
Gerücht [gəˈrʏçt] (-(e)s, -e) *nt* rumour
geruhen [gəˈruːən] *vi* to deign
geruhsam *adj* (*Leben*) peaceful; (*Nacht,*
Zeit) peaceful, restful; (*langsam*:
Arbeitsweise, Spaziergang) leisurely
Gerümpel [gəˈrʏmpəl] (-s) *nt* junk
Gerüst [gəˈrʏst] (-(e)s, -e) *nt* (*Bau~*)
scaffold(ing); frame
gesalzen [gəˈzaltsən] *pp von* **salzen**
♦ *adj* (*umg: Preis, Rechnung*) steep
gesamt [gəˈzamt] *adj* whole, entire;
(*Kosten*) total; (*Werke*) complete; **im** ~**en**
all in all; ~**deutsch** *adj* all-German;
G~eindruck *m* general impression;
G~heit *f* totality, whole; **G~schule** *f*
≈ comprehensive school
gesandt [gəˈzant] *vb siehe* **senden**
Gesandte(r) *m* envoy
Gesandtschaft [gəˈzantʃaft] *f* legation
Gesang [gəˈzaŋ] (-(e)s, ⸚e) *m* song;
(*Singen*) singing; ~**buch** *nt* (*REL*) hymn
book
Gesangverein *m* choral society
Gesäß [gəˈzɛːs] (-es, -e) *nt* seat, bottom
Geschäft [gəˈʃɛft] (-(e)s, -e) *nt* business;
(*Laden*) shop; (*~sabschluß*) deal; **g~ig** *adj*
active, busy; (*pej*) officious; **g~lich** *adj*
commercial ♦ *adv* on business
Geschäfts- *zW*: ~**bericht** *m* financial
report; ~**führer** *m* manager; (*Klub*)
secretary; ~**geheimnis** *nt* trade secret;
~**jahr** *nt* financial year; ~**lage** *f* business
conditions *pl*; ~**mann** *m* businessman;
g~mäßig *adj* businesslike; ~**partner** *m*

business partner; ~**reise** *f* business trip;
~**schluß** *m* closing time; ~**stelle** *f* office,
place of business; **g~tüchtig** *adj*
business-minded; ~**viertel** *nt* business
quarter; shopping centre; ~**wagen** *m*
company car; ~**zeit** *f* business hours
geschehen [gəˈʃeːən] (*unreg*) *vi* to
happen; **es war um ihn** ~ that was the
end of him
gescheit [gəˈʃait] *adj* clever
Geschenk [gəˈʃɛŋk] (-(e)s, -e) *nt* present,
gift
Geschichte [gəˈʃɪçtə] *f* story; (*Sache*)
affair; (*Historie*) history
geschichtlich *adj* historical
Geschick [gəˈʃɪk] (-(e)s, -e) *nt* aptitude;
(*Schicksal*) fate; ~**lichkeit** *f* skill,
dexterity; **g~t** *adj* skilful
geschieden [gəˈʃiːdən] *adj* divorced
geschienen [gəˈʃiːnən] *vb siehe*
scheinen
Geschirr [gəˈʃɪr] (-(e)s, -e) *nt* crockery;
pots and pans *pl*; (*Pferde~*) harness;
~**spülmaschine** *f* dishwasher; ~**tuch** *nt*
dish cloth
Geschlecht [gəˈʃlɛçt] (-(e)s, -er) *nt* sex;
(*GRAM*) gender; (*Gattung*) race; family;
g~lich *adj* sexual
Geschlechts- *zW*: ~**krankheit** *f*
venereal disease; ~**teil** *nt* genitals *pl*;
~**verkehr** *m* sexual intercourse
geschlossen [gəˈʃlɔsən] *adj* shut ♦ *vb*
siehe **schließen**
Geschmack [gəˈʃmak] (-(e)s, ⸚e) *m* taste;
nach jds ~ to sb's taste; ~ **finden an etw**
dat to (come to) like sth; **g~los** *adj*
tasteless; (*fig*) in bad taste; ~**(s)sache** *f*
matter of taste; ~**ssinn** *m* sense of taste;
g~voll *adj* tasteful
geschmeidig [gəˈʃmaidɪç] *adj* supple;
(*formbar*) malleable
Geschnetzelte(s) [gəˈʃnɛtsəltə(s)] *nt*
(*KOCH*) strips of meat stewed to produce a
thick sauce
geschnitten [gəˈʃnɪtən] *vb siehe*
schneiden
Geschöpf [gəˈʃœpf] (-(e)s, -e) *nt* creature
Geschoß [gəˈʃɔs] (-sses, -sse) *nt* (*MIL*)
projectile, missile; (*Stockwerk*) floor

geschossen *vb siehe* **schießen**

geschraubt [gəˈʃraupt] *adj* stilted, artificial

Geschrei [gəˈʃrai] (-s) *nt* cries *pl*, shouting; *(fig: Aufheben)* noise, fuss

geschrieben [gəˈʃriːbən] *vb siehe* **schreiben**

Geschütz [gəˈʃyts] (-es, -e) *nt* gun, cannon; **ein schweres ~ auffahren** *(fig)* to bring out the big guns; **~feuer** *nt* artillery fire, gunfire

geschützt *adj* protected

Geschw. *abk siehe* **Geschwister**

Geschwafel [gəˈʃvaːfəl] (-s) *nt* silly talk

Geschwätz [gəˈʃvɛts] (-es) *nt* chatter, gossip; **g~ig** *adj* talkative

geschweige [gəˈʃvaigə] *adv*: **~ (denn)** let alone, not to mention

geschwind [gəˈʃvint] *adj* quick, swift; **G~igkeit** [-dɪçkait] *f* speed, velocity; **G~igkeitsbeschränkung** *f* speed limit; **G~igkeitsüberschreitung** *f* exceeding the speed limit

Geschwister [gəˈʃvistər] *pl* brothers and sisters

geschwollen [gəˈʃvɔlən] *adj* pompous

geschwommen [gəˈʃvɔmən] *vb siehe* **schwimmen**

Geschworene(r) [gəˈʃvoːrənə(r)] *mf* juror; **~n** *pl* jury

Geschwulst [gəˈʃvulst] (-, ⸚e) *f* swelling; growth, tumour

geschwungen [gəˈʃvuŋən] *pp von* **schwingen** ♦ *adj* curved, arched

Geschwür [gəˈʃvyːr] (-(e)s, -e) *nt* ulcer

Gesell- [gəˈzɛl] *zW*: **~e** (-n, -n) *m* fellow; *(Handwerk~)* journeyman; **g~ig** *adj* sociable; **~igkeit** *f* sociability; **~schaft** *f* society; *(Begleitung, COMM)* company; *(Abendgesellschaft etc)* party; **g~schaftlich** *adj* social; **~schaftsordnung** *f* social structure; **~schaftsschicht** *f* social stratum; **~schaftsspiel** *nt* party game

gesessen [gəˈzɛsən] *vb siehe* **sitzen**

Gesetz [gəˈzɛts] (-es, -e) *nt* law; **~buch** *nt* statute book; **~gebung** *f* legislation; **g~lich** *adj* legal, lawful; **g~licher Feiertag** *m* statutory holiday; **g~los** *adj*

lawless; **g~mäßig** *adj* lawful; **g~t** *adj* *(Mensch)* sedate; **g~widrig** *adj* illegal, unlawful

Gesicht [gəˈzɪçt] (-(e)s, -er) *nt* face; **das zweite ~** second sight; **das ist mir nie zu ~ gekommen** I've never laid eyes on that

Gesichts- *zW*: **~ausdruck** *m* (facial) expression; **~farbe** *f* complexion; **~punkt** *m* point of view; **~züge** *pl* features

Gesindel [gəˈzɪndəl] (-s) *nt* rabble

gesinnt [gəˈzɪnt] *adj* disposed, minded

Gesinnung [gəˈzɪnʊŋ] *f* disposition; *(Ansicht)* views *pl*

gesittet [gəˈzɪtət] *adj* well-mannered

Gespann [gəˈʃpan] (-(e)s, -e) *nt* team; *(umg)* couple

gespannt *adj* tense, strained; *(begierig)* eager; **ich bin ~, ob** I wonder if *od* whether; **auf etw/jdn ~ sein** to look forward to sth/meeting sb

Gespenst [gəˈʃpɛnst] (-(e)s, -er) *nt* ghost, spectre

gesperrt [gəˈʃpɛrt] *adj* closed off

Gespött [gəˈʃpœt] (-(e)s) *nt* mockery; **zum ~ werden** to become a laughing stock

Gespräch [gəˈʃprɛːç] (-(e)s, -e) *nt* conversation; discussion(s); *(Anruf)* call; **g~ig** *adj* talkative

gesprochen [gəˈʃprɔxən] *vb siehe* **sprechen**

gesprungen [gəˈʃprʊŋən] *vb siehe* **springen**

Gespür [gəˈʃpyːr] (-s) *nt* feeling

Gestalt [gəˈʃtalt] (-, -en) *f* form, shape; *(Person)* figure; **in ~ von** in the form of; **~ annehmen** to take shape; **g~en** *vt* *(formen)* to shape, to form; *(organisieren)* to arrange, to organize ♦ *vr*: **sich g~en (zu)** to turn out (to be); **~ung** *f* formation; organization

gestanden [gəˈʃtandən] *vb siehe* **stehen**

Geständnis [gəˈʃtɛntnɪs] (-ses, -se) *nt* confession

Gestank [gəˈʃtaŋk] (-(e)s) *m* stench

gestatten [gəˈʃtatən] *vt* to permit, to allow; **~ Sie?** may I?; **sich** *dat* **~, etw zu tun** to take the liberty of doing sth

Geste ['gɛstə] f gesture

gestehen [gə'ʃteːən] (*unreg*) *vt* to confess

Gestein [gə'ʃtaɪn] (-(e)s, -e) *nt* rock

Gestell [gə'ʃtɛl] (-(e)s, -e) *nt* frame; (*Regal*) rack, stand

gestern ['gɛstərn] *adv* yesterday; ~ **abend/morgen** yesterday evening/morning

Gestirn [gə'ʃtɪrn] (-(e)s, -e) *nt* star; (*Sternbild*) constellation

gestohlen [gə'ʃtoːlən] *vb siehe* **stehlen**

gestorben [gə'ʃtɔrbən] *vb siehe* **sterben**

gestört [gə'ʃtøːrt] *adj* disturbed

gestreift [gə'ʃtraɪft] *adj* striped

gestrichen [gə'ʃtrɪçən] *adj* cancelled

gestrig ['gɛstrɪç] *adj* yesterday's

Gestrüpp [gə'ʃtrʏp] (-(e)s, -e) *nt* undergrowth

Gestüt [gə'ʃtyːt] (-(e)s, -e) *nt* stud farm

Gesuch [gə'zuːx] (-(e)s, -e) *nt* petition; (*Antrag*) application; **g~t** *adj* (*COMM*) in demand; wanted; (*fig*) contrived

gesund [gə'zʊnt] *adj* healthy; **wieder ~ werden** to get better; **G~heit** f health(iness); **G~heit!** bless you!; ~**heitlich** *adj* health *attrib*, physical ♦ *adv*: **wie geht es Ihnen ~heitlich?** how's your health?; ~**heitsschädlich** *adj* unhealthy; **G~heitswesen** *nt* health service; **G~heitszustand** *m* state of health

gesungen [gə'zʊŋən] *vb siehe* **singen**

getan [gə'taːn] *vb siehe* **tun**

Getöse [gə'tøːzə] (-s) *nt* din, racket

Getränk [gə'trɛŋk] (-(e)s, -e) *nt* drink; ~**ekarte** f wine list

getrauen [gə'trauən] *vr* to dare, to venture

Getreide [gə'traɪdə] (-s, -) *nt* cereals *pl*, grain; ~**speicher** *m* granary

getrennt [gə'trɛnt] *adj* separate

Getriebe [gə'triːbə] (-s, -) *nt* (*Leute*) bustle; (*AUT*) gearbox

getrieben *vb siehe* **treiben**

getroffen [gə'trɔfən] *vb siehe* **treffen**

getrost [gə'troːst] *adv* without any bother

getrunken [gə'trʊŋkən] *vb siehe* **trinken**

Getue [gə'tuːə] (-s) *nt* fuss

geübt [gə'ʔyːpt] *adj* experienced

Gewächs [gə'vɛks] (-es, -e) *nt* growth; (*Pflanze*) plant

gewachsen [gə'vaksən] *adj*: **jdm/etw ~ sein** to be sb's equal/equal to sth

Gewächshaus *nt* greenhouse

gewagt [gə'vaːkt] *adj* daring, risky

gewählt [gə'vɛːlt] *adj* (*Sprache*) refined, elegant

Gewähr [gə'vɛːr] (-) f guarantee; **keine ~ übernehmen für** to accept no responsibility for; **g~en** *vt* to grant; (*geben*) to provide; **g~leisten** *vt* to guarantee

Gewahrsam [gə'vaːrzaːm] (-s, -e) *m* safekeeping; (*Polizei~*) custody

Gewährsmann *m* informant, source

Gewalt [gə'valt] (-, -en) f power; (*große Kraft*) force; (*~taten*) violence; **mit aller ~** with all one's might; ~**anwendung** f use of force; **g~ig** *adj* tremendous; (*Irrtum*) huge; ~**marsch** *m* forced march; **g~sam** *adj* forcible; **g~tätig** *adj* violent

Gewand [gə'vant] (-(e)s, ̈er) *nt* gown, robe

gewandt [gə'vant] *adj* deft, skilful; (*erfahren*) experienced; **G~heit** f dexterity, skill

gewann *etc* [gə'van] *vb siehe* **gewinnen**

Gewässer [gə'vɛsər] (-s, -) *nt* waters *pl*

Gewebe [gə'veːbə] (-s, -) *nt* (*Stoff*) fabric; (*BIOL*) tissue

Gewehr [gə'veːr] (-(e)s, -e) *nt* gun; rifle; ~**lauf** *m* rifle barrel

Geweih [gə'vaɪ] (-(e)s, -e) *nt* antlers *pl*

Gewerb- [gə'vɛrb] *zW*: ~**e** (-s, -) *nt* trade, occupation; **Handel und ~e** trade and industry; ~**eschule** f technical school; ~**szweig** *m* line of trade

Gewerkschaft [gə'vɛrkʃaft] f trade union; ~**ler** (-s, -) *m* trade unionist; ~**sbund** *m* trade unions federation

gewesen [gə'veːzən] *pp von* **sein**

Gewicht [gə'vɪçt] (-(e)s, -e) *nt* weight; (*fig*) importance

gewieft [gə'viːft] *adj* shrewd, cunning

gewillt [gə'vɪlt] *adj* willing, prepared

Gewimmel [gə'vɪməl] (-s) *nt* swarm

Gewinde [gə'vɪndə] (**-s**, **-**) *nt* (*Kranz*) wreath; (*von Schraube*) thread

Gewinn [gə'vɪn] (**-(e)s**, **-e**) *m* profit; (*bei Spiel*) winnings *pl*; **etw mit ~ verkaufen** to sell sth at a profit; **~- und Verlustrechnung** (*COMM*) profit and loss account; **~beteiligung** *f* profit-sharing; **g~bringend** *adj* profitable; **g~en** (*unreg*) *vt* to win; (*erwerben*) to gain; (*Kohle, Öl*) to extract ♦ *vi* to win; (*profitieren*) to gain; **an etw** *dat* **g~en** to gain (in) sth; **g~end** *adj* (*Lächeln, Aussehen*) winning, charming; **~er(in)** (**-s**, **-**) *m(f)* winner; **~spanne** *f* profit margin; **~ung** *f* winning; gaining; (*von Kohle etc*) extraction

Gewirr [gə'vɪr] (**-(e)s**, **-e**) *nt* tangle; (*von Straßen*) maze

gewiß [gə'vɪs] *adj* certain ♦ *adv* certainly

Gewissen [gə'vɪsən] (**-s**, **-**) *nt* conscience; **g~haft** *adj* conscientious; **g~los** *adj* unscrupulous

Gewissens- *zW*: **~bisse** *pl* pangs of conscience, qualms; **~frage** *f* matter of conscience; **~freiheit** *f* freedom of conscience; **~konflikt** *m* moral conflict

gewissermaßen [gəvɪsər'ma:sən] *adv* more or less, in a way

Gewißheit [gə'vɪshaɪt] *f* certainty

Gewitter [gə'vɪtər] (**-s**, **-**) *nt* thunderstorm; **g~n** *vi unpers*: **es g~t** there's a thunderstorm

gewitzt [gə'vɪtst] *adj* shrewd, cunning

gewogen [gə'vo:gən] *adj* (+*dat*) well-disposed (towards)

gewöhnen [gə'vø:nən] *vt*: **jdn an etw** *akk* **~** to accustom sb to sth; (*erziehen zu*) to teach sb sth; **sich an etw** *akk* **~** to get used *od* accustomed to sth

Gewohnheit [gə'vo:nhaɪt] *f* habit; (*Brauch*) custom; **aus ~** from habit; **zur ~ werden** to become a habit

Gewohnheitsmensch *m* creature of habit

Gewohnheitsrecht *nt* common law

gewöhnlich [gə'vø:nlɪç] *adj* usual; ordinary; (*pej*) common; **wie ~** as usual

gewohnt [gə'vo:nt] *adj* usual; **etw ~ sein** to be used to sth

Gewöhnung *f*: **~ (an** +*akk*) getting accustomed (to)

Gewölbe [gə'vœlbə] (**-s**, **-**) *nt* vault

gewollt [gə'vɔlt] *adj* affected, artificial

gewonnen [gə'vɔnən] *vb siehe* **gewinnen**

geworden [gə'vɔrdən] *vb siehe* **werden**

geworfen [gə'vɔrfən] *vb siehe* **werfen**

Gewühl [gə'vy:l] (**-(e)s**) *nt* throng

Gewürz [gə'vʏrts] (**-es**, **-e**) *nt* spice, seasoning; **~nelke** *f* clove; **g~t** *adj* spiced

gewußt [gə'vʊst] *vb siehe* **wissen**

Gezeiten [gə'tsaɪtən] *pl* tides

gezielt [gə'tsi:lt] *adj* with a particular aim in mind, purposeful; (*Kritik*) pointed

geziert [gə'tsi:rt] *adj* affected

gezogen [gə'tso:gən] *vb siehe* **ziehen**

Gezwitscher [gə'tsvɪtʃər] (**-s**) *nt* twitter(ing), chirping

gezwungen [gə'tsvʊŋən] *adj* forced; **~ermaßen** *adv* of necessity

ggf *abk von* **gegebenenfalls**

gibst *etc* [gi:pst] *vb siehe* **geben**

Gicht [gɪçt] (**-**) *f* gout; **g~isch** *adj* gouty

Giebel ['gi:bəl] (**-s**, **-**) *m* gable; **~dach** *nt* gable(d) roof; **~fenster** *nt* gable window

Gier [gi:r] (**-**) *f* greed; **g~ig** *adj* greedy

gießen ['gi:sən] (*unreg*) *vt* to pour; (*Blumen*) to water; (*Metall*) to cast; (*Wachs*) to mould

Gießkanne *f* watering can

Gift [gɪft] (**-(e)s**, **-e**) *nt* poison; **g~ig** *adj* poisonous; (*fig: boshaft*) venomous; **~müll** *m* toxic waste; **~stoff** *m* toxic substance; **~zahn** *m* fang

ging *etc* [gɪŋ] *vb siehe* **gehen**

Ginster ['gɪnstər] (**-s**, **-**) *m* broom

Gipfel ['gɪpfəl] (**-s**, **-**) *m* summit, peak; (*fig: Höhepunkt*) height; **g~n** *vi* to culminate; **~treffen** *nt* summit (meeting)

Gips [gɪps] (**-es**, **-e**) *m* plaster; (*MED*) plaster (of Paris); **~abdruck** *m* plaster cast; **g~en** *vt* to plaster; **~verband** *m* plaster (cast)

Giraffe [gi'rafə] *f* giraffe

Girlande [gɪr'landə] *f* garland

Giro ['ʒi:ro] (**-s**, **-s**) *nt* giro; **~konto** *nt* current account

Gischt [gɪʃt] (-(e)s, -e) *m* spray

Gitarre [gi'tarə] *f* guitar

Gitter ['gɪtər] (-s, -) *nt* grating, bars *pl*; (*für Pflanzen*) trellis; (*Zaun*) railing(s); **~bett** *nt* cot; **~fenster** *nt* barred window; **~zaun** *m* railing(s)

Glacéhandschuh [gla'se:hantʃuː] *m* kid glove

Glanz [glants] (-es) *m* shine, lustre; (*fig*) splendour

glänzen ['glɛntsən] *vi* to shine (*also fig*), to gleam ♦ *vt* to polish; **~d** *adj* shining; (*fig*) brilliant

Glanz- *zW*: **~leistung** *f* brilliant achievement; **g~los** *adj* dull; **~zeit** *f* heyday

Glas [glaːs] (-es, ⁻er) *nt* glass; **~er** (-s, -) *m* glazier; **~faser** *f* fibreglass; **g~ieren** [gla'ziːrən] *vt* to glaze; **g~ig** *adj* glassy; **~scheibe** *f* pane; **~ur** [gla'zuːr] *f* glaze; (*KOCH*) icing

glatt [glat] *adj* smooth; (*rutschig*) slippery; (*Absage*) flat; (*Lüge*) downright

Glätte ['glɛtə] *f* smoothness; slipperiness

Glatteis *nt* (black) ice; **jdn aufs ~ führen** (*fig*) to take sb for a ride

glätten *vt* to smooth out

Glatze ['glatsə] *f* bald head; **eine ~ bekommen** to go bald

Glaube ['glaubə] (-ns, -n) *m*: **~ (an +akk)** faith (in; belief (in); **g~n** *vt, vi* to believe; to think; **jdm g~n** to believe sb; **an etw** *akk* **g~n** to believe in sth; **daran g~n müssen** (*umg*) to be for it; **~nsbekenntnis** *nt* creed

glaubhaft ['glaubhaft] *adj* credible

gläubig ['glɔybɪç] *adj* (*REL*) devout; (*vertrauensvoll*) trustful; **G~e(r)** *mf* believer; **die G~en** the faithful; **G~er** (-s, -) *m* creditor

glaubwürdig ['glaubvyrdɪç] *adj* credible; (*Mensch*) trustworthy; **G~keit** *f* credibility; trustworthiness

gleich [glaɪç] *adj* equal; (*identisch*) (the) same, identical ♦ *adv* equally; (*sofort*) straight away; (*bald*) in a minute; **es ist mir ~** it's all the same to me; **2 mal 2 ~ 4** 2 times 2 is *od* equals 4; **~ groß** the same size; **~ nach/an** right after/at;

~altrig *adj* of the same age; **~artig** *adj* similar; **~bedeutend** *adj* synonymous; **G~berechtigung** *f* equal rights *pl*; **~bleibend** *adj* constant; **~en** (*unreg*) *vi*: **jdm/etw ~en** to be like sb/sth ♦ *vr* to be alike; **~falls** *adv* likewise; **danke ~falls!** the same to you; **G~förmigkeit** *f* uniformity; **~gesinnt** *adj* like-minded; **G~gewicht** *nt* equilibrium, balance; **~gültig** *adj* indifferent; (*unbedeutend*) unimportant; **G~gültigkeit** *f* indifference; **G~heit** *f* equality; **~kommen** (*unreg*) *vi* +*dat* to be equal to; **~mäßig** *adj* even, equal; **G~nis** (-ses, -se) *nt* parable; **~sam** *adv* as it were; **G~schritt** *m*: **im G~schritt gehen** to walk in step; **~stellen** *vt* (*rechtlich etc*) to treat as (an) equal; **G~strom** *m* (*ELEK*) direct current; **~tun** (*unreg*) *vi*: **es jdm ~tun** to match sb; **G~ung** *f* equation; **~viel** *adv* no matter; **~wertig** *adj* (*Geld*) of the same value; (*Gegner*) evenly-matched; **~zeitig** *adj* simultaneous

Gleis [glaɪs] (-es, -e) *nt* track, rails *pl*; (*Bahnsteig*) platform

gleiten ['glaɪtən] (*unreg*) *vi* to glide; (*rutschen*) to slide

Gletscher ['glɛtʃər] (-s, -) *m* glacier; **~spalte** *f* crevasse

Glied [gliːt] (-(e)s, -er) *nt* member; (*Arm, Bein*) limb; (*von Kette*) link; (*MIL*) rank(s); **g~ern** [-dərn] *vt* to organize, to structure; **~erung** *f* structure, organization

glimmen ['glɪmən] (*unreg*) *vi* to glow, to gleam

glimpflich ['glɪmpflɪç] *adj* mild, lenient; **~ davonkommen** to get off lightly

glitschig ['glɪtʃɪç] *adj* (*Fisch, Weg*) slippery

glitzern ['glɪtsərn] *vi* to glitter; to twinkle

global [glo'baːl] *adj* global

Globus ['gloːbʊs] (- *od* -ses, Globen *od* -se) *m* globe

Glocke ['glɔkə] *f* bell; **etw an die große ~ hängen** (*fig*) to shout sth from the rooftops

Glockenblume *f* bellflower

Glocken- *zW*: **~geläut** *nt* peal of bells; **~spiel** *nt* chime(s); (*MUS*) glockenspiel;

~turm *m* bell tower
Glosse ['glɔsə] *f* comment
glotzen ['glɔtsən] (*umg*) *vi* to stare
Glück [glʏk] **(-(e)s)** *nt* luck, fortune; (*Freude*) happiness; **~ haben** to be lucky; **viel ~!** good luck!; **zum ~** fortunately; **g~en** *vi* to succeed; **es g~te ihm, es zu bekommen** he succeeded in getting it
gluckern ['glʊkərn] *vi* to glug
Glück- *zW*: **g~lich** *adj* fortunate; (*froh*) happy; **g~licherweise** *adv* fortunately; **g~'selig** *adj* blissful
Glücks- *zW*: **~fall** *m* stroke of luck; **~kind** *nt* lucky person; **~sache** *f* matter of luck; **~spiel** *nt* game of chance
Glückwunsch *m* congratulations *pl*, best wishes *pl*
Glüh- [glyː] *zW*: **~birne** *f* light bulb; **g~en** *vi* to glow; **~wein** *m* mulled wine; **~würmchen** *nt* glow-worm
Glut [gluːt] **(-, -en)** *f* (*Röte*) glow; (*Feuers~*) fire; (*Hitze*) heat; (*fig*) ardour
Glyzerin [glʏtsə'riːn] *nt* glycerine
Gnade ['gnaːdə] *f* (*Gunst*) favour; (*Erbarmen*) mercy; (*Milde*) clemency
Gnaden- *zW*: **~frist** *f* reprieve, respite; **g~los** *adj* merciless; **~stoß** *m* coup de grâce
gnädig ['gnɛːdɪç] *adj* gracious; (*voll Erbarmen*) merciful
Gold [gɔlt] **(-(e)s)** *nt* gold; **g~en** ['gɔldən] *adj* golden; **~fisch** *m* goldfish; **~grube** *f* goldmine; **g~ig** ['gɔldɪç] (*umg*) *adj* (*fig: allerliebst*) sweet, adorable; **~regen** *m* laburnum; **G~schmied** *m* goldsmith
Golf¹ [gɔlf] **(-(e)s, -e)** *m* gulf
Golf² **(-s)** *nt* golf; **~platz** *m* golf course; **~schläger** *m* golf club
Golfstrom *m* Gulf Stream
Gondel ['gɔndəl] **(-, -n)** *f* gondola; (*Seilbahn*) cable-car
gönnen ['gœnən] *vt*: **jdm etw ~** not to begrudge sb sth; **sich** *dat* **etw ~** to allow o.s. sth
Gönner **(-s, -)** *m* patron; **g~haft** *adj* patronizing
Gosse ['gɔsə] *f* gutter
Gott [gɔt] **(-es, ⁻er)** *m* god; **mein ~!** for heaven's sake!; **um ~es willen!** for

heaven's sake!; **grüß ~!** hello; **~ sei Dank!** thank God!; **~heit** *f* deity
Göttin ['gœtɪn] *f* goddess
göttlich *adj* divine
gottlos *adj* godless
Götze ['gœtsə] **(-n, -n)** *m* idol
Grab [graːp] **(-(e)s, ⁻er)** *nt* grave; **g~en** ['graːbən] (*unreg*) *vt* to dig; **~en (-s, ⁻)** *m* ditch; (*MIL*) trench; **~stein** *m* gravestone
Grad [graːt] **(-(e)s, -e)** *m* degree; **~einteilung** *f* graduation
Graf [graːf] **(-en, -en)** *m* count, earl
Gram [graːm] **(-(e)s)** *m* grief, sorrow
grämen ['grɛːmən] *vr* to grieve
Gramm [gram] **(-s, -e)** *nt* gram(me)
Grammatik [gra'matɪk] *f* grammar
Grammophon [gramo'foːn] **(-s, -e)** *nt* gramophone
Granat [gra'naːt] **(-(e)s, -e)** *m* (*Stein*) garnet
Granate *f* (*MIL*) shell; (*Hand~*) grenade
Granit [gra'niːt] **(-s, -e)** *m* granite
Graphiker(in) ['graːfɪkər(ɪn)] **(-s, -)** *m(f)* graphic designer
graphisch ['graːfɪʃ] *adj* graphic
Gras [graːs] **(-es, ⁻er)** *nt* grass; **g~en** ['graːzən] *vi* to graze; **~halm** *m* blade of grass
grassieren [gra'siːrən] *vi* to be rampant, to rage
gräßlich ['grɛslɪç] *adj* horrible
Grat [graːt] **(-(e)s, -e)** *m* ridge
Gräte ['grɛːtə] *f* fishbone
gratis ['graːtɪs] *adj, adv* free (of charge); **G~probe** *f* free sample
Gratulation [gratulatsi'oːn] *f* congratulation(s)
gratulieren [gratu'liːrən] *vi*: **jdm ~ (zu etw)** to congratulate sb (on sth); **(ich) gratuliere!** congratulations!
grau [grau] *adj* grey
Grauen **(-s)** *nt* horror; **g~** *vi unpers*: **es graut jdm vor etw** sb dreads sth, sb is afraid of sth; **sich g~ vor** to dread, to have a horror of; **g~haft** *adj* horrible
grauhaarig *adj* grey-haired
grausam ['grauzaːm] *adj* cruel; **G~keit** *f* cruelty
Grausen ['grauzən] **(-s)** *nt* horror; **g~** *vb*

= **grauen**

gravieren [gra'viːrən] *vt* to engrave; **~d** *adj* grave

graziös [gratsi'øːs] *adj* graceful

greifbar *adj* tangible, concrete; **in ~er Nähe** within reach

greifen ['graɪfən] (*unreg*) *vt* to seize; to grip; **nach etw ~** to reach for sth; **um sich ~** (*fig*) to spread; **zu etw ~** to turn to sth

Greis [graɪs] (**-es, -e**) *m* old man; **g~enhaft** ['graɪzən-] *adj* senile; **~in** *f* old woman

grell [grɛl] *adj* harsh

Grenz- ['grɛnts] *zW*: **~beamte(r)** *m* frontier official; **~e** *f* boundary; (*Staats~*) frontier; (*Schranke*) limit; **g~en** *vi*: **g~en (an** +*akk*) to border (on); **g~enlos** *adj* boundless; **~fall** *m* borderline case; **~übergang** *m* frontier crossing

Greuel ['grɔyəl] (**-s, -**) *m* horror, revulsion; **etw ist jdm ein ~** sb loathes sth

greulich ['grɔylɪç] *adj* horrible

Griech- ['griːç] *zW*: **~e** (**-n, -n**) *m* Greek; **~enland** *nt* Greece; **~in** *f* Greek; **g~isch** *adj* Greek

griesgrämig ['griːsgrɛːmɪç] *adj* grumpy

Grieß [griːs] (**-es, -e**) *m* (*KOCH*) semolina

Griff [grɪf] (**-(e)s, -e**) *m* grip; (*Vorrichtung*) handle; **g~bereit** *adj* handy

Grill [grɪl] *m* grill; **~e** *f* cricket; **g~en** *vt* to grill

Grimasse [gri'masə] *f* grimace

grimmig ['grɪmɪç] *adj* furious; (*heftig*) fierce, severe

grinsen ['grɪnzən] *vi* to grin

Grippe ['grɪpə] *f* influenza, flu

grob [groːp] *adj* coarse, gross; (*Fehler, Verstoß*) gross; **G~heit** *f* coarseness; coarse expression

grölen ['grøːlən] (*pej*) *vt* to bawl, to bellow

Groll [grɔl] (**-(e)s**) *m* resentment; **g~en** *vi* (*Donner*) to rumble; **g~en (mit** *od* +*dat*) to bear ill will (towards)

groß [groːs] *adj* big, large; (*hoch*) tall; (*fig*) great ♦ *adv* greatly; **im ~en und ganzen** on the whole; **~artig** *adj* great,

splendid; **G~aufnahme** *f* (*CINE*) close-up; **G~britannien** *nt* Great Britain

Größe ['grøːsə] *f* size; (*Höhe*) height; (*fig*) greatness

Groß- *zW*: **~einkauf** *m* bulk purchase; **~eltern** *pl* grandparents; **g~enteils** *adv* mostly; **~format** *nt* large size; **~handel** *m* wholesale trade; **~händler** *m* wholesaler; **~macht** *f* great power; **g~mütig** *adj* magnanimous; **~mutter** *f* grandmother; **~rechner** *m* mainframe (computer); **g~schreiben** (*unreg*) *vt* to write in block capitals; **bei jdm g~schreiben werden** to be high on sb's list of priorities; **g~spurig** *adj* pompous; **~stadt** *f* city, large town

größte(r, s) [grøːstə(r, s)] *adj superl von* **groß**; **~nteils** *adv* for the most part

Groß- *zW*: **g~tun** (*unreg*) *vi* to boast; **~vater** *m* grandfather; **g~ziehen** (*unreg*) *vt* to raise; **g~zügig** *adj* generous; (*Planung*) on a large scale

grotesk [gro'tɛsk] *adj* grotesque

Grotte ['grɔtə] *f* grotto

Grübchen ['gryːpçən] *nt* dimple

Grube ['gruːbə] *f* pit; mine

grübeln ['gryːbəln] *vi* to brood

Grubengas *nt* firedamp

Gruft [gruft] (**-, ̈e**) *f* tomb, vault

grün [gryːn] *adj* green; **G~anlage** *f* park

Grund [grunt] (**-(e)s, ̈e**) *m* ground; (*von See, Gefäß*) bottom; (*fig*) reason; **im ~e genommen** basically; **~ausbildung** *f* basic training; **~besitz** *m* land(ed) property), real estate; **~buch** *nt* land register

gründen ['gryndən] *vt* to found ♦ *vr*: **sich ~ (auf** +*dat*) to be based (on); **~ auf** +*akk* to base on

Gründer (**-s, -**) *m* founder

Grund- *zW*: **~gebühr** *f* basic charge; **~gesetz** *nt* constitution; **~lage** *f* foundation; **g~legend** *adj* fundamental

gründlich *adj* thorough

Grund- *zW*: **g~los** *adj* groundless; **~regel** *f* basic rule; **~riß** *m* plan; (*fig*) outline; **~satz** *m* principle; **g~sätzlich** *adj* fundamental; (*Frage*) of principle ♦ *adv* fundamentally; (*prinzipiell*) on principle; **~schule** *f* elementary school; **~stein** *m* foundation stone; **~stück** *nt* estate; plot

Grundwasser *nt* ground water

Grünen *pl* (*POL*): **die ~** the Greens

Grünspan *m* verdigris

Grünstreifen *m* central reservation

grunzen ['grʊntsən] *vi* to grunt

Gruppe ['grʊpə] *f* group; **g~nweise** *adv* in groups

gruppieren [grʊ'piːrən] *vt, vr* to group

gruselig *adj* creepy

gruseln ['gruːzəln] *vi unpers*: **es gruselt jdm vor etw** sth gives sb the creeps ♦ *vr* to have the creeps

Gruß [gruːs] (**-es, ⸚e**) *m* greeting; (*MIL*) salute; **viele Grüße** best wishes; **mit freundlichen Grüßen** yours sincerely; **Grüße an** +*akk* regards to

grüßen ['gryːsən] *vt* to greet; (*MIL*) to salute; **jdn von jdm ~** to give sb sb's regards; **jdn ~ lassen** to send sb one's regards

gucken ['gʊkən] *vi* to look

gültig ['gʏltɪç] *adj* valid; **G~keit** *f* validity

Gummi ['gʊmi] (**-s, -s**) *nt od m* rubber; (**~harze**) gum; **~band** *nt* rubber *od* elastic band; (*Hosen~*) elastic; **~bärchen** ≈ jelly baby (*BRIT*); **~baum** *m* rubber plant; **g~eren** [gʊ'miːrən] *vt* to gum; **~knüppel** *m* rubber truncheon; **~strumpf** *m* elastic stocking

günstig ['gʏnstɪç] *adj* convenient; (*Gelegenheit*) favourable; **das habe ich ~ bekommen** it was a bargain

Gurgel ['gʊrgəl] (**-, -n**) *f* throat; **g~n** *vi* to gurgle; (*im Mund*) to gargle

Gurke ['gʊrkə] *f* cucumber; **saure ~** pickled cucumber, gherkin

Gurt [gʊrt] (**-(e)s, -e**) *m* belt

Gürtel ['gʏrtəl] (**-s, -**) *m* belt; (*GEOG*) zone; **~reifen** *m* radial tyre

GUS *f abk* (= *Gemeinschaft unabhängiger Staaten*) CIS

Guß [gʊs] (**-sses, Güsse**) *m* casting; (*Regen~*) downpour; (*KOCH*) glazing; **~eisen** *nt* cast iron

gut [guːt] *adj* good; **alles Gute** all the best; **also gut** all right then
♦ *adv* well; **gut schmecken** to taste good; **gut, aber ...** OK, but ...; **(na) gut, ich komme** all right, I'll come; **gut drei Stunden** a good three hours; **das kann gut sein** that may well be; **laß es gut sein** that'll do

Gut [guːt] (**-(e)s, ⸚er**) *nt* (*Besitz*) possession; **Güter** *pl* (*Waren*) goods; **~achten** (**-s, -**) *nt* (expert) opinion; **~achter** (**-s, -**) *m* expert; **g~artig** *adj* good-natured; (*MED*) benign; **g~bürgerlich** *adj* (*Küche*) (good) plain; **~dünken** *nt*: **nach ~dünken** at one's discretion

Güte ['gyːtə] *f* goodness, kindness; (*Qualität*) quality

Güter- *zW*: **~abfertigung** *f* (*EISENB*) goods office; **~bahnhof** *m* goods station; **~wagen** *m* goods waggon (*BRIT*), freight car (*US*); **~zug** *m* goods train (*BRIT*), freight train (*US*)

Gütezeichen *nt* quality mark, ≈ kite mark

gut- *zW*: **~gehen** (*unreg*) *vi unpers* to work, to come off; **es geht jdm ~** sb's doing fine; **~gemeint** *adj* well meant; **~gläubig** *adj* trusting; **G~haben** (**-s**) *nt* credit; **~heißen** (*unreg*) *vt* to approve (of)

gütig ['gyːtɪç] *adj* kind

Gut- *zW*: **g~mütig** *adj* good-natured; **~mütigkeit** *f* good nature; **~schein** *m* voucher; **g~schreiben** (*unreg*) *vt* to credit; **g~tun** (*unreg*) *vi*: **jdm g~tun** to do sb good; **g~willig** *adj* willing

Gymnasium [gʏm'naːziʊm] *nt* grammar school (*BRIT*), high school (*US*)

Gymnastik [gʏm'nastɪk] *f* exercises *pl*, keep fit

H h

Haag [haːg] *m*: **Den ~** the Hague

Haar [haːr] (**-(e)s, -e**) *nt* hair; **um ein ~** nearly; **an den ~en herbeigezogen** (*umg*:

Vergleich) very far-fetched; **~bürste** *f* hairbrush; **h~en** *vi, vr* to lose hair; **~esbreite** *f*: **um ~esbreite** by a hair's-breadth; **h~genau** *adv* precisely; **h~ig** *adj* hairy; (*fig*) nasty; **~klammer** *f* hairgrip; **~klemme** *f* hair grip; **~nadel** *f* hairpin; **h~scharf** *adv* (*beobachten*) very sharply; (*daneben*) by a hair's breadth; **~schnitt** *m* haircut; **~spange** *f* hair slide; **h~sträubend** *adj* hair-raising; **~teil** *nt* hairpiece; **~waschmittel** *nt* shampoo

Habe ['ha:bə] (-) *f* property

haben ['ha:bən] (*unreg*) *vt, vb aux* to have; **Hunger/Angst ~** to be hungry/afraid; **woher hast du das?** where did you get that from?; **was hast du denn?** what's the matter (with you)?; **du hast zu schweigen** you're to be quiet; **ich hätte gern** I would like; **H~** (-s, -) *nt* credit

Habgier *f* avarice; **h~ig** *adj* avaricious

Habicht ['ha:bɪçt] (-s, -e) *m* hawk

Habseligkeiten *pl* belongings

Hachse ['haksə] *f* (*KOCH*) knuckle

Hacke ['hakə] *f* hoe; (*Ferse*) heel; **h~n** *vt* to hack, to chop; (*Erde*) to hoe

Hackfleisch *nt* mince, minced meat

Hafen ['ha:fən] (-s, ⏑) *m* harbour, port; **~arbeiter** *m* docker; **~stadt** *f* port

Hafer ['ha:fər] (-s, -) *m* oats *pl*; **~flocken** *pl* rolled oats; **~schleim** *m* gruel

Haft [haft] (-) *f* custody; **h~bar** *adj* liable, responsible; **~befehl** *m* warrant (for arrest); **h~en** *vi* to stick, to cling; **h~en für** to be liable *od* responsible for; **h~enbleiben** (*unreg*) *vi*: **h~enbleiben (an** +*dat*) to stick (to); **Häftling** *m* prisoner; **~pflicht** *f* liability; **~pflichtversicherung** *f* (*AUT*) third party insurance; **~schalen** *pl* contact lenses; **~ung** *f* liability

Hagebutte ['ha:gəbʊtə] *f* rose hip

Hagel ['ha:gəl] (-s) *m* hail; **h~n** *vi unpers* to hail

hager ['ha:gər] *adj* gaunt

Hahn [ha:n] (-(e)s, ⏑e) *m* cock; (*Wasser~*) tap, faucet (*US*)

Hähnchen ['hɛ:nçən] *nt* cockerel; (*KOCH*) chicken

Hai(fisch) ['haɪ(fɪʃ)] (-(e)s, -e) *m* shark

häkeln ['hɛ:kəln] *vt* to crochet

Häkelnadel *f* crochet hook

Haken ['ha:kən] (-s, -) *m* hook; (*fig*) catch; **~kreuz** *nt* swastika; **~nase** *f* hooked nose

halb [halp] *adj* half; **~ eins** half past twelve; **ein ~es Dutzend** half a dozen; **H~dunkel** *nt* semi-darkness

halber ['halbər] *präp* +*gen* (*wegen*) on account of; (*für*) for the sake of

Halb- *zW*: **~heit** *f* half-measure; **h~ieren** *vt* to halve; **~insel** *f* peninsula; **~jahr** *nt* six months; (*auch: Komm*) half-year; **h~jährlich** *adj* half-yearly; **~kreis** *m* semicircle; **~leiter** *m* semiconductor; **~links** (-, -) *m* (*SPORT*) inside left; **~mond** *m* half-moon; (*fig*) crescent; **h~offen** *adj* half-open; **~pension** *f* half-board; **~rechts** (-, -) *m* (*SPORT*) inside right; **~schuh** *m* shoe; **h~tags** *adv*: **h~tags arbeiten** to work part-time, to work mornings/afternoons; **h~wegs** *adv* halfway; **h~wegs besser** more or less better; **~zeit** *f* (*SPORT*) half; (*Pause*) half-time

Halde ['haldə] *f* (*Kohlen*) heap

half [half] *vb siehe* **helfen**

Hälfte ['hɛlftə] *f* half

Halfter[1] ['halftər] (-s, -) *m od nt* (*für Tiere*) halter

Halfter[2] (-, -n *od* -s, -) *f od nt* (*Pistolen~*) holster

Halle ['halə] *f* hall; (*AVIAT*) hangar; **h~n** *vi* to echo, to resound; **~nbad** *nt* indoor swimming pool

hallo [ha'lo:] *excl* hello

Halluzination [halutsinatsi'o:n] *f* hallucination

Halm [halm] (-(e)s, -e) *m* blade; stalk

Hals [hals] (-es, ⏑e) *m* neck; (*Kehle*) throat; **~ über Kopf** in a rush; **~band** *nt* (*von Hund*) collar; **~kette** *f* necklace; **~- Nasen-Ohren-Arzt** *m* ear, nose and throat specialist; **~schmerzen** *pl* sore throat *sg*; **~tuch** *nt* scarf

Halt [halt] (-(e)s, -e) *m* stop; (*fester ~*) hold; (*innerer ~*) stability; **h~** *excl* stop!, halt!; **h~bar** *adj* durable; (*Lebensmittel*) non-perishable; (*MIL, fig*) tenable; **~barkeit**

f durability; (non-)perishability
halten ['haltən] (*unreg*) *vt* to keep; (*fest~*) to hold ♦ *vi* to hold; (*frisch bleiben*) to keep; (*stoppen*) to stop ♦ *vr* (*frisch bleiben*) to keep; (*sich behaupten*) to hold out; **~ für** to regard as; **~ von** to think of; **an sich ~** to restrain o.s.; **sich rechts/ links ~** to keep to the right/left
Haltestelle *f* stop
Halteverbot *nt*: **hier ist ~** there's no waiting here
Halt- *zW*: **h~los** *adj* unstable; **h~machen** *vi* to stop; **~ung** *f* posture; (*fig*) attitude; (*Selbstbeherrschung*) composure
Halunke [ha'luŋkə] (**-n, -n**) *m* rascal
hämisch ['hɛːmɪʃ] *adj* malicious
Hammel ['haməl] (**-s, ⸚ od -**) *m* wether; **~fleisch** *nt* mutton
Hammer ['hamər] (**-s, ⸚**) *m* hammer
hämmern ['hɛmərn] *vt, vi* to hammer
Hämorrhoiden [hɛmɔroˈiːdən] *pl* haemorrhoids
Hampelmann ['hampəlman] *m* (*auch fig*) puppet
Hamster ['hamstər] (**-s, -**) *m* hamster; **~ei** ['-raɪ] *f* hoarding; **h~n** *vi* to hoard
Hand [hant] (**-, ⸚e**) *f* hand; **~arbeit** *f* manual work; (*Nadelarbeit*) needlework; **~ball** *m* (*SPORT*) handball; **~bremse** *f* handbrake; **~buch** *nt* handbook, manual; **~creme** *f* handcream
Händedruck ['hɛndədrʊk] *m* handshake
Handel ['handəl] (**-s**) *m* trade; (*Geschäft*) transaction
Handeln ['handəln] (**-s**) *nt* action
handeln *vi* to trade; (*agieren*) to act ♦ *vr unpers*: **sich ~ um** to be a question of, to be about; **~ von** to be about
Handels- *zW*: **~bilanz** *f* balance of trade; **~kammer** *f* chamber of commerce; **~reisende(r)** *m* commercial traveller; **~schule** *f* business school; **h~üblich** *adj* customary; (*Preis*) going *attrib*; **~vertreter** *m* sales representative
Hand- *zW*: **~feger** (**-s, -**) *m* handbrush; **h~fest** *adj* hefty; **h~gearbeitet** *adj* handmade; **~gemenge** *nt* scuffle; **~gepäck** *nt* hand-luggage;

h~geschrieben *adj* handwritten; **h~greiflich** *adj* palpable; **h~greiflich werden** to become violent; **~granate** *f* hand grenade; **~griff** *m* flick of the wrist; **h~haben** *vt insep* to handle
Händler ['hɛndlər] (**-s, -**) *m* trader, dealer
handlich ['hantlɪç] *adj* handy
Handlung ['handlʊŋ] *f* act(ion); (*in Buch*) plot; (*Geschäft*) shop
Hand- *zW*: **~pflege** *f* manicure; **~schelle** *f* handcuff; **~schrift** *f* handwriting; (*Text*) manuscript; **~schuh** *m* glove; **~stand** *m* (*SPORT*) handstand; **~tasche** *f* handbag; **~tuch** *nt* towel; **~umdrehen** *nt*: **im ~umdrehen** in the twinkling of an eye; **~werk** *nt* trade, craft; **~werker** (**-s, -**) *m* craftsman, artisan; **~werkzeug** *nt* tools *pl*
Hanf [hanf] (**-(e)s**) *m* hemp
Hang [haŋ] (**-(e)s, ⸚e**) *m* inclination; (*Ab~*) slope
Hänge- ['hɛŋə] *in zW* hanging; **~brücke** *f* suspension bridge; **~matte** *f* hammock
hängen ['hɛŋən] *vi* (*unreg*) to hang ♦ *vt*: **etw (an etw *akk*) ~** to hang sth (on sth); **~ an** +*dat* (*fig*) to be attached to; **sich ~ an** +*akk* to hang on to, to cling to; **~bleiben** (*unreg*) *vi* to be caught; (*fig*) to remain, to stick; **~bleiben an** +*dat* to catch *od* get caught on; **~lassen** (*unreg*) *vt* (*vergessen*) to leave; **den Kopf ~lassen** to get downhearted
Hannover [ha'noːfər] (**-s**) *nt* Hanover
hänseln ['hɛnzəln] *vt* to tease
Hansestadt ['hanzəʃtat] *f* Hanse town
hantieren [han'tiːrən] *vi* to work, to be busy; **mit etw ~** to handle sth
hapern ['haːpərn] *vi unpers*: **es hapert an etw** *dat* there is a lack of sth
Happen ['hapən] (**-s, -**) *m* mouthful
Harfe ['harfə] *f* harp
Harke ['harkə] *f* rake; **h~n** *vt, vi* to rake
harmlos ['harmloːs] *adj* harmless; **H~igkeit** *f* harmlessness
Harmonie [harmoˈniː] *f* harmony; **h~ren** *vi* to harmonize
Harmonika [har'moːnika] (**-, -s**) *f* (*Zieh~*) concertina
harmonisch [har'moːnɪʃ] *adj*

harmonious

Harmonium [har'mo:niʊm] (-s, -nien *od* -s) *nt* harmonium

Harn [harn] (-(e)s, -e) *m* urine; **~blase** *f* bladder

Harpune [har'pu:nə] *f* harpoon

harren ['harən] *vi:* ~ **(auf** +*akk*) to wait (for)

hart [hart] *adj* hard; *(fig)* harsh

Härte ['hɛrtə] *f* hardness; *(fig)* harshness

hart- *zW:* **~gekocht** *adj* hard-boiled; **~herzig** *adj* hard-hearted; **~näckig** *adj* stubborn; **H~näckigkeit** *f* stubbornness; **H~platte** *f* hard disk

Harz [ha:rts] (-es, -e) *nt* resin

Haschee [ha'ʃe:] (-s, -s) *nt* hash

Haschisch ['haʃɪʃ] (-) *nt* hashish

Hase ['ha:zə] (-n, -n) *m* hare

Haselnuß ['ha:zəlnʊs] *f* hazelnut

Hasenfuß *m* coward

Hasenscharte *f* harelip

Haß [has] (-sses) *m* hate, hatred

hassen ['hasən] *vt* to hate

häßlich ['hɛslɪç] *adj* ugly; *(gemein)* nasty; **H~keit** *f* ugliness; nastiness

Hast [hast] *f* haste

hast *vb siehe* **haben**

hasten *vi* to rush

hastig *adj* hasty

hat [hat] *vb siehe* **haben**

hatte *etc* ['hatə] *vb siehe* **haben**

Haube ['haʊbə] *f* hood; *(Mütze)* cap; *(AUT)* bonnet, hood *(US)*

Hauch [haʊx] (-(e)s, -e) *m* breath; *(Luft~)* breeze; *(fig)* trace; **h~dünn** *adj* extremely thin; **h~en** *vi* to breathe

Haue ['haʊə] *f* hoe, pick; *(umg)* hiding; **h~n** *(unreg) vt* to hew, to cut; *(umg)* to thrash

Haufen ['haʊfən] (-s, -) *m* heap; *(Leute)* crowd; **ein** ~ **(x)** *(umg)* loads *od* a lot (of x); **auf einem** ~ in one heap

häufen ['hɔyfən] *vt* to pile up ♦ *vr* to accumulate

haufenweise *adv* in heaps; in droves; **etw** ~ **haben** to have piles of sth

häufig ['hɔyfɪç] *adj* frequent ♦ *adv* frequently; **H~keit** *f* frequency

Haupt [haʊpt] (-(e)s, **Häupter**) *nt* head;

(Ober~) chief ♦ *in zW* main; **~bahnhof** *m* central station; **h~beruflich** *adv* as one's main occupation; **~darsteller(in)** *m(f)* leading actor (actress); **~eingang** *m* main entrance; **~fach** *nt* (*SCH, UNIV*) main subject, major *(US)*; **~film** *m* main film; **~gericht** *nt* (*KOCH*) main course

Häuptling ['hɔyptlɪŋ] *m* chief(tain)

Haupt- *zW:* **~mann** *(pl* **-leute)** *m* (*MIL*) captain; **~person** *f* central figure; **~quartier** *nt* headquarters *pl*; **~rolle** *f* leading part; **~sache** *f* main thing; **h~sächlich** *adj* chief ♦ *adv* chiefly; **~saison** *f* high season, peak season; **~schule** *f* ≈ secondary school; **~stadt** *f* capital; **~straße** *f* main street; **~verkehrszeit** *f* rush-hour, peak traffic hours *pl*; **~wort** *nt* noun

Haus [haʊs] (-es, **Häuser**) *nt* house; **nach ~e** home; **zu ~e** at home; **~angestellte** *f* domestic servant; **~apotheke** *f* medicine cabinet; **~arbeit** *f* housework; *(SCH)* homework; **~arzt** *m* family doctor; **~aufgabe** *f* (*SCH*) homework; **~besitzer(in)** *m(f)* house-owner; **~besuch** *m* (*von Arzt*) house call

Häuserblock ['hɔyzərblɔk] *m* block (of houses)

Häusermakler ['hɔyzər-] *m* estate agent *(BRIT)*, real estate agent *(US)*

Haus- *zW:* **~frau** *f* housewife; **~flur** *m* hallway; **h~gemacht** *adj* home-made; **~halt** *m* household; *(POL)* budget; **h~halten** *(unreg) vi (sparen)* to economize; **~hälterin** *f* housekeeper; **~haltsgeld** *nt* housekeeping (money); **~haltsgerät** *nt* domestic appliance; **~herr** *m* host; *(Vermieter)* landlord; **h~hoch** *adv:* **h~hoch verlieren** to lose by a mile

hausieren [haʊ'zi:rən] *vi* to peddle

Hausierer (-s, -) *m* peddlar

häuslich ['hɔyslɪç] *adj* domestic

Haus- *zW:* **~meister** *m* caretaker, janitor; **~nummer** *f* street number; **~ordnung** *f* house rules *pl*; **~putz** *m* house cleaning; **~schlüssel** *m* front-door key; **~schuh** *m* slipper; **~suchung** *f* police raid; **~tier** *nt* pet; **~tür** *f* front door; **~wirt** *m* landlord; **~wirtschaft** *f* domestic science

Haut [haut] (-, **Häute**) *f* skin; (*Tier~*) hide; **~creme** *f* skin cream; **h~eng** *adj* skin-tight; **~farbe** *f* complexion; **~krebs** *m* skin cancer

Haxe ['haksə] *f* = **Hachse**

Hbf *abk* = **Hauptbahnhof**

Hebamme ['he:p'amə] *f* midwife

Hebel ['he:bəl] (-s, -) *m* lever

heben ['he:bən] (*unreg*) *vt* to raise, to lift

Hecht [hɛçt] (-(e)s, -e) *m* pike

Heck [hɛk] (-(e)s, -e) *nt* stern; (*von Auto*) rear

Hecke ['hɛkə] *f* hedge

Heckenrose *f* dog rose

Heckenschütze *m* sniper

Heer [he:r] (-(e)s, -e) *nt* army

Hefe ['he:fə] *f* yeast

Heft [hɛft] (-(e)s, -e) *nt* exercise book; (*Zeitschrift*) number; (*von Messer*) haft

heften *vt*: **~ (an** +*akk*) to fasten (to); (*nähen*) to tack ((on) to); **etw an etw** *akk* **~** to fasten sth to sth

Hefter (-s, -) *m* folder

heftig *adj* fierce, violent; **H~keit** *f* fierceness, violence

Heft- *zW:* **~klammer** *f* paper clip; **~maschine** *f* stapling machine; **~pflaster** *nt* sticking plaster; **~zwecke** *f* drawing pin

hegen ['he:gən] *vt* (*Wild, Bäume*) to care for, to tend; (*fig, geh: empfinden: Wunsch*) to cherish; (: *Mißtrauen*) to feel

Hehl [he:l] *m od nt*: **kein(en) ~ aus etw machen** to make no secret of sth; **~er** (-s, -) *m* receiver (of stolen goods), fence

Heide[1] ['haidə] *f* heath, moor; (*~kraut*) heather

Heide[2] (-n, -n) *m* heathen, pagan

Heidekraut *nt* heather

Heidelbeere *f* bilberry

Heidentum *nt* paganism

Heidin *f* heathen, pagan

heikel ['haikəl] *adj* awkward, thorny; (*wählerisch*) fussy

Heil [hail] (-(e)s) *nt* well-being; (*Seelen~*) salvation; **h~** *adj* in one piece, intact; **~and** (-(e)s, -e) *m* saviour; **h~bar** *adj*

curable; **h~en** *vt* to cure ♦ *vi* to heal; **h~froh** *adj* very relieved

heilig ['hailiç] *adj* holy; **H~abend** *m* Christmas Eve; **H~e(r)** *mf* saint; **~en** *vt* to sanctify, to hallow; **H~enschein** *m* halo; **H~keit** *f* holiness; **~sprechen** (*unreg*) *vt* to canonize; **H~tum** *nt* shrine; (*Gegenstand*) relic

Heil- *zW:* **h~los** *adj* unholy; (*fig*) hopeless; **~mittel** *nt* remedy; **~praktiker(in)** *m(f)* non-medical practitioner; **h~sam** *adj* (*fig*) salutary; **~sarmee** *f* Salvation Army; **~ung** *f* cure

Heim [haim] (-(e)s, -e) *nt* home; **h~** *adv* home

Heimat ['haima:t] (-, -en) *f* home (town/country *etc*); **~land** *nt* homeland; **h~lich** *adj* native; (*Gefühle*) nostalgic; **h~los** *adj* homeless; **~ort** *m* home town/area; **~vertriebene(r)** *mf* displaced person

Heim- *zW:* **~computer** *m* home computer; **h~elig** *adj* cosy; **h~fahren** (*unreg*) *vi* to drive home; **~fahrt** *f* journey home; **h~gehen** (*unreg*) *vi* to go home; (*sterben*) to pass away; **h~isch** *adj* (*gebürtig*) native; **sich h~isch fühlen** to feel at home; **~kehr** (-, -en) *f* homecoming; **h~kehren** *vi* to return home; **h~lich** *adj* secret; **~lichkeit** *f* secrecy; **~reise** *f* journey home; **~spiel** *nt* (*SPORT*) home game; **h~suchen** *vt* to afflict; (*Geist*) to haunt; **~trainer** *m* exercise bike; **h~tückisch** *adj* malicious; **~weg** *m* way home; **~weh** *nt* homesickness; **h~zahlen** *vt*: **jdm etw h~zahlen** to pay sb back for sth

Heirat ['haira:t] (-, -en) *f* marriage; **h~en** *vt* to marry ♦ *vi* to marry, to get married ♦ *vr* to get married; **~santrag** *m* proposal

heiser ['haizər] *adj* hoarse; **H~keit** *f* hoarseness

heiß [hais] *adj* hot; **~e(s) Eisen** (*umg*) hot potato; **h~blütig** *adj* hot-blooded

heißen ['haisən] (*unreg*) *vi* to be called; (*bedeuten*) to mean ♦ *vt* to command; (*nennen*) to name ♦ *vi unpers*: **es heißt** it says; it is said; **das heißt** that is (to say)

Heißhunger *m* ravenous hunger
heißlaufen (*unreg*) *vi, vr* to overheat
Heißmangel *f* rotary iron
heiter ['haɪtər] *adj* cheerful; (*Wetter*)
bright; **H~keit** *f* cheerfulness;
(*Belustigung*) amusement
Heiz- ['haɪts] *zW:* **h~bar** *adj* heated;
(*Raum*) with heating; **h~en** *vt* to heat;
~er (*-s, -*) *m* stoker; **~körper** *m* radiator;
~öl *nt* fuel oil; **~sonne** *f* electric fire;
~ung *f* heating; **~ungsanlage** *f* heating
system
hektisch ['hɛktɪʃ] *adj* hectic
Held [hɛlt] (*-en, -en*) *m* hero; **h~enhaft**
adj heroic; **~in** *f* heroine
helfen ['hɛlfən] (*unreg*) *vi* to help;
(*nützen*) to be of use ♦ *vb unpers:* **es hilft
nichts, du mußt ...** it's no use, you'll
have to ...; **jdm (bei etw) ~** to help sb
(with sth); **sich** *dat* **zu ~ wissen** to be
resourceful
Helfer (*-s, -*) *m* helper, assistant;
Helfershelfer *m* accomplice
hell [hɛl] *adj* clear, bright; (*Farbe, Bier*)
light; (*Haar*) light blue; **~blond** *adj*
ash-blond; **H~e** (*-*) *f* clearness, brightness;
~hörig *adj* (*Wand*) paper-thin; **~hörig
werden** (*fig*) to prick up one's ears;
H~seher *m* clairvoyant; **~wach** *adj*
wide-awake
Helm [hɛlm] (*-(e)s, -e*) *m* (*auf Kopf*)
helmet
Hemd [hɛmt] (*-(e)s, -en*) *nt* shirt;
(*Unter~*) vest; **~bluse** *f* blouse
hemmen ['hɛmən] *vt* to check, to hold
up; **gehemmt sein** to be inhibited
Hemmung *f* check; (*PSYCH*) inhibition;
h~slos *adj* unrestrained, without
restraint
Hengst [hɛŋst] (*-es, -e*) *m* stallion
Henkel ['hɛŋkəl] (*-s, -*) *m* handle
Henker (*-s, -*) *m* hangman
Henne ['hɛnə] *f* hen

SCHLÜSSELWORT

her [heːr] *adv* **1** (*Richtung*): **komm her zu
mir** come here (to me); **von England her**
from England; **von weit her** from a long
way away; **her damit!** hand it over!; **wo**

hat er das her? where did he get that
from?
2 (*Blickpunkt*): **von der Form her** as far
as the form is concerned
3 (*zeitlich*): **das ist 5 Jahre her** that was
5 years ago; **wo bist du her?** where do
you come from?; **ich kenne ihn von
früher her** I know him from before

herab [hɛ'rap] *adv* down(ward(s));
~hängen (*unreg*) *vi* to hang down;
~lassen (*unreg*) *vi* to let down ♦ *vr* to
condescend; **~lassend** *adj* condescending;
~setzen *vt* to lower, to reduce; (*fig*) to
belittle, to disparage
heran [hɛ'ran] *adv:* **näher ~!** come up
closer!; **~ zu mir!** come up to me!;
~bringen (*unreg*) *vt:* **~bringen (an** +*akk*)
to bring up (to); **~fahren** (*unreg*) *vi:*
~fahren (an +*akk*) to drive up (to);
~kommen (*unreg*) *vi:* **(an jdn/etw)
~kommen** to approach (sb/sth), to come
near (to sb/sth); **~machen** *vr:* **sich an
jdn ~machen** to make up to sb; **~treten**
(*unreg*) *vi:* **mit etw an jdn ~treten** to
approach sb with sth; **~wachsen** (*unreg*)
vi to grow up; **~ziehen** (*unreg*) *vt* to pull
nearer; (*aufziehen*) to raise; (*ausbilden*) to
train; **jdn zu etw ~ziehen** to call upon sb
to help in sth
herauf [hɛ'raʊf] *adv* up(ward(s)), up here;
~beschwören (*unreg*) *vt* to conjure up,
to evoke; **~bringen** (*unreg*) *vt* to bring
up; **~setzen** *vt* (*Preise, Miete*) to raise,
put up
heraus [hɛ'raʊs] *adv* out; **~bekommen**
(*unreg*) *vt* to get out; (*fig*) to find *od* figure
out; **~bringen** (*unreg*) *vt* to bring out;
(*Geheimnis*) to elicit; **~finden** (*unreg*) *vt*
to find out; **~fordern** *vt* to challenge;
H~forderung *f* challenge; provocation;
~geben (*unreg*) *vt* to hand over, to
surrender; (*zurückgeben*) to give back;
(*Buch*) to edit; (*veröffentlichen*) to publish;
H~geber (*-s, -*) *m* editor; (*Verleger*)
publisher; **~gehen** (*unreg*) *vi:* **aus sich
~gehen** to come out of one's shell;
~halten (*unreg*) *vr:* **sich aus etw
~halten** to keep out of sth; **~hängen**[1] *vt*

to hang out; **~hängen**[2] (*unreg*) *vi* to hang out; **~holen** *vt*: **~holen (aus)** to get out (of); **~kommen** (*unreg*) *vi* to come out; **dabei kommt nichts ~** nothing will come of it; **~nehmen** (*unreg*) *vt* to remove (from), take out (of); **sich** *dat* **etw ~nehmen** to take liberties; **~reißen** (*unreg*) *vt* to tear out; to pull out; **~rücken** *vt* (*Geld*) to fork out, to hand over; **mit etw ~rücken** (*fig*) to come out with sth; **~stellen** *vr*: **sich ~stellen (als)** to turn out (to be); **~suchen** *vt*: **sich** *dat* **jdn/etw ~suchen** to pick sb/sth out; **~ziehen** (*unreg*) *vt* to pull out, to extract

herb [hɛrp] *adj* (slightly) bitter, acid; (*Wein*) dry; (*fig: schmerzlich*) bitter; (: *streng*) stern, austere

herbei [hɛr'baɪ] *adv* (over) here; **~führen** *vt* to bring about; **~schaffen** *vt* to procure

herbemühen ['heːrbəmyːən] *vr* to take the trouble to come

Herberge ['hɛrbɛrgə] *f* shelter; hostel, inn

Herbergsmutter *f* warden

Herbergsvater *m* warden

herbitten (*unreg*) *vt* to ask to come (here)

herbringen (*unreg*) *vt* to bring here

Herbst [hɛrpst] (**-(e)s, -e**) *m* autumn, fall (*US*); **h~lich** *adj* autumnal

Herd [heːrt] (**-(e)s, -e**) *m* cooker; (*fig, MED*) focus, centre

Herde ['heːrdə] *f* herd; (*Schaf~*) flock

herein [hɛ'raɪn] *adv* in (here), here; **~!** come in!; **~bitten** (*unreg*) *vt* to ask in; **~brechen** (*unreg*) *vi* to set in; **~bringen** (*unreg*) *vt* to bring in; **~fallen** (*unreg*) *vi* to be caught, to be taken in; **~fallen auf** +*akk* to fall for; **~kommen** (*unreg*) *vi* to come in; **~lassen** (*unreg*) *vt* to admit; **~legen** *vt*: **jdn ~legen** to take sb in; **~platzen** (*umg*) *vi* to burst in

Her- *zW*: **~fahrt** *f* journey here; **h~fallen** (*unreg*) *vi*: **h~fallen über** +*akk* to fall upon; **~gang** *m* course of events; **h~geben** (*unreg*) *vt* to give, to hand (over); **sich zu etw h~geben** to lend one's name to sth; **h~gehen** (*unreg*) *vi*:

hinter jdm hergehen to follow sb; **es geht hoch h~** there are a lot of goings-on; **h~halten** (*unreg*) *vt* to hold out; **h~halten müssen** (*umg*) to have to suffer; **h~hören** *vi* to listen

Hering ['heːrɪŋ] (**-s, -e**) *m* herring

her- [hɛr] *zW*: **~kommen** (*unreg*) *vi* to come; **komm mal ~!** come here!; **~kömmlich** *adj* traditional; **H~kunft** (**-, -künfte**) *f* origin; **~laufen** (*unreg*) *vi*: **~laufen hinter** +*dat* to run after

Hermelin [hɛrmə'liːn] (**-s, -e**) *m od nt* ermine

hermetisch [hɛr'meːtɪʃ] *adj* hermetic ♦ *adv* hermetically

her'nach *adv* afterwards

Heroin [hero'iːn] (**-s**) *nt* heroin

Herr [hɛr] (**-(e)n, -en**) *m* master; (*Mann*) gentleman; (*REL*) Lord; (*vor Namen*) Mr.; **mein ~!** sir!; **meine ~en!** gentlemen!; **~endoppel** *nt* men's doubles; **~eneinzel** *nt* men's singles; **~enhaus** *nt* mansion; **~enkonfektion** *f* menswear; **h~enlos** *adj* ownerless

herrichten ['hɛrrɪçtən] *vt* to prepare

Herr- *zW*: **~in** *f* mistress; **h~isch** *adj* domineering; **h~lich** *adj* marvellous, splendid; **~lichkeit** *f* splendour, magnificence; **~schaft** *f* power, rule; (*Herr und Herrin*) master and mistress; **meine ~schaften!** ladies and gentlemen!

herrschen ['hɛrʃən] *vi* to rule; (*bestehen*) to prevail, to be

Herrscher(in) (**-s, -**) *m(f)* ruler

her- *zW*: **~rühren** *vi* to arise, to originate; **~sagen** *vt* to recite; **~stellen** *vt* to make, to manufacture; **H~steller** (**-s, -**) *m* manufacturer; **H~stellung** *f* manufacture

herüber [hɛ'ryːbər] *adv* over (here), across

herum [hɛ'rʊm] *adv* about, (a)round; **um etw ~** around sth; **~führen** *vt* to show around; **~gehen** (*unreg*) *vi* to walk about; **um etw ~gehen** to walk *od* go round sth; **~kommen** (*unreg*) *vi* (*um Kurve etc*) to come round, to turn (round); **~kriegen** (*umg*) *vt* to bring *od* talk around; **~lungern** (*umg*) *vi* to hang about *od* around; **~sprechen** (*unreg*) *vr* to get around, to be spread; **~treiben** *vi, vr* to drift about; **~ziehen** *vi, vr* to wander about

herunter [hɛ'rʊntər] *adv* downward(s), down (there); **~gekommen** *adj* rundown; **~kommen** (*unreg*) *vi* to come down; (*fig*) to come down in the world; **~machen** *vt* to take down; (*schimpfen*) to have a go at

hervor [hɛr'foːr] *adv* out, forth; **~bringen** (*unreg*) *vt* to produce; (*Wort*) to utter; **~gehen** (*unreg*) *vi* to emerge, to result; **~heben** (*unreg*) *vt* to stress; (*als Kontrast*) to set off; **~ragend** *adj* (*fig*) excellent; **~rufen** (*unreg*) *vt* to cause, to give rise to; **~treten** (*unreg*) *vi* to come out (from behind/between/below); (*Adern*) to be prominent

Herz [hɛrts] (**-ens, -en**) *nt* heart; (*KARTEN*) hearts *pl*; **~anfall** *m* heart attack; **~enslust** *f*: **nach ~enslust** to one's heart's content; **~fehler** *m* heart defect; **h~haft** *adj* hearty

herziehen ['hɛr'tsiːən] (*unreg*) *vi*: **über jdn/etw ~** (*umg: auch fig*) to pull sb/sth to pieces (*inf*)

Herz- zW: ~infarkt *m* heart attack; **~klopfen** *nt* palpitation; **h~lich** *adj* cordial; **h~lichen Glückwunsch** congratulations *pl*; **h~liche Grüße** best wishes; **~los** *adj* heartless

Herzog ['hɛrtsoːk] (**-(e)s, ⁻e**) *m* duke; **~tum** *nt* duchy

Herzschlag *m* heartbeat; (*MED*) heart attack

herzzerreißend *adj* heartrending

Hessen ['hɛsən] (**-s**) *nt* Hesse

hessisch *adj* Hessian

Hetze ['hɛtsə] *f* (*Eile*) rush; **h~n** *vt* to hunt; (*verfolgen*) to chase ♦ *vi* (*eilen*) to rush; **jdn/etw auf jdn/etw h~n** to set sb/sth on sb/sth; **h~n gegen** to stir up feeling against; **h~n zu** to agitate for; **~'rei** *f* agitation; (*Eile*) rush

Heu [hɔy] (**-(e)s**) *nt* hay; **Geld wie ~** stacks of money; **~boden** *m* hayloft

Heuchelei [hɔyçə'laɪ] *f* hypocrisy

heucheln ['hɔyçəln] *vt* to pretend, to feign ♦ *vi* to be hypocritical

Heuchler(in) ['hɔyçlər(ɪn)] (**-s, -**) *m(f)* hypocrite; **h~isch** *adj* hypocritical

heulen ['hɔylən] *vi* to howl; to cry; **das ~de Elend bekommen** to get the blues

Heurige(r) ['hɔyrɪɡə(r)] *m* new wine

Heuschnupfen *m* hay fever

Heuschrecke ['hɔyʃrɛkə] *f* grasshopper; locust

heute ['hɔytə] *adv* today; **~ abend/früh** this evening/morning

heutig ['hɔytɪç] *adj* today's

heutzutage ['hɔyttsutaːɡə] *adv* nowadays

Hexe ['hɛksə] *f* witch; **h~n** *vi* to practise witchcraft; **ich kann doch nicht h~n** I can't work miracles; **~nschuß** *m* lumbago; **~'rei** *f* witchcraft

Hieb [hiːp] (**-(e)s, -e**) *m* blow; (*Wunde*) cut, gash; (*Stichelei*) cutting remark; **~e bekommen** to get a thrashing

hielt *etc* [hiːlt] *vb siehe* **halten**

hier [hiːr] *adv* here; **~auf** *adv* thereupon; (*danach*) after that; **~behalten** (*unreg*) *vt* to keep here; **~bei** *adv* herewith, enclosed; **~bleiben** (*unreg*) *vi* to stay here; **~durch** *adv* by this means; (*örtlich*) through here; **~her** *adv* this way, here; **~hin** *adv* here; **~lassen** (*unreg*) *vt* to leave here; **~mit** *adv* hereby; **~nach** *adv* hereafter; **~von** *adv* about this, hereof; **~zulande** *adv* in this country

hiesig ['hiːzɪç] *adj* of this place, local

hieß *etc* [hiːs] *vb siehe* **heißen**

Hilfe ['hɪlfə] *f* help; aid; **Erste ~** first aid; **~!** help!

Hilf- zW: h~los *adj* helpless; **~losigkeit** *f* helplessness; **h~reich** *adj* helpful

Hilfs- zW: ~arbeiter *m* labourer; **h~bedürftig** *adj* needy; **h~bereit** *adj* ready to help; **~kraft** *f* assistant, helper

hilfst [hɪlfst] *vb siehe* **helfen**

Himbeere ['hɪmbeːrə] *f* raspberry

Himmel ['hɪməl] (**-s, -**) *m* sky; (*REL, liter*) heaven; **~bett** *nt* four-poster bed; **h~blau** *adj* sky-blue; **~fahrt** *f* Ascension; **~srichtung** *f* direction

himmlisch ['hɪmlɪʃ] *adj* heavenly

SCHLÜSSELWORT

hin [hɪn] *adv* **1** (*Richtung*): **hin und zurück** there and back; **hin und her** to and fro; **bis zur Mauer hin** up to the wall; **wo ist er hin?** where has he gone?; **Geld hin, Geld her** money or no money **2** (*auf ... hin*): **auf meine Bitte hin** at my request; **auf seinen Rat hin** on the basis of his advice **3**: **mein Glück ist hin** my happiness has gone

---

hinab [hɪˈnap] *adv* down; **~gehen** (*unreg*) *vi* to go down; **~sehen** (*unreg*) *vi* to look down

hinauf [hɪˈnauf] *adv* up; **~arbeiten** *vr* to work one's way up; **~steigen** (*unreg*) *vi* to climb

hinaus [hɪˈnaʊs] *adv* out; **~gehen** (*unreg*) *vi* to go out; **~gehen über** +*akk* to exceed; **~laufen** (*unreg*) *vi* to run out; **~laufen auf** +*akk* to come to, to amount to; **~schieben** (*unreg*) *vt* to put off, to postpone; **~werfen** (*unreg*) *vt* (*Gegenstand, Person*) to throw out; **~wollen** *vi* to want to go out; **~wollen auf** +*akk* to drive at, to get at

Hinblick [ˈhɪnblɪk] *m*: **in** *od* **im ~ auf** +*akk* in view of

hinder- [ˈhɪndər] *zW*: **~lich** *adj* to be a hindrance *od* nuisance; **~n** *vt* to hinder, to hamper; **jdn an etw** *dat* **~n** to prevent sb from doing sth; **H~nis** (-ses, -se) *nt* obstacle; **H~nisrennen** *nt* steeplechase

hindeuten [ˈhɪndɔʏtən] *vi*: **~ auf** +*akk* to point to

hindurch [hɪnˈdʊrç] *adv* through; across; (*zeitlich*) through(out)

hinein [hɪˈnaɪn] *adv* in; **~fallen** (*unreg*) *vi* to fall in; **~fallen in** +*akk* to fall into; **~gehen** (*unreg*) *vi* to go in; **~gehen in** +*akk* to go into, to enter; **~geraten** (*unreg*) *vi*: **~geraten in** +*akk* to get into; **~passen** *vi* to fit in; **~passen in** +*akk* to fit into; (*fig*) to fit in with; **~steigern** *vr* to get worked up; **~versetzen** *vr*: **sich ~versetzen in** +*akk* to put o.s. in the position of; **~ziehen** (*unreg*) *vt* to pull in

♦ *vi* to go in

hin- [ˈhɪn] *zW*: **~fahren** (*unreg*) *vi* to go; to drive **♦** *vt* to take; to drive; **H~fahrt** *f* journey there; **~fallen** (*unreg*) *vi* to fall (down); **~fällig** *adj* frail; (*fig: ungültig*) invalid; **H~flug** *m* outward flight; **~gabe** *f* devotion; **~geben** (*unreg*) *vr* +*dat* to give o.s. up to, to devote o.s. to; **~gehen** (*unreg*) *vi* to go; (*Zeit*) to pass; **~halten** (*unreg*) *vt* to hold out; (*warten lassen*) to put off, to stall

hinken [ˈhɪŋkən] *vi* to limp; (*Vergleich*) to be unconvincing

hinkommen (*unreg*) *vi* (*an Ort*) to arrive

hin- [ˈhɪn] *zW*: **~legen** *vt* to put down **♦** *vr* to lie down; **~nehmen** (*unreg*) *vt* (*fig*) to put up with, to take; **H~reise** *f* journey out; **~reißen** (*unreg*) *vt* to carry away, to enrapture; **sich ~reißen lassen, etw zu tun** to get carried away and do sth; **~richten** *vt* to execute; **H~richtung** *f* execution; **~setzen** *vt* to put down **♦** *vr* to sit down; **~sichtlich** *präp* +*gen* with regard to; **~stellen** *vt* to put (down) **♦** *vr* to place o.s.

hinanstellen [hɪntˈʔanʃtɛlən] *vt* (*fig*) to ignore

hinten [ˈhɪntən] *adv* at the back; behind; **~herum** *adv* round the back; (*fig*) secretly

hinter [ˈhɪntər] *präp* (+*dat od akk*) behind; (: *nach*) after; **~ jdm hersein** to be after sb; **H~achse** *f* rear axle; **H~bliebene(r)** *mf* surviving relative; **~e(r, s)** *adj* rear, back; **~einander** *adv* one after the other; **H~gedanke** *m* ulterior motive; **~'gehen** (*unreg*) *vt untr* to deceive; **H~grund** *m* background; **H~halt** *m* ambush; **~hältig** *adj* underhand, sneaky; **~her** *adv* afterwards, after; **H~hof** *m* backyard; **H~kopf** *m* back of one's head; **~'lassen** (*unreg*) *vt* to leave; **~'legen** *vt* to deposit; **H~list** *f* cunning, trickery; (*Handlung*) trick, dodge; **~listig** *adj* cunning, crafty; **H~mann** *m* person behind; **H~rad** *nt* back wheel; **H~radantrieb** *m* (*AUT*) rear wheel drive; **~rücks** *adv* from behind; **H~tür** *f* back door; (*fig: Ausweg*) loophole;

~'ziehen (*unreg*) *vt* (*Steuern*) to evade
hinüber [hɪ'nyːbər] *adv* across, over;
~**gehen** (*unreg*) *vi* to go over *od* across
hinunter [hɪ'nʊntər] *adv* down; ~**bringen**
(*unreg*) *vt* to take down; ~**schlucken** *vt*
(*auch fig*) to swallow; ~**steigen** (*unreg*) *vi*
to descend
Hinweg ['hɪnveːk] *m* journey out
hinweghelfen [hɪn'vɛk-] (*unreg*) *vi*: jdm
über etw *akk* ~ to help sb to get over sth
hinwegsetzen [hɪn'vɛk-] *vr*: sich ~
über +*akk* to disregard
hin- ['hɪn] *zW*: **H~weis** (**-es, -e**) *m*
(*Andeutung*) hint; (*Anweisung*)
instruction; (*Verweis*) reference; ~**weisen**
(*unreg*) *vi*: ~**weisen auf** +*akk* (*anzeigen*)
to point to; (*sagen*) to point out, to refer
to; ~**werfen** (*unreg*) *vt* to throw down;
~**ziehen** (*unreg*) *vr* (*fig*) to drag on
hinzu [hɪn'tsuː] *adv* in addition; ~**fügen**
vt to add; ~**kommen** (*unreg*) *vi* (*Mensch*)
to arrive, to turn up; (*Umstand*) to ensue
Hirn [hɪrn] (**-(e)s, -e**) *nt* brain(s);
~**gespinst** (**-(e)s, -e**) *nt* fantasy
Hirsch [hɪrʃ] (**-(e)s, -e**) *m* stag
Hirse ['hɪrzə] *f* millet
Hirt [hɪrt] (**-en, -en**) *m* herdsman; (*Schaf~*,
fig) shepherd
Hirte (**-n, -n**) *m* (*lit*) **siehe Hirt**
hissen ['hɪsən] *vt* to hoist
Historiker [hɪs'toːrikər] (**-s, -**) *m*
historian
historisch [hɪs'toːrɪʃ] *adj* historical
Hitze ['hɪtsə] (**-**) *f* heat; h~**beständig** *adj*
heat-resistant; h~**frei** *adj*: h~**frei haben**
to have time off school because of
excessively hot weather; ~**welle** *f* heat
wave
hitzig ['hɪtsɪç] *adj* hot-tempered; (*Debatte*)
heated
Hitzkopf *m* hothead
Hitzschlag *m* heatstroke
hl. *abk von* **heilig**
hm [(h)m] *excl* hm
Hobby ['hɔbɪ] *nt* hobby
Hobel ['hoːbəl] (**-s, -**) *m* plane; ~**bank** *f*
carpenter's bench; h~**n** *vt, vi* to plane;
~**späne** *pl* wood shavings
Hoch (**-s, -s**) *nt* (*Ruf*) cheer; (*MET*)
anticyclone

hoch [hoːx] (*attrib* **hohe(r, s)**) *adj* high;
~**achten** *vt* to respect; **H~achtung** *f*
respect, esteem; ~**achtungsvoll** *adv*
yours faithfully; **H~amt** *nt* high mass;
~**arbeiten** *vr* to work one's way up;
~**begabt** *adj* extremely gifted;
H~betrieb *m* intense activity; (*COMM*)
peak time; **H~burg** *f* stronghold;
H~deutsch *nt* High German; ~**dotiert**
adj highly paid; **H~druck** *m* high
pressure; **H~ebene** *f* plateau; **H~form** *f*
top form; **H~glanz** *m* (*PHOT*) high gloss
print; **etw auf H~glanz bringen** to make
sth sparkle like new; ~**halten** (*unreg*) *vt*
to hold up; (*fig*) to uphold, to cherish;
H~haus *nt* multi-storey building;
~**heben** (*unreg*) *vt* to lift (up);
H~konjunktur *f* boom; **H~land** *nt*
highlands *pl*; ~**leben** *vi*: **jdn ~leben**
lassen to give sb three cheers; **H~mut** *m*
pride; ~**mütig** *adj* proud, haughty;
~**näsig** *adj* stuck-up, snooty; **H~ofen** *m*
blast furnace; ~**prozentig** *adj* (*Alkohol*)
strong; **H~rechnung** *f* projection;
H~saison *f* high season; **H~schule** *f*
college; university; **H~sommer** *m* middle
of summer; **H~spannung** *f* high tension;
H~sprung *m* high jump
höchst [høːçst] *adv* highly, extremely
Hochstapler ['hoːxʃtaːplər] (**-s, -**) *m*
swindler
höchste(r, s) *adj* highest; (*äußerste*)
extreme
Höchst- *zW*: h~**ens** *adv* at the most;
~**geschwindigkeit** *f* maximum speed;
h~**persönlich** *adv* in person; ~**preis** *m*
maximum price; h~**wahrscheinlich** *adv*
most probably
Hoch- *zW*: ~**verrat** *m* high treason;
~**wasser** *nt* high water; (*Überschwem-*
mung) floods *pl*; ~**zahl** *f* (*MATH*) exponent
Hochzeit ['hɔxtsaɪt] (**-, -en**) *f* wedding;
~**sreise** *f* honeymoon
hocken ['hɔkən] *vi, vr* to squat, to crouch
Hocker (**-s, -**) *m* stool
Höcker ['hœkər] (**-s, -**) *m* hump
Hoden ['hoːdən] (**-s, -**) *m* testicle
Hof [hoːf] (**-(e)s, ⁻e**) *m* (*Hinter~*) yard;

(*Bauern~*) farm; (*Königs~*) court
hoffen ['hɔfən] *vi*: ~ **(auf** +*akk*) to hope (for)
hoffentlich ['hɔfəntlɪç] *adv* I hope, hopefully
Hoffnung ['hɔfnʊŋ] *f* hope
Hoffnungs- *zW*: **h~los** *adj* hopeless; **~losigkeit** *f* hopelessness; **~schimmer** *m* glimmer of hope; **h~voll** *adj* hopeful
höflich ['hø:flɪç] *adj* polite, courteous; **H~keit** *f* courtesy, politeness
hohe(r, s) ['ho:ə(r, s)] *adj attrib siehe* **hoch**
Höhe ['hø:ə] *f* height; (*An~*) hill
Hoheit ['ho:haɪt] *f* (*POL*) sovereignty; (*Titel*) Highness
Hoheitsgebiet *nt* sovereign territory
Hoheitsgewässer *nt* territorial waters *pl*
Höhen- ['hø:ən] *zW*: **~luft** *f* mountain air; **~messer** (**-s**, **-**) *m* altimeter; **~sonne** *f* sun lamp; **~unterschied** *m* difference in altitude
Höhepunkt *m* climax
höher *adj, adv* higher
hohl [ho:l] *adj* hollow
Höhle ['hø:lə] *f* cave, hole; (*Mund~*) cavity; (*fig, ZOOL*) den
Hohlmaß *nt* measure of volume
Hohn [ho:n] (**-(e)s**) *m* scorn
höhnisch *adj* scornful, taunting
holen ['ho:lən] *vt* to get, to fetch; (*Atem*) to take; **jdn/etw ~ lassen** to send for sb/sth
Holland ['hɔlant] *nt* Holland; **Holländer** ['hɔlɛndər] *m* Dutchman
holländisch ['hɔlɛndɪʃ] *adj* Dutch
Hölle ['hœlə] *f* hell
höllisch ['hœlɪʃ] *adj* hellish, infernal
holperig ['hɔlpərɪç] *adj* rough, bumpy
Holunder [ho'lʊndər] (**-s**, **-**) *m* elder
Holz [hɔlts] (**-es**, **-er**) *nt* wood
hölzern ['hœltsərn] *adj* (*auch fig*) wooden
Holz- *zW*: **~fäller** (**-s**, **-**) *m* lumberjack, woodcutter; **h~ig** *adj* woody; **~kohle** *f* charcoal; **~scheit** *nt* log; **~schuh** *m* clog; **~weg** *m* (*fig*) wrong track; **~wolle** *f* fine wood shavings *pl*
Homöopathie [homøopa'ti:] *f* homeopathy
homosexuell [homozɛksu'ɛl] *adj* homosexual
Honig ['ho:nɪç] (**-s**, **-e**) *m* honey; **~melone** *f* (*BOT, KOCH*) honeydew melon; **~wabe** *f* honeycomb
Honorar [hono'ra:r] (**-s**, **-e**) *nt* fee
Hopfen ['hɔpfən] (**-s**, **-**) *m* hops *pl*
hopsen ['hɔpsən] *vi* to hop
Hörapparat *m* hearing aid
hörbar *adj* audible
horchen ['hɔrçən] *vi* to listen; (*pej*) to eavesdrop
Horde ['hɔrdə] *f* horde
hören ['hø:rən] *vt, vi* to hear; **Musik/ Radio ~** to listen to music/the radio
Hörer (**-s**, **-**) *m* hearer; (*RADIO*) listener; (*UNIV*) student; (*Telefon~*) receiver
Hörfunk (**-s**) *m* radio
Horizont [hori'tsɔnt] (**-(e)s**, **-e**) *m* horizon; **h~al** [-'ta:l] *adj* horizontal
Hormon [hɔr'mo:n] (**-s**, **-e**) *nt* hormone
Hörmuschel *f* (*TEL*) earpiece
Horn [hɔrn] (**-(e)s**, **-er**) *nt* horn; **~haut** *f* horny skin
Hornisse [hɔr'nɪsə] *f* hornet
Horoskop [horo'sko:p] (**-s**, **-e**) *nt* horoscope
Hörspiel *nt* radio play
Hort [hɔrt] (**-(e)s**, **-e**) *m* (*SCH*) day centre *for schoolchildren whose parents are at work*
horten ['hɔrtən] *vt* to hoard
Hose ['ho:zə] *f* trousers *pl*, pants *pl* (*US*)
Hosen- *zW*: **~anzug** *m* trouser suit; **~rock** *m* culottes *pl*; **~tasche** *f* (trouser) pocket; **~träger** *m* braces *pl* (*BRIT*), suspenders *pl* (*US*)
Hostie ['hɔstiə] *f* (*REL*) host
Hotel [ho'tɛl] (**-s**, **-s**) *nt* hotel
Hotelier [hotɛli'e:] (**-s**, **-s**) *m* hotelkeeper, hotelier
Hubraum ['hu:p-] *m* (*AUT*) cubic capacity
hübsch [hypʃ] *adj* pretty, nice
Hubschrauber ['hu:pʃraʊbər] (**-s**, **-**) *m* helicopter
Huf [hu:f] (**-(e)s**, **-e**) *m* hoof; **~eisen** *nt* horseshoe
Hüft- ['hyft] *zW*: **~e** *f* hip; **~gürtel** *m*

girdle; **~halter** (-s, -) *m* girdle
Hügel ['hy:gəl] (-s, -) *m* hill; **h~ig** *adj*
hilly
Huhn [hu:n] (-(e)s, ⁼er) *nt* hen; (*KOCH*)
chicken
Hühnerauge ['hy:nər-] *nt* corn
Hühnerbrühe ['hy:nər-] *f* chicken broth
Hülle ['hylə] *f* cover(ing); wrapping; **in ~
und Fülle** galore; **h~n** *vt*: **h~n (in** +*akk*)
to cover (with); to wrap (in)
Hülse ['hylzə] *f* husk, shell; **~nfrucht** *f*
pulse
human [hu'ma:n] *adj* humane; **~i'tär** *adj*
humanitarian; **H~i'tät** *f* humanity
Hummel ['homəl] (-, -n) *f* bumblebee
Hummer ['homər] (-s, -) *m* lobster
Humor [hu'mo:r] (-s, -e) *m* humour; **~
haben** to have a sense of humour; **~ist**
[-'rɪst] *m* humorist; **h~istisch** *adj*
humorous; **h~voll** *adj* humorous
humpeln ['hompəln] *vi* to hobble
Humpen ['hompən] (-s, -) *m* tankard
Hund [hont] (-(e)s, -e) *m* dog
Hunde- ['hondə] *zW*: **~hütte** *f* (dog)
kennel; **~kuchen** *m* dog biscuit;
h~müde (*umg*) *adj* dog-tired
hundert ['hondərt] *num* hundred;
H~'jahrfeier *f* centenary; **~prozentig**
adj, adv one hundred per cent
Hundesteuer *f* dog licence fee
Hündin ['hyndɪn] *f* bitch
Hunger ['hoŋər] (-s) *m* hunger; **~ haben**
to be hungry; **h~n** *vi* to starve; **~snot** *f*
famine; **~streik** *m* hunger strike
hungrig ['hoŋrɪç] *adj* hungry
Hupe ['hu:pə] *f* horn; **h~n** *vi* to hoot, to
sound one's horn
hüpfen ['hypfən] *vi* to hop; to jump
Hürde ['hyrdə] *f* hurdle; (*für Schafe*) pen;
~nlauf *m* hurdling
Hure ['hu:rə] *f* whore
hurtig ['hortɪç] *adj* brisk, quick ♦ *adv*
briskly, quickly
huschen ['hoʃən] *vi* to flit; to scurry
Husten ['hu:stən] (-s) *m* cough; **h~** *vi* to
cough; **~anfall** *m* coughing fit; **~bonbon**
m od nt cough drop; **~saft** *m* cough
mixture
Hut¹ [hu:t] (-(e)s, ⁼e) *m* hat

Hut² (-) *f* care; **auf der ~ sein** to be on
one's guard
hüten ['hy:tən] *vt* to guard ♦ *vr* to watch
out; **sich ~, zu** to take care not to; **sich ~
(vor)** to beware (of), to be on one's guard
(against)
Hütte ['hytə] *f* hut; cottage; (*Eisen~*) forge
Hüttenkäse *m* (*KOCH*) cottage cheese
Hüttenschuh *m* slipper-sock
Hyäne [hy'ɛ:nə] *f* hyena
Hyazinthe [hya'tsɪntə] *f* hyacinth
Hydrant [hy'drant] *m* hydrant
hydraulisch [hy'draulɪʃ] *adj* hydraulic
Hygiene [hygi'e:nə] (-) *f* hygiene
hygienisch [hygi'e:nɪʃ] *adj* hygienic
Hymne ['hymnə] *f* hymn; anthem
hyper- ['hypɛr] *präfix* hyper-
Hypno- [hyp'no:] *zW*: **~se** *f* hypnosis;
h~tisch *adj* hypnotic; **~tiseur** [-ti'zø:r]
m hypnotist; **h~ti'sieren** *vt* to hypnotize
Hypothek [hypo'te:k] (-, -en) *f* mortgage
Hypothese [hypo'te:zə] *f* hypothesis
Hysterie [hyste'ri:] *f* hysteria
hysterisch [hys'te:rɪʃ] *adj* hysterical

I i

Ich (-(s), -(s)) *nt* self; (*PSYCH*) ego
ich [ɪç] *pron* I; **~ bin's!** it's me!
Ideal [ide'a:l] (-s, -e) *nt* ideal; **i~** *adj* ideal;
i~istisch [-'lɪstɪʃ] *adj* idealistic
Idee [i'de:, *pl* i'de:ən] *f* idea
identifizieren [identifi'tsi:rən] *vt* to
identify
identisch [i'dentɪʃ] *adj* identical
Identität [identi'tɛ:t] *f* identity
Ideo- [ideo] *zW*: **~loge** [-'lo:gə] (-n, -n) *m*
ideologist; **~logie** [-lo'gi:] *f* ideology;
i~logisch [-'lo:gɪʃ] *adj* ideological
Idiot [idi'o:t] (-en, -en) *m* idiot; **i~isch**
adj idiotic
idyllisch [i'dylɪʃ] *adj* idyllic
Igel ['i:gəl] (-s, -) *m* hedgehog
ignorieren [ɪgno'ri:rən] *vt* to ignore
ihm [i:m] (*dat von* **er, es**) *pron* (to) him;
(to) it
ihn [i:n] (*akk von* **er**) *pron* him; it; **~en**
(*dat von* **sie** *pl*) *pron* (to) them; **i~en** (*dat*

von **Sie** *pl*) *pron* (to) you

ihr [iːr] *pron* **1** (*nom pl*) you; **ihr seid es**
it's you
2 (*dat von sie*) to her; **gib es ihr** give it
to her; **er steht neben ihr** he is standing
beside her

♦ *possessiv pron* **1** (*sg*) her; (: *bei Tieren,*
Dingen) its; **ihr Mann** her husband
2 (*pl*) their; **die Bäume und ihre Blätter**
the trees and their leaves

ihr(e) *adj* (*sg*) her; its; (*pl*) their; **I~(e)** *adj*
your
ihre(r, s) *pron* (*sg*) hers; its (*pl*) theirs;
I~(r, s) *pron* yours; **~r** (*gen von* **sie** *sg/pl*)
pron of her/them; **I~r** (*gen von* **Sie**) *pron*
of you; **~rseits** *adv* for her/their part;
~sgleichen *pron* people like her/them;
(*von Dingen*) others like it; **~twegen** *adv*
(*für sie*) for her/its/their sake; (*wegen ihr*)
on her/its/their account; **~twillen** *adv*:
um ~twillen = **~twegen**
ihrige *pron*: **der/die/das ~** hers; its;
theirs
illegal ['ɪlega:l] *adj* illegal
Illusion [ɪluzi'oːn] *f* illusion
illusorisch [ɪlu'zoːrɪʃ] *adj* illusory
illustrieren [ɪlus'triːrən] *vt* to illustrate
Illustrierte *f* magazine
Iltis ['ɪltɪs] (*-ses, -se*) *m* polecat
im [ɪm] = **in dem**
Imbiß ['ɪmbɪs] (*-sses, -sse*) *m* snack;
~halle *f* snack bar; **~stube** *f* snack bar
imitieren [ɪmɪ'tiːrən] *vt* to imitate
Imker ['ɪmkər] (*-s, -*) *m* beekeeper
immatrikulieren [ɪmatriku'liːrən] *vi, vr*
to register
immer ['ɪmər] *adv* always; **~ wieder**
again and again; **~ noch** still; **~ noch**
nicht still not; **für ~** forever; **~ wenn ich**
... every time I ...; **~ schöner/trauriger**
more and more beautiful/sadder and
sadder; **was/wer (auch) ~** whatever/
whoever; **~hin** *adv* all the same; **~zu** *adv*
all the time
Immobilien [ɪmo'biːliən] *pl* real estate *sg*
immun [ɪ'muːn] *adj* immune; **I~ität**

[-i'tɛːt] *f* immunity; **I~system** *nt* immune
system
Imperfekt ['ɪmpɛrfɛkt] (*-s, -e*) *nt*
imperfect (tense)
Impf- ['ɪmpf] *zW*: **i~en** *vt* to vaccinate;
~stoff *m* vaccine, serum; **~ung** *f*
vaccination
imponieren [ɪmpo'niːrən] *vi* +*dat* to
impress
Import [ɪm'pɔrt] (*-(e)s, -e*) *m* import;
~eur *m* importer; **i~ieren** *vt* to import
imposant [ɪmpo'zant] *adj* imposing
impotent ['ɪmpotɛnt] *adj* impotent
imprägnieren [ɪmprɛ'gniːrən] *vt* to
(water)proof
improvisieren [ɪmprovi'ziːrən] *vt, vi* to
improvise
Impuls [ɪm'pʊls] (*-es, -e*) *m* impulse; **i~iv**
[-'ziːf] *adj* impulsive
imstande [ɪm'ʃtandə] *adj*: **~ sein** to be
in a position; (*fähig*) to be able

in [ɪn] *präp* +*akk* **1** (*räumlich: wohin?*) in,
into; **in die Stadt** to town; **in die**
Schule gehen to go to school
2 (*zeitlich*): **bis ins 20. Jahrhundert** into
od up to the 20th century

♦ *präp* +*dat* **1** (*räumlich: wo*) in; **in der**
Stadt in town; **in der Schule sein** to be
at school
2 (*zeitlich: wann*): **in diesem Jahr** this
year; (*in jenem Jahr*) in that year; **heute**
in zwei Wochen two weeks today

Inanspruchnahme [ɪn''anʃpruxnaːmə] *f*
(+*gen*) demands *pl* (on)
Inbegriff ['ɪnbəgrɪf] *m* embodiment,
personification; **i~en** *adv* included
indem [ɪn'deːm] *konj* while; **~ man etw**
macht (*dadurch*) by doing sth
Inder(in) ['ɪndər(ɪn)] *m(f)* Indian
indes(sen) [ɪn'dɛs(ən)] *adv* however;
(*inzwischen*) meanwhile ♦ *konj* while
Indianer(in) [ɪndi'aːnər(ɪn)] (*-s, -*) *m(f)*
American Indian, native American
indianisch *adj* Red Indian
Indien ['ɪndiən] *nt* India
indirekt ['ɪndirɛkt] *adj* indirect

indisch ['ındıʃ] *adj* Indian

indiskret ['ındıskre:t] *adj* indiscreet

indiskutabel ['ındıskuta:bəl] *adj* out of the question

individuell [ındividu'ɛl] *adj* individual

Individuum [ındi'vi:duɔm] (**-s, -duen**) *nt* individual

Indiz [ın'di:ts] (**-es, -ien**) *nt* (*JUR*) clue; ~ **(für)** sign (of)

industrialisieren [ındʊstriali'zi:rən] *vt* to industrialize

Industrie [ındʊs'tri:] *f* industry ♦ *in zW* industrial; **~gebiet** *nt* industrial area; **~zweig** *m* branch of industry

ineinander [ın'aı'nandər] *adv* in(to) one another *od* each other

Infarkt [ın'farkt] (**-(e)s, -e**) *m* coronary (thrombosis)

Infektion [ınfɛktsi'o:n] *f* infection; **~skrankheit** *f* infectious disease

Infinitiv ['ınfiniti:f] (**-s, -e**) *m* infinitive

infizieren [ınfi'tsi:rən] *vt* to infect ♦ *vr*: **sich (bei jdm)** ~ to be infected (by sb)

Inflation [ınflatsi'o:n] *f* inflation

inflationär [ınflatsio'nɛ:r] *adj* inflationary

infolge [ın'fɔlgə] *präp +gen* as a result of, owing to; **~dessen** [-'dɛsən] *adv* consequently

Informatik [ınfɔr'ma:tık] *f* information studies *pl*

Information [ınfɔrmatsi'o:n] *f* information *no pl*

informieren [ınfɔr'mi:rən] *vt* to inform ♦ *vr*: **sich** ~ **(über** +*akk*) to find out (about)

Infusion [ınfuzi'o:n] *f* infusion

Ingenieur [ınʒeni'ø:r] *m* engineer; **~schule** *f* school of engineering

Ingwer ['ıŋvər] (**-s**) *m* ginger

Inh. *abk* (= *Inhaber*) prop.; (= *Inhalt*) contents

Inhaber(in) ['ınha:bər(ın)] (**-s, -**) *m(f)* owner; (*Haus~*) occupier; (*Lizenz~*) licensee, holder; (*FIN*) bearer

inhaftieren *vt* to take into custody

inhalieren [ınha'li:rən] *vt, vi* to inhale

Inhalt ['ınhalt] (**-(e)s, -e**) *m* contents *pl*; (*eines Buchs etc*) content; (*MATH*) area;

volume; **i~lich** *adj* as regards content

Inhalts- *zW*: **~angabe** *f* summary; **~verzeichnis** *nt* table of contents

inhuman ['ınhuma:n] *adj* inhuman

Initiative [initsia'ti:və] *f* initiative

Injektion [ınjɛktsi'o:n] *f* injection

inklusive [ınklu'zi:və] *präp +gen* inclusive of ♦ *adv* inclusive

inkognito [ın'kɔgnito] *adv* incognito

Inkrafttreten [ın'krafttre:tən] (**-s**) *nt* coming into force

Inland ['ınlant] (**-(e)s**) *nt* (*GEOG*) inland; (*POL, COMM*) home (country)

inmitten [ın'mıtən] *präp +gen* in the middle of; ~ **von** amongst

innehaben ['ınəha:bən] (*unreg*) *vt* to hold

innen ['ınən] *adv* inside; **I~architekt** *m* interior designer; **I~einrichtung** *f* (interior) furnishings *pl*; **I~hof** *m* inner courtyard; **I~minister** *m* minister of the interior, Home Secretary (*BRIT*); **I~politik** *f* domestic policy; **~politisch** *adj* (*Entwicklung, Lage*) internal, domestic; **I~stadt** *f* town/city centre

inner- ['ınər] *zW*: **~e(s)** *adj* inner; (*im Körper, inländisch*) internal; **I~e(s)** *nt* inside; (*Mitte*) centre; (*fig*) heart; **I~eien** [-'raıən] *pl* innards; **~halb** *adv* within; (*räumlich*) inside ♦ *präp +gen* within; inside; **~lich** *adj* internal; (*geistig*) inward; **~ste(r, s)** *adj* innermost; **I~ste(s)** *nt* heart

innig *adj* (*Freundschaft*) close

inoffiziell ['ın'ɔfitsiɛl] *adj* unofficial

ins [ıns] = **in das**

Insasse ['ınzasə] (**-n, -n**) *m* (*Anstalt*) inmate; (*AUT*) passenger

insbesondere [ınsbə'zɔndərə] *adv* (e)specially

Inschrift ['ınʃrıft] *f* inscription

Insekt [ın'zɛkt] (**-(e)s, -en**) *nt* insect

Insel ['ınzəl] (**-, -n**) *f* island

Inser- *zW*: **~at** [ınze'ra:t] (**-(e)s, -e**) *nt* advertisement; **~ent** [ınze'rɛnt] *m* advertiser; **i~ieren** [ınze'ri:rən] *vt, vi* to advertise

insgeheim [ınsgə'haım] *adv* secretly

insgesamt [ınsgə'zamt] *adv* altogether, all in all

insofern ['ɪnzo'fɛrn] *adv* in this respect
♦ *konj* if; *(deshalb)* (and) so; ~ **als** in so
far as

insoweit ['ɪnzo'vaɪt] = **insofern**

Installateur [ɪnstala'tøːr] *m* electrician;
plumber

Instandhaltung [ɪn'ʃtant-] *f*
maintenance

instandig [ɪn'ʃtɛndɪç] *adj* urgent

Instandsetzung [ɪn'ʃtant-] *f* overhaul;
(eines Gebäudes) restoration

Instanz [ɪn'stants] *f* authority; *(JUR)* court

Instinkt [ɪn'stɪŋkt] **(-(e)s, -e)** *m* instinct;
i~iv [-'tiːf] *adj* instinctive

Institut [ɪnsti'tuːt] **(-(e)s, -e)** *nt* institute

Instrument [ɪnstru'mɛnt] *nt* instrument

Intell- [ɪntɛl] *zW:* **i~ektuell** [-ɛktu'ɛl] *adj*
intellectual; **i~igent** [-i'gɛnt] *adj*
intelligent; **~igenz** [-i'gɛnts] *f*
intelligence; *(Leute)* intelligentsia *pl*

Intendant [ɪntɛn'dant] *m* director

intensiv [ɪntɛn'ziːf] *adj* intensive

Interess- [ɪntɛrɛs] *zW:* **i~ant** [ɪntɛrɛ'sant] *adj*
interesting; **i~anterweise** *adv*
interestingly enough; **~e** [ɪntɛ'rɛsə] **(-s,
-n)** *nt* interest; **~e haben an** *+dat* to be
interested in; **~ent** [ɪntɛrɛ'sɛnt] *m*
interested party; **i~ieren** [ɪntɛrɛ'siːrən] *vt*
to interest ♦ *vr:* **sich i~ieren für** to be
interested in

intern *adj (Angelegenheiten, Regelung)*
internal; *(Besprechung)* private

Internat [ɪntɛr'naːt] **(-(e)s, -e)** *nt* boarding
school

inter- [ɪntɛr] *zW:* **~national** [-natsio'naːl]
adj international; **~pretieren** [-pre'tiːrən]
vt to interpret; **i~vall** [-'val] **(-s, -e)** *nt*
interval; **i~view** ['-vjuː] **(-s, -s)** *nt*
interview; **~viewen** [-'vjuːən] *vt* to
interview

intim [ɪn'tiːm] *adj* intimate; **i~ität** *f*
intimacy

intolerant ['ɪntolerant] *adj* intolerant

intransitiv ['ɪntranzitiːf] *adj (GRAM)*
intransitive

Intrige [ɪn'triːgə] *f* intrigue, plot

Invasion [ɪnvazi'oːn] *f* invasion

Inventar [ɪnvɛn'taːr] **(-s, -e)** *nt* inventory

Inventur [ɪnvɛn'tuːr] *f* stocktaking; ~

machen to stocktake

investieren [ɪnvɛs'tiːrən] *vt* to invest

inwiefern [ɪnvi'fɛrn] *adv* how far, to
what extent

inwieweit [ɪnvi'vaɪt] *adv* how far, to
what extent

inzwischen [ɪn'tsvɪʃən] *adv* meanwhile

Irak [i'raːk] **(-s)** *m:* **der ~** Iraq; **i~isch** *adj*
Iraqi

Iran [i'raːn] **(-s)** *m:* **der ~** Iran; **i~isch** *adj*
Iranian

irdisch ['ɪrdɪʃ] *adj* earthly

Ire ['iːrə] **(-n, -n)** *m* Irishman

irgend ['ɪrgənt] *adv* at all; **wann/was/
wer** ~ whenever/whatever/whoever; ~
jemand/etwas somebody/something;
anybody/anything; **~ein(e, s)** *adj* some,
any; **~einmal** *adv* sometime or other;
(fragend) ever; **~wann** *adv* sometime;
~wie *adv* somehow; **~wo** *adv*
somewhere; anywhere; **~wohin** *adv*
somewhere; anywhere

Irin ['iːrɪn] *f* Irishwoman

Irland ['ɪrlant] **(-s)** *nt* Ireland

Ironie [iro'niː] *f* irony

ironisch [i'roːnɪʃ] *adj* ironic(al)

irre ['ɪrə] *adj* crazy, mad; **I~(r)** *mf* lunatic;
~führen *vt* to mislead; **~machen** *vt* to
confuse; **~n** *vi* to be mistaken;
(umherirren) to wander, to stray ♦ *vr* to
be mistaken; **I~nanstalt** *f* lunatic asylum

Irrgarten *m* maze

irrig ['ɪrɪç] *adj* incorrect, wrong

irritieren [ɪri'tiːrən] *vt (verwirren)* to
confuse; *(ärgern)* to irritate; *(stören)* to
annoy

Irr- *zW:* **i~sinnig** *adj* mad, crazy; *(umg)*
terrific; **~tum** **(-s, -tümer)** *m* mistake,
error; **i~tümlich** *adj* mistaken

Islam ['ɪslam] **(-s)** *m* Islam

Island ['iːslant] **(-s)** *nt* Iceland

Isolation [izolatsi'oːn] *f* isolation; *(ELEK)*
insulation

Isolier- [izo'liːr] *zW:* **~band** *nt* insulating
tape; **i~en** *vt* to isolate; *(ELEK)* to insulate;
~station *f (MED)* isolation ward; **~ung** *f*
isolation; *(ELEK)* insulation

Israel ['ɪsraeːl] **(-s)** *nt* Israel; **~i** [-'eːli] **(-s,
-s)** *m* Israeli; **i~isch** *adj* Israeli

ißt [ɪst] *vb siehe* **essen**
ist [ɪst] *vb siehe* **sein**
Italien [i'ta:liən] (-s) *nt* Italy; **~er(in)** (-s) *m(f)* Italian; **i~isch** *adj* Italian
i.V. *abk* = **in Vertretung**

J j

ja [ja:] *adv* **1** yes; **haben Sie das gesehen? - ja** did you see it? - yes(, I did); **ich glaube ja** (yes) I think so
2 (*fragend*) really?; **ich habe gekündigt - ja?** I've quit - have you?; **du kommst, ja?** you're coming, aren't you?
3: **sei ja vorsichtig** do be careful; **Sie wissen ja, daß ...** as you know, ...; **tu das ja nicht!** don't do that!; **ich habe es ja gewußt** I just knew it; **ja, also ...** well you see ...

Jacht [jaxt] (-, -en) *f* yacht
Jacke [jakə] *f* jacket; (*Woll~*) cardigan
Jackett [ʒa'kɛt] (-s, -s *od* -e) *nt* jacket
Jagd [ja:kt] (-, -en) *f* hunt; (*Jagen*) hunting; **~beute** *f* kill; **~flugzeug** *nt* fighter; **~gewehr** *nt* sporting gun; **~hund** *m* hunting dog
jagen ['ja:gən] *vi* to hunt; (*eilen*) to race ♦ *vt* to hunt; (*weg~*) to drive (off); (*verfolgen*) to chase
Jäger ['jɛ:gər] (-s, -) *m* hunter
Jägerschnitzel *nt* (*KOCH*) pork in a spicy sauce with mushrooms
jäh [jɛ:] *adj* sudden, abrupt; (*steil*) steep, precipitous
Jahr [ja:r] (-(e)s, -e) *nt* year; **j~elang** *adv* for years
Jahres- *zW*: **~abonnement** *nt* annual subscription; **~abschluß** *m* end of the year; (*COMM*) annual statement of account; **~beitrag** *m* annual subscription; **~karte** *f* yearly season ticket; **~tag** *m* anniversary; **~wechsel** *m* turn of the year; **~zahl** *f* date; year; **~zeit** *f* season
Jahrgang *m* age group; (*von Wein*) vintage

Jahr'hundert (-s, -e) *nt* century
jährlich ['jɛ:rlɪç] *adj, adv* yearly
Jahrmarkt *m* fair
Jahrtausend *nt* millennium
Jahr'zehnt *nt* decade
Jähzorn *m* sudden anger; hot temper; **j~ig** *adj* hot-tempered
Jalousie [ʒalu'zi:] *f* venetian blind
Jammer ['jamər] (-s) *m* misery; **es ist ein ~, daß ...** it is a crying shame that ...
jämmerlich ['jɛmərlɪç] *adj* wretched, pathetic
jammern *vi* to wail ♦ *vt unpers*: **es jammert jdn** it makes sb feel sorry
jammerschade *adj*: **es ist ~** it is a crying shame
Januar ['janua:r] (-(s), -e) *m* January
Japan ['ja:pan] (-s) *nt* Japan; **~er(in)** [-'pa:nər(ɪn)] (-s) *m(f)* Japanese; **j~isch** *adj* Japanese
Jargon [ʒar'gõ:] (-s, -s) *m* jargon
jäten ['jɛ:tən] *vt*: **Unkraut ~** to weed
jauchzen ['jauxtsən] *vi* to rejoice, to shout (with joy)
jaulen ['jaulən] *vi* to howl
jawohl [ja'vo:l] *adv* yes (of course)
Jawort ['ja:vɔrt] *nt* consent
Jazz [dʒɛs] (-) *m* Jazz

je [je:] *adv* **1** (*jemals*) ever; **hast du so was je gesehen?** did you ever see anything like it?
2 (*jeweils*) every; each; **sie zahlten je 3 Mark** they paid 3 marks each ♦ *konj* **1**: **je nach** depending on; **je nachdem** it depends; **je nachdem, ob ...** depending on whether ...
2: **je eher, desto** *od* **um so besser** the sooner the better

Jeans [dʒi:nz] *pl* jeans
jede(r, s) ['je:də(r, s)] *adj* every, each ♦ *pron* everybody; (*~ einzelne*) each; **ohne ~ x** without any x
jedenfalls *adv* in any case
jedermann *pron* everyone
jederzeit *adv* at any time
jedesmal *adv* every time, each time

jedoch [je'dɔx] *adv* however
jeher ['je:he:r] *adv:* **von/seit ~** always
jemals ['je:ma:ls] *adv* ever
jemand ['je:mant] *pron* somebody; anybody
jene(r, s) ['je:nə(r, s)] *adj* that ♦ *pron* that one
jenseits ['je:nzaits] *adv* on the other side ♦ *präp +gen* on the other side of, beyond
Jenseits *nt:* **das ~** the hereafter, the beyond
jetzig ['jɛtsiç] *adj* present
jetzt [jɛtst] *adv* now
jeweilig *adj* respective
jeweils *adv:* **~ zwei zusammen** two at a time; **zu ~ 5 DM** at 5 marks each; **~ das erste** the first each time
Jh. *abk* = **Jahrhundert**
Jockei ['dʒɔke] (-s, -s) *m* jockey
Jod [jo:t] (-(e)s) *nt* iodine
jodeln ['jo:dəln] *vi* to yodel
joggen ['dʒɔgən] *vi* to jog
Joghurt ['jo:gʊrt] (-s, -s) *m od nt* yogurt
Johannisbeere [jo'hanisbe:rə] *f* redcurrant; **schwarze ~** blackcurrant
johlen ['jo:lən] *vi* to yell
jonglieren [ʒɔ̃'gli:rən] *vi* to juggle
Journal- [ʒʊrnal] *zW:* **~ismus** [-'lismʊs] *m* journalism; **~ist(in)** [-'list(in)] *m(f)* journalist; **journa'listisch** *adj* journalistic
Jubel ['ju:bəl] (-s) *m* rejoicing; **j~n** *vi* to rejoice
Jubiläum [jubi'lɛːʊm] (-s, Jubiläen) *nt* anniversary; jubilee
jucken ['jʊkən] *vi* to itch ♦ *vt:* **es juckt mich am Arm** my arm is itching; **das juckt mich** that's itchy
Juckreiz ['jʊkraits] *m* itch
Jude ['ju:də] (-n, -n) *m* Jew
Judentum (-) *nt* Judaism; Jewry
Judenverfolgung *f* persecution of the Jews
Jüdin ['jy:din] *f* Jewess
jüdisch ['jy:dɪʃ] *adj* Jewish
Judo ['ju:do] (-(s)) *nt* judo
Jugend ['ju:gənt] (-) *f* youth; **j~frei** *adj* (*CINE*) U (*BRIT*), G (*US*), suitable for children; **~herberge** *f* youth hostel;

j~lich *adj* youthful; **~liche(r)** *mf* teenager, young person
Jugoslaw- [jugo'sla:v] *zW:* **~e** *m* Yugoslavian; **~ien** (-s) *nt* Yugoslavia; **~in** *f* Yugoslavian; **~isch** *adj* Yugoslavian
Juli ['ju:li] (-(s), -s) *m* July
jun. *abk* (= *junior*) jr.
jung [jʊŋ] *adj* young; **J~e** (-n, -n) *m* boy, lad; **J~e(s)** *nt* young animal; **J~en** *pl* (*von Tier*) young *pl*
Jünger ['jʏŋər] (-s, -) *m* disciple
jünger *adj* younger
Jung- *zW:* **~frau** *f* virgin; (*ASTROL*) Virgo; **~geselle** *m* bachelor; **~gesellin** *f* unmarried woman; **Jüngling** *m* youth
jüngst [jʏŋst] *adv* lately, recently; **~e(r, s)** *adj* youngest; (*neueste*) latest
Juni ['ju:ni] (-(s), -s) *m* June
Junior ['ju:niɔr, *pl* -'o:rən] (-s, -en) *m* junior
Jurist [ju'rist] *m* jurist, lawyer; **j~isch** *adj* legal
Justiz [jʊs'ti:ts] (-) *f* justice; **~beamte(r)** *m* judicial officer; **~irrtum** *m* miscarriage of justice; **~minister** *m* ≈ Lord (High) Chancellor (*BRIT*), ≈ Attorney General (*US*)
Juwel [ju've:l] (-s, -en) *nt od m* jewel
Juwelier [juve'li:r] (-s, -e) *m* jeweller; **~geschäft** *nt* jeweller's (shop)
Jux [jʊks] (-es, -e) *m* joke, lark

K k

Kabarett [kaba'rɛt] (-s, -e *od* -s) *nt* cabaret; **~ist** [-'tist] *m* cabaret artiste
Kabel ['ka:bəl] (-s, -) *nt* (*ELEK*) wire; (*stark*) cable; **~fernsehen** *nt* cable television
Kabeljau ['ka:bəljau] (-s, -e *od* -s) *m* cod
kabeln *vt, vi* to cable
Kabine [ka'bi:nə] *f* cabin; (*Zelle*) cubicle
Kabinett [kabi'nɛt] (-s, -e) *nt* (*POL*) cabinet
Kachel ['kaxəl] (-, -n) *f* tile; **k~n** *vt* to tile; **~ofen** *m* tiled stove
Käfer ['kɛːfər] (-s, -) *m* beetle
Kaffee ['kafe] (-s, -s) *m* coffee; **~kanne** *f* coffeepot; **~löffel** *m* coffee spoon

Käfig ['kɛːfɪç] (-s, -e) m cage

kahl [kaːl] adj bald; **~geschoren** adj shaven, shorn; **~köpfig** adj bald-headed

Kahn [kaːn] (-(e)s, ⸚e) m boat, barge

Kai [kaɪ] (-s, -e od -s) m quay

Kaiser ['kaɪzər] (-s, -) m emperor; **~in** f empress; **k~lich** adj imperial; **~reich** nt empire; **~schnitt** m (MED) Caesarian (section)

Kajak ['kaːjak] (-s, -s) m (SPORT) kayak

Kakao [ka'kaʊ] (-s, -s) m cocoa

Kaktee [kak'teː(ə)] (-, -n) f cactus

Kaktus ['kaktʊs] (-, -teen) m cactus

Kalb [kalp] (-(e)s, ⸚er) nt calf; **k~en** ['kalbən] vi to calve; **~fleisch** nt veal; **~sleder** nt calf(skin)

Kalender [ka'lɛndər] (-s, -) m calendar; (Taschen~) diary

Kaliber [ka'liːbər] (-s, -) nt (auch fig) calibre

Kalk [kalk] (-(e)s, -e) m lime; (BIOL) calcium; **~stein** m limestone

kalkulieren [kalku'liːrən] vt to calculate

Kalorie [kalo'riː] f calorie

kalt [kalt] adj cold; **mir ist (es)** ~ I am cold; **~bleiben** (unreg) vi to remain unmoved; **~blütig** adj cold-blooded; (ruhig) cool

Kälte ['kɛltə] (-) f cold; coldness; **~grad** m degree of frost od below zero; **~welle** f cold spell

kalt- zW: **~herzig** adj cold-hearted; **~schnäuzig** adj cold, unfeeling; **~stellen** vt to chill; (fig) to leave out in the cold

kam etc [kaːm] vb siehe **kommen**

Kamel [ka'meːl] (-(e)s, -e) m camel

Kamera ['kamera] (-, -s) f camera

Kamerad [kamə'raːt] (-en, -en) m comrade, friend; **~schaft** f comradeship; **k~schaftlich** adj comradely

Kameramann (-(e)s, -männer) m cameraman

Kamille [ka'mɪlə] f camomile; **~ntee** m camomile tea

Kamin [ka'miːn] (-s, -e) m (außen) chimney; (innen) fireside, fireplace; **~feger** (-s, -) m chimney sweep; **~kehrer** (-s, -) m chimney sweep

Kamm [kam] (-(e)s, ⸚e) m comb; (Berg~)

ridge; (Hahnen~) crest

kämmen ['kɛmən] vt to comb ♦ vr to comb one's hair

Kammer ['kamər] (-, -n) f chamber; small bedroom; **~diener** m valet

Kampagne [kam'panjə] f campaign

Kampf [kampf] (-(e)s, ⸚e) m fight, battle; (Wettbewerb) contest; (fig: Anstrengung) struggle; **k~bereit** adj ready for action

kämpfen ['kɛmpfən] vi to fight

Kämpfer (-s, -) m fighter, combatant

Kampf- zW: **~handlung** f action; **k~los** adj without a fight; **~richter** m (SPORT) referee; (TENNIS) umpire; **~stoff** m: **chemischer/biologischer ~stoff** chemical/biological weapon

Kanada ['kanada] (-s) nt Canada

Kanadier(in) [ka'naːdiər(ɪn)] (-s, -) m(f) Canadian

kanadisch [ka'naːdɪʃ] adj Canadian

Kanal [ka'naːl] (-s, Kanäle) m (Fluß) canal; (Rinne, Ärmel~) channel; (für Abfluß) drain; **~inseln** pl Channel Islands; **~isation** [-izatsi'oːn] f sewage system; **~tunnel** m: **der ~** the Channel Tunnel

Kanarienvogel [ka'naːriənfoːgəl] m canary

kanarisch [ka'naːrɪʃ] adj: **K~e Inseln** Canary Islands, Canaries

Kandi- [kandi] zW: **~dat** [-'daːt] (-en, -en) m candidate; **~datur** [-da'tuːr] f candidature, candidacy; **k~dieren** [-'diːrən] vi to stand, to run

Kandis(zucker) ['kandɪs(tsʊkər)] (-) m candy

Känguruh ['kɛŋguru] (-s, -s) nt kangaroo

Kaninchen [ka'niːnçən] nt rabbit

Kanister [ka'nɪstər] (-s, -) m can, canister

Kännchen ['kɛnçən] nt pot

Kanne ['kanə] f (Krug) jug; (Kaffee~) pot; (Milch~) churn; (Gieß~) can

kannst etc [kanst] vb siehe **können**

Kanon ['kaːnɔn] (-s, -s) m canon

Kanone [ka'noːnə] f gun; (HIST) cannon; (fig: Mensch) ace

Kantate [kan'taːtə] f cantata

Kante ['kantə] f edge

Kantine [kan'tiːnə] f canteen

Kanu ['ka:nu] (-s, -s) *nt* canoe
Kanzel ['kantsəl] (-, -n) *f* pulpit
Kanzler ['kantslər] (-s, -) *m* chancellor
Kap [kap] (-s, -s) *nt* cape (*GEOG*); ~ **der Guten Hoffnung** Cape of Good Hope
Kapazität [kapatsi'tɛ:t] *f* capacity; (*Fachmann*) authority
Kapelle [ka'pɛlə] *f* (*Gebäude*) chapel; (*MUS*) band
kapieren [ka'pi:rən] (*umg*) *vt, vi* to get, to understand
Kapital [kapi'ta:l] (-s, -e *od* -ien) *nt* capital; ~**anlage** *f* investment; ~**ismus** [-'lɪsmʊs] *m* capitalism; ~**ist** [-'lɪst] *m* capitalist; **k~istisch** *adj* capitalist
Kapitän [kapi'tɛ:n] (-s, -e) *m* captain
Kapitel [ka'pɪtəl] (-s, -) *nt* chapter
Kapitulation [kapitulatsi'o:n] *f* capitulation
kapitulieren [kapitu'li:rən] *vi* to capitulate
Kaplan [ka'pla:n] (-s, **Kapläne**) *m* chaplain
Kappe ['kapə] *f* cap; (*Kapuze*) hood
kappen *vt* to cut
Kapsel ['kapsəl] (-, -n) *f* capsule
kaputt [ka'pʊt] (*umg*) *adj* kaput, broken; (*Person*) exhausted, finished; **am Auto ist etwas ~** there's something wrong with the car; ~**gehen** (*unreg*) *vi* to break; (*Schuhe*) to fall apart; (*Firma*) to go bust; (*Stoff*) to wear out; (*sterben*) to cop it (*umg*); ~**machen** *vt* to break; (*Mensch*) exhaust, to wear out
Kapuze [ka'pu:tsə] *f* hood
Karaffe [ka'rafə] *f* carafe; (*geschliffen*) decanter
Karamel [kara'mɛl] (-s) *m* caramel; ~**bonbon** *m od nt* toffee
Karat [ka'ra:t] (-(e)s, -e) *nt* carat
Karate [ka'ra:tə] (-s) *nt* karate
Karawane [kara'va:nə] *f* caravan
Kardinal [kardi'na:l] (-s, **Kardinäle**) *m* cardinal; ~**zahl** *f* cardinal number
Karfreitag [ka:r'fraita:k] *m* Good Friday
karg [kark] *adj* (*Landschaft, Boden*) barren; (*Lohn*) meagre
kärglich ['kɛrklɪç] *adj* poor, scanty
Karibik [ka'ri:bɪk] (-) *f*: **die ~** the

Caribbean
karibisch [ka'ri:bɪʃ] *adj*: **K~e Inseln** Caribbean Islands
kariert [ka'ri:rt] *adj* (*Stoff*) checked; (*Papier*) squared
Karies ['ka:ries] (-) *f* caries
Karikatur [karika'tu:r] *f* caricature; ~**ist** [-'rɪst] *m* cartoonist
Karneval ['karnəval] (-s, -e *od* -s) *m* carnival
Karo ['ka:ro] (-s, -s) *nt* square; (*KARTEN*) diamonds; ~**-As** *nt* ace of diamonds
Karosserie [karəsə'ri:] *f* (*AUT*) body(work)
Karotte [ka'rɔtə] *f* carrot
Karpfen ['karpfən] (-s, -) *m* carp
Karre ['karə] *f* cart, barrow
Karren (-s, -) *m* cart, barrow
Karriere [kari'ɛ:rə] *f* career; ~ **machen** to get on, to get to the top; ~**macher** (-s, -) *m* careerist
Karte ['kartə] *f* card; (*Land~*) map; (*Speise~*) menu; (*Eintritts~, Fahr~*) ticket; **alles auf eine ~ setzen** to put all one's eggs in one basket
Kartei [kar'tai] *f* card index; ~**karte** *f* index card
Kartell [kar'tɛl] (-s, -e) *nt* cartel
Kartenspiel *nt* card game; pack of cards
Kartoffel [kar'tɔfəl] (-, -n) *f* potato; ~**brei** *m* mashed potatoes *pl*; ~**mus** *nt* mashed potatoes *pl*; ~**püree** *nt* mashed potatoes *pl*; ~**salat** *m* potato salad
Karton [kar'tõ:] (-s, -s) *m* cardboard; (*Schachtel*) cardboard box; **k~iert** [karto'ni:rt] *adj* hardback
Karussell [karʊ'sɛl] (-s, -s) *nt* roundabout (*BRIT*), merry-go-round
Karwoche ['ka:rvɔxə] *f* Holy Week
Käse ['kɛ:zə] (-s, -) *m* cheese; ~**glocke** *f* cheese(-plate) cover; ~**kuchen** *m* cheesecake
Kaserne [ka'zɛrnə] *f* barracks *pl*; ~**nhof** *m* parade ground
Kasino [ka'zi:no] (-s, -s) *nt* club; (*MIL*) officers' mess; (*Spiel~*) casino
Kasper ['kaspər] (-s, -) *m* Punch; (*fig*) fool
Kasse ['kasə] *f* (*Geldkasten*) cashbox; (*in Geschäft*) till, cash register; cash desk, checkout; (*Kino~, Theater~ etc*) box office;

ticket office; (*Kranken~*) health insurance; (*Spar~*) savings bank; ~ **machen** to count the money; **getrennte ~ führen** to pay separately; **an der ~** (*in Geschäft*) at the desk; **gut bei ~ sein** to be in the money

Kassen- *zW*: **~arzt** *m* panel doctor (*BRIT*); **~bestand** *m* cash balance; **~patient** *m* panel patient (*BRIT*); **~prüfung** *f* audit; **~sturz** *m*: **~sturz machen** to check one's money; **~zettel** *m* receipt

Kassette [ka'sɛtə] *f* small box; (*Tonband, PHOT*) cassette; (*Bücher~*) case

Kassettenrecorder (**-s, -**) *m* cassette recorder

kassieren [ka'si:rən] *vt* to take ♦ *vi*: **darf ich ~?** would you like to pay now?

Kassierer [ka'si:rər] (**-s, -**) *m* cashier; (*von Klub*) treasurer

Kastanie [kas'ta:niə] *f* chestnut; (*Baum*) chestnut tree

Kasten ['kastən] (**-s, ⁻**) *m* (*auch SPORT*) box; case; (*Truhe*) chest; **~wagen** *m* van

kastrieren [kas'tri:rən] *vt* to castrate

Katalog [kata'lo:k] (**-(e)s, -e**) *m* catalogue

Katalysator [kataly'za:tor] *m* catalyst; (*AUT*) catalytic converter

Katarrh [ka'tar] (**-s, -e**) *m* catarrh

katastrophal [katastro'fa:l] *adj* catastrophic

Katastrophe [kata'stro:fə] *f* catastrophe, disaster

Kat-Auto ['kat'auto] *n* car fitted with a catalytic converter

Kategorie [katego'ri:] *f* category

kategorisch [kate'go:rɪʃ] *adj* categorical

Kater ['ka:tər] (**-s, -**) *m* tomcat; (*umg*) hangover

kath. *abk* (= *katholisch*) Cath.

Kathedrale [kate'dra:lə] *f* cathedral

Kathode [ka'to:də] *f* cathode

Katholik [kato'li:k] (**-en, -en**) *m* Catholic

katholisch [ka'to:lɪʃ] *adj* Catholic

Kätzchen ['kɛtsçən] *nt* kitten

Katze ['katsə] *f* cat; **für die Katz** (*umg*) in vain, for nothing

Katzen- *zW*: **~auge** *nt* cat's eye; (*Fahrrad*) rear light; **~jammer** (*umg*) *m* hangover; **~sprung** (*umg*) *m* stone's throw; short journey

Kauderwelsch ['kaudərvɛlʃ] (**-(s)**) *nt* jargon; (*umg*) double Dutch

kauen ['kauən] *vt, vi* to chew

kauern ['kauərn] *vi* to crouch down; (*furchtsam*) to cower

Kauf [kauf] (**-(e)s, Käufe**) *m* purchase, buy; (*Kaufen*) buying; **ein guter ~** a bargain; **etw in ~ nehmen** to put up with sth; **k~en** *vt* to buy

Käufer(in) ['kɔyfər(ɪn)] (**-s, -**) *m(f)* buyer

Kauffrau *f* businesswoman

Kaufhaus *nt* department store

Kaufkraft *f* purchasing power

käuflich ['kɔyflɪç] *adj* purchasable, for sale; (*pej*) venal ♦ *adv*: **~ erwerben** to purchase

Kauf- *zW*: **k~lustig** *adj* interested in buying; **~mann** (*pl* **-leute**) *m* businessman; shopkeeper; **k~männisch** *adj* commercial; **k~männischer Angestellter** office worker

Kaugummi ['kaugumi] *m* chewing gum

Kaulquappe ['kaulkvapə] *f* tadpole

kaum [kaum] *adv* hardly, scarcely

Kaution [kautsi'o:n] *f* deposit; (*JUR*) bail

Kauz [kauts] (**-es, Käuze**) *m* owl; (*fig*) queer fellow

Kavalier [kava'li:r] (**-s, -e**) *m* gentleman, cavalier; **~sdelikt** *nt* peccadillo

Kaviar ['ka:viar] *m* caviar

keck [kɛk] *adj* daring, bold; **K~heit** *f* daring, boldness

Kegel ['ke:gəl] (**-s, -**) *m* skittle; (*MATH*) cone; **~bahn** *f* skittle alley; bowling alley; **k~n** *vi* to play skittles

Kehle ['ke:lə] *f* throat

Kehlkopf *m* larynx

Kehre ['ke:rə] *f* turn(ing), bend; **k~n** *vt, vi* to turn; (*mit Besen*) to sweep; **sich an etw** *dat* **nicht k~n** not to heed sth

Kehricht ['ke:rɪçt] (**-s**) *m* sweepings *pl*

Kehrmaschine *f* sweeper

Kehrseite *f* reverse, other side; wrong side; bad side

kehrtmachen *vi* to turn about, to about-turn

keifen ['kaifən] *vi* to scold, to nag

Keil [kail] (**-(e)s, -e**) *m* wedge; (*MIL*)

arrowhead; **~riemen** *m* (*AUT*) fan belt
Keim [kaım] (-(e)s, -e) *m* bud; (*MED, fig*)
germ; **k~en** *vi* to germinate; **k~frei** *adj*
sterile; **~zelle** *f* (*fig*) nucleus
kein [kaın] *adj* no, not ... any; **~e(r, s)**
pron no one, nobody; none; **~erlei** *adj*
attrib no ... whatsoever
keinesfalls *adv* on no account
keineswegs *adv* by no means
keinmal *adv* not once
Keks [ke:ks] (-es, -e) *m od nt* biscuit
Kelch [kɛlç] (-(e)s, -e) *m* cup, goblet,
chalice
Kelle ['kɛlə] *f* (*Suppen~*) ladle; (*Maurer~*)
trowel
Keller ['kɛlər] (-s, -) *m* cellar
Kellner(in) ['kɛlnər(ın)] (-s, -) *m(f)*
waiter(tress)
keltern ['kɛltərn] *vt* to press
kennen ['kɛnən] (*unreg*) *vt* to know;
~lernen *vt* to get to know; **sich ~lernen**
to get to know each other; (*zum
erstenmal*) to meet
Kenner (-s, -) *m* connoisseur
kenntlich *adj* distinguishable,
discernible; **etw ~ machen** to mark sth
Kenntnis (-, -se) *f* knowledge *no pl; etw*
zur ~ nehmen to note sth; **von etw ~**
nehmen to take notice of sth; **jdn in ~**
setzen to inform sb
Kenn- *zW:* **~zeichen** *nt* mark,
characteristic; **k~zeichnen** *vt insep* to
characterize; **~ziffer** *f* reference number
kentern ['kɛntərn] *vi* to capsize
Keramik [ke'ra:mık] (-, -en) *f* ceramics
pl, pottery
Kerbe ['kɛrbə] *f* notch, groove
Kerker ['kɛrkər] (-s, -) *m* prison
Kerl [kɛrl] (-s, -e) *m* chap, bloke (*BRIT*),
guy; **sie ist ein netter ~** she's a good
sort
Kern [kɛrn] (-(e)s, -e) *m* (*Obst~*) pip,
stone; (*Nuß~*) kernel; (*Atom~*) nucleus;
(*fig*) heart, core; **~energie** *f* nuclear
energy; **~forschung** *f* nuclear research;
~frage *f* central issue; **k~gesund** *adj*
thoroughly healthy, fit as a fiddle; **k~ig**
adj (*kraftvoll*) robust; (*Ausspruch*) pithy;
~kraftwerk *nt* nuclear power station;

k~los *adj* seedless, pipless; **~physik** *f*
nuclear physics *sg;* **~spaltung** *f* nuclear
fission; **~waffen** *pl* nuclear weapons
Kerze ['kɛrtsə] *f* candle; (*Zünd~*) plug;
k~ngerade *adj* straight as a die;
~nständer *m* candle holder
keß [kɛs] *adj* saucy
Kessel ['kɛsəl] (-s, -) *m* kettle; (*von
Lokomotive etc*) boiler; (*GEOG*) depression;
(*MIL*) encirclement
Kette ['kɛtə] *f* chain; **k~n** *vt* to chain
Ketten- *zW:* **~laden** *m* chain store;
~rauchen *nt* chain smoking; **~reaktion**
f chain reaction
Ketzer ['kɛtsər] (-s, -) *m* heretic
keuchen ['kɔʏçən] *vi* to pant, to gasp
Keuchhusten *m* whooping cough
Keule ['kɔʏlə] *f* club; (*KOCH*) leg
keusch [kɔʏʃ] *adj* chaste; **K~heit** *f*
chastity
kfm. *abk* = **kaufmännisch**
KG [ka:'ge:] (-, -s) *f abk*
(= *Kommanditgesellschaft*) limited
partnership
kg *abk* = **Kilogramm**
kichern ['kıçərn] *vi* to giggle
kidnappen ['kıdnɛpən] *vt* to kidnap
Kiefer¹ ['ki:fər] (-s, -) *m* jaw
Kiefer² (-, -n) *f* pine; **~nzapfen** *m* pine
cone
Kiel [ki:l] (-(e)s, -e) *m* (*Feder~*) quill;
(*NAUT*) keel
Kieme ['ki:mə] *f* gill
Kies [ki:s] (-es, -e) *m* gravel
Kilo ['ki:lo] *nt* kilo; **~gramm** [kilo'gram]
nt kilogram; **~meter** [kilo'me:tər] *m*
kilometre; **~meterzähler** *m* ≈ milometer
Kind [kınt] (-(e)s, -er) *nt* child; **von ~ auf**
from childhood
Kinder- ['kındər] *zW:* **~ei** [-'raı] *f*
childishness; **~garten** *m* nursery school,
playgroup; **~gärtnerin** *f* nursery school
teacher; **~geld** *nt* child benefit (*BRIT*);
~heim *nt* children's home; **~krippe** *f*
crèche; **~lähmung** *f* poliomyelitis;
k~leicht *adj* childishly easy; **k~los** *adj*
childless; **~mädchen** *nt* nursemaid;
k~reich *adj* with a lot of children;
~sendung *f* (*RUNDF, TV*) children's

programme; **~spiel** nt (fig) child's play;
~tagesstätte f day-nursery; **~wagen** m
pram, baby carriage (US); **~zimmer** nt
(für Kinder) children's room; (für
Säugling) nursery

Kind- zW: **~heit** f childhood; **k~isch** adj
childish; **k~lich** adj childlike

Kinn [kɪn] (-(e)s, -e) nt chin; **~haken** m
(BOXEN) uppercut

Kino ['ki:no] (-s, -s) nt cinema;
~besucher m cinema-goer; **~programm**
nt film programme

Kiosk ['ki:ɔsk] (-(e)s, -e) m kiosk

Kippe ['kɪpə] f cigarette end; (umg) fag;
auf der ~ stehen (fig) to be touch and go

kippen vi to topple over, to overturn ♦ vt
to tilt

Kirch- [kɪrç] zW: **~e** f church; **~enlied**
nt hymn; **~ensteuer** f church tax;
~gänger (-s, -) m churchgoer; **~hof** m
churchyard; **k~lich** adj ecclesiastical;
~turm m church tower, steeple

Kirmes ['kɪrmɛs] (-, -sen) f fair

Kirsche ['kɪrʃə] f cherry

Kissen ['kɪsən] (-s, -) nt cushion; (Kopf~)
pillow; **~bezug** m pillowslip

Kiste ['kɪstə] f box; chest

Kitsch [kɪtʃ] (-(e)s) m kitsch; **k~ig** adj
kitschy

Kitt [kɪt] (-(e)s, -e) m putty

Kittel (-s, -) m overall, smock

kitten vt to putty; (fig: Ehe etc) to cement

Kitz [kɪts] (-es, -e) nt kid; (Reh~) fawn

kitzelig ['kɪtsəlɪç] adj (auch fig) ticklish

kitzeln vt to tickle

Kiwi ['ki:vi] (-, -s) f (BOT, KOCH) kiwi fruit

KKW [ka:ka:'ve:] nt abk = **Kernkraftwerk**

kläffen ['klɛfən] vi to yelp

Klage ['kla:gə] f complaint; (JUR) action;
k~n vi (wehklagen) to lament, to wail;
(sich beschweren) to complain; (JUR) to
take legal action

Kläger(in) ['klɛ:gər(ɪn)] (-s, -) m(f)
plaintiff

kläglich ['klɛ:klɪç] adj wretched

klamm [klam] adj (Finger) numb; (feucht)
damp

Klammer ['klamər] (-, -n) f clamp; (in

Text) bracket; (Büro~) clip; (Wäsche~)
peg; (Zahn~) brace; **k~n** vr: **sich k~n an**
+akk to cling to

Klang [klaŋ] (-(e)s, ⁻e) m sound; **k~voll**
adj sonorous

Klappe ['klapə] f valve; (Ofen~) damper;
(umg: Mund) trap; **k~n** vi (Geräusch) to
click; (Sitz etc) to tip ♦ vt to tip ♦ vb
unpers to work

Klapper ['klapər] (-, -n) f rattle; **k~ig** adj
run-down, worn-out; **k~n** vi to clatter, to
rattle; **~schlange** f rattlesnake; **~storch**
m stork

Klapp- zW: **~messer** nt jack-knife; **~rad**
nt collapsible bicycle; **~stuhl** m folding
chair; **~tisch** m folding table

Klaps [klaps] (-es, ⁻e) m slap

klar [kla:r] adj clear; (NAUT) ready for sea;
(MIL) ready for action; **sich dat im ~en
sein über** +akk to be clear about; **ins ~e
kommen** to get clear; **(na) ~!** of course!

Kläranlage f purification plant

klären ['klɛ:rən] vt (Flüssigkeit) to purify;
(Probleme) to clarify ♦ vr to clear (itself)
up

Klarheit f clarity

Klarinette [klari'nɛtə] f clarinet

klar- zW: **~legen** vt to clear up, to
explain; **~machen** vt (Schiff) to get ready
for sea; **jdm etw ~machen** to make sth
clear to sb; **~sehen** (unreg) vi to see
clearly; **K~sichtfolie** f transparent film;
~stellen vt to clarify

Klärung ['klɛ:rʊŋ] f (von Flüssigkeit)
purification; (von Probleme) clarification

klarwerden (unreg) vr: **sich dat (über
etw akk) ~** to get (sth) clear in one's
mind

Klasse ['klasə] f class; (SCH) class, form;
k~ (umg) adj smashing

Klassen- zW: **~arbeit** f test;
~bewußtsein nt class consciousness;
~gesellschaft f class society; **~kampf** m
class conflict; **~lehrer** m form master;
k~los adj classless; **~sprecher(in)** m(f)
form prefect; **~zimmer** nt classroom

klassifizieren [klasifi'tsi:rən] vt to
classify

Klassik ['klasɪk] f (Zeit) classical period;

(*Stil*) classicism; ~**er** (-s, -) *m* classic

klassisch *adj* (*auch fig*) classical

Klatsch [klatʃ] (-(e)s, -e) *m* smack, crack; (*Gerede*) gossip; ~**base** *f* gossip, scandalmonger; ~**e** (*umg*) *f* crib; k~**en** *vi* (*Geräusch*) to clash; (*reden*) to gossip; (*applaudieren*) to applaud, to clap ♦ *vt*: **jdm Beifall k~en** to applaud sb; ~**mohn** *m* (corn) poppy; k~**naß** *adj* soaking wet

Klaue [ˈklaʊə] *f* claw; (*umg: Schrift*) scrawl; k~**n** (*umg*) *vt* to pinch

Klausel [ˈklaʊzəl] (-, -n) *f* clause

Klausur [klaʊˈzuːr] *f* seclusion; ~**arbeit** *f* examination paper

Klaviatur [klaviaˈtuːr] *f* keyboard

Klavier [klaˈviːr] (-s, -e) *nt* piano

Kleb- [ˈkleːb] *zW*: k~**en** *vt, vi*: k~**en (an** +*akk*) to stick (to); k~**rig** *adj* sticky; ~**stoff** *m* glue; ~**streifen** *m* adhesive tape

kleckern [ˈklɛkərn] *vi* to make a mess ♦ *vt* to spill

Klecks [klɛks] (-es, -e) *m* blot, stain

Klee [kleː] (-s) *m* clover; ~**blatt** *nt* cloverleaf; (*fig*) trio

Kleid [klaɪt] (-(e)s, -er) *nt* garment; (*Frauen~*) dress; ~**er** *pl* (*Kleidung*) clothes; k~**en** [ˈklaɪdən] *vt* to clothe, to dress; to suit ♦ *vr* to dress

Kleider [ˈklaɪdər] *zW*: ~**bügel** *m* coat hanger; ~**bürste** *f* clothes brush; ~**schrank** *m* wardrobe

Kleid- *zW*: k~**sam** *adj* flattering; ~**ung** *f* clothing; ~**ungsstück** *nt* garment

Kleie [ˈklaɪə] *f* bran

klein [klaɪn] *adj* little, small; K~**e(r, s)** *mf* little one; K~**format** *nt* small size; **im K~format** small-scale; K~**geld** *nt* small change; ~**hacken** *vt* to chop up, to mince; K~**igkeit** *f* trifle; K~**kind** *nt* infant; K~**kram** *m* details *pl*; ~**laut** *adj* dejected, quiet; ~**lich** *adj* petty, paltry; K~**od** [ˈklaɪnoːt] (-s, -odien) *nt* gem, jewel; treasure; ~**schneiden** (*unreg*) *vt* to chop up; ~**städtisch** *adj* provincial; ~**stmöglich** *adj* smallest possible

Kleister [ˈklaɪstər] (-s, -) *m* paste; k~**n** *vt* to paste

Klemme [ˈklɛmə] *f* clip; (*MED*) clamp; (*fig*)

jam; k~**n** *vt* (*festhalten*) to jam; (*quetschen*) to pinch, to nip ♦ *vr* to catch o.s.; (*sich hineinzwängen*) to squeeze o.s. ♦ *vi* (*Tür*) to stick, to jam; **sich hinter jdn/etw k~n** to get on to sb/down to sth

Klempner [ˈklɛmpnər] (-s, -) *m* plumber

Klerus [ˈkleːrʊs] (-) *m* clergy

Klette [ˈklɛtə] *f* burr

Kletter- [ˈklɛtər] *zW*: ~**er** (-s, -) *m* climber; k~**n** *vi* to climb; ~**pflanze** *f* creeper

Klient(in) [kliˈɛnt(ɪn)] *m(f)* client

Klima [ˈkliːma, *pl* kliˈmaːtə] (-s, -s *od* -te) *nt* climate; ~**anlage** *f* air conditioning; ~**wechsel** *m* change of air

klimpern [ˈklɪmpərn] (*umg*) *vi* (*mit Münzen, Schlüsseln*) to jingle; (*auf Klavier*) to plonk (away)

Klinge [ˈklɪŋə] *f* blade; sword

Klingel [ˈklɪŋəl] (-, -n) *f* bell; ~**beutel** *m* collection bag; k~**n** *vi* to ring

klingen [ˈklɪŋən] (*unreg*) *vi* to sound; (*Gläser*) to clink

Klinik [ˈkliːnɪk] *f* hospital, clinic

Klinke [ˈklɪŋkə] *f* handle

Klippe [ˈklɪpə] *f* cliff; (*im Meer*) reef; (*fig*) hurdle

klipp und klar [ˈklɪpˈʊntklaːr] *adj* clear and concise

klirren [ˈklɪrən] *vi* to clank, to jangle; (*Gläser*) to clink; ~**de Kälte** biting cold

Klischee [klɪˈʃeː] (-s, -s) *nt* (*Druckplatte*) plate, block; (*fig*) cliché; ~**vorstellung** *f* stereotyped idea

Klo [kloː] (-s, -s; *umg*) *nt* loo (*BRIT*), john (*US*)

Kloake [kloˈaːkə] *f* sewer

klobig [ˈkloːbɪç] *adj* clumsy

Klopapier (*umg*) *nt* loo paper (*BRIT*)

klopfen [ˈklɔpfən] *vi* to knock; (*Herz*) to thump ♦ *vt* to beat; **es klopft** somebody's knocking; **jdm auf die Schulter ~** to tap sb on the shoulder

Klopfer (-s, -) *m* (*Teppich~*) beater; (*Tür~*) knocker

Klops [klɔps] (-es, -e) *m* meatball

Klosett [kloˈzɛt] (-s, -e *od* -s) *nt* lavatory, toilet; ~**papier** *nt* toilet paper

Kloß [kloːs] (-es, ⁼e) *m* (*im Hals*) lump;

(*KOCH*) dumpling

Kloster ['klo:stər] (-s, ‥) *nt* (*Männer~*) monastery; (*Frauen~*) convent

klösterlich ['klø:stərlıç] *adj* monastic; convent *cpd*

Klotz [klɔts] (-es, ‥e) *m* log; (*Hack~*) block; **ein ~ am Bein** (*fig*) a drag, a millstone round (sb's) neck

Klub [klʊp] (-s, -s) *m* club; **~sessel** *m* easy chair

Kluft [klʊft] (-, ‥e) *f* cleft, gap; (*GEOG*) gorge, chasm

klug [klu:k] *adj* clever, intelligent; **K~heit** *f* cleverness, intelligence

Klumpen ['klʊmpən] (-s, -) *m* (*Erd~*) clod; (*Blut~*) clot; (*Gold~*) nugget; (*KOCH*) lump; **k~** *vi* to go lumpy; to clot

km *abk* = **Kilometer**

knabbern ['knabərn] *vt, vi* to nibble

Knabe ['kna:bə] (-n, -n) *m* boy; **k~nhaft** *adj* boyish

Knäckebrot ['knɛkəbro:t] *nt* crispbread

knacken ['knakən] *vt, vi* (*auch fig*) to crack

Knacks [knaks] (-es, -e) *m* crack; (*fig*) defect

Knall [knal] (-(e)s, -e) *m* bang; (*Peitschen~*) crack; **~ und Fall** (*umg*) unexpectedly; **~bonbon** *nt* cracker; **k~en** *vi* to bang; to crack; **k~rot** *adj* bright red

knapp [knap] *adj* tight; (*Geld*) scarce; (*Sprache*) concise; **eine ~e Stunde** just under an hour; **~ unter/neben** just under/by; **~halten** (*unreg*) *vt*: **jdn (mit etw) ~halten** to keep sb short (of sth); **K~heit** *f* tightness; scarcity; conciseness

knarren ['knarən] *vi* to creak

Knast [knast] (-(e)s; *umg*) *m* (*Haftstrafe*) porridge (*inf*), time (*inf*); (*Gefängnis*) slammer (*inf*), clink (*inf*)

knattern ['knatərn] *vi* to rattle; (*Maschinengewehr*) to chatter

Knäuel ['knɔʏəl] (-s, -) *m od nt* (*Woll~*) ball; (*Menschen~*) knot

Knauf [knaʊf] (-(e)s, **Knäufe**) *m* knob; (*Schwert~*) pommel

knautschen ['knaʊtʃən] *vt, vi* to crumple

Knebel ['kne:bəl] (-s, -) *m* gag; **k~n** *vt* to gag; (*NAUT*) to fasten

kneifen ['knaɪfən] (*unreg*) *vt* to pinch ♦ *vi* to pinch; (*sich drücken*) to back out; **vor etw ~** to dodge sth

Kneipe ['knaɪpə] (*umg*) *f* pub

kneten ['kne:tən] *vt* to knead; (*Wachs*) to mould

Knick [knɪk] (-(e)s, -e) *m* (*Sprung*) crack; (*Kurve*) bend; (*Falte*) fold; **k~en** *vt, vi* (*springen*) to crack; (*brechen*) to break; (*Papier*) to fold; **gek~t sein** to be downcast

Knicks [knɪks] (-es, -e) *m* curtsey; **k~en** *vi* to curtsey

Knie [kni:] (-s, -) *nt* knee; **~beuge** *f* knee bend; **~bundhose** *m* knee breeches; **~gelenk** *nt* knee joint; **~kehle** *f* back of the knee; **k~n** *vi* to kneel; **~scheibe** *f* kneecap; **~strumpf** *m* knee-length sock

Kniff [knɪf] (-(e)s, -e) *m* (*fig*) trick, knack; **k~elig** *adj* tricky

knipsen ['knɪpsən] *vt* (*Fahrkarte*) to punch; (*PHOT*) to take a snap of, to snap ♦ *vi* to take a snap *od* snaps

Knirps [knɪrps] (-es, -e) *m* little chap; (®: *Schirm*) telescopic umbrella

knirschen ['knɪrʃən] *vi* to crunch; **mit den Zähnen ~** to grind one's teeth

knistern ['knɪstərn] *vi* to crackle

Knitter- ['knɪtər] *zW:* **~falte** *f* crease; **k~frei** *adj* non-crease; **k~n** *vi* to crease

Knoblauch ['kno:plaʊx] (-(e)s) *m* garlic

Knoblauchzehe *f* (*KOCH*) clove of garlic

Knöchel ['knœçəl] (-s, -) *m* knuckle; (*Fuß~*) ankle

Knochen ['knɔxən] (-s, -) *m* bone; **~bruch** *m* fracture; **~gerüst** *nt* skeleton; **~mark** *nt* bone marrow

knöchern ['knœçərn] *adj* bone

knochig ['knɔxıç] *adj* bony

Knödel ['knø:dəl] (-s, -) *m* dumpling

Knolle ['knɔlə] *f* tuber

Knopf [knɔpf] (-(e)s, ‥e) *m* button; (*Kragen~*) stud

knöpfen ['knœpfən] *vt* to button

Knopfloch *nt* buttonhole

Knorpel ['knɔrpəl] (-s, -) *m* cartilage, gristle; **k~ig** *adj* gristly

Knospe ['knɔspə] *f* bud

Knoten ['kno:tən] (-s, -) *m* knot; (*BOT*)

node; (*MED*) lump; **k~** *vt* to knot; **~punkt** *m* junction

Knüller ['knʏlər] (-s, -; *umg*) *m* hit; (*Reportage*) scoop

knüpfen ['knʏpfən] *vt* to tie; (*Teppich*) to knot; (*Freundschaft*) to form

Knüppel ['knʏpəl] (-s, -) *m* cudgel; (*Polizei~*) baton, truncheon; (*AVIAT*) (joy)stick; **~schaltung** *f* (*AUT*) floor-mounted gear change

knurren ['knʊrən] *vi* (*Hund*) to snarl; to growl; (*Magen*) to rumble; (*Mensch*) to mutter

knusperig ['knʊspərɪç] *adj* crisp; (*Keks*) crunchy

k.o. [ka:'o:] *adj* knocked out; (*fig*) done in

Koalition [koalitsi'o:n] *f* coalition

Kobalt ['ko:balt] (-s) *nt* cobalt

Kobold ['ko:bɔlt] (-(e)s, -e) *m* goblin, imp

Kobra ['ko:bra] (-, -s) *f* cobra

Koch [kɔx] (-(e)s, ⁺e) *m* cook; **~buch** *nt* cook(ery) book; **k~en** *vt, vi* to cook; (*Wasser*) to boil; **~er** (-s, -) *m* stove, cooker

Köcher ['kœçər] (-s, -) *m* quiver

Kochgelegenheit ['kɔxgəle:gənhaɪt] *f* cooking facilities *pl*

Köchin ['kœçɪn] *f* cook

Koch- *zW*: **~löffel** *m* kitchen spoon; **~nische** *f* kitchenette; **~platte** *f* hotplate; **~salz** *nt* cooking salt; **~topf** *m* saucepan, pot

Köder ['kø:dər] (-s, -) *m* bait, lure

ködern *vt* (*Tier*) to trap with bait; (*Person*) to entice, to tempt

Koexistenz [koɛksɪs'tɛnts] *f* coexistence

Koffein [kɔfe'i:n] (-s) *nt* caffeine; **k~frei** *adj* decaffeinated

Koffer ['kɔfər] (-s, -) *m* suitcase; (*Schrank~*) trunk; **~radio** *nt* portable radio; **~raum** *m* (*AUT*) boot (*BRIT*), trunk (*US*)

Kognak ['kɔnjak] (-s, -s) *m* brandy, cognac

Kohl [ko:l] (-(e)s, -e) *m* cabbage

Kohle ['ko:lə] *f* coal; (*Holz~*) charcoal; (*CHEM*) carbon; **~hydrat** (-(e)s, -e) *nt* carbohydrate

Kohlen- *zW*: **~dioxyd** (-(e)s, -e) *nt*

carbon dioxide; **~händler** *m* coal merchant, coalman; **~säure** *f* carbon dioxide; **~stoff** *m* carbon

Kohlepapier *nt* carbon paper

Koje ['ko:jə] *f* cabin; (*Bett*) bunk

Kokain [koka'i:n] (-s) *nt* cocaine

kokett [ko'kɛt] *adj* coquettish, flirtatious

Kokosnuß ['ko:kɔsnʊs] *f* coconut

Koks [ko:ks] (-es, -e) *m* coke

Kolben ['kɔlbən] (-s, -) *m* (*Gewehr~*) rifle butt; (*Keule*) club; (*CHEM*) flask; (*TECH*) piston; (*Mais~*) cob

Kolchose [kɔl'ço:zə] *f* collective farm

Kolik ['ko:lɪk] *f* colic, the gripes *pl*

Kollaps [kɔ'laps] (-es, -e) *m* collapse

Kolleg [kɔ'le:k] (-s, -s *od* -ien) *nt* lecture course; **~e** [kɔ'le:gə] (-n, -n) *m* colleague; **~in** *f* colleague; **~ium** *nt* working party; (*SCH*) staff

Kollekte [kɔ'lɛktə] *f* (*REL*) collection

kollektiv [kɔlɛk'ti:f] *adj* collective

Köln [kœln] (-s) *nt* Cologne

Kolonie [kolo'ni:] *f* colony

kolonisieren [koloni'zi:rən] *vt* to colonize

Kolonne [ko'lɔnə] *f* column; (*von Fahrzeugen*) convoy

Koloß [ko'lɔs] (-sses, -sse) *m* colossus

kolossal [kolo'sa:l] *adj* colossal

Kombi- ['kɔmbi] *zW*: **~nation** [-natsi'o:n] *f* combination; (*Vermutung*) conjecture; (*Hemdhose*) combinations *pl*; **~nationsschloß** *nt* combination lock; **k~nieren** [-'ni:rən] *vt* to combine ♦ *vi* to deduce, to work out; (*vermuten*) to guess; **~wagen** *m* station wagon; **~zange** *f* (pair of) pliers *pl*

Komet [ko'me:t] (-en, -en) *m* comet

Komfort [kɔm'fo:r] (-s) *m* luxury

Komik ['ko:mɪk] *f* humour, comedy; **~er** (-s, -) *m* comedian

komisch ['ko:mɪʃ] *adj* funny

Komitee [komi'te:] (-s, -s) *nt* committee

Komma ['kɔma] (-s, -s *od* -ta) *nt* comma; 2 ~ 3 2 point 3

Kommand- [kɔ'mand] *zW*: **~ant** [-'dant] *m* commander, commanding officer; **k~ieren** [-'di:rən] *vt, vi* to command; **~o** (-s, -s) *nt* command, order; (*Truppe*)

detachment, squad; **auf ~o** to order
kommen [ˈkɔmən] (*unreg*) *vi* to come;
(*näher~*) to approach; (*passieren*) to
happen; (*gelangen, geraten*) to get;
(*Blumen, Zähne, Tränen etc*) to appear; (*in
die Schule, das Zuchthaus etc*) to go; **~
lassen** to send for; **das kommt in den
Schrank** that goes in the cupboard; **zu
sich ~** to come round *od* to; **zu etw ~** to
acquire sth; **um etw ~** to lose sth; **nichts
auf jdn/etw ~ lassen** to have nothing
said against sb/sth; **jdm frech ~** to get
cheeky with sb; **auf jeden vierten
kommt ein Platz** there's one place for
every fourth person; **wer kommt zuerst?**
who's first?; **unter ein Auto ~** to be run
over by a car; **wie hoch kommt das?**
what does that cost?; **komm gut nach
Hause!** safe journey (home); **~den
Sonntag** next Sunday; **K~** (-s) *nt* coming
Kommentar [kɔmɛnˈtaːr] *m*
commentary; **kein ~** no comment; **k~los**
adj without comment
Kommentator [kɔmɛnˈtaːtɔr] *m* (*TV*)
commentator
kommentieren [kɔmɛnˈtiːrən] *vt* to
comment on
kommerziell [kɔmɛrtsiˈɛl] *adj*
commercial
Kommilitone [kɔmiliˈtoːnə] (-n, -n) *m*
fellow student
Kommissar [kɔmɪˈsaːr] *m* police
inspector
Kommission [kɔmɪsiˈoːn] *f* (*COMM*)
commission; (*Ausschuß*) committee
Kommode [kɔˈmoːdə] *f* (chest of)
drawers
kommunal [kɔmuˈnaːl] *adj* local; (*von
Stadt auch*) municipal
Kommune [kɔˈmuːnə] *f* commune
Kommunikation [kɔmunɪkatsiˈoːn] *f*
communication
Kommunion [kɔmuniˈoːn] *f* communion
Kommuniqué [kɔmyniˈkeː] (-s, -s) *nt*
communiqué
Kommunismus [kɔmuˈnɪsmʊs] *m*
communism
Kommunist(in) *m(f)* communist; **k~isch**
adj communist

kommunizieren [kɔmuniˈtsiːrən] *vi* to
communicate; (*REL*) to receive
Communion
Komödie [koˈmøːdiə] *f* comedy
Kompagnon [kɔmpanˈjõː] (-s, -s) *m*
(*COMM*) partner
kompakt [kɔmˈpakt] *adj* compact
Kompanie [kɔmpaˈniː] *f* company
Kompaß [ˈkɔmpas] (-sses, -sse) *m*
compass
kompatibel [kɔmpaˈtiːbəl] *adj*
compatible
kompetent [kɔmpeˈtɛnt] *adj* competent
Kompetenz *f* competence, authority
komplett [kɔmˈplɛt] *adj* complete
Komplex [kɔmˈplɛks] (-es, -e) *m*
(*Gebäude~*) complex
Komplikation [kɔmplikatsiˈoːn] *f*
complication
Kompliment [kɔmpliˈmɛnt] *nt*
compliment
Komplize [kɔmˈpliːtsə] (-n, -n) *m*
accomplice
kompliziert [kɔmpliˈtsiːrt] *adj*
complicated
komponieren [kɔmpoˈniːrən] *vt* to
compose
Komponist [kɔmpoˈnɪst] *m* composer
Komposition [kɔmpozitsiˈoːn] *f*
composition
Kompost [kɔmˈpɔst] (-(e)s, -e) *m*
compost
Kompott [kɔmˈpɔt] (-(e)s, -e) *nt* stewed
fruit
Kompromiß [kɔmproˈmɪs] (-sses, -sse) *m*
compromise; **k~bereit** *adj* willing to
compromise; **~lösung** *f* compromise
solution
Kondens- [kɔnˈdɛns] *zW*: **~ation**
[kɔndɛnzatsiˈoːn] *f* condensation; **k~ieren**
[kɔndɛnˈziːrən] *vt* to condense; **~milch** *f*
condensed milk
Kondition [kɔndɪtsiˈoːn] *f* (*WIRTS, FINANZ*)
condition; (*Durchhaltevermögen*) stamina;
(*körperliche Verfassung*) physical
condition, state of health
Konditionstraining
[kɔndɪtsiˈoːnstrɛːnɪŋ] *nt* fitness training
Konditor [kɔnˈdiːtɔr] *m* pastrycook; **~ei**

[-'raɪ] *f* café; cake shop
Kondom [kɔn'do:m] (**-s, -e**) *nt* condom
Konferenz [kɔnfe'rɛnts] *f* conference, meeting
Konfession [kɔnfɛsi'o:n] *f* (religious) denomination; **k~ell** [-'nɛl] *adj* denominational; **k~slos** *adj* non-denominational
Konfetti [kɔn'fɛti] (**-(s)**) *nt* confetti
Konfirmand [kɔnfɪr'mant] *m* candidate for confirmation
Konfirmation [kɔnfɪrmatsi'o:n] *f* (*REL*) confirmation
konfirmieren [kɔnfɪr'mi:rən] *vt* to confirm
konfiszieren [kɔnfɪs'tsi:rən] *vt* to confiscate
Konfitüre [kɔnfi'ty:rə] *f* jam
Konflikt [kɔn'flɪkt] (**-(e)s, -e**) *m* conflict
konfrontieren [kɔnfrɔn'ti:rən] *vt* to confront
konfus [kɔn'fu:s] *adj* confused
Kongreß [kɔn'grɛs] (**-sses, -sse**) *m* congress
Kongruenz [kɔngru'ɛnts] *f* agreement, congruence
König ['kø:nɪç] (**-(e)s, -e**) *m* king; **~in** ['kø:nɪgɪn] *f* queen; **k~lich** *adj* royal; **~reich** *nt* kingdom; **~tum** (**-(e)s**) *nt* kingship
Konjugation [kɔnjugatsi'o:n] *f* conjugation
konjugieren [kɔnju'gi:rən] *vt* to conjugate
Konjunktion [kɔnjuŋktsi'o:n] *f* conjunction
Konjunktiv ['kɔnjuŋkti:f] (**-s, -e**) *m* subjunctive
Konjunktur [kɔnjuŋk'tu:r] *f* economic situation; (*Hoch~*) boom
konkav [kɔn'ka:f] *adj* concave
konkret [kɔn'kre:t] *adj* concrete
Konkurrent(in) [kɔnku'rɛnt(ɪn)] *m(f)* competitor
Konkurrenz [kɔnku'rɛnts] *f* competition; **k~fähig** *adj* competitive; **~kampf** *m* competition; rivalry, competitive situation
konkurrieren [kɔnku'ri:rən] *vi* to

compete
Konkurs [kɔn'kurs] (**-es, -e**) *m* bankruptcy
Können (**-s**) *nt* ability

können ['kœnən] (*pt* **konnte**, *pp* **gekonnt** *od* (*als Hilfsverb*) **können**) *vt, vi* **1** to be able to; **ich kann es machen** I can do it, I am able to do it; **ich kann es nicht machen** I can't do it, I'm not able to do it; **ich kann nicht ...** I can't ..., I cannot ...; **ich kann nicht mehr** I can't go on
2 (*wissen, beherrschen*) to know; **können Sie Deutsch?** can you speak German?; **er kann gut Englisch** he speaks English well; **sie kann keine Mathematik** she can't do mathematics
3 (*dürfen*) to be allowed to; **kann ich gehen?** can I go?; **könnte ich ...?** could I ...?; **kann ich mit?** (*umg*) can I come with you?
4 (*möglich sein*): **Sie könnten recht haben** you may be right; **das kann sein** that's possible; **kann sein** maybe

Könner *m* expert
konnte *etc* ['kɔntə] *vb siehe* **können**
konsequent [kɔnze'kvɛnt] *adj* consistent
Konsequenz [kɔnze'kvɛnts] *f* consistency; (*Folgerung*) conclusion
Konserv- [kɔn'zɛrv] *zW:* **k~ativ** [-a'ti:f] *adj* conservative; **~ative(r)** [-a'ti:və(r)] *mf* (*POL*) conservative; **~e** *f* tinned food; **~enbüchse** *f* tin, can; **k~ieren** [-'vi:rən] *vt* to preserve; **~ierung** *f* preservation; **~ierungsmittel** *nt* preservative; **~ierungsstoff** *m* preservatives
Konsonant [kɔnzo'nant] *m* consonant
konstant [kɔn'stant] *adj* constant
konstruieren [kɔnstru'i:rən] *vt* to construct
Konstrukteur [kɔnstrok'tø:r] *m* designer
Konstruktion [kɔnstroktsi'o:n] *f* construction
konstruktiv [kɔnstrok'ti:f] *adj* constructive
Konsul ['kɔnzol] (**-s, -n**) *m* consul; **~at** [-'la:t] *nt* consulate

konsultieren [kɔnzʊl'tiːrən] *vt* to consult
Konsum [kɔn'zuːm] (-s) *m* consumption;
~**artikel** *m* consumer article; ~**ent**
[-'mɛnt] *m* consumer; **k~ieren** [-'miːrən]
vt to consume
Kontakt [kɔn'takt] (-(e)s, -e) *m* contact;
k~arm *adj* unsociable; **k~freudig** *adj*
sociable; ~**linsen** *pl* contact lenses
kontern ['kɔntərn] *vt, vi* to counter
Kontinent ['kɔntinɛnt] *m* continent
Kontingent [kɔntɪŋ'gɛnt] (-(e)s, -e) *nt*
quota; (*Truppen~*) contingent
kontinuierlich [kɔntinu'iːrlɪç] *adj*
continuous
Konto ['kɔntoː] (-s, **Konten**) *nt* account;
~**auszug** *m* statement (of account);
~**inhaber(in)** *m(f)* account holder;
~**stand** *m* balance
Kontra ['kɔntra] (-s, -s) *nt* (*KARTEN*)
double; **jdm** ~ **geben** (*fig*) to contradict
sb; ~**baß** *m* double bass
Kontrahent [-'hɛnt] *m* (*COMM*)
contracting party
Kontrapunkt *m* counterpoint
Kontrast [kɔn'trast] (-(e)s, -e) *m* contrast
Kontroll- [kɔn'trɔl] *zW:* ~**e** *f* control,
supervision; (*Paß~*) passport control;
~**eur** [-'løːr] *m* inspector; **k~ieren**
[-'liːrən] *vt* to control, to supervise;
(*nachprüfen*) to check
Konvention [kɔnvɛntsi'oːn] *f* convention;
k~ell [-'nɛl] *adj* conventional
Konversation [kɔnvɛrzatsi'oːn] *f*
conversation; ~**slexikon** *nt*
encyclop(a)edia
konvex [kɔn'vɛks] *adj* convex
Konvoi ['kɔnvɔy] (-s, -s) *m* convoy
Konzentration [kɔntsɛntratsi'oːn] *f*
concentration
Konzentrationslager *nt* concentration
camp
konzentrieren [kɔntsɛn'triːrən] *vt, vr* to
concentrate
konzentriert *adj* concentrated ♦ *adv*
(*zuhören, arbeiten*) intently
Konzern [kɔn'tsɛrn] (-s, -e) *m* combine
Konzert [kɔn'tsɛrt] (-(e)s, -e) *nt* concert;
(*Stück*) concerto; ~**saal** *m* concert hall
Konzession [kɔntsɛsi'oːn] *f* licence;

(*Zugeständnis*) concession
Konzil [kɔn'tsiːl] (-s, -e *od* -ien) *nt* council
kooperativ [ko'ɔpera'tiːf] *adj*
cooperative
koordinieren [ko'ɔrdɪ'niːrən] *vt* to
coordinate
Kopf [kɔpf] (-(e)s, ⁼e) *m* head; ~**haut** *f*
scalp; ~**hörer** *m* headphones *pl*; ~**kissen**
nt pillow; **k~los** *adj* panic-stricken;
k~rechnen *vi* to do mental arithmetic;
~**salat** *m* lettuce; ~**schmerzen** *pl*
headache *sg*; ~**sprung** *m* header, dive;
~**stand** *m* headstand; ~**stütze** *f* (*im Auto*
etc) headrest, head restraint; ~**tuch** *nt*
headscarf; ~**weh** *nt* headache;
~**zerbrechen** *nt*: **jdm** ~**zerbrechen**
machen to be a headache for sb
Kopie [ko'piː] *f* copy; **k~ren** *vt* to copy
Kopiergerät *nt* photocopier
Koppel¹ ['kɔpəl] (-, -n) *f* (*Weide*)
enclosure
Koppel² (-s, -) *nt* (*Gürtel*) belt
koppeln *vt* to couple
Koppelung *f* coupling
Koralle [ko'ralə] *f* coral; ~**nriff** *nt* coral
reef
Koran [ko'raːn] (-s, -e) *m* Koran
Korb [kɔrp] (-(e)s, ⁼e) *m* basket; **jdm**
einen ~ **geben** (*fig*) to turn sb down;
~**ball** *m* basketball; ~**stuhl** *m* wicker
chair
Kord [kɔrt] (-(e)s, -e) *m* corduroy
Kordel ['kɔrdəl] (-, -n) *f* cord, string
Kork [kɔrk] (-(e)s, -e) *m* cork; ~**en** (-s, -)
m stopper, cork; ~**enzieher** (-s, -) *m*
corkscrew
Korn [kɔrn] (-(e)s, ⁼er) *nt* corn, grain;
(*Gewehr*) sight; ~**blume** *f* cornflower
Körper ['kœrpər] (-s, -) *m* body; ~**bau** *m*
build; **k~behindert** *adj* disabled;
~**geruch** *m* body odour; ~**gewicht** *nt*
weight; ~**größe** *f* height; **k~lich** *adj*
physical; ~**pflege** *f* personal hygiene;
~**schaft** *f* corporation; ~**schaftssteuer** *f*
corporation tax; ~**teil** *m* part of the body
korpulent [kɔrpu'lɛnt] *adj* corpulent
korrekt [kɔ'rɛkt] *adj* correct; **K~ur**
[-'tuːr] *f* (*eines Textes*) proofreading; (*Text*)
proof; (*SCH*) marking, correction

Korrespond- [kɔrɛspɔnd] *zW:* **~ent(in)**
[-'dɛnt(ɪn)] *m(f)* correspondent; **~enz**
[-'dɛnts] *f* correspondence; **k~ieren**
[-'diːrən] *vi* to correspond
Korridor ['kɔridoːr] *(-s, -e) m* corridor
korrigieren [kɔri'giːrən] *vt* to correct
Korruption [kɔrʊptsi'oːn] *f* corruption
Korsett [kɔr'zɛt] *(-(e)s, -e) nt* corset
Kose- ['koːzə] *zW:* **~form** *f* pet form;
~name *m* pet name; **~wort** *nt* term of
endearment
Kosmetik [kɔs'meːtɪk] *f* cosmetics *pl*;
~erin *f* beautician
kosmetisch *adj* cosmetic; *(Chirurgie)*
plastic
kosmisch ['kɔsmɪʃ] *adj* cosmic
Kosmo- [kɔsmo] *zW:* **~naut** [-'naʊt] *(-en,*
-en) m cosmonaut; **k~po'litisch** *adj*
cosmopolitan; **'~s** *(-) m* cosmos
Kost [kɔst] *(-) f (Nahrung)* food;
(Verpflegung) board; **k~bar** *adj* precious;
(teuer) costly, expensive; **~barkeit** *f*
preciousness; costliness, expensiveness;
(Wertstück) valuable
Kosten *pl* cost(s); *(Ausgaben)* expenses;
auf ~ von at the expense of; **k~** *vt* to
cost; *(versuchen)* to taste ♦ *vi* to taste;
was kostet ...? what does ... cost?, how
much is ...?; **~anschlag** *m* estimate;
k~los *adj* free (of charge)
köstlich ['kœstlɪç] *adj* precious; *(Einfall)*
delightful; *(Essen)* delicious; **sich ~**
amüsieren to have a marvellous time
Kostprobe *f* taste; *(fig)* sample
kostspielig *adj* expensive
Kostüm [kɔs'tyːm] *(-s, -e) nt* costume;
(Damen~) suit; **~fest** *nt* fancy-dress
party; **k~ieren** [kɔsty'miːrən] *vt, vr* to
dress up; **~verleih** *m* costume agency
Kot [koːt] *(-(e)s) m* excrement
Kotelett [kɔtə'lɛt] *(-(e)s, -e od -s) nt*
cutlet, chop
Koteletten *pl (Bart)* sideboards
Köter ['køːtər] *(-s, -) m* cur
Kotflügel *m (AUT)* wing
kotzen ['kɔtsən] *(umg!) vi* to puke *(inf)*,
to throw up *(inf)*
Krabbe ['krabə] *f* shrimp; **k~ln** *vi* to
crawl

Krach [krax] *(-(e)s, -s od -e) m* crash;
(andauernd) noise; *(umg: Streit)* quarrel,
argument; **k~en** *vi* to crash; *(beim*
Brechen) to crack ♦ *vr (umg)* to argue, to
quarrel
krächzen ['krɛçtsən] *vi* to croak
Kraft [kraft] *(-, ⁺e) f* strength; power;
force; *(Arbeits~)* worker; **in ~ treten** to
come into force; **k~ präp +gen** by virtue
of; **~fahrer** *m* (motor) driver; **~fahrzeug**
nt motor vehicle; **~fahrzeugbrief** *m*
logbook; **~fahrzeugsteuer** *f* ≈ road tax;
~fahrzeugversicherung *f* car insurance
kräftig ['krɛftɪç] *adj* strong; **~en** [-gən] *vt*
to strengthen
Kraft- *zW:* **k~los** *adj* weak; powerless;
(JUR) invalid; **~probe** *f* trial of strength;
k~voll *adj* vigorous; **~werk** *nt* power
station
Kragen ['kraːgən] *(-s, -) m* collar; **~weite**
f collar size
Krähe ['krɛːə] *f* crow; **k~n** *vi* to crow
Kralle ['kralə] *f* claw; *(Vogel~)* talon; **k~n**
vt to clutch; *(krampfhaft)* to claw
Kram [kraːm] *(-(e)s) m* stuff, rubbish;
k~en *vi* to rummage; **~laden** *(pej) m*
small shop
Krampf [krampf] *(-(e)s, ⁺e) m* cramp;
(zuckend) spasm; **~ader** *f* varicose vein;
k~haft *adj* convulsive; *(fig: Versuche)*
desperate
Kran [kraːn] *(-(e)s, ⁺e) m* crane; *(Wasser~)*
tap, faucet *(US)*
Kranich ['kraːnɪç] *(-s, -e) m (ZOOL)* crane
krank [kraŋk] *adj* ill, sick; **K~e(r)** *mf* sick
person, invalid; patient
kranken ['kraŋkən] *vi:* **an etw** *dat* **~** *(fig)*
to suffer from sth
kränken ['krɛŋkən] *vt* to hurt
Kranken- *zW:* **~geld** *nt* sick pay;
~gymnastik *f* physiotherapy; **~haus** *nt*
hospital; **~kasse** *f* health insurance;
~pfleger *m* nursing orderly; **~schein** *m*
health insurance card; **~schwester** *f*
nurse; **~versicherung** *f* health
insurance; **~wagen** *m* ambulance
Krank- *zW:* **k~haft** *adj* diseased; *(Angst*
etc) morbid; **~heit** *f* illness; disease;
~heitserreger *m* disease-causing agent

kränklich → *kritisch*

kränklich *adj* sickly

Kränkung *f* insult, offence

Kranz [krants] (-es, ⁼e) *m* wreath, garland

kraß [kras] *adj* crass

Krater ['kra:tər] (-s, -) *m* crater

Kratz- ['krats] *zW*: **~bürste** *f* (*fig*) crosspatch; **k~en** *vt, vi* to scratch; **~er** (-s, -) *m* scratch; (*Werkzeug*) scraper

Kraul [kraʊl] (-s) *nt* crawl; **~ schwimmen** to do the crawl; **k~en** *vi* (*schwimmen*) to do the crawl ♦ *vt* (*streicheln*) to fondle

kraus [kraʊs] *adj* crinkly; (*Haar*) frizzy; (*Stirn*) wrinkled; **K~e** ['kraʊzə] *f* frill, ruffle

Kraut [kraʊt] (-(e)s, Kräuter) *nt* plant; (*Gewürz*) herb; (*Gemüse*) cabbage

Krawall [kra'val] (-s, -e) *m* row, uproar

Krawatte [kra'vatə] *f* tie

kreativ [krea'ti:f] *adj* creative

Krebs [kre:ps] (-es, -e) *m* crab; (*MED, ASTROL*) cancer

krebskrank *adj* suffering from cancer

Kredit [kre'di:t] (-(e)s, -e) *m* credit

Kreditinstitut *nt* bank

Kreditkarte *f* credit card

Kreide ['kraɪdə] *f* chalk; **k~bleich** *adj* as white as a sheet

Kreis [kraɪs] (-es, -e) *m* circle; (*Stadt~ etc*) district; **im ~ gehen** (*auch fig*) to go round in circles

kreischen ['kraɪʃən] *vi* to shriek, to screech

Kreis- *zW*: **~el** ['kraɪzəl] (-s, -) *m* top; (*Verkehrs~*) roundabout (*BRIT*), traffic circle (*US*); **k~en** ['kraɪzən] *vi* to spin; **~lauf** *m* (*MED*) circulation; (*fig: der Natur etc*) cycle; **~säge** *f* circular saw

Kreisstadt *f* county town

Kreisverkehr *m* roundabout traffic

Krematorium [krema'to:rɪʊm] *nt* crematorium

Kreml ['krɛm(ə)l] (-s) *m* Kremlin

krepieren [kre'pi:rən] (*umg*) *vi* (*sterben*) to die, to kick the bucket

Krepp [krɛp] (-s, -s *od* -e) *m* crepe; **~(p)apier** *nt* crepe paper; **~sohle** *f* crepe sole

Kresse ['krɛsə] *f* cress

Kreta ['kre:ta] (-s) *nt* Crete

Kreuz [krɔyts] (-es, -e) *nt* cross; (*ANAT*) small of the back; (*KARTEN*) clubs; **k~en** *vt, vr* to cross ♦ *vi* (*NAUT*) to cruise; **~er** (-s, -) *m* (*Schiff*) cruiser; **~fahrt** *f* cruise; **~feuer** *nt* (*fig*): **ins ~feuer geraten** to be under fire from all sides; **~gang** *m* cloisters *pl*; **~igen** *vt* to crucify; **~igung** *f* crucifixion; **~ung** *f* (*Verkehrskreuzung*) crossing, junction; (*Züchten*) cross; **~verhör** *nt* cross-examination; **~weg** *m* crossroads; (*REL*) Way of the Cross; **~worträtsel** *nt* crossword puzzle; **~zug** *m* crusade

Kriech- ['kri:ç] *zW*: **k~en** (*unreg*) *vi* to crawl, to creep; (*pej*) to grovel, to crawl; **~er** (-s, -) *m* crawler; **~spur** *f* crawler lane; **~tier** *nt* reptile

Krieg [kri:k] (-(e)s, -e) *m* war

kriegen ['kri:gən] (*umg*) *vt* to get

Kriegs- *zW*: **~erklärung** *f* declaration of war; **~fuß** *m*: **mit jdm/etw auf ~fuß stehen** to be at loggerheads with sb/to have difficulties with sth; **~gefangene(r)** *m* prisoner of war; **~gefangenschaft** *f* captivity; **~gericht** *nt* court-martial; **~schiff** *nt* warship; **~verbrecher** *m* war criminal; **~versehrte(r)** *m* person disabled in the war; **~zustand** *m* state of war

Krim [krɪm] (-) *f* Crimea

Krimi ['kri:mi] (-s, -s; *umg*) *m* thriller

Kriminal- [krimi'na:l] *zW*: **~beamte(r)** *m* detective; **~ität** *f* criminality; **~polizei** *f* ≈ Criminal Investigation Department (*BRIT*), Federal Bureau of Investigation (*US*); **~roman** *m* detective story

kriminell [krimi'nɛl] *adj* criminal; **K~e(r)** *f(m)* criminal

Krippe ['krɪpə] *f* manger, crib; (*Kinder~*) crèche

Krise ['kri:zə] *f* crisis; **k~ln** *vi*: **es k~lt** there's a crisis

Kristall [krɪs'tal] (-s, -e) *m* crystal ♦ *nt* (*Glas*) crystal

Kriterium [kri'te:rɪʊm] *nt* criterion

Kritik [kri'ti:k] *f* criticism; (*Zeitungs~*) review, write-up; **~er** ['kri:tikər] (-s, -) *m* critic; **k~los** *adj* uncritical

kritisch ['kri:tɪʃ] *adj* critical

kritisieren [kriti'tsi:rən] *vt, vi* to criticize

kritzeln ['krɪtsəln] *vt, vi* to scribble, to scrawl

Kroatien [kro'a:tiən] *nt* Croatia

Krokodil [kroko'di:l] (-s, -e) *nt* crocodile

Krokus ['kro:kʊs] (-, -od -se) *m* crocus

Krone ['kro:nə] *f* crown; (*Baum~*) top

krönen ['krø:nən] *vt* to crown

Kron- *zW*: **~korken** *m* bottle top; **~leuchter** *m* chandelier; **~prinz** *m* crown prince

Krönung ['krø:nʊŋ] *f* coronation

Kropf [krɔpf] (-(e)s, ⁼e) *m* (*MED*) goitre; (*von Vogel*) crop

Kröte ['krø:tə] *f* toad

Krücke ['krʏkə] *f* crutch

Krug [kru:k] (-(e)s, ⁼e) *m* jug; (*Bier~*) mug

Krümel ['kry:məl] (-s, -) *m* crumb; **k~n** *vt, vi* to crumble

krumm [krʊm] *adj* (*auch fig*) crooked; (*kurvig*) curved; **~beinig** *adj* bandy-legged; **~lachen** (*umg*) *vr* to laugh o.s. silly; **~nehmen** (*unreg; umg*) *vt*: **jdm etw ~nehmen** to take sth amiss

Krümmung ['krʏmʊŋ] *f* bend, curve

Krüppel ['krʏpəl] (-s, -) *m* cripple

Kruste ['krʊstə] *f* crust

Kruzifix [krutsi'fɪks] (-es, -e) *nt* crucifix

Kübel ['ky:bəl] (-s, -) *m* tub; (*Eimer*) pail

Kubikmeter [ku'bi:kme:tər] *m* cubic metre

Küche ['kʏçə] *f* kitchen; (*Kochen*) cooking, cuisine

Kuchen ['ku:xən] (-s, -) *m* cake; **~form** *f* baking tin; **~gabel** *f* pastry fork

Küchen- *zW*: **~herd** *m* cooker, stove; **~schabe** *f* cockroach; **~schrank** *m* kitchen cabinet

Kuckuck ['kʊkʊk] (-s, -e) *m* cuckoo; **~suhr** *f* cuckoo clock

Kufe ['ku:fə] *f* (*Faß*) vat; (*Schlitten~*) runner; (*AVIAT*) skid

Kugel ['ku:gəl] (-, -n) *f* ball; (*MATH*) sphere; (*MIL*) bullet; (*Erd~*) globe; (*SPORT*) shot; **k~förmig** *adj* spherical; **~kopf** *m* golf ball; **~lager** *nt* ball bearing; **k~rund** *adj* (*Gegenstand*) round; (*umg: Person*) tubby; **~schreiber** *m* ball-point (pen), Biro ®; **k~sicher** *adj* bulletproof;

~stoßen (-s) *nt* shot-put

Kuh [ku:] (-, ⁼e) *f* cow

kühl [ky:l] *adj* (*auch fig*) cool; **K~anlage** *f* refrigeration plant; **K~e** (-) *f* coolness; **~en** *vt* to cool; **K~er** (-s, -) *m* (*AUT*) radiator; **K~erhaube** *f* (*AUT*) bonnet (*BRIT*), hood (*US*); **K~raum** *m* cold-storage chamber; **K~schrank** *m* refrigerator; **K~truhe** *f* freezer; **K~ung** *f* cooling; **K~wasser** *nt* radiator water

kühn [ky:n] *adj* bold, daring; **K~heit** *f* boldness

Kuhstall *m* byre, cattle shed

Küken ['ky:kən] (-s, -) *nt* chicken

kulant [ku'lant] *adj* obliging

Kuli ['ku:li] (-s, -s) *m* coolie; (*umg: Kugelschreiber*) Biro ®

Kulisse [ku'lɪsə] *f* scenery

kullern ['kʊlərn] *vi* to roll

Kult [kʊlt] (-(e)s, -e) *m* worship, cult; **mit etw einen ~ treiben** to make a cult out of sth

kultivieren [kʊlti'vi:rən] *vt* to cultivate

kultiviert *adj* cultivated, refined

Kultur [kʊl'tu:r] *f* culture; civilization; (*des Bodens*) cultivation; **~banause** (*umg*) *m* philistine, low-brow; **~beutel** *m* toilet bag; **k~ell** [-'ʊrɛl] *adj* cultural; **~ministerium** *nt* ministry of education and the arts

Kümmel ['kʏməl] (-s, -) *m* caraway seed; (*Branntwein*) kümmel

Kummer ['kʊmər] (-s) *m* grief, sorrow

kümmerlich *adj* miserable, wretched

kümmern ['kʏmərn] *vt* to concern ♦ *vr*: **sich um jdn ~** to look after sb; **das kümmert mich nicht** that doesn't worry me; **sich um etw ~** to see to sth

Kumpel ['kʊmpəl] (-s, -; *umg*) *m* mate

kündbar ['kʏntba:r] *adj* redeemable, recallable; (*Vertrag*) terminable

Kunde¹ ['kʊndə] (-n, -n) *m* customer

Kunde² *f* (*Botschaft*) news

Kundendienst *m* after-sales service

Kundenkonto *nt* charge account

Kund- *zW*: **~geben** (*unreg*) *vt* to announce; **~gebung** *f* announcement; (*Versammlung*) rally

kündigen ['kʏndɪgən] *vi* to give in one's

notice ♦ *vt* to cancel; **jdm ~igen** to give sb his notice; **die Stellung/Wohnung ~igen** to give notice that one is leaving one's job/house; **jdm die Stellung/ Wohnung ~igen** to give sb notice to leave his/her job/house

Kund- *zW:* **~igung** *f* notice; **~igungsfrist** *f* period of notice

Kundin *f* customer

Kundschaft *f* customers *pl*, clientele

künftig ['kʏnftɪç] *adj* future ♦ *adv* in future

Kunst [kʊnst] *(-, -̈e)* *f* art; *(Können)* skill; **das ist doch keine ~** it's easy; **~dünger** *m* artificial manure; **~faser** *f* synthetic fibre; **~fertigkeit** *f* skilfulness; **~gegenstand** *m* art object; **k~gerecht** *adj* skilful; **~geschichte** *f* history of art; **~gewerbe** *nt* arts and crafts *pl*; **~griff** *m* trick, knack; **~händler** *m* art dealer

Künstler(in) ['kʏnstlər(ɪn)] *(-s, -)* *m(f)* artist; **k~isch** *adj* artistic; **~name** *m* pseudonym

künstlich ['kʏnstlɪç] *adj* artificial

Kunst- *zW:* **~sammler** *(-s, -)* *m* art collector; **~seide** *f* artificial silk; **~stoff** *m* synthetic material; **~stück** *nt* trick; **~turnen** *nt* gymnastics *sg*; **k~voll** *adj* artistic; **~werk** *nt* work of art

kunterbunt ['kʊntərbʊnt] *adj* higgledy-piggledy

Kupfer ['kʊpfər] *(-s)* *nt* copper; **k~n** *adj* copper

Kuppe ['kʊpə] *f (Berg~)* top; *(Finger~)* tip

Kuppe'lei *f (JUR)* procuring

Kuppel *(-, -n)* *f* dome; **k~n** *vi (JUR)* to procure; *(AUT)* to declutch ♦ *vt* to join

Kupplung *f* coupling; *(AUT)* clutch

Kur [kuːr] *(-, -en)* *f* cure, treatment

Kür [kyːr] *(-, -en)* *f (SPORT)* free exercises *pl*

Kurbel ['kʊrbəl] *(-, -n)* *f* crank, winder; *(AUT)* starting handle; **~welle** *f* crankshaft

Kürbis ['kʏrbɪs] *(-ses, -se)* *m* pumpkin; *(exotisch)* gourd

Kurgast *m* visitor (to a health resort)

kurieren [ku'riːrən] *vt* to cure

kurios [kuri'oːs] *adj* curious, odd; **K~i'tät** *f* curiosity

Kurort *m* health resort

Kurpfuscher *m* quack

Kurs [kʊrs] *(-es, -e)* *m* course; *(FIN)* rate; **~buch** *nt* timetable; **k~ieren** [kʊr'ziːrən] *vi* to circulate; **k~iv** [kʊr'ziːf] *adv* in italics; **~us** ['kʊrzʊs] *(-, Kurse)* *m* course; **~wagen** *m (EISENB)* through carriage

Kurve ['kʊrvə] *f* curve; *(Straßen~)* curve, bend; **kurvig** *adj (Straße)* bendy

kurz [kʊrts] *adj* short; **~ gesagt** in short; **zu ~ kommen** to come off badly; **den kürzeren ziehen** to get the worst of it; **K~arbeit** *f* short-time work; **~ärm(e)lig** *adj* short-sleeved

Kürze ['kʏrtsə] *f* shortness, brevity; **k~n** *vt* to cut short; *(in der Länge)* to shorten; *(Gehalt)* to reduce

kurz- *zW:* **~erhand** *adv* on the spot; **~fristig** *adj* short-term; **K~geschichte** *f* short story; **~halten** *(unreg) vt* to keep short; **~lebig** *adj* short-lived

kürzlich ['kʏrtslɪç] *adv* lately, recently

Kurz- *zW:* **~schluß** *m (ELEK)* short circuit; **~schrift** *f* shorthand; **k~sichtig** *adj* short-sighted

Kürzung *f (eines Textes)* abridgement; *(eines Theaterstück, des Gehalts)* cut

Kurzwelle *f* shortwave

kuscheln ['kʊʃəln] *vr* to snuggle up

Kusine [ku'ziːnə] *f* cousin

Kuß [kʊs] *(-sses, -̈sse)* *m* kiss

küssen ['kʏsən] *vt, vr* to kiss

Küste ['kʏstə] *f* coast, shore

Kutsche ['kʊtʃə] *f* coach, carriage; **~r** *(-s, -)* *m* coachman

Kutte ['kʊtə] *f* habit

Kuvert [ku'veːr] *(-s, -e od -s)* *nt* envelope; cover

Kybernetik [kybɛr'neːtɪk] *f* cybernetics *sg*

KZ *nt abk von* **Konzentrationslager**

L I

l. *abk* = **Liter**

labil [la'biːl] *adj (MED: Konstitution)* delicate

Labor [la'boːr] *(-s, -e od -s)* *nt* lab;

~ant(in) [labo'rant(ɪn)] *m(f)* lab(oratory) assistant

Labyrinth [laby'rɪnt] (-s, -e) *nt* labyrinth

Lache ['laxə] *f (Flüssigkeit)* puddle; *(von Blut, Benzin etc)* pool

lächeln ['lɛçəln] *vi* to smile; **L~** (-s) *nt* smile

lachen ['laxən] *vi* to laugh

lächerlich ['lɛçərlɪç] *adj* ridiculous

Lachgas *nt* laughing gas

lachhaft *adj* laughable

Lachs [laks] (-es, -e) *m* salmon

Lack [lak] (-(e)s, -e) *m* lacquer, varnish; *(von Auto)* paint; **l~ieren** [la'ki:rən] *vt* to varnish; *(Auto)* to spray; **~ierer** [la'ki:rər] (-s, -) *m* varnisher

Lackmus ['lakmʊs] (-) *m od nt* litmus

Laden ['la:dən] (-s, ⸚) *m* shop; *(Fenster~)* shutter

laden ['la:dən] *(unreg) vt (Lasten)* to load; *(JUR)* to summon; *(einladen)* to invite

Laden- *zW:* **~dieb** *m* shoplifter; **~diebstahl** *m* shoplifting; **~schluß** *m* closing time; **~tisch** *m* counter

Laderaum *m* freight space; *(FLUG, NAUT)* hold

Ladung ['la:dʊŋ] *f (Last)* cargo, load; *(Beladen)* loading; *(JUR)* summons; *(Einladung)* invitation; *(Spreng~)* charge

Lage ['la:gə] *f* position, situation; *(Schicht)* layer; **in der ~ sein** to be in a position

Lageplan *m* ground plan

Lager ['la:gər] (-s, -) *nt* camp; *(COMM)* warehouse; *(Schlaf~)* bed; *(von Tier)* lair; *(TECH)* bearing; **~bestand** *m* stocks *pl*; **~feuer** *nt* campfire; **~haus** *nt* warehouse, store

lagern ['la:gərn] *vi (Dinge)* to be stored; *(Menschen)* to camp ♦ *vt* to store; *(betten)* to lay down; *(Maschine)* to bed

Lagune [la'gu:nə] *f* lagoon

lahm [la:m] *adj* lame; **~en** *vi* to be lame

lähmen ['lɛ:mən] *vt* to paralyse

lahmlegen *vt* to paralyse

Lähmung *f* paralysis

Laib [laɪp] (-s, -e) *m* loaf

Laie ['laɪə] (-n, -n) *m* layman; **l~nhaft** *adj* amateurish

Laken ['la:kən] (-s, -) *nt* sheet

Lakritz *m od nt* = **Lakritze**

Lakritze [la'krɪtsə] *f* liquorice

lallen ['lalən] *vt, vi* to slur; *(Baby)* to babble

Lama ['la:ma] (-s, -s) *nt (ZOOL)* llama

Lamelle [la'mɛlə] *f* lamella; *(ELEK)* lamina; *(TECH)* plate

Lametta [la'mɛta] (-s) *nt* tinsel

Lamm [lam] (-(e)s, ⸚er) *nt* lamb

Lampe ['lampə] *f* lamp; **~nfieber** *nt* stage fright; **~nschirm** *m* lampshade

Lampion [lampi'õ:] (-s, -s) *m* Chinese lantern

Land [lant] (-(e)s, ⸚er) *nt* land; *(Nation, nicht Stadt)* country; *(Bundes~)* state; **auf dem ~(e)** in the country; **~besitz** *m* landed property; **~ebahn** *f* runway; **l~en** ['landən] *vt, vi* to land

Landes- ['landəs] *zW:* **~farben** *pl* national colours; **~innere(s)** *nt* inland region; **~sprache** *f* national language; **l~üblich** *adj* customary; **~verrat** *m* high treason; **~währung** *f* national currency

landesweit *adj* nationwide

Land- *zW:* **~haus** *nt* country house; **~karte** *f* map; **~kreis** *m* administrative region; **l~läufig** *adj* customary

ländlich ['lɛntlɪç] *adj* rural

Land- *zW:* **~schaft** *f* countryside; *(KUNST)* landscape; **~sitz** *m* country seat; **~straße** *f* country road; **~streicher** (-s, -) *m* tramp; **~strich** *m* region

Landung ['landʊŋ] *f* landing; **~sbrücke** *f* jetty, pier

Land- *zW:* **~wirt** *m* farmer; **~weg** *m*: **etw auf dem ~weg befördern** to transport sth by land; **~wirtschaft** *f* agriculture; **~zunge** *f* spit

lang [laŋ] *adj* long; *(Mensch)* tall; **~atmig** *adj* long-winded; **~e** *adv* for a long time; *(dauern, brauchen)* a long time

Länge ['lɛŋə] *f* length; *(GEOG)* longitude

langen ['laŋən] *vi (ausreichen)* to do, to suffice; *(fassen)*: **~ (nach)** to reach (for) ♦ *vt*: **jdm etw ~** to hand od pass sb sth; **es langt mir** I've had enough

Längengrad *m* longitude

Längenmaß *nt* linear measure

lang- *zW*: **L~eweile** *f* boredom; **~fristig** *adj* long-term; **~jährig** *adj* (*Freundschaft, Gewohnheit*) long-standing; **L~lauf** *m* (*SKI*) cross-country skiing
länglich *adj* longish
längs [lɛŋs] *präp* (+*gen od dat*) along
♦ *adv* lengthwise
lang- *zW*: **~sam** *adj* slow; **L~samkeit** *f* slowness; **L~schläfer(in)** *m(f)* late riser; **L~spielplatte** *f* long-playing record
längst [lɛŋst] *adv*: **das ist ~ fertig** that was finished a long time ago, that has been finished for a long time; **~e(r, s)** *adj* longest
lang- *zW*: **~weilen** *vt* to bore ♦ *vr* to be bored; **~weilig** *adj* boring, tedious; **L~welle** *f* long wave; **~wierig** *adj* lengthy, long-drawn-out
Lanze ['lantsə] *f* lance
Lappalie [la'pa:liə] *f* trifle
Lappen ['lapən] (-s, -) *m* cloth, rag; (*ANAT*) lobe
läppisch ['lɛpɪʃ] *adj* foolish
Lapsus ['lapsʊs] (-, -) *m* slip
Laptop ['lɛptɔp] (-s, -s) *m* laptop (computer)
Lärche ['lɛrçə] *f* larch
Lärm [lɛrm] (-(e)s) *m* noise; **l~en** *vi* to be noisy, to make a noise
Larve ['larfə] *f* (*BIOL*) larva
lasch [laʃ] *adj* slack
Lasche ['laʃə] *f* (*Schuh~*) tongue
Laser ['leɪzər] (-s, -) *m* laser

SCHLÜSSELWORT

lassen ['lasən] (*pt* **ließ**, *pp* **gelassen** *od* (*als Hilfsverb*) **lassen**) *vt* **1** (*unterlassen*) to stop; (*momentan*) to leave; **laß das (sein)!** don't (do it)!; (*hör auf*) stop it!; **laß mich!** leave me alone; **lassen wir das!** let's leave it; **er kann das Trinken nicht lassen** he can't stop drinking
2 (*zurücklassen*) to leave; **etw lassen, wie es ist** to leave sth (just) as it is
3 (*überlassen*): **jdn ins Haus lassen** to let sb into the house
♦ *vi*: **laß mal, ich mache das schon** leave it, I'll do it
♦ *Hilfsverb* **1** (*veranlassen*): **etw machen**

lassen to have *od* get sth done; **sich** *dat* **etw schicken lassen** to have sth sent (to one)
2 (*zulassen*): **jdn etw wissen lassen** to let sb know sth; **das Licht brennen lassen** to leave the light on; **jdn warten lassen** to keep sb waiting; **das läßt sich machen** that can be done
3: **laß uns gehen** let's go

lässig ['lɛsɪç] *adj* casual; **L~keit** *f* casualness
Last [last] (-, -en) *f* load, burden; (*NAUT, AVIAT*) cargo; (*meist pl: Gebühr*) charge; **jdm zur ~ fallen** to be a burden to sb; **~auto** *nt* lorry, truck; **l~en** *vi*: **l~en auf** +*dat* to weigh on
Laster ['lastər] (-s, -) *nt* vice
lästern ['lɛstərn] *vt, vi* (*Gott*) to blaspheme; (*schlecht sprechen*) to mock
Lästerung *f* jibe; (*Gottes~*) blasphemy
lästig ['lɛstɪç] *adj* troublesome, tiresome
Last- *zW*: **~kahn** *m* barge; **~kraftwagen** *m* heavy goods vehicle; **~schrift** *f* debit; **~wagen** *m* lorry, truck; **~zug** *m* articulated lorry
Latein [la'taɪn] (-s) *nt* Latin; **~amerika** *nt* Latin America
latent [la'tɛnt] *adj* latent
Laterne [la'tɛrnə] *f* lantern; (*Straßen~*) lamp, light; **~npfahl** *m* lamppost
latschen ['la:tʃən] (*umg*) *vi* (*gehen*) to wander, to go; (*lässig*) to slouch
Latte ['latə] *f* lath; (*SPORT*) goalpost; (*quer*) crossbar
Latzhose ['latsho:zə] *f* dungarees *pl*
lau [lau] *adj* (*Nacht*) balmy; (*Wasser*) lukewarm
Laub [laup] (-(e)s) *nt* foliage; **~baum** *m* deciduous tree; **~frosch** *m* tree frog; **~säge** *f* fretsaw
Lauch [laux] (-(e)s, -e) *m* leek
Lauer ['lauər] *f*: **auf der ~ sein** *od* **liegen** to lie in wait; **l~n** *vi* to lie in wait; (*Gefahr*) to lurk
Lauf [lauf] (-(e)s, Läufe) *m* run; (*Wett~*) race; (*Entwicklung, ASTRON*) course; (*Gewehr~*) barrel; **einer Sache** *dat* **ihren ~ lassen** to let sth take its course; **~bahn**

f career

laufen ['laʊfən] (*unreg*) *vt, vi* to run; (*umg: gehen*) to walk; **~d** *adj* running; (*Monat, Ausgaben*) current; **auf dem ~den sein/halten** to be/keep up to date; **am ~den Band** (*fig*) continuously

Läufer ['lɔʏfər] (**-s, -**) *m* (*Teppich, SPORT*) runner; (*Fußball*) half-back; (*Schach*) bishop

Lauf- *zW*: **~masche** *f* run, ladder (*BRIT*); **~paß** *m*: **jdm den ~paß geben** (*umg*) to send sb packing (*inf*); **~stall** *m* playpen; **~steg** *m* catwalk; **~werk** *nt* (*COMPUT*) disk drive

Lauge ['laʊgə] *f* soapy water; (*CHEM*) alkaline solution

Laune ['laʊnə] *f* mood, humour; (*Einfall*) caprice; (*schlechte*) temper; **l~nhaft** *adj* capricious, changeable

launisch *adj* moody; bad-tempered

Laus [laʊs] (**-, Läuse**) *f* louse; **~bub** *m* rascal, imp

lauschen ['laʊʃən] *vi* to eavesdrop, to listen in

lauschig ['laʊʃɪç] *adj* snug

lausig ['laʊzɪç] (*umg: pej*) *adj* measly; (*Kälte*) perishing

laut [laʊt] *adj* loud ♦ *adv* loudly; (*lesen*) aloud ♦ *präp* (+*gen od dat*) according to; **L~** (**-(e)s, -e**) *m* sound

Laute ['laʊtə] *f* lute

lauten ['laʊtən] *vi* to say; (*Urteil*) to be

läuten ['lɔʏtən] *vt, vi* to ring, to sound

lauter ['laʊtər] *adj* (*Wasser*) clear, pure; (*Wahrheit, Charakter*) honest ♦ *adj inv* (*Freude, Dummheit etc*) sheer ♦ *adv* nothing but, only

laut- *zW*: **~hals** *adv* at the top of one's voice; **~los** *adj* noiseless, silent; **L~schrift** *f* phonetics *pl*; **L~sprecher** *m* loudspeaker; **~stark** *adj* vociferous; **L~stärke** *f* (*RADIO*) volume

lauwarm ['laʊvarm] *adj* (*auch fig*) lukewarm

Lava ['laːva] (**-, Laven**) *f* lava

Lavendel [la'vɛndəl] (**-s, -**) *m* lavender

Lawine [la'viːnə] *f* avalanche; **~ngefahr** *f* danger of avalanches

lax [laks] *adj* lax

Lazarett [latsa'rɛt] (**-(e)s, -e**) *nt* (*MIL*) hospital, infirmary

leasen ['liːzən] *vt* to lease

Leben (**-s, -**) *nt* life

leben ['leːbən] *vt, vi* to live; **~d** *adj* living; **~dig** [le'bɛndɪç] *adj* living, alive; (*lebhaft*) lively; **L~digkeit** *f* liveliness

Lebens- *zW*: **~art** *f* way of life; **~erwartung** *f* life expectancy; **l~fähig** *adj* able to live; **~freude** *f* zest for life; **~gefahr** *f*: **~gefahr!** danger!; **in ~gefahr** dangerously ill; **l~gefährlich** *adj* dangerous; (*Verletzung*) critical; **~haltungskosten** *pl* cost of living *sg*; **~jahr** *nt* year of life; **l~länglich** *adj* (*Strafe*) for life; **~lauf** *m* curriculum vitae; **~mittel** *pl* food *sg*; **~mittelgeschäft** *nt* grocer's (shop); **~mittelvergiftung** *f* (*MED*) food poisoning; **l~müde** *adj* tired of life; **~retter** *m* lifesaver; **~standard** *m* standard of living; **~unterhalt** *m* livelihood; **~versicherung** *f* life insurance; **~wandel** *m* way of life; **~weise** *f* lifestyle, way of life; **l~wichtig** *adj* vital, essential; **~zeichen** *nt* sign of life

Leber ['leːbər] (**-, -n**) *f* liver; **~fleck** *m* mole; **~tran** *m* cod-liver oil; **~wurst** *f* liver sausage

Lebewesen *nt* creature

leb- ['leːp] *zW*: **~haft** *adj* lively, vivacious; **L~kuchen** *m* gingerbread; **~los** *adj* lifeless

Leck [lɛk] (**-(e)s, -e**) *nt* leak; **l~** *adj* leaky, leaking; **l~en** *vi* (*Loch haben*) to leak; (*schlecken*) to lick ♦ *vt* to lick

lecker ['lɛkər] *adj* delicious, tasty; **L~bissen** *m* dainty morsel

Leder ['leːdər] (**-s, -**) *nt* leather; **~hose** *f* lederhosen; **l~n** *adj* leather; **~waren** *pl* leather goods

ledig ['leːdɪç] *adj* single; **einer Sache** *gen* **~ sein** to be free of sth; **~lich** *adv* merely, solely

leer [leːr] *adj* empty; vacant; **~ machen** to empty; **L~e** (**-**) *f* emptiness; **~en** *vt, vr* to empty; **L~gewicht** *nt* weight when empty; **L~lauf** *m* neutral; **~stehend** *adj* empty; **L~ung** *f* emptying; (*Post*) collection

legal [le'ga:l] *adj* legal, lawful; **~i'sieren** *vt* to legalize

legen ['le:gən] *vt* to lay, to put, to place; (*Ei*) to lay ♦ *vr* to lie down; (*fig*) to subside

Legende [le'gɛndə] *f* legend

leger [le'ʒɛːr] *adj* casual

Legierung [le'gi:ruŋ] *f* alloy

Legislative [legisla'ti:və] *f* legislature

legitim [legi'ti:m] *adj* legitimate

legitimieren [legiti'mi:rən] *vt* to legitimate ♦ *vr* to prove one's identity

Lehm [le:m] (**-(e)s**₋ **-e**) *m* loam; **l~ig** *adj* loamy

Lehne ['le:nə] *f* arm; back; **l~n** *vt, vr* to lean

Lehnstuhl *m* armchair

Lehr- *zW:* **~amt** *nt* teaching profession; **~buch** *nt* textbook

Lehre ['le:rə] *f* teaching, doctrine; (*beruflich*) apprenticeship; (*moralisch*) lesson; (*TECH*) gauge; **l~n** *vt* to teach; **~r(in)** (**-s**, **-**) *m(f)* teacher; **~rzimmer** *nt* staff room

Lehr- *zW:* **~gang** *m* course; **~jahre** *pl* apprenticeship *sg*; **~kraft** *f* (*förmlich*) teacher; **~ling** *m* apprentice; **~plan** *m* syllabus; **l~reich** *adj* instructive; **~stelle** *f* apprenticeship; **~zeit** *f* apprenticeship

Leib [laip] (**-(e)s**, **-er**) *m* body; **halt ihn mir vom ~!** keep him away from me!; **l~haftig** *adj* personified; (*Teufel*) incarnate; **l~lich** *adj* bodily; (*Vater etc*) own

Leibschmerzen *pl* stomach pains

Leibwache *f* bodyguard

Leiche ['laiçə] *f* corpse; **~nhalle** *f* mortuary; **~nwagen** *m* hearse

Leichnam ['laiçna:m] (**-(e)s**, **-e**) *m* corpse

leicht [laiçt] *adj* light; (*einfach*) easy; **L~athletik** *f* athletics *sg*; **~fallen** (*unreg*) *vi*: **jdm ~fallen** to be easy for sb; **~fertig** *adj* frivolous; **~gläubig** *adj* gullible, credulous; **~hin** *adv* lightly; **L~igkeit** *f* easiness; **mit L~igkeit** with ease; **~machen** *vt*: **sich *dat* ~machen** to make things easy for o.s.; **L~sinn** *m* carelessness; **~sinnig** *adj* careless

Leid [lait] (**-(e)s**) *nt* grief, sorrow; **l~** *adj*: **etw l~ haben** *od* **sein** to be tired of sth; **es tut mir/ihm l~** I am sorry for him/it; **er/ das tut mir l~** I am sorry; **l~en** ['laidən] (*unreg*) *vt* to suffer; (*erlauben*) to permit ♦ *vi* to suffer; **jdn/ etw nicht l~en können** not to be able to stand sb/sth; **~en** (**-s**, **-**) *nt* suffering; (*Krankheit*) complaint; **~enschaft** *f* passion; **l~enschaftlich** *adj* passionate

leider ['laidər] *adv* unfortunately; **ja, ~** yes, I'm afraid so; **~ nicht** I'm afraid not

leidig *adj* worrying, troublesome

leidlich *adj* tolerable ♦ *adv* tolerably

Leidtragende(r) *mf* bereaved; (*Benachteiligter*) one who suffers

Leidwesen *nt*: **zu jds ~** to sb's disappointment

Leier ['laiər] (**-**, **-n**) *f* lyre; (*fig*) old story; **~kasten** *m* barrel organ

Leihbibliothek *f* lending library

Leihbücherei *f* lending library

leihen ['laiən] (*unreg*) *vt* to lend; **sich *dat* etw ~** to borrow sth

Leih- *zW:* **~gebühr** *f* hire charge; **~haus** *nt* pawnshop; **~schein** *m* pawn ticket; (*Buchleihschein etc*) borrowing slip; **~wagen** *m* hired car

Leim [laim] (**-(e)s**, **-e**) *m* glue; **l~en** *vt* to glue

Leine ['lainə] *f* line, cord; (*Hunde~*) leash, lead

Leinen *nt* linen; **l~** *adj* linen

Leintuch *nt* (*Bett~*) sheet; linen cloth

Leinwand *f* (*KUNST*) canvas; (*CINE*) screen

leise ['laizə] *adj* quiet; (*sanft*) soft, gentle

Leiste ['laistə] *f* ledge; (*Zier~*) strip; (*ANAT*) groin

leisten ['laistən] *vt* (*Arbeit*) to do; (*Gesellschaft*) to keep; (*Ersatz*) to supply; (*vollbringen*) to achieve; **sich *dat* etw ~ können** to be able to afford sth

Leistung *f* performance; (*gute*) achievement; **~sdruck** *m* pressure; **l~sfähig** *adj* efficient

Leitartikel *m* leading article

Leitbild *nt* model

leiten ['laitən] *vt* to lead; (*Firma*) to manage; (*in eine Richtung*) to direct;

(*ELEK*) to conduct
Leiter[1] ['laɪtər] (**-s, -**) *m* leader, head; (*ELEK*) conductor
Leiter[2] (**-, -n**) *f* ladder
Leitfaden *m* guide
Leitplanke *f* crash barrier
Leitung *f* (*Führung*) direction; (*CINE, THEAT etc*) production; (*von Firma*) management; directors *pl*; (*Wasser~*) pipe; (*Kabel*) cable; **eine lange ~ haben** to be slow on the uptake
Leitungs- *zW:* **~draht** *m* wire; **~rohr** *nt* pipe; **~wasser** *nt* tap water
Lektion [lɛktsi'oːn] *f* lesson
Lektüre [lɛk'tyːrə] *f* (*Lesen*) reading; (*Lesestoff*) reading matter
Lende ['lɛndə] *f* loin; **~nstück** *nt* fillet
lenk- ['lɛŋk] *zW:* **~bar** *adj* (*Fahrzeug*) steerable; (*Kind*) manageable; **~en** *vt* to steer; (*Kind*) to guide; (*Blick, Aufmerksamkeit*) to direct (at); **L~rad** *nt* steering wheel; **L~stange** *f* handlebars *pl*
Leopard [leo'part] (**-en, -en**) *m* leopard
Lepra ['leːpra] (**-**) *f* leprosy
Lerche ['lɛrçə] *f* lark
lernbegierig *adj* eager to learn
lernen ['lɛrnən] *vt* to learn
lesbar ['leːsbaːr] *adj* legible
Lesbierin ['lɛsbiərɪn] *f* lesbian
lesbisch ['lɛsbɪʃ] *adj* lesbian
Lese ['leːzə] *f* (*Wein*) harvest
Lesebrille *f* reading glasses
Lesebuch *nt* reading book, reader
lesen (*unreg*) *vt, vi* to read; (*ernten*) to gather, to pick
Leser(in) (**-s, -**) *m(f)* reader; **~brief** *m* reader's letter; **l~lich** *adj* legible
Lesezeichen *nt* bookmark
Lesung ['leːzʊŋ] *f* (*PARL*) reading
letzte(r, s) ['lɛtstə(r, s)] *adj* last; (*neueste*) latest; **zum ~nmal** for the last time; **~ns** *adv* lately; **~re(r, s)** *adj* latter
Leuchte ['lɔʏçtə] *f* lamp, light; **l~n** *vi* to shine, to gleam; **~r** (**-s, -**) *m* candlestick
Leucht- *zW:* **~farbe** *f* fluorescent colour; **~rakete** *f* flare; **~reklame** *f* neon sign; **~röhre** *f* strip light; **~turm** *m* lighthouse; **~zifferblatt** *nt* luminous dial

leugnen ['lɔʏgnən] *vt* to deny
Leukämie [lɔʏkɛ'miː] *f* leukaemia
Leukoplast [lɔʏko'plast] (®; **-(e)s, -e**) *nt* Elastoplast ®
Leumund ['lɔʏmʊnt] (**-(e)s, -e**) *m* reputation
Leumundszeugnis *nt* character reference
Leute ['lɔʏtə] *pl* people *pl*
Leutnant ['lɔʏtnant] (**-s, -s** *od* **-e**) *m* lieutenant
leutselig ['lɔʏtzeːlɪç] *adj* amiable
Lexikon ['lɛksikɔn] (**-s, Lexiken** *od* **Lexika**) *nt* encyclop(a)edia
Libelle [li'bɛlə] *f* dragonfly; (*TECH*) spirit level
liberal [libe'raːl] *adj* liberal; **L~e(r)** *mf* liberal
Libero ['liːbero] (**-s, -s**) *m* (*Fußball*) sweeper
Licht [lɪçt] (**-(e)s, -er**) *nt* light; **~bild** *nt* photograph; (*Dia*) slide; **~blick** *m* cheering prospect; **l~empfindlich** *adj* sensitive to light; **l~en** *vt* to clear; (*Anker*) to weigh ♦ *vr* to clear up; (*Haar*) to thin; **l~erloh** *adv*: **l~erloh brennen** to be ablaze; **~hupe** *f* flashing of headlights; **~jahr** *nt* light year; **~maschine** *f* dynamo; **~schalter** *m* light switch
Lichtung *f* clearing, glade
Lid [liːt] (**-(e)s, -er**) *nt* eyelid; **~schatten** *m* eyeshadow
lieb [liːp] *adj* dear; **das ist ~ von dir** that's kind of you; **l~äugeln** ['liːbɔʏgəln] *vi insep*: **mit etw ~äugeln** to have one's eye on sth; **mit dem Gedanken ~äugeln, etw zu tun** to toy with the idea of doing sth
Liebe ['liːbə] *f* love; **l~bedürftig** *adj*: **l~bedürftig sein** to need love; **l~n** *vt* to love; to fall in love
liebens- *zW:* **~wert** *adj* loveable; **~würdig** *adj* kind; **~würdigerweise** *adv* kindly; **L~würdigkeit** *f* kindness
lieber ['liːbər] *adv* rather, preferably; **ich gehe ~ nicht** I'd rather not go; *siehe auch* **gern; lieb**
Liebes- *zW:* **~brief** *m* love letter; **~kummer** *m*: **~kummer haben** to be

lovesick; **~paar** nt courting couple, lovers pl

liebevoll adj loving

lieb- ['li:p] zW: **~gewinnen** (unreg) vt to get fond of; **~haben** (unreg) vt to be fond of; **L~haber** (-s, -) m lover; **L~habe'rei** f hobby; **~kosen** ['li:pko:zən] vt insep to caress; **~lich** adj lovely, charming; **L~ling** m darling; **L~lings-** in zW favourite; **~los** adj unloving; **L~schaft** f love affair

Lied [li:t] (-(e)s, -er) nt song; (REL) hymn; **~erbuch** ['li:dər-] nt songbook; hymn book

liederlich ['li:dərlıç] adj slovenly; (Lebenswandel) loose, immoral; **L~keit** f slovenliness; immorality

lief etc [li:f] vb siehe **laufen**

Lieferant [li:fə'rant] m supplier

Lieferbedingungen pl terms of delivery

liefern ['li:fərn] vt to deliver; (versorgen mit) to supply; (Beweis) to produce

Liefer- zW: **~schein** m delivery note; **~termin** m delivery date; **~ung** f delivery; supply; **~wagen** m van; **~zeit** f delivery period

Liege ['li:gə] f bed

liegen ['li:gən] (unreg) vi to lie; (sich befinden) to be; **mir liegt nichts/viel daran** it doesn't matter to me/it matters a lot to me; **es liegt bei Ihnen, ob ...** it's up to you whether ...; **Sprachen ~ mir nicht** languages are not my line; **woran liegt es?** what's the cause?; **~bleiben** (unreg) vi (im Bett) to stay in bed; (nicht aufstehen) to stay lying down; (vergessen werden) to be left (behind); **~lassen** (unreg) vt (vergessen) to leave behind

Liege- zW: **~sitz** m (AUT) reclining seat; **~stuhl** m deck chair; **~wagen** m (EISENB) couchette

Lift [lıft] (-(e)s, -e od -s) m lift

Likör [li'kø:r] (-s, -e) m liqueur

lila ['li:la] adj inv purple, lilac; **L~** (-s, -s) nt (Farbe) purple, lilac

Lilie ['li:liə] f lily

Limonade [limo'na:də] f lemonade

Limone [li'mo:nə] f lime

Linde ['lındə] f lime tree, linden

lindern ['lındərn] vt to alleviate, to soothe

Linderung f alleviation

Lineal [line'a:l] (-s, -e) nt ruler

Linie ['li:niə] f line

Linien- zW: **~blatt** nt ruled sheet; **~flug** m scheduled flight; **~richter** m linesman

linieren [lin'i:rən] vt to line

Linke ['lıŋkə] f left side; left hand; (POL) left

linkisch adj awkward, gauche

links [lıŋks] adv left; **to** od **on the left**; **~ von mir** on od to my left; **L~außen** [lıŋks'auʂən] (-s, -) m (SPORT) outside left; **L~händer(in)** (-s, -) m(f) left-handed person; **L~kurve** f left-hand bend; **L~verkehr** m driving on the left

Linoleum [li'no:leum] (-s) nt lino(leum)

Linse ['lınzə] f lentil; (optisch) lens sg

Lippe ['lıpə] f lip; **~nstift** m lipstick

lispeln ['lıspəln] vi to lisp

Lissabon ['lısabɔn] (-s) nt Lisbon

List [lıst] (-, -en) f cunning; trick, ruse

Liste ['lıstə] f list

listig ['lıstıç] adj cunning, sly

Litanei [lita'nai] f litany

Liter ['li:tər] (-s, -) nt od m litre

literarisch [lite'ra:rıʃ] adj literary

Literatur [litera'tu:r] f literature

Litfaßsäule ['lıtfaszɔylə] f advertising pillar

Lithographie [litogra'fi:] f lithography

Liturgie [litʊr'gi:] f liturgy

liturgisch [li'tʊrgıʃ] adj liturgical

Litze ['lıtsə] f braid; (ELEK) flex

live [laıf] adv (RADIO, TV) live

Livree [li'vre:] (-, -n) f livery

Lizenz [li'tsɛnts] f licence

Lkw [ɛlka:'ve:] (-(s), -(s)) m abk = **Lastkraftwagen**

Lob [lo:p] (-(e)s) nt praise

Lobby ['lɔbı] f lobby

loben ['lo:bən] vt to praise; **~swert** adj praiseworthy

löblich ['lø:plıç] adj praiseworthy, laudable

Loch [lɔx] (-(e)s, ⸚er) nt hole; **l~en** vt to punch holes in; **~er** (-s, -) m punch

löcherig ['lœçərıç] adj full of holes

Lochkarte f punch card

Lochstreifen *m* punch tape
Locke ['lɔkə] *f* lock, curl; **l~n** *vt* to entice; (*Haare*) to curl; **~nwickler** (-s, -) *m* curler
locker ['lɔkər] *adj* loose; **~lassen** (*unreg*) *vi*: **nicht ~lassen** not to let up; **~n** *vt* to loosen
lockig ['lɔkɪç] *adj* curly
Lodenmantel ['loːdənmantəl] *m* thick woollen coat
lodern ['loːdərn] *vi* to blaze
Löffel ['lœfəl] (-s, -) *m* spoon
löffeln *vt* to spoon
Logarithmus [loga'rɪtmʊs] *m* logarithm
Loge ['loːʒə] *f* (*THEAT*) box; (*Freimaurer*) (masonic) lodge; (*Pförtner~*) office
Logik ['loːgɪk] *f* logic
logisch ['loːgɪʃ] *adj* logical
Logopäde [logo'pɛːdə] (-n, -n) *m* speech therapist
Lohn [loːn] (-(e)s, ⁼e) *m* reward; (*Arbeits~*) pay, wages *pl*; **~büro** *nt* wages office; **~empfänger** *m* wage earner
lohnen ['loːnən] *vr unpers* to be worth it ♦ *vt* (*liter*): **(jdm etw)** ~ to reward (sb for sth); **~d** *adj* worthwhile
Lohnerhöhung *f* pay rise
Lohn- *zW*: **~steuer** *f* income tax; **~streifen** *m* pay slip; **~tüte** *f* pay packet
Lokal [lo'kaːl] (-(e)s, -e) *nt* pub(lic house)
lokal *adj* local; **~i'sieren** *vt* to localize
Lokomotive [lokomo'tiːvə] *f* locomotive
Lokomotivführer *m* engine driver
Lorbeer ['lɔrbeːr] (-s, -en) *m* (*auch fig*) laurel; **~blatt** *nt* (*KOCH*) bay leaf
Lore ['loːrə] *f* (*MIN*) truck
Los [loːs] (-es, -e) *nt* (*Schicksal*) lot, fate; (*Lotterie~*) lottery ticket
los [loːs] *adj* (*locker*) loose; **~!** go on!; **etw ~ sein** to be rid of sth; **was ist ~?** what's the matter?; **dort ist nichts/viel ~** there's nothing/a lot going on there; **etw ~ haben** (*umg*) to be clever; **~binden** (*unreg*) *vt* to untie
Löschblatt *nt* sheet of blotting paper
löschen ['lœʃən] *vt* (*Feuer, Licht*) to put out, to extinguish; (*Durst*) to quench; (*COMM*) to cancel; (*COMPUT*) to delete; (*Tonband*) to erase; (*Fracht*) to unload

♦ *vi* (*Feuerwehr*) to put out a fire; (*Tinte*) to blot
Lösch- *zW*: **~fahrzeug** *nt* fire engine; fire boat; **~gerät** *nt* fire extinguisher; **~papier** *nt* blotting paper; **~taste** *f* delete key
lose ['loːzə] *adj* loose
Lösegeld *nt* ransom
losen ['loːzən] *vi* to draw lots
lösen ['løːzən] *vt* to loosen; (*Rätsel etc*) to solve; (*Verlobung*) to call off; (*CHEM*) to dissolve; (*Partnerschaft*) to break up; (*Fahrkarte*) to buy ♦ *vr* (*aufgehen*) to come loose; (*Zucker etc*) to dissolve; (*Problem, Schwierigkeit*) to (re)solve itself
los- *zW*: **~fahren** (*unreg*) *vi* to leave; **~gehen** (*unreg*) *vi* to set out; (*anfangen*) to start; (*Bombe*) to go off; **auf jdn ~gehen** to go for sb; **~kaufen** *vt* (*Gefangene, Geißeln*) to pay ransom for; **~kommen** (*unreg*) *vi*: **von etw ~kommen** to get away from sth; **~lassen** (*unreg*) *vt* (*Seil*) to let go of; (*Schimpfe*) to let loose; **~laufen** (*unreg*) *vi* to run off
löslich ['løːslɪç] *adj* soluble; **L~keit** *f* solubility
los- *zW*: **~lösen** *vt*: **(sich) ~lösen** to free (o.s.); **~machen** *vt* to loosen; (*Boot*) to unmoor ♦ *vr* to get away; **~schrauben** *vt* to unscrew
Losung ['loːzʊŋ] *f* watchword, slogan
Lösung ['løːzʊŋ] *f* (*Lockermachen*) loosening; (*eines Rätsels, CHEM*) solution; **~smittel** *nt* solvent
loswerden (*unreg*) *vt* to get rid of
losziehen (*unreg; umg*) *vi* (*sich aufmachen*) to set off
Lot [loːt] (-(e)s, -e) *nt* plumbline; **im ~** vertical; (*fig*) on an even keel
löten ['løːtən] *vt* to solder
Lothringen ['loːtrɪŋən] (-s) *nt* Lorraine
Lötkolben *m* soldering iron
Lotse ['loːtsə] (-n, -n) *m* pilot; (*AVIAT*) air traffic controller; **l~n** *vt* to pilot; (*umg*) to lure
Lotterie [lɔtə'riː] *f* lottery
Lotto ['lɔto] (-s, -s) *nt* national lottery; **~zahlen** *pl* winning lottery numbers
Löwe ['løːvə] (-n, -n) *m* lion; (*ASTROL*) Leo;

~**nanteil** *m* lion's share; ~**nzahn** *m*
dandelion
loyal [loa'jaːl] *adj* loyal
Loyali'tät *f* loyalty
Luchs [lʊks] (-es, -e) *m* lynx
Lücke ['lʏkə] *f* gap; ~**nbüßer** (-s, -) *m*
stopgap; **l~nhaft** *adj* full of gaps; (*care,
supplies etc*) inadequate; **l~nlos** *adj*
complete
Luft [lʊft] (-, ̈e) *f* air; (*Atem*) breath; **in
der ~ liegen** to be in the air; **jdn wie ~
behandeln** to ignore sb; ~**angriff** *m* air
raid; ~**ballon** *m* balloon; ~**blase** *f* air
bubble; **l~dicht** *adj* airtight; ~**druck** *m*
atmospheric pressure
lüften ['lʏftən] *vt* to air; (*Hut*) to lift, to
raise ♦ *vi* to let some air in
Luft- *zW*: ~**fahrt** *f* aviation; **l~gekühlt**
adj air-cooled; ~**gewehr** *nt* air-rifle,
airgun; **l~ig** *adj* (*Ort*) breezy; (*Raum*)
airy; (*Kleider*) summery;
~**kissenfahrzeug** *nt* hovercraft; ~**kurort**
m health resort; **l~leer** *adj*: **luftleerer
Raum** vacuum; ~**linie** *f*: **in der ~linie as
the crow flies**; ~**loch** *nt* air-hole; (*AVIAT*)
air-pocket; ~**matratze** *f* lilo (®: *BRIT*), air
mattress; ~**pirat** *m* hijacker; ~**post** *f*
airmail; ~**röhre** *f* (*ANAT*) windpipe;
~**schlange** *f* streamer; ~**schutzkeller** *m*
air-raid shelter; ~**verkehr** *m* air traffic;
~**verschmutzung** *f* air pollution;
~**waffe** *f* air force; ~**zug** *m* draught
Lüge ['lyːgə] *f* lie; **jdn/etw ~n strafen** to
give the lie to sb/sth; **l~n** (*unreg*) *vi* to lie
Lügner(in) (-s, -) *m(f)* liar
Luke ['luːkə] *f* dormer window; hatch
Lump [lʊmp] (-en, -en) *m* scamp, rascal
Lumpen ['lʊmpən] (-s, -) *m* rag
lumpen *vi*: **sich nicht ~ lassen** not to be
mean
lumpig ['lʊmpɪç] *adj* shabby
Lupe ['luːpə] *f* magnifying glass; **unter
die ~ nehmen** (*fig*) to scrutinize
Lupine [lu'piːnə] *f* lupin
Lust [lʊst] (-, ̈e) *f* joy, delight; (*Neigung*)
desire; **~ haben zu** *od* **auf etw** *akk*/**etw
zu tun** to feel like sth/doing sth
lüstern ['lʏstərn] *adj* lustful, lecherous
lustig ['lʊstɪç] *adj* (*komisch*) amusing,

funny; (*fröhlich*) cheerful
Lüstling *m* lecher
Lust- *zW*: **l~los** *adj* unenthusiastic;
~**mord** *m* sex(ual) murder; ~**spiel** *nt*
comedy
lutschen ['lʊtʃən] *vt, vi* to suck; **am
Daumen ~** to suck one's thumb
Lutscher (-s, -) *m* lollipop
luxuriös [lʊksuri'øːs] *adj* luxurious
Luxus ['lʊksʊs] (-) *m* luxury; ~**artikel** *pl*
luxury goods; ~**hotel** *nt* luxury hotel
Lymphe ['lʏmfə] *f* lymph
lynchen ['lʏnçən] *vt* to lynch
Lyrik ['lyːrɪk] *f* lyric poetry; ~**er** (-s, -) *m*
lyric poet
lyrisch ['lyːrɪʃ] *adj* lyrical

M m

m *abk* = **Meter**
Machart *f* make
machbar *adj* feasible

SCHLÜSSELWORT

machen ['maxən] *vt* **1** to do; (*herstellen,
zubereiten*) to make; **was machst du da?**
what are you doing (there)?; **das ist
nicht zu machen** that can't be done; **das
Radio leiser machen** to turn the radio
down; **aus Holz gemacht** made of wood
2 (*verursachen, bewirken*) to make; **jdm
Angst machen** to make sb afraid; **das
macht die Kälte** it's the cold that does
that
3 (*ausmachen*) to matter; **das macht
nichts** that doesn't matter; **die Kälte
macht mir nichts** I don't mind the cold
4 (*kosten, ergeben*) to be; **3 und 5 macht
8** 3 and 5 is *od* are 8; **was** *od* **wieviel
macht das?** how much does that make?
5: **was macht die Arbeit?** how's the
work going?; **was macht dein Bruder?**
how is your brother doing?; **das Auto
machen lassen** to have the car done;
mach's gut! take care!; (*viel Glück*) good
luck!
♦ *vi*: **mach schnell!** hurry up!; **Schluß
machen** to finish (off); **mach schon!**

come on!; **das macht müde** it makes you tired; **in etw** *dat* **machen** to be *od* deal in sth

♦ *vr* to come along (nicely); **sich an etw** *akk* **machen** to set about sth; **sich verständlich machen** to make o.s. understood; **sich** *dat* **viel aus jdm/etw machen** to like sb/sth

Macht [maxt] (-, ⸚e) *f* power; **~haber** (-s, -) *m* ruler

mächtig ['mɛçtɪç] *adj* powerful, mighty; (*umg: ungeheuer*) enormous

Macht- *zW:* **m~los** *adj* powerless; **~probe** *f* trial of strength; **~wort** *nt:* **ein ~wort sprechen** to exercise one's authority

Mädchen ['mɛːtçən] *nt* girl; **m~haft** *adj* girlish; **~name** *m* maiden name

Made ['maːdə] *f* maggot

madig ['maːdɪç] *adj* maggoty; **jdm etw ~ machen** to spoil sth for sb

mag *etc* [maːk] *vb siehe* **mögen**

Magazin [maga'tsiːn] (-s, -e) *nt* magazine

Magen ['maːgən] (-s, - *od* ⸚) *m* stomach; **~geschwür** *nt* (*MED*) stomach ulcer; **~schmerzen** *pl* stomachache *sg*

mager ['maːgər] *adj* lean; (*dünn*) thin; **M~keit** *f* leanness; thinness

Magie [ma'giː] *f* magic

magisch ['maːgɪʃ] *adj* magical

Magnet [ma'gneːt] (-s *od* -en, -en) *m* magnet; **m~isch** *adj* magnetic; **~nadel** *f* magnetic needle

Mahagoni [maha'goːni] (-s) *nt* mahogany

mähen ['mɛːən] *vt, vi* to mow

Mahl [maːl] (-(e)s, -e) *nt* meal; **m~en** (*unreg*) *vt* to grind; **~zeit** *f* meal ♦ *excl* enjoy your meal

Mahnbrief *m* reminder

Mähne ['mɛːnə] *f* mane

mahnen ['maːnən] *vt* to remind; (*warnend*) to warn; (*wegen Schuld*) to demand payment from

Mahnung *f* reminder; admonition, warning

Mai [maɪ] (-(e)s, -e) *m* May; **~glöckchen** *nt* lily of the valley; **~käfer** *m* cockchafer

Mailand *nt* Milan

mailändisch *adj* Milanese

Mais [maɪs] (-es, -e) *m* maize, corn (*US*); **~kolben** *m* corncob; **~mehl** *nt* (*KOCH*) corn meal

Majestät [majɛs'tɛːt] *f* majesty; **m~isch** *adj* majestic

Major [ma'joːr] (-s, -e) *m* (*MIL*) major; (*AVIAT*) squadron leader

Majoran [majo'raːn] (-s, -e) *m* marjoram

makaber [ma'kaːbər] *adj* macabre

Makel ['maːkəl] (-s, -) *m* blemish; (*moralisch*) stain; **m~los** *adj* immaculate, spotless

mäkeln ['mɛːkəln] *vi* to find fault

Makkaroni [maka'roːni] *pl* macaroni *sg*

Makler(in) ['maːklər(ɪn)] (-s, -) *m(f)* broker

Makrele [ma'kreːlə] *f* mackerel

Makrone [ma'kroːnə] *f* macaroon

Mal [maːl] (-(e)s, -e) *nt* mark, sign; (*Zeitpunkt*) time; **m~** *adv* times; (*umg*) *siehe* **einmal** ♦ *suffix:* **-m~** -times

Malaria [ma'laːrja] (-) *f* (*MED*) malaria

malen *vt, vi* to paint

Maler (-s, -) *m* painter

Male'rei *f* painting

malerisch *adj* picturesque

Malkasten *m* paintbox

Mallorca [ma'lɔrka] (-s) *nt* Majorca

malnehmen (*unreg*) *vt, vi* to multiply

Malz [malts] (-es) *nt* malt; **~bier** *nt* (*KOCH*) malt beer; **~bonbon** *nt* cough drop; **~kaffee** *m* malt coffee

Mama ['mama:] (-, -s; *umg*) *f* mum(my) (*BRIT*), mom(my) (*US*)

Mami ['mami] (-, -s; *umg*) *f* mum(my) (*BRIT*), mom(my) (*US*)

Mammut ['mamʊt] (-s, -e *od* -s) *nt* mammoth

man [man] *pron* one, you; **~ sagt, ...** they *od* people say ...; **wie schreibt ~ das?** how do you write it?, how is it written?

manch [manç] (*unver*) *pron* many a

manche(r, s) ['mançə(r, s)] *adj* many a; (*pl: einige*) a number of ♦ *pron* some

mancherlei *adj inv* various ♦ *pron inv* a variety of things

manchmal *adv* sometimes

Mandant(in) [man'dant(ɪn)] *m(f)* (*JUR*)

client

Mandarine [manda'ri:nə] *f* mandarin, tangerine

Mandat [man'da:t] (-(e)s, -e) *nt* mandate

Mandel ['mandəl] (-, -n) *f* almond; (*ANAT*) tonsil

Mandelentzündung *f* (*MED*) tonsillitis

Manege [ma'ne:ʒə] *f* ring, arena

Mangel[1] ['maŋəl] (-, -n) *f* mangle

Mangel[2] (-s, ·) *m* lack; (*Knappheit*) shortage; (*Fehler*) defect, fault; **~ an** +*dat* shortage of; **~erscheinung** *f* deficiency symptom; **m~haft** *adj* poor; (*fehlerhaft*) defective, faulty; **m~n** *vi unpers*: **es m~t jdm an etw** *dat* sb lacks sth ♦ *vt* (*Wäsche*) to mangle

mangels *präp* +*gen* for lack of

Mango ['maŋgo] (-, -s) *f* (*BOT, KOCH*) mango

Manie [ma'ni:] *f* mania

Manier [ma'ni:r] (-) *f* manner; style; (*pej*) mannerism; **~en** *pl* (*Umgangsformen*) manners

manierlich *adj* well-mannered

Manifest [mani'fɛst] (-es, -e) *nt* manifesto

Maniküre [mani'ky:rə] *f* manicure; **m~n** *vt* to manicure

manipulieren [manipu'li:rən] *vt* to manipulate

Manko ['maŋko] (-s, -s) *nt* deficiency; (*COMM*) deficit

Mann [man] (-(e)s, ·er) *m* man; (*Ehe~*) husband; (*NAUT*) hand; **seinen ~ stehen** to hold one's own

Männchen ['mɛnçən] *nt* little man; (*Tier*) male

Mannequin [manə'kɛ̃] (-s, -s) *nt* fashion model

männlich ['mɛnlıç] *adj* (*BIOL*) male; (*fig, GRAM*) masculine

Mannschaft *f* (*SPORT, fig*) team; (*AVIAT, NAUT*) crew; (*MIL*) other ranks *pl*

Manöver [ma'nø:vər] (-s, -) *nt* manoeuvre

manövrieren [manø'vri:rən] *vt, vi* to manoeuvre

Mansarde [man'zardə] *f* attic

Manschette [man'ʃɛtə] *f* cuff; (*TECH*)

collar; sleeve; **~nknopf** *m* cufflink

Mantel ['mantəl] (-s, ·) *m* coat; (*TECH*) casing, jacket

Manuskript [manu'skrıpt] (-(e)s, -e) *nt* manuscript

Mappe ['mapə] *f* briefcase; (*Akten~*) folder

Märchen ['mɛːrçən] *nt* fairy tale; **m~haft** *adj* fabulous; **~prinz** *m* Prince Charming

Marder ['mardər] (-s, -) *m* marten

Margarine [marga'ri:nə] *f* margarine

Margerite [margə'ri:tə] *f* (*BOT*) marguerite

Maria [ma'ri:a] (-) *f* (*REL*) Mary

Marienkäfer [ma'ri:ənkɛːfər] *m* ladybird

Marine [ma'ri:nə] *f* navy; **m~blau** *adj* navy-blue

marinieren [mari'ni:rən] *vt* to marinate

Marionette [mario'nɛtə] *f* puppet

Mark[1] [mark] (-, -) *f* (*Münze*) mark

Mark[2] (-(e)s) *nt* (*Knochen~*) marrow; **jdm durch ~ und Bein gehen** to go right through sb

markant [mar'kant] *adj* striking

Marke ['markə] *f* mark; (*Warensorte*) brand; (*Fabrikat*) make; (*Rabatt~, Brief~*) stamp; (*Essens~*) ticket; (*aus Metall etc*) token, disc

markieren [mar'ki:rən] *vt* to mark; (*umg*) to act ♦ *vi* to act it

Markierung *f* marking

Markise [mar'ki:zə] *f* awning

Markstück *nt* one-mark piece

Markt [markt] (-(e)s, ·e) *m* market; **~lücke** *f* (*WIRTS*) opening, gap in the market; **~platz** *m* market place; **m~üblich** *adj* (*Preise, Mieten*) standard, usual; **~wert** *m* (*WIRTS*) market value; **~wirtschaft** *f* market economy

Marmelade [marmə'la:də] *f* jam

Marmor ['marmor] (-s, -e) *m* marble; **m~ieren** [-'ri:rən] *vt* to marble; **m~n** *adj* marble

Marokko [ma'rɔko] (-s) *nt* Morocco

Marone [ma'ro:nə] (-, -n *od* **Maroni**) *f* chestnut

Marotte [ma'rɔtə] *f* fad, quirk

Marsch[1] [marʃ] (-(e)s, ·e) *m* march ♦ *excl*

march!

Marsch² (-, -en) f marsh

Marsch- [marʃ] *zW*: **~befehl** *m* marching orders *pl*; **m~bereit** *adj* ready to move; **m~ieren** [mar'ʃiːrən] *vi* to march

Märtyrer(in) ['mɛrtyrər(ɪn)] (-s, -) *m(f)* martyr

März [mɛrts] (-(es), -e) *m* March

Marzipan [martsi'paːn] (-s, -e) *nt* marzipan

Masche ['maʃə] f mesh; (*Strick~*) stitch; **das ist die neueste ~** that's the latest thing; **~ndraht** *m* wire mesh; **m~nfest** *adj* runproof

Maschine [ma'ʃiːnə] f machine; (*Motor*) engine; (*Schreib~*) typewriter; **m~ll** [maʃi'nɛl] *adj* machine(-); mechanical

Maschinen- *zW*: **~bauer** *m* mechanical engineer; **~gewehr** *nt* machine gun; **~pistole** f submachine gun; **~schaden** *m* mechanical fault; **~schlosser** *m* fitter; **~schrift** f typescript

maschineschreiben (*unreg*) *vi* to type

Maschinist [maʃi'nɪst] *m* engineer

Maser ['maːzər] (-, -n) f (*von Holz*) grain; **~n** *pl* (*MED*) measles *sg*; **~ung** f grain(ing)

Maske ['maskə] f mask; **~nball** *m* fancy-dress ball; **~rade** [maskə'raːdə] f masquerade

maskieren [mas'kiːrən] *vt* to mask; (*verkleiden*) to dress up ♦ *vr* to disguise o.s.; to dress up

Maskottchen [mas'kɔtçən] *nt* (lucky) mascot

Maß¹ [maːs] (-es, -e) *nt* measure; (*Mäßigung*) moderation; (*Grad*) degree, extent

Maß² (-, -(e)) f litre of beer

Massage [ma'saːʒə] f massage

Maßanzug *m* made-to-measure suit

Maßarbeit f (*fig*) neat piece of work

Masse ['masə] f mass

Massen- *zW*: **~artikel** *m* mass-produced article; **~grab** *nt* mass grave; **m~haft** *adj* loads of; **~medien** *pl* mass media *pl*; **~veranstaltung** f mass meeting

massenweise *adv* on a large scale

Masseur [ma'søːr] *m* masseur

Masseurin f masseuse

maßgebend *adj* authoritative

maßhalten (*unreg*) *vi* to exercise moderation

massieren [ma'siːrən] *vt* to massage; (*MIL*) to mass

massig ['masɪç] *adj* massive; (*umg*) massive amount of

mäßig ['mɛːsɪç] *adj* moderate; **~en** ['mɛːsɪgən] *vt* to restrain, to moderate; **M~keit** f moderation

Massiv (-s, -e) *nt* massif

massiv [ma'siːf] *adj* solid; (*fig*) heavy, rough

Maß- *zW*: **~krug** *m* tankard; **m~los** *adj* extreme; **~nahme** f measure, step; **~stab** *m* rule, measure; (*fig*) standard; (*GEOG*) scale; **m~voll** *adj* moderate

Mast [mast] (-(e)s, -e(n)) *m* mast; (*ELEK*) pylon

mästen ['mɛstən] *vt* to fatten

Material [materi'aːl] (-s, -ien) *nt* material(s); **~fehler** *m* material defect; **~ismus** [-'lɪsmʊs] *m* materialism; **m~istisch** [-'lɪstɪʃ] *adj* materialistic

Materie [ma'teːriə] f matter, substance

materiell [materi'ɛl] *adj* material

Mathematik [matema'tiːk] f mathematics *sg*; **~er(in)** [mate'maː-tikər(ɪn)] (-s, -) *m(f)* mathematician

mathematisch [mate'maːtɪʃ] *adj* mathematical

Matjeshering ['matjəsheːrɪŋ] *m* (*KOCH*) young herring

Matratze [ma'tratsə] f mattress

Matrixdrucker ['maːtrɪks-] *m* dot-matrix printer

Matrize [ma'triːtsə] f matrix; (*zum Abziehen*) stencil

Matrose [ma'troːzə] (-n, -n) *m* sailor

Matsch [matʃ] (-(e)s) *m* mud; (*Schnee~*) slush; **m~ig** *adj* muddy; slushy

matt [mat] *adj* weak; (*glanzlos*) dull; (*PHOT*) matt; (*SCHACH*) mate

Matte ['matə] f mat

Mattscheibe f (*TV*) screen; **~ haben** (*umg*) not to be quite with it

Mauer ['mauər] (-, -n) f wall; **m~n** *vi* to build; to lay bricks ♦ *vt* to build

Maul [maʊl] (-(e)s, Mäuler) *nt* mouth; **m~en** (*umg*) *vi* to grumble; **~esel** *m* mule; **~korb** *m* muzzle; **~sperre** *f* lockjaw; **~tasche** *f* (*KOCH*) *pasta envelopes stuffed and used in soup*; **~tier** *nt* mule; **~wurf** *m* mole

Maurer ['maʊrər] (-s, -) *m* bricklayer

Maus [maʊs] (-, Mäuse) *f* (*auch COMPUT*) mouse

Mause- ['maʊzə] *zW*: **~falle** *f* mousetrap; **m~n** *vi* to catch mice ♦ *vt* (*umg*) to pinch; **m~tot** *adj* stone dead

maximal [maksi'maːl] *adj* maximum ♦ *adv* at most

Mayonnaise [majo'nɛːzə] *f* mayonnaise

Mechan- [me'çaːn] *zW*: **~ik** *f* mechanics *sg*; (*Getriebe*) mechanics *pl*; **~iker** (-s, -) *m* mechanic, engineer; **m~isch** *adj* mechanical; **~ismus** [meça'nɪsmʊs] *m* mechanism

meckern ['mɛkərn] *vi* to bleat; (*umg*) to moan

Medaille [me'daljə] *f* medal

Medaillon [medal'jõː] (-s, -s) *nt* (*Schmuck*) locket

Medikament [medika'mɛnt] *nt* medicine

Meditation [meditatsi'oːn] *f* meditation

meditieren [medi'tiːrən] *vi* to meditate

Medizin [medi'tsiːn] (-, -en) *f* medicine; **m~isch** *adj* medical

Meer [meːr] (-(e)s, -e) *nt* sea; **~enge** *f* straits *pl*; **~esspiegel** *m* sea level; **~rettich** *m* horseradish; **~schweinchen** *nt* guinea-pig; **~wasser** *nt* sea water

Megaphon [mega'foːn] (-s, -e) *nt* megaphone

Mehl [meːl] (-(e)s, -e) *nt* flour; **m~ig** *adj* floury; **~schwitze** *f* (*KOCH*) roux; **~speise** *f* (*KOCH*) flummery

mehr [meːr] *adj, adv* more; **~deutig** *adj* ambiguous; **~ere** *adj* several; **~eres** *pron* several things; **~fach** *adj* multiple; (*wiederholt*) repeated; **M~heit** *f* majority; **~malig** *adj* repeated; **~mals** *adv* repeatedly; **~stimmig** *adj* for several voices; **~stimmig singen** to harmonize; **M~wertsteuer** *f* value added tax; **M~zahl** *f* majority; (*GRAM*) plural

Mehrzweck- *in zW* multipurpose

meiden ['maɪdən] (*unreg*) *vt* to avoid

Meile ['maɪlə] *f* mile; **~nstein** *m* milestone; **m~nweit** *adj* for miles

mein(e) [maɪn(ə)] *adj* my; **~e(r, s)** *pron* mine

Meineid ['maɪnʔaɪt] *m* perjury

meinen ['maɪnən] *vi* to think ♦ *vt* to think; (*sagen*) to say; (*sagen wollen*) to mean; **das will ich ~** I should think so

mein- *zW*: **~erseits** *adv* for my part; **~etwegen** *adv* (*für mich*) for my sake; (*wegen mir*) on my account; (*von mir aus*) as far as I'm concerned; I don't care *od* mind; **~etwillen** *adv*: **um ~etwillen** for my sake, on my account

Meinung ['maɪnʊŋ] *f* opinion; **ganz meine ~** I quite agree; **jdm die ~ sagen** to give sb a piece of one's mind

Meinungs- *zW*: **~austausch** *m* exchange of views; **~umfrage** *f* opinion poll; **~verschiedenheit** *f* difference of opinion

Meise ['maɪzə] *f* tit(mouse)

Meißel ['maɪsəl] (-s, -) *m* chisel; **m~n** *vt* to chisel

meist [maɪst] *adj* most ♦ *adv* mostly; **am ~en** the most; **~ens** *adv* generally, usually

Meister ['maɪstər] (-s, -) *m* master; (*SPORT*) champion; **m~haft** *adj* masterly; **m~n** *vt* (*Schwierigkeiten etc*) to overcome, conquer; **~schaft** *f* mastery; (*SPORT*) championship; **~stück** *nt* masterpiece; **~werk** *nt* masterpiece

Melancholie [melaŋko'liː] *f* melancholy

melancholisch [melaŋ'koːlɪʃ] *adj* melancholy

Melde- ['mɛldə] *zW*: **~frist** *f* registration period; **m~n** *vt* to report ♦ *vr* to report; (*SCH*) to put one's hand up; (*freiwillig*) to volunteer; (*auf etw, am Telefon*) to answer; **sich m~n bei** to report to; to register with; **sich zu Wort m~n** to ask to speak; **~pflicht** *f* obligation to register with the police; **~stelle** *f* registration office

Meldung ['mɛldʊŋ] *f* announcement; (*Bericht*) report

meliert [me'liːrt] *adj* (*Haar*) greying;

(*Wolle*) flecked
melken ['mɛlkən] (*unreg*) *vt* to milk
Melodie [melo'di:] *f* melody, tune
melodisch [me'lo:dɪʃ] *adj* melodious, tuneful
Melone [me'lo:nə] *f* melon; (*Hut*) bowler (hat)
Membran [mem'bra:n] (-, -en) *f* (*TECH*) diaphragm
Membrane *f* (*TECH*) diaphragm
Memoiren [memo'a:rən] *pl* memoirs
Menge ['mɛŋə] *f* quantity; (*Menschen~*) crowd; (*große Anzahl*) lot (of); **m~n** *vt* to mix ♦ *vr*: **sich m~n in** +*akk* to meddle with; **~nlehre** *f* (*MATH*) set theory; **~nrabatt** *m* bulk discount
Mensch [mɛnʃ] (-en, -en) *m* human being, man; person ♦ *excl* hey!; **kein ~** nobody
Menschen- *zW*: **~affe** *m* (*ZOOL*) ape; **~feind** *m* misanthrope; **m~freundlich** *adj* philanthropical; **~kenner** *m* judge of human nature; **m~leer** *adj* deserted; **m~möglich** *adj* humanly possible; **~rechte** *pl* human rights; **m~unwürdig** *adj* beneath human dignity; **~verstand** *m*: **gesunder ~verstand** common sense
Mensch- *zW*: **~heit** *f* humanity, mankind; **m~lich** *adj* human; (*human*) humane; **~lichkeit** *f* humanity
Menstruation [mɛnstruatsi'o:n] *f* menstruation
Mentalität [mɛntali'tɛ:t] *f* mentality
Menü [me'ny:] (-s, -s) *nt* (*auch COMPUT*) menu
Merk- ['mɛrk] *zW*: **~blatt** *nt* instruction sheet *od* leaflet; **m~en** *vt* to notice; **sich** *dat* **etw m~en** to remember sth; **m~lich** *adj* noticeable; **~mal** *nt* sign, characteristic; **m~würdig** *adj* odd
meßbar ['mɛsba:r] *adj* measurable
Meßbecher *m* measuring jug
Messe ['mɛsə] *f* fair; (*ECCL*) mass; **~halle** *f* pavilion at a fair
messen (*unreg*) *vt* to measure ♦ *vr* to compete
Messer (-s, -) *nt* knife; **~spitze** *f* knife point; (*in Rezept*) pinch

Messestand *m* stall at a fair
Meßgerät *nt* measuring device, gauge
Messing ['mɛsɪŋ] (-s) *nt* brass
Metall [me'tal] (-s, -e) *nt* metal; **m~isch** *adj* metallic
Meteor [mete'o:r] (-s, -e) *nt* meteor
Meter ['me:tər] (-s, -) *nt od m* metre; **~maß** *nt* tape measure
Methode [me'to:də] *f* method
methodisch [me'to:dɪʃ] *adj* methodical
Metropole [metro'po:lə] *f* metropolis
Metzger ['mɛtsgər] (-s, -) *m* butcher; **~ei** [-'rai] *f* butcher's (shop)
Meute ['mɔʏtə] *f* pack; **~'rei** *f* mutiny; **m~rn** *vi* to mutiny
miauen [mi'aʊən] *vi* to miaow
mich [mɪç] (*akk von* **ich**) *pron* me; myself
Miene ['mi:nə] *f* look, expression
mies [mi:s] (*umg*) *adj* lousy
Miet- ['mi:t] *zW*: **~auto** *nt* hired car; **~e** *f* rent; **zur ~e wohnen** to live in rented accommodation; **m~en** *vt* to rent; (*Auto*) to hire; **~er(in)** (-s, -) *m(f)* tenant; **~shaus** *nt* tenement, block of (rented) flats; **~vertrag** *m* lease
Migräne [mi'grɛ:nə] *f* migraine
Mikro- ['mikro] *zW*: **~fon** [-'fo:n] (-s, -e) *nt* microphone; **~phon** (-s, -e) [-'fo:n] *nt* microphone; **~skop** [-'sko:p] (-s, -e) *nt* microscope; **m~skopisch** *adj* microscopic; **~wellenherd** *m* microwave (oven)
Milch [mɪlç] (-) *f* milk; **~glas** *nt* frosted glass; **m~ig** *adj* milky; **~kaffee** *m* white coffee; **~mann** (*pl* -männer) *m* milkman; **~mixgetränk** *m* (*KOCH*) milkshake; **~pulver** *nt* powdered milk; **~straße** *f* Milky Way; **~zahn** *m* milk tooth
mild [mɪlt] *adj* mild; (*Richter*) lenient; (*freundlich*) kind, charitable; **M~e** ['mɪldə] *f* mildness; leniency; **~ern** *vt* to mitigate, to soften; (*Schmerz*) to alleviate; **~ernde Umstände** extenuating circumstances
Milieu [mili'ø:] (-s, -s) *nt* background, environment; **m~geschädigt** *adj* maladjusted
Mili- [mili] *zW*: **m~tant** [-'tant] *adj* militant; **~tär** [-'tɛ:r] (-s) *nt* military,

army; ~'tärgericht *nt* military court;
m~'tärisch *adj* military
Milli- ['mɪli] *zW:* ~ardär [-ar'dɛːr] *m*
multimillionaire; ~arde [-'ardə] *f*
milliard; billion (*bes US*); ~meter *m*
millimetre; ~meterpapier *nt* graph
paper
Million [mɪli'oːn] (-, -en) *f* million; ~är
[-o'nɛːr] *m* millionaire
Milz [mɪlts] (-, -en) *f* spleen
Mimik ['miːmɪk] *f* mime
Mimose [mi'moːzə] *f* mimosa; (*fig*)
sensitive person
minder ['mɪndər] *adj* inferior ♦ *adv* less;
M~heit *f* minority; ~jährig *adj* minor;
M~jährige(r) *mf* minor; ~n *vt, vr* to
decrease, to diminish; M~ung *f* decrease;
~wertig *adj* inferior; M~wer-
tigkeitskomplex *m* inferiority
complex
Mindest- ['mɪndəst] *zW:* ~alter *nt*
minimum age; ~betrag *m* minimum
amount; m~e(r, s) *adj* least; zum ~en
at least; m~ens *adv* at least; ~lohn *m*
minimum wage; ~maß *nt* minimum
Mine ['miːnə] *f* mine; (*Bleistift~*) lead;
(*Kugelschreiber~*) refill; ~nfeld *nt*
minefield
Mineral [mine'raːl] (-s, -e *od* -ien) *nt*
mineral; m~isch *adj* mineral; ~wasser
nt mineral water
Miniatur [miniatu:r] *f* miniature
Minigolf ['miːnigɔlf] *nt* miniature golf,
crazy golf
minimal [mini'maːl] *adj* minimal
Minimum ['miːnimʊm] *nt* minimum
Minirock *m* miniskirt
Minister [mi'nɪstər] (-s, -) *m* minister;
m~iell [minɪsteri'ɛl] *adj* ministerial;
~ium [minɪs'teːriʊm] *nt* ministry;
~präsident *m* prime minister
Minus ['miːnʊs] (-, -) *nt* deficit
minus *adv* minus; M~zeichen *nt* minus
sign
Minute [mi'nuːtə] *f* minute; ~nzeiger *m*
minute hand
Minze ['mɪntsə] *f* mint
mir [miːr] (*dat von* ich) *pron* (to) me; ~
nichts, dir nichts just like that

Misch- ['mɪʃ] *zW:* ~ehe *f* mixed
marriage; m~en *vt* to mix; ~ling *m* half-
caste; ~ung *f* mixture
miserabel [mizə'raːbəl] (*umg*) *adj* (*Essen,
Film*) dreadful
Miß- ['mɪs] *zW:* ~behagen *nt* discomfort,
uneasiness; ~bildung *f* deformity;
m~'billigen *vt insep* to disapprove of;
~brauch *m* abuse; (*falscher Gebrauch*)
misuse; m~'brauchen *vt insep* to abuse;
jdn zu *od* für etw m~brauchen to use
sb for *od* to do sth; ~erfolg *m* failure;
~fallen (-s) *nt* displeasure; m~'fallen
(*unreg*) *vi insep:* jdm m~fallen to
displease sb; ~geburt *f* freak; (*fig*)
abortion; ~geschick *nt* misfortune;
m~glücken [mɪs'glʏkən] *vi insep* to fail;
jdm m~glückt etw sb does not succeed
with sth; ~griff *m* mistake; ~gunst *f*
envy; m~günstig *adj* envious; m~'handeln *vt insep* to ill-treat; ~'handlung *f*
ill-treatment
Mission [mɪsi'oːn] *f* mission; ~ar(in)
[mɪsio'naːr(ɪn)] *m(f)* missionary
Miß- *zW:* ~klang *m* discord; ~kredit *m*
discredit; m~lingen [mɪs'lɪŋən] (*unreg*) *vi
insep* to fail; ~mut *m* sullenness;
m~mutig *adj* sullen; m~'raten (*unreg*)
vi insep to turn out badly ♦ *adj* ill-bred;
~stand *m* bad state of affairs; abuse;
~stimmung *f* ill-humour, discord;
m~'trauen *vi insep* to mistrust; ~trauen
(-s) *nt* distrust, suspicion;
~trauensantrag *m* (*POL*) motion of no
confidence; m~trauisch *adj* distrustful,
suspicious; ~verhältnis *nt* disproportion;
~verständnis *nt* misunderstanding;
m~verstehen (*unreg*) *vt insep* to
misunderstand; ~wirtschaft *f*
mismanagement
Mist [mɪst] (-(e)s) *m* dung; dirt; (*umg*)
rubbish
Mistel (-, -n) *f* mistletoe
Misthaufen *m* dungheap
mit [mɪt] *präp +dat* with; (*mittels*) by
♦ *adv* along, too; ~ der Bahn by train; ~
10 Jahren at the age of 10; wollen Sie
~? do you want to come along?
Mitarbeit ['mɪt'arbaɪt] *f* cooperation;

m~en *vi* to cooperate, to collaborate;
~er(in) *m(f)* collaborator; co-worker ♦ *pl*
(*Personal*) staff
Mit- *zW:* **~bestimmung** *f* participation
in decision-making; **m~bringen** (*unreg*)
vt to bring along
miteinander [mɪt'aɪ'nandər] *adv*
together, with one another
miterleben *vt* to see, to witness
Mitesser ['mɪt'ɛsər] (**-s, -**) *m* blackhead
mitfahren *vi* to accompany; (*auf Reise auch*) to travel with
mitfühlend *adj* sympathetic,
compassionate
Mit- *zW:* **m~geben** (*unreg*) *vt* to give;
~gefühl *nt* sympathy; **m~gehen** (*unreg*)
vi to go/come along; **m~genommen** *adj*
done in, in a bad way; **~gift** *f* dowry
Mitglied ['mɪtɡliːt] *nt* member;
~beitrag *m* membership fee; **~schaft** *f*
membership
Mit- *zW:* **m~halten** (*unreg*) *vi* to keep up;
m~helfen (*unreg*) *vi* to help; **~hilfe** *f*
help, assistance; **m~hören** *vt* to listen in
to; **m~kommen** (*unreg*) *vi* to come
along; (*verstehen*) to keep up, to follow;
~läufer *m* hanger-on; (*POL*) fellow-
traveller
Mitleid *nt* sympathy; (*Erbarmen*)
compassion; **m~ig** *adj* sympathetic;
m~slos *adj* pitiless, merciless
Mit- *zW:* **m~machen** *vt* to join in, to
take part in; **~mensch** *m* fellow man;
m~nehmen (*unreg*) *vt* to take along/
away; (*anstrengen*) to wear out, to
exhaust; **zum ~nehmen** to take away;
m~reden *vi*: **bei etw m~reden** to have a
say in sth; **m~reißen** (*unreg*) *vt* to carry
away/along; (*fig*) to thrill, captivate
mitsamt *präp +dat* together with
Mitschuld *f* complicity; **m~ig** *adj*: **m~ig**
(**an** *+dat*) implicated (in); (*an Unfall*)
partly responsible (for)
Mit- *zW:* **~schüler(in)** *m(f)* schoolmate;
m~spielen *vi* to join in, to take part;
~spieler(in) *m(f)* partner;
~spracherecht ['mɪtʃpraːxərɛçt] *nt*
voice, say
Mittag ['mɪtaːk] (**-(e)s, -e**) *m* midday,

lunchtime; (**zu**) **~ essen** to have lunch;
m~ *adv* at lunchtime *od* noon; **~essen** *nt*
lunch, dinner
mittags *adv* at lunchtime *od* noon;
M~pause *f* lunch break; **M~schlaf** *m*
early afternoon nap, siesta
Mittäter(in) ['mɪttɛːtər(ɪn)] *m(f)*
accomplice
Mitte ['mɪtə] *f* middle; (*POL*) centre; **aus**
unserer ~ from our midst
mitteilen ['mɪttaɪlən] *vt*: **jdm etw ~** to
inform sb of sth, to communicate sth to
sb
Mitteilung *f* communication
Mittel ['mɪtəl] (**-s -**) *nt* means; method;
(*MATH*) average; (*MED*) medicine; **ein ~**
zum Zweck a means to an end; **~alter** *nt*
Middle Ages *pl*; **m~alterlich** *adj*
mediaeval; **~ding** *nt* cross; **~europa** *nt*
Central Europe; **m~mäßig** *adj* mediocre,
middling; **~mäßigkeit** *f* mediocrity;
~meer *nt* Mediterranean; **~punkt** *m*
centre; **~stand** *m* middle class; **~streifen**
m central reservation; **~stürmer** *m*
centre-forward; **~weg** *m* middle course;
~welle *f* (*RADIO*) medium wave
mitten ['mɪtən] *adv* in the middle; **~ auf**
der Straße/in der Nacht in the middle
of the street/night
Mitternacht ['mɪtərnaxt] *f* midnight
mittlere(r, s) ['mɪtlərə(r, s)] *adj* middle;
(*durchschnittlich*) medium, average
mittlerweile ['mɪtlər'vaɪlə] *adv*
meanwhile
Mittwoch ['mɪtvɔx] (**-(e)s, -e**) *m*
Wednesday; **m~s** *adv* on Wednesdays
mitunter [mɪt'ʊntər] *adv* occasionally,
sometimes
Mit- *zW:* **m~verantwortlich** *adj* jointly
responsible; **m~wirken** *vi*: **m~wirken**
(**bei**) to contribute (to); (*THEAT*) to take
part (in); **~wirkung** *f* contribution;
participation
Möbel ['møːbəl] *pl* furniture *sg*; **~wagen**
m furniture *od* removal van
mobil [mo'biːl] *adj* mobile; (*MIL*)
mobilized; **M~iar** [mobiliˈaːr] (**-s, -e**) *nt*
furnishings *pl*; **M~machung** *f*
mobilization; **M~telefon** *nt* mobile phone

möblieren [mø'bli:rən] *vt* to furnish; **möbliert wohnen** to live in furnished accommodation

möchte *etc* ['mœçtə] *vb siehe* **mögen**

Mode ['mo:də] *f* fashion

Modell [mo'dɛl] (-s, -e) *nt* model; **m~ieren** [-'li:rən] *vt* to model

Modenschau *f* fashion show

moderig ['mo:dərɪç] *adj* (*Keller*) musty; (*Luft*) stale

modern [mo'dɛrn] *adj* modern; (*modisch*) fashionable; **~isieren** *vt* to modernize

Mode- *zW:* **~schau** *f* fashion show; **~schmuck** *m* fashion jewellery; **~schöpfer(in)** *m(f)* fashion designer; **~wort** *nt* fashionable word, buzz word

modisch ['mo:dɪʃ] *adj* fashionable

Mofa ['mo:fa] (-s, -s) *nt* small moped

mogeln ['mo:gəln] (*umg*) *vi* to cheat

SCHLÜSSELWORT
---

mögen ['mø:gən] (*pt* **mochte**, *pp* **gemocht** *od* (*als Hilfsverb*) **mögen**) *vt, vi* to like; **magst du/mögen Sie ihn?** do you like him?; **ich möchte ...** I would like ..., I'd like ...; **er möchte in die Stadt** he'd like to go into town; **ich möchte nicht, daß du ...** I wouldn't like you to ...; **ich mag nicht mehr** I've had enough

♦ *Hilfsverb* to like to; (*wollen*) to want; **möchtest du etwas essen?** would you like something to eat?; **sie mag nicht bleiben** she doesn't want to stay; **das mag wohl sein** that may well be; **was mag das heißen?** what might that mean?; **Sie möchten zu Hause anrufen** could you please call home?

möglich ['mø:klɪç] *adj* possible; **~erweise** *adv* possibly; **M~keit** *f* possibility; **nach M~keit** if possible; **~st** *adv* as ... as possible

Mohn [mo:n] (-(e)s, -e) *m* (*~blume*) poppy; (*~samen*) poppy seed

Möhre ['mø:rə] *f* carrot

Mohrrübe ['mo:rry:bə] *f* carrot

mokieren [mo'ki:rən] *vr:* **sich ~ über** +*akk* to make fun of

Mole ['mo:lə] *f* (harbour) mole

Molekül [mole'ky:l] (-s, -e) *nt* molecule

Molkerei [mɔlkə'raɪ] *f* dairy

Moll [mɔl] (-, -) *nt* (*MUS*) minor (key)

mollig *adj* cosy; (*dicklich*) plump

Moment [mo'mɛnt] (-(e)s, -e) *m* moment ♦ *nt* factor; **im ~** at the moment; **~ (mal)!** just a moment; **m~an** [-'ta:n] *adj* momentary ♦ *adv* at the moment

Monarch [mo'narç] (-en, -en) *m* monarch; **~ie** [monar'çi:] *f* monarchy

Monat ['mo:nat] (-(e)s, -e) *m* month; **m~elang** *adv* for months; **m~lich** *adj* monthly; **~sgehalt** *nt:* **das dreizehnte ~sgehalt** Christmas bonus (*of one month's salary*); **~skarte** *f* monthly ticket

Mönch [mœnç] (-(e)s, -e) *m* monk

Mond [mo:nt] (-(e)s, -e) *m* moon; **~finsternis** *f* eclipse of the moon; **m~hell** *adj* moonlit; **~landung** *f* moon landing; **~schein** *m* moonlight; **~sonde** *f* moon probe

Mono- [mono] *in zW* mono; **~log** [-'lo:k] (-s, -e) *m* monologue; **~pol** [-'po:l] (-s, -e) *nt* monopoly; **m~polisieren** [-poli'zi:rən] *vt* to monopolize; **m~ton** [-'to:n] *adj* monotonous; **~tonie** [-to'ni:] *f* monotony

Montag ['mo:nta:k] (-(e)s, -e) *m* Monday

Montage [mɔn'ta:ʒə] *f* (*PHOT etc*) montage; (*TECH*) assembly; (*Einbauen*) fitting

Monteur [mɔn'tø:r] *m* fitter

montieren [mɔn'ti:rən] *vt* to assemble

Monument [monu'mɛnt] *nt* monument; **m~al** [-'ta:l] *adj* monumental

Moor [mo:r] (-(e)s, -e) *nt* moor

Moos [mo:s] (-es, -e) *nt* moss

Moped ['mo:pɛt] (-s, -s) *nt* moped

Mops [mɔps] (-es, ⁇e) *m* pug

Moral [mo'ra:l] (-, -en) *f* morality; (*einer Geschichte*) moral; **m~isch** *adj* moral

Moräne [mo'rɛ:nə] *f* moraine

Morast [mo'rast] (-(e)s, -e) *m* morass, mire; **m~ig** *adj* boggy

Mord [mɔrt] (-(e)s, -e) *m* murder; **~anschlag** *m* murder attempt

Mörder(in) ['mœrdər(ɪn)] (-s, -) *m(f)* murderer/murderess

mörderisch *adj* (*fig: schrecklich*) terrible,

dreadful ◆ *adv* (*umg*: *entsetzlich*) terribly, dreadfully

Mord- *zW*: **~kommission** *f* murder squad; **~sglück** (*umg*) *nt* amazing luck; **m~smäßig** (*umg*) *adj* terrific, enormous; **~verdacht** *m* suspicion of murder; **~waffe** *f* murder weapon

morgen ['mɔrgən] *adv* tomorrow; ~ **früh** tomorrow morning; **M~** (**-s, -**) *m* morning; **M~mantel** *m* dressing gown; **M~rock** *m* dressing gown; **M~röte** *f* dawn; **~s** *adv* in the morning

morgig ['mɔrgɪç] *adj* tomorrow's; **der ~e Tag** tomorrow

Morphium ['mɔrfiʊm] *nt* morphine

morsch [mɔrʃ] *adj* rotten

Morsealphabet ['mɔrzə-] *nt* Morse code

morsen *vi* to send a message by Morse code

Mörtel ['mœrtəl] (**-s, -**) *m* mortar

Mosaik [moza'i:k] (**-s, -en** *od* **-e**) *nt* mosaic

Moschee [mɔ'ʃe:] (**-, -n**) *f* mosque

Moskito [mɔs'ki:to] (**-s, -s**) *m* mosquito

Most [mɔst] (**-(e)s, -e**) *m* (unfermented) fruit juice; (*Apfelwein*) cider

Motel [mo'tel] (**-s, -s**) *nt* motel

Motiv [mo'ti:f] (**-s, -e**) *nt* motive; (*MUS*) theme; **~ation** [-vatsi'o:n] *f* motivation; **m~ieren** [moti'vi:rən] *vt* to motivate

Motor ['mo:tɔr, *pl* mo'to:rən] (**-s, -en**) *m* engine; (*bes ELEK*) motor; **~boot** *nt* motorboat; **~haube** *f* (*von Auto*) bonnet (*BRIT*), hood (*US*); **m~isieren** [motori'zi:rən] *vt* to motorize; **~öl** *nt* engine oil; **~rad** *nt* motorcycle; **~schaden** *m* engine trouble *od* failure

Motte ['mɔtə] *f* moth; **~nkugel** *f* mothball(s)

Motto ['mɔto] (**-s, -s**) *nt* motto

Möwe ['mø:və] *f* seagull

Mücke ['mʏkə] *f* midge, gnat; **~nstich** *m* midge *od* gnat bite

müde ['my:də] *adj* tired

Müdigkeit ['my:dɪçkaɪt] *f* tiredness

Muff [mʊf] (**-(e)s, -e**) *m* (*Handwärmer*) muff

Muffel (**-s, -**; *umg*) *m* killjoy, sourpuss

muffig *adj* (*Luft*) musty

Mühe ['my:ə] *f* trouble, pains *pl*; **mit Müh und Not** with great difficulty; **sich** *dat* ~ **geben** to go to a lot of trouble; **m~los** *adj* without trouble, easy; **m~voll** *adj* laborious, arduous

Mühle ['my:lə] *f* mill; (*Kaffee~*) grinder

Müh- *zW*: **~sal** (**-, -e**) *f*, tribulation; **m~sam** *adj* arduous, troublesome; **m~selig** *adj* arduous, laborious

Mulde ['mʊldə] *f* hollow, depression

Mull [mʊl] (**-(e)s, -e**) *m* thin muslin; **~binde** *f* gauze bandage

Müll [mʏl] (**-(e)s, -e**) *m* refuse; **~abfuhr** *f* rubbish disposal; (*Leute*) dustmen *pl*; **~abladeplatz** *m* rubbish dump; **~eimer** *m* dustbin, garbage can (*US*); **~haufen** *m* rubbish heap; **~schlucker** (**-s, -**) *m* garbage disposal unit; **~tonne** *f* dustbin; **~verbrennungsanlage** *f* incinerator

mulmig ['mʊlmɪç] *adj* rotten; (*umg*) dodgy; **jdm ist** ~ sb feels funny

multiplizieren [mʊltipli'tsi:rən] *vt* to multiply

Mumie ['mu:miə] *f* mummy

Mumm [mʊm] (**-s**; *umg*) *m* gumption, nerve

Mumps [mʊmps] (**-**) *m od f* (*MED*) mumps

München ['mʏnçən] (**-s**) *nt* Munich

Mund [mʊnt, *pl* 'mʏndər] (**-(e)s, ¨er**) *m* mouth; **~art** *f* dialect

Mündel ['mʏndəl] (**-s, -**) *nt* ward

münden ['mʏndən] *vi*: ~ **in** +*akk* to flow into

Mund- *zW*: **m~faul** *adj* taciturn; **~geruch** *m* bad breath; **~harmonika** *f* mouth organ

mündig ['mʏndɪç] *adj* of age; **M~keit** *f* majority

mündlich ['mʏntlɪç] *adj* oral

Mundstück *nt* mouthpiece; (*Zigaretten~*) tip

Mündung ['mʏndʊŋ] *f* (*von Fluß*) mouth; (*Gewehr*) muzzle

Mund- *zW*: **~wasser** *nt* mouthwash; **~werk** *nt*: **ein großes ~werk haben** to have a big mouth; **~winkel** *m* corner of the mouth

Munition [munitsi'o:n] *f* ammunition; **~slager** *nt* ammunition dump

munkeln ['muŋkəln] *vi* to whisper, to mutter

Münster ['mʏnstər] (**-s, -**) *nt* minster

munter ['muntər] *adj* lively

Münze ['mʏntsə] *f* coin; **m~n** *vt* to coin, to mint; **auf jdn gemünzt sein** to be aimed at sb

Münzfernsehen *nt* pay television

Münzfernsprecher ['mʏntsfɛrnʃpreçər] *m* callbox (*BRIT*), pay phone

mürb(e) ['mʏrb(ə)] *adj* (*Gestein*) crumbly; (*Holz*) rotten; (*Gebäck*) crisp; **jdn ~ machen** to wear sb down; **M~teig** ['mʏrbətaɪç] *m* shortcrust pastry

murmeln ['murməln] *vt, vi* to murmur, to mutter

Murmeltier ['murməltiːr] *nt* marmot

murren ['murən] *vi* to grumble, to grouse

mürrisch ['mʏrɪʃ] *adj* sullen

Mus [muːs] (**-es, -e**) *nt* purée

Muschel ['muʃəl] (**-, -n**) *f* mussel; (*~schale*) shell; (*Telefon~*) receiver

Muse ['muːzə] *f* Muse

Museum [mu'zeːum] (**-s, Museen**) *nt* museum

Musik [mu'ziːk] *f* music; (*Kapelle*) band; **m~alisch** [-'kaːlɪʃ] *adj* musical; **~ant(in)** [-'kant(ɪn)] (**-en, -en**) *m(f)* musician; **~box** *f* jukebox; **~er** (**-s, -**) *m* musician; **~hochschule** *f* college of music; **~instrument** *nt* musical instrument

musisch *adj* (*Mensch*) artistic

musizieren [muzi'tsiːrən] *vi* to make music

Muskat [mus'kaːt] (**-(e)s, -e**) *m* nutmeg

Muskel ['muskəl] (**-s, -n**) *m* muscle

Muskulatur [muskula'tuːr] *f* muscular system

muskulös [musku'løːs] *adj* muscular

Müsli ['myːsli] (**-s, -**) *nt* (*KOCH*) muesli

Muß [mus] (**-**) *nt* necessity, must

Muße ['muːsə] (**-**) *f* leisure

müssen ['mʏsən] (*pt* **mußte**, *pp* **gemußt** *od* (*als Hilfsverb*) **müssen**) *vi* 1 (*Zwang*) must (*nur im Präsens*), to have to; **ich muß es tun** I must do it, I have to do it; **ich mußte es tun** I had to do it; **er muß**

es nicht tun he doesn't have to do it; **muß ich?** must I?, do I have to?; **wann müßt ihr zur Schule?** when do you have to go to school?; **er hat gehen müssen** he (has) had to go; **muß das sein?** is that really necessary?; **ich muß mal** (*umg*) I need the toilet

2 (*sollen*): **das mußt du nicht tun!** you oughtn't to *od* shouldn't do that; **Sie hätten ihn fragen müssen** you should have asked him

3: **es muß geregnet haben** it must have rained; **es muß nicht wahr sein** it needn't be true

müßig ['myːsɪç] *adj* idle

Muster ['mustər] (**-s, -**) *nt* model; (*Dessin*) pattern; (*Probe*) sample; **m~gültig** *adj* exemplary; **m~n** *vt* (*Tapete*) to pattern; (*fig, MIL*) to examine; (*Truppen*) to inspect; **~ung** *f* (*von Stoff*) pattern; (*MIL*) inspection

Mut [muːt] *m* courage; **nur ~!** cheer up!; **jdm ~ machen** to encourage sb; **m~ig** *adj* courageous; **m~los** *adj* discouraged, despondent

mutmaßlich ['muːtmaːslɪç] *adj* presumed ♦ *adv* probably

Mutprobe *f* test *or* trial of courage

Mutter¹ ['mutər] (**-, ⁿ**) *f* mother

Mutter² (**-, Muttern**) *f* (*Schrauben~*) nut

mütterlich ['mʏtərlɪç] *adj* motherly; **~erseits** *adv* on the mother's side

Mutter- *zW*: **~liebe** *f* motherly love; **~mal** *nt* birthmark; **~milch** *f* mother's milk; **~schaft** *f* motherhood, maternity; **~schutz** *m* maternity regulations; **'m~'seelen'llein** *adj* all alone; **~sprache** *f* native language; **~tag** *m* Mother's Day

Mutti ['muti] (**-, -s**) *f* mum(my) (*BRIT*), mom(my) (*US*)

mutwillig ['muːtvɪlɪç] *adj* malicious, deliberate

Mütze ['mʏtsə] *f* cap

MwSt *abk* (= *Mehrwertsteuer*) VAT

mysteriös [mʏsteri'øːs] *adj* mysterious

Mythos ['myːtɔs] (**-, Mythen**) *m* myth

N n

na [na] *excl* well; ~ **gut** okay then
Nabel ['na:bəl] (**-s**, **-**) *m* navel; ~**schnur** *f* umbilical cord

SCHLÜSSELWORT

nach [na:x] *präp +dat* **1** (*örtlich*) to; **nach Berlin** to Berlin; **nach links/rechts** (to the) left/right; **nach oben/hinten** up/back
2 (*zeitlich*) after; **einer nach dem anderen** one after the other; **nach Ihnen!** after you!; **zehn (Minuten) nach drei** ten (minutes) past three
3 (*gemäß*) according to; **nach dem Gesetz** according to the law; **dem Namen nach** judging by his/her name; **nach allem, was ich weiß** as far as I know
♦ *adv*: **ihm nach!** after him!; **nach und nach** gradually, little by little; **nach wie vor** still

nachahmen ['na:x'a:mən] *vt* to imitate
Nachbar(in) ['na:xba:r(ɪn)] (**-s**, **-n**) *m(f)* neighbour; ~**haus** *nt*: **im ~haus** next door; **n~lich** *adj* neighbourly; ~**schaft** *f* neighbourhood; ~**staat** *m* neighbouring state
nach- *zW*: ~**bestellen** *vt*: **50 Stück ~bestellen** to order another 50; **N~bestellung** *f* (*COMM*) repeat order; **N~bildung** *f* imitation, copy; ~**blicken** *vi* to gaze after; ~**datieren** *vt* to postdate
nachdem [na:x'de:m] *konj* after; (*weil*) since; **je ~ (ob)** it depends (whether)
nach- *zW*: ~**denken** (*unreg*) *vi*: ~**denken über** +*akk* to think about; **N~denken** (**-s**) *nt* reflection, meditation; ~**denklich** *adj* thoughtful, pensive
Nachdruck ['na:xdrʊk] *m* emphasis; (*TYP*) reprint, reproduction
nachdrücklich ['na:xdrʏklɪç] *adj* emphatic
nacheinander [na:x'aɪ'nandər] *adv* one after the other
nachempfinden ['na:x'ɛmpfɪndən]

(*unreg*) *vt*: **jdm etw ~** to feel sth with sb
Nacherzählung ['na:x'ɛrtsɛ:lʊŋ] *f* reproduction (of a story)
Nachfahr ['na:xfa:r] (**-en**, **-en**) *m* descendant
Nachfolge ['na:xfɔlgə] *f* succession; **n~n** *vi +dat* to follow; ~**r(in)** (**-s**, **-**) *m(f)* successor
nachforschen *vt*, *vi* to investigate
Nachforschung *f* investigation
Nachfrage ['na:xfra:gə] *f* inquiry; (*COMM*) demand; **n~n** *vi* to inquire
nach- *zW*: ~**fühlen** *vt* = ~**empfinden**; ~**füllen** *vt* to refill; ~**geben** (*unreg*) *vi* to give way, to yield; **N~gebühr** *f* (*POST*) excess postage
nachgehen ['na:xge:ən] (*unreg*) *vi* (+*dat*) to follow; (*erforschen*) to inquire (into); (*Uhr*) to be slow
Nachgeschmack ['na:xgəʃmak] *m* aftertaste
nachgiebig ['na:xgi:bɪç] *adj* soft, accommodating; **N~keit** *f* softness
nachhaltig ['na:xhaltɪç] *adj* lasting; (*Widerstand*) persistent
nachhelfen ['na:xhɛlfən] (*unreg*) *vi +dat* to assist, to help
nachher [na:x'he:r] *adv* afterwards
Nachhilfeunterricht ['na:xhɪlfə'ʊntərɪçt] *m* extra tuition
nachholen ['na:xho:lən] *vt* to catch up with; (*Versäumtes*) to make up for
Nachkomme ['na:xkɔmə] (**-**, **-n**) *m* descendant
nachkommen (*unreg*) *vi* to follow; (*einer Verpflichtung*) to fulfil; **N~schaft** *f* descendants *pl*
Nachkriegszeit ['na:xkri:kstsaɪt] *f* postwar period
Nach- *zW*: ~**laß** (**-lasses**, **-lässe**) *m* (*COMM*) discount, rebate; (*Erbe*) estate; **n~lassen** (*unreg*) *vt* (*Strafe*) to remit; (*Summe*) to take off; (*Schulden*) to cancel ♦ *vi* to decrease, to ease off; (*Sturm*) to die down, to ease off; (*schlechter werden*) to deteriorate; **er hat n~gelassen** he has got worse; **n~lässig** *adj* negligent, careless
nachlaufen ['na:xlaʊfən] (*unreg*) *vi +dat*

to run after, to chase

nachlösen ['na:xlø:zən] *vi* (*Zuschlag*) to pay on the train, pay at the other end; (*zur Weiterfahrt*) to pay the supplement

nachmachen ['na:xmaxən] *vt* to imitate (*jdm etw* from sb), to copy; (*fälschen*) to counterfeit

Nachmittag ['na:xmɪta:k] *m* afternoon; **am ~** in the afternoon; **n~s** *adv* in the afternoon

Nach- *zW*: **~nahme** *f* cash on delivery; **per ~nahme** C.O.D.; **~name** *m* surname; **~porto** *nt* excess postage

nachprüfen ['na:xpry:fən] *vt* to check

nachrechnen ['na:xrɛçnən] *vt* to check

nachreichen ['na:xraɪçən] *vt* (*Unterlagen*) to hand in later

Nachricht ['na:xrɪçt] (-, **-en**) *f* (piece of) news; (*Mitteilung*) message; **~en** *pl* (*Neuigkeiten*) news; **~enagentur** *f* news agency; **~endienst** *m* (*MIL*) intelligence service; **~ensprecher(in)** *m(f)* newsreader; **~entechnik** *f* telecommunications *sg*

Nachruf ['na:xru:f] *m* obituary

nachsagen ['na:xza:gən] *vt* to repeat; **jdm etw ~** to say sth of sb

nachschicken ['na:xʃɪkən] *vt* to forward

nachschlagen ['na:xʃla:gən] (*unreg*) *vt* to look up

Nachschlagewerk *nt* reference book

Nachschlüssel *m* duplicate key

Nachschub *m* supplies *pl*; (*Truppen*) reinforcements *pl*

nachsehen ['na:xze:ən] (*unreg*) *vt* (*prüfen*) to check ♦ *vi* (*erforschen*) to look and see; **jdm etw ~** to forgive sb sth; **das N~ haben** to come off worst

nachsenden ['na:xzɛndən] (*unreg*) *vt* to send on, to forward

nachsichtig *adj* indulgent, lenient

nachsitzen ['na:xzɪtsən] (*unreg*) *vi*: **~ (müssen)** (*SCH*) to be kept in

Nachspeise ['na:xʃpaɪzə] *f* dessert, sweet, pudding

Nachspiel ['na:xʃpi:l] *nt* epilogue; (*fig*) sequel

nachsprechen ['na:xʃprɛçən] (*unreg*) *vt*: **(jdm) ~** to repeat (after sb)

nächst [nɛːçst] *präp +dat* (*räumlich*) next to; (*außer*) apart from; **~beste(r, s)** *adj* first that comes along; (*zweitbeste*) next best; **N~e(r)** *mf* neighbour; **~e(r, s)** *adj* next; (*nächstgelegen*) nearest

nachstellen *vt* (*TECH*: *neu einstellen*) to adjust

nächst- *zW*: **N~enliebe** *f* love for one's fellow men; **~ens** *adv* shortly, soon; **~liegend** *adj* nearest; (*fig*) obvious; **~möglich** *adj* next possible

nachsuchen ['na:xzu:xən] *vi*: **um etw ~** to ask *od* apply for sth

Nacht [naxt] (-, **-e**) *f* night; **~dienst** *m* nightshift

Nachteil ['na:xtaɪl] *m* disadvantage; **n~ig** *adj* disadvantageous

Nachthemd *nt* (*Herren~*) nightshirt; (*Damen~*) nightdress

Nachtigall ['naxtɪgal] (-, **-en**) *f* nightingale

Nachtisch ['na:xtɪʃ] *m* = **Nachspeise**

Nachtleben *nt* nightlife

nächtlich ['nɛçtlɪç] *adj* nightly

Nachtlokal *nt* night club

Nacht- *zW*: **~s** *adv* at *od* by night; **~schicht** *f* nightshift; **~schwester** *f* night nurse; **n~süber** *adv* during the night; **~tarif** *m* off-peak tariff; **~tisch** *m* bedside table; **~wächter** *m* night watchman

Nach- *zW*: **~untersuchung** *f* checkup; **n~wachsen** (*unreg*) *vi* to grow again; **~wahl** *f* (*POL*) ≈ by-election

Nachweis ['na:xvaɪs] (-es, **-e**) *m* proof; **n~bar** *adj* provable, demonstrable; **n~en** (*unreg*) *vt* to prove; **jdm etw n~en** to point sth out to sb; **n~lich** *adj* evident, demonstrable

nach- *zW*: **~wirken** *vi* to have after-effects; **N~wirkung** *f* aftereffect;

Nach- *zW*: **~trag** (-(e)s, **-träge**) *m* supplement; **n~tragen** (*unreg*) *vt* to carry; (*zufügen*) to add; **jdm etw n~tragen** to hold sth against sb; **n~träglich** *adj* later, subsequent; additional ♦ *adv* later, subsequently; additionally; **n~trauern** *vi*: **jdm/etw n~trauern** to mourn the loss of sb/sth

N~wort *nt* epilogue; **N~wuchs** *m* offspring; (*beruflich etc*) new recruits *pl*; **~zahlen** *vt, vi* to pay extra; **N~zahlung** *f* additional payment; (*zurückdatiert*) back pay; **~ziehen** (*unreg*) *vt* (*hinter sich herziehen: Bein*) to drag; **N~zügler (-s, -)** *m* straggler

Nacken ['nakən] **(-s, -)** *m* nape of the neck

nackt [nakt] *adj* naked; (*Tatsachen*) plain, bare; **N~heit** *f* nakedness

Nadel ['na:dəl] **(-, -n)** *f* needle; (*Steck~*) pin; **~öhr** *nt* eye of a needle; **~wald** *m* coniferous forest

Nagel ['na:gəl] **(-s, ⸚)** *m* nail; **~bürste** *f* nailbrush; **~feile** *f* nailfile; **~lack** *m* nail varnish *od* polish (*BRIT*); **n~n** *vt, vi* to nail; **n~neu** *adj* brand-new; **~schere** *f* nail scissors *pl*

nagen ['na:gən] *vt, vi* to gnaw

Nagetier ['na:gəti:r] *nt* rodent

nah(e) ['na:(ə)] *adj* (*räumlich*) near(by); (*Verwandte*) near; (*Freunde*) close; (*zeitlich*) near, close ♦ *adv* near(by); near, close; (*verwandt*) closely ♦ *präp +dat* near (to), close to; **der Nahe Osten** the Near East; **Nahaufnahme** *f* close-up

Nähe ['nɛ:ə] **(-)** *f* nearness, proximity; (*Umgebung*) vicinity; **in der ~** close by; at hand; **aus der ~** from close to

nahe- *zW:* **~bei** *adv* nearby; **~gehen** (*unreg*) *vi +dat* to grieve; **~kommen** (*unreg*) *vi (+dat*) to get close (to); **~legen** *vt:* **jdm etw ~legen** to suggest sth to sb; **~liegen** (*unreg*) *vi* to be obvious; **~liegend** *adj* obvious; **~n** *vi, vr* to approach, to draw near

nähen ['nɛ:ən] *vt, vi* to sew

näher *adj, adv* nearer; (*Erklärung, Erkundigung*) more detailed; **N~e(s)** *nt* details *pl*, particulars *pl*

Näherei *f* sewing, needlework

näherkommen (*unreg*) *vi, vr* to get closer

nähern *vr* to approach

nahe- *zW:* **~stehen** (*unreg*) *vi (+dat*) to be close (to); **einer Sache ~stehen** to sympathize with sth; **~stehend** *adj* close; **~treten** (*unreg*) *vi:* **jdm (zu) ~treten** to

offend sb; **~zu** *adv* nearly

Nähgarn *nt* thread

Nahkampf *m* hand-to-hand fighting

Nähkasten *m* sewing basket, workbox

nahm *etc* [na:m] *vb siehe* **nehmen**

Nähmaschine *f* sewing machine

Nähnadel *f* needle

nähren ['nɛ:rən] *vt* to feed ♦ *vr* (*Person*) to feed o.s.; (*Tier*) to feed

nahrhaft ['na:rhaft] *adj* nourishing, nutritious

Nahrung ['na:ruŋ] *f* food; (*fig auch*) sustenance

Nahrungs- *zW:* **~mittel** *nt* foodstuffs *pl*; **~mittelindustrie** *f* food industry; **~suche** *f* search for food

Nährwert *m* nutritional value

Naht [na:t] **(-, ⸚e)** *f* seam; (*MED*) suture; (*TECH*) join; **n~los** *adj* seamless; **n~los ineinander übergehen** to follow without a gap

Nah- *zW:* **~verkehr** *m* local traffic; **~verkehrszug** *m* local train; **~ziel** *nt* immediate objective

Name ['na:mə] **(-ns, -n)** *m* name; **im ~n von** on behalf of; **n~ns** *adv* by the name of; **~nstag** *m* name day, saint's day; **n~ntlich** *adj* by name ♦ *adv* particularly, especially

namhaft ['na:mhaft] *adj* (*berühmt*) famed, renowned; (*beträchtlich*) considerable; **~ machen** to name

nämlich ['nɛ:mlɪç] *adv* that is to say, namely; (*denn*) since

nannte *etc* ['nantə] *vb siehe* **nennen**

nanu [na'nu:] *excl* well, well!

Napf [napf] **(-(e)s, ⸚e)** *m* bowl, dish

Narbe ['narbə] *f* scar

narbig ['narbɪç] *adj* scarred

Narkose [nar'ko:zə] *f* anaesthetic

Narr [nar] **(-en, -en)** *m* fool; **n~en** *vt* to fool

Närrin ['nɛrɪn] *f* fool

närrisch *adj* foolish, crazy

Narzisse [nar'tsɪsə] *f* narcissus; daffodil

naschen ['naʃən] *vt, vi* to nibble; (*heimlich kosten*) to pinch a bit

naschhaft *adj* sweet-toothed

Nase ['na:zə] *f* nose

Nasen- *zW:* **~bluten** (-s) *nt* nosebleed;
~loch *nt* nostril; **~tropfen** *pl* nose drops
naseweis *adj* pert, cheeky; *(neugierig)*
nosey
Nashorn ['naːshɔrn] *nt* rhinoceros
naß [nas] *adj* wet
Nässe ['nɛsə] (-) *f* wetness; **n~n** *vt* to wet
naßkalt *adj* wet and cold
Naßrasur *f* wet shave
Nation [natsiˈoːn] *f* nation
national [natsioˈnaːl] *adj* national;
N~feiertag *m* national holiday;
~hymne *f* national anthem; **~isieren**
[-iˈziːrən] *vt* to nationalize; **N~i'sierung** *f*
nationalization; **N~ismus** [-'lɪsmʊs] *m*
nationalism; **~istisch** [-'lɪstɪʃ] *adj*
nationalistic; **N~i'tät** *f* nationality; **N~-
mannschaft** *f* national team; **N~-
sozialismus** *m* national socialism
Natron [naːtrɔn] (-s) *nt* soda
Natter ['natər] (-, -n) *f* adder
Natur [naˈtuːr] *f* nature; *(körperlich)*
constitution; **~ell** [natuˈrɛl] (-es, -e) *nt*
disposition; **~erscheinung** *f* natural
phenomenon *od* event; **n~farben** *adj*
natural coloured; **n~gemäß** *adj* natural;
~gesetz *nt* law of nature; **~getreu** *adj*
true to life; **~katastrophe** *f* natural
disaster
natürlich [naˈtyːrlɪç] *adj* natural ♦ *adv*
naturally; **ja, ~!** yes, of course; **N~keit** *f*
naturalness
Natur- *zW:* **~park** *m* ≈ national park;
~produkt *nt* natural product; **n~rein** *adj*
natural, pure; **~schutzgebiet** *nt* nature
reserve; **~wissenschaft** *f* natural
science; **~wissenschaftler(in)** *m(f)*
scientist; **~zustand** *m* natural state
nautisch ['naʊtɪʃ] *adj* nautical
Nazi ['naːtsi] (-s, -s) *m* Nazi
NB *abk* (= *nota bene*) nb
n.Chr. *abk* (= *nach Christus*) A.D.
Nebel ['neːbəl] (-s, -) *m* fog, mist; **n~ig**
adj foggy, misty; **~scheinwerfer** *m*
foglamp
neben ['neːbən] *präp* (+*akk od dat*) next
to; (+*dat: außer*) apart from, besides; **~an**
[neːbənˈʔan] *adv* next door; **N~anschluß**
m *(TEL)* extension; **N~ausgang** *m* side

exit; **~bei** [neːbənˈbaɪ] *adv* at the same
time; *(außerdem)* additionally; *(beiläufig)*
incidentally; **N~beruf** *m* second job;
N~beschäftigung *f* second job;
N~buhler(in) (-s, -) *m(f)* rival;
~einander [neːbənʔaɪˈnandər] *adv* side by
side; **~einanderlegen** *vt* to put next to
each other; **N~eingang** *m* side entrance;
N~erscheinung *f* side effect; **N~fach** *nt*
subsidiary subject; **N~fluß** *m* tributary;
N~gebäude *nt* annexe; **N~geräusch** *nt*
(RADIO) atmospherics *pl*, interference;
~her [neːbənˈheːr] *adv* (*zusätzlich*)
besides; *(gleichzeitig)* at the same time;
(daneben) alongside; **~herfahren** (*unreg*)
vi to drive alongside; **N~kosten** *pl* extra
charges, extras; **N~produkt** *nt* by-
product; **N~sache** *f* trifle, side issue;
~sächlich *adj* minor, peripheral;
N~saison *f* low season; **N~straße** *f* side
street; **N~verdienst** *m* secondary
income; **N~zimmer** *nt* adjoining room
neblig ['neːblɪç] *adj* foggy, misty
Necessaire [nesɛˈsɛːr] (-s, -s) *nt* (*Näh~*)
needlework box; *(Nagel~)* manicure case
necken ['nɛkən] *vt* to tease
Neckerei [nɛkəˈraɪ] *f* teasing
Neffe ['nɛfə] (-n, -n) *m* nephew
negativ [negaˈtiːf] *adj* negative; **N~** (-s,
-e) *nt* *(PHOT)* negative
Neger ['neːgər] (-s, -) *m* negro; **~in** *f*
negress
nehmen ['neːmən] (*unreg*) *vt* to take; **jdn
zu sich ~** to take sb in; **sich ernst ~** to
take o.s. seriously; **nimm dir doch bitte**
please help yourself
Neid [naɪt] (-(e)s) *m* envy; **~er** (-s, -) *m*
envier; **n~isch** ['naɪdɪʃ] *adj* envious,
jealous
neigen ['naɪgən] *vt* to incline, to lean;
(Kopf) to bow ♦ *vi:* **zu etw ~** to tend to
sth
Neigung *f* (*des Geländes*) slope; *(Tendenz)*
tendency, inclination; *(Vorliebe)* liking;
(Zuneigung) affection
nein [naɪn] *adv* no
Nektarine [nɛktaˈriːnə] *f* (*Frucht*)
nectarine
Nelke ['nɛlkə] *f* carnation, pink; *(Gewürz)*

clove

Nenn- ['nɛn] *zW:* **n~en** (*unreg*) *vt* to name; (*mit Namen*) to call; **wie n~t man ...?** what do you call ...?; **n~enswert** *adj* worth mentioning; **~er** (-s, -) *m* denominator; **~wert** *m* nominal value; (*COMM*) par

Neon ['neːɔn] (-s) *nt* neon; **~licht** *nt* neon light; **~röhre** *f* neon tube

Nerv [nɛrf] (-s, -en) *m* nerve; **jdm auf die ~en gehen** to get on sb's nerves; **n~enaufreibend** *adj* nerve-racking; **~enbündel** *nt* bundle of nerves; **~enheilanstalt** *f* mental home; **n~enkrank** *adj* mentally ill; **~ensäge** (*umg*) *f* pain (in the neck) (*inf*); **~ensystem** *nt* nervous system; **~enzusammenbruch** *m* nervous breakdown; **n~lich** *adj* (*Belastung*) affecting the nerves; **n~ös** [nɛr'vøːs] *adj* nervous; **~osi'tät** *f* nervousness; **n~tötend** *adj* nerve-racking; (*Arbeit*) soul-destroying

Nerz [nɛrts] (-es, -e) *m* mink

Nessel ['nɛsəl] (-, -n) *f* nettle

Nest [nɛst] (-(e)s, -er) *nt* nest; (*umg: Ort*) dump

nett [nɛt] *adj* nice; (*freundlich*) nice, kind; **~erweise** *adv* kindly

netto ['nɛto] *adv* net

Netz [nɛts] (-es, -e) *nt* net; (*Gepäck~*) rack; (*Einkaufs~*) string bag; (*Spinnen~*) web; (*System*) network; **jdm ins ~ gehen** (*fig*) to fall into sb's trap; **~anschluß** *m* mains connection; **~haut** *f* retina

neu [nɔy] *adj* new; (*Sprache, Geschichte*) modern; **seit ~estem** (since) recently; **die ~esten Nachrichten** the latest news; **~ schreiben** to rewrite, to write again; **N~anschaffung** *f* new purchase of, acquisition; **~artig** *adj* new kind of; **N~bau** *m* new building; **N~e(r)** *mf* the new man/woman; **~erdings** *adv* (*kürzlich*) (since) recently; (*von neuem*) again; **N~erscheinung** *f* (*Buch*) new publication; (*Schallplatte*) new release; **N~erung** *f* innovation, new departure; **N~gier** *f* curiosity; **~gierig** *adj* curious; **N~heit** *f* newness; novelty; **N~igkeit** *f*

news *sg*; **N~jahr** *nt* New Year; **~lich** *adv* recently, the other day; **N~ling** *m* novice; **N~mond** *m* new moon

neun [nɔyn] *num* nine; **~zehn** *num* nineteen; **~zig** *num* ninety

neureich *adj* nouveau riche; **N~e(r)** *mf* nouveau riche

neurotisch *adj* neurotic

Neu- *zW:* **~seeland** [nɔy'zeːlant] *nt* New Zealand; **~seeländer(in)** [nɔy'zeːlɛndər(ɪn)] *m(f)* New Zealander

neutral [nɔy'traːl] *adj* neutral; **~i'sieren** *vt* to neutralize

Neutrum ['nɔytrʊm] (-s, -a *od* -en) *nt* neuter

Neu- *zW:* **~wert** *m* purchase price; **n~wertig** *adj* (as) new, not used; **~zeit** *f* modern age; **n~zeitlich** *adj* modern, recent

---

nicht [nɪçt] *adv* **1** (*Verneinung*) not; **er ist es nicht** it's not him, it isn't him; **er raucht nicht** (*gerade*) he isn't smoking; (*gewöhnlich*) he doesn't smoke; **ich kann das nicht - ich auch nicht** I can't do it - neither *od* nor can I; **es regnet nicht mehr** it's not raining any more

2 (*Bitte, Verbot*): **nicht!** don't!, no!; **nicht berühren!** do not touch!; **nicht doch!** don't!

3 (*rhetorisch*): **du bist müde, nicht (wahr)?** you're tired, aren't you?; **das ist schön, nicht (wahr)?** it's nice, isn't it?

4: **was du nicht sagst!** the things you say!

Nichtangriffspakt [nɪçt''angrɪfspakt] *m* non-aggression pact

Nichte ['nɪçtə] *f* niece

nichtig ['nɪçtɪç] *adj* (*ungültig*) null, void; (*wertlos*) futile; **N~keit** *f* nullity, invalidity; (*Sinnlosigkeit*) futility

Nichtraucher(in) *m(f)* non-smoker

nichtrostend *adj* stainless

nichts [nɪçts] *pron* nothing; **für ~ und wieder ~** for nothing at all; **N~** (-) *nt* nothingness; (*pej: Person*) nonentity

Nichtschwimmer *m* nonswimmer

nichts- *zW:* **~desto'weniger** *adv* nevertheless; **N~nutz** (**-es, -e**) *m* good-for-nothing; **~nutzig** *adj* worthless, useless; **~sagend** *adj* meaningless; **N~tun** (**-s**) *nt* idleness

Nichtzutreffende(s) *nt:* **~s (bitte) streichen!** (please) delete where appropriate

Nickel ['nɪkəl] (**-s**) *nt* nickel

nicken ['nɪkən] *vi* to nod

Nickerchen ['nɪkərçən] *nt* nap

nie [ni:] *adv* never; **~ wieder** *od* **mehr** never again; **~ und nimmer** never ever

nieder ['ni:dər] *adj* low; (*gering*) inferior ♦ *adv* down; **N~gang** *m* decline; **~gedrückt** *adj* (*deprimiert*) dejected, depressed; **~gehen** (*unreg*) *vi* to descend; (*AVIAT*) to come down; (*Regen*) to fall; (*Boxer*) to go down; **~geschlagen** *adj* depressed, dejected; **N~lage** *f* defeat; **N~lande** *pl* Netherlands; **N~länder(in)** *m(f)* Dutchman(woman); **~ländisch** *adj* Dutch; **~lassen** (*unreg*) *vr* (*sich setzen*) to sit down; (*an Ort*) to settle (down); (*Arzt, Rechtsanwalt*) to set up a practice; **N~lassung** *f* settlement; (*COMM*) branch; **~legen** *vt* to lay down; (*Arbeit*) to stop; (*Amt*) to resign; **N~schlag** *m* (*MET*) precipitation; rainfall; **~schlagen** (*unreg*) *vt* (*Gegner*) to beat down; (*Gegenstand*) to knock down; (*Augen*) to lower; (*Aufstand*) to put down ♦ *vr* (*CHEM*) to precipitate; **~schreiben** (*unreg*) *vt* to put down in writing; **~trächtig** *adj* base, mean; **N~trächtigkeit** *f* meanness, baseness; outrage; **N~ung** *f* (*GEOG*) depression; (*Mündungsgebiet*) flats *pl*

niedlich ['ni:tlɪç] *adj* sweet, cute

niedrig ['ni:drɪç] *adj* low; (*Stand*) lowly, humble; (*Gesinnung*) mean

niemals ['ni:ma:ls] *adv* never

niemand ['ni:mant] *pron* nobody, no one

Niemandsland *nt* no-man's land

Niere ['ni:rə] *f* kidney

nieseln ['ni:zəln] *vi* to drizzle

niesen ['ni:zən] *vi* to sneeze

Niete ['ni:tə] *f* (*TECH*) rivet; (*Los*) blank; (*Reinfall*) flop; (*Mensch*) failure; **n~n** *vt* to rivet

Nikotin [niko'ti:n] (**-s**) *nt* nicotine

Nilpferd [ni:l-] *nt* hippopotamus

Nimmersatt ['nɪmərzat] (**-(e)s, -e**) *m* glutton

nimmst *etc* [nɪmst] *vb siehe* **nehmen**

nippen ['nɪpən] *vt, vi* to sip

nirgend- ['nɪrgənt] *zW:* **~s** *adv* nowhere; **~wo** *adv* nowhere; **~wohin** *adv* nowhere

Nische ['ni:ʃə] *f* niche

nisten ['nɪstən] *vi* to nest

Nitrat [ni'tra:t] (**-(e)s, -e**) *nt* nitrate

Niveau [ni'vo:] (**-s, -s**) *nt* level

Nixe ['nɪksə] *f* water nymph

nobel ['no:bəl] *adj* (*großzügig*) generous; (*elegant*) posh (*inf*)

SCHLÜSSELWORT

---

noch [nɔx] *adv* **1** (*weiterhin*) still; **noch nicht** not yet; **noch nie** never (yet); **noch immer** *od* **immer noch** still; **bleiben Sie doch noch** stay a bit longer

2 (*in Zukunft*) still, yet; **das kann noch passieren** that might still happen; **er wird noch kommen** he'll come (yet)

3 (*nicht später als*): **noch vor einer Woche** only a week ago; **noch am selben Tag** the very same day; **noch im 19. Jahrhundert** as late as the 19th century; **noch heute** today

4 (*zusätzlich*): **wer war noch da?** who else was there?; **noch einmal** once more, again; **noch dreimal** three more times; **noch einer** another one

5 (*bei Vergleichen*): **noch größer** even bigger; **das ist noch besser** that's better still; **und wenn es noch so schwer ist** however hard it is

6: **Geld noch und noch** heaps (and heaps) of money; **sie hat noch und noch versucht, ...** she tried again and again to ...

♦ *konj:* **weder A noch B** neither A nor B

---

noch- *zW:* **~mal** ['nɔxma:l] *adv* again, once more; **~malig** ['nɔxma:lɪç] *adj* repeated; **~mals** *adv* again, once more

Nominativ ['no:minati:f] (**-s, -e**) *m* nominative

nominell [nomi'nɛl] *adj* nominal

Nonne ['nɔnə] *f* nun
Nord(en) ['nɔrd(ən)] (-s) *m* north
Nordirland *nt* Northern Ireland
nordisch *adj* northern
nördlich ['nœrtlɪç] *adj* northerly,
northern ♦ *präp +gen* (to the) north of; ~
von (to the) north of
Nord- *zW:* **~pol** *m* North Pole; **~rhein-
Westfalen** *nt* North Rhine-Westphalia;
~see *f* North Sea; **n~wärts** *adv*
northwards
nörgeln ['nœrgəln] *vi* to grumble;
Nörgler (**-s,** -) *m* grumbler
Norm [nɔrm] (-, -en) *f* norm;
(*Größenvorschrift*) standard; **n~al**
[nɔr'ma:l] *adj* normal; **~al(benzin)** *nt*
≈ 2-star petrol (*BRIT*), regular petrol (*US*);
n~alerweise *adv* normally; **n~ali'sieren**
vt to normalize ♦ *vr* to return to normal
normen *vt* to standardize
Norweg- ['nɔrve:g] *zW:* **~en** *nt* Norway;
~er(in) (**-s,** -) *m(f)* Norwegian; **n~isch** *adj*
Norwegian
Nostalgie [nɔstal'gi:] *f* nostalgia
Not [no:t] (-, ⸚e) *f* need; (*Mangel*) want;
(*Mühe*) trouble; (*Zwang*) necessity; **zur ~**
if necessary; (*gerade noch*) just about
Notar [no'ta:r] (-s, -e) *m* notary; **n~i'ell**
adj notarial
Not- *zW:* **~ausgang** *m* emergency exit;
~behelf (**-s,** -e) *m* makeshift; **~bremse** *f*
emergency brake; **~dienst** *m*
(*Bereitschaftsdienst*) emergency service;
n~dürftig *adj* scanty; (*behelfsmäßig*)
makeshift
Note ['no:tə] *f* note; (*SCH*) mark (*BRIT*),
grade (*US*)
Noten- *zW:* **~blatt** *nt* sheet of music;
~schlüssel *m* clef; **~ständer** *m* music
stand
Not- *zW:* **~fall** *m* (case of) emergency;
n~falls *adv* if need be; **n~gedrungen**
adj necessary, unavoidable; **etw**
n~gedrungen machen to be forced to do
sth
notieren [no'ti:rən] *vt* to note; (*COMM*) to
quote
Notierung *f* (*COMM*) quotation
nötig ['nø:tɪç] *adj* necessary; **etw ~**

haben to need sth; **~en** [-gən] *vt* to compel,
to force; **~enfalls** *adv* if necessary
Notiz [no'ti:ts] (-, -en) *f* note; (*Zeitungs~*)
item; **~ nehmen** to take notice; **~block** *m*
notepad; **~buch** *nt* notebook
Not- *zW:* **~lage** *f* crisis, emergency;
n~landen *vi* to make a forced *od*
emergency landing; **n~leidend** *adj*
needy; **~lösung** *f* temporary solution;
~lüge *f* white lie
notorisch [no'to:rɪʃ] *adj* notorious
Not- *zW:* **~ruf** *m* emergency call;
~rufsäule *f* emergency telephone; **~stand**
m state of emergency;
~unterkunft *f* emergency
accommodation; **~verband** *m* emergency
dressing; **~wehr** (-) *f* self-defence;
n~wendig *adj* necessary; **~wendigkeit**
f necessity
Novelle [no'vɛlə] *f* short novel; (*JUR*)
amendment
November [no'vɛmbər] (**-s,** -) *m*
November
Nu [nu:] *m:* **im ~** in an instant
Nuance [ny'ã:sə] *f* nuance
nüchtern ['nʏçtərn] *adj* sober; (*Magen*)
empty; (*Urteil*) prudent; **N~heit** *f* sobriety
Nudel ['nu:dəl] (-, -n) *f* noodle; **~n** *pl*
(*Teigwaren*) pasta *sg*; (*in Suppe*) noodles
Null [nʊl] (-, -en) *f* nought, zero; (*pej:
Mensch*) washout; **n~** *num* zero; (*Fehler*)
no; **n~ Uhr** midnight; **n~ und nichtig**
null and void; **~punkt** *m* zero; **auf dem**
~punkt at zero; **~tarif** *m* (*für*
Verkehrsmittel) free travel
numerieren [nume'ri:rən] *vt* to number
numerisch [nu'me:rɪʃ] *adj* numerical
Nummer ['nʊmər] (-, -n) *f* number;
(*Größe*) size; **~nschild** *nt* (*AUT*) number *od*
license (*US*) plate
nun [nu:n] *adv* now ♦ *excl* well; **das ist ~**
mal so that's the way it is
nur [nu:r] *adv* just, only; **wo bleibt er ~?**
(just) where is he?
Nürnberg ['nʏrnbɛrk] (**-s**) *nt* Nuremberg
Nuß [nʊs] (-, **Nüsse**) *f* nut; **~baum** *m*
walnut tree; **~knacker** (**-s,** -) *m*
nutcracker
Nüster ['ny:stər] (-, -n) *f* nostril

nutz [nʊts] *adj*: **zu nichts ~ sein** to be no use for anything
nutzbringend *adj* (*Verwendung*) profitable
nütze ['nʏtsə] *adj* = **nutz**
Nutzen (-s) *m* usefulness; (*Gewinn*) profit; **von ~** useful; **n~** *vi* to be of use ♦ *vt*: **etw zu etw n~** to use sth for sth; **was nutzt es?** what's the use?, what use is it?
nützen *vi*, *vt* = **nutzen**
nützlich ['nʏtslɪç] *adj* useful; **N~keit** *f* usefulness
Nutz- *zW*: **n~los** *adj* useless; **~losigkeit** *f* uselessness; **~nießer** (-s, -) *m* beneficiary
Nylon ['naɪlɔn] (-(s)) *nt* nylon

O o

Oase [o'a:zə] *f* oasis
ob [ɔp] *konj* if, whether; **~ das wohl wahr ist?** can that be true?; **und ~!** you bet!
obdachlos *adj* homeless
Obdachlose(r) *mf* homeless person; **~nasyl** *nt* shelter for the homeless
Obduktion [ɔpdʊktsi'o:n] *f* post-mortem
obduzieren [ɔpdu'tsi:rən] *vt* to do a post-mortem on
O-Beine ['o:baɪnə] *pl* bow *od* bandy legs
oben ['o:bən] *adv* above; (*in Haus*) upstairs; **nach ~** up; **von ~** down; **~ ohne** topless; **jdn von ~ bis unten ansehen** to look sb up and down; **Befehl von ~** orders from above; **~an** *adv* at the top; **~auf** *adv* up above, on the top ♦ *adj* (*munter*) in form; **~drein** *adv* into the bargain; **~erwähnt** *adj* above-mentioned; **~genannt** *adj* above-mentioned
Ober ['o:bər] (-s, -) *m* waiter; **die ~en** *pl* (*umg*) the bosses; (*ECCL*) the superiors; **~arm** *m* upper arm; **~arzt** *m* senior physician; **~aufsicht** *f* supervision; **~bayern** *nt* Upper Bavaria; **~befehl** *m* supreme command; **~befehlshaber** *m* commander-in-chief; **~bekleidung** *f* outer clothing; **~'bürgermeister** *m* lord mayor; **~deck** *nt* upper *od* top deck;

o~e(r, s) *adj* upper; **~fläche** *f* surface; **o~flächlich** *adj* superficial; **~geschoß** *nt* upper storey; **o~halb** *adv* above ♦ *präp* +*gen* above; **~haupt** *nt* head, chief; **~haus** *nt* (*POL*) upper house, House of Lords (*BRIT*); **~hemd** *nt* shirt; **~herrschaft** *f* supremacy, sovereignty; **~in** *f* matron; (*ECCL*) Mother Superior; **~kellner** *m* head waiter; **~kiefer** *m* upper jaw; **~körper** *m* upper part of body; **~leitung** *f* direction; (*ELEK*) overhead cable; **~licht** *nt* skylight; **~lippe** *f* upper lip; **~schenkel** *m* thigh; **~schicht** *f* upper classes *pl*; **~schule** *f* grammar school (*BRIT*), high school (*US*); **~schwester** *f* (*MED*) matron
Oberst ['o:bərst] (-en *od* -s, -en *od* -e) *m* colonel; **o~e(r, s)** *adj* very top, topmost
Ober- *zW*: **~stufe** *f* upper school; **~teil** *nt* upper part; **~weite** *f* bust/chest measurement
obgleich [ɔp'glaɪç] *konj* although
Obhut ['ɔphu:t] (-) *f* care, protection; **in jds ~ sein** to be in sb's care
obig ['o:bɪç] *adj* above
Objekt [ɔp'jɛkt] (-(e)s, -e) *nt* object; **~iv** [-'ti:f] (-s, -e) *nt* lens; **o~iv** *adj* objective; **~ivi'tät** *f* objectivity
Oblate [o'bla:tə] *f* (*Gebäck*) wafer; (*ECCL*) host
obligatorisch [obliga'to:rɪʃ] *adj* compulsory, obligatory
Oboe [o'bo:ə] *f* oboe
Obrigkeit ['o:brɪçkaɪt] *f* (*Behörden*) authorities *pl*, administration; (*Regierung*) government
obschon [ɔp'ʃo:n] *konj* although
Observatorium [ɔpzɛrva'to:rium] *nt* observatory
obskur [ɔps'ku:r] *adj* obscure; (*verdächtig*) dubious
Obst [o:pst] (-(e)s) *nt* fruit; **~baum** *m* fruit tree; **~garten** *m* orchard; **~händler** *m* fruiterer, fruit merchant; **~kuchen** *m* fruit tart; **~salat** *m* (*KOCH*) fruit salad
obszön [ɔps'tsø:n] *adj* obscene; **O~i'tät** *f* obscenity
obwohl [ɔp'vo:l] *konj* although
Ochse ['ɔksə] (-n, -n) *m* ox; **o~n** (*umg*)

vt, vi to cram, to swot (*BRIT*);
~nschwanzsuppe *f* oxtail soup;
~nzunge *f* oxtongue
öd(e) ['øːd(ə)] *adj* (*Land*) waste, barren;
(*fig*) dull; **Öde** *f* desert, waste(land); (*fig*)
tedium
oder ['oːdər] *konj* or; **das stimmt, ~?**
that's right, isn't it?
Ofen ['oːfən] (**-s,** ˝) *m* oven; (*Heiz~*) fire,
heater; (*Kohlen~*) stove; (*Hoch~*) furnace;
(*Herd*) cooker, stove; **~rohr** *nt* stovepipe
offen ['ɔfən] *adj* open; (*aufrichtig*) frank;
(*Stelle*) vacant; **~ gesagt** to be honest;
~bar *adj* obvious; **~baren** [ɔfən'baːrən]
vt to reveal, to manifest; **O~'barung** *f*
(*REL*) revelation; **~bleiben** (*unreg*) *vi*
(*Fenster*) to stay open; (*Frage,
Entscheidung*) to remain open; **~halten**
(*unreg*) *vt* to keep open; **O~heit** *f*
candour, frankness; **~herzig** *adj* candid,
frank; (*Kleid*) revealing; **~kundig** *adj*
well-known; (*klar*) evident; **~lassen**
(*unreg*) *vt* to leave open; **~sichtlich** *adj*
evident, obvious
offensiv [ɔfɛn'ziːf] *adj* offensive; **O~e**
[-'ziːvə] *f* offensive
offenstehen (*unreg*) *vi* to be open;
(*Rechnung*) to be unpaid; **es steht Ihnen
offen, es zu tun** you are at liberty to do
it
öffentlich ['œfəntlɪç] *adj* public; **Ö~keit**
f (*Leute*) public; (*einer Versammlung etc*)
public nature; **in aller Ö~keit** in public;
an die Ö~keit dringen to reach the
public ear
offiziell [ɔfitsi'ɛl] *adj* official
Offizier [ɔfi'tsiːr] (**-s, -e**) *m* officer;
~skasino *nt* officers' mess
öffnen ['œfnən] *vt, vr* to open; **jdm die
Tür ~** to open the door for sb
Öffner ['œfnər] (**-s, -**) *m* opener
Öffnung ['œfnʊŋ] *f* opening; **~szeiten** *pl*
opening times
oft [ɔft] *adv* often
öfter ['œftər] *adv* more often *od*
frequently; **~s** *adv* often, frequently
oh [oː] *excl* oh; **~ je!** oh dear
OHG [oːhaːˈɡeː] *abk* (= *Offene
Handelsgesellschaft*) general partnership

ohne ['oːnə] *präp +akk* without ♦ *konj*
without; **das ist nicht ~** (*umg*) it's not
bad; **~ weiteres** without a second
thought; (*sofort*) immediately; **~ zu
fragen** without asking; **~ daß er es
wußte** without him knowing it; **~dies**
[oːnəˈdiːs] *adv* anyway; **~einander**
[oːnəˈaɪˈnandər] *adv* without each other;
~gleichen [oːnəˈɡlaɪçən] *adj*
unsurpassed, without equal; **~hin**
[oːnəˈhɪn] *adv* anyway, in any case
Ohnmacht ['oːnmaxt] *f* faint; (*fig*)
impotence; **in ~ fallen** to faint
ohnmächtig ['oːnmɛçtɪç] *adj* in a faint,
unconscious; (*fig*) weak, impotent; **sie ist
~** she has fainted
Ohr [oːr] (**-(e)s, -en**) *nt* ear; (*Gehör*)
hearing
Öhr [øːr] (**-(e)s, -e**) *nt* eye
Ohren- *zW:* **~arzt** *m* ear specialist;
o~betäubend *adj* deafening; **~schmalz**
nt earwax; **~schmerzen** *pl* earache *sg*;
~schützer (**-s, -**) *m* earmuff
Ohr- *zW:* **~feige** *f* slap on the face; box
on the ears; **o~feigen** *vt*: **jdn o~feigen**
to slap sb's face; to box sb's ears;
~läppchen *nt* ear lobe; **~ring** *m* earring;
~wurm *m* earwig; (*MUS*) catchy tune
ökologisch [økoˈloːɡɪʃ] *adj* ecological
ökonomisch [økoˈnoːmɪʃ] *adj*
economical
Oktan [ɔkˈtaːn] (**-s, -e**) *nt* (*bei Benzin*)
octane
Oktave [ɔkˈtaːvə] *f* octave
Oktober [ɔkˈtoːbər] (**-s, -**) *m* October
ökumenisch [økuˈmeːnɪʃ] *adj*
ecumenical
Öl [øːl] (**-(e)s, -e**) *nt* oil; **~baum** *m* olive
tree; **ö~en** *vt* to oil; (*TECH*) to lubricate;
~farbe *f* oil paint; **~feld** *nt* oilfield;
~film *m* film of oil; **~heizung** *f* oil-fired
central heating; **ö~ig** *adj* oily;
~industrie *f* oil industry
oliv [oˈliːf] *adj* olive-green; **O~e** *f* olive
Öl- *zW:* **~meßstab** *m* dipstick; **~sardine**
f sardine; **~standanzeiger** *m* (*AUT*) oil
gauge; **~tanker** *m* oil tanker; **~ung** *f*
lubrication; oiling; (*ECCL*) anointment; **die
Letzte ~ung** Extreme Unction; **~wechsel**

m oil change

Olymp- [o'lʏmp] *zW:* **~iade** [olʏmpi'a:də] *f* Olympic Games *pl;* **~iasieger(in)** [-iazi:gər(ɪn)] *m(f)* Olympic champion; **~iateilnehmer(in)** *m(f)* Olympic competitor; **o~isch** *adj* Olympic

Ölzeug *nt* oilskins *pl*

Oma ['o:ma] (-, -s; *umg*) *f* granny

Omelett [ɔm(ə)'lɛt] (-(e)s, -s) *nt* omelet(te)

Omen ['o:mɛn] (-s, -) *nt* omen

ominös [omi'nø:s] *adj* (*unheilvoll*) ominous

Omnibus ['ɔmnibʊs] *m* (omni)bus

Onanie [ona'ni:] *f* masturbation; **o~ren** *vi* to masturbate

Onkel ['ɔŋkəl] (-s, -) *m* uncle

Opa ['o:pa] (-s, -s; *umg*) *m* grandpa

Opal [o'pa:l] (-s, -e) *m* opal

Oper ['o:pər] (-, -n) *f* opera; opera house

Operation [operatsi'o:n] *f* operation; **~ssaal** *m* operating theatre

Operette [ope'rɛtə] *f* operetta

operieren [ope'ri:rən] *vt* to operate on ♦ *vi* to operate

Opern- *zW:* **~glas** *nt* opera glasses *pl;* **~haus** *nt* opera house; **~sänger(in)** *m(f)* opera singer

Opfer ['ɔpfər] (-s, -) *nt* sacrifice; (*Mensch*) victim; **o~n** *vt* to sacrifice; **~ung** *f* sacrifice

Opium ['o:piʊm] (-s) *nt* opium

opponieren [ɔpo'ni:rən] *vi:* **gegen jdn/ etw ~** to oppose sb/sth

Opportunist [ɔpɔrtu'nɪst] *m* opportunist

Opposition [ɔpozitsi'o:n] *f* opposition; **o~ell** *adj* opposing

Optik ['ɔptɪk] *f* optics *sg;* **~er** (-s, -) *m* optician

optimal [ɔpti'ma:l] *adj* optimal, optimum

Optimismus [ɔpti'mɪsmʊs] *m* optimism

Optimist [ɔpti'mɪst] *m* optimist; **o~isch** *adj* optimistic

optisch ['ɔptɪʃ] *adj* optical

Orakel [o'ra:kəl] (-s, -) *nt* oracle

oral [o'ra:l] *adj* (*MED*) oral

Orange [o'rãːʒə] *f* orange; **o~** *adj* orange; **~ade** [orã'ʒa:də] *f* orangeade; **~at** [orã'ʒa:t] (-s, -e) *nt* candied peel

Orchester [ɔr'kɛstər] (-s, -) *nt* orchestra

Orchidee [ɔrçi'de:ə] *f* orchid

Orden ['ɔrdən] (-s, -) *m* (*ECCL*) order; (*MIL*) decoration; **~sschwester** *f* nun

ordentlich ['ɔrdəntlɪç] *adj* (*anständig*) decent, respectable; (*geordnet*) tidy, neat; (*umg: annehmbar*) not bad; (: *tüchtig*) real, proper ♦ *adv* properly; **~er Professor** (full) professor; **O~keit** *f* respectability; tidiness, neatness

ordinär [ɔrdi'nɛ:r] *adj* common, vulgar

ordnen ['ɔrdnən] *vt* to order, to put in order

Ordner (-s, -) *m* steward; (*COMM*) file

Ordnung *f* order; (*Ordnen*) ordering; (*Geordnetsein*) tidiness; **~ machen** to tidy up; **in ~!** okay!

Ordnungs- *zW:* **o~gemäß** *adj* proper, according to the rules; **o~liebend** *adj* orderly, methodical; **~strafe** *f* fine; **o~widrig** *adj* contrary to the rules, irregular; **~zahl** *f* ordinal number

Organ [ɔr'ga:n] (-s, -e) *nt* organ; (*Stimme*) voice; **~isation** [-izatsi'o:n] *f* organization; **~isator** [-i'za:tɔr] *m* organizer; **o~isch** *adj* organic; **o~isieren** [-i'zi:rən] *vt* to organize, to arrange; (*umg: beschaffen*) to acquire ♦ *vr* to organize; **~ismus** [-'nɪsmʊs] *m* organism; **~ist** [-'nɪst] *m* organist

Orgasmus [ɔr'gasmʊs] *m* orgasm

Orgel ['ɔrgəl] (-, -n) *f* organ

Orgie ['ɔrgiə] *f* orgy

Orient ['o:riɛnt] (-s) *m* Orient, east; **~ale** [-'ta:lə] (-n, -n) *m* Oriental; **o~alisch** [-'ta:lɪʃ] *adj* oriental

orientier- *zW:* **~en** [-'ti:rən] *vt* (*örtlich*) to locate; (*fig*) to inform ♦ *vr* to find one's way *od* bearings; to inform o.s.; **O~ung** [-'ti:rʊŋ] *f* orientation; (*fig*) information; **O~ungssinn** *m* sense of direction

Origano [ori:'ga:no] (-) *m* (*KOCH*) oregano

original [origi'na:l] *adj* original; **O~** (-s, -e) *nt* original; **O~fassung** *f* original version; **O~i'tät** *f* originality

originell [origi'nɛl] *adj* original

Orkan [ɔr'ka:n] (-(e)s, -e) *m* hurricane; **o~artig** *adj* (*Wind*) gale-force; (*Beifall*) thunderous

Ornament [ɔrna'mɛnt] *nt* decoration,

ornament; **o~al** [-'taːl] *adj* decorative, ornamental

Ort [ɔrt] **(-(e)s, -e** *od* **ᵉer)** *m* place; **an ~ und Stelle** on the spot; **o~en** *vt* to locate

ortho- [ɔrto] *zW:* **~dox** [-'dɔks] *adj* orthodox; **O~graphie** [-graˈfiː] *f* spelling, orthography; **~'graphisch** *adj* orthographic; **O~päde** [-'pɛːdə] **(-n, -n)** *m* orthopaedic specialist, orthopaedist; **O~pädie** [-pɛˈdiː] *f* orthopaedics *sg*; **~'pädisch** *adj* orthopaedic

örtlich ['œrtlɪç] *adj* local; **Ö~keit** *f* locality

ortsansässig *adj* local

Ortschaft *f* village, small town

Orts- *zW:* **o~fremd** *adj* non-local; **~gespräch** *nt* local (phone)call; **~name** *m* place-name; **~netz** *nt* (*TEL*) local telephone exchange area; **~tarif** *m* (*TEL*) tariff for local calls; **~zeit** *f* local time

Ortung *f* locating

Öse ['øːzə] *f* loop, eye

Ost'asien [ɔsˈtaːziən] *nt* Eastern Asia

Osten **(-s)** *m* east

Oster- ['oːstər] *zW:* **~ei** *nt* Easter egg; **~fest** *nt* Easter; **~glocke** *f* daffodil; **~hase** *m* Easter bunny; **~montag** *m* Easter Monday; **~n** **(-s, -)** *nt* Easter

Österreich ['øːstərraɪç] **(-s)** *nt* Austria; **~er(in)** **(-s, -)** *m(f)* Austrian; **ö~isch** *adj* Austrian

Ostküste *f* east coast

östlich ['œstlɪç] *adj* eastern, easterly

Otter¹ ['ɔtər] **(-s, -)** *m* otter

Otter² **(-s, -)** *f* (*Schlange*) adder

Ouvertüre [uverˈtyːrə] *f* overture

oval [oˈvaːl] *adj* oval

Ovation [ovatsiˈoːn] *f* ovation

Ovulation [ovulatsiˈoːn] *f* ovulation

Oxyd [ɔˈksyːt] **(-(e)s, -e)** *nt* oxide; **o~ieren** *vt, vi* to oxidize; **~ierung** *f* oxidization

Ozean ['oːtseaːn] **(-s, -e)** *m* ocean; **~dampfer** *m* (ocean-going) liner

Ozon [oˈtsoːn] **(-s)** *nt* ozone; **~loch** *nt* ozone hole; **~schicht** *f* ozone layer

P p

Paar [paːr] **(-(e)s, -e)** *nt* pair; (*Ehe~*) couple; **ein p~** a few; **p~en** *vt, vr* to couple; (*Tiere*) to mate; **~lauf** *m* pair skating; **p~mal** *adv:* **ein p~mal** a few times; **~ung** *f* combination; mating; **p~weise** *adv* in pairs; in couples

Pacht [paxt] **(-, -en)** *f* lease; **p~en** *vt* to lease

Pächter ['pɛçtər] **(-s, -)** *m* leaseholder, tenant

Pack¹ [pak] **(-(e)s, -e** *od* **ᵉe)** *m* bundle, pack

Pack² **(-(e)s)** *nt* (*pej*) mob, rabble

Päckchen ['pɛkçən] *nt* small package; (*Zigaretten*) packet; (*Post~*) small parcel

Pack- *zW:* **p~en** *vt* to pack; (*fassen*) to grasp, to seize; (*umg: schaffen*) to manage; (*fig: fesseln*) to grip; **~en** **(-s, -)** *m* bundle; (*fig: Menge*) heaps of; **~esel** *m* (*auch fig*) packhorse; **~papier** *nt* brown paper, wrapping paper; **~ung** *f* packet; (*Pralinenpackung*) box; (*MED*) compress

Pädagog- [pedaˈgoːg] *zW:* **~e** **(-n, -n)** *m* teacher; **~ik** *f* education; **p~isch** *adj* educational, pedagogical

Paddel ['padəl] **(-s, -)** *nt* paddle; **~boot** *nt* canoe; **p~n** *vi* to paddle

Page ['paːʒə] **(-n, -n)** *m* page; **~nkopf** *m* pageboy (cut)

Paket [paˈkeːt] **(-(e)s, -e)** *nt* packet; (*Post~*) parcel; **~karte** *f* dispatch note; **~post** *f* parcel post; **~schalter** *m* parcels counter

Pakt [pakt] **(-(e)s, -e)** *m* pact

Palast [paˈlast] **(-es, Paläste)** *m* palace

Palästina [palɛsˈtiːna] **(-s)** *nt* Palestine

Palme ['palmə] *f* palm (tree)

Palmsonntag *m* Palm Sunday

Pampelmuse ['pampəlmuːzə] *f* grapefruit

pampig ['pampɪç] (*umg*) *adj* (*frech*) fresh

panieren [paˈniːrən] *vt* (*KOCH*) to bread

Paniermehl [paˈniːrmeːl] *nt* breadcrumbs *pl*

Panik ['paːnɪk] *f* panic

panisch ['pa:nɪʃ] *adj* panic-stricken
Panne ['panə] *f* (*AUT etc*) breakdown; (*Mißgeschick*) slip; **~nhilfe** *f* breakdown service
panschen ['panʃən] *vi* to splash about ♦ *vt* to water down
Panther ['pantər] (**-s**, **-**) *m* panther
Pantoffel [pan'tɔfəl] (**-s**, **-n**) *m* slipper
Pantomime [panto'mi:mə] *f* mime
Panzer ['pantsər] (**-s**, **-**) *m* armour; (*Platte*) armour plate; (*Fahrzeug*) tank; **~glas** *nt* bulletproof glass; **p~n** *vt* to armour ♦ *vr* (*fig*) to arm o.s.
Papa [pa'pa:] (**-s**, **-s**; *umg*) *m* dad, daddy
Papagei [papa'gai] (**-s**, **-en**) *m* parrot
Papier [pa'pi:r] (**-s**, **-e**) *nt* paper; (*Wert~*) security; **~fabrik** *f* paper mill; **~geld** *nt* paper money; **~korb** *m* wastepaper basket; **~tüte** *f* paper bag
Papp- ['pap] *zW*: **~deckel** *m* cardboard; **~e** *f* cardboard; **~el** (**-**, **-n**) *f* poplar; **p~en** (*umg*) *vt*, *vi* to stick; **p~ig** *adj* sticky; **~maché** [-ma'ʃe:] (**-s**, **-s**) *nt* papier-mâché
Paprika ['paprika] (**-s**, **-s**) *m* (*Gewürz*) paprika; (*~schote*) pepper
Papst [pa:pst] (**-(e)s**, *̈e*) *m* pope
päpstlich ['pɛ:pstlɪç] *adj* papal
Parabel [pa'ra:bəl] (**-**, **-n**) *f* parable; (*MATH*) parabola
Parabolantenne [para'bo:l-] *f* satellite dish
Parade [pa'ra:də] *f* (*MIL*) parade, review; (*SPORT*) parry
Paradies [para'di:s] (**-es**, **-e**) *nt* paradise; **p~isch** *adj* heavenly
Paradox [para'dɔks] (**-es**, **-e**) *nt* paradox; **p~** *adj* paradoxical
Paragraph [para'gra:f] (**-en**, **-en**) *m* paragraph; (*JUR*) section
parallel [para'le:l] *adj* parallel; **P~e** *f* parallel
Paranuß ['pa:ranus] *f* Brazil nut
Parasit [para'zi:t] (**-en**, **-en**) *m* (*auch fig*) parasite
parat [pa'ra:t] *adj* ready
Pärchen ['pɛ:rçən] *nt* couple
Parfüm [par'fy:m] (**-s**, **-s** *od* **-e**) *nt* perfume; **~erie** [-ə'ri:] *f* perfumery; **p~ieren** *vt* to scent, to perfume

parieren [pa'ri:rən] *vt* to parry ♦ *vi* (*umg*) to obey
Paris [pa'ri:s] (**-**) *nt* Paris; **~er** *adj* Parisian ♦ *m* Parisian; **~erin** *f* Parisian
Park [park] (**-s**, **-s**) *m* park; **~anlage** *f* park; (*um Gebäude*) grounds *pl*; **p~en** *vt*, *vi* to park
Parkett [par'ket] (**-(e)s**, **-e**) *nt* parquet (floor); (*THEAT*) stalls *pl*
Park- *zW*: **~haus** *nt* multi-storey car park; **~lücke** *f* parking space; **~platz** *m* parking place; car park, parking lot (*US*); **~scheibe** *f* parking disc; **~uhr** *f* parking meter; **~verbot** *nt* parking ban
Parlament [parla'mɛnt] *nt* parliament; **~arier** [-'ta:riər] (**-s**, **-**) *m* parliamentarian; **p~arisch** [-'ta:rɪʃ] *adj* parliamentary
Parlaments- *zW*: **~beschluß** *m* vote of parliament; **~mitglied** *nt* member of parliament; **~sitzung** *f* sitting (of parliament)
Parodie [paro'di:] *f* parody; **p~ren** *vt* to parody
Parole [pa'ro:lə] *f* password; (*Wahlspruch*) motto
Partei [par'tai] *f* party; **~ ergreifen für jdn** to take sb's side; **p~isch** *adj* partial, bias(s)ed; **p~los** *adj* neutral, impartial; **~mitglied** *nt* party member; **~programm** *nt* (party) manifesto; **~tag** *m* party conference
Parterre [par'tɛr(ə)] (**-s**, **-s**) *nt* ground floor; (*THEAT*) stalls *pl*
Partie [par'ti:] *f* part; (*Spiel*) game; (*Ausflug*) outing; (*Mann, Frau*) catch; (*COMM*) lot; **mit von der ~ sein** to join in
Partisan [parti'za:n] (**-s** *od* **-en**, **-en**) *m* partisan
Partitur [parti'tu:r] *f* (*MUS*) score
Partizip [parti'tsi:p] (**-s**, **-ien**) *nt* participle
Partner(in) ['partnər(ɪn)] (**-s**, **-**) *m(f)* partner; **p~schaftlich** *adj* as partners; **~stadt** *f* twin town
Party ['pa:rti] (**-**, **-s** *od* **Parties**) *f* party
Paß [pas] (**-sses**, *̈sse*) *m* pass; (*Ausweis*) passport
passabel [pa'sa:bəl] *adj* passable, reasonable

Passage [pa'saːʒə] *f* passage
Passagier [pasaˈʒiːr] (-s, -e) *m* passenger; **~flugzeug** *nt* airliner
Paßamt *nt* passport office
Passant [pa'sant] *m* passer-by
Paßbild *nt* passport photograph
passen [ˈpasən] *vi* to fit; (*Farbe*) to go; (*auf Frage, KARTEN, SPORT*) to pass; **das paßt mir nicht** that doesn't suit me; **~ zu** (*Farbe, Kleider*) to go with; **er paßt nicht zu dir** he's not right for you; **~d** *adj* suitable; (*zusammenpassend*) matching; (*angebracht*) fitting; (*Zeit*) convenient
passier- [pa'siːr] *zW:* **~bar** *adj* passable; **~en** *vt* to pass; (*durch Sieb*) to strain ♦ *vi* to happen; **P~schein** *m* pass, permit
Passion [pasi'oːn] *f* passion; **p~iert** [-'niːrt] *adj* enthusiastic, passionate; **~sspiel** *nt* Passion Play
passiv [ˈpasiːf] *adj* passive; **P~** (-s, -e) *nt* passive; **P~a** *pl* (*COMM*) liabilities; **P~rauchen** *nt* passive smoking; **P~i'tät** *f* passiveness
Paß- *zW:* **~kontrolle** *f* passport control; **~stelle** *f* passport office; **~straße** *f* (mountain) pass
Paste [ˈpastə] *f* paste
Pastell [pas'tɛl] (-(e)s, -e) *nt* pastel
Pastete [pas'teːtə] *f* pie
pasteurisieren [pastøriˈziːrən] *vt* to pasteurize
Pastor [ˈpastɔr] *m* vicar; pastor, minister
Pate [ˈpaːtə] (-n, -n) *m* godfather; **~nkind** *nt* godchild
Patent [pa'tɛnt] (-(e)s, -e) *nt* patent; (*MIL*) commission; **p~** *adj* clever; **~amt** *nt* patent office
Patentante *f* godmother
patentieren *vt* to patent
Patentinhaber *m* patentee
Pater [ˈpaːtər] (-s, - *od* **Patres**) *m* (*ECCL*) Father
pathetisch [pa'teːtɪʃ] *adj* emotional; bombastic
Pathologe [patoˈloːgə] (-n, -n) *m* pathologist
pathologisch *adj* pathological
Pathos [ˈpaːtɔs] (-) *nt* emotiveness,

emotionalism
Patient(in) [patsiˈɛnt(ɪn)] *m(f)* patient
Patin [ˈpaːtɪn] *f* godmother
Patina [ˈpaːtina] (-) *f* patina
Patriot [patriˈoːt] (-en, -en) *m* patriot; **p~isch** *adj* patriotic; **~ismus** [-ˈtɪsmʊs] *m* patriotism
Patrone [paˈtroːnə] *f* cartridge
Patrouille [paˈtrʊljə] *f* patrol
patrouillieren [patrʊlˈjiːrən] *vi* to patrol
patsch [patʃ] *excl* splash; **P~e** (*umg*) *f* (*Bedrängnis*) mess, jam; **~en** *vi* to smack, to slap; (*im Wasser*) to splash; **~naß** *adj* soaking wet
patzig [ˈpatsɪç] (*umg*) *adj* cheeky, saucy
Pauke [ˈpaʊkə] *f* kettledrum; **auf die ~ hauen** to live it up
pauken *vt* (*intensiv lernen*) to swot up (*inf*) ♦ *vi* to swot (*inf*), cram (*inf*)
pausbäckig [ˈpaʊsbɛkɪç] *adj* chubby-cheeked
pauschal [paʊˈʃaːl] *adj* (*Kosten*) inclusive; (*Urteil*) sweeping; **P~e** *f* flat rate; **P~gebühr** *f* flat rate; **P~preis** *m* all-in price; **P~reise** *f* package tour; **P~summe** *f* lump sum
Pause [ˈpaʊzə] *f* break; (*THEAT*) interval; (*Innehalten*) pause; (*Kopie*) tracing
pausen *vt* to trace; **~los** *adj* non-stop; **P~zeichen** *nt* call sign; (*MUS*) rest
Pauspapier [ˈpaʊspapiːr] *nt* tracing paper
Pavian [ˈpaːviaːn] (-s, -e) *m* baboon
Pavillon (-s, -s) *m* pavilion
Pazif- [paˈtsiːf] *zW:* **~ik** (-s) *m* Pacific; **p~istisch** *adj* pacifist
Pech [pɛç] (-s, -e) *nt* pitch; (*fig*) bad luck; **~ haben** to be unlucky; **p~schwarz** *adj* pitch-black; **~strähne** (*umg*) *m* unlucky patch; **~vogel** (*umg*) *m* unlucky person
Pedal [pe'daːl] (-s, -e) *nt* pedal
Pedant [pe'dant] *m* pedant; **~e'rie** *f* pedantry; **p~isch** *adj* pedantic
Pediküre [pediˈkyːrə] *f* (*Fußpflege*) pedicure
Pegel [ˈpeːgəl] (-s, -) *m* water gauge; **~stand** *m* water level
peilen [ˈpaɪlən] *vt* to get a fix on
Pein [paɪn] (-) *f* agony, pain; **p~igen** *vt* to

torture; (*plagen*) to torment; **p~lich** *adj* (*unangenehm*) embarrassing, awkward, painful; (*genau*) painstaking; **~lichkeit** *f* painfulness, awkwardness; scrupulousness

Peitsche ['paɪtʃə] *f* whip; **p~n** *vt* to whip; (*Regen*) to lash

Pelikan ['peːlikaːn] (**-s, -e**) *m* pelican

Pelle ['pɛlə] *f* skin; **p~n** *vt* to skin, to peel

Pellkartoffeln *pl* jacket potatoes

Pelz [pɛlts] (**-es, -e**) *m* fur

Pendel ['pɛndəl] (**-s, -**) *nt* pendulum

pendeln *vi* (*Zug, Fähre etc*) to operate a shuttle service; (*Mensch*) to commute

Pendelverkehr *m* shuttle traffic; (*für Pendler*) commuter traffic

Pendler ['pɛndlər] (**-s, -**) *m* commuter

penetrant [pene'trant] *adj* sharp; (*Person*) pushing

Penis ['peːnɪs] (**-, -se**) *m* penis

pennen ['pɛnən] (*umg*) *vi* to kip

Penner (*umg: pej*) *m* (*Landstreicher*) tramp

Pension [pɛnzi'oːn] *f* (*Geld*) pension; (*Ruhestand*) retirement; (*für Gäste*) boarding *od* guest-house; **~är(in)** [-'nɛːr(ɪn)] (**-s, -e**) *m(f)* pensioner; **p~ieren** *vt* to pension off; **p~iert** *adj* retired; **~ierung** *f* retirement; **~sgast** *m* boarder, paying guest

Pensum ['pɛnzʊm] (**-s, Pensen**) *nt* quota; (*SCH*) curriculum

per [pɛr] *präp +akk* by, per; (*pro*) per; (*bis*) by

Perfekt ['pɛrfɛkt] (**-(e)s, -e**) *nt* perfect; **p~** [pɛr'fɛkt] *adj* perfect

perforieren [pɛrfo'riːrən] *vt* to perforate

Pergament [pɛrga'mɛnt] *nt* parchment; **~papier** *nt* greaseproof paper

Periode [peri'oːdə] *f* period

periodisch [peri'oːdɪʃ] *adj* periodic; (*dezimal*) recurring

Perle ['pɛrlə] *f* (*auch fig*) pearl; **p~n** *vi* to sparkle; (*Tropfen*) to trickle

Perlmutt ['pɛrlmʊt] (**-s**) *nt* mother-of-pearl

Perlwein *m* sparkling wine

perplex [pɛr'plɛks] *adj* dumbfounded

Person [pɛr'zoːn] (**-, -en**) *f* person; **ich**

für meine ~ ... personally I ...

Personal [pɛrzo'naːl] (**-s**) *nt* personnel; (*Bedienung*) servants *pl*; **~ausweis** *m* identity card; **~computer** *m* personal computer; **~ien** [-iən] *pl* particulars; **~mangel** *m* undermanning; **~pronomen** *nt* personal pronoun

Personen- *zW:* **~aufzug** *m* lift, elevator (*US*); **~kraftwagen** *m* private motorcar; **~schaden** *m* injury to persons; **~zug** *m* stopping train; passenger train

personifizieren [pɛrzonifi'tsiːrən] *vt* to personify

persönlich [pɛr'zøːnlɪç] *adj* personal ♦ *adv* in person; personally; **P~keit** *f* personality

personell [pɛrzo'nɛl] *adj* (*Veränderungen*) personnel

Perspektive [pɛrspɛk'tiːvə] *f* perspective

Perücke [pe'rʏkə] *f* wig

pervers [pɛr'vɛrs] *adj* perverse

Pessimismus [pɛsi'mɪsmʊs] *m* pessimism

Pessimist [pɛsi'mɪst] *m* pessimist; **p~isch** *adj* pessimistic

Pest [pɛst] (**-**) *f* plague

Petersilie [petər'ziːliə] *f* parsley

Petroleum [pe'troːleʊm] (**-s**) *nt* paraffin, kerosene (*US*)

Petunie *f* (*BOT*) petunia

Pfad [pfaːt] (**-(e)s, -e**) *m* path; **~finder** (**-s, -**) *m* boy scout; **~finderin** *f* girl guide

Pfahl [pfaːl] (**-(e)s, ⁓e**) *m* post, stake

Pfand [pfant] (**-(e)s, ⁓er**) *nt* pledge, security; (*Flaschen~*) deposit; (*im Spiel*) forfeit; **~brief** *m* bond

pfänden ['pfɛndən] *vt* to seize, to distrain

Pfänderspiel *nt* game of forfeits

Pfandschein *m* pawn ticket

Pfändung ['pfɛndʊŋ] *f* seizure, distraint

Pfanne ['pfanə] *f* (frying) pan

Pfannkuchen *m* pancake; (*Berliner*) doughnut

Pfarr- ['pfar] *zW:* **~ei** *f* parish; **~er** (**-s, -**) *m* priest; (*evangelisch*) vicar; minister; **~haus** *nt* vicarage; manse

Pfau [pfaʊ] (**-(e)s, -en**) *m* peacock; **~enauge** *nt* peacock butterfly

Pfeffer ['pfɛfər] (**-s, -**) *m* pepper; **~korn** *nt* peppercorn; **~kuchen** *m* gingerbread;

~minz (-es, -e) *nt* peppermint; **~mühle** *f* pepper-mill; **p~n** *vt* to pepper; (*umg: werfen*) to fling; **gep~te Preise/Witze** steep prices/spicy jokes

Pfeife ['pfaɪfə] *f* whistle; (*Tabak~, Orgel~*) pipe; **p~n** (*unreg*) *vt, vi* to whistle; **~r** (-s, -) *m* piper

Pfeil [pfaɪl] (-(e)s, -e) *m* arrow

Pfeiler ['pfaɪlər] (-s, -) *m* pillar, prop; (*Brücken~*) pier

Pfennig ['pfɛnɪç] (-(e)s, -e) *m* pfennig (*hundredth part of a mark*)

Pferd [pfeːrt] (-(e)s, -e) *nt* horse

Pferde- ['pfeːrdə] *zW:* **~rennen** *nt* horse-race; horse-racing; **~schwanz** *m* (*Frisur*) ponytail; **~stall** *m* stable

Pfiff [pfɪf] (-(e)s, -e) *m* whistle

Pfifferling ['pfɪfərlɪŋ] *m* yellow chanterelle (*mushroom*); **keinen ~ wert** not worth a thing

pfiffig *adj* sly, sharp

Pfingsten ['pfɪŋstən] (-, -) *nt* Whitsun (*BRIT*), Pentecost

Pfingstrose ['pfɪŋstroːzə] *f* peony

Pfirsich ['pfɪrzɪç] (-s, -e) *m* peach

Pflanz- ['pflants] *zW:* **~e** *f* plant; **p~en** *vt* to plant; **~enfett** *nt* vegetable fat; **p~lich** *adj* vegetable; **~ung** *f* plantation

Pflaster ['pflastər] (-s, -) *nt* plaster; (*Straße*) pavement; **p~n** *vt* to pave; **~stein** *m* paving stone

Pflaume ['pflaʊmə] *f* plum

Pflege ['pfleːgə] *f* care; (*von Idee*) cultivation; (*Kranken~*) nursing; **in ~ sein** (*Kind*) to be fostered out; **p~bedürftig** *adj* needing care; **~eltern** *pl* foster parents; **~heim** *nt* nursing home; **~kind** *nt* foster child; **p~leicht** *adj* easy-care; **~mutter** *f* foster mother; **p~n** *vt* to look after; (*Kranke*) to nurse; (*Beziehungen*) to foster; **~r** (-s, -) *m* orderly; male nurse; **~rin** *f* nurse, attendant; **~vater** *m* foster father

Pflicht [pflɪçt] (-, -en) *f* duty; (*SPORT*) compulsory section; **p~bewußt** *adj* conscientious; **~fach** *nt* (*SCH*) compulsory subject; **~gefühl** *nt* sense of duty; **p~gemäß** *adj* dutiful ♦ *adv* as in duty bound; **~versicherung** *f* compulsory insurance

pflücken ['pflʏkən] *vt* to pick; (*Blumen*) to pick, to pluck

Pflug [pfluːk] (-(e)s, ~e) *m* plough

pflügen ['pflyːgən] *vt* to plough

Pforte ['pfɔrtə] *f* gate; door

Pförtner ['pfœrtnər] (-s, -) *m* porter, doorkeeper, doorman

Pfosten ['pfɔstən] (-s, -) *m* post

Pfote ['pfoːtə] *f* paw; (*umg: Schrift*) scrawl

Pfropfen ['pfrɔpfən] (-s, -) *m* (*Flaschen~*) stopper; (*Blut~*) clot; **p~** *vt* (*stopfen*) to cram; (*Baum*) to graft

pfui [pfʊi] *excl* ugh!

Pfund [pfʊnt] (-(e)s, -e) *nt* pound; **p~ig** (*umg*) *adj* great

pfuschen ['pfʊʃən] (*umg*) *vi* to be sloppy; **jdm ins Handwerk ~** to interfere in sb's business

Pfuscher ['pfʊʃər] (-s, -; *umg*) *m* sloppy worker; (*Kur~*) quack; **~ei** (*umg*) *f* sloppy work; quackery

Pfütze ['pfʏtsə] *f* puddle

Phänomen [fɛnoˈmeːn] (-s, -e) *nt* phenomenon; **p~al** [-ˈnaːl] *adj* phenomenal

Phantasie [fantaˈziː] *f* imagination; **p~los** *adj* unimaginative; **p~ren** *vi* to fantasize; **p~voll** *adj* imaginative

phantastisch [fanˈtastɪʃ] *adj* fantastic

Phase ['faːzə] *f* phase

Philologe [filoˈloːgə] (-n, -n) *m* philologist

Philologie [filoloˈgiː] *f* philology

Philosoph [filoˈzoːf] (-en, -en) *m* philosopher; **~ie** [-ˈfiː] *f* philosophy; **p~isch** *adj* philosophical

phlegmatisch [flɛˈgmaːtɪʃ] *adj* lethargic

Phonetik [foˈneːtɪk] *f* phonetics *sg*

phonetisch *adj* phonetic

Phosphor ['fɔsfɔr] (-s) *m* phosphorus

Photo *etc* ['foːto] (-s, -s) *nt* = **Foto** *etc*

Phrase ['fraːzə] *f* phrase; (*pej*) hollow phrase

pH-Wert *m* pH-value

Physik [fyˈziːk] *f* physics *sg*; **p~alisch** [-ˈkaːlɪʃ] *adj* of physics; **~er(in)** ['fyːzɪkər(ɪn)] (-s, -) *m(f)* physicist

Physiologie [fyzioloʹgiː] f physiology
physisch [ʹfyːzɪʃ] adj physical
Pianist(in) [piaʹnɪst(ɪn)] m(f) pianist
Pickel [ʹpɪkəl] (-s, -) m pimple; (*Werkzeug*) pickaxe; (*Berg~*) ice-axe; **p~ig** adj pimply, spotty
picken [ʹpɪkən] vi to pick, to peck
Picknick [ʹpɪknɪk] (-s, -e *od* -s) nt picnic; **~ machen** to have a picnic
piepen [ʹpiːpən] vi to chirp
piepsen [ʹpiːpsən] vi to chirp
Piepser (*umg*) m pager, paging device
Pier [piːər] (-s, -s *od* -e) m *od* f pier
Pietät [pieʹtɛːt] f piety, reverence; **p~los** adj impious, irreverent
Pigment [pɪʹgmɛnt] nt pigment
Pik [piːk] (-s, -s) nt (*KARTEN*) spades
pikant [piʹkant] adj spicy, piquant; (*anzüglich*) suggestive
Pilger [ʹpɪlgər] (-s, -) m pilgrim; **~fahrt** f pilgrimage
Pille [ʹpɪlə] f pill
Pilot [piʹloːt] (-en, -en) m pilot
Pilz [pɪlts] (-es, -e) m fungus; (*eßbar*) mushroom; (*giftig*) toadstool; **~krankheit** f fungal disease
Pinguin [ʹpɪŋguiːn] (-s, -e) m penguin
Pinie [ʹpiːniə] f pine
pinkeln [ʹpɪŋkəln] (*umg*) vi to pee
Pinnwand f noticeboard
Pinsel [ʹpɪnzəl] (-s, -) m paintbrush
Pinzette [pɪnʹtsɛtə] f tweezers pl
Pionier [pioʹniːr] (-s, -e) m pioneer; (*MIL*) sapper, engineer
Pirat [piʹraːt] (-en, -en) m pirate; **~ensender** m pirate radio station
Piste [ʹpɪstə] f (*SKI*) run, piste; (*AVIAT*) runway
Pistole [pɪsʹtoːlə] f pistol
Pizza [ʹpɪtsa] (-, -s) f pizza
Pkw [peːkaːʹveː] (-(s), -(s)) m abk = **Personenkraftwagen**
pl. abk = **pluralisch; Plural**
plädieren [plɛʹdiːrən] vi to plead
Plädoyer [plɛdoaʹjeː] (-s, -s) nt speech for the defence; (*fig*) plea
Plage [ʹplaːgə] f plague; (*Mühe*) nuisance; **~geist** m pest, nuisance; **p~n** vt to torment ♦ vr to toil, to slave

Plakat [plaʹkaːt] (-(e)s, -e) nt placard; poster
Plan [plaːn] (-(e)s, ~e) m plan; (*Karte*) map
Plane f tarpaulin
planen vt to plan; (*Mord etc*) to plot
Planer (-s, -) m planner
Planet [plaʹneːt] (-en, -en) m planet
planieren [plaʹniːrən] vt to plane, to level
Planke [ʹplaŋkə] f plank
Plankton [ʹplaŋktən] (-s) nt plankton
planlos adj (*Vorgehen*) unsystematic; (*Umherlaufen*) aimless
planmäßig adj according to plan; systematic; (*EISENB*) scheduled
Planschbecken nt paddling pool
planschen [ʹplanʃən] vi to splash
Plansoll (-s) nt output target
Plantage [planʹtaːʒə] f plantation
Planung f planning
Planwirtschaft f planned economy
plappern [ʹplapərn] vi to chatter
plärren [ʹplɛrən] vi (*Mensch*) to cry, to whine; (*Radio*) to blare
Plasma [ʹplasma] (-s, **Plasmen**) nt plasma
Plastik¹ [ʹplastɪk] f sculpture
Plastik² (-s) nt (*Kunststoff*) plastic; **~beutel** m plastic bag, carrier bag; **~folie** f plastic film; **~tüte** f plastic bag
plastisch [ʹplastɪʃ] adj plastic; **stell dir das ~ vor!** just picture it!
Platane [plaʹtaːnə] f plane (tree)
Platin [ʹplaːtiːn] (-s) nt platinum
platonisch [plaʹtoːnɪʃ] adj platonic
platsch [platʃ] excl splash; **~en** vi to splash
plätschern [ʹplɛtʃərn] vi to babble
platschnaß adj drenched
platt [plat] adj flat; (*umg: überrascht*) flabbergasted; (*fig: geistlos*) flat, boring; **~deutsch** adj low German; **P~e** f (*Speisen~, PHOT, TECH*) plate; (*Steinplatte*) flag; (*Kachel*) tile; (*Schallplatte*) record; **P~enspieler** m record player; **P~enteller** m turntable; **P~fuß** m flat foot
Platz [plats] (-es, ~e) m place; (*Sitz~*) seat; (*Raum*) space, room; (*in Stadt*) square; (*Sport~*) playing field; **~ nehmen** to take

a seat; **jdm ~ machen** to make room for sb; **~angst** f (MED) agoraphobia; (umg) claustrophobia; **~anweiser(in)** (-s, -) m(f) usher(ette)

Plätzchen ['plɛtsçən] nt spot; (Gebäck) biscuit

Platz- zW: **p~en** vi to burst; (Bombe) to explode; **vor Wut p~en** (umg) to be bursting with anger; **~karte** f seat reservation; **~mangel** m lack of space; **~patrone** f blank cartridge; **~regen** m downpour; **~wunde** f cut

Plauderei [plaudə'rai] f chat, conversation; (RADIO) talk

plaudern ['plaudərn] vi to chat, to talk

plausibel [plau'zi:bəl] adj plausible

plazieren [pla'tsi:rən] vt to place ♦ vr (SPORT) to be placed; (TENNIS) to be seeded

Pleite ['plaitə] f bankruptcy; (umg: Reinfall) flop; **~ machen** to go bust; **p~** (umg) adj broke

Plenum ['ple:nʊm] (-s) nt plenum

Plombe ['plɔmbə] f lead seal; (Zahn~) filling

plombieren [plɔm'bi:rən] vt to seal; (Zahn) to fill

plötzlich ['plœtslɪç] adj sudden ♦ adv suddenly

plump [plʊmp] adj clumsy; (Hände) coarse; (Körper) shapeless; **~sen** (umg) vi to plump down, to fall

Plunder ['plʊndər] (-s) m rubbish

plündern ['plʏndərn] vt to plunder; (Stadt) to sack ♦ vi to plunder

Plünderung ['plʏndərʊŋ] f plundering, sack, pillage

Plural ['plu:ra:l] (-s, -e) m plural; **p~istisch** adj pluralistic

Plus [plʊs] (-, -) nt plus; (FIN) profit; (Vorteil) advantage; **p~** adv plus

Plüsch [ply:ʃ] (-(e)s, -e) m plush

Pluspol m (ELEK) positive pole

Pluspunkt m point; (fig) point in sb's favour

Plutonium (-s) nt plutonium

PLZ abk = **Postleitzahl**

Po [po:] (-s, -s; umg) m bottom, bum

Pöbel ['pø:bəl] (-s) m mob, rabble; **~ei** f vulgarity; **p~haft** adj low, vulgar

pochen ['pɔxən] vi to knock; (Herz) to pound; **auf etw** akk **~** (fig) to insist on sth

Pocken ['pɔkən] pl smallpox sg

Podium ['po:diʊm] nt podium; **~sdiskussion** f panel discussion

Poesie [poe'zi:] f poetry

Poet [po'e:t] (-en, -en) m poet; **p~isch** adj poetic

Pointe [po'ɛ̃:tə] f point

Pokal [po'ka:l] (-s, -e) m goblet; (SPORT) cup; **~spiel** nt cup-tie

Pökelfleisch nt salt meat

pökeln ['pø:kəln] vt to pickle, to salt

Poker (-s) nt od m poker

Pol [po:l] (-s, -e) m pole; **p~ar** adj polar; **~arkreis** m Arctic circle

Pole (-n, -n) m Pole

polemisch [po'le:mɪʃ] adj polemical

Polen (-s) nt Poland

Police [po'li:s(ə)] f insurance policy

Polier [po'li:r] (-s, -e) m foreman

polieren vt to polish

Poliklinik ['po:likli:nɪk] f outpatients (department) sg

Polin f Pole

Politik [poli'ti:k] f politics sg; (eine bestimmte) policy; **~er(in)** [poli'ti:kər(ɪn)] (-s, -) m(f) politician

politisch [po'li:tɪʃ] adj political

Politur [poli'tu:r] f polish

Polizei [poli'tsai] f police; **~beamte(r)** m police officer; **p~lich** adj police; **sich p~lich melden** to register with the police; **~revier** nt police station; **~staat** m police state; **~streife** f police patrol; **~stunde** f closing time; **~wache** f police station

Polizist(in) [poli'tsɪst(ɪn)] (-en, -en) m(f) policeman(woman)

Pollen ['pɔlən] (-s, -) m pollen

polnisch ['pɔlnɪʃ] adj Polish

Polohemd nt polo shirt

Polster ['pɔlstər] (-s, -) nt cushion; (~ung) upholstery; (in Kleidung) padding; (fig: Geld) reserves pl; **~er** (-s, -) m upholsterer; **~möbel** pl upholstered furniture sg; **p~n** vt to upholster; to pad

Polterabend m party on eve of wedding

poltern ['pɔltərn] *vi* (*Krach machen*) to crash; (*schimpfen*) to rant
Polyp [po'ly:p] (-en, -en) *m* polyp; (*umg*) cop; **~en** *pl* (*MED*) adenoids
Pomade [po'ma:də] *f* pomade
Pommes frites [pɔm'frit] *pl* chips, French fried potatoes
Pomp [pɔmp] (-(e)s) *m* pomp
pompös [pɔm'pø:s] *adj* (*Auftritt, Fest, Haus*) ostentatious, showy
Pony ['pɔni] (-s, -s) *nt* (*Pferd*) pony ♦ *m* (*Frisur*) fringe
Popmusik ['pɔpmuzi:k] *f* pop music
Popo [po'po:] (-s, -s; *umg*) *m* bottom, bum
poppig ['pɔpiç] *adj* (*Farbe etc*) gaudy
populär [popu'lɛ:r] *adj* popular
Popularität [populari'tɛ:t] *f* popularity
Pore ['po:rə] *f* pore
Pornographie [pɔrnogra'fi:] *f* pornography
pornographisch [pɔrno'gra:fiʃ] *adj* pornographic
porös [po'rø:s] *adj* porous
Porree ['pɔre] (-s, -s) *m* leek
Portal [pɔr'ta:l] (-s, -e) *nt* portal
Portefeuille [pɔrt'fø:j] *nt* (*POL, FIN*) portfolio
Portemonnaie [pɔrtmɔ'ne:] (-s, -s) *nt* purse
Portier [pɔrti'e:] (-s, -s) *m* porter
Portion [pɔrtsi'o:n] *f* portion, helping; (*umg: Anteil*) amount
Porto ['pɔrto] (-s, -s) *nt* postage; **p~frei** *adj* post-free, (postage) prepaid
Portrait (-s, -s) *nt* = **Porträt**; **p~ieren** *vt* = **porträtieren**
Porträt [pɔr'trɛ:] (-s, -s) *nt* portrait; **p~ieren** [pɔrtrɛ'ti:rən] *vt* to paint, to portray
Portugal ['pɔrtugal] (-s) *nt* Portugal
Portugiese [pɔrtu'gi:zə] (-n, -n) *m* Portuguese
Portugiesin *f* Portuguese
portugiesisch *adj* Portuguese
Porzellan [pɔrtsɛ'la:n] (-s, -e) *nt* china, porcelain; (*Geschirr*) china
Posaune [po'zaunə] *f* trombone
Pose ['po:zə] *f* pose

Position [pozitsi'o:n] *f* position
positiv ['po:ziti:f] *adj* positive; **P~** (-s, -e) *nt* (*PHOT*) positive
possessiv ['pɔsɛsi:f] *adj* possessive; **P~pronomen** (-s, -e) *nt* possessive pronoun
possierlich [pɔ'si:rliç] *adj* funny
Post [pɔst] (-, -en) *f* post (office); (*Briefe*) post, mail; **~amt** *nt* post office; **~anweisung** *f* postal order, money order; **~bote** *m* postman; **~en** (-s, -) *m* post, position; (*COMM*) item; (*auf Liste*) entry; (*MIL*) sentry; (*Streik~*) picket; **~er** (-s, -(s)) *nt* poster; **~fach** *nt* post-office box; **~karte** *f* postcard; **p~lagernd** *adv* poste restante (*BRIT*), general delivery (*US*); **~leitzahl** *f* postal code; **~scheckkonto** *nt* postal giro account; **~sparbuch** *nt* post office savings book; **~sparkasse** *f* post office savings bank; **~stempel** *m* postmark; **p~wendend** *adv* by return of post; **~wertzeichen** *nt* postage stamp
potent [po'tɛnt] *adj* potent
Potential [potɛntsi'a:l] (-s, -e) *nt* potential
potentiell [potɛntsi'ɛl] *adj* potential
Potenz [po'tɛnts] *f* power; (*eines Mannes*) potency
Pracht [praxt] (-) *f* splendour, magnificence
prächtig ['prɛçtiç] *adj* splendid
Prachtstück *nt* showpiece
prachtvoll *adj* splendid, magnificent
Prädikat [prɛdi'ka:t] (-(e)s, -e) *nt* title; (*GRAM*) predicate; (*Zensur*) distinction
prägen ['prɛ:gən] *vt* to stamp; (*Münze*) to mint; (*Ausdruck*) to coin; (*Charakter*) to form
prägnant [prɛ'gnant] *adj* precise, terse
Prägung ['prɛ:guŋ] *f* minting; forming; (*Eigenart*) character, stamp
prahlen ['pra:lən] *vi* to boast, to brag
Prahlerei [pra:lə'rai] *f* boasting
Praktik ['praktik] *f* practice; **p~abel** [-'ka:bəl] *adj* practicable; **~ant(in)** [-'kant(in)] *m(f)* trainee; **~um** (-s, **Praktika** *od* **Praktiken**) *nt* practical training
praktisch ['praktiʃ] *adj* practical, handy; **~er Arzt** general practitioner

praktizieren [prakti'tsi:rən] *vt, vi* to practise

Praline [pra'li:nə] *f* chocolate

prall [pral] *adj* firmly rounded; (*Segel*) taut; (*Arme*) plump; (*Sonne*) blazing; **~en** *vi* to bounce, to rebound; (*Sonne*) to blaze

Prämie ['prɛːmiə] *f* premium; (*Belohnung*) award, prize; **p~ren** *vt* to give an award to

Präparat [prɛpa'raːt] (-(e)s, -e) *nt* (*BIOL*) preparation; (*MED*) medicine

Präposition [prɛpozitsi'o:n] *f* preposition

Prärie [prɛ'riː] *f* prairie

Präsens ['prɛːzɛns] (-) *nt* present tense

präsentieren [prɛzɛn'tiːrən] *vt* to present

Präservativ [prɛzɛrva'tiːf] (-s, -e) *nt* contraceptive

Präsident(in) [prɛzi'dɛnt(ɪn)] *m(f)* president; **~schaft** *f* presidency

Präsidium [prɛ'ziːdium] *nt* presidency, chair(manship); (*Polizei~*) police headquarters *pl*

prasseln ['prasəln] *vi* (*Feuer*) to crackle; (*Hagel*) to drum; (*Wörter*) to rain down

Praxis ['praksɪs] (-, **Praxen**) *f* practice; (*Behandlungsraum*) surgery; (*von Anwalt*) office

präzis [prɛ'tsiːs] *adj* precise; **P~ion** [prɛtsizi'o:n] *f* precision

predigen ['preːdɪgən] *vt, vi* to preach

Prediger (-s, -) *m* preacher

Predigt ['preːdɪçt] (-, **-en**) *f* sermon

Preis [praɪs] (-es, -e) *m* price; (*Sieges~*) prize; **um keinen ~** not at any price

preisbewußt *adj* price-conscious

Preiselbeere *f* cranberry

preis- ['praɪz] *zW:* **~en** (*unreg*) *vi* to praise; **~geben** (*unreg*) *vt* to abandon; (*opfern*) to sacrifice; (*zeigen*) to expose; **~gekrönt** *adj* prize-winning; **P~gericht** *nt* jury; **~günstig** *adj* inexpensive; **P~lage** *f* price range; **~lich** *adj* (*Lage, Unterschied*) price, in price; **P~liste** *f* price list; **P~richter** *m* judge (*in a competition*); **P~schild** *nt* price tag; **P~träger(in)** *m(f)* prizewinner; **~wert** *adj* inexpensive

prekär [pre'kɛːr] *adj* precarious

Prell- [prɛl] *zW:* **~bock** *m* buffers *pl*;

p~en *vt* to bump; (*fig*) to cheat, to swindle; **~ung** *f* bruise

Premiere [prəmi'ɛːrə] *f* premiere

Premierminister [prəmi'eːmɪnɪstər] *m* prime minister, premier

Presse ['prɛsə] *f* press; **~agentur** *f* press agency; **~freiheit** *f* freedom of the press; **p~n** *vt* to press

pressieren [prɛ'siːrən] *vi* to (be in a) hurry

Preßluft ['prɛsluft] *f* compressed air; **~bohrer** *m* pneumatic drill

Prestige [prɛs'tiːʒə] (-s) *nt* prestige

prickeln ['prɪkəln] *vt, vi* to tingle; to tickle

Priester ['priːstər] (-s, -) *m* priest

Prima ['priːma] (-, **Primen**) *f* sixth form, top class

prima *adj inv* first-class, excellent

primär [pri'mɛːr] *adj* primary

Primel ['priːməl] (-, **-n**) *f* primrose

primitiv [primi'tiːf] *adj* primitive

Prinz [prɪnts] (-en, -en) *m* prince; **~essin** *f* princess

Prinzip [prɪn'tsiːp] (-s, -ien) *nt* principle; **p~iell** [-i'ɛl] *adj, adv* on principle; **p~ienlos** *adj* unprincipled

Priorität [priori'tɛːt] *f* priority

Prise ['priːzə] *f* pinch

Prisma ['prɪsma] (-s, **Prismen**) *nt* prism

privat [pri'vaːt] *adj* private; **P~patient(in)** *m(f)* private patient; **P~schule** *f* public school

Privileg [privi'leːk] (-(e)s, -ien) *nt* privilege

Pro (-) *nt* pro

pro [proː] *präp +akk* per

Probe ['proːbə] *f* test; (*Teststück*) sample; (*THEAT*) rehearsal; **jdn auf die ~ stellen** to put sb to the test; **~exemplar** *nt* specimen copy; **~fahrt** *f* test drive; **p~n** *vt* to try; (*THEAT*) to rehearse; **p~weise** *adv* on approval; **~zeit** *f* probation period

probieren [pro'biːrən] *vt* to try; (*Wein, Speise*) to taste, to sample ♦ *vi* to try; to taste

Problem [pro'bleːm] (-s, -e) *nt* problem; **~atik** [-'maːtɪk] *f* problem; **p~atisch** [-'maːtɪʃ] *adj* problematic; **p~los** *adj*

problem-free

Produkt [pro'dukt] (-(e)s, -e) *nt* product; (*AGR*) produce *no pl*; ~**ion** [produktsi'o:n] *f* production; output; **p~iv** [-'ti:f] *adj* productive; ~**ivität** *f* productivity

Produzent [produ'tsɛnt] *m* manufacturer; (*Film*) producer

produzieren [produ'tsi:rən] *vt* to produce

Professor [pro'fɛsɔr] *m* professor

Profi ['pro:fi] (-s, -s) *m* (*umg, SPORT*) pro

Profil [pro'fi:l] (-s, -e) *nt* profile; (*fig*) image

Profit [pro'fi:t] (-(e)s, -e) *m* profit; **p~ieren** [profi'ti:rən] *vi*: **p~ieren (von)** to profit (from)

Prognose [pro'gno:zə] *f* prediction, prognosis

Programm [pro'gram] (-s, -e) *nt* programme; (*COMPUT*) program; **p~ieren** [-'mi:rən] *vt* to programme; (*COMPUT*) to program; ~**ierer(in)** (-s, -) *m(f)* programmer

progressiv [progrɛ'si:f] *adj* progressive

Projekt [pro'jɛkt] (-(e)s, -e) *nt* project; ~**or** [pro'jɛktɔr] *m* projector

proklamieren [prokla'mi:rən] *vt* to proclaim

Prokurist(in) [proku'rɪst(ɪn)] *m(f)* ≈ company secretary

Prolet [pro'le:t] (-en, -en) *m* prole, pleb; ~**arier** [-'ta:riər] (-s, -) *m* proletarian

Prolog [pro'lo:k] (-(e)s, -e) *m* prologue

Promenade [promə'na:də] *f* promenade

Promille [pro'milə] (-(s), -) *nt* alcohol level

prominent [promi'nɛnt] *adj* prominent

Prominenz [promi'nɛnts] *f* VIPs *pl*

Promotion [promotsi'o:n] *f* doctorate, Ph.D.

promovieren [promo'vi:rən] *vi* to do a doctorate *od* Ph.D.

prompt [prɔmpt] *adj* prompt

Pronomen [pro'no:mɛn] (-s, -) *nt* pronoun

Propaganda [propa'ganda] (-) *f* propaganda

Propeller [pro'pɛlər] (-s, -) *m* propeller

Prophet [pro'fe:t] (-en, -en) *m* prophet

prophezeien [profe'tsaɪən] *vt* to prophesy

Prophezeiung *f* prophecy

Proportion [proportsi'o:n] *f* proportion; **p~al** [-'na:l] *adj* proportional

proportioniert *adj*: **gut/schlecht ~** well-/badly-proportioned

Prosa ['pro:za] (-) *f* prose; **p~isch** [pro'za:ɪʃ] *adj* prosaic

prosit ['pro:zɪt] *excl* cheers

Prospekt [pro'spɛkt] (-(e)s, -e) *m* leaflet, brochure

prost [pro:st] *excl* cheers

Prostituierte [prostitu'i:rtə] *f* prostitute

Prostitution [prostitutsi'o:n] *f* prostitution

Protein (-s, -e) *nt* protein

Protest [pro'tɛst] (-(e)s, -e) *m* protest; ~**ant(in)** [protɛs'tant(ɪn)] *m(f)* Protestant; **p~antisch** [protɛs'tantɪʃ] *adj* Protestant; **p~ieren** [protɛs'ti:rən] *vi* to protest

Prothese [pro'te:zə] *f* artificial limb; (*Zahn~*) dentures *pl*

Protokoll [proto'kɔl] (-s, -e) *nt* register; (*von Sitzung*) minutes *pl*; (*diplomatisch*) protocol; (*Polizei~*) statement; **p~ieren** [-'li:rən] *vt* to take down in the minutes

protzen ['prɔtsən] *vi* to show off

protzig *adj* ostentatious

Proviant [provi'ant] (-s, -e) *m* provisions *pl*, supplies *pl*

Provinz [pro'vɪnts] (-, -en) *f* province; **p~iell** [-'ɛl] *adj* provincial

Provision [provizi'o:n] *f* (*COMM*) commission

provisorisch [provi'zo:rɪʃ] *adj* provisional

Provokation [provokatsi'o:n] *f* provocation

provozieren [provo'tsi:rən] *vt* to provoke

Prozedur [protse'du:r] *f* procedure; (*pej*) carry-on

Prozent [pro'tsɛnt] (-(e)s, -e) *nt* per cent, percentage; ~**satz** *m* percentage; **p~ual** [-u'a:l] *adj* percentage *cpd*; as a percentage

Prozeß [pro'tsɛs] (-sses, -sse) *m* trial, case

Prozession [protsɛsi'o:n] *f* procession

prüde ['pry:də] *adj* prudish; **P~rie** [-'ri:] *f*

prudery

Prüf- ['pry:f] *zW:* **p~en** *vt* to examine, to test; (*nach~*) to check; **~er** (-s, -) *m* examiner; **~ling** *m* examinee; **~ung** *f* examination; checking; **~ungsausschuß** *m* examining board

Prügel ['pry:gəl] (-s, -) *m* cudgel ♦ *pl* (*Schläge*) beating; **~ei** [-'laɪ] *f* fight; **p~n** *vt* to beat ♦ *vr* to fight; **~strafe** *f* corporal punishment

Prunk [prʊŋk] (-(e)s) *m* pomp, show; **p~voll** *adj* splendid, magnificent

PS [pe:'ɛs] *abk* (= *Pferdestärke*) H.P.

Psalm [psalm] (-s, -en) *m* psalm

pseudo- ['psɔydɔ] *in zW* pseudo

pst [pst] *excl* psst!

Psych- ['psyç] *zW:* **~iater** [-i'a:tər] (-s, -) *m* psychiatrist; **p~iatrisch** *adj* (*MED*) psychiatric; **p~isch** *adj* psychological; **~oanalyse** [-o'ana'ly:zə] *f* psychoanalysis; **~ologe** [-o'lo:gə] (-n, -n) *m* psychologist; **~olo'gie** *f* psychology; **p~ologisch** *adj* psychological; **~otherapeut(in)** (-en, -en) *m(f)* psychotherapist

Pubertät [puber'tɛ:t] *f* puberty

Publikum ['pu:blikʊm] (-s) *nt* audience; (*SPORT*) crowd

publizieren [publi'tsi:rən] *vt* to publish, to publicize

Pudding ['pʊdɪŋ] (-s, -e *od* -s) *m* blancmange

Pudel ['pu:dəl] (-s, -) *m* poodle

Puder ['pu:dər] (-s, -) *m* powder; **~dose** *f* powder compact; **p~n** *vt* to powder; **~zucker** *m* icing sugar

Puff¹ [pʊf] (-(e)s, -e) *m* (*Wäsche~*) linen basket; (*Sitz~*) pouf

Puff² (-(e)s, *-e; umg*) *m* (*Stoß*) push

Puff³ (-s, -s; *umg*) *m od nt* (*Bordell*) brothel

Puffer (-s, -) *m* buffer; **~speicher** *m* (*COMPUT*) buffer

Pullover [pʊ'lo:vər] (-s, -) *m* pullover, jumper

Puls [pʊls] (-es, -e) *m* pulse; **~ader** *f* artery; **p~ieren** *vi* to throb, to pulsate

Pult [pʊlt] (-(e)s, -e) *nt* desk

Pulver ['pʊlfər] (-s, -) *nt* powder; **p~ig**

adj powdery; **~schnee** *m* powdery snow

pummelig ['pʊmǝlɪç] *adj* chubby

Pumpe ['pʊmpə] *f* pump; **p~n** *vt* to pump; (*umg*) to lend; to borrow

Punkt [pʊŋkt] (-(e)s, -e) *m* point; (*bei Muster*) dot; (*Satzzeichen*) full stop; **p~ieren** [-'ti:rən] *vt* to dot; (*MED*) to aspirate

pünktlich ['pʏŋktlɪç] *adj* punctual; **P~keit** *f* punctuality

Punktsieg *m* victory on points

Punktzahl *f* score

Punsch [pʊnʃ] (-(e)s, -e) *m* punch

Pupille [pu'pɪlə] *f* pupil

Puppe ['pʊpə] *f* doll; (*Marionette*) puppet; (*Insekten~*) pupa, chrysalis; **~nspieler** *m* puppeteer; **~nstube** *f* doll's house; **~ntheater** *nt* puppet theatre

pur [pu:r] *adj* pure; (*völlig*) sheer; (*Whisky*) neat

Püree [py're:] (-s, -s) *nt* mashed potatoes *pl*

Purzelbaum *m* somersault

purzeln ['pʊrtsəln] *vi* to tumble

Puste ['pu:stə] (-; *umg*) *f* puff; (*fig*) steam; **p~n** *vi* to puff, to blow

Pute ['pu:tə] *f* turkey-hen; **~r** (-s, -) *m* turkey-cock

Putsch [pʊtʃ] (-(e)s, -e) *m* revolt, putsch

Putz [pʊts] (-es) *m* (*Mörtel*) plaster, roughcast

putzen *vt* to clean; (*Nase*) to wipe, to blow ♦ *vr* to clean o.s.; to dress o.s. up

Putz- *zW:* **~frau** *f* charwoman; **p~ig** *adj* quaint, funny; **~lappen** *m* cloth

Puzzle ['pasəl] (-s, -s) *nt* jigsaw

PVC *nt abk* PVC

Pyjama [py'dʒa:ma] (-s, -s) *m* pyjamas *pl*

Pyramide [pyra'mi:də] *f* pyramid

Pyrenäen [pyre'nɛ:ən] *pl* Pyrenees

Q q

Quacksalber ['kvakzalbər] (-s, -) *m* quack (doctor)

Quader ['kva:dər] (-s, -) *m* square stone; (*MATH*) cuboid

Quadrat [kva'dra:t] (-(e)s, -e) *nt* square;

q~isch *adj* square; ~meter *m* square
metre
quaken ['kva:kən] *vi* to croak; (*Ente*) to
quack
quäken ['kvɛ:kən] *vi* to screech
Qual [kva:l] (-, -en) *f* pain, agony;
(*seelisch*) anguish
quälen ['kvɛ:lən] *vt* to torment ♦ *vr* to
struggle; (*geistig*) to torment o.s.
Quälerei [kvɛlə'raı] *f* torture, torment
Qualifikation [kvalifikatsi'o:n] *f*
qualification
qualifizieren [kvalifi'tsi:rən] *vt* to
qualify; (*einstufen*) to label ♦ *vr* to qualify
Qualität [kvali'tɛ:t] *f* quality; ~sware *f*
article of high quality
Qualle ['kvalə] *f* jellyfish
Qualm [kvalm] (-(e)s) *m* thick smoke;
q~en *vt, vi* to smoke
qualvoll ['kva:lfɔl] *adj* excruciating,
painful, agonizing
Quant- ['kvant] *zW:* ~entheorie *f*
quantum theory; ~ität [-i'tɛ:t] *f* quantity;
q~itativ [-ita'ti:f] *adj* quantitative; ~um
(-s) *nt* quantity, amount
Quarantäne [karan'tɛ:nə] *f* quarantine
Quark [kvark] (-s) *m* curd cheese; (*umg*)
rubbish
Quartal [kvar'ta:l] (-s, -e) *nt* quarter
(year)
Quartier [kvar'ti:r] (-s, -e) *nt*
accommodation; (*MIL*) quarters *pl*; (*Stadt~*)
district
Quarz [kva:rts] (-es, -e) *m* quartz
quasseln ['kvasəln] (*umg*) *vi* to natter
Quatsch [kvatʃ] (-es) *m* rubbish; q~en
vi to chat, to natter
Quecksilber ['kvɛkzılbər] *nt* mercury
Quelle ['kvɛlə] *f* spring; (*eines Flusses*)
source; q~n (*unreg*) *vi* (*hervor~*) to pour
od gush forth; (*schwellen*) to swell
quer [kve:r] *adv* crossways, diagonally;
(*rechtwinklig*) at right angles; ~ **auf dem
Bett** across the bed; Q~balken *m*
crossbeam; Q~feldein *adv* across country;
Q~flöte *f* flute; Q~format *nt* (*PHOT*)
oblong format; Q~schnitt *m* cross-
section; ~schnittsgelähmt *adj* paralysed
below the waist; Q~straße *f* intersecting

road
quetschen ['kvɛtʃən] *vt* to squash, to
crush; (*MED*) to bruise
Quetschung *f* bruise, contusion
quieken ['kvi:kən] *vi* to squeak
quietschen ['kvi:tʃən] *vi* to squeak
Quint- ['kvınt] *zW:* ~a (-, **Quinten**) *f*
second year of secondary school;
~essenz [-ɛsɛnts] *f* quintessence; ~ett
[-'tɛt] (-(e)s, -e) *nt* quintet
Quirl [kvırl] (-(e)s, -e) *m* whisk
quitt [kvıt] *adj* quits, even
Quitte *f* quince
quittieren [kvı'ti:rən] *vt* to give a receipt
for; (*Dienst*) to leave
Quittung *f* receipt
Quiz [kvıs] (-, -) *nt* quiz
quoll *etc* [kvɔl] *vb siehe* **quellen**
Quote ['kvo:tə] *f* number, rate

R r

Rabatt [ra'bat] (-(e)s, -e) *m* discount
Rabatte *f* flowerbed, border
Rabattmarke *f* trading stamp
Rabe ['ra:bə] (-n, -n) *m* raven
rabiat [rabi'a:t] *adj* furious
Rache ['raxə] (-) *f* revenge, vengeance
Rachen (-s, -) *m* throat
rächen ['rɛçən] *vt* to avenge, to revenge
♦ *vr* to take (one's) revenge; **das wird
sich ~** you'll pay for that
Rachitis [ra'xi:tıs] (-) *f* rickets *sg*
Rad [ra:t] (-(e)s, -er) *nt* wheel; (*Fahr~*)
bike
Radar ['ra:da:r] (-s) *m od nt* radar; ~falle
f speed trap; ~kontrolle *f* radar-
controlled speed trap
Radau [ra'dau] (-s; *umg*) *m* row
radebrechen *vi insep:* **deutsch** *etc* ~ to
speak broken German *etc*
radeln ['ra:dəln] (*umg*) *vi* to cycle
radfahr- *zW:* ~en (*unreg*) *vi* to cycle;
R~er(in) *m(f)* cyclist; R~weg *m* cycle
track *od* path
Radier- [ra'di:r] *zW:* r~en *vt* to rub out,
to erase; (*ART*) to etch; ~gummi *m*
rubber, eraser; ~ung *f* etching

Radieschen [ra'di:sçən] *nt* radish
radikal [radi'ka:l] *adj* radical; **R~e(r)** *mf* radical
Radio ['ra:dio] (**-s, -s**) *nt* radio, wireless; **r~ak'tiv** *adj* radioactive; **~aktivi'tät** *f* radioactivity; **~apparat** *m* radio, wireless set
Radius ['ra:diʊs] (**-, Radien**) *m* radius
Rad- *zW:* **~kappe** *f* (*AUT*) hub cap; **~ler(in)** (*umg*) *m(f)* cyclist; **~rennen** *nt* cycle race; cycle racing; **~sport** *m* cycling
raffen ['rafən] *vt* to snatch, to pick up; (*Stoff*) to gather (up); (*Geld*) to pile up, to rake in
Raffinade [rafi'na:də] *f* refined sugar
raffi'niert *adj* crafty, cunning
ragen ['ra:gən] *vi* to tower, to rise
Rahm [ra:m] (**-s**) *m* cream
Rahmen (**-s, -**) *m* frame(work); **im ~ des Möglichen** within the bounds of possibility; **r~** *vt* to frame
Rakete [ra'ke:tə] *f* rocket; **~nstützpunkt** *m* missile base
rammen ['ramən] *vt* to ram
Rampe ['rampə] *f* ramp; **~nlicht** *nt* (*THEAT*) footlights *pl*
ramponieren [rampo'ni:rən] (*umg*) *vt* to damage
Ramsch [ramʃ] (**-(e)s, -e**) *m* junk
ran [ran] (*umg*) *adv* = **heran**
Rand [rant] (**-(e)s, er**) *m* edge; (*von Brille, Tasse etc*) rim; (*Hut~*) brim; (*auf Papier*) margin; (*Schmutz~, unter Augen*) ring; (*fig*) verge, brink; **außer ~ und Band** wild; **am ~e bemerkt** mentioned in passing
randalieren [randa'li:rən] *vi* to (go on the) rampage
Rang [raŋ] (**-(e)s, e**) *m* rank; (*Stand*) standing; (*Wert*) quality; (*THEAT*) circle
Rangier- [rãʒi:r] *zW:* **~bahnhof** *m* marshalling yard; **r~en** *vt* (*EISENB*) to shunt, to switch (*US*) ♦ *vi* to rank, to be classed; **~gleis** *nt* siding
Ranke ['raŋkə] *f* tendril, shoot
ranzig ['rantsɪç] *adj* rancid
Rappe ['rapə] (**-n, -n**) *m* black horse
Rappen ['rapən] *m* (*FIN*) rappen, centime

rar [ra:r] *adj* rare; **sich ~ machen** (*umg*) to keep o.s. to o.s.; **R~i'tät** *f* rarity; (*Sammelobjekt*) curio
rasant [ra'zant] *adj* quick, rapid
rasch [raʃ] *adj* quick
rascheln *vi* to rustle
Rasen ['ra:zən] (**-s, -**) *m* lawn; grass
rasen *vi* to rave; (*schnell*) to race; **~d** *adj* furious; **~de Kopfschmerzen** a splitting headache
Rasenmäher (**-s, -**) *m* lawnmower
Rasier- [ra'zi:r] *zW:* **~apparat** *m* shaver; **~creme** *f* shaving cream; **r~en** *vt, vr* to shave; **~klinge** *f* razor blade; **~messer** *nt* razor; **~pinsel** *m* shaving brush; **~seife** *f* shaving soap *od* stick; **~wasser** *nt* shaving lotion
Rasse ['rasə] *f* race; (*Tier~*) breed; **~hund** *m* thoroughbred dog
rasseln ['rasəln] *vi* to clatter
Rass- *zW:* **~enhaß** *m* race *od* racial hatred; **~entrennung** *f* racial segregation; **~ismus** [ra'sɪsmʊs] *m* racism
Rast [rast] (**-, -en**) *f* rest; **r~en** *vi* to rest; **~hof** *m* (*AUT*) service station; **r~los** *adj* tireless; (*unruhig*) restless; **~platz** *m* (*AUT*) layby; **~stätte** *f* (*AUT*) service station
Rasur [ra'zu:r] *f* shaving
Rat [ra:t] (**-(e)s, -schläge**) *m* advice *no pl*; **ein ~** a piece of advice; **jdn zu ~e ziehen** to consult sb; **keinen ~ wissen** not to know what to do
Rate *f* instalment
raten (*unreg*) *vt, vi* to guess; (*empfehlen*): **jdm ~** to advise sb
Ratenzahlung *f* hire purchase
Ratgeber (**-s, -**) *m* adviser
Rathaus *nt* town hall
ratifizieren [ratifi'tsi:rən] *vt* to ratify
Ration [ratsi'o:n] *f* ration; **r~al** [-'na:l] *adj* rational; **r~ali'sieren** *vt* to rationalize; **r~ell** [-'nɛl] *adj* efficient; **r~ieren** [-'ni:rən] *vt* to ration
Rat- *zW:* **r~los** *adj* at a loss, helpless; **r~sam** *adj* advisable; **~schlag** *m* (piece of) advice
Rätsel ['rɛ:tsəl] (**-s, -**) *nt* puzzle; (*Wort~*)

riddle; **r~haft** *adj* mysterious; **es ist mir r~haft** it's a mystery to me

Ratte ['ratə] *f* rat; **~nfänger** (-s, -) *m* ratcatcher

rattern ['ratərn] *vi* to rattle, to clatter

Raub [raup] (-(e)s) *m* robbery; (*Beute*) loot, booty; **~bau** *m* ruthless exploitation; **r~en** ['raubən] *vt* to rob; (*Mensch*) to kidnap, to abduct

Räuber ['rɔybər] (-s, -) *m* robber

Raub- *zW*: **~mord** *m* robbery with murder; **~tier** *nt* predator; **~überfall** *m* robbery with violence; **~vogel** *m* bird of prey

Rauch [raux] (-(e)s) *m* smoke; **r~en** *vt, vi* to smoke; **~er(in)** (-s, -) *m(f)* smoker; **~erabteil** *nt* (*EISENB*) smoker

räuchern ['rɔyçərn] *vt* to smoke, to cure

Rauchfleisch *nt* smoked meat

rauchig *adj* smoky

rauf [rauf] (*umg*) *adv* = **herauf; hinauf**

raufen *vt* (*Haare*) to pull out ♦ *vi, vr* to fight; **Raufe'rei** *f* brawl, fight

rauh [rau] *adj* rough, coarse; (*Wetter*) harsh; **R~reif** *m* hoarfrost

Raum [raum] (-(e)s, **Räume**) *m* space; (*Zimmer, Platz*) room; (*Gebiet*) area

räumen ['rɔymən] *vt* to clear; (*Wohnung, Platz*) to vacate; (*wegbringen*) to shift, to move; (*in Schrank etc*) to put away

Raum- *zW*: **~fähre** *f* space shuttle; **~fahrt** *f* space travel; **~inhalt** *m* cubic capacity, volume

räumlich ['rɔymlɪç] *adj* spatial; **R~keiten** *pl* premises

Raum- *zW*: **~mangel** *m* lack of space; **~pflegerin** *f* cleaner; **~schiff** *nt* spaceship; **~schiffahrt** *f* space travel

Räumung ['rɔymʊŋ] *f* vacating, evacuation; clearing (away); **~sverkauf** *m* clearance sale; (*bei Geschäftsaufgabe*) closing down sale

raunen ['raunən] *vt, vi* to whisper

Raupe ['raupə] *f* caterpillar; (*~nkette*) (caterpillar) track; **~nschlepper** *m* caterpillar tractor

raus [raus] (*umg*) *adv* = **heraus; hinaus**

Rausch [rauʃ] (-(e)s, **Räusche**) *m* intoxication

rauschen *vi* (*Wasser*) to rush; (*Baum*) to rustle; (*Radio etc*) to hiss; (*Mensch*) to sweep, to sail; **~d** *adj* (*Beifall*) thunderous; (*Fest*) sumptuous

Rauschgift *nt* drug; **~süchtige(r)** *mf* drug addict

räuspern ['rɔyspərn] *vr* to clear one's throat

Razzia ['ratsia] (-, **Razzien**) *f* raid

Reagenzglas [rea'gɛntsglaːs] *nt* test tube

reagieren [rea'giːrən] *vi*: **~ (auf +akk)** to react (to)

Reakt- *zW*: **~ion** [reaktsi'oːn] *f* reaction; **r~io'när** *adj* reactionary; **~or** [re'aktɔr] *m* reactor

real [re'aːl] *adj* real, material

reali'sieren *vt* (*verwirklichen: Pläne*) to carry out

Realismus [rea'lɪsmʊs] *m* realism

rea'listisch *adj* realistic

Realschule *f* secondary school

Rebe ['reːbə] *f* vine

rebellieren [rebɛ'liːrən] *vi* to rebel; **Rebelli'on** *f* rebellion; **re'bellisch** *adj* rebellious

Rebhuhn ['rɛphuːn] *nt* (*KOCH, ZOOL*) partridge

Rechen ['rɛçən] (-s, -) *m* rake; **r~** *vt, vi* to rake

Rechen- *zW*: **~fehler** *m* miscalculation; **~maschine** *f* calculating machine; **~schaft** *f* account; **für etw ~schaft ablegen** to account for sth; **~schieber** *m* slide rule

Rech- ['rɛç] *zW*: **r~nen** *vt, vi* to calculate; **jdn/etw r~nen zu** to count sb/sth among; **r~nen mit** to reckon with; **r~nen auf +akk** to count on; **~nen** *nt* arithmetic; **~ner** (-s, -) *m* calculator; (*COMPUT*) computer; **~nung** *f* calculation(s); (*COMM*) bill, check (*US*); **jdm/etw ~nung tragen** to take sb/sth into account; **~nungsjahr** *nt* financial year; **~nungsprüfer** *m* auditor

Recht [rɛçt] (-(e)s, -e) *nt* right; (*JUR*) law; **mit ~** rightly, justly; **von ~s wegen** by rights

recht *adj* right ♦ *adv* (*vor Adjektiv*) really, quite; **das ist mir ~** that suits me;

jetzt erst ~ now more than ever; **~ haben** to be right; **jdm ~ geben** to agree with sb

Rechte f right (hand); (*POL*) Right; **r~(r, s)** adj right; (*POL*) right-wing; **ein ~r** a right-winger; **~(s)** nt right thing; **etwas/ nichts ~s** something/nothing proper

recht- zW: **~eckig** adj rectangular; **~fertigen** vt insep to justify ♦ vr insep to justify o.s.; **R~fertigung** f justification

rechthaberisch (*pej*) adj (*Mensch*) opinionated

rechtlich adj (*gesetzlich: Gleichstellung, Anspruch*) legal

rechtlos adj with no rights

rechtmäßig adj legal, lawful

rechts [rɛçts] adv on/to the right; **R~anwalt** m lawyer, barrister; **R~anwältin** f lawyer, barrister

rechtschaffen adj upright

Rechtschreibung f spelling

Rechts- zW: **~fall** m (law) case; **~händer (-s, -)** m right-handed person; **r~kräftig** adj valid, legal; **~kurve** f right-hand bend; **r~verbindlich** adj legally binding; **~verkehr** m driving on the right; **r~widrig** adj illegal; **~wissenschaft** f jurisprudence

rechtwinklig adj right-angled

rechtzeitig adj timely ♦ adv in time

Reck [rɛk] (-(e)s, -e) nt horizontal bar; **r~en** vt, vr to stretch

Redakteur [redak'tøːr] m editor

Redaktion [redaktsi'oːn] f editing; (*Leute*) editorial staff; (*Büro*) editorial office(s)

Rede ['reːdə] f speech; (*Gespräch*) talk; **jdn zur ~ stellen** to take sb to task; **~freiheit** f freedom of speech; **r~gewandt** adj eloquent; **r~n** vi to talk, to speak ♦ vt to say; (*Unsinn etc*) to talk; **~nsart** f set phrase; **~wendung** f expression, idiom

redlich ['reːtlɪç] adj honest

Redner (-s, -) m speaker, orator

redselig adj talkative, loquacious

reduzieren [redu'tsiːrən] vt to reduce

Reede ['reːdə] f protected anchorage; **~r (-s, -)** m shipowner; **~'rei** f shipping line od firm

reell [re'ɛl] adj fair, honest; (*MATH*) real

Refer- zW: **~at** [refe'raːt] (-(e)s, -e) nt report; (*Vortrag*) paper; (*Gebiet*) section; **~ent** [refe'rɛnt] m speaker; (*Berichterstatter*) reporter; (*Sachbearbeiter*) expert; **r~ieren** [refe'riːrən] vi: **r~ieren über** +*akk* to speak od talk on

reflektieren [reflɛk'tiːrən] vt (*Licht*) to reflect

Reflex [re'flɛks] (-es, -e) m reflex; **r~iv** [-'ksiːf] adj (*GRAM*) reflexive

Reform [re'fɔrm] (-, -en) f reform; **~ati'on** f reformation; **~haus** nt health food shop; **r~ieren** [-'miːrən] vt to reform

Regal [re'gaːl] (-s, -e) nt (book)shelves pl, bookcase; stand, rack

rege ['reːgə] adj (*lebhaft: Treiben*) lively; (*wach, lebendig: Geist*) keen

Regel ['reːgəl] (-, -n) f rule; (*MED*) period; **r~mäßig** adj regular; **~mäßigkeit** f regularity; **r~n** vt to regulate, to control; (*Angelegenheit*) to settle ♦ vr: **sich von selbst r~n** to take care of itself; **r~recht** adj regular, proper, thorough; **~ung** f regulation; settlement; **r~widrig** adj irregular, against the rules

Regen ['reːgən] (-s, -) m rain; **~bogen** m rainbow; **~bogenpresse** f tabloids pl

regenerierbar [regene'riːrbaːr] adj renewable

Regen- zW: **~mantel** m raincoat, mac(kintosh); **~schauer** m shower (of rain); **~schirm** m umbrella; **~wald** m (*GEOG*) rainforest; **~wurm** m earthworm; **~zeit** f rainy season

Regie [re'ʒiː] f (*Film etc*) direction; (*THEAT*) production

Regier- zW: **r~en** [re'giːr] vt, vi to govern, to rule; **~ung** f government; (*Monarchie*) reign; **~ungswechsel** m change of government; **~ungszeit** f period in government; (*von König*) reign

Regiment [regi'mɛnt] (-s, -er) nt regiment

Region [regi'oːn] f region

Regisseur [reʒi'søːr] m director; (*THEAT*) (stage) producer

Register [re'gɪstər] (-s, -) nt register; (*in*

Buch) table of contents, index

registrieren [regɪs'triːrən] *vt* to register

Regler ['reːglər] (**-s, -**) *m* regulator, governor

reglos ['reːkloːs] *adj* motionless

regnen *vi unpers* to rain

regnerisch *adj* rainy

regulär [regu'lɛːr] *adj* regular

regulieren [regu'liːrən] *vt* to regulate; (*COMM*) to settle

Regung ['reːgʊŋ] *f* motion; (*Gefühl*) feeling, impulse; **r~slos** *adj* motionless

Reh [reː] (**-(e)s, -e**) *nt* deer, roe; **~bock** *m* roebuck; **~kitz** *nt* fawn

Reib- ['raɪb] *zW:* **~e** *f* grater; **~eisen** *nt* grater; **r~en** (*unreg*) *vt* to rub; (*KOCH*) to grate; **~fläche** *f* rough surface; **~ung** *f* friction; **r~ungslos** *adj* smooth

Reich [raɪç] (**-(e)s, -e**) *nt* empire, kingdom; (*fig*) realm; **das Dritte ~** the Third Reich

reich *adj* rich

reichen *vi* to reach; (*genügen*) to be enough *od* sufficient ♦ *vt* to hold out; (*geben*) to pass, to hand; (*anbieten*) to offer; **jdm ~** to be enough *od* sufficient for sb

reich- *zW:* **~haltig** *adj* ample, rich; **~lich** *adj* ample, plenty of; **R~tum** (**-s**) *m* wealth; **R~weite** *f* range

Reif (**-(e)s, -e**) *m* (*Ring*) ring, hoop

reif [raɪf] *adj* ripe; (*Mensch, Urteil*) mature

Reife (**-**) *f* ripeness; maturity; **r~n** *vi* to mature; to ripen

Reifen (**-s, -**) *m* ring, hoop; (*Fahrzeug~*) tyre; **~druck** *m* tyre pressure; **~panne** *f* puncture

Reihe ['raɪə] *f* row; (*von Tagen etc, umg: Anzahl*) series *sg*; **der ~ nach** in turn; **er ist an der ~** it's his turn; **an die ~ kommen** to have one's turn; **~nfolge** *f* sequence; **alphabetische ~nfolge** alphabetical order; **~nhaus** *nt* terraced house

Reiher (**-s, -**) *m* (*ZOOL*) heron

reihum [raɪ'ʊm] *adv:* **es geht/wir machen das ~** we take turns

Reim [raɪm] (**-(e)s, -e**) *m* rhyme; **r~en** *vt* to rhyme

rein¹ [raɪn] (*umg*) *adv* = **herein; hinein**

rein² *adj* pure; (*sauber*) clean ♦ *adv* purely; **etw ins ~ schreiben** to make a fair copy of sth; **etw ins ~ bringen** to clear up sth; **R~fall** (*umg*) *m* let-down; **R~gewinn** *m* net profit; **R~heit** *f* purity; cleanness; **~igen** *vt* to clean; (*Wasser*) to purify; **R~igung** *f* cleaning; purification; (*Geschäft*) cleaner's; **chemische R~igung** dry cleaning; dry cleaner's; **~rassig** *adj* pedigree; **R~schrift** *f* fair copy

Reis [raɪs] (**-es, -e**) *m* rice

Reise ['raɪzə] *f* journey; (*Schiffs~*) voyage; **~n** *pl* (*Herum~*) travels; **gute ~!** have a good journey; **~andenken** *nt* souvenir; **~büro** *nt* travel agency; **r~fertig** *adj* ready to start; **~führer** *m* guide(book); (*Mensch*) travel guide; **~gepäck** *nt* luggage; **~gesellschaft** *f* party of travellers; **~kosten** *pl* travelling expenses; **~leiter** *m* courier; **~lektüre** *f* reading matter for the journey; **r~n** *vi* to travel; **r~n nach** to go to; **~nde(r)** *mf* traveller; **~paß** *m* passport; **~proviant** *m* food and drink for the journey; **~route** *f* route; itinerary; **~scheck** *m* traveller's cheque; **~ziel** *nt* destination

reißen ['raɪsən] (*unreg*) *vt* to tear; (*ziehen*) to pull, to drag; (*Witz*) to crack ♦ *vi* to tear; to pull, to drag; **etw an sich ~** to snatch sth up; (*fig*) to take over sth; **sich um etw ~** to scramble for sth

reißend *adj* (*Fluß*) raging; (*WIRTS: Verkauf*) rapid

Reißnagel *m* drawing pin (*BRIT*), thumbtack (*US*)

Reißverschluß *m* zip(per), zip fastener

Reit- ['raɪt] *zW:* **r~en** (*unreg*) *vt, vi* to ride; **~er** (**-s, -**) *m* rider; (*MIL*) cavalryman, trooper; **~erin** *f* rider; **~hose** *f* riding breeches *pl*; **~pferd** *nt* saddle horse; **~stiefel** *m* riding boot; **~weg** *n* bridle path; **~zeug** *nt* riding outfit

Reiz [raɪts] (**-es, -e**) *m* stimulus; (*angenehm*) charm; (*Verlockung*) attraction; **r~bar** *adj* irritable; **~barkeit** *f* irritability; **r~en** *vt* to stimulate; (*unangenehm*) to irritate; (*verlocken*) to appeal to, to attract; **r~end** *adj* charming; **r~voll** *adj* attractive

rekeln ['re:kəln] *vr* to stretch out; (*lümmeln*) to lounge *od* loll about

Reklamation [reklamatsi'o:n] *f* complaint

Reklame [re'kla:mə] *f* advertising; advertisement; ~ **machen für etw** to advertise sth

rekonstruieren [rekɔnstru'i:rən] *vt* to reconstruct

Rekord [re'kɔrt] (-(e)s, -e) *m* record; ~**leistung** *f* record performance

Rektor ['rɛktɔr] *m* (*UNIV*) rector, vice-chancellor; (*SCH*) headteacher (*BRIT*), principal (*US*); ~**at** [-'ra:t] (-(e)s, -e) *nt* rectorate, vice-chancellorship; headship; (*Zimmer*) rector's *etc* office

Relais [rə'lɛ:] (-, -) *nt* relay

relativ [rela'ti:f] *adj* relative; **R~ität** [relativi'tɛ:t] *f* relativity

relevant [rele'vant] *adj* relevant

Relief [reli'ɛf] (-s, -s) *nt* relief

Religion [religi'o:n] *f* religion

religiös [religi'ø:s] *adj* religious

Reling ['re:lɪŋ] (-, -s) *f* (*NAUT*) rail

Remoulade [remu'la:də] *f* remoulade

Rendezvous [rãde'vu:] (-, -) *nt* rendezvous

Renn- ['rɛn] *zW*: ~**bahn** *f* racecourse; (*AUT*) circuit, race track; **r~en** (*unreg*) *vt*, *vi* to run, to race; ~**en** (-s, -) *nt* running; (*Wettbewerb*) race; ~**fahrer** *m* racing driver; ~**pferd** *nt* racehorse; ~**wagen** *m* racing car

renommiert [reno'mi:rt] *adj* renowned

renovieren [reno'vi:rən] *vt* to renovate

Renovierung *f* renovation

rentabel [rɛn'ta:bəl] *adj* profitable, lucrative

Rentabilität [rɛntabili'tɛ:t] *f* profitability

Rente ['rɛntə] *f* pension

Rentier ['rɛnti:r] *nt* reindeer

rentieren [rɛn'ti:rən] *vr* to pay, to be profitable

Rentner(in) ['rɛntnər(ɪn)] (-s, -) *m(f)* pensioner

Reparatur [repara'tu:r] *f* repairing; repair; ~**werkstatt** *f* repair shop; (*AUT*) garage

reparieren [repa'ri:rən] *vt* to repair

Reportage [repɔr'ta:ʒə] *f* (on-the-spot) report; (*TV, RADIO*) live commentary *od* coverage

Reporter [re'pɔrtər] (-s, -) *m* reporter, commentator

repräsentativ [reprɛzɛnta'ti:f] *adj* (*stellvertretend, typisch: Menge, Gruppe*) representative; (*beeindruckend: Haus, Auto etc*) impressive

repräsentieren [reprɛzɛn'ti:rən] *vt* (*Staat, Firma*) to represent; (*darstellen: Wert*) to constitute ♦ *vi* (*gesellschaftlich*) to perform official duties

Repressalie [reprɛ'sa:liə] *f* reprisal

Reprivatisierung [reprivati'zi:rʊŋ] *f* denationalization

Reproduktion [reprodʊktsi'o:n] *f* reproduction

reproduzieren [reprodu'tsi:rən] *vt* to reproduce

Reptil [rɛp'ti:l] (-s, -ien) *nt* reptile

Republik [repu'bli:k] *f* republic; **r~anisch** [-'ka:nɪʃ] *adj* republican

Reservat [rezɛr'va:t] (-(e)s, -e) *nt* reservation

Reserve [re'zɛrvə] *f* reserve; ~**rad** *nt* (*AUT*) spare wheel; ~**spieler** *m* reserve; ~**tank** *m* reserve tank

reservieren [rezɛr'vi:rən] *vt* to reserve

Reservoir [rezɛrvo'a:r] (-s, -e) *nt* reservoir

Residenz [rezi'dɛnts] *f* residence, seat

resignieren [rezɪ'gni:rən] *vi* to resign

resolut [rezo'lu:t] *adj* resolute

Resonanz [rezo'nants] *f* resonance; (*fig*) response

Resopal [rezo'pa:l] (®; -s) *nt* Formica ®

Resozialisierung [rezotsiali'zi:rʊŋ] *f* rehabilitation

Respekt [re'spɛkt] (-(e)s) *m* respect; **r~ieren** [-'ti:rən] *vt* to respect; **r~los** *adj* disrespectful; **r~voll** *adj* respectful

Ressort [rɛ'so:r] (-s, -s) *nt* department

Rest [rɛst] (-(e)s, -e) *m* remainder, rest; (*Über~*) remains *pl*

Restaurant [rɛsto'rã:] (-s, -s) *nt* restaurant

restaurieren [rɛstau'ri:rən] *vt* to restore

Rest- *zW:* **~betrag** *m* remainder, outstanding sum; **r~lich** *adj* remaining; **r~los** *adj* complete
Resultat [rezul'ta:t] (-(e)s, -e) *nt* result
Retorte [re'tortə] *f* retort
Retouren [re'tu:rən] *pl (COMM)* returns
retten ['rɛtən] *vt* to save, to rescue
Retter(in) *m(f)* rescuer
Rettich ['rɛtɪç] (-s, -e) *m* radish
Rettung *f* rescue; *(Hilfe)* help; **seine letzte ~** his last hope
Rettungs- *zW:* **~boot** *nt* lifeboat; **r~los** *adj* hopeless; **~ring** *m* lifebelt, life preserver *(US)*; **~wagen** *m* ambulance
retuschieren [retu'ʃi:rən] *vt (PHOT)* to retouch
Reue ['rɔʏə] (-) *f* remorse; *(Bedauern)* regret; **r~n** *vt:* **es reut ihn** he regrets it *od* is sorry about it
reuig ['rɔʏɪç] *adj* penitent
Revanche [re'vã:ʃə] *f* revenge; *(SPORT)* return match
revanchieren [revã'ʃi:rən] *vr (sich rächen)* to get one's own back, to have one's revenge; *(erwidern)* to reciprocate, to return the compliment
Revier [re'vi:r] (-s, -e) *nt* district; *(Jagd~)* preserve; *(Polizei~)* police station; beat
Revolte [re'vɔltə] *f* revolt
revol'tieren *vi (gegen jdn/etw)* to rebel
Revolution [revolutsi'o:n] *f* revolution; **~är** [-'nɛ:r] (-s, -e) *m* revolutionary; **r~ieren** [-'ni:rən] *vt* to revolutionize
Revolver [re'vɔlvər] (-s, -) *m* revolver
Rezept [re'tsɛpt] (-(e)s, -e) *nt* recipe; *(MED)* prescription; **r~frei** *adj* available without prescription
Rezeption [retsɛptsi'o:n] *f* reception
rezeptflichtig *adj* available only on prescription
rezitieren [retsi'ti:rən] *vt* to recite
R-Gespräch ['ɛrgəʃprɛ:ç] *nt* reverse charge call *(BRIT)*, collect call *(US)*
Rhabarber [ra'barbər] (-s) *m* rhubarb
Rhein [raɪn] (-s) *m* Rhine; **r~isch** *adj* Rhenish
Rheinland-Pfalz *nt (GEOG)* Rheinland-Pfalz, Rhineland-Palatinate
Rhesusfaktor ['re:zusfaktɔr] *m* rhesus factor

rhetorisch [re'to:rɪʃ] *adj* rhetorical
Rheuma ['rɔʏma] (-s) *nt* rheumatism; **r~tisch** [-'ma:tɪʃ] *adj* rheumatic; **~tismus** [-'tɪsmus] *m* rheumatism
Rhinozeros [ri'no:tserɔs] (- *od* -ses, -se) *nt* rhinoceros
rhythmisch ['rʏtmɪʃ] *adj* rhythmical
Rhythmus ['rʏtmus] *m* rhythm
richt- ['rɪçt] *zW:* **~en** *vt* to direct; *(Waffe)* to aim; *(einstellen)* to adjust; *(instand setzen)* to repair; *(zurechtmachen)* to prepare; *(bestrafen)* to pass judgement on ♦ *vr:* **sich ~en nach** to go by; **~en an** +*akk* to direct at; *(fig)* to direct to; **~en auf** +*akk* to aim at; **R~er(in)** (-s, -) *m(f)* judge; **~erlich** *adj* judicial
richtig *adj* right, correct; *(echt)* proper ♦ *adv (umg: sehr)* really; **bin ich hier ~?** am I in the right place?; **der/die R~e** the right one/person; **das R~e** the right thing; **R~keit** *f* correctness
Richtpreis *m* recommended price
Richtung *f* direction; tendency, orientation
rieb *etc* [ri:p] *vb siehe* **reiben**
riechen ['ri:çən] *(unreg) vt, vi* to smell; **an etw** *dat* **~** to smell sth; **nach etw ~** to smell of sth; **ich kann das/ihn nicht ~** *(umg)* I can't stand it/him
rief *etc* [ri:f] *vb siehe* **rufen**
Riegel ['ri:gəl] (-s, -) *m* bolt; *(Schokolade usw)* bar
Riemen ['ri:mən] (-s, -) *m* strap; *(Gürtel, TECH)* belt; *(NAUT)* oar
Riese ['ri:zə] (-n, -n) *m* giant
rieseln *vi* to trickle; *(Schnee)* to fall gently
Riesenerfolg *m* enormous success
riesengroß *adj* colossal, gigantic, huge
Riesenrad *nt* big wheel
riesig ['ri:zɪç] *adj* enormous, huge, vast
riet *etc* [ri:t] *vb siehe* **raten**
Riff [rɪf] (-(e)s, -e) *nt* reef
Rille ['rɪlə] *f* groove
Rind [rɪnt] (-(e)s, -er) *nt* ox; cow; cattle *pl*; *(KOCH)* beef
Rinde ['rɪndə] *f* rind; *(Baum~)* bark; *(Brot~)* crust

Rindfleisch *nt* beef

Rindvieh *nt* cattle *pl*; (*umg*) blockhead, stupid oaf

Ring [rɪŋ] (-(e)s, -e) *m* ring; ~**buch** *nt* ring binder; ~**elnatter** *f* grass snake; **r~en** (*unreg*) *vi* to wrestle; ~**en** (-s) *nt* wrestling; ~**finger** *m* ring finger; ~**kampf** *m* wrestling bout; ~**richter** *m* referee; **r~s** *adv*: **r~s um** round; **r~sherum** *adv* round about; ~**straße** *f* ring road; **r~sum** *adv* (*rundherum*) round about; (*überall*) all round; **r~sum'her** = **r~sum**

Rinn- [rɪn] *zW*: ~**e** *f* gutter, drain; **r~en** (*unreg*) *vi* to run, to trickle; ~**stein** *m* gutter

Rippchen ['rɪpçən] *nt* small rib; cutlet

Rippe ['rɪpə] *f* rib; ~**nfellentzündung** *f* pleurisy

Risiko ['riːziko] (-s, -s *od* Risiken) *nt* risk

riskant [rɪs'kant] *adj* risky, hazardous

riskieren [rɪs'kiːrən] *vt* to risk

Riß [rɪs] (-sses, -sse) *m* tear; (*in Mauer, Tasse etc*) crack; (*in Haut*) scratch; (*TECH*) design

rissig ['rɪsɪç] *adj* torn; cracked; scratched

Ritt [rɪt] (-(e)s, -e) *m* ride

ritt *etc vb siehe* **reiten**

Ritter (-s, -) *m* knight; **r~lich** *adj* chivalrous

Ritze ['rɪtsə] *f* crack, chink

Rivale [ri'vaːlə] (-n, -n) *m* rival

Rivalität [rivali'tɛːt] *f* rivalry

Riviera [rivi'eːra] *f*: **die ~** the Riviera

Robbe ['rɔbə] *f* seal

Roboter ['rɔbɔtər] (-s, -) *m* robot

robust [ro'bʊst] *adj* (*kräftig: Mensch, Gesundheit*) robust

roch *etc* [rɔx] *vb siehe* **riechen**

Rock [rɔk] (-(e)s, -e) *m* skirt; (*Jackett*) jacket; (*Uniform~*) tunic

Rodel ['roːdəl] (-s, -) *m* toboggan; ~**bahn** *f* toboggan run; **r~n** *vi* to toboggan

roden ['roːdən] *vt, vi* to clear

Rogen ['roːgən] (-s, -) *m* roe, spawn

Roggen ['rɔgən] (-s, -) *m* rye

Roggenbrot *nt* (*KOCH*) rye bread

roh [roː] *adj* raw; (*Mensch*) coarse, crude; **R~bau** *m* shell of a building;

R~material *nt* raw material; **R~öl** *nt* crude oil

Rohr [roːr] (-(e)s, -e) *nt* pipe, tube; (*BOT*) cane; (*Schilf*) reed; (*Gewehr~*) barrel; ~**bruch** *m* burst pipe

Röhre ['røːrə] *f* tube, pipe; (*RADIO etc*) valve; (*Back~*) oven

Rohr- *zW*: ~**leitung** *f* pipeline; ~**post** *f* pneumatic postal system; ~**zucker** *m* cane sugar

Rohstoff *m* raw material

Rokoko ['rɔkoko] (-s) *nt* rococo

Roll- ['rɔl] *zW*: ~**(l)aden** *m* shutter; ~**bahn** *f* (*AVIAT*) runway

Rolle ['rɔlə] *f* roll; (*THEAT, soziologisch*) role; (*Garn~ etc*) reel, spool; (*Walze*) roller; (*Wäsche~*) mangle; **keine ~ spielen** not to matter; **eine (wichtige) ~ spielen bei** to play a (major) part *od* role in; **r~n** *vt, vi* to roll; (*AVIAT*) to taxi; ~**r** (-s, -) *m* scooter; (*Welle*) roller

Roll- *zW*: ~**kragen** *m* rollneck, polo neck; ~**(l)aden** *m* shutter; ~**mops** *m* pickled herring; ~**schuh** *m* roller skate; ~**stuhl** *m* wheelchair; ~**treppe** *f* escalator

Rom [roːm] (-s) *nt* Rome

Roman [ro'maːn] (-s, -e) *m* novel; ~**tik** *f* romanticism; ~**tiker** [ro'mantɪkər] (-s, -) *m* romanticist; **r~tisch** [ro'mantɪʃ] *adj* romantic; ~**ze** [ro'mantsə] *f* romance

Römer ['røːmər] (-s, -) *m* wineglass; (*Mensch*) Roman

römisch *adj* Roman; ~**-katholisch** *adj* (*REL*) Roman Catholic

röntgen ['rœntgən] *vt* to X-ray; **R~bild** *nt* X-ray; **R~strahlen** *pl* X-rays

rosa ['roːza] *adj inv* pink, rose(-coloured)

Rose ['roːzə] *f* rose; ~**nkohl** *m* Brussels sprouts *pl*; ~**nkranz** *m* rosary; ~**nmontag** *m* Monday before Ash Wednesday

rosig ['roːzɪç] *adj* rosy

Rosine [ro'ziːnə] *f* raisin, currant

Rosmarin ['rɔsmariːn] (-s) *m* (*BOT, KOCH*) rosemary

Roß [rɔs] (-sses, -sse) *nt* horse, steed; ~**kastanie** *f* horse chestnut

Rost [rɔst] (-(e)s, -e) *m* rust; (*Gitter*) grill, gridiron; (*Bett~*) springs *pl*

Rostbraten *m* roast(ed) meat, roast
rosten *vi* to rust
rösten ['rø:stən] *vt* to roast; to toast; to grill
Rost- *zW:* **r~frei** *adj* rust-free; rustproof; stainless; **r~ig** *adj* rusty; **~schutz** *m* rust-proofing
rot [ro:t] *adj* red; **in den ~en Zahlen** in the red; **das R~e Meer** the Red Sea
Röte ['rø:tə] (-) *f* redness; **~ln** *pl* German measles *sg*; **r~n** *vt, vr* to redden
rothaarig *adj* red-haired
rotieren [ro'ti:rən] *vi* to rotate
Rot- *zW:* **~kehlchen** *nt* robin; **~stift** *m* red pencil; **~wein** *m* red wine
Rouge [ru:ʒ] *nt* blusher
Roulade [ru'la:də] *f (KOCH)* beef olive
Route ['ru:tə] *f* route
Routine [ru'ti:nə] *f* experience; routine
Rübe ['ry:bə] *f* turnip; **gelbe ~** carrot; **rote ~** beetroot *(BRIT),* beet *(US)*
rüber ['ry:bər] *(umg) adv* = **herüber; hinüber**
Rubin [ru'bi:n] (**-s, -e**) *m* ruby
Rubrik [ru'bri:k] *f* heading; *(Spalte)* column
Ruck [rʊk] (**-(e)s, -e**) *m* jerk, jolt
Rück- ['rʏk] *zW:* **~antwort** *f* reply, answer; **r~bezüglich** *adj* reflexive
Rücken ['rʏkən] (**-s, -**) *m* back; *(Berg~)* ridge
rücken *vt, vi* to move
Rücken- *zW:* **~mark** *nt* spinal cord; **~schwimmen** *nt* backstroke
Rück- *zW:* **~erstattung** *f* return, restitution; **~fahrkarte** *f* return (ticket); **~fahrt** *f* return journey; **~fall** *m* relapse; **r~fällig** *adj* relapsing; **r~fällig werden** to relapse; **~flug** *m* return flight; **~frage** *f* question; **r~fragen** *vi* to check, to inquire (further); **~gabe** *f* return; **~gang** *m* decline, fall; **r~gängig** *adj:* **etw r~gängig machen** to cancel sth; **~grat** (**-(e)s, -e**) *nt* spine, backbone; **~halt** *m (Unterstützung)* backing, support; **~kehr** (**-, -en**) *f* return; **~licht** *nt* back light; **r~lings** *adv* from behind; backwards; **~nahme** *f* taking back; **~porto** *nt* return postage; **~reise** *f* return journey; *(NAUT)*

home voyage; **~ruf** *m* recall
Rucksack ['rʊkzak] *m* rucksack
Rück- *zW:* **~schau** *f* reflection; **~schlag** *m (plötzliche Verschlechterung)* setback; **~schluß** *m* conclusion; **~schritt** *m* retrogression; **r~schrittlich** *adj* reactionary; retrograde; **~seite** *f* back; *(von Münze etc)* reverse; **~sicht** *f* consideration; **~sicht nehmen auf** +*akk* to show consideration for; **r~sichtslos** *adj* inconsiderate; *(Fahren)* reckless; *(unbarmherzig)* ruthless; **r~sichtsvoll** *adj* considerate; **~sitz** *m* back seat; **~spiegel** *m (AUT)* rear-view mirror; **~spiel** *nt* return match; **~sprache** *f* further discussion *od* talk; **~stand** *m* arrears *pl;* **r~ständig** *adj* backward, out-of-date; *(Zahlungen)* in arrears; **~strahler** (**-s, -**) *m* rear reflector; **~tritt** *m* resignation; **~trittbremse** *f* pedal brake; **~vergütung** *f* repayment; *(COMM)* refund; **~versicherung** *f* reinsurance; **r~wärtig** *adj* rear; **r~wärts** *adv* backward(s), back; **~wärtsgang** *m (AUT)* reverse gear; **~weg** *m* return journey, way back; **r~wirkend** *adj* retroactive; **~wirkung** *f* reaction; retrospective effect; **~zahlung** *f* repayment; **~zug** *m* retreat
Rudel ['ru:dəl] (**-s, -**) *nt* pack; herd
Ruder ['ru:dər] (**-s, -**) *nt* oar; *(Steuer)* rudder; **~boot** *nt* rowing boat; **r~n** *vt, vi* to row
Ruf [ru:f] (**-(e)s, -e**) *m* call, cry; *(Ansehen)* reputation; **r~en** *(unreg) vt, vi* to call; to cry; **~name** *m* usual (first) name; **~nummer** *f* (tele)phone number; **~säule** *f (an Autobahn)* emergency telephone; **~zeichen** *nt (RADIO)* call sign; *(TEL)* ringing tone
rügen ['ry:gən] *vt* to rebuke
Ruhe ['ru:ə] (-) *f* rest; *(Ungestörtheit)* peace, quiet; *(Gelassenheit, Stille)* calm; *(Schweigen)* silence; **jdn in ~ lassen** to leave sb alone; **sich zur ~ setzen** to retire; **~! be quiet!, silence!; r~n** *vi* to rest; **~pause** *f* break; **~stand** *m* retirement; **~stätte** *f:* **letzte ~stätte** final resting place; **~störung** *f* breach of the peace; **~tag** *m (von Geschäft)* closing day

ruhig ['ruːɪç] *adj* quiet; *(bewegungslos)* still; *(Hand)* steady; *(gelassen, friedlich)* calm; *(Gewissen)* clear; **kommen Sie ~ herein** just come on in; **tu das ~** feel free to do that

Ruhm [ruːm] (-(e)s) *m* fame, glory

rühmen ['ryːmən] *vt* to praise ♦ *vr* to boast

Ruhr [ruːr] (-) *f* dysentery

Rühr- ['ryːr] *zW:* **~ei** *nt* scrambled egg; **r~en** *vt, vr (auch fig)* to move, to stir ♦ *vi:* **r~en von** to come *od* stem from; **r~en an** +*akk* to touch; *(fig)* to touch on; **r~end** *adj* touching, moving; **r~ig** *adj* active, lively; **r~selig** *adj* sentimental, emotional; **~ung** *f* emotion

Ruin [ru'iːn] (-s, -e) *m* ruin; **~e** *f* ruin; **r~ieren** [-'niːrən] *vt* to ruin

rülpsen ['rʏlpsən] *vi* to burp, to belch

Rum [rʊm] (-s, -s) *m* rum

Rumän- [ru'mɛːn] *zW:* **~e** (-n, -n) *m* Ro(u)manian; **~ien** (-s) *nt* Ro(u)mania; **~in** *f* Ro(u)manian; **r~isch** *adj* Ro(u)manian

Rummel ['rʊməl] (-s; *umg*) *m* hubbub; *(Jahrmarkt)* fair; **~platz** *m* fairground, fair

Rumpf [rʊmpf] (-(e)s, ⁻e) *m* trunk, torso; *(AVIAT)* fuselage; *(NAUT)* hull

rümpfen ['rʏmpfən] *vt (Nase)* to turn up

rund [rʊnt] *adj* round ♦ *adv (etwa)* around; **~ um etw** round sth; **R~brief** *m* circular; **R~e** ['rʊndə] *f* round; *(in Rennen)* lap; *(Gesellschaft)* circle; **R~fahrt** *f* (round) trip

Rundfunk ['rʊntfʊŋk] (-(e)s) *m* broadcasting; **im ~** on the radio; **~gerät** *nt* wireless set; **~sendung** *f* broadcast, radio programme

Rund- *zW:* **r~heraus** *adv* straight out, bluntly; **r~herum** *adv* round about; all round; **r~lich** *adj* plump, rounded; **~reise** *f* round trip; **~schreiben** *nt (COMM)* circular; **~(wander)weg** *m* circular path *od* route

runter ['rʊntər] *(umg) adv* = **herunter; hinunter**

Runzel ['rʊntsəl] (-, -n) *f* wrinkle; **r~ig** *adj* wrinkled; **r~n** *vt* to wrinkle; **die Stirn r~n** to frown

Rupfen ['rʊpfən] (-s, -) *m* sackcloth

rupfen *vt* to pluck

ruppig ['rʊpɪç] *adj* rough, gruff

Rüsche ['ryːʃə] *f* frill

Ruß [ruːs] (-es) *m* soot

Russe ['rʊsə] (-n, -n) *m* Russian

Rüssel ['rʏsəl] (-s, -) *m* snout; *(Elefanten~)* trunk

rußig ['ruːsɪç] *adj* sooty

Russin ['rʊsɪn] *f* Russian

russisch *adj* Russian

Rußland ['rʊslant] (-s) *nt* Russia

rüsten ['rʏstən] *vt* to prepare ♦ *vi* to prepare; *(MIL)* to arm ♦ *vr* to prepare (o.s.); to arm o.s.

rüstig ['rʏstɪç] *adj* sprightly, vigorous

Rüstung ['rʏstʊŋ] *f* preparation; arming; *(Ritter~)* armour; *(Waffen etc)* armaments *pl*; **~skontrolle** *f* arms control

Rute ['ruːtə] *f* rod

Rutsch [rʊtʃ] (-(e)s, -e) *m* slide; *(Erd~)* landslide; **~bahn** *f* slide; **r~en** *vi* to slide; *(ausrutschen)* to slip; **r~ig** *adj* slippery

rütteln ['rʏtəln] *vt, vi* to shake, to jolt

S s

S. *abk* (= *Seite*) p.; = **Schilling**

s. *abk* (= *siehe*) see

Saal [zaːl] (-(e)s, **Säle**) *m* hall; room

Saarland ['zaːrlant] *nt:* **das ~** the Saar(land)

Saat [zaːt] (-, -en) *f* seed; *(Pflanzen)* crop; *(Säen)* sowing

Säbel ['zɛːbəl] (-s, -) *m* sabre, sword

Sabotage [zabo'taːʒə] *f* sabotage

Sach- ['zax] *zW:* **~bearbeiter** *m* specialist; **s~dienlich** *adj* relevant, helpful; **~e** *f* thing; *(Angelegenheit)* affair, business; *(Frage)* matter; *(Pflicht)* task; **zur ~e** to the point; **s~kundig** *adj* expert; **s~lich** *adj* matter-of-fact; objective; *(Irrtum, Angabe)* factual

sächlich ['zɛçlɪç] *adj* neuter

Sachschaden *m* material damage

Sachsen ['zaksən] (-s) *nt* Saxony

sächsisch ['zɛksɪʃ] *adj* Saxon

sacht(e) ['zaxt(ə)] *adv* softly, gently
Sachverständige(r) *mf* expert
Sack [zak] **(-(e)s, ᵈe)** *m* sack; **~gasse** *f* cul-de-sac, dead-end street (*US*)
Sadismus [za'dɪsmʊs] *m* sadism
Sadist [za'dɪst] *m* sadist
säen ['zɛːən] *vt, vi* to sow
Safe(r) Sex *m* safe sex
Saft [zaft] **(-(e)s, ᵈe)** *m* juice; (*BOT*) sap; **s~ig** *adj* juicy; **s~los** *adj* dry
Sage ['zaːgə] *f* saga
Säge ['zɛːgə] *f* saw; **~mehl** *nt* sawdust
sagen ['zaːgən] *vt, vi* to say; (*mitteilen*): **jdm ~** to tell sb; **~ Sie ihm, daß ...** tell him ...
sägen *vt, vi* to saw
sagenhaft *adj* legendary; (*umg*) great, smashing
sah *etc* [zaː] *vb siehe* **sehen**
Sahne ['zaːnə] **(-)** *f* cream
Saison [zɛ'zõː] **(-, -s)** *f* season
Saite ['zaɪtə] *f* string; **~ninstrument** *nt* string instrument
Sakko ['zako] **(-s, -s)** *m od nt* jacket
Sakrament [zakra'mɛnt] *nt* sacrament
Sakristei [zakrɪs'taɪ] *f* sacristy
Salat [za'laːt] **(-(e)s, -e)** *m* salad; (*Kopf~*) lettuce; **~soße** *f* salad dressing
Salbe ['zalbə] *f* ointment
Salbei [zal'baɪ] **(-s** *od* **-)** *m od f* sage
Saldo ['zaldo] **(-s, Salden)** *m* balance
Salmiak [zalmi'ak] **(-s)** *m* sal ammoniac; **~geist** *m* liquid ammonia
salopp [za'lɔp] *adj* casual
Salpeter [zal'peːtər] **(-s)** *m* saltpetre; **~säure** *f* nitric acid
Salz [zalts] **(-es, -e)** *nt* salt; **s~en** (*unreg*) *vt* to salt; **s~ig** *adj* salty; **~kartoffeln** *pl* boiled potatoes; **~säure** *f* hydrochloric acid; **~streuer** *m* salt cellar; **~wasser** *nt* (*Meerwasser*) salt water
Samen ['zaːmən] **(-s, -)** *m* seed; (*ANAT*) sperm
Sammelband *m* anthology
sammeln ['zaməln] *vt* to collect ♦ *vr* to assemble, to gather; (*konzentrieren*) to concentrate
Sammlung ['zamlʊŋ] *f* collection; assembly, gathering; concentration

Samstag ['zamstaːk] *m* Saturday; **s~s** *adv* (on) Saturdays
Samt [zamt] **(-(e)s, -e)** *m* velvet
samt *präp +dat* (along) with, together with; **~ und sonders** each and every one (of them)
sämtlich ['zɛmtlɪç] *adj* all (the), entire
Sand [zant] **(-(e)s, -e)** *m* sand
Sandale [zan'daːlə] *f* sandal
Sand- *zW:* **~bank** *f* sandbank; **s~ig** ['zandɪç] *adj* sandy; **~kasten** *m* sandpit; **~kuchen** *m* Madeira cake; **~papier** *nt* sandpaper; **~stein** *m* sandstone; **s~strahlen** *vt insep* to sandblast ♦ *vi insep* to sandblast; **~strand** *m* sandy beach
sandte *etc* ['zantə] *vb siehe* **senden**
Sanduhr *f* hourglass
sanft [zanft] *adj* soft, gentle; **~mütig** *adj* gentle, meek
sang *etc* [zaŋ] *vb siehe* **singen**
Sänger(in) ['zɛŋər(ɪn)] **(-s, -)** *m(f)* singer
Sani- *zW:* **s~eren** [za'niːrən] *vt* to redevelop; (*Betrieb*) to make financially sound ♦ *vr* to line one's pockets; to become financially sound; **s~tär** [zani'tɛːr] *adj* sanitary; **s~täre Anlagen** sanitation *sg*; **~täter** [zani'tɛːtər] **(-s, -)** *m* first-aid attendant; (*MIL*) (medical) orderly
sanktionieren [zaŋktsio'niːrən] *vt* to sanction
Saphir ['zaːfiːr] **(-s, -e)** *m* sapphire
Sardelle [zar'dɛlə] *f* anchovy
Sardine [zar'diːnə] *f* sardine
Sardinien [zar'diːniən] **(-s)** *nt* Sardinia
Sarg [zark] **(-(e)s, ᵈe)** *m* coffin
Sarkasmus [zar'kasmʊs] *m* sarcasm
saß *etc* [zaːs] *vb siehe* **sitzen**
Satan ['zaːtan] **(-s, -e)** *m* Satan; devil
Satellit [zatɛ'liːt] **(-en, -en)** *m* satellite; **~enfernsehen** *nt* satellite television
Satire [za'tiːrə] *f* satire
satirisch [za'tiːrɪʃ] *adj* satirical
satt [zat] *adj* full; (*Farbe*) rich, deep; **jdn/etw ~ sein** *od* **haben** to be fed up with sb/sth; **sich ~ hören/sehen an** +*dat* to hear/see enough of; **sich ~ essen** to eat one's fill; **~ machen** to be filling
Sattel ['zatəl] **(-s, ᵈ)** *m* saddle; (*Berg*)

ridge; **s~n** *vt* to saddle; **~schlepper** *m* articulated lorry

sättigen ['zɛtɪgən] *vt* to satisfy; (*CHEM*) to saturate

Satz [zats] **(-es, ˟e)** *m* (*GRAM*) sentence; (*Neben~, Adverbial~*) clause; (*Theorem*) theorem; (*MUS*) movement; (*TENNIS, Briefmarken etc*) set; (*Kaffee*) grounds *pl*; (*COMM*) rate; (*Sprung*) jump; **~teil** *m* part of a sentence; **~ung** *f* (*Statut*) statute, rule; **~zeichen** *nt* punctuation mark

Sau [zau] **(-, Säue)** *f* sow; (*umg*) dirty pig

sauber ['zaubər] *adj* clean; (*ironisch*) fine; **~halten** (*unreg*) *vt* to keep clean; **S~keit** *f* cleanness; (*einer Person*) cleanliness

säuberlich ['zɔybərlɪç] *adv* neatly

säubern *vt* to clean; (*POL etc*) to purge

Säuberung *f* cleaning; purge

Sauce ['zo:sə] *f* sauce, gravy

sauer ['zauər] *adj* sour; (*CHEM*) acid; (*umg*) cross; **saurer Regen** acid rain

Sauerei [zauə'rai] (*umg*) *f* rotten state of affairs, scandal; (*Schmutz etc*) mess; (*Unanständigkeit*) obscenity

säuerlich *adj* (*Geschmack*) sour; (*mißvergnügt: Gesicht*) dour

Sauer- *zW*: **~milch** *f* sour milk; **~rahm** *m* (*KOCH*) sour cream; **~stoff** *m* oxygen; **~teig** *m* leaven

saufen ['zaufən] (*unreg; umg*) *vt, vi* to drink, to booze

Säufer ['zɔyfər] **(-s, -;** *umg*) *m* boozer

saugen ['zaugən] (*unreg*) *vt, vi* to suck

säugen ['zɔygən] *vt* to suckle

Sauger ['zaugər] **(-s, -)** *m* dummy, comforter (*US*); (*auf Flasche*) teat; (*Staub~*) vacuum cleaner, Hoover ®

Säugetier ['zɔygə-] *nt* mammal

Säugling *m* infant, baby

Säule ['zɔylə] *f* column, pillar

Saum [zaum] **(-(e)s, Säume)** *m* hem; (*Naht*) seam

säumen ['zɔymən] *vt* to hem; to seam ♦ *vi* to delay, to hesitate

Sauna ['zauna] **(-, -s)** *f* sauna

Säure ['zɔyrə] *f* acid; (*Geschmack*) sourness, acidity

sausen ['zauzən] *vi* to blow; (*umg: eilen*) to rush; (*Ohren*) to buzz; **etw ~ lassen**

(*umg*) not to bother with sth

Saxophon [zakso'fo:n] **(-s, -e)** *nt* saxophone

SB *abk* = **Selbstbedienung**

S-Bahn *f abk* (= *Schnellbahn*) high speed railway; (= *Stadtbahn*) suburban railway

schaben ['ʃa:bən] *vt* to scrape

schäbig ['ʃɛ:bɪç] *adj* shabby

Schablone [ʃa'blo:nə] *f* stencil; (*Muster*) pattern; (*fig*) convention

Schach [ʃax] **(-s, -s)** *nt* chess; (*Stellung*) check; **~brett** *nt* chessboard; **~figur** *f* chessman; **s~'matt** *adj* checkmate; **~spiel** *nt* game of chess

Schacht [ʃaxt] **(-(e)s, ˟e)** *m* shaft

Schachtel **(-, -n)** *f* box; (*pej: Frau*) bag, cow

schade ['ʃa:də] *adj* a pity *od* shame ♦ *excl*: **(wie) ~!** (what a) pity *od* shame; **sich** *dat* **zu ~ sein für etw** to consider o.s. too good for sth

Schädel ['ʃɛ:dəl] **(-s, -)** *m* skull; **~bruch** *m* fractured skull

Schaden ['ʃa:dən] **(-s, ˟)** *m* damage; (*Verletzung*) injury; (*Nachteil*) disadvantage; **s~** *vi* +*dat* to hurt; **einer Sache s~** to damage sth; **~ersatz** *m* compensation, damages *pl*; **~freude** *f* malicious glee; **s~froh** *adj* (*Mensch, Lachen*) gloating

schadhaft ['ʃa:thaft] *adj* faulty, damaged

schäd- ['ʃɛ:t] *zW*: **~igen** ['ʃɛdɪgən] *vt* to damage; (*Person*) to do harm to, to harm; **~lich** *adj*: **~lich (für)** harmful (to); **S~lichkeit** *f* harmfulness; **S~ling** *m* pest

Schadstoff ['ʃa:tʃtɔf] *m* harmful substance

Schaf [ʃa:f] **(-(e)s, -e)** *nt* sheep; **~bock** *m* ram

Schäfer ['ʃɛ:fər] **(-s, -)** *m* shepherd; **~hund** *m* Alsatian (dog) (*BRIT*), German shepherd (dog) (*US*)

Schaffen ['ʃafən] **(-s)** *nt* (creative) activity

schaffen¹ (*unreg*) *vt* to create; (*Platz*) to make

schaffen² *vt* (*erreichen*) to manage, to do; (*erledigen*) to finish; (*Prüfung*) to pass; (*transportieren*) to take ♦ *vi* (*umg*:

arbeiten) to work; **sich** *dat* **etw ~** to get o.s. sth; **sich an etw** *dat* **zu ~ machen** to busy o.s. with sth

Schaffner(in) ['ʃafnər(ɪn)] **(-s, -)** *m(f)* (*Bus~*) conductor(tress); (*EISENB*) guard

Schaft [ʃaft] **(-(e)s, ⁼e)** *m* shaft; (*von Gewehr*) stock; (*von Stiefel*) leg; (*BOT*) stalk; tree trunk; **~stiefel** *m* high boot

Schakal [ʃa'ka:l] **(-s, -e)** *m* jackal

Schal [ʃa:l] **(-s, -e** *od* **-s)** *m* scarf

schal *adj* flat; (*fig*) insipid

Schälchen ['ʃɛːlçən] *nt* cup, bowl

Schale ['ʃa:lə] *f* skin; (*abgeschält*) peel; (*Nuß~, Muschel~, Ei~*) shell; (*Geschirr*) dish, bowl

schälen ['ʃɛːlən] *vt* to peel; to shell ♦ *vr* to peel

Schall [ʃal] **(-(e)s, -e)** *m* sound; **~dämpfer** **(-s, -)** *m* (*AUT*) silencer; **s~dicht** *adj* soundproof; **s~en** *vi* to (re)sound; **s~end** *adj* resounding, loud; **~mauer** *f* sound barrier; **~platte** *f* (gramophone) record

Schalt- ['ʃalt] *zW:* **~bild** *nt* circuit diagram; **~brett** *nt* switchboard; **s~en** *vt* to switch, to turn ♦ *vi* (*AUT*) to change (gear); (*umg: begreifen*) to catch on; **~er** **(-s, -)** *m* counter; (*an Gerät*) switch; **~beamte(r)** *m* counter clerk; **~erstunden** *pl* hours of business; **~hebel** *m* switch; (*AUT*) gear-lever; **~jahr** *nt* leap year; **~ung** *f* switching; (*ELEK*) circuit; (*AUT*) gear change

Scham [ʃaːm] **(-)** *f* shame; (*~gefühl*) modesty; (*Organe*) private parts *pl*

schämen ['ʃɛːmən] *vr* to be ashamed

schamlos *adj* shameless

Schande ['ʃandə] **(-)** *f* disgrace

schändlich ['ʃɛntlɪç] *adj* disgraceful, shameful

Schändung ['ʃɛndʊŋ] *f* violation, defilement

Schanktisch ['ʃaŋktɪʃ] *m* bar

Schanze ['ʃantsə] *f* (*Sprung~*) skijump

Schar [ʃaːr] **(-, -en)** *f* band, company; (*Vögel*) flock; (*Menge*) crowd; **in ~en** in droves; **s~en** *vr* to assemble, to rally

scharf [ʃarf] *adj* sharp; (*Essen*) hot, spicy; (*Munition*) live; **~ nachdenken** to think

hard; **auf etw** *akk* **~ sein** (*umg*) to be keen on sth

Schärfe ['ʃɛrfə] *f* sharpness; (*Strenge*) rigour; **s~n** *vt* to sharpen

Scharf- *zW:* **s~machen** (*umg*) *vt* to stir up; **~richter** *m* executioner; **~schütze** *m* marksman, sharpshooter; **s~sinnig** *adj* astute, shrewd

Scharlach ['ʃarlax] **(-s, -e)** *m* (*~fieber*) scarlet fever

Scharnier [ʃar'niːr] **(-s, -e)** *nt* hinge

Schärpe ['ʃɛrpə] *f* sash

scharren ['ʃarən] *vt, vi* to scrape, to scratch

Schaschlik ['ʃaʃlɪk] **(-s, -s)** *m od nt* (shish) kebab

Schatten ['ʃatən] **(-s, -)** *m* shadow; **~riß** *m* silhouette; **~seite** *f* shady side, dark side

schattieren [ʃa'tiːrən] *vt, vi* to shade

schattig ['ʃatɪç] *adj* shady

Schatulle [ʃa'tʊlə] *f* casket; (*Geld~*) coffer

Schatz [ʃats] **(-es, ⁼e)** *m* treasure; (*Person*) darling

schätz- ['ʃɛts] *zW:* **~bar** *adj* assessable; **S~chen** *nt* darling, love; **~en** *vt* (*abschätzen*) to estimate; (*Gegenstand*) to value; (*würdigen*) to value, to esteem; (*vermuten*) to reckon; **S~ung** *f* estimate; estimation; valuation; **nach meiner S~ung ...** I reckon that ...

Schau [ʃaʊ] **(-)** *f* show; (*Ausstellung*) display, exhibition; **etw zur ~ stellen** to make a show of sth, to show sth off; **~bild** *nt* diagram

Schauder ['ʃaʊdər] **(-s, -)** *m* shudder; (*wegen Kälte*) shiver; **s~haft** *adj* horrible; **s~n** *vi* to shudder; to shiver

schauen ['ʃaʊən] *vi* to look

Schauer ['ʃaʊər] **(-s, -)** *m* (*Regen~*) shower; (*Schreck*) shudder; **~geschichte** *f* horror story; **s~lich** *adj* horrific, spine-chilling

Schaufel ['ʃaʊfəl] **(-, -n)** *f* shovel; (*NAUT*) paddle; (*TECH*) scoop; **s~n** *vt* to shovel, to scoop

Schau- *zW:* **~fenster** *nt* shop window; **~fensterbummel** *m* window shopping (expedition); **~kasten** *m* showcase

Schaukel ['ʃaukəl] (-, -n) *f* swing; **s~n** *vi* to swing, to rock; **~pferd** *nt* rocking horse; **~stuhl** *m* rocking chair

Schaulustige(r) *mf* onlooker

Schaum [ʃaum] (-(e)s, **Schäume**) *m* foam; (*Seifen~*) lather

schäumen ['ʃɔymən] *vi* to foam

Schaum- ~gummi *m* foam (rubber); **s~ig** *adj* frothy, foamy; **~stoff** *m* foam material; **~wein** *m* sparkling wine

Schauplatz *m* scene

schaurig ['ʃaurɪç] *adj* horrific, dreadful

Schau- zW: ~spiel *nt* spectacle; (*THEAT*) play; **~spieler(in)** *m(f)* actor (actress); **s~spielern** *vi insep* to act; **~spielhaus** *nt* theatre

Scheck [ʃɛk] (-s, -s) *m* cheque; **~heft** *nt* cheque book; **~karte** *f* cheque card

scheffeln ['ʃɛfəln] *vt* to amass

Scheibe ['ʃaibə] *f* disc; (*Brot etc*) slice; (*Glas~*) pane; (*MIL*) target

Scheiben- zW: ~bremse *f* (*AUT*) disc brake; **~wischer** *m* (*AUT*) windscreen wiper

Scheich [ʃaiç] (-s, -e *od* -s) *m* sheik(h)

Scheide ['ʃaidə] *f* sheath; (*Grenze*) boundary; (*ANAT*) vagina; **s~n** (*unreg*) *vt* to separate; (*Ehe*) to dissolve ♦ *vi* to depart; to part; **sich s~n lassen** to get a divorce

Scheidung *f* (*Ehe~*) divorce

Schein [ʃain] (-(e)s, -e) *m* light; (*An~*) appearance; (*Geld*) (bank)note; (*Bescheinigung*) certificate; **zum ~** in pretence; **s~bar** *adj* apparent; **s~en** (*unreg*) *vi* to shine; (*Anschein haben*) to seem; **s~heilig** *adj* hypocritical; **~werfer** (-s, -) *m* floodlight; spotlight; (*Suchwerfer*) searchlight; (*AUT*) headlamp

Scheiß- ['ʃais] (*umg*) *in zW* bloody

Scheiße (-; *umg*) *f* shit

Scheit [ʃait] (-(e)s, -e *od* -er) *nt* log

Scheitel ['ʃaitəl] (-s, -) *m* top; (*Haar~*) parting; **s~n** *vt* to part

scheitern ['ʃaitərn] *vi* to fail

Schelle ['ʃɛlə] *f* small bell; **s~n** *vi* to ring

Schellfisch ['ʃɛlfɪʃ] *m* haddock

Schelm [ʃɛlm] (-(e)s, -e) *m* rogue; **s~isch** *adj* mischievous, roguish

Schelte ['ʃɛltə] *f* scolding; **s~n** (*unreg*) *vt* to scold

Schema ['ʃeːma] (-s, -s *od* -ta) *nt* scheme, plan; (*Darstellung*) schema; **nach ~** quite mechanically; **s~tisch** [ʃe'maːtɪʃ] *adj* schematic; (*pej*) mechanical

Schemel ['ʃeːməl] (-s, -) *m* (foot)stool

Schenkel ['ʃɛŋkəl] (-s, -) *m* thigh

schenken ['ʃɛŋkən] *vt* (*auch fig*) to give; (*Getränk*) to pour; **sich** *dat* **etw ~** (*umg*) to skip sth; **das ist geschenkt!** (*billig*) that's a giveaway!; (*nichts wert*) that's worthless!

Scherbe ['ʃɛrbə] *f* broken piece, fragment; (*archäologisch*) potsherd

Schere ['ʃeːrə] *f* scissors *pl*; (*groß*) shears *pl*; **s~n** (*unreg*) *vt* to cut; (*Schaf*) to shear; (*kümmern*) to bother ♦ *vr* to care; **scher dich zum Teufel!** get lost!; **~'rei** (*umg*) *f* bother, trouble

Scherz [ʃɛrts] (-es, -e) *m* joke; fun; **~frage** *f* conundrum; **s~haft** *adj* joking, jocular

Scheu [ʃɔy] (-) *f* shyness; (*Angst*) fear; (*Ehrfurcht*) awe; **s~** *adj* shy; **s~en** *vr*: **sich s~en vor** +*dat* to be afraid of, to shrink from ♦ *vt* to shun ♦ *vi* (*Pferd*) to shy

scheuern ['ʃɔyərn] *vt* to scour, to scrub

Scheuklappe *f* blinker

Scheune ['ʃɔynə] *f* barn

Scheusal ['ʃɔyzaːl] (-s, -e) *nt* monster

scheußlich ['ʃɔyslɪç] *adj* dreadful, frightful

Schi [ʃiː] *m* = **Ski**

Schicht [ʃɪçt] (-, -en) *f* layer; (*Klasse*) class, level; (*in Fabrik etc*) shift; **~arbeit** *f* shift work; **s~en** *vt* to layer, to stack

schick [ʃɪk] *adj* stylish, chic

schicken *vt* to send ♦ *vr*: **sich ~** (**in** +*akk*) to resign o.s. (to) ♦ *vb unpers* (*anständig sein*) to be fitting

schicklich *adj* proper, fitting

Schicksal (-s, -e) *nt* fate; **~sschlag** *m* great misfortune, blow

Schieb- ['ʃiːb] *zW:* **~edach** *nt* (*AUT*) sun roof; **s~en** (*unreg*) *vt* (*auch Drogen*) to push; (*Schuld*) to put ♦ *vi* to push; **~etür** *f* sliding door; **~ung** *f* fiddle

Schieds- ['ʃiːts] *zW:* **~gericht** *nt* court of arbitration; **~richter** *m* referee; umpire; (*Schlichter*) arbitrator

schief [ʃiːf] *adj* crooked; (*Ebene*) sloping; (*Turm*) leaning; (*Winkel*) oblique; (*Blick*) funny; (*Vergleich*) distorted ♦ *adv* crooked(ly); (*ansehen*) askance; **etw ~ stellen** to slope sth

Schiefer ['ʃiːfər] (**-s, -**) *m* slate; **~dach** *nt* slate roof

schiefgehen (*unreg; umg*) *vi* to go wrong

schielen ['ʃiːlən] *vi* to squint; **nach etw ~** (*fig*) to eye sth

schien *etc* [ʃiːn] *vb siehe* **scheinen**

Schienbein *nt* shinbone

Schiene ['ʃiːnə] *f* rail; (*MED*) splint; **s~n** *vt* to put in splints

schier [ʃiːr] *adj* (*fig*) sheer ♦ *adv* nearly, almost

Schieß- ['ʃiːs] *zW:* **~bude** *f* shooting gallery; **s~en** (*unreg*) *vt* to shoot; (*Ball*) to kick; (*Geschoß*) to fire ♦ *vi* to shoot; (*Salat etc*) to run to seed; **s~en auf** +*akk* to shoot at; **~e'rei** *f* shooting incident, shoot-up; **~pulver** *nt* gunpowder; **~scharte** *f* embrasure

Schiff [ʃɪf] (**-(e)s, -e**) *nt* ship, vessel; (*Kirchen~*) nave; **s~bar** *adj* (*Fluß*) navigable; **~bruch** *m* shipwreck; **s~brüchig** *adj* shipwrecked; **~chen** *nt* small boat; (*Weben*) shuttle; (*Mütze*) forage cap; **~er** (**-s, -**) *m* bargeman, boatman; **~(f)ahrt** *f* shipping; (*Reise*) voyage; **~(fahrts)linie** *f* shipping route

Schikane [ʃiˈkaːnə] *f* harassment; dirty trick; **mit allen ~n** with all the trimmings

schikanieren [ʃikaˈniːrən] *vt* to harass, to torment

Schild¹ [ʃɪlt] (**-(e)s, -e**) *m* shield; **etw im Schilde führen** to be up to sth

Schild² (**-(e)s, -er**) *nt* sign; nameplate; (*Etikett*) label

Schilddrüse *f* thyroid gland

schildern ['ʃɪldərn] *vt* to depict, to portray

Schildkröte *f* tortoise; (*Wasser~*) turtle

Schilf [ʃɪlf] (**-(e)s, -e**) *nt* (*Pflanze*) reed; (*Material*) reeds *pl*, rushes *pl*; **~rohr** *nt*

(*Pflanze*) reed

schillern ['ʃɪlərn] *vi* to shimmer; **~d** *adj* iridescent

Schilling ['ʃɪlɪŋ] *m* shilling

Schimmel ['ʃɪməl] (**-s, -**) *m* mould; (*Pferd*) white horse; **s~ig** *adj* mouldy; **s~n** *vi* to go mouldy

Schimmer ['ʃɪmər] (**-s**) *m* (*Lichtsein*) glimmer; (*Glanz*) shimmer

schimmern ['ʃɪmərn] *vi* to glimmer, to shimmer

Schimpanse [ʃɪmˈpanzə] (**-n, -n**) *m* chimpanzee

schimpfen ['ʃɪmpfən] *vt* to scold ♦ *vi* to curse, to complain; to scold

Schimpfwort *nt* term of abuse

schinden ['ʃɪndən] (*unreg*) *vt* to maltreat, to drive too hard ♦ *vr:* **sich ~ (mit)** to sweat and strain (at), to toil away (at); **Eindruck ~** (*umg*) to create an impression

Schinde'rei *f* grind, drudgery

Schinken ['ʃɪŋkən] (**-s, -**) *m* ham

Schippe ['ʃɪpə] *f* shovel; **s~n** *vt* to shovel

Schirm [ʃɪrm] (**-(e)s, -e**) *m* (*Regen~*) umbrella; (*Sonnen~*) parasol, sunshade; (*Wand~, Bild~*) screen; (*Lampen~*) (lamp)shade; (*Mützen~*) peak; (*Pilz~*) cap; **~mütze** *f* peaked cap; **~ständer** *m* umbrella stand

schizophren [ʃitsoˈfreːn] *adj* schizophrenic

Schlacht [ʃlaxt] (**-, -en**) *f* battle; **s~en** *vt* to slaughter, to kill; **~er** (**-s, -**) *m* butcher; **~feld** *nt* battlefield; **~hof** *m* slaughterhouse, abattoir; **~schiff** *nt* battleship; **~vieh** *nt* animals kept for meat; beef cattle

Schlacke ['ʃlakə] *f* slag

Schlaf [ʃlaːf] (**-(e)s**) *m* sleep; **~anzug** *m* pyjamas *pl*

Schläfe ['ʃlɛːfə] *f* (*ANAT*) temple

schlafen ['ʃlaːfən] (*unreg*) *vi* to sleep; **~ gehen** to go to bed; **S~gehen** (**-s**) *nt* going to bed; **S~szeit** *f* bedtime

schlaff [ʃlaf] *adj* slack; (*energielos*) limp; (*erschöpft*) exhausted

Schlaf- *zW:* **~gelegenheit** *f* sleeping accommodation; **~lied** *nt* lullaby; **s~los**

adj sleepless; **~losigkeit** *f* sleeplessness, insomnia; **~mittel** *nt* sleeping pill
schläfrig [ˈʃlɛːfrɪç] *adj* sleepy
Schlaf- *zW*: **~saal** *m* dormitory; **~sack** *m* sleeping bag; **~tablette** *f* sleeping pill; **~wagen** *m* sleeping car, sleeper; **s~wandeln** *vi insep* to sleepwalk; **~zimmer** *nt* bedroom
Schlag [ʃlaːk] **(-(e)s, ⸚e)** *m* (*auch fig*) blow; (*auch MED*) stroke; (*Puls~, Herz~*) beat; (*ELEK*) shock; (*Blitz~*) bolt, stroke; (*Autotür*) car door; (*umg: Portion*) helping; (*Art*) kind, type; **Schläge** *pl* (*Tracht Prügel*) beating *sg*; **mit einem ~** all at once; **~ auf ~** in rapid succession; **~ader** *f* artery; **~anfall** *m* stroke; **s~artig** *adj* sudden, without warning; **~baum** *m* barrier; **s~en** [ˈʃlaːgən] (*unreg*) *vt, vi* to strike, to hit; (*wiederholt schlagen, besiegen*) to beat; (*Glocke*) to ring; (*Stunde*) to strike; (*Sahne*) to whip; (*Schlacht*) to fight ♦ *vr* to fight; **nach jdm s~en** (*fig*) to take after sb; **sich gut s~en** (*fig*) to do well; **~er** [ˈʃlaːgər] **(-s, -)** *m* (*auch fig*) hit
Schläger [ˈʃlɛːgər] *m* brawler; (*SPORT*) bat; (*TENNIS etc*) racket; (*GOLF*) club; hockey stick; (*Waffe*) rapier; **Schläge'rei** *f* fight, punch-up
Schlagersänger(in) *m(f)* pop singer
Schlag- *zW*: **s~fertig** *adj* quick-witted; **~fertigkeit** *f* ready wit, quickness of repartee; **~loch** *nt* pothole; **~obers** (*ÖSTERR*) *nt*, **~sahne** *f* (whipped) cream; **~seite** *f* (*NAUT*) list; **~wort** *nt* slogan, catch phrase; **~zeile** *f* headline; **~zeug** *nt* percussion; drums *pl*; **~zeuger** **(-s, -)** *m* drummer
Schlamassel [ʃlaˈmasəl] **(-s, -;** *umg*) *m* mess
Schlamm [ʃlam] **(-(e)s, -e)** *m* mud; **s~ig** *adj* muddy
Schlamp- *zW*: **~e** (*umg*) *f* slut; **s~en** (*umg*) *vi* to be sloppy; **~e'rei** (*umg*) *f* disorder, untidiness; sloppy work; **s~ig** (*umg*) *adj* (*Mensch, Arbeit*) sloppy, messy
Schlange [ˈʃlaŋə] *f* snake; (*Menschen~*) queue (*BRIT*), line-up (*US*); **~ stehen** to (form a) queue, to line up

schlängeln [ˈʃlɛŋəln] *vr* (*Schlange*) to wind; (*Weg*) to wind, twist; (*Fluß*) to meander
Schlangen- *zW*: **~biß** *m* snake bite; **~gift** *nt* snake venom; **~linie** *f* wavy line
schlank [ʃlaŋk] *adj* slim, slender; **S~heit** *f* slimness, slenderness; **S~heitskur** *f* diet
schlapp [ʃlap] *adj* limp; (*locker*) slack; **S~e** (*umg*) *f* setback
Schlaraffenland [ʃlaˈrafənlant] *nt* land of milk and honey
schlau [ʃlaʊ] *adj* crafty, cunning
Schlauch [ʃlaʊx] **(-(e)s, Schläuche)** *m* hose; (*in Reifen*) inner tube; (*umg: Anstrengung*) grind; **~boot** *nt* rubber dinghy; **s~en** (*umg*) *vt* to tell on, to exhaust; **s~los** *adj* (*Reifen*) tubeless
Schläue [ˈʃlɔʏə] **(-)** *f* cunning
Schlaufe [ˈʃlaʊfə] *f* loop; (*Aufhänger*) hanger
Schlauheit *f* cunning
Schlaukopf *m* clever dick
schlecht [ʃlɛçt] *adj* bad ♦ *adv* badly; **~ gelaunt** in a bad mood; **~ und recht** after a fashion; **jdm ist ~** sb feels sick *od* bad; **~gehen** *vi unpers*: **jdm geht es ~** sb is in a bad way; **S~igkeit** *f* badness; bad deed; **~machen** *vt* to run down
schlecken [ˈʃlɛkən] *vt, vi* to lick
Schlegel [ˈʃleːgəl] **(-s, -)** *m* (drum)stick; (*Hammer*) mallet, hammer; (*KOCH*) leg
schleichen [ˈʃlaɪçən] (*unreg*) *vi* to creep, to crawl; **~d** *adj* gradual; creeping
Schleichwerbung *f* (*KOMM*) plug
Schleier [ˈʃlaɪər] **(-s, -)** *m* veil; **s~haft** (*umg*) *adj*: **jdm s~haft sein** to be a mystery to sb
Schleif- [ʃlaɪf] *zW*: **~e** *f* loop; (*Band*) bow; **s~en¹** *vt, vi* to drag; **s~en²** (*unreg*) *vt* to grind; (*Edelstein*) to cut; (*MIL: Soldaten*) to drill; **~stein** *m* grindstone
Schleim [ʃlaɪm] **(-(e)s, -e)** *m* slime; (*MED*) mucus; (*KOCH*) gruel; **~haut** *f* (*ANAT*) mucous membrane; **s~ig** *adj* slimy
Schlemm- [ʃlɛm] *zW*: **s~en** *vi* to feast; **~er** **(-s, -)** *m* gourmet; **~e'rei** *f* gluttony, feasting
schlendern [ˈʃlɛndərn] *vi* to stroll

schlenkern ['ʃlɛŋkərn] *vt, vi* to swing, to dangle

Schlepp- ['ʃlɛp] *zW:* ~**e** *f* train; **s~en** *vt* to drag; (*Auto, Schiff*) to tow; (*tragen*) to lug; **s~end** *adj* dragging, slow; ~**er** (-s, -) *m* tractor; (*Schiff*) tug

Schlesien ['ʃleːziən] (-s) *nt* (*GEOG*) Silesia

Schleuder ['ʃlɔydər] (-, -n) *f* catapult; (*Wäsche~*) spin-drier; (*Butter~ etc*) centrifuge; **s~n** *vt* to hurl; (*Wäsche*) to spin-dry ♦ *vi* (*AUT*) to skid; ~**preis** *m* give-away price; ~**sitz** *m* (*AVIAT*) ejector seat; (*fig*) hot seat; ~**ware** *f* cheap *od* cut-price goods *pl*

schleunigst ['ʃlɔynɪçst] *adv* straight away

Schleuse ['ʃlɔyzə] *f* lock; (*~ntor*) sluice

schlicht [ʃlɪçt] *adj* simple, plain; ~**en** *vt* (*glätten*) to smooth, to dress; (*Streit*) to settle; **S~er** (-s, -) *m* mediator, arbitrator; **S~ung** *f* settlement; arbitration

Schlick [ʃlɪk] (-(e)s, -e) *m* mud; (*Öl~*) slick

schlief *etc* [ʃliːf] *vb siehe* **schlafen**

Schließ- ['ʃliːs] *zW:* ~**e** *f* fastener; **s~en** (*unreg*) *vt* to close, to shut; (*beenden*) to close; (*Freundschaft, Bündnis, Ehe*) to enter into; (*folgern*): **s~en (aus)** to infer (from) ♦ *vi, vr* to close, to shut; **etw in sich s~en** to include sth; ~**fach** *nt* locker; **s~lich** *adv* finally; **s~lich doch** after all

Schliff [ʃlɪf] (-(e)s, -e) *m* cut(ting); (*fig*) polish

schlimm [ʃlɪm] *adj* bad; ~**er** *adj* worse; ~**ste(r, s)** *adj* worst; ~**stenfalls** *adv* at (the) worst

Schlinge ['ʃlɪŋə] *f* loop; (*bes Henker~*) noose; (*Falle*) snare; (*MED*) sling; ~**l** (-s, -) *m* rascal; **s~n** (*unreg*) *vt* to wind; (*essen*) to bolt, to gobble ♦ *vi* to bolt one's food, to gobble; **s~rn** *vi* to roll

Schlips [ʃlɪps] (-es, -e) *m* tie

Schlitten ['ʃlɪtən] (-s, -) *m* sledge, sleigh; ~**fahren** (-s) *nt* tobogganing

schlittern ['ʃlɪtərn] *vi* to slide

Schlittschuh ['ʃlɪtʃuː] *m* skate; ~ **laufen** to skate; ~**bahn** *f* skating rink; ~**läufer(in)** *m(f)* skater

Schlitz [ʃlɪts] (-es, -e) *m* slit; (*für Münze*) slot; (*Hosen~*) flies *pl*; **s~äugig** *adj* slant-eyed; **s~en** *vt* to slit

Schloß [ʃlɔs] (-sses, =sser) *nt* lock; (*an Schmuck etc*) clasp; (*Bau*) castle; chateau

schloß *etc vb siehe* **schließen**

Schlosser ['ʃlɔsər] (-s, -) *m* (*Auto~*) fitter; (*für Schlüssel etc*) locksmith; ~**ei** [-'raɪ] *f* metal (working) shop

Schlot [ʃloːt] (-(e)s, -e) *m* chimney; (*NAUT*) funnel

schlottern ['ʃlɔtərn] *vi* to shake, to tremble; (*Kleidung*) to be baggy

Schlucht [ʃlʊxt] (-, -en) *f* gorge, ravine

schluchzen ['ʃlʊxtsən] *vi* to sob

Schluck [ʃlʊk] (-(e)s, -e) *m* swallow; (*Menge*) drop; ~**auf** (-s, -s) *m* hiccups *pl*; **s~en** *vt, vi* to swallow

schludern ['ʃluːdərn] *vi* to skimp, to do sloppy work

schlug *etc* [ʃluːk] *vb siehe* **schlagen**

Schlummer ['ʃlʊmər] (-s) *m* slumber; **s~n** *vi* to slumber

Schlund [ʃlʊnt] (-(e)s, =e) *m* gullet; (*fig*) jaw

schlüpfen ['ʃlʏpfən] *vi* to slip; (*Vogel etc*) to hatch (out)

Schlüpfer ['ʃlʏpfər] (-s, -) *m* panties *pl*, knickers *pl*

schlüpfrig ['ʃlʏpfrɪç] *adj* slippery; (*fig*) lewd; **S~keit** *f* slipperiness; (*fig*) lewdness

schlurfen ['ʃlʊrfən] *vi* to shuffle

schlürfen ['ʃlʏrfən] *vt, vi* to slurp

Schluß [ʃlʊs] (-sses, =sse) *m* end; (*~folgerung*) conclusion; **am ~** at the end; **~ machen mit** to finish with

Schlüssel ['ʃlʏsəl] (-s, -) *m* (*auch fig*) key; (*Schraub~*) spanner, wrench; (*MUS*) clef; ~**bein** *nt* collarbone; ~**blume** *f* cowslip, primrose; ~**bund** *m* bunch of keys; ~**loch** *nt* keyhole; ~**position** *f* key position; ~**wort** *nt* keyword

schlüssig ['ʃlʏsɪç] *adj* conclusive

Schluß- *zW:* ~**licht** *nt* taillight; (*fig*) tailender; ~**strich** *m* (*fig*) final stroke; ~**verkauf** *m* clearance sale

schmächtig ['ʃmɛçtɪç] *adj* slight

schmackhaft ['ʃmakhaft] *adj* tasty

schmal [ʃmaːl] *adj* narrow; (*Person, Buch*

etc) slender, slim; (*karg*) meagre

schmälern ['ʃmɛːlərn] *vt* to diminish; (*fig*) to belittle

Schmalfilm *m* cine film

Schmalz [ʃmalts] (*-es, -e*) *nt* dripping, lard; (*fig*) sentiment, schmaltz; **s~ig** *adj* (*fig*) schmaltzy

schmarotzen [ʃmaˈrɔtsən] *vi* to sponge; (*BOT*) to be parasitic

Schmarotzer (*-s, -*) *m* parasite; sponger

Schmarren ['ʃmarən] (*-s, -*) *m* (*ÖSTERR*) small piece of pancake; (*fig*) rubbish, tripe

schmatzen ['ʃmatsən] *vi* to smack one's lips; to eat noisily

schmecken ['ʃmɛkən] *vt, vi* to taste; **es schmeckt ihm** he likes it

Schmeichel- ['ʃmaɪçəl] *zW:* **~ei** [-'laɪ] *f* flattery; **s~haft** *adj* flattering; **s~n** *vi* to flatter

schmeißen ['ʃmaɪsən] (*unreg; umg*) *vt* to throw, to chuck

Schmeißfliege *f* bluebottle

Schmelz [ʃmɛlts] (*-es, -e*) *m* enamel; (*Glasur*) glaze; (*von Stimme*) melodiousness; **s~en** (*unreg*) *vt* to melt; (*Erz*) to smelt ♦ *vi* to melt; **~punkt** *m* melting point; **~wasser** *nt* melted snow

Schmerz [ʃmɛrts] (*-es, -en*) *m* pain; (*Trauer*) grief; **s~empfindlich** *adj* sensitive to pain; **s~en** *vt, vi* to hurt; **~ensgeld** *nt* compensation; **s~haft** *adj* painful; **s~lich** *adj* painful; **s~los** *adj* painless; **~mittel** *nt* painkiller; **s~stillend** *adj* soothing; **~tablette** *f* painkiller

Schmetterling ['ʃmɛtərlɪŋ] *m* butterfly

schmettern ['ʃmɛtərn] *vt* (*werfen*) to hurl; (*TENNIS: Ball*) to smash; (*singen*) to belt out (*inf*)

Schmied [ʃmiːt] (*-(e)s, -e*) *m* blacksmith; **~e** ['ʃmiːdə] *f* smithy, forge; **~eeisen** *nt* wrought iron; **s~en** *vt* to forge; (*Pläne*) to devise, to concoct

schmiegen ['ʃmiːgən] *vt* to press, to nestle ♦ *vr:* **sich ~ (an** +*akk*) to cuddle up (to), to nestle (up to)

Schmier- ['ʃmiːr] *zW:* **~e** *f* grease; (*THEAT*) greasepaint, make-up; **s~en** *vt* to smear;

(*ölen*) to lubricate, to grease; (*bestechen*) to bribe; (*schreiben*) to scrawl ♦ *vi* to scrawl; **~fett** *nt* grease; **~geld** *nt* bribe; **s~ig** *adj* greasy; **~seife** *f* soft soap

Schminke ['ʃmɪŋkə] *f* make-up; **s~n** *vt, vr* to make up

schmirgeln ['ʃmɪrgəln] *vt* to sand (down)

Schmirgelpapier *nt* emery paper

schmollen ['ʃmɔlən] *vi* to sulk, to pout

Schmorbraten *m* stewed *od* braised meat

schmoren ['ʃmoːrən] *vt* to stew, to braise

Schmuck [ʃmʊk] (*-(e)s, -e*) *m* jewellery; (*Verzierung*) decoration

schmücken ['ʃmʏkən] *vt* to decorate

Schmuck- *zW:* **s~los** *adj* unadorned, plain; **~sachen** *pl* jewels, jewellery *sg*

Schmuggel ['ʃmʊgəl] (*-s*) *m* smuggling; **s~n** *vt, vi* to smuggle

Schmuggler (*-s, -*) *m* smuggler

schmunzeln ['ʃmʊntsəln] *vi* to smile benignly

schmusen ['ʃmuːzən] (*umg*) *vi* (*zärtlich sein*) to cuddle, canoodle (*inf*)

Schmutz [ʃmʊts] (*-es*) *m* dirt, filth; **~fink** *m* filthy creature; **~fleck** *m* stain; **s~ig** *adj* dirty

Schnabel ['ʃnaːbəl] (*-s, ˝*) *m* beak, bill; (*Ausguß*) spout

Schnake ['ʃnaːkə] *f* cranefly; (*Stechmücke*) gnat

Schnalle ['ʃnalə] *f* buckle, clasp; **s~n** *vt* to buckle

Schnapp- ['ʃnap] *zW:* **s~en** *vt* to grab, to catch ♦ *vi* to snap; **~schloß** *nt* spring lock; **~schuß** *m* (*PHOT*) snapshot

Schnaps [ʃnaps] (*-es, ˝e*) *m* spirits *pl*; schnapps

schnarchen ['ʃnarçən] *vi* to snore

schnattern ['ʃnatərn] *vi* (*Gänse*) to gabble; (*Ente*) to quack; (*zittern*) to shiver

schnauben ['ʃnaʊbən] *vi* to snort ♦ *vr* to blow one's nose

schnaufen ['ʃnaʊfən] *vi* to puff, to pant

Schnauze ['ʃnaʊtsə] *f* snout, muzzle; (*Ausguß*) spout; (*umg*) gob

Schnecke ['ʃnɛkə] *f* snail; **~nhaus** *nt* snail's shell

Schnee [ʃneː] (*-s*) *m* snow; (*Ei~*) beaten

egg white; **~ball** *m* snowball; **~flocke** *f* snowflake; **~gestöber** *nt* snowstorm; **~glöckchen** *nt* snowdrop; **~kette** *f* (AUT) snow chain; **~mann** *m* snowman; **~pflug** *m* snowplough; **~schmelze** *f* thaw

Schneid [ʃnait] (-(e)s; *umg*) *m* pluck

Schneide ['ʃnaidə] *f* edge; (*Klinge*) blade; **s~n** (*unreg*) *vt* to cut; (*kreuzen*) to cross, to intersect with ♦ *vr* to cut o.s.; to cross, to intersect; **s~nd** *adj* cutting; **~r** (-s, -) *m* tailor; **~rei** *f* (*Geschäft*) tailor's; **~rin** *f* dressmaker; **s~rn** *vt* to make ♦ *vi* to be a tailor; **~zahn** *m* incisor

schneien ['ʃnaiən] *vi unpers* to snow

Schneise ['ʃnaizə] *f* clearing

schnell [ʃnɛl] *adj* quick, fast ♦ *adv* quick, quickly, fast; **S~hefter** (-s, -) *m* loose-leaf binder; **S~igkeit** *f* speed; **S~imbiß** *m* (*Lokal*) snack bar; **S~kochtopf** *m* (*Dampfkochtopf*) pressure cooker; **S~reinigung** *f* dry cleaner's; **~stens** *adv* as quickly as possible; **S~straße** *f* expressway; **S~zug** *m* fast *od* express train

schneuzen ['ʃnɔytsən] *vr* to blow one's nose

schnippeln (*umg*) *vt*: **~(an** +*dat*) to snip (at)

schnippisch ['ʃnɪpɪʃ] *adj* sharp-tongued

Schnitt [ʃnɪt] (-(e)s, -e) *m* cut(ting); (*~punkt*) intersection; (*Quer~*) (cross) section; (*Durch~*) average; (*~muster*) pattern; (*an Buch*) edge; (*umg: Gewinn*) profit

schnitt *etc vb siehe* **schneiden**

Schnitt- *zW*: **~blumen** *pl* cut flowers; **~e** *f* slice; (*belegt*) sandwich; **~fläche** *f* section; **~lauch** *m* chive; **~muster** *nt* pattern; **~punkt** *m* (point of) intersection; **~stelle** *f* (COMPUT) interface; **~wunde** *f* cut

Schnitz- ['ʃnɪts] *zW*: **~arbeit** *f* wood carving; **~el** (-s, -) *nt* chip; (KOCH) escalope; **s~en** *vt* to carve; **~er** (-s, -) *m* carver; (*umg*) blunder; **~e'rei** *f* carving; carved woodwork

schnodderig ['ʃnɔdərɪç] (*umg*) *adj* snotty

Schnorchel ['ʃnɔrçəl] (-s, -) *m* snorkel

Schnörkel ['ʃnœrkəl] (-s, -) *m* flourish; (ARCHIT) scroll

schnorren ['ʃnɔrən] *vt, vi* to cadge

schnüffeln ['ʃnyfəln] *vi* to sniff; **S~** (*umg*) *nt* (*von Klebstoff etc*) glue-sniffing *etc*

Schnüffler (-s, -) *m* snooper

Schnuller ['ʃnulər] (-s, -) *m* dummy, comforter (US)

Schnupfen ['ʃnupfən] (-s, -) *m* cold

schnuppern ['ʃnupərn] *vi* to sniff

Schnur [ʃnuːr] (-, ~e) *f* string, cord; (ELEK) flex

schnüren ['ʃnyːrən] *vt* to tie

schnurgerade *adj* straight (as a die)

Schnurrbart *m* moustache

schnurren ['ʃnurən] *vi* to purr; (*Kreisel*) to hum

Schnürschuh *m* lace-up (shoe)

Schnürsenkel *m* shoelace

schnurstracks *adv* straight (away)

Schock [ʃɔk] (-(e)s, -e) *m* shock; **s~ieren** [ʃɔ'kiːrən] *vt* to shock, to outrage

Schöffe ['ʃœfə] (-n, -n) *m* lay magistrate

Schöffin *f* lay magistrate

Schokolade [ʃoko'laːdə] *f* chocolate

Scholle ['ʃɔlə] *f* clod; (*Eis~*) ice floe; (*Fisch*) plaice

---

SCHLÜSSELWORT

schon [ʃoːn] *adv* **1** (*bereits*) already; **er ist schon da** he's there already, he's already there; **ist er schon da?** is he there yet?; **warst du schon einmal da?** have you ever been there?; **ich war schon einmal da** I've been there before; **das war schon immer so** that has always been the case; **schon oft** often; **hast du schon gehört?** have you heard?
2 (*bestimmt*) all right; **du wirst schon sehen** you'll see (all right); **das wird schon noch gut** that'll be OK
3 (*bloß*) just; **allein schon das Gefühl ...** just the very feeling ...; **schon der Gedanke** the very thought; **wenn ich das schon höre** I only have to hear that
4 (*einschränkend*): **ja schon, aber ...** yes (well), but ...
5: **schon möglich** possible; **schon gut!**

OK!; **du weißt schon** you know; **komm schon!** come on!

schön [ʃøːn] *adj* beautiful; (*nett*) nice; **~e Grüße** best wishes; **~e Ferien** have a nice holiday; **~en Dank** (many) thanks
schonen [ˈʃoːnən] *vt* to look after ♦ *vr* to take it easy; **~d** *adj* careful, gentle
Schön- *zW*: **~heit** *f* beauty; **~heitsfehler** *m* blemish, flaw; **~heitsoperation** *f* cosmetic surgery
Schonkost (-) *f* light diet; (*Spezialdiät*) special diet
schönmachen *vr* to make o.s. look nice
Schon- *zW*: **~ung** *f* good care; (*Nachsicht*) consideration; (*Forst*) plantation of young trees; **s~ungslos** *adj* unsparing, harsh; **~zeit** *f* close season
Schöpf- [ˈʃœpf] *zW*: **s~en** *vt* to scoop, to ladle; (*Mut*) to summon up; (*Luft*) to breathe in; **~er** (-s, -) *m* creator; **s~erisch** *adj* creative; **~kelle** *f* ladle; **~ung** *f* creation
Schorf [ʃɔrf] (-(e)s, -e) *m* scab
Schornstein [ˈʃɔrnʃtain] *m* chimney; (*NAUT*) funnel; **~feger** (-s, -) *m* chimney sweep
Schoß [ʃoːs] (-es, ⁓e) *m* lap; (*Rock~*) coat tail
schoß *etc vb siehe* **schießen**
Schoßhund *m* pet dog, lapdog
Schote [ˈʃoːtə] *f* pod
Schotte [ˈʃɔtə] *m* Scot, Scotsman
Schotter [ˈʃɔtər] (-s) *m* broken stone, road metal; (*EISENB*) ballast
Schott- [ʃɔt] *zW*: **~in** *f* Scot, Scotswoman; **s~isch** *adj* Scottish, Scots; **~land** *nt* Scotland
schraffieren [ʃraˈfiːrən] *vt* to hatch
schräg [ʃrɛːk] *adj* slanting, not straight; **etw ~ stellen** to put sth at an angle; **~ gegenüber** diagonally opposite; **S~e** [ˈʃrɛːgə] *f* slant; **S~strich** *m* oblique stroke
Schramme [ˈʃramə] *f* scratch; **s~n** *vt* to scratch
Schrank [ʃraŋk] (-(e)s, ⁓e) *m* cupboard; (*Kleider~*) wardrobe; **~e** *f* barrier; **~enwärter** *m* (*EISENB*) level crossing

attendant; **~koffer** *m* trunk
Schraube [ˈʃraubə] *f* screw; **s~n** *vt* to screw; **~nschlüssel** *m* spanner; **~nzieher** (-s, -) *m* screwdriver
Schraubstock [ˈʃraupʃtɔk] *m* (*TECH*) vice
Schreck [ʃrɛk] (-(e)s, -e) *m* terror; fright; **~en** (-s, -) *m* terror; fright; **s~en** *vt* to frighten, to scare; **~gespenst** *nt* spectre, nightmare; **s~haft** *adj* jumpy, easily frightened; **s~lich** *adj* terrible, dreadful
Schrei [ʃrai] (-(e)s, -e) *m* scream; (*Ruf*) shout
Schreib- [ˈʃraib] *zW*: **~block** *m* writing pad; **s~en** (*unreg*) *vt, vi* to write; (*buchstabieren*) to spell; **~en** (-s, -) *nt* letter, communication; **s~faul** *adj* bad about writing letters; **~kraft** *f* typist; **~maschine** *f* typewriter; **~papier** *nt* notepaper; **~tisch** *m* desk; **~ung** *f* spelling; **~waren** *pl* stationery *sg*; **~weise** *f* spelling; way of writing; **~zentrale** *f* typing pool; **~zeug** *nt* writing materials *pl*
schreien [ˈʃraiən] (*unreg*) *vt, vi* to scream; (*rufen*) to shout; **~d** *adj* (*fig*) glaring; (*Farbe*) loud
Schrein (-(e)s, -e) *m* shrine
Schreiner [ˈʃrainər] (-s, -) *m* joiner; (*Zimmermann*) carpenter; (*Möbel~*) cabinetmaker; **~ei** [-ˈrai] *f* joiner's workshop
schreiten [ˈʃraitən] (*unreg*) *vi* to stride
schrieb *etc* [ʃriːp] *vb siehe* **schreiben**
Schrift [ʃrift] (-, -en) *f* writing; handwriting; (*~art*) script; (*Gedrucktes*) pamphlet, work; **~deutsch** *nt* written German; **~führer** *m* secretary; **s~lich** *adj* written ♦ *adv* in writing; **~sprache** *f* written language; **~steller(in)** (-s, -) *m(f)* writer; **~stück** *nt* document; **~wechsel** *m* correspondence
schrill [ʃril] *adj* shrill
Schritt [ʃrit] (-(e)s, -e) *m* step; (*Gangart*) walk; (*Tempo*) pace; (*von Hose*) crutch; **~ fahren** to drive at walking pace; **~macher** (-s, -) *m* pacemaker; **~(t)empo** *nt*: **im ~(t)empo** at a walking pace
schroff [ʃrɔf] *adj* steep; (*zackig*) jagged; (*fig*) brusque; (*ungeduldig*) abrupt

schröpfen ['ʃrœpfən] vt (fig) to fleece
Schrot [ʃroːt] (-(e)s, -e) m od nt (Blei) (small) shot; (Getreide) coarsely ground grain, groats pl; ~**flinte** f shotgun
Schrott [ʃrɔt] (-(e)s, -e) m scrap metal; ~**haufen** m scrap heap; s~**reif** adj ready for the scrap heap
schrubben ['ʃrʊbən] vt to scrub
Schrubber (-s, -) m scrubbing brush
schrumpfen ['ʃrʊmpfən] vi to shrink; (Apfel) to shrivel
Schub- ['ʃuːb] zW: ~**fach** nt drawer; ~**karren** m wheelbarrow; ~**lade** f drawer
Schubs [ʃʊps] (-es, -e) (umg) m shove (inf), push
schüchtern ['ʃʏçtərn] adj shy; **S~heit** f shyness
Schuft [ʃʊft] (-(e)s, -e) m scoundrel
schuften (umg) vi to graft, to slave away
Schuh [ʃuː] (-(e)s, -e) m shoe; ~**band** nt shoelace; ~**creme** f shoe polish; ~**größe** f shoe size; ~**löffel** m shoehorn; ~**macher** (-s, -) m shoemaker
Schul- zW: ~**arbeit** f homework (no pl); ~**aufgaben** pl homework sg; ~**besuch** m school attendance; ~**buch** nt school book
Schuld [ʃʊlt] (-, -en) f guilt; (FIN) debt; (Verschulden) fault; **s~** adj: **s~ sein od haben** (an +dat) to be to blame (for); **er ist od hat s~** it's his fault; **jdm s~ geben** to blame sb; **s~en** ['ʃʊldən] vt to owe; **s~enfrei** adj free from debt; ~**gefühl** nt feeling of guilt; **s~ig** adj guilty; (gebührend) due; **s~ig an etw** dat **sein** to be guilty of sth; **jdm etw s~ig sein** to owe sb sth; **jdm etw s~ig bleiben** not to provide sb with sth; **s~los** adj innocent, without guilt; ~**ner** (-s, -) m debtor; ~**schein** m promissory note, IOU
Schule ['ʃuːlə] f school; **s~n** vt to train, to school
Schüler(in) ['ʃyːlər(ɪn)] (-s, -) m(f) pupil
Schul- zW: ~**ferien** pl school holidays; **s~frei** adj: **s~freier Tag** holiday; **s~frei sein** to be a holiday; ~**hof** m playground; ~**jahr** nt school year; ~**junge** m schoolboy; ~**kind** nt schoolchild; ~**mädchen** nt schoolgirl; **s~pflichtig** adj of school age; ~**schiff** nt (NAUT) training ship; ~**stunde** f period, lesson; ~**tasche** f school bag

Schulter ['ʃʊltər] (-, -n) f shoulder; ~**blatt** nt shoulder blade; **s~n** vt to shoulder
Schulung f education, schooling
Schulzeugnis nt school report
Schund [ʃʊnt] (-(e)s) m trash, garbage
Schuppe ['ʃʊpə] f scale; ~**n** pl (Haarschuppen) dandruff sg
Schuppen (-s, -) m shed
schuppen vt to scale ♦ vr to peel
schuppig ['ʃʊpɪç] adj scaly
Schur [ʃuːr] (-, -en) f shearing
schüren ['ʃyːrən] vt to rake; (fig) to stir up
schürfen ['ʃʏrfən] vt, vi to scrape, to scratch; (MIN) to prospect
Schurke ['ʃʊrkə] (-n, -n) m rogue
Schurwolle f: „**reine ~**" "pure new wool"
Schürze ['ʃʏrtsə] f apron
Schuß [ʃʊs] (-sses, ⁻sse) m shot; (WEBEN) woof; ~**bereich** m effective range
Schüssel ['ʃʏsəl] (-, -n) f bowl
Schuß- zW: ~**linie** f line of fire; ~**verletzung** f bullet wound; ~**waffe** f firearm
Schuster ['ʃuːstər] (-s, -) m cobbler, shoemaker
Schutt [ʃʊt] (-(e)s) m rubbish; (Bau~) rubble; ~**abladeplatz** m refuse dump
Schüttelfrost m shivering
schütteln ['ʃʏtəln] vt, vr to shake
schütten ['ʃʏtən] vt to pour; (Zucker, Kies etc) to tip; (ver~) to spill ♦ vi unpers to pour (down)
Schutthalde f dump
Schutthaufen m heap of rubble
Schutz [ʃʊts] (-es) m protection; (Unterschlupf) shelter; **jdn in ~ nehmen** to stand up for sb; ~**anzug** m overalls pl; ~**blech** nt mudguard
Schütze ['ʃʏtsə] (-n, -n) m gunman; (Gewehr~) rifleman; (Scharf~, Sport~) marksman; (ASTROL) Sagittarius
schützen vt to protect; **~ vor** +dat od **gegen** to protect from
Schützenfest nt fair featuring shooting

matches

Schutz- *zW:* **~engel** *m* guardian angel; **~gebiet** *nt* protectorate; (*Naturschutzgebiet*) reserve; **~impfung** *f* immunization

Schützling *m* protégé(e); (*bes Kind*) charge

Schütz- *zW:* **s~los** *adj* defenceless; **~mann** *m* policeman; **~patron** *m* patron saint

Schwabe ['ʃvaːbə] (**-n, -n**) *m* (*GEOG*) Swabian (*male*)

Schwaben ['ʃvaːbən] *nt* Swabia; **Schwäbin** *f* (*GEOG*) Swabian (*female*); **schwäbisch** ['ʃvɛːbɪʃ] *adj* Swabian

schwach [ʃvax] *adj* weak, feeble

Schwäche ['ʃvɛçə] *f* weakness; **s~n** *vt* to weaken

Schwachheit *f* weakness

schwächlich *adj* weakly, delicate

Schwächling *m* weakling

Schwach- *zW:* **~sinn** *m* imbecility; **s~sinnig** *adj* mentally deficient; (*Idee*) idiotic; **~strom** *m* weak current

Schwächung ['ʃvɛçʊŋ] *f* weakening

Schwager ['ʃvaːgər] (**-s, ⸚**) *m* brother-in-law

Schwägerin ['ʃvɛːgərɪn] *f* sister-in-law

Schwalbe ['ʃvalbə] *f* swallow

Schwall [ʃval] (**-(e)s, -e**) *m* surge, (*Worte*) flood, torrent

Schwamm [ʃvam] (**-(e)s, ⸚e**) *m* sponge; (*Pilz*) fungus

schwamm *etc vb siehe* **schwimmen**

schwammig *adj* spongy; (*Gesicht*) puffy

Schwan [ʃvaːn] (**-(e)s, ⸚e**) *m* swan

schwanger ['ʃvaŋər] *adj* pregnant

Schwangerschaft *f* pregnancy

Schwank [ʃvaŋk] (**-(e)s, ⸚e**) *m* funny story

schwanken *vi* to sway; (*taumeln*) to stagger, to reel; (*Preise, Zahlen*) to fluctuate; (*zögern*) to hesitate, to vacillate

Schwankung *f* fluctuation

Schwanz [ʃvants] (**-es, ⸚e**) *m* tail

schwänzen ['ʃvɛntsən] (*umg*) *vt* to skip, to cut ♦ *vi* to play truant

Schwarm [ʃvarm] (**-(e)s, ⸚e**) *m* swarm; (*umg*) heart-throb, idol

schwärm- ['ʃvɛrm] *zW:* **~en** *vi* to swarm; **~en für** to be mad *od* wild about; **S~erei** [-ə'raɪ] *f* enthusiasm; **~erisch** *adj* impassioned, effusive

Schwarte ['ʃvartə] *f* hard skin; (*Speck~*) rind

schwarz [ʃvarts] *adj* black; **~es Brett** notice board; **ins S~e treffen** (*auch fig*) to hit the bull's eye; **in den ~en Zahlen** in the black; **S~arbeit** *f* illicit work, moonlighting; **S~brot** *nt* black bread; **S~e(r)** *mf* black (man/woman)

Schwärze ['ʃvɛrtsə] *f* blackness; (*Farbe*) blacking; (*Drucker~*) printer's ink; **s~n** *vt* to blacken

Schwarz- *zW:* **s~fahren** (*unreg*) *vi* to travel without paying; to drive without a licence; **~handel** *m* black-market (trade); **s~hören** *vi* to listen to the radio without a licence; **~markt** *m* black market; **s~sehen** (*unreg*; *umg*) *vi* to see the gloomy side of things; (*TV*) to watch TV without a licence; **~seher** *m* pessimist; (*TV*) viewer without a licence; **~wald** *m* Black Forest; **s~weiß** *adj* black and white

schwatzen ['ʃvatsən] *vi* to chatter

schwätzen ['ʃvɛtsən] *vi* to chatter

Schwätzer ['ʃvɛtsər] (**-s, -**) *m* gasbag

schwatzhaft *adj* talkative, gossipy

Schwebe ['ʃveːbə] *f:* **in der ~** (*fig*) in abeyance; **~bahn** *f* overhead railway; **~balken** *m* (*SPORT*) beam; **s~n** *vi* to drift, to float; (*hoch*) to soar

Schwed- ['ʃveːd] *zW:* **~e** *m* Swede; **~en** *nt* Sweden; **~in** *f* Swede; **s~isch** *adj* Swedish

Schwefel ['ʃveːfəl] (**-s**) *m* sulphur; **s~ig** *adj* sulphurous; **~säure** *f* sulphuric acid

Schweig- ['ʃvaɪg] *zW:* **~egeld** *nt* hush money; **~en** (**-s**) *nt* silence; **s~en** (*unreg*) *vi* to be silent; to stop talking; **s~sam** ['ʃvaɪkzaːm] *adj* silent, taciturn; **~samkeit** *f* taciturnity, quietness

Schwein [ʃvaɪn] (**-(e)s, -e**) *nt* pig; (*umg*) (good) luck

Schweine- *zW:* **~fleisch** *nt* pork; **~'rei** *f* mess; (*Gemeinheit*) dirty trick; **~stall** *m* pigsty

schweinisch *adj* filthy
Schweinsleder *nt* pigskin
Schweiß [ʃvaɪs] (-es) *m* sweat, perspiration; **s~en** *vt, vi* to weld; **~er** (-s, -) *m* welder; (*abspülen*) to rinse **~füße** *pl* sweaty feet; **~naht** *f* weld
Schweiz [ʃvaɪts] *f* Switzerland; **~er(in)** *m(f)* Swiss; **s~erisch** *adj* Swiss
schwelgen [ʃvɛlɡən] *vi* to indulge
Schwelle [ʃvɛlə] *f* (*auch fig*) threshold; doorstep; (*EISENB*) sleeper (*BRIT*), tie (*US*)
schwellen (*unreg*) *vi* to swell
Schwellung *f* swelling
Schwemme [ʃvɛmə] *f* (*WIRTS*: *Überangebot*) surplus
Schwenk- [ʃvɛŋk] *zW*: **s~bar** *adj* swivel-mounted; **s~en** *vt* to swing; (*Fahne*) to wave; (*abspülen*) to rinse **♦** *vi* to turn, to swivel; (*MIL*) to wheel; **~ung** *f* turn; wheel
schwer [ʃveːr] *adj* heavy; (*schwierig*) difficult, hard; (*schlimm*) serious, bad **♦** *adv* (*sehr*) very (much); (*verletzt etc*) seriously, badly; **S~arbeiter** *m* manual worker, labourer; **S~behinderte(r)** *mf* seriously handicapped person; **S~e** *f* weight, heaviness; (*PHYS*) gravity; **~elos** *adj* weightless; (*Kammer*) zero-G; **~erziehbar** *adj* difficult (to bring up); **~fallen** (*unreg*) *vi*: **jdm ~fallen** to be difficult for sb; **~fällig** *adj* ponderous; **S~gewicht** *nt* heavyweight; (*fig*) emphasis; **~hörig** *adj* hard of hearing; **S~industrie** *f* heavy industry; **S~kraft** *f* gravity; **S~kranke(r)** *mf* person who is seriously ill; **~lich** *adv* hardly; **~machen** *vt*: **jdm/sich etw ~machen** to make sth difficult for sb/o.s.; **~mütig** *adj* melancholy; **~nehmen** (*unreg*) *vt* to take to heart; **S~punkt** *m* centre of gravity; (*fig*) emphasis, crucial point
Schwert [ʃveːrt] (-(e)s, -er) *nt* sword; **~lilie** *f* iris
schwer- *zW*: **~tun** (*unreg*) *vi*: **sich** *dat od akk* **~tun** to have difficulties; **S~verbrecher(in)** *m(f)* criminal, serious offender; **~verdaulich** *adj* indigestible, heavy; **~verletzt** *adj* badly injured; **S~verletzte(r)** *mf* serious casualty; (*bei*

Unfall usw auch) seriously injured person; **~wiegend** *adj* weighty, important
Schwester [ʃvɛstər] (-, -n) *f* sister; (*MED*) nurse; **s~lich** *adj* sisterly
Schwieger- [ʃviːɡər] *zW*: **~eltern** *pl* parents-in-law; **~mutter** *f* mother-in-law; **~sohn** *m* son-in-law; **~tochter** *f* daughter-in-law; **~vater** *m* father-in-law
Schwiele [ʃviːlə] *f* callus
schwierig [ʃviːrɪç] *adj* difficult, hard; **S~keit** *f* difficulty
Schwimm- [ʃvɪm] *zW*: **~bad** *nt* swimming baths *pl*; **~becken** *nt* swimming pool; **s~en** (*unreg*) *vi* to swim; (*treiben, nicht sinken*) to float; (*fig: unsicher sein*) to be all at sea; **~er** (-s, -) *m* swimmer; (*Angeln*) float; **~erin** *f* (female) swimmer; **~lehrer** *m* swimming instructor; **~weste** *f* life jacket
Schwindel [ʃvɪndəl] (-s) *m* giddiness; dizzy spell; (*Betrug*) swindle, fraud; (*Zeug*) stuff; **s~frei** *adj*: **s~frei sein** to have a good head for heights; **s~n** (*umg*) *vi* (*lügen*) to fib; **jdm s~t es** sb feels dizzy
schwinden [ʃvɪndən] (*unreg*) *vi* to disappear; (*sich verringern*) to decrease; (*Kräfte*) to decline
Schwindler [ʃvɪndlər] *m* swindler; (*Lügner*) liar
schwindlig *adj* dizzy; **mir ist ~** I feel dizzy
Schwing- [ʃvɪŋ] *zW*: **s~en** (*unreg*) *vt* to swing; (*Waffe etc*) to brandish **♦** *vi* to swing; (*vibrieren*) to vibrate; (*klingen*) to sound; **~tür** *f* swing door(s); **~ung** *f* vibration; (*PHYS*) oscillation
Schwips [ʃvɪps] (-es, -e) *m*: **einen ~ haben** to be tipsy
schwirren [ʃvɪrən] *vi* to buzz
schwitzen [ʃvɪtsən] *vi* to sweat, to perspire
schwören [ʃvøːrən] (*unreg*) *vt, vi* to swear
schwul [ʃvuːl] (*umg*) *adj* gay, queer
schwül [ʃvyːl] *adj* sultry, close; **S~e** (-) *f* sultriness
Schwule(r) (*umg*) *mf* gay (man/ woman)

schwülstig ['ʃvylstɪç] *adj* pompous
Schwung [ʃvʊŋ] (-(e)s, ⁓e) *m* swing; (*Triebkraft*) momentum; (*fig: Energie*) verve, energy; (*umg: Menge*) batch; **s~haft** *adj* brisk, lively; **s~voll** *adj* vigorous
Schwur [ʃvuːr] (-(e)s, ⁓e) *m* oath; **~gericht** *nt* court with a jury
sechs [zɛks] *num* six; **~hundert** *num* six hundred; **~te(r, s)** *adj* sixth; **S~tel** (-s, -) *nt* sixth
sechzehn ['zɛçtseːn] *num* sixteen
sechzig ['zɛçtsɪç] *num* sixty
See¹ [zeː] (-, -n) *f* sea
See² (-s, -n) *m* lake
See- [zeː] *zW:* **~bad** *nt* seaside resort; **~hund** *m* seal; **~igel** ['zeːʔiːgəl] *m* sea urchin; **s~krank** *adj* seasick; **~krankheit** *f* seasickness; **~lachs** *m* rock salmon
Seele ['zeːlə] *f* soul; **s~nruhig** *adv* calmly
Seeleute ['zeːlɔʏtə] *pl* seamen
Seel- *zW:* **s~isch** *adj* mental; **~sorge** *f* pastoral duties *pl*; **~sorger** (-s, -) *m* clergyman
See- *zW:* **~macht** naval power; **~mann** (*pl* -leute) *m* seaman, sailor; **~meile** *f* nautical mile; **~möwe** *f* (*ZOOL*) seagull; **~not** *f* distress; **~räuber** *m* pirate; **~rose** *f* water lily; **~stern** *m* starfish; **~tang** *m* (*BOT*) seaweed; **s~tüchtig** *adj* seaworthy; **~weg** *m* sea route; **auf dem ~weg** by sea; **~zunge** *f* sole
Segel ['zeːgəl] (-s, -) *nt* sail; **~boot** *nt* yacht; **~fliegen** (-s) *nt* gliding; **~flieger** *m* glider pilot; **~flugzeug** *nt* glider; **s~n** *vt, vi* to sail; **~schiff** *nt* sailing vessel; **~sport** *m* sailing; **~tuch** *nt* canvas
Segen ['zeːgən] (-s, -) *m* blessing; **s~sreich** *adj* beneficial
Segler ['zeːglər] (-s, -) *m* sailor, yachtsman
segnen ['zeːgnən] *vt* to bless
Seh- ['zeː] *zW:* **s~en** (*unreg*) *vt, vi* to see; (*in bestimmte Richtung*) to look; **mal s~en(, ob ...)** let's see (if ...); **siehe Seite 5** see page 5; **s~enswert** *adj* worth seeing; **~enswürdigkeiten** *pl* sights (of a town); **~er** (-s, -) *m* seer; **~fehler** *m*

sight defect
Sehne ['zeːnə] *f* sinew; (*an Bogen*) string
sehnen *vr:* **sich ~ nach** to long *od* yearn for
sehnig *adj* sinewy
Sehn- *zW:* **s~lich** *adj* ardent; **~sucht** *f* longing; **s~süchtig** *adj* longing
sehr [zeːr] *adv* very; (*mit Verben*) a lot, (very) much; **zu ~** too much; **~ geehrte(r) ...** dear ...
seicht [zaɪçt] *adj* (*auch fig*) shallow
Seide ['zaɪdə] *f* silk; **s~n** *adj* silk; **~npapier** *nt* tissue paper
seidig ['zaɪdɪç] *adj* silky
Seife ['zaɪfə] *f* soap
Seifen- *zW:* **~lauge** *f* soapsuds *pl*; **~schale** *f* soap dish; **~schaum** *m* lather
seihen ['zaɪən] *vt* to strain, to filter
Seil [zaɪl] (-(e)s, -e) *nt* rope; cable; **~bahn** *f* cable railway; **~hüpfen** (-s) *nt* skipping; **~springen** (-s) *nt* skipping; **~tänzer(in)** *m(f)* tightrope walker

---
SCHLÜSSELWORT
---

sein [zaɪn] (*pt* war, *pp* gewesen) *vi* **1** to be; **ich bin** I am; **du bist** you are; **er/sie/es ist** he/she/it is; **wir sind/ihr seid/sie sind** we/you/they are; **wir waren** we were; **wir sind gewesen** we have been

2: **seien Sie nicht böse** don't be angry; **sei so gut und ...** be so kind as to ...; **das wäre gut** that would *od* that'd be a good thing; **wenn ich Sie wäre** if I were *od* was you; **das wär's** that's all, that's it; **morgen bin ich in Rom** tomorrow I'll *od* I will *od* I shall be in Rome; **waren Sie mal in Rom?** have you ever been to Rome?

3: **wie ist das zu verstehen?** how is that to be understood?; **er ist nicht zu ersetzen** he cannot be replaced; **mit ihr ist nicht zu reden** you can't talk to her

4: **mir ist kalt** I'm cold; **was ist?** what's the matter?, what is it?; **ist was?** is something the matter?; **es sei denn, daß ...** unless ...; **wie dem auch sei** be that as it may; **wie wäre es mit ...?** how *od*

what about ...?; **laß das sein!** stop that!

sein(e) ['zaɪn(ə)] *adj* his; its; **~e(r, s)**
pron his; its; **~er** (*gen von* **er**) *pron* of
him; **~erseits** *adv* for his part; **~erzeit**
adv in those days, formerly; **~esgleichen**
pron people like him; **~etwegen** *adv* (*für
ihn*) for his sake; (*wegen ihm*) on his
account; (*von ihm aus*) as far as he is
concerned; **~etwillen** *adv*: **um ~etwillen**
= **~etwegen**; **~ige** *pron*: **der/die/das
~ige** his

Seismograph [zaɪsmo'graːf] (-en, -en) *m*
seismograph

seit [zaɪt] *präp +dat* since ♦ *konj* since;
er ist ~ einer Woche hier he has been
here for a week; **~ langem** for a long
time; **~dem** [zaɪt'deːm] *adv, konj* since

Seite ['zaɪtə] *f* side; (*Buch~*) page; (*MIL*)
flank

Seiten- *zW*: **~ansicht** *f* side view; **~hieb**
m (*fig*) passing shot, dig; **~s** *präp +gen*
on the part of; **~schiff** *nt* aisle; **~sprung**
m extramarital escapade; **~stechen** *nt* (a)
stitch; **~straße** *f* side road; **~streifen** *m*
verge; (*der Autobahn*) hard shoulder

seither [zaɪt'heːr] *adv, konj* since (then)

seitlich *adj* on one *od* the side; side *cpd*

seitwärts *adv* sideways

Sekretär [zekre'tɛːr] *m* secretary; (*Möbel*)
bureau; **~in** *f* secretary

Sekretariat [zekretari'aːt] (-(e)s, -e) *nt*
secretary's office, secretariat

Sekt [zɛkt] (-(e)s, -e) *m* champagne

Sekte ['zɛktə] *f* sect

Sekunde [ze'kʊndə] *f* second

selber ['zɛlbər] = **selbst**

Selbst [zɛlpst] (-) *nt* self

SCHLÜSSELWORT
---

selbst *pron* **1**: **ich/er/wir selbst** I
myself/he himself/we ourselves; **sie ist
die Tugend selbst** she's virtue itself; **er
braut sein Bier selbst** he brews his own
beer; **wie geht's? - gut, und selbst?** how
are things? - fine, and yourself?
2 (*ohne Hilfe*) alone, on my/his/one's *etc*
own; **von selbst** by itself; **er kam von
selbst** he came of his own accord

♦ *adv* even; **selbst wenn** even if; **selbst
Gott** even God (himself)

selbständig ['zɛlpʃtɛndɪç] *adj*
independent; **S~keit** *f* independence

Selbst- *zW*: **~auslöser** *m* (*PHOT*) delayed-
action shutter release; **~bedienung** *f*
self-service; **~befriedigung** *f*
masturbation; **~beherrschung** *f* self-
control; **~bestimmung** *f* (*POL*) self-
determination; **~beteiligung** *f*
(*VERSICHERUNG: bei Kosten*) (voluntary)
excess; **s~bewußt** *adj* (self-)confident;
~bewußtsein *nt* self-confidence;
~erhaltung *f* self-preservation;
~erkenntnis *f* self-knowledge; **s~gefällig**
adj smug, self-satisfied; **s~gemacht** *adj*
home-made; **~gespräch** *nt* conversation
with o.s.; **~kostenpreis** *m* cost price;
s~los *adj* unselfish, selfless; **~mord** *m*
suicide; **~mörder(in)** *m(f)* suicide;
s~mörderisch *adj* suicidal; **s~sicher**
adj self-assured; **s~süchtig** *adj* (*Mensch*)
selfish; **s~verständlich** ['zɛlpstfɛr-
ʃtɛntlɪç] *adj* obvious ♦ *adv* naturally; **ich
halte das für s~verständlich** I take that
for granted; **~verteidigung** *f* self-
defence; **~vertrauen** *nt* self-confidence;
~verwaltung *f* autonomy, self-
government

selig ['zeːlɪç] *adj* happy, blissful; (*REL*)
blessed; (*tot*) late; **S~keit** *f* bliss

Sellerie ['zɛləriː] (-s, -(s) *od* -, -) *m od f*
celery

selten ['zɛltən] *adj* rare ♦ *adv* seldom,
rarely; **S~heit** *f* rarity

Selterswasser ['zɛltərsvasər] *nt* soda
water

seltsam ['zɛltzaːm] *adj* strange, curious;
S~keit *f* strangeness

Semester [ze'mɛstər] (-s, -) *nt* semester

Semi- [zemi] *in zW* semi-; **~kolon**
[-'koːlon] (-s, -s) *nt* semicolon

Seminar [-'naːr] (-s, -e) *nt* seminary;
(*Kurs*) seminar; (*UNIV: Ort*) department
building

Semmel ['zɛməl] (-, -n) *f* roll

Senat [ze'naːt] (-(e)s, -e) *m* senate,
council

Sende- ['zɛndə] *zW:* **~bereich** *m* transmission range; **~folge** *f* (*Serie*) series; **s~n** (*unreg*) *vt* to send; (*RADIO, TV*) to transmit, to broadcast ♦ *vi* to transmit, to broadcast; **~r** (-s, -) *m* station; (*Anlage*) transmitter; **~reihe** *f* series (of broadcasts)

Sendung ['zɛnduŋ] *f* consignment; (*Aufgabe*) mission; (*RADIO, TV*) transmission; (*Programm*) programme

Senf [zɛnf] (-(e)s, -e) *m* mustard

senil [ze'ni:l] (*pej*) *adj* senile

Senior(in) ['ze:niɔr, -ɪn] (-s, -en) *m(f)* (*Mensch im Rentenalter*) (old age) pensioner; **~enheim** [zeni'o:rənhaɪm] *nt* old people's home

Senk- ['zɛŋk] *zW:* **~blei** *nt* plumb; **~e** *f* depression; **s~en** *vt* to lower ♦ *vr* to sink, to drop gradually; **s~recht** *adj* vertical, perpendicular; **~rechte** *f* perpendicular; **~rechtstarter** *m* (*AVIAT*) vertical take-off plane; (*fig*) high-flyer

Sensation [zɛnzatsi'o:n] *f* sensation; **s~ell** [-'nɛl] *adj* sensational

Sense ['zɛnzə] *f* scythe

sensibel [zɛn'zi:bəl] *adj* sensitive

sentimental [zɛntimɛn'ta:l] *adj* sentimental; **S~ität** *f* sentimentality

separat [zepa'ra:t] *adj* separate

September [zɛp'tɛmbər] (-(s), -) *m* September

Serie ['ze:riə] *f* series; **~nmörder(in)** *m(f)* serial killer; **s~nweise** *adv* in series

seriös [zeri'ø:s] *adj* serious, bona fide

Serum ['ze:rʊm] (-s, Seren) *nt* serum

Service[1] [zɛr'vi:s] (-(s), -) *nt* (*Geschirr*) set, service

Service[2] (-, -s) *m* service

servieren [zɛr'vi:rən] *vt, vi* to serve

Serviererin *f* waitress

Serviette [zɛrvi'ɛtə] *f* napkin, serviette

Servobremse ['zɛrvo-] *f* (*AUT*) servo (-assisted) brake

Servolenkung *f* (*AUT*) power steering

Sessel ['zɛsəl] (-s, -) *m* armchair; **~lift** *m* chairlift

seßhaft ['zɛshaft] *adj* settled; (*ansässig*) resident

setzen ['zɛtsən] *vt* to put, to set; (*Baum*

etc) to plant; (*Segel, TYP*) to set ♦ *vr* to settle; (*Person*) to sit down ♦ *vi* (*springen*) to leap; (*wetten*) to bet

Setz- ['zɛts] *zW:* **~er** (-s, -) *m* (*TYP*) compositor; **~ling** *m* young plant

Seuche ['zɔʏçə] *f* epidemic; **~ngebiet** *nt* infected area

seufzen ['zɔʏftsən] *vt, vi* to sigh

Seufzer ['zɔʏftsər] (-s, -) *m* sigh

Sex [zɛks] (-(es)) *m* sex; **~ualität** [-uali'tɛt] *f* sex, sexuality; **~ualkunde** [zɛksu'a:l-] *f* (*SCH*) sex education; **s~uell** [-u'ɛl] *adj* sexual

sezieren [ze'tsi:rən] *vt* to dissect

Shampoo [ʃam'pu:] (-s, -s) *nt* shampoo

Sibirien [zi'bi:riən] *nt* Siberia

sibirisch [zi'bi:rɪʃ] *adj* Siberian

SCHLÜSSELWORT

sich [zɪç] *pron* **1** (*akk*): **er/sie/es ... sich** he/she/it ... himself/herself/itself; **sie** *pl*/**man ... sich** they/one ... themselves/oneself; **Sie ... sich** you ... yourself/yourselves *pl*; **sich wiederholen** to repeat oneself/itself

2 (*dat*): **er/sie/es ... sich** he/she/it ... to himself/herself/itself; **sie** *pl*/**man ... sich** they/one ... to themselves/oneself; **Sie ... sich** you ... to yourself/yourselves *pl*; **sie hat sich einen Pullover gekauft** she bought herself a jumper; **sich die Haare waschen** to wash one's hair

3 (*mit Präposition*): **haben Sie Ihren Ausweis bei sich?** do you have your pass on you?; **er hat nichts bei sich** he's got nothing on him; **sie bleiben gern unter sich** they keep themselves to themselves

4 (*einander*) each other, one another; **sie bekämpfen sich** they fight each other *od* one another

5: **dieses Auto fährt sich gut** this car drives well; **hier sitzt es sich gut** it's good to sit here

---

Sichel ['zɪçəl] (-, -n) *f* sickle; (*Mond~*) crescent

sicher ['zɪçər] *adj* safe; (*gewiß*) certain; (*zuverlässig*) secure, reliable; (*selbst~*)

confident; **vor jdm/etw ~ sein** to be safe from sb/sth; **ich bin nicht ~** I'm not sure *od* certain; **~ nicht** surely not; **aber ~!** of course!; **~gehen** (*unreg*) *vi* to make sure
Sicherheit ['zɪçɐhaɪt] *f* safety; (*auch FIN*) security; (*Gewißheit*) certainty; (*Selbst~*) confidence
Sicherheits- *zW:* **~abstand** *m* safe distance; **~glas** *nt* safety glass; **~gurt** *m* safety belt; **s~halber** *adv* for safety; to be on the safe side; **~nadel** *f* safety pin; **~schloß** *nt* safety lock; **~vorkehrung** *f* safety precaution
sicher- *zW:* **~lich** *adv* certainly, surely; **~n** *vt* to secure; (*schützen*) to protect; (*Waffe*) to put the safety catch on; **jdm etw ~n** to secure sth for sb; **sich** *dat* **etw ~n** to secure sth (for o.s.); **~stellen** *vt* to impound; (*COMPUT*) to save; **S~ung** *f* (*Sichern*) securing; (*Vorrichtung*) safety device; (*an Waffen*) safety catch; (*ELEK*) fuse; **S~ungskopie** *f* back-up copy
Sicht [zɪçt] (-) *f* sight; (*Aus~*) view; **auf** *od* **nach ~** (*FIN*) at sight; **auf lange ~** on a long-term basis; **s~bar** *adj* visible; **s~en** *vt* to sight; (*auswählen*) to sort out; **s~lich** *adj* evident, obvious; **~verhältnisse** *pl* visibility *sg*; **~vermerk** *m* visa; **~weite** *f* visibility
sickern ['zɪkɐrn] *vi* to trickle, to seep
Sie [zi:] (*nom, akk*) *pron* you
sie [zi:] *pron* (*sg: nom*) she; it; (: *akk*) her; it; (*pl: nom*) they; (: *akk*) them
Sieb [zi:p] (-(e)s, -e) *nt* sieve; (*KOCH*) strainer; **s~en**[1] [zi:bən] *vt* to sift; (*Flüssigkeit*) to strain
sieben[2] *num* seven; **~hundert** *num* seven hundred; **S~sachen** *pl* belongings
siebte(r, s) ['zi:ptə(r, s)] *adj* seventh; **S~l** (-s, -) *nt* seventh
siebzehn ['zi:ptse:n] *num* seventeen
siebzig ['zi:ptsɪç] *num* seventy
siedeln *vi* to settle
sieden ['zi:dən] *vt, vi* to boil, to simmer
Siedepunkt *m* boiling point
Siedler (-s, -) *m* settler
Siedlung *f* settlement; (*Häuser~*) housing estate
Sieg [zi:k] (-(e)s, -e) *m* victory

Siegel ['zi:gəl] (-s, -) *nt* seal; **~ring** *m* signet ring
Sieg- *zW:* **s~en** *vi* to be victorious; (*SPORT*) to win; **~er** (-s, -) *m* victor; (*SPORT etc*) winner; **s~essicher** *adj* sure of victory; **s~reich** *adj* victorious
siehe *etc* ['zi:ə] *vb siehe* **sehen**
siezen ['zi:tsən] *vt* to address as "Sie"
Signal [zɪ'gna:l] (-s, -e) *nt* signal
Silbe ['zɪlbə] *f* syllable
Silber ['zɪlbɐ] (-s) *nt* silver; **s~n** *adj* silver; **~papier** *nt* silver paper
Silhouette [zilu'ɛtə] *f* silhouette
Silo ['zi:lo] (-s, -s) *nt od m* silo
Silvester [zɪl'vɛstɐ] (-s, -) *nt* New Year's Eve, Hogmanay (*SCOTTISH*); **~abend** *m* = **Silvester**
simpel ['zɪmpəl] *adj* simple
Sims [zɪms] (-es, -e) *nt od m* (*Kamin~*) mantelpiece; (*Fenster~*) (window)sill
simulieren [zimu'li:rən] *vt* to simulate; (*vortäuschen*) to feign ♦ *vi* to feign illness
simultan [zimul'ta:n] *adj* simultaneous
Sinfonie [zɪnfo'ni:] *f* symphony
singen ['zɪŋən] (*unreg*) *vt, vi* to sing
Singular ['zɪŋgula:r] *m* singular
Singvogel ['zɪŋfo:gəl] *m* songbird
sinken ['zɪŋkən] (*unreg*) *vi* to sink; (*Preise etc*) to fall, to go down
Sinn [zɪn] (-(e)s, -e) *m* mind; (*Wahrnehmungs~*) sense; (*Bedeutung*) sense, meaning; **~ für etw** sense of sth; **von ~en sein** to be out of one's mind; **es hat keinen ~** there's no point; **~bild** *nt* symbol; **s~en** (*unreg*) *vi* to ponder; **auf etw** *akk* **s~en** to contemplate sth; **~estäuschung** *f* illusion; **s~gemäß** *adj* faithful; (*Wiedergabe*) in one's own words; **s~ig** *adj* clever; **s~lich** *adj* sensual, sensuous; (*Wahrnehmung*) sensory; **~lichkeit** *f* sensuality; **s~los** *adj* senseless; meaningless; **~losigkeit** *f* senselessness; meaninglessness; **s~voll** *adj* meaningful; (*vernünftig*) sensible
Sintflut ['zɪntflu:t] *f* Flood
Sippe ['zɪpə] *f* clan, kin
Sippschaft ['zɪpʃaft] (*pej*) *f* relations *pl*, tribe; (*Bande*) gang
Sirene [zi're:nə] *f* siren

Sirup ['ziːrʊp] (-s, -e) *m* syrup

Sitt- ['zɪt] *zW:* **~e** *f* custom; **~en** *pl* (*Sittlichkeit*) morals; **~enpolizei** *f* vice squad; **s~sam** *adj* modest, demure

Situation [zituatsi'oːn] *f* situation

Sitz [zɪts] (-es, -e) *m* seat; **der Anzug hat einen guten ~** the suit is a good fit; **s~en** (*unreg*) *vi* to sit; (*Bemerkung, Schlag*) to strike home, to tell; (*Gelerntes*) to have sunk in; **s~en bleiben** to remain seated; **s~enbleiben** (*unreg*) *vi* (*SCH*) to have to repeat a year; (*Gegenstand*) **auf etw** *dat* **s~enbleiben** to be lumbered with sth; **s~end** *adj* (*Tätigkeit*) sedentary; **s~enlassen** (*unreg*) *vt* (*SCH*) to make (sb) repeat a year; (*Mädchen*) to jilt; (*Wartenden*) to stand up; **etw auf sich** *dat* **s~enlassen** to take sth lying down; **~gelegenheit** *f* place to sit down; **~platz** *m* seat; **~streik** *m* sit-down strike; **~ung** *f* meeting

Sizilien [zi'tsiːliən] *nt* Sicily

Skala ['skaːla] (-, Skalen) *f* scale

Skalpell [skal'pɛl] (-s, -e) *nt* scalpel

Skandal [skan'daːl] (-s, -e) *m* scandal; **s~ös** [-'løːs] *adj* scandalous

Skandinav- [skandi'naːv] *zW:* **~ien** *nt* Scandinavia; **~ier(in)** *m(f)* Scandinavian; **s~isch** *adj* Scandinavian

Skelett [ske'lɛt] (-(e)s, -e) *nt* skeleton

Skepsis ['skɛpsɪs] (-) *f* scepticism

skeptisch ['skɛptɪʃ] *adj* sceptical

Ski [ʃiː] (-s, -er) *m* ski; **~ laufen** *od* **fahren** to ski; **~fahrer** *m* skier; **~läufer** *m* skier; **~lehrer** *m* ski instructor; **~lift** *m* ski-lift; **~springen** *nt* ski-jumping; **~stock** *m* ski-pole

Skizze ['skɪtsə] *f* sketch

skizzieren [skɪ'tsiːrən] *vt, vi* to sketch

Sklave ['sklaːvə] (-n, -n) *m* slave; **~'rei** *f* slavery; **Sklavin** *f* slave

Skonto ['skɔnto] (-s, -s) *m od nt* discount

Skorpion [skɔrpi'oːn] (-s, -e) *m* scorpion; (*ASTROL*) Scorpio

Skrupel ['skruːpəl] (-s, -) *m* scruple; **s~los** *adj* unscrupulous

Skulptur [skʊlp'tuːr] *f* (*Gegenstand*) sculpture

Slalom ['slaːlɔm] (-s, -s) *m* slalom

Slip (-s, -s) *m* (under)pants

Slowenien [slo'veːniən] *nt* Slovenia

Smaragd [sma'rakt] (-(e)s, -e) *m* emerald

Smoking ['smoːkɪŋ] (-s, -s) *m* dinner jacket

SCHLÜSSELWORT

---

so [zoː] *adv* **1** (*sosehr*) so; **so groß/schön** *etc* so big/nice *etc*; **so groß/schön wie ...** as big/nice as ...; **das hat ihn so geärgert, daß ...** that annoyed him so much that ...; **so einer wie ich** somebody like me; **na so was!** well, well!

2 (*auf diese Weise*) like this; **mach es nicht so** don't do it like that; **so oder so** in one way or the other; **und so weiter** and so on; **... oder so was** ... or something like that; **das ist gut so** that's fine

3 (*umg: umsonst*): **ich habe es so bekommen** I got it for nothing

♦ *konj:* **so daß** so that; **so wie es jetzt ist** as things are at the moment

♦ *excl:* **so?** really?; **so, das wär's** so, that's it then

---

s.o. *abk* = **siehe oben**

Söckchen ['zœkçən] *nt* ankle sock

Socke ['zɔkə] *f* sock

Sockel ['zɔkəl] (-s, -) *m* pedestal, base

Sodawasser ['zoːdavasər] *nt* soda water

Sodbrennen ['zoːtbrɛnən] (-s, -) *nt* heartburn

soeben [zo'eːbən] *adv* just (now)

Sofa ['zoːfa] (-s, -s) *nt* sofa

sofern [zo'fɛrn] *konj* if, provided (that)

sofort [zo'fɔrt] *adv* immediately, at once; **~ig** *adj* immediate

Sog [zoːk] (-(e)s, -e) *m* (*Strömung*) undertow

sogar [zo'gaːr] *adv* even

sogenannt ['zoːgənant] *adj* so-called

sogleich [zo'glaiç] *adv* straight away, at once

Sohle ['zoːlə] *f* sole; (*Tal- etc*) bottom; (*MIN*) level

Sohn [zoːn] (-(e)s, ⸚e) *m* son

Solar- [zo'laːr] *in zW* solar; **~zelle** *f* solar cell

solch [zɔlç] *pron* such; **ein ~e(r, s)** ... such a ...

Soldat [zɔl'daːt] (**-en, -en**) *m* soldier

Söldner ['zœldnər] (**-s, -**) *m* mercenary

solidarisch [zoli'daːrɪʃ] *adj* in *od* with solidarity; **sich ~ erklären** to declare one's solidarity

Solidari'tät *f* solidarity

solid(e) [zo'liːd(ə)] *adj* solid; (*Leben, Person*) respectable

Solist(in) [zo'lɪst(ɪn)] *m(f)* soloist

Soll [zɔl] (**-(s), -(s)**) *nt* (FIN) debit (side); (*Arbeitsmenge*) quota, target

---

SCHLÜSSELWORT

sollen ['zɔlən] (*pt* **sollte**, *pp* **gesollt** *od* (*als Hilfsverb*) **sollen**) *Hilfsverb* **1** (*Pflicht, Befehl*) to be supposed to; **du hättest nicht gehen sollen** you shouldn't have gone, you oughtn't to have gone; **soll ich?** shall I?; **soll ich dir helfen?** shall I help you?; **sag ihm, er soll warten** tell him he's to wait; **was soll ich machen?** what should I do?

2 (*Vermutung*): **sie soll verheiratet sein** she's said to be married; **was soll das heißen?** what's that supposed to mean?; **man sollte glauben, daß ...** you would think that ...; **sollte das passieren, ...** if that should happen ...

♦ *vt, vi*: **was soll das?** what's all this?; **das sollst du nicht** you shouldn't do that; **was soll's?** what the hell!

Solo ['zoːlo] (**-s, -s** *od* **Soli**) *nt* solo

somit [zo'mɪt] *konj* and so, therefore

Sommer ['zɔmər] (**-s, -**) *m* summer; **s~lich** *adj* summery; summer; **~schlußverkauf** *m* summer sale; **~sprossen** *pl* freckles

Sonate [zo'naːtə] *f* sonata

Sonde ['zɔndə] *f* probe

Sonder- ['zɔndər] *in zW* special; **~angebot** *nt* special offer; **s~bar** *adj* strange, odd; **~fahrt** *f* special trip; **~fall** *m* special case; **s~lich** *adj* particular; (*außergewöhnlich*) remarkable; (*eigenartig*) peculiar; **~marke** *f* special issue stamp; **s~n** *konj* but ♦ *vt* to

separate; **nicht nur ..., s~n auch** not only ..., but also; **~zug** *m* special train

Sonnabend ['zɔn'aːbənt] *m* Saturday

Sonne ['zɔnə] *f* sun; **s~n** *vr* to sun o.s.

Sonnen- *zW:* **~aufgang** *m* sunrise; **s~baden** *vi* to sunbathe; **~brand** *m* sunburn; **~brille** *f* sunglasses *pl*; **~creme** *f* suntan lotion; **~energie** *f* solar energy, solar power; **~finsternis** *f* solar eclipse; **~kollektor** *m* solar panel; **~schein** *m* sunshine; **~schirm** *m* parasol, sunshade; **~stich** *m* sunstroke; **~uhr** *f* sundial; **~untergang** *m* sunset; **~wende** *f* solstice

sonnig ['zɔnɪç] *adj* sunny

Sonntag ['zɔntaːk] *m* Sunday

sonst [zɔnst] *adv* otherwise; (*mit pron, in Fragen*) else; (*zu anderer Zeit*) at other times, normally ♦ *konj* otherwise; **~ noch etwas?** anything else?; **~ nichts** nothing else; **~ig** *adj* other; **~jemand** *pron* anybody (at all); **~wo** *adv* somewhere else; **~woher** *adv* from somewhere else; **~wohin** *adv* somewhere else

sooft [zo''ɔft] *konj* whenever

Sopran [zo'praːn] (**-s, -e**) *m* soprano

Sopra'nistin *f* soprano

Sorge ['zɔrgə] *f* care, worry

sorgen *vi*: **für jdn ~** to look after sb ♦ *vr*: **sich ~ (um)** to worry (about); **für etw ~** to take care of *od* see to sth; **~frei** *adj* carefree; **~voll** *adj* troubled, worried

Sorgerecht *nt* custody (of a child)

Sorg- [zɔrk] *zW:* **~falt** (**-**) *f* care(fulness); **s~fältig** *adj* careful; **s~los** *adj* careless; (*ohne Sorgen*) carefree; **s~sam** *adj* careful

Sorte ['zɔrtə] *f* sort; (*Waren~*) brand; **~n** *pl* (FIN) foreign currency *sg*

sortieren [zɔr'tiːrən] *vt* to sort (out)

Sortiment [zɔrti'mɛnt] *nt* assortment

sosehr [zo'zeːr] *konj* as much as

Soße ['zoːsə] *f* sauce; (*Braten~*) gravy

Souffleur [zu'fløːr] *m* prompter

Souffleuse [zu'fløːzə] *f* prompter

soufflieren [zu'fliːrən] *vt, vi* to prompt

Souterrain [zutɛ'rɛ̃ː] (**-s, -s**) *nt* basement

souverän [zuvə'rɛːn] *adj* sovereign; (*überlegen*) superior

so- *zW:* **~viel** [zo'fiːl] *konj:* **~viel ich weiß** as far as I know; **~viel (wie)** as much as; **rede nicht ~viel** don't talk so much; **~weit** [zo'vaɪt] *konj* as far as ♦ *adj:* **~weit sein** to be ready; **~weit wie** *od* **als möglich** as far as possible; **ich bin ~weit zufrieden** by and large I'm quite satisfied; **~wenig** [zo'veːnɪç] *konj* little as ♦ *pron:* **~wenig (wie)** as little as; **~wie** [zo'viː] *konj (sobald)* as soon as; *(ebenso)* as well as; **~wieso** [zovi'zoː] *adv* anyway

sowjetisch [zɔ'vjɛtɪʃ] *adj* Soviet

Sowjetunion *f* Soviet Union

sowohl [zo'voːl] *konj:* **~ ... als** *od* **wie auch** both ... and

sozial [zotsi'aːl] *adj* social; **S~abgaben** *pl* national insurance contributions; **S~arbeiter(in)** *m(f)* social worker; **S~demokrat** *m* social democrat; **~demokratisch** *adj* social democratic; **~isieren** *vt* to socialize; **S~ismus** [-'lɪsmʊs] *m* socialism; **S~ist** [-'lɪst] *m* socialist; **~istisch** *adj* socialist; **S~politik** *f* social welfare policy; **S~produkt** *nt* (net) national product; **S~staat** *m* welfare state; **S~wohnung** *f* council flat

soziologisch [zotsio'loːɡɪʃ] *adj* sociological

sozusagen [zotsu'zaːɡən] *adv* so to speak

Spachtel ['ʃpaxtəl] (-s, -) *m* spatula

spähen ['ʃpɛːən] *vi* to peep, to peek

Spalier [ʃpa'liːr] (-s, -e) *nt (Gerüst)* trellis; *(Leute)* guard of honour

Spalt [ʃpalt] (-(e)s, -e) *m* crack; *(Tür~)* chink; *(fig: Kluft)* split; **~e** *f* crack, fissure; *(Gletscherspalte)* crevasse; *(in Text)* column; **s~en** *vt, vr (auch fig)* to split; **~ung** *f* splitting

Span [ʃpaːn] (-(e)s, ꞏe) *m* shaving

Spanferkel *nt* sucking-pig

Spange ['ʃpaŋə] *f* clasp; *(Haar~)* hair slide; *(Schnalle)* buckle; *(Armreif)* bangle

Spanien ['ʃpaːniən] *nt* Spain

Spanier(in) *m(f)* Spaniard

spanisch *adj* Spanish

Spann- ['ʃpan] *zW:* **~beton** *m* prestressed concrete; **~bettuch** *nt* fitted sheet; **~e** *f (Zeitspanne)* space; *(Differenz)* gap; **s~en** *vt (straffen)* to tighten, to tauten; *(befestigen)* to brace ♦ *vi* to be tight; **s~end** *adj* exciting, gripping; **~ung** *f* tension *(ELEK)* voltage; *(fig)* suspense; *(unangenehm)* tension

Spar- ['ʃpaːr] *zW:* **~buch** *nt* savings book; **~büchse** *f* moneybox; **s~en** *vt, vi* to save; **sich** *dat* **etw s~en** to save o.s. sth; *(Bemerkung)* to keep sth to o.s.; **mit etw s~en** to be sparing with sth; **an etw** *dat* **s~en** to economize on sth; **~er** (-s, -) *m* saver

Spargel ['ʃparɡəl] (-s, -) *m* asparagus

Sparkasse *f* savings bank

Sparkonto *nt* savings account

spärlich ['ʃpɛːrlɪç] *adj* meagre; *(Bekleidung)* scanty

Spar- *zW:* **s~sam** *adj* economical, thrifty; **~samkeit** *f* thrift, economizing; **~schwein** *nt* piggy bank

Sparte ['ʃpartə] *f* field; line of business; *(PRESSE)* column

Spaß [ʃpaːs] (-es, ꞏe) *m* joke; *(Freude)* fun; **jdm ~ machen** to be fun (for sb); **viel ~!** have fun!; **s~en** *vi* to joke; **mit ihm ist nicht zu s~en** you can't take liberties with him; **s~haft** *adj* funny, droll; **s~ig** *adj* funny, droll; **~verderber** (-s, -) *m* spoilsport

spät [ʃpɛːt] *adj, adv* late; **wie ~ ist es?** what's the time?

Spaten ['ʃpaːtən] (-s, -) *m* spade

später *adj, adv* later

spätestens *adv* at the latest

Spatz [ʃpats] (-en, -en) *m* sparrow

spazier- [ʃpa'tsiːr] *zW:* **~en** *vi* to stroll, to walk; **~enfahren** *(unreg)* *vi* to go for a drive; **~engehen** *(unreg)* *vi* to go for a walk; **S~gang** *m* walk; **S~stock** *m* walking stick; **S~weg** *m* path, walk

Specht [ʃpɛçt] (-(e)s, -e) *m* woodpecker

Speck [ʃpɛk] (-(e)s, -e) *m* bacon

Spediteur [ʃpedi'tøːr] *m* carrier; *(Möbel~)* furniture remover

Spedition [ʃpeditsi'oːn] *f* carriage; *(Speditionsfirma)* road haulage contractor; removal firm

Speer [ʃpeːr] (-(e)s, -e) *m* spear; *(SPORT)*

javelin

Speiche ['ʃpaɪçə] f spoke

Speichel ['ʃpaɪçəl] (-s) m saliva, spit(tle)

Speicher ['ʃpaɪçər] (-s, -) m storehouse; (*Dach~*) attic, loft; (*Korn~*) granary; (*Wasser~*) tank; (*TECH*) store; (*COMPUT*) memory; **s~n** vt to store; (*COMPUT*) to save

speien ['ʃpaɪən] (*unreg*) vt, vi to spit; (*erbrechen*) to vomit; (*Vulkan*) to spew

Speise ['ʃpaɪzə] f food; **~eis** [-'aɪs] nt ice-cream; **~kammer** f larder, pantry; **~karte** f menu; **s~n** vt to feed; to eat ♦ vi to dine; **~röhre** f gullet, oesophagus; **~saal** m dining room; **~wagen** m dining car

Speku- [ʃpeku] zW: **~lant** m speculator; **~lation** [-latsi'oːn] f speculation; **s~lieren** [-'liːrən] vi (*fig*) to speculate; **auf etw** akk **s~lieren** to have hopes of sth

Spelunke [ʃpe'lʊŋkə] f dive

Spende ['ʃpɛndə] f donation; **s~n** vt to donate, to give; **~r** (-s, -) m donor, donator

spendieren [ʃpɛn'diːrən] vt to pay for, to buy; **jdm etw ~** to treat sb to sth, to stand sb sth

Sperling ['ʃpɛrlɪŋ] m sparrow

Sperma ['ʃpɛrma] (-s, **Spermen**) nt sperm

Sperr- ['ʃpɛr] zW: **~e** f barrier; (*Verbot*) ban; **s~en** vt to block; (*SPORT*) to suspend, to bar; (*vom Ball*) to obstruct; (*einschließen*) to lock; (*verbieten*) to ban ♦ vr to baulk, to jib(e); **~gebiet** nt prohibited area; **~holz** nt plywood; **s~ig** adj bulky; **~müll** m bulky refuse; **~sitz** m (*THEAT*) stalls pl; **~stunde** f closing time

Spesen ['ʃpeːzən] pl expenses

Spezial- [ʃpetsi'aːl] in zW special; **~gebiet** nt specialist field; **s~i'sieren** vr to specialize; **~i'sierung** f specialization; **~ist** [-'lɪst] m specialist; **~i'tät** f speciality

speziell [ʃpetsi'ɛl] adj special

spezifisch [ʃpe'tsiːfɪʃ] adj specific

Sphäre ['sfɛːrə] f sphere

Spiegel ['ʃpiːgəl] (-s, -) m mirror; (*Wasser~*) level; (*MIL*) tab; **~bild** nt reflection; **s~bildlich** adj reversed; **~ei** nt fried egg; **s~n** vt to mirror, to reflect ♦ vr to be reflected ♦ vi to gleam; (*widerspiegeln*) to be reflective; **~ung** f reflection

Spiel [ʃpiːl] (-(e)s, -e) nt game; (*Schau~*) play; (*Tätigkeit*) play(ing); (*KARTEN*) deck; (*TECH*) (free) play; **s~en** vt, vi to play; (*um Geld*) to gamble; (*THEAT*) to perform, to act; **s~end** adv easily; **~er** (-s, -) m player; (*um Geld*) gambler; **~e'rei** f trifling pastime; **~feld** nt pitch, field; **~film** m feature film; **~kasino** nt casino; **~plan** m (*THEAT*) programme; **~platz** m playground; **~raum** m room to manoeuvre, scope; **~regel** f rule; **~sachen** pl toys; **~uhr** f musical box; **~verderber** (-s, -) m spoilsport; **~waren** pl toys; **~zeug** nt toy(s)

Spieß [ʃpiːs] (-es, -e) m spear; (*Brat~*) spit; **~bürger** m bourgeois; **~er** (-s, -; umg) m bourgeois

spießig (*pej*) adj (petit) bourgeois

Spikes [spaɪks] pl spikes; (*AUT*) studs

Spinat [ʃpi'naːt] (-(e)s, -e) m spinach

Spind [ʃpɪnt] (-(e)s, -e) m od nt locker

Spinn- [ʃpɪn] zW: **~e** f spider; **s~en** (*unreg*) vt, vi to spin; (umg) to talk rubbish; (*verrückt sein*) to be crazy od mad; **~e'rei** f spinning mill; **~rad** nt spinning-wheel; **~webe** f cobweb

Spion [ʃpi'oːn] (-s, -e) m spy; (*in Tür*) spyhole; **~age** [ʃpio'naːʒə] f espionage; **s~ieren** [ʃpio'niːrən] vi to spy; **~in** f (female) spy

Spirale [ʃpi'raːlə] f spiral

Spirituosen [ʃpiritu'oːzən] pl spirits

Spiritus ['ʃpiːritus] (-, -se) m (methylated) spirit

Spital [ʃpi'taːl] (-s, ⁻er) nt hospital

spitz [ʃpɪts] adj pointed; (*Winkel*) acute; (*fig: Zunge*) sharp; (: *Bemerkung*) caustic

Spitze f point, tip; (*Berg~*) peak; (*Bemerkung*) taunt, dig; (*erster Platz*) lead, top; (*meist pl: Gewebe*) lace

Spitzel (-s, -) m police informer

spitzen vt to sharpen

Spitzenmarke f brand leader

spitzfindig adj (over)subtle

Spitzname *m* nickname
Splitter ['ʃplɪtər] (**-s, -**) *m* splinter
sponsern ['spɔnzərn, 'ʃpɔnzərn] *vt* to sponsor
spontan [ʃpɔn'taːn] *adj* spontaneous
Sport [ʃpɔrt] (**-(e)s, -e**) *m* sport; (*fig*) hobby; **~lehrer(in)** *m(f)* games *od* P.E. teacher; **~ler(in)** (**-s, -**) *m(f)* sportsman(woman); **s~lich** *adj* sporting; (*Mensch*) sporty; **~platz** *m* playing *od* sports field; **~schuh** *m* (*Turnschuh*) training shoe, trainer; **~stadion** *nt* sports stadium; **~verein** *m* sports club; **~wagen** *m* sports car
Spott [ʃpɔt] (**-(e)s**) *m* mockery, ridicule; **s~billig** *adj* dirt-cheap; **s~en** *vi* to mock; **s~en (über** +*akk*) to mock (at), to ridicule
spöttisch ['ʃpœtɪʃ] *adj* mocking
sprach *etc* [ʃpraːx] *vb siehe* **sprechen**
Sprach- *zW*: **s~begabt** *adj* good at languages; **~e** *f* language; **~enschule** *f* language school; **~fehler** *m* speech defect; **~führer** *m* phrasebook; **~gefühl** *nt* feeling for language; **~kurs** *m* language course; **~labor** *nt* language laboratory; **s~lich** *adj* linguistic; **s~los** *adj* speechless
sprang *etc* [ʃpraŋ] *vb siehe* **springen**
Spray [spreː] (**-s, -s**) *m od nt* spray
Sprech- ['ʃprɛç] *zW*: **~anlage** *f* intercom; **s~en** (*unreg*) *vi* to speak, to talk ♦ *vt* to say; (*Sprache*) to speak; (*Person*) to speak to; **mit jdm s~en** to speak to sb; **das spricht für ihn** that's a point in his favour; **~er(in)** (**-s, -**) *m(f)* speaker; (*für Gruppe*) spokesman(woman); (*RADIO, TV*) announcer; **~stunde** *f* consultation (hour); (*doctor's*) surgery; **~stundenhilfe** *f* (doctor's) receptionist; **~zimmer** *nt* consulting room, surgery, office (*US*)
spreizen ['ʃpraɪtsən] *vt* (*Beine*) to open, to spread; (*Finger, Flügel*) to spread
Spreng- ['ʃprɛŋ] *zW*: **s~en** *vt* to sprinkle; (*mit Sprengstoff*) to blow up; (*Gestein*) to blast; (*Versammlung*) to break up; **~stoff** *m* explosive(s)
sprichst *etc* [ʃprɪçst] *vb siehe* **sprechen**
Sprichwort *nt* proverb

sprichwörtlich *adj* proverbial
Spring- ['ʃprɪŋ] *zW*: **~brunnen** *m* fountain; **s~en** (*unreg*) *vi* to jump; (*Glas*) to crack; (*mit Kopfsprung*) to dive; **~er** (**-s, -**) *m* jumper; (*Schach*) knight
Sprit [ʃprɪt] (**-(e)s, -e**; *umg*) *m* juice, gas
Spritz- ['ʃprɪts] *zW*: **~e** *f* syringe; injection; (*an Schlauch*) nozzle; **s~en** *vt* to spray; (*MED*) to inject ♦ *vi* to splash; (*heraus~*) to spurt; (*MED*) to give injections; **~pistole** *f* spray gun
spröde ['ʃprøːdə] *adj* brittle; (*Person*) reserved, coy
Sprosse ['ʃprɔsə] *f* rung
Sprößling ['ʃprœslɪŋ] (*umg*) *m* (*Kind*) offspring (*pl inv*)
Spruch [ʃprʊx] (**-(e)s, ⁀e**) *m* saying, maxim; (*JUR*) judgement
Sprudel ['ʃpruːdəl] (**-s, -**) *m* mineral water; lemonade; **s~n** *vi* to bubble; **~wasser** *nt* (*KOCH*) sparkling *od* fizzy mineral water
Sprüh- ['ʃpryː] *zW*: **~dose** *f* aerosol (can); **s~en** *vi* to spray; (*fig*) to sparkle ♦ *vt* to spray; **~regen** *m* drizzle
Sprung [ʃprʊŋ] (**-(e)s, ⁀e**) *m* jump; (*Riß*) crack; **~brett** *nt* springboard; **s~haft** *adj* erratic; (*Aufstieg*) rapid; **~schanze** *f* skijump
Spucke ['ʃpʊkə] (**-**) *f* spit; **s~n** *vt, vi* to spit
Spuk [ʃpuːk] (**-(e)s, -e**) *m* haunting; (*fig*) nightmare; **s~en** *vi* (*Geist*) to walk; **hier s~t es** this place is haunted
Spülbecken *nt* (*in Küche*) sink
Spule ['ʃpuːlə] *f* spool; (*ELEK*) coil
Spül- ['ʃpyːl] *zW*: **~e** *f* (kitchen) sink; **s~en** *vt, vi* to rinse; (*Geschirr*) to wash up; (*Toilette*) to flush; **~maschine** *f* dishwasher; **~mittel** *nt* washing-up liquid; **~stein** *m* sink; **~ung** *f* rinsing; flush; (*MED*) irrigation
Spur [ʃpuːr] (**-, -en**) *f* trace; (*Fuß~, Rad~, Tonband~*) track; (*Fährte*) trail; (*Fahr~*) lane
spürbar *adj* noticeable, perceptible
spüren ['ʃpyːrən] *vt* to feel
spurlos *adv* without (a) trace
Spurt [ʃpʊrt] (**-(e)s, -s** *od* **-e**) *m* spurt

spurten *vi* to spurt

sputen ['ʃpuːtən] *vr* to make haste

St. *abk* = **Stück**; (= *Sankt*) St.

Staat [ʃtaːt] (-(e)s, -en) *m* state; (*Prunk*) show; (*Kleidung*) finery; **mit etw ~ machen** to show off *od* parade sth; **s~enlos** *adj* stateless; **s~lich** *adj* state(-); state-run

Staats- *zW*: **~angehörige(r)** *f(m)* national; **~angehörigkeit** *f* nationality; **~anwalt** *m* public prosecutor; **~bürger** *m* citizen; **~dienst** *m* civil service; **~examen** *nt* (*UNIV*) state exam(ination); **s~feindlich** *adj* subversive; **~mann** (*pl* **-männer**) *m* statesman; **~oberhaupt** *nt* head of state

stämmig ['ʃtɛmɪç] *adj* sturdy; (*Mensch*) stocky

Stab [ʃtaːp] (-(e)s, ÷e) *m* rod; (*Gitter~*) bar; (*Menschen*) staff; **~hochsprung** *m* pole vault

stabil [ʃtaˈbiːl] *adj* stable; (*Möbel*) sturdy; **~i'sieren** *vt* to stabilize

Stachel ['ʃtaxəl] (-s, -n) *m* spike; (*von Tier*) spine; (*von Insekten*) sting; **~beere** *f* gooseberry; **~draht** *m* barbed wire; **s~ig** *adj* prickly; **~schwein** *nt* porcupine

Stadion ['ʃtaːdiɔn] (-s, **Stadien**) *nt* stadium

Stadium ['ʃtaːdiʊm] *nt* stage, phase

Stadt [ʃtat] (-, ÷e) *f* town; **~bücherei** *f* municipal library

Städt- ['ʃtɛːt] *zW*: **~ebau** *m* town planning; **~er(in)** (-s, -) *m(f)* town dweller; **s~isch** *adj* municipal; (*nicht ländlich*) urban

Stadt- *zW*: **~kern** *m* town centre, city centre; **~mauer** *f* city wall(s); **~mitte** *f* town centre; **~plan** *m* street map; **~rand** *m* outskirts *pl*; **~rat** *m* (*Behörde*) town council, city council; **~rundfahrt** *f* tour of a/the city; **~teil** *m* district, part of town; **~zentrum** *nt* town centre

Staffel ['ʃtafəl] (-, -n) *f* rung; (*SPORT*) relay (team); (*AVIAT*) squadron; **~lauf** *m* (*SPORT*) relay (race); **s~n** *vt* to graduate

Stahl [ʃtaːl] (-(e)s, ÷e) *m* steel

stahl *etc vb siehe* **stehlen**

stak *etc* [ʃtaːk] *vb siehe* **stecken**

Stall [ʃtal] (-(e)s, ÷e) *m* stable; (*Kaninchen~*) hutch; (*Schweine~*) sty;

(*Hühner~*) henhouse

Stamm [ʃtam] (-(e)s, ÷e) *m* (*Baum~*) trunk; (*Menschen~*) tribe; (*GRAM*) stem; **~baum** *m* family tree; (*von Tier*) pedigree; **s~eln** *vt*, *vi* to stammer; **s~en** *vi*: **s~en von** *od* **aus** to come from; **~gast** *m* regular (customer)

Stammtisch ['ʃtamtɪʃ] *m* table for the regulars

stampfen ['ʃtampfən] *vt*, *vi* to stamp; (*stapfen*) to tramp; (*mit Werkzeug*) to pound

Stand [ʃtant] (-(e)s, ÷e) *m* position; (*Wasser~, Benzin~ etc*) level; (*Stehen*) standing position; (*Zu~*) state; (*Spiel~*) score; (*Messe~ etc*) stand; (*Klasse*) class; (*Beruf*) profession

stand *etc vb siehe* **stehen**

Standard ['ʃtandart] (-s, -s) *m* standard

Ständer ['ʃtɛndər] (-s, -) *m* stand

Standes- ['ʃtandəs] *zW*: **~amt** *nt* registry office; **~beamte(r)** *m* registrar; **s~gemäß** *adj*, *adv* according to one's social position; **~unterschied** *m* social difference

Stand- *zW*: **s~haft** *adj* steadfast; **s~halten** (*unreg*) *vi*: (**jdm/etw**) **s~halten** to stand firm (against sb/sth), to resist (sb/sth)

ständig ['ʃtɛndɪç] *adj* permanent; (*ununterbrochen*) constant, continual

Stand- *zW*: **~licht** *nt* sidelights *pl*, parking lights *pl* (*US*); **~ort** *m* location; (*MIL*) garrison; **~punkt** *m* standpoint

Stange ['ʃtaŋə] *f* stick; (*Stab*) pole, bar; rod; (*Zigaretten*) carton; **von der ~** (*COMM*) off the peg; **eine ~ Geld** (*umg*) quite a packet

Stanniol [ʃtaniˈoːl] (-s, -e) *nt* tinfoil

Stapel ['ʃtaːpəl] (-s, -) *m* pile; (*NAUT*) stocks *pl*; **~lauf** *m* launch; **s~n** *vt* to pile (up)

Star[1] [ʃtaːr] (-(e)s, -e) *m* starling; (*MED*) cataract

Star[2] (-s, -s) *m* (*Film~ etc*) star

starb *etc* [ʃtarp] *vb siehe* **sterben**

stark [ʃtark] *adj* strong; (*heftig, groß*)

heavy; (*Maßangabe*) thick

Stärke ['ʃtɛrkə] *f* strength; heaviness; thickness; (*KOCH, Wäsche~*) starch; **s~n** *vt* to strengthen; (*Wäsche*) to starch

Starkstrom *m* heavy current

Stärkung ['ʃtɛrkʊŋ] *f* strengthening; (*Essen*) refreshment

starr [ʃtar] *adj* stiff; (*unnachgiebig*) rigid; (*Blick*) staring; **~en vor** *od* **von** to be covered in; (*Waffen*) to be bristling with; **S~heit** *f* rigidity; **~köpfig** *adj* stubborn; **S~sinn** *m* obstinacy

Start [ʃtart] **(-(e)s, -e)** *m* start; (*AVIAT*) takeoff; **~automatik** *f* (*AUT*) automatic choke; **~bahn** *f* runway; **s~en** *vt* to start ♦ *vi* to start; to take off; **~er (-s, -)** *m* starter; **~erlaubnis** *f* takeoff clearance

Station [ʃtatsi'oːn] *f* station; hospital ward; **S~är** [ʃtatsio'nɛːr] *adj* (*MED*) in-patient *attr*; **s~ieren** [-'niːrən] *vt* to station

Statist [ʃta'tɪst] *m* extra, supernumerary

Statistik *f* statistics *sg*; **~er (-s, -)** *m* statistician

statistisch *adj* statistical

Stativ [ʃta'tiːf] **(-s, -e)** *nt* tripod

statt [ʃtat] *konj* instead of ♦ *präp* (+*gen od dat*) instead of

Stätte ['ʃtɛtə] *f* place

statt- *zW*: **~finden** (*unreg*) *vi* to take place; **~haft** *adj* admissible; **~lich** *adj* imposing, handsome

Statue ['ʃtaːtuə] *f* statue

Status ['ʃtaːtʊs] **(-, -)** *m* status; **~symbol** *nt* status symbol

Stau [ʃtau] **(-(e)s, -e)** *m* blockage; (*Verkehrs~*) (traffic) jam

Staub [ʃtaup] **(-(e)s)** *m* dust; **s~en** ['ʃtaubən] *vi* to be dusty; **s~ig** *adj* dusty; **s~saugen** *vi* to vacuum, to hoover ®; **~sauger** *m* vacuum cleaner; **~tuch** *nt* duster

Staudamm *m* dam

Staude ['ʃtaudə] *f* shrub

stauen ['ʃtauən] *vt* (*Wasser*) to dam up; (*Blut*) to stop the flow of ♦ *vr* (*Wasser*) to become dammed up; (*MED, Verkehr*) to become congested; (*Menschen*) to collect; (*Gefühle*) to build up

staunen ['ʃtaunən] *vi* to be astonished; **S~ (-s)** *nt* amazement

Stausee **(-s, -n)** *m* reservoir, man-made lake

Stauung ['ʃtauʊŋ] *f* (*von Wasser*) damming-up; (*von Blut, Verkehr*) congestion

Std. *abk* (= *Stunde*) hr.

Steak [steːk] *nt* steak

Stech- ['ʃtɛç] *zW*: **s~en** (*unreg*) *vt* (*mit Nadel etc*) to prick; (*mit Messer*) to stab; (*mit Finger*) to poke; (*Biene etc*) to sting; (*Mücke*) to bite; (*Sonne*) to burn; (*KARTEN*) to take; (*ART*) to engrave; (*Torf, Spargel*) to cut; **in See s~en** to put to sea; **~en (-s, -)** *nt* (*SPORT*) play-off; jump-off; **s~end** *adj* piercing, stabbing; (*Geruch*) pungent; **~palme** *f* holly; **~uhr** *f* time clock

Steck- ['ʃtɛk] *zW*: **~brief** *m* "wanted" poster; **~dose** *f* (wall) socket; **s~en** *vt* to put, to insert; (*Nadel*) to stick; (*Pflanzen*) to plant; (*beim Nähen*) to pin ♦ *vi* (*auch unreg*) to be; (*festsitzen*) to be stuck; (*Nadeln*) to stick; **s~enbleiben** (*unreg*) *vi* to get stuck; **s~enlassen** (*unreg*) *vt* to leave in; **~enpferd** *nt* hobby-horse; **~er (-s, -)** *m* plug; **~nadel** *f* pin

Steg [ʃteːk] **(-(e)s, -e)** *m* small bridge; (*Anlege~*) landing stage; **~reif** *m*: **aus dem ~reif** just like that

stehen ['ʃteːən] (*unreg*) *vi* to stand; (*sich befinden*) to be; (*in Zeitung*) to say; (*still~*) to have stopped ♦ *vi unpers*: **es steht schlecht um jdn/etw** things are bad for sb/sth; **zu jdm/etw ~** to stand by sb/sth; **jdm ~** to suit sb; **wie steht's?** how are things?; (*SPORT*) what's the score?; **~ bleiben** to remain standing; **~bleiben** (*unreg*) *vi* (*Uhr*) to stop; (*Fehler*) to stay as it is; **~lassen** (*unreg*) *vt* to leave; (*Bart*) to grow

Stehlampe ['ʃteːlampə] *f* standard lamp

stehlen ['ʃteːlən] (*unreg*) *vt* to steal

Stehplatz ['ʃteːplats] *m* standing place

steif [ʃtaɪf] *adj* stiff; **S~heit** *f* stiffness

Steig- ['ʃtaɪk] *zW*: **~bügel** *m* stirrup; **~eisen** *nt* crampon; **s~en** ['ʃtaɪgən] (*unreg*) *vi* to rise; (*klettern*) to climb; **s~en in** +*akk*/**auf** +*akk* to get in/on; **s~ern** *vt* to raise; (*GRAM*) to compare ♦ *vi* (*Auktion*) to bid ♦ *vr* to increase; **~erung** *f* raising; (*GRAM*) comparison; **~ung** *f* incline, gradient, rise

steil [ʃtail] *adj* steep

Stein [ʃtain] (**-(e)s, -e**) *m* stone; (*in Uhr*) jewel; **~bock** *m* (*ASTROL*) Capricorn; **~bruch** *m* quarry; **s~ern** *adj* (*made of*) stone; (*fig*) stony; **~gut** *nt* stoneware; **s~ig** [ʃtainiç] *adj* stony; **s~igen** *vt* to stone; **~kohle** *f* mineral coal; **~zeit** *f* Stone Age

Stelle [ˈʃtɛlə] *f* place; (*Arbeit*) post, job; (*Amt*) office; **an Ihrer/meiner ~** in your/my place

stellen *vt* to put; (*Uhr etc*) to set; (*zur Verfügung ~*) to supply; (*fassen: Dieb*) to apprehend ♦ *vr* (*sich aufstellen*) to stand; (*sich einfinden*) to present o.s.; (*bei Polizei*) to give o.s. up; (*vorgeben*) to pretend (to be); **sich zu etw ~** to have an opinion of sth

Stellen- *zW*: **~angebot** *nt* offer of a post; (*in Zeitung*) "vacancies"; **~gesuch** *nt* application for a post; **~vermittlung** *f* employment agency

Stell- *zW*: **~ung** *f* position; (*MIL*) line; **~ung nehmen zu** to comment on; **~ungnahme** *f* comment; **s~vertretend** *adj* deputy, acting; **~vertreter** *m* deputy

Stelze [ˈʃtɛltsə] *f* stilt

Stemmbogen *m* (*SKI*) stem turn

stemmen [ˈʃtɛmən] *vt* to lift (up); (*drücken*) to press; **sich ~ gegen** (*fig*) to resist, to oppose

Stempel [ˈʃtɛmpəl] (**-s, -**) *m* stamp; (*BOT*) pistil; **~kissen** *nt* inkpad; **s~n** *vt* to stamp; (*Briefmarke*) to cancel; **s~n gehen** (*umg*) to be *od* go on the dole

Stengel [ˈʃtɛŋəl] (**-s, -**) *m* stalk

Steno- [ʃteno] *zW*: **~gramm** [-ˈgram] *nt* shorthand report; **~graphie** [-graˈfiː] *f* shorthand; **s~graphieren** [-graˈfiːrən] *vt, vi* to write (in) shorthand; **~typist(in)** [-tyˈpist(in)] *m(f)* shorthand typist

Stepp- [ˈʃtɛp] *zW*: **~decke** *f* quilt; **~e** *f* prairie; steppe; **s~en** *vt* to stitch ♦ *vi* to tap-dance

Sterb- [ˈʃtɛrb] *zW*: **~efall** *m* death;

~ehilfe *f* euthanasia; **s~en** (*unreg*) *vi* to die; **s~lich** [ˈʃtɛrpliç] *adj* mortal; **~lichkeit** *f* mortality; **~lichkeitsziffer** *f* death rate

stereo- [ˈsteːreo] *in zW* stereo(-); **S~anlage** *f* stereo (system); **~typ** [ʃtereoˈtyːp] *adj* stereotype

steril [ʃteˈriːl] *adj* sterile; **~isieren** *vt* to sterilize; **S~isierung** *f* sterilization

Stern [ʃtɛrn] (**-(e)s, -e**) *m* star; **~bild** *nt* constellation; **~schnuppe** *f* meteor, falling star; **~stunde** *f* historic moment

stet [ʃteːt] *adj* steady; **~ig** *adj* constant, continual; **~s** *adv* continually, always

Steuer[1] [ˈʃtɔyər] (**-s, -**) *nt* (*NAUT*) helm; (*~ruder*) rudder; (*AUT*) steering wheel

Steuer[2] (**-, -n**) *f* tax; **~berater(in)** *m(f)* tax consultant

Steuerbord *nt* (*NAUT, FLUG*) starboard

Steuer- [ˈʃtɔyər] *zW*: **~erklärung** *f* tax return; **~freibetrag** *m* tax allowance; **~klasse** *f* tax group; **~knüppel** *m* control column; (*AVIAT, COMPUT*) joystick; **~mann** (*pl* **-männer** *od* **-leute**) *m* helmsman; **s~n** *vt, vi* to steer; (*Flugzeug*) to pilot; (*Entwicklung, Tonstärke*) to control; **~rad** *nt* steering wheel; **~ung** *f* (*auch AUT*) steering; piloting; control; (*Vorrichtung*) controls *pl*; **~zahler** (**-s, -**) *m* taxpayer

Steward [ˈstjuːərt] (**-s, -s**) *m* steward; **~eß** [ˈstjuːərdɛs] (**-, -essen**) *f* stewardess; air hostess

Stich [ʃtiç] (**-(e)s, -e**) *m* (*Insekten~*) sting; (*Messer~*) stab; (*beim Nähen*) stitch; (*Färbung*) tinge; (*KARTEN*) trick; (*ART*) engraving; **jdn im ~ lassen** to leave sb in the lurch; **s~eln** *vi* (*fig*) to jibe; **s~haltig** *adj* sound, tenable; **~probe** *f* spot check; **~straße** *f* cul-de-sac; **~wahl** *f* final ballot; **~wort** *nt* cue; (*in Wörterbuch*) headword; (*für Vortrag*) note

sticken [ˈʃtikən] *vt, vi* to embroider

Stickeˈrei *f* embroidery

stickig *adj* stuffy, close

Stickstoff *m* nitrogen

Stief- [ˈʃtiːf] *in zW* step

Stiefel [ˈʃtiːfəl] (**-s, -**) *m* boot

Stief- *zW*: **~kind** *nt* stepchild; (*fig*)

Cinderella; **~mutter** *f* stepmother;
~mütterchen *nt* pansy; **s~mütterlich**
adj (*fig*): jdn/etw s~mütterlich
behandeln to pay little attention to sb/
sth; **~vater** *m* stepfather
Stiege ['ʃtiːɡə] *f* staircase
stiehlst *etc* [ʃtiːlst] *vb siehe* **stehlen**
Stiel [ʃtiːl] (-(e)s, -e) *m* handle; (*BOT*) stalk
Stier (-(e)s, -e) *m* bull; (*ASTROL*) Taurus
stier [ʃtiːr] *adj* staring, fixed; **~en** *vi* to
stare
Stierkampf *m* bullfight
Stierkämpfer *m* bullfighter
Stift [ʃtɪft] (-(e)s, -e) *m* peg; (*Nagel*) tack;
(*Farb~*) crayon; (*Blei~*) pencil ♦ *nt*
(charitable) foundation; (*ECCL*) religious
institution; **s~en** *vt* to found; (*Unruhe*) to
cause; (*spenden*) to contribute; **~er(in)**
(-s, -) *m(f)* founder; **~ung** *f* donation;
(*Organisation*) foundation; **~zahn** *m* post
crown
Stil [ʃtiːl] (-(e)s, -e) *m* style
still [ʃtɪl] *adj* quiet; (*unbewegt*) still;
(*heimlich*) secret; **S~er Ozean** Pacific;
S~e *f* stillness, quietness; **in aller S~e**
quietly; **~en** *vt* to stop; (*befriedigen*) to
satisfy; (*Säugling*) to breast-feed; **~halten**
(*unreg*) *vi* to keep still; **~(l)egen** *vt* to
close down; **~schweigen** (*unreg*) *vi* to be
silent; **S~schweigen** *nt* silence;
~schweigend *adj* silent;
(*Einverständnis*) tacit ♦ *adv* silently;
tacitly; **S~stand** *m* standstill; **~stehen**
(*unreg*) *vi* to stand still
Stimm- [ʃtɪm] *zW*: **~bänder** *pl* vocal
cords; **s~berechtigt** *adj* entitled to vote;
~e *f* voice; (*Wahlstimme*) vote; **s~en** *vt*
(*MUS*) to tune ♦ *vi* to be right; **das s~te**
ihn traurig that made him feel sad; **s~en**
für/gegen to vote for/against; **s~t so!**
that's right; **~enmehrheit** *f* majority (of
votes); **~enthaltung** *f* abstention;
~gabel *f* tuning fork; **~recht** *nt* right to
vote; **~ung** *f* mood; atmosphere;
s~ungsvoll *adj* enjoyable; full of
atmosphere; **~zettel** *m* ballot paper
stinken ['ʃtɪŋkən] (*unreg*) *vi* to stink
Stipendium [ʃtiˈpɛndiʊm] *nt* grant
stirbst *etc* [ʃtɪrpst] *vb siehe* **sterben**

Stirn [ʃtɪrn] (-, -en) *f* forehead, brow;
(*Frechheit*) impudence; **~band** *nt*
headband; **~höhle** *f* sinus
stöbern ['ʃtøːbərn] *vi* to rummage
stochern ['ʃtɔxərn] *vi* to poke (about)
Stock¹ [ʃtɔk] (-(e)s, ːe) *m* stick; (*BOT*)
stock
Stock² (-(e)s, - *od* **~werke**) *m* storey
stocken *vi* to stop, to pause; **~d** *adj*
halting
Stockung *f* stoppage
Stockwerk *nt* storey, floor
Stoff [ʃtɔf] (-(e)s, -e) *m* (*Gewebe*)
material, cloth; (*Materie*) matter; (*von
Buch etc*) subject (matter); **s~lich** *adj*
material; **~tier** *nt* soft toy; **~wechsel** *m*
metabolism
stöhnen ['ʃtøːnən] *vi* to groan
stoisch ['ʃtoːɪʃ] *adj* stoical
Stollen ['ʃtɔlən] (-s, -) *m* (*MIN*) gallery;
(*KOCH*) cake eaten at Christmas; (*von
Schuhen*) stud
stolpern ['ʃtɔlpərn] *vi* to stumble, to trip
Stolz [ʃtɔlts] (-es) *m* pride; **s~** *adj* proud;
s~ieren [ʃtɔlˈtsiːrən] *vi* to strut
stopfen ['ʃtɔpfən] *vt* (*hinein~*) to stuff;
(*voll~*) to fill (up); (*nähen*) to darn ♦ *vi*
(*MED*) to cause constipation
Stopfgarn *nt* darning thread
Stoppel ['ʃtɔpəl] (-, -n) *f* stubble
Stopp- ['ʃtɔp] *zW*: **s~en** *vt* to stop; (*mit
Uhr*) to time ♦ *vi* to stop; **~schild** *nt* stop
sign; **~uhr** *f* stopwatch
Stöpsel ['ʃtœpsəl] (-s, -) *m* plug; (*für
Flaschen*) stopper
Storch [ʃtɔrç] (-(e)s, ːe) *m* stork
Stör- ['ʃtøːr] *zW*: **s~en** *vt* to disturb;
(*behindern, RADIO*) to interfere with ♦ *vr*:
sich an etw *dat* **s~en** to let sth bother
one; **s~end** *adj* disturbing, annoying;
~enfried (-(e)s, -e) *m* troublemaker
störrisch ['ʃtœrɪʃ] *adj* stubborn, perverse
Störung *f* disturbance; interference
Stoß [ʃtoːs] (-es, ːe) *m* (*Schub*) push;
(*Schlag*) blow; knock; (*mit Schwert*)
thrust; (*mit Fuß*) kick; (*Erd~*) shock;
(*Haufen*) pile; **~dämpfer** (-s, -) *m* shock
absorber; **s~en** (*unreg*) *vt* (*mit Druck*) to
shove, to push; (*mit Schlag*) to knock, to

bump; (*mit Fuß*) to kick; (*Schwert etc*) to thrust; (*anstoßen: Kopf etc*) to bump ♦ *vr* to get a knock ♦ *vi:* **s~en an** *od* **auf** +*akk* to bump into; (*finden*) to come across; (*angrenzen*) to be next to; **sich s~en an** +*dat* (*fig*) to take exception to; **~stange** *f* (*AUT*) bumper

stottern ['ʃtɔtərn] *vt, vi* to stutter

Str. *abk* (= *Straße*) St.

Straf- ['ʃtraːf] *zW:* **~anstalt** *f* penal institution; **~arbeit** *f* (*SCH*) punishment; lines *pl*; **s~bar** *adj* punishable; **~e** *f* punishment; (*JUR*) penalty; (*Gefängnisstrafe*) sentence; (*Geldstrafe*) fine; **s~en** *vt* to punish

straff [ʃtraf] *adj* tight; (*streng*) strict; (*Stil etc*) concise; (*Haltung*) erect; **~en** *vt* to tighten, to taut

Strafgefangene(r) *mf* prisoner, convict

Strafgesetzbuch *nt* penal code

sträflich ['ʃtrɛːflɪç] *adj* criminal

Sträfling *m* convict

Straf- *zW:* **~porto** *nt* excess postage (charge); **~predigt** *f* telling-off; **~raum** *m* (*SPORT*) penalty area; **~recht** *nt* criminal law; **~stoß** *m* (*SPORT*) penalty (kick); **~tat** *f* punishable act; **~zettel** *m* ticket

Strahl [ʃtraːl] (-s, -en) *m* ray, beam; (*Wasser~*) jet; **s~en** *vi* to radiate; (*fig*) to beam; **~ung** *f* radiation

Strähne ['ʃtrɛːnə] *f* strand

stramm [ʃtram] *adj* tight; (*Haltung*) erect; (*Mensch*) robust

strampeln ['ʃtrampəln] *vi* to kick (about), to fidget

Strand [ʃtrant] (-(e)s, ̈e) *m* shore; (*mit Sand*) beach; **~bad** *nt* open-air swimming pool, lido; **s~en** ['ʃtrandən] *vi* to run aground; (*fig: Mensch*) to fail; **~gut** *nt* flotsam; **~korb** *m* beach chair

Strang [ʃtraŋ] (-(e)s, ̈e) *m* cord, rope; (*Bündel*) skein

Strapaz- *zW:* **~e** [ʃtra'paːtsə] *f* strain, exertion; **s~ieren** [ʃtrapa'tsiːrən] *vt* (*Material*) to treat roughly, to punish; (*Mensch, Kräfte*) to wear out, to exhaust; **s~ierfähig** *adj* hard-wearing; **s~iös** [ʃtrapatsi'øːs] *adj* exhausting, tough

Straße ['ʃtraːsə] *f* street, road

Straßen- *zW:* **~bahn** *f* tram, streetcar (*US*); **~beleuchtung** *f* street lighting; **~karte** *f* road map; **~kehrer** (-s, -) *m* roadsweeper; **~sperre** *f* roadblock; **~verkehr** *m* (road) traffic; **~verkehrsordnung** *f* highway code

Strateg- [ʃtra'teːg] *zW:* **~e** (-n, -n) *m* strategist; **~ie** [ʃtrate'giː] *f* strategy; **s~isch** *adj* strategic

sträuben ['ʃtrɔybən] *vt* to ruffle ♦ *vr* to bristle; (*Mensch*): **sich (gegen etw)** ~ to resist (sth)

Strauch [ʃtraʊx] (-(e)s, Sträucher) *m* bush, shrub

Strauß[1] [ʃtraʊs] (-es, Sträuße) *m* bunch; bouquet

Strauß[2] (-es, -e) *m* ostrich

Streb- [ʃtreːb] *zW:* **s~en** *vi* to strive, to endeavour; **s~en nach** to strive for; **~er** (-s, -; *pej*) *m* pusher, climber; (*SCH*) swot (*BRIT*); **s~sam** *adj* industrious

Strecke ['ʃtrɛkə] *f* stretch; (*Entfernung*) distance; (*EISENB, MATH*) line; **s~n** *vt* to stretch; (*Waffen*) to lay down; (*KOCH*) to eke out ♦ *vr* to stretch (o.s.)

Streich [ʃtraɪç] (-(e)s, -e) *m* trick, prank; (*Hieb*) blow; **s~eln** *vt* to stroke; **s~en** (*unreg*) *vt* (*berühren*) to stroke; (*auftragen*) to spread; (*anmalen*) to paint; (*durchstreichen*) to delete; (*nicht genehmigen*) to cancel ♦ *vi* (*berühren*) to brush; (*schleichen*) to prowl; **~holz** *nt* match; **~instrument** *nt* string instrument

Streif- [ʃtraɪf] *zW:* **~e** *f* patrol; **s~en** *vt* (*leicht berühren*) to brush against, to graze; (*Blick*) to skim over; (*Thema, Problem*) to touch on; (*abstreifen*) to take off ♦ *vi* (*gehen*) to roam; **~en** (-s, -) *m* (*Linie*) stripe; (*Stück*) strip; (*Film*) film; **~schuß** *m* graze, grazing shot; **~zug** *m* scouting trip

Streik [ʃtraɪk] (-(e)s, -s) *m* strike; **~brecher** (-s, -) *m* blackleg, strikebreaker; **s~en** *vi* to strike; **~posten** *m* (strike) picket

Streit [ʃtraɪt] (-(e)s, -e) *m* argument; dispute; **s~en** (*unreg*) *vi, vr* to argue; to dispute; **~frage** *f* point at issue; **s~ig** *adj:*

jdm etw s~ig machen to dispute sb's right to sth; **~igkeiten** *pl* quarrel *sg*, dispute *sg*; **~kräfte** *pl* (*MIL*) armed forces
streng [ʃtrɛŋ] *adj* severe; (*Lehrer, Maßnahme*) strict; (*Geruch etc*) sharp; **S~e** (-) *f* severity, strictness, sharpness; **~genommen** *adv* strictly speaking; **~gläubig** *adj* orthodox, strict; **~stens** *adv* strictly
Streß [ʃtrɛs] (-sses, -sse) *m* stress
stressen *vt* to put under stress
streuen [ˈʃtrɔʏən] *vt* to strew, to scatter, to spread; **Streuung** *f* dispersion
Strich [ʃtrɪç] (-(e)s, -e) *m* (*Linie*) line; (*Feder~, Pinsel~*) stroke; (*von Geweben*) nap; (*von Fell*) pile; **auf den ~ gehen** (*umg*) to walk the streets; **jdm gegen den ~ gehen** to rub sb up the wrong way; **einen ~ machen durch** to cross out; (*fig*) to foil; **~kode** *m* (*auf Waren*) barcode; **~mädchen** *nt* streetwalker; **~punkt** *m* semicolon; **s~weise** *adv* here and there
Strick [ʃtrɪk] (-(e)s, -e) *m* rope; **s~en** *vt*, *vi* to knit; **~jacke** *f* cardigan; **~leiter** *f* rope ladder; **~nadel** *f* knitting needle; **~waren** *pl* knitwear *sg*
striegeln [ˈʃtriːɡəln] *vt* (*Tiere, Fell*) to groom
strikt [ˈstrɪkt] *adj* strict
strittig [ˈʃtrɪtɪç] *adj* disputed, in dispute
Stroh [ʃtroː] (-(e)s) *nt* straw; **~blume** *f* everlasting flower; **~dach** *nt* thatched roof; **~halm** *m* (drinking) straw
Strom [ʃtroːm] (-(e)s, ⁀e) *m* river; (*fig*) stream; (*ELEK*) current; **s~'abwärts** *adv* downstream; **s~'aufwärts** *adv* upstream
strömen [ˈʃtrøːmən] *vi* to stream, to pour
Strom- *zW*: **~kreis** *m* circuit; **s~linienförmig** *adj* streamlined; **~sperre** *f* power cut
Strömung [ˈʃtrøːmʊŋ] *f* current
Strophe [ˈʃtroːfə] *f* verse
strotzen [ˈʃtrɔtsən] *vi*: **~ vor** *od* **von** to abound in, to be full of
Strudel [ˈʃtruːdəl] (-s, -) *m* whirlpool, vortex; (*KOCH*) strudel
Struktur [ʃtrʊkˈtuːr] *f* structure
Strumpf [ʃtrʊmpf] (-(e)s, ⁀e) *m* stocking; **~band** *nt* garter; **~hose** *f* (pair of) tights

Stube [ˈʃtuːbə] *f* room
Stuben- *zW*: **~arrest** *m* confinement to one's room; (*MIL*) confinement to quarters; **~hocker** (*umg*) *m* stay-at-home; **s~rein** *adj* house-trained
Stuck [ʃtʊk] (-(e)s) *m* stucco
Stück [ʃtʏk] (-(e)s, -e) *nt* piece; (*etwas*) bit; (*THEAT*) play; **~chen** *nt* little piece; **~lohn** *m* piecework wages *pl*; **s~weise** *adv* bit by bit, piecemeal; (*COMM*) individually
Student(in) [ʃtuˈdɛnt(ɪn)] *m(f)* student; **s~isch** *adj* student, academic
Studie [ˈʃtuːdiə] *f* study
studieren [ʃtuˈdiːrən] *vt*, *vi* to study
Studio [ˈʃtuːdio] (-s, -s) *nt* studio
Studium [ˈʃtuːdiʊm] *nt* studies *pl*
Stufe [ˈʃtuːfə] *f* step; (*Entwicklungs~*) stage; **s~nweise** *adv* gradually
Stuhl [ʃtuːl] (-(e)s, ⁀e) *m* chair; **~gang** *m* bowel movement
stülpen [ˈʃtʏlpən] *vt* (*umdrehen*) to turn upside down; (*bedecken*) to put
stumm [ʃtʊm] *adj* silent; (*MED*) dumb
Stummel [ˈʃtʊməl] (-s, -) *m* stump; (*Zigaretten~*) stub
Stummfilm *m* silent film
Stümper [ˈʃtʏmpər] (-s, -) *m* incompetent, duffer; **s~haft** *adj* bungling, incompetent; **s~n** *vi* to bungle
Stumpf [ʃtʊmpf] (-(e)s, ⁀e) *m* stump; **s~** *adj* blunt; (*teilnahmslos, glanzlos*) dull; (*Winkel*) obtuse; **~sinn** *m* tediousness; **s~sinnig** *adj* dull
Stunde [ˈʃtʊndə] *f* hour; (*SCH*) lesson
stunden *vt*: **jdm etw ~** to give sb time to pay sth; **S~geschwindigkeit** *f* average speed per hour; **S~kilometer** *pl* kilometres per hour; **~lang** *adj* for hours; **S~lohn** *m* hourly wage; **S~plan** *m* timetable; **~weise** *adv* by the hour; every hour
stündlich [ˈʃtʏntlɪç] *adj* hourly
Stups [ʃtʊps] (-es, -e; *umg*) *m* push; **~nase** *f* snub nose
stur [ʃtuːr] *adj* obstinate, pigheaded
Sturm [ʃtʊrm] (-(e)s, ⁀e) *m* storm, gale; (*MIL etc*) attack, assault
stürm- [ˈʃtʏrm] *zW*: **~en** *vi* (*Wind*) to

blow hard, to rage; (*rennen*) to storm ♦ *vt* (*MIL, fig*) to storm ♦ *vb unpers*: **es ~t** there's a gale blowing; **S~er** (-s, -) *m* (*SPORT*) forward, striker; **~isch** *adj* stormy

Sturmwarnung *f* gale warning

Sturz [ʃtʊrts] (-es, ⸚e) *m* fall; (*POL*) overthrow

stürzen ['ʃtʏrtsən] *vt* (*werfen*) to hurl; (*POL*) to overthrow; (*umkehren*) to overturn ♦ *vr* to rush; (*hinein~*) to plunge ♦ *vi* to fall; (*AVIAT*) to dive; (*rennen*) to dash

Sturzflug *m* nose-dive

Sturzhelm *m* crash helmet

Stute ['ʃtuːtə] *f* mare

Stützbalken *m* brace, joist

Stütze ['ʃtʏtsə] *f* support; help

stutzen ['ʃtʊtsən] *vt* to trim; (*Ohr, Schwanz*) to dock; (*Flügel*) to clip ♦ *vi* to hesitate; to become suspicious

stützen *vt* (*auch fig*) to support; (*Ellbogen etc*) to prop up

stutzig *adj* perplexed, puzzled; (*mißtrauisch*) suspicious

Stützpunkt *m* point of support; (*von Hebel*) fulcrum; (*MIL, fig*) base

Styropor [ʃtyro'poːr] (®; -s) *nt* polystyrene

s.u. *abk* = **siehe unten**

Subjekt [zʊp'jɛkt] (-(e)s, -e) *nt* subject; **s~iv** [-'tiːf] *adj* subjective; **~ivi'tät** *f* subjectivity

Subsidiarität *f* subsidiarity

Substantiv ['zʊpstantiːf] (-s, -e) *nt* noun

Substanz [zʊp'stants] *f* substance

subtil [zʊp'tiːl] *adj* subtle

subtrahieren [zʊptra'hiːrən] *vt* to subtract

subtropisch ['zʊptroːpɪʃ] *adj* subtropical

Subvention [zʊpvɛntsi'oːn] *f* subsidy; **s~ieren** [-'niːrən] *vt* to subsidize

Such- ['zuːx] *zW*: **~aktion** *f* search; **~e** *f* search; **s~en** *vt* to look (for), to seek; (*versuchen*) to try ♦ *vi* to seek, to search; **~er** (-s, -) *m* seeker, searcher; (*PHOT*) viewfinder

Sucht [zʊxt] (-, ⸚e) *f* mania; (*MED*) addiction, craving

süchtig ['zʏçtɪç] *adj* addicted; **S~e(r)** *mf* addict

Süd- ['zyːt] *zW*: **~en** ['zyːdən] (-s) *m* south; **~früchte** *pl* Mediterranean fruit *sg*; **s~lich** *adj* southern; **s~lich von** (to the) south of; **~pol** *m* South Pole; **s~wärts** *adv* southwards

süffig ['zʏfɪç] *adj* (*Wein*) pleasant to the taste

süffisant [zyfi'zant] *adj* smug

suggerieren [zʊɡe'riːrən] *vt* to suggest

Sühne ['zyːnə] *f* atonement, expiation; **s~n** *vt* to atone for, to expiate

Sultan ['zʊltan] (-s, -e) *m* sultan; **~ine** [zʊlta'niːnə] *f* sultana

Sülze ['zʏltsə] *f* brawn

Summe ['zʊmə] *f* sum, total

summen *vt*, *vi* to buzz; (*Lied*) to hum

Sumpf [zʊmpf] (-(e)s, ⸚e) *m* swamp, marsh; **s~ig** *adj* marshy

Sünde ['zʏndə] *f* sin; **~nbock** (*umg*) *m* scapegoat; **~nfall** *m* Fall (of man); **~r(in)** (-s, -) *m(f)* sinner; **sündigen** *vi* to sin

Super ['zuːpər] (-s) *nt* (*Benzin*) four star (petrol) (*BRIT*), premium (*US*); **~lativ** [-latiːf] (-s, -e) *m* superlative; **~macht** *f* superpower; **~markt** *m* supermarket

Suppe ['zʊpə] *f* soup; **~nteller** *m* soup plate

süß [zyːs] *adj* sweet; **S~e** (-) *f* sweetness; **~en** *vt* to sweeten; **S~igkeit** *f* sweetness; (*Bonbon etc*) sweet (*BRIT*), candy (*US*); **~lich** *adj* sweetish; (*fig*) sugary; **~sauer** *adj* (*Gurke*) pickled; (*Sauce etc*) sweet-and-sour; **S~speise** *f* pudding, sweet; **S~stoff** *m* sweetener; **S~waren** *pl* confectionery (*sing*); **S~wasser** *nt* fresh water

Sylvester [zyl'vɛstər] (-s, -) *nt* = **Silvester**

Symbol [zym'boːl] (-s, -e) *nt* symbol; **s~isch** *adj* symbolic(al)

Symmetrie [zyme'triː] *f* symmetry

symmetrisch [zy'meːtrɪʃ] *adj* symmetrical

Sympathie [zympa'tiː] *f* liking, sympathy; **sympathisch** [zym'paːtɪʃ] *adj* likeable; **er ist mir sympathisch** I like him; **sympathi'sieren** *vi* to sympathize

Symphonie [zymfo'niː] *f* (*MUS*)

symphony

Symptom [zʏmpˈtoːm] (-s, -e) *nt* symptom; **s~atisch** [zʏmptoˈmaːtɪʃ] *adj* symptomatic

Synagoge [zynaˈɡoːɡə] *f* synagogue

synchron [zʏnˈkroːn] *adj* synchronous; **S~getriebe** *nt* synchromesh (gears *pl*); **~i'sieren** *vt* to synchronize; (*Film*) to dub

Synonym [zynoˈnyːm] (-s, -e) *nt* synonym; **s~** *adj* synonymous

Synthese [zʏnˈteːzə] *f* synthesis

synthetisch [zʏnˈteːtɪʃ] *adj* synthetic

Syphilis [ˈzyːfilɪs] (-) *f* syphilis

System [zʏsˈteːm] (-s, -e) *nt* system; **s~atisch** [zʏsteˈmaːtɪʃ] *adj* systematic; **s~ati'sieren** *vt* to systematize

Szene [ˈstseːnə] *f* scene; **~rie** [stsenəˈriː] *f* scenery

T t

t *abk* (= *Tonne*) t

Tabak [ˈtaːbak] (-s, -e) *m* tobacco

Tabell- [taˈbɛl] *zW*: **t~arisch** [tabɛˈlaːrɪʃ] *adj* tabular; **~e** *f* table

Tablett [taˈblɛt] *nt* tray; **~e** *f* tablet, pill

Tabu [taˈbuː] *nt* taboo; **t~** *adj* taboo

Tachometer [taxoˈmeːtər] (-s, -) *m* (*AUT*) speedometer

Tadel [ˈtaːdəl] (-s, -) *m* censure; scolding; (*Fehler*) fault, blemish; **t~los** *adj* faultless, irreproachable; **t~n** *vt* to scold

Tafel [ˈtaːfəl] (-, -n) *f* (*auch MATH*) table; (*Anschlag~*) board; (*Wand~*) blackboard; (*Schiefer~*) slate; (*Gedenk~*) plaque; (*Illustration*) plate; (*Schalt~*) panel; (*Schokolade etc*) bar

Taft [taft] (-(e)s, -e) *m* taffeta

Tag [taːk] (-(e)s, -e) *m* day; daylight; **unter/über ~e** (*MIN*) underground/on the surface; **an den ~ kommen** to come to light; **guten ~!** good morning/afternoon!; **t~aus** *adv*: **t~aus, t~ein** day in, day out; **~dienst** *m* day duty

Tage- [ˈtaːɡə] *zW*: **~buch** [ˈtaːɡəbuːx] *nt* diary, journal; **~geld** *nt* daily allowance; **t~lang** *adv* for days; **t~n** *vi* to sit, to meet ♦ *vb unpers*: **es tagt** dawn is breaking

Tages- *zW*: **~ablauf** *m* course of the day; **~anbruch** *m* dawn; **~fahrt** *f* day trip; **~karte** *f* menu of the day; (*Fahrkarte*) day ticket; **~licht** *nt* daylight; **~ordnung** *f* agenda; **~zeit** *f* time of day; **~zeitung** *f* daily (paper)

täglich [ˈtɛːklɪç] *adj, adv* daily

tagsüber [ˈtaːksyːbər] *adv* during the day

Tagung *f* conference

Taille [ˈtaljə] *f* waist

Takt [takt] (-(e)s, -e) *m* tact; (*MUS*) time; **~gefühl** *nt* tact

Taktik *f* tactics *pl*

taktisch *adj* tactical

Takt- *zW*: **t~los** *adj* tactless; **~losigkeit** *f* tactlessness; **~stock** *m* (conductor's) baton; **t~voll** *adj* tactful

Tal [taːl] (-(e)s, ⁼er) *nt* valley

Talent [taˈlɛnt] (-(e)s, -e) *nt* talent; **t~iert** [talɛnˈtiːrt] *adj* talented, gifted

Talisman [ˈtaːlɪsman] (-s, -e) *m* talisman

Talsohle *f* bottom of a valley

Talsperre *f* dam

Tamburin [tambuˈriːn] (-s, -e) *nt* tambourine

Tampon [ˈtampɔn] (-s, -s) *m* tampon

Tandem (-s, -s) *nt* tandem

Tang [taŋ] (-(e)s, -e) *m* seaweed

Tangente [taŋˈɡɛntə] *f* tangent

Tango (-s, -s) *m* tango

Tank [taŋk] (-s, -s) *m* tank; **t~en** *vi* to fill up with petrol (*BRIT*) *od* gas (*US*); (*AVIAT*) to (re)fuel; **~er** (-s, -) *m* tanker; **~schiff** *nt* tanker; **~stelle** *f* petrol (*BRIT*) *od* gas (*US*) station; **~wart** *m* petrol pump (*BRIT*) *od* gas station (*US*) attendant

Tanne [ˈtanə] *f* fir; **~nbaum** *m* fir tree; **~nzapfen** *m* fir cone

Tante [ˈtantə] *f* aunt

Tanz [tants] (-es, ⁼e) *m* dance; **t~en** *vt, vi* to dance

Tänzer(in) [ˈtɛntsər(ɪn)] (-s, -) *m(f)* dancer

Tanzfläche *f* (dance) floor

Tanzschule *f* dancing school

Tapete [taˈpeːtə] *f* wallpaper; **~nwechsel** *m* (*fig*) change of scenery

tapezieren [tape'tsi:rən] *vt* to (wall)paper

Tapezierer [tape'tsi:rər] (**-s**, **-**) *m* (interior) decorator

tapfer ['tapfər] *adj* brave; **T~keit** *f* courage, bravery

Tarif [ta'ri:f] (**-s**, **-e**) *m* tariff, (scale of) fares *od* charges; **~lohn** *m* standard wage rate; **~verhandlungen** *pl* wage negotiations

Tarn- ['tarn] *zW*: **t~en** *vt* to camouflage; (*Person, Absicht*) to disguise; **~farbe** *f* camouflage paint; **~ung** *f* camouflaging; disguising

Tasche ['taʃə] *f* pocket; handbag

Taschen- *in zW* pocket; **~buch** *nt* paperback; **~dieb** *m* pickpocket; **~geld** *nt* pocket money; **~lampe** *f* (electric) torch, flashlight (*US*); **~messer** *nt* penknife; **~tuch** *nt* handkerchief

Tasse ['tasə] *f* cup

Tastatur [tasta'tu:r] *f* keyboard

Taste ['tastə] *f* push-button control; (*an Schreibmaschine*) key; **t~en** *vt* to feel, to touch ♦ *vi* to feel, to grope ♦ *vr* to feel one's way

Tat [ta:t] (**-**, **-en**) *f* act, deed, action; **in der ~** indeed, as a matter of fact; **t~** *etc vb siehe* **tun**; **~bestand** *m* facts *pl* of the case; **t~enlos** *adj* inactive

Tät- ['tɛ:t] *zW*: **~er(in)** (**-s**, **-**) *m(f)* perpetrator, culprit; **t~ig** *adj* active; **in einer Firma t~ig sein** to work for a firm; **~igkeit** *f* activity; (*Beruf*) occupation; **t~lich** *adj* violent; **~lichkeit** *f* violence; **~lichkeiten** *pl* (*Schläge*) blows

tätowieren [tɛto'vi:rən] *vt* to tattoo

Tatsache *f* fact

tatsächlich *adj* actual ♦ *adv* really

Tau[1] [tau] (**-(e)s**, **-e**) *nt* rope

Tau[2] (**-(e)s**) *m* dew

taub [taup] *adj* deaf; (*Nuß*) hollow

Taube ['taubə] *f* dove; pigeon; **~nschlag** *m* dovecote; **hier geht es zu wie in einem ~nschlag** it's a hive of activity here

taub- *zW*: **T~heit** *f* deafness; **~stumm** *adj* deaf-and-dumb

Tauch- ['taux] *zW*: **t~en** *vt* to dip ♦ *vi* to dive; (*NAUT*) to submerge; **~er** (**-s**, **-**) *m*

diver; **~eranzug** *m* diving suit; **~erbrille** *f* diving goggles *pl*; **~sieder** (**-s**, **-**) *m* immersion coil (*for boiling water*)

tauen ['tauən] *vt*, *vi* to thaw ♦ *vb unpers*: **es taut** it's thawing

Tauf- ['tauf] *zW*: **~becken** *nt* font; **~e** *f* baptism; **t~en** *vt* to christen, to baptize; **~name** *m* Christian name; **~pate** *m* godfather; **~patin** *f* godmother; **~schein** *m* certificate of baptism

taug- ['taug] *zW*: **~en** *vi* to be of use; **~en für** to do for, to be good for; **nicht ~en** to be no good *od* useless; **T~enichts** (**-es**, **-e**) *m* good-for-nothing; **~lich** ['tauklɪç] *adj* suitable; (*MIL*) fit (for service)

Taumel ['tauməl] (**-s**) *m* dizziness; (*fig*) frenzy; **t~n** *vi* to reel, to stagger

Tausch [tauʃ] (**-(e)s**, **-e**) *m* exchange; **t~en** *vt* to exchange, to swap

täuschen ['tɔyʃən] *vt* to deceive ♦ *vi* to be deceptive ♦ *vr* to be wrong; **~d** *adj* deceptive

Tauschhandel *m* barter

Täuschung *f* deception; (*optisch*) illusion

tausend ['tauzənt] *num* (a) thousand; **T~füßler** (**-s**, **-**) *m* centipede; millipede

Tauwetter *nt* thaw

Taxi ['taksi] (**-(s)**, **-(s)**) *nt* taxi; **~fahrer** *m* taxi driver; **~stand** *m* taxi rank

Tech- ['tɛç] *zW*: **~nik** *f* technology; (*Methode, Kunstfertigkeit*) technique; **~niker** (**-s**, **-**) *m* technician; **t~nisch** *adj* technical; **~nolo'gie** *f* technology; **t~no'logisch** *adj* technological

TEE [te:'e:'e:] (**-**, **-(s)**) *m abk* (= *Trans-Europ-Express*) Trans-European Express

Tee [te:] (**-s**, **-s**) *m* tea; **~beutel** *m* tea bag; **~kanne** *f* teapot; **~löffel** *m* teaspoon

Teer [te:r] (**-(e)s**, **-e**) *m* tar; **t~en** *vt* to tar

Teesieb *nt* tea strainer

Teich [taıç] (**-(e)s**, **-e**) *m* pond

Teig [taık] (**-(e)s**, **-e**) *m* dough; **t~ig** ['taıgıç] *adj* doughy; **~waren** *pl* pasta *sg*

Teil [taıl] (**-(e)s**, **-e**) *m od nt* part; (*An~*) share; (*Bestand~*) component; **zum ~** partly; **t~bar** *adj* divisible; **~betrag** *m* instalment; **~chen** *nt* (atomic) particle; **t~en** *vt*, *vr* to divide; (*mit jdm*) to share; **t~haben** (*unreg*) *vi*: **t~haben an** +*dat* to

share in; **~haber** (-s, -) *m* partner;
~kaskoversicherung *f* third party, fire
and theft insurance; **~nahme** *f*
participation; (*Mitleid*) sympathy;
t~nahmslos *adj* disinterested, apathetic;
t~nehmen (*unreg*) *vi*: **t~nehmen an**
+*dat* to take part in; **~nehmer** (-s, -) *m*
participant; **t~s** *adv* partly; **~ung** *f*
division; **t~weise** *adv* partially, in part;
~zahlung *f* payment by instalments;
~zeitarbeit *f* part-time work

Teint [tɛ:] (-s, -s) *m* complexion

Telefax ['telefaks] *nt* fax

Telefon [tele'fo:n] (-s, -e) *nt* telephone;
~anruf *m* (tele)phone call; **~at**
[telefo'na:t] (-(e)s, -e) *nt* (tele)phone call;
~buch *nt* telephone directory; **~hörer** *m*
(telephone) receiver; **t~ieren**
[telefo'ni:rən] *vi* to telephone; **t~isch** [-ɪʃ]
adj telephone; (*Benachrichtigung*) by
telephone; **~ist(in)** [telefo'nɪst(ɪn)] *m(f)*
telephonist; **~karte** *f* phonecard;
~nummer *f* (tele)phone number; **~zelle** *f*
telephone kiosk, callbox; **~zentrale** *f*
telephone exchange

Telegraf [tele'gra:f] (-en, -en) *m*
telegraph; **~enmast** *m* telegraph pole;
~ie [-'fi:] *f* telegraphy; **t~ieren** [-'fi:rən]
vt, vi to telegraph, to wire; **t~isch** *adj*
telegraphic

Telegramm [tele'gram] (-s, -e) *nt*
telegram, cable; **~adresse** *f* telegraphic
address

Tele- *zW*: **~objektiv** ['te:le'ɔpjɛkti:f] *nt*
telephoto lens; **t~pathisch** [tele'pa:tɪʃ]
adj telepathic; **~skop** [tele'sko:p] (-s, -e)
nt telescope

Telex ['te:leks] (-es, -e) *nt* telex

Teller ['tɛlər] (-s, -) *m* plate

Tellergericht *nt* (*KOCH*) one-course meal

Tempel ['tɛmpəl] (-s, -) *m* temple

Temperament [tɛmpera'mɛnt] *nt*
temperament; (*Schwung*) vivacity,
liveliness; **t~voll** *adj* high-spirited, lively

Temperatur [tɛmpera'tu:r] *f* temperature

Tempo[1] ['tɛmpo] (-s, -s) *nt* speed, pace;
~! get a move on!

Tempo[2] (-s, **Tempi**) *nt* (*MUS*) tempo

Tendenz [tɛn'dɛnts] *f* tendency; (*Absicht*)

intention; **t~iös** [-i'ø:s] *adj* biased,
tendentious

tendieren [tɛn'di:rən] *vi*: **~ zu** to show a
tendency to, to incline towards

Tennis ['tɛnɪs] (-) *nt* tennis; **~ball** *m*
tennis ball; **~platz** *m* tennis court;
~schläger *m* tennis racket; **~schuh** *m*
tennis shoe; **~spieler(in)** *m(f)* tennis
player

Tenor [te'no:r] (-s, ⸚e) *m* tenor

Teppich ['tɛpɪç] (-s, -e) *m* carpet;
~boden *m* wall-to-wall carpeting

Termin [tɛr'mi:n] (-s, -e) *m* (*Zeitpunkt*)
date; (*Frist*) time limit, deadline; (*Arzt~
etc*) appointment; **~kalender** *m* diary,
appointments book; **~planer** *m* personal
organizer

Termite [tɛr'mi:tə] *f* termite

Terpentin [tɛrpɛn'ti:n] (-s, -e) *nt*
turpentine, turps *sg*

Terrasse [tɛ'rasə] *f* terrace

Terrine [tɛ'ri:nə] *f* tureen

territorial [tɛritori'a:l] *adj* territorial

Territorium [tɛri'to:rium] *nt* territory

Terror ['tɛrɔr] (-s) *m* terror; reign of
terror; **t~isieren** [tɛrori'zi:rən] *vt* to
terrorize; **~ismus** [-'rɪsmus] *m* terrorism;
~ist [-'rɪst] *m* terrorist

Terz [tɛrts] (-, -en) *f* (*MUS*) third; **~ett**
[tɛr'tsɛt] (-(e)s, -e) *nt* trio

Tesafilm ['te:zafɪlm] ® *m* Sellotape ®
(*BRIT*), Scotch tape ® (*US*)

Test [tɛst] (-s, -s) *m* test

Testament [tɛsta'mɛnt] *nt* will,
testament; (*REL*) Testament; **t~arisch**
[-'ta:rɪʃ] *adj* testamentary; **~svoll-
strecker** *m* executor (of a will)

testen *vt* to test

Tetanus ['te:tanus] (-) *nt* tetanus;
~impfung *f* (anti-)tetanus injection

teuer ['tɔyər] *adj* dear, expensive; **T~ung**
f increase in prices; **T~ungszulage** *f*
cost of living bonus

Teufel ['tɔyfəl] (-s, -) *m* devil

teuflisch ['tɔyflɪʃ] *adj* fiendish, diabolical

Text [tɛkst] (-(e)s, -e) *m* text; (*Lieder~*)
words *pl*; **t~en** *vi* to write the words

textil [tɛks'ti:l] *adj* textile; **T~ien** *pl*
textiles; **T~industrie** *f* textile industry;

T~waren *pl* textiles

Textverarbeitung *f* word processing

Theater [te'a:tər] (-s, -) *nt* theatre; (*umg*) fuss; ~ **spielen** (*auch fig*) to playact; ~**besucher** *m* playgoer; ~**kasse** *f* box office; ~**stück** *nt* (stage-)play

Theke ['te:kə] *f* (*Schanktisch*) bar; (*Ladentisch*) counter

Thema ['te:ma] (-s, Themen *od* -ta) *nt* theme, topic, subject

Themse ['tɛmzə] *f* Thames

Theo- [teo] *zW:* ~**loge** [-'lo:gə] (-n, -n) *m* theologian; ~**logie** [-lo'gi:] *f* theology; **t~logisch** [-'lo:gɪʃ] *adj* theological; ~**retiker** [-'re:tikər] (-s, -) *m* theorist; **t~retisch** [-'re:tɪʃ] *adj* theoretical; ~**rie** [-'ri:] *f* theory

Thera- [tera] *zW:* ~**peut** [-'pɔyt] (-en, -en) *m* therapist; **t~peutisch** [-'pɔytɪʃ] *adj* therapeutic; ~**pie** [-'pi:] *f* therapy

Therm- *zW:* ~**albad** [tɛr'ma:lba:t] *nt* thermal bath; thermal spa; ~**odrucker** ['tɛrmo-] *m* thermal printer; ~**ometer** [tɛrmo'me:tər] (-s, -) *nt* thermometer; ~**osflasche** ® ['tɛrmɔsflaʃə] *f* Thermos ® flask; ~**ostat** [tɛrmo'sta:t] (-(e)s *od* -en, -e(n)) *m* thermostat

These ['te:zə] *f* thesis

Thrombose [trɔm'bo:zə] *f* thrombosis

Thron [tro:n] (-(e)s, -e) *m* throne; **t~en** *vi* to sit enthroned (*fig*) to sit in state; ~**folge** *f* succession (to the throne)

Thunfisch ['tu:nfɪʃ] *m* tuna

Thymian ['ty:mia:n] (-s, -e) *m* thyme

Tick [tɪk] (-(e)s, -s) *m* tic; (*Eigenart*) quirk; (*Fimmel*) craze

ticken *vi* to tick

tief [ti:f] *adj* deep; (*~sinnig*) profound; (*Ausschnitt, Preis, Ton*) low; **T~** (-s, -s) *nt* (*MET*) depression; **T~druck** *m* low pressure; **T~e** *f* depth; **T~ebene** *f* plain; **T~enpsychologie** *f* depth psychology; **T~enschärfe** *f* (*PHOT*) depth of focus; **T~garage** *f* underground garage; ~**gekühlt** *adj* frozen; ~**greifend** *adj* far-reaching; **T~kühlfach** *nt* deep-freeze compartment; **T~kühlkost** *f* (deep) frozen food; **T~kühltruhe** *f* deep-freeze, freezer; **T~punkt** *m* low point; (*fig*) low ebb

T~schlag *m* (*BOXEN, fig*) blow below the belt; ~**schürfend** *adj* profound; **T~see** *f* deep sea; ~**sinnig** *adj* profound; melancholy; **T~stand** *m* low level; **T~stwert** *m* minimum *od* lowest value

Tier [ti:r] (-(e)s, -e) *nt* animal; ~**arzt** *m* vet(erinary surgeon); ~**garten** *m* zoo(logical gardens *pl*); ~**heim** *nt* cat/dog home; **t~isch** *adj* animal; (*auch fig*) brutish; (*fig: Ernst etc*) deadly; ~**kreis** *m* zodiac; ~**kunde** *f* zoology; **t~liebend** *adj* fond of animals; ~**park** *m* zoo; ~**quälerei** [-kvɛ:lə'raɪ] *f* cruelty to animals; ~**schutzverein** *m* society for the prevention of cruelty to animals

Tiger(in) ['ti:gər(ɪn)] (-s, -) *m(f)* tiger(gress)

tilgen ['tɪlgən] *vt* to erase; (*Sünden*) to expiate; (*Schulden*) to pay off

Tinte ['tɪntə] *f* ink; ~**nfisch** *m* cuttlefish; ~**nstift** *m* copying *od* indelible pencil

Tip [tɪp] *m* tip; **t~pen** *vt, vi* to tap, to touch; (*umg: schreiben*) to type; (*im Lotto etc*) to bet (on); **auf jdn t~pen** (*umg: raten*) to tip sb, to put one's money on sb (*fig*)

Tipp- [tɪp] *zW:* ~**fehler** (*umg*) *m* typing error; **t~topp** (*umg*) *adj* tip-top; ~**zettel** *m* (pools) coupon

Tirol [ti'ro:l] *nt* the Tyrol; ~**er(in)** *m(f)* Tyrolean; **t~isch** *adj* Tyrolean

Tisch [tɪʃ] (-(e)s, -e) *m* table; **bei ~** at table; **vor/nach ~** before/after eating; **unter den ~ fallen** (*fig*) to be dropped; ~**decke** *f* tablecloth; ~**ler** (-s, -) *m* carpenter, joiner; ~**le'rei** *f* joiner's workshop; (*Arbeit*) carpentry, joinery; **t~lern** *vi* to do carpentry *etc*; ~**rede** *f* after-dinner speech; ~**tennis** *nt* table tennis; ~**tuch** *nt* tablecloth

Titel ['ti:təl] (-s, -) *m* title; ~**bild** *nt* cover (picture); (*von Buch*) frontispiece; ~**rolle** *f* title role; ~**seite** *f* cover; (*Buch~*) title page; ~**verteidiger** *m* defending champion, title holder

Toast [to:st] (-(e)s, -s *od* -e) *m* toast; ~**brot** *nt* bread for toasting; ~**er** (-s, -) *m* toaster

tob- ['to:b] *zW:* ~**en** *vi* to rage; (*Kinder*) to romp about; ~**süchtig** *adj* maniacal

Tochter ['tɔxtər] (-, ¨) *f* daughter; **~gesellschaft** *f* subsidiary (company)

Tod [to:t] (-(e)s, -e) *m* death; **t~ernst** *adj* deadly serious ♦ *adv* in dead earnest

Todes- ['to:dəs] *zW:* **~angst** [-aŋst] *f* mortal fear; **~anzeige** *f* obituary (notice); **~fall** *m* death; **~strafe** *f* death penalty; **~ursache** *f* cause of death; **~urteil** *nt* death sentence; **~verachtung** *f* utter disgust

todkrank *adj* dangerously ill

tödlich ['tø:tlɪç] *adj* deadly, fatal

tod- *zW:* **~müde** *adj* dead tired; **~schick** *(umg) adj* smart, classy; **~sicher** *(umg) adj* absolutely *od* dead certain; **T~sünde** *f* deadly sin

Toilette [toa'lɛtə] *f* toilet, lavatory; *(Frisiertisch)* dressing table; *(Kleidung)* outfit

Toiletten- *zW:* **~artikel** *pl* toiletries, toilet articles; **~papier** *nt* toilet paper; **~tisch** *m* dressing table

toi, toi, toi ['tɔy 'tɔy 'tɔy] *excl* touch wood

tolerant [tole'rant] *adj* tolerant

Toleranz [tole'rants] *f* tolerance

tolerieren [tole'ri:rən] *vt* to tolerate

toll [tɔl] *adj* mad; *(Treiben)* wild; *(umg)* terrific; **~en** *vi* to romp; **T~kirsche** *f* deadly nightshade; **~kühn** *adj* daring; **T~wut** *f* rabies

Tomate [to'ma:tə] *f* tomato; **~nmark** *nt* tomato purée

Tombola ['tɔmbola] *f* tombola

Ton¹ [to:n] (-(e)s, -e) *m (Erde)* clay

Ton² (-(e)s, ¨e) *m (Laut)* sound; *(MUS)* note; *(Redeweise)* tone; *(Farb~, Nuance)* shade; *(Betonung)* stress; **~abnehmer** *m* pick-up; **t~angebend** *adj* leading; **~art** *f* (musical) key; **~band** *nt* tape; **~bandgerät** *nt* tape recorder

tönen ['tø:nən] *vi* to sound ♦ *vt* to shade; *(Haare)* to tint

tönern ['tø:nərn] *adj* clay

Ton- *zW:* **~fall** *m* intonation; **~film** *m* sound film; **~leiter** *f (MUS)* scale; **t~los** *adj* soundless

Tonne ['tɔnə] *f* barrel; *(Maß)* ton

Tontaube *f* clay pigeon

Tonwaren *pl* pottery *sg*, earthenware *sg*

Topf [tɔpf] (-(e)s, ¨e) *m* pot; **~blume** *f* pot plant

Töpfer ['tœpfər] (-s, -) *m* potter; **~ei** [-'rai] *f* piece of pottery; potter's workshop; **~scheibe** *f* potter's wheel

topographisch [topo'gra:fɪʃ] *adj* topographic

Tor¹ [to:r] (-en, -en) *m* fool

Tor² (-(e)s, -e) *nt* gate; *(SPORT)* goal; **~bogen** *m* archway

Torf [tɔrf] (-(e)s) *m* peat

Torheit *f* foolishness; foolish deed

töricht ['tø:rɪçt] *adj* foolish

torkeln ['tɔrkəln] *vi* to stagger, to reel

Torpedo [tɔr'pe:do] (-s, -s) *m* torpedo

Torte ['tɔrtə] *f* cake; *(Obst~)* flan, tart

Tortur [tɔr'tu:r] *f* ordeal

Torwart (-(e)s, -e) *m* goalkeeper

tosen ['to:zən] *vi* to roar

tot [to:t] *adj* dead

total [to'ta:l] *adj* total; **~itär** [totali'tɛ:r] *adj* totalitarian; **T~schaden** *m (AUT)* complete write-off

Tote(r) *mf* dead person

töten ['tø:tən] *vt, vi* to kill

Toten- ['to:tən] *zW:* **~bett** *nt* death bed; **t~blaß** *adj* deathly pale, white as a sheet; **~kopf** *m* skull; **~schein** *m* death certificate; **~stille** *f* deathly silence

tot- *zW:* **~fahren** *(unreg) vt* to run over; **~geboren** *adj* stillborn; **~lachen** *(umg) vr* to laugh one's head off

Toto ['to:to] (-s, -s) *m od nt* pools *pl*; **~schein** *m* pools coupon

tot- *zW:* **T~schlag** *m* manslaughter; **~schlagen** *(unreg) vt (auch fig)* to kill; **~schweigen** *(unreg) vt* to hush up; **~stellen** *vr* to pretend to be dead

Tötung ['tø:tʊŋ] *f* killing

Toupet [tu'pe:] (-s, -s) *nt* toupee

toupieren [tu'pi:rən] *vt* to back-comb

Tour [tu:r] (-, -en) *f* tour, trip; *(Umdrehung)* revolution; *(Verhaltensart)* way; **in einer ~** incessantly; **~enzähler** *m* rev counter; **~ismus** [tu'rɪsmʊs] *m* tourism; **~ist** [tu'rɪst] *m* tourist; **~istenklasse** *f* tourist class; **~nee** [tʊr'ne:] (-, -n) *f (THEAT etc)* tour; **auf ~nee**

gehen to go on tour
Trab [traːp] (-(e)s) *m* trot
Trabantenstadt *f* satellite town
traben ['traːbən] *vi* to trot
Tracht [traxt] (-, -en) *f* (*Kleidung*) costume, dress; **eine ~ Prügel** a sound thrashing; **t~en** *vi*: **t~en (nach)** to strive (for); **jdm nach dem Leben t~en** to seek to kill sb; **danach t~en, etw zu tun** to strive *od* endeavour to do sth
trächtig ['trɛçtɪç] *adj* (*Tier*) pregnant
Tradition [traditsiˈoːn] *f* tradition; **t~ell** [-'nɛl] *adj* traditional
traf *etc* [traːf] *vb siehe* **treffen**
Tragbahre *f* stretcher
tragbar *adj* (*Gerät*) portable; (*Kleidung*) wearable; (*erträglich*) bearable
träge ['trɛːgə] *adj* sluggish, slow; (*PHYS*) inert
tragen ['traːgən] (*unreg*) *vt* to carry; (*Kleidung, Brille*) to wear; (*Namen, Früchte*) to bear; (*erdulden*) to endure ♦ *vi* (*schwanger sein*) to be pregnant; (*Eis*) to hold; **sich mit einem Gedanken ~** to have an idea in mind; **zum T~ kommen** to have an effect
Träger ['trɛːgər] (-s, -) *m* carrier; wearer; bearer; (*Ordens~*) holder; (*an Kleidung*) (shoulder) strap; (*Körperschaft etc*) sponsor; **~rakete** *f* launch vehicle
Tragetasche *f* carrier bag
Tragfläche *f* (*AVIAT*) wing
Tragflügelboot *nt* hydrofoil
Trägheit ['trɛːkhaɪt] *f* laziness; (*PHYS*) inertia
Tragik ['traːgɪk] *f* tragedy
tragisch ['traːgɪʃ] *adj* tragic
Tragödie [traˈgøːdiə] *f* tragedy
Tragweite *f* range; (*fig*) scope
Train- ['trɛːn] *zW:* **~er** (-s, -) *m* (*SPORT*) trainer, coach; (*Fußball*) manager; **t~ieren** [trɛˈniːrən] *vt, vi* to train; (*Mensch*) to train, to coach; (*Übung*) to practise; **~ing** (-s, -s) *nt* training; **~ingsanzug** *m* track suit
Traktor ['traktɔr] *m* tractor; (*von Drucker*) tractor feed
trällern ['trɛlərn] *vt, vi* to trill, to sing
Tram (-, -s) *f* tram

trampeln ['trampəln] *vt, vi* to trample, to stamp
trampen ['trɛmpən] *vi* to hitch-hike
Tramper(in) (-s, -) *m(f)* hitch-hiker
Tran [traːn] (-(e)s, -e) *m* train oil, blubber
tranchieren [trãˈʃiːrən] *vt* to carve
Träne ['trɛːnə] *f* tear; **t~n** *vi* to water; **~ngas** *nt* teargas
trank *etc* [traŋk] *vb siehe* **trinken**
tränken ['trɛŋkən] *vt* (*Tiere*) to water
Trans- *zW:* **~formator** [transfɔrˈmaːtɔr] *m* transformer; **~istor** [tranˈzɪstɔr] *m* transistor; **~itverkehr** [tranˈziːtfɛrkeːr] *m* transit traffic; **~itvisum** *nt* transit visa; **t~parent** [transpaˈrɛnt] *adj* transparent; **~parent** (-(e)s, -e) *nt* (*Bild*) transparency; (*Spruchband*) banner; **~plantation** [transplantatsiˈoːn] *f* transplantation; (*Hauttransplantation*) graft(ing)
Transport [transˈpɔrt] (-(e)s, -e) *m* transport; **t~ieren** [transpɔrˈtiːrən] *vt* to transport; **~kosten** *pl* transport charges, carriage *sg*; **~mittel** *nt* means *sg* of transportation; **~unternehmen** *nt* carrier
Trapez [traˈpeːts] (-es, -e) *nt* trapeze; (*MATH*) trapezium
Traube ['traubə] *f* grape; bunch (of grapes); **~nzucker** *m* glucose
trauen ['trauən] *vi*: **jdm/etw ~** to trust sb/sth ♦ *vr* to dare ♦ *vt* to marry
Trauer ['trauər] (-) *f* sorrow; (*für Verstorbenen*) mourning; **~fall** *m* death, bereavement; **~feier** *f* funeral service; **~kleidung** *f* mourning; **t~n** *vi* to mourn; **um jdn t~n** to mourn (for) sb; **~rand** *m* black border; **~spiel** *nt* tragedy
traulich ['traulɪç] *adj* cosy, intimate
Traum [traum] (-(e)s, Träume) *m* dream
Trauma (-s, -men) *nt* trauma
träum- ['trɔym] *zW:* **~en** *vt, vi* to dream; **T~er** (-s, -) *m* dreamer; **T~e'rei** *f* dreaming; **~erisch** *adj* dreamy
traumhaft *adj* dreamlike; (*fig*) wonderful
traurig ['trauɾɪç] *adj* sad; **T~keit** *f* sadness
Trau- ['trau] *zW:* **~ring** *m* wedding ring; **~schein** *m* marriage certificate; **~ung** *f* wedding ceremony; **~zeuge** *m* witness

(to a marriage); **~zeugin** *f* witness (at a marriage ceremony)

treffen ['trɛfən] (*unreg*) *vt* to strike, to hit; (*Bemerkung*) to hurt; (*begegnen*) to meet; (*Entscheidung etc*) to make; (*Maßnahmen*) to take ♦ *vi* to hit ♦ *vr* to meet; **er hat es gut getroffen** he did well; **~ auf** +*akk* to come across, to meet with; **es traf sich, daß ...** it so happened that ...; **es trifft sich gut** it's convenient; **wie es so trifft** as these things happen; **T~** (-s, -) *nt* meeting; **~d** *adj* pertinent, apposite

Treffer (-s, -) *m* hit; (*Tor*) goal; (*Los*) winner

Treffpunkt *m* meeting place

Treib- ['traɪb] *zW*: **~eis** *nt* drift ice; **t~en** (*unreg*) *vt* to drive; (*Studien etc*) to pursue; (*Sport*) to do, to go in for ♦ *vi* (*Schiff etc*) to drift; (*Pflanzen*) to sprout; (*KOCH: aufgehen*) to rise; (*Tee, Kaffee*) to be diuretic; **Unsinn t~en** to fool around; **~haus** *nt* greenhouse; **~hauseffekt** *m* greenhouse effect; **~hausgas** *nt* greenhouse gas; **~stoff** *m* fuel

trenn- ['trɛn] *zW*: **~bar** *adj* separable; **~en** *vt* to separate; (*teilen*) to divide ♦ *vr* to separate; **sich ~en von** to part with; **T~ung** *f* separation; **T~wand** *f* partition (wall)

Trepp- ['trɛp] *zW*: **t~ab** *adv* downstairs; **t~auf** *adv* upstairs; **~e** *f* stair(case); **~engeländer** *nt* banister; **~enhaus** *nt* staircase

Tresor [tre'zoːr] (-s, -e) *m* safe

Tretboot *nt* pedalo, pedal boat

treten ['treːtən] (*unreg*) *vi* to step; (*Tränen, Schweiß*) to appear ♦ *vt* (*mit Fußtritt*) to kick; (*nieder~*) to tread, to trample; **~ nach** to kick at; **~ in** +*akk* to step in(to); **in Verbindung ~** to get in contact; **in Erscheinung ~** to appear

treu [trɔy] *adj* faithful, true; **T~e** (-) *f* loyalty, faithfulness; **T~händer** (-s, -) *m* trustee; **T~handgesellschaft** *f* trust company; **~herzig** *adj* innocent; **~los** *adj* faithless

Tribüne [tri'byːnə] *f* grandstand; (*Redner~*) platform

Trichter ['trɪçtər] (-s, -) *m* funnel; (*in Boden*) crater

Trick [trɪk] (-s, -e *od* -s) *m* trick; **~film** *m* cartoon

Trieb [triːp] (-(e)s, -e) *m* urge, drive; (*Neigung*) inclination; (*an Baum etc*) shoot; **t~** *etc vb siehe* **treiben**; **~feder** *f* (*fig*) motivating force; **~kraft** *f* (*fig*) drive; **~täter** *m* sex offender; **~werk** *nt* engine

triefen ['triːfən] *vi* to drip

triffst *etc* [trɪfst] *vb siehe* **treffen**

triftig ['trɪftɪç] *adj* good, convincing

Trikot [tri'koː] (-s, -s) *nt* vest; (*SPORT*) shirt

Trimester [tri'mɛstər] (-s, -) *nt* term

trimmen ['trɪmən] *vr* to do keep fit exercises

trink- ['trɪŋk] *zW*: **~bar** *adj* drinkable; **~en** (*unreg*) *vt, vi* to drink; **T~er** (-s, -) *m* drinker; **T~geld** *nt* tip; **T~halle** *f* refreshment kiosk; **T~wasser** *nt* drinking water

Tripper ['trɪpər] (-s, -) *m* gonorrhoea

Tritt [trɪt] (-(e)s, -e) *m* step; (*Fuß~*) kick; **~brett** *nt* (*EISENB*) step; (*AUT*) running-board

Triumph [tri'ʊmf] (-(e)s, -e) *m* triumph; **~bogen** *m* triumphal arch; **t~ieren** [trium'fiːrən] *vi* to triumph; (*jubeln*) to exult

trocken ['trɔkən] *adj* dry; **T~element** *nt* dry cell; **T~haube** *f* hair-dryer; **T~heit** *f* dryness; **~legen** *vt* (*Sumpf*) to drain; (*Kind*) to put a clean nappy on; **T~milch** *f* dried milk; **T~rasur** *f* dry shave, electric shave

trocknen ['trɔknən] *vt, vi* to dry

Trödel ['trøːdəl] (-s; *umg*) *m* junk; **~markt** *m* flea market; **t~n** (*umg*) *vi* to dawdle

Trog [troːk] (-(e)s, ⁺e) *m* trough

Trommel ['trɔməl] (-, -n) *f* drum; **~fell** *nt* eardrum; **t~n** *vt, vi* to drum

Trompete [trɔm'peːtə] *f* trumpet; **~r** (-s, -) *m* trumpeter

Tropen ['troːpən] *pl* tropics; **~helm** *m* sun helmet

tröpfeln ['trœpfəln] *vi* to drop, to trickle

Tropfen ['trɔpfən] (-s, -) *m* drop; **t~** *vt, vi*

to drip ♦ *vb unpers*: **es tropft** a few
raindrops are falling; **t~weise** *adv* in
drops
Tropfsteinhöhle *f* stalactite cave
tropisch ['tro:pɪʃ] *adj* tropical
Trost [tro:st] (-es) *m* consolation, comfort
trösten ['trø:stən] *vt* to console, to
comfort
trost- *zW*: **~los** *adj* bleak; (*Verhältnisse*)
wretched; **T~preis** *m* consolation prize;
~reich *adj* comforting
Trott [trɔt] (-(e)s, -e) *m* trot; (*Routine*)
routine; **~el** (-s, -; *umg*) *m* fool, dope;
t~en *vi* to trot; **~oir** [trɔto'a:r] (-s, -s *od*
-e) *nt* pavement, sidewalk (*US*)
Trotz [trɔts] (-es) *m* pigheadedness; **etw
aus ~ tun** to do sth just to show them;
jdm zum ~ in defiance of sb; **t~** *präp*
(+*gen od dat*) in spite of; **t~dem** *adv*
nevertheless, all the same ♦ *konj* although; **t~en** *vi* (+*dat*) to defy; (*der Kälte,
Klima etc*) to withstand; (*der Gefahr*) to
brave; (*trotzig sein*) to be awkward; **t~ig**
adj defiant, pig-headed; **~kopf** *m*
obstinate child
trüb [try:p] *adj* dull; (*Flüssigkeit, Glas*)
cloudy; (*fig*) gloomy
Trubel ['tru:bəl] (-s) *m* hurly-burly
trüb- *zW*: **~en** ['try:bən] *vt* to cloud ♦ *vr*
to become clouded; **T~heit** *f* dullness;
cloudiness; gloom; **T~sal** (-, -e) *f* distress;
~selig *adj* sad, melancholy; **T~sinn** *m*
depression; **~sinnig** *adj* depressed,
gloomy
Trüffel ['tryfəl] (-, -n) *f* truffle
trug *etc* [tru:k] *vb siehe* **tragen**
trügen ['try:gən] (*unreg*) *vt* to deceive
♦ *vi* to be deceptive
trügerisch *adj* deceptive
Trugschluß ['tru:gʃlʊs] *m* false
conclusion
Truhe ['tru:ə] *f* chest
Trümmer ['trʏmər] *pl* wreckage *sg*;
(*Bau~*) ruins; **~haufen** *m* heap of rubble
Trumpf [trʊmpf] (-(e)s, ̈-e) *m* (*auch fig*)
trump; **t~en** *vt, vi* to trump
Trunk [trʊŋk] (-(e)s, ̈-e) *m* drink; **t~en**
adj intoxicated; **~enheit** *f* intoxication;
~enheit am Steuer drunken driving;

~sucht *f* alcoholism
Trupp [trʊp] (-s, -s) *m* troop; **~e** *f* troop;
(*Waffengattung*) force; (*Schauspiel~*)
troupe; **~en** *pl* (MIL) troops;
~enübungsplatz *m* training area
Truthahn ['tru:tha:n] *m* turkey
Tschech- ['tʃɛç] *zW*: **~e** *m* Czech,
Czechoslovak(ian); **~in** *f* Czech, Czecho-
slovak(ian); **t~isch** *adj* Czech,
Czechoslovak(ian); **~oslowake**
[-oslo'va:kə] *m* Czech, Czechoslovak(ian);
~oslowakei [-oslova'kaɪ] *f*: **die**
~oslowakei Czechoslovakia;
t~oslowakisch [-oslo'va:kɪʃ] *adj* Czech,
Czechoslovak(ian)
tschüs [tʃy:s] *excl* cheerio
T-Shirt ['ti:ʃœrt] *nt* T-shirt
Tube ['tu:bə] *f* tube
Tuberkulose [tubɛrku'lo:zə] *f*
tuberculosis
Tuch [tu:x] (-(e)s, ̈er) *nt* cloth; (*Hals~*)
scarf; (*Kopf~*) headscarf; (*Hand~*) towel
tüchtig ['tʏçtɪç] *adj* efficient, (cap)able;
(*umg*: *kräftig*) good, sound; **T~keit** *f*
efficiency, ability
Tücke ['tʏkə] *f* (*Arglist*) malice; (*Trick*)
trick; (*Schwierigkeit*) difficulty, problem;
seine ~n haben to be temperamental
tückisch ['tʏkɪʃ] *adj* treacherous;
(*böswillig*) malicious
Tugend ['tu:gənt] (-, -en) *f* virtue; **t~haft**
adj virtuous
Tüll [tʏl] (-s, -e) *m* tulle
Tülle *f* spout
Tulpe ['tʊlpə] *f* tulip
Tumor ['tu:mɔr] (-s, -e) *m* tumour
Tümpel ['tʏmpəl] (-s, -) *m* pool, pond
Tumult [tu'mʊlt] (-(e)s, -e) *m* tumult
tun [tu:n] (*unreg*) *vt* (*machen*) to do;
(*legen*) to put ♦ *vi* to act ♦ *vr*: **es tut sich
etwas/viel** something/a lot is happening;
jdm etw ~ (*antun*) to do sth to sb; **etw
tut es auch** sth will do; **das tut nichts**
that doesn't matter; **das tut nichts zur
Sache** that's neither here nor there; **so ~,
als ob** to act as if
tünchen ['tʏnçən] *vt* to whitewash
Tunke ['tʊŋkə] *f* sauce; **t~n** *vt* to dip, to
dunk

tunlichst ['tu:nlɪçst] *adv* if at all possible; **~ bald** as soon as possible

Tunnel ['tʊnəl] (**-s, -s** *od* **-**) *m* tunnel

Tupfen ['tʊpfən] (**-s, -**) *m* dot, spot; **t~** *vt, vi* to dab; (*mit Farbe*) to dot

Tür [ty:r] (**-, -en**) *f* door

Turban ['tʊrba:n] (**-s, -e**) *m* turban

Turbine [tʊr'bi:nə] *f* turbine

Türk- [tyrk] *zW:* **~e** *m* Turk; **~ei** [tyr'kaɪ] *f:* **die ~ei** Turkey; **~in** *f* Turk

Türkis [tyr'ki:s] (**-es, -e**) *m* turquoise; **t~** *adj* turquoise

türkisch ['tyrkɪʃ] *adj* Turkish

Türklinke *f* doorknob, door handle

Turm [tʊrm] (**-(e)s, -e**) *m* tower; (*Kirch~*) steeple; (*Sprung~*) diving platform; (*SCHACH*) castle, rook

türmen ['tyrmən] *vr* to tower up ♦ *vt* to heap up ♦ *vi* (*umg*) to scarper, to bolt

Turn- ['tʊrn] *zW:* **t~en** *vi* to do gymnastic exercises ♦ *vt* to perform; **~en** (**-s**) *nt* gymnastics; (*SCH*) physical education, P.E.; **~er(in)** (**-s, -**) *m(f)* gymnast; **~halle** *f* gym (**-nasium**); **~hose** *f* gym shorts *pl*

Turnier [tʊr'ni:r] (**-s, -e**) *nt* tournament

Turn- *zW:* **~schuh** *m* gym shoe; **~verein** *m* gymnastics club; **~zeug** *nt* gym things *pl*

Tusche ['tʊʃə] *f* Indian ink

tuscheln ['tʊʃəln] *vt, vi* to whisper

Tuschkasten *m* paintbox

Tüte ['ty:tə] *f* bag

tuten ['tu:tən] *vi* (*AUT*) to hoot (*BRIT*), to honk (*US*)

TÜV [tyf] (**-s, -s**) *m abk* (= *Technischer Überwachungsverein*) ≈ MOT

Typ [ty:p] (**-s, -en**) *m* type; **~e** *f* (*TYP*) type

Typhus ['ty:fʊs] (**-**) *m* typhoid (fever)

typisch ['ty:pɪʃ] *adj:* **~ (für)** typical (of)

Tyrann [ty'ran] (**-en, -en**) *m* tyrant; **~ei** [-'naɪ] *f* tyranny; **t~isch** *adj* tyrannical; **t~i'sieren** *vt* to tyrannize

U u

u.a. *abk* = **unter anderem**

U-Bahn ['u:ba:n] *f* underground, tube

übel ['y:bəl] *adj* bad; (*moralisch*) bad,
wicked; **jdm ist ~** sb feels sick; **Ü~** (**-s, -**) *nt* evil; (*Krankheit*) disease; **~gelaunt** *adj* bad-tempered; **Ü~keit** *f* nausea; **~nehmen** (*unreg*) *vt:* **jdm eine Bemerkung** *etc* **~nehmen** to be offended at sb's remark *etc*

üben ['y:bən] *vt, vi* to exercise, to practise

SCHLÜSSELWORT

über ['y:bər] *präp +dat* **1** (*räumlich*) over, above; **zwei Grad über Null** two degrees above zero

2 (*zeitlich*) over; **über der Arbeit einschlafen** to fall asleep over one's work

♦ *präp +akk* **1** (*räumlich*) over; (*hoch über auch*) above; (*quer über auch*) across

2 (*zeitlich*) over; **über Weihnachten** over Christmas; **über kurz oder lang** sooner or later

3 (*mit Zahlen*): **Kinder über 12 Jahren** children over *od* above 12 years of age; **ein Scheck über 200 Mark** a cheque for 200 marks

4 (*auf dem Wege*) via; **nach Köln über Aachen** to Cologne via Aachen; **ich habe es über die Auskunft erfahren** I found out from information

5 (*betreffend*) about; **ein Buch über ...** a book about *od* on ...; **über jdn/etw lachen** to laugh about *od* at sb/sth

6: **Macht über jdn haben** to have power over sb; **sie liebt ihn über alles** she loves him more than everything

♦ *adv* over; **über und über** over and over; **den ganzen Tag über** all day long; **jdm in etw** *dat* **über sein** to be superior to sb in sth

überall [y:bər'al] *adv* everywhere; **~'hin** *adv* everywhere

überanstrengen [y:bər''anʃtrɛŋən] *vt insep* to overexert ♦ *vr insep* to overexert o.s.

überarbeiten [y:bər''arbaɪtən] *vt insep* to revise, to rework ♦ *vr insep* to overwork (o.s.)

überaus ['y:bər'aʊs] *adv* exceedingly

überbelichten → *überlaufen*

überbelichten ['y:bərbəliçtən] *vt (PHOT)* to overexpose

über'bieten *(unreg) vt insep* to outbid; *(übertreffen)* to surpass; *(Rekord)* to break

Überbleibsel ['y:bərblaipsəl] *(-s, -) nt* residue, remainder

Überblick ['y:bərblɪk] *m* view; *(fig: Darstellung)* survey, overview; *(Fähigkeit)*: ~ **(über** +*akk*) grasp (of), overall view (of); **ü~en** [-'blɪkən] *vt insep* to survey

überbring- [y:bər'brɪŋ] *zW*: ~**en** *(unreg) vt insep* to deliver, to hand over; **Ü~er** *(-s, -) m* bearer

überbrücken [y:bər'brʏkən] *vt insep* to bridge

über'dauern *vt insep* to outlast

über'denken *(unreg) vt insep* to think over

überdies [y:bər'di:s] *adv* besides

überdimensional ['y:bərdimɛnzɪona:l] *adj* oversize

Überdruß ['y:bərdrʊs] *(-sses) m* weariness; **bis zum** ~ ad nauseam

übereifrig ['y:bər'aifrɪç] *adj* overkeen

übereilt [y:bər'ailt] *adj* (over)hasty, premature

überein- [y:bər'ain] *zW*: ~**ander** [y:bər'ai'nandər] *adv* one upon the other; *(sprechen)* about each other; ~**kommen** *(unreg) vi* to agree; **Ü~kunft** *(-, -künfte) f* agreement; ~**stimmen** *vi* to agree; **Ü~stimmung** *f* agreement

überempfindlich ['y:bər'ɛmpfɪntlɪç] *adj* hypersensitive

überfahren [y:bər'fa:rən] *(unreg) vt insep (AUT)* to run over; *(fig)* to walk all over

Überfahrt ['y:bərfa:rt] *f* crossing

Überfall ['y:bərfal] *m (Bank~, MIL)* raid; *(auf jdn)* assault; **ü~en** [-'falən] *(unreg) vt insep* to attack; *(Bank)* to raid; *(besuchen)* to drop in on, to descend on

überfällig ['y:bərfɛlɪç] *adj* overdue

über'fliegen *(unreg) vt insep* to fly over, to overfly; *(Buch)* to skim through

Überfluß ['y:bərflʊs] *m*: ~ **(an** +*dat)* (super)abundance (of), excess (of)

überflüssig ['y:bərflʏsɪç] *adj* superfluous

über'fordern *vt insep* to demand too

much of; *(Kräfte etc)* to overtax

über'führen *vt insep (Leiche etc)* to transport; *(Täter)* to have convicted

Über'führung *f* transport; conviction; *(Brücke)* bridge, overpass

über'füllt *adj (Schulen, Straßen)* overcrowded; *(Kurs)* oversubscribed

Übergabe ['y:bərga:bə] *f* handing over; *(MIL)* surrender

Übergang ['y:bərgaŋ] *m* crossing; *(Wandel, Überleitung)* transition

Übergangs- *zW*: ~**lösung** *f* provisional solution, stopgap; ~**stadium** *nt* transitional stage; ~**zeit** *f* transitional period

über'geben *(unreg) vt insep* to hand over; *(MIL)* to surrender ♦ *vr insep* to be sick; **dem Verkehr** ~ to open to traffic

übergehen ['y:bərge:ən] *(unreg) vi (Besitz)* to pass; *(zum Feind etc)* to go over, to defect; ~ **in** +*akk* to turn into; **über'gehen** *(unreg) vt insep* to pass over, to omit

Übergewicht ['y:bərgəvɪçt] *nt* excess weight; *(fig)* preponderance

überglücklich ['y:bərglʏklɪç] *adj* overjoyed

überhaupt [y:bər'haupt] *adv* at all; *(im allgemeinen)* in general; *(besonders)* especially; ~ **nicht/keine** not/none at all

überheblich [y:bər'he:plɪç] *adj* arrogant; **Ü~keit** *f* arrogance

über'holen *vt insep* to overtake; *(TECH)* to overhaul

über'holt *adj* out-of-date, obsolete

Überholverbot *nt* restriction on overtaking

über'hören *vt insep* not to hear; *(absichtlich)* to ignore

überirdisch ['y:bər'ɪrdɪʃ] *adj* supernatural, unearthly

über'laden *(unreg) vt insep* to overload ♦ *adj (fig)* cluttered

über'lassen *(unreg) vt insep*: **jdm etw** ~ to leave sth to sb ♦ *vr insep*: **sich einer Sache** *dat* ~ to give o.s. over to sth

über'lasten *vt insep* to overload; *(Mensch)* to overtax

überlaufen ['y:bərlaufən] *(unreg) vi*

(*Flüssigkeit*) to flow over; (*zum Feind etc*) to go over, to defect; **~ sein** to be inundated *od* besieged; **über'laufen** (*unreg*) *vt insep* (*Schauer*) to come over

Überläufer ['y:bərlɔyfər] (**-s, -**) *m* deserter

über'leben *vt insep* to survive; **Ü~de(r)** *mf* survivor

über'legen *vt insep* to consider ♦ *adj* superior; **ich muß es mir ~** I'll have to think about it; **Ü~heit** *f* superiority

Über'legung *f* consideration, deliberation

über'liefern *vt insep* to hand down, to transmit

Überlieferung *f* tradition

überlisten [y:bər'lɪstən] *vt insep* to outwit

überm ['y:bərm] = **über dem**

Übermacht ['y:bərmaxt] *f* superior force, superiority

übermächtig ['y:bərmɛçtɪç] *adj* superior (in strength); (*Gefühl etc*) overwhelming

übermannen [y:bər'manən] *vt insep* to overcome

übermäßig ['y:bərmɛ:sɪç] *adj* excessive

Übermensch ['y:bərmɛnʃ] *m* superman; **ü~lich** *adj* superhuman

übermitteln [y:bər'mɪtəln] *vt insep* to convey

übermorgen ['y:bərmɔrgən] *adv* the day after tomorrow

Übermüdung [y:bər'my:duŋ] *f* fatigue, overtiredness

Übermut ['y:bərmu:t] *m* exuberance

übermütig ['y:bərmy:tɪç] *adj* exuberant, high-spirited; **~ werden** to get overconfident

übernächste(r, s) *adj* next but one

übernachten [y:bər'naxtən] *vi insep*: **(bei jdm) ~** to spend the night (at sb's place)

Übernahme ['y:bərna:mə] *f* taking over *od* on, acceptance

über'nehmen (*unreg*) *vt insep* to take on, to accept; (*Amt, Geschäft*) to take over ♦ *vr insep* to take on too much

über'prüfen *vt insep* to examine, to check

überqueren [y:bər'kve:rən] *vt insep* to cross

überragen [y:bər'ra:gən] *vt insep* to tower above; (*fig*) to surpass

überraschen [y:bər'raʃən] *vt insep* to surprise

Überraschung *f* surprise

überreden [y:bər're:dən] *vt insep* to persuade

überreichen [y:bər'raiçən] *vt insep* to present, to hand over

'Überrest *m* remains, remnants

überrumpeln [y:bər'rumpəln] *vt insep* to take by surprise

überrunden [y:bər'rundən] *vt insep* to lap

übers ['y:bərs] = **über das**

Überschallflugzeug ['y:bərʃal-] *nt* supersonic jet

Überschallgeschwindigkeit *f* supersonic speed

über'schätzen *vt insep* to overestimate

'überschäumen *vi* (*Bier*) to foam over, bubble over; (*Temperament*) to boil over

Überschlag ['y:bərʃla:k] *m* (*FIN*) estimate; (*SPORT*) somersault; **ü~en** [-'ʃla:gən] (*unreg*) *vt insep* (*berechnen*) to estimate; (*auslassen: Seite*) to omit ♦ *vr insep* to somersault; (*Stimme*) to crack; (*AVIAT*) to loop the loop; **'überschlagen** (*unreg*) *vt* (*Beine*) to cross ♦ *vi* (*Wellen*) to break; (*Funken*) to flash

überschnappen ['y:bərʃnapən] *vi* (*Stimme*) to crack; (*umg: Mensch*) to flip one's lid

über'schneiden (*unreg*) *vr insep* (*auch fig*) to overlap; (*Linien*) to intersect

über'schreiben (*unreg*) *vt insep* to provide with a heading; **jdm etw ~** to transfer *od* make over sth to sb

über'schreiten (*unreg*) *vt insep* to cross over; (*fig*) to exceed; (*verletzen*) to transgress

Überschrift ['y:bərʃrɪft] *f* heading, title

Überschuß ['y:bərʃus] *m*: **~ (an** +*dat*) surplus (of)

überschüssig ['y:bərʃʏsɪç] *adj* surplus, excess

über'schütten *vt insep*: **jdn/etw mit**

etw ~ to pour sth over sb/sth; **jdn mit etw** ~ to shower sb with sth
überschwemmen [y:bər'ʃvɛmən] *vt insep* to flood
Überschwemmung *f* flood
überschwenglich ['y:bərʃvɛŋlɪç] *adj* effusive
Übersee ['y:bərze:] *f*: **nach/in** ~ overseas; **ü~isch** *adj* overseas
über'sehen (*unreg*) *vt insep* to look (out) over; (*fig: Folgen*) to see, to get an overall view of; (: *nicht beachten*) to overlook
über'senden (*unreg*) *vt insep* to send, to forward
übersetz- *zW:* **~en** [y:bər'zɛtsən] *vt insep* to translate; '**übersetzen** *vi* to cross; **Ü~er(in)** [-'zɛtsər(ɪn)] (**-s, -**) *m(f)* translator; **Ü~ung** [-'zɛtsʊŋ] *f* translation; (*TECH*) gear ratio
Übersicht ['y:bərzɪçt] *f* overall view; (*Darstellung*) survey; **ü~lich** *adj* clear; (*Gelände*) open; **~lichkeit** *f* clarity, lucidity
übersiedeln ['y:bərzi:dəln] *vi sep* to move; **über'siedeln** *vi* to move
über'spannen *vt insep* (*zu sehr spannen*) to overstretch; (*überdecken*) to cover
über'spannt *adj* eccentric; (*Idee*) wild, crazy
überspitzt [y:bər'ʃpɪtst] *adj* exaggerated
über'springen (*unreg*) *vt insep* to jump over; (*fig*) to skip
überstehen [y:bər'ʃte:ən] (*unreg*) *vt insep* to overcome, to get over; (*Winter etc*) to survive, to get through; '**überstehen** (*unreg*) *vi* to project
über'steigen (*unreg*) *vt insep* to climb over; (*fig*) to exceed
über'stimmen *vt insep* to outvote
Überstunden ['y:bərʃtʊndən] *pl* overtime *sg*
über'stürzen *vt insep* to rush ♦ *vr insep* to follow (one another) in rapid succession
überstürzt *adj* (over)hasty
über'tönen *vt insep* to drown (out)
Übertrag ['y:bərtra:k] (-(e)s, -träge) *m* (*COMM*) amount brought forward; **ü~bar** [-'tra:kba:r] *adj* transferable; (*MED*)

infectious; **ü~en** [-'tra:gən] (*unreg*) *vt insep* to transfer; (*RADIO*) to broadcast; (*übersetzen*) to render; (*Krankheit*) to transmit ♦ *vr insep* to spread ♦ *adj* figurative; **jdm etw ü~en** to assign sth to sb; **sich ü~en auf** +*akk* to spread to; **~ung** [-'tra:gʊŋ] *f* transfer(ence); (*RADIO*) broadcast; rendering; transmission
über'treffen (*unreg*) *vt insep* to surpass
über'treiben (*unreg*) *vt insep* to exaggerate
Übertreibung *f* exaggeration
übertreten [y:bər'tre:tən] (*unreg*) *vt insep* to cross; (*Gebot etc*) to break; '**übertreten** (*unreg*) *vi* (*über Linie, Gebiet*) to step (over); (*SPORT*) to overstep; (*zu anderem Glauben*) to be converted; '**übertreten (in** +*akk*) (*POL*) to go over (to)
Über'tretung *f* violation, transgression
übertrieben [y:bər'tri:bən] *adj* exaggerated, excessive
übervölkert [y:bər'fœlkərt] *adj* overpopulated
übervoll ['y:bərfɔl] *adj* overfull
übervorteilen [y:bər'fortaɪlən] *vt insep* to dupe, to cheat
über'wachen *vt insep* to supervise; (*Verdächtigen*) to keep under surveillance
Überwachung *f* supervision; surveillance
überwältigen [y:bər'vɛltɪgən] *vt insep* to overpower; **~d** *adj* overwhelming
überweisen [y:bər'vaɪzən] (*unreg*) *vt insep* to transfer
Überweisung *f* transfer
über'wiegen (*unreg*) *vi insep* to predominate; **~d** *adj* predominant
über'winden (*unreg*) *vt insep* to overcome ♦ *vr insep* to make an effort, to bring o.s. (to do sth)
Überwindung *f* effort, strength of mind
Überzahl ['y:bərtsa:l] *f* superiority, superior numbers *pl*; **in der** ~ **sein** to be numerically superior
überzählig [y:bərtsɛ:lɪç] *adj* surplus
über'zeugen *vt insep* to convince; **~d** *adj* convincing
Überzeugung *f* conviction

überziehen ['y:bərtsi:ən] (*unreg*) *vt* to put on to cover; (*Konto*) to overdraw
Überzug ['y:bərtsu:k] *m* cover; (*Belag*) coating
üblich ['y:plɪç] *adj* usual
U-Boot ['u:bo:t] *nt* submarine
übrig ['y:brɪç] *adj* remaining; **für jdn etwas ~ haben** (*umg*) to be fond of sb; **die ~en** the others; **das ~e** the rest; **im ~en** besides; **~bleiben** (*unreg*) *vi* to remain, to be left (over); **~ens** ['y:brɪgəns] *adv* besides; (*nebenbei bemerkt*) by the way; **~lassen** (*unreg*) *vt* to leave (over)
Übung ['y:bʊŋ] *f* practice; (*Turn~, Aufgabe etc*) exercise; **~ macht den Meister** practice makes perfect
Ufer ['u:fər] (**-s, -**) *nt* bank; (*Meeres~*) shore
Uhr [u:r] (**-, -en**) *f* clock; (*Armband~*) watch; **wieviel ~ ist es?** what time is it?; **1 ~** 1 o'clock; **20 ~** 8 o'clock, 20.00 (twenty hundred) hours; **~armband** *nt* watch strap; **~band** *nt* watch strap; **~kette** *f* watch chain; **~macher** (**-s, -**) *m* watchmaker; **~werk** *nt* clockwork; works of a watch; **~zeiger** *m* hand; **~zeigersinn** *m*: **im ~zeigersinn** clockwise; **entgegen dem ~zeigersinn** anticlockwise; **~zeit** *f* time (of day)
Uhu ['u:hu] (**-s, -s**) *m* eagle owl
UKW [u:ka:'ve:] *abk* (= *Ultrakurzwelle*) VHF
ulkig ['ʊlkɪç] *adj* funny
Ulme ['ʊlmə] *f* elm
Ultimatum [ʊlti'ma:tʊm] (**-s, Ultimaten**) *nt* ultimatum
Ultraschall ['ʊltraʃal] *m* ultrasound
ultraviolett ['ʊltravio'lɛt] *adj* ultraviolet

SCHLÜSSELWORT
---

um [ʊm] *präp +akk* **1** (*um herum*) (a)round; **um Weihnachten** around Christmas; **er schlug um sich** he hit about him
2 (*mit Zeitangabe*) at; **um acht (Uhr)** at eight (o'clock)
3 (*mit Größenangabe*) by; **etw um 4 cm kürzen** to shorten sth by 4 cm; **um 10% teurer** 10% more expensive; **um vieles**

besser better by far; **um nichts besser** not in the least bit better; **um so besser** so much the better
4: **der Kampf um den Titel** the battle for the title; **um Geld spielen** to play for money; **Stunde um Stunde** hour after hour; **Auge um Auge** an eye for an eye
♦ *präp +gen*: **um ... willen** for the sake of ...; **um Gottes willen** for goodness *od* (*stärker*) God's sake
♦ *konj*: **um ... zu** (in order) to ...; **zu klug, um zu ...** too clever to ...; **um so besser/schlimmer** so much the better/worse
♦ *adv* **1** (*ungefähr*) about; **um (die) 30 Leute** about *od* around 30 people
2 (*vorbei*): **die 2 Stunden sind um** the two hours are up

---

umändern ['ʊm'ɛndərn] *vt* to alter
Umänderung *f* alteration
umarbeiten ['ʊm'arbaıtən] *vt* to remodel; (*Buch etc*) to revise, to rework
umarmen [ʊm'armən] *vt insep* to embrace
Umbau ['ʊmbaʊ] (**-(e)s, -e** *od* **-ten**) *m* reconstruction, alteration(s); **u~en** *vt* to rebuild, to reconstruct
umbilden ['ʊmbɪldən] *vt* to reorganize; (*POL: Kabinett*) to reshuffle
umbinden ['ʊmbɪndən] (*unreg*) *vt* (*Krawatte etc*) to put on
umblättern ['ʊmblɛtərn] *vt* to turn over
umblicken ['ʊmblɪkən] *vr* to look around
umbringen ['ʊmbrɪŋən] (*unreg*) *vt* to kill
umbuchen ['ʊmbu:xən] *vi* to change one's reservation/flight *etc* ♦ *vt* to change
umdenken ['ʊmdɛŋkən] (*unreg*) *vi* to adjust one's views
umdrehen ['ʊmdre:ən] *vt* to turn (round); (*Hals*) to wring ♦ *vr* to turn (round)
Um'drehung *f* revolution; rotation
umeinander [ʊm'aı'nandər] *adv* round one another; (*füreinander*) for one another
umfahren ['ʊmfa:rən] (*unreg*) *vt* to run over; **um'fahren** (*unreg*) *vt insep* to drive round; to sail round

umfallen ['ʊmfalən] (*unreg*) *vi* to fall down *od* over

Umfang ['ʊmfaŋ] *m* extent; (*von Buch*) size; (*Reichweite*) range; (*Fläche*) area; (*MATH*) circumference; **u~reich** *adj* extensive; (*Buch etc*) voluminous

um'fassen *vt insep* to embrace; (*umgeben*) to surround; (*enthalten*) to include; **~d** *adj* comprehensive, extensive

umformen ['ʊmfɔrmən] *vi* to transform

Umformer (**-s, -**) *m* (*ELEK*) transformer, converter

Umfrage ['ʊmfra:gə] *f* poll

umfüllen ['ʊmfʏlən] *vt* to transfer; (*Wein*) to decant

umfunktionieren ['ʊmfʊŋktsioni:rən] *vt* to convert, to transform

Umgang ['ʊmgaŋ] *m* company; (*mit jdm*) dealings *pl*; (*Behandlung*) way of behaving

umgänglich ['ʊmgɛŋlɪç] *adj* sociable

Umgangsformen *pl* manners

Umgangssprache *f* colloquial language

umgeben [ʊm'ge:bən] (*unreg*) *vt insep* to surround

Umgebung *f* surroundings *pl*; (*Milieu*) environment; (*Personen*) people in one's circle

umgehen ['ʊmge:ən] (*unreg*) *vi* to go (a)round; **im Schlosse ~** to haunt the castle; **mit jdm grob** *etc* **~** to treat sb roughly *etc*; **mit Geld sparsam ~** to be careful with one's money; **um'gehen** (*unreg*) *vt insep* to bypass; (*MIL*) to outflank; (*Gesetz etc*) to circumvent; (*vermeiden*) to avoid; **'umgehend** *adj* immediate

Um'gehung *f* bypassing; outflanking; circumvention; avoidance;

Umgehungsstraße *f* bypass

umgekehrt ['ʊmgəke:rt] *adj* reverse(d); (*gegenteilig*) opposite ♦ *adv* the other way around; **und ~** and vice versa

umgraben ['ʊmgra:bən] (*unreg*) *vt* to dig up

Umhang ['ʊmhaŋ] *m* wrap, cape

umhauen ['ʊmhauən] *vt* to fell; (*fig*) to bowl over

umher [ʊm'he:r] *adv* about, around; **~gehen** (*unreg*) *vi* to walk about;

~ziehen (*unreg*) *vi* to wander from place to place

umhinkönnen [ʊm'hɪnkœnən] (*unreg*) *vi*: **ich kann nicht umhin, das zu tun** I can't help doing it

umhören ['ʊmhø:rən] *vr* to ask around

Umkehr ['ʊmke:r] (**-**) *f* turning back; (*Änderung*) change; **u~en** *vi* to turn back ♦ *vt* to turn round, to reverse; (*Tasche etc*) to turn inside out; (*Gefäß etc*) to turn upside down

umkippen ['ʊmkɪpən] *vt* to tip over ♦ *vi* to overturn; (*umg: Mensch*) to keel over; (*fig: Meinung ändern*) to change one's mind

Umkleidekabine *f* (*im Schwimmbad*) (changing) cubicle

Umkleideraum ['ʊmklaɪdəraʊm] *m* changing *od* dressing room

umkommen ['ʊmkɔmən] (*unreg*) *vi* to die, to perish; (*Lebensmittel*) to go bad

Umkreis ['ʊmkraɪs] *m* neighbourhood; **im ~ von** within a radius of

Umlage ['ʊmla:gə] *f* share of the costs

Umlauf ['ʊmlaʊf] *m* (*Geld~*) circulation; (*von Gestirn*) revolution; **~bahn** *f* orbit

Umlaut ['ʊmlaʊt] *m* umlaut

umlegen ['ʊmle:gən] *vt* to put on; (*verlegen*) to move, to shift; (*Kosten*) to share out; (*umkippen*) to tip over; (*umg: töten*) to bump off

umleiten ['ʊmlaɪtən] *vt* to divert

Umleitung *f* diversion

umliegend ['ʊmli:gənt] *adj* surrounding

um'rahmen *vt insep* to frame

um'randen *vt insep* to border, to edge

umrechnen ['ʊmrɛçnən] *vt* to convert

Umrechnung *f* conversion; **~skurs** *m* rate of exchange

um'reißen (*unreg*) *vt insep* to outline, to sketch

Umriß ['ʊmrɪs] *m* outline

umrühren ['ʊmry:rən] *vt, vi* to stir

ums [ʊms] = **um das**

Umsatz ['ʊmzats] *m* turnover

Umsatzsteuer *f* sales tax

umschalten ['ʊmʃaltən] *vt* to switch

Umschau ['ʊmʃaʊ] *f* look(ing) round; **~ halten nach** to look around for; **u~en** *vr*

to look round
Umschlag ['ʊmʃlaːk] *m* cover; (*Buch~ auch*) jacket; (*MED*) compress; (*Brief~*) envelope; (*Wechsel*) change; (*von Hose*) turn-up; **u~en** [-gən] (*unreg*) *vi* to change; (*NAUT*) to capsize ♦ *vt* to knock over; (*Ärmel*) to turn up; (*Seite*) to turn over; (*Waren*) to transfer; **~platz** *m* (*COMM*) distribution centre
umschreiben ['ʊmʃraibən] (*unreg*) *vt* (*neu~*) to rewrite; (*übertragen*) to transfer; **~ auf** +*akk* to transfer to; to paraphrase; (*abgrenzen*) to define
umschulen ['ʊmʃuːlən] *vt* to retrain; (*Kind*) to send to another school
Umschweife ['ʊmʃvaifə] *pl*: **ohne ~** without beating about the bush, straight out
Umschwung ['ʊmʃvʊŋ] *m* change (around), revolution
umsehen ['ʊmzeːən] (*unreg*) *vr* to look around *od* about; (*suchen*): **sich ~ (nach)** to look out (for)
umseitig ['ʊmzaitiç] *adv* overleaf
umsichtig ['ʊmzɪçtiç] *adj* cautious, prudent
umsonst [ʊm'zɔnst] *adv* in vain; (*gratis*) for nothing
umspringen ['ʊmʃprɪŋən] (*unreg*) *vi* to change; (*Wind auch*) to veer; **mit jdm ~** to treat sb badly
Umstand ['ʊmʃtant] *m* circumstance; **Umstände** *pl* (*fig: Schwierigkeiten*) fuss; **in anderen Umständen sein** to be pregnant; **Umstände machen** to go to a lot of trouble; **unter Umständen** possibly
umständlich ['ʊmʃtɛntliç] *adj* (*Methode*) cumbersome, complicated; (*Ausdrucksweise, Erklärung*) long-winded; (*Mensch*) ponderous
Umstandskleid *nt* maternity dress
Umstehende(n) ['ʊmʃteːəndə(n)] *pl* bystanders
umsteigen ['ʊmʃtaigən] (*unreg*) *vi* (*EISENB*) to change
umstellen ['ʊmʃtɛlən] *vt* (*an anderen Ort*) to change round, to rearrange; (*TECH*) to convert ♦ *vr* to adapt (o.s.); **sich auf etw** *akk* **~** to adapt to sth; **um'stellen** *vt*

insep to surround
Umstellung ['ʊmʃtɛlʊŋ] *f* change; (*Umgewöhnung*) adjustment; (*TECH*) conversion
umstimmen ['ʊmʃtɪmən] *vt* (*MUS*) to retune; **jdn ~** to make sb change his mind
umstoßen ['ʊmʃtoːsən] (*unreg*) *vt* to overturn; (*Plan etc*) to change, to upset
umstritten [ʊm'ʃtrɪtən] *adj* disputed
Umsturz ['ʊmʃtʊrts] *m* overthrow
umstürzen ['ʊmʃtʏrtsən] *vt* (*umwerfen*) to overturn ♦ *vi* to collapse, to fall down; (*Wagen*) to overturn
Umtausch ['ʊmtauʃ] *m* exchange; **u~en** *vt* to exchange
umtun ['ʊmtuːn] (*unreg*, *umg*) *vr* (*suchen*): **sich nach jdm/etw ~** to look (around) for sb/sth
umwandeln ['ʊmvandəln] *vt* to change, to convert; (*ELEK*) to transform
umwechseln ['ʊmvɛksəln] *vt* to change
Umweg ['ʊmveːk] *m* detour, roundabout way
Umwelt ['ʊmvɛlt] *f* environment; **u~feindlich** *adj* ecologically harmful; **u~freundlich** *adj* not harmful to the environment, environment-friendly; **~schützer** *m* environmentalist; **~verschmutzung** *f* environmental pollution
umwenden ['ʊmvɛndən] (*unreg*) *vt, vr* to turn (round)
umwerfen ['ʊmvɛrfən] (*unreg*) *vt* to upset, to overturn; (*Mantel*) to throw on; (*fig: erschüttern*) to upset, to throw
umwerfend (*umg*) *adj* fantastic
umziehen ['ʊmtsiːən] (*unreg*) *vt, vr* to change ♦ *vi* to move
Umzug ['ʊmtsuːk] *m* procession; (*Wohnungs~*) move, removal
unab- ['ʊn'ap] *zW*: **~änderlich** *adj* irreversible, unalterable; **~hängig** *adj* independent; **U~hängigkeit** *f* independence; **~kömmlich** *adj* indispensable; **zur Zeit ~kömmlich** not free at the moment; **~lässig** *adj* incessant, constant; **~sehbar** *adj* immeasurable; (*Folgen*) unforeseeable;

(*Kosten*) incalculable; **~sichtlich** adj unintentional; **~'wendbar** adj inevitable
unachtsam ['ʊn'axtza:m] adj careless; **U~keit** f carelessness
unan- ['ʊn'an] zW: **~'fechtbar** adj indisputable; **~gebracht** adj uncalled-for; **~gemessen** adj inadequate; **~genehm** adj unpleasant; **U~nehmlichkeit** f inconvenience; **U~nehmlichkeiten** pl (*Ärger*) trouble sg; **~sehnlich** adj unsightly; **~ständig** adj indecent, improper
unappetitlich ['ʊn'apeti:tlɪç] adj unsavoury
Unart ['ʊn'a:rt] f bad manners pl; (*Angewohnheit*) bad habit; **u~ig** adj naughty, badly behaved
unauf- ['ʊn'aʊf] zW: **~fällig** adj unobtrusive; (*Kleidung*) inconspicuous; **~'findbar** adj not to be found; **~gefordert** adj unasked ♦ adv spontaneously; **~haltsam** adj irresistible; **~'hörlich** adj incessant, continuous; **~merksam** adj inattentive; **~richtig** adj insincere
unaus- ['ʊn'aʊs] zW: **~geglichen** adj unbalanced; **~'sprechlich** adj inexpressible; **~'stehlich** adj intolerable
unbarmherzig ['ʊnbarmhɛrtsɪç] adj pitiless, merciless
unbeabsichtigt ['ʊnbə'apzɪçtɪçt] adj unintentional
unbeachtet ['ʊnbə'axtət] adj unnoticed, ignored
unbedenklich ['ʊnbədɛŋklɪç] adj (*Plan*) unobjectionable ♦ adv without hesitation
unbedeutend ['ʊnbədɔytənt] adj insignificant, unimportant; (*Fehler*) slight
unbedingt ['ʊnbədɪŋt] adj unconditional ♦ adv absolutely; **mußt du ~ gehen?** do you really have to go?
unbefangen ['ʊnbəfaŋən] adj impartial, unprejudiced; (*ohne Hemmungen*) uninhibited; **U~heit** f impartiality; uninhibitedness
unbefriedigend ['ʊnbəfri:dɪgənt] adj unsatisfactory
unbefriedigt [-dɪçt] adj unsatisfied, dissatisfied
unbefugt ['ʊnbəfu:kt] adj unauthorized

unbegreiflich [ʊnbə'graɪflɪç] adj inconceivable
unbegrenzt ['ʊnbəgrɛntst] adj unlimited
unbegründet ['ʊnbəgryndət] adj unfounded
Unbehagen ['ʊnbəha:gən] nt discomfort
unbehaglich [-klɪç] adj uncomfortable; (*Gefühl*) uneasy
unbeholfen ['ʊnbəhɔlfən] adj awkward, clumsy
unbeirrt ['ʊnbə'ɪrt] adj imperturbable
unbekannt ['ʊnbəkant] adj unknown
unbekümmert ['ʊnbəkʏmərt] adj unconcerned
unbeliebt ['ʊnbəli:pt] adj unpopular
unbequem ['ʊnbəkve:m] adj (*Stuhl*) uncomfortable; (*Mensch*) bothersome; (*Regelung*) inconvenient
unberechenbar [ʊnbə'rɛçənba:r] adj incalculable; (*Mensch, Verhalten*) unpredictable
unberechtigt ['ʊnbərɛçtɪçt] adj unjustified; (*nicht erlaubt*) unauthorized
unberührt ['ʊnbəry:rt] adj untouched, intact; **sie ist noch ~** she is still a virgin
unbescheiden ['ʊnbəʃaɪdən] adj presumptuous
unbeschreiblich [ʊnbə'ʃraɪplɪç] adj indescribable
unbesonnen ['ʊnbəzɔnən] adj unwise, rash, imprudent
unbeständig ['ʊnbəʃtɛndɪç] adj (*Mensch*) inconstant; (*Wetter*) unsettled; (*Lage*) unstable
unbestechlich [ʊnbə'ʃtɛçlɪç] adj incorruptible
unbestimmt ['ʊnbəʃtɪmt] adj indefinite; (*Zukunft auch*) uncertain
unbeteiligt [ʊnbə'taɪlɪçt] adj unconcerned, indifferent
unbewacht ['ʊnbəvaxt] adj unguarded, unwatched
unbeweglich ['ʊnbəve:klɪç] adj immovable
unbewußt ['ʊnbəvʊst] adj unconscious
unbezahlt ['ʊnbətsa:lt] adj (*Rechnung*) outstanding, unsettled; (*Urlaub*) unpaid
unbrauchbar ['ʊnbraʊxba:r] adj (*Arbeit*) useless; (*Gerät auch*) unusable

und [ʊnt] *konj* and; **~ so weiter** and so on

Undank ['ʊndaŋk] *m* ingratitude; **u~bar** *adj* ungrateful

undefinierbar [ʊndefi'niːrbaːr] *adj* indefinable

undenkbar [ʊn'dɛŋkbaːr] *adj* inconceivable

undeutlich ['ʊndɔʏtlɪç] *adj* indistinct

undicht ['ʊndɪçt] *adj* leaky

Unding ['ʊndɪŋ] *nt* absurdity

undurch- ['ʊndʊrç] *zW:* **~führbar** [-'fyːrbaːr] *adj* impracticable; **~lässig** [-lɛsɪç] *adj* waterproof, impermeable; **~sichtig** [-zɪçtɪç] *adj* opaque; *(fig)* obscure

uneben ['ʊn'eːbən] *adj* uneven

unecht ['ʊn'ɛçt] *adj* (*Schmuck*) fake (*vorgetäuscht: Freundlichkeit*) false

unehelich ['ʊn'eːəlɪç] *adj* illegitimate

uneinig ['ʊn'aɪnɪç] *adj* divided; **~ sein** to disagree; **U~keit** *f* discord, dissension

uneins ['ʊn'aɪns] *adj* at variance, at odds

unempfindlich ['ʊn'ɛmpfɪntlɪç] *adj* insensitive; (*Stoff*) practical

unendlich [ʊn''ɛntlɪç] *adj* infinite

unent- ['ʊn'ɛnt] *zW:* **~behrlich** [-'beːrlɪç] *adj* indispensable; **~geltlich** [-gɛltlɪç] *adj* free (of charge); **~schieden** [-ʃiːdən] *adj* undecided; **~schieden enden** (*SPORT*) to end in a draw; **~schlossen** [-ʃlɔsən] *adj* undecided; irresolute; **~wegt** [-'veːkt] *adj* unswerving; (*unaufhörlich*) incessant

uner- ['ʊn'ɛr] *zW:* **~bittlich** [-'bɪtlɪç] *adj* unyielding, inexorable; **~fahren** [-faːrən] *adj* inexperienced; **~freulich** [-frɔʏlɪç] *adj* unpleasant; **~'gründlich** *adj* unfathomable; **~hört** [-høːrt] *adj* unheard-of; (*Bitte*) outrageous; **~läßlich** [-'lɛslɪç] *adj* indispensable; **~laubt** *adj* unauthorized; **~'meßlich** *adj* immeasurable, immense; **~müdlich** [-'myːtlɪç] *adj* indefatigable; **~reichbar** *adj* (*Ziel*) unattainable; (*Ort*) inaccessible; (*telefonisch*) unobtainable; **~schöpflich** [-'ʃœpflɪç] *adj* inexhaustible; **~schütterlich** [-'ʃʏtərlɪç] *adj* unshakeable; **~schwinglich** [-'ʃvɪŋlɪç] *adj* (*Preis*) exorbitant; too expensive;

~träglich [-'trɛːklɪç] *adj* unbearable; (*Frechheit*) insufferable; **~wartet** *adj* unexpected; **~wünscht** *adj* undesirable, unwelcome

unfähig ['ʊnfɛːɪç] *adj* incapable, incompetent; **zu etw ~ sein** to be incapable of sth; **U~keit** *f* incapacity; incompetence

unfair ['ʊnfɛːr] *adj* unfair

Unfall ['ʊnfal] *m* accident; **~flucht** *f* hit-and-run (driving); **~stelle** *f* scene of the accident; **~versicherung** *f* accident insurance

unfaßbar [ʊn'fasbaːr] *adj* inconceivable

unfehlbar [ʊn'feːlbaːr] *adj* infallible ♦ *adv* inevitably; **U~keit** *f* infallibility

unförmig ['ʊnfœrmɪç] *adj* (*formlos*) shapeless

unfrei ['ʊnfraɪ] *adj* not free, unfree; (*Paket*) unfranked; **~willig** *adj* involuntary, against one's will

unfreundlich ['ʊnfrɔʏntlɪç] *adj* unfriendly; **U~keit** *f* unfriendliness

Unfriede(n) ['ʊnfriːdə(n)] *m* dissension, strife

unfruchtbar ['ʊnfrʊxtbaːr] *adj* infertile; (*Gespräche*) unfruitful; **U~keit** *f* infertility; unfruitfulness

Unfug ['ʊnfuːk] (*-s*) *m* (*Benehmen*) mischief; (*Unsinn*) nonsense; **grober ~** (*JUR*) gross misconduct; malicious damage

Ungar(in) ['ʊŋgar(ɪn)] *m(f)* Hungarian; **u~isch** *adj* Hungarian; **~n** *nt* Hungary

ungeachtet ['ʊŋgə'axtət] *präp +gen* notwithstanding

ungeahnt ['ʊŋgə'aːnt] *adj* unsuspected, undreamt-of

ungebeten ['ʊŋgəbeːtən] *adj* uninvited

ungebildet ['ʊŋgəbɪldət] *adj* uneducated; uncultured

ungedeckt ['ʊŋgədɛkt] *adj* (*Scheck*) uncovered

Ungeduld ['ʊŋgədʊlt] *f* impatience; **u~ig** [-dɪç] *adj* impatient

ungeeignet ['ʊŋgə'aɪgnət] *adj* unsuitable

ungefähr ['ʊŋgəfɛːr] *adj* rough, approximate; **das kommt nicht von ~** that's hardly surprising

ungefährlich *adj* not dangerous,

harmless

ungehalten ['ʊngəhaltən] *adj* indignant

ungeheuer ['ʊngəhɔʏər] *adj* huge ♦ *adv*
(*umg*) enormously; **U~** (**-s, -**) *nt* monster;
~lich [-'hɔʏərlɪç] *adj* monstrous

ungehobelt ['ʊngəhoːbəlt] *adj* (*fig*)
uncouth

ungehörig ['ʊngəhøːrɪç] *adj* impertinent,
improper

ungehorsam ['ʊngəhoːrzaːm] *adj*
disobedient; **U~** *m* disobedience

ungeklärt ['ʊngəkleːrt] *adj* not cleared
up; (*Rätsel*) unsolved

ungeladen ['ʊngəlaːdən] *adj* not loaded;
(*Gast*) uninvited

ungelegen ['ʊngəleːgən] *adj*
inconvenient

ungelernt ['ʊngəlernt] *adj* unskilled

ungelogen ['ʊngəloːgən] *adv* really,
honestly

ungemein ['ʊngəmaɪn] *adj* uncommon

ungemütlich ['ʊngəmyːtlɪç] *adj*
uncomfortable; (*Person*) disagreeable

ungenau ['ʊngənaʊ] *adj* inaccurate;
U~igkeit *f* inaccuracy

ungeniert ['ʊnʒeniːrt] *adj* free and easy,
unceremonious ♦ *adv* without
embarrassment, freely

ungenießbar ['ʊngəniːsbaːr] *adj*
inedible; undrinkable; (*umg*) unbearable

ungenügend ['ʊngənyːgənt] *adj*
insufficient, inadequate

ungepflegt ['ʊngəpfleːkt] *adj* (*Garten
etc*) untended; (*Person*) unkempt; (*Hände*)
neglected

ungerade ['ʊngəraːdə] *adj* odd, uneven
(*US*)

ungerecht ['ʊngərɛçt] *adj* unjust;
~fertigt *adj* unjustified; **U~igkeit** *f*
injustice, unfairness

ungern ['ʊngern] *adv* unwillingly,
reluctantly

ungerührt ['ʊngəryːrt] *adj* unmoved

ungeschehen ['ʊngəʃeːən] *adj*: ~
machen to undo

Ungeschicklichkeit ['ʊngəʃɪklɪçkaɪt] *f*
clumsiness

ungeschickt *adj* awkward, clumsy

ungeschminkt ['ʊngəʃmɪŋkt] *adj*
without make-up; (*fig*) unvarnished

ungesetzlich ['ʊngəzɛtslɪç] *adj* illegal

ungestört ['ʊngəʃtøːrt] *adj* undisturbed

ungestraft ['ʊngəʃtraːft] *adv* with
impunity

ungestüm ['ʊngəʃtyːm] *adj* impetuous;
tempestuous; **U~** (**-(e)s**) *nt* impetuosity;
passion

ungesund ['ʊngəzʊnt] *adj* unhealthy

ungetrübt ['ʊngətryːpt] *adj* clear; (*fig*)
untroubled; (*Freude*) unalloyed

Ungetüm ['ʊngətyːm] *nt* (**-(e)s, -e**) *nt*
monster

ungewiß ['ʊngəvɪs] *adj* uncertain;
U~heit *f* uncertainty

ungewöhnlich ['ʊngəvøːnlɪç] *adj*
unusual

ungewohnt ['ʊngəvoːnt] *adj*
unaccustomed

Ungeziefer ['ʊngətsiːfər] (**-s**) *nt* vermin

ungezogen ['ʊngətsoːgən] *adj* rude,
impertinent; **U~heit** *f* rudeness,
impertinence

ungezwungen ['ʊngətsvʊŋən] *adj*
natural, unconstrained

ungläubig ['ʊnglɔʏbɪç] *adj* unbelieving;
die U~en the infidel(s)

unglaublich [ʊn'glaʊblɪç] *adj* incredible

ungleich ['ʊnglaɪç] *adj* dissimilar;
unequal ♦ *adv* incomparably; **~artig** *adj*
different; **U~heit** *f* dissimilarity;
inequality; **~mäßig** *adj* irregular, uneven

Unglück ['ʊnglʏk] (**-(e)s, -e**) *nt*
misfortune; (*Pech*) bad luck; (*~sfall*)
calamity, disaster; (*Verkehrs~*) accident;
u~lich *adj* unhappy; (*erfolglos*) unlucky;
(*unerfreulich*) unfortunate;
u~licherweise [-'vaɪzə] *adv*
unfortunately; **u~selig** *adj* calamitous;
(*Person*) unfortunate; **~sfall** *m* accident,
calamity

ungültig ['ʊngʏltɪç] *adj* invalid; **U~keit** *f*
invalidity

ungünstig ['ʊngʏnstɪç] *adj* unfavourable

ungut ['ʊnguːt] *adj* (*Gefühl*) uneasy;
nichts für ~ no offence

unhaltbar ['ʊnhaltbaːr] *adj* untenable

Unheil ['ʊnhaɪl] *nt* evil; (*Unglück*)
misfortune; **~ anrichten** to cause

mischief; **u~bar** *adj* incurable
unheimlich ['ʊnhaɪmlɪç] *adj* weird,
uncanny ♦ *adv* (*umg*) tremendously
unhöflich ['ʊnhøːflɪç] *adj* impolite;
U~keit *f* impoliteness
unhygienisch ['ʊnhygi'eːnɪʃ] *adj*
unhygienic
Uni ['ʊni] (-, -s; *umg*) *f* university
uni [y'niː] *adj* self-coloured
Uniform [uni'fɔrm] *f* uniform; **u~iert**
[-'miːrt] *adj* uniformed
uninteressant ['ʊn'ɪnteresant] *adj*
uninteresting
Universität [univerzi'tɛːt] *f* university
Universum [uni'vɛrzʊm] (-s) *nt* universe
unkenntlich ['ʊnkɛntlɪç] *adj*
unrecognizable
Unkenntnis ['ʊnkɛntnɪs] *f* ignorance
unklar ['ʊnklaːr] *adj* unclear; **im ~en
sein über** +*akk* to be in the dark about;
U~heit *f* unclarity; (*Unentschiedenheit*)
uncertainty
unklug ['ʊnkluːk] *adj* unwise
Unkosten ['ʊnkɔstən] *pl* expense(s)
Unkostenbeitrag *m* contribution to
costs *or* expenses
Unkraut ['ʊnkraʊt] *nt* weed; weeds *pl*
unkündbar *adj* (*Stelle*) permanent;
(*Vertrag*) binding
unlängst ['ʊnlɛŋst] *adv* not long ago
unlauter ['ʊnlaʊtər] *adj* unfair
unleserlich ['ʊnleːzərlɪç] *adj* illegible
unlogisch ['ʊnloːgɪʃ] *adj* illogical
unlösbar [ʊn'løːsbar] *adj* insoluble
unlöslich [ʊn'løːslɪç] *adj* insoluble
Unlust ['ʊnlʊst] *f* lack of enthusiasm
unmäßig ['ʊnmɛːsɪç] *adj* immoderate
Unmenge ['ʊnmɛŋə] *f* tremendous
number, hundreds *pl*
Unmensch ['ʊnmɛnʃ] *m* ogre, brute;
u~lich *adj* inhuman, brutal; (*ungeheuer*)
awful
unmerklich [ʊn'mɛrklɪç] *adj* imperceptible
unmißverständlich ['ʊnmɪsfɛrʃtɛntlɪç]
adj unmistakable
unmittelbar ['ʊnmɪtəlbaːr] *adj* immediate
unmöbliert ['ʊnmøbliːrt] *adj* un-

furnished
unmodern *adj* old-fashioned
unmöglich ['ʊnmøːklɪç] *adj* impossible;
U~keit *f* impossibility
unmoralisch ['ʊnmoraːlɪʃ] *adj* immoral
Unmut ['ʊnmuːt] *m* ill humour
unnachgiebig ['ʊnnaːxgiːbɪç] *adj*
unyielding
unnahbar [ʊn'naːbaːr] *adj*
unapproachable
unnötig ['ʊnnøːtɪç] *adj* unnecessary
unnütz ['ʊnnʏts] *adj* useless
unordentlich ['ʊn'ɔrdəntlɪç] *adj* untidy
Unordnung ['ʊn'ɔrdnʊŋ] *f* disorder
unparteiisch ['ʊnpartaɪʃ] *adj* impartial;
U~e(r) *mf* umpire; (*FUSSBALL*) referee
unpassend ['ʊnpasənt] *adj*
inappropriate; (*Zeit*) inopportune
unpäßlich ['ʊnpɛslɪç] *adj* unwell
unpersönlich ['ʊnpɛrzøːnlɪç] *adj*
impersonal
unpolitisch ['ʊnpoliːtɪʃ] *adj* apolitical
unpraktisch ['ʊnpraktɪʃ] *adj* unpractical
unpünktlich ['ʊnpʏŋktlɪç] *adj*
unpunctual
unrationell ['ʊnratsionɛl] *adj* inefficient
unrealistisch *adj* unrealistic
unrecht ['ʊnrɛçt] *adj* wrong; **U~** *nt*
wrong; **zu U~** wrongly; **U~ haben** to be
wrong; **~mäßig** *adj* unlawful, illegal
unregelmäßig ['ʊnreːgəlmɛsɪç] *adj*
irregular; **U~keit** *f* irregularity
unreif ['ʊnraɪf] *adj* (*Obst*) unripe; (*fig*)
immature
unrentabel ['ʊnrɛntabəl] *adj*
unprofitable
unrichtig ['ʊnrɪçtɪç] *adj* incorrect, wrong
Unruhe ['ʊnruːə] *f* unrest; **~stifter** *m*
troublemaker
unruhig ['ʊnruːɪç] *adj* restless
uns [ʊns] (*akk, dat von* **wir**) *pron* us;
ourselves
unsachlich ['ʊnzaxlɪç] *adj* not to the
point, irrelevant
unsagbar [ʊn'zaːkbaːr] *adj* indescribable
unsanft ['ʊnzanft] *adj* rough
unsauber ['ʊnzaʊbər] *adj* unclean, dirty;
(*fig*) crooked; (*MUS*) fuzzy
unschädlich ['ʊnʃɛːtlɪç] *adj* harmless;

jdn/etw ~ **machen** to render sb/sth harmless
unscharf ['ʊnʃarf] adj indistinct; (*Bild etc*) out of focus, blurred
unscheinbar ['ʊnʃaɪnbaːr] adj insignificant; (*Aussehen, Haus etc*) unprepossessing
unschlagbar [ʊn'ʃlaːkbaːr] adj invincible
unschlüssig ['ʊnʃlʏsɪç] adj undecided
unschön ['ʊnʃøːn] adj (*häßlich: Anblick*) ugly, unattractive; (*unfreundlich: Benehmen*) unpleasant, ugly
Unschuld ['ʊnʃʊlt] f innocence; **u~ig** [-dɪç] adj innocent
unselbständig ['ʊnzɛlpʃtɛndɪç] adj dependent, over-reliant on others
unser(e) ['ʊnzər(ə)] adj our; ~**e(r, s)** pron ours; ~**einer** pron people like us; ~**eins** pron = unsereiner; ~**erseits** adv on our part; ~**twegen** adv (*für uns*) for our sake; (*wegen uns*) on our account; ~**twillen** adv: **um ~twillen** = unsertwegen
unsicher ['ʊnzɪçər] adj uncertain; (*Mensch*) insecure; **U~heit** f uncertainty; insecurity
unsichtbar ['ʊnzɪçtbaːr] adj invisible
Unsinn ['ʊnzɪn] m nonsense; **u~ig** adj nonsensical
Unsitte ['ʊnzɪtə] f deplorable habit
unsittlich ['ʊnzɪtlɪç] adj indecent
unsozial ['ʊnzotsiaːl] adj (*Verhalten*) antisocial
unsportlich ['ʊnʃpɔrtlɪç] adj not sporty; unfit; (*Verhalten*) unsporting
unsre ['ʊnzrə] = unsere
unsterblich [ʊn'ʃtɛrplɪç] adj immortal
Unstimmigkeit ['ʊnʃtɪmɪçkaɪt] f inconsistency; (*Streit*) disagreement
unsympathisch ['ʊnzʏmpaːtɪʃ] adj unpleasant; **er ist mir ~** I don't like him
untätig ['ʊntɛːtɪç] adj idle
untauglich ['ʊntaʊklɪç] adj unsuitable; (*MIL*) unfit
unteilbar [ʊn'taɪlbaːr] adj indivisible
unten ['ʊntən] adv below; (*im Haus*) downstairs; (*an der Treppe etc*) at the bottom; **nach ~** down; ~ **am Berg** etc at the bottom of the mountain *etc*; **ich bin**

bei ihm ~ durch (*umg*) he's through with me

SCHLÜSSELWORT

unter ['ʊntər] präp +dat **1** (*räumlich, mit Zahlen*) under; (*drunter*) underneath, below; **unter 18 Jahren** under 18 years **2** (*zwischen*) among(st); **sie waren unter sich** they were by themselves; **einer unter ihnen** one of them; **unter anderem** among other things
♦ präp +akk under, below

Unterarm ['ʊntərarm] m forearm
unter- zW: ~**belichten** vt (*PHOT*) to underexpose; **U~bewußtsein** nt subconscious; ~**bezahlt** adj underpaid
unterbieten [ʊntər'biːtən] (*unreg*) vt insep (*COMM*) to undercut; (*Rekord*) to lower
unterbrechen [ʊntər'brɛçən] (*unreg*) vt insep to interrupt
Unterbrechung f interruption
unterbringen ['ʊntərbrɪŋən] (*unreg*) vt (*in Koffer*) to stow; (*in Zeitung*) to place; (*Person: in Hotel etc*) to accommodate, to put up; (*: beruflich*): **jdn in einer Stellung** od **auf einem Posten ~** to fix sb up with a job
unterdessen [ʊntər'dɛsən] adv meanwhile
Unterdruck ['ʊntərdrʊk] m low pressure
unterdrücken [ʊntər'drʏkən] vt insep to suppress; (*Leute*) to oppress
untere(r, s) ['ʊntərə(r, s)] adj lower
untereinander [ʊntəraɪ'nandər] adv with each other; among themselves *etc*
unterentwickelt ['ʊntərɛntvɪkəlt] adj underdeveloped
unterernährt ['ʊntərɛrnɛːrt] adj undernourished, underfed
Unterernährung f malnutrition
Unter'führung f subway, underpass
Untergang ['ʊntərgaŋ] m (down)fall, decline; (*NAUT*) sinking; (*von Gestirn*) setting
unter'geben adj subordinate
untergehen ['ʊntərgeːən] (*unreg*) vi to go down; (*Sonne auch*) to set; (*Staat*) to

fall; (*Volk*) to perish; (*Welt*) to come to an end; (*im Lärm*) to be drowned

Untergeschoß ['ʊntərgəʃɔs] *nt* basement

Untergewicht *nt* underweight

unter'gliedern *vt insep* to subdivide

Untergrund ['ʊntərgrʊnt] *m* foundation; (*POL*) underground; **~bahn** *f* underground, tube, subway (*US*); **~bewegung** *f* underground (movement)

unterhalb ['ʊntərhalp] *präp +gen* below ♦ *adv* below; **~** below

Unterhalt ['ʊntərhalt] *m* maintenance; **u~en** [ʊntər'haltən] (*unreg*) *vt insep* to maintain; (*belustigen*) to entertain ♦ *vr insep* to talk; (*sich belustigen*) to enjoy o.s.; **u~sam** *adj* (*Abend, Person*) entertaining, amusing; **~ung** *f* maintenance; (*Belustigung*) entertainment, amusement; (*Gespräch*) talk

Unterhändler ['ʊntərhɛntlər] *m* negotiator

Unterhemd ['ʊntərhɛmt] *nt* vest, undershirt (*US*)

Unterhose ['ʊntərhoːzə] *f* underpants *pl*

Unterkiefer ['ʊntərkiːfər] *m* lower jaw

unterkommen ['ʊntərkɔmən] (*unreg*) *vi* to find shelter; to find work; **das ist mir noch nie untergekommen** I've never met with that

unterkühlt [ʊntər'kyːlt] *adj* (*Körper*) affected by hypothermia

Unterkunft ['ʊntərkʊnft] (*-, -künfte*) *f* accommodation

Unterlage ['ʊntərlaːgə] *f* foundation; (*Beleg*) document; (*Schreib~ etc*) pad

unter'lassen (*unreg*) *vt insep* (*versäumen*) to fail to do; (*sich enthalten*) to refrain from

unterlaufen [ʊntər'laʊfən] (*unreg*) *vi insep* to happen ♦ *adj*: **mit Blut ~** suffused with blood; (*Augen*) bloodshot

unterlegen ['ʊntərleːgən] *vt* to lay *od* put under; **unter'legen** *adj* inferior; (*besiegt*) defeated

Unterleib ['ʊntərlaɪp] *m* abdomen

unter'liegen (*unreg*) *vi insep* (*+dat*) to be defeated *od* overcome (by); (*unterworfen*

sein) to be subject (to)

Untermiete ['ʊntərmiːtə] *f*: **zur ~ wohnen** to be a subtenant *od* lodger; **~r(in)** *m(f)* subtenant, lodger

unter'nehmen (*unreg*) *vt insep* to undertake; **U~** (*-s, -*) *nt* undertaking, enterprise (*auch COMM*)

Unternehmer [ʊntər'neːmər] (*-s, -*) *m* entrepreneur, businessman

unterordnen ['ʊntərɔrdnən] *vr +dat* to submit o.s. (to) ♦ *vr* to give o.s. second place to

Unterredung [ʊntər'reːdʊŋ] *f* discussion, talk

Unterricht ['ʊntərrɪçt] (*-(e)s, -e*) *m* instruction, lessons *pl*; **u~en** [ʊntər'rɪçtən] *vt insep* to instruct; (*SCH*) to teach ♦ *vr insep*: **sich u~en (über +***akk***)** to inform o.s. (about), to obtain information (about); **~sfach** *nt* subject (on school *etc* curriculum)

Unterrock ['ʊntərrɔk] *m* petticoat, slip

unter'sagen *vt insep* to forbid; **jdm etw ~** to forbid sb to do sth

Untersatz ['ʊntərzats] *m* coaster, saucer

unter'schätzen *vt insep* to underestimate

unter'scheiden (*unreg*) *vt insep* to distinguish ♦ *vr insep* to differ

Unter'scheidung *f* (*Unterschied*) distinction; (*Unterscheiden*) differentiation

Unterschied ['ʊntərʃiːt] (*-(e)s, -e*) *m* difference, distinction; **im ~ zu** as distinct from; **u~lich** *adj* varying, differing; (*diskriminierend*) discriminatory; **u~slos** *adv* indiscriminately

unter'schlagen (*unreg*) *vt insep* to embezzle; (*verheimlichen*) to suppress

Unter'schlagung *f* embezzlement

Unterschlupf ['ʊntərʃlʊpf] (*-(e)s, -schlüpfe*) *m* refuge

unter'schreiben (*unreg*) *vt insep* to sign

Unterschrift ['ʊntərʃrɪft] *f* signature

Unterseeboot ['ʊntərzeːboːt] *nt* submarine

Untersetzer ['ʊntərzɛtsər] *m* tablemat; (*für Gläser*) coaster

untersetzt [ʊntər'zɛtst] *adj* stocky

unterste(r, s) ['ʊntərstə(r, s)] *adj* lowest, bottom

unterstehen [ʊntər'ʃteːən] (*unreg*) *vi insep* (+*dat*) to be under ♦ *vr insep* to dare; '**unterstehen** (*unreg*) *vi* to shelter

unterstellen [ʊntər'ʃtɛlən] *vt insep* to subordinate; (*fig*) to impute; '**unterstellen** *vt* (*Auto*) to garage, to park ♦ *vr* to take shelter

unter'streichen (*unreg*) *vt insep* (*auch fig*) to underline

Unterstufe ['ʊntərʃtuːfə] *f* lower grade

unter'stützen *vt insep* to support

Unter'stützung *f* support, assistance

unter'suchen *vt insep* (*MED*) to examine; (*Polizei*) to investigate

Unter'suchung *f* examination; investigation, inquiry; **~sausschuß** *m* committee of inquiry; **~shaft** *f* imprisonment on remand

Untertan ['ʊntərtaːn] (**-s, -en**) *m* subject

Untertasse ['ʊntərtasə] *f* saucer

untertauchen ['ʊntərtauxən] *vi* to dive; (*fig*) to disappear, to go underground

Unterteil ['ʊntərtail] *nt od m* lower part, bottom; **~en** [ʊntər'tailən] *vt insep* to divide up

Untertitel ['ʊntərtiːtəl] *m* subtitle

Unterwäsche ['ʊntərvɛʃə] *f* underwear

unterwegs [ʊntər'veːks] *adv* on the way

unter'werfen (*unreg*) *vt insep* to subject; (*Volk*) to subjugate ♦ *vr insep* (+*dat*) to submit (to)

unterwürfig [ʊntər'vʏrfɪç] *adj* obsequious, servile

unter'zeichnen *vt insep* to sign

unter'ziehen (*unreg*) *vt insep* to subject ♦ *vr insep* (+*dat*) to undergo; (*einer Prüfung*) to take

untragbar [ʊn'traːkbaːr] *adj* unbearable, intolerable

untreu ['ʊntrɔy] *adj* unfaithful; **U~e** *f* unfaithfulness

untröstlich [ʊn'trøːstlɪç] *adj* inconsolable

unüberlegt ['ʊn'yːbərleːkt] *adj* ill-considered ♦ *adv* without thinking

unübersichtlich *adj* (*Gelände*) broken; (*Kurve*) blind

unumgänglich [ʊn'ʊm'gɛnlɪç] *adj* indispensable, vital; absolutely necessary

unumwunden ['ʊn'ʊmvʊndən] *adj* candid ♦ *adv* straight out

ununterbrochen ['ʊn'ʊntərbrɔxən] *adj* uninterrupted

unver- [ʊnfɛr] *zW*: **~änderlich** [-'ɛndərlɪç] *adj* unchangeable; **~antwortlich** [-'antvɔrtlɪç] *adj* irresponsible; (*unentschuldbar*) inexcusable; **~'besserlich** *adj* incorrigible; **~bindlich** *adj* not binding; (*Antwort*) curt ♦ *adv* (*COMM*) without obligation; **~bleit** *adj* (*Benzin usw*) unleaded; **ich fahre ~bleit** I use unleaded; **~blümt** [-'blyːmt] *adj* plain, blunt ♦ *adv* plainly, bluntly; **~daulich** *adj* indigestible; **~'einbar** *adj* incompatible; **~fänglich** [-'fɛŋlɪç] *adj* harmless; **~froren** *adj* impudent; **~'geßlich** *adj* (*Tag, Erlebnis*) unforgettable; **~hofft** [-'hɔft] *adj* unexpected; **~meidlich** [-'maitlɪç] *adj* unavoidable; **~mutet** *adj* unexpected; **~nünftig** [-'nʏnftɪç] *adj* foolish; **~schämt** *adj* impudent; **U~schämtheit** *f* impudence, insolence; **~sehens** [-'zeːəns] *adv* all of a sudden; **~sehrt** *adj* uninjured; **~söhnlich** [-'zøːnlɪç] *adj* irreconcilable; **~ständlich** [-'ʃtɛntlɪç] *adj* unintelligible; **~träglich** *adj* quarrelsome; (*Meinungen, MED*) incompatible; **~wüstlich** [-'vyːstlɪç] *adj* indestructible; (*Mensch*) irrepressible; **~'zeihlich** *adj* unpardonable; **~züglich** [-'tsyːklɪç] *adj* immediate

unvollkommen ['ʊnfɔlkɔmən] *adj* imperfect

unvollständig *adj* incomplete

unvor- ['ʊnfoːr] *zW*: **~bereitet** *adj* unprepared; **~eingenommen** *adj* unbiased; **~hergesehen** [-heːrgezeːən] *adj* unforeseen; **~sichtig** [-zɪçtɪç] *adj* careless, imprudent; **~stellbar** [-'ʃtɛlbaːr] *adj* inconceivable; **~teilhaft** *adj* disadvantageous

unwahr ['ʊnvaːr] *adj* untrue; **~scheinlich** *adj* improbable, unlikely ♦ *adv* (*umg*) incredibly

unweigerlich [ʊn'vaigərlɪç] *adj* unquestioning ♦ *adv* without fail

Unwesen ['ʊnveːzən] *nt* nuisance; (*Unfug*) mischief; **sein ~ treiben** to wreak havoc; **u~tlich** *adj* inessential, unimportant; **u~tlich besser** marginally better

Unwetter ['ʊnvɛtər] *nt* thunderstorm

unwichtig ['ʊnvɪçtɪç] *adj* unimportant

unwider- [ʊnviːdər] *zW:* **~'legbar** *adj* irrefutable; **~'ruflich** *adj* irrevocable; **~'stehlich** *adj* irresistible

unwill- ['ʊnvɪl] *zW:* **U~e(n)** *m* indignation; **~ig** *adj* indignant; (*widerwillig*) reluctant; **~kürlich** [-kyːrlɪç] *adj* involuntary ♦ *adv* instinctively; (*lachen*) involuntarily

unwirklich ['ʊnvɪrklɪç] *adj* unreal

unwirksam *adj* (*Mittel, Methode*) ineffective

unwirsch ['ʊnvɪrʃ] *adj* cross, surly

unwirtschaftlich ['ʊnvɪrtʃaftlɪç] *adj* uneconomical

unwissen- ['ʊnvɪsən] *zW:* **~d** *adj* ignorant; **U~heit** *f* ignorance; **~tlich** *adv* unknowingly, unwittingly

unwohl ['ʊnvoːl] *adj* unwell, ill; **U~sein** (*-s*) *nt* indisposition

unwürdig ['ʊnvʏrdɪç] *adj* unworthy

unzählig [ʊn'tsɛːlɪç] *adj* innumerable, countless

unzer- [ʊntsɛr] *zW:* **~'brechlich** *adj* unbreakable; **~'störbar** *adj* indestructible; **~'trennlich** *adj* inseparable

Unzucht ['ʊntsʊxt] *f* sexual offence

unzüchtig ['ʊntsʏçtɪç] *adj* immoral; lewd

unzu- ['ʊntsu] *zW:* **~frieden** *adj* dissatisfied; **U~friedenheit** *f* discontent; **~länglich** *adj* inadequate; **~lässig** *adj* inadmissible; **~rechnungsfähig** *adj* irresponsible; **~treffend** *adj* incorrect; **~verlässig** *adj* unreliable

unzweideutig ['ʊntsvaɪdɔʏtɪç] *adj* unambiguous

üppig ['ʏpɪç] *adj* (*Frau*) curvaceous; (*Busen*) full, ample; (*Essen*) sumptuous; (*Vegetation*) luxuriant, lush

Ur- ['uːr] *in zW* original

uralt ['uːr'alt] *adj* ancient, very old

Uran [u'raːn] (*-s*) *nt* uranium

Ur- *zW:* **~aufführung** *f* first performance; **~einwohner** *m* original inhabitant; **~eltern** *pl* ancestors; **~enkel(in)** *m(f)* great-grandchild, great-grandson (daughter); **~großeltern** *pl* great-grandparents; **~großmutter** *f* great-grandmother; **~großvater** *m* great-grandfather; **~heber** (*-s, -*) *m* originator; (*Autor*) author

Urin [u'riːn] (*-s, -e*) *m* urine

Urkunde ['uːrkʊndə] *f* document, deed

Urlaub ['uːrlaʊp] (*-(e)s, -e*) *m* holiday(s*pl*) (*BRIT*), vacation (*US*); (*MIL etc*) leave; **~er** [-laʊbər] (*-s, -*) *m* holiday-maker (*BRIT*), vacationer (*US*); **~sort** *m* holiday resort

Urne ['ʊrnə] *f* urn

Urologe [uro'loːgə] *m* (*MED*) urologist

Ursache ['uːrzaxə] *f* cause; **keine ~** that's all right

Ursprung ['uːrʃprʊŋ] *m* origin, source; (*von Fluß*) source

ursprünglich ['uːrʃprʏŋlɪç] *adj* original ♦ *adv* originally

Urteil ['ʊrtaɪl] (*-s, -e*) *nt* opinion; (*JUR*) sentence, judgement; **u~en** *vi* to judge; **~sspruch** *m* sentence, verdict

Urwald *m* jungle

Urzeit *f* prehistoric times *pl*

USA [uː'ɛs''aː] *pl abk* (= *Vereinigte Staaten von Amerika*) USA

usw. *abk* (= *und so weiter*) etc

Utensilien [ʊtɛn'ziːliən] *pl* utensils

Utopie [ʊto'piː] *f* pipedream

utopisch [u'toːpɪʃ] *adj* utopian

V v

vag(e) [vaːk, vaːgə] *adj* vague

Vagina [va'giːna] (*-, Vaginen*) *f* vagina

Vakuum ['vaːkuʊm] (*-s, Vakua od Vakuen*) *nt* vacuum

Vampir (*-s, -e*) *m* vampire

Vanille [va'nɪljə] (*-*) *f* vanilla

Variation [variatsi'oːn] *f* variation

variieren [vari'iːrən] *vt, vi* to vary

Vase ['vaːzə] *f* vase

Vater ['faːtər] (*-s, ⸚*) *m* father; **~land** *nt* native country; Fatherland

väterlich ['fɛːtərlɪç] *adj* fatherly
Vaterschaft *f* paternity
Vaterunser (-s, -) *nt* Lord's prayer
Vati ['faːti] *m* daddy
v.Chr. *abk* (= *vor Christus*) B.C.
Vegetarier(in) [vegeˈtaːriər(ɪn)] (-s, -) *m(f)* vegetarian
Veilchen ['faɪlçən] *nt* violet
Vene ['veːnə] *f* vein
Ventil [vɛnˈtiːl] (-s, -e) *nt* valve
Ventilator [vɛntiˈlaːtɔr] *m* ventilator
verab- [fɛrˈʔap] *zW*: **~reden** *vt* to agree, to arrange ♦ *vr*: **sich mit jdm ~reden** to arrange to meet sb; **mit jdm ~redet sein** to have arranged to meet sb; **V~redung** *f* arrangement; (*Treffen*) appointment; **~scheuen** *vt* to detest, to abhor; **~schieden** *vt* (*Gäste*) to say goodbye to; (*entlassen*) to discharge; (*Gesetz*) to pass ♦ *vr* to take one's leave; **V~schiedung** *f* leave-taking; discharge; passing
ver- [fɛr] *zW*: **~achten** *vt* to despise; **~ächtlich** [-"ɛçtlɪç] *adj* contemptuous; (*verachtenswert*) contemptible; **jdn ~ächtlich machen** to run sb down; **V~achtung** *f* contempt
verallgemeinern [fɛrʔalgəˈmaɪnərn] *vt* to generalize
Verallgemeinerung *f* generalization
veralten [fɛrˈʔaltən] *vi* to become obsolete *od* out-of-date
Veranda [veˈranda] (-, **Veranden**) *f* veranda
veränder- [fɛrˈʔɛndər] *zW*: **~lich** *adj* changeable; **~n** *vt, vr* to change, to alter; **V~ung** *f* change, alteration
veran- [fɛrˈʔan] *zW*: **~lagt** *adj* with a ... nature; **V~lagung** *f* disposition; **~lassen** *vt* to cause; **Maßnahmen ~lassen** to take measures; **sich ~laßt sehen** to feel prompted; **~schaulichen** *vt* to illustrate; **~schlagen** *vt* to estimate; **~stalten** *vt* to organize, to arrange; **V~stalter** (-s, -) *m* organizer; **V~staltung** *f* (*Veranstalten*) organizing; (*Konzert etc*) event, function
verantwort- [fɛrˈʔantvɔrt] *zW*: **~en** *vt* to answer ♦ *vr* to justify o.s.; **~lich** *adj* responsible; **V~ung** *f* responsibility; **~ungsbewußt** *adj* responsible;

~ungslos *adj* irresponsible
verarbeiten [fɛrˈʔarbaɪtən] *vt* to process; (*geistig*) to assimilate; **etw zu etw ~** to make sth into sth
Verarbeitung *f* processing; assimilation
verärgern [fɛrˈʔɛrgərn] *vt* to annoy
verausgaben [fɛrˈʔausgaːbən] *vr* to run out of money; (*fig*) to exhaust o.s.
Verb [vɛrp] (-s, -en) *nt* verb
Verband [fɛrˈbant] (-(e)s, ⁀e) *m* (*MED*) bandage, dressing; (*Bund*) association, society; (*MIL*) unit; **~skasten** *m* medicine chest, first-aid box; **~szeug** *nt* bandage
verbannen [fɛrˈbanən] *vt* to banish
Verbannung *f* exile
verbergen [fɛrˈbɛrgən] (*unreg*) *vt, vr*: **(sich) ~ (vor** +*dat*) to hide (from)
verbessern [fɛrˈbɛsərn] *vt, vr* to improve; (*berichtigen*) to correct (o.s.)
Verbesserung *f* improvement; correction
verbeugen [fɛrˈbɔygən] *vr* to bow
Verbeugung *f* bow
ver'biegen (*unreg*) *vi* to bend
ver'bieten (*unreg*) *vt* to forbid; **jdm etw verbieten** to forbid sb to do sth
ver'binden (*unreg*) *vt* to connect; (*kombinieren*) to combine; (*MED*) to bandage ♦ *vr* (*auch CHEM*) to combine, to join; **jdm die Augen ~** to blindfold sb
verbindlich [fɛrˈbɪntlɪç] *adj* binding; (*freundlich*) friendly
Ver'bindung *f* connection; (*Zusammensetzung*) combination; (*CHEM*) compound; (*UNIV*) club
verbissen [fɛrˈbɪsən] *adj* (*Kampf*) bitter; (*Gesichtsausdruck*) grim
ver'bitten (*unreg*) *vt*: **sich** *dat* **etw ~** not to tolerate sth, not to stand for sth
verblassen [fɛrˈblasən] *vi* to fade
Verbleib [fɛˈblaɪp] (-(e)s) *m* whereabouts; **v~en** [-bən] (*unreg*) *vi* to remain
verbleit [fɛrˈblaɪt] *adj* (*Benzin*) leaded
verblüffen [fɛrˈblʏfən] *vt* to stagger, to amaze
Verblüffung *f* stupefaction
ver'blühen *vi* to wither, to fade
ver'bluten *vi* to bleed to death
verborgen [fɛrˈbɔrgən] *adj* hidden

Verbot [fɛr'boːt] (-(e)s, -e) *nt* prohibition, ban; **v~en** *adj* forbidden; **Rauchen v~en!** no smoking; **~sschild** *nt* prohibitory sign

Verbrauch [fɛr'braʊx] (-(e)s) *m* consumption; **v~en** *vt* to use up; **~er** (-s, -) *m* consumer; **v~t** *adj* used up, finished; (*Luft*) stale; (*Mensch*) worn-out

Verbrechen [fɛr'brɛçən] (-s, -) *nt* crime

Verbrecher [fɛr'brɛçər] (-s, -) *m* criminal; **v~isch** *adj* criminal

ver'breiten *vt, vr* to spread; **sich über etw** *akk* ~ to expound on sth

verbreitern [fɛr'braɪtərn] *vt* to broaden

Verbreitung *f* spread(ing), propagation

verbrenn- [fɛr'brɛn] *zW:* **~bar** *adj* combustible; **~en** (*unreg*) *vt* to burn; (*Leiche*) to cremate; **V~ung** *f* burning; (*in Motor*) combustion; (*von Leiche*) cremation; **V~ungsmotor** *m* internal combustion engine

verbringen [fɛr'brɪŋən] (*unreg*) *vt* to spend

verbrühen [fɛr'bryːən] *vt* to scald

verbuchen [fɛr'buːxən] *vt* (*FIN*) to register; (*Erfolg*) to enjoy; (*Mißerfolg*) to suffer

verbunden [fɛr'bʊndən] *adj* connected; **jdm** ~ **sein** to be obliged *od* indebted to sb; „**falsch ~**" (*TEL*) "wrong number"

verbünden [fɛr'byndən] *vr* to ally o.s.

Verbündete(r) [fɛr'byndətə(r)] *mf* ally

ver'bürgen *vr:* **sich ~ für** to vouch for

ver'büßen *vt:* **eine Strafe ~** to serve a sentence

Verdacht [fɛr'daxt] (-(e)s) *m* suspicion

verdächtig [fɛr'dɛçtɪç] *adj* suspicious, suspect; **~en** [fɛr'dɛçtɪgən] *vt* to suspect

verdammen [fɛr'damən] *vt* to damn, to condemn; **verdammt!** damn!

verdammt (*umg*) *adj, adv* damned; ~ **noch mal!** damn!; dammit!

ver'dampfen *vi* to vaporize, to evaporate

ver'danken *vt:* **jdm etw ~** to owe sb sth

verdauen [fɛr'daʊən] *vt* (*auch fig*) to digest

verdaulich [fɛr'daʊlɪç] *adj* digestible; **das ist schwer ~** that is hard to digest

Verdauung *f* digestion

Verdeck [fɛr'dɛk] (-(e)s, -e) *nt* (*AUT*) hood; (*NAUT*) deck; **v~en** *vt* to cover (up); (*verbergen*) to hide

Verderb- [fɛr'dɛrp] *zW:* **~en** [-'dɛrbən] (-s) *nt* ruin; **v~en** (*unreg*) *vt* to spoil; (*schädigen*) to ruin; (*moralisch*) to corrupt ♦ *vi* (*Essen*) to spoil, to rot; (*Mensch*) to go to the bad; **es mit jdm v~en** to get into sb's bad books; **v~lich** *adj* (*Einfluß*) pernicious; (*Lebensmittel*) perishable

verdeutlichen [fɛr'dɔʏtlɪçən] *vt* to make clear

ver'dichten *vt, vr* to condense

ver'dienen *vt* to earn; (*moralisch*) to deserve

Ver'dienst (-(e)s, -e) *m* earnings *pl* ♦ *nt* merit; (*Leistung*): ~ (**um**) service (to)

verdient [fɛr'diːnt] *adj* well-earned; (*Person*) deserving of esteem; **sich um etw ~ machen** to do a lot for sth

verdoppeln [fɛr'dɔpəln] *vt* to double

verdorben [fɛr'dɔrbən] *adj* spoilt; (*geschädigt*) ruined; (*moralisch*) corrupt

verdrängen [fɛr'drɛŋən] *vt* to oust, to displace (*auch PHYS*); (*PSYCH*) to repress

ver'drehen *vt* (*auch fig*) to twist; (*Augen*) to roll; **jdm den Kopf ~** (*fig*) to turn sb's head

verdreifachen [fɛr'draɪfaxən] *vt* to treble

verdrießlich [fɛr'driːslɪç] *adj* peevish, annoyed

Verdruß [fɛr'drʊs] (-sses, -sse) *m* annoyance, worry

verdummen [fɛr'dʊmən] *vt* to make stupid ♦ *vi* to grow stupid

verdunkeln [fɛr'dʊŋkəln] *vt* to darken; (*fig*) to obscure ♦ *vr* to darken

Verdunk(e)lung *f* blackout; (*fig*) obscuring

verdünnen [fɛr'dʏnən] *vt* to dilute

verdunsten [fɛr'dʊnstən] *vi* to evaporate

verdursten [fɛr'dʊrstən] *vi* to die of thirst

verdutzt [fɛr'dʊtst] *adj* nonplussed, taken aback

verehr- [fɛr'ʔeːr] *zW:* **~en** *vt* to venerate, to worship (*auch REL*); **jdm etw ~en** to present sb with sth; **V~er(in)** (-s, -) *m(f)* admirer, worshipper (*auch REL*); **~t** *adj* esteemed; **V~ung** *f* respect; (*REL*) worship

Verein [fɛrˈʔaɪn] (-(e)s, -e) *m* club, association; **v~bar** *adj* compatible; **v~baren** *vt* to agree upon; **~barung** *f* agreement; **v~en** *vt* (*Menschen, Länder*) to unite; (*Prinzipien*) to reconcile; **mit v~ten Kräften** having pooled resources, having joined forces; **v~fachen** *vt* to simplify; **v~igen** *vt, vr* to unite; **~igung** *f* union; (*Verein*) association; **v~t** *adj* united; **V~te Nationen** United Nations

vereinzelt [fɛrˈʔaɪntsəlt] *adj* isolated

vereiteln [fɛrˈʔaɪtəln] *vt* to frustrate

ver'eitern *vi* to suppurate, to fester

verengen [fɛrˈʔɛŋən] *vr* to narrow

vererb- [fɛrˈʔɛrb] *zW:* **~en** *vt* to bequeath; (*BIOL*) to transmit ♦ *vr* to be hereditary; **~lich** [fɛrˈʔɛrplɪç] *adj* hereditary; **V~ung** *f* bequeathing; (*BIOL*) transmission; (*Lehre*) heredity

verewigen [fɛrˈʔeːvɪgən] *vt* to immortalize ♦ *vr* (*umg*) to immortalize o.s.

ver'fahren (*unreg*) *vi* to act ♦ *vr* to get lost ♦ *adj* tangled; **~ mit** to deal with; **V~** (-s, -) *nt* procedure; (*TECH*) process; (*JUR*) proceedings *pl*

Verfall [fɛrˈfal] (-(e)s, -e) *m* decline; (*von Haus*) dilapidation; (*FIN*) expiry; **v~en** (*unreg*) *vi* to decline; (*Haus*) to be falling down; (*FIN*) to lapse; **v~en in** *+akk* to lapse into; **v~en auf** *+akk* to hit upon; **einem Laster v~en sein** to be addicted to a vice; **~sdatum** *nt* expiry date; (*der Haltbarkeit*) sell-by date

verfänglich [fɛrˈfɛŋlɪç] *adj* (*Frage, Situation*) awkward, tricky

ver'färben *vr* to change colour

verfassen [fɛrˈfasən] *vt* (*Rede*) to prepare, work out

Verfasser(in) [fɛrˈfasər(ɪn)] (-s, -) *m(f)* author, writer

Verfassung *f* (*auch POL*) constitution

Verfassungs- *zW:* **~gericht** *nt* constitutional court; **v~widrig** *adj* unconstitutional

ver'faulen *vi* to rot

ver'fehlen *vt* to miss; **etw für verfehlt halten** to regard sth as mistaken

verfeinern [fɛrˈfaɪnərn] *vt* to refine

ver'filmen *vt* to film

verflixt [fɛrˈflɪkst] (*umg*) *adj* damned, damn

ver'fluchen *vt* to curse

verfolg- [fɛrˈfɔlg] *zW:* **~en** *vt* to pursue; (*gerichtlich*) to prosecute; (*grausam, bes POL*) to persecute; **V~er** (-s, -) *m* pursuer; **V~ung** *f* pursuit; prosecution; persecution

verfrüht [fɛrˈfryːt] *adj* premature

verfüg- [fɛrˈfyːg] *zW:* **~bar** *adj* available; **~en** *vt* to direct, to order ♦ *vr* to proceed ♦ *vi:* **~en über** *+akk* to have at one's disposal; **V~ung** *f* direction, order; **zur V~ung** at one's disposal; **jdm zur V~ung stehen** to be available to sb

verführ- [fɛrˈfyːr] *zW:* **~en** *vt* to tempt; (*sexuell*) to seduce; **V~er** *m* tempter; seducer; **~erisch** *adj* seductive; **V~ung** *f* seduction; (*Versuchung*) temptation

ver'gammeln (*umg*) *vi* to go to seed; (*Nahrung*) to go off

vergangen [fɛrˈgaŋən] *adj* past; **V~heit** *f* past

vergänglich [fɛrˈgɛŋlɪç] *adj* transitory; **V~keit** *f* transitoriness, impermanence

vergasen [fɛrˈgaːzən] *vt* (*töten*) to gas

Vergaser (-s, -) *m* (*AUT*) carburettor

vergaß *etc* [fɛrˈgaːs] *vb siehe* **vergessen**

vergeb- [fɛrˈgeːb] *zW:* **~en** (*unreg*) *vt* (*verzeihen*) to forgive; (*weggeben*) to give away; **jdm etw ~en** to forgive sb (for) sth; **~ens** *adv* in vain; **~lich** [fɛrˈgeːplɪç] *adv* in vain ♦ *adj* vain, futile; **V~ung** *f* forgiveness

ver'gehen (*unreg*) *vi* to pass by *od* away ♦ *vr* to commit an offence; **jdm vergeht etw** sb loses sth; **sich an jdm ~** to (sexually) assault sb; **V~** (-s, -) *nt* offence

ver'gelten (*unreg*) *vt:* **jdm etw ~** to pay sb back for sth, to repay sb for sth

Ver'geltung *f* retaliation, reprisal; **Vergeltungsschlag** *m* (*MIL*) reprisal

vergessen [fɛrˈgɛsən] (*unreg*) *vt* to forget; **V~heit** *f* oblivion

vergeßlich [fɛrˈgɛslɪç] *adj* forgetful; **V~keit** *f* forgetfulness

vergeuden [fɛrˈgɔʏdən] *vt* to squander,

to waste

vergewaltigen [fɛrgə'valtɪgən] *vt* to rape; (*fig*) to violate

Vergewaltigung *f* rape

vergewissern [fɛrgə'vɪsərn] *vr* to make sure

ver'gießen (*unreg*) *vt* to shed

vergiften [fɛr'gɪftən] *vt* to poison

Vergiftung *f* poisoning

Vergißmeinnicht [fɛr'gɪsmaɪnnɪçt] (-(e)s, -e) *nt* forget-me-not

vergißt *etc* [fɛr'gɪst] *vb siehe* **vergessen**

Vergleich [fɛr'glaɪç] (-(e)s, -e) *m* comparison; (*JUR*) settlement; **im ~ mit** *od* **zu** compared with *od* to; **v~bar** *adj* comparable; **v~en** (*unreg*) *vt* to compare ♦ *vr* to reach a settlement

vergnügen [fɛr'gny:gən] *vr* to enjoy *od* amuse o.s.; **V~** (-s, -) *nt* pleasure; **viel V~!** enjoy yourself!

vergnügt [fɛr'gny:kt] *adj* cheerful

Vergnügung *f* pleasure, amusement; **~spark** *m* amusement park

vergolden [fɛr'gɔldən] *vt* to gild

vergöttern [fɛr'gœtərn] *vt* to idolize

ver'graben *vt* to bury

ver'greifen (*unreg*) *vr*: **sich an jdm ~** to lay hands on sb; **sich an etw ~** to misappropriate sth; **sich im Ton ~** to say the wrong thing

vergriffen [fɛr'grɪfən] *adj* (*Buch*) out of print; (*Ware*) out of stock

vergrößern [fɛr'grø:sərn] *vt* to enlarge; (*mengenmäßig*) to increase; (*Lupe*) to magnify

Vergrößerung *f* enlargement; increase; magnification; **~sglas** *nt* magnifying glass

Vergünstigung [fɛr'gʏnstɪgʊŋ] *f* concession, privilege

Vergütung *f* compensation

verhaften [fɛr'haftən] *vt* to arrest

Verhaftung *f* arrest

ver'hallen *vi* to die away

ver'halten (*unreg*) *vr* to be, to stand; (*sich benehmen*) to behave ♦ *vt* to hold *od* keep back; (*Schritt*) to check; **sich ~ (zu)** (*MATH*) to be in proportion (to); **V~** (-s) *nt* behaviour

Verhältnis [fɛr'hɛltnɪs] (-ses, -se) *nt* relationship; (*MATH*) proportion, ratio; **~se** *pl* (*Umstände*) conditions; **über seine ~se leben** to live beyond one's means; **v~mäßig** *adj* relative, comparative ♦ *adv* relatively, comparatively

verhandeln [fɛr'handəln] *vi* to negotiate; (*JUR*) to hold proceedings ♦ *vt* to discuss; (*JUR*) to hear; **über etw** *akk* **~** to negotiate sth *od* about sth

Verhandlung *f* negotiation; (*JUR*) proceedings *pl*; **~sbasis** *f* (*FINANZ*) basis for negotiations

ver'hängen *vt* (*fig*) to impose, to inflict

Verhängnis [fɛr'hɛŋnɪs] (-ses, -se) *nt* fate, doom; **jdm zum ~ werden** to be sb's undoing; **v~voll** *adj* fatal, disastrous

verharmlosen [fɛr'harmlo:zən] *vt* to make light of, to play down

verhärten [fɛr'hɛrtən] *vr* to harden

verhaßt [fɛr'hast] *adj* odious, hateful

verhauen [fɛr'hauən] (*unreg; umg*) *vt* (*verprügeln*) to beat up

verheerend [fɛr'he:rənt] *adj* disastrous, devastating

verheimlichen [fɛr'haɪmlɪçən] *vt*: **jdm etw ~** to keep sth secret from sb

verheiratet [fɛr'haɪra:tət] *adj* married

ver'helfen (*unreg*) *vi*: **jdm ~ zu** to help sb to get

ver'hexen *vt* to bewitch; **es ist wie verhext** it's jinxed

ver'hindern *vt* to prevent; **verhindert sein** to be unable to make it

verhöhnen [fɛr'hø:nən] *vt* to mock, to sneer at

Verhör [fɛr'hø:r] (-(e)s, -e) *nt* interrogation; (*gerichtlich*) (cross-) examination; **v~en** *vt* to interrogate; to (cross-)examine ♦ *vr* to misunderstand, to mishear

ver'hungern *vi* to starve, to die of hunger

ver'hüten *vt* to prevent, to avert

Ver'hütung *f* prevention; **Verhütungsmittel** *nt* contraceptive

verirren [fɛr'ɪrən] *vr* to go astray

ver'jagen *vt* to drive away *od* out

verkalken [fɛr'kalkən] *vi* to calcify;

(*umg*) to become senile
verkannt [fɛrˈkant] *adj* unappreciated
Verkauf [fɛrˈkaʊf] *m* sale; **v~en** *vt* to sell
Verkäufer(in) [fɛrˈkɔʏfər(ɪn)] (-s, -) *m(f)*
seller; salesman(woman); (*in Laden*) shop
assistant
verkaufsoffen *adj*: **~er Samstag**
Saturday when the shops stay open all day
Verkehr [fɛrˈkeːr] (-s, -e) *m* traffic;
(*Umgang, bes sexuell*) intercourse;
(*Umlauf*) circulation; **v~en** *vi* (*Fahrzeug*)
to ply, to run ♦ *vt, vr* to turn, to
transform; **v~en mit** to associate with;
bei jdm v~en (*besuchen*) to visit sb
regularly
Verkehrs- *zW*: **~ampel** *f* traffic lights *pl*;
~amt *nt* tourist office; **~delikt** *nt* traffic
offence; **v~günstig** *adj* convenient;
~mittel *nt* means of transport; **~schild**
nt road sign; **~stauung** *f* traffic jam,
stoppage; **~stockung** *f* traffic jam,
stoppage; **~unfall** *m* traffic accident;
~verein *m* tourist information office;
~zeichen *nt* traffic sign
verkehrt *adj* wrong; (*umgekehrt*) the
wrong way round
ver'kennen (*unreg*) *vt* to misjudge, not
to appreciate
ver'klagen *vt* to take to court
verkleiden [fɛrˈklaɪdən] *vr* to disguise
(o.s.); (*sich kostümieren*) to get dressed up
♦ *vt* (*Wand*) to cover
Verkleidung *f* disguise; (*ARCHIT*)
wainscoting
verkleinern [fɛrˈklaɪnərn] *vt* to make
smaller, to reduce in size
verklemmt [fɛrˈklɛmt] *adj* (*fig*) inhibited
ver'kneifen (*umg*) *vt*: **sich** *dat* **etw ~**
(*Lachen*) to stifle sth; (*Schmerz*) to hide
sth; (*sich versagen*) to do without sth
verknüpfen [fɛrˈknʏpfən] *vt* to tie (up),
to knot; (*fig*) to connect
ver'kommen (*unreg*) *vi* to deteriorate, to
decay; (*Mensch*) to go downhill, to come
down in the world ♦ *adj* (*moralisch*)
dissolute, depraved
verkörpern [fɛrˈkœrpərn] *vt* to embody,
to personify
verkraften [fɛrˈkraftən] *vt* to cope with

ver'kriechen (*unreg*) *vr* to creep away,
to creep into a corner
Ver'krümmung *f* bend, warp; (*ANAT*)
curvature
verkrüppelt [fɛrˈkrʏpəlt] *adj* crippled
ver'kühlen *vr* to get a chill
ver'kümmern *vi* to waste away
verkünden [fɛrˈkʏndən] *vt* to proclaim;
(*Urteil*) to pronounce
verkürzen [fɛrˈkʏrtsən] *vt* to shorten;
(*Wort*) to abbreviate; **sich** *dat* **die Zeit ~**
to while away the time
Verkürzung *f* shortening; abbreviation
verladen [fɛrˈlaːdən] (*unreg*) *vt* (*Waren,
Vieh*) to load; (*Truppen*) to embark,
entrain, enplane
Verlag [fɛrˈlaːk] (-(e)s, -e) *m* publishing
firm
verlangen [fɛrˈlaŋən] *vt* to demand; to
desire ♦ *vi*: **~ nach** to ask for, to desire;
~ Sie Herrn X ask for Mr X; **V~** (-s, -)
nt: **V~** (**nach**) desire (for); **auf jds V~**
(**hin**) at sb's request
verlängern [fɛrˈlɛŋərn] *vt* to extend;
(*länger machen*) to lengthen
Verlängerung *f* extension; (*SPORT*) extra
time; **~sschnur** *f* extension cable
verlangsamen [fɛrˈlaŋzaːmən] *vt, vr* to
decelerate, to slow down
Verlaß [fɛrˈlas] *m*: **auf ihn/das ist kein
~** he/it cannot be relied upon
ver'lassen (*unreg*) *vt* to leave ♦ *vr*: **sich
~ auf** +*akk* to depend on ♦ *adj* desolate;
(*Mensch*) abandoned
verläßlich [fɛrˈlɛslɪç] *adj* reliable
Verlauf [fɛrˈlaʊf] *m* course; **v~en** (*unreg*)
vi (*zeitlich*) to pass; (*Farben*) to run ♦ *vr*
to get lost; (*Menschenmenge*) to disperse
ver'lauten *vi*: **etw ~ lassen** to disclose
sth; **wie verlautet** as reported
ver'legen *vt* to move; (*verlieren*) to
mislay; (*Buch*) to publish ♦ *vr*: **sich auf
etw** *akk* **~** to take up *od* to sth ♦ *adj*
embarrassed; **nicht ~ um** never at a loss
for; **V~heit** *f* embarrassment; (*Situation*)
difficulty, scrape
Verleger [fɛrˈleːgər] (-s, -) *m* publisher
Verleih [fɛrˈlaɪ] (-(e)s, -e) *m* hire service;
v~en (*unreg*) *vt* to lend; (*Kraft, Anschein*)

to confer, to bestow; (*Preis, Medaille*) to award; **~ung** *f* lending; bestowal; award

ver'leiten *vt* to lead astray; **~ zu** to talk into, to tempt into

ver'lernen *vt* to forget, to unlearn

ver'lesen (*unreg*) *vt* to read out; (*aussondern*) to sort out ♦ *vr* to make a mistake in reading

verletz- [fɛr'lɛts] *zW*: **~en** *vt* (*auch fig*) to injure, to hurt; (*Gesetz etc*) to violate; **~end** *adj* (*fig: Worte*) hurtful; **~lich** *adj* vulnerable, sensitive; **V~te(r)** *mf* injured person; **V~ung** *f* injury; (*Verstoß*) violation, infringement

verleugnen [fɛr'lɔygnən] *vt* (*Herkunft, Glauben*) to belie; (*Menschen*) to disown

verleumden [fɛr'lɔymdən] *vt* to slander

Verleumdung *f* slander, libel

ver'lieben *vr*: **sich ~ (in** +*akk*) to fall in love (with)

verliebt [fɛr'li:pt] *adj* in love

verlieren [fɛr'li:rən] (*unreg*) *vt, vi* to lose ♦ *vr* to get lost

Verlierer *m* loser

verlob- [fɛr'lo:b] *zW*: **~en** *vr* to get engaged (to); **V~te(r)** [fɛr'lo:ptə(r)] *mf* fiancé(e); **V~ung** *f* engagement

ver'locken *vt* to entice, to lure

Ver'lockung *f* temptation, attraction

verlogen [fɛr'lo:gən] *adj* untruthful

verlor *etc vb siehe* **verlieren**

verloren [fɛr'lo:rən] *adj* lost; (*Eier*) poached ♦ *vb siehe* **verlieren**; **etw ~ geben** to give sth up for lost; **~gehen** (*unreg*) *vi* to get lost

verlosen [fɛr'lo:zən] *vt* to raffle, to draw lots for

Verlosung *f* raffle, lottery

verlottern [fɛr'lɔtərn] (*umg*) *vi* to go to the dogs

verludern [fɛr'lu:dərn] (*umg*) *vi* to go to the dogs

Verlust [fɛr'lʊst] (**-(e)s, -e**) *m* loss; (*MIL*) casualty

ver'machen *vt* to bequeath, to leave

Vermächtnis [fɛr'mɛçtnɪs] (**-ses, -se**) *nt* legacy

Vermählung [fɛr'mɛ:lʊŋ] *f* wedding, marriage

vermarkten [fɛr'marktən] *vt* (*WIRTS: Artikel*) to market

vermehren [fɛr'me:rən] *vt, vr* to multiply; (*Menge*) to increase

Vermehrung *f* multiplying; increase

ver'meiden (*unreg*) *vt* to avoid

vermeintlich [fɛr'maɪntlɪç] *adj* supposed

Vermerk [fɛr'mɛrk] (**-(e)s, -e**) *m* note; (*in Ausweis*) endorsement; **v~en** *vt* to note

ver'messen (*unreg*) *vt* to survey ♦ *adj* presumptuous, bold; **V~heit** *f* presumptuousness; recklessness

Ver'messung *f* survey(ing)

ver'mieten *vt* to let, to rent (out); (*Auto*) to hire out, to rent

Ver'mieter(in) (**-s, -**) *m(f)* landlord(lady)

Ver'mietung *f* letting, renting (out); (*von Autos*) hiring (out)

vermindern [fɛr'mɪndərn] *vt, vr* to lessen, to decrease; (*Preise*) to reduce

Verminderung *f* reduction

ver'mischen *vt, vr* to mix, to blend

vermissen [fɛr'mɪsən] *vt* to miss

vermitteln [fɛr'mɪtəln] *vi* to mediate ♦ *vt* (*Gespräch*) to connect; **jdm etw ~** to help sb to obtain sth

Vermittler [fɛr'mɪtlər] (**-s, -**) *m* (*Schlichter*) agent, mediator

Vermittlung [fɛr'mɪtlʊŋ] *f* procurement; (*Stellen~*) agency; (*TEL*) exchange; (*Schlichtung*) mediation

ver'mögen (*unreg*) *vt* to be capable of; **~ zu** to be able to; **V~** (**-s, -**) *nt* wealth; (*Fähigkeit*) ability; **ein V~ kosten** to cost a fortune; **~d** *adj* wealthy

vermuten [fɛr'mu:tən] *vt* to suppose, to guess; (*argwöhnen*) to suspect

vermutlich *adj* supposed, presumed ♦ *adv* probably

Vermutung *f* supposition; suspicion

vernachlässigen [fɛr'na:xlɛsɪgən] *vt* to neglect

ver'nehmen (*unreg*) *vt* to perceive, to hear; (*erfahren*) to learn; (*JUR*) to (cross-) examine; **dem V~ nach** from what I/we *etc* hear

Vernehmung *f* (cross-)examination

verneigen [fɛr'naɪgən] *vr* to bow

verneinen [fɛr'naɪnən] *vt* (*Frage*) to

answer in the negative; (*ablehnen*) to deny; (*GRAM*) to negate; **~d** *adj* negative

Verneinung *f* negation

vernichten [fɛrˈnɪçtən] *vt* to annihilate, to destroy; **~d** *adj* (*fig*) crushing; (*Blick*) withering; (*Kritik*) scathing

Vernunft [fɛrˈnʊnft] (-) *f* reason, understanding

vernünftig [fɛrˈnʏnftɪç] *adj* sensible, reasonable

veröffentlichen [fɛrˈˈœfəntlɪçən] *vt* to publish

Veröffentlichung *f* publication

verordnen [fɛrˈˈɔrdnən] *vt* (*MED*) to prescribe

Verordnung *f* order, decree; (*MED*) prescription

ver'pachten *vt* to lease (out)

ver'packen *vt* to pack

Ver'packung *f* packing, wrapping; **~smaterial** *nt* packing, wrapping

ver'passen *vt* to miss; **jdm eine Ohrfeige ~** (*umg*) to give sb a clip round the ear

verpfänden [fɛrˈpfɛndən] *vt* (*Besitz*) to mortgage

ver'pflanzen *vt* to transplant

Ver'pflanzung *f* transplant(ing)

ver'pflegen *vt* to feed, to cater for

Ver'pflegung *f* feeding, catering; (*Kost*) food; (*in Hotel*) board

verpflichten [fɛrˈpflɪçtən] *vt* to oblige, to bind; (*anstellen*) to engage ♦ *vr* to undertake; (*MIL*) to sign on ♦ *vi* to carry obligations; **jdm zu Dank verpflichtet sein** to be obliged to sb

Verpflichtung *f* obligation, duty

verpönt [fɛrˈpøːnt] *adj* disapproved (of), taboo

ver'prügeln (*umg*) *vt* to beat up, to do over

Verputz [fɛrˈpʊts] *m* plaster, roughcast; **v~en** *vt* to plaster; (*umg: Essen*) to put away

Verrat [fɛrˈraːt] (-(e)s) *m* treachery; (*POL*) treason; **v~en** (*unreg*) *vt* to betray; (*Geheimnis*) to divulge ♦ *vr* to give o.s. away

Verräter [fɛrˈrɛːtər(ɪn)] (-s, -) *m*

traitor(tress); **v~isch** *adj* treacherous

ver'rechnen *vt*: **~ mit** to set off against ♦ *vr* to miscalculate

Verrechnungsscheck [fɛrˈrɛçnʊŋsʃɛk] *m* crossed cheque

verregnet [fɛrˈreːgnət] *adj* spoilt by rain, rainy

ver'reisen *vi* to go away (on a journey)

verrenken [fɛrˈrɛŋkən] *vt* to contort; (*MED*) to dislocate; **sich** *dat* **den Knöchel ~** to sprain one's ankle

ver'richten *vt* to do, to perform

verriegeln [fɛrˈriːgəln] *vt* to bolt up, to lock

verringern [fɛrˈrɪŋərn] *vt* to reduce ♦ *vr* to diminish

Verringerung *f* reduction; lessening

ver'rinnen (*unreg*) *vi* to run out *od* away; (*Zeit*) to elapse

ver'rosten *vi* to rust

verrotten [fɛrˈrɔtən] *vi* to rot

ver'rücken *vt* to move, to shift

verrückt [fɛrˈrʏkt] *adj* crazy, mad; **V~e(r)** *mf* lunatic; **V~heit** *f* madness, lunacy

Verruf [fɛrˈruːf] *m*: **in ~ geraten/bringen** to fall/bring into disrepute; **v~en** *adj* notorious, disreputable

Vers [fɛrs] (-es, -e) *m* verse

ver'sagen *vt*: **jdm/sich etw ~** to deny sb/o.s. sth ♦ *vi* to fail; **V~** (-s) *nt* failure

Versager [fɛrˈzaːgər] (-s, -) *m* failure

ver'salzen (*unreg*) *vt* to put too much salt in; (*fig*) to spoil

ver'sammeln *vt*, *vr* to assemble, to gather

Ver'sammlung *f* meeting, gathering

Versand [fɛrˈzant] (-(e)s) *m* forwarding; dispatch; (*~abteilung*) dispatch department; **~haus** *nt* mail-order firm

versäumen [fɛrˈzɔymən] *vt* to miss; (*unterlassen*) to neglect, to fail

ver'schaffen *vt*: **jdm/sich etw ~** to get *od* procure sth for sb/o.s.

verschämt [fɛrˈʃɛːmt] *adj* bashful

verschandeln [fɛrˈʃandəln] (*umg*) *vt* to spoil

verschärfen [fɛrˈʃɛrfən] *vt* to intensify; (*Lage*) to aggravate ♦ *vr* to intensify; to become aggravated

ver'schätzen *vr* to be out in one's reckoning

ver'schenken *vt* to give away

verscheuchen [fɛrˈʃɔʏçən] *vt* (*Tiere*) to chase off *or* away

ver'schicken *vt* to send off

ver'schieben (*unreg*) *vt* to shift; (*EISENB*) to shunt; (*Termin*) to postpone

verschieden [fɛrˈʃiːdən] *adj* different; (*pl: mehrere*) various; **sie sind ~ groß** they are of different sizes; **~tlich** *adv* several times

verschimmeln [fɛrˈʃɪməln] *vi* (*Nahrungsmittel*) to go mouldy

verschlafen [fɛrˈʃlaːfən] (*unreg*) *vt* to sleep through; (*fig: versäumen*) to miss ♦ *vi*, *vr* to oversleep ♦ *adj* sleepy

Verschlag [fɛrˈʃlaːk] *m* shed; **v~en** [-gən] (*unreg*) *vt* to board up ♦ *adj* cunning; **jdm den Atem v~en** to take sb's breath away; **an einen Ort v~en werden** to wind up in a place

verschlechtern [fɛrˈʃlɛçtərn] *vt* to make worse ♦ *vr* to deteriorate, to get worse

Verschlechterung *f* deterioration

Verschleiß [fɛrˈʃlaɪs] (**-es, -e**) *m* wear and tear; **v~en** (*unreg*) *vt* to wear out

ver'schleppen *vt* to carry off, to abduct; (*Krankheit*) to protract; (*zeitlich*) to drag out

ver'schleudern *vt* to squander; (*COMM*) to sell dirt-cheap

verschließbar *adj* lockable

verschließen [fɛrˈʃliːsən] (*unreg*) *vt* to close; to lock ♦ *vr*: **sich einer Sache** *dat* ~ to close one's mind to sth

verschlimmern [fɛrˈʃlɪmərn] *vt* to make worse, to aggravate ♦ *vr* to get worse, to deteriorate

verschlingen [fɛrˈʃlɪŋən] (*unreg*) *vt* to devour, to swallow up; (*Fäden*) to twist

verschlossen [fɛrˈʃlɔsən] *adj* locked; (*fig*) reserved; **V~heit** *f* reserve

ver'schlucken *vt* to swallow ♦ *vr* to choke

Verschluß [fɛrˈʃlʊs] *m* lock; (*von Kleid etc*) fastener; (*PHOT*) shutter; (*Stöpsel*) plug; **unter ~ halten** to keep under lock and key

verschlüsseln [fɛrˈʃlʏsəln] *vt* to encode

verschmähen [fɛrˈʃmɛːən] *vt* to disdain, to scorn

verschmerzen [fɛrˈʃmɛrtsən] *vt* to get over

verschmieren [fɛrˈʃmiːrən] *vt* (*verstreichen: Gips, Mörtel*) to apply, spread on; (*schmutzig machen: Wand etc*) to smear

verschmutzen [fɛrˈʃmʊtsən] *vt* to soil; (*Umwelt*) to pollute

verschneit [fɛrˈʃnaɪt] *adj* snowed up, covered in snow

verschollen [fɛrˈʃɔlən] *adj* lost, missing

ver'schonen *vt*: **jdn mit etw** ~ to spare sb sth

verschönern [fɛrˈʃøːnərn] *vt* to decorate; (*verbessern*) to improve

ver'schreiben (*unreg*) *vt* (*MED*) to prescribe ♦ *vr* to make a mistake (in writing); **sich einer Sache** *dat* ~ to devote o.s. to sth

verschreibungspflichtig *adj* (*Medikament*) available on prescription only

verschroben [fɛrˈʃroːbən] *adj* eccentric, odd

verschrotten [fɛrˈʃrɔtən] *vt* to scrap

verschuld- [fɛrˈʃʊld] *zW*: **~en** *vt* to be guilty of; **V~en** (**-s**) *nt* fault, guilt; **~et** *adj* in debt; **V~ung** *f* fault; (*Geld*) debts *pl*

ver'schütten *vt* to spill; (*zuschütten*) to fill; (*unter Trümmer*) to bury

ver'schweigen (*unreg*) *vt* to keep secret; **jdm etw** ~ to keep sth from sb

verschwend- [fɛrˈʃvɛnd] *zW*: **~en** *vt* to squander; **V~er** (**-s, -**) *m* spendthrift; **~erisch** *adj* wasteful, extravagant; **V~ung** *f* waste; extravagance

verschwiegen [fɛrˈʃviːgən] *adj* discreet; (*Ort*) secluded; **V~heit** *f* discretion; seclusion

ver'schwimmen (*unreg*) *vi* to grow hazy, to become blurred

ver'schwinden (*unreg*) *vi* to disappear, to vanish; **V~** (**-s**) *nt* disappearance

verschwitzt [fɛrˈʃvɪtst] *adj* (*Mensch*) sweaty

verschwommen [fɛr'ʃvomən] *adj* hazy, vague

verschwör- [fɛr'ʃvøːr] *zW*: **~en** (*unreg*) *vr* to plot, to conspire; **V~er** (**-s, -**) *m* conspirator; **V~ung** *f* conspiracy, plot

ver'sehen (*unreg*) *vt* to supply, to provide; (*Pflicht*) to carry out; (*Amt*) to fill; (*Haushalt*) to keep ♦ *vr* (*fig*) to make a mistake; **ehe er (es) sich ~ hatte ...** before he knew it ...; **V~** (**-s, -**) *nt* oversight; **aus V~** by mistake; **v~tlich** *adv* by mistake

Versehrte(r) [fɛr'zeːrtə(r)] *mf* disabled person

ver'senden (*unreg*) *vt* to forward, to dispatch

ver'senken *vt* to sink ♦ *vr*: **sich ~ in** +*akk* to become engrossed in

versessen [fɛr'zɛsən] *adj*: **~ auf** +*akk* mad about

ver'setzen *vt* to transfer; (*verpfänden*) to pawn; (*umg*) to stand up ♦ *vr*: **sich in jdn** *od* **in jds Lage ~** to put o.s. in sb's place; **jdm einen Tritt/Schlag ~** to kick/hit sb; **etw mit etw ~** to mix sth with sth; **jdn in gute Laune ~** to put sb in a good mood

Ver'setzung *f* transfer

verseuchen [fɛr'zɔʏçən] *vt* to contaminate

versichern [fɛr'zɪçərn] *vt* to assure; (*mit Geld*) to insure

Versicherung *f* assurance; insurance; **~sgesellschaft** *f* insurance company; **~spolice** *f* insurance policy

ver'siegen *vi* to dry up

ver'sinken (*unreg*) *vi* to sink

versöhnen [fɛr'zøːnən] *vt* to reconcile ♦ *vr* to become reconciled

Versöhnung *f* reconciliation

ver'sorgen *vt* to provide, to supply; (*Familie etc*) to look after

Ver'sorgung *f* provision; (*Unterhalt*) maintenance; (*Alters~ etc*) benefit, assistance

verspäten [fɛr'ʃpɛːtən] *vr* to be late

verspätet *adj* (*Zug, Abflug, Ankunft*) late; (*Glückwünsche*) belated

Verspätung *f* delay; **~ haben** to be late

ver'sperren *vt* to bar, to obstruct

verspielt [fɛr'ʃpiːlt] *adj* (*Kind, Tier*) playful

ver'spotten *vt* to ridicule, to scoff at

ver'sprechen (*unreg*) *vt* to promise; **sich** *dat* **etw von etw ~** to expect sth from sth; **V~** (**-s, -**) *nt* promise

verstaatlichen [fɛr'ʃtaːtlɪçən] *vt* to nationalize

Verstand [fɛr'ʃtant] *m* intelligence; mind; **den ~ verlieren** to go out of one's mind; **über jds ~ gehen** to go beyond sb

verständig [fɛr'ʃtɛndɪç] *adj* sensible; **~en** [fɛr'ʃtɛndɪgən] *vt* to inform ♦ *vr* to communicate; (*sich einigen*) to come to an understanding; **V~ung** *f* communication; (*Benachrichtigung*) informing; (*Einigung*) agreement

verständ- [fɛr'ʃtɛnt] *zW*: **~lich** *adj* understandable, comprehensible; **V~lichkeit** *f* clarity, intelligibility; **V~nis** (**-ses, -se**) *nt* understanding; **~nislos** *adj* uncomprehending; **~nisvoll** *adj* understanding, sympathetic

verstärk- [fɛr'ʃtɛrk] *zW*: **~en** *vt* to strengthen; (*Ton*) to amplify; (*erhöhen*) to intensify ♦ *vr* to intensify; **V~er** (**-s, -**) *m* amplifier; **V~ung** *f* strengthening; (*Hilfe*) reinforcements *pl*; (*von Ton*) amplification

verstauchen [fɛr'ʃtauxən] *vt* to sprain

verstauen [fɛr'ʃtauən] *vt* to stow away

Versteck [fɛr'ʃtɛk] (**-(e)s, -e**) *nt* hiding (place); **v~en** *vt, vr* to hide; **v~t** *adj* hidden

ver'stehen (*unreg*) *vt* to understand ♦ *vr* to get on; **das versteht sich (von selbst)** that goes without saying

versteigern [fɛr'ʃtaɪgərn] *vt* to auction

Versteigerung *f* auction

verstell- [fɛr'ʃtɛl] *zW*: **~bar** *adj* adjustable, variable; **~en** *vt* to move, to shift; (*Uhr*) to adjust; (*versperren*) to block; (*fig*) to disguise ♦ *vr* to pretend, to put on an act; **V~ung** *f* pretence

versteuern [fɛr'ʃtɔʏərn] *vt* to pay tax on

verstiegen [fɛr'ʃtiːgən] *adj* exaggerated

verstimmt [fɛr'ʃtɪmt] *adj* out of tune; (*fig*) cross, put out; (*Magen*) upset

verstohlen [fɛr'ʃtoːlən] *adj* stealthy

ver'stopfen *vt* to block, to stop up; (*MED*) to constipate

Ver'stopfung *f* obstruction; (*MED*) constipation

verstorben [fɛr'ʃtɔrbən] *adj* deceased, late

verstört [fɛr'ʃtøːrt] *adj* (*Mensch*) distraught

Verstoß [fɛr'ʃtoːs] *m*: ~ (gegen) infringement (of), violation (of); v~en (*unreg*) *vt* to disown, to reject ♦ *vi*: v~en gegen to offend against

ver'streichen (*unreg*) *vt* to spread ♦ *vi* to elapse

ver'streuen *vt* to scatter (about)

verstümmeln [fɛr'ʃtyməln] *vt* to maim, to mutilate (*auch fig*)

verstummen [fɛr'ʃtumən] *vi* to go silent; (*Lärm*) to die away

Versuch [fɛr'zuːx] (-(e)s, -e) *m* attempt; (*SCI*) experiment; v~en *vt* to try; (*verlocken*) to tempt ♦ *vr*: sich an etw *dat* v~en to try one's hand at sth; ~skaninchen *nt* (*fig*) guinea-pig; ~ung *f* temptation

versunken [fɛr'zuŋkən] *adj* sunken; ~ sein in +*akk* to be absorbed *od* engrossed in

vertagen [fɛr'taːgən] *vt, vi* to adjourn

ver'tauschen *vt* to exchange; (*versehentlich*) to mix up

verteidig- [fɛr'taɪdɪg] *zW*: ~en *vt* to defend; V~er (-s, -) *m* defender; (*JUR*) defence counsel; V~ung *f* defence

ver'teilen *vt* to distribute; (*Rollen*) to assign; (*Salbe*) to spread

Verteilung *f* distribution, allotment

vertiefen [fɛr'tiːfən] *vt* to deepen ♦ *vr*: sich in etw *akk* ~ to become engrossed *od* absorbed in sth

Vertiefung *f* depression

vertikal [vɛrti'kaːl] *adj* vertical

vertilgen [fɛr'tɪlgən] *vt* to exterminate; (*umg*) to eat up, to consume

vertonen [fɛr'toːnən] *vt* to set to music

Vertrag [fɛr'traːk] (-(e)s, ⁼e) *m* contract, agreement; (*POL*) treaty; v~en [-gən] (*unreg*) *vt* to tolerate, to stand ♦ *vr* to get along; (*sich aussöhnen*) to become

reconciled; v~lich *adj* contractual

verträglich [fɛr'trɛːklɪç] *adj* good-natured, sociable; (*Speisen*) easily digested; (*MED*) easily tolerated; V~keit *f* sociability; good nature; digestibility

Vertrags- *zW*: ~bruch *m* breach of contract; ~partner *m* party to a contract; v~widrig *adj* contrary to contract

vertrauen [fɛr'trauən] *vi*: jdm ~ to trust sb; ~ auf +*akk* to rely on; V~ (-s) *nt* confidence; ~erweckend [fɛr'trauənɛrvɛkənd] *adj* inspiring trust; ~svoll *adj* trustful; ~swürdig *adj* trustworthy

vertraulich [fɛr'traulɪç] *adj* familiar; (*geheim*) confidential

vertraut [fɛr'traut] *adj* familiar; V~heit *f* familiarity

ver'treiben (*unreg*) *vt* to drive away; (*aus Land*) to expel; (*COMM*) to sell; (*Zeit*) to pass

vertret- [fɛr'treːt] *zW*: ~en (*unreg*) *vt* to represent; (*Ansicht*) to hold, to advocate; sich *dat* die Beine ~en to stretch one's legs; V~er (-s, -) *m* representative; (*Verfechter*) advocate; V~ung *f* representation; advocacy

Vertrieb [fɛr'triːp] (-(e)s, -e) *m* marketing (department)

ver'trocknen *vi* to dry up

ver'trösten *vt* to put off

vertun [fɛr'tuːn] (*unreg*) *vt* to waste ♦ *vr* (*umg*) to make a mistake

vertuschen [fɛr'tuʃən] *vt* to hush *od* cover up

verübeln [fɛr''yːbəln] *vt*: jdm etw ~ to be cross *od* offended with sb on account of sth

verüben [fɛr''yːbən] *vt* to commit

verun- [fɛr''un] *zW*: ~glimpfen *vt* to disparage; ~glücken *vi* to have an accident; tödlich ~glücken to be killed in an accident; (*Umwelt*) to pollute; ~sichern *vt* to rattle; ~treuen [-trɔyən] *vt* to embezzle

verur- [fɛr''uːr] *zW*: ~sachen *vt* to cause; ~teilen [-taɪlən] *vt* to condemn; V~teilung *f* condemnation; (*JUR*) sentence

verviel- [fɛr'fiːl] *zW*: ~fachen *vt* to

multiply; **~fältigen** [-fɛltɪgən] *vt* to duplicate, to copy; **V~fältigung** *f* duplication, copying

vervollkommnen [fɛrˈfɔlkɔmnən] *vt* to perfect

vervollständigen *vt* to complete

ver'wackeln *vt* (*Foto*) to blur

ver'wählen *vr* (*TEL*) to dial the wrong number

verwahren [fɛrˈvaːrən] *vt* to keep, to lock away ♦ *vr* to protest

verwalt- [fɛrˈvalt] *zW*: **~en** *vt* to manage; to administer; **V~er** (**-s, -**) *m* manager; (*Vermögensverwalter*) trustee; **V~ung** *f* administration; management

ver'wandeln *vt* to change, to transform ♦ *vr* to change; to be transformed

Ver'wandlung *f* change, transformation

verwandt [fɛrˈvant] *adj*: **~ (mit)** related (to); **V~e(r)** *mf* relative, relation; **V~schaft** *f* relationship; (*Menschen*) relations *pl*

ver'warnen *vt* to caution

Ver'warnung *f* caution

ver'wechseln *vt*: **~ mit** to confuse with; to mistake for; **zum V~ ähnlich** as like as two peas

Ver'wechslung *f* confusion, mixing up

verwegen [fɛrˈveːgən] *adj* daring, bold

Verwehung [fɛrˈveːʊŋ] *f* snowdrift; sanddrift

verweichlicht [fɛrˈvaɪçlɪçt] *adj* effeminate, soft

ver'weigern *vt*: **jdm etw ~** to refuse sb sth; **den Gehorsam/die Aussage ~** to refuse to obey/testify

Ver'weigerung *f* refusal

Verweis [fɛrˈvaɪs] (**-es, -e**) *m* reprimand, rebuke; (*Hinweis*) reference; **v~en** [fɛrˈvaɪzən] (*unreg*) *vt* to refer; **jdn von der Schule v~en** to expel sb (from school); **jdn des Landes v~en** to deport *od* expel sb

ver'welken *vi* to fade

verwendbar [fɛrˈvɛntbaːr] *adj* usable

ver'wenden (*unreg*) *vt* to use; (*Mühe, Zeit, Arbeit*) to spend ♦ *vr* to intercede

Ver'wendung *f* use

ver'werfen (*unreg*) *vt* to reject

verwerflich [fɛrˈvɛrflɪç] *adj* reprehensible

ver'werten *vt* to utilize

Ver'wertung *f* utilization

verwesen [fɛrˈveːzən] *vi* to decay

ver'wickeln *vt* to tangle (up); (*fig*) to involve ♦ *vr* to get tangled (up); **jdn in etw** *akk* **~** to involve sb in sth; **sich in etw** *akk* **~** to get involved in sth

verwickelt [fɛrˈvɪkəlt] *adj* (*Situation, Fall*) difficult, complicated

verwildern [fɛrˈvɪldərn] *vi* to run wild

ver'winden (*unreg*) *vt* to get over

verwirklichen [fɛrˈvɪrklɪçən] *vt* to realize, to put into effect

Verwirklichung *f* realization

verwirren [fɛrˈvɪrən] *vt* to tangle (up); (*fig*) to confuse

Verwirrung *f* confusion

verwittern [fɛrˈvɪtərn] *vi* to weather

verwitwet [fɛrˈvɪtvət] *adj* widowed

verwöhnen [fɛrˈvøːnən] *vt* to spoil

verworfen [fɛrˈvɔrfən] *adj* depraved

verworren [fɛrˈvɔrən] *adj* confused

verwundbar [fɛrˈvʊntbaːr] *adj* vulnerable

verwunden [fɛrˈvʊndən] *vt* to wound

verwunderlich [fɛrˈvʊndərlɪç] *adj* surprising

Verwunderung [fɛrˈvʊndərʊŋ] *f* astonishment

Verwundete(r) *mf* injured person

Verwundung *f* wound, injury

ver'wünschen *vt* to curse

verwüsten [fɛrˈvyːstən] *vt* to devastate

verzagen [fɛrˈtsaːgən] *vi* to despair

ver'zählen *vr* to miscount

verzehren [fɛrˈtseːrən] *vt* to consume

ver'zeichnen *vt* to list; (*Niederlage, Verlust*) to register

Verzeichnis [fɛrˈtsaɪçnɪs] (**-ses, -se**) *nt* list, catalogue; (*in Buch*) index

verzeih- [fɛrˈtsaɪ] *zW*: **~en** (*unreg*) *vt, vi* to forgive; **jdm etw ~en** to forgive sb for sth; **~lich** *adj* pardonable; **V~ung** *f* forgiveness, pardon; **V~ung!** sorry!, excuse me!

verzichten [fɛrˈtsɪçtən] *vi*: **~ auf** *+akk* to forgo, to give up ver'ziehen (*unreg*) *vi* to move ♦ *vt* to put out of shape; (*Kind*) to spoil; (*Pflanzen*) to thin out ♦ *vr* to go out of shape; (*Gesicht*) to contort; (*verschwinden*) to disappear; **das Gesicht ~** to pull a face

verzieren [fɛr'tsiːrən] *vt* to decorate, to ornament

Verzierung *f* decoration

verzinsen [fɛr'tsɪnzən] *vt* to pay interest on

ver'zögern *vt* to delay

Ver'zögerung *f* delay, time-lag;
Verzögerungstaktik *f* delaying tactics *pl*

verzollen [fɛr'tsɔlən] *vt* to pay duty on

verzückt [fɛr'tsʏkt] *adj* enraptured

Verzug [fɛr'tsuːk] *m* delay

verzweif- [fɛr'tsvaɪf] *zW*: **~eln** *vi* to despair; **~elt** *adj* desperate; **V~lung** *f* despair

verzwickt [fɛr'tsvɪkt] (*umg*) *adj* awkward, complicated

Vesuv [ve'zuːf] (**-(s)**) *m* Vesuvius

Veto ['veːto] (**-s, -s**) *nt* veto

Vetter ['fɛtər] (**-s, -n**) *m* cousin

vgl. *abk* (= *vergleiche*) cf.

v.H. *abk* (= *vom Hundert*) p.c.

vibrieren [vi'briːrən] *vi* to vibrate

Video ['viːdeo] *nt* video; **~gerät** *nt* video recorder; **~recorder** *m* video recorder

Vieh [fiː] (**-(e)s**) *nt* cattle *pl*; **v~isch** *adj* bestial

viel [fiːl] *adj* a lot of, much ♦ *adv* a lot, much; **~e** *pron pl* a lot of, many; **~ zuwenig** much too little; **~erlei** *adj* a great variety of; **~es** *pron* a lot; **~fach** *adj, adv* many times; **auf ~fachen Wunsch** at the request of many people; **V~falt** (**-**) *f* variety; **~fältig** *adj* varied, many-sided

vielleicht [fi'laɪçt] *adv* perhaps

viel- *zW*: **~mal(s)** *adv* many times; **danke ~mals** many thanks; **~mehr** *adv* rather, on the contrary; **~sagend** *adj* significant; **~seitig** *adj* many-sided; **~versprechend** *adj* promising

vier [fiːr] *num* four; **V~eck** (**-(e)s, -e**) *nt* four-sided figure; (*gleichseitig*) square; **~eckig** *adj* four-sided; square; **V~takt-**

motor *m* four-stroke engine; **~te(r, s)** ['fɪrtə(r, s)] *adj* fourth; **V~tel** (**-s, -**) ['fɪrtəl] *nt* quarter; **V~teljahr** *nt* quarter; **~teljährlich** *adj* quarterly; **~teln** *vt* to divide into four; (*Kuchen usw*) to divide into quarters; **V~telnote** *f* crotchet; **V~tel'stunde** *f* quarter of an hour; **~zehn** ['fɪrtseːn] *num* fourteen; **in ~zehn Tagen** in a fortnight; **~zehntägig** *adj* fortnightly; **~zig** ['fɪrtsɪç] *num* forty

Villa ['vɪla] (**-, Villen**) *f* villa

violett [vio'lɛt] *adj* violet

Violin- [vio'liːn] *zW*: **~e** *f* violin; **~schlüssel** *m* treble clef

virtuell [vɪrtu'ɛl] *adj* (*COMPUT*) virtual; **~e Realität** virtual reality

Virus ['viːrus] (**-, Viren**) *m od nt* (*auch COMPUT*) virus

Visa ['viːza] *pl von* Visum

vis-à-vis [viza'viː] *adv* opposite

Visen ['viːzən] *pl von* Visum

Visier [vi'ziːr] (**-s, -e**) *nt* gunsight; (*am Helm*) visor

Visite [vi'ziːtə] *f* (*MED*) visit; **~nkarte** *f* visiting card

Visum ['viːzum] (**-s, Visa od Visen**) *nt* visa

vital [vi'taːl] *adj* lively, full of life, vital

Vitamin [vita'miːn] (**-s, -e**) *nt* vitamin

Vogel ['foːgəl] (**-s, ¨**) *m* bird; **einen ~ haben** (*umg*) to have bats in the belfry; **jdm den ~ zeigen** to tap one's forehead (*meaning that one thinks sb stupid*); **~bauer** *nt* birdcage; **~häuschen** *nt* bird house; **~perspektive** *f* bird's-eye view; **~scheuche** *f* scarecrow

Vokabel [vo'kaːbəl] (**-, -n**) *f* word

Vokabular [vokabu'laːr] (**-s, -e**) *nt* vocabulary

Vokal [vo'kaːl] (**-s, -e**) *m* vowel

Volk [fɔlk] (**-(e)s, ¨er**) *nt* people; nation

Völker- ['fœlkər] *zW*: **~recht** *nt* international law; **v~rechtlich** *adj* according to international law; **~verständigung** *f* international understanding

Volks- *zW*: **~entscheid** *m* referendum; **~fest** *nt* fair; **~hochschule** *f* adult education classes *pl*; **~lied** *nt* folksong;

~**republik** f people's republic; **die ~republik China** the People's Republic of China; ~**schule** f elementary school; ~**tanz** m folk dance; ~**vertreter(in)** m(f) people's representative; ~**wirtschaft** f economics sg; ~**zählung** f (national) census

voll [fɔl] adj full; **etw ~ machen** to fill sth up; ~ **und ganz** completely; **jdn für ~ nehmen** (umg) to take sb seriously; ~**auf** [fɔl'?auf] adv amply; **V~bart** m full beard; ~'**bringen** (unreg) vt insep to accomplish; ~'**enden** vt insep to finish, to complete; ~**endet** adj (vollkommen) completed; ~**ends** ['fɔlɛnts] adv completely; **V~'endung** f completion; ~**er adj** fuller; ~**er einer Sache** gen full of sth

Volleyball ['vɔlibal] m volleyball

Vollgas nt: **mit ~** at full throttle; ~ **geben** to step on it

völlig ['fœlɪç] adj complete ♦ adv completely

voll- zW: ~**jährig** adj of age; **V~kaskoversicherung** ['fɔlkasko-fɛrzɪçərʊŋ] f fully comprehensive insurance; ~'**kommen** adj perfect; **V~'kommenheit** f perfection; **V~kornbrot** nt wholemeal bread; **V~macht** (-, -en) f authority, full powers pl; **V~milch** f (KOCH) full-cream milk; **V~mond** m full moon; **V~pension** f full board; ~**ständig** ['fɔlʃtɛndɪç] adj complete; ~'**strecken** vt insep to execute; ~**tanken** vt, vi to fill up; **V~wertkost** f wholefood; ~**zählig** ['fɔltsɛːlɪç] adj complete, in full number; ~'**ziehen** (unreg) vt insep to carry out ♦ vr insep to happen; **V~'zug** m execution

Volt [vɔlt] (- od -(e)s, -) nt volt

Volumen [vo'luːmən] (-s, - od **Volumina**) nt volume

vom [fɔm] = **von dem**

von [fɔn] präp +dat 1 (Ausgangspunkt) from; **von ... bis** from ... to; **von morgens bis abends** from morning till night; **von ... nach ...** from ... to ...; **von ... an** from ...; **von ... aus** from ...; **von**

dort aus from there; **etw von sich aus tun** tó do sth of one's own accord; **von mir aus** (umg) if you like, I don't mind; **von wo/wann ...?** where/when ... from?

2 (Ursache, im Passiv) by; **ein Gedicht von Schiller** a poem by Schiller; **von etw müde** tired from sth

3 (als Genitiv) of; **ein Freund von mir** a friend of mine; **nett von dir** nice of you; **jeweils zwei von zehn** two out of every ten

4 (über) about; **er erzählte vom Urlaub** he talked about his holiday

5: von wegen! (umg) no way!

voneinander adv from each other

vor [foːr] präp +dat 1 (räumlich) in front of; **vor der Kirche links abbiegen** turn left before the church

2 (zeitlich) before; **ich war vor ihm da** I was there before him; **vor 2 Tagen** 2 days ago; **5 (Minuten) vor 4** 5 (minutes) to 4; **vor kurzem** a little while ago

3 (Ursache) with; **vor Wut/Liebe** with rage/love; **vor Hunger sterben** to die of hunger; **vor lauter Arbeit** because of work

4: vor allem, vor allen Dingen most of all

♦ präp +akk (räumlich) in front of

♦ adv: **vor und zurück** backwards and forwards

Vorabend ['foːr'?aːbənt] m evening before, eve

voran [fo'ran] adv before, ahead; **mach ~!** get on with it!; ~**gehen** (unreg) vi to go ahead; **einer Sache** dat ~**gehen** to precede sth; ~**kommen** (unreg) vi to come along, to make progress

Voranschlag m estimate

Vorarbeiter m foreman

voraus [fo'raus] adv ahead; (zeitlich) in advance; **jdm ~ sein** to be ahead of sb; **im ~** in advance; ~**gehen** (unreg) vi to go (on) ahead; (fig) to precede; ~**haben** (unreg) vt: **jdm etw ~haben** to have the

edge on sb in sth; **V~sage** *f* prediction;
~sagen *vt* to predict; **~sehen** (*unreg*) *vt*
to foresee; **~setzen** *vt* to assume;
~gesetzt, daß ... provided that ...;
V~setzung *f* requirement, prerequisite;
V~sicht *f* foresight; **aller V~sicht nach**
in all probability; **~sichtlich** *adv*
probably

Vorbehalt ['fo:rbəhalt] (**-(e)s, -e**) *m*
reservation, proviso; **v~en** (*unreg*) *vt*:
sich/jdm etw v~en to reserve sth (for
o.s.)/for sb; **v~los** *adj* unconditional
♦ *adv* unconditionally

vorbei [fɔr'baɪ] *adv* by, past; **das ist ~**
that's over; **~gehen** (*unreg*) *vi* to pass by,
to go past; **~kommen** (*unreg*) *vi*: **bei
jdm ~kommen** to drop in *od* call in on
sb

vor- *zW*: **~belastet** ['fo:rbəlastət] *adj*
(*fig*) handicapped; **~bereiten** *vt* to
prepare; **V~bereitung** *f* preparation;
~bestraft ['fo:rbəʃtra:ft] *adj* previously
convicted, with a record

vorbeugen ['fo:rbɔygən] *vt, vr* to lean
forward ♦ *vi* +*dat* to prevent; **~d** *adj*
preventive

Vorbeugung *f* prevention; **zur ~ gegen**
for the prevention of

Vorbild ['fo:rbɪlt] *nt* model; **sich** *dat* **jdn
zum ~ nehmen** to model o.s. on sb;
v~lich *adj* model, ideal

vorbringen ['fo:rbrɪŋən] (*unreg*) *vt* to
advance, to state

Vorder- ['fɔrdər] *zW*: **~achse** *f* front
axle; **v~e(r, s)** *adj* front; **~grund** *m*
foreground; **~mann** (*pl* **-männer**) *m* man
in front; **jdn auf ~mann bringen** (*umg*)
to get sb to shape up; **~seite** *f* front
(side); **v~ste(r, s)** *adj* front

vordrängen ['fo:rdrɛŋən] *vr* to push to
the front

voreilig ['fo:r'aɪlɪç] *adj* hasty, rash

voreinander [fo:r'aɪ'nandər] *adv*
(*räumlich*) in front of each other

voreingenommen ['fo:r'aɪŋənɔmən]
adj biased; **V~heit** *f* bias

vorenthalten ['fo:r'ɛnthaltən] (*unreg*) *vt*:
jdm etw ~ to withhold sth from sb

vorerst ['fo:r'e:rst] *adv* for the moment

od present

Vorfahr ['fo:rfa:r] (**-en, -en**) *m* ancestor

vorfahren (*unreg*) *vi* to drive (on) ahead;
(*vors Haus etc*) to drive up

Vorfahrt *f* (*AUT*) right of way; **~ achten!**
give way!

Vorfahrts- *zW*: **~regel** *f* right of way;
~schild *nt* give way sign

Vorfall ['fo:rfal] *m* incident; **v~en**
(*unreg*) *vi* to occur

vorfinden ['fo:rfɪndən] (*unreg*) *vt* to find

Vorfreude ['fo:rfrɔydə] *f* (joyful)
anticipation

vorführen ['fo:rfy:rən] *vt* to show, to
display; **dem Gericht ~** to bring before
the court

Vorgabe ['fo:rga:bə] *f* (*SPORT*) start,
handicap ♦ *in zW* (*COMPUT*) default

Vorgang ['fo:rgaŋ] *m* course of events;
(*bes SCI*) process

Vorgänger(in) ['fo:rgɛŋər(ɪn)] (**-s, -**) *m(f)*
predecessor

vorgeben ['fo:rge:bən] (*unreg*) *vt* to
pretend, to use as a pretext; (*SPORT*) to
give an advantage *od* a start of

vorgefaßt ['fo:rgəfast] *adj* preconceived

vorgefertigt ['fo:rgəfɛrtɪçt] *adj*
prefabricated

vorgehen ['fo:rge:ən] (*unreg*) *vi* (*voraus*)
to go (on) ahead; (*nach vorn*) to go up
front; (*handeln*) to act, to proceed; (*Uhr*)
to be fast; (*Vorrang haben*) to take
precedence; (*passieren*) to go on; **V~** (**-s**)
nt action

Vorgeschichte ['fo:rgəʃɪçtə] *f* past
history

Vorgeschmack ['fo:rgəʃmak] *m*
foretaste

Vorgesetzte(r) ['fo:rgəzɛtstə(r)] *mf*
superior

vorgestern ['fo:rgɛstərn] *adv* the day
before yesterday

vorhaben ['fo:rha:bən] (*unreg*) *vt* to
intend; **hast du schon was vor?** have
you got anything on?; **V~** (**-s, -**) *nt*
intention

vorhalten ['fo:rhaltən] (*unreg*) *vt* to hold
od put up ♦ *vi* to last; **jdm etw ~** (*fig*) to
reproach sb for sth

vorhanden [fo:r'handən] *adj* existing; (*erhältlich*) available

Vorhang ['fo:rhaŋ] *m* curtain

Vorhängeschloß ['fo:rhɛŋəʃlɔs] *nt* padlock

vorher [fo:r'he:r] *adv* before(hand); **~bestimmen** *vt* (*Schicksal*) to preordain; **~gehen** (*unreg*) *vi* to precede; **~ig** [-ɪç] *adj* previous

Vorherrschaft ['fo:rhɛrʃaft] *f* predominance, supremacy

vorherrschen ['fo:rhɛrʃən] *vi* to predominate

vorher- [fo:r'he:r] *zW:* **V~sage** *f* forecast; **~sagen** *vt* to forecast, to predict; **~sehbar** *adj* predictable; **~sehen** (*unreg*) *vt* to foresee

vorhin [fo:r'hɪn] *adv* not long ago, just now; **~ein** ['fo:r-] *adv:* **im ~ein** beforehand

vorig ['fo:rɪç] *adj* previous, last

Vorkämpfer(in) ['fo:rkɛmpfər(ɪn)] *m(f)* pioneer

Vorkaufsrecht ['fo:rkaufsrɛçt] *nt* option to buy

Vorkehrung ['fo:rke:ruŋ] *f* precaution

vorkommen ['fo:rkɔmən] (*unreg*) *vi* to come forward; (*geschehen, sich finden*) to occur; (*scheinen*) to seem (to be); **sich** *dat* **dumm** *etc* **~** to feel stupid *etc*; **V~** (**-s, -**) *nt* occurrence

Vorkriegs- ['fo:rkri:ks] *in zW* prewar

Vorladung ['fo:rla:duŋ] *f* summons *sg*

Vorlage ['fo:rla:gə] *f* model, pattern; (*Gesetzes~*) bill; (*SPORT*) pass

vorlassen ['fo:rlasən] (*unreg*) *vt* to admit; (*vorgehen lassen*) to allow to go in front

vorläufig ['fo:rlɔyfɪç] *adj* temporary, provisional

vorlaut ['fo:rlaut] *adj* impertinent, cheeky

vorlesen ['fo:rle:zən] (*unreg*) *vt* to read (out)

Vorlesung *f* (*UNIV*) lecture

vorletzte(r, s) ['fo:rlɛtstə(r, s)] *adj* last but one

Vorliebe ['fo:rli:bə] *f* preference, partiality

vorliebnehmen [fo:r'li:pne:mən] (*unreg*)

vi: **~ mit** to make do with

vorliegen ['fo:rli:gən] (*unreg*) *vi* to be (here); **etw liegt jdm vor** sb has sth; **~d** *adj* present, at issue

vormachen ['fo:rmaxən] *vt:* **jdm etw ~** to show sb how to do sth; (*fig*) to fool sb; to have sb on

Vormachtstellung ['fo:rmaxtʃtɛluŋ] *f* supremacy, hegemony

Vormarsch ['fo:rmarʃ] *m* advance

vormerken ['fo:rmɛrkən] *vt* to book

Vormittag ['fo:rmɪta:k] *m* morning; **v~s** *adv* in the morning, before noon

Vormund ['fo:rmʊnt] (**-(e)s, -e** *od* **-münder**) *m* guardian

vorn ['fɔrn] *adv* in front; **von ~ anfangen** to start at the beginning; **nach ~** to the front

Vorname ['fo:rna:mə] *m* first name, Christian name

vornehm ['fo:rne:m] *adj* distinguished; refined; elegant

vornehmen (*unreg*) *vt* (*fig*) to carry out; **sich** *dat* **etw ~** to start on sth; (*beschließen*) to decide to do sth; **sich** *dat* **jdn ~** to tell sb off

vornherein ['fɔrnhɛraɪn] *adv:* **von ~** from the start

Vorort ['fo:r'ɔrt] *m* suburb

Vorrang ['fo:rraŋ] *m* precedence, priority; **v~ig** *adj* of prime importance, primary

Vorrat ['fo:rra:t] *m* stock, supply

vorrätig ['fo:rrɛ:tɪç] *adj* in stock

Vorratskammer *f* pantry

Vorrecht ['fo:rrɛçt] *nt* privilege

Vorrichtung ['fo:rrɪçtuŋ] *f* device, contrivance

vorrücken ['fo:rrykən] *vi* to advance ♦ *vt* to move forward

Vorsatz ['fo:rzats] *m* intention; (*JUR*) intent; **einen ~ fassen** to make a resolution

vorsätzlich ['fo:rzɛtslɪç] *adj* intentional; (*JUR*) premeditated ♦ *adv* intentionally

Vorschau ['fo:rʃau] *f* (*RADIO, TV*) (programme) preview; (*Film*) trailer

Vorschlag ['fo:rʃla:k] *m* suggestion,

proposal; **v~en** [-gən] (*unreg*) *vt* to suggest, to propose

vorschreiben ['foːrʃraɪbən] (*unreg*) *vt* to prescribe, to specify

Vorschrift ['foːrʃrɪft] *f* regulation(s); rule(s); (*Anweisungen*) instruction(s); **Dienst nach ~** work-to-rule; **v~smäßig** *adj* as per regulations/instructions

Vorschuß ['foːrʃʊs] *m* advance

vorsehen ['foːrzeːən] (*unreg*) *vt* to provide for, to plan ♦ *vr* to take care, to be careful ♦ *vi* to be visible

Vorsehung *f* providence

vorsetzen ['foːrzɛtsən] *vt* to move forward; (*anbieten*) to offer; **~ vor** +*akk* to put in front of

Vorsicht ['foːrzɪçt] *f* caution, care; **~!** look out!, take care!; (*auf Schildern*) caution!, danger!; **~, Stufe!** mind the step!; **v~ig** *adj* cautious, careful; **v~shalber** *adv* just in case

Vorsilbe ['foːrzɪlbə] *f* prefix

vorsingen *vt* (*vor Zuhörern*) to sing (to); (*in Prüfung, für Theater etc*) to audition (for) ♦ *vi* to sing

Vorsitz ['foːrzɪts] *m* chair(manship); **~ende(r)** *mf* chairman(woman)

Vorsorge ['foːrzɔrgə] *f* precaution(s), provision(s); **v~n** *vi*: **v~n für** to make provision(s) for; **~untersuchung** *f* check-up

vorsorglich ['foːrzɔrklɪç] *adv* as a precaution

Vorspeise ['foːrʃpaɪzə] *f* hors d'oeuvre, appetizer

Vorspiel ['foːrʃpiːl] *nt* prelude

vorspielen *vt*: **jdm etw ~** (*MUS*) to play sth for *or* to sb ♦ *vi* (*zur Prüfung etc*) to play for *or* to sb

vorsprechen ['foːrʃprɛçən] (*unreg*) *vt* to say out loud, to recite ♦ *vi*: **bei jdm ~** to call on sb

Vorsprung ['foːrʃprʊŋ] *m* projection, ledge; (*fig*) advantage, start

Vorstadt ['foːrʃtat] *f* suburbs *pl*

Vorstand ['foːrʃtant] *m* executive committee; (*COMM*) board (of directors); (*Person*) director, head

vorstehen ['foːrʃteːən] (*unreg*) *vi* to

project; **einer Sache** *dat* **~** (*fig*) to be the head of sth

vorstell- ['foːrʃtɛl] *zW*: **~bar** *adj* conceivable; **~en** *vt* to put forward (*bekannt machen*) to introduce; (*darstellen*) to represent; **~en vor** +*akk* to put in front of; **sich** *dat* **etw ~en** to imagine sth; **V~ung** *f* (*Bekanntmachen*) introduction; (*THEAT etc*) performance; (*Gedanke*) idea, thought

vorstoßen ['foːrʃtoːsən] (*unreg*) *vi* (*ins Unbekannte*) to venture (forth)

Vorstrafe ['foːrʃtraːfə] *f* previous conviction

Vortag ['foːrtaːk] *m*: **am ~ einer Sache** *gen* on the day before sth

vortäuschen ['foːrtɔʏʃən] *vt* to feign, to pretend

Vorteil ['fɔrtaɪl] (-**s**, -**e**) *m*: **~ (gegenüber)** advantage (over); **im ~ sein** to have the advantage; **v~haft** *adj* advantageous

Vortrag ['foːrtraːk] (-(**e**)**s**, **Vorträge**) *m* talk, lecture; **v~en** [-gən] (*unreg*) *vt* to carry forward; (*fig*) to recite; (*Rede*) to deliver; (*Lied*) to perform; (*Meinung etc*) to express

vortrefflich ['foːrtrɛflɪç] *adj* excellent

vortreten ['foːrtreːtən] (*unreg*) *vi* to step forward; (*Augen etc*) to protrude

vorüber [fo'ryːbər] *adv* past, over; **~gehen** (*unreg*) *vi* to pass (by); **~gehen an** +*dat* (*fig*) to pass over; **~gehend** *adj* temporary, passing

Vorurteil [fo'rʔʊrtaɪl] *nt* prejudice

Vorverkauf ['foːrfɛrkaʊf] *m* advance booking

Vorwahl ['foːrvaːl] *f* preliminary election; (*TEL*) dialling code

Vorwand ['foːrvant] (-(**e**)**s**, **Vorwände**) *m* pretext

vorwärts ['foːrvɛrts] *adv* forward; **V~gang** *m* (*AUT etc*) forward gear; **~gehen** (*unreg*) *vi* to progress; **~kommen** (*unreg*) *vi* to get on, to make progress

Vorwäsche *f* prewash

vorweg [foːr'vɛk] *adv* in advance; **~nehmen** (*unreg*) *vt* to anticipate

vorweisen ['foːrvaɪzən] (*unreg*) *vt* to

show, to produce
vorwerfen ['fo:rverfən] (*unreg*) *vt*: **jdm etw ~** to reproach sb for sth, to accuse sb of sth; **sich** *dat* **nichts vorzuwerfen haben** to have nothing to reproach o.s. with
vorwiegend ['fo:rvi:gənt] *adj* predominant ♦ *adv* predominantly
vorwitzig ['fo:rvɪtsɪç] *adj* (*Mensch, Bemerkung*) cheeky
Vorwort ['fo:rvɔrt] (-(e)s, -e) *nt* preface
Vorwurf ['fo:rvʊrf] *m* reproach; **jdm/ sich Vorwürfe machen** to reproach sb/ o.s.; **v~svoll** *adj* reproachful
vorzeigen ['fo:rtsaɪgən] *vt* to show, to produce
vorzeitig ['fo:rtsaɪtɪç] *adj* premature
vorziehen ['fo:rtsi:ən] (*unreg*) *vt* to pull forward; (*Gardinen*) to draw; (*lieber haben*) to prefer
Vorzimmer ['fo:rtsɪmər] *nt* (*Büro*) outer office
Vorzug ['fo:rtsu:k] *m* preference; (*gute Eigenschaft*) merit, good quality; (*Vorteil*) advantage
vorzüglich [fo:r'tsy:klɪç] *adj* excellent
vulgär [vʊl'gɛ:r] *adj* vulgar
Vulkan [vʊl'ka:n] (-s, -e) *m* volcano

W w

Waage ['va:gə] *f* scales *pl*; (*ASTROL*) Libra; **w~recht** *adj* horizontal
Wabe ['va:bə] *f* honeycomb
wach [vax] *adj* awake; (*fig*) alert; **W~e** *f* guard, watch; **W~e halten** to keep watch; **W~e stehen** to stand guard; **~en** *vi* to be awake; (*Wache halten*) to guard
Wacholder [va'xɔldər] (-s, -) *m* juniper
Wachs [vaks] (-es, -e) *nt* wax
wachsam ['vaxza:m] *adj* watchful, vigilant, alert
wachsen (*unreg*) *vi* to grow
Wachstuch *nt* oilcloth
Wachstum (-s) *nt* growth
Wächter ['vɛçtər] (-s, -) *m* guard, warden, keeper; (*Parkplatz~*) attendant
wackel- ['vakəl] *zW*: **~ig** *adj* shaky,

wobbly; **W~kontakt** *m* loose connection; **~n** *vi* to shake; (*fig*: *Position*) to be shaky
wacker ['vakər] *adj* valiant, stout ♦ *adv* well, bravely
Wade ['va:də] *f* (*ANAT*) calf
Waffe ['vafə] *f* weapon
Waffel (-, -n) *f* waffle; wafer
Waffen- *zW*: **~schein** *m* gun licence; **~stillstand** *m* armistice, truce
Wagemut ['va:gəmu:t] *m* daring
wagen ['va:gən] *vt* to venture, to dare
Wagen ['va:gən] (-s, -) *m* vehicle; (*Auto*) car; (*EISENB*) carriage; (*Pferde~*) cart; **~heber** (-s, -) *m* jack
Waggon [va'gõ:] (-s, -s) *m* carriage; (*Güter~*) goods van, freight truck (*US*)
waghalsig ['va:khalzɪç] *adj* foolhardy
Wagnis ['va:knɪs] (-ses, -se) *nt* risk
Wahl ['va:l] (-, -en) *f* choice; (*POL*) election; **zweite ~** (*COMM*) seconds *pl*
wähl- ['vɛ:l] *zW*: **~bar** *adj* eligible; **~en** *vt*, *vi* to choose; (*POL*) to elect, to vote (for); (*TEL*) to dial; **W~er(in)** (-s, -) *m(f)* voter; **~erisch** *adj* fastidious, particular
Wahl- *zW*: **~fach** *nt* optional subject; **~gang** *m* ballot; **~kabine** *f* polling booth; **~kampf** *m* election campaign; **~kreis** *m* constituency; **~lokal** *nt* polling station; **w~los** *adv* at random; **~recht** *nt* franchise; **~spruch** *m* motto; **~urne** *f* ballot box
Wahn [va:n] (-(e)s) *m* delusion; folly; **~sinn** *m* madness; **w~sinnig** *adj* insane, mad ♦ *adv* (*umg*) incredibly
wahr [va:r] *adj* true
wahren *vt* to maintain, to keep
während ['vɛ:rənt] *präp* +*gen* during ♦ *konj* while; **~dessen** *adv* meanwhile
wahr- *zW*: **~haben** (*unreg*) *vt*: **etw nicht ~haben wollen** to refuse to admit sth; **~haft** *adv* (*tatsächlich*) truly; **~haftig** [va:r'haftɪç] *adj* true, real ♦ *adv* really; **W~heit** *f* truth; **~nehmen** (*unreg*) *vt* to perceive, to observe; **W~nehmung** *f* perception; **~sagen** *vi* to prophesy, to tell fortunes; **W~sager(in)** (-s, -) *m(f)* fortune teller; **~scheinlich** [va:r'ʃaɪnlɪç] *adj* probable ♦ *adv* probably; **W~'scheinlichkeit** *f* probability; **aller**

W~scheinlichkeit nach in all probability

Währung ['vɛːrʊŋ] *f* currency

Waise ['vaizə] *f* orphan; **~nhaus** *nt* orphanage

Wald [valt] (-(e)s, ¨er) *m* wood(s); (*groß*) forest; **~brand** *m* forest fire; **~sterben** *nt* trees dying due to pollution

Wal(fisch) ['vaːl(fɪʃ)] (-(e)s, -e) *m* whale

Walkman ['wɔːkman] ® *m* Walkman ®, personal stereo

Wall [val] (-(e)s, ¨e) *m* embankment; (*Bollwerk*) rampart

Wallfahr- *zW*: **~er(in)** *m(f)* pilgrim; **~t** *f* pilgrimage

Walnuß ['valnʊs] *f* walnut

Walroß ['valrɔs] *nt* walrus

Walze ['valtsə] *f* (*Gerät*) cylinder; (*Fahrzeug*) roller; **w~n** *vt* to roll (out)

wälzen ['vɛltsən] *vt* to roll (over); (*Bücher*) to hunt through; (*Probleme*) to deliberate on ♦ *vr* to wallow; (*vor Schmerzen*) to roll about; (*im Bett*) to toss and turn

Walzer ['valtsər] (-s, -) *m* waltz

Wand [vant] (-, ¨e) *f* wall; (*Trenn~*) partition; (*Berg~*) precipice

Wandel ['vandəl] (-s) *m* change; **w~bar** *adj* changeable, variable; **w~n** *vt, vr* to change ♦ *vi* (*gehen*) to walk

Wander- ['vandər] *zW*: **~er** (-s, -) *m* hiker, rambler; **~karte** *f* map of country walks; **w~n** *vi* to hike; (*Blick*) to wander; (*Gedanken*) to stray; **~schaft** *f* travelling; **~ung** *f* walk, hike; **~weg** *m* trail, walk

Wandlung *f* change, transformation

Wange ['vaŋə] *f* cheek

wankelmütig ['vaŋkəlmyːtɪç] *adj* vacillating, inconstant

wanken ['vaŋkən] *vi* to stagger; (*fig*) to waver

wann [van] *adv* when

Wanne ['vanə] *f* tub

Wanze ['vantsə] *f* bug

Wappen ['vapən] (-s, -) *nt* coat of arms, crest; **~kunde** *f* heraldry

war *etc* [vaːr] *vb siehe* **sein**

Ware ['vaːrə] *f* ware

Waren- *zW*: **~haus** *nt* department store;

~lager *nt* stock, store; **~probe** *f* sample; **~zeichen** *nt*: (**eingetragenes**) **~zeichen** (registered) trademark

warf *etc* [varf] *vb siehe* **werfen**

warm [varm] *adj* warm; (*Essen*) hot

Wärm- ['vɛrm] *zW*: **~e** *f* warmth; **w~en** *vt, vr* to warm (up), to heat (up); **~flasche** *f* hot-water bottle

warnen ['varnən] *vt* to warn

Warnung *f* warning

warten ['vartən] *vi*: **~ (auf** +*akk*) to wait (for); **auf sich ~ lassen** to take a long time

Wärter(in) ['vɛrtər(ɪn)] (-s, -) *m(f)* attendant

Warte- ['vartə] *zW*: **~raum** *m* (*EISENB*) waiting room; **~saal** *m* (*EISENB*) waiting room; **~zimmer** *nt* waiting room

Wartung *f* servicing; service; **~ und Instandhaltung** maintenance

warum [va'rʊm] *adv* why

Warze ['vartsə] *f* wart

was [vas] *pron* what; (*umg: etwas*) something; **~ für (ein)** ... what sort of ...

waschbar *adj* washable

Waschbecken *nt* washbasin

Wäsche ['vɛʃə] *f* wash(ing); (*Bett~*) linen; (*Unter~*) underclothing

waschecht *adj* colourfast; (*fig*) genuine

Wäscheklammer *f* clothes peg (*BRIT*), clothespin (*US*)

Wäscheleine *f* washing line (*BRIT*)

waschen ['vaʃən] (*unreg*) *vt, vi* to wash ♦ *vr* to (have a) wash; **sich** *dat* **die Hände ~** to wash one's hands

Wäsche'rei *f* laundry

Waschgelegenheit *f* washing facilities

Wasch- *zW*: **~küche** *f* laundry room; **~lappen** *m* face flannel, washcloth (*US*); (*umg*) sissy; **~maschine** *f* washing machine; **~mittel** *nt* detergent, washing powder; **~pulver** *nt* detergent, washing powder; **~raum** *m* washroom; **~salon** *m* Launderette ®

Wasser ['vasər] (-s, -) *nt* water; **~ball** *m* water polo; **w~dicht** *adj* waterproof; **~fall** *m* waterfall; **~farbe** *f* watercolour; **~hahn** *m* tap, faucet (*US*); **~kraftwerk** *nt* hydroelectric power station; **~leitung** *f*

water pipe; **~mann** n (*ASTROL*) Aquarius;
~melone f (*BOT*) water melon
wässern ['vɛsərn] vt, vi to water
Wasser- zW: **w~scheu** adj afraid of
(the) water; **~ski** ['vasərʃiː] nt water-
skiing; **~stoff** m hydrogen; **~waage** f
spirit level; **~zeichen** nt watermark
wäßrig ['vɛsrɪç] adj watery
waten ['vaːtən] vi to wade
watscheln ['vaːtʃəln] vi to waddle
Watt[1] [vat] (-(e)s, -en) nt mud flats pl
Watt[2] (-s, -) nt (*ELEK*) watt
Watte f cotton wool, absorbent cotton
(*US*)
WC ['veː'tseː] (-(s), -s) nt abk (= *water
closet*) W.C.
Web- ['veːb] zW: **w~en** (*unreg*) vt to
weave; **~er** (-s, -) m weaver; **~e'rei** f
(*Betrieb*) weaving mill; **~stuhl** m loom
Wechsel ['vɛksəl] (-s, -) m change;
(*COMM*) bill of exchange; **~geld** nt change;
w~haft adj (*Wetter*) variable; **~jahre** pl
change of life sg; **~kurs** m rate of
exchange; **w~n** vt to change; (*Blicke*) to
exchange ♦ vi to change; to vary;
(*Geldwechseln*) to have change; **~strom** m
alternating current; **~stube** f bureau de
change; **~wirkung** f interaction
wecken ['vɛkən] vt to wake (up); to call
Wecker ['vɛkər] (-s, -) m alarm clock
wedeln ['veːdəln] vi (*mit Schwanz*) to
wag; (*mit Fächer etc*) to wave
weder ['veːdər] konj neither; **~ ... noch**
... neither ... nor ...
Weg [veːk] (-(e)s, -e) m way; (*Pfad*) path;
(*Route*) route; **sich auf den ~ machen** to
be on one's way; **jdm aus dem ~ gehen**
to keep out of sb's way
weg [vɛk] adv away, off; **über etw** akk **~
sein** to be over sth; **er war schon ~** he
had already left; **Finger ~!** hands off!
wegbleiben (*unreg*) vi to stay away
wegen ['veːgən] präp +gen (*umg*: +dat)
because of
weg- ['vɛk] zW: **~fallen** (*unreg*) vi to be
left out; (*Ferien, Bezahlung*) to be
cancelled; (*aufhören*) to cease; **~gehen**
(*unreg*) vi to go away; to leave; **~lassen**
(*unreg*) vt to leave out; **~laufen** (*unreg*)

vi to run away od off; **~legen** vt to put
aside; **~machen** (*umg*) vt to get rid of;
~müssen (*unreg*; *umg*) vi to have to go;
~nehmen (*unreg*) vt to take away; **~tun**
(*unreg*) vt to put away
Wegweiser ['veːgvaɪzər] (-s, -) m road
sign, signpost
weg- zW: **~werfen** (*unreg*) vt to throw
away; **~werfend** adj disparaging
weh [veː] adj sore; **~ tun** to hurt, to be
sore; **jdm/sich ~ tun** to hurt sb/o.s.; **~(e)**
excl: **~(e), wenn du ...** woe betide you if
...; **o ~!** oh dear!; **~e!** just you dare!
wehen vt, vi to blow; (*Fahnen*) to flutter
weh- zW: **~leidig** adj whiny, whining;
~mütig adj melancholy
Wehr[1] [veːr] (-(e)s, -e) nt weir
Wehr[2] (-, -en) f: **sich zur ~ setzen** to
defend o.s.; **~dienst** m military service;
~dienstverweigerer m ≈ conscientious
objector; **w~en** vr to defend o.s.; **w~los**
adj defenceless; **~pflicht** f compulsory
military service; **w~pflichtig** adj liable
for military service
Weib [vaɪp] (-(e)s, -er) nt woman, female;
wife; **~chen** nt female; **w~lich** adj
feminine
weich [vaɪç] adj soft; **W~e** f (*EISENB*)
points pl; **~en** (*unreg*) vi to yield, to give
way; **W~heit** f softness; **~lich** adj soft,
namby-pamby; **W~ling** m weakling
Weide ['vaɪdə] f (*Baum*) willow; (*Gras*)
pasture; **w~n** vi to graze ♦ vr: **sich an
etw** dat **w~n** to delight in sth
weidlich ['vaɪtlɪç] adv thoroughly
weigern ['vaɪgərn] vr to refuse
Weigerung ['vaɪgərʊŋ] f refusal
Weihe ['vaɪə] f consecration; (*Priester~*)
ordination; **w~n** vt to consecrate; to
ordain
Weiher (-s, -) m pond
Weihnacht- zW: **~en** (-) nt Christmas;
w~lich adj Christmas cpd
Weihnachts- zW: **~abend** m Christmas
Eve; **~lied** nt Christmas carol; **~mann** m
Father Christmas, Santa Claus; **~markt**
m Christmas fair; **~tag** m Christmas
Day; **zweiter ~tag** Boxing Day
Weihrauch m incense

Weihwasser *nt* holy water
weil [vaɪl] *konj* because
Weile ['vaɪlə] (-) *f* while, short time
Wein [vaɪn] (-(e)s, -e) *m* wine; (*Pflanze*) vine; **~bau** *m* cultivation of vines; **~berg** *m* vineyard; **~bergschnecke** *f* snail; **~brand** *m* brandy
weinen *vt, vi* to cry; **das ist zum W~** it's enough to make you cry *od* weep
Wein- *zW:* **~glas** *nt* wine glass; **~karte** *f* wine list; **~lese** *f* vintage; **~probe** *f* wine-tasting; **~rebe** *f* vine; **w~rot** *adj* burgundy, claret, wine-red; **~stock** *m* vine; **~stube** *f* wine bar; **~traube** *f* grape
weise [vaɪzə] *adj* wise
Weise *f* manner, way; (*Lied*) tune; **auf diese ~** in this way
weisen (*unreg*) *vt* to show
Weisheit ['vaɪshaɪt] *f* wisdom; **Weisheitszahn** *m* wisdom tooth
weiß [vaɪs] *adj* white ♦ *vb siehe* **wissen**; **W~brot** *nt* white bread; **~en** *vt* to whitewash; **W~glut** *f* (*TECH*) incandescence; **jdn bis zur W~glut bringen** (*fig*) to make sb see red; **W~kohl** *m* (white) cabbage; **W~wein** *m* white wine
weit [vaɪt] *adj* wide; (*Begriff*) broad; (*Reise, Wurf*) long ♦ *adv* far; **wie ~ ist es ...?** how far is it ...?; **in ~er Ferne** in the far distance; **das geht zu ~** that's going too far; **~aus** *adv* by far; **~blickend** *adj* far-seeing; **W~e** *f* width; (*Raum*) space; (*von Entfernung*) distance; **~en** *vt, vr* to widen
weiter ['vaɪtər] *adj* wider; broader; farther (away); (*zusätzlich*) further ♦ *adv* further; **ohne ~es** without further ado; just like that; **~ nichts/niemand** nothing/nobody else; **~arbeiten** *vi* to go on working; **~bilden** *vr* to continue one's education; **~empfehlen** (*unreg*) *vt* to recommend (to others); **W~fahrt** *f* continuation of the journey; **~führen** *vi* (*Straße*) to lead on (to) ♦ *vt* (*fortsetzen*) to continue, carry on; **~gehen** (*unreg*) *vi* to go on; **~hin** *adv:* **etw ~hin tun** to go on doing sth; **~kommen** (*unreg*) *vi* (*fig: mit*

Arbeit) to make progress; **~leiten** *vt* to pass on; **~machen** *vt, vi* to continue
weit- *zW:* **~gehend** *adj* considerable ♦ *adv* largely; **~läufig** *adj* (*Gebäude*) spacious; (*Erklärung*) lengthy; (*Verwandter*) distant; **~reichend** *adj* long-range; (*fig*) far-reaching; **~schweifig** *adj* long-winded; **~sichtig** *adj* (*MED*) long-sighted; (*fig*) far-sighted; **W~sprung** *m* long jump; **~verbreitet** *adj* widespread; **W~winkelobjektiv** *nt* (*PHOT*) wide-angle lens
Weizen ['vaɪtsən] (-s, -) *m* wheat

welche(r, s) ['vɛlçə(r, s)] *interrogativ pron* which; **welcher von beiden?** which (one) of the two?; **welchen hast du genommen?** which (one) did you take?; **welche eine ...!** what a ...!; **welche Freude!** what joy!
♦ *indef pron* some; (*in Fragen*) any; **ich habe welche** I have some; **haben Sie welche?** do you have any?
♦ *relativ pron* (*bei Menschen*) who; (*bei Sachen*) which, that; **welche(r, s) auch immer** whoever/whichever/whatever

welk [vɛlk] *adj* withered; **~en** *vi* to wither
Wellblech *nt* corrugated iron
Welle ['vɛlə] *f* wave; (*TECH*) shaft; **~nbereich** *m* waveband; **~nlänge** *f* (*auch fig*) wavelength; **~nlinie** *f* wavy line; **~nsittich** *m* budgerigar
Welt [vɛlt] (-, -en) *f* world; **~all** *nt* universe; **~anschauung** *f* philosophy of life; **w~berühmt** *adj* world-famous; **~krieg** *m* world war; **w~lich** *adj* worldly; (*nicht kirchlich*) secular; **~macht** *f* world power; **~meister** *m* world champion; **~raum** *m* space; **~reise** *f* trip round the world; **~stadt** *f* metropolis; **w~weit** *adj* world-wide
wem [ve:m] (*dat von* **wer**) *pron* to whom
wen [ve:n] (*akk von* **wer**) *pron* whom
Wende ['vɛndə] *f* turn; (*Veränderung*) change; **~kreis** *m* (*GEOG*) tropic; (*AUT*)

turning circle; **~ltreppe** f spiral staircase; **w~n** (unreg) vt, vi, vr to turn; **sich an jdn w~n** to go/come to sb; **~punkt** m turning point

wendig ['vɛndɪç] adj (Auto etc) manoeuvrable; (fig) agile

Wendung f turn; (Rede~) idiom

wenig ['veːnɪç] adj, adv little; **~e** pron pl few pl; **~er** adj less; (mit pl) fewer ♦ adv less; **~ste(r, s)** adj least; **am ~sten** least; **~stens** adv at least

wenn [vɛn] konj 1 (falls, bei Wünschen) if; **wenn auch ..., selbst wenn ...** even if ...; **wenn ich doch ...** if only I ...

2 (zeitlich) when; **immer wenn** whenever

wennschon ['vɛnʃoːn] adv: **na ~** so what?; **~, dennschon!** in for a penny, in for a pound

wer [veːr] pron who

Werbe- ['vɛrbə] zW: **~fernsehen** nt commercial television; **w~n** (unreg) vt to win; (Mitglied) to recruit ♦ vi to advertise; **um jdn/etw w~n** to try to win sb/sth; **für jdn/etw w~n** to promote sb/sth

Werbung f advertising; (von Mitgliedern) recruitment; **~ um jdn/etw** promotion of sb/sth

Werdegang ['veːrdəgaŋ] m (Laufbahn) development; (beruflich) career

werden ['veːrdən] (pt **wurde**, pp **geworden** od (bei Passiv) **worden**) vi to become; **was ist aus ihm/aus der Sache geworden?** what became of him/it?; **es ist nichts/gut geworden** it came to nothing/turned out well; **es wird Nacht/Tag** it's getting dark/light; **mir wird kalt** I'm getting cold; **mir wird schlecht** I feel ill; **Erster werden** to come od to be first; **das muß anders werden** that'll have to change; **rot/zu Eis werden** to turn red/to ice; **was willst du (mal) werden?** what do you want to be?; **die Fotos sind gut geworden** the photos

have come out nicely

♦ als Hilfsverb 1 (bei Futur): **er wird es tun** he will od he'll do it; **er wird das nicht tun** he will not od he won't do it; **es wird gleich regnen** it's going to rain

2 (bei Konjunktiv): **ich würde ...** I would ...; **er würde gern ...** he would od he'd like to ...; **ich würde lieber ...** I would od I'd rather ...

3 (bei Vermutung): **sie wird in der Küche sein** she will be in the kitchen

4 (bei Passiv): **gebraucht werden** to be used; **er ist erschossen worden** he has od he's been shot; **mir wurde gesagt, daß ...** I was told that ...

werfen ['vɛrfən] (unreg) vt to throw

Werft [vɛrft] (-, -en) f shipyard, dockyard

Werk [vɛrk] (-(e)s, -e) nt work; (Tätigkeit) job; (Fabrik, Mechanismus) works pl; **ans ~ gehen** to set to work; **~statt** (-, -stätten) f workshop; (AUT) garage; **~tag** m working day; **~tags** adv on working days; **w~tätig** adj working; **~zeug** nt tool

Wermut ['veːrmuːt] (-(e)s) m wormwood; (Wein) vermouth

Wert [veːrt] (-(e)s, -e) m worth; (FIN) value; **~ legen auf** +akk to attach importance to; **es hat doch keinen ~** it's useless; **w~** adj worth; (geschätzt) dear; worthy; **das ist nichts/viel w~** it's not worth anything/it's worth a lot; **das ist es/er mir w~** it's/he's worth that to me; **w~en** vt to rate; **~gegenstände** mpl valuables; **w~los** adj worthless; **~papier** nt security; **w~voll** adj valuable

Wesen ['veːzən] (-s, -) nt (Geschöpf) being; (Natur, Character) nature; **w~tlich** adj significant; (beträchtlich) considerable

weshalb [vɛs'halp] adv why

Wespe ['vɛspə] f wasp

wessen ['vɛsən] (gen von **wer**) pron whose

Weste ['vɛstə] f waistcoat, vest (US); (Woll~) cardigan

West- zW: **~en** (-s) m west; **~europa** nt Western Europe; **~indien** nt the West Indies; **w~lich** adj western ♦ adv to the west

weswegen [vɛs'veːgən] *adv* why

wett [vɛt] *adj* even; **W~bewerb** *m*
competition; **W~e** *f* bet, wager; **~en** *vt, vi*
to bet

Wetter ['vɛtər] **(-s, -)** *nt* weather;
~bericht *m* weather report; **~dienst** *m*
meteorological service; **~lage** *f* (weather)
situation; **~vorhersage** *f* weather
forecast; **~warte** *f* weather station

Wett- *zW:* **~kampf** *m* contest; **~lauf** *m*
race; **w~machen** *vt* to make good

wichtig ['vɪçtɪç] *adj* important; **W~keit** *f*
importance

wickeln ['vɪkəln] *vt* to wind; (*Haare*) to
set; (*Kind*) to change; **jdn/etw in etw**
akk ~ to wrap sb/sth in sth

Widder ['vɪdər] **(-s, -)** *m* ram; (*ASTROL*)
Aries

wider ['viːdər] *präp +akk* against;
~'fahren (*unreg*) *vi* to happen; **~'legen**
vt to refute

widerlich ['viːdərlɪç] *adj* disgusting,
repulsive

wider- ['viːdər] *zW:* **~rechtlich** *adj*
unlawful; **W~rede** *f* contradiction;
W~ruf *m* retraction; countermanding;
~'rufen (*unreg*) *vt insep* to retract;
(*Anordnung*) to revoke; (*Befehl*) to
countermand; **~'setzen** *vr insep:* **sich**
jdm/etw ~setzen to oppose sb/sth

widerspenstig ['viːdərʃpɛnstɪç] *adj*
wilful

widerspiegeln ['viːdərʃpiːgəln] *vt*
(*Entwicklung, Erscheinung*) to mirror,
reflect ♦ *vr* to be reflected

wider'sprechen (*unreg*) *vi insep:* **jdm ~**
to contradict sb

Widerspruch ['viːdərʃprʊx] *m*
contradiction; **w~slos** *adv* without
arguing

Widerstand ['viːdərʃtant] *m* resistance

Widerstands- *zW:* **~bewegung** *f*
resistance (movement); **w~fähig** *adj*
resistant, tough; **w~los** *adj* unresisting

wider'stehen (*unreg*) *vi insep:* **jdm/etw**
~ to withstand sb/sth

wider- ['viːdər] *zW:* **~wärtig** *adj* nasty,
horrid; **W~wille** *m:* **W~wille (gegen)**

aversion (to); **~willig** *adj* unwilling,
reluctant

widmen ['vɪtmən] *vt* to dedicate; to
devote ♦ *vr* to devote o.s.

widrig ['viːdrɪç] *adj* (*Umstände*) adverse

SCHLÜSSELWORT

wie [viː] *adv* how; **wie groß/schnell?**
how big/fast?; **wie wär's?** how about it?;
wie ist er? what's he like?; **wie gut du**
das kannst! you're very good at it; **wie**
bitte? pardon?; (*entrüstet*) I beg your
pardon!; **und wie!** and how!
♦ *konj* **1** (*bei Vergleichen*): **so schön wie**
... as beautiful as ...; **wie ich schon sagte**
as I said; **wie du** like you; **singen wie**
ein ... to sing like a ...; **wie (zum**
Beispiel) such as (for example)
2 (*zeitlich*): **wie er das hörte, ging er**
when he heard that he left; **er hörte, wie**
der Regen fiel he heard the rain falling

---

wieder ['viːdər] *adv* again; ~ **da sein** to
be back (again); **gehst du schon ~?** are
you off again?; ~ **ein(e) ...** another ...;
W~aufbau [-'aufbau] *m* rebuilding;
~aufbereiten *vt sep* to recycle;
~aufnehmen (*unreg*) *vt* to resume;
~bekommen (*unreg*) *vt* to get back;
~bringen (*unreg*) *vt* to bring back;
~erkennen (*unreg*) *vt* to recognize;
W~gabe *f* reproduction; **~geben** (*unreg*)
vt (*zurückgeben*) to return; (*Erzählung*
etc) to repeat; (*Gefühle etc*) to convey;
~gutmachen *vt* to make up for; (*Fehler*)
to put right; **W~'gutmachung** *f*
reparation; **~'herstellen** *vt* to restore;
~'holen *vt insep* to repeat; **W~'holung** *f*
repetition; **W~hören** *nt:* **auf W~hören**
(*TEL*) goodbye; **W~kehr** **(-)** *f* return; (*von*
Vorfall) repetition, recurrence; **~sehen**
(*unreg*) *vt* to see again; **auf W~sehen**
goodbye; **~um** *adv* again; (*andererseits*)
on the other hand; **~vereinigen** *vt* to
reunite; (*POL*) to reunify; **~verwerten** *vt*
sep to recycle; **W~wahl** *f* re-election

Wiege ['viːgə] *f* cradle; **w~n¹** *vt*
(*schaukeln*) to rock

wiegen² (*unreg*) *vt, vi* (*Gewicht*) to weigh

wiehern ['vi:ərn] *vi* to neigh, to whinny

Wien [vi:n] *nt* Vienna

Wiese ['vi:zə] *f* meadow

Wiesel ['vi:zəl] (-s, -) *nt* weasel

wieso [vi:'zo:] *adv* why

wieviel [vi:'fi:l] *adj* how much; ~
Menschen how many people; ~**mal** *adv*
how often; ~**te(r, s)** *adj*: **zum ~ten Mal?**
how many times?; **den W~ten haben
wir?** what's the date?; **an ~ter Stelle?** in
what place?; **der ~te Besucher war er?**
how many visitors were there before
him?

wieweit [vi:'vait] *adv* to what extent

wild [vɪlt] *adj* wild; **W~** (-(e)s) *nt* game;
W~e(r) ['vɪldə(r)] *mf* savage; **w~ern** *vi* to
poach; ~'**fremd** (*umg*) *adj* quite strange
od unknown; **W~heit** *f* wildness;
W~leder *nt* suede; **W~nis** (-, -se) *f*
wilderness; **W~schwein** *nt* (wild) boar

will *etc* [vɪl] *vb siehe* **wollen**

Wille ['vɪlə] (-ns, -n) *m* will; **w~n** *präp*
+*gen*: **um ... w~n** for the sake of ...;
w~nsstark *adj* strong-willed

will- *zW*: ~**ig** *adj* willing; **W~kommen**
[vɪl'kɔmən] (-s, -) *nt* welcome; **~kommen**
adj welcome; **jdn ~kommen heißen** to
welcome sb; ~**kürlich** *adj* arbitrary;
(*Bewegung*) voluntary

wimmeln ['vɪməln] *vi*: ~ (**von**) to swarm
(with)

wimmern ['vɪmərn] *vi* to whimper

Wimper ['vɪmpər] (-, -n) *f* eyelash

Wimperntusche *f* mascara

Wind [vɪnt] (-(e)s, -e) *m* wind; ~**beutel** *m*
cream puff; (*fig*) rake; ~**e** *f* (*TECH*) winch,
windlass; (*BOT*) bindweed; ~**el** ['vɪndəl]
(-, -n) *f* nappy, diaper (*US*); **w~en** *vi*
unpers to be windy ♦ *vt* (*unreg*) to wind;
(*Kranz*) to weave; (*entwinden*) to twist
♦ *vr* (*unreg*) to wind; (*Person*) to writhe;
~**energie** *f* wind energy; ~**hund** *m*
greyhound; (*Mensch*) fly-by-night; **w~ig**
['vɪndɪç] *adj* windy; (*fig*) dubious;
~**mühle** *f* windmill; ~**pocken** *pl*
chickenpox *sg*; ~**schutzscheibe** *f* (*AUT*)
windscreen (*BRIT*), windshield (*US*);
~**stärke** *f* wind-force; **w~still** *adj* (*Tag*)
still, windless; (*Platz*) sheltered; ~**stille** *f*

calm; ~**stoß** *m* gust of wind

Wink [vɪŋk] (-(e)s, -e) *m* (*mit Hand*) wave;
(*mit Kopf*) nod; (*Hinweis*) hint

Winkel ['vɪnkəl] (-s, -) *m* (*MATH*) angle;
(*Gerät*) set square; (*in Raum*) corner

winken ['vɪŋkən] *vt, vi* to wave

winseln ['vɪnzəln] *vi* to whine

Winter ['vɪntər] (-s, -) *m* winter; **w~fest**
adj (*Pflanze*) hardy; ~**garten** *m*
conservatory; **w~lich** *adj* wintry; ~**reifen**
m winter tyre; ~**sport** *m* winter sports *pl*

Winzer ['vɪntsər] (-s, -) *m* vine grower

winzig ['vɪntsɪç] *adj* tiny

Wipfel ['vɪpfəl] (-s, -) *m* treetop

wir [vi:r] *pron we*; ~ **alle** all of us, we all

Wirbel ['vɪrbəl] (-s, -) *m* whirl, swirl;
(*Trubel*) hurly-burly; (*Aufsehen*) fuss;
(*ANAT*) vertebra; **w~n** *vi* to whirl, to swirl;
~**säule** *f* spine

wird [vɪrt] *vb siehe* **werden**

wirfst *etc* [vɪrfst] *vb siehe* **werfen**

wirken ['vɪrkən] *vi* to have an effect;
(*erfolgreich sein*) to work; (*scheinen*) to
seem ♦ *vt* (*Wunder*) to work

wirklich ['vɪrklɪç] *adj* real ♦ *adv* really;
W~keit *f* reality

wirksam ['vɪrkza:m] *adj* effective

Wirkstoff *m* (*biologisch, chemisch,
pflanzlich*) active substance

Wirkung ['vɪrkʊŋ] *f* effect; **w~slos** *adj*
ineffective; **w~slos bleiben** to have no
effect; **w~svoll** *adj* effective

wirr [vɪr] *adj* confused, wild; **W~warr**
(-s) *m* disorder, chaos

Wirsing ['vɪrzɪŋ] (-s) *m* savoy cabbage

wirst [vɪrst] *vb siehe* **werden**

Wirt(in) ['vɪrt(ɪn)] (-(e)s, -e) *m(f)*
landlord(lady); ~**schaft** *f* (*Gaststätte*) pub;
(*Haushalt*) housekeeping; (*eines Landes*)
economy; (*umg: Durcheinander*) mess;
w~schaftlich *adj* economical; (*POL*)
economic

Wirtschafts- *zW*: ~**krise** *f* economic
crisis; ~**politik** *f* economic policy;
~**prüfer** *m* chartered accountant;
~**wunder** *nt* economic miracle

Wirtshaus *nt* inn

wischen ['vɪʃən] *vt* to wipe

Wischer (-s, -) *m* (*AUT*) wiper

wispern ['vɪspərn] *vt, vi* to whisper
Wißbegier(de) ['vɪsbəgiːr(də)] *f* thirst
for knowledge; **wißbegierig** *adj*
inquisitive, eager for knowledge
wissen ['vɪsən] (*unreg*) *vt* to know; **was
weiß ich!** I don't know!; **W~ (-s)** *nt*
knowledge; **W~schaft** *f* science;
W~schaftler(in) (-s, -) *m(f)* scientist;
~schaftlich *adj* scientific; **~swert** *adj*
worth knowing; **~tlich** *adj* knowing
wittern ['vɪtərn] *vt* to scent; (*fig*) to
suspect
Witterung *f* weather; (*Geruch*) scent
Witwe ['vɪtvə] *f* widow; **~r (-s, -)** *m*
widower
Witz [vɪts] **(-es, -e)** *m* joke; **~bold (-(e)s,
-e)** *m* joker, wit; **w~ig** *adj* funny
wo [voː] *adv* where; (*umg: irgendwo*)
somewhere; **im Augenblick, ~ ...** the
moment (that) ...; **die Zeit, ~ ...** the time
when ...; **~anders** [voː'andərs] *adv*
elsewhere; **~bei** [-'baɪ] *adv* (*relativ*) by/
with which; (*interrogativ*) what ... in/by/
with
Woche ['vɔxə] *f* week
Wochen- *zW:* **~ende** *nt* weekend;
w~lang *adj, adv* for weeks; **~schau** *f*
newsreel
wöchentlich ['vœçəntlɪç] *adj, adv*
weekly
wodurch [voː'dʊrç] *adv* (*relativ*) through
which; (*interrogativ*) what ... through
wofür [voː'fyːr] *adv* (*relativ*) for which;
(*interrogativ*) what ... for
wog *etc* [voːk] *vb siehe* **wiegen**
wo- [voː] *zW:* **~'gegen** *adv* (*relativ*)
against which; (*interrogativ*) what ...
against; **~her** [-'heːr] *adv* where ... from;
~hin [-'hɪn] *adv* where ... to

wohl [voːl] *adv* **1: sich wohl fühlen**
(*zufrieden*) to feel happy; (*gesundheitlich*)
to feel well; **wohl oder übel** whether one
likes it or not
2 (*wahrscheinlich*) probably; (*gewiß*)
certainly; (*vielleicht*) perhaps; **sie ist
wohl zu Hause** she's probably at home;
das ist doch wohl nicht dein Ernst!

surely you're not serious!; **das mag wohl
sein** that may well be; **ob das wohl
stimmt?** I wonder if that's true; **er weiß
das sehr wohl** he knows that perfectly
well

Wohl [voːl] **(-(e)s)** *nt* welfare; **zum ~!**
cheers!; **w~'auf** *adv* well; **~behagen** *nt*
comfort; **~fahrt** *f* welfare; **~fahrtsstaat**
m welfare state; **w~habend** *adj* wealthy;
w~ig *adj* contented, comfortable;
w~schmeckend *adj* delicious; **~stand**
m prosperity; **~standsgesellschaft** *f*
affluent society; **~tat** *f* relief; act of
charity; **~täter(in)** *m(f)* benefactor;
w~tätig *adj* charitable; **~tätigkeits-** *zW*
charity, charitable; **w~tun** (*unreg*) *vi*:
jdm w~tun to do sb good; **w~verdient**
adj well-earned, well-deserved;
w~weislich *adv* prudently; **~wollen (-s)**
nt good will; **w~wollend** *adj* benevolent
wohn- ['voːn] *zW:* **~en** *vi* to live;
W~gemeinschaft *f* (*Menschen*) people
sharing a flat; **~haft** *adj* resident;
W~heim *nt* (*für Studenten*) hall of
residence; (*für Senioren*) home; (*bes für
Arbeiter*) hostel; **~lich** *adj* comfortable;
W~ort *m* domicile; **W~sitz** *m* place of
residence; **W~ung** *f* house;
(*Etagenwohnung*) flat, apartment (*US*);
W~wagen *m* caravan; **W~zimmer** *nt*
living room
wölben ['vœlbən] *vt, vr* to curve
Wölbung *f* curve
Wolf [vɔlf] **(-(e)s, ⁻e)** *m* wolf
Wolke ['vɔlkə] *f* cloud; **~nkratzer** *m*
skyscraper
wolkig ['vɔlkɪç] *adj* cloudy
Wolle ['vɔlə] *f* wool; **w~n¹** *adj* woollen

wollen² ['vɔlən] (*pt* **wollte**, *pp* **gewollt**
od (*als Hilfsverb*) **wollen**) *vt, vi* to want;
ich will nach Hause I want to go home;
er will nicht he doesn't want to; **er
wollte das nicht** he didn't want it; **wenn
du willst** if you like; **ich will, daß du
mir zuhörst** I want you to listen to me
♦ *Hilfsverb*: **er will ein Haus kaufen** he

wants to buy a house; **ich wollte, ich
wäre ...** I wish I were ...; **etw gerade tun
wollen** to be going to do sth

wollüstig ['vɔlystɪç] *adj* lusty, sensual
wo- *zW:* **~mit** [voː'mɪt] *adv* (*relativ*) with
which; (*interrogativ*) what ... with;
~'möglich *adv* probably, I suppose;
~'nach *adv* (*relativ*) after/for which;
(*interrogativ*) what ... for/after; **~'ran** *adv*
(*relativ*) on/at; (*interrogativ*) what
... on/at; **~'rauf** *adv* (*relativ*) on which;
(*interrogativ*) what ... on; **~'raus** *adv*
(*relativ*) from/out of which; (*interrogativ*)
what ... from/out of; **~'rin** *adv* (*relativ*) in
which; (*interrogativ*) what ... in
Wort [vɔrt] (*-(e)s, -er* *od* *-e*) *nt* word; **jdn
beim ~ nehmen** to take sb at his word;
mit anderen ~en in other words;
w~brüchig *adj* not true to one's word
Wörterbuch ['vœrtərbuːx] *nt* dictionary
Wort- *zW:* **~führer** *m* spokesman;
w~karg *adj* taciturn; **~laut** *m* wording
wörtlich ['vœrtlɪç] *adj* literal
Wort- *zW:* **w~los** *adj* mute; **w~reich** *adj*
wordy, verbose; **~schatz** *m* vocabulary;
~spiel *nt* play on words, pun
wo- *zW:* **~rüber** [voː'ryːbər] *adv* (*relativ*)
over/about which; (*interrogativ*) what ...
over/about; **~'rum** *adv* (*relativ*) about/
round which; (*interrogativ*) what ...
about/round; **~'runter** *adv* (*relativ*) under
which; (*interrogativ*) what ... under;
~'von *adv* (*relativ*) from which;
(*interrogativ*) what ... from; **~'vor** *adv*
(*relativ*) in front of/before which;
(*interrogativ*) in front of/before what; of
what; **~'zu** *adv* (*relativ*) to/for which;
(*interrogativ*) what ... for/to; (*warum*) why
Wrack [vrak] (*-(e)s, -s*) *nt* wreck
wringen ['vrɪŋən] (*unreg*) *vt* to wring
Wucher ['vuːxər] (*-s*) *m* profiteering; **~er**
(*-s, -*) *m* profiteer; **w~isch** *adj*
profiteering; **w~n** *vi* (*Pflanzen*) to grow
wild; **~ung** *f* (*MED*) tumour, growth
Wuchs [vuːks] (*-es*) *m* (*Wachstum*)
growth; (*Statur*) build
Wucht [vʊxt] (*-*) *f* force
wühlen ['vyːlən] *vi* to scrabble; (*Tier*) to

root; (*Maulwurf*) to burrow; (*umg:
arbeiten*) to slave away ♦ *vt* to dig
Wulst [vʊlst] (*-es, ⁓e*) *m* bulge; (*an
Wunde*) swelling
wund [vʊnt] *adj* sore, raw; **W~e** *f* wound
Wunder ['vʊndər] (*-s, -*) *nt* miracle; **es ist
kein ~** it's no wonder; **w~bar** *adj*
wonderful, marvellous; **~kerze** *f* sparkler;
~kind *nt* infant prodigy; **w~lich** *adj* odd,
peculiar; **w~n** *vr* to be surprised ♦ *vt* to
surprise; **sich w~n über** *+akk* to be
surprised at; **w~schön** *adj* beautiful;
w~voll *adj* wonderful
Wundstarrkrampf ['vʊntʃtarkrampf] *m*
tetanus, lockjaw
Wunsch [vʊnʃ] (*-(e)s, ⁓e*) *m* wish
wünschen ['vynʃən] *vt* to wish; **sich** *dat*
etw ~ to want sth, to wish for sth;
~swert *adj* desirable
wurde *etc* ['vʊrdə] *vb siehe* **werden**
Würde ['vyrdə] *f* dignity; (*Stellung*)
honour; **w~voll** *adj* dignified
würdig ['vyrdɪç] *adj* worthy; (*würdevoll*)
dignified; **~en** ['vyrdɪgən] *vt* to
appreciate; **jdn keines Blickes ~en** not
to so much as look at sb
Wurf [vʊrf] (*-(e)s, ⁓e*) *m* throw; (*Junge*)
litter
Würfel ['vyrfəl] (*-s, -*) *m* dice; (*MATH*) cube;
~becher *m* (dice) cup; **w~n** *vi* to play
dice ♦ *vt* to dice; **~zucker** *m* lump sugar
würgen ['vyrgən] *vt, vi* to choke
Wurm [vʊrm] (*-(e)s, ⁓er*) *m* worm
wurmstichig *adj* worm-ridden
Wurst [vʊrst] (*-, ⁓e*) *f* sausage; **das ist
mir ~** (*umg*) I don't care, I don't give a
damn
Würstchen ['vyrstçən] *nt* sausage
Würze ['vyrtsə] *f* seasoning, spice
Wurzel ['vʊrtsəl] (*-, -n*) *f* root
würzen ['vyrtsən] *vt* to season, to spice
würzig *adj* spicy
wusch *etc* [vuʃ] *vb siehe* **waschen**
wußte *etc* ['vʊstə] *vb siehe* **wissen**
wüst [vyːst] *adj* untidy, messy;
(*ausschweifend*) wild; (*öde*) waste; (*umg:
heftig*) terrible; **W~e** *f* desert
Wut [vuːt] (*-*) *f* rage, fury; **~anfall** *m* fit
of rage

wüten ['vy:tən] *vi* to rage; **~d** *adj* furious, mad

X x

X-Beine ['ɪksbaɪnə] *pl* knock-knees
x-beliebig [ɪksbə'li:bɪç] *adj* any (whatever)
xerokopieren [kseroko'pi:rən] *vt* to xerox, to photocopy
x-mal ['ɪksma:l] *adv* any number of times, n times
Xylophon [ksylo'fo:n] (-s, -e) *nt* xylophone

Y y

Ypsilon ['ʏpsilɔn] (-(s), -s) *nt* the letter Y

Z z

Zacke ['tsakə] *f* point; (*Berg~*) jagged peak; (*Gabel~*) prong; (*Kamm~*) tooth
zackig ['tsakɪç] *adj* jagged; (*umg*) smart; (*Tempo*) brisk
zaghaft ['tsa:khaft] *adj* timid
zäh [tsɛ:] *adj* tough; (*Mensch*) tenacious; (*Flüssigkeit*) thick; (*schleppend*) sluggish; **Z~igkeit** *f* toughness; tenacity
Zahl [tsa:l] (-, -en) *f* number; **z~bar** *adj* payable; **z~en** *vt, vi* to pay; **z~en bitte!** the bill please!
zählen ['tsɛ:lən] *vt, vi* to count; **~ auf** +*akk* to count on; **~ zu** to be numbered among
Zahlenschloß *nt* combination lock
Zähler ['tsɛ:lər] (-s, -) *m* (*TECH*) meter; (*MATH*) numerator
Zahl- *zW*: **z~los** *adj* countless; **z~reich** *adj* numerous; **~tag** *m* payday; **~ung** *f* payment; **z~ungsfähig** *adj* solvent; **~wort** *nt* numeral
zahm [tsa:m] *adj* tame
zähmen ['tsɛ:mən] *vt* to tame; (*fig*) to curb
Zahn [tsa:n] (-(e)s, ⁼e) *m* tooth; **~arzt** *m*

dentist; **~ärztin** *f* (female) dentist; **~bürste** *f* toothbrush; **~fleisch** *nt* gums *pl*; **~pasta** *f* toothpaste; **~rad** *nt* cog(wheel); **~schmerzen** *pl* toothache *sg*; **~stein** *m* tartar; **~stocher** (-s, -) *m* toothpick
Zange ['tsaŋə] *f* pliers *pl*; (*Zucker~ etc*) tongs *pl*; (*Beiß~, ZOOL*) pincers *pl*; (*MED*) forceps *pl*
zanken ['tsaŋkən] *vi, vr* to quarrel
zänkisch ['tsɛŋkɪʃ] *adj* quarrelsome
Zäpfchen ['tsɛpfçən] *nt* (*ANAT*) uvula; (*MED*) suppository
Zapfen ['tsapfən] (-s, -) *m* plug; (*BOT*) cone; (*Eis~*) icicle
zappeln ['tsapəln] *vi* to wriggle; to fidget
zart [tsart] *adj* (*weich, leise*) soft; (*Fleisch*) tender; (*fein, schwächlich*) delicate; **Z~heit** *f* softness; tenderness; delicacy
zärtlich ['tsɛ:rtlɪç] *adj* tender, affectionate
Zauber ['tsaʊbər] (-s, -) *m* magic; (*~bann*) spell; **~ei** [-'raɪ] *f* magic; **~er** (-s, -) *m* magician; conjuror; **z~haft** *adj* magical, enchanting; **~künstler** *m* conjuror; **~kunststück** *nt* conjuring trick; **z~n** *vi* to conjure, to practise magic
zaudern ['tsaʊdərn] *vi* to hesitate
Zaum [tsaʊm] (-(e)s, Zäume) *m* bridle; **etw im ~ halten** to keep sth in check
Zaun [tsaʊn] (-(e)s, Zäune) *m* fence; **~könig** *m* wren
z.B. *abk* (= *zum Beispiel*) e.g.
Zebra ['tse:bra] *nt* zebra; **~streifen** *m* zebra crossing
Zeche ['tsɛçə] *f* (*Rechnung*) bill; (*Bergbau*) mine
Zeh [tse:] (-s, -en) *m* toe
Zehe ['tse:ə] *f* toe; (*Knoblauch~*) clove
zehn [tse:n] *num* ten; **~te(r, s)** *adj* tenth; **Z~tel** (-s, -) *nt* tenth (part)
Zeich- ['tsaɪç] *zW*: **~en** (-s, -) *nt* sign; **z~nen** *vt* to draw; (*kennzeichnen*) to mark; (*unterzeichnen*) to sign ♦ *vi* to draw; to sign; **~ner** (-s, -) *m* artist; **technischer ~ner** draughtsman; **~nung** *f* drawing; (*Markierung*) markings *pl*
Zeige- ['tsaɪgə] *zW*: **~finger** *m* index finger; **z~n** *vt* to show ♦ *vi* to point ♦ *vr*

to show o.s.; **z~n auf** +*akk* to point to; to
point at; **es wird sich z~n** time will tell;
es zeigte sich, daß ... it turned out that
...; **~r (-s, -)** *m* pointer; (*Uhrzeiger*) hand
Zeile ['tsaɪlə] *f* line; (*Häuser~*) row
Zeit [tsaɪt] **(-, -en)** *f* time; (*GRAM*) tense;
zur ~ at the moment; **sich** *dat* **~ lassen**
to take one's time; **von ~ zu ~** from time
to time; **~alter** *nt* age; **~arbeit** *f* (*WIRTS*)
temporary job; **z~gemäß** *adj* in keeping
with the times; **~genosse** *m*
contemporary; **z~ig** *adj* early; **z~lich** *adj*
temporal; **~lupe** *f* slow motion;
z~raubend *adj* time-consuming; **~raum**
m period; **~rechnung** *f* time, era; **nach/
vor unserer ~rechnung** A.D./B.C.;
~schrift *f* periodical; **~ung** *f* newspaper;
~verschwendung *f* waste of time;
~vertreib *m* pastime, diversion;
z~weilig *adj* temporary; **z~weise** *adv*
for a time; **~wort** *nt* verb; **~zünder** *m*
time fuse
Zelle ['tsɛlə] *f* cell; (*Telefon~*) callbox
Zellstoff *m* cellulose
Zelt [tsɛlt] **(-(e)s, -e)** *nt* tent; **z~en** *vi* to
camp; **~platz** *m* camp site
Zement [tse'mɛnt] **(-(e)s, -e)** *m* cement;
z~ieren [-'tiːrən] *vt* to cement
zensieren [tsɛn'ziːrən] *vt* to censor; (*SCH*)
to mark
Zensur [tsɛn'zuːr] *f* censorship; (*SCH*)
mark
Zentimeter [tsɛnti'meːtər] *m od nt*
centimetre
Zentner ['tsɛntnər] **(-s, -)** *m*
hundredweight
zentral [tsɛn'traːl] *adj* central; **Z~e** *f*
central office; (*TEL*) exchange; **Z~heizung**
f central heating
Zentrum ['tsɛntrʊm] **(-s, Zentren)** *nt*
centre
zerbrechen [tsɛr'brɛçən] (*unreg*) *vt, vi* to
break
zerbrechlich *adj* fragile
zer'drücken *vt* to squash, to crush;
(*Kartoffeln*) to mash
Zeremonie [tseremo'niː] *f* ceremony
Zerfall [tsɛr'fal] *m* decay; **z~en** (*unreg*) *vi*
to disintegrate, to decay; (*sich gliedern*):

z~en (in +*akk*) to fall (into)
zer'gehen (*unreg*) *vi* to melt, to dissolve
zerkleinern [tsɛr'klaɪnərn] *vt* to reduce
to small pieces
zerlegbar *adj* able to be dismantled
zerlegen [tsɛr'leːgən] *vt* to take to pieces;
(*Fleisch*) to carve; (*Satz*) to analyse
zermürben [tsɛr'mʏrbən] *vt* to wear
down
zerquetschen [tsɛr'kvɛtʃən] *vt* to
squash
Zerrbild ['tsɛrbɪlt] *nt* caricature, distorted
picture
zer'reißen (*unreg*) *vt* to tear to pieces
♦ *vi* to tear, to rip
zerren ['tsɛrən] *vt* to drag ♦ *vi:* **~ (an**
+*dat*) to tug (at)
zer'rinnen (*unreg*) *vi* to melt away
zerrissen [tsɛr'rɪsən] *adj* torn, tattered;
Z~heit *f* tattered state; (*POL*) disunion,
discord; (*innere Zerrissenheit*)
disintegration
Zerrung *f* (*MED*): **eine ~** a pulled muscle
zerrütten [tsɛr'rʏtən] *vt* to wreck, to
destroy
zerrüttet *adj* wrecked, shattered
zer'schlagen (*unreg*) *vt* to shatter, to
smash ♦ *vr* to fall through
zer'schneiden (*unreg*) *vt* to cut up
zer'setzen *vt, vr* to decompose, to
dissolve
zer'springen (*unreg*) *vi* to shatter, to
burst
Zerstäuber [tsɛr'ʃtɔʏbər] **(-s, -)** *m*
atomizer
zerstören [tsɛr'ʃtøːrən] *vt* to destroy
Zerstörung *f* destruction
zerstreu- [tsɛr'ʃtrɔʏ] *zW:* **~en** *vt* to
disperse, to scatter; (*unterhalten*) to
divert; (*Zweifel etc*) to dispel ♦ *vr* to
disperse, to scatter; to be dispelled; **~t** *adj*
scattered; (*Mensch*) absent-minded;
Z~theit *f* absent-mindedness; **Z~ung** *f*
dispersion; (*Ablenkung*) diversion
zerstückeln [tsɛr'ʃtʏkəln] *vt* to cut into
pieces
zer'teilen *vt* to divide into parts
Zertifikat [tsɛrtifi'kaːt] **(-(e)s, -e)** *nt*
certificate

zer'treten (*unreg*) *vt* to crush underfoot

zertrümmern [tsɛr'trymərn] *vt* to shatter; (*Gebäude etc*) to demolish

zetern ['tseːtərn] *vi* to shout, to shriek

Zettel ['tsɛtəl] (**-s, -**) *m* piece of paper, slip; (*Notiz*~) note; (*Formular*) form

Zeug [tsɔʏk] (**-(e)s, -e**; *umg*) *nt* stuff; (*Ausrüstung*) gear; **dummes ~** (*stupid*) nonsense; **das ~ haben zu** to have the makings of; **sich ins ~ legen** to put one's shoulder to the wheel

Zeuge ['tsɔʏgə] (**-n, -n**) *m* witness; **z~n** *vi* to bear witness, to testify ♦ *vt* (*Kind*) to father; **es zeugt von ...** it testifies to ...; **~naussage** *f* evidence; **Zeugin** ['tsɔʏgɪn] *f* witness

Zeugnis ['tsɔʏgnɪs] (**-ses, -se**) *nt* certificate; (*SCH*) report; (*Referenz*) reference; (*Aussage*) evidence, testimony; **~ geben von** to be evidence of, to testify to

z.H(d). *abk* (= *zu Händen*) attn.

Zickzack ['tsɪktsak] (**-(e)s, -e**) *m* zigzag

Ziege ['tsiːgə] *f* goat

Ziegel ['tsiːgəl] (**-s, -**) *m* brick; (*Dach*~) tile

ziehen ['tsiːən] (*unreg*) *vt* to draw; (*zerren*) to pull; (*SCHACH etc*) to move; (*züchten*) to rear ♦ *vi* to draw; (*um*~, *wandern*) to move; (*Rauch, Wolke etc*) to drift; (*reißen*) to pull ♦ *vb unpers*: **es zieht** there is a draught, it's draughty ♦ *vr* (*Gummi*) to stretch; (*Grenze etc*) to run; (*Gespräche*) to be drawn out; **etw nach sich ~** to lead to sth, to entail sth

Ziehharmonika ['tsiːharmoːnika] *f* concertina; accordion

Ziehung ['tsiːʊŋ] *f* (*Los*~) drawing

Ziel [tsiːl] (**-(e)s, -e**) *nt* (*einer Reise*) destination; (*SPORT*) finish; (*MIL*) target; (*Absicht*) goal; **z~bewußt** *adj* decisive; **z~en** *vi*: **z~en (auf** +*akk*) to aim (at); **z~los** *adj* aimless; **~scheibe** *f* target; **z~strebig** *adj* purposeful

ziemlich ['tsiːmlɪç] *adj* quite a; fair ♦ *adv* rather; quite a bit

zieren ['tsiːrən] *vr* to act coy

zierlich ['tsiːrlɪç] *adj* dainty

Ziffer ['tsɪfər] (**-, -n**) *f* figure, digit; **~blatt** *nt* dial, clock-face

zig [tsɪç] (*umg*) *adj* umpteen

Zigarette [tsiga'rɛtə] *f* cigarette

Zigaretten- *zW*: **~automat** *m* cigarette machine; **~schachtel** *f* cigarette packet; **~spitze** *f* cigarette holder

Zigarillo [tsiga'rɪlo] (**-s, -s**) *nt od m* cigarillo

Zigarre [tsi'garə] *f* cigar

Zigeuner(in) [tsi'gɔʏnər(ɪn)] (**-s, -**) *m(f)* gipsy

Zimmer ['tsɪmər] (**-s, -**) *nt* room; **~lautstärke** *f* reasonable volume; **~mädchen** *nt* chambermaid; **~mann** *m* carpenter; **z~n** *vt* to make (from wood); **~nachweis** *m* accommodation office; **~pflanze** *f* indoor plant

zimperlich ['tsɪmpərlɪç] *adj* squeamish; (*pingelig*) fussy, finicky

Zimt [tsɪmt] (**-(e)s, -e**) *m* cinnamon

Zink [tsɪŋk] (**-(e)s**) *nt* zinc

Zinn [tsɪn] (**-(e)s**) *nt* (*Element*) tin; (*in* ~*waren*) pewter; **~soldat** *m* tin soldier

Zins [tsɪns] (**-es, -en**) *m* interest

Zinseszins *m* compound interest

Zins- *zW*: **~fuß** *m* rate of interest; **z~los** *adj* interest-free; **~satz** *m* rate of interest

Zipfel ['tsɪpfəl] (**-s, -**) *m* corner; (*spitz*) tip; (*Hemd*~) tail; (*Wurst*~) end; **~mütze** *f* stocking cap; nightcap

zirka ['tsɪrka] *adv* (round) about

Zirkel ['tsɪrkəl] (**-s, -**) *m* circle; (*MATH*) pair of compasses

Zirkus ['tsɪrkʊs] (**-, -se**) *m* circus

zischen ['tsɪʃən] *vi* to hiss

Zitat [tsi'taːt] (**-(e)s, -e**) *nt* quotation, quote

zitieren [tsi'tiːrən] *vt* to quote

Zitronat [tsitro'naːt] (**-(e)s, -e**) *nt* candied lemon peel

Zitrone [tsi'troːnə] *f* lemon; **~nlimonade** *f* lemonade; **~nsaft** *m* lemon juice

zittern ['tsɪtərn] *vi* to tremble

zivil [tsi'viːl] *adj* civil; (*Preis*) moderate; **Z~** (**-s**) *nt* plain clothes *pl*; (*MIL*) civilian clothing; **Z~bevölkerung** *f* civilian population; **Z~courage** *f* courage of one's convictions; **Z~dienst** *m* community service; **Z~isation** [tsivilizatsi'oːn] *f*

civilization; **Z~isationskrankheit** *f*
disease peculiar to civilization; **~i'sieren**
vt to civilize; **Z~ist** [tsivi'lɪst] *m* civilian
zögern ['tsøːgərn] *vi* to hesitate
Zoll [tsɔl] **(-(e)s, ⁀e)** *m* customs *pl*;
(*Abgabe*) duty; **~abfertigung** *f* customs
clearance; **~amt** *nt* customs office;
~beamte(r) *m* customs official;
~erklärung *f* customs declaration; **z~frei**
adj duty-free; **~kontrolle** *f* customs
check; **z~pflichtig** *adj* liable to duty,
dutiable
Zone ['tsoːnə] *f* zone
Zoo [tsoː] **(-s, -s)** *m* zoo; **~loge**
[tsoo'loːgə] **(-n, -n)** *m* zoologist; **~lo'gie** *f*
zoology; **z~'logisch** *adj* zoological
Zopf [tsɔpf] **(-(e)s, ⁀e)** *m* plait; pigtail;
alter ~ antiquated custom
Zorn [tsɔrn] **(-(e)s)** *m* anger; **z~ig** *adj*
angry
zottig ['tsɔtɪç] *adj* shaggy
z.T. *abk* = **zum Teil**

SCHLÜSSELWORT
---

zu [tsuː] *präp +dat* **1** (*örtlich*) to; **zum
Bahnhof/Arzt gehen** to go to the
station/doctor; **zur Schule/Kirche gehen**
to go to school/church; **sollen wir zu
euch gehen?** shall we go to your place?;
sie sah zu ihm hin she looked towards
him; **zum Fenster herein** through the
window; **zu meiner Linken** to *od* on my
left
2 (*zeitlich*) at; **zu Ostern** at Easter; **bis
zum 1. Mai** until May 1st; (*nicht später
als*) by May 1st; **zu meiner Zeit** in my
time
3 (*Zusatz*) with; **Wein zum Essen
trinken** to drink wine with one's meal;
sich zu jdm setzen to sit down beside sb;
setz dich doch zu uns (come and) sit
with us; **Anmerkungen zu etw** notes on
sth
4 (*Zweck*) for; **Wasser zum Waschen**
water for washing; **Papier zum
Schreiben** paper to write on; **etw zum
Geburtstag bekommen** to get sth for
one's birthday
5 (*Veränderung*) into; **zu etw werden** to

turn into sth; **jdn zu etw machen** to
make sb (into) sth; **zu Asche
verbrennen** to burn to ashes
6 (*mit Zahlen*): **3 zu 2** (*SPORT*) 3-2; **das
Stück zu 2 Mark** at 2 marks each; **zum
ersten Mal** for the first time
7: **zu meiner Freude** *etc* to my joy *etc*;
zum Glück luckily; **zu Fuß** on foot; **es
ist zum Weinen** it's enough to make you
cry
♦ *konj* to; **etw zu essen** sth to eat; **um
besser sehen zu können** in order to see
better; **ohne es zu wissen** without
knowing it; **noch zu bezahlende
Rechnungen** bills that are still to be paid
♦ *adv* **1** (*allzu*) too; **zu sehr** too much
2 (*örtlich*) toward(s); **er kam auf mich
zu** he came up to me
3 (*geschlossen*) shut; closed; **die
Geschäfte haben zu** the shops are
closed; **auf/zu** (*Wasserhahn etc*) on/off
4 (*umg: los*): **nur zu!** just keep on!; **mach
zu!** hurry up!

zuallererst [tsuʔalərʔeːrst] *adv* first of
all
zuallerletzt [tsuʔalərʔlɛtst] *adv* last of all
Zubehör ['tsuːbəhøːr] **(-(e)s, -e)** *nt*
accessories *pl*
zubereiten ['tsuːbəraɪtən] *vt* to prepare
zubilligen ['tsuːbɪlɪgən] *vt* to grant
zubinden ['tsuːbɪndən] (*unreg*) *vt* to tie
up
zubringen ['tsuːbrɪŋən] (*unreg*) *vt* (*Zeit*)
to spend
Zubringer **(-s, -)** *m* (*Straße*) approach *od*
slip road
Zucchini [tsu'kiːniː] *pl* (*BOT, KOCH*)
courgette (*BRIT*), zucchini (*US*)
Zucht [tsʊxt] **(-, -en)** *f* (*von Tieren*)
breeding; (*von Pflanzen*) cultivation;
(*Rasse*) breed; (*Erziehung*) raising;
(*Disziplin*) discipline
züchten ['tsʏçtən] *vt* (*Tiere*) to breed;
(*Pflanzen*) to cultivate, to grow
Züchter **(-s, -)** *m* breeder; grower
Zuchthaus *nt* prison, penitentiary (*US*)
züchtigen ['tsʏçtɪgən] *vt* to chastise
Züchtung *f* (*Zuchtart, Sorte: von Tier*)

breed; (: *von Pflanze*) variety

zucken ['tsʊkən] *vi* to jerk, to twitch; (*Strahl etc*) to flicker ♦ *vt* (*Schultern*) to shrug

Zucker ['tsʊkər] (**-s**, **-**) *m* sugar; (*MED*) diabetes; **~guß** *m* icing; **z~krank** *adj* diabetic; **~krankheit** *f* (*MED*) diabetes; **z~n** *vt* to sugar; **~rohr** *nt* sugar cane; **~rübe** *f* sugar beet

Zuckung ['tsʊkʊŋ] *f* convulsion, spasm; (*leicht*) twitch

zudecken ['tsuːdɛkən] *vt* to cover (up)

zudem [tsuː'deːm] *adv* in addition (to this)

zudringlich ['tsuːdrɪŋlɪç] *adj* forward, pushing, obtrusive

zudrücken ['tsuːdrʏkən] *vt* to close; **ein Auge ~** to turn a blind eye

zueinander [tsuːaɪ'nandər] *adv* to one other; (*in Verbindung*) together

zuerkennen ['tsuː'ɛrkɛnən] (*unreg*) *vt* to award; **jdm etw ~** to award sth to sb, to award sb sth

zuerst [tsuː'eːrst] *adv* first; (*zu Anfang*) at first; **~ einmal** first of all

Zufahrt ['tsuːfaːrt] *f* approach; **~sstraße** *f* approach road; (*von Autobahn etc*) slip road

Zufall ['tsuːfal] *m* chance; (*Ereignis*) coincidence; **durch ~** by accident; **so ein ~** what a coincidence; **z~en** (*unreg*) *vi* to close, to shut; (*Anteil, Aufgabe*) to fall

zufällig [tsuː'fɛlɪç] *adj* chance ♦ *adv* by chance; (*in Frage*) by any chance

Zuflucht ['tsuːflʊxt] *f* recourse; (*Ort*) refuge

zufolge [tsuː'fɔlgə] *präp* (+*dat od gen*) judging by; (*laut*) according to

zufrieden [tsuː'friːdən] *adj* content(ed), satisfied; **~geben** (*unreg*) *vr* to be content *od* satisfied (with); **~stellen** *vt* to satisfy

zufrieren ['tsuːfriːrən] (*unreg*) *vi* to freeze up *od* over

zufügen ['tsuːfyːgən] *vt* to add; (*Leid etc*): **(jdm) etw ~** to cause (sb) sth

Zufuhr ['tsuːfuːr] (**-**, **-en**) *f* (*Herbeibringen*) supplying; (*MET*) influx

Zug [tsuːk] (**-(e)s**, **ːe**) *m* (*EISENB*) train; (*Luft~*) draught; (*Ziehen*) pull(ing); (*Gesichts~*) feature; (*SCHACH etc*) move; (*Klingel~*) pull; (*Schrift~*) stroke; (*Atem~*) breath; (*Charakter~*) trait; (*an Zigarette*) puff, pull, drag; (*Schluck*) gulp; (*Menschengruppe*) procession; (*von Vögeln*) flight; (*MIL*) platoon; **etw in vollen Zügen genießen** to enjoy sth to the full

Zu- [tsuː] *zW*: **~gabe** *f* extra; (*in Konzert etc*) encore; **~gang** *m* access, approach; **z~gänglich** *adj* accessible; (*Mensch*) approachable

zugeben ['tsuːgeːbən] (*unreg*) *vt* (*beifügen*) to add, to throw in; (*zugestehen*) to admit; (*erlauben*) to permit

zugehen ['tsuːgeːən] (*unreg*) *vi* (*schließen*) to shut; **es geht dort seltsam zu** there are strange goings-on there; **auf jdn/etw ~** to walk towards sb/sth; **dem Ende ~** to be finishing

Zugehörigkeit ['tsuːgəhøːrɪçkaɪt] *f*: **~ (zu)** membership (of), belonging (to)

Zügel ['tsyːgəl] (**-s**, **-**) *m* rein(s); (*fig*) curb

zuge- ['tsuːgə] *zW*: **Z~ständnis** (**-ses**, **-se**) *nt* concession; **~stehen** (*unreg*) *vt* to admit; (*Rechte*) to concede

Zugführer *m* (*EISENB*) guard

zugig ['tsuːgɪç] *adj* draughty

zügig ['tsyːgɪç] *adj* speedy, swift

zugreifen ['tsuːgraɪfən] (*unreg*) *vi* to seize *od* grab at; (*helfen*) to help; (*beim Essen*) to help o.s.

zugrunde [tsuː'grʊndə] *adv*: **~ gehen** to collapse; (*Mensch*) to perish; **einer Sache** *dat* **etw ~ legen** to base sth on sth; **einer Sache** *dat* **~ liegen** to be based on sth; **~ richten** to ruin, to destroy

zugunsten [tsuː'gʊnstən] *präp* (+*gen od dat*) in favour of

zugute [tsuː'guːtə] *adv*: **jdm etw ~ halten** to concede sth to sb; **jdm ~ kommen** to be of assistance to sb

Zugvogel *m* migratory bird

zuhalten ['tsuːhaltən] (*unreg*) *vt* to keep closed ♦ *vi*: **auf jdn/etw ~** to make a beeline for sb/sth

Zuhälter ['tsuːhɛltər] (**-s**, **-**) *m* pimp

Zuhause [tsuː'hauzə] (**-**) *nt* home

zuhören ['tsu:hø:rən] *vi* to listen
Zuhörer (-s, -) *m* listener
zukleben ['tsu:kle:bən] *vt* to paste up
zukommen ['tsu:kɔmən] (*unreg*) *vi* to come up to sb; **auf jdn ~** to come up to sb; **jdm etw ~ lassen** to give sb sth; **etw auf sich ~ lassen** to wait and see; **jdm ~** (*sich gehören*) to be fitting for sb
Zukunft ['tsu:kunft] (-, **Zukünfte**) *f* future; **zukünftig** ['tsu:kynftɪç] *adj* future ♦ *adv* in future; **mein zukünftiger Mann** my husband to be
Zulage ['tsu:la:gə] *f* bonus
zulassen ['tsu:lasən] (*unreg*) *vt* (*hereinlassen*) to admit; (*erlauben*) to permit; (*Auto*) to license; (*umg: nicht öffnen*) to (keep) shut
zulässig ['tsu:lɛsɪç] *adj* permissible, permitted
Zulassung *f* (*amtlich*) authorization; (*von Kfz*) licensing
zulaufen ['tsu:laufən] (*unreg*) *vi* (*subj: Mensch*): **~ auf jdn/etw** to run up to sb/sth; (: *Straße*): **~ auf** to lead towards
zuleide ['tsu:laidə] *adv*: **jdm etw ~ tun** to hurt *od* harm sb
zuletzt [tsu'lɛtst] *adv* finally, at last
zuliebe [tsu'li:bə] *adv*: **jdm ~** to please sb
zum [tsum] = **zu dem**; **~ dritten Mal** for the third time; **~ Scherz** as a joke; **~ Trinken** for drinking
zumachen ['tsu:maxən] *vt* to shut; (*Kleidung*) to do up, to fasten ♦ *vi* to shut; (*umg*) to hurry up
zumal [tsu'ma:l] *konj* especially (as)
zumeist [tsu'maist] *adv* mostly
zumindest [tsu'mɪndəst] *adv* at least
zumut- *zW*: **~bar** ['tsu:mu:tba:r] *adj* reasonable; **~e** *adv*: **wie ist ihm ~e**? how does he feel?; **~en** ['tsu:mu:tən] *vt*: **(jdm) etw ~en** to expect *od* ask sth (of sb); **Z~ung** ['tsu:mu:tuŋ] *f* unreasonable expectation *od* demand, impertinence
zunächst [tsu'nɛ:çst] *adv* first of all; **~ einmal** to start with
Zunahme ['tsu:na:mə] *f* increase
Zuname ['tsu:na:mə] *m* surname
Zünd- [tsynd] *zW*: **z~en** *vi* (*Feuer*) to light, to ignite; (*Motor*) to fire;

(*begeistern*): **bei jdm z~en** to fire sb (with enthusiasm); **z~end** *adj* fiery; **~er** (-s, -) *m* fuse; (*MIL*) detonator; **~holz** ['tsynt-] *nt* match; **~kerze** *f* (*AUT*) spark(ing) plug; **~schlüssel** *m* ignition key; **~schnur** *f* fuse wire; **~stoff** *m* (*fig*) inflammatory stuff; **~ung** *f* ignition
zunehmen ['tsu:ne:mən] (*unreg*) *vi* to increase, to grow; (*Mensch*) to put on weight
Zuneigung ['tsu:naigun] *f* affection
Zunft [tsunft] (-, **-e**) *f* guild
zünftig ['tsynftɪç] *adj* proper, real; (*Handwerk*) decent
Zunge ['tsuŋə] *f* tongue
zunichte [tsu'nɪçtə] *adv*: **~ machen** to ruin, to destroy; **~ werden** to come to nothing
zunutze [tsu'nutsə] *adv*: **sich** *dat* **etw ~ machen** to make use of sth
zuoberst [tsu'o:bərst] *adv* at the top
zupfen ['tsupfən] *vt* to pull, to pick, to pluck; (*Gitarre*) to pluck
zur [tsu:r] = **zu der**
zurechnungsfähig ['tsu:rɛçnuŋsfɛ:ɪç] *adj* responsible, accountable
zurecht- [tsu'rɛçt] *zW*: **~finden** (*unreg*) *vr* to find one's way (about); **~kommen** (*unreg*) *vi* to (be able to) cope, to manage; **~legen** *vt* to get ready; (*Ausrede etc*) to have ready; **~machen** *vt* to prepare ♦ *vr* to get ready; **~weisen** (*unreg*) *vt* to reprimand; **Z~weisung** *f* reprimand, rebuff
zureden ['tsu:re:dən] *vi*: **jdm ~** to persuade *od* urge sb
zurück [tsu'ryk] *adv* back; **~behalten** (*unreg*) *vt* to keep back; **~bekommen** (*unreg*) *vt* to get back; **~bleiben** (*unreg*) *vi* (*Mensch*) to remain behind; (*nicht nachkommen*) to fall behind, to lag; (*Schaden*) to remain; **~bringen** (*unreg*) *vt* to bring back; **~fahren** (*unreg*) *vi* to travel back; (*vor Schreck*) to recoil, to start ♦ *vt* to drive back; **~finden** (*unreg*) *vi* to find one's way back; **~fordern** *vt* to demand back; **~führen** *vt* to lead back; **etw auf etw** *akk* **~führen** to trace sth back to sth; **~geben** (*unreg*) *vt* to give

back; (*antworten*) to retort with;
~**geblieben** *adj* retarded; ~**gehen**
(*unreg*) *vi* to go back; (*fallen*) to go down,
to fall; (*zeitlich*): ~**gehen (auf** +*akk*) to
date back (to); ~**gezogen** *adj* retired,
withdrawn; ~**halten** (*unreg*) *vt* to hold
back; (*Mensch*) to restrain; (*hindern*) to
prevent ♦ *vr* (*reserviert sein*) to be
reserved; (*im Essen*) to hold back;
~**haltend** *adj* reserved; **Z~haltung** *f*
reserve; ~**kehren** *vi* to return; ~**kommen**
(*unreg*) *vi* to come back; **auf**
etw *akk* ~**kommen** to return to sth;
~**lassen** (*unreg*) *vt* to leave behind;
~**legen** *vt* to put back; (*Geld*) to put by;
(*reservieren*) to keep back; (*Strecke*) to
cover; ~**nehmen** (*unreg*) *vt* to take back;
~**schrecken** *vi*: ~**schrecken (vor** +*dat*)
to shrink (from); ~**stellen** *vt* to put back,
to replace; (*aufschieben*) to put off, to
postpone; (*MIL*) to turn down; (*Interessen*)
to defer; (*Ware*) to keep; ~**treten** (*unreg*)
vi to step back; (*vom Amt*) to retire;
gegenüber etw *od* **hinter etw** *dat*
~**treten** to diminish in importance in
view of sth; ~**weisen** (*unreg*) *vt* to turn
down; (*Mensch*) to reject; ~**zahlen** *vt* to
repay, to pay back; ~**ziehen** (*unreg*) *vt* to
pull back; (*Angebot*) to withdraw ♦ *vr* to
retire
Zuruf ['tsu:ru:f] *m* shout, cry
Zusage ['tsu:za:gə] *f* promise; (*Annahme*)
consent; **z~n** *vt* to promise ♦ *vi* to accept;
jdm z~n (*gefallen*) to agree with *od*
please sb
zusammen [tsu'zamən] *adv* together;
Z~arbeit *f* cooperation; ~**arbeiten** *vi* to
cooperate; ~**beißen** (*unreg*) *vt* (*Zähne*) to
clench; ~**bleiben** (*unreg*) *vi* to stay
together; ~**brechen** (*unreg*) *vi* to collapse;
(*Mensch auch*) to break down; ~**bringen**
(*unreg*) *vt* to bring *od* get together; (*Geld*)
to get; (*Sätze*) to put together; **Z~bruch**
m collapse; ~**fassen** *vt* to summarize;
(*vereinigen*) to unite; **Z~fassung** *f*
summary, résumé; ~**fügen** *vt* to join
(together), to unite; ~**halten** (*unreg*) *vi* to
stick together; **Z~hang** *m* connection;
im/aus dem Z~hang in/out of context;

~**hängen** (*unreg*) *vi* to be connected *od*
linked; ~**kommen** (*unreg*) *vi* to meet, to
assemble; (*sich ereignen*) to occur at once
od together; ~**legen** *vt* to put together;
(*stapeln*) to pile up; (*falten*) to fold;
(*verbinden*) to combine, to unite;
(*Termine, Fest*) to amalgamate; (*Geld*) to
collect; ~**nehmen** (*unreg*) *vt* to summon
up ♦ *vr* to pull o.s. together; **alles**
~**genommen** all in all; ~**passen** *vi* to go
well together, to match; ~**schließen**
(*unreg*) *vt, vr* to join (together); **Z~schluß**
m amalgamation; ~**schreiben** (*unreg*) *vt*
to write as one word; (*Bericht*) to put
together; **Z~sein** (**-s**) *nt* get-together;
~**setzen** *vt* to put together ♦ *vr* (*Stoff*) to
be composed of; (*Menschen*) to get
together; **Z~setzung** *f* composition;
~**stellen** *vt* to put together; to compile;
Z~stoß *m* collision; ~**stoßen** (*unreg*) *vi*
to collide; ~**treffen** (*unreg*) *vi* to coincide;
(*Menschen*) to meet; ~**zählen** *vt* to add
up; ~**ziehen** (*unreg*) *vt* (*verengern*) to
draw together; (*vereinigen*) to bring
together; (*addieren*) to add up ♦ *vr* to
shrink; (*sich bilden*) to form, to develop
zusätzlich ['tsu:zɛtslɪç] *adj* additional
♦ *adv* in addition
zuschauen ['tsu:ʃauən] *vi* to watch, to
look on
Zuschauer(in) (**-s, -**) *m(f)* spectator ♦ *pl*
(*THEAT*) audience *sg*
zuschicken ['tsu:ʃɪkən] *vt*: (**jdm etw**) ~
to send *od* to forward (sth to sb)
Zuschlag ['tsu:ʃlak] *m* extra charge,
surcharge; **z~en** [-gən] (*unreg*) *vt* (*Tür*) to
slam; (*Ball*) to hit; (*bei Auktion*) to knock
down; (*Steine etc*) to knock into shape
♦ *vi* (*Fenster, Tür*) to shut; (*Mensch*) to
hit, to punch; ~**karte** *f* (*EISENB*) surcharge
ticket; **z~pflichtig** *adj* subject to
surcharge
zuschneiden ['tsu:ʃnaidən] (*unreg*) *vt* to
cut out; to cut to size
zuschrauben ['tsu:ʃraubən] *vt* to screw
down *od* up
zuschreiben ['tsu:ʃraibən] (*unreg*) *vt*
(*fig*) to ascribe, to attribute; (*COMM*) to
credit

Zuschrift ['tsu:ʃrɪft] *f* letter, reply

zuschulden [tsu'ʃʊldən] *adv*: **sich** *dat* **etw ~ kommen lassen** to make o.s. guilty of sth

Zuschuß ['tsu:ʃʊs] *m* subsidy, allowance

zusehen ['tsu:ze:ən] (*unreg*) *vi* to watch; (*dafür sorgen*) to take care; **jdm/etw ~** to watch sb/sth; **~ds** *adv* visibly

zusenden ['tsu:zɛndən] (*unreg*) *vt* to forward, to send on

zusichern ['tsu:zɪçərn] *vt*: **jdm etw ~** to assure sb of sth

zuspielen ['tsu:ʃpi:lən] *vt, vi* to pass

zuspitzen ['tsu:ʃpɪtsən] *vt* to sharpen ♦ *vr* (*Lage*) to become critical

zusprechen ['tsu:ʃprɛçən] (*unreg*) *vt* (*zuerkennen*) to award ♦ *vi* to speak; **jdm etw ~** to award sb sth *od* sth to sb; **jdm Trost ~** to comfort sb; **dem Essen/ Alkohol ~** to eat/drink a lot

Zustand ['tsu:ʃtant] *m* state, condition; **z~e** ['tsu:ʃtandə] *adv*: **z~e bringen** to bring about; **z~e kommen** to come about

zuständig ['tsu:ʃtɛndɪç] *adj* responsible; **Z~keit** *f* competence, responsibility

zustehen ['tsu:ʃte:ən] (*unreg*) *vi*: **jdm ~** to be sb's right

zustellen ['tsu:ʃtɛlən] *vt* (*verstellen*) to block; (*Post etc*) to send

zustimmen ['tsu:ʃtɪmən] *vi* to agree

Zustimmung *f* agreement, consent

zustoßen ['tsu:ʃto:sən] (*unreg*) *vi* (*fig*) to happen

zutage [tsu'ta:gə] *adv*: **~ bringen** to bring to light; **~ treten** to come to light

Zutaten ['tsu:ta:tən] *pl* ingredients

zuteilen ['tsu:taɪlən] *vt* (*Arbeit, Rolle*) to designate, assign; (*Aktien, Wohnung*) to allocate

zutiefst [tsu'ti:fst] *adv* deeply

zutragen ['tsu:tra:gən] (*unreg*) *vt* to bring; (*Klatsch*) to tell ♦ *vr* to happen

zutrauen ['tsu:trau] *zW*: **Z~en** (**-s**) *nt*: **Z~en (zu)** trust (in); **~en** *vt*: **jdm etw ~en** to credit sb with sth; **~lich** *adj* trusting, friendly

zutreffen ['tsu:trɛfən] (*unreg*) *vi* to be correct; to apply

zutreffend *adj* (*richtig*) accurate; **Z~es**

bitte unterstreichen please underline where applicable

Zutritt ['tsu:trɪt] *m* access, admittance

Zutun ['tsu:tu:n] (**-s**) *nt* assistance

zuverlässig ['tsu:fɛrlɛsɪç] *adj* reliable; **Z~keit** *f* reliability

zuversichtlich ['tsu:fɛrzɪçtlɪç] *adj* confident

zuviel [tsu'fi:l] *adv* too much

zuvor [tsu'fo:r] *adv* before, previously; **~kommen** (*unreg*) *vi* +*dat* to anticipate; **jdm ~kommen** to beat sb to it; **~kommend** *adj* obliging, courteous

Zuwachs ['tsu:vaks] (**-es**) *m* increase, growth; (*umg*) addition; **z~en** (*unreg*) *vi* to become overgrown; (*Wunde*) to heal (up)

zuwege [tsu've:gə] *adv*: **etw ~ bringen** to accomplish sth

zuweilen [tsu'vaɪlən] *adv* at times, now and then

zuweisen ['tsu:vaɪzən] (*unreg*) *vt* to assign, to allocate

zuwenden ['tsu:vɛndən] (*unreg*) *vt* (+*dat*) to turn (towards) ♦ *vr*: **sich jdm/ etw ~** to devote o.s. to sb/sth; to turn to sb/sth; **jdm seine Aufmerksamkeit ~** to give sb one's attention

zuwenig [tsu've:nɪç] *adv* too little

zuwider [tsu'vi:dər] *adv*: **etw ist jdm ~** sb loathes sth, sb finds sth repugnant: **~handeln** *vi*: **einer Sache** *dat* **~handeln** to act contrary to sth; **einem Gesetz ~handeln** to contravene a law

zuziehen ['tsu:tsi:ən] (*unreg*) *vt* (*schließen: Vorhang*) to draw, to close; (*herbeirufen: Experten*) to call in ♦ *vi* to move in, to come; **sich** *dat* **etw ~** (*Krankheit*) to catch sth; (*Zorn*) to incur sth

zuzüglich ['tsu:tsy:klɪç] *präp* +*gen* plus, with the addition of

Zwang [tsvaŋ] (**-(e)s, ⁼e**) *m* compulsion, coercion

zwängen ['tsvɛŋən] *vt, vr* to squeeze

zwanglos *adj* informal

Zwangs- *zW*: **~arbeit** *f* forced labour; (*Strafe*) hard labour; **~lage** *f* predicament, tight corner; **z~läufig** *adj* necessary, inevitable

zwanzig ['tsvantsıç] *num* twenty

zwar [tsva:r] *adv* to be sure, indeed; **das ist ~ ..., aber ...** that may be ... but ...; **und ~ am Sonntag** on Sunday to be precise; **und ~ so schnell, daß ...** in fact so quickly that ...

Zweck ['tsvɛk] (**-(e)s, -e**) *m* purpose, aim; **es hat keinen ~** there's no point; **z~dienlich** *adj* practical; expedient

Zwecke *f* hobnail; (*Heft~*) drawing pin, thumbtack (*US*)

Zweck- *zW:* **z~los** *adj* pointless; **z~mäßig** *adj* suitable, appropriate; **z~s** *präp* +*gen* for the purpose of

zwei [tsvaı] *num* two; **~deutig** *adj* ambiguous; (*unanständig*) suggestive; **~erlei** *adj:* **~erlei Stoff** two different kinds of material; **~erlei Meinung** of differing opinions; **~fach** *adj* double

Zweifel ['tsvaıfəl] (**-s, -**) *m* doubt; **z~haft** *adj* doubtful, dubious; **z~los** *adj* doubtless; **z~n** *vi:* **(an etw** *dat***) z~n** to doubt (sth)

Zweig [tsvaık] (**-(e)s, -e**) *m* branch; **~stelle** *f* branch (office)

zwei- *zW:* **~hundert** *num* two hundred; **Z~kampf** *m* duel; **~mal** *adv* twice; **~sprachig** *adj* bilingual; **~spurig** *adj* (*AUT*) two-lane; **~stimmig** *adj* for two voices

zweit [tsvaıt] *adv:* **zu ~** together; (*bei mehreren Paaren*) in twos

Zweitaktmotor *m* two-stroke engine

zweitbeste(r, s) *adj* second best

zweite(r, s) *adj* second

zweiteilig *adj* (*Gruppe*) two-piece; (*Fernsehfilm*) two-part; (*Kleidung*) two-piece

zweit- *zW:* **~ens** *adv* secondly; **~größte(r, s)** *adj* second largest; **~klassig** *adj* second-class; **~letzte(r, s)** *adj* last but one, penultimate; **~rangig** *adj* second-rate

Zwerchfell ['tsvɛrçfɛl] *nt* diaphragm

Zwerg [tsvɛrk] (**-(e)s, -e**) *m* dwarf

Zwetsch(g)e ['tsvɛtʃ(g)ə] *f* plum

Zwieback ['tsvi:bak] (**-(e)s, -e**) *m* rusk

Zwiebel ['tsvi:bəl] (**-, -n**) *f* onion; (*Blumen~*) bulb

Zwie- ['tsvi:] *zW:* **z~lichtig** *adj* shady, dubious; **z~spältig** *adj* (*Gefühle*) conflicting; (*Charakter*) contradictory; **~tracht** *f* discord, dissension

Zwilling ['tsvılıŋ] (**-s, -e**) *m* twin; **~e** *pl* (*ASTROL*) Gemini

zwingen ['tsvıŋən] (*unreg*) *vt* to force; **~d** *adj* (*Grund etc*) compelling

zwinkern ['tsvıŋkərn] *vi* to blink; (*absichtlich*) to wink

Zwirn [tsvırn] (**-(e)s, -e**) *m* thread

zwischen ['tsvıʃən] *präp* (+*akk od dat*) between; **Z~bemerkung** *f* (incidental) remark; **Z~ding** *nt* cross; **~'durch** *adv* in between; (*räumlich*) here and there; **Z~ergebnis** *nt* intermediate result; **Z~fall** *m* incident; **Z~frage** *f* question; **Z~handel** *m* middlemen *pl*; middleman's trade; **Z~landung** *f* (*AVIAT*) stopover; **~menschlich** *adj* interpersonal; **Z~raum** *m* space; **Z~ruf** *m* interjection; **Z~zeit** *f* interval; **in der Z~zeit** in the interim, meanwhile

zwitschern ['tsvıtʃərn] *vt, vi* to twitter, to chirp

zwo [tsvo:] *num* two

zwölf [tsvœlf] *num* twelve

Zyklus ['tsy:klʊs] (**-, Zyklen**) *m* cycle

Zylinder [tsi'lındər] (**-s, -**) *m* cylinder; (*Hut*) top hat

Zyniker ['tsy:nikər] (**-s, -**) *m* cynic

zynisch ['tsy:nıʃ] *adj* cynical

Zypern ['tsy:pərn] *nt* Cyprus

Zyste ['tsystə] *f* cyst

z.Z(t). *abk* = **zur Zeit**

PUZZLES AND WORDGAMES

Introduction

We are delighted that you have decided to invest in this Collins Pocket Dictionary! Whether you intend to use it in school, at home, on holiday or at work, we are sure that you will find it very useful.

In the pages which follow you will find explanations and wordgames (not too difficult!) designed to give you practice in exploring the dictionary's contents and in retrieving information for a variety of purposes. Answers are provided at the end. If you spend a little time on these pages you should be able to use your dictionary more efficiently and effectively. Have fun!

Supplement by
Roy Simon
reproduced by kind permission of
Tayside Region Education Department

HOW INFORMATION IS PRESENTED IN YOUR DICTIONARY

A great deal of information is packed into your Collins Pocket Dictionary using colour, various typefaces, sizes of type, symbols, abbreviations and brackets. The purpose of this section is to acquaint you with the conventions used in presenting information.

Headwords

A headword is the word you look up in a dictionary. Headwords are listed in alphabetical order throughout the dictionary. They are printed in colour so that they stand out clearly from all the other words on the dictionary page.

Note that at the top of each page two headwords appear. These are guides to the alphabetical order of words on the page. They are there to help you scan through the dictionary more quickly to find the word you want.

The German alphabet consists of the same 26 letters as the English alphabet, plus the letter ß, which is used in some words instead of ss. Although certain letters in the German alphabet take umlaut (ä, ö, ü), this does not affect the order of words in the German-English section of the dictionary.

A Dictionary Entry

An entry is made up of a headword and all the information about that headword. Entries will be short or long depending on how frequently a word is used in either English or German and how many meanings it has. Inevitably, the fuller the dictionary entry the more care is needed in sifting through it to find the information you require.

Meanings

The translations of a headword are given in ordinary type. Where there is more than one meaning or usage, a semi-colon separates one from the other.

abladen ['apla:dən] (*unreg*) *vt* to unload
Ablage ['apla:gə] *f* (*für Akten*) tray; (*für Kleider*) cloakroom
ablassen ['aplasən] (*unreg*) *vt* (*Wasser, Dampf*) to let off; (*vom Preis*) to knock off
♦ *vi*: **von etw ~** to give sth up, to abandon sth

nt flashlight; **b~schnell** *adj* lightning
♦ *adv* (as) quick as a flash

Ohnmacht ['o:nmaxt] *f* faint; (*fig*) impotence; **in ~ fallen** to faint
ohnmächtig ['o:nmɛçtɪç] *adj* in a faint, unconscious; (*fig*) weak, impotent; **sie ist ~** she has fainted
Ohr [o:r] (**-(e)s, -en**) *nt* ear; (*Gehör*) hearing
Öhr [ø:r] (**-(e)s, -e**) *nt* eye

Zug [tsu:k] (**-(e)s, ⁻e**) *m* (*EISENB*) train; (*Luft~*) draught; (*Ziehen*) pull(ing); (*Gesichts~*) feature; (*SCHACH etc*) move; (*Klingel~*) pull; (*Schrift~*) stroke; (*Atem~*) breath; (*Charakter~*) trait; (*an Zigarette*) puff, pull, drag; (*Schluck*) gulp; (*Menschengruppe*) procession; (*von Vögeln*) flight; (*MIL*) platoon; **etw in vollen Zügen genießen** to enjoy sth to the full

Blut- *zW*: **~gruppe** *f* blood group; **b~ig** *adj* bloody; **b~jung** *adj* very young;

Gurt [gʊrt] (**-(e)s, -e**) *m* belt

klar [kla:r] *adj* clear; (*NAUT*) ready for sea; (*MIL*) ready for action; **sich** *dat* **im ~en sein über** +*akk* to be clear about; **ins ~e kommen** to get clear; **(na) ~!** of course!

279

In addition, you will often find other words appearing in *italics* in brackets before the translations. These either give some notion of the contexts in which the headword might appear (as with 'scharf' opposite — 'scharfes Essen', 'scharfe Munition', etc.) or else they provide synonyms (as with 'fremd' opposite — 'unvertraut', 'ausländisch', etc.).

Phonetic Spellings

In square brackets immediately after most headwords you will find the phonetic spelling of the word — i.e. its pronunciation. The phonetic transcription of German and English vowels and consonants is given on page xv near the front of your dictionary.

Additional Information About Headwords

Information about the usage or form of certain headwords is given in brackets between the phonetics and the translation or translations. Have a look at the entries for 'KG', 'Filiale', 'löschen' and 'Bruch' opposite.

This information is usually given in abbreviated form. A helpful list of abbreviations is given on pages xi to xiii at the front of your dictionary.

You should be particularly careful with colloquial words or phrases. Words labelled '(*umg*)' would not normally be used in formal speech, while those labelled '(*umg!*)' would be considered offensive.

Careful consideration of such style labels will provide indications as to the degree of formality and appropriateness of a word and could help you avoid many an embarrassing situation when using German!

Expressions in which the Headword Appears

An entry will often feature certain common expressions in which the headword appears. These expressions are in **bold** type but in black as opposed to colour. A swung dash (~) is used instead of repeating a headword in an entry. 'Schikane' and 'man' opposite illustrate this point.

Related Words

In the Pocket Dictionary words related to certain headwords are sometimes given at the end of an entry, as with 'Lohn' and 'accept' opposite. These are easily picked out as they are also in colour. To help you find these words, they are placed in alphabetical order after the headword to which they belong — see 'acceptable', 'acceptance' etc. opposite.

scharf [ʃarf] *adj* sharp; (*Essen*) hot, spicy; (*Munition*) live; ~ **nachdenken** to think hard; **auf etw** *akk* ~ **sein** (*umg*) to be keen on sth

fremd [frɛmt] *adj* (*unvertraut*) strange; (*ausländisch*) foreign; (*nicht eigen*) someone else's; **etw ist jdm** ~ sth is foreign to sb; **~artig** *adj* strange;

gänzlich ['gɛntslɪç] *adj* complete, entire ♦ *adv* completely, entirely

Teufel ['tɔyfəl] (-s, -) *m* devil

KG [kaː'geː] (-, -s) *f abk* (= *Kommanditgesellschaft*) limited partnership

Filiale [fili'aːlə] *f* (*COMM*) branch

löschen ['lœʃən] *vt* (*Feuer, Licht*) to put out, to extinguish; (*Durst*) to quench; (*COMM*) to cancel; (*COMPUT*) to delete; (*Tonband*) to erase; (*Fracht*) to unload ♦ *vi* (*Feuerwehr*) to put out a fire; (*Tinte*) to blot

Bruch [brʊx] (-(e)s, ⸚e) *m* breakage; (*zerbrochene Stelle*) break; (*fig*) split, breach; (*MED: Eingeweide~*) rupture, hernia; (*Bein~ etc*) fracture; (*MATH*) fraction

schenken ['ʃɛŋkən] *vt* (*auch fig*) to give; (*Getränk*) to pour; **sich** *dat* **etw** ~ (*umg*) to skip sth; **das ist geschenkt!** (*billig*) that's a giveaway!; (*nichts wert*) that's worthless!

fuchsen (*umg*) *vt* to rile, to annoy

Arsch [arʃ] (-es, ⸚e; *umg!*) *m* arse (*BRIT!*), ass (*US!*)

Schikane [ʃi'kaːnə] *f* harassment; dirty trick; **mit allen ~n** with all the trimmings

man [man] *pron* one, you; ~ **sagt, ...** they *od* people say ...; **wie schreibt** ~ **das?** how do you write it?, how is it written?

Lohn [loːn] (-(e)s, ⸚e) *m* reward; (*Arbeits~*) pay, wages *pl*; **~büro** *nt* wages office; **~empfänger** *m* wage earner

accept [ək'sɛpt] *vt* (*take*) annehmen; (*agree to*) akzeptieren; **~able** *adj* annehmbar; **~ance** *n* Annahme *f*

'Key' Words

Your Collins Pocket Dictionary gives special status to certain German and English words which can be looked on as 'key' words in each language. These are words which have many different usages. 'Werden', 'alle(r, s)' and 'sich' opposite are typical examples in German. You are likely to become familiar with them in your day-to-day language studies.

There will be occasions, however, when you want to check on a particular usage. Your dictionary can be very helpful here. Note how different parts of speech and different usages are clearly indicated by a combination of lozenges (♦) and numbers. In addition, further guides to usage are given in italics in brackets in the language of the user who needs them.

werden ['ve:rdən] (*pt* **wurde,** *pp* **geworden** *od* (*bei Passiv*) **worden**) *vi* to become; **was ist aus ihm/aus der Sache geworden?** what became of him/it?; **es ist nichts/gut geworden** it came to nothing/turned out well; **es wird Nacht/Tag** it's getting dark/light; **mir wird kalt** I'm getting cold; **Erster werden** to come *od* be first; **das muß anders werden** that'll have to change; **rot/zu Eis werden** to turn red/to ice; **was willst du (mal) werden?** what do you want to be?; **die Fotos sind gut geworden** the photos have come out nicely

♦ *als Hilfsverb* **1** (*bei Futur*): **er wird es tun** he will *od* he'll do it; **er wird das nicht tun** he will not *od* he won't do it; **es wird gleich regnen** it's going to rain

2 (*bei Konjunktiv*): **ich würde ...** I would ...; **er würde gern ...** he would *od* he'd like to ...; **ich würde lieber ...** I would *od* I'd rather ...

3 (*bei Vermutung*): **sie wird in der Küche sein** she will be in the kitchen

4 (*bei Passiv*): **gebraucht werden** to be used; **er ist erschossen worden** he has *od* he's been shot; **mir wurde gesagt, daß ...** I was told that ...

alle(r, s) ['alə(r, s)] *adj* **1** (*sämtliche*) all; **wir alle** all of us; **alle Kinder waren da** all the children were there; **alle Kinder mögen ...** all children like ...; **alle beide** both of us/them; **sie kamen alle** they all came; **alles Gute** all the best; **alles in allem** all in all

2 (*mit Zeit- oder Maßangaben*) every; **alle vier Jahre** every four years; **alle fünf Meter** every five metres

♦ *pron* everything; **alles was er sagt** everything he says, all that he says

♦ *adv* (*zu Ende, aufgebraucht*) finished; **die Milch ist alle** the milk's all gone, there's no milk left; **etw alle machen** to finish sth up

sich [zɪç] *pron* **1** (*akk*): **er/sie/es ... sich** he/she/it ... himself/herself/itself; **sie** *pl*/**man ... sich** they/one ... themselves/oneself; **Sie ... sich** you ... yourself/yourselves *pl*; **sich wiederholen** to repeat oneself/itself

2 (*dat*): **er/sie/es ... sich** he/she/it ... to himself/herself/itself; **sie** *pl*/**man ... sich** they/one ... to themselves/oneself; **Sie ... sich** you ... to yourself/yourselves *pl*; **sie hat sich einen Pullover gekauft** she bought herself a jumper; **sich die Haare waschen** to wash one's hair

3 (*mit Präposition*): **haben Sie Ihren Ausweis bei sich?** do you have your pass on you?; **er hat nichts bei sich** he's got nothing on him; **sie bleiben gern unter sich** they keep themselves to themselves

4 (*einander*) each other, one another; **sie bekämpfen sich** they fight each other *od* one another

5: **dieses Auto fährt sich gut** this car drives well; **hier sitzt es sich gut** it's good to sit here

WORDGAME 1

HEADWORDS

Study the following sentences. In each sentence a wrong word spelt very similarly to the correct word has deliberately been put in and the sentence doesn't make sense. This word is shaded each time. Write out the correct word, which you will find in your dictionary near the wrong word.

Example   Raufen verboten

['Raufen' (= 'to pull out') is the wrong word and should be replaced by 'rauchen' (= 'to smoke')]

1. Hast du das Buch schon gekonnt?
2. Ich habe ein paar VW-Akten gekauft.
3. Wir waren gestern im Kilo.
4. Sollen wir die Theaterkarten schon kauen?
5. Unser Nachbar hat einen kleinen schwarzen Puder.
6. Ich zähle heute die Rechnung.
7. Der Student muß sich für den Kurs einschreiten.
8. Das neue Restaurant ist gar nicht über.
9. Gans viele Leute standen am Unfallort.
10. Ich habe meiner Tanne einen Brief geschrieben.

WORDGAME 2
DICTIONARY ENTRIES

Complete the crossword below by looking up the English words in the list and finding the correct German translations. There is a slight catch, however! All the English words can be translated several ways into German, but only one translation will fit correctly into each part of the crossword. So look carefully through the entries in the English-German section of your dictionary.

1. FAIR
2. CATCH
3. LEARN
4. FALL
5. HIT
6. HARD
7. CALF
8. PLACE
9. HOLD
10. PLACE
11. TRACK
12. HOME

285

WORDGAME 3

FINDING MEANINGS

In this list there are eight pairs of words that have some sort of connection with each other. For example, 'Diplom' (= 'diploma') and 'Student' (= 'student') are linked. Find the other pairs by looking up the words in your dictionary.

1. Morgenrock
2. Handtasche
3. Bett
4. Kirchturm
5. Fisch
6. Nest
7. Diplom
8. Lederwaren
9. Hausschuhe
10. Glockengeläut
11. Student
12. Decke
13. Elster
14. Buch
15. Schuppe
16. Regal

WORDGAME 4

SYNONYMS

Complete the crossword by supplying synonyms of the words below. You will sometimes find the words you are looking for in italics in brackets in the entries for the words in the list. Sometimes you will have to turn to the English-German section for help.

1. Art
2. sich bemühen
3. Feuer
4. sich ereignen
5. Arroganz
6. namhaft
7. Ladung
8. Plan
9. begegnen
10. Neigung

287

WORDGAME 5

SPELLING

You will often use your dictionary to check spellings. The person who has compiled this list of ten German words has made <u>three</u> spelling mistakes. Find the three words which have been misspelt and write them out correctly.

1. nachsehen
2. nacht
3. Nagetier
4. Name
5. Nature
6. neuriech
7. Nickerchen
8. Nimmersatt
9. nördlich
10. nötig

WORDGAME 6
ANTONYMS

Complete the crossword by supplying ANTONYMS (i.e. opposites) in German of the words below. Use your dictionary to help.

1. gestehen
2. enthüllen
3. unschuldig
4. kaufen
5. verbieten
6. Reichtum
7. ruhig
8. ankommen
9. ängstlich
10. schmutzig

WORDGAME 7
PHONETIC SPELLINGS

The phonetic transcriptions of ten German words are given below. If you study page xv near the front of your dictionary you should be able to work out what the words are.

1. frikaˈdɛlə

2. ʃpuːr

3. faɪn

4. ˈlyːgə

5. ˈʃtaxəl

6. ˈnaʊtɪʃ

7. gəˈvœlbə

8. ˈkɔyçən

9. ˈmøːgən

10. ˈglaʊbvʏrdɪç

WORDGAME 8
EXPRESSIONS IN WHICH THE HEADWORD APPEARS

If you look up the headword 'Satz' in the German-English section of your dictionary you will find that the word can have many meanings. Study the entry carefully and translate the following sentences into English.

1. Der Satz ist viel zu lang.

2. Unterstreicht jeden Satz, der mit einer Konjunktion beginnt.

3. Den Satz von Pythagoras kennt jeder.

4. Das Orchester hat den letzten Satz ganz ausgezeichnet gespielt.

5. Steffi Graf hat in der Meisterschaft keinen Satz verloren.

6. Der ganze Satz war in der Tasse.

7. Bei Lieferungen ins Ausland gilt ein anderer Satz.

8. Sie hat vor lauter Begeisterung einen großen Satz gemacht.

WORDGAME 9
RELATED WORDS

Fill in the blanks in the pairs of sentences below. The missing words are related to the headwords on the left. Choose the correct "relative" each time. You will find it in your dictionary near the headword provided.

HEADWORD	RELATED WORDS
Stellung	1. Ich habe die Uhr auf 1/2 6 _____. 2. Das Auto steht an der gleichen _____.
Hoffnung	3. _____ bleibt das Wetter so. 4. Sie _____, daß sie bald wieder gesund ist.
Betrug	5. Von ihm lassen wir uns nicht mehr _____. 6. Er ist als _____ bekannt.
sprechen	7. Hat er schon mit seiner Mutter _____? 8. Das Buch wurde in fünf _____ übersetzt.
Student	9. Er hat letztes Semester mit dem _____ begonnen. 10. Sie _____ Medizin.
kurz	11. Ich habe _____ noch mit ihm gesprochen. 12. Der Rock muß _____ werden.

WORDGAME 10
'KEY' WORDS

Study carefully the entry 'machen' in your dictionary and find translations for the following:

1. what are you doing (there)?

2. it's the cold that does that

3. that doesn't matter

4. I don't mind the cold

5. 3 and 5 are 8

6. to have the car done

7. how's the work going?

8. hurry up!

9. to set about sth

10. to turn the radio down

THE DICTIONARY AND GRAMMAR

While it is true that a dictionary can never be a substitute for a detailed grammar book, it nevertheless provides a great deal of grammatical information. If you know how to extract this information you will be able to use German more accurately both in speech and in writing.

The Collins Pocket Dictionary presents grammatical information as follows.

Parts of Speech

Parts of speech are given in italics immediately after the phonetic spellings of headwords. Abbreviated forms are used. Abbreviations can be checked on pages xi to xiii.

Changes in parts of speech within an entry — for example, from adjective to pronoun to adverb, or from noun to intransitive verb to transitive verb — are indicated by means of lozenges (♦), as with the German 'alle(r, s)' and the English 'fast' opposite.

German Nouns

The gender of each noun in the German-English section of the dictionary is indicated in the following way:

> m = Maskulinum
>
> f = Femininum
>
> nt = Neutrum

You will occasionally see *'m od nt'* or *'m od f'* beside an entry. This indicates that the noun can be either masculine or neuter (see 'Knäuel' opposite) or masculine or feminine (see 'Sellerie' opposite).

Feminine forms of nouns are shown, as with 'Lehrer(in)' opposite. This is marked *m(f)* to show that the feminine form has the ending '-in'. Nouns which have the ending '-(r)', like 'Angeklagte(r)' opposite, are formed from adjectives and are marked *mf* to show that they can be either masculine or feminine. Their spelling changes in the same way as adjectives, depending on their article and position in the sentence.

prosit ['pro:zɪt] *excl* cheers

leiten ['laɪtən] *vt* to lead; (*Firma*) to manage; (*in eine Richtung*) to direct; (*ELEK*) to conduct

Knäuel ['knɔʏəl] (*-s, -*) *m od nt* (*Woll~*) ball; (*Menschen~*) knot

Sellerie ['zɛləri:] (*-s, -(s) od -, -*) *m od f* celery

SCHLÜSSELWORT

alle(r, s) ['alə(r, s)] *adj* **1** (*sämtliche*) all; **wir alle** all of us; **alle Kinder waren da** all the children were there; **alle Kinder mögen ...** all children like ...; **alle beide** both of us/them; **sie kamen alle** they all came; **alles Gute** all the best; **alles in allem** all in all
2 (*mit Zeit- oder Maßangaben*) every; **alle vier Jahre** every four years; **alle fünf Meter** every five metres
♦ *pron* everything; **alles was er sagt** everything he says, all that he says
♦ *adv* (*zu Ende, aufgebraucht*) finished; **die Milch ist alle** the milk's all gone, there's no milk left; **etw alle machen** to finish sth up

---

fast [fɑːst] *adj* schnell; (*firm*) fest ♦ *adv* schnell; fest ♦ *n* Fasten *nt* ♦ *vi* fasten; **to be ~** (*clock*) vorgehen

Lehre ['leːrə] *f* teaching, doctrine; (*beruflich*) apprenticeship; (*moralisch*) lesson; (*TECH*) gauge; **l~n** *vt* to teach; **~r(in)** (*-s, -*) *m(f)* teacher; **~rzimmer** *nt* staff room

Angeklagte(r) ['angəklɑːktə(r)] *mf* accused

295

So many things depend on you knowing the correct gender of a German noun — whether you use 'er', 'sie' or 'es' to translate 'it'; whether you use 'er' or 'es' to translate 'he', 'sie' or 'es' to translate 'she'; the spelling of adjectives etc. If you are in any doubt as to the gender of a noun, it is always best to check it in your dictionary.

Genitive singular and nominative plural forms of many nouns are also given (see 'Bube' and 'Scheitel' opposite). A list of regular noun endings is given on page xiv and nouns which have these forms will not show genitive singular and nominative plural at the headword (see 'Rasur' and 'Genesung' opposite). Nouns formed from two or more words do not have genitive singular and nominative plural shown if the last element appears in the dictionary as a headword. For example, if you want to know how to decline 'Backenzahn', you will find the necessary information at 'Zahn'.

Adjectives

Adjectives are given in the form used when they come after a verb. If the adjective comes before a noun, the spelling changes, depending on the gender of the noun and on the article (if any) which comes before the adjective. Compare 'der Hund ist schwarz' with 'der schwarze Hund'. If you find an unfamiliar adjective in a text and want to look it up in the dictionary, you will have to decide what spelling changes have been made before you can know how it will appear in the dictionary.

Some adjectives are never used after a verb. In these cases, the dictionary shows all the possible nominative singular endings.

Adverbs

German adverbs come in three main types.

Some are just adjectives in their after-verb form, used as adverbs. Sometimes the meaning is similar to the meaning of the adjective (see 'laut'), sometimes it is rather different (see 'richtig').

Some adverbs are formed by adding '-weise', '-sweise' or 'erweise' to the adjective.

Other adverbs are not considered to be derived from particular adjectives.

In your dictionary, adjective-adverbs may be shown by a change of part of speech or by the mention 'adj, adv' at the beginning of the entry.

Fuß [fuːs] (**-es**, **ᵉe**) *m* foot; (*von Glas, Säule etc*) base; (*von Möbel*) leg; **zu ~** on

Stube ['ʃtuːbə] *f* room

Mädchen ['mɛːtçən] *nt* girl; **m~haft** *adj* girlish; **~name** *m* maiden name

Bube ['buːbə] (**-n**, **-n**) *m* (*Schurke*) rogue; (*KARTEN*) jack

Scheitel ['ʃaɪtəl] (**-s**, **-**) *m* top; (*Haar~*) parting; **s~n** *vt* to part

Rasur [ra'zuːr] *f* shaving

Genesung *f* recovery, convalescence

Backenzahn *m* molar

Zahn [tsaːn] (**-(e)s**, **ᵉe**) *m* tooth; **~arzt** *m* dentist; **~ärztin** *f* (female) dentist; **~bürste** *f* toothbrush; **~fleisch** *nt* gums *pl*; **~pasta** *f* toothpaste; **~rad** *nt*

schwarz [ʃvarts] *adj* black; **~es Brett** notice board; **ins S~e treffen** (*auch fig*) to hit the bull's eye; **in den ~en Zahlen** in the black; **S~arbeit** *f* illicit work, moonlighting; **S~brot** *nt* black bread; **S~e(r)** *mf* black (man/woman)

besondere(r, s) [bə'zɔndərə(r, s)] *adj* special; (*eigen*) particular; (*gesondert*) separate; (*eigentümlich*) peculiar

letzte(r, s) ['lɛtstə(r, s)] *adj* last; (*neueste*) latest; **zum ~nmal** for the last time; **~ns** *adv* lately; **~re(r, s)** *adj* latter

laut [laʊt] *adj* loud ♦ *adv* loudly; (*lesen*) aloud ♦ *präp* (*+gen od dat*) according to; **L~** (**-(e)s**, **-e**) *m* sound

richtig *adj* right, correct; (*echt*) proper ♦ *adv* (*umg: sehr*) really; **bin ich hier ~?** am I in the right place?; **der/die R~e** the right one/person; **das R~e** the right thing; **R~keit** *f* correctness

beispielsweise *adv* for instance *od* example

leider ['laɪdər] *adv* unfortunately; **ja, ~** yes, I'm afraid so; **~ nicht** I'm afraid not

Glück- *zW*: **g~lich** *adj* fortunate; (*froh*) happy; **g~licherweise** *adv* fortunately; **g~'selig** *adj* blissful

oben ['oːbən] *adv* above; (*in Haus*) upstairs;

297

Adjective-plus-ending adverbs will usually appear as subentries.

Adverbs like 'oben' and 'leider' will usually appear as separate headwords.

Where a word in your text seems to be an adverb but does not appear in the dictionary, you should be able to work out a translation from the word it is related to, once you have found that in the dictionary.

Information about Verbs

A major problem facing language learners is that the form of a verb will change according to the subject and/or the tense being used. A typical German verb can take on many different forms — too many to list in a dictionary entry.

Yet, although verbs are listed in your dictionary in their infinitive forms only, this does not mean that the dictionary is of limited value when it comes to handling the verb system of the German language. On the contrary, it contains much valuable information.

First of all, your dictionary will help you with the meanings of unfamiliar verbs. If you came across the word 'füllt' in a text and looked it up in your dictionary you wouldn't find it. What you must do is assume that it is part of a verb and look for the infinitive form. Thus you will deduce that 'füllt' is a form of the verb 'füllen'. You now have the basic meaning of the word you are concerned with — something to do with the English verb 'fill' — and this should be enough to help you understand the text you are reading.

It is usually an easy task to make the connection between the form of a verb and the infinitive. For example, 'füllten', 'füllst', 'füllte' and 'gefüllt' are all recognizable as parts of the infinitive 'füllen'. However, sometimes it is less obvious — for example, 'hilft', 'halfen' and 'geholfen' are all parts of 'helfen'. The only real solution to this problem is to learn the various forms of the main German irregular verbs.

And this is the second source of help offered by your dictionary as far as verbs are concerned. The irregular verb lists on pages 614 to 618 at the back of the Collins Pocket Dictionary provide the main forms of the main tenses of the basic irregular verbs. (Verbs which consist of a basic verb with prefix usually follow the rules for the basic verb.) Consider the verb 'sehen' below where the following information is given:

infinitive	present indicative (2nd, 3rd sg.)	imperfect	past participle
sehen	siehst, sieht	sah	gesehen

In order to make maximum use of the information contained in these pages, a good working knowledge of the various rules affecting German verbs is required. You will acquire this in the course of your German studies and your Collins dictionary will serve as a useful 'aide-mémoire'. If you happen to forget how to form the second person singular form of the Past Tense of 'sehen' (i.e. how to translate 'You saw'), there will be no need to panic — your dictionary contains the information!

In addition, the main parts of the most common irregular verbs are listed in the body of the dictionary.

WORDGAME 11
PARTS OF SPEECH

In each sentence below a word has been shaded. Put a tick in the appropriate box to indicate the **part of speech** each time.

SENTENCE	Noun	Adj	Adv	Verb
1. Das Essen ist fertig.				
2. Er hat kein Recht dazu.				
3. Warum fahren wir nicht in die Stadt zum Essen?				
4. Ich gehe nicht mit essen.				
5. Rauchen ist strengstens verboten.				
6. Gehen Sie geradeaus und dann die erste Straße links.				
7. Das war aber ein interessanter Vortrag.				
8. Die Schauspielerin trug ein herrliches Kleid.				
9. Hast du schon von deiner Freundin gehört?				
10. Es ist immer noch recht sommerlich.				

WORDGAME 12

MEANING CHANGING WITH GENDER

Some German nouns change meaning according to their gender. Look at the pairs of sentences below and fill in the blanks with either 'ein, einen, eine' or 'der, den, die, das'.

1. Ist das _____ erste Band der Schillerausgabe?
   _____ Band ist nicht lang genug.

2. _____ Mark ist in letzter Zeit wieder gestiegen.
   Der Metzger löst _____ Mark aus den Knochen.

3. Was kostet _____ Bund Petersilie?
   _____ Bund an der Hose ist zu weit.

4. _____ Tau lag noch auf den Wiesen.
   Der Mann konnte _____ Tau nicht heben.

5. Wie steht mir _____ Hut?
   Wir müssen wirklich auf _____ Hut sein.

6. Vor vielen Jahren wurde hier _____ Wehr gebaut.
   _____ Wehr machte den Angriff unmöglich.

WORDGAME 13
ADJECTIVES

Try to work out how the adjectives in the following phrases will appear in the dictionary. Write your answer beside the phrase, then check in the dictionary.

1. ein englisches Buch

2. der rote Traktor

3. letzte Nacht

4. mein kleiner Bruder

5. eine lange Reise

6. guter Käse

7. das alte Trikot

8. schwarzes Brot

9. die große Kommode

10. ein heftiger Schlag

11. der siebte Sohn

12. die neuen Nachbarn

WORDGAME 14
VERB TENSES

Use your dictionary to help you fill in the blanks in the table below.
(Remember the important pages at the front of your dictionary.)

INFINITIVE	PRESENT TENSE	IMPERFECT	PERFECT TENSE
sehen		ich	
schlafen	du		
sein			ich
schlagen		ich	
anrufen			ich
abfahren	er		
studieren			ich
haben		ich	
anfangen	du		
waschen	er		
werden		ich	
nehmen			ich

WORDGAME 15
PAST PARTICIPLES

Use your dictionary to find the past participle of these verbs.

INFINITIVE	PAST PARTICIPLE
singen	
beißen	
bringen	
frieren	
reiben	
gewinnen	
helfen	
geschehen	
liegen	
lügen	
schneiden	
kennen	
mögen	
wissen	
können	

WORDGAME 16

IDENTIFYING INFINITIVES

In the sentences below you will see various German verbs shaded. Use your dictionary to help you find the INFINITIVE form of each verb.

1. Leider habe ich Ihren Namen vergessen.

2. Bitte ruf mich doch morgen früh mal an.

3. Er ist um 16 Uhr angekommen.

4. Sie hielt an ihrem Argument fest.

5. Wir waren im Sommer in Italien.

6. Ich würde gerne kommen, wenn ich nur könnte.

7. Die Maschine flog über den Nordpol.

8. Ich würde es ja machen, aber ich habe keine Zeit.

9. Wohin fährst du diesen Winter zum Skilaufen?

10. Wen habt ihr sonst noch eingeladen?

11. Er hat deinen Brief erst gestern bekommen.

12. Liest du das Buch nicht zu Ende?

13. Meine Mutter ist letztes Jahr gestorben.

14. Er hat den Zettel aus Versehen weggeworfen.

15. Ich nahm ihn jeden Tag mit nach Hause.

MORE ABOUT MEANING

In this section we will consider some of the problems associated with using a bilingual dictionary.

Overdependence on your dictionary

That the dictionary is an invaluable tool for the language learner is beyond dispute. Nevertheless, it is possible to become overdependent on your dictionary, turning to it in an almost automatic fashion every time you come up against a new German word or phrase. Tackling an unfamiliar text in this way will turn reading in German into an extremely tedious activity. If you stop to look up every new word you may actually be *hindering* your ability to read in German — you are so concerned with the individual words that you pay no attention to the text as a whole and to the context which gives them meaning. It is therefore important to develop appropriate reading skills — using clues such as titles, headlines, illustrations, etc., understanding relations within a sentence, etc. to predict or infer what a text is about.

A detailed study of the development of reading skills is not within the scope of this supplement; we are concerned with knowing how to use a dictionary, which is only one of several important skills involved in reading. Nevertheless, it may be instructive to look at one example. You see the following text in a German newspaper and are interested in working out what it is about.

Contextual clues here include the word in large type which you would probably recognize as a German name, something that looks like a date below, and the name and address at the bottom. Some 'form' words such as 'wir', 'sind', 'und' and 'Tochter' will be familiar to you from your general studies in German. Given that we are dealing with

> *Wir sind glücklich*
> *über die Geburt*
> *unserer Tochter*
>
> ## Julia
>
> am 5. November 1989
>
> *Christine und Artur Landgraf*
> *Vacher Straße 50 B, Köln*

a newspaper, you will probably have worked out by now that this could be an announcement placed in the 'Personal Column'.

So you have used a series of cultural, contextual and word-formation clues to get you to the point where you have understood that Christine and Artur Landgraf have placed this notice in the 'Personal Column' of the newspaper and that something happened to Julia on 5 November 1989. And you have reached this point *without* opening your dictionary once. Common sense and your knowledge of newspaper contents in this country might suggest that this must be an announcement of someone's birth or death. Thus 'glücklich' ('happy') and 'Geburt' ('birth') become the only words that you might have to look up in order to confirm that this is indeed a birth announcement.

When learning German we are helped by the fact that some German and English words look and sound alike and have exactly the same meaning. Such words are called 'COGNATES' i.e. words derived from the same root. Many words come from a common Latin root. Other words are the same or nearly the same in both languages because the German language has borrowed a word from English or vice versa. The dictionary should not be necessary where cognates are concerned — provided you know the English word that the German word resembles!

Words With More Than One Meaning

The need to examine with care *all* the information contained in a dictionary entry must be stressed. This is particularly important with the many German words which have more than one meaning. For example, the German 'Zeit' can mean 'grammatical tense' as well as 'time'. How you translated the word would depend on the context in which you found it.

Similarly, if you were trying to translate a phrase such as 'sich vor etwas drücken', you would have to look through the whole entry for 'drücken' to get the right translation. If you restricted your search to the first couple of lines of the entry and saw that the first meaning given is 'press', you might be tempted to assume that the idiom meant 'to press o.s. in front of sth'. But if you examined the entry closely you would see that 'sich vor etwas drücken' means 'to get out of (doing) sth', as in the sentence 'Sie drückt sich immer vor dem Abwasch'.

The same need for care applies when you are using the English-German section of your dictionary to translate a word from English into German. Watch out in particular for the lozenges indicating changes in parts of speech.

307

If you want to translate 'You can't fool me', the capital letters at 'Narr' and 'Närrin' will remind you that these words are nouns. But watch what you are doing with the verbs or you could end up with a mistranslation like 'Sie können mich nicht herumalbern'!

Phrasal Verbs

Another potential source of difficulty is English phrasal verbs. These consist of a common verb ('go', 'make', etc.) plus an adverb and/or a preposition to give English expressions such as 'to take after', 'to make out', etc. Entries for such verbs tend to be fairly full; therefore close examination of the contents is required. Note how these verbs appear in colour within the entry.

fool [fuːl] *n* Narr *m*, Närrin *f* ♦ *vt* (*deceive*) hereinlegen ♦ *vi* (*also*: ~ *around*) (herum)albern; **~hardy** *adj* tollkühn; **~ish** *adj* albern; **~proof** *adj* idiotensicher

make [meɪk] (*pt*, *pp* **made**) *vt* machen; (*appoint*) ernennen (zu); (*cause to do sth*) veranlassen; (*reach*) erreichen; (*in time*) schaffen; (*earn*) verdienen ♦ *n* Marke *f*; **to ~ sth happen** etw geschehen lassen; **to ~ it** es schaffen; **what time do you ~ it?** wie spät hast du es?; **to ~ do with** auskommen mit; **~ for** *vi* gehen/fahren nach; **~ out** *vt* (*write out*) ausstellen; (*understand*) verstehen; (*write*: *cheque*) ausstellen; **~ up** *vt* machen; (*face*) schminken; (*quarrel*) beilegen; (*story etc*) erfinden ♦ *vi* sich versöhnen; **~ up for** *vt* wiedergutmachen; (*COMM*) vergüten; **~believe** *n* Phantasie *f*; **~r** *n* (*COMM*) Hersteller *m*; **~shift** *adj* behelfsmäßig, Not-; **~-up** *n* Schminke *f*, Make-up *nt*; **~-up remover** *n* Make-up-Entferner *m*

False Friends

Some German and English words have similar forms *and* meanings. There are, however, German words which *look* like English words but have a completely *different* meaning. For example, 'blank' in German means 'bright'; 'Sense' means 'scythe'; 'bilden' means 'to educate'. This can easily lead to serious mistranslations.

Sometimes the meaning of the German word is close to the English. For example, 'die Chips' are 'potato crisps' rather than 'chips'; 'der Hund' means a dog of any sort, not just a 'hound'. But some German words have two meanings, one the same as the English, the other completely different! 'Golf' can mean 'gulf' as well as 'golf'; 'senden' can mean 'to send' but can also mean 'to transmit/broadcast'.

Such words are often referred to as 'false friends'. You will have to look at the context in which they appear in order to arrive at the correct meaning. If they seem to fit with the sense of the passage as a whole, it will probably not be necessary to look them up. If they don't make sense, however, you may be dealing with 'false friends'

WORDGAME 17
WORDS IN CONTEXT

Study the sentences below. Translations of the underlined words are given at the bottom. Match the number of the sentence and the letter of the translation correctly each time.

1. Sprich bitte etwas lauter, ich kann dich nicht hören.

2. Er hört den ganzen Tag Radio.

3. Kannst du das Licht ausmachen, wenn du ins Bett gehst?

4. Können wir heute schon einen Termin ausmachen?

5. Seine Frau saß am Steuer, als der Unfall passierte.

6. Ich muß dieses Jahr viel Steuern nachzahlen.

7. Die Nachfrage nach japanischen Autos ist groß.

8. Aufgrund meiner Nachfrage konnte ich dann doch etwas erfahren.

9. Das Haus wird auf meinen Namen umgeschrieben.

10. Das Referat mußt du völlig umschreiben.

11. Sind die Äpfel schon reif?

12. Für ihr Alter wirkt sie schon ziemlich reif.

a. demand	e. ripe	i. steering wheel
b. transferred	f. inquiry	j. listens to
c. turn off	g. mature	k. agree
d. hear	h. rewrite	l. tax

WORDGAME 18
FALSE FRIENDS

Look at the advertisements below. The words which have been shaded resemble English words but have different meanings here. Find a correct translation for each word in the context.

1

Reformhaus
Neustr. 23
Sonderangebot:
Vollkornbrot 2,78 DM

2

Hotel Olympia
Alle Zimmer mit Dusche/WC
Gemütliche Atmosphäre
Bitte Prospekt anfordern

Heinrichstraße 51 –
7000 STUTTGART 25
Tel. 0711/21 56 93

3

KP-Chef Italiens fliegt morgen nach New York

4

W. Meinzer   Lebensmittel
Heute Chips
im
Sonderangebot

310

5

Der Mann im Smoking

6

Reagan
will weiter Präsident der USA werden

7

Nach der Jahrtausendwende erst mit 65 in Rente

8

Europaparlament

Fraktions-Flanke abdecken

9

Reise sorgenfrei mit diesen Drei

Reisescheck
Devisen
Sparkassenbuch

BEZIRKSSPARKASSE HAUSACH
Hauptstr. 14

WORDGAME 19

WORDS WITH MORE THAN ONE MEANING

Look at the advertisements and headlines below. The words which have been shaded can have more than one meaning. Use your dictionary to help you work out the correct translation in the context.

1

Landespräsident
tritt
zurück

2

Vermögen:
Vom kleinen zum großen Geld

3

Ich weiß, wie ich
Schmerzen schnell los werde

Parazetamol
Von Apotheken

4

Heinrich Wohnmobile GmbH
Spezialisten bieten günstige Preise

5

Hotel Restaurant Seeberger

Alle Preise inklusive Bedienung

Marktplatz 12
Loßurg   Telefon (07165) 33 14

6

Müsli - Riegel

von Cadbury

– gibt Kraft und Energie!

7

Hotel - Pension Miramar

Behagliche Atmosphäre
Günstige Nachsaisonpreise

*Strandstr. 6,
2356 Eckernförde
Telefon (04269) 29 51*

8

Das Blatt
Finanz- und
Wirtschaftszeitung

HAVE FUN WITH YOUR DICTIONARY

Here are some word games for you to try. You will find your dictionary helpful as you attempt the activities.

WORDGAME 20
CODED WORDS

In the boxes below the letters of eight German words have been replaced by numbers. A number represents the same letter each time.

Try to crack the code and find the eight words. If you need help, use your dictionary.

Here is a clue: all the words you are looking for have something to do with TRANSPORT.

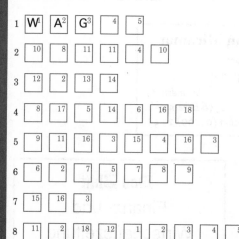

1 | W¹ | A² | G³ | 4 | 5 |

2 | 10 | 8 | 11 | 11 | 4 | 10 |

3 | 12 | 2 | 13 | 14 |

4 | 8 | 17 | 5 | 14 | 6 | 16 | 18 |

5 | 9 | 11 | 16 | 3 | 15 | 4 | 16 | 3 |

6 | 6 | 2 | 7 | 5 | 7 | 8 | 9 |

7 | 15 | 16 | 3 |

8 | 11 | 2 | 18 | 12 | 1 | 2 | 3 | 4 | 5 |

WORDGAME 21

BEHEADED WORDS

If you 'behead' certain German words, i.e. take away their first letter, you are left with another German word. For example, if you behead 'Kleider' (= 'clothes'), you get 'leider' (= 'unfortunately'), and 'dort' (= 'there') gives 'Ort' (= 'place').

The following words have their heads chopped off, i.e. the first letter has been removed. Use your dictionary to help you form a new German word by adding one letter to the start of each word below. Write down the new German word and its meaning.

1. ragen (= to tower)
2. tollen (= to romp)
3. nie (= never)
4. Rand (= edge)
5. oben (= above)
6. ich (= I)
7. Rad (= wheel)
8. innen (= inside)
9. raten (= to guess)
10. indisch (= Indian)
11. eigen (= own)
12. eben (= level)
13. Ohr (= ear)
14. pur (= pure)

WORDGAME 22
CROSSWORD

Complete this crossword by looking up the words listed below in the English-German section of your dictionary. Remember to read through the entry carefully to find the word that will fit.

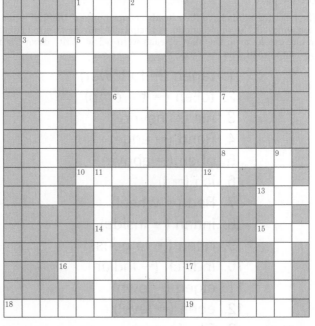

1. Heavily
2. Tearful
3. Meal
4. To record
5. Mood
6. Sad
7. Smooth
8. Deaf
9. To reassure
10. (A piece of) news
11. To start up (a car)
12. Tap
13. Place
14. To withdraw
15. Time
16. To dirty
17. Day
18. To fold
19. Profit

WORDGAME 23

There are twelve German words hidden in the grid below. Each word is made up of five letters but has been split into two parts.

Find the German words. Each group of letters can only be used once.

Use your dictionary to help you.

re	ten	cke	er	Lad	Na
rbe	Sch	tr	Sip	eh	wei
unt	en	He	am	ank	pe
ren	be	ne	cht	se	ben

WORDGAME 24

Here is a list of German words for things you will find in the kitchen.
Unfortunately, they have all been jumbled up. Try to work out what each
word is and put the word in the boxes on the right. You will see that there are
six shaded boxes below. With the six letters in the shaded boxes make up
<u>another</u> German word for an object you can find in the kitchen.

1 CSIHT   Die Kinder   ☐☐■☐☐
decken den ____

2 DERH   Die Kasserolle   ☐■☐☐
steht auf dem
____

3 RSNAHCK   Ist die   ☐☐☐☐☐☐☐■
Kaffeekanne in
diesem ____?

4 SAETS   Sie gießt den   ☐☐☐■☐
Tee in die ____

5 SRIGHCRE   Das ____ liegt   ☐■☐☐☐☐☐☐
im Spülbecken

6 HKRÜHNSKCLA Hol die Milch   ☐☐☐■☐☐☐☐☐☐☐
aus dem ____
heraus

The word you are looking for is:

☐☐☐☐☐☐

318

WORDGAME 25

Take the four letters given each time and put them in the four empty boxes in the centre of each grid. Arrange them in such a way that you form four six-letter words. Use your dictionary to check the words.

ANSWERS

WORDGAME 1

1 gekannt
2 Aktien
3 Kino
4 kaufen
5 Pudel
6 zahle
7 einschreiben
8 übel
9 Ganz
10 Tante

WORDGAME 2

1 gerecht
2 erreichen
3 erfahren
4 Herbst
5 treffen
6 schwer
7 Wade
8 Ort
9 fassen
10 Stelle
11 Gleis
12 Heim

WORDGAME 3

Morgenrock + Hausschuhe
Handtasche + Lederwaren
Bett + Decke
Kirchturm + Glockengeläut
Fisch + Schuppe
Nest + Elster
Diplom + Student
Buch + Regal

WORDGAME 4

1 Weise
2 versuchen
3 Brand
4 passieren
5 Überheblichkeit
6 berühmt
7 Last
8 Karte
9 treffen
10 Tendenz

WORDGAME 5

2 Nacht   5 Natur   6 neureich

WORDGAME 6

1 leugnen
2 verstecken
3 schuldig
4 verkaufen
5 erlauben
6 Armut
7 lärmend
8 abreisen
9 tapfer
10 sauber

WORDGAME 7

1 Frikadelle
2 Spur
3 fein
4 Lüge
5 Stachel
6 nautisch
7 Gewölbe
8 keuchen
9 mögen
10 glaubwürdig

WORDGAME 8

1 The sentence is much too long.
2 Underline every sentence which starts with a conjunction.
3 Everybody knows Pythagoras' theorem.
4 The orchestra performed the last movement really well.
5 Steffi Graf hasn't lost a set in the championships.
6 All the grounds were in the cup.
7 For deliveries abroad there is a different rate.
8 She jumped for joy.

320

WORDGAME 9

1	gestellt	7	gesprochen
2	Stelle	8	Sprachen
3	hoffentlich	9	Studium
4	hofft	10	studiert
5	betrügen	11	kürzlich
6	Betrüger	12	gekürzt

WORDGAME 11

1	adj	6	adv
2	noun	7	adj
3	noun	8	verb
4	verb	9	verb
5	adv	10	adj

WORDGAME 12

1 der/das
2 die/das
3 das (or ein)/der
4 der/das
5 der/der
6 ein/die

WORDGAME 13

1	englisch	7	alt
2	rot	8	schwarz
3	letzte(r,s)	9	groß
4	klein	10	heftig
5	lang	11	siebte(r,s)
6	gut	12	neu

WORDGAME 14

ich sah
du schläfst
ich bin gewesen
ich schlug
ich habe angerufen
er fährt ab
ich habe studiert
ich hatte
du fängst an
er wäscht
ich wurde
ich habe genommen

WORDGAME 15

gesungen	gelegen
gebissen	gelogen
gebracht	geschnitten
gefroren	gekannt
gerieben	gemocht
gewonnen	gewußt
geholfen	gekonnt
geschehen	

WORDGAME 16

1	vergessen	9	fahren
2	anrufen	10	einladen
3	ankommen	11	bekommen
4	festhalten	12	lesen
5	sein	13	sterben
6	können	14	wegwerfen
7	fliegen	15	mitnehmen
8	werden		

WORDGAME 17

1	d	5	i	9	b
2	j	6	l	10	h
3	c	7	a	11	e
4	k	8	f	12	g

WORDGAME 18

1 health food shop 6 wants
2 brochure 7 pension
3 boss 8 parliamentary party
4 crisps 9 foreign currency
5 dinner jacket

WORDGAME 19

1 resigns
2 wealth
3 know
4 offer
5 service
6 bar
7 guesthouse
8 newspaper

WORDGAME 20

1 Wagen
2 Roller
3 Taxi
4 Omnibus
5 Flugzeug
6 Bahnhof
7 Zug
8 Lastwagen

WORDGAME 21

1 tragen (= to carry)
2 Stollen (= gallery)
3 Knie (= knee)
4 Brand (= fire)
5 loben (= to praise)
6 dich (= you);
sich (= oneself);
mich (= me)
7 Grad (= degree)
8 sinnen (= to ponder)
9 braten (= to roast)
10 kindisch (= childish)
11 zeigen (= to show);
neigen (= to incline)
12 geben (= to give);
leben (= to live);
neben (= next to)
13 Rohr (= pipe, tube)
14 Spur (= trace)

WORDGAME 22

1 schwer
2 weinerlich
3 Mahlzeit
4 aufnehmen
5 Laune
6 traurig
7 glatt
8 taub
9 beruhigen
10 Nachricht
11 anlassen
12 Hahn
13 Ort
14 abheben
15 Uhr
16 beschmutzen
17 Tag
18 falten
19 Gewinn

WORDGAME 23

1 recht 7 neben
2 Laden 8 Sippe
3 Hecke 9 unter
4 ehren 10 Scham
5 beten 11 weise
6 Narbe 12 trank

WORDGAME 24

1 Tisch   4 Tasse
2 Herd   5 Geschirr
3 Schrank   6 Kühlschrank

Hidden word — KESSEL

WORDGAME 25

1

```
    U N
    M I
E I G E L B
K L A S S E
    N E
    G N
```

2

```
      B W
      E Ä
M A C H E N
U N K L A R
      E E
      N R
```

3

```
      F W
      Ü I
S C H E L M
W E R D E N
      E E
      N R
```

323

ENGLISH - GERMAN
ENGLISCH - DEUTSCH

A a

A [eɪ] n (MUS) A nt; **~ road** Hauptverkehrsstraße f

KEYWORD

a [eɪ, ə] (before vowel or silent h: **an**) indef art **1** ein; eine; **a woman** eine Frau; **a book** ein Buch; **an eagle** ein Adler; **she's a doctor** sie ist Ärztin

2 (instead of the number 'one') ein; eine; **a year ago** vor einem Jahr; **a hundred/thousand etc pounds** (ein) hundert/(ein) tausend etc Pfund

3 (in expressing ratios, prices etc) pro; **3 a day/week** 3 pro Tag/Woche, 3 am Tag/in der Woche; **10 km an hour** 10 km pro Stunde/in der Stunde

A.A. n abbr = **Alcoholics Anonymous**; (BRIT) = **Automobile Association**

A.A.A. (US) n abbr = **American Automobile Association**

aback [ə'bæk] adv: **to be taken ~** verblüfft sein

abandon [ə'bændən] vt (give up) aufgeben; (desert) verlassen ♦ n Hingabe f

abate [ə'beɪt] vi nachlassen, sich legen

abattoir ['æbətwɑ:*] (BRIT) n Schlachthaus nt

abbey ['æbɪ] n Abtei f

abbot ['æbət] n Abt m

abbreviate [ə'bri:vɪeɪt] vt abkürzen

abbreviation [əbri:vɪ'eɪʃən] n Abkürzung f

abdicate ['æbdɪkeɪt] vt aufgeben ♦ vi abdanken

abdomen ['æbdəmən] n Unterleib m

abduct [æb'dʌkt] vt entführen

aberration [æbə'reɪʃən] n (geistige) Verwirrung f

abet [ə'bet] vt see **aid**

abeyance [ə'beɪəns] n: **in ~** in der Schwebe; (disuse) außer Kraft

abhor [əb'hɔ:*] vt verabscheuen

abide [ə'baɪd] vt vertragen; leiden; **~ by** vt sich halten an +acc

ability [ə'bɪlɪtɪ] n (power) Fähigkeit f; (skill) Geschicklichkeit f

abject ['æbdʒekt] adj (liar) übel; (poverty) größte(r, s); (apology) zerknirscht

ablaze [ə'bleɪz] adj in Flammen

able ['eɪbl] adj geschickt, fähig; **to be ~ to do sth** etw tun können; **~-bodied** adj kräftig; (seaman) Voll-

ably ['eɪblɪ] adv geschickt

abnormal [æb'nɔ:məl] adj regelwidrig, abnorm

aboard [ə'bɔ:d] adv an Bord ♦ prep an Bord +gen

abode [ə'bəud] n: **of no fixed ~** ohne festen Wohnsitz

abolish [ə'bɒlɪʃ] vt abschaffen

abolition [æbə'lɪʃən] n Abschaffung f

abominable [ə'bɒmɪnəbl] adj scheußlich

aborigine [æbə'rɪdʒɪni:] n Ureinwohner m

abort [ə'bɔ:t] vt abtreiben; fehlgebären; **~ion** [ə'bɔ:ʃən] n Abtreibung f; (miscarriage) Fehlgeburt f; **~ive** adj mißlungen

abound [ə'baund] vi im Überfluß vorhanden sein; **to ~ in** Überfluß haben an +dat

KEYWORD

about [ə'baut] adv **1** (approximately) etwa, ungefähr; **about a hundred/thousand etc** etwa hundert/tausend etc; **at about 2 o'clock** etwa um 2 Uhr; **I've just about finished** ich bin gerade fertig

2 (referring to place) herum, umher; **to leave things lying about** Sachen herumliegen lassen; **to run/walk etc**

about herumrennen/gehen *etc*
3: **to be about to do sth** im Begriff sein,
etw zu tun; **he was about to go to bed**
er wollte gerade ins Bett gehen
♦ *prep* 1 (*relating to*) über +*acc*; **a book
about London** ein Buch über London;
what is it about? worum geht es?; (*book
etc*) wovon handelt es?; **we talked about
it** wir haben darüber geredet; **what *or*
how about doing this?** wollen wir das
machen?
2 (*referring to place*) um (... herum); **to
walk about the town** in der Stadt
herumgehen; **her clothes were scattered
about the room** ihre Kleider waren über
das ganze Zimmer verstreut

about-face [ə'baut'feɪs] *n* Kehrtwendung
f
about-turn [ə'baut'tɜːn] *n* Kehrtwendung
f
above [ə'bʌv] *adv* oben ♦ *prep* über; ~
all vor allem; ~ **board** *adj* offen, ehrlich
abrasive [ə'breɪzɪv] *adj* Abschleif-;
(*personality*) zermürbend, aufreibend
abreast [ə'brest] *adv* nebeneinander; **to
keep ~ of** Schritt halten mit
abridge [ə'brɪdʒ] *vt* (ab)kürzen
abroad [ə'brɔːd] *adv* (*be*) im Ausland;
(*go*) ins Ausland
abrupt [ə'brʌpt] *adj* (*sudden*) abrupt, jäh;
(*curt*) schroff
abscess ['æbsɪs] *n* Geschwür *nt*
abscond [əb'skɒnd] *vi* flüchten, sich
davonmachen
abseil ['æbsaɪl] *vi* (*also*: ~ **down**) sich
abseilen
absence ['æbsəns] *n* Abwesenheit *f*
absent ['æbsənt] *adj* abwesend, nicht da;
(*lost in thought*) geistesabwesend; ~**ee**
[æbsən'tiː] *n* Abwesende(r) *m*; ~**eeism**
[æbsən'tiːzəm] *n* Fehlen *nt* (am
Arbeitsplatz/in der Schule); ~**-minded**
adj zerstreut
absolute ['æbsəluːt] *adj* (*all*) absolut; (*power*)
unumschränkt; (*rubbish*) vollkommen,
rein; ~**ly** [æbsə'luːtlɪ] *adv* absolut,
vollkommen; ~**ly!** ganz bestimmt!
absolve [əb'zɒlv] *vt* entbinden;

freisprechen
absorb [əb'zɔːb] *vt* aufsaugen,
absorbieren; (*fig*) ganz in Anspruch
nehmen, fesseln; **to be ~ed in a book** in
ein Buch vertieft sein; ~**ent cotton** (*US*)
n Verbandwatte *f*; ~**ing** *adj* aufsaugend;
(*fig*) packend
absorption [əb'zɔːpʃən] *n* Aufsaugung *f*,
Absorption *f*; (*fig*) Versunkenheit *f*
abstain [əb'steɪn] *vi* (*in vote*) sich
enthalten; **to ~ from** (*keep from*) sich
enthalten +*gen*
abstemious [əb'stiːmɪəs] *adj* enthaltsam
abstention [əb'stenʃən] *n* (*in vote*)
(Stimm)enthaltung *f*
abstinence ['æbstɪnəns] *n*
Enthaltsamkeit *f*
abstract ['æbstrækt] *adj* abstrakt
absurd [əb'sɜːd] *adj* absurd
abundance [ə'bʌndəns] *n*: ~ **(of)**
Überfluß *m* (an +*dat*)
abundant [ə'bʌndənt] *adj* reichlich
abuse [*n* ə'bjuːs, *vb* ə'bjuːz] *n* (*rude
language*) Beschimpfung *f*; (*ill usage*) Miß-
brauch *m*; (*bad practice*) (Amts)miß-
brauch *m* ♦ *vt* (*misuse*) mißbrauchen
abusive [ə'bjuːsɪv] *adj* beleidigend,
Schimpf-
abysmal [ə'bɪzməl] *adj* scheußlich;
(*ignorance*) bodenlos
abyss [ə'bɪs] *n* Abgrund *m*
AC *abbr* (= *alternating current*)
Wechselstrom *m*
academic [ækə'demɪk] *adj* akademisch;
(*theoretical*) theoretisch ♦ *n*
Akademiker(in) *m(f)*
academy [ə'kædəmɪ] *n* (*school*)
Hochschule *f*; (*society*) Akademie *f*
accelerate [æk'seləreɪt] *vi* schneller
werden; (*AUT*) Gas geben ♦ *vt*
beschleunigen
acceleration [ækselə'reɪʃən] *n*
Beschleunigung *f*
accelerator [ək'seləreɪtə*] *n* Gas(pedal)
nt
accent ['æksent] *n* Akzent *m*, Tonfall *m*;
(*mark*) Akzent *m*; (*stress*) Betonung *f*
accept [ək'sept] *vt* (*take*) annehmen;
(*agree to*) akzeptieren; ~**able** *adj*

annehmbar; **~ance** *n* Annahme *f*

access ['ækses] *n* Zugang *m*; **~ible** [æk'sesɪbl] *adj (easy to approach)* zugänglich; *(within reach)* (leicht) erreichbar

accessory [æk'sesərɪ] *n* Zubehörteil *nt*; **toilet accessories** Toilettenartikel *pl*

accident ['æksɪdənt] *n* Unfall *m*; *(coincidence)* Zufall *m*; **by ~** zufällig; **~al** [æksɪ'dentl] *adj* unbeabsichtigt; **~ally** [æksɪ'dentəlɪ] *adv* zufällig; **~-prone** *adj*: **to be ~-prone** zu Unfällen neigen

acclaim [ə'kleɪm] *vt* zujubeln +*dat* ♦ *n* Beifall *m*

acclimate [ə'klaɪmət] *(US) vt* = **acclimatize**

acclimatize [ə'klaɪmətaɪz] *vt*: **to become ~d (to)** sich gewöhnen (an +*acc*), sich akklimatisieren (in +*dat*)

accolade ['ækəleɪd] *n* Auszeichnung *f*

accommodate [ə'kɒmədeɪt] *vt* unterbringen; *(hold)* Platz haben für; *(oblige)* (aus)helfen +*dat*

accommodating [ə'kɒmədeɪtɪŋ] *adj* entgegenkommend

accommodation [ə'kɒmə'deɪʃən] *(US* **~s**) *n* Unterkunft *f*

accompany [ə'kʌmpənɪ] *vt* begleiten

accomplice [ə'kʌmplɪs] *n* Helfershelfer *m*, Komplize *m*

accomplish [ə'kʌmplɪʃ] *vt (fulfil)* durchführen; *(finish)* vollenden; *(aim)* erreichen; **~ed** *adj* vollendet, ausgezeichnet; **~ment** *n (skill)* Fähigkeit *f*; *(completion)* Vollendung *f*; *(feat)* Leistung *f*

accord [ə'kɔːd] *n* Übereinstimmung *f* ♦ *vt* gewähren; **of one's own ~** freiwillig; **~ing to** nach, laut +*gen*; **~ance** *n*: **in ~ance with** in Übereinstimmung mit; **~ingly** *adv* danach, dementsprechend

accordion [ə'kɔːdɪən] *n* Akkordeon *nt*

accost [ə'kɒst] *vt* ansprechen

account [ə'kaʊnt] *n (bill)* Rechnung *f*; *(narrative)* Bericht *m*; *(report)* Rechenschaftsbericht *m*; *(in bank)* Konto *nt*; *(importance)* Geltung *f*; **~s** *npl (FIN)* Bücher *pl*; **on ~** auf Rechnung; **of no ~** ohne Bedeutung; **on no ~** keinesfalls; **on**

~ of wegen; **to take into ~** berücksichtigen; **~ for** *vt fus (expenditure)* Rechenschaft ablegen für; **how do you ~ for that?** wie erklären Sie (sich) das?; **~able** *adj* verantwortlich; **~ancy** [ə'kaʊntənsɪ] *n* Buchhaltung *f*; **~ant** [ə'kaʊntənt] *n* Wirtschaftsprüfer(in) *m(f)*; **~ number** *n* Kontonummer *f*

accredited [ə'kredɪtɪd] *adj* (offiziell) zugelassen

accrue [ə'kruː] *vi* sich ansammeln

accumulate [ə'kjuːmjʊleɪt] *vt* ansammeln ♦ *vi* sich ansammeln

accuracy ['ækjʊrəsɪ] *n* Genauigkeit *f*

accurate ['ækjʊrɪt] *adj* genau; **~ly** *adv* genau, richtig

accusation [ækjuː'zeɪʃən] *n* Anklage *f*, Beschuldigung *f*

accuse [ə'kjuːz] *vt* anklagen, beschuldigen; **~d** *n* Angeklagte(r) *mf*

accustom [ə'kʌstəm] *vt*: **to ~ sb (to sth)** jdn (an etw *acc*) gewöhnen; **~ed** *adj* gewohnt

ace [eɪs] *n* As *nt*; *(inf)* As *nt*, Kanone *f*

ache [eɪk] *n* Schmerz *m* ♦ *vi (be sore)* schmerzen, weh tun

achieve [ə'tʃiːv] *vt* zustande bringen; *(aim)* erreichen; **~ment** *n* Leistung *f*; *(act)* Erreichen *nt*

acid ['æsɪd] *n* Säure *f* ♦ *adj* sauer, scharf; **~ rain** *n* saure(r) Regen *m*

acknowledge [ək'nɒlɪdʒ] *vt (receipt)* bestätigen; *(admit)* zugeben; **~ment** *n* Anerkennung *f*; *(letter)* Empfangsbestätigung *f*

acne ['æknɪ] *n* Akne *f*

acorn ['eɪkɔːn] *n* Eichel *f*

acoustic [ə'kuːstɪk] *adj* akustisch; **~s** *npl* Akustik *f*

acquaint [ə'kweɪnt] *vt* vertraut machen; **to be ~ed with sb** mit jdm bekannt sein; **~ance** *n (person)* Bekannte(r) *mf*; *(knowledge)* Kenntnis *f*

acquiesce [ækwɪ'es] *vi*: **to ~ (in)** sich abfinden (mit)

acquire [ə'kwaɪə*] *vt* erwerben

acquisition [ækwɪ'zɪʃən] *n* Errungenschaft *f*; *(act)* Erwerb *m*

acquisitive [ə'kwɪzɪtɪv] *adj*

gewinnsüchtig

acquit [ə'kwɪt] *vt* (*free*) freisprechen; **to ~ o.s. well** sich bewähren; **~tal** *n* Freispruch *m*

acre ['eɪkə*] *n* Morgen *m*

acrid ['ækrɪd] *adj* (*smell, taste*) bitter; (*smoke*) beißend

acrimonious [ækrɪ'məʊnɪəs] *adj* bitter

acrobat ['ækrəbæt] *n* Akrobat *m*

across [ə'krɒs] *prep* über +*acc* ♦ *adv* hinüber, herüber; **he lives ~ the river** er wohnt auf der anderen Seite des Flusses; **ten metres ~** zehn Meter breit; **he lives ~ from us** er wohnt uns gegenüber; **to run/swim ~** hinüberlaufen/schwimmen

acrylic [ə'krɪlɪk] *adj* Acryl-

act [ækt] *n* (*deed*) Tat *f*; (*JUR*) Gesetz *nt*; (*THEAT*) Akt *m*; (: *turn*) Nummer *f* ♦ *vi* (*take action*) handeln; (*behave*) sich verhalten; (*pretend*) vorgeben; (*THEAT*) spielen ♦ *vt* (*in play*) spielen; **to ~ as** fungieren als; **~ing** *adj* stellvertretend ♦ *n* Schauspielkunst *f*; (*performance*) Aufführung *f*

action ['ækʃən] *n* (*deed*) Tat *f*; Handlung *f*; (*motion*) Bewegung *f*; (*way of working*) Funktionieren *nt*; (*battle*) Einsatz *m*, Gefecht *nt*; (*lawsuit*) Klage *f*, Prozeß *m*; **out of ~** (*person*) nicht einsatzfähig; (*thing*) außer Betrieb; **to take ~** etwas unternehmen; **~ replay** *n* (*TV*) Wiederholung *f*

activate ['æktɪveɪt] *vt* (*mechanism*) betätigen; (*CHEM, PHYS*) aktivieren

active ['æktɪv] *adj* (*brisk*) rege, tatkräftig; (*working*) aktiv, Tätigkeits-; **~ly** *adv* aktiv; (*dislike*) offen

activity [æk'tɪvɪtɪ] *n* Aktivität *f*; (*doings*) Unternehmungen *pl*; (*occupation*) Tätigkeit *f*

actor ['æktə*] *n* Schauspieler *m*

actress ['æktrɪs] *n* Schauspielerin *f*

actual ['æktjʊəl] *adj* wirklich; **~ly** *adv* tatsächlich; **~ly no** eigentlich nicht

acumen ['ækjʊmen] *n* Scharfsinn *m*

acute [ə'kjuːt] *adj* (*severe*) heftig, akut; (*keen*) scharfsinnig

ad [æd] *n abbr* = **advertisement**

A.D. *adv abbr* (= *Anno Domini*) n.Chr.

Adam ['ædəm] *n* Adam *m*

adamant ['ædəmənt] *adj* eisern; hartnäckig

adapt [ə'dæpt] *vt* anpassen ♦ *vi*: **to ~ (to)** sich anpassen (an +*acc*); **~able** *adj* anpassungsfähig; **~ation** [ædæp'teɪʃən] *n* (*THEAT etc*) Bearbeitung *f*; (*adjustment*) Anpassung *f*; **~er** *n* (*ELEC*) Zwischenstecker *m*; **~or** *n* (*ELEC*) Zwischenstecker *m*

add [æd] *vt* (*join*) hinzufügen; (*numbers: also*: ~ *up*) addieren; **~ up** *vi* (*make sense*) stimmen; **~ up to** *vt fus* ausmachen

adder ['ædə*] *n* Kreuzotter *f*, Natter *f*

addict ['ædɪkt] *n* Süchtige(r) *mf*; **~ed** [ə'dɪktɪd] *adj*: **~ed to** -süchtig; **~ion** [ə'dɪkʃən] *n* Sucht *f*; **~ive** *adj*: **to be ~ive** süchtig machen.

addition [ə'dɪʃən] *n* Anhang *m*, Addition *f*; (*MATH*) Addition *f*, Zusammenzählen *nt*; **in ~** zusätzlich, außerdem; **~al** *adj* zusätzlich, weiter

additive ['ædɪtɪv] *n* Zusatz *m*

address [ə'dres] *n* Adresse *f*; (*speech*) Ansprache *f* ♦ *vt* (*letter*) adressieren; (*speak to*) ansprechen; (*make speech to*) eine Ansprache halten an +*acc*

adept ['ædept] *adj* geschickt; **to be ~ at** gut sein in +*dat*

adequate ['ædɪkwɪt] *adj* angemessen

adhere [əd'hɪə*] *vi*: **to ~ to** haften an +*dat*; (*fig*) festhalten an +*dat*

adhesive [əd'hiːzɪv] *adj* klebend; Kleb(e)- ♦ *n* Klebstoff *m*; **~ tape** *n* (*BRIT*) Klebestreifen *m*; (*US*) Heftpflaster *nt*

ad hoc [æd'hɒk] *adj* (*decision, committee*) Ad-hoc- ♦ *adv* (*decide, appoint*) ad hoc

adjacent [ə'dʒeɪsənt] *adj* benachbart; **~ to** angrenzend an +*acc*

adjective ['ædʒəktɪv] *n* Adjektiv *nt*, Eigenschaftswort *nt*

adjoining [ə'dʒɔɪnɪŋ] *adj* benachbart, Neben-

adjourn [ə'dʒɜːn] *vt* vertagen ♦ *vi* abbrechen

adjudicate [ə'dʒuːdɪkeɪt] *vi* entscheiden, ein Urteil fällen

adjust [ə'dʒʌst] *vt* (*alter*) anpassen; (*put right*) regulieren, richtig stellen ♦ *vi* sich

anpassen; **~able** *adj* verstellbar
ad-lib [æd'lɪb] *vt*, *vi* improvisieren ♦ *adv*:
ad lib aus dem Stegreif
administer [æd'mɪnɪstə*] *vt* (*manage*)
verwalten; (*dispense*) ausüben; (*justice*)
sprechen; (*medicine*) geben
administration [ədmɪnɪs'treɪʃən] *n*
Verwaltung *f*; (*POL*) Regierung *f*
administrative [əd'mɪnɪstrətɪv] *adj*
Verwaltungs-
administrator [əd'mɪnɪstreɪtə*] *n*
Verwaltungsbeamte(r) *m*
admiral [ˈædmərəl] *n* Admiral *m*
Admiralty [ˈædmərəltɪ] (*BRIT*) *n*
Admiralität *f*
admiration [ædmɪˈreɪʃən] *n*
Bewunderung *f*
admire [əd'maɪə*] *vt* (*respect*) bewundern;
(*love*) verehren; **~r** *n* Bewunderer *m*
admission [əd'mɪʃən] *n* (*entrance*) Einlaß
m; (*fee*) Eintritt(spreis *m*) *m*; (*confession*)
Geständnis *nt*
admit [əd'mɪt] *vt* (*let in*) einlassen;
(*confess*) gestehen; (*accept*) anerkennen;
~tance *n* Zulassung *f*; **~tedly** *adv*
zugegebenermaßen
admonish [əd'mɒnɪʃ] *vt* ermahnen
ad nauseam [æd'nɔːsɪæm] *adv* (*repeat*,
talk) endlos
ado [ə'duː] *n*: **without more ~** ohne
weitere Umstände
adolescence [ædə'lesns] *n* Jugendalter
nt
adolescent [ædə'lesnt] *adj* jugendlich
♦ *n* Jugendliche(r) *mf*
adopt [ə'dɒpt] *vt* (*child*) adoptieren; (*idea*)
übernehmen; **~ion** [ə'dɒpʃən] *n* Adoption
f; Übernahme *f*
adore [ə'dɔː*] *vt* anbeten; verehren
adorn [ə'dɔːn] *vt* schmücken
Adriatic [eɪdrɪ'ætɪk] *n*: **the ~ (Sea)** die
Adria
adrift [ə'drɪft] *adv* Wind und Wellen
preisgegeben
adult [ˈædʌlt] *n* Erwachsene(r) *mf*
adultery [ə'dʌltərɪ] *n* Ehebruch *m*
advance [əd'vɑːns] *n* (*progress*)
Vorrücken *nt*; (*money*) Vorschuß *m* ♦ *vt*
(*move forward*) vorrücken; (*money*)

vorschießen; (*argument*) vorbringen ♦ *vi*
vorwärtsgehen; **in ~** im voraus; **~d** *adj*
(*ahead*) vorgerückt; (*modern*) fortgeschrit-
ten; (*study*) für Fortgeschrittene; **~ment**
n Förderung *f*; (*promotion*) Beförderung *f*
advantage [əd'vɑːntɪdʒ] *n* Vorteil *m*; **to
have an ~ over sb** jdm gegenüber im
Vorteil sein; **to take ~ of** (*misuse*)
ausnutzen; (*profit from*) Nutzen ziehen
aus; **~ous** [ædvən'teɪdʒəs] *adj* vorteilhaft
advent [ˈædvent] *n* Ankunft *f*; **A~** Advent
m
adventure [əd'ventʃə*] *n* Abenteuer *nt*
adventurous [əd'ventʃərəs] *adj*
abenteuerlich, waghalsig
adverb [ˈædvɜːb] *n* Adverb *nt*,
Umstandswort *nt*
adversary [ˈædvəsərɪ] *n* Gegner *m*
adverse [ˈædvɜːs] *adj* widrig
adversity [əd'vɜːsɪtɪ] *n* Widrigkeit *f*,
Mißgeschick *nt*
advert [ˈædvɜːt] *n* Anzeige *f*
advertise [ˈædvətaɪz] *vt* werben für ♦ *vi*
annoncieren; **to ~ for sth** etw (per
Anzeige) suchen
advertisement [əd'vɜːtɪsmənt] *n*
Anzeige *f*, Inserat *nt*
advertiser [ˈædvətaɪzə*] *n* (*in newspaper
etc*) Inserent *m*
advertising [ˈædvətaɪzɪŋ] *n* Werbung *f*
advice [əd'vaɪs] *n* Rat(schlag) *m*;
(*notification*) Benachrichtigung *f*
advisable [əd'vaɪzəbl] *adj* ratsam
advise [əd'vaɪz] *vt*: **to ~ (sb)** (jdm) raten
advisedly [əd'vaɪzədlɪ] *adv* (*deliberately*)
bewußt
adviser *n* Berater *m*
advisory [əd'vaɪzərɪ] *adj* beratend,
Beratungs-
advocate [*vb* ˈædvəkeɪt, *n* ˈædvəkət] *vt*
vertreten ♦ *n* Befürworter(in) *m(f)*
Aegean [iː'dʒiːən] *n*: **the ~ (Sea)** die
Ägäis
aerial [ˈeərɪəl] *n* Antenne *f* ♦ *adj* Luft-
aerobics [eə'rəubɪks] *n* Aerobic *nt*
aerodynamic [ˈeərəudaɪ'næmɪk] *adj*
aerodynamisch
aeroplane [ˈeərəpleɪn] *n* Flugzeug *nt*
aerosol [ˈeərəsɒl] *n* Aerosol *nt*;

Sprühdose *f*

aesthetic [ɪs'θetɪk] *adj* ästhetisch

afar [ə'fɑː*] *adv*: **from ~** aus der Ferne

affable ['æfəbl] *adj* umgänglich

affair [ə'fɛə*] *n* (*concern*) Angelegenheit *f*; (*event*) Ereignis *nt*; (*love ~*) Verhältnis *nt*; **~s** *npl* (*business*) Geschäfte *pl*

affect [ə'fekt] *vt* (*influence*) (ein)wirken auf +*acc*; (*move deeply*) bewegen; **this change doesn't ~ us** diese Änderung betrifft uns nicht; **~ed** *adj* affektiert, gekünstelt

affection [ə'fekʃən] *n* Zuneigung *f*; **~ate** [ə'fekʃənɪt] *adj* liebevoll

affiliated [ə'fɪlɪeɪtɪd] *adj* angeschlossen

affinity [ə'fɪnɪtɪ] *n* (*attraction*) gegenseitige Anziehung *f*; (*relationship*) Verwandtschaft *f*

affirmation [æfə'meɪʃən] *n* Behauptung *f*

affirmative [ə'fɜːmətɪv] *adj* bestätigend

affix [ə'fɪks] *vt* aufkleben, anheften

afflict [ə'flɪkt] *vt* quälen, heimsuchen

affluence [ə'fluːəns] *n* (*wealth*) Wohlstand *m*

affluent ['æfluənt] *adj* wohlhabend, Wohlstands-

afford [ə'fɔːd] *vt* sich *dat* leisten; (*yield*) bieten, einbringen

affront [ə'frʌnt] *n* Beleidigung *f*

Afghanistan [æf'gænɪstɑːn] *n* Afghanistan *nt*

afield [ə'fiːld] *adv*: **far ~** weit fort

afloat [ə'fləut] *adv*: **to be ~** schwimmen

afoot [ə'fut] *adv* im Gang

afraid [ə'freɪd] *adj* ängstlich; **to be ~ of** Angst haben vor +*dat*; **to be ~ to do sth** sich scheuen, etw zu tun; **I am ~ I have ...** ich habe leider ...; **I'm ~ so/not** leider/leider nicht; **I am ~ that ...** ich fürchte(, daß) ...

afresh [ə'freʃ] *adv* von neuem

Africa ['æfrɪkə] *n* Afrika *nt*; **~n** *adj* afrikanisch ♦ *n* Afrikaner(in) *m(f)*

aft [ɑːft] *adv* achtern

after ['ɑːftə*] *prep* nach; (*following, seeking*) hinter ... *dat* ... her; (*in imitation*) nach, im Stil von ♦ *adv*: **soon ~** bald danach ♦ *conj* nachdem; **what are you ~?** was wollen Sie?; **~ he left** nachdem er

gegangen war; **~ you!** nach Ihnen!; **~ all** letzten Endes; **~ having shaved** als er sich rasiert hatte; **~-effects** *npl* Nachwirkungen *pl*; **~math** *n* Auswirkungen *pl*; **~noon** *n* Nachmittag *m*; **~s** (*inf*) *n* (*dessert*) Nachtisch *m*; **~- sales service** (*BRIT*) *n* Kundendienst *m*; **~-shave (lotion)** *n* Rasierwasser *nt*; **~thought** *n* nachträgliche(r) Einfall *m*; **~wards** *adv* danach, nachher

again [ə'gen] *adv* wieder, noch einmal; (*besides*) außerdem, ferner; **~ and ~** immer wieder

against [ə'genst] *prep* gegen

age [eɪdʒ] *n* (*of person*) Alter *nt*; (*in history*) Zeitalter *nt* ♦ *vi* altern, alt werden ♦ *vt* älter machen; **to come of ~** mündig werden; **20 years of ~** 20 Jahre alt; **it's been ~s since ...** es ist ewig her, seit ...

aged[1] [eɪdʒd] *adj* ... Jahre alt, -jährig

aged[2] ['eɪdʒɪd] *adj* (*elderly*) betagt ♦ *npl*: **the ~** die Alten *pl*

age: **~ group** *n* Altersgruppe *f*; **~ limit** *n* Altersgrenze *f*

agency ['eɪdʒənsɪ] *n* Agentur *f*; Vermittlung *f*; (*CHEM*) Wirkung *f*; **through** *or* **by the ~ of ...** mit Hilfe von ...

agenda [ə'dʒendə] *n* Tagesordnung *f*

agent ['eɪdʒənt] *n* (*COMM*) Vertreter *m*; (*spy*) Agent *m*

aggravate ['ægrəveɪt] *vt* (*make worse*) verschlimmern; (*irritate*) reizen

aggregate ['ægrɪgɪt] *n* Summe *f*

aggression [ə'greʃən] *n* Aggression *f*

aggressive [ə'gresɪv] *adj* aggressiv

aggrieved [ə'griːvd] *adj* bedrückt, verletzt

aghast [ə'gɑːst] *adj* entsetzt

agile ['ædʒaɪl] *adj* flink, agil; (*mind*) rege

agitate ['ædʒɪteɪt] *vt* rütteln; **to ~ for** sich starkmachen für

ago [ə'gəu] *adv*: **two days ~** vor zwei Tagen; **not long ~** vor kurzem; **it's so long ~** es ist schon so lange her

agog [ə'gɒg] *adj* gespannt

agonizing ['ægənaɪzɪŋ] *adj* quälend

agony ['ægənɪ] *n* Qual *f*; **to be in ~** Qualen leiden

agree [ə'gri:] vt (*date*) vereinbaren ♦ vi (*have same opinion, correspond*) übereinstimmen; (*consent*) zustimmen; (*be in harmony*) sich vertragen; **to ~ to sth** einer Sache *dat* zustimmen; **to ~ that ...** (*admit*) zugeben, daß ...; **to ~ to do sth** sich bereit erklären, etw zu tun; **garlic doesn't ~ with me** Knoblauch vertrage ich nicht; **I ~** einverstanden, ich stimme zu; **to ~ on sth** sich auf etw *acc* einigen; **~able** *adj* (*pleasing*) liebenswürdig; (*willing to consent*) einverstanden; **~d** *adj* vereinbart; **~ment** n (*agreeing*) Übereinstimmung f; (*contract*) Vereinbarung f, Vertrag m; **to be in ~ment** übereinstimmen

agricultural [ægrɪ'kʌltʃərəl] *adj* landwirtschaftlich, Landwirtschafts-
agriculture ['ægrɪkʌltʃə*] n Landwirtschaft f

aground [ə'graund] *adv*: **to run ~** auf Grund laufen

ahead [ə'hed] *adv* vorwärts; **to be ~** voraus sein; **~ of time** der Zeit voraus; **go right** *or* **straight ~** gehen Sie geradeaus; fahren Sie geradeaus

aid [eɪd] n (*assistance*) Hilfe f, Unterstützung f; (*person*) Hilfe f; (*thing*) Hilfsmittel nt ♦ vt unterstützen, helfen +*dat*; **in ~ of** zugunsten +*gen*; **to ~ and abet sb** jdm Beihilfe leisten

aide [eɪd] n (*person*) Gehilfe m; (MIL) Adjutant m

AIDS [eɪdz] n *abbr* (= *acquired immune deficiency syndrome*) Aids nt

ailing ['eɪlɪŋ] *adj* kränkelnd
ailment ['eɪlmənt] n Leiden nt

aim [eɪm] vt (*gun, camera*) richten ♦ vi (*with gun: also:* **take ~**) zielen; (*intend*) beabsichtigen ♦ n (*intention*) Absicht f, Ziel nt; (*pointing*) Zielen nt, Richten nt; **to ~ at sth** auf etw *dat* richten; (*fig*) etw anstreben; **to ~ to do sth** vorhaben, etw zu tun; **~less** *adj* ziellos; **~lessly** *adv* ziellos

ain't [eɪnt] (*inf*) = **am not; are not; is not; has not; have not**

air [ɛə*] n Luft f; (*manner*) Miene f, Anschein m; (MUS) Melodie f ♦ vt lüften; (*fig*) an die Öffentlichkeit bringen ♦ *cpd* Luft-; **by ~** (*travel*) auf dem Luftweg; **to be on the ~** (RADIO, TV: *programme*) gesendet werden; **~bed** (BRIT) n Luftmatratze f; **~-borne** *adj* in der Luft; **~-conditioned** *adj* mit Klimaanlage; **~-conditioning** n Klimaanlage f; **~craft** n Flugzeug nt, Maschine f; **~craft carrier** n Flugzeugträger m; **~field** n Flugplatz m; **~ force** n Luftwaffe f; **~ freshener** n Raumspray nt; **~gun** n Luftgewehr nt; **~ hostess** (BRIT) n Stewardeß f; **~ letter** (BRIT) n Luftpostbrief m; **~lift** n Luftbrücke f; **~line** n Luftverkehrsgesellschaft f; **~liner** n Verkehrsflugzeug nt; **~lock** n Luftblase f; **~mail** n: **by ~mail** mit Luftpost; **~plane** (US) n Flugzeug nt; **~port** n Flughafen m, Flugplatz m; **~ raid** n Luftangriff m; **~sick** *adj* luftkrank; **~space** n Luftraum m; **~strip** n Landestreifen m; **~ terminal** n Terminal m; **~tight** *adj* luftdicht; **~ traffic controller** n Fluglotse m; **~y** *adj* luftig; (*manner*) leichtfertig

aisle [aɪl] n Gang m

ajar [ə'dʒɑ:*] *adv* angelehnt; einen Spalt offen

akin [ə'kɪn] *adj*: **~ to** ähnlich +*dat*

alacrity [ə'lækrɪtɪ] n Bereitwilligkeit f

alarm [ə'lɑ:m] n (*warning*) Alarm m; (*bell etc*) Alarmanlage f; (*anxiety*) Sorge f ♦ vt erschrecken; **~ call** n (*in hotel etc*) Weckruf m; **~ clock** n Wecker m

alas [ə'læs] *excl* ach

Albania [æl'beɪnɪə] n Albanien nt

albeit [ɔːl'biːɪt] *conj* obgleich

album ['ælbəm] n Album nt

alcohol ['ælkəhɒl] n Alkohol m; **~ic** [ælkə'hɒlɪk] *adj* (*drink*) alkoholisch ♦ n Alkoholiker(in) m(f); **~ism** n Alkoholismus m

ale [eɪl] n Ale nt

alert [ə'lɜ:t] *adj* wachsam ♦ n Alarm m ♦ vt alarmieren; **to be on the ~** wachsam sein

algebra ['ældʒɪbrə] n Algebra f

Algeria [æl'dʒɪərɪə] n Algerien nt

alias ['eɪlɪəs] *adv* alias ♦ n Deckname m

alibi ['ælɪbaɪ] n Alibi nt

alien ['eɪlɪən] *n* Ausländer *m* ♦ *adj*
(*foreign*) ausländisch; (*strange*) fremd; ~
to fremd +*dat*; **~ate** *vt* entfremden

alight [ə'laɪt] *adj* brennend; (*of building*)
in Flammen ♦ *vi* (*descend*) aussteigen;
(*bird*) sich setzen

align [ə'laɪn] *vt* ausrichten

alike [ə'laɪk] *adj* gleich, ähnlich ♦ *adv*
gleich, ebenso; **to look ~** sich *dat* ähnlich
sehen

alimony ['ælɪmənɪ] *n* Unterhalt *m*,
Alimente *pl*

alive [ə'laɪv] *adj* (*living*) lebend; (*lively*)
lebendig, aufgeweckt; **~ (with)** (*full of*)
voll (von), wimmelnd (von)

---KEYWORD---

all [ɔːl] *adj* alle(r, s); **all day/night** den
ganzen Tag/die ganze Nacht; **all men are
equal** alle Menschen sind gleich; **all five
came** alle fünf kamen; **all the books/
food** die ganzen Bücher/das ganze Essen;
all the time die ganze Zeit (über); **all his
life** sein ganzes Leben (lang)
♦ *pron* 1 alles; **I ate it all, I ate all of it**
ich habe alles gegessen; **all of us/the
boys went** wir gingen alle/alle Jungen
gingen; **we all sat down** wir setzten uns
alle
2 (*in phrases*): **above all** vor allem; **after
all** schließlich; **at all: not at all** (*in
answer to question*) überhaupt nicht; (*in
answer to thanks*) gern geschehen; **I'm
not at all tired** ich bin überhaupt nicht
müde; **anything at all will do** es ist
egal, welche(r, s); **all in all** in allem
♦ *adv* ganz; **all alone** ganz allein; **it's not
as hard as all that** so schwer ist es nun
auch wieder nicht; **all the more/better** um so mehr/besser; **all but** fast;
the score is 2 all es steht 2 zu 2

allay [ə'leɪ] *vt* (*fears*) beschwichtigen

all clear ['ɔːl'klɪə*] *n* Entwarnung *f*

allegation [ælɪ'geɪʃən] *n* Behauptung *f*

allege [ə'ledʒ] *vt* (*declare*) behaupten;
(*falsely*) vorgeben; **~dly** [ə'ledʒɪdlɪ] *adv*
angeblich

allegiance [ə'liːdʒəns] *n* Treue *f*

allergic [ə'lɜːdʒɪk] *adj*: **~ (to)** allergisch
(gegen)

allergy ['ælədʒɪ] *n* Allergie *f*

alleviate [ə'liːvɪeɪt] *vt* lindern

alley ['ælɪ] *n* Gasse *f*, Durchgang *m*

alliance [ə'laɪəns] *n* Bund *m*, Allianz *f*

allied ['ælaɪd] *adj* vereinigt; (*powers*)
alliiert; **~ (to)** verwandt (mit)

alligator ['ælɪgeɪtə*] *n* Alligator *m*

all-in ['ɔːlɪn] (*BRIT*) *adj*, *adv* (*charge*) alles
inbegriffen, Gesamt-; **~ wrestling** *n*
Freistilringen *nt*

all-night ['ɔːl'naɪt] *adj* (*café, cinema*) die
ganze Nacht geöffnet, Nacht-

allocate ['æləkeɪt] *vt* zuteilen

allot [ə'lɒt] *vt* zuteilen; **~ment** *n* (*share*)
Anteil *m*; (*plot*) Schrebergarten *m*

all-out ['ɔːl'aʊt] *adj* total; **all out** *adv* mit
voller Kraft

allow [ə'laʊ] *vt* (*permit*) erlauben (*sb*
jdm), gestatten; (*grant*) bewilligen;
(*deduct*) abziehen; (*concede*): **to ~ that ...**
annehmen, daß ...; **to ~ sb sth** jdm etw
erlauben, jdm etw gestatten; **to ~ sb to
do sth** jdm erlauben *or* gestatten, etw zu
tun; **~ for** *vt fus* berücksichtigen,
einplanen; **~ance** *n* Beihilfe *f*; **to make
~ances for** berücksichtigen

alloy ['ælɔɪ] *n* Metallegierung *f*

all right *adv* (*well*) gut; (*correct*) richtig;
(*as answer*) okay

all-round ['ɔːl'raʊnd] *adj* (*sportsman*)
allseitig, Allround-; (*view*) Rundum-

all-time ['ɔːl'taɪm] *adj* (*record, high*) ...
aller Zeiten, Höchst-

allude [ə'luːd] *vi*: **to ~ to** hinweisen auf
+*acc*, anspielen auf +*acc*

alluring [ə'ljʊərɪŋ] *adj* verlockend

allusion [ə'luːʒən] *n* Anspielung *f*

ally [*n* 'ælaɪ, *vb* ə'laɪ] *n* Verbündete(r) *mf*;
(*POL*) Alliierte(r) *m* ♦ *vr*: **to ~ o.s. with**
sich verbünden mit

almighty [ɔːl'maɪtɪ] *adj* allmächtig

almond ['ɑːmənd] *n* Mandel *f*

almost ['ɔːlməʊst] *adv* fast, beinahe

alms [ɑːmz] *npl* Almosen *nt*

aloft [ə'lɒft] *adv* (*be*) in der Luft; (*throw*)
in die Luft

alone [ə'ləʊn] *adj*, *adv* allein; **to leave**

sth ~ etw sein lassen; **let** ~ ... geschweige denn ...

along [ə'lɒŋ] *prep* entlang, längs ♦ *adv* (*onward*) vorwärts, weiter; ~ **with** zusammen mit; **he was limping** ~ er humpelte einher; **all** ~ (*all the time*) die ganze Zeit; ~**side** *adv* (*walk*) nebenher; (*come*) nebendran; (*be*) daneben ♦ *prep* (*walk, compared with*) neben +*dat*; (*come*) neben +*acc*; (*be*) entlang, neben +*dat*; (*of ship*) längsseits +*gen*

aloof [ə'luːf] *adj* zurückhaltend ♦ *adv* fern; **to stand** ~ abseits stehen

aloud [ə'laud] *adv* laut

alphabet ['ælfəbet] *n* Alphabet *nt*; ~**ical** [ælfə'betɪkəl] *adj* alphabetisch

alpine ['ælpaɪn] *adj* alpin, Alpen-

Alps [ælps] *npl*: **the** ~ die Alpen *pl*

already [ɔːl'redɪ] *adv* schon, bereits

alright ['ɔːl'raɪt] (*BRIT*) *adv* = **all right**

Alsatian [æl'seɪʃən] *n* (*dog*) Schäferhund *m*

also ['ɔːlsəu] *adv* auch, außerdem

altar ['ɔːltə*] *n* Altar *m*

alter ['ɔːltə*] *vt* ändern; (*dress*) umändern; ~**ation** [ɒltə'reɪʃən] *n* Änderung *f*; Umänderung *f*; (*to building*) Umbau *m*

alternate [*adj* ɒl'tɜːnɪt, *vb* 'ɒltɜːneɪt] *adj* abwechselnd ♦ *vi* abwechseln; **on** ~ **days** jeden zweiten Tag

alternating ['ɒltɜːneɪtɪŋ] *adj*: ~ **current** Wechselstrom *m*

alternative [ɒl'tɜːnətɪv] *adj* andere(r, s) ♦ *n* Alternative *f*; ~ **medicine** Alternativmedizin *f*; ~**ly** *adv* im anderen Falle; ~**ly one could** ... oder man könnte ...

alternator ['ɒltɜːneɪtə*] *n* (*AUT*) Lichtmaschine *f*

although [ɔːl'ðəu] *conj* obwohl

altitude ['æltɪtjuːd] *n* Höhe *f*

alto ['æltəu] *n* Alt *m*

altogether [ɔːltə'geðə*] *adv* (*on the whole*) im ganzen genommen; (*entirely*) ganz und gar

aluminium [ælju'mɪnɪəm] (*BRIT*) *n* Aluminium *nt*

aluminum [ə'luːmɪnəm] (*US*) *n* Aluminium *nt*

always ['ɔːlweɪz] *adv* immer

Alzheimer's (disease) ['æltshaɪməz-] *n* (*MED*) Alzheimer-Krankheit *f*

am [æm] *see* **be**

a.m. *adv abbr* (= *ante meridiem*) vormittags

amalgamate [ə'mælgəmeɪt] *vi* (*combine*) sich vereinigen ♦ *vt* (*mix*) amalgamieren

amass [ə'mæs] *vt* anhäufen

amateur ['æmətɜː*] *n* Amateur *m*; (*pej*) Amateur *m*, Stümper *m*; ~**ish** (*pej*) *adj* dilettantisch, stümperhaft

amaze [ə'meɪz] *vt* erstaunen; **to be** ~**d** (**at**) erstaunt sein (über); ~**ment** *n* höchste(s) Erstaunen

amazing [ə'meɪzɪŋ] *adj* höchst erstaunlich

Amazon ['æməzən] *n* (*GEOG*) Amazonas *m*

ambassador [æm'bæsədə*] *n* Botschafter *m*

amber ['æmbə*] *n* Bernstein *m*; **at** ~ (*BRIT: AUT*) (auf) gelb

ambiguous [æm'bɪgjuəs] *adj* zweideutig; (*not clear*) unklar

ambition [æm'bɪʃən] *n* Ehrgeiz *m*

ambitious [æm'bɪʃəs] *adj* ehrgeizig

ambivalent [æm'bɪvələnt] *adj* (*attitude*) zwiespältig

amble ['æmbl] *vi* (*usu*: ~ **along**) schlendern

ambulance ['æmbjuləns] *n* Krankenwagen *m*; ~**man** (*irreg*) *n* Sanitäter *m*

ambush ['æmbuʃ] *n* Hinterhalt *m* ♦ *vt* (aus dem Hinterhalt) überfallen

amenable [ə'miːnəbl] *adj* gefügig; ~ (**to**) (*reason*) zugänglich (+*dat*); (*flattery*) empfänglich (für); (*law*) unterworfen (+*dat*)

amend [ə'mend] *vt* (*law etc*) abändern, ergänzen; **to make** ~**s** etw wiedergutmachen; ~**ment** *n* Abänderung *f*

amenities [ə'miːnɪtɪz] *npl* Einrichtungen *pl*

America [ə'merɪkə] *n* Amerika *nt*; ~**n** *adj* amerikanisch ♦ *n* Amerikaner(in) *m(f)*

amiable ['eɪmɪəbl] *adj* liebenswürdig

amicable [ˈæmɪkəbl] *adj*
freundschaftlich; *(settlement)* gütlich
amid(st) [əˈmɪd(st)] *prep* mitten in *or*
unter +*dat*
amiss [əˈmɪs] *adv*: **to take sth ~** etw
übelnehmen; **there's something ~** da
stimmt irgend etwas nicht
ammonia [əˈməʊnɪə] *n* Ammoniak *nt*
ammunition [æmjʊˈnɪʃən] *n* Munition *f*
amnesia [æmˈniːzɪə] *n* Gedächtnisverlust
m
amnesty [ˈæmnɪstɪ] *n* Amnestie *f*
amok [əˈmɔk] *adv*: **to run ~** Amok laufen
among(st) [əˈmʌŋ(st)] *prep* unter
amoral [eɪˈmɒrəl] *adj* unmoralisch
amorous [ˈæmərəs] *adj* verliebt
amount [əˈmaʊnt] *n (of money)* Betrag *m*;
(of water, sand) Menge *f* ♦ *vi*: **to ~ to**
(total) sich belaufen auf +*acc*; **a great ~
of time/energy** ein großer Aufwand an
Zeit/Energie *(dat)*; **this ~s to treachery**
das kommt Verrat gleich; **it ~s to the
same** es läuft aufs gleiche hinaus; **he
won't ~ to much** aus ihm wird nie was
amp(ere) [ˈæmp(ɛəˀ)] *n* Ampere *nt*
amphibian [æmˈfɪbɪən] *n* Amphibie *f*
amphibious [æmˈfɪbɪəs] *adj* amphibisch,
Amphibien-
ample [ˈæmpl] *adj (portion)* reichlich;
(dress) weit, groß; **~ time** genügend Zeit
amplifier [ˈæmplɪfaɪəˀ] *n* Verstärker *m*
amuse [əˈmjuːz] *vt (entertain)*
unterhalten; *(make smile)* belustigen;
~ment *n (feeling)* Unterhaltung *f*;
(recreation) Zeitvertreib *m*; **~ment
arcade** *n* Spielhalle *f*
an [æn] *see* **a**
anaemia [əˈniːmɪə] *n* Anämie *f*
anaemic [əˈniːmɪk] *adj* blutarm
anaesthetic [ænɪsˈθetɪk] *n*
Betäubungsmittel *nt*; **under ~** unter
Narkose
anaesthetist [æˈniːsθɪtɪst] *n*
Anästhesist(in) *m(f)*
analgesic [ænəlˈdʒiːsɪk] *n*
schmerzlindernde(s) Mittel *nt*
analog(ue) [ˈænəlɒg] *adj* Analog-
analogy [əˈnælədʒɪ] *n* Analogie *f*
analyse [ˈænəlaɪz] *(BRIT) vt* analysieren

analyses [əˈnælɪsiːz] *(BRIT) npl of* **analysis**
analysis [əˈnælɪsɪs] *(pl* **analyses)** *n*
Analyse *f*
analyst [ˈænəlɪst] *n* Analytiker(in) *m(f)*
analytic(al) [ænəˈlɪtɪk(əl)] *adj* analytisch
analyze [ˈænəlaɪz] *(US) vt =* **analyse**
anarchy [ˈænəkɪ] *n* Anarchie *f*
anathema [əˈnæθɪmə] *n (fig)* Greuel *nt*
anatomy [əˈnætəmɪ] *n (structure)*
anatomische(r) Aufbau *m*; *(study)*
Anatomie *f*
ancestor [ˈænsestəˀ] *n* Vorfahr *m*
anchor [ˈæŋkəˀ] *n* Anker *m* ♦ *vi (also: to
drop ~)* ankern, vor Anker gehen ♦ *vt*
verankern; **to weigh ~** den Anker lichten
anchovy [ˈæntʃəvɪ] *n* Sardelle *f*
ancient [ˈeɪnʃənt] *adj* alt; *(car etc)* uralt
ancillary [ænˈsɪlərɪ] *adj* Hilfs-
and [ænd] *conj* und; **~ so on** und so
weiter; **try ~ come** versuche zu kommen;
better ~ better immer besser
Andes [ˈændiːz] *npl*: **the ~** die Anden *pl*
anemia [əˈniːmɪə] *etc (US) n =* **anaemia**
etc
anesthetic [ænɪsˈθetɪk] *etc (US) n*
= **anaesthetic** *etc*
anew [əˈnjuː] *adv* von neuem
angel [ˈeɪndʒəl] *n* Engel *m*
anger [ˈæŋgəˀ] *n* Zorn *m* ♦ *vt* ärgern
angina [ænˈdʒaɪnə] *n* Angina *f*
angle [ˈæŋgl] *n* Winkel *m*; *(point of view)*
Standpunkt *m*
angler *n* Angler *m*
Anglican [ˈæŋglɪkən] *adj* anglikanisch
♦ *n* Anglikaner(in) *m(f)*
angling [ˈæŋglɪŋ] *n* Angeln *nt*
Anglo- [ˈæŋgləʊ] *prefix* Anglo-
angrily [ˈæŋgrɪlɪ] *adv* ärgerlich, böse
angry [ˈæŋgrɪ] *adj* ärgerlich, ungehalten,
böse; *(wound)* entzündet; **to be ~ with sb**
auf jdn böse sein; **to be ~ at sth** über
etw *acc* verärgert sein
anguish [ˈæŋgwɪʃ] *n* Qual *f*
angular [ˈæŋgjʊləˀ] *adj* eckig,
winkelförmig; *(face)* kantig
animal [ˈænɪməl] *n* Tier *nt*; *(living
creature)* Lebewesen *n* ♦ *adj* tierisch
animate [*vb* ˈænɪmeɪt, *adj* ˈænɪmət] *vt*
beleben ♦ *adj* lebhaft; **~d** *adj* lebendig;

(film) Zeichentrick-
animosity [ænɪ'mɒsɪtɪ] *n* Feindseligkeit
f, Abneigung *f*
aniseed ['ænɪsiːd] *n* Anis *m*
ankle ['æŋkl] *n* (Fuß)knöchel *m*; ~ **sock**
n Söckchen *nt*
annex [*n* 'æneks, *vb* ə'neks] *n* (*also*: *BRIT*:
annexe) Anbau *m* ♦ *vt* anfügen; (*POL*)
annektieren, angliedern
annihilate [ə'naɪəleɪt] *vt* vernichten
anniversary [ænɪ'vɜːsərɪ] *n* Jahrestag *m*
annotate ['ænəteɪt] *vt* kommentieren
announce [ə'naʊns] *vt* ankündigen,
anzeigen; **~ment** *n* Ankündigung *f*;
(*official*) Bekanntmachung *f*; **~r** *n*
Ansager(in) *m(f)*
annoy [ə'nɔɪ] *vt* ärgern; **don't get ~ed!**
reg' dich nicht auf!; **~ance** *n* Ärgernis *nt*,
Störung *f*; **~ing** *adj* ärgerlich; (*person*)
lästig
annual ['ænjʊəl] *adj* jährlich; (*salary*)
Jahres- ♦ *n* (*plant*) einjährige Pflanze *f*;
(*book*) Jahrbuch *nt*; **~ly** *adv* jährlich
annul [ə'nʌl] *vt* aufheben, annullieren
annum ['ænəm] *n see* **per**
anomaly [ə'nɒməlɪ] *n* Abweichung *f* von
der Regel
anonymous [ə'nɒnɪməs] *adj* anonym
anorak ['ænəræk] *n* Anorak *m*,
Windjacke *f*
anorexia [ænə'reksɪə] *n* (*MED*)
Magersucht *f*
another [ə'nʌðə*] *adj, pron* (*different*)
ein(e) andere(r, s); (*additional*) noch
eine(r, s); *see also* **one**
answer ['ɑːnsə*] *n* Antwort *f* ♦ *vi*
antworten; (*on phone*) sich melden ♦ *vt*
(*person*) antworten +*dat*; (*letter, question*)
beantworten; (*telephone*) gehen an +*acc*,
abnehmen; (*door*) öffnen; **in ~ to your
letter** in Beantwortung Ihres Schreibens;
to ~ the phone ans Telefon gehen; **to ~
the bell** *or* **the door** aufmachen; **~ back**
vi frech sein; **~ for** *vt fus*: **to ~ for sth**
für etw verantwortlich sein; **~able** *adj*:
to be ~able to sb for sth jdm gegenüber
für etw verantwortlich sein; **~ing
machine** *n* Anrufbeantworter *m*
ant [ænt] *n* Ameise *f*

antagonism [æn'tægənɪzəm] *n*
Antagonismus *m*
antagonize [æn'tægənaɪz] *vt* reizen
Antarctic [ænt'ɑːktɪk] *adj* antarktisch
♦ *n*: **the ~** die Antarktis
antelope ['æntɪləʊp] *n* Antilope *f*
antenatal [æntɪ'neɪtl] *adj* vor der
Geburt; ~ **clinic** *n* Sprechstunde *f* für
werdende Mütter
antenna [æn'tenə] *n* (*BIOL*) Fühler *m*;
(*RADIO*) Antenne *f*
antennae [æn'teniː] *npl of* **antenna**
anthem ['ænθəm] *n* Hymne *f*; **national ~**
Nationalhymne *f*
anthology [æn'θɒlədʒɪ] *n* Gedicht-
sammlung *f*, Anthologie *f*
anti- ['æntɪ] *prefix* Gegen-, Anti-
anti-aircraft ['æntɪ'ɛəkrɑːft] *adj*
Flugabwehr-
antibiotic ['æntɪbaɪ'ɒtɪk] *n* Antibiotikum
nt
antibody ['æntɪbɒdɪ] *n* Antikörper *m*
anticipate [æn'tɪsɪpeɪt] *vt* (*expect:
trouble, question*) erwarten, rechnen mit;
(*look forward to*) sich freuen auf +*acc*; (*do
first*) vorwegnehmen; (*foresee*) ahnen,
vorhersehen
anticipation [æntɪsɪ'peɪʃən] *n* Erwartung
f; (*foreshadowing*) Vorwegnahme *f*
anticlimax ['æntɪ'klaɪmæks] *n*
Ernüchterung *f*
anticlockwise ['æntɪ'klɒkwaɪz] *adv*
entgegen dem Uhrzeigersinn
antics ['æntɪks] *npl* Possen *pl*
anticyclone ['æntɪ'saɪkləʊn] *n* Hoch *nt*,
Hochdruckgebiet *nt*
antidote ['æntɪdəʊt] *n* Gegenmittel *nt*
antifreeze ['æntɪfriːz] *n*
Frostschutzmittel *nt*
antihistamine [æntɪ'hɪstəmiːn] *n*
Antihistamin *nt*
antiquated ['æntɪkweɪtɪd] *adj* antiquiert
antique [æn'tiːk] *n* Antiquität *f* ♦ *adj*
antik; (*old-fashioned*) altmodisch; ~ **shop**
n Antiquitätenladen *m*
antiquity [æn'tɪkwɪtɪ] *n* Altertum *nt*
antiseptic [æntɪ'septɪk] *n* Antiseptikum
nt ♦ *adj* antiseptisch
antisocial [æntɪ'səʊʃl] *adj* (*person*)

ungesellig; *(law)* unsozial

antlers ['æntləz] *npl* Geweih *nt*

anus ['eɪnəs] *n* After *m*

anvil ['ænvɪl] *n* Amboß *m*

anxiety [æŋ'zaɪətɪ] *n* Angst *f*; *(worry)* Sorge *f*

anxious ['æŋkʃəs] *adj* ängstlich; *(worried)* besorgt; **to be ~ to do sth** etw unbedingt tun wollen

any ['enɪ] *adj* **1** *(in questions etc)*: **have you any butter?** haben Sie (etwas) Butter?; **have you any children?** haben Sie Kinder?; **if there are any tickets left** falls noch Karten da sind

2 *(with negative)*: **I haven't any money/ books** ich habe kein Geld/keine Bücher

3 *(no matter which)* jede(r, s) (beliebige); **any colour (at all)** jede beliebige Farbe; **choose any book you like** nehmen Sie ein beliebiges Buch

4 *(in phrases)*: **in any case** in jedem Fall; **any day now** jeden Tag; **at any moment** jeden Moment; **at any rate** auf jeden Fall

♦ *pron* **1** *(in questions etc)*: **have you got any?** haben Sie welche?; **can any of you sing?** kann (irgend)einer von euch singen?

2 *(with negative)*: **I haven't any (of them)** ich habe keinen/keines (davon)

3 *(no matter which one(s))*: **take any of those books (you like)** nehmen Sie irgendeines dieser Bücher

♦ *adv* **1** *(in questions etc)*: **do you want any more soup/sandwiches?** möchten Sie noch Suppe/Brote?; **are you feeling any better?** fühlen Sie sich etwas besser?

2 *(with negative)*: **I can't hear him any more** ich kann ihn nicht mehr hören

anybody ['enɪbɒdɪ] *pron (no matter who)* jede(r); *(in questions etc)* (irgend) jemand, (irgend) eine(r); *(with negative)*: **I can't see ~** ich kann niemanden sehen

anyhow ['enɪhaʊ] *adv (at any rate)*: **I shall go ~** ich gehe sowieso; *(haphazardly)*: **do it ~** machen Sie es, wie Sie wollen

anyone ['enɪwʌn] *pron* = **anybody**

anything ['enɪθɪŋ] *pron* **1** *(in questions etc)* (irgend) etwas; **can you see anything?** können Sie etwas sehen?

2 *(with negative)*: **I can't see anything** ich kann nichts sehen

3 *(no matter what)*: **you can say anything you like** Sie können sagen, was Sie wollen; **anything will do** irgend etwas(, wird genügen), irgendeine(r, s) (wird genügen); **he'll eat anything** er ißt alles

anyway ['enɪweɪ] *adv (at any rate)* auf jeden Fall; *(besides)*: **~, I couldn't come even if I wanted to** jedenfalls könnte ich nicht kommen, selbst wenn ich wollte; **why are you phoning, ~?** warum rufst du überhaupt an?

anywhere ['enɪwɛə*] *adv (in questions etc)* irgendwo; *(: with direction)* irgendwohin; *(no matter where)* überall; *(: with direction)* überallhin; *(with negative)*: **I can't see him ~** ich kann ihn nirgendwo *or* nirgends sehen; **can you see him ~?** siehst du ihn irgendwo?; **put the books down ~** leg die Bücher irgendwohin

apart [ə'pɑːt] *adv (parted)* auseinander; *(away)* beiseite, abseits; **10 miles ~** 10 Meilen auseinander; **to take ~** auseinandernehmen; **~ from** *prep* außer

apartheid [ə'pɑːteɪt] *n* Apartheid *f*

apartment [ə'pɑːtmənt] *(US) n* Wohnung *f*; **~ building** *(US) n* Wohnhaus *nt*

apathy ['æpəθɪ] *n* Teilnahmslosigkeit *f*, Apathie *f*

ape [eɪp] *n* (Menschen)affe *m* ♦ *vt* nachahmen

aperitif *n* Aperitif *m*

aperture ['æpətjʊə*] *n* Öffnung *f*; *(PHOT)* Blende *f*

apex ['eɪpeks] *n* Spitze *f*

apiece [ə'piːs] *adv* pro Stück; *(per person)* pro Kopf

apologetic [əpɒlə'dʒetɪk] *adj* entschuldigend; **to be ~** sich sehr entschuldigen

apologize [ə'pɒlədʒaɪz] *vi*: **to ~ (for sth to sb)** sich (für etw bei jdm) entschuldigen

apology [ə'pɒlədʒɪ] *n* Entschuldigung *f*

apostle [ə'pɒsl] *n* Apostel *m*

apostrophe [ə'pɒstrəfɪ] *n* Apostroph *m*

appal [ə'pɔːl] *vt* erschrecken; **~ling** [ə'pɔːlɪŋ] *adj* schrecklich

apparatus [æpə'reɪtəs] *n* Gerät *nt*

apparel [ə'pærəl] (*US*) *n* Kleidung *f*

apparent [ə'pærənt] *adj* offenbar; **~ly** *adv* anscheinend

apparition [æpə'rɪʃən] *n* (*ghost*) Erscheinung *f*, Geist *m*; (*appearance*) Erscheinen *nt*

appeal [ə'piːl] *vi* dringend ersuchen; (*JUR*) Berufung einlegen ♦ *n* Aufruf *m*; (*JUR*) Berufung *f*; **to ~ for** dringend bitten um; **to ~ to** sich wenden an +*acc*; (*to public*) appellieren an +*acc*; **it doesn't ~ to me** es gefällt mir nicht; **~ing** *adj* ansprechend

appear [ə'pɪə*] *vi* (*come into sight*) erscheinen; (*be seen*) auftauchen; (*seem*) scheinen; **it would ~ that ...** anscheinend ...; **~ance** *n* (*coming into sight*) Erscheinen *nt*; (*outward show*) Äußere(s) *nt*

appease [ə'piːz] *vt* beschwichtigen

appendices [ə'pendɪsɪːz] *npl of* **appendix**

appendicitis [əpendɪ'saɪtɪs] *n* Blinddarmentzündung *f*

appendix [ə'pendɪks] (*pl* **appendices**) *n* (*in book*) Anhang *m*; (*MED*) Blinddarm *m*

appetite ['æpɪtaɪt] *n* Appetit *m*; (*fig*) Lust *f*

appetizer ['æpətaɪzə*] *n* Appetitanreger *m*

appetizing ['æpɪtaɪzɪŋ] *adj* appetitanregend

applaud [ə'plɔːd] *vi* Beifall klatschen, applaudieren ♦ *vt* Beifall klatschen +*dat*

applause [ə'plɔːz] *n* Beifall *m*, Applaus *m*

apple ['æpl] *n* Apfel *m*; **~ tree** *n* Apfelbaum *m*

appliance [ə'plaɪəns] *n* Gerät *nt*

applicable [ə'plɪkəbl] *adj* anwendbar; (*in forms*) zutreffend

applicant ['æplɪkənt] *n* Bewerber(in) *m(f)*

application [æplɪ'keɪʃən] *n* (*request*) Antrag *m*; (*for job*) Bewerbung *f*; (*putting into practice*) Anwendung *f*; (*hard work*) Fleiß *m*; **~ form** *n* Bewerbungsformular *nt*

applied [ə'plaɪd] *adj* angewandt

apply [ə'plaɪ] *vi* (*be suitable*) zutreffen; (*ask*): **to ~ (to)** sich wenden (an +*acc*); (*request*): **to ~ for** sich melden für ♦ *vt* (*place on*) auflegen; (*cream*) auftragen; (*put into practice*) anwenden; **to ~ for sth** sich um etw bewerben; **to ~ o.s. to sth** sich bei etw anstrengen

appoint [ə'pɔɪnt] *vt* (*to office*) ernennen, berufen; (*settle*) festsetzen; **~ment** *n* (*meeting*) Verabredung *f*; (*at hairdresser etc*) Bestellung *f*; (*in business*) Termin *m*; (*choice for a position*) Ernennung *f*; (*UNIV*) Berufung *f*

appraisal [ə'preɪzl] *n* Beurteilung *f*

appreciable [ə'priːʃəbl] *adj* (*perceptible*) merklich; (*able to be estimated*) abschätzbar

appreciate [ə'priːʃɪeɪt] *vt* (*value*) zu schätzen wissen; (*understand*) einsehen ♦ *vi* (*increase in value*) im Wert steigen

appreciation [əpriːʃɪ'eɪʃən] *n* Wertschätzung *f*; (*COMM*) Wertzuwachs *m*

appreciative [ə'priːʃɪətɪv] *adj* (*showing thanks*) dankbar; (*showing liking*) anerkennend

apprehend [æprɪ'hend] *vt* (*arrest*) festnehmen; (*understand*) erfassen

apprehension [æprɪ'henʃən] *n* Angst *f*

apprehensive [æprɪ'hensɪv] *adj* furchtsam

apprentice [ə'prentɪs] *n* Lehrling *m*; **~ship** *n* Lehrzeit *f*

approach [ə'prəʊtʃ] *vi* sich nähern ♦ *vt* herantreten an +*acc*; (*problem*) herangehen an +*acc* ♦ *n* Annäherung *f*; (*to problem*) Ansatz *m*; (*path*) Zugang *m*, Zufahrt *f*; **~able** *adj* zugänglich

appropriate [*adj* ə'prəʊprɪət, *vb* ə'prəʊprɪeɪt] *adj* angemessen; (*remark*) angebracht ♦ *vt* (*take for o.s.*) sich

aneignen; (*set apart*) bereitstellen
approval [ə'pruːvəl] *n* (*show of
satisfaction*) Beifall *m*; (*permission*)
Billigung *f*; **on ~** (*COMM*) bei Gefallen
approve [ə'pruːv] *vt, vi* billigen; **I don't
~ of it/him** ich halte nichts davon/von
ihm; **~d school** (*BRIT*) *n* Erziehungsheim
nt
approximate [*adj* ə'prɒksɪmɪt, *vb*
ə'prɒksɪmeɪt] *adj* annähernd, ungefähr
♦ *vt* nahekommen +*dat*; **~ly** *adv* rund,
ungefähr
apricot ['eɪprɪkɒt] *n* Aprikose *f*
April ['eɪprəl] *n* April *m*; **~ Fools' Day** *n*
der erste April
apron ['eɪprən] *n* Schürze *f*
apt [æpt] *adj* (*suitable*) passend; (*able*)
begabt; (*likely*): **to be ~ to do sth** dazu
neigen, etw zu tun
aptitude ['æptɪtjuːd] *n* Begabung *f*
aqualung ['ækwəlʌŋ] *n*
Unterwasseratmungsgerät *nt*
aquarium [ə'kweərɪəm] *n* Aquarium *nt*
Aquarius [ə'kweərɪəs] *n* Wassermann *m*
aquatic [ə'kwætɪk] *adj* Wasser-
Arab ['ærəb] *n* Araber(in) *m(f)*
Arabia [ə'reɪbɪə] *n* Arabien *nt*
Arabian [ə'reɪbɪən] *adj* arabisch
Arabic ['ærəbɪk] *adj* arabisch ♦ *n*
Arabisch *nt*
arable ['ærəbl] *adj* bebaubar, Kultur-
arbitrary ['aːbɪtrəri] *adj* willkürlich
arbitration [aːbɪ'treɪʃən] *n* Schlichtung *f*
arc [aːk] *n* Bogen *m*
arcade [aː'keɪd] *n* Säulengang *m*
arch [aːtʃ] *n* Bogen *m* ♦ *vt* überwölben;
(*back*) krumm machen
archaeologist [aːkɪ'ɒlədʒɪst] *n*
Archäologe *m*
archaeology [aːkɪ'ɒlədʒɪ] *n* Archäologie *f*
archaic [aː'keɪɪk] *adj* altertümlich
archbishop ['aːtʃ'bɪʃəp] *n* Erzbischof *m*
archenemy ['aːtʃ'enəmɪ] *n* Erzfeind *m*
archeology [aːkɪ'ɒlədʒɪ] *etc* (*US*)
= **archaeology** *etc*
archer ['aːtʃə*] *n* Bogenschütze *m*; **~y** *n*
Bogenschießen *nt*
archipelago [aːkɪ'pelɪgəʊ] *n* Archipel *m*;
(*sea*) Inselmeer *nt*

architect ['aːkɪtekt] *n* Architekt(in) *m(f)*;
~ural [aːkɪ'tektʃərəl] *adj* architektonisch;
~ure ['aːkɪtektʃə*] *n* Architektur *f*
archives ['aːkaɪvz] *npl* Archiv *nt*
archway ['aːtʃweɪ] *n* Bogen *m*
Arctic ['aːktɪk] *adj* arktisch ♦ *n*: **the ~**
die Arktis
ardent ['aːdənt] *adj* glühend
arduous ['aːdjuəs] *adj* mühsam
are [aː*] *see* be
area ['eərɪə] *n* Fläche *f*; (*of land*) Gebiet
nt; (*part of sth*) Teil *m*, Abschnitt *m*
arena [ə'riːnə] *n* Arena *f*
aren't [aːnt] = **are not**
Argentina [aːdʒən'tiːnə] *n* Argentinien
nt
Argentinian [aːdʒən'tɪnɪən] *adj*
argentinisch ♦ *n* Argentinier(in) *m(f)*
arguably ['aːgjʊəblɪ] *adv* wohl
argue ['aːgjuː] *vi* diskutieren; (*angrily*)
streiten
argument ['aːgjʊmənt] *n* (*theory*)
Argument *nt*; (*reasoning*) Argumentation
f; (*row*) Auseinandersetzung *f*, Streit *m*;
to have an ~ sich streiten; **~ative**
[aːgjʊ'mentətɪv] *adj* streitlustig
aria ['aːrɪə] *n* Arie *f*
arid ['ærɪd] *adj* trocken
Aries ['eərɪːz] *n* Widder *m*
arise [ə'raɪz] (*pt* arose, *pp* arisen) *vi*
aufsteigen; (*get up*) aufstehen; (*difficulties
etc*) entstehen; (*case*) vorkommen; **to ~
from sth** herrühren von etw; **arisen**
[ə'rɪzn] *pp* of **arise**
aristocracy [ærɪs'tɒkrəsɪ] *n* Adel *m*,
Aristokratie *f*
aristocrat ['ærɪstəkræt] *n* Adlige(r) *mf*,
Aristokrat(in) *m(f)*
arithmetic [ə'rɪθmətɪk] *n* Rechnen *nt*,
Arithmetik *f*
ark [aːk] *n*: **Noah's A~** die Arche Noah
arm [aːm] *n* Arm *m*; (*branch of military
service*) Zweig *m* ♦ *vt* bewaffnen; **~s** *npl*
(*weapons*) Waffen *pl*
armaments ['aːməmənts] *npl*
Ausrüstung *f*
armchair *n* Lehnstuhl *m*
armed *adj* (*forces*) Streit-, bewaffnet; **~
robbery** *n* bewaffnete(r) Raubüberfall *m*

armistice ['ɑːmɪstɪs] *n* Waffenstillstand *m*

armour ['ɑːmə*] (*US* **armor**) *n* (*knight's*) Rüstung *f*; (*MIL*) Panzerplatte *f*; **~ed car** *n* Panzerwagen *m*; **~y** *n* Waffenlager *nt*; (*factory*) Waffenfabrik *f*

armpit ['ɑːmpɪt] *n* Achselhöhle *f*

armrest ['ɑːmrest] *n* Armlehne *f*

army ['ɑːmɪ] *n* Armee *f*, Heer *nt*; (*host*) Heer *nt*

aroma [ə'rəʊmə] *n* Duft *m*, Aroma *nt*; **~therapy** *n* Aromatherapie *f*; **~tic** [ærə'mætɪk] *adj* aromatisch, würzig

arose [ə'rəʊz] *pt of* **arise**

around [ə'raʊnd] *adv* ringsherum; (*almost*) ungefähr ♦ *prep* um ... herum; **is he ~?** ist er hier?

arouse [ə'raʊz] *vt* wecken

arrange [ə'reɪndʒ] *vt* (*time, meeting*) festsetzen; (*holidays*) festlegen; (*flowers, hair, objects*) anordnen; **I ~d to meet him** ich habe mit ihm ausgemacht, ihn zu treffen; **it's all ~d** es ist alles arrangiert; **~ment** *n* (*order*) Reihenfolge *f*; (*agreement*) Vereinbarung *f*, **~ments** *npl* (*plans*) Pläne *pl*

array [ə'reɪ] *n* (*collection*) Ansammlung *f*

arrears [ə'rɪəz] *npl* (*of debts*) Rückstand *m*; (*of work*) Unerledigte(s) *nt*; **in ~** im Rückstand

arrest [ə'rest] *vt* (*person*) verhaften; (*stop*) aufhalten ♦ *n* Verhaftung *f*; **under ~** in Haft

arrival [ə'raɪvəl] *n* Ankunft *f*

arrive [ə'raɪv] *vi* ankommen; **to ~ at** ankommen in +*dat*, ankommen bei

arrogance ['ærəgəns] *n* Überheblichkeit *f*, Arroganz *f*

arrogant ['ærəgənt] *adj* überheblich, arrogant

arrow ['ærəʊ] *n* Pfeil *m*

arse [ɑːs] (*inf!*) *n* Arsch *m* (*!*)

arsenal ['ɑːsɪnl] *n* Waffenlager *nt*, Zeughaus *nt*

arsenic ['ɑːsnɪk] *n* Arsen *nt*

arson ['ɑːsn] *n* Brandstiftung *f*

art [ɑːt] *n* Kunst *f*, **A~s** *npl* (*UNIV*) Geisteswissenschaften *pl*

artery ['ɑːtərɪ] *n* Schlagader *f*, Arterie *f*

artful ['ɑːtfʊl] *adj* verschlagen

art gallery *n* Kunstgalerie *f*

arthritis [ɑː'θraɪtɪs] *n* Arthritis *f*

artichoke ['ɑːtɪtʃəʊk] *n* Artischocke *f*; **Jerusalem ~** Erdartischocke *f*

article ['ɑːtɪkl] *n* (*PRESS, GRAM*) Artikel *m*; (*thing*) Gegenstand *m*, Artikel *m*; (*clause*) Abschnitt *m*, Paragraph *m*; **~ of clothing** Kleidungsstück *nt*

articulate [*adj* ɑː'tɪkjʊlɪt, *vb* ɑː'tɪkjʊleɪt] *adj* (*able to express o.s.*) redegewandt; (*speaking clearly*) deutlich, verständlich ♦ *vt* (*connect*) zusammenfügen, gliedern; **to be ~** sich gut ausdrücken können; **~d vehicle** *n* Sattelschlepper *m*

artificial [ɑːtɪ'fɪʃəl] *adj* künstlich, Kunst-; **~ respiration** [respɪ'reɪʃən] *n* künstliche Atmung *f*

artisan ['ɑːtɪzæn] *n* gelernte(r) Handwerker *m*

artist ['ɑːtɪst] *n* Künstler(in) *m(f)*; **~ic** [ɑː'tɪstɪk] *adj* künstlerisch; **~ry** *n* künstlerische(s) Können *nt*

artless ['ɑːtlɪs] *adj* ungekünstelt; (*character*) arglos

art school *n* Kunsthochschule *f*

KEYWORD

as [æz] *conj* **1** (*referring to time*) als; **as the years went by** mit den Jahren; **he came in as I was leaving** als er hereinkam, ging ich gerade; **as from tomorrow** ab morgen

2 (*in comparisons*): **as big as** so groß wie; **twice as big as** zweimal so groß wie; **as much/many as** soviel/so viele wie; **as soon as** sobald

3 (*since, because*) da; **he left early as he had to be home by 10** er ging früher, da er um 10 zu Hause sein mußte

4 (*referring to manner, way*) wie; **do as you wish** mach was du willst; **as she said** wie sie sagte

5 (*concerning*): **as for** *or* **to that** was das betrifft *or* angeht

6: **as if** *or* **though** als ob

♦ *prep* als; *see also* **long**; **he works as a driver** er arbeitet als Fahrer; *see also* **such**; **he gave it to me as a present** er hat es mir als Geschenk gegeben; *see also* **well**

a.s.a.p. *abbr* = **as soon as possible**
ascend [ə'sɛnd] *vi* aufsteigen ♦ *vt* besteigen; ~**ancy** *n* Oberhand *f*
ascent [ə'sɛnt] *n* Aufstieg *m*; Besteigung *f*
ascertain [æsə'teɪn] *vt* feststellen
ascribe [əs'kraɪb] *vt*: **to ~ sth to sth/sb** to sb etw einer Sache/jdm etw zuschreiben
ash [æʃ] *n* Asche *f*; (*tree*) Esche *f*
ashamed [ə'ʃeɪmd] *adj* beschämt; **to be ~ of sth** sich für etw schämen
ashen ['æʃən] *adj* (*pale*) aschfahl
ashore [ə'ʃɔː*] *adv* an Land
ashtray ['æʃtreɪ] *n* Aschenbecher *m*
Ash Wednesday *n* Aschermittwoch *m*
Asia ['eɪʃə] *n* Asien *nt*; ~**n** *adj* asiatisch ♦ *n* Asiat(in) *m(f)*
aside [ə'saɪd] *adv* beiseite ♦ *n* beiseite gesprochene Worte *pl*
ask [ɑːsk] *vt* fragen; (*permission*) bitten um; ~ **him his name** frage ihn nach seinem Namen; **he ~ed to see you** er wollte dich sehen; **to ~ sb to do sth** jdn bitten, etw zu tun; **to ~ sb about sth** jdn nach etw fragen; **to ~ (sb) a question** jdn etwas fragen; **to ~ sb out to dinner** jdn zum Essen einladen; ~ **after** *vt fus* fragen nach; ~ **for** *vt fus* bitten um
askance [əs'kɑːns] *adv*: **to look ~ at sb** jdn schief ansehen
askew [əs'kjuː] *adv* schief
asking price ['ɑːskɪŋ-] *n* Verkaufspreis *m*
asleep [ə'sliːp] *adj*: **to be ~** schlafen; **to fall ~** einschlafen
asparagus [əs'pærəgəs] *n* Spargel *m*
aspect ['æspɛkt] *n* Aspekt *m*
aspersions [əs'pɜːʃənz] *npl*: **to cast ~ on sb/sth** sich abfällig über jdn/etw äußern
asphyxiation [əsfɪksɪ'eɪʃən] *n* Erstickung *f*
aspirations [æspə'reɪʃənz] *npl*: **to have ~ towards sth** etw anstreben
aspire [əs'paɪə*] *vi*: **to ~ to** streben nach
aspirin ['æsprɪn] *n* Aspirin *nt*

ass [æs] *n* (*also fig*) Esel *m*; (*US: inf!*) Arsch *m* (*!*)
assailant [ə'seɪlənt] *n* Angreifer *m*
assassin [ə'sæsɪn] *n* Attentäter(in) *m(f)*; ~**ate** [ə'sæsɪneɪt] *vt* ermorden
assassination [əsæsɪ'neɪʃən] *n* (geglückte(s)) Attentat *nt*
assault [ə'sɔːlt] *n* Angriff *m* ♦ *vt* überfallen; (*woman*) herfallen über +*acc*
assemble [ə'sɛmbl] *vt* versammeln; (*parts*) zusammensetzen ♦ *vi* sich versammeln
assembly [ə'sɛmblɪ] *n* (*meeting*) Versammlung *f*; (*construction*) Zusammensetzung *f*, Montage *f*; ~ **line** *n* Fließband *nt*
assent [ə'sɛnt] *n* Zustimmung *f*
assert [ə'sɜːt] *vt* erklären; ~**ion** [ə'sɜːʃən] *n* Behauptung *f*
assess [ə'sɛs] *vt* schätzen; ~**ment** *n* Bewertung *f*, Einschätzung *f*; ~**or** *n* Steuerberater *m*
asset ['æsɛt] *n* Vorteil *m*, Wert *m*; ~**s** *npl* (*FIN*) Vermögen *nt*; (*estate*) Nachlaß *m*
assiduous [ə'sɪdjʊəs] *adj* fleißig, aufmerksam
assign [ə'saɪn] *vt* zuweisen
assignment [ə'saɪnmənt] *n* Aufgabe *f*, Auftrag *m*
assimilate [ə'sɪmɪleɪt] *vt* sich aneignen, aufnehmen
assist [ə'sɪst] *vt* beistehen +*dat*; ~**ance** *n* Unterstützung *f*, Hilfe *f*; ~**ant** *n* Assistent(in) *m(f)*, Mitarbeiter(in) *m(f)*; (*BRIT: also: shop ~ant*) Verkäufer(in) *m(f)*
assizes [ə'saɪzɪz] *npl* Landgericht *nt*
associate [*n* ə'səʊʃɪɪt, *vb* ə'səʊʃɪeɪt] *n* (*partner*) Kollege *m*, Teilhaber *m*; (*member*) außerordentliche(s) Mitglied *nt* ♦ *vt* verbinden ♦ *vi* (*keep company*) verkehren
association [əsəʊsɪ'eɪʃən] *n* Verband *m*, Verein *m*; (*PSYCH*) Assoziation *f*; (*link*) Verbindung *f*
assorted [ə'sɔːtɪd] *adj* gemischt
assortment [ə'sɔːtmənt] *n* Sammlung *f*; (*COMM*): ~ **(of)** Sortiment *nt* (von), Auswahl *f* (an +*dat*)
assume [ə'sjuːm] *vt* (*take for granted*)

annehmen; (*put on*) annehmen, sich
geben; ~**d name** n Deckname m
assumption [ə'sʌmpʃən] n Annahme f
assurance [ə'ʃʊərəns] n (*firm statement*)
Versicherung f; (*confidence*)
Selbstsicherheit f; (*insurance*)
(Lebens)versicherung f
assure [ə'ʃʊə*] vt (*make sure*)
sicherstellen; (*convince*) versichern +dat;
(*life*) versichern
asterisk ['æstərɪsk] n Sternchen nt
astern [əs'tɜːn] adv achtern
asthma ['æsmə] n Asthma nt
astonish [əs'tɒnɪʃ] vt erstaunen; ~**ment**
n Erstaunen nt
astound [əs'taʊnd] vt verblüffen
astray [əs'treɪ] adv in die Irre; auf
Abwege; **to go ~** (*go wrong*) sich vertun;
to lead ~ irreführen
astride [əs'traɪd] adv rittlings ♦ prep
rittlings auf
astrologer [əs'trɒlədʒə*] n Astrologe m,
Astrologin f
astrology [əs'trɒlədʒɪ] n Astrologie f
astronaut ['æstrənɔːt] n Astronaut(in)
m(f)
astronomer [əs'trɒnəmə*] n Astronom
m
astronomical [æstrə'nɒmɪkəl] adj
astronomisch; (*success*) riesig
astronomy [əs'trɒnəmɪ] n Astronomie f
astute [əs'tjuːt] adj scharfsinnig; schlau,
gerissen
asylum [ə'saɪləm] n (*home*) Heim nt;
(*refuge*) Asyl nt

KEYWORD

at [æt] prep 1 (*referring to position,
direction*) an +dat, bei +dat; (*with place*)
in +dat; **at the top** an der Spitze; **at
home/school** zu Hause/in der Schule; **at
the baker's** beim Bäcker; **to look at sth**
auf etw acc blicken; **to throw sth at sb**
etw nach jdm werfen
2 (*referring to time*): **at 4 o'clock** um 4
Uhr; **at night** bei Nacht; **at Christmas**
zu Weihnachten; **at times** manchmal
3 (*referring to rates, speed etc*): **at £1 a
kilo** zu £1 pro Kilo; **two at a time** zwei

auf einmal; **at 50 km/h** mit 50 km/h
4 (*referring to manner*): **at a stroke** mit
einem Schlag; **at peace** in Frieden
5 (*referring to activity*): **to be at work** bei
der Arbeit sein; **to play at cowboys**
Cowboy spielen; **to be good at sth** gut in
etw dat sein
6 (*referring to cause*): **shocked/
surprised/annoyed at sth** schockiert/
überrascht/verärgert über etw acc; **I
went at his suggestion** ich ging auf
seinen Vorschlag hin

ate [et, eɪt] pt of **eat**
atheist ['eɪθɪɪst] n Atheist(in) m(f)
Athens ['æθɪnz] n Athen nt
athlete ['æθliːt] n Athlet m, Sportler m
athletic [æθ'letɪk] adj sportlich,
athletisch; ~**s** n Leichtathletik f
Atlantic [ət'læntɪk] adj atlantisch ♦ n:
the ~ (Ocean) der Atlantik
atmosphere ['ætməsfɪə*] n Atmosphäre
f
atom ['ætəm] n Atom nt; (*fig*) bißchen nt;
~**ic** [ə'tɒmɪk] adj atomar, Atom-; ~**(ic)
bomb** n Atombombe f; ~**izer**
['ætəmaɪzə*] n Zerstäuber m
atone [ə'təʊn] vi sühnen; **to ~ for sth**
etw sühnen
atrocious [ə'trəʊʃəs] adj gräßlich
atrocity [ə'trɒsɪtɪ] n Scheußlichkeit f;
(*deed*) Greueltat f
attach [ə'tætʃ] vt (*fasten*) befestigen; **to
be ~ed to sb/sth** an jdm/etw hängen; **to
~ importance etc to sth** Wichtigkeit etc
auf etw acc legen, einer Sache dat
Wichtigkeit etc beimessen
attaché case [ə'tæʃeɪ-] n Aktenkoffer m
attachment [ə'tætʃmənt] n (*tool*)
Zubehörteil nt; (*love*): ~ **(to sb)** Zuneigung
f (zu jdm)
attack [ə'tæk] vt angreifen ♦ n Angriff m;
(*MED*) Anfall m; ~**er** n Angreifer(in) m(f)
attain [ə'teɪn] vt erreichen; ~**ments** npl
Kenntnisse pl
attempt [ə'tempt] n Versuch m ♦ vt
versuchen; ~**ed murder** Mordversuch m
attend [ə'tend] vt (*go to*) teilnehmen (an
+dat); (*lectures*) besuchen; **to ~ to** (*needs*)

nachkommen +*dat*; (*person*) sich kümmern um; ~ance *n* (*presence*) Anwesenheit *f*; (*people present*) Besucherzahl *f*; good ~ance gute Teilnahme; ~ant *n* (*companion*) Begleiter(in) *m(f)*; Gesellschafter(in) *m(f)*; (*in car park etc*) Wächter(in) *m(f)*; (*servant*) Bedienstete(r) *mf* ♦ *adj* begleitend; (*fig*) damit verbunden

attention [ə'tenʃən] *n* Aufmerksamkeit *f*; (*care*) Fürsorge *f*; (*for machine etc*) Pflege *f* ♦ *excl* (*MIL*) Achtung!; for the ~ of ... zu Händen (von) ...

attentive [ə'tentɪv] *adj* aufmerksam

attest [ə'test] *vi*: to ~ to sich verbürgen für

attic ['ætɪk] *n* Dachstube *f*, Mansarde *f*

attitude ['ætɪtjuːd] *n* (*mental*) Einstellung *f*

attorney [ə'tɜːnɪ] *n* (*solicitor*) Rechtsanwalt *m*; A~ General *n* Justizminister *m*

attract [ə'trækt] *vt* anziehen; (*attention*) erregen; ~ion [ə'trækʃən] *n* Anziehungskraft *f*; (*thing*) Attraktion *f*; ~ive *adj* attraktiv

attribute [*n* 'ætrɪbjuːt, *vb* ə'trɪbjuːt] *n* Eigenschaft *f*, Attribut *nt* ♦ *vt* zuschreiben

attrition [ə'trɪʃən] *n*: war of ~ Zermürbungskrieg *m*

aubergine ['əʊbəʒiːn] *n* Aubergine *f*

auburn ['ɔːbən] *adj* kastanienbraun

auction ['ɔːkʃən] *n* (*also: sale by ~*) Versteigerung *f*, Auktion *f* ♦ *vt* versteigern; ~eer [ɔːkʃə'nɪə*] *n* Versteigerer *m*

audacity [ɔː'dæsɪtɪ] *n* (*boldness*) Wagemut *m*; (*impudence*) Unverfrorenheit *f*

audible ['ɔːdɪbl] *adj* hörbar

audience ['ɔːdɪəns] *n* Zuhörer *pl*, Zuschauer *pl*; (*with king etc*) Audienz *f*

audiotypist ['ɔːdɪəʊ'taɪpɪst] *n* Phonotypistin *f*

audiovisual ['ɔːdɪəʊ'vɪzjʊəl] *adj* audiovisuell

audit ['ɔːdɪt] *vt* prüfen

audition [ɔː'dɪʃən] *n* Probe *f*

auditor ['ɔːdɪtə*] *n* (*accountant*) Rechnungsprüfer(in) *m(f)*, Buchprüfer *m*

auditorium [ɔːdɪ'tɔːrɪəm] *n* Zuschauerraum *m*

augment [ɔːg'ment] *vt* vermehren

augur ['ɔːgə*] *vi* bedeuten, voraussagen; this ~s well das ist ein gutes Omen

August ['ɔːgəst] *n* August *m*

aunt [ɑːnt] *n* Tante *f*; ~ie *n* Tantchen *nt*; ~y *n* = auntie

au pair ['əʊ'peə*] *n* (*also: ~ girl*) Aupair-Mädchen *nt*

aura ['ɔːrə] *n* Nimbus *m*

auspices ['ɔːspɪsɪz] *npl*: under the ~ of unter der Schirmherrschaft von

auspicious [ɔːs'pɪʃəs] *adj* günstig; verheißungsvoll

austere [ɒs'tɪə*] *adj* streng; (*room*) nüchtern

austerity [ɒs'terɪtɪ] *n* Strenge *f*; (*POL*) wirtschaftliche Einschränkung *f*

Australia [ɒs'treɪlɪə] *n* Australien *nt*; ~n *adj* australisch ♦ *n* Australier(in) *m(f)*

Austria ['ɒstrɪə] *n* Österreich *nt*; ~n *adj* österreichisch ♦ *n* Österreicher(in) *m(f)*

authentic [ɔː'θentɪk] *adj* echt, authentisch

author ['ɔːθə*] *n* Autor *m*, Schriftsteller *m*; (*beginner*) Urheber *m*, Schöpfer *m*

authoritarian [ɔːθɒrɪ'teərɪən] *adj* autoritär

authoritative [ɔː'θɒrɪtətɪv] *adj* (*account*) maßgeblich; (*manner*) herrisch

authority [ɔː'θɒrɪtɪ] *n* (*power*) Autorität *f*; (*expert*) Autorität *f*, Fachmann *m*; the authorities *npl* (*ruling body*) die Behörden *pl*

authorize ['ɔːθəraɪz] *vt* bevollmächtigen; (*permit*) genehmigen

auto ['ɔːtəʊ] *n* (*US*) Auto *nt*, Wagen *m*

autobiography [ɔːtəʊbaɪ'ɒɡrəfɪ] *n* Autobiographie *f*

autograph ['ɔːtəɡrɑːf] *n* (*of celebrity*) Autogramm *nt* ♦ *vt* mit Autogramm versehen

automatic [ɔːtə'mætɪk] *adj* automatisch ♦ *n* (*gun*) Selbstladepistole *f*; (*car*) Automatik *m*; ~ally *adv* automatisch

automation [ɔːtə'meɪʃən] *n*

Automatisierung *f*

automobile ['ɔːtəməbiːl] (*US*) *n* Auto(mobil) *nt*

autonomous [ɔː'tɒnəməs] *adj* autonom

autumn ['ɔːtəm] *n* Herbst *m*

auxiliary [ɔːg'zɪlɪərɪ] *adj* Hilfs-

Av. *abbr* = **avenue**

avail [ə'veɪl] *vt*: **to ~ o.s. of sth** sich einer Sache *gen* bedienen ♦ *n*: **to no ~** nutzlos

availability [əveɪlə'bɪlɪtɪ] *n* Erhältlichkeit *f*, Vorhandensein *nt*

available [ə'veɪləbl] *adj* erhältlich; zur Verfügung stehend; (*person*) erreichbar, abkömmlich

avalanche ['ævəlɑːnʃ] *n* Lawine *f*

avarice ['ævərɪs] *n* Habsucht *f*, Geiz *m*

Ave. *abbr* = **avenue**

avenge [ə'vendʒ] *vt* rächen, sühnen

avenue ['ævənjuː] *n* Allee *f*

average ['ævərɪdʒ] *n* Durchschnitt *m* ♦ *adj* durchschnittlich, Durchschnitts- ♦ *vt* (*figures*) den Durchschnitt nehmen von; (*perform*) durchschnittlich leisten; (*in car etc*) im Schnitt fahren; **on ~** durchschnittlich, im Durchschnitt; **~ out** *vi*: **to ~ out at** im Durchschnitt betragen

averse [ə'vɜːs] *adj*: **to be ~ to doing sth** eine Abneigung dagegen haben, etw zu tun

avert [ə'vɜːt] *vt* (*turn away*) abkehren; (*prevent*) abwehren

aviary ['eɪvɪərɪ] *n* Vogelhaus *nt*

aviation [eɪvɪ'eɪʃən] *n* Luftfahrt *f*, Flugwesen *nt*

avid ['ævɪd] *adj*: **~ (for)** gierig (auf +*acc*)

avocado [ævə'kɑːdəʊ] *n* (*also*: *BRIT*: **~ pear**) Avocado(birne) *f*

avoid [ə'vɔɪd] *vt* vermeiden

await [ə'weɪt] *vt* erwarten, entgegensehen +*dat*

awake [ə'weɪk] (*pt* awoke, *pp* awoken *or* awaked) *adj* wach ♦ *vt* (auf)wecken ♦ *vi* aufwachen; **to be ~** wach sein; **~ning** *n* Erwachen *nt*

award [ə'wɔːd] *n* (*prize*) Preis *m* ♦ *vt*: **to ~ (sb sth)** (jdm etw) zuerkennen

aware [ə'wɛə*] *adj* bewußt; **to be ~** sich bewußt sein; **~ness** *n* Bewußtsein *nt*

awash [ə'wɒʃ] *adj* überflutet

away [ə'weɪ] *adv* weg, fort; **two hours ~ by car** zwei Autostunden entfernt; **the holiday was two weeks ~** es war noch zwei Wochen bis zum Urlaub; **two kilometres ~** zwei Kilometer entfernt; **~ match** *n* (*SPORT*) Auswärtsspiel *nt*

awe [ɔː] *n* Ehrfurcht *f*; **~-inspiring** *adj* ehrfurchtgebietend; **~some** *adj* ehrfurchtgebietend

awful ['ɔːfʊl] *adj* (*very bad*) furchtbar; **~ly** *adv* furchtbar, sehr

awhile [ə'waɪl] *adv* eine Weile

awkward ['ɔːkwəd] *adj* (*clumsy*) ungeschickt, linkisch; (*embarrassing*) peinlich

awning ['ɔːnɪŋ] *n* Markise *f*

awoke [ə'wəʊk] *pt of* awake; **awoken** [ə'wəʊkən] *pp of* awake

awry [ə'raɪ] *adv* schief; **to go ~** (*person*) fehlgehen; (*plans*) schiefgehen

axe [æks] (*US* **ax**) *n* Axt *f*, Beil *nt* ♦ *vt* (*end suddenly*) streichen

axes[1] ['æksɪz] *npl of* **axe**

axes[2] ['æksiːz] *npl of* **axis**

axis ['æksɪs] (*pl* **axes**) *n* Achse *f*

axle ['æksl] *n* Achse *f*

ay(e) [aɪ] *excl* (*yes*) ja

azalea [ə'zeɪlɪə] *n* Azalee *f*

B b

B [biː] *n* (*MUS*) H *nt*

B.A. *n abbr* = **Bachelor of Arts**

babble ['bæbl] *vi* schwätzen; (*stream*) murmeln

baby ['beɪbɪ] *n* Baby *nt*; **~ carriage** (*US*) *n* Kinderwagen *m*; **~-sit** *vi* Kinder hüten, babysitten; **~-sitter** *n* Babysitter *m*

bachelor ['bætʃələ*] *n* Junggeselle *m*; **B~ of Arts** Bakkalaureus *m* der philosophischen Fakultät; **B~ of Science** Bakkalaureus *m* der Naturwissenschaften

back [bæk] *n* (*of person, horse*) Rücken *m*; (*of house*) Rückseite *f*; (*of train*) Ende *nt*; (*FOOTBALL*) Verteidiger *m* ♦ *vt* (*support*) unterstützen; (*wager*) wetten auf +*acc*; (*car*) rückwärts fahren ♦ *vi* (*go*

backwards) rückwärts gehen *or* fahren
♦ *adj* hintere(r, s) ♦ *adv* zurück; (*to the
rear*) nach hinten; ~ **down** *vi*
zurückstecken; ~ **out** *vi* sich
zurückziehen; (*inf*) kneifen; ~ **up** *vt*
(*support*) unterstützen; (*car*) zurücksetzen; (*COMPUT*) eine Sicherungskopie machen
von; ~**bencher** (*BRIT*) *n*
Parlamentarier(in) *m(f)*; ~**bone** *n*
Rückgrat *nt*; (*support*) Rückhalt *m*;
~**cloth** *n* Hintergrund *m*; ~**date** *vt*
rückdatieren; ~**drop** *n* (*THEAT*)
= **backcloth**; (*background*) Hintergrund
m; ~**fire** *vi* (*plan*) fehlschlagen; (*TECH*)
fehlzünden; ~**ground** *n* Hintergrund *m*;
(*person's education*) Vorbildung *f*; **family
~ground** Familienverhältnisse *pl*; ~**hand**
n (*TENNIS*: *also*: ~**hand stroke**) Rückhand *f*;
~**hander** (*BRIT*) *n* (*bribe*) Schmiergeld *nt*;
~**ing** *n* (*support*) Unterstützung *f*; ~**lash**
n (*fig*) Gegenschlag *m*; ~**log** *n* (*of work*)
Rückstand *m*; ~ **number** *n* (*PRESS*) alte
Nummer *f*; ~**pack** *n* Rucksack *m*; ~ **pay**
n (*Gehalts- or Lohn*)nachzahlung *f*; ~
payments *npl* Zahlungsrückstände *pl*; ~
seat *n* (*AUT*) Rücksitz *m*; ~**side** (*inf*) *n*
Hintern *m*; ~**stage** *adv* hinter den
Kulissen; ~**stroke** *n* Rückenschwimmen
nt; ~**up** *adj* (*train*) Zusatz-; (*plane*)
Sonder-; (*COMPUT*) Sicherungs- ♦ *n* (*see
adj*) Zusatzzug *m*; Sondermaschine *f*;
Sicherungskopie *f*; ~**ward** *adj* (*less
developed*) zurückgeblieben; (*primitive*)
rückständig; ~**wards** *adv* rückwärts;
~**water** *n* (*fig*) Kaff *nt*; ~**yard** *n*
Hinterhof *m*

bacon ['beɪkən] *n* Schinkenspeck *m*
bacteria [bæk'tɪərɪə] *npl* Bakterien *pl*
bad [bæd] *adj* schlecht, schlimm; **to go ~**
schlecht werden
bade [bæd] *pt of* **bid**
badge [bædʒ] *n* Abzeichen *nt*
badger ['bædʒə*] *n* Dachs *m*
badly ['bædlɪ] *adv* schlecht, schlimm; ~
wounded schwerverwundet; **he needs it
~** er braucht es dringend; **to be ~ off** (*for
money*) dringend Geld nötig haben
badminton ['bædmɪntən] *n* Federball *m*,
Badminton *nt*

bad-tempered ['bæd'tempəd] *adj*
schlecht gelaunt
baffle ['bæfl] *vt* (*puzzle*) verblüffen
bag [bæg] *n* (*sack*) Beutel *m*; (*paper*) Tüte
f; (*hand~*) Tasche *f*; (*suitcase*) Koffer *m*;
(*booty*) Jagdbeute *f*; (*inf*: *old woman*) alte
Schachtel *f* ♦ *vt* (*put in sack*) in einen
Sack stecken; (*hunting*) erlegen; ~**s of**
(*inf*: *lots of*) eine Menge +*acc*; ~**gage**
['bægɪdʒ] *n* Gepäck *nt*; ~**gy** ['bægɪ] *adj*
bauschig, sackartig; ~**pipes** ['bægpaɪps]
npl Dudelsack *m*
Bahamas [bə'hɑːməz] *npl*: **the ~** die
Bahamas *pl*
bail [beɪl] *n* (*money*) Kaution *f* ♦ *vt*
(*prisoner*: *usu*: *grant ~ to*) gegen Kaution
freilassen; (*boat*: *also*: ~ **out**) ausschöpfen;
on ~ (*prisoner*) gegen Kaution
freigelassen; **to ~ sb out** die Kaution für
jdn stellen; *see also* **bale**
bailiff ['beɪlɪf] *n* Gerichtsvollzieher(in)
m(f)
bait [beɪt] *n* Köder *m* ♦ *vt* mit einem
Köder versehen; (*fig*) ködern
bake [beɪk] *vt*, *vi* backen; ~**d beans**
gebackene Bohnen *pl*; ~**r** *n* Bäcker *m*; ~**ry**
n Bäckerei *f*
baking ['beɪkɪŋ] *n* Backen *nt*; ~ **powder**
n Backpulver *nt*
balance ['bæləns] *n* (*scales*) Waage *f*;
(*equilibrium*) Gleichgewicht *nt*; (*FIN*: *state
of account*) Saldo *m*; (*difference*) Bilanz *f*;
(*amount remaining*) Restbetrag *m* ♦ *vt*
(*weigh*) wägen; (*make equal*) ausgleichen;
~ **of trade/payments** Handels-/Zahlungs-
bilanz *f*; ~**d** *adj* ausgeglichen; ~ **sheet** *n*
Bilanz *f*, Rechnungsabschluß *m*
balcony ['bælkənɪ] *n* Balkon *m*
bald [bɔːld] *adj* kahl; (*statement*) knapp
bale [beɪl] *n* Ballen *m*; ~ **out** *vi* (*from a
plane*) abspringen
ball [bɔːl] *n* Ball *m*; ~ **bearing** *n*
Kugellager *nt*
ballet ['bæleɪ] *n* Ballett *nt*; ~ **dancer** *n*
Ballettänzer(in) *m(f)*
balloon [bə'luːn] *n* (*Luft*)ballon *m*
ballot ['bælət] *n* (*geheime*) Abstimmung *f*
ballpoint (pen) ['bɔːlpɔɪnt-] *n*
Kugelschreiber *m*

ballroom ['bɔːlrʊm] *n* Tanzsaal *m*
Baltic ['bɔːltɪk] *n*: **the ~ (Sea)** die Ostsee
bamboo [bæm'buː] *n* Bambus *m*
ban [bæn] *n* Verbot *nt* ♦ *vt* verbieten
banana [bə'nɑːnə] *n* Banane *f*
band [bænd] *n* Band *nt*; (*group*) Gruppe *f*;
(*of criminals*) Bande *f*; (MUS) Kapelle *f*,
Band *f*; **~ together** *vi* sich zusammentun
bandage ['bændɪdʒ] *n* Verband *m*;
(*elastic*) Bandage *f* ♦ *vt* (*cut*) verbinden;
(*broken limb*) bandagieren
Bandaid ['bændeɪd] (® US) *n* Heftpflaster
nt
bandwagon ['bændwægən] *n*: **to jump**
on the ~ (*fig*) auf den fahrenden Zug
aufspringen
bandy ['bændɪ] *vt* wechseln; **~-legged**
['bændɪ'legɪd] *adj* o-beinig
bang [bæŋ] *n* (*explosion*) Knall *m*; (*blow*)
Hieb *m* ♦ *vt, vi* knallen
Bangladesh [bæŋglə'deʃ] *n* Bangladesch
nt
bangle ['bæŋgl] *n* Armspange *f*
bangs [bæŋz] (US) *npl* (*fringe*) Pony *m*
banish ['bænɪʃ] *vt* verbannen
banister(s) ['bænɪstə(z)] *n(pl)*
(Treppen)geländer *nt*
bank [bæŋk] *n* (*raised ground*) Erdwall *m*;
(*of lake etc*) Ufer *nt*; (FIN) Bank *f* ♦ *vt* (*tilt:*
AVIAT) in die Kurve bringen; (*money*)
einzahlen; **~ on** *vt fus*: **to ~ on sth** mit
etw rechnen; **~ account** *n* Bankkonto *nt*;
~ card *n* Scheckkarte *f*; **~er** *n* Bankier
m; **~er's card** (BRIT) *n* = **bank card**; **B~**
holiday (BRIT) *n* gesetzliche(r) Feiertag *m*;
~ing *n* Bankwesen *nt*; **~note** *n* Banknote
f; **~ rate** *n* Banksatz *m*
bank statement *n* Kontoauszug *m*
banner ['bænə*] *n* Banner *nt*
banns [bænz] *npl* Aufgebot *nt*
baptism ['bæptɪzəm] *n* Taufe *f*
baptize [bæp'taɪz] *vt* taufen
bar [bɑː*] *n* (*rod*) Stange *f*; (*obstacle*)
Hindernis *nt*; (*of chocolate*) Tafel *f*; (*of*
soap) Stück *nt*; (*for food, drink*) Buffet *nt*,
Bar *f*; (*pub*) Wirtschaft *f*; (MUS)

Takt(strich) *m* ♦ *vt* (*fasten*) verriegeln;
(*hinder*) versperren; (*exclude*)
ausschließen; **behind ~s** hinter Gittern;
the B~: to be called to the B~ als
Anwalt zugelassen werden; **~ none** ohne
Ausnahme
barbaric [bɑː'bærɪk] *adj* primitiv,
unkultiviert
barbecue ['bɑːbɪkjuː] *n* Barbecue *nt*
barbed wire ['bɑːbd-] *n* Stacheldraht *m*
barber ['bɑːbə*] *n* Herrenfriseur *m*
bar code *n* (*on goods*) Registrierkode *f*
bare [bɛə*] *adj* nackt; (*trees, country*)
kahl; (*mere*) bloß ♦ *vt* entblößen; **~back**
adv ungesattelt; **~faced** *adj* unverfroren;
~foot *adj, adv* barfuß; **~ly** *adv* kaum,
knapp
bargain ['bɑːgɪn] *n* (*sth cheap*) günstiger
Kauf; (*agreement: written*) Kaufvertrag *m*;
(: *oral*) Geschäft *nt*; **into the ~** obendrein;
~ for *vt*: **he got more than he ~ed for**
er erlebte sein blaues Wunder
barge [bɑːdʒ] *n* Lastkahn *m*; **~ in** *vi*
hereinplatzen; **~ into** *vt* rennen gegen
bark [bɑːk] *n* (*of tree*) Rinde *f*; (*of dog*)
Bellen *nt* ♦ *vi* (*dog*) bellen
barley ['bɑːlɪ] *n* Gerste *f*; **~ sugar** *n*
Malzbonbon *nt*
barmaid ['bɑːmeɪd] *n* Bardame *f*
barman ['bɑːmən] (*irreg*) *n* Barkellner *m*
barn [bɑːn] *n* Scheune *f*
barometer [bə'rɒmɪtə*] *n* Barometer *nt*
baron ['bærən] *n* Baron *m*; **~ess** *n*
Baronin *f*
barracks ['bærəks] *npl* Kaserne *f*
barrage ['bærɑːʒ] *n* (*gunfire*) Sperrfeuer
nt; (*dam*) Staudamm *m*; Talsperre *f*
barrel ['bærəl] *n* Faß *nt*; (*of gun*) Lauf *m*
barren ['bærən] *adj* unfruchtbar
barricade [bærɪ'keɪd] *n* Barrikade *f* ♦ *vt*
verbarrikadieren
barrier ['bærɪə*] *n* (*obstruction*) Hindernis
nt; (*fence*) Schranke *f*
barring ['bɑːrɪŋ] *prep* außer im Falle
+*gen*
barrister ['bærɪstə*] (BRIT) *n*
Rechtsanwalt *m*
barrow ['bærəʊ] *n* (*cart*) Schubkarren *m*
bartender ['bɑːtendə*] (US) *n* Barmann

or -kellner *m*

barter ['bɑːtə*] *vt* handeln

base [beɪs] *n* (*bottom*) Boden *m*, Basis *f*; (*MIL*) Stützpunkt *m* ♦ *vt* gründen; (*opinion, theory*): **to be ~d on** basieren auf +*dat* ♦ *adj* (*low*) gemein; **~ball** ['beɪsbɔːl] *n* Baseball *m*; **~ment** ['beɪsmənt] *n* Kellergeschoß *nt*

bases[1] ['beɪsɪz] *npl of* **base**

bases[2] ['beɪsiːz] *npl of* **basis**

bash [bæʃ] (*inf*) *vt* (heftig) schlagen

bashful ['bæʃful] *adj* schüchtern

basic ['beɪsɪk] *adj* grundlegend; **~s** *npl*: **the ~s** das Wesentliche (*sg*); **~ally** *adv* im Grunde

basil ['bæzl] *n* Basilikum *nt*

basin ['beɪsn] *n* (*dish*) Schüssel *f*; (*for washing, also valley*) Becken *nt*; (*dock*) (Trocken)becken *nt*

basis ['beɪsɪs] (*pl* **bases**) *n* Basis *f*, Grundlage *f*

bask [bɑːsk] *vi*: **to ~ in the sun** sich sonnen

basket ['bɑːskɪt] *n* Korb *m*; **~ball** *n* Basketball *m*

bass [beɪs] *n* (*MUS, also instrument*) Baß *m*; (*voice*) Baßstimme *f*

bassoon [bə'suːn] *n* Fagott *nt*

bastard ['bɑːstəd] *n* Bastard *m*; (*inf!*) Arschloch *m* (*!*)

bastion ['bæstɪən] *n* (*also fig*) Bollwerk *nt*

bat [bæt] *n* (*SPORT*) Schlagholz *nt*; Schläger *m*; (*ZOOL*) Fledermaus *f* ♦ *vt*: **he didn't ~ an eyelid** er hat nicht mit der Wimper gezuckt

batch [bætʃ] *n* (*of letters*) Stoß *m*; (*of samples*) Satz *m*

bated ['beɪtɪd] *adj*: **with ~ breath** mit angehaltenem Atem

bath [bɑːθ, *pl* bɑːðz] *n* Bad *nt*; (*~ tub*) Badewanne *f* ♦ *vt* baden; **to have a ~** baden; *see also* **baths**

bathe [beɪð] *vt, vi* baden; **~r** *n* Badende(r) *mf*

bathing ['beɪðɪŋ] *n* Baden *nt*; **~ cap** *n* Badekappe *f*; **~ costume** *n* Badeanzug *m*; **~ suit** (*US*) *n* Badeanzug *m*; **~ trunks** (*BRIT*) *npl* Badehose *f*

bathrobe ['bɑːθrəub] *n* Bademantel *m*

bathroom ['bɑːθrʊm] *n* Bad(ezimmer *nt*) *nt*

baths [bɑːðz] *npl* (Schwimm)bad *nt*

bath towel *n* Badetuch *nt*

baton ['bætən] *n* (*of police*) Gummiknüppel *m*; (*MUS*) Taktstock *m*

batter ['bætə*] *vt* verprügeln ♦ *n* Schlagteig *m*; (*for cake*) Biskuitteig *m*; **~ed** *adj* (*hat, pan*) verbeult

battery ['bætərɪ] *n* (*ELEC*) Batterie *f*; (*MIL*) Geschützbatterie *f*

battle ['bætl] *n* Schlacht *f*; (*small*) Gefecht *nt* ♦ *vi* kämpfen; **~field** *n* Schlachtfeld *nt*; **~ship** *n* Schlachtschiff *nt*

Bavaria *n* Bayern *nt*; **~n** *adj* bay(e)risch ♦ *n* (*person*) Bayer(in) *m(f)*; (*LING*) Bay(e)risch *nt*

bawdy ['bɔːdɪ] *adj* unflätig

bawl [bɔːl] *vi* brüllen

bay [beɪ] *n* (*of sea*) Bucht *f* ♦ *vi* bellen; **to keep at ~** unter Kontrolle halten

bay window *n* Erkerfenster *nt*

bazaar [bə'zɑː*] *n* Basar *m*

B. & B. *abbr* = **bed and breakfast**

BBC *n abbr* (= *British Broadcasting Corporation*) BBC *f or* m

B.C. *adv abbr* (= *before Christ*) v.Chr.

KEYWORD

be [biː] (*pt* **was**, **were**, *pp* **been**) *aux vb* **1** (*with present participle: forming continuous tenses*): **what are you doing?** was machst du (gerade)?; **it is raining** es regnet; **I've been waiting for you for hours** ich warte schon seit Stunden auf dich

2 (*with pp: forming passives*): **to be killed** getötet werden; **the thief was nowhere to be seen** der Dieb war nirgendwo zu sehen

3 (*in tag questions*): **it was fun, wasn't it?** es hat Spaß gemacht, nicht wahr?

4 (*+to +infin*): **the house is to be sold** das Haus soll verkauft werden; **he's not to open it** er darf es nicht öffnen

♦ *vb* +*complement* **1** (*with n/num complement*) sein; **I'm tired** ich bin müde; **I'm hot/cold** mir ist heiß/kalt; **he's a doctor** er ist Arzt; **2** and 2 are 4 2 und 2 ist *or* sind 4; **she's tall/pretty** sie ist groß/hübsch; **be careful/quiet** sei vorsichtig/ruhig **2** (*of health*): **how are you?** wie geht es dir?; **he's very ill** er ist sehr krank; **I'm fine now** jetzt geht es mir gut **3** (*of age*): **how old are you?** wie alt bist du?; **I'm sixteen (years old)** ich bin sechzehn (Jahre alt) **4** (*cost*): **how much was the meal?** was *or* wieviel hat das Essen gekostet?; **that'll be £5.75, please** das macht £5.75, bitte ♦ *vi* **1** (*exist, occur etc*) sein; **is there a God?** gibt es einen Gott?; **be that as it may** wie dem auch sei; **so be it** also gut **2** (*referring to place*) sein; **I won't be here tomorrow** ich werde morgen nicht hier sein **3** (*referring to movement*): **where have you been?** wo bist du gewesen?; **I've been in the garden** ich war im Garten ♦ *impers vb* **1** (*referring to time, distance, weather*): **it's 5 o'clock** es ist 5 Uhr; **it's 10 km to the village** es sind 10 km bis zum Dorf; **it's too hot/cold** es ist zu heiß/kalt **2** (*emphatic*): **it's me** ich bin's; **it's the postman** es ist der Briefträger

beach [biːtʃ] *n* Strand *m* ♦ *vt* (*ship*) auf den Strand setzen

beacon ['biːkən] *n* (*signal*) Leuchtfeuer *nt*; (*traffic ~*) Bake *f*

bead [biːd] *n* Perle *f*; (*drop*) Tropfen *m*

beak [biːk] *n* Schnabel *m*

beaker ['biːkə*] *n* Becher *m*

beam [biːm] *n* (*of wood*) Balken *m*; (*of light*) Strahl *m*; (*smile*) strahlende(s) Lächeln *nt* ♦ *vi* strahlen

bean [biːn] *n* Bohne *f*; **~ sprouts** *npl* Sojasprossen *pl*

bear [beə*] (*pt* bore, *pp* borne) *n* Bär *m* ♦ *vt* (*weight, crops*) tragen; (*tolerate*) ertragen; (*young*) gebären ♦ *vi*: **to ~ right/left** sich rechts/links halten; **~ out** *vt* (*suspicions etc*) bestätigen; **~ up** *vi* sich halten

beard [biəd] *n* Bart *m*; **~ed** *adj* bärtig

bearer ['beərə*] *n* Träger *m*

bearing ['beərɪŋ] *n* (*posture*) Haltung *f*; (*relevance*) Relevanz *f*; (*relation*) Bedeutung *f*; (*TECH*) Kugellager *nt*; **~s** *npl* (*direction*) Orientierung *f*; (*also*: **ball ~s**) (Kugel)lager *nt*

beast [biːst] *n* Tier *nt*, Vieh *nt*; (*person*) Biest *nt*; **~ly** *adj* viehisch; (*inf*) scheußlich

beat [biːt] (*pt* beat, *pp* beaten) *n* (*stroke*) Schlag *m*; (*pulsation*) (Herz)schlag *m*; (*police round*) Runde *f*; Revier *nt*; (*MUS*) Takt *m*; Beat *m* ♦ *vt, vi* schlagen; **to ~ it** abhauen; **off the ~en track** abgelegen; **~ off** *vt* abschlagen; **~ up** *vt* zusammenschlagen; **beaten** *pp* of **beat**; **~ing** *n* Prügel *pl*

beautiful ['bjuːtɪful] *adj* schön; **~ly** *adv* ausgezeichnet

beauty ['bjuːtɪ] *n* Schönheit *f*; **~ salon** *n* Schönheitssalon *m*; **~ spot** *n* Schönheitsfleck *m*; (*BRIT: TOURISM*) (besonders) schöne(r) Ort *m*

beaver ['biːvə*] *n* Biber *m*

became [bɪ'keɪm] *pt* of **become**

because [bɪ'kɒz] *conj* weil ♦ *prep*: **~ of** wegen +*gen*, wegen +*dat* (*inf*)

beck [bek] *n*: **to be at the ~ and call of sb** nach jds Pfeife tanzen

beckon ['bekən] *vt, vi*: **to ~ to sb** jdm ein Zeichen geben

become [bɪ'kʌm] (*irreg: like* come) *vi* werden ♦ *vt* werden; (*clothes*) stehen +*dat*

becoming [bɪ'kʌmɪŋ] *adj* (*suitable*) schicklich; (*clothes*) kleidsam

bed [bed] *n* Bett *nt*; (*of river*) Flußbett *nt*; (*foundation*) Schicht *f*; (*in garden*) Beet *nt*; **to go to ~** zu Bett gehen; **~ and breakfast** *n* Übernachtung *f* mit Frühstück; **~clothes** *npl* Bettwäsche *f*; **~ding** *n* Bettzeug *nt*

bedlam ['bedləm] *n* (*uproar*) tolle(s) Durcheinander *nt*

bedraggled [bɪ'dræɡld] *adj* ramponiert

bed: ~ridden *adj* bettlägerig; **~room** *n* Schlafzimmer *nt*; **~side** *n*: **at the ~side** am Bett; **~sit(ter)** (*BRIT*) *n* Einzimmerwohnung *f*, möblierte(s) Zimmer *nt*; **~spread** *n* Tagesdecke *f*; **~time** *n* Schlafenszeit *f*

bee [biː] *n* Biene *f*

beech [biːtʃ] *n* Buche *f*

beef [biːf] *n* Rindfleisch *nt*; **roast ~** Roastbeef *nt*; **~burger** *n* Hamburger *m*

beehive ['biːhaɪv] *n* Bienenstock *m*

beeline ['biːlaɪn] *n*: **to make a ~ for** schnurstracks zugehen auf +*acc*

been [biːn] *pp of* **be**

beer [bɪə*] *n* Bier *nt*

beet [biːt] *n* (*vegetable*) Rübe *f*; (*US: also:* **red ~**) rote Bete *f or* Rübe *f*

beetle ['biːtl] *n* Käfer *m*

beetroot ['biːtruːt] (*BRIT*) *n* rote Bete *f*

before [bɪ'fɔː*] *prep* vor ♦ *conj* bevor ♦ *adv* (*of time*) zuvor; früher; **the week ~** die Woche zuvor *or* vorher; **I've done it ~** das hab' ich schon mal getan; **~ going** bevor er/sie *etc* geht/ging; **~ she goes** bevor sie geht; **~hand** *adv* im voraus

beg [beg] *vt, vi* (*implore*) dringend bitten; (*alms*) betteln

began [bɪ'gæn] *pt of* **begin**

beggar ['begə*] *n* Bettler(in) *m(f)*

begin [bɪ'gɪn] (*pt* **began**, *pp* **begun**) *vt, vi* anfangen, beginnen; (*found*) gründen; **to ~ doing** *or* **to do sth** anfangen *or* beginnen, etw zu tun; **to ~ with** zunächst (einmal); **~ner** *n* Anfänger *m*; **~ning** *n* Anfang *m*

begun [bɪ'gʌn] *pp of* **begin**

behalf [bɪ'hɑːf] *n*: **on ~ of** im Namen +*gen*; **on my ~** für mich

behave [bɪ'heɪv] *vi* sich benehmen

behaviour [bɪ'heɪvjə*] (*US* **behavior**) *n* Benehmen *nt*

behead [bɪ'hed] *vt* enthaupten

beheld [bɪ'held] *pt, pp of* **behold**

behind [bɪ'haɪnd] *prep* hinter ♦ *adv* (*late*) im Rückstand; (*in the rear*) hinten ♦ *n* (*inf*) Hinterteil *nt*; **~ the scenes** (*fig*) hinter den Kulissen

behold [bɪ'həʊld] (*irreg: like* **hold**) *vt* erblicken

beige [beɪʒ] *adj* beige

Beijing ['beɪ'dʒɪŋ] *n* Peking *nt*

being ['biːɪŋ] *n* (*existence*) (Da)sein *nt*; (*person*) Wesen *nt*; **to come into ~** entstehen

belated [bɪ'leɪtɪd] *adj* verspätet

belch [beltʃ] *vi* rülpsen ♦ *vt* (*smoke*) ausspeien

belfry ['belfrɪ] *n* Glockenturm *m*

Belgian ['beldʒən] *adj* belgisch ♦ *n* Belgier(in) *m(f)*

Belgium ['beldʒəm] *n* Belgien *nt*

belie [bɪ'laɪ] *vt* Lügen strafen +*acc*

belief [bɪ'liːf] *n* Glaube *m*; (*conviction*) Überzeugung *f*; **~ in sb/sth** Glaube an jdn/etw

believe [bɪ'liːv] *vt* glauben +*dat*; (*think*) glauben, meinen, denken ♦ *vi* (*have faith*) glauben; **to ~ in sth** an etw *acc* glauben; **~r** *n* Gläubige(r) *mf*

belittle [bɪ'lɪtl] *vt* herabsetzen

bell [bel] *n* Glocke *f*

belligerent [bɪ'lɪdʒərənt] *adj* (*person*) streitsüchtig; (*country*) kriegsführend

bellow ['beləʊ] *vt, vi* brüllen

bellows ['beləʊz] *npl* (*TECH*) Gebläse *nt*; (*for fire*) Blasebalg *m*

belly ['belɪ] *n* Bauch *m*

belong [bɪ'lɒŋ] *vi* gehören; **to ~ to sb** jdm gehören; **to ~ to a club** *etc* einem Club *etc* angehören; **it does not ~ here** es gehört nicht hierher; **~ings** *npl* Habe *f*

beloved [bɪ'lʌvɪd] *adj* innig geliebt ♦ *n* Geliebte(r) *mf*

below [bɪ'ləʊ] *prep* unter ♦ *adv* unten

belt [belt] *n* (*band*) Riemen *m*; (*round waist*) Gürtel *m* ♦ *vt* (*fasten*) mit Riemen befestigen; (*inf: beat*) schlagen; **~way** (*US*) *n* (*AUT: ring road*) Umgehungsstraße *f*

bemused [bɪ'mjuːzd] *adj* verwirrt

bench [bentʃ] *n* (*seat*) Bank *f*; (*workshop*) Werkbank *f*; (*judge's seat*) Richterbank *f*; (*judges*) Richter *pl*

bend [bend] (*pt, pp* **bent**) *vt* (*curve*) biegen; (*stoop*) sich biegen ♦ *vi* sich biegen; sich beugen ♦ *n* Biegung *f*; (*BRIT: in road*) Kurve *f*; **~ down** *or* **over** *vi* sich bücken

beneath [bɪ'niːθ] *prep* unter ♦ *adv* darunter

benefactor ['benɪfæktə*] *n* Wohltäter(in) *m(f)*

beneficial [benɪ'fɪʃl] *adj* vorteilhaft; (*to health*) heilsam

benefit ['benɪfɪt] *n* (*advantage*) Nutzen *m* ♦ *vt* fördern ♦ *vi*: **to ~ (from)** Nutzen ziehen (aus)

Benelux ['benɪlʌks] n Beneluxstaaten pl

benevolent [bɪ'nevələnt] adj
wohlwollend

benign [bɪ'naɪn] adj (person) gütig;
(climate) mild

bent [bent] pt, pp of **bend** ♦ n
(inclination) Neigung f ♦ adj (inf:
dishonest) unehrlich; **to be ~ on**
versessen sein auf +acc

bequest [bɪ'kwest] n Vermächtnis nt

bereaved [bɪ'riːvd] npl: **the ~** die
Hinterbliebenen pl

bereft [bɪ'reft] adj: **~ of** bar +gen

beret ['bereɪ] n Baskenmütze f

Berlin [bɜː'lɪn] n Berlin nt

berm [bɜːm] (US) n (AUT) Seitenstreifen m

Bermuda [bɜː'mjuːdə] n Bermuda nt

berry ['berɪ] n Beere f

berserk [bə'sɜːk] adj: **to go ~** wild
werden

berth [bɜːθ] n (for ship) Ankerplatz m; (in
ship) Koje f; (in train) Bett nt ♦ vt am Kai
festmachen ♦ vi anlegen

beseech [bɪ'siːtʃ] (pt, pp **besought**) vt
anflehen

beset [bɪ'set] (pt, pp **beset**) vt bedrängen

beside [bɪ'saɪd] prep neben, bei; (except)
außer; **to be ~ o.s. (with)** außer sich sein
(vor +dat); **that's ~ the point** das tut
nichts zur Sache

besides [bɪ'saɪdz] prep außer, neben
♦ adv außerdem

besiege [bɪ'siːdʒ] vt (MIL) belagern;
(surround) umlagern, bedrängen

besought [bɪ'sɔːt] pt, pp of **beseech**

best [best] adj beste(r, s) ♦ adv am
besten; **the ~ part of** (quantity) das
meiste +gen; **at ~** höchstens; **to make the
~ of it** das Beste daraus machen; **to do
one's ~** sein Bestes tun; **to the ~ of my
knowledge** meines Wissens; **to the ~ of
my ability** so gut ich kann; **for the ~**
zum Besten; **~ man** n Trauzeuge m

bestow [bɪ'stəʊ] vt verleihen

bet [bet] (pt, pp **bet** or **betted**) n Wette f
♦ vt, vi wetten

betray [bɪ'treɪ] vt verraten

better ['betə*] adj, adv besser ♦ vt

verbessern ♦ n: **to get the ~ of sb** jdn
überwinden; **he thought ~ of it** er hat
sich eines Besseren besonnen; **you had ~
leave** Sie gehen jetzt wohl besser; **to get
~** (MED) gesund werden; **~ off** adj (richer)
wohlhabender

betting ['betɪŋ] n Wetten nt; **~ shop**
(BRIT) n Wettbüro nt

between [bɪ'twiːn] prep zwischen;
(among) unter ♦ adv dazwischen

beverage ['bevərɪdʒ] n Getränk nt

bevy ['bevɪ] n Schar f

beware [bɪ'wɛə*] vt, vi sich hüten vor
+dat; **"~ of the dog"** „Vorsicht, bissiger
Hund!"

bewildered [bɪ'wɪldəd] adj verwirrt

bewitching [bɪ'wɪtʃɪŋ] adj bestrickend

beyond [bɪ'jɒnd] prep (place) jenseits
+gen; (time) über ... hinaus; (out of reach)
außerhalb +gen ♦ adv darüber hinaus; **~
doubt** ohne Zweifel; **~ repair** nicht mehr
zu reparieren

bias ['baɪəs] n (slant) Neigung f;
(prejudice) Vorurteil nt; **~(s)ed** adj
voreingenommen

bib [bɪb] n Latz m

Bible ['baɪbl] n Bibel f

bicarbonate of soda [baɪ'kɑːbənɪt-] n
Natron nt

bicker ['bɪkə*] vi zanken

bicycle ['baɪsɪkl] n Fahrrad nt

bid [bɪd] (pt **bade** or **bid, bid**(den)) n
(offer) Gebot nt; (attempt) Versuch m
♦ vt, vi (offer) bieten; **to ~ farewell**
Lebewohl sagen; **bidden** ['bɪdn] pp of
bid; ~der n (person) Steigerer m; **the
highest ~der** der Meistbietende; **~ding** n
(command) Geheiß nt

bide [baɪd] vt: **to ~ one's time** abwarten

bifocals [baɪ'fəʊkəlz] npl Bifokalbrille f

big [bɪg] adj groß

big dipper [-'dɪpə*] n Achterbahn f

bigheaded ['bɪg'hedɪd] adj eingebildet

bigot ['bɪgət] n Frömmler m; **~ed** adj
bigott; **~ry** n Bigotterie f

big top n Zirkuszelt nt

bike [baɪk] n Rad nt

bikini [bɪ'kiːnɪ] n Bikini m

bile [baɪl] n (BIOL) Galle f

bilingual [baɪˈlɪŋgwəl] *adj* zweisprachig

bill [bɪl] *n* (*account*) Rechnung *f*; (*POL*) Gesetzentwurf *m*; (*US: FIN*) Geldschein *m*; **to fit** *or* **fill the ~** (*fig*) der/die/das richtige sein; **"post no ~s"** „Plakate ankleben verboten"; **~board** [ˈbɪlbɔːd] *n* Reklameschild *nt*

billet [ˈbɪlɪt] *n* Quartier *nt*

billfold [ˈbɪlfəʊld] *n* (*US*) Geldscheintasche *f*

billiards [ˈbɪljədz] *n* Billard *nt*

billion [ˈbɪljən] *n* (*BRIT*) Billion *f*; (*US*) Milliarde *f*

bimbo [ˈbɪmbəʊ] *n* (*inf: pej*) Puppe *f*, Häschen *nt*

bin [bɪn] *n* Kasten *m*; (*dust~*) (Abfall)eimer *m*

bind [baɪnd] (*pt, pp* **bound**) *vt* (*tie*) binden; (*tie together*) zusammenbinden; (*oblige*) verpflichten; **~ing** *n* (*Buch*)einband *m* ♦ *adj* verbindlich

binge [bɪndʒ] (*inf*) *n* Sauferei *f*

bingo [ˈbɪŋgəʊ] *n* Bingo *nt*

binoculars [bɪˈnɒkjʊləz] *npl* Fernglas *nt*

bio... [baɪəʊ] *prefix*: **~chemistry** *n* Biochemie *f*; **~graphy** *n* Biographie *f*; **~logical** [baɪəˈlɒdʒɪkəl] *adj* biologisch; **~logy** [baɪˈɒlədʒɪ] *n* Biologie *f*

birch [bɜːtʃ] *n* Birke *f*

bird [bɜːd] *n* Vogel *m*; (*BRIT: inf: girl*) Mädchen *nt*; **~'s-eye view** *n* Vogelschau *f*; **~ watcher** *n* Vogelbeobachter(in) *m(f)*

Biro [ˈbaɪrəʊ] ® *n* Kugelschreiber *m*

birth [bɜːθ] *n* Geburt *f*; **to give ~ to** zur Welt bringen; **~ certificate** *n* Geburtsurkunde *f*; **~ control** *n* Geburtenkontrolle *f*; **~day** *n* Geburtstag *m*; **~day card** *n* Geburtstagskarte *f*; **~place** *n* Geburtsort *m*; **~ rate** *n* Geburtenrate *f*

biscuit [ˈbɪskɪt] *n* Keks *m*

bisect [baɪˈsekt] *vt* halbieren

bishop [ˈbɪʃəp] *n* Bischof *m*

bit [bɪt] *pt of* **bite** ♦ *n* bißchen, Stückchen *nt*; (*horse's*) Gebiß *nt*; (*COMPUT*) Bit *nt*; **a ~ tired** etwas müde

bitch [bɪtʃ] *n* (*dog*) Hündin *f*; (*unpleasant woman*) Weibsstück *nt*

bite [baɪt] (*pt* **bit**, *pp* **bitten**) *vt, vi* beißen

♦ *n* Biß *m*; (*mouthful*) Bissen *m*; **to ~ one's nails** Nägel kauen; **let's have a ~ to eat** laß uns etwas essen

biting [ˈbaɪtɪŋ] *adj* beißend

bitten [ˈbɪtn] *pp of* **bite**

bitter [ˈbɪtə*] *adj* bitter; (*memory etc*) schmerzlich; (*person*) verbittert ♦ *n* (*BRIT: beer*) dunkle(s) Bier *nt*; **~ness** *n* Bitterkeit *f*

blab [blæb] *vi* klatschen ♦ *vt* (*also:* ~ *out*) ausplaudern

black [blæk] *adj* schwarz; (*night*) finster ♦ *vt* schwärzen; (*shoes*) wichsen; (*eye*) blau schlagen; (*BRIT: INDUSTRY*) boykottieren; **to give sb a ~ eye** jdm ein blaues Auge schlagen; **in the ~** (*bank account*) in den schwarzen Zahlen; **~ and blue** *adj* grün und blau; **~berry** *n* Brombeere *f*; **~bird** *n* Amsel *f*; **~board** *n* (Wand)tafel *f*; **~ coffee** *n* schwarze(r) Kaffee *m*; **~currant** *n* schwarze Johannisbeere *f*; **~en** *vt* schwärzen; (*fig*) verunglimpfen; **B~ Forest** *n* Schwarzwald *m*; **~ ice** *n* Glatteis *nt*; **~jack** (*US*) *n* Siebzehn und Vier; **~leg** (*BRIT*) *n* Streikbrecher(in) *m(f)*; **~list** *n* schwarze Liste *f*; **~mail** *n* Erpressung *f* ♦ *vt* erpressen; **~ market** *n* Schwarzmarkt *m*; **~out** *n* Verdunklung *f*; (*MED*): **to have a ~out** bewußtlos werden; **B~ Sea** *n*: **the B~ Sea** das Schwarze Meer; **~ sheep** *n* schwarze(s) Schaf *nt*; **~smith** *n* Schmied *m*; **~ spot** *n* (*AUT*) Gefahrenstelle *f*; (*for unemployment etc*) schwer betroffene(s) Gebiet *nt*

bladder [ˈblædə*] *n* Blase *f*

blade [bleɪd] *n* (*of weapon*) Klinge *f*; (*of grass*) Halm *m*; (*of oar*) Ruderblatt *nt*

blame [bleɪm] *n* Tadel *m*, Schuld *f* ♦ *vt* Vorwürfe machen +*dat*; **to ~ sb for sth** jdm die Schuld an etw *dat* geben; **he is to ~** er ist daran schuld

bland [blænd] *adj* mild

blank [blæŋk] *adj* leer, unbeschrieben; (*look*) verdutzt; (*verse*) Blank- ♦ *n* (*space*) Lücke *f*; (*cartridge*) Platzpatrone *f*, **~ cheque** *n* Blankoscheck *m*; (*fig*) Freibrief *m*

blanket [ˈblæŋkɪt] *n* (Woll)decke *f*

blare [blɛə*] vi (*radio*) plärren; (*horn*)
tuten; (*MUS*) schmettern

blasé ['blɑːzeɪ] adj blasiert

blast [blɑːst] n Explosion f; (*of wind*)
Windstoß m ♦ vt (*blow up*) sprengen; ~!
(*inf*) verflixt!; **~-off** n (*SPACE*)
(Raketen)abschuß m

blatant ['bleɪtənt] adj offenkundig

blaze [bleɪz] n (*fire*) lodernde(s) Feuer nt
♦ vi lodern ♦ vt: **to ~ a trail** Bahn
brechen

blazer ['bleɪzə*] n Blazer m

bleach [bliːtʃ] n (*also: household ~*)
Bleichmittel nt ♦ vt bleichen

bleachers ['bliːtʃəz] (*US*) npl (*SPORT*)
unüberdachte Tribüne f

bleak [bliːk] adj kahl, rauh; (*future*)
trostlos

bleary-eyed ['blɪərɪ'aɪd] adj triefäugig;
(*on waking up*) mit verschlafenen Augen

bleat [bliːt] vi blöken; (*fig: complain*)
meckern

bled [bled] pt, pp of **bleed**

bleed [bliːd] (pt, pp **bled**) vi bluten ♦ vt
(*draw blood*) zur Ader lassen; **to ~ to
death** verbluten

bleeper ['bliːpə*] n (*of doctor etc*)
Funkrufempfänger m

blemish ['blemɪʃ] n Makel m ♦ vt
verunstalten

blend [blend] n Mischung f ♦ vt mischen
♦ vi sich mischen

bless [bles] (pt, pp **blessed** or **blest**) vt
segnen; (*give thanks*) preisen; (*make happy*) glücklich machen; **~ you!** Gesundheit!; **~ing** n Segen m; (*at table*) Tischgebet nt; (*happiness*) Wohltat f; Segen m;
(*good wish*) Glück nt

blest [blest] pt, pp of **bless**

blew [bluː] pt of **blow**

blight [blaɪt] vt zunichte machen

blimey ['blaɪmɪ] (*BRIT: inf*) excl verflucht

blind [blaɪnd] adj blind; (*corner*)
unübersichtlich ♦ n (*for window*) Rouleau
nt ♦ vt blenden; **~ alley** n Sackgasse f;
~fold n Augenbinde f ♦ adj, adv mit
verbundenen Augen ♦ vt: **to ~fold sb** jdm
die Augen verbinden; **~ly** adv blind; (*fig*)
blindlings; **~ness** n Blindheit f; **~ spot** n

(*AUT*) tote(r) Winkel m; (*fig*) schwache(r)
Punkt m

blink [blɪŋk] vi blinzeln; **~ers** npl
Scheuklappen pl

bliss [blɪs] n (Glück)seligkeit f

blister ['blɪstə*] n Blase f ♦ vi Blasen
werfen

blithe [blaɪð] adj munter

blitz [blɪts] n Luftkrieg m

blizzard ['blɪzəd] n Schneesturm m

bloated ['bləʊtɪd] adj aufgedunsen; (*inf:
full*) nudelsatt

blob [blɒb] n Klümpchen nt

bloc [blɒk] n (*POL*) Block m

block [blɒk] n (*of wood*) Block m, Klotz
m; (*of houses*) Häuserblock m ♦ vt
hemmen; **~ade** [blɒ'keɪd] n Blockade f
♦ vt blockieren; **~age** n Verstopfung f;
~buster n Knüller m; **~ letters** npl
Blockbuchstaben pl; **~ of flats** (*BRIT*) n
Häuserblock m

bloke [bləʊk] (*BRIT: inf*) n Kerl m, Typ m

blond(e) [blɒnd] adj blond ♦ n Blondine f

blood [blʌd] n Blut nt; **~ donor** n
Blutspender m; **~ group** n Blutgruppe f;
~ pressure n Blutdruck m; **~shed** n
Blutvergießen nt; **~shot** adj
blutunterlaufen; **~stained** adj
blutbefleckt; **~stream** n Blut nt,
Blutkreislauf m; **~ test** n Blutprobe f;
~thirsty adj blutrünstig; **~y** adj blutig;
(*BRIT: inf*) verdammt; **~y-minded** (*BRIT:
inf*) adj stur

bloom [bluːm] n Blüte f; (*freshness*) Glanz
m ♦ vi blühen

blossom ['blɒsəm] n Blüte f ♦ vi blühen

blot [blɒt] n Klecks m ♦ vt beklecksen;
(*ink*) (ab)löschen; **~ out** vt auslöschen

blotchy ['blɒtʃɪ] adj fleckig

blotting paper ['blɒtɪŋ-] n Löschpapier
nt

blouse [blaʊz] n Bluse f

blow [bləʊ] (pt **blew**, pp **blown**) n Schlag
m ♦ vi blasen ♦ vi (*wind*) wehen; **to ~
one's nose** sich dat die Nase putzen; **~
away** vt wegblasen; **~ down** vt
unwehen; **~ out** vi ausgehen ♦ vt
ausblasen; **~ over** vi vorübergehen; **~ up**
vi explodieren ♦ vt sprengen; **~-dry** n: **to**

have a ~-dry sich fönen lassen ♦ *vt* fönen; **~lamp** (*BRIT*) *n* Lötlampe *f*; **~n** [bləun] *pp* of **blow**; **~-out** *n* (*AUT*) geplatzte(r) Reifen *m*; **~torch** *n* = **blowlamp**

blue [blu:] *adj* blau; (*inf*: *unhappy*) niedergeschlagen; (*obscene*) pornographisch; (*joke*) anzüglich ♦ *n* **out of the ~** (*fig*) aus heiterem Himmel; **to have the ~s** traurig sein; **~bell** *n* Glockenblume *f*; **~bottle** *n* Schmeißfliege *f*; **~ film** *n* Pornofilm *m*; **~print** *n* (*fig*) Entwurf *m*

bluff [blʌf] *vi* bluffen, täuschen ♦ *n* (*deception*) Bluff *m*; **to call sb's ~** es darauf ankommen lassen

blunder ['blʌndə*] *n* grobe(r) Fehler *m*, Schnitzer *m* ♦ *vi* einen groben Fehler machen

blunt [blʌnt] *adj* (*knife*) stumpf; (*talk*) unverblümt ♦ *vt* abstumpfen

blur [blə:*] *n* Fleck *m* ♦ *vt* verschwommen machen

blurb [blə:b] *n* Waschzettel *m*

blurt [blə:t] *vt*: **to ~ out** herausplatzen mit

blush [blʌʃ] *vi* erröten ♦ *n* (Scham)röte *f*

blustery ['blʌstəri] *adj* stürmisch

boar [bɔ:*] *n* Keiler *m*, Eber *m*

board [bɔ:d] *n* (*of wood*) Brett *nt*; (*of card*) Pappe *f*; (*committee*) Ausschuß *m*; (*of firm*) Aufsichtsrat *m*; (*SCH*) Direktorium *nt* ♦ *vt* (*train*) einsteigen in +*acc*; (*ship*) an Bord gehen +*gen*; **on ~** (*AVIAT, NAUT*) an Bord; **~ and lodging** Unterkunft *f* und Verpflegung; **full/half ~** (*BRIT*) Voll-/Halbpension *f*; **to go by the ~** flachfallen, über Bord gehen; **~ up** *vt* mit Brettern vernageln; **~er** *n* Kostgänger *m*; (*SCH*) Internatsschüler(in) *m(f)*; **~ing card** *n* (*AVIAT, NAUT*) Bordkarte *f*; **~ing house** *n* Pension *f*; **~ing school** *n* Internat *nt*; **~ room** *n* Sitzungszimmer *nt*

boast [bəust] *vi* prahlen ♦ *vt* sich rühmen +*gen* ♦ *n* Großtuerei *f*; Prahlerei *f*; **to ~ about** *or* **of sth** mit etw prahlen

boat [bəut] *n* Boot *nt*; (*ship*) Schiff *nt*; **~er** *n* (*hat*) Kreissäge *f*; **~swain** *n* = **bosun**

bob [bɔb] *vi* sich auf und nieder bewegen ♦ *n* (*BRIT*: *inf*) = **shilling**; **~ up** *vi* auftauchen

bobbin ['bɔbin] *n* Spule *f*

bobby ['bɔbi] (*BRIT*: *inf*) *n* Bobby *m*

bobsleigh ['bɔbslei] *n* Bob *m*

bode [bəud] *vi*: **to ~ well/ill** ein gutes/ schlechtes Zeichen sein

bodily ['bɔdili] *adj, adv* körperlich

body ['bɔdi] *n* Körper *m*; (*dead*) Leiche *f*; (*group*) Mannschaft *f*; (*AUT*) Karosserie *f*; (*trunk*) Rumpf *m*; **~guard** *n* Leibwache *f*; **~work** *n* Karosserie *f*

bog [bɔg] *n* Sumpf *m* ♦ *vt*: **to get ~ged down** sich festfahren

boggle ['bɔgl] *vi* stutzen; **the mind ~s** es ist kaum auszumalen

bogus ['bəugəs] *adj* unecht, Schein-

boil [bɔil] *vt, vi* kochen ♦ *n* (*MED*) Geschwür *nt*; **to come to the** (*BRIT*) *or* **a** (*US*) **~** zu kochen anfangen; **to ~ down to** (*fig*) hinauslaufen auf +*acc*; **~ over** *vi* überkochen; **~ed egg** *n* gekochte(s) Ei *nt*; **~ed potatoes** *npl* Salzkartoffeln *pl*; **~er** *n* Boiler *m*; **~er suit** (*BRIT*) *n* Arbeitsanzug *m*; **~ing point** *n* Siedepunkt *m*

boisterous ['bɔistərəs] *adj* ungestüm

bold [bəuld] *adj* (*fearless*) unerschrocken; (*handwriting*) fest und klar

bollard ['bɔləd] *n* (*NAUT*) Poller *m*; (*BRIT*: *AUT*) Pfosten *m*

bolster ['bəulstə*] *vt*: **~ up** *vt* unterstützen

bolt [bəult] *n* Bolzen *m*; (*lock*) Riegel *m* ♦ *adv*: **~ upright** kerzengerade ♦ *vt* verriegeln; (*swallow*) verschlingen ♦ *vi* (*horse*) durchgehen

bomb [bɔm] *n* Bombe *f* ♦ *vt* bombardieren; **~ard** [bɔm'ba:d] *vt* bombardieren; **~ardment** [bɔm'ba:d-mənt] *n* Beschießung *f*; **~ disposal** *n*: **~ disposal unit** Bombenräumkommando *nt*; **~shell** *n* (*fig*) Bombe *f*

bona fide ['bəunə'faidi] *adj* echt

bond [bɔnd] *n* (*link*) Band *nt*; (*FIN*) Schuldverschreibung *f*

bondage ['bɔndidʒ] *n* Sklaverei *f*

bone [bəun] *n* Knochen *m*; (*of fish*) Gräte *f*; (*piece of* ~) Knochensplitter *m* ♦ *vt* die

Knochen herausnehmen +*dat*; (*fish*) entgräten; ~ **idle** *adj* stinkfaul; ~ **marrow** *n* (*ANAT*) Knochenmark *nt*

bonfire ['bɒnfaɪə*] *n* Feuer *nt* im Freien

bonnet ['bɒnɪt] *n* Haube *f*; (*for baby*) Häubchen *nt*; (*BRIT: AUT*) Motorhaube *f*

bonus ['bəʊnəs] *n* Bonus *m*; (*annual* ~) Prämie *f*

bony ['bəʊnɪ] *adj* knochig, knochendürr

boo [buː] *vt* auspfeifen

booby trap ['buːbɪ-] *n* Falle *f*

book [bʊk] *n* Buch *nt* ♦ *vt* (*ticket etc*) vorbestellen; (*person*) verwarnen; ~**s** *npl* (*COMM*) Bücher *pl*; ~**case** *n* Bücherregal *nt*, Bücherschrank *m*; ~**ing office** (*BRIT*) *n* (*RAIL*) Fahrkartenschalter *m*; (*THEAT*) Vorverkaufsstelle *f*; ~**-keeping** *n* Buchhaltung *f*; ~**let** *n* Broschüre *f*; ~**maker** *n* Buchmacher *m*; ~**seller** *n* Buchhändler *m*; ~**shop**, ~**store** *n* Buchhandlung *f*

boom [buːm] *n* (*noise*) Dröhnen *nt*; (*busy period*) Hochkonjunktur *f* ♦ *vi* dröhnen

boon [buːn] *n* Wohltat *f*, Segen *m*

boost [buːst] *n* Auftrieb *m*; (*fig*) Reklame *f* ♦ *vt* Auftrieb geben +*dat*; ~**er** *n* (*MED*) Wiederholungsimpfung *f*

boot [buːt] *n* Stiefel *m*; (*BRIT: AUT*) Kofferraum *m* ♦ *vt* (*kick*) einen Fußtritt geben +*dat*; (*COMPUT*) laden; **to** ~ (*in addition*) obendrein

booth [buːð] *n* (*at fair*) Bude *f*; (*telephone* ~) Zelle *f*; (*voting* ~) Kabine *f*

booze [buːz] (*inf*) *n* Alkohol *m*, Schnaps *m* ♦ *vi* saufen

border ['bɔːdə*] *n* Grenze *f*; (*edge*) Kante *f*; (*in garden*) (Blumen)rabatte *f* ♦ *adj* Grenz-; **the B**~**s** *Grenzregion f zwischen England und Schottland*; ~ **on** *vt* grenzen an +*acc*; ~**line** *n* Grenze *f*; ~**line case** *n* Grenzfall *m*

bore [bɔː*] *pt of* **bear** ♦ *vt* bohren; (*weary*) langweilen ♦ *n* (*person*) Langweiler *m*; (*thing*) langweilige Sache *f*; (*of gun*) Kaliber *nt*; **I am ~d** ich langweile mich; ~**dom** *n* Langeweile *f*

boring ['bɔːrɪŋ] *adj* langweilig

born [bɔːn] *adj*: **to be ~** geboren werden

borne [bɔːn] *pp of* **bear**

borough ['bʌrə] *n* Stadt(gemeinde) *f*, Stadtbezirk *m*

borrow ['bɒrəʊ] *vt* borgen

Bosnia (and) Herzegovina ['bɒznɪə (ənd) hɜːtsəgəʊ'viːnə] *n* Bosnien und Herzegowina *nt*

bosom ['bʊzəm] *n* Busen *m*

boss [bɒs] *n* Chef *m*, Boß *m* ♦ *vt*: **to ~ around** herumkommandieren; ~**y** *adj* herrisch

bosun ['bəʊsn] *n* Bootsmann *m*

botany ['bɒtənɪ] *n* Botanik *f*

botch [bɒtʃ] *vt* (*also:* ~ **up**) verpfuschen

both [bəʊθ] *adj* beide(s) ♦ *pron* beide(s) ♦ *adv*: ~ **X and Y** sowohl X wie *or* als auch Y; ~ (**of**) **the books** beide Bücher; ~ **of us went, we ~ went** wir gingen beide

bother ['bɒðə*] *vt* (*pester*) quälen ♦ *vi* (*fuss*) sich aufregen ♦ *n* Mühe *f*, Umstand *m*; **to ~ doing sth** sich *dat* die Mühe machen, etw zu tun; **what a ~!** wie ärgerlich!

bottle ['bɒtl] *n* Flasche *f* ♦ *vt* (in Flaschen) abfüllen; ~ **up** *vt* aufstauen; ~ **bank** *n* Altglascontainer *m*; ~**neck** *n* (*also fig*) Engpaß *m*; ~**-opener** *n* Flaschenöffner *m*

bottom ['bɒtəm] *n* Boden *m*; (*of person*) Hintern *m*; (*riverbed*) Flußbett *nt* ♦ *adj* unterste(r, s)

bough [baʊ] *n* Zweig *m*, Ast *m*

bought [bɔːt] *pt, pp of* **buy**

boulder ['bəʊldə*] *n* Felsbrocken *m*

bounce [baʊns] *vi* (*ball*) hochspringen; (*person*) herumhüpfen; (*cheque*) platzen ♦ *vt* (auf)springen lassen ♦ *n* (*rebound*) Aufprall *m*; ~**r** *n* Rausschmeißer *m*

bound [baʊnd] *pt, pp of* **bind** ♦ *n* Grenze *f*; (*leap*) Sprung *m* ♦ *vi* (*spring, leap*) (auf)springen ♦ *adj* (*obliged*) gebunden, verpflichtet; **out of ~s** Zutritt verboten; **to be ~ to do sth** verpflichtet sein, etw zu tun; **it's ~ to happen** es muß so kommen; **to be ~ for ...** nach ... fahren

boundary ['baʊndərɪ] *n* Grenze *f*

bouquet [buˈkeɪ] *n* Strauß *m*; (*of wine*) Blume *f*

bourgeois ['bʊəʒwɑː] *adj* kleinbürgerlich, bourgeois ♦ *n*

Spießbürger(in) *m(f)*

bout [baʊt] *n (of illness)* Anfall *m*; *(of contest)* Kampf *m*

bow[1] [bəʊ] *n (ribbon)* Schleife *f*; *(weapon, MUS)* Bogen *m*

bow[2] [baʊ] *n (with head, body)* Verbeugung *f*; *(of ship)* Bug *m* ♦ *vi* sich verbeugen; *(submit)*: **to bow to** sich beugen +*dat*

bowels [ˈbaʊəlz] *npl* Darm *m*; *(centre)* Innere *nt*

bowl [bəʊl] *n (basin)* Schüssel *f*; *(of pipe)* (Pfeifen)kopf *m*; *(wooden ball)* (Holz)kugel *f* ♦ *vt, vi* (die Kugel) rollen

bow-legged [ˈbəʊˈlegɪd] *adj* o-beinig

bowler [ˈbəʊlə*] *n* Werfer *m*; *(BRIT: also:* ~ **hat)** Melone *f*

bowling [ˈbəʊlɪŋ] *n* Kegeln *nt*; ~ **alley** *n* Kegelbahn *f*; ~ **green** *n* Rasen *m* zum Bowling-Spiel

bowls *n (game)* Bowls-Spiel *nt*

bow tie [ˈbəʊ-] *n* Fliege *f*

box [bɒks] *n (also: cardboard* ~) Schachtel *f*; *(bigger)* Kasten *m*; *(THEAT)* Loge *f* ♦ *vt* einpacken ♦ *vi* boxen; ~**er** *n* Boxer *m*; ~**ing** *n (SPORT)* Boxen *nt*; **B**~**ing Day** *(BRIT)* *n* zweite(r) Weihnachtsfeiertag *m*; ~**ing gloves** *npl* Boxhandschuhe *pl*; ~**ing ring** *n* Boxring *m*; ~ **office** *n* (Theater)kasse *f*; ~**room** *n* Rumpelkammer *f*

boy [bɔɪ] *n* Junge *m*

boycott [ˈbɔɪkɒt] *n* Boykott *m* ♦ *vt* boykottieren

boyfriend [ˈbɔɪfrend] *n* Freund *m*

boyish [ˈbɔɪʃ] *adj* jungenhaft

B.R. *n abbr* = **British Rail**

bra [brɑː] *n* BH *m*

brace [breɪs] *n (TECH)* Stütze *f*; *(MED)* Klammer *f* ♦ *vt* stützen; ~**s** *npl (BRIT)* Hosenträger *pl*; **to** ~ **o.s. for sth** *(fig)* sich auf etw *acc* gefaßt machen

bracelet [ˈbreɪslɪt] *n* Armband *nt*

bracing [ˈbreɪsɪŋ] *adj* kräftigend

bracken [ˈbrækən] *n* Farnkraut *nt*

bracket [ˈbrækɪt] *n* Halter *m*, Klammer *f*; *(in punctuation)* Klammer *f*; *(group)* Gruppe *f* ♦ *vt* einklammern; *(fig)* in dieselbe Gruppe einordnen

brag [bræg] *vi* sich rühmen

braid [breɪd] *n (hair)* Flechte *f*; *(trim)* Borte *f*

Braille [breɪl] *n* Blindenschrift *f*

brain [breɪn] *n (ANAT)* Gehirn *nt*; *(intellect)* Intelligenz *f*, Verstand *m*; *(person)* kluge(r) Kopf *m*; ~**s** *npl (intelligence)* Verstand *m*; ~**child** *n* Erfindung *f*; ~**wash** *vt* eine Gehirnwäsche vornehmen bei; ~**wave** *n* Geistesblitz *m*; ~**y** *adj* gescheit

braise [breɪz] *vt* schmoren

brake [breɪk] *n* Bremse *f* ♦ *vt, vi* bremsen; ~ **fluid** *n* Bremsflüssigkeit *f*; ~ **light** *n* Bremslicht *nt*

bramble [ˈbræmbl] *n* Brombeere *f*

bran [bræn] *n* Kleie *f*; *(food)* Frühstückflocken *pl*

branch [brɑːntʃ] *n* Ast *m*; *(division)* Zweig *m* ♦ *vi (also:* ~ **out: road)** sich verzweigen

brand [brænd] *n (COMM)* Marke *f*, Sorte *f*; *(on cattle)* Brandmal *nt* ♦ *vt* brandmarken; *(COMM)* ein Warenzeichen geben +*dat*

brandish [ˈbrændɪʃ] *vt* (drohend) schwingen

brand-new [ˈbrændˈnjuː] *adj* funkelnagelneu

brandy [ˈbrændɪ] *n* Weinbrand *m*, Kognak *m*

brash [bræʃ] *adj* unverschämt

brass [brɑːs] *n* Messing *nt*; **the** ~ *(MUS)* das Blech; ~ **band** *n* Blaskapelle *f*

brassière [ˈbræsɪə*] *n* Büstenhalter *m*

brat [bræt] *n* Gör *nt*

bravado [brəˈvɑːdəʊ] *n* Tollkühnheit *f*

brave [breɪv] *adj* tapfer ♦ *n* indianische(r) Krieger *m* ♦ *vt* die Stirn bieten +*dat*

bravery [ˈbreɪvərɪ] *n* Tapferkeit *f*

brawl [brɔːl] *n* Rauferei *f*

brawn [brɔːn] *n (ANAT)* Muskeln *pl*; *(strength)* Muskelkraft *f*

bray [breɪ] *vi* schreien

brazen [ˈbreɪzn] *adj (shameless)* unverschämt ♦ *vt*: **to** ~ **it out** sich mit Lügen und Betrügen durchsetzen

brazier [ˈbreɪzɪə*] *n (of workmen)*

offene(r) Kohlenofen m

Brazil [brə'zɪl] n Brasilien nt; **~ian** adj brasilianisch ♦ n Brasilianer(in) m(f)

breach [briːtʃ] n (gap) Lücke f; (MIL) Durchbruch m; (of discipline) Verstoß m (gegen die Disziplin); (of faith) Vertrauensbruch m ♦ vt durchbrechen; **~ of contract** Vertragsbruch m; **~ of the peace** öffentliche Ruhestörung f

bread [bred] n Brot nt; **~ and butter** Butterbrot nt; **~bin** n Brotkasten m; **~box** (US) n Brotkasten m; **~crumbs** npl Brotkrumen pl; (COOK) Paniermehl nt; **~line** n: **to be on the ~line** sich gerade so durchschlagen

breadth [bretθ] n Breite f

breadwinner ['bredwɪnə*] n Ernährer m

break [breɪk] (pt broke, pp broken) vt (destroy) (ab- or zer)brechen; (promise) brechen, nicht einhalten ♦ vi (fall apart) auseinanderbrechen; (collapse) zusammenbrechen; (dawn) anbrechen ♦ n (gap) Lücke f; (chance) Chance f, Gelegenheit f; (fracture) Bruch m; (rest) Pause f; **~ down** vt (figures, data) aufschlüsseln; (undermine) überwinden ♦ vi (car) eine Panne haben; (person) zusammenbrechen; **~ even** vi die Kosten decken; **~ free** vi sich losreißen; **~ in** vt (animal) abrichten; (horse) zureiten ♦ vi (burglar) einbrechen; **~ into** vt fus (house) einbrechen in +acc; **~ loose** vi sich losreißen; **~ off** vi abbrechen; **~ open** vt (door etc) aufbrechen; **~ out** vi ausbrechen; **to ~ out in spots** Pickel bekommen; **~ up** vi zerbrechen; (fig) sich zerstreuen; (BRIT: SCH) in die Ferien gehen ♦ vt brechen; **~age** n Bruch m, Beschädigung f; **~down** n (TECH) Panne f; (MED: also: nervous ~down) Zusammenbruch m; **~down van** (BRIT) n Abschleppwagen m; **~er** n Brecher m

breakfast ['brekfəst] n Frühstück nt

break: ~-in n Einbruch m; **~ing** n: **~ing and entering** (JUR) Einbruch m; **~through** n Durchbruch m; **~water** n Wellenbrecher m

breast [brest] n Brust f; **~-feed** (irreg: like feed) vt, vi stillen; **~-stroke** n Brustschwimmen nt

breath [breθ] n Atem m; **out of ~** außer Atem; **under one's ~** flüsternd

Breathalyzer ['breθəlaɪzə*] ® n Röhrchen nt

breathe [briːð] vt, vi atmen; **~ in** vt, vi einatmen; **~ out** vt, vi ausatmen; **~r** n Verschnaufpause f

breathing ['briːðɪŋ] n Atmung f

breathless ['breθlɪs] adj atemlos

breathtaking ['breθteɪkɪŋ] adj atemberaubend

bred [bred] pt, pp of **breed**

breed [briːd] (pt, pp bred) vi sich vermehren ♦ vt züchten ♦ n (race) Rasse f, Zucht f; **~er** n (person) Züchter m; **~ing** n Züchtung f; (upbringing) Erziehung f; (education) Bildung f

breeze [briːz] n Brise f

breezy ['briːzɪ] adj windig; (manner) munter

brevity ['brevɪtɪ] n Kürze f

brew [bruː] vt brauen; (plot) anzetteln ♦ vi (storm) sich zusammenziehen; **~ery** n Brauerei f

bribe [braɪb] n Bestechungsgeld nt, Bestechungsgeschenk nt ♦ vt bestechen; **~ry** ['braɪbərɪ] n Bestechung f

bric-a-brac ['brɪkəbræk] n Nippes pl

brick [brɪk] n Backstein m; **~layer** n Maurer m; **~works** n Ziegelei f

bridal ['braɪdl] adj Braut-

bride [braɪd] n Braut f; **~groom** n Bräutigam m; **~smaid** n Brautjungfer f

bridge [brɪdʒ] n Brücke f; (NAUT) Kommandobrücke f; (CARDS) Bridge nt; (ANAT) Nasenrücken m ♦ vt eine Brücke schlagen über +acc; (fig) überbrücken

bridle ['braɪdl] n Zaum m ♦ vt (fig) zügeln; (horse) aufzäumen; **~ path** n Reitweg m

brief [briːf] adj kurz ♦ n (JUR) Akten pl ♦ vt instruieren; **~s** npl (underwear) Schlüpfer m, Slip m; **~case** n Aktentasche f; **~ing** n (genaue) Anweisung f; **~ly** adv kurz

brigadier [brɪgə'dɪə*] n Brigadegeneral m

bright [braɪt] adj hell; (cheerful) heiter;

(idea) klug; **~en (up)** ['braɪtn-] *vt*
aufhellen; *(person)* aufheitern ♦ *vi* sich
aufheitern

brilliance ['brɪljəns] *n* Glanz *m*; *(of person)* Scharfsinn *m*

brilliant ['brɪljənt] *adj* glänzend

brim [brɪm] *n* Rand *m*

brine [braɪn] *n* Salzwasser *nt*

bring [brɪŋ] *(pt, pp* **brought)** *vt* bringen;
~ about *vt* zustande bringen; **~ back** *vt*
zurückbringen; **~ down** *vt (price)*
senken; **~ forward** *vt (meeting)*
vorverlegen; *(COMM)* übertragen; **~ in** *vt*
hereinbringen; *(harvest)* einbringen; **~ off**
vt davontragen; *(success)* erzielen; **~ out**
vt (object) herausbringen; **~ round** *or* **to**
vt wieder zu sich bringen; **~ up** *vt*
aufziehen; *(question)* zur Sprache bringen

brink [brɪŋk] *n* Rand *m*

brisk [brɪsk] *adj* lebhaft

brisket ['brɪskɪt] *n* Bruststück *nt*

bristle ['brɪsl] *n* Borste *f* ♦ *vi* sich
sträuben; **bristling with** strotzend vor
+*dat*

Britain ['brɪtən] *n (also:* **Great ~)**
Großbritannien *nt*

British ['brɪtɪʃ] *adj* britisch ♦ *npl:* **the ~**
die Briten *pl;* **the ~ Isles** *npl* die
Britischen Inseln *pl;* **~ Rail** *n die
Britischen Eisenbahnen pl*

Briton ['brɪtən] *n* Brite *m*, Britin *f*

brittle ['brɪtl] *adj* spröde

broach [brəʊtʃ] *vt (subject)* anschneiden

broad [brɔːd] *adj* breit; *(hint)* deutlich;
(daylight) hellicht; *(general)* allgemein;
(accent) stark; **in ~ daylight** am
hellichten Tag; **~cast** *(pt, pp* **broadcast)**
n Rundfunkübertragung *f* ♦ *vt, vi*
übertragen, senden; **~en** *vt* erweitern ♦ *vi*
sich erweitern; **~ly** *adv* allgemein gesagt;
~-minded *adj* tolerant

broccoli ['brɒkəlɪ] *n* Brokkoli *pl*

brochure ['brəʊfʊə*] *n* Broschüre *f*

broil [brɔɪl] *vt (grill)* grillen

broke [brəʊk] *pt of* **break** ♦ *adj (inf)*
pleite

broken ['brəʊkən] *pp of* **break** ♦ *adj:* **~ leg** gebrochenes Bein; **in ~ English** in
gebrochenem Englisch; **~-hearted** *adj*

untröstlich

broker ['brəʊkə*] *n* Makler *m*

brolly ['brɒlɪ] *(BRIT: inf) n* Schirm *m*

bronchitis [brɒŋ'kaɪtɪs] *n* Bronchitis *f*

bronze [brɒnz] *n* Bronze *f*

brooch [brəʊtʃ] *n* Brosche *f*

brood [bruːd] *n* Brut *f* ♦ *vi* brüten

brook [brʊk] *n* Bach *m*

broom [bruːm] *n* Besen *m;* **~stick** *n*
Besenstiel *m*

Bros. *abbr =* **Brothers**

broth [brɒθ] *n* Suppe *f*, Fleischbrühe *f*

brothel ['brɒθl] *n* Bordell *nt*

brother ['brʌðə*] *n* Bruder *m;* **~-in-law**
n Schwager *m*

brought [brɔːt] *pt, pp of* **bring**

brow [braʊ] *n (eyebrow)* (Augen)braue *f;*
(forehead) Stirn *f; (of hill)* Bergkuppe *f*

brown [braʊn] *adj* braun ♦ *n* Braun *nt*
♦ *vt* bräunen; **~ bread** *n* Mischbrot *nt;*
B~ie *n* Wichtel *m;* **~ paper** *n* Packpapier
nt; **~ sugar** *n* braune(r) Zucker *m*

browse [braʊz] *vi (in books)* blättern; *(in shop)* schmökern, herumschauen

bruise [bruːz] *n* Bluterguß *m*, blaue(r)
Fleck *m* ♦ *vt* einen blauen Fleck geben
♦ *vi* einen blauen Fleck bekommen

brunt [brʌnt] *n* volle Wucht *f*

brush [brʌʃ] *n* Bürste *f; (for sweeping)*
Handbesen *m; (for painting)* Pinsel *m;*
(fight) kurze(r) Kampf *m; (MIL)*
Scharmützel *nt; (fig)* Auseinandersetzung
f ♦ *vt (clean)* bürsten; *(sweep)* fegen; *(usu:*
~ past, ~ against) streifen; **~ aside** *vt*
abtun; **~ up** *vt (knowledge)* auffrischen;
~wood *n* Gestrüpp *nt*

brusque [bruːsk] *adj* schroff

Brussels ['brʌslz] *n* Brüssel *nt;* **~ sprout**
n Rosenkohl *m*

brutal ['bruːtl] *adj* brutal

brute [bruːt] *n (person)* Scheusal *nt* ♦ *adj:*
by ~ force mit roher Kraft

B.Sc. *n abbr =* **Bachelor of Science**

BSE *n abbr (= bovine spongiform encephalopathy)* BSE *f*

bubble ['bʌbl] *n* (Luft)blase *f* ♦ *vi*
sprudeln; *(with joy)* übersprudeln; **~ bath**
n Schaumbad *nt;* **~gum** *n* Kaugummi *m or nt*

buck [bʌk] n Bock m; (US: inf) Dollar m
♦ vi bocken; **to pass the ~ (to sb)** die
Verantwortung (auf jdn) abschieben; **~
up** (inf) vi sich zusammenreißen
bucket ['bʌkɪt] n Eimer m
buckle ['bʌkl] n Schnalle f ♦ vt (an- or
zusammen)schnallen ♦ vi (bend) sich
verziehen
bud [bʌd] n Knospe f ♦ vi knospen,
keimen
Buddhism ['budɪzəm] n Buddhismus m
budding ['bʌdɪŋ] adj angehend
buddy ['bʌdɪ] (inf) n Kumpel m
budge [bʌdʒ] vt, vi (sich) von der Stelle
rühren
budgerigar ['bʌdʒərɪgɑ:*] n
Wellensittich m
budget ['bʌdʒɪt] n Budget nt; (POL)
Haushalt m ♦ vi: **to ~ for sth** etw
einplanen
budgie ['bʌdʒɪ] n = **budgerigar**
buff [bʌf] adj (colour) lederfarben ♦ n
(enthusiast) Fan m
buffalo ['bʌfələu] (pl ~ or **~es**) n (BRIT)
Büffel m; (US: bison) Bison m
buffer ['bʌfə*] n Puffer m; (COMPUT)
Pufferspeicher m
buffet¹ ['bʌfɪt] n (blow) Schlag m ♦ vt
(herum)stoßen
buffet² ['bufeɪ] (BRIT) n (bar) Imbißraum
m, Erfrischungsraum m; (food) (kaltes)
Büfett nt; **~ car** (BRIT) n Speisewagen m
bug [bʌg] n (also fig) Wanze f ♦ vt
verwanzen
bugle ['bju:gl] n Jagdhorn nt; (MIL: MUS)
Bügelhorn nt
build [bɪld] (pt, pp **built**) vt bauen ♦ n
Körperbau m; **~ up** vt aufbauen; **~er** n
Bauunternehmer m; **~ing** n Gebäude nt;
~ing society (BRIT) n Bausparkasse f
built [bɪlt] pt, pp of **build**
built-in adj (cupboard) eingebaut
built-up area n Wohngebiet nt
bulb [bʌlb] n (BOT) (Blumen)zwiebel f;
(ELEC) Glühlampe f, Birne f
Bulgaria [bʌl'gɛərɪə] n Bulgarien nt; **~n**
adj bulgarisch ♦ n Bulgare m, Bulgarin f;
(LING) Bulgarisch nt
bulge [bʌldʒ] n (Aus)bauchung f ♦ vi sich

(aus)bauchen
bulk [bʌlk] n Größe f, Masse f; (greater
part) Großteil m; **in ~** (COMM) en gros; **the
~ of** der größte Teil +gen; **~head** n
Schott nt; **~y** adj (sehr) umfangreich;
(goods) sperrig
bull [bul] n (animal) Bulle m; (cattle) Stier
m; (papal) Bulle f; **~dog** n Bulldogge f
bulldozer ['buldəuzə*] n Planierraupe f
bullet ['bulɪt] n Kugel f
bulletin ['bulɪtɪn] n Bulletin nt,
Bekanntmachung f
bulletproof ['bulɪtpru:f] adj kugelsicher
bullfight ['bulfaɪt] n Stierkampf m; **~er** n
Stierkämpfer m
bullion ['buliən] n Barren m
bullock ['bulək] n Ochse m
bullring ['bulrɪŋ] n Stierkampfarena f
bull's-eye ['bulzaɪ] n Zentrum nt
bully ['bulɪ] n Raufbold m ♦ vt
einschüchtern
bum [bʌm] n (inf: backside) Hintern m;
(tramp) Landstreicher m
bumblebee ['bʌmblbi:] n Hummel f
bump [bʌmp] n (blow) Stoß m; (swelling)
Beule f ♦ vt, vi stoßen, prallen; **~ into** vt
fus stoßen gegen ♦ vt (person) treffen; **~
cars** (US) npl (dodgems) Autoskooter pl;
~er n (AUT) Stoßstange f ♦ adj (edition)
dick; (harvest) Rekord-
bumptious ['bʌmpʃəs] adj aufgeblasen
bumpy ['bʌmpɪ] adj holprig
bun [bʌn] n Korinthenbrötchen nt
bunch [bʌntʃ] n (of flowers) Strauß m; (of
keys) Bund m; (of people) Haufen m
bundle ['bʌndl] n Bündel nt ♦ vt (also: ~
up) bündeln
bungalow ['bʌŋgələu] n einstöckige(s)
Haus nt, Bungalow m
bungle ['bʌŋgl] vt verpfuschen
bunion ['bʌnjən] n entzündete(r)
Fußballen m
bunk [bʌŋk] n Schlafkoje f; **~ beds** npl
Etagenbett nt
bunker ['bʌŋkə*] n (coal store)
Kohlenbunker m; (GOLF) Sandloch nt
bunny ['bʌnɪ] n (also: ~ rabbit) Häschen
nt
bunting ['bʌntɪŋ] n Fahnentuch nt

buoy [bɔɪ] *n* Boje *f*; (*life~*) Rettungsboje *f*; **~ up** *vt* Auftrieb geben +*dat*; **~ant** *adj* (*floating*) schwimmend; (*fig*) heiter

burden ['bɜːdn] *n* (*weight*) Ladung *f*, Last *f*; (*fig*) Bürde *f* ♦ *vt* belasten

bureau ['bjuərəu] (*pl* **~x**) *n* (*BRIT: writing desk*) Sekretär *m*; (*US: chest of drawers*) Kommode *f*; (*for information etc*) Büro *nt*

bureaucracy [bjuˈrɒkrəsɪ] *n* Bürokratie *f*

bureaucrat ['bjuərəkræt] *n* Bürokrat(in) *m(f)*

bureaux ['bjuərəuz] *npl of* **bureau**

burglar ['bɜːglə*] *n* Einbrecher *m*; **~ alarm** *n* Einbruchssicherung *f*; **~y** *n* Einbruch *m*

burial ['berɪəl] *n* Beerdigung *f*

burly ['bɜːlɪ] *adj* stämmig

Burma ['bɜːmə] *n* Birma *nt*

burn [bɜːn] (*pt, pp* **burned** *or* **burnt**) *vt* verbrennen ♦ *vi* brennen ♦ *n* Brandwunde *f*; **~ down** *vt, vi* abbrennen; **~er** *n* Brenner *m*; **~ing** *adj* brennend; **~t** [bɜːnt] *pt, pp of* **burn**

burrow ['bʌrəu] *n* (*of fox*) Bau *m*; (*of rabbit*) Höhle *f* ♦ *vt* eingraben

bursar ['bɜːsə*] *n* Kassenverwalter *m*, Quästor *m*; **~y** *n* (*BRIT*) Stipendium *nt*

burst [bɜːst] (*pt, pp* **burst**) *vt* zerbrechen ♦ *vi* platzen ♦ *n* Explosion *f*; (*outbreak*) Ausbruch *m*; (*in pipe*) Bruch(stelle *f*) *m*; **to ~ into flames** in Flammen aufgehen; **to ~ into tears** in Tränen ausbrechen; **to ~ out laughing** in Gelächter ausbrechen; **~ into** *vt fus* (*room etc*) platzen in +*acc*; **~ open** *vi* aufbrechen

bury ['berɪ] *vt* vergraben; (*in grave*) beerdigen

bus [bʌs] *n* (*Auto*)bus *m*, Omnibus *m*

bush [buʃ] *n* Busch *m*; **to beat about the ~** wie die Katze um den heißen Brei herumgehen

bushy ['buʃɪ] *adj* buschig

busily ['bɪzɪlɪ] *adv* geschäftig

business ['bɪznɪs] *n* Geschäft *nt*; (*concern*) Angelegenheit *f*; **it's none of your ~** es geht dich nichts an; **to mean ~** es ernst meinen; **to be away on ~** geschäftlich verreist sein; **it's my ~ to ...** es ist meine Sache, zu ...; **~like** *adj* geschäftsmäßig; **~man** (*irreg*) *n* Geschäftsmann *m*; **~ trip** *n* Geschäftsreise *f*; **~woman** (*irreg*) *n* Geschäftsfrau *f*

busker ['bʌskə*] (*BRIT*) *n* Straßenmusikant *m*

bus stop *n* Bushaltestelle *f*

bust [bʌst] *n* Büste *f* ♦ *adj* (*broken*) kaputt(gegangen); (*business*) pleite; **to go ~** pleite machen

bustle ['bʌsl] *n* Getriebe *nt* ♦ *vi* hasten

bustling ['bʌslɪŋ] *adj* geschäftig

busy ['bɪzɪ] *adj* beschäftigt; (*road*) belebt ♦ *vt*: **to ~ o.s.** sich beschäftigen; **~body** *n* Übereifrige(r) *mf*; **~ signal** (*US*) *n* (*TEL*) Besetztzeichen *nt*

KEYWORD

but [bʌt] *conj* **1** (*yet*) aber; **not X but Y** nicht X sondern Y

2 (*however*): **I'd love to come, but I'm busy** ich würde gern kommen, bin aber beschäftigt

3 (*showing disagreement, surprise etc*): **but that's fantastic!** (aber) das ist ja fantastisch!

♦ *prep* (*apart from, except*): **nothing but trouble** nichts als Ärger; **no-one but him can do it** niemand außer ihn kann es machen; **but for you/your help** ohne dich/deine Hilfe; **anything but that** alles, nur das nicht

♦ *adv* (*just, only*): **she's but a child** sie ist noch ein Kind; **had I but known** wenn ich es nur gewußt hätte; **I can but try** ich kann es immerhin versuchen; **all but finished** so gut wie fertig

---

butcher ['butʃə*] *n* Metzger *m*; (*murderer*) Schlächter *m* ♦ *vt* schlachten; (*kill*) abschlachten; **~'s (shop)** *n* Metzgerei *f*

butler ['bʌtlə*] *n* Butler *m*

butt [bʌt] *n* (*cask*) große(s) Faß *nt*; (*BRIT: fig: target*) Zielscheibe *f*; (*thick end*) dicke(s) Ende *nt*; (*of gun*) Kolben *m*; (*of cigarette*) Stummel *m* ♦ *vt* (mit dem Kopf) stoßen; **~ in** *vi* (*interrupt*) sich einmischen

butter ['bʌtə*] n Butter f ♦ vt buttern; **~ bean** n Wachsbohne f; **~cup** n Butterblume f

butterfly ['bʌtəflaɪ] n Schmetterling m; (SWIMMING: also ~ **stroke**) Butterflystil m

buttocks ['bʌtəks] npl Gesäß nt

button ['bʌtn] n Knopf m ♦ vt, vi (also: ~ up) zuknöpfen

buttress ['bʌtrɪs] n Strebepfeiler m; Stützbogen m

buxom ['bʌksəm] adj drall

buy [baɪ] (pt, pp bought) vt kaufen ♦ n Kauf m; **to ~ sb a drink** jdm einen Drink spendieren; **~er** n Käufer(in) m(f)

buzz [bʌz] n Summen nt ♦ vi summen

buzzer ['bʌzə*] n Summer m

buzz word n Modewort nt

KEYWORD

by [baɪ] prep 1 (referring to cause, agent) von, durch; **killed by lightning** vom Blitz getötet; **a painting by Picasso** ein Gemälde von Picasso

2 (referring to method, manner, means): **by bus/car/train** mit dem Bus/Auto/Zug; **to pay by cheque** per Scheck bezahlen; **by moonlight** bei Mondschein; **by saving hard, he ...** indem er eisern sparte, ... er ...

3 (via, through) über +acc; **he came in by the back door** er kam durch die Hintertür herein

4 (close to, past) bei, an +dat; **a holiday by the sea** ein Urlaub am Meer; **she rushed by me** sie eilte an mir vorbei

5 (not later than): **by 4 o'clock** bis 4 Uhr; **by this time tomorrow** morgen um diese Zeit; **by the time I got here it was too late** als ich hier ankam, war es zu spät

6 (during): **by day** bei Tag

7 (amount): **by the kilo/metre** kiloweise/meterweise; **paid by the hour** stundenweise bezahlt

8 (MATH, measure): **to divide by 3** durch 3 teilen; **to multiply by 3** mit 3 malnehmen; **a room 3 metres by 4** ein Zimmer 3 mal 4 Meter; **it's broader by a metre** es ist (um) einem Meter breiter

9 (according to) nach; **it's all right by me** von mir aus gern

10: **(all) by oneself** etc ganz allein

11: **by the way** übrigens

♦ adv 1 see go; pass etc

2: **by and by** irgendwann; (with past tenses) nach einiger Zeit; **by and large** (on the whole) im großen und ganzen

bye(-bye) ['baɪ('baɪ)] excl (auf) Wiedersehen

by(e)-law ['baɪlɔː] n Verordnung f

by-election ['baɪɪ'lekʃən] (BRIT) n Nachwahl f

bygone ['baɪgɒn] adj vergangen ♦ n: let ~s be ~s laß(t) das Vergangene vergangen sein

bypass ['baɪpɑːs] n Umgehungsstraße f ♦ vt umgehen

by-product ['baɪprɒdʌkt] n Nebenprodukt nt

bystander ['baɪstændə*] n Zuschauer m

byte [baɪt] n (COMPUT) Byte nt

byword ['baɪwɜːd] n Inbegriff m

C c

C [siː] n (MUS) C nt

C. abbr (= centigrade) C

C.A. abbr = **chartered accountant**

cab [kæb] n Taxi nt; (of train) Führerstand m; (of truck) Führersitz m

cabaret ['kæbəreɪ] n Kabarett nt

cabbage ['kæbɪdʒ] n Kohl(kopf) m

cabin ['kæbɪn] n Hütte f; (NAUT) Kajüte f; (AVIAT) Kabine f; ~ **cruiser** n Motorjacht f

cabinet ['kæbɪnɪt] n Schrank m; (for china) Vitrine f; (POL) Kabinett nt; **~-maker** n Kunsttischler m

cable ['keɪbl] n Drahtseil nt, Tau nt; (TEL) (Leitungs)kabel nt; (telegram) Kabel nt ♦ vt kabeln, telegraphieren; **~-car** n Seilbahn f; ~ **television** n Kabelfernsehen nt

cache [kæʃ] n geheime(s) (Waffen)lager nt; (provisions) (Proviant)lager nt

cackle ['kækl] vi gacken

cacti ['kæktaɪ] npl of **cactus**

cactus ['kæktəs] (*pl* **cacti**) *n* Kaktus *m*, Kaktee *f*

caddie ['kædɪ] *n* (GOLF) Golfjunge *m*

caddy *n* = **caddie**

cadet [kə'det] *n* Kadett *m*

cadge [kædʒ] *vt* schmarotzen

Caesarean [siː'zɛərɪən] *adj*: ~ **(section)** Kaiserschnitt *m*

café ['kæfɪ] *n* Café *nt*, Restaurant *nt*

cafeteria [kæfɪ'tɪərɪə] *n* Selbstbedienungsrestaurant *nt*

caffein(e) ['kæfiːn] *n* Koffein *nt*

cage [keɪdʒ] *n* Käfig *m* ♦ *vt* einsperren

cagey ['keɪdʒɪ] *adj* geheimnistuerisch, zurückhaltend

cagoule [kə'guːl] *n* Windhemd *nt*

Cairo ['kaɪərəʊ] *n* Kairo *nt*

cajole [kə'dʒəʊl] *vt* überreden

cake [keɪk] *n* Kuchen *m*; (*of soap*) Stück *nt*; ~**d** *adj* verkrustet

calamity [kə'læmɪtɪ] *n* Unglück *nt*, (Schicksals)schlag *m*

calcium ['kælsɪəm] *n* Kalzium *nt*

calculate ['kælkjʊleɪt] *vt* berechnen, kalkulieren; **calculating** *adj* berechnend; **calculation** [kælkjʊ'leɪʃən] *n* Berechnung *f*; **calculator** *n* Rechner *m*

calculus ['kælkjʊləs] *n* Infinitesimalrechnung *f*

calendar ['kælɪndə*] *n* Kalender *m*; ~ **month** *n* Kalendermonat *m*

calf [kɑːf] (*pl* **calves**) *n* Kalb *nt*; (*also:* ~*skin*) Kalbsleder *nt*; (ANAT) Wade *f*

calibre ['kælɪbə*] (*US* **caliber**) *n* Kaliber *nt*

call [kɔːl] *vt* rufen; (*name*) nennen; (*meeting*) einberufen; (*awaken*) wecken; (TEL) anrufen ♦ *vi* (*shout*) rufen; (*visit: also:* ~ **in**, ~ **round**) vorbeikommen ♦ *n* (*shout*) Ruf *m*; (TEL) Anruf *m*; **to be** ~**ed** heißen; **on** ~ in Bereitschaft; ~ **back** *vi* (*return*) wiederkommen; (TEL) zurückrufen; ~ **for** *vt fus* (*demand*) erfordern, verlangen; (*fetch*) abholen; ~ **off** *vt* (*cancel*) absagen; ~ **on** *vt fus* (*visit*) besuchen; (*turn to*) bitten; ~ **out** *vi* rufen; ~ **up** *vt* (MIL) einberufen; ~**box** (BRIT) *n* Telefonzelle *f*; ~**er** *n* Besucher(in) *m(f)*; (TEL) Anrufer *m*; ~ **girl** *n* Call-Girl *nt*; ~-

in (US) *n* (*phone-in*) Phone-in *nt*; ~**ing** *n* (*vocation*) Berufung *f*; ~**ing card** (US) *n* Visitenkarte *f*

callous ['kæləs] *adj* herzlos

calm [kɑːm] *n* Ruhe *f*; (NAUT) Flaute *f* ♦ *vt* beruhigen ♦ *adj* ruhig; (*person*) gelassen; ~ **down** *vi* sich beruhigen ♦ *vt* beruhigen

Calor gas ['kælə-] ® *n* Propangas *nt*

calorie ['kælərɪ] *n* Kalorie *f*

calves [kɑːvz] *npl of* **calf**

camber ['kæmbə*] *n* Wölbung *f*

Cambodia [kæm'bəʊdjə] *n* Kambodscha *nt*

camcorder ['kæmkɔːdə*] *n* Camcorder *m*

came [keɪm] *pt of* **come**

cameo ['kæmɪəʊ] *n* Kamee *f*

camera ['kæmərə] *n* Fotoapparat *m*; (CINE, TV) Kamera *f*; **in** ~ unter Ausschluß der Öffentlichkeit; ~**man** (*irreg*) *n* Kameramann *m*

camouflage ['kæməflɑːʒ] *n* Tarnung *f* ♦ *vt* tarnen

camp [kæmp] *n* Lager *nt* ♦ *vi* zelten, campen ♦ *adj* affektiert

campaign [kæm'peɪn] *n* Kampagne *f*; (MIL) Feldzug *m* ♦ *vi* Krieg führen; (*fig*) werben, Propaganda machen; (POL) den Wahlkampf führen

campbed ['kæmp'bed] (BRIT) *n* Campingbett *nt*

camper ['kæmpə*] *n* Camper(in) *m(f)*; (*vehicle*) Camping-wagen *m*

camping ['kæmpɪŋ] *n*: **to go** ~ zelten, Camping machen

campsite ['kæmpsaɪt] *n* Campingplatz *m*

campus ['kæmpəs] *n* Universitätsgelände *nt*, Campus *m*

can¹ [kæn] *n* Büchse *f*, Dose *f*; (*for water*) Kanne *f* ♦ *vt* konservieren, in Büchsen einmachen

---

KEYWORD

---

can² [kæn] (*negative* **cannot**, **can't**; *conditional* **could**) *aux vb* **1** (*be able to*, *know how to*) können; **I can see you tomorrow, if you like** ich könnte Sie morgen sehen, wenn Sie wollen; **I can swim** ich kann schwimmen; **can you**

speak German? sprechen Sie Deutsch?
2 (*may*) können, dürfen; **could I have a
word with you?** könnte ich Sie kurz
sprechen?

Canada ['kænədə] n Kanada nt
Canadian [kə'neɪdɪən] adj kanadisch ♦ n
Kanadier(in) m(f)
canal [kə'næl] n Kanal m
canary [kə'neərɪ] n Kanarienvogel m
cancel ['kænsəl] vt absagen; (*delete*)
durchstreichen; (*train*) streichen; **~lation**
[kænsə'leɪʃən] n Absage f; Streichung f
cancer ['kænsə*] n (*also*: ASTROL: C~)
Krebs m
candid ['kændɪd] adj offen, ehrlich
candidate ['kændɪdeɪt] n Kandidat(in)
m(f)
candle ['kændl] n Kerze f; **~light** n
Kerzenlicht nt; **~stick** n (*also*: ~ holder)
Kerzenhalter m
candour ['kændə*] (US **candor**) n
Offenheit f
candy ['kændɪ] n Kandis(zucker) m; (US)
Bonbons pl; **~-floss** [-flɒs] (BRIT) n
Zuckerwatte f
cane [keɪn] n (BOT) Rohr nt; (*stick*) Stock
m ♦ vt (BRIT: SCH) schlagen
canine ['kænaɪn] adj Hunde-
canister ['kænɪstə*] n Blechdose f
cannabis ['kænəbɪs] n Hanf m, Haschisch
nt
canned [kænd] adj Büchsen-, eingemacht
cannibal ['kænɪbəl] n Menschenfresser m
cannon ['kænən] (pl ~ or ~s) n Kanone f
cannot ['kænɒt] = **can not**
canny ['kænɪ] adj schlau
canoe [kə'nu:] n Kanu nt
canon ['kænən] n (*clergyman*) Domherr
m; (*standard*) Grundsatz m
canonize ['kænənaɪz] vt heiligsprechen
can-opener [-'əʊpnə*] n Büchsenöffner
m
canopy ['kænəpɪ] n Baldachin m
can't [kɑːnt] = **can not**
cantankerous [kæn'tæŋkərəs] adj
zänkisch, mürrisch
canteen [kæn'tiːn] n Kantine f; (BRIT: of
cutlery) Besteckkasten m; (*bottle*)

Feldflasche f
canter ['kæntə*] n Kanter m ♦ vi in
kurzem Galopp reiten
canvas ['kænvəs] n Segeltuch nt; (*sail*)
Segel nt; (*for painting*) Leinwand f; **under
~** (*camping*) in Zelten
canvass ['kænvəs] vi um Stimmen
werben; **~ing** n Wahlwerbung f
canyon ['kænjən] n Felsenschlucht f
cap [kæp] n Mütze f; (*of pen*) Kappe f; (*of
bottle*) Deckel m ♦ vt (*surpass*)
übertreffen; (SPORT) aufstellen; (*put limit
on*) einen Höchstsatz festlegen für
capability [keɪpə'bɪlɪtɪ] n Fähigkeit f
capable ['keɪpəbl] adj fähig
capacity [kə'pæsɪtɪ] n Fassungsvermögen
nt; (*ability*) Fähigkeit f; (*position*)
Eigenschaft f
cape [keɪp] n (*garment*) Cape nt, Umhang
m; (GEOG) Kap nt
caper ['keɪpə*] n (COOK: usu: ~s) Kaper f;
(*prank*) Kapriole f
capital ['kæpɪtl] n (~ *city*) Hauptstadt f;
(FIN) Kapital nt; (~ *letter*) Großbuchstabe
m; **~ gains tax** n Kapitalertragssteuer f;
~ism n Kapitalismus m; **~ist** adj
kapitalistisch ♦ n Kapitalist(in) m(f); **~ize**
vi: **to ~ize on** Kapital schlagen aus; **~
punishment** n Todesstrafe f
capitulate [kə'pɪtjuleɪt] vi kapitulieren
capricious [kə'prɪʃəs] adj launisch
Capricorn ['kæprɪkɔːn] n Steinbock m
capsize [kæp'saɪz] vt, vi kentern
capsule ['kæpsjuːl] n Kapsel f
captain ['kæptɪn] n Kapitän m; (MIL)
Hauptmann m ♦ vt anführen
caption ['kæpʃən] n (*heading*) Überschrift
f; (*to picture*) Unterschrift f
captivate ['kæptɪveɪt] vt fesseln
captive ['kæptɪv] n Gefangene(r) mf ♦ adj
gefangen(gehalten)
captivity [kæp'tɪvɪtɪ] n Gefangenschaft f
capture ['kæptʃə*] vt gefangennehmen;
(*place*) erobern; (*attention*) erregen ♦ n
Gefangennahme f; (*data ~*) Erfassung f
car [kɑː*] n Auto nt, Wagen m; (RAIL)
Wagen m
carat ['kærət] n Karat nt
caravan ['kærəvæn] n (BRIT) Wohnwagen

m; (*in desert*) Karawane *f*; ~ **site** (*BRIT*) *n* Campingplatz *m* für Wohnwagen

carbohydrate [kɑːbəʊˈhaɪdreɪt] *n* Kohlenhydrat *nt*

carbon [ˈkɑːbən] *n* Kohlenstoff *m*; ~ **copy** *n* Durchschlag *m*; ~ **paper** *n* Kohlepapier *nt*

carburettor [ˈkɑːbjʊretə*] (*US* **carburetor**) *n* Vergaser *m*

carcass [ˈkɑːkəs] *n* Kadaver *m*

card [kɑːd] *n* Karte *f*; ~**board** *n* Pappe *f*; ~ **game** *n* Kartenspiel *nt*

cardiac [ˈkɑːdɪæk] *adj* Herz-

cardigan [ˈkɑːdɪgən] *n* Strickjacke *f*

cardinal [ˈkɑːdɪnl] *adj*: ~ **number** Kardinalzahl *f* ♦ *n* (*REL*) Kardinal *m*

card index *n* Kartei *f*; (*in library*) Katalog *m*

care [keə*] *n* (*of teeth, car etc*) Pflege *f*; (*of children*) Fürsorge *f*; (*carefulness*) Sorgfalt *f*; (*worry*) Sorge *f* ♦ *vi*: to ~ **about** sich kümmern um; ~ **of** bei; **in sb's** ~ in jds Obhut; **I don't** ~ das ist mir egal; **I couldn't** ~ **less** es ist mir doch völlig egal; **to take** ~ aufpassen; **to take** ~ **of** sorgen für; **to take** ~ **to do sth** sich bemühen, etw zu tun; ~ **for** *vt* sorgen für; (*like*) mögen

career [kəˈrɪə*] *n* Karriere *f*, Laufbahn *f* ♦ *vi* (*also*: ~ **along**) rasen

carefree [ˈkeəfriː] *adj* sorgenfrei

careful [ˈkeəfʊl] *adj* sorgfältig; (**be**) ~! paß auf!

careless [ˈkeəlɪs] *adj* nachlässig; ~**ness** *n* Nachlässigkeit *f*

carer [ˈkeərə*] *n* (*MED*) Betreuer(in) *m(f)*

caress [kəˈres] *n* Liebkosung *f* ♦ *vt* liebkosen

caretaker [ˈkeəteɪkə*] *n* Hausmeister *m*

car-ferry [ˈkɑːferɪ] *n* Autofähre *f*

cargo [ˈkɑːgəʊ] (*pl* ~**es**) *n* Schiffsladung *f*

car hire *n* Autovermietung *f*

Caribbean [kærɪˈbiːən] *n*: **the** ~ (**Sea**) die Karibik

caricature [ˈkærɪkətjʊə*] *n* Karikatur *f*

caring [ˈkeərɪŋ] *adj* (*society, organization*) sozial eingestellt; (*person*) liebevoll

carnage [ˈkɑːnɪdʒ] *n* Blutbad *nt*

carnal [ˈkɑːnl] *adj* fleischlich

carnation [kɑːˈneɪʃən] *n* Nelke *f*

carnival [ˈkɑːnɪvəl] *n* Karneval *m*, Fasching *m*; (*US: fun fair*) Kirmes *f*

carnivorous [kɑːˈnɪvərəs] *adj* fleischfressend

carol [ˈkærəl] *n*: (**Christmas**) ~ (Weihnachts)lied *nt*

carp [kɑːp] *n* (*fish*) Karpfen *m*; ~ **at** *vt* herumnörgeln an +*dat*

car park (*BRIT*) *n* Parkplatz *m*; (*covered*) Parkhaus *n*

carpenter [ˈkɑːpɪntə*] *n* Zimmermann *m*

carpentry [ˈkɑːpɪntrɪ] *n* Zimmerei *f*

carpet [ˈkɑːpɪt] *n* Teppich *m* ♦ *vt* mit einem Teppich auslegen; ~ **bombing** *n* Flächenbombardierung *f*; ~ **slippers** *npl* Pantoffeln *pl*; ~ **sweeper** [-swiːpə*] *n* Teppichkehrer *m*

car phone *n* (*TEL*) Autotelefon *nt*

carriage [ˈkærɪdʒ] *n* Kutsche *f*; (*RAIL: of typewriter*) Wagen *m*; (*of goods*) Beförderung *f*; (*bearing*) Haltung *f*; ~ **return** *n* (*on typewriter*) Rücklauftaste *f*; ~**way** (*BRIT*) *n* (*part of road*) Fahrbahn *f*

carrier [ˈkærɪə*] *n* Träger(in) *m(f)*; (*COMM*) Spediteur *m*; ~ **bag** (*BRIT*) *n* Tragetasche *m*

carrot [ˈkærət] *n* Möhre *f*, Karotte *f*

carry [ˈkærɪ] *vt, vi* tragen; **to get carried away** (*fig*) sich nicht mehr bremsen können; ~ **on** *vi* (*continue*) weitermachen; (*inf: complain*) Theater machen; ~ **out** *vt* (*orders*) ausführen; (*investigation*) durchführen; ~**cot** (*BRIT*) *n* Babytragetasche *f*; ~**-on** (*inf*) *n* (*fuss*) Theater *nt*

cart [kɑːt] *n* Wagen *m*, Karren *m* ♦ *vt* schleppen

cartilage [ˈkɑːtɪlɪdʒ] *n* Knorpel *m*

carton [ˈkɑːtən] *n* Karton *m*; (*of milk*) Tüte *f*

cartoon [kɑːˈtuːn] *n* (*PRESS*) Karikatur *f*; (*comic strip*) Comics *pl*; (*CINE*) (Zeichen)trickfilm *m*

cartridge [ˈkɑːtrɪdʒ] *n* Patrone *f*

carve [kɑːv] *vt* (*wood*) schnitzen; (*stone*) meißeln; (*meat*) (vor)schneiden; ~ **up** *vt* aufschneiden

carving [ˈkɑːvɪŋ] *n* Schnitzerei *f*; ~ **knife**

n Tranchiermesser *nt*

car wash *n* Autowäsche *f*

cascade [kæsˈkeɪd] *n* Wasserfall *m* ♦ *vi* kaskadenartig herabfallen

case [keɪs] *n* (*box*) Kasten *m*; (*BRIT: also: suit~*) Koffer *m*; (*JUR, matter*) Fall *m*; **in ~** falls, im Falle; **in any ~** jedenfalls, auf jeden Fall

cash [kæʃ] *n* (Bar)geld *nt* ♦ *vt* einlösen; **~ on delivery** per Nachnahme; **~ book** *n* Kassenbuch *nt*; **~ card** *n* Scheckkarte *f*; **~ desk** (*BRIT*) *n* Kasse *f*; **~ dispenser** *n* Geldautomat *m*

cashew [kæˈʃuː] *n* (*also: ~ nut*) Cashewnuß *f*

cash flow *n* Cash-flow *m*

cashier [kæˈʃɪə*] *n* Kassierer(in) *m(f)*

cashmere [ˈkæʃmɪə*] *n* Kaschmirwolle *f*

cash register *n* Registrierkasse *f*

casing [ˈkeɪsɪŋ] *n* Gehäuse *nt*

casino [kəˈsiːnəʊ] *n* Kasino *nt*

cask [kɑːsk] *n* Faß *nt*

casket [ˈkɑːskɪt] *n* Kästchen *nt*; (*US: coffin*) Sarg *m*

casserole [ˈkæsərəʊl] *n* Kasserolle *f*; (*food*) Auflauf *m*

cassette [kæˈset] *n* Kassette *f*; **~ player** *n* Kassettengerät *nt*

cast [kɑːst] (*pt, pp* **cast**) *vt* werfen; (*horns*) verlieren; (*metal*) gießen; (*THEAT*) besetzen; (*vote*) abgeben ♦ *n* (*THEAT*) Besetzung *f*; (*also: plaster ~*) Gipsverband *m*; **~ off** *vi* (*NAUT*) losmachen

castaway [ˈkɑːstəweɪ] *n* Schiffbrüchige(r) *mf*

caste [kɑːst] *n* Kaste *f*

caster sugar [ˈkɑːstə-] (*BRIT*) *n* Raffinade *f*

casting vote [ˈkɑːstɪŋ-] (*BRIT*) *n* entscheidende Stimme *f*

cast iron *n* Gußeisen *nt*

castle [ˈkɑːsl] *n* Burg *f*; Schloß *nt*; (*CHESS*) Turm *m*

castor [ˈkɑːstə*] *n* (*wheel*) Laufrolle *f*

castor oil *n* Rizinusöl *nt*

castrate [kæsˈtreɪt] *vt* kastrieren

casual [ˈkæʒjʊl] *adj* (*attitude*) nachlässig; (*dress*) leger; (*meeting*) zufällig; (*work*) Gelegenheits-; **~ly** *adv* (*dress*) zwanglos,

leger; (*remark*) beiläufig

casualty [ˈkæʒjʊltɪ] *n* Verletzte(r) *mf*; (*dead*) Tote(r) *mf*; (*also: ~ department*) Unfallstation *f*

cat [kæt] *n* Katze *f*

catalogue [ˈkætələɡ] (*US* **catalog**) *n* Katalog *m* ♦ *vt* katalogisieren

catalyst [ˈkætəlɪst] *n* Katalysator *m*

catalytic converter [kætəˈlɪtɪkkənˈvɜːtə*] *n* Katalysator *m*

catapult [ˈkætəpʌlt] *n* Schleuder *f*

cataract [ˈkætərækt] *n* (*MED*) graue(r) Star *m*

catarrh [kəˈtɑː*] *n* Katarrh *m*

catastrophe [kəˈtæstrəfɪ] *n* Katastrophe *f*

catch [kætʃ] (*pt, pp* **caught**) *vt* fangen; (*arrest*) fassen; (*train*) erreichen; (*person: by surprise*) ertappen; (*also: ~ up*) einholen ♦ *vi* (*fire*) in Gang kommen; (*in branches etc*) hängenbleiben ♦ *n* (*fish etc*) Fang *m*; (*trick*) Haken *m*; (*of lock*) Sperrhaken *m*; **to ~ an illness** sich *dat* eine Krankheit holen; **to ~ fire** Feuer fangen; **~ on** *vi* (*understand*) begreifen; (*grow popular*) ankommen; **~ up** *vi* (*fig*) aufholen

catching [ˈkætʃɪŋ] *adj* ansteckend

catchment area [ˈkætʃmənt-] (*BRIT*) *n* Einzugsgebiet *nt*

catch phrase *n* Slogan *m*

catchy [ˈkætʃɪ] *adj* (*tune*) eingängig

catechism [ˈkætɪkɪzəm] *n* Katechismus *m*

categoric(al) [kætəˈɡɒrɪk(l)] *adj* kategorisch

category [ˈkætɪɡərɪ] *n* Kategorie *f*

cater [ˈkeɪtə*] *vi* versorgen; **~ for** (*BRIT*) *vt fus* (*party*) ausrichten; (*needs*) eingestellt sein auf *+acc*; **~er** *n* Lieferant(in) *m(f)* von Speisen und Getränken; **~ing** *n* Gastronomie *f*

caterpillar [ˈkætəpɪlə*] *n* Raupe *f*; **~ track** ® *n* Gleiskette *f*

cathedral [kəˈθiːdrəl] *n* Kathedrale *f*, Dom *m*

catholic [ˈkæθəlɪk] *adj* (*tastes etc*) vielseitig; **C~** *adj* (*REL*) katholisch ♦ *n* Katholik(in) *m(f)*

Catseye ['kætsaɪ] (*BRIT*:®) *n* (*AUT*) Katzenauge *nt*

cattle ['kætl] *npl* Vieh *nt*

catty ['kætɪ] *adj* gehässig

caucus ['kɔːkəs] *n* (*POL*) Gremium *nt*; (*US: meeting*) Sitzung *f*

caught [kɔːt] *pt, pp of* catch

cauliflower ['kɒlɪflaʊə*] *n* Blumenkohl *m*

cause [kɔːz] *n* Ursache *f*; (*purpose*) Sache *f* ♦ *vt* verursachen

causeway ['kɔːzweɪ] *n* Damm *m*

caustic ['kɔːstɪk] *adj* ätzend; (*fig*) bissig

caution ['kɔːʃən] *n* Vorsicht *f*; (*warning*) Verwarnung *f* ♦ *vt* verwarnen

cautious ['kɔːʃəs] *adj* vorsichtig

cavalier [kævə'lɪə*] *adj* blasiert

cavalry ['kævəlrɪ] *n* Kavallerie *f*

cave [keɪv] *n* Höhle *f*; ~ **in** *vi* einstürzen; **~man** (*irreg*) *n* Höhlenmensch *m*

cavern ['kævən] *n* Höhle *f*

caviar(e) ['kævɪɑː*] *n* Kaviar *m*

cavity ['kævɪtɪ] *n* Loch *nt*

cavort [kə'vɔːt] *vi* umherspringen

C.B. *n abbr* (= *Citizens' Band (Radio)*) CB

C.B.I. *n abbr* (= *Confederation of British Industry*) ≈ BDI *m*

cc *n abbr* = **carbon copy; cubic centimetres**

CD *n abbr* (= *compact disc*) CD *f*; (: *player*) CD-Spieler *m*

CD-ROM *n abbr* (= *compact disk read-only memory*) CD-Rom *f*

cease [siːs] *vi* aufhören ♦ *vt* beenden; **~fire** *n* Feuereinstellung *f*; **~less** *adj* unaufhörlich

cedar ['siːdə*] *n* Zeder *f*

cede [siːd] *vt* abtreten

ceiling ['siːlɪŋ] *n* Decke *f*; (*fig*) Höchstgrenze *f*

celebrate ['selɪbreɪt] *vt, vi* feiern; **~d** *adj* gefeiert

celebration [selɪ'breɪʃən] *n* Feier *f*

celebrity [sɪ'lebrɪtɪ] *n* gefeierte Persönlichkeit *f*

celery ['selərɪ] *n* Sellerie *m or f*

celestial [sɪ'lestɪəl] *adj* himmlisch

celibacy ['selɪbəsɪ] *n* Zölibat *nt or m*

cell [sel] *n* Zelle *f*; (*ELEC*) Element *nt*

cellar ['selə*] *n* Keller *m*

'cello ['tʃeləʊ] *n* Cello *nt*

cellophane ['seləfeɪn] ® *n* Cellophan *nt* ®

cellphone ['selfəʊn] *n* Funktelefon *nt*

cellular ['seljʊlə*] *adj* zellular

cellulose ['seljʊləʊs] *n* Zellulose *f*

Celt [kelt, selt] *n* Kelte *m*, Keltin *f*; **~ic** ['keltɪk, 'seltɪk] *adj* keltisch

cement [sɪ'ment] *n* Zement *m* ♦ *vt* zementieren; **~ mixer** *n* Betonmischmaschine *f*

cemetery ['semɪtrɪ] *n* Friedhof *m*

cenotaph ['senətɑːf] *n* Ehrenmal *nt*

censor ['sensə*] *n* Zensor *m* ♦ *vt* zensieren; **~ship** *n* Zensur *f*

censure ['senʃə*] *vt* rügen

census ['sensəs] *n* Volkszählung *f*

cent [sent] *n* (*US: coin*) Cent *m*; *see also* **per cent**

centenary [sen'tiːnərɪ] *n* Jahrhundertfeier *f*

center ['sentə*] (*US*) *n* = **centre**

centigrade ['sentɪgreɪd] *adj* Celsius

centimetre ['sentɪmiːtə*] (*US* **centimeter**) *n* Zentimeter *nt*

centipede ['sentɪpiːd] *n* Tausendfüßler *m*

central ['sentrəl] *adj* zentral; **C~ America** *n* Mittelamerika *nt*; **~ heating** *n* Zentralheizung *f*; **~ize** *vt* zentralisieren; **~ reservation** (*BRIT*) *n* (*AUT*) Mittelstreifen *m*

centre ['sentə*] (*US* **center**) *n* Zentrum *nt* ♦ *vt* zentrieren; **~-forward** *n* (*SPORT*) Mittelstürmer *m*; **~-half** *n* (*SPORT*) Stopper *m*

century ['sentjʊrɪ] *n* Jahrhundert *nt*

ceramic [sɪ'ræmɪk] *adj* keramisch; **~s** *npl* Keramiken *pl*

cereal ['sɪərɪəl] *n* (*grain*) Getreide *nt*; (*at breakfast*) Getreideflocken *pl*

cerebral ['serɪbrəl] *adj* zerebral; (*intellectual*) geistig

ceremony ['serɪmənɪ] *n* Zeremonie *f*; **to stand on ~** förmlich sein

certain ['sɜːtən] *adj* sicher; (*particular*) gewiß; **for ~** ganz bestimmt; **~ly** *adv* sicher, bestimmt; **~ty** *n* Gewißheit *f*

certificate [sə'tɪfɪkɪt] *n* Bescheinigung *f*;

(*SCH etc*) Zeugnis *nt*

certified mail ['sɜ:tɪfaɪd-] (*US*) *n* Einschreiben *nt*

certified public accountant ['sɜ:tɪfaɪd-] (*US*) *n* geprüfte(r) Buchhalter *m*

certify ['sɜ:tɪfaɪ] *vt* bescheinigen

cervical ['sɜ:vɪkl] *adj* (*smear, cancer*) Gebärmutterhals-

cervix ['sɜ:vɪks] *n* Gebärmutterhals *m*

cessation [se'seɪʃən] *n* Einstellung *f*, Ende *nt*

cf. *abbr* (= *compare*) vgl.

CFC *n abbr* (= *chlorofluorocarbon*) FCKW *m*

ch. *abbr* (= *chapter*) Kap.

chafe [tʃeɪf] *vt* scheuern

chaffinch ['tʃæfɪntʃ] *n* Buchfink *m*

chagrin ['ʃægrɪn] *n* Verdruß *m*

chain [tʃeɪn] *n* Kette *f* ♦ *vt* (*also:* ~ *up*) anketten; ~ **reaction** *n* Kettenreaktion *f*; ~-**smoke** *vi* kettenrauchen; ~ **store** *n* Kettenladen *m*

chair [tʃeə*] *n* Stuhl *m*; (*arm*~) Sessel *m*; (*UNIV*) Lehrstuhl *m* ♦ *vt* (*meeting*) den Vorsitz führen bei; ~**lift** *n* Sessellift *m*; ~**man** (*irreg*) *n* Vorsitzende(r) *m*

chalet ['ʃæleɪ] *n* Chalet *nt*

chalice ['tʃælɪs] *n* Kelch *m*

chalk ['tʃɔ:k] *n* Kreide *f*

challenge ['tʃælɪndʒ] *n* Herausforderung *f* ♦ *vt* herausfordern; (*contest*) bestreiten

challenging ['tʃælɪndʒɪŋ] *adj* (*tone*) herausfordernd; (*work*) anspruchsvoll

chamber ['tʃeɪmbə*] *n* Kammer *f*; ~ **of commerce** Handelskammer *f*; ~**maid** *n* Zimmermädchen *nt*; ~ **music** *n* Kammermusik *f*

chamois ['ʃæmwɑ:] *n* Gemse *f*

champagne [ʃæm'peɪn] *n* Champagner *m*, Sekt *m*

champion ['tʃæmpɪən] *n* (*SPORT*) Meister(in) *m(f)*; (*of cause*) Verfechter(in) *m(f)*; ~**ship** *n* Meisterschaft *f*

chance [tʃɑ:ns] *n* (*luck*) Zufall *m*; (*possibility*) Möglichkeit *f*; (*opportunity*) Gelegenheit *f*, Chance *f*; (*risk*) Risiko *nt* ♦ *adj* zufällig ♦ *vt*: **to** ~ **it** es darauf ankommen lassen; **by** ~ zufällig; **to take**

a ~ ein Risiko eingehen

chancellor ['tʃɑ:nsələ*] *n* Kanzler *m*; **C~ of the Exchequer** (*BRIT*) *n* Schatzkanzler *m*

chandelier [ʃændɪ'lɪə*] *n* Kronleuchter *m*

change [tʃeɪndʒ] *vt* ändern; (*replace, COMM: money*) wechseln; (*exchange*) umtauschen; (*transform*) verwandeln ♦ *vi* sich ändern; (~ *trains*) umsteigen; (~ *clothes*) sich umziehen ♦ *n* Veränderung *f*; (*money returned*) Wechselgeld *nt*; (*coins*) Kleingeld *nt*; **to** ~ **one's mind** es sich *dat* anders überlegen; **to** ~ **into sth** (*be transformed*) sich in etw *acc* verwandeln; **for a** ~ zur Abwechslung; ~**able** *adj* (*weather*) wechselhaft; ~ **machine** *n* Geldwechselautomat *m*; ~**over** *n* Umstellung *f*

changing ['tʃeɪndʒɪŋ] *adj* veränderlich; ~ **room** (*BRIT*) *n* Umkleideraum *m*

channel ['tʃænl] *n* (*stream*) Bachbett *nt*; (*NAUT*) Straße *f*; (*TV*) Kanal *m*; (*fig*) Weg *m* ♦ *vt* (*efforts*) lenken; **the (English)** C~ der Ärmelkanal; **C~ Islands** *npl*: **the C~ Islands** die Kanalinseln *pl*; **C~ Tunnel** *n*: **the C~ Tunnel** der Kanaltunnel

chant [tʃɑ:nt] *n* Gesang *m*; (*of football fans etc*) Sprechchor *m* ♦ *vt* intonieren

chaos ['keɪɒs] *n* Chaos *nt*

chap [tʃæp] (*inf*) *n* Kerl *m*

chapel ['tʃæpəl] *n* Kapelle *f*

chaperon ['ʃæpərəʊn] *n* Anstandsdame *f*

chaplain ['tʃæplɪn] *n* Kaplan *m*

chapped ['tʃæpt] *adj* (*skin, lips*) spröde

chapter ['tʃæptə*] *n* Kapitel *nt*

char [tʃɑ:*] *vt* (*burn*) verkohlen ♦ *n* (*BRIT*) = **charlady**

character ['kærɪktə*] *n* Charakter *m*, Wesen *nt*; (*in novel, film*) Figur *f*; ~**istic** [kærɪktə'rɪstɪk] *adj*: ~**istic (of sb/sth)** (für jdn/etw) charakteristisch ♦ *n* Kennzeichen *nt*; ~**ize** *vt* charakterisieren, kennzeichnen

charade [ʃə'rɑ:d] *n* Scharade *f*

charcoal ['tʃɑ:kəʊl] *n* Holzkohle *f*

charge [tʃɑ:dʒ] *n* (*cost*) Preis *m*; (*JUR*) Anklage *f*; (*explosive*) Ladung *f*; (*attack*) Angriff *m* ♦ *vt* (*gun, battery*) laden; (*price*) verlangen; (*JUR*) anklagen; (*MIL*) angreifen

♦ *vi* (*rush*) (an)stürmen; **bank ~s** Bankgebühren *pl*; **free of ~** kostenlos; **to reverse the ~s** (*TEL*) ein R-Gespräch führen; **to be in ~ of** verantwortlich sein für; **to take ~** (die Verantwortung) übernehmen; **to ~ sth (up) to sb's account** jdm etw in Rechnung stellen; **~ card** *n* Kundenkarte *f*

charitable ['tʃærɪtəbl] *adj* wohltätig; (*lenient*) nachsichtig

charity ['tʃærɪtɪ] *n* (*institution*) Hilfswerk *nt*; (*attitude*) Nächstenliebe *f*

charlady ['tʃɑːleɪdɪ] (*BRIT*) *n* Putzfrau *f*

charlatan ['ʃɑːlətən] *n* Scharlatan *m*

charm [tʃɑːm] *n* Charme *m*; (*spell*) Bann *m*; (*object*) Talisman *m* ♦ *vt* bezaubern; **~ing** *adj* reizend

chart [tʃɑːt] *n* Tabelle *f*; (*NAUT*) Seekarte *f* ♦ *vt* (*course*) abstecken

charter ['tʃɑːtə*] *vt* chartern ♦ *n* Schutzbrief *m*; **~ed accountant** *n* Wirtschaftsprüfer(in) *m(f)*; **~ flight** *n* Charterflug *m*

charwoman ['tʃɑːwʊmən] *n* = **charlady**

chase [tʃeɪs] *vt* jagen, verfolgen ♦ *n* Jagd *f*

chasm ['kæzəm] *n* Kluft *f*

chassis ['ʃæsɪ] *n* Fahrgestell *nt*

chastity ['tʃæstɪtɪ] *n* Keuschheit *f*

chat [tʃæt] *vi* (*also: have a ~*) plaudern ♦ *n* Plauderei *f*; **~ show** (*BRIT*) *n* Talkshow *f*

chatter ['tʃætə*] *vi* schwatzen; (*teeth*) klappern ♦ *n* Geschwätz *nt*; **~box** *n* Quasselstrippe *f*

chatty ['tʃætɪ] *adj* geschwätzig

chauffeur ['ʃəʊfə*] *n* Chauffeur *m*

chauvinist ['ʃəʊvɪnɪst] *n* (*male ~*) Chauvi *m* (*inf*); (*nationalist*) Chauvinist(in) *m(f)*

cheap [tʃiːp] *adj, adv* billig; **~ly** *adv* billig

cheat [tʃiːt] *vt, vi* betrügen; (*SCH*) mogeln ♦ *n* Betrüger(in) *m(f)*

check [tʃek] *vt* (*examine*) prüfen; (*make sure*) nachsehen; (*control*) kontrollieren; (*restrain*) zügeln; (*stop*) anhalten ♦ *n* (*examination, restraint*) Kontrolle *f*; (*bill*) Rechnung *f*; (*pattern*) Karo(muster) *nt*; (*US*) = **cheque** ♦ *adj* (*pattern, cloth*)

kariert; **~ in** *vi* (*in hotel, airport*) einchecken ♦ *vt* (*luggage*) abfertigen lassen; **~ out** *vi* (*of hotel*) abreisen; **~ up** *vi* nachschauen; **~ up on** *vt* kontrollieren; **~ered** (*US*) *adj* = **chequered**; **~ers** (*US*) *n* (*draughts*) Damespiel *nt*; **~-in (desk)** *n* Abfertigung *f*; **~ing account** (*US*) *n* (*current account*) Girokonto *nt*; **~mate** *n* Schachmatt *nt*; **~point** *n* Kontrollpunkt *m*; **~ room** (*US*) *n* (*left-luggage office*) Gepäckaufbewahrung *f*; **~up** *n* (*Nach*)prüfung *f*; (*MED*) (ärztliche) Untersuchung *f*

cheek [tʃiːk] *n* Backe *f*; (*fig*) Frechheit *f*; **~bone** *n* Backenknochen *m*; **~y** *adj* frech

cheep [tʃiːp] *vi* piepsen

cheer [tʃɪə*] *n* (*usu pl*) Hurra- *or* Beifallsruf *m* ♦ *vt* zujubeln; (*encourage*) aufmuntern ♦ *vi* jauchzen; **~s!** Prost!; **~ up** *vi* bessere Laune bekommen ♦ *vt* aufmuntern; **~ up!** nun lach doch mal!; **~ful** *adj* fröhlich

cheerio ['tʃɪərɪ'əʊ] (*BRIT*) *excl* tschüs!

cheese [tʃiːz] *n* Käse *m*; **~board** *n* (gemischte) Käseplatte *f*

cheetah ['tʃiːtə] *n* Gepard *m*

chef [ʃef] *n* Küchenchef *m*

chemical ['kemɪkəl] *adj* chemisch ♦ *n* Chemikalie *f*

chemist ['kemɪst] *n* (*BRIT: pharmacist*) Apotheker *m*, Drogist *m*; (*scientist*) Chemiker *m*; **~ry** *n* Chemie *f*; **~'s (shop)** (*BRIT*) *n* Apotheke *f*, Drogerie *f*

cheque [tʃek] (*BRIT*) *n* Scheck *m*; **~book** *n* Scheckbuch *nt*; **~ card** *n* Scheckkarte *f*

chequered ['tʃekəd] *adj* (*fig*) bewegt

cherish ['tʃerɪʃ] *vt* (*person*) lieben; (*hope*) hegen

cherry ['tʃerɪ] *n* Kirsche *f*

chess [tʃes] *n* Schach *nt*; **~board** *n* Schachbrett *nt*; **~man** (*irreg*) *n* Schachfigur *f*

chest [tʃest] *n* (*ANAT*) Brust *f*; (*box*) Kiste *f*; **~ of drawers** Kommode *f*

chestnut ['tʃesnʌt] *n* Kastanie *f*; **~ tree** *n* Kastanienbaum *m*

chew [tʃuː] *vt, vi* kauen; **~ing gum** *n* Kaugummi *m*

chic [ʃi:k] *adj* schick, elegant

chick [tʃɪk] *n* Küken *nt*; (*US: inf: girl*) Biene *f*

chicken ['tʃɪkɪn] *n* Huhn *nt*; (*food*) Hähnchen *nt*; ~ **out** (*inf*) *vi* kneifen (*inf*)

chickenpox ['tʃɪkɪnpɒks] *n* Windpocken *pl*

chicory ['tʃɪkərɪ] *n* (*in coffee*) Zichorie *f*; (*plant*) Chicorée *f*

chief [tʃi:f] *n* (*of tribe*) Häuptling *m*; (*COMM*) Chef *m* ♦ *adj* Haupt-; ~ **executive** *n* Geschäftsführer(in) *m(f)*; ~**ly** *adv* hauptsächlich

chiffon ['ʃɪfɒn] *n* Chiffon *m*

chilblain ['tʃɪlbleɪn] *n* Frostbeule *f*

child [tʃaɪld] *n* (*pl* **children**) Kind *nt*; ~**birth** *n* Entbindung *f*; ~**hood** *n* Kindheit *f*; ~**ish** *adj* kindisch; ~**like** *adj* kindlich; ~ **minder** (*BRIT*) *n* Tagesmutter *f*

children ['tʃɪldrən] *npl of* **child**

Chile ['tʃɪlɪ] *n* Chile *nt*; ~**an** *adj* chilenisch

chill [tʃɪl] *n* Kühle *f*; (*MED*) Erkältung *f* ♦ *vt* (*CULIN*) kühlen

chilli ['tʃɪlɪ] *n* Peperoni *pl*; (*meal, spice*) Chili *m*

chilly ['tʃɪlɪ] *adj* kühl, frostig

chime [tʃaɪm] *n* Geläut *nt* ♦ *vi* ertönen

chimney ['tʃɪmnɪ] *n* Schornstein *m*; ~ **sweep** *n* Schornsteinfeger(in) *m(f)*

chimpanzee [tʃɪmpæn'zi:] *n* Schimpanse *m*

chin [tʃɪn] *n* Kinn *nt*

China ['tʃaɪnə] *n* China *nt*

china ['tʃaɪnə] *n* Porzellan *nt*

Chinese [tʃaɪ'ni:z] *adj* chinesisch ♦ *n* (*inv*) Chinese *m*, Chinesin *f*; (*LING*) Chinesisch *nt*

chink [tʃɪŋk] *n* (*opening*) Ritze *f*; (*noise*) Klirren *n*

chip [tʃɪp] *n* (*of wood etc*) Splitter *m* (*in poker etc: US: crisp*) Chip *m* ♦ *vt* absplittern; ~**s** *npl* (*BRIT: COOK*) Pommes frites *pl*; ~ **in** *vi* Zwischenbemerkungen machen

chiropodist [kɪ'rɒpədɪst] (*BRIT*) *n* Fußpfleger(in) *m(f)*

chirp [tʃɜ:p] *vi* zwitschern

chisel ['tʃɪzl] *n* Meißel *m*

chit [tʃɪt] *n* Notiz *f*

chitchat ['tʃɪttʃæt] *n* Plauderei *f*

chivalrous ['ʃɪvəlrəs] *adj* ritterlich

chivalry ['ʃɪvəlrɪ] *n* Ritterlichkeit *f*

chives [tʃaɪvz] *npl* Schnittlauch *m*

chlorine ['klɔ:ri:n] *n* Chlor *nt*

chock [tʃɒk] *n* Bremsklotz *m*; ~-**a-block** *adj* vollgepfropft; ~-**full** *adj* vollgepfropft

chocolate ['tʃɒklɪt] *n* Schokolade *f*

choice [tʃɔɪs] *n* Wahl *f*; (*of goods*) Auswahl *f* ♦ *adj* Qualitäts-

choir ['kwaɪə*] *n* Chor *m*; ~**boy** *n* Chorknabe *m*

choke [tʃəuk] *vi* ersticken ♦ *vt* erdrosseln; (*block*) (ab)drosseln ♦ *n* (*AUT*) Starterklappe *f*

cholera ['kɒlərə] *n* Cholera *f*

cholesterol [kɒ'lestərəl] *n* Cholesterin *nt*

choose [tʃu:z] (*pt* **chose**, *pp* **chosen**) *vt* wählen

choosy ['tʃu:zɪ] *adj* wählerisch

chop [tʃɒp] *vt* (*wood*) spalten; (*COOK: also*: ~ *up*) (zer)hacken ♦ *n* Hieb *m*; (*COOK*) Kotelett *nt*; ~**s** *npl* (*jaws*) Lefzen *pl*

chopper ['tʃɒpə*] *n* (*helicopter*) Hubschrauber *m*

choppy ['tʃɒpɪ] *adj* (*sea*) bewegt

chopsticks ['tʃɒpstɪks] *npl* (Eß)stäbchen *pl*

choral ['kɔ:rəl] *adj* Chor-

chord [kɔ:d] *n* Akkord *m*

chore [tʃɔ:*] *n* Pflicht *f*; ~**s** *npl* (*housework*) Hausarbeit *f*

choreographer [kɒrɪ'ɒgrəfə*] *n* Choreograph(in) *m(f)*

chorister ['kɒrɪstə*] *n* Chorsänger(in) *m(f)*

chortle ['tʃɔ:tl] *vi* glucksen

chorus ['kɔ:rəs] *n* Chor *m*; (*in song*) Refrain *m*

chose [tʃəuz] *pt of* **choose**

chosen ['tʃəuzn] *pp of* **choose**

Christ [kraɪst] *n* Christus *m*

christen ['krɪsn] *vt* taufen

Christian ['krɪstɪən] *adj* christlich ♦ *n* Christ(in) *m(f)*; ~**ity** [krɪstɪ'ænɪtɪ] *n* Christentum *nt*; ~ **name** *n* Vorname *m*

Christmas ['krɪsməs] *n* Weihnachten *pl*; **Happy** *or* **Merry** ~! Frohe *or* fröhliche

Weihnachten!; ~ **card** *n* Weihnachtskarte
f; ~ **Day** *n* der erste Weihnachtstag; ~
Eve *n* Heiligabend *m*; ~ **tree** *n*
Weihnachtsbaum *m*

chrome [krəʊm] *n* Verchromung *f*

chromium ['krəʊmɪəm] *n* Chrom *nt*

chronic ['krɒnɪk] *adj* chronisch

chronicle ['krɒnɪkl] *n* Chronik *f*

chronological [krɒnə'lɒdʒɪkəl] *adj*
chronologisch

chubby ['tʃʌbɪ] *adj* rundlich

chuck [tʃʌk] *vt* werfen; (*BRIT: also:* ~ **up**)
hinwerfen; ~ **out** *vt* (*person*) rauswerfen;
(*old clothes etc*) wegwerfen

chuckle ['tʃʌkl] *vi* in sich hineinlachen

chug [tʃʌg] *vi* tuckern

chum [tʃʌm] *n* Kumpel *m*

chunk [tʃʌŋk] *n* Klumpen *m*; (*of food*)
Brocken *m*

church [tʃɜːtʃ] *n* Kirche *f*; ~**yard** *n*
Kirchhof *m*

churlish ['tʃɜːlɪʃ] *adj* grob

churn [tʃɜːn] *n* (*for butter*) Butterfaß *nt*;
(*for milk*) Milchkanne *f*; ~ **out** (*inf*) *vt*
produzieren

chute [ʃuːt] *n* Rutsche *f*; (*rubbish* ~)
Müllschlucker *m*

CIA (*US*) *n abbr* (= *Central Intelligence
Agency*) CIA *m*

CID (*BRIT*) *n abbr* (= *Criminal
Investigation Department*) ≈ Kripo *f*

cider ['saɪdə*] *n* Apfelwein *m*

cigar [sɪ'gɑː*] *n* Zigarre *f*

cigarette [sɪgə'ret] *n* Zigarette *f*; ~ **case**
n Zigarettenetui *nt*; ~ **end** *n*
Zigarettenstummel *m*

Cinderella [sɪndə'relə] *n* Aschenbrödel *nt*

cinders ['sɪndəz] *npl* Asche *f*

cine-camera ['sɪnɪkæmərə] (*BRIT*) *n*
Filmkamera *f*

cine-film ['sɪnɪfɪlm] (*BRIT*) *n* Schmalfilm *m*

cinema ['sɪnəmə] *n* Kino *nt*

cinnamon ['sɪnəmən] *n* Zimt *m*

cipher ['saɪfə*] *n* (*code*) Chiffre *f*

circle ['sɜːkl] *n* Kreis *m*; (*in cinema etc*)
Rang *m* ♦ *vi* kreisen ♦ *vt* (*surround*)
umgeben; (*move round*) kreisen um

circuit ['sɜːkɪt] *n* (*track*) Rennbahn *f*;
(*lap*) Runde *f*; (*ELEC*) Stromkreis *m*; ~**ous**

[sɜː'kjuːɪtəs] *adj* weitschweifig

circular ['sɜːkjʊlə*] *adj* rund ♦ *n*
Rundschreiben *nt*

circulate ['sɜːkjʊleɪt] *vi* zirkulieren ♦ *vt*
in Umlauf setzen; **circulation**
[sɜːkjʊ'leɪʃən] *n* (*of blood*) Kreislauf *m*; (*of
newspaper*) Auflage *f*; (*of money*) Umlauf
m

circumcise ['sɜːkəmsaɪz] *vt* beschneiden

circumference [sə'kʌmfərəns] *n*
(Kreis)umfang *m*

circumspect ['sɜːkəmspekt] *adj*
umsichtig

circumstances ['sɜːkəmstənsəz] *npl*
Umstände *pl*; (*financial condition*)
Verhältnisse *pl*

circumvent [sɜːkəm'vent] *vt* umgehen

circus ['sɜːkəs] *n* Zirkus *m*

CIS *n abbr* (= *Commonwealth of
Independent States*) GUS *f*

cistern ['sɪstən] *n* Zisterne *f*; (*of W.C.*)
Spülkasten *m*

cite [saɪt] *vt* zitieren, anführen

citizen ['sɪtɪzn] *n* Bürger(in) *m(f)*; ~**ship**
n Staatsbürgerschaft *f*

citrus fruit ['sɪtrəs fruːt] *n* Zitrusfrucht *f*

city ['sɪtɪ] *n* Großstadt *f*; **the C~** die City,
das Finanzzentrum Londons

civic ['sɪvɪk] *adj* (*of town*) städtisch; (*of
citizen*) Bürger-; ~ **centre** (*BRIT*) *n*
Stadtverwaltung *f*

civil ['sɪvɪl] *adj* bürgerlich; (*not military*)
zivil; (*polite*) höflich; ~ **engineer** *n*
Bauingenieur *m*; ~**ian** [sɪ'vɪlɪən] *n*
Zivilperson *f* ♦ *adj* zivil, Zivil-

civilization [sɪvɪlaɪ'zeɪʃən] *n* Zivilisation
f

civilized ['sɪvɪlaɪzd] *adj* zivilisiert

civil: ~ **law** *n* Zivilrecht *nt*; ~ **servant** *n*
Staatsbeamte(r) *m*; **C~ Service** *n*
Staatsdienst *m*; ~ **war** *n* Bürgerkrieg *m*

clad [klæd] *adj*: ~ **in** gehüllt in +*acc*

claim [kleɪm] *vt* beanspruchen; (*have
opinion*) behaupten ♦ *vi* (*for insurance*)
Ansprüche geltend machen ♦ *n* (*demand*)
Forderung *f*; (*right*) Anspruch *m*;
(*pretension*) Behauptung *f*; ~**ant** *n*
Antragsteller(in) *m(f)*

clairvoyant [kleə'vɔɪənt] *n* Hellseher(in)

m(f)

clam [klæm] *n* Venusmuschel *f*

clamber ['klæmbə*] *vi* kraxeln

clammy ['klæmɪ] *adj* klamm

clamour ['klæmə*] *vi*: **to ~ for sth** nach etw verlangen

clamp [klæmp] *n* Schraubzwinge *f* ♦ *vt* einspannen; **~ down on** *vt fus* Maßnahmen ergreifen gegen

clan [klæn] *n* Clan *m*

clandestine [klæn'destɪn] *adj* geheim

clang [klæŋ] *vi* scheppern

clap [klæp] *vi* klatschen ♦ *vt* Beifall klatschen +*dat* ♦ *n* (*of hands*) Klatschen *nt*; (*of thunder*) Donnerschlag *m*; **~ping** *n* Klatschen *nt*

claret ['klærɪt] *n* rote(r) Bordeaux(wein) *m*

clarify ['klærɪfaɪ] *vt* klären, erklären

clarinet [klærɪ'net] *n* Klarinette *f*

clarity ['klærɪtɪ] *n* Klarheit *f*

clash [klæʃ] *n* (*fig*) Konflikt *m* ♦ *vi* zusammenprallen; (*colours*) sich beißen; (*argue*) sich streiten

clasp [klɑːsp] *n* Griff *m*; (*on jewels, bag*) Verschluß *m* ♦ *vt* umklammern

class [klɑːs] *n* Klasse *f* ♦ *vt* einordnen; **~-conscious** *adj* klassenbewußt

classic ['klæsɪk] *n* Klassiker *m* ♦ *adj* klassisch; **~al** *adj* klassisch

classified ['klæsɪfaɪd] *adj* (*information*) Geheim-; **~ advertisement** *n* Kleinanzeige *f*

classify ['klæsɪfaɪ] *vt* klassifizieren

classmate ['klɑːsmeɪt] *n* Klassenkamerad(in) *m(f)*

classroom ['klɑːsrʊm] *n* Klassenzimmer *nt*

clatter ['klætə*] *vi* klappern; (*feet*) trappeln

clause [klɔːz] *n* (*JUR*) Klausel *f*; (*GRAM*) Satz *m*

claustrophobia [klɒstrə'fəʊbɪə] *n* Platzangst *f*

claw [klɔː] *n* Kralle *f* ♦ *vt* (zer)kratzen

clay [kleɪ] *n* Lehm *m*; (*for pots*) Ton *m*

clean [kliːn] *adj* sauber ♦ *vt* putzen; (*clothes*) reinigen; **~ out** *vt* gründlich putzen; **~ up** *vt* aufräumen; **~-cut** *adj* (*per-*

son) adrett; (*clear*) klar; **~er** *n* (*person*) Putzfrau *f*; **~ing** *n* Putzen *nt*; (*clothes*) Reinigung *f*; **~liness** ['klenlɪnɪs] *n* Reinlichkeit *f*

cleanse [klenz] *vt* reinigen; **~r** *n* (*for face*) Reinigungsmilch *f*

clean-shaven ['kliːn'ʃeɪvn] *adj* glattrasiert

cleansing department ['klenzɪŋ-] (*BRIT*) *n* Stadtreinigung *f*

clear ['klɪə*] *adj* klar; (*road*) frei ♦ *vt* (*road etc*) freimachen; (*obstacle*) beseitigen; (*JUR: suspect*) freisprechen ♦ *vi* klarwerden; (*fog*) sich lichten ♦ *adv*: **~ of** von ... entfernt; **to ~ the table** den Tisch abräumen; **~ up** *vt* aufräumen; (*solve*) aufklären; **~ance** *n* (*removal*) Räumung *f*; (*free space*) Lichtung *f*; (*permission*) Freigabe *f*; **~-cut** *adj* (*case*) eindeutig; **~ing** *n* Lichtung *f*; **~ing bank** (*BRIT*) *n* Clearingbank *f*; **~ly** *adv* klar; (*obviously*) eindeutig; **~way** (*BRIT*) *n* (Straße *f* mit) Halteverbot *nt*

cleaver ['kliːvə*] *n* Hackbeil *f*

clef [klef] *n* Notenschlüssel *m*

cleft [kleft] *n* (*in rock*) Spalte *f*

clemency ['klemənsɪ] *n* Milde *f*

clench [klentʃ] *vt* (*teeth*) zusammenbeißen; (*fist*) ballen

clergy ['klɜːdʒɪ] *n* Geistliche(n) *pl*; **~man** (*irreg*) *n* Geistliche(r) *m*

clerical ['klerɪkəl] *adj* (*office*) Schreib-, Büro-; (*REL*) geistlich

clerk [klɑːk, (*US*) klɜːk] *n* (*in office*) Büroangestellte(r) *mf*; (*US: sales person*) Verkäufer(in) *m(f)*

clever ['klevə*] *adj* klug; (*crafty*) schlau

cliché ['kliːʃeɪ] *n* Klischee *nt*

click [klɪk] *vt* (*heels*) zusammenklappen; (*tongue*) schnalzen mit

client ['klaɪənt] *n* Klient(in) *m(f)*; **~ele** [kliːɒn'tel] *n* Kundschaft *f*

cliff [klɪf] *n* Klippe *f*

climate ['klaɪmɪt] *n* Klima *nt*

climax ['klaɪmæks] *n* Höhepunkt *m*

climb [klaɪm] *vt* besteigen ♦ *vi* steigen, klettern ♦ *n* Aufstieg *m*; **~-down** *n* Abstieg *m*; **~er** *n* Bergsteiger(in) *m(f)*; **~ing** *n* Bergsteigen *nt*

clinch [klɪntʃ] *vt* (*decide*) entscheiden; (*deal*) festmachen

cling [klɪŋ] (*pt, pp* **clung**) *vi* (*clothes*) eng anliegen; **to ~ to** sich festklammern an +*dat*

clinic ['klɪnɪk] *n* Klinik *f*; **~al** *adj* klinisch

clink [klɪŋk] *vi* klimpern

clip [klɪp] *n* Spange *f*; (*also: paper ~*) Klammer *f* ♦ *vt* (*papers*) heften; (*hair, hedge*) stutzen; **~pers** *npl* (*for hedge*) Heckenschere *f*; (*for hair*) Haarschneidemaschine *f*; **~ping** *n* Ausschnitt *m*

cloak [kləʊk] *n* Umhang *m* ♦ *vt* hüllen; **~room** *n* (*for coats*) Garderobe *f*; (*BRIT: W.C.*) Toilette *f*

clock [klɒk] *n* Uhr *f*; **~ in** *or* **on** *vi* stempeln; **~ off** *or* **out** *vi* stempeln; **~wise** *adv* im Uhrzeigersinn; **~work** *n* Uhrwerk *nt* ♦ *adj* zum Aufziehen

clog [klɒg] *n* Holzschuh *m* ♦ *vt* verstopfen

cloister ['klɔɪstə*] *n* Kreuzgang *m*

clone [kləʊn] *n* Klon *m*

close¹ [kləʊs] *adj* (*near*) in der Nähe; (*friend, connection, print*) eng; (*relative*) nahe; (*result*) knapp; (*examination*) eingehend; (*weather*) schwül; (*room*) stickig ♦ *adv* nahe, dicht; **~ by** in der Nähe; **~ at hand** in der Nähe; **to have a ~ shave** (*fig*) mit knapper Not davorkommen

close² [kləʊz] *vt* (*shut*) schließen; (*end*) beenden ♦ *vi* (*shop etc*) schließen; (*door etc*) sich schließen ♦ *n* Ende *nt*; **~ down** *vi* schließen; **~d** *adj* (*shop etc*) geschlossen; **~d shop** *n* Gewerkschaftszwang *m*

close-knit [kləʊs'nɪt] *adj* eng zusammengewachsen

closely ['kləʊslɪ] *adv* eng; (*carefully*) genau

closet ['klɒzɪt] *n* Schrank *m*

close-up ['kləʊsʌp] *n* Nahaufnahme *f*

closure ['kləʊʒə*] *n* Schließung *f*

clot [klɒt] *n* (*of blood*) Blutgerinnsel *nt*; (*fool*) Blödmann *m* ♦ *vi* gerinnen

cloth [klɒθ] *n* (*material*) Tuch *nt*; (*rag*) Lappen *m*

clothe [kləʊð] *vt* kleiden; **~s** *npl* Kleider

pl; **~s brush** *n* Kleiderbürste *f*; **~s line** *n* Wäscheleine *f*; **~s peg** (*US* **~s pin**) *n* Wäscheklammer *f*

clothing ['kləʊðɪŋ] *n* Kleidung *f*

cloud [klaʊd] *n* Wolke *f*; **~burst** *n* Wolkenbruch *m*; **~y** *adj* bewölkt; (*liquid*) trüb

clout [klaʊt] *vt* hauen

clove [kləʊv] *n* Gewürznelke *f*; **~ of garlic** Knoblauchzehe *f*

clover ['kləʊvə*] *n* Klee *m*

clown [klaʊn] *n* Clown *m* ♦ *vi* (*also: ~ about, ~ around*) kaspern

cloying ['klɔɪɪŋ] *adj* (*taste, smell*) übersüß

club [klʌb] *n* (*weapon*) Knüppel *m*; (*society*) Klub *m*; (*also: golf ~*) Golfschläger *m* ♦ *vt* prügeln ♦ *vi*: **to ~ together** zusammenlegen; **~s** *npl* (*CARDS*) Kreuz *nt*; **~ car** (*US*) *n* (*RAIL*) Speisewagen *m*; **~ class** *n* (*AVIAT*) Club-Klasse *f*; **~house** *n* Klubhaus *nt*

cluck [klʌk] *vi* glucken

clue [kluː] *n* Anhaltspunkt *m*; (*in crosswords*) Frage *f*; **I haven't a ~** (ich hab') keine Ahnung

clump [klʌmp] *n* Gruppe *f*

clumsy ['klʌmzɪ] *adj* (*person*) unbeholfen; (*shape*) unförmig

clung [klʌŋ] *pt, pp* of **cling**

cluster ['klʌstə*] *n* (*of trees etc*) Gruppe *f* ♦ *vi* sich drängen, sich scharen

clutch [klʌtʃ] *n* Griff *m*; (*AUT*) Kupplung *f* ♦ *vt* sich festklammern an +*dat*

clutter ['klʌtə*] *vt* vollpfropfen; (*desk*) übersäen

CND *n abbr* = **Campaign for Nuclear Disarmament**

Co. *abbr* = **county; company**

c/o *abbr* (= *care of*) c/o

coach [kəʊtʃ] *n* (*bus*) Reisebus *m*; (*horse-drawn*) Kutsche *f*; (*RAIL*) (Personen)wagen *m*; (*trainer*) Trainer *m* ♦ *vt* (*SCH*) Nachhilfeunterricht geben +*dat*; (*SPORT*) trainieren; **~ trip** *n* Busfahrt *f*

coagulate [kəʊ'ægjʊleɪt] *vi* gerinnen

coal [kəʊl] *n* Kohle *f*; **~ face** *n* Streb *m*; **~ field** *n* Kohlengebiet *nt*

coalition [kəʊə'lɪʃən] *n* Koalition *f*

coalman ['kəʊlmən] (*irreg*) *n*

Kohlenhändler m
coal merchant n = **coalman**
coal mine n Kohlenbergwerk nt
coarse [kɔːs] adj grob; (*fig*) ordinär
coast [kəʊst] n Küste f ♦ vi dahinrollen;
(*AUT*) im Leerlauf fahren; **~al** adj Küsten-;
~guard n Küstenwache f; **~line** n
Küste(nlinie) f
coat [kəʊt] n Mantel m; (*on animals*) Fell
nt; (*of paint*) Schicht f ♦ vt überstreichen;
~hanger n Kleiderbügel m; **~ing** n
Überzug m; (*of paint*) Schicht f; **~ of
arms** n Wappen nt
coax [kəʊks] vt beschwatzen
cob [kɒb] n see **corn**
cobbler ['kɒblə*] n Schuster m
cobbles ['kɒblz] npl Pflastersteine pl
cobblestones ['kɒblstəʊnz] npl
Pflastersteine pl
cobweb ['kɒbweb] n Spinnennetz nt
cocaine [kə'keɪn] n Kokain nt
cock [kɒk] n Hahn m ♦ vt (*gun*)
entsichern; **~erel** n ['kɒkərl] n junge(r)
Hahn m; **~-eyed** adj (*fig*) verrückt
cockle ['kɒkl] n Herzmuschel f
cockney ['kɒknɪ] n echte(r) Londoner m
cockpit ['kɒkpɪt] n (*AVIAT*) Pilotenkanzel f
cockroach ['kɒkrəʊtʃ] n Küchenschabe f
cocktail ['kɒkteɪl] n Cocktail m; **~
cabinet** n Hausbar f; **~ party** n
Cocktailparty f
cocoa ['kəʊkəʊ] n Kakao m
coconut ['kəʊkənʌt] n Kokosnuß f
cocoon [kə'kuːn] n Kokon m
cod [kɒd] n Kabeljau m
C.O.D. abbr = **cash on delivery**
code [kəʊd] n Kode m; (*JUR*) Kodex m
cod-liver oil ['kɒdlɪvər-] n Lebertran m
coercion [kəʊ'ɜːʃən] n Zwang m
coffee ['kɒfɪ] n Kaffee m; **~ bar** (*BRIT*) n
Café nt; **~ bean** n Kaffeebohne f; **~
break** n Kaffeepause f; **~pot** n
Kaffeekanne f; **~ table** n Couchtisch m
coffin ['kɒfɪn] n Sarg m
cog [kɒg] n (Rad)zahn m
cogent ['kəʊdʒənt] adj triftig,
überzeugend, zwingend
cognac ['kɒnjæk] n Kognak m
coherent [kəʊ'hɪərənt] adj

zusammenhängend; (*person*) verständlich
cohesion [kəʊ'hiːʒən] n Zusammenhang
m
coil [kɔɪl] n Rolle f; (*ELEC*) Spule f;
(*contraceptive*) Spirale f ♦ vt aufwickeln
coin [kɔɪn] n Münze f ♦ vt prägen; **~age**
['kɔɪnɪdʒ] n (*word*) Prägung f; **~-box**
(*BRIT*) n Münzfernsprecher m
coincide [kəʊɪn'saɪd] vi (*happen together*)
zusammenfallen; (*agree*) übereinstimmen
coincidence [kəʊ'ɪnsɪdəns] n Zufall m
Coke [kəʊk] ® n (*drink*) Coca-Cola f ®
coke n Koks m
colander ['kʌləndə*] n Durchschlag m
cold [kəʊld] adj kalt ♦ n Kälte f; (*MED*)
Erkältung f; **I'm ~** mir ist kalt; **to catch
~** sich erkälten; **in ~ blood** kaltblütig; **to
give sb the ~ shoulder** jdm aufwickeln
Schulter zeigen; **~ly** adv kalt; **~-
shoulder** vt die kalte Schulter zeigen
+dat; **~ sore** n Erkältungsbläschen nt
coleslaw ['kəʊlslɔː] n Krautsalat m
colic ['kɒlɪk] n Kolik f
collaborate [kə'læbəreɪt] vi
zusammenarbeiten
collaboration [kəlæbə'reɪʃən] n
Zusammenarbeit f; (*POL*) Kollaboration f
collapse [kə'læps] vi (*people*)
zusammenbrechen; (*things*) einstürzen
♦ n Zusammenbruch m; Einsturz m
collapsible [kə'læpsəbl] adj
zusammenklappbar, Klapp-
collar ['kɒlə*] n Kragen m; **~bone** n
Schlüsselbein nt
collateral [kɒ'lætərəl] n (zusätzliche)
Sicherheit f
colleague ['kɒliːg] n Kollege m, Kollegin
f
collect [kə'lekt] vt sammeln; (*BRIT*: *call
and pick up*) abholen ♦ vi sich sammeln
♦ adv: **to call ~** (*US*: *TEL*) ein R-Gespräch
führen; **~ion** [kə'lekʃən] n Sammlung f;
(*REL*) Kollekte f; (*of post*) Leerung f
collective [kə'lektɪv] adj gemeinsam;
(*POL*) kollektiv
collector [kə'lektə*] n Sammler m; (*tax
~*) (Steuer)einnehmer m
college ['kɒlɪdʒ] n (*UNIV*) College nt;
(*TECH*) Fach-, Berufsschule f

collide [kə'laɪd] *vi* zusammenstoßen

colliery ['kɒlɪərɪ] (*BRIT*) *n* Zeche *f*

collision [kə'lɪʒən] *n* Zusammenstoß *m*

colloquial [kə'ləʊkwɪəl] *adj* umgangssprachlich

collusion [kə'lu:ʒən] *n* geheime(s) Einverständnis *nt*

colon ['kəʊlɒn] *n* Doppelpunkt *m*; (*MED*) Dickdarm *m*

colonel ['kɜ:nl] *n* Oberst *m*

colonial [kə'ləʊnɪəl] *adj* Kolonial-

colonize ['kɒlənaɪz] *vt* kolonisieren

colony ['kɒlənɪ] *n* Kolonie *f*

colour ['kʌlə*] (*US* **color**) *n* Farbe *f* ♦ *vt* (*also fig*) färben ♦ *vi* sich verfärben; **~s** *npl* (*of club*) Fahne *f*; **~ bar** *n* Rassenschranke *f*; **~-blind** *adj* farbenblind; **~ed** *adj* farbig; **~ film** *n* Farbfilm *m*; **~ful** *adj* bunt; (*personality*) schillernd; **~ing** *n* (*complexion*) Gesichtsfarbe *f*; (*substance*) Farbstoff *m*; **~ scheme** *n* Farbgebung *f*; **~ television** *n* Farbfernsehen *nt*

colt [kəʊlt] *n* Fohlen *nt*

column ['kɒləm] *n* Säule *f*; (*MIL*) Kolonne *f*; (*of print*) Spalte *f*; **~ist** ['kɒləmnɪst] *n* Kolumnist *m*

coma ['kəʊmə] *n* Koma *nt*

comb [kəʊm] *n* Kamm *m* ♦ *vt* kämmen; (*search*) durchkämmen

combat ['kɒmbæt] *n* Kampf *m* ♦ *vt* bekämpfen

combination [kɒmbɪ'neɪʃən] *n* Kombination *f*

combine [*vb* kəm'baɪn, *n* 'kɒmbaɪn] *vt* verbinden ♦ *vi* sich vereinigen ♦ *n* (*COMM*) Konzern *m*; **~ (harvester)** *n* Mähdrescher *m*

combustion [kəm'bʌstʃən] *n* Verbrennung *f*

come [kʌm] (*pt* **came**, *pp* **come**) *vi* kommen; **to ~ undone** aufgehen; **~ about** *vi* geschehen; **~ across** *vt fus* (*find*) stoßen auf +*acc*; **~ away** *vi* (*person*) weggehen; (*handle etc*) abgehen; **~ back** *vi* zurückkommen; **~ by** *vt fus* (*find*): **to ~ by sth** zu etw kommen; **~ down** *vi* (*price*) fallen; **~ forward** *vi* (*volunteer*) sich melden; **~ from** *vt fus*

(*result*) kommen von; **where do you ~ from?** wo kommen Sie her?; **I ~ from London** ich komme aus London; **~ in** *vi* hereinkommen; (*train*) einfahren; **~ in for** *vt fus* abkriegen; **~ into** *vt fus* (*inherit*) erben; **~ off** *vi* (*handle*) abgehen; (*succeed*) klappen; **~ on** *vi* (*progress*) vorankommen; **~ on!** komm!; (*hurry*) beeil dich!; **~ out** *vi* herauskommen; **~ round** *vi* (*MED*) wieder zu sich kommen; **~ to** *vi* (*MED*) wieder zu sich kommen ♦ *vt fus* (*bill*) sich belaufen auf +*acc*; **~ up** *vi* hochkommen; (*sun*) aufgehen; (*problem*) auftauchen; **~ up against** *vt fus* (*resistance, difficulties*) stoßen auf +*acc*; **~ upon** *vt fus* stoßen auf +*acc*; **~ up with** *vt fus* sich einfallen lassen

comedian [kə'mi:dɪən] *n* Komiker *m*

comedienne [kəmi:dɪ'en] *n* Komikerin *f*

comedown ['kʌmdaʊn] *n* Abstieg *m*

comedy ['kɒmədɪ] *n* Komödie *f*

comet ['kɒmɪt] *n* Komet *m*

comeuppance [kʌm'ʌpəns] *n*: **to get one's ~** seine Quittung bekommen

comfort ['kʌmfət] *n* Komfort *m*; (*consolation*) Trost *m* ♦ *vt* trösten; **~able** *adj* bequem; **~ably** *adv* (*sit etc*) bequem; (*live*) angenehm; **~ station** (*US*) *n* öffentliche Toilette *f*

comic ['kɒmɪk] *n* Comic(heft) *nt*; (*comedian*) Komiker *m* ♦ *adj* (*also*: **~al**) komisch

coming ['kʌmɪŋ] *n* Kommen *nt*; **~(s) and going(s)** *n(pl)* Kommen und Gehen *nt*

comma ['kɒmə] *n* Komma *nt*

command [kə'mɑ:nd] *n* Befehl *m*; (*control*) Führung *f*; (*MIL*) Kommando *nt*; (*mastery*) Beherrschung *f* ♦ *vt* befehlen +*dat*; (*MIL*) kommandieren; (*be able to get*) verfügen über +*acc*; **~eer** [kɒmən'dɪə*] *vt* requirieren; **~er** *n* Kommandant *m*

commandment [kə'mɑ:ndmənt] *n* (*REL*) Gebot *nt*

commando [kə'mɑ:ndəʊ] *n* Kommandotruppe *nt*; (*person*) Mitglied *nt* einer Kommandotruppe

commemorate [kə'meməreɪt] *vt* gedenken +*gen*

commence [kə'mens] *vt*, *vi* beginnen

commend → compensate

commend [kə'mend] vt (recommend)
empfehlen; (praise) loben

commensurate [kə'mensjʊrɪt] adj: ~
with sth einer Sache dat entsprechend

comment ['kɒment] n Bemerkung f ♦ vi:
to ~ (on) sich äußern (zu); ~**ary**
['kɒmentrı] n Kommentar m; ~**ator**
['kɒmenteıtə*] n Kommentator m; (TV)
Reporter(in) m(f)

commerce ['kɒmɜːs] n Handel m

commercial [kə'mɜːʃəl] adj kommerziell,
geschäftlich; (training) kaufmännisch ♦ n
(TV) Fernsehwerbung f; ~ **break** n
Werbespot m; ~**ize** vt kommerzialisieren

commiserate [kə'mɪzəreɪt] vi: to ~ with
Mitleid haben mit

commission [kə'mɪʃən] n (act) Auftrag
m; (fee) Provision f; (body) Kommission f
♦ vt beauftragen; (MIL) zum Offizier
ernennen; (work of art) in Auftrag geben;
out of ~ außer Betrieb; ~**aire**
[kəmɪʃə'nɛə*] (BRIT) n Portier m; ~**er** n
(POLICE) Polizeipräsident m

commit [kə'mɪt] vt (crime) begehen;
(entrust) anvertrauen; to ~ o.s. sich festlegen; ~**ment** n Verpflichtung f

committee [kə'mɪtı] n Ausschuß m

commodity [kə'mɒdɪtı] n Ware f

common ['kɒmən] adj (cause)
gemeinsam; (pej) gewöhnlich;
(widespread) üblich, häufig ♦ n
Gemeindeland nt; C~s npl (BRIT): the C~s
das Unterhaus; ~**er** n Bürgerliche(r) mf;
~ **law** n Gewohnheitsrecht nt; ~**ly** adv
gewöhnlich; C~ **Market** n
Gemeinsame(r) Markt m; ~**place** adj
alltäglich; ~**room** n Gemeinschaftsraum
m; ~ **sense** n gesunde(r)
Menschenverstand m; C~**wealth** n: the
C~**wealth** das Commonwealth

commotion [kə'məʊʃən] n Aufsehen nt

communal ['kɒmjuːnl] adj Gemeinde-;
Gemeinschafts-

commune [n 'kɒmjuːn, vb kə'mjuːn] n
Kommune f ♦ vi: to ~ with sich mitteilen
+dat

communicate [kə'mjuːnɪkeɪt] vt
(transmit) übertragen ♦ vi (be in touch) in
Verbindung stehen; (make self understood)
sich verständigen

communication [kəmjuːnɪ'keɪʃən] n
(message) Mitteilung f; (making
understood) Kommunikation f; ~ **cord**
(BRIT) n Notbremse f

communion [kə'mjuːnɪən] n (also: Holy
C~) Abendmahl nt, Kommunion f

communism ['kɒmjʊnɪzəm] n
Kommunismus m

communist ['kɒmjʊnɪst] n
Kommunist(in) m(f) ♦ adj kommunistisch

community [kə'mjuːnɪtı] n
Gemeinschaft f; ~ **centre** n
Gemeinschaftszentrum nt; ~ **chest** (US) n
Wohltätigkeitsfonds m; ~ **home** (BRIT) n
Erziehungsheim nt

commutation ticket [kɒmjʊ'teɪʃən-]
(US) n Zeitkarte f

commute [kə'mjuːt] vi pendeln ♦ vt
umwandeln; ~**r** n Pendler m

compact [adj kəm'pækt, n 'kɒmpækt] adj
kompakt ♦ n (for make-up) Puderdose f; ~
disc n Compact-disc f; ~ **disc player** n
CD-Spieler m

companion [kəm'pænɪən] n Begleiter(in)
m(f); ~**ship** n Gesellschaft f

company ['kʌmpənɪ] n Gesellschaft f;
(COMM) Firma f, Gesellschaft f; to keep sb
~ jdm Gesellschaft leisten; ~ **secretary**
(BRIT) n ≈ Prokurist(in) m(f)

comparable ['kɒmpərəbl] adj
vergleichbar

comparative [kəm'pærətɪv] adj (relative)
relativ; ~**ly** adv verhältnismäßig

compare [kəm'pɛə*] vt vergleichen ♦ vi
sich vergleichen lassen

comparison [kəm'pærɪsn] n Vergleich m;
in ~ **(with)** im Vergleich (mit or zu)

compartment [kəm'pɑːtmənt] n (RAIL)
Abteil nt; (in drawer etc) Fach nt

compass ['kʌmpəs] n Kompaß m; ~**es**
npl (MATH etc: also: pair of ~es) Zirkel m

compassion [kəm'pæʃən] n Mitleid nt;
~**ate** adj mitfühlend

compatible [kəm'pætɪbl] adj vereinbar;
(COMPUT) kompatibel

compel [kəm'pel] vt zwingen

compensate ['kɒmpenseɪt] vt
entschädigen ♦ vi: to ~ for Ersatz

leisten für

compensation [kɒmpen'seɪʃən] *n*
Entschädigung *f*

compère ['kɒmpɛə*] *n* Conférencier *m*

compete [kəm'piːt] *vi (take part)*
teilnehmen; *(vie with)* konkurrieren

competent ['kɒmpɪtənt] *adj* kompetent

competition [kɒmpɪ'tɪʃən] *n (contest)*
Wettbewerb *m; (COMM, rivalry)*
Konkurrenz *f*

competitive [kəm'petɪtɪv] *adj*
Konkurrenz-; *(COMM)* konkurrenzfähig

competitor [kəm'petɪtə*] *n (COMM)*
Konkurrent(in) *m(f); (participant)*
Teilnehmer(in) *m(f)*

compile [kəm'paɪl] *vt* zusammenstellen

complacency [kəm'pleɪsnsɪ] *n*
Selbstzufriedenheit *f*

complacent [kəm'pleɪsnt] *adj*
selbstzufrieden

complain [kəm'pleɪn] *vi* sich beklagen;
(formally) sich beschweren; **~t** *n* Klage *f*;
(formal ~t) Beschwerde *f*; *(MED)* Leiden *nt*

complement [*n* 'kɒmplɪmənt, *vb*
'kɒmplɪment] *n* Ergänzung *f; (ship's crew
etc)* Bemannung *f* ♦ *vt* ergänzen; **~ary**
[kɒmplɪ'mentərɪ] *adj* (sich) ergänzend

complete [kəm'pliːt] *adj (full)*
vollkommen, ganz; *(finished)* fertig ♦ *vt*
vervollständigen; *(finish)* beenden; *(fill in:
form)* ausfüllen; **~ly** *adv* ganz

completion [kəm'pliːʃən] *n*
Fertigstellung *f; (of contract etc)* Abschluß
m

complex ['kɒmpleks] *adj* kompliziert

complexion [kəm'plekʃən] *n*
Gesichtsfarbe *f; (fig)* Aspekt *m*

complexity [kəm'pleksɪtɪ] *n*
Kompliziertheit *f*

compliance [kəm'plaɪəns] *n* Fügsamkeit
f, Einwilligung *f;* **in ~ with sth** einer
Sache *dat* gemäß

complicate ['kɒmplɪkeɪt] *vt*
komplizieren; **~d** *adj* kompliziert

complication [kɒmplɪ'keɪʃən] *n*
Komplikation *f*

complicity [kəm'plɪsɪtɪ] *n:* **~ (in)**
Mittäterschaft *f* (bei)

compliment [*n* 'kɒmplɪmənt, *vb*
'kɒmplɪment] *n* Kompliment *nt* ♦ *vt* ein
Kompliment machen +*dat;* **~s** *npl (greetings)* Grüße *pl;* **to pay sb a ~** jdm ein
Kompliment machen; **~ary** [kɒmplɪ'men-
tərɪ] *adj* schmeichelhaft; *(free)* Frei-,
Gratis-

comply [kəm'plaɪ] *vi:* **to ~ with** erfüllen
+*acc;* entsprechen +*dat*

component [kəm'pəʊnənt] *adj* Teil- ♦ *n*
Bestandteil *m*

compose [kəm'pəʊz] *vt (music)*
komponieren; *(poetry)* verfassen; **to ~ o.s.**
sich sammeln; **~d** *adj* gefaßt; **~r** *n*
Komponist(in) *m(f)*

composite ['kɒmpəzɪt] *adj*
zusammengesetzt

composition [kɒmpə'zɪʃən] *n (MUS)*
Komposition *f; (SCH)* Aufsatz *m; (structure)*
Zusammensetzung *f*, Aufbau *m*

compost ['kɒmpɒst] *n* Kompost *m*

composure [kəm'pəʊʒə*] *n* Fassung *f*

compound ['kɒmpaʊnd] *n (CHEM)*
Verbindung *f; (enclosure)* Lager *nt; (LING)*
Kompositum *nt* ♦ *adj* zusammengesetzt;
(fracture) kompliziert; **~ interest** *n*
Zinseszins *m*

comprehend [kɒmprɪ'hend] *vt* begreifen

comprehension [kɒmprɪ'henʃən] *n*
Verständnis *nt*

comprehensive [kɒmprɪ'hensɪv] *adj*
umfassend ♦ *n* = **comprehensive school;**
~ insurance *n* Vollkasko *nt;* **~ school**
(BRIT) *n* Gesamtschule *f*

compress [*vb* kəm'pres, *n* 'kɒmpres] *vt*
komprimieren ♦ *n (MED)* Kompresse *f*

comprise [kəm'praɪz] *vt (also:* be ~d of)
umfassen, bestehen aus

compromise ['kɒmprəmaɪz] *n*
Kompromiß *m* ♦ *vt* kompromittieren ♦ *vi*
einen Kompromiß schließen

compulsion [kəm'pʌlʃən] *n* Zwang *m*

compulsive [kəm'pʌlsɪv] *adj* zwanghaft

compulsory [kəm'pʌlsərɪ] *adj*
obligatorisch

computer [kəm'pjuːtə*] *n* Computer *m*,
Rechner *m;* **~ game** *n* Computerspiel *nt;*
~ize *vt (information)* computerisieren;
(company, accounts) auf Computer
umstellen; **~ programmer** *n*

Programmierer(in) *m(f)*; ~
programming *n* Programmieren *nt*; ~
science *n* Informatik *f*
computing [kəm'pju:tɪŋ] *n* (*science*)
Informatik *f*; (*work*) Computerei *f*
comrade ['kɒmrɪd] *n* Kamerad *m*; (*POL*)
Genosse *m*
con [kɒn] *vt* hereinlegen ♦ *n* Schwindel *nt*
concave [kɒn'keɪv] *adj* konkav
conceal [kən'si:l] *vt* (*secret*)
verschweigen; (*hide*) verbergen
concede [kən'si:d] *vt* (*grant*) gewähren;
(*point*) zugeben ♦ *vi* (*admit defeat*)
nachgeben
conceit [kən'si:t] *n* Einbildung *f*; **~ed** *adj*
eingebildet
conceivable [kən'si:vəbl] *adj* vorstellbar
conceive [kən'si:v] *vt* (*idea*) ausdenken;
(*imagine*) sich vorstellen; (*baby*)
empfangen ♦ *vi* empfangen
concentrate ['kɒnsəntreɪt] *vi* sich
konzentrieren ♦ *vt* konzentrieren; **to ~ on**
sth sich auf etw *acc* konzentrieren
concentration [kɒnsən'treɪʃən] *n*
Konzentration *f*; **~ camp** *n*
Konzentrationslager *nt*, KZ *nt*
concept ['kɒnsept] *n* Begriff *m*
conception [kən'sepʃən] *n* (*idea*)
Vorstellung *f*; (*BIOL*) Empfängnis *f*
concern [kən'sɜ:n] *n* (*affair*)
Angelegenheit *f*, (*COMM*) Unternehmen *nt*;
(*worry*) Sorge *f* ♦ *vt* (*interest*) angehen; (*be
about*) handeln von; (*have connection
with*) betreffen; **to be ~ed (about)** sich
Sorgen machen (um); **~ing** *prep*
hinsichtlich +*gen*
concert ['kɒnsət] *n* Konzert *nt*
concerted [kən'sɜ:tɪd] *adj* gemeinsam
concert hall *n* Konzerthalle *f*
concertina [kɒnsə'ti:nə] *n*
Handharmonika *f*
concerto [kən'tʃɜ:təʊ] *n* Konzert *nt*
concession [kən'seʃən] *n* (*yielding*)
Zugeständnis *nt*; **tax ~** Steuer-Konzession
f
conciliation [kənsɪlɪ'eɪʃən] *n*
Versöhnung *f*; (*official*) Schlichtung *f*
concise [kən'saɪs] *adj* präzis
conclude [kən'klu:d] *vt* (*end*) beenden;

(*treaty*) (ab)schließen; (*decide*) schließen,
folgern
conclusion [kən'klu:ʒən] *n* (Ab)schluß *m*;
(*deduction*) Schluß *m*
conclusive [kən'klu:sɪv] *adj* schlüssig
concoct [kən'kɒkt] *vt* zusammenbrauen;
~ion [kən'kɒkʃən] *n* Gebräu *nt*
concourse ['kɒŋkɔ:s] *n* (Bahnhofs)halle
f, Vorplatz *m*
concrete ['kɒŋkri:t] *n* Beton *m* ♦ *adj*
konkret
concur [kən'kɜ:*] *vi* übereinstimmen
concurrently [kən'kʌrəntlɪ] *adv*
gleichzeitig
concussion [kən'kʌʃən] *n* (Gehirn)er-
schütterung *f*
condemn [kən'dem] *vt* (*JUR*) verurteilen;
(*building*) abbruchreif erklären
condensation [kɒnden'seɪʃən] *n*
Kondensation *f*
condense [kən'dens] *vi* (*CHEM*)
kondensieren ♦ *vt* (*fig*)
zusammendrängen; **~d milk** *n*
Kondensmilch *f*
condescending [kɒndɪ'sendɪŋ] *adj*
herablassend
condition [kən'dɪʃən] *n* (*state*) Zustand
m; (*presupposition*) Bedingung *f* ♦ *vt* (*hair
etc*) behandeln; (*accustom*) gewöhnen; **~s**
npl (*circumstances*) Verhältnisse *pl*; **on ~
that ...** unter der Bedingung, daß ...; **~al**
adj bedingt; (*LING*) Bedingungs-; **~er** *n* (*for
hair*) Spülung *f*; (*for fabrics*) Weichspüler
m
condolences [kən'dəʊlənsɪz] *npl* Beileid
nt
condom ['kɒndəm] *n* Kondom *nt or m*
condominium [kɒndə'mɪnɪəm] (*US*) *n*
Eigentumswohnung *f*; (*block*)
Eigentumsblock *m*
condone [kən'dəʊn] *vt* gutheißen
conducive [kən'dju:sɪv] *adj*: **~ to**
dienlich +*dat*
conduct [*n* 'kɒndʌkt, *vb* kən'dʌkt] *n*
(*behaviour*) Verhalten *nt*; (*management*)
Führung *f* ♦ *vt* führen; (*MUS*) dirigieren;
~ed tour *n* Führung *f*; **~or** [kən'dʌktə*]
n (*of orchestra*) Dirigent *m*; (*in bus, US: on
train*) Schaffner *m*; (*ELEC*) Leiter *m*; **~ress**

[kən'dʌktrɪs] n (*in bus*) Schaffnerin f
cone [kəun] n (MATH) Kegel m; (*for ice cream*) (Waffel)tüte f; (BOT) Tannenzapfen m
confectioner [kən'fekʃənə*] n Konditor m; ~'s (**shop**) n Konditorei f; ~y [kən'fekʃənrɪ] n Süßigkeiten pl
confederation [kənfedə'reɪʃən] n Bund m
confer [kən'fɜ:*] vt (*degree*) verleihen
♦ vi (*discuss*) konferieren, verhandeln; ~**ence** ['kɒnfərəns] n Konferenz f
confess [kən'fes] vt, vi gestehen; (ECCL) beichten; ~**ion** [kən'feʃən] n Geständnis nt; (ECCL) Beichte f; ~**ional** [kən'feʃənl] n Beichtstuhl m
confetti [kən'fetɪ] n Konfetti nt
confide [kən'faɪd] vi: **to ~ in** (sich) anvertrauen +dat
confidence ['kɒnfɪdəns] n Vertrauen nt; (*assurance*) Selbstvertrauen nt; (*secret*) Geheimnis nt; **in ~** (*speak, write*) vertraulich; **~ trick** n Schwindel m
confident ['kɒnfɪdənt] adj (*sure*) überzeugt; (*self-assured*) selbstsicher
confidential [kɒnfɪ'denʃəl] adj vertraulich
confine [kən'faɪn] vt (*limit*) beschränken; (*lock up*) einsperren; ~**d** adj (*space*) eng; ~**ment** n (*in prison*) Haft f; (MED) Wochenbett nt; ~**s** ['kɒnfaɪnz] npl Grenzen pl
confirm [kən'fɜ:m] vt bestätigen; ~**ation** [kɒnfə'meɪʃən] n Bestätigung f; (REL) Konfirmation f; ~**ed** adj unverbesserlich; (*bachelor*) eingefleischt
confiscate ['kɒnfɪskeɪt] vt beschlagnahmen
conflict [n 'kɒnflɪkt, vb kən'flɪkt] n Konflikt m ♦ vi im Widerspruch stehen; ~**ing** [kən'flɪktɪŋ] adj widersprüchlich
conform [kən'fɔ:m] vi: **to ~ to** (*things*) entsprechen +dat; (*people*) sich anpassen +dat; (*to rules*) sich richten (nach)
confound [kən'faund] vt verblüffen; (*throw into confusion*) durcheinanderbringen
confront [kən'frʌnt] vt (*enemy*) entgegentreten +dat; (*problems*) sich

stellen +dat; **to ~ sb with sth** jdn mit etw konfrontieren; ~**ation** [kɒnfrən-'teɪʃən] n Konfrontation f
confuse [kən'fju:z] vt verwirren; (*sth with sth*) verwechseln; ~**d** adj verwirrt; **confusing** adj verwirrend; **confusion** [kən'fju:ʒən] n (*perplexity*) Verwirrung f; (*mixing up*) Verwechslung f; (*tumult*) Aufruhr m
congeal [kən'dʒi:l] vi (*freeze*) gefrieren; (*clot*) gerinnen
congenial [kən'dʒi:nɪəl] adj angenehm
congenital [kən'dʒenɪtəl] adj angeboren
congested [kən'dʒestɪd] adj überfüllt
congestion [kən'dʒestʃən] n Stau m
conglomerate [kən'glɒmərət] n (COMM, GEOL) Konglomerat nt
conglomeration [kənglɒmə'reɪʃən] n Anhäufung f
congratulate [kən'grætjʊleɪt] vt: **to ~ sb (on sth)** jdn (zu etw) beglückwünschen
congratulations [kəngrætjʊ'leɪʃənz] npl Glückwünsche pl; ~**!** gratuliere!, herzlichen Glückwunsch!
congregate ['kɒŋgrɪgeɪt] vi sich versammeln
congregation [kɒŋgrɪ'geɪʃən] n Gemeinde f
congress ['kɒŋgres] n Kongreß m; **C~man** (US: irreg) n Mitglied nt des amerikanischen Repräsentantenhauses
conical ['kɒnɪkəl] adj kegelförmig
conifer ['kɒnɪfə*] n Nadelbaum m
conjecture [kən'dʒektʃə*] n Vermutung f
conjugal ['kɒndʒʊgəl] adj ehelich
conjugate ['kɒndʒʊgeɪt] vt konjugieren
conjunction [kən'dʒʌŋkʃən] n Verbindung f; (GRAM) Konjunktion f
conjunctivitis [kəndʒʌŋktɪ'vaɪtɪs] n Bindehautentzündung f
conjure ['kʌndʒə*] vi zaubern; **~ up** vt heraufbeschwören; **~r** n Zauberkünstler(in) m(f)
conk out [kɒŋk-] (inf) vi den Geist aufgeben
con man (irreg) n Schwindler m
connect [kə'nekt] vt verbinden; (ELEC) anschließen; **to be ~ed with** ein Beziehung haben zu; (*be related to*)

verwandt sein mit; **~ion** [kəˈnekʃən] *n*
Verbindung *f*; (*relation*) Zusammenhang
m; (*ELEC, TEL, RAIL*) Anschluß *m*
connive [kəˈnaɪv] *vi*: **to ~ at**
stillschweigend dulden
connoisseur [kɒnɪˈsɜː*] *n* Kenner *m*
conquer [ˈkɒŋkə*] *vt* (*feelings*)
überwinden; (*enemy*) besiegen; (*country*)
erobern; **~or** *n* Eroberer *m*
conquest [ˈkɒŋkwest] *n* Eroberung *f*
cons [kɒnz] *npl see* **convenience; pro**
conscience [ˈkɒnʃəns] *n* Gewissen *nt*
conscientious [kɒnʃɪˈenʃəs] *adj*
gewissenhaft
conscious [ˈkɒnʃəs] *adj* bewußt; (*MED*)
bei Bewußtsein; **~ness** *n* Bewußtsein *nt*
conscript [ˈkɒnskrɪpt] *n*
Wehrpflichtige(r) *m*; **~ion** [kənˈskrɪpʃən]
n Wehrpflicht *f*
consecrate [ˈkɒnsɪkreɪt] *vt* weihen
consecutive [kənˈsekjʊtɪv] *adj*
aufeinanderfolgend
consensus [kənˈsensəs] *n* allgemeine
Übereinstimmung *f*
consent [kənˈsent] *n* Zustimmung *f* ♦ *vi*
zustimmen
consequence [ˈkɒnsɪkwəns] *n*
(*importance*) Bedeutung *f*; (*effect*) Folge *f*
consequently [ˈkɒnsɪkwəntlɪ] *adv*
folglich
conservation [kɒnsəˈveɪʃən] *n*
Erhaltung *f*; (*nature ~*) Umweltschutz *m*
conservative [kənˈsɜːvətɪv] *adj*
konservativ; **C~** (*BRIT*) *adj* konservativ
♦ *n* Konservative(r) *mf*
conservatory [kənˈsɜːvətrɪ] *n* (*room*)
Wintergarten *m*
conserve [kənˈsɜːv] *vt* erhalten
consider [kənˈsɪdə*] *vt* überlegen; (*take*
into account) in Betracht ziehen; (*regard*
as) halten für; **to ~ doing sth** daran
denken, etw zu tun
considerable [kənˈsɪdərəbl] *adj*
beträchtlich
considerably [kənˈsɪdərəblɪ] *adv*
beträchtlich
considerate [kənˈsɪdərɪt] *adj*
rücksichtsvoll
consideration [kənsɪdəˈreɪʃən] *n*

Rücksicht(nahme) *f*; (*thought*) Erwägung
f; (*reward*) Entgelt *nt*
considering [kənˈsɪdərɪŋ] *prep* in
Anbetracht +*gen*
consign [kənˈsaɪn] *vt* übergeben; **~ment**
n Sendung *f*
consist [kənˈsɪst] *vi*: **to ~ of** bestehen aus
consistency [kənˈsɪstənsɪ] *n* (*of material*)
Konsistenz *f*; (*of argument, person*)
Konsequenz *f*
consistent [kənˈsɪstənt] *adj* (*person*)
konsequent; (*argument*) folgerichtig
consolation [kɒnsəˈleɪʃən] *n* Trost *m*
console¹ [kənˈsəʊl] *vt* trösten
console² [ˈkɒnsəʊl] *n* Kontroll(pult) *nt*
consolidate [kənˈsɒlɪdeɪt] *vt* festigen
consommé [kənˈsɒmeɪ] *n* Fleischbrühe *f*
consortium [kənˈsɔːtɪəm] *n* (*COMM*)
Konsortium *nt*
conspicuous [kənˈspɪkjʊəs] *adj*
(*prominent*) auffällig; (*visible*) deutlich
sichtbar
conspiracy [kənˈspɪrəsɪ] *n* Verschwörung
f
conspire [kənˈspaɪə*] *vi* sich
verschwören
constable [ˈkʌnstəbl] (*BRIT*) *n* Polizist(in)
m(f); **chief ~** Polizeipräsident *m*
constabulary [kənˈstæbjʊlərɪ] *n* Polizei *f*
constant [ˈkɒnstənt] *adj* (*continuous*)
ständig; (*unchanging*) konstant; **~ly** *adv*
ständig
constellation [kɒnstəˈleɪʃən] *n* Sternbild
nt
consternation [kɒnstəˈneɪʃən] *n*
Bestürzung *f*
constipated [ˈkɒnstɪpeɪtəd] *adj* verstopft
constipation [kɒnstɪˈpeɪʃən] *n*
Verstopfung *f*
constituency [kənˈstɪtjʊənsɪ] *n*
Wahlkreis *m*
constituent [kənˈstɪtjʊənt] *n* (*person*)
Wähler *m*; (*part*) Bestandteil *m*
constitute [ˈkɒnstɪtjuːt] *vt* (*make up*)
bilden; (*amount to*) darstellen
constitution [kɒnstɪˈtjuːʃən] *n*
Verfassung *f*; **~al** *adj* Verfassungs-
constraint [kənˈstreɪnt] *n* Zwang *m*;
(*shyness*) Befangenheit *f*

construct [kən'strʌkt] *vt* bauen; **~ion** [kən'strʌkʃən] *n* Konstruktion *f*; *(building)* Bau *m*; **~ive** *adj* konstruktiv

construe [kən'struː] *vt* deuten

consul ['kɒnsl] *n* Konsul *m*; **~ate** ['kɒnsjulət] *n* Konsulat *nt*

consult [kən'sʌlt] *vt* um Rat fragen; *(doctor)* konsultieren; *(book)* nachschlagen in +*dat*; **~ant** *n* (MED) Facharzt *m*; *(other specialist)* Gutachter *m*; **~ation** [kɒnsəl'teɪʃən] *n* Beratung *f*; (MED) Konsultation *f*; (MED) Sprechzimmer *nt*

consume [kən'sjuːm] *vt* verbrauchen; *(food)* konsumieren; **~r** *n* Verbraucher *m*; **~r goods** *npl* Konsumgüter *pl*; **~rism** *n* Konsum *m*; **~r society** *n* Konsumgesellschaft *f*

consummate ['kɒnsʌmeɪt] *vt* (*marriage*) vollziehen

consumption [kən'sʌmpʃən] *n* Verbrauch *m*; *(of food)* Konsum *m*

cont. *abbr* (= *continued*) Forts.

contact ['kɒntækt] *n* (*touch*) Berührung *f*; *(connection)* Verbindung *f*; *(person)* Kontakt *m* ♦ *vt* sich in Verbindung setzen mit; **~ lenses** *npl* Kontaktlinsen *pl*

contagious [kən'teɪdʒəs] *adj* ansteckend

contain [kən'teɪn] *vt* enthalten; **to ~ o.s.** sich zügeln; **~er** *n* Behälter *m*; *(transport)* Container *m*

contaminate [kən'tæmɪneɪt] *vt* verunreinigen

contamination [kəntæmɪ'neɪʃən] *n* Verunreinigung *f*

cont'd *abbr* (= *continued*) Forts.

contemplate ['kɒntəmpleɪt] *vt* (*look at*) (nachdenklich) betrachten; *(think about)* überdenken; *(plan)* vorhaben

contemporary [kən'tempərərɪ] *adj* zeitgenössisch ♦ *n* Zeitgenosse *m*

contempt [kən'tempt] *n* Verachtung *f*; **~ of court** (JUR) Mißachtung *f* des Gerichts; **~ible** *adj* verachtenswert; **~uous** *adj* verächtlich

contend [kən'tend] *vt* (*argue*) behaupten ♦ *vi* kämpfen; **~er** *n* (*for post*) Bewerber(in) *m(f)*; (SPORT) Wettkämpfer(in) *m(f)*

content [*adj, vb* kən'tent, *n* 'kɒntent] *adj* zufrieden ♦ *vt* befriedigen ♦ *n* (*also:* ~s) Inhalt *m*; **~ed** *adj* zufrieden

contention [kən'tenʃən] *n* (*dispute*) Streit *m*; *(argument)* Behauptung *f*

contentment [kən'tentmənt] *n* Zufriedenheit *f*

contest [*n* 'kɒntest, *vb* kən'test] *n* (Wett)kampf *m* ♦ *vt* (*dispute*) bestreiten; (JUR) anfechten; (POL) kandidieren in +*dat*; **~ant** [kən'testənt] *n* Bewerber(in) *m(f)*

context ['kɒntekst] *n* Zusammenhang *m*

continent ['kɒntɪnənt] *n* Kontinent *m*; **the C~** (BRIT) das europäische Festland; **~al** [kɒntɪ'nentl] *adj* kontinental; **~al quilt** (BRIT) *n* Federbett *nt*

contingency [kən'tɪndʒənsɪ] *n* Möglichkeit *f*

contingent [kən'tɪndʒənt] *n* Kontingent *nt*

continual [kən'tɪnjuəl] *adj* (*endless*) fortwährend; *(repeated)* immer wiederkehrend; **~ly** *adv* immer wieder

continuation [kəntɪnju'eɪʃən] *n* Fortsetzung *f*

continue [kən'tɪnjuː] *vi* (*person*) weitermachen; *(thing)* weitergehen ♦ *vt* fortsetzen

continuity [kɒntɪ'njuɪtɪ] *n* Kontinuität *f*

continuous [kən'tɪnjuəs] *adj* ununterbrochen; **~ stationery** *n* Endlospapier *nt*

contort [kən'tɔːt] *vt* verdrehen; **~ion** [kən'tɔːʃən] *n* Verzerrung *f*

contour ['kɒntuə*] *n* Umriß *m*; *(also:* ~ *line)* Höhenlinie *f*

contraband ['kɒntrəbænd] *n* Schmuggelware *f*

contraception [kɒntrə'sepʃən] *n* Empfängnisverhütung *f*

contraceptive [kɒntrə'septɪv] *n* empfängnisverhütende(s) Mittel *nt* ♦ *adj* empfängnisverhütend

contract [*n* 'kɒntrækt, *vb* kən'trækt] *n* Vertrag *m* ♦ *vi* (*muscle, metal*) sich zusammenziehen ♦ *vt* zusammenziehen; **to ~ to do sth** (COMM) sich vertraglich verpflichten, etw zu tun; **~ion** [kən'trækʃən] *n* (*shortening*) Verkürzung

f; **~or** [kənˈtræktə*] *n* Unternehmer *m*
contradict [kɒntrəˈdɪkt] *vt*
widersprechen +*dat*; **~ion** [kɒntrəˈdɪkʃən]
n Widerspruch *m*; **~ory** *adj*
widersprüchlich
contraption [kənˈtræpʃən] (*inf*) *n*
Apparat *m*
contrary[1] [ˈkɒntrərɪ] *adj* (*opposite*)
entgegengesetzt ♦ *n* Gegenteil *nt*; **on the**
~ im Gegenteil
contrary[2] [kənˈtrɛərɪ] *adj* (*obstinate*)
widerspenstig
contrast [*n* ˈkɒntrɑːst, *vb* kənˈtrɑːst] *n*
Kontrast *m* ♦ *vt* entgegensetzen; **~ing**
[kənˈtrɑːstɪŋ] *adj* Kontrast-
contravene [kɒntrəˈviːn] *vt* verstoßen
gegen
contribute [kənˈtrɪbjuːt] *vt, vi*: **to ~ to**
beitragen zu
contribution [kɒntrɪˈbjuːʃən] *n* Beitrag
m
contributor [kənˈtrɪbjutə*] *n*
Beitragende(r) *mf*
contrive [kənˈtraɪv] *vt* ersinnen ♦ *vi*: **to ~**
to do sth es schaffen, etw zu tun
control [kənˈtrəul] *vt* (*direct, test*)
kontrollieren ♦ *n* Kontrolle *f*; **~s** *npl* (*of*
vehicle) Steuerung *f*; (*of engine*) Schalttafel
f; **to be in ~ of** (*business, office*) leiten;
(*group of children*) beaufsichtigen; **out of**
~ außer Kontrolle; **under ~** unter
Kontrolle; **~ panel** *n* Schalttafel *f*; **~**
room *n* Kontrollraum *m*; **~ tower** *n*
(*AVIAT*) Kontrollturm *m*
controversial [kɒntrəˈvɜːʃəl] *adj*
umstritten
controversy [ˈkɒntrəvɜːsɪ] *n*
Kontroverse *f*
conurbation [kɒnɜːˈbeɪʃən] *n*
Ballungsgebiet *nt*
convalesce [kɒnvəˈles] *vi* genesen; **~nce**
[kɒnvəˈlesns] *n* Genesung *f*
convector [kənˈvektə*] *n* Heizlüfter *m*
convene [kənˈviːn] *vt* zusammenrufen
♦ *vi* sich versammeln
convenience [kənˈviːnɪəns] *n*
Annehmlichkeit *f*; **all modern ~s** mit
allem Komfort; **all mod cons** (*BRIT*) mit
allem Komfort; **at your ~** wann es Ihnen

paßt
convenient [kənˈviːnɪənt] *adj* günstig
convent [ˈkɒnvənt] *n* Kloster *nt*
convention [kənˈvenʃən] *n*
Versammlung *f*; (*custom*) Konvention *f*;
~al *adj* konventionell
converge [kənˈvɜːdʒ] *vi* zusammenlaufen
conversant [kənˈvɜːsənt] *adj*: **to be ~**
with bewandert sein in +*dat*
conversation [kɒnvəˈseɪʃən] *n* Gespräch
nt; **~al** *adj* Unterhaltungs-
converse [*n* ˈkɒnvɜːs, *vb* kənˈvɜːs] *n*
Gegenteil *nt* ♦ *vi* sich unterhalten
conversion [kənˈvɜːʃən] *n* Umwandlung
f; (*esp REL*) Bekehrung *f*
convert [*vb* kənˈvɜːt, *n* ˈkɒnvɜːt] *vt*
(*change*) umwandeln; (*REL*) bekehren ♦ *n*
Bekehrte(r) *mf*; Konvertit(in) *m(f)*; **~ible**
n (*AUT*) Kabriolett *nt* ♦ *adj* umwandelbar;
(*FIN*) konvertierbar
convex [kɒnˈveks] *adj* konvex
convey [kənˈveɪ] *vt* (*carry*) befördern;
(*feelings*) vermitteln; **~or belt** *n*
Fließband *nt*
convict [*vb* kənˈvɪkt, *n* ˈkɒnvɪkt] *vt*
verurteilen ♦ *n* Häftling *m*; **~ion**
[kənˈvɪkʃən] *n* (*verdict*) Verurteilung *f*;
(*belief*) Überzeugung *f*
convince [kənˈvɪns] *vt* überzeugen; **~d**
adj: **~d that** überzeugt davon, daß;
convincing *adj* überzeugend
convoluted [ˈkɒnvəˈluːtɪd] *adj*
verwickelt; (*style*) gewunden
convoy [ˈkɒnvɔɪ] *n* (*of vehicles*) Kolonne
f; (*protected*) Konvoi *m*
convulse [kənˈvʌls] *vt* zusammenzucken
lassen; **to be ~d with laughter** sich vor
Lachen krümmen
convulsion [kənˈvʌlʃən] *n* (*esp MED*)
Zuckung *f*, Krampf *m*
coo [kuː] *vi* gurren
cook [kuk] *vt, vi* kochen ♦ *n* Koch *m*,
Köchin *f*; **~ book** *n* Kochbuch *nt*; **~er** *n*
Herd *m*; **~ery** *n* Kochkunst *f*; **~ery book**
(*BRIT*) *n* = **cook book**; **~ie** (*US*) *n*
Plätzchen *nt*; **~ing** *n* Kochen *nt*
cool [kuːl] *adj* kühl ♦ *vt, vi* (ab)kühlen; **~**
down *vt, vi* (*fig*) (sich) beruhigen; **~ness**
n Kühle *f*; (*of temperament*) kühle(r)

Kopf *m*

coop [kuːp] *n* Hühnerstall *m* ♦ *vt*: ~ **up**
(*fig*) einpferchen

cooperate [kəʊˈɒpəreɪt] *vi*
zusammenarbeiten; **cooperation**
[kəʊɒpəˈreɪʃən] *n* Zusammenarbeit *f*

cooperative [kəʊˈɒpərətɪv] *adj*
hilfsbereit; (*COMM*) genossenschaftlich ♦ *n*
(*of farmers*) Genossenschaft *f*; (~ *store*)
Konsumladen *m*

coordinate [*vb* kəʊˈɔːdɪneɪt, *n* kəʊˈɔːdɪnət]
vt koordinieren ♦ *n* (*MATH*) Koordinate *f*;
~**s** *npl* (*clothes*) Kombinationen *pl*

coordination [kəʊɔːdɪˈneɪʃən] *n*
Koordination *f*

cop [kɒp] (*inf*) *n* Polyp *m*, Bulle *m*

cope [kəʊp] *vi*: **to** ~ **with** fertig werden
mit

copious [ˈkəʊpɪəs] *adj* reichhaltig

copper [ˈkɒpə*] *n* (*metal*) Kupfer *nt*; (*inf:
policeman*) Polyp *m*, Bulle *m*; ~**s** *npl*
(*money*) Kleingeld *nt*

coppice [ˈkɒpɪs] *n* Unterholz *nt*

copse [kɒps] *n* Unterholz *nt*

copulate [ˈkɒpjʊleɪt] *vi* sich paaren

copy [ˈkɒpɪ] *n* (*imitation*) Kopie *f*; (*of
book etc*) Exemplar *nt*; (*of newspaper*)
Nummer *f* ♦ *vt* kopieren, abschreiben;
~**right** *n* Copyright *nt*

coral [ˈkɒrəl] *n* Koralle *f*; ~ **reef** *n*
Korallenriff *nt*

cord [kɔːd] *n* Schnur *f*; (*ELEC*) Kabel *nt*

cordial [ˈkɔːdɪəl] *adj* herzlich ♦ *n*
Fruchtsaft *m*

cordon [ˈkɔːdn] *n* Absperrkette *f*; ~ **off**
vt abriegeln

corduroy [ˈkɔːdərɔɪ] *n* Kord(samt) *m*

core [kɔː*] *n* Kern *m* ♦ *vt* entkernen

cork [kɔːk] *n* (*bark*) Korkrinde *f*; (*stopper*)
Korken *m*; ~**screw** *n* Korkenzieher *m*

corn [kɔːn] *n* (*BRIT: wheat*) Getreide *nt*,
Korn *nt*; (*US: maize*) Mais *m*; (*on foot*)
Hühnerauge *nt*; ~ **on the cob** Maiskolben
m

cornea [ˈkɔːnɪə] *n* Hornhaut *f*

corned beef [ˈkɔːnd-] *n* Corned Beef *nt*

corner [ˈkɔːnə*] *n* Ecke *f*; (*on road*)
Kurve *f* ♦ *vt* in die Enge treiben; (*market*)
monopolisieren ♦ *vi* (*AUT*) in die Kurve

gehen; ~**stone** *n* Eckstein *m*

cornet [ˈkɔːnɪt] *n* (*MUS*) Kornétt *nt*; (*BRIT:
of ice cream*) Eistüte *f*

cornflakes [ˈkɔːnfleɪks] *npl* Cornflakes *pl*
®

cornflour [ˈkɔːnflaʊə*] (*BRIT*) *n* Maizena
nt ®

cornstarch [ˈkɔːnstɑːtʃ] (*US*) *n* Maizena
nt ®

Cornwall [ˈkɔːnwəl] *n* Cornwall *nt*

corny [ˈkɔːnɪ] *adj* (*joke*) blöd(e)

corollary [kəˈrɒlərɪ] *n* Folgesatz *m*

coronary [ˈkɒrənərɪ] *n* (*also*: ~
thrombosis) Herzinfarkt *m*

coronation [kɒrəˈneɪʃən] *n* Krönung *f*

coroner [ˈkɒrənə*] *n*
Untersuchungsrichter *m*

coronet [ˈkɒrənɪt] *n* Adelskrone *f*

corporal [ˈkɔːpərəl] *n* Obergefreite(r) *m*
♦ *adj*: ~ **punishment** Prügelstrafe *f*

corporate [ˈkɔːpərɪt] *adj*
gemeinschaftlich, korporativ

corporation [kɔːpəˈreɪʃən] *n* (*of town*)
Gemeinde *f*; (*COMM*) Körperschaft *f*,
Aktiengesellschaft *f*

corps [kɔː*, *pl* kɔːz] (*pl* **corps**) *n*
(Armee)korps *nt*

corpse [kɔːps] *n* Leiche *f*

corpuscle [ˈkɔːpʌsl] *n* Blutkörperchen *nt*

corral [kəˈrɑːl] *n* Pferch *m*, Korral *m*

correct [kəˈrekt] *adj* (*accurate*) richtig;
(*proper*) korrekt ♦ *vt* korrigieren; ~**ion**
[kəˈrekʃən] *n* Berichtigung *f*

correlation [kɒrɪˈleɪʃən] *n*
Wechselbeziehung *f*

correspond [kɒrɪsˈpɒnd] *vi* (*agree*)
übereinstimmen; (*exchange letters*)
korrespondieren; ~**ence** *n* (*similarity*)
Entsprechung *f*; (*letters*) Briefwechsel *m*,
Korrespondenz *f*; ~**ence course** *n* Fern-
kurs *m*; ~**ent** *n* (*PRESS*) Berichterstatter *m*

corridor [ˈkɒrɪdɔː*] *n* Gang *m*

corroborate [kəˈrɒbəreɪt] *vt* bestätigen

corrode [kəˈrəʊd] *vt* zerfressen ♦ *vi*
rosten

corrosion [kəˈrəʊʒən] *n* Korrosion *f*

corrugated [ˈkɒrəgeɪtɪd] *adj* gewellt; ~
iron *n* Wellblech *nt*

corrupt [kəˈrʌpt] *adj* korrupt ♦ *vt*

verderben; (*bribe*) bestechen; **~ion**
[kə'rʌpʃən] *n* (*of society*) Verdorbenheit *f*;
(*bribery*) Bestechung *f*
corset ['kɔːsɪt] *n* Korsett *nt*
Corsica ['kɔːsɪkə] *n* Korsika *nt*
cortège [kɔː'teɪʒ] *n* Zug *m*; (*of funeral*)
Leichenzug *m*
cosh [kɒʃ] (*BRIT*) *n* Totschläger *m*
cosmetics [kɒz'metɪks] *npl* Kosmetika *pl*
cosmic ['kɒzmɪk] *adj* kosmisch
cosmonaut ['kɒzmənɔːt] *n*
Kosmonaut(in) *m(f)*
cosmopolitan [kɒzmə'pɒlɪtən] *adj*
international; (*city*) Welt-
cosmos ['kɒzmɒs] *n* Kosmos *m*
cosset ['kɒsɪt] *vt* verwöhnen
cost [kɒst] (*pt, pp* cost) *n* Kosten *pl*, Preis
m ♦ *vt, vi* kosten; **~s** *npl* (*JUR*) Kosten *pl*;
how much does it ~? wieviel kostet
das?; **at all ~s** um jeden Preis
co-star ['kəʊstɑː*] *n* zweite(r) *or*
weitere(r) Hauptdarsteller(in) *m(f)*
cost-effective ['kɒstɪ'fektɪv] *adj*
rentabel
costly ['kɒstlɪ] *adj* kostspielig
cost-of-living ['kɒstəv'lɪvɪŋ] *adj*
(*allowance, index*) Lebenshaltungskosten-
cost price (*BRIT*) *n* Selbstkostenpreis *m*
costume ['kɒstjuːm] *n* Kostüm *nt*; (*fancy
dress*) Maskenkostüm *nt*; (*BRIT: also:
swimming ~*) Badeanzug *m*; **~ jewellery**
n Modeschmuck *m*
cosy ['kəʊzɪ] (*BRIT*) *adj* behaglich; (*atmosphere*) gemütlich
cot [kɒt] *n* (*BRIT: child's*) Kinderbett(chen)
nt; (*US: campbed*) Feldbett *nt*
cottage ['kɒtɪdʒ] *n* kleine(s) Haus *nt*; **~
cheese** *n* Hüttenkäse *m*; **~ industry** *n*
Heimindustrie *f*; **~ pie** *n* Auflauf mit
Hackfleisch und Kartoffelbrei
cotton ['kɒtn] *n* Baumwolle *f*; (*thread*)
Garn *nt*; **~ on to** (*inf*) *vt* kapieren; **~
candy** (*US*) *n* Zuckerwatte *f*; **~ wool**
(*BRIT*) *n* Watte *f*
couch [kaʊtʃ] *n* Couch *f*
couchette [kuː'ʃet] *n* (*on train, boat*)
Liegewagenplatz *m*
cough [kɒf] *vi* husten ♦ *n* Husten *m*; **~
drop** *n* Hustenbonbon *nt*

could [kʊd] *pt of* **can²**; **~n't** = could not
council ['kaʊnsl] *n* (*of town*) Stadtrat *m*;
~ estate (*BRIT*) *n* Siedlung *f* des sozialen
Wohnungsbaus; **~ house** (*BRIT*) *n* Haus *nt*
des sozialen Wohnungsbaus; **~lor**
['kaʊnsɪlə*] *n* Stadtrat *m*/-rätin *f*
counsel ['kaʊnsl] *n* (*barrister*) Anwalt *m*;
(*advice*) Rat(schlag) *m* ♦ *vt* beraten; **~lor**
n Berater *m*
count [kaʊnt] *vt, vi* zählen ♦ *n*
(*reckoning*) Abrechnung *f*; (*nobleman*)
Graf *m*; **~ on** *vt* zählen auf +*acc*; **~down**
n Countdown *m*
countenance ['kaʊntɪnəns] *n* (*old*)
Antlitz *nt* ♦ *vt* (*tolerate*) gutheißen
counter ['kaʊntə*] *n* (*in shop*) Ladentisch
m; (*in café*) Theke *f*; (*in bank, post office*)
Schalter *m* ♦ *vt* entgegnen; **~act**
[kaʊntə'rækt] *vt* entgegenwirken +*dat*; **~-
espionage** *n* Spionageabwehr *f*
counterfeit ['kaʊntəfiːt] *n* Fälschung *f*
♦ *vt* fälschen ♦ *adj* gefälscht
counterfoil ['kaʊntəfɔɪl] *n*
(Kontroll)abschnitt *m*
countermand ['kaʊntəmɑːnd] *vt* rück-
gängig machen
counterpart ['kaʊntəpɑːt] *n* (*object*)
Gegenstück *nt*; (*person*) Gegenüber *nt*
counterproductive ['kaʊntəprə'dʌktɪv]
adj destruktiv
countersign ['kaʊntəsaɪn] *vt*
gegenzeichnen
countess ['kaʊntɪs] *n* Gräfin *f*
countless ['kaʊntlɪs] *adj* zahllos,
unzählig
country ['kʌntrɪ] *n* Land *nt*; **~ dancing**
(*BRIT*) *n* Volkstanz *m*; **~ house** *n*
Landhaus *nt*; **~man** (*irreg*) *n* (*national*)
Landsmann *m*; (*rural*) Bauer *m*; **~side**
n Landschaft *f*
county ['kaʊntɪ] *n* Landkreis *m*; (*BRIT*)
Grafschaft *f*
coup [kuː] (*pl* **~s**) *n* Coup *m*; (*also: ~
d'état*) Staatsstreich *m*, Putsch *m*
coupé ['kuːpeɪ] *n* (*AUT*) Coupé *nt*
couple ['kʌpl] *n* Paar *nt* ♦ *vt* koppeln; **a
~ of** ein paar
coupon ['kuːpɒn] *n* Gutschein *m*
coups [kuːz] *npl of* **coup**

courage ['kʌrɪdʒ] *n* Mut *m*; **~ous** [kə'reɪdʒəs] *adj* mutig
courgette [kuə'ʒet] (*BRIT*) *n* Zucchini *f*
courier ['kʊrɪə*] *n* (*for holiday*) Reiseleiter *m*; (*messenger*) Kurier *m*
course [kɔːs] *n* (*race*) Bahn *f*; (*of stream*) Lauf *m*; (*golf* ~) Platz *m*; (*NAUT, SCH*) Kurs *m*; (*in meal*) Gang *m*; **of** ~ natürlich
court [kɔːt] *n* (*royal*) Hof *m*; (*JUR*) Gericht *nt* ♦ *vt* (*woman*) gehen mit; (*danger*) herausfordern; **to take to** ~ vor Gericht bringen
courteous ['kɔːtɪəs] *adj* höflich
courtesan [kɔːtɪ'zæn] *n* Kurtisane *f*
courtesy ['kɔːtəsɪ] *n* Höflichkeit *f*
court-house ['kɔːthaus] (*US*) *n* Gerichtsgebäude *nt*
courtier ['kɔːtɪə*] *n* Höfling *m*
court-martial ['kɔːt'mɑːʃəl] (*pl* **courts-martial**) *n* Kriegsgericht *nt* ♦ *vt* vor ein Kriegsgericht stellen
courtroom ['kɔːtrʊm] *n* Gerichtssaal *m*
courts-martial ['kɔːts'mɑːʃəl] *npl of* **court-martial**
courtyard ['kɔːtjɑːd] *n* Hof *m*
cousin ['kʌzn] *n* Cousin *m*, Vetter *m*; Kusine *f*
cove [kəʊv] *n* kleine Bucht *f*
covenant ['kʌvənənt] *n* (*ECCL*) Bund *m*; (*JUR*) Verpflichtung *f*
cover ['kʌvə*] *vt* (*spread over*) bedecken; (*shield*) abschirmen; (*include*) sich erstrecken über +*acc*; (*protect*) decken; (*distance*) zurücklegen; (*report on*) berichten über +*acc* ♦ *n* (*for bed*) Decke *f*; (*lid*) Deckel *m*; (*for book*) Einband *m*; (*of magazine*) Umschlag *m*; (*insurance*) Versicherung *f*; **to take** ~ (*from rain*) sich unterstellen; (*MIL*) in Deckung gehen; **under** ~ (*indoors*) drinnen; **under** ~ **of** im Schutze +*gen*; **under separate** ~ (*COMM*) mit getrennter Post; **to** ~ **up for sb** jdn decken; **~age** (*PRESS: reports*) Berichterstattung *f*; (*distribution*) Verbreitung *f*; ~ **charge** *n* Bedienungsgeld *nt*; **~ing** *n* Bedeckung *f*; **~ing letter** (*US* ~ **letter**) *n* Begleitbrief *m*; ~ **note** *n* (*INSURANCE*) vorläufige(r) Versicherungsschein *m*

covert ['kʌvət] *adj* geheim
cover-up ['kʌvərʌp] *n* Vertuschung *f*
covet ['kʌvɪt] *vt* begehren
cow [kaʊ] *n* Kuh *f* ♦ *vt* einschüchtern
coward ['kaʊəd] *n* Feigling *m*; **~ice** ['kaʊədɪs] *n* Feigheit *f*; **~ly** *adj* feige
cowboy ['kaʊbɔɪ] *n* Cowboy *m*
cower ['kaʊə*] *vi* kauern
coxswain ['kɒksn] *n* (*abbr*: **cox**) Steuermann *m*
coy [kɔɪ] *adj* schüchtern
coyote [kɔɪ'əʊtɪ] *n* Präriewolf *m*
cozy ['kəʊzɪ] (*US*) *adj* = **cosy**
CPA (*US*) *n abbr* = **certified public accountant**
crab [kræb] *n* Krebs *m*; ~ **apple** *n* Holzapfel *m*
crack [kræk] *n* Riß *m*, Sprung *m*; (*noise*) Knall *m*; (*drug*) Crack *nt* ♦ *vt* (*break*) springen lassen; (*joke*) reißen; (*nut, safe*) knacken; (*whip*) knallen lassen ♦ *vi* springen ♦ *adj* erstklassig; (*troops*) Elite-; ~ **down** *vi*: **to** ~ **down (on)** hart durchgreifen (bei); ~ **up** *vi* (*fig*) zusammenbrechen; **~er** *n* (*firework*) Knallkörper *m*, Kracher *m*; (*biscuit*) Keks *m*; (*Christmas ~er*) Knallbonbon *nt*
crackle ['krækl] *vi* knistern; (*fire*) prasseln
cradle ['kreɪdl] *n* Wiege *f*
craft [krɑːft] *n* (*skill*) (*Hand- or Kunst*)fertigkeit *f*; (*trade*) Handwerk *nt*; (*NAUT*) Schiff *nt*; **~sman** (*irreg*) *n* Handwerker *m*; **~smanship** *n* (*quality*) handwerkliche Ausführung *f*; (*ability*) handwerkliche(s) Können *nt*; **~y** *adj* schlau
crag [kræg] *n* Klippe *f*
cram [kræm] *vt* vollstopfen ♦ *vi* (*learn*) pauken; **to** ~ **sth into sth** etw in etw *acc* stopfen
cramp [kræmp] *n* Krampf *m* ♦ *vt* (*limit*) einengen; (*hinder*) hemmen; **~ed** *adj* (*position*) verkrampft; (*space*) eng
crampon ['kræmpən] *n* Steigeisen *nt*
cranberry ['krænbərɪ] *n* Preiselbeere *f*
crane [kreɪn] *n* (*machine*) Kran *m*; (*bird*) Kranich *m*
crank [kræŋk] *n* (*lever*) Kurbel *f*; (*person*)

Spinner *m*; **~shaft** *n* Kurbelwelle *f*
cranny ['krænɪ] *n see* **nook**
crash [kræʃ] *n* (*noise*) Krachen *nt*; (*with cars*) Zusammenstoß *m*; (*with plane*) Absturz *m*; (*COMM*) Zusammenbruch *m* ♦ *vt* (*plane*) abstürzen mit ♦ *vi* (*cars*) zusammenstoßen; (*plane*) abstürzen; (*economy*) zusammenbrechen; (*noise*) knallen; **~ course** *n* Schnellkurs *m*; **~ helmet** *n* Sturzhelm *m*; **~ landing** *n* Bruchlandung *f*
crass [kræs] *adj* kraß
crate [kreɪt] *n* (*also fig*) Kiste *f*
crater ['kreɪtə*] *n* Krater *m*
cravat(e) [krə'væt] *n* Halstuch *nt*
crave [kreɪv] *vt* verlangen nach
crawl [krɔːl] *vi* kriechen; (*baby*) krabbeln ♦ *n* Kriechen *nt*; (*swim*) Kraul *m*
crayfish ['kreɪfɪʃ] *n inv* (*freshwater*) Krebs *m*; (*saltwater*) Languste *f*
crayon ['kreɪən] *n* Buntstift *m*
craze [kreɪz] *n* Fimmel *m*
crazy ['kreɪzɪ] *adj* verrückt; **~ paving** *n* Mosaikpflaster *nt*
creak [kriːk] *vi* knarren
cream [kriːm] *n* (*from milk*) Rahm *m*, Sahne *f*; (*polish, cosmetic*) Creme *f*; (*fig: people*) Elite *f* ♦ *adj* cremfarbig; **~ cake** *n* Sahnetorte *f*; **~ cheese** *n* Rahmquark *m*; **~y** *adj* sahnig
crease [kriːs] *n* Falte *f* ♦ *vt* falten; (*untidy*) zerknittern ♦ *vi* (*wrinkle up*) knittern
create [krɪ'eɪt] *vt* erschaffen; (*cause*) verursachen
creation [krɪ'eɪʃən] *n* Schöpfung *f*
creative [krɪ'eɪtɪv] *adj* kreativ
creator [krɪ'eɪtə*] *n* Schöpfer *m*
creature ['kriːtʃə*] *n* Geschöpf *nt*
crèche [kreʃ] *n* Krippe *f*
credence ['kriːdəns] *n*: **to lend** *or* **give ~ to sth** etw *dat* Glauben schenken
credentials [krɪ'denʃəlz] *npl* Beglaubigungsschreiben *nt*
credibility [kredɪ'bɪlɪtɪ] *n* Glaubwürdigkeit *f*
credible ['kredɪbl] *adj* (*person*) glaubwürdig; (*story*) glaubhaft
credit ['kredɪt] *n* (*also COMM*) Kredit *m*

♦ *vt* Glauben schenken +*dat*; (*COMM*) gutschreiben; **~s** *npl* (*of film*) Mitwirkenden *pl*; **~able** *adj* rühmlich; **~ card** *n* Kreditkarte *f*; **~or** *n* Gläubiger *m*
creed [kriːd] *n* Glaubensbekenntnis *nt*
creek [kriːk] *n* (*inlet*) kleine Bucht *f*; (*US: river*) kleine(r) Wasserlauf *m*
creep [kriːp] (*pt, pp* **crept**) *vi* kriechen; **~er** *n* Kletterpflanze *f*; **~y** *adj* (*frightening*) gruselig
cremate [krɪ'meɪt] *vt* einäschern
cremation [krɪ'meɪʃən] *n* Einäscherung *f*
crêpe [kreɪp] *n* Krepp *m*; **~ bandage** (*BRIT*) *n* Elastikbinde *f*
crept [krept] *pt, pp of* **creep**
crescent ['kresnt] *n* (*of moon*) Halbmond *m*
cress [kres] *n* Kresse *f*
crest [krest] *n* (*of cock*) Kamm *m*; (*of wave*) Wellenkamm *m*; (*coat of arms*) Wappen *nt*; **~fallen** *adj* niedergeschlagen
Crete [kriːt] *n* Kreta *nt*
crevice ['krevɪs] *n* Riß *m*
crew [kruː] *n* Besatzung *f*, Mannschaft *f*; **~-cut** *n* Bürstenschnitt *m*; **~-neck** *n* runde(r) Ausschnitt *m*
crib [krɪb] *n* (*bed*) Krippe *f* ♦ *vt* (*inf*) spicken
crick [krɪk] *n* Muskelkrampf *m*
cricket ['krɪkɪt] *n* (*insect*) Grille *f*; (*game*) Kricket *nt*
crime [kraɪm] *n* Verbrechen *nt*
criminal ['krɪmɪnl] *n* Verbrecher *m* ♦ *adj* kriminell; (*act*) strafbar
crimson ['krɪmzn] *adj* leuchtend rot
cringe [krɪndʒ] *vi* sich ducken
crinkle ['krɪŋkl] *vt* zerknittern
cripple ['krɪpl] *n* Krüppel *m* ♦ *vt* lahmlegen; (*MED*) verkrüppeln
crises ['kraɪsiːz] *npl of* **crisis**
crisis ['kraɪsɪs] (*pl* **crises**) *n* Krise *f*
crisp [krɪsp] *adj* knusprig; **~s** (*BRIT*) *npl* Chips *pl*
crisscross ['krɪskrɒs] *adj* gekreuzt, Kreuz-
criteria [kraɪ'tɪərɪə] *npl of* **criterion**
criterion [kraɪ'tɪərɪən] (*pl* **criteria**) *n* Kriterium *nt*
critic ['krɪtɪk] *n* Kritiker(in) *m(f)*; **~al** *adj*

kritisch; **~ally** *adv* kritisch; (*ill*)
gefährlich; **~ism** ['krɪtɪsɪzəm] *n* Kritik *f*;
~ize ['krɪtɪsaɪz] *vt* kritisieren
croak [krəʊk] *vi* krächzen; (*frog*) quaken
Croatia [krəʊ'eɪʃə] *n* Kroatien *nt*
crochet ['krəʊʃeɪ] *n* Häkelei *f*
crockery ['krɒkərɪ] *n* Geschirr *nt*
crocodile ['krɒkədaɪl] *n* Krokodil *nt*
crocus ['krəʊkəs] *n* Krokus *m*
croft [krɒft] (*BRIT*) *n* kleine(s) Pachtgut *nt*
crony ['krəʊnɪ] (*inf*) *n* Kumpel *m*
crook [krʊk] *n* (*criminal*) Gauner *m*;
(*stick*) Hirtenstab *m*; **~ed** ['krʊkɪd] *adj*
krumm
crop [krɒp] *n* (*harvest*) Ernte *f*; (*riding ~*)
Reitpeitsche *f* ♦ *vt* ernten; **~ up** *vi*
passieren
croquet ['krəʊkeɪ] *n* Krocket *nt*
croquette [krə'ket] *n* Krokette *f*
cross [krɒs] *n* Kreuz *nt* ♦ *vt* (*road*)
überqueren; (*legs*) übereinander legen;
kreuzen ♦ *adj* (*annoyed*) böse; **~ out** *vt*
streichen; **~ over** *vi* hinübergehen; **~bar**
n Querstange *f*; **~country (race)** *n*
Geländelauf *m*; **~-examine** *vt* ins
Kreuzverhör nehmen; **~-eyed** *adj*: to be
~-eyed schielen; **~fire** *n* Kreuzfeuer *nt*;
~ing *n* (*crossroads*) (Straßen)kreuzung *f*;
(*of ship*) Überfahrt *f*; (*for pedestrians*)
Fußgängerüberweg *m*; **~ing guard** (*US*) *n*
Schülerlotse *m*; **~ purposes** *npl*: to be
at **~ purposes** aneinander vorbeireden;
~-reference *n* Querverweis *m*; **~roads** *n*
Straßenkreuzung *f*; (*fig*) Scheideweg *m*; **~
section** *n* Querschnitt *m*; **~walk** (*US*) *n*
Fußgängerüberweg *m*; **~wind** *n*
Seitenwind *m*; **~word (puzzle)** *n*
Kreuzworträtsel *nt*
crotch [krɒtʃ] *n* Zwickel *m*; (*ANAT*)
Unterleib *nt*
crotchet ['krɒtʃɪt] *n* Viertelnote *f*
crotchety ['krɒtʃɪtɪ] *adj* launenhaft
crouch [kraʊtʃ] *vi* hocken
croupier ['kruːpɪeɪ] *n* Croupier *m*
crow [krəʊ] *n* (*bird*) Krähe *f*; (*of cock*)
Krähen *nt* ♦ *vi* krähen
crowbar ['krəʊbɑː*] *n* Stemmeisen *nt*
crowd [kraʊd] *n* Menge *f* ♦ *vt* (*fill*)
überfüllen ♦ *vi* drängen; **~ed** *adj*
überfüllt

crown [kraʊn] *n* Krone *f*; (*of head, hat*)
Kopf *m* ♦ *vt* krönen; **~ jewels** *npl*
Kronjuwelen *pl*; **~ prince** *n* Kronprinz *m*
crow's-feet ['krəʊzfiːt] *npl* Krähenfüße
pl
crucial ['kruːʃəl] *adj* entscheidend
crucifix ['kruːsɪfɪks] *n* Kruzifix *nt*; **~ion**
[kruːsɪ'fɪkʃən] *n* Kreuzigung *f*
crude [kruːd] *adj* (*raw*) roh; (*humour,
behaviour*) grob; (*basic*) primitiv; **~ (oil)**
n Rohöl *nt*
cruel ['krʊəl] *adj* grausam; **~ty** *n*
Grausamkeit *f*
cruet ['kruːɪt] *n* Gewürzständer *m*
cruise [kruːz] *n* Kreuzfahrt *f* ♦ *vi*
kreuzen; **~r** *n* (*MIL*) Kreuzer *m*
crumb [krʌm] *n* Krume *f*
crumble ['krʌmbl] *vt, vi* zerbröckeln
crumbly ['krʌmblɪ] *adj* krümelig
crumpet ['krʌmpɪt] *n* Tee(pfann)kuchen
m
crumple ['krʌmpl] *vt* zerknittern
crunch [krʌntʃ] *n*: the **~** (*fig*) der
Knackpunkt ♦ *vt* knirschen; **~y** *adj*
knusprig
crusade [kruː'seɪd] *n* Kreuzzug *m*
crush [krʌʃ] *n* Gedränge *nt* ♦ *vt*
zerdrücken; (*rebellion*) unterdrücken
crust [krʌst] *n* Kruste *f*
crutch [krʌtʃ] *n* Krücke *f*
crux [krʌks] *n* springende(r) Punkt *m*
cry [kraɪ] *vi* (*shout*) schreien; (*weep*)
weinen ♦ *n* (*call*) Schrei *m*; **~ off** *vi*
(plötzlich) absagen
crypt [krɪpt] *n* Krypta *f*
cryptic ['krɪptɪk] *adj* hintergründig
crystal ['krɪstl] *n* Kristall *m*; (*glass*)
Kristallglas *nt*; (*mineral*) Bergkristall *m*;
~-clear *adj* kristallklar
crystallize ['krɪstəlaɪz] *vt, vi*
kristallisieren; (*fig*) klären
cub [kʌb] *n* Junge(s) *nt*; (*also*: C~ *scout*)
Wölfling *m*
Cuba ['kjuːbə] *n* Kuba *nt*; **~n** *adj*
kubanisch ♦ *n* Kubaner(in) *m(f)*
cubbyhole ['kʌbɪhəʊl] *n* Eckchen *nt*
cube [kjuːb] *n* Würfel *m* ♦ *vt* (*MATH*) hoch
drei nehmen; **~ root** *n* Kubikwurzel *f*

cubic ['kju:bɪk] *adj* würfelförmig; (*centimetre etc*) Kubik-; ~ **capacity** *n* Fassungsvermögen *nt*

cubicle ['kju:bɪkl] *n* Kabine *f*

cuckoo ['kʊku:] *n* Kuckuck *m*; ~ **clock** *n* Kuckucksuhr *f*

cucumber ['kju:kʌmbə*] *n* Gurke *f*

cuddle ['kʌdl] *vt, vi* herzen, drücken (*inf*)

cue [kju:] *n* (THEAT) Stichwort *nt*; (*snooker* ~) Billardstock *m*

cuff [kʌf] *n* (BRIT: *of shirt, coat etc*) Manschette *f*; Aufschlag *m*; (US) = **turn-up**; off the ~ aus dem Handgelenk; ~**link** *n* Manschettenknopf *m*

cuisine [kwɪ'zi:n] *n* Kochkunst *f*, Küche *f*

cul-de-sac ['kʌldəsæk] *n* Sackgasse *f*

culinary ['kʌlɪnərɪ] *adj* Koch-

cull [kʌl] *vt* (*flowers*) pflücken; (*select*) auswählen

culminate ['kʌlmɪneɪt] *vi* gipfeln

culmination [kʌlmɪ'neɪʃən] *n* Höhepunkt *m*

culottes [kju:'lɒts] *npl* Hosenrock *m*

culpable ['kʌlpəbl] *adj* schuldig

culprit ['kʌlprɪt] *n* Täter *m*

cult [kʌlt] *n* Kult *m*

cultivate ['kʌltɪveɪt] *vt* (AGR) bebauen; (*mind*) bilden

cultivation [kʌltɪ'veɪʃən] *n* (AGR) Bebauung *f*; (*of person*) Bildung *f*

cultural ['kʌltʃərəl] *adj* kulturell, Kultur-

culture ['kʌltʃə*] *n* Kultur *f*; ~**d** *adj* gebildet

cumbersome ['kʌmbəsəm] *adj* (*object*) sperrig

cumulative ['kju:mjʊlətɪv] *adj* gehäuft

cunning ['kʌnɪŋ] *n* Verschlagenheit *f* ♦ *adj* schlau

cup [kʌp] *n* Tasse *f*; (*prize*) Pokal *m*

cupboard ['kʌbəd] *n* Schrank *m*

Cupid ['kju:pɪd] *n* Amor *m*

cup tie (BRIT) *n* Pokalspiel *nt*

curate ['kjʊərɪt] *n* (*Catholic*) Kurat *m*; (*Protestant*) Vikar *m*

curator [kjʊ'reɪtə*] *n* Kustos *m*

curb [kɜ:b] *vt* zügeln ♦ *n* (*on spending etc*) Einschränkung *f*; (US) Bordstein *m*

curdle ['kɜ:dl] *vi* gerinnen

cure [kjʊə*] *n* Heilmittel *nt*; (*process*) Heilverfahren *nt* ♦ *vt* heilen

curfew ['kɜ:fju:] *n* Ausgangssperre *f*; Sperrstunde *f*

curio ['kjʊərɪəʊ] *n* Kuriosität *f*

curiosity [kjʊərɪ'ɒsɪtɪ] *n* Neugier *f*

curious ['kjʊərɪəs] *adj* neugierig; (*strange*) seltsam

curl [kɜ:l] *n* Locke *f* ♦ *vt* locken ♦ *vi* sich locken; ~ **up** *vi* sich zusammenrollen; (*person*) sich ankuscheln; ~**er** *n* Lockenwickler *m*; ~**y** ['kɜ:lɪ] *adj* lockig

currant ['kʌrənt] *n* Korinthe *f*

currency ['kʌrənsɪ] *n* Währung *f*; to gain ~ an Popularität gewinnen

current ['kʌrənt] *n* Strömung *f* ♦ *adj* (*expression*) gängig, üblich; (*issue*) neueste; ~ **account** (BRIT) *n* Girokonto *nt*; ~ **affairs** *npl* Zeitgeschehen *nt*; ~**ly** *adv* zur Zeit

curricula [kə'rɪkjʊlə] *npl of* **curriculum**

curriculum [kə'rɪkjʊləm] (*pl* ~**s** *or* **curricula**) *n* Lehrplan *m*; ~ **vitae** *n* Lebenslauf *m*

curry ['kʌrɪ] *n* Currygericht *nt* ♦ *vt*: to ~ **favour** with sich einschmeicheln bei; ~ **powder** *n* Curry(pulver) *nt*

curse [kɜ:s] *vi* (*swear*): to ~ (at) fluchen (auf *or* über +*acc*) ♦ *vt* (*insult*) verwünschen ♦ *n* Fluch *m*

cursor ['kɜ:sə*] *n* (COMPUT) Cursor *m*

cursory ['kɜ:sərɪ] *adj* flüchtig

curt [kɜ:t] *adj* schroff

curtail [kɜ:'teɪl] *vt* abkürzen; (*rights*) einschränken

curtain ['kɜ:tn] *n* Vorhang *m*

curts(e)y ['kɜ:tsɪ] *n* Knicks *m* ♦ *vi* knicksen

curve [kɜ:v] *n* Kurve *f*; (*of body, vase etc*) Rundung *f* ♦ *vi* sich biegen; (*hips, breasts*) sich runden; (*road*) einen Bogen machen

cushion ['kʊʃən] *n* Kissen *nt* ♦ *vt* dämpfen

custard ['kʌstəd] *n* Vanillesoße *f*

custodian [kʌs'təʊdɪən] *n* Kustos *m*, Verwalter(in) *m(f)*

custody ['kʌstədɪ] *n* Aufsicht *f*; (*police* ~) Haft *f*; to take into ~ verhaften

custom ['kʌstəm] *n* (*tradition*) Brauch *m*; (COMM) Kundschaft *f*; ~**ary** *adj* üblich

customer ['kʌstəmə*] *n* Kunde *m*, Kundin *f*
customized ['kʌstəmaɪzd] *adj* (*car etc*) mit Spezialausrüstung
custom-made ['kʌstəm'meɪd] *adj* speziell angefertigt
customs ['kʌstəmz] *npl* Zoll *m*; ~ **duty** *n* Zollabgabe *f*; ~ **officer** *n* Zollbeamte(r) *m*, Zollbeamtin *f*
cut [kʌt] (*pt, pp* cut) *vt* schneiden; (*wages*) kürzen; (*prices*) heruntersetzen ♦ *vi* schneiden; (*intersect*) sich schneiden ♦ *n* Schnitt *m*; (*wound*) Schnittwunde *f*; (*in book, income etc*) Kürzung *f*; (*share*) Anteil *m*; **to ~ a tooth** zahnen; ~ **down** *vt* (*tree*) fällen; (*reduce*) einschränken; ~ **off** *vt* (*also fig*) abschneiden; (*allowance*) sperren; ~ **out** *vt* (*shape*) ausschneiden; (*delete*) streichen; ~ **up** *vt* (*meat*) aufschneiden; ~**back** *n* Kürzung *f*; (*CINE*) Rückblende *f*
cute [kjuːt] *adj* niedlich
cuticle ['kjuːtɪkl] *n* Nagelhaut *f*
cutlery ['kʌtlərɪ] *n* Besteck *nt*
cutlet ['kʌtlɪt] *n* (*pork*) Kotelett *nt*; (*veal*) Schnitzel *nt*
cut: ~**out** *n* (*cardboard ~out*) Ausschneidemodell *nt*; ~-**price** (*US* ~-**rate**) *adj* verbilligt; ~-**throat** *n* Verbrechertyp *m* ♦ *adj* mörderisch
cutting ['kʌtɪŋ] *adj* schneidend ♦ *n* (*BRIT: PRESS*) Ausschnitt *m*; (: *RAIL*) Durchstich *m*
CV *n abbr* = **curriculum vitae**
cwt *abbr* = **hundredweight(s)**
cyanide ['saɪənaɪd] *n* Zyankali *nt*
cycle ['saɪkl] *n* Fahrrad *nt*; (*series*) Reihe *f* ♦ *vi* radfahren; **cycling** ['saɪklɪŋ] *n* Radfahren *nt*; **cyclist** ['saɪklɪst] *n* Radfahrer(in) *m(f)*
cyclone ['saɪkləʊn] *n* Zyklon *m*
cygnet ['sɪgnɪt] *n* junge(r) Schwan *m*
cylinder ['sɪlɪndə*] *n* Zylinder *m*; (*TECH*) Walze *f*; ~-**head gasket** *n* Zylinderkopfdichtung *f*
cymbals ['sɪmbəlz] *npl* Becken *nt*
cynic ['sɪnɪk] *n* Zyniker(in) *m(f)*; ~**al** *adj* zynisch; ~**ism** ['sɪnɪsɪzəm] *n* Zynismus *m*
cypress ['saɪprəs] *n* Zypresse *f*
Cyprus ['saɪprəs] *n* Zypern *nt*

cyst [sɪst] *n* Zyste *f*
cystitis [sɪs'taɪtɪs] *n* Blasenentzündung *f*
czar [zɑː*] *n* Zar *m*
Czech [tʃek] *adj* tschechisch ♦ *n* Tscheche *m*, Tschechin *f*
Czechoslovakia [tʃekəslə'vækɪə] *n* die Tschechoslowakei; ~**n** *adj* tschechoslowakisch ♦ *n* Tschechoslowake *m*, Tchechoslowakin *f*

D d

D [diː] *n* (*MUS*) D *nt*
dab [dæb] *vt* (*wound, paint*) betupfen ♦ *n* (*little bit*) bißchen *nt*; (*of paint*) Tupfer *m*
dabble ['dæbl] *vi*: **to ~ in sth** in etw *dat* machen
dad [dæd] *n* Papa *m*, Vati *m*; ~**dy** ['dædɪ] *n* Papa *m*, Vati *m*; ~**dy-long-legs** *n* Weberknecht *m*
daffodil ['dæfədɪl] *n* Osterglocke *f*
daft [dɑːft] (*inf*) *adj* blöd(e), doof
dagger ['dægə*] *n* Dolch *m*
daily ['deɪlɪ] *adj* täglich ♦ *n* (*PRESS*) Tageszeitung *f*; (*BRIT: cleaning woman*) Haushaltshilfe *f* ♦ *adv* täglich
dainty ['deɪntɪ] *adj* zierlich
dairy ['dɛərɪ] *n* (*shop*) Milchgeschäft *nt*; (*on farm*) Molkerei *f* ♦ *adj* Milch-; ~ **farm** *n* Hof *m* mit Milchwirtschaft; ~ **produce** *n* Molkereiprodukte *pl*; ~ **store** (*US*) *n* Milchgeschäft *nt*
dais ['deɪɪs] *n* Podium *nt*
daisy ['deɪzɪ] *n* Gänseblümchen *nt*; ~ **wheel** *n* (*on printer*) Typenrad *nt*
dale [deɪl] *n* Tal *nt*
dam [dæm] *n* (Stau)damm *m* ♦ *vt* stauen
damage ['dæmɪdʒ] *n* Schaden *m* ♦ *vt* beschädigen; ~**s** *npl* (*JUR*) Schaden(s)ersatz *m*
damn [dæm] *vt* verdammen ♦ *n* (*inf*): **I don't give a ~** das ist mir total egal ♦ *adj* (: *also*: ~**ed**) verdammt; ~ **it!** verflucht!; ~**ing** *adj* vernichtend
damp [dæmp] *adj* feucht ♦ *n* Feuchtigkeit *f* ♦ *vt* (*also*: ~**en**) befeuchten; (*discourage*) dämpfen
damson ['dæmzən] *n* Damaszener-

pflaume *f*

dance [dɑːns] *n* Tanz *m* ♦ *vi* tanzen; **~ hall** *n* Tanzlokal *nt*; **~r** *n* Tänzer(in) *m(f)*

dancing ['dɑːnsɪŋ] *n* Tanzen *nt*

dandelion ['dændɪlaɪən] *n* Löwenzahn *m*

dandruff ['dændrəf] *n* (Kopf)schuppen *pl*

Dane [deɪn] *n* Däne *m*, Dänin *f*

danger ['deɪndʒə*] *n* Gefahr *f*; **~!** *(sign)* Achtung!; **to be in ~ of doing sth** Gefahr laufen, etw zu tun; **~ous** *adj* gefährlich

dangle ['dæŋgl] *vi* baumeln ♦ *vt* herabhängen lassen

Danish ['deɪnɪʃ] *adj* dänisch ♦ *n* Dänisch *nt*

dapper ['dæpə*] *adj* elegant

dare [dɛə*] *vt* herausfordern ♦ *vi*: **to ~ (to) do sth** es wagen, etw zu tun; **I ~ say** ich würde sagen; **~devil** *n* Draufgänger(in) *m(f)*

daring ['dɛərɪŋ] *adj* (*audacious*) verwegen; (*bold*) wagemutig; (*dress*) gewagt ♦ *n* Mut *m*

dark [dɑːk] *adj* dunkel; (*fig*) düster, trübe; (*deep colour*) dunkel- ♦ *n* Dunkelheit *f*; **to be left in the ~ about** im dunkeln sein über +*acc*; **after ~** nach Anbruch der Dunkelheit; **~en** *vt, vi* verdunkeln; **~ glasses** *npl* Sonnenbrille *f*; **~ness** *n* Finsternis *nt*; **~room** *n* Dunkelkammer *f*

darling ['dɑːlɪŋ] *n* Liebling *m* ♦ *adj* lieb

darn [dɑːn] *vt* stopfen

dart [dɑːt] *n* (*weapon*) Pfeil *m*; (*in sewing*) Abnäher *m* ♦ *vi* sausen; **~s** *n* (*game*) Pfeilwerfen *nt*; **~board** *n* Zielscheibe *f*

dash [dæʃ] *n* Sprung *m*; (*mark*) (Gedanken)strich *m*; (*small amount*) bißchen *nt* ♦ *vt* (*hopes*) zunichte machen ♦ *vi* stürzen; **~ away** *vi* davonstürzen; **~ off** *vi* davonstürzen

dashboard ['dæʃbɔːd] *n* Armaturenbrett *nt*

dashing ['dæʃɪŋ] *adj* schneidig

data ['deɪtə] *npl* Einzelheiten *pl*, Daten *pl*; **~ base** *n* Datenbank *f*; **~ processing** *n* Datenverarbeitung *f*

date [deɪt] *n* Datum *nt*; (*for meeting etc*) Termin *m*; (*with person*) Verabredung *f*; (*fruit*) Dattel *f* ♦ *vt* (*letter etc*) datieren; (*person*) gehen mit; **~ of birth**

Geburtsdatum *nt*; **to ~** bis heute; **out of ~** überholt; **up to ~** (*clothes*) modisch; (*report*) up-to-date; (*with news*) auf dem laufenden; **~d** *adj* altmodisch; **~ rape** *n* Vergewaltigung *f* nach einem Rendezvous

daub [dɔːb] *vt* beschmieren; (*paint*) schmieren

daughter ['dɔːtə*] *n* Tochter *f*; **~-in-law** *n* Schwiegertochter *f*

daunting ['dɔːntɪŋ] *adj* entmutigend

dawdle ['dɔːdl] *vi* trödeln

dawn [dɔːn] *n* Morgendämmerung *f* ♦ *vi* dämmern; (*fig*): **it ~ed on him that ...** es dämmerte ihm, daß ...

day [deɪ] *n* Tag *m*; **the ~ before/after** am Tag zuvor/danach; **the ~ after tomorrow** übermorgen; **the ~ before yesterday** vorgestern; **by ~** am Tage; **~break** *n* Tagesanbruch *m*; **~dream** *vi* mit offenen Augen träumen; **~light** *n* Tageslicht *nt*; **~ return** *n* (*BRIT*) Tagesrückfahrkarte *f*; **~time** *n* Tageszeit *f*; **~-to-~** *adj* alltäglich

daze [deɪz] *vt* betäuben ♦ *n* Betäubung *f*; **in a ~** benommen

dazzle ['dæzl] *vt* blenden

DC *abbr* (= *direct current*) Gleichstrom *m*

D-day ['diːdeɪ] *n* (*HIST*) Tag der Invasion durch die Alliierten (6.6.44); (*fig*) der Tag X

deacon ['diːkən] *n* Diakon *m*

dead [ded] *adj* tot; (*without feeling*) gefühllos ♦ *adv* (*exactly*) genau ♦ *npl*: **the ~** die Toten *pl*; **to shoot sb ~** jdn erschießen; **~ tired** todmüde; **to stop ~** abrupt stehenbleiben; **~en** *vt* (*pain*) abtöten; (*sound*) ersticken; **~ end** *n* Sackgasse *f*; **~ heat** *n* tote(s) Rennen *nt*; **~line** *n* Stichtag *m*; **~lock** *n* Stillstand *m*; **~ loss** (*inf*) *n*: **to be a ~ loss** ein hoffnungsloser Fall sein; **~ly** *adj* tödlich; **~pan** *adj* undurchdringlich; **D~ Sea** *n*: **the D~ Sea** das Tote Meer

deaf [def] *adj* taub; **~en** *vt* taub machen; **~-mute** *n* Taubstumme(r) *mf*; **~ness** *n* Taubheit *f*

deal [diːl] (*pt, pp* **dealt**) *n* Geschäft *nt* ♦ *vt* austeilen; (*CARDS*) geben; **a great ~ of** sehr viel; **~ in** *vt fus* handeln mit; **~ with** *vt fus* (*person*) behandeln; (*subject*) sich befassen mit; (*problem*) in Angriff nehmen; **~er** n (*COMM*) Händler m; (*CARDS*) Kartengeber m; **~ings** npl (*FIN*) Geschäfte pl; (*relations*) Beziehungen pl; **~t** [delt] pt, pp of **deal**

dean [di:n] n (*Protestant*) Superintendent m; (*Catholic*) Dechant m; (*UNIV*) Dekan m

dear [dɪə*] adj lieb; (*expensive*) teuer ♦ n Liebling m ♦ excl: **~ me!** du liebe Zeit!; **D~ Sir** Sehr geehrter Herr!; **D~ John** Lieber John!; **~ly** adv (*love*) herzlich; (*pay*) teuer

death [deθ] n Tod m; (*statistic*) Todesfall m; **~ certificate** n Totenschein m; **~ duties** npl (*BRIT*) Erbschaftssteuer f; **~ly** adj totenähnlich, Toten-; **~ penalty** n Todesstrafe f; **~ rate** n Sterblichkeitsziffer f

debar [dɪ'bɑ:*] vt ausschließen

debase [dɪ'beɪs] vt entwerten

debatable [dɪ'beɪtəbl] adj anfechtbar

debate [dɪ'beɪt] n Debatte f ♦ vt debattieren, diskutieren; (*consider*) überlegen

debauchery [dɪ'bɔ:tʃərɪ] n Ausschweifungen pl

debilitating [dɪ'bɪlɪteɪtɪŋ] adj schwächend

debit ['debɪt] n Schuldposten m ♦ vt belasten

debris ['debri:] n Trümmer pl

debt [det] n Schuld f; **to be in ~** verschuldet sein; **~or** n Schuldner m

debunk [di:'bʌŋk] vt entlarven

decade ['dekeɪd] n Jahrzehnt nt

decadence ['dekədəns] n Dekadenz f

decaffeinated [di:'kæfɪneɪtɪd] adj koffeinfrei

decanter [dɪ'kæntə*] n Karaffe f

decay [dɪ'keɪ] n Verfall m; (*tooth ~*) Karies m ♦ vi verfallen; (*teeth, meat etc*) faulen; (*leaves etc*) verrotten

deceased [dɪ'si:st] adj verstorben

deceit [dɪ'si:t] n Betrug m; **~ful** adj falsch

deceive [dɪ'si:v] vt täuschen

December [dɪ'sembə*] n Dezember m

decency ['di:sənsɪ] n Anstand m

decent ['di:sənt] adj (*respectable*) anständig; (*pleasant*) annehmbar

deception [dɪ'sepʃən] n Betrug m

deceptive [dɪ'septɪv] adj irreführend

decibel ['desɪbel] n Dezibel nt

decide [dɪ'saɪd] vt entscheiden ♦ vi sich entscheiden; **to ~ on sth** etw beschließen; **~d** adj entschieden; **~dly** [dɪ'saɪdɪdlɪ] adv entschieden

deciduous [dɪ'sɪdjuəs] adj Laub-

decimal ['desɪməl] adj dezimal ♦ n Dezimalzahl f; **~ point** n Komma nt

decimate ['desɪmeɪt] vt dezimieren

decipher [dɪ'saɪfə*] vt entziffern

decision [dɪ'sɪʒən] n Entscheidung f, Entschluß m

decisive [dɪ'saɪsɪv] adj entscheidend; (*person*) entschlossen

deck [dek] n (*NAUT*) Deck nt; (*of cards*) Pack m; **~chair** n Liegestuhl m

declaration [deklə'reɪʃən] n Erklärung f

declare [dɪ'klɛə*] vt erklären; (*CUSTOMS*) verzollen

decline [dɪ'klaɪn] n (*decay*) Verfall m; (*lessening*) Rückgang m ♦ vt (*invitation*) ablehnen ♦ vi (*of strength*) nachlassen; (*say no*) ablehnen

declutch ['di:'klʌtʃ] vi auskuppeln

decode ['di:'kəʊd] vt entschlüsseln

decoder ['di:'kəʊdə*] n (*TV*) decoder m

decompose [di:kəm'pəʊz] vi (sich) zersetzen

décor ['deɪkɔ:*] n Ausstattung f

decorate ['dekəreɪt] vt (*room: paper*) tapezieren; (: *paint*) streichen; (*adorn*) (aus)schmücken; (*cake*) verzieren; (*honour*) auszeichnen

decoration [dekə'reɪʃən] n (*of house*) (Wand)dekoration f; (*medal*) Orden m

decorator ['dekəreɪtə*] n Maler m, Anstreicher m

decorum [dɪ'kɔ:rəm] n Anstand m

decoy ['di:kɔɪ] n Lockvogel m

decrease [n 'di:kri:s, vb di:'kri:s] n Abnahme f ♦ vt vermindern ♦ vi abnehmen

decree [dɪ'kri:] n Erlaß m; **~ nisi** [-'naɪsaɪ] n vorläufige(s) Scheidungsurteil nt

decrepit [dɪ'krepɪt] adj hinfällig

dedicate ['dedɪkeɪt] vt widmen

dedication [dedɪ'keɪʃən] n (*devotion*) Ergebenheit f; (*in book*) Widmung f

deduce [dɪ'djuːs] vt: **to ~ sth (from sth)** etw (aus etw) ableiten, etw (aus etw) schließen

deduct [dɪ'dʌkt] vt abziehen; **~ion** [dɪ'dʌkʃən] n (*of money*) Abzug m; (*conclusion*) (Schluß)folgerung f

deed [diːd] n Tat f; (*document*) Urkunde f

deem [diːm] vt: **to ~ sb/sth (to be) sth** jdn/etw für etw halten

deep [diːp] adj tief ♦ adv: **the spectators stood 20 ~** die Zuschauer standen in 20 Reihen hintereinander; **to be 4m ~** 4 Meter tief sein; **~en** vt vertiefen ♦ vi (*darkness*) tiefer werden; **~-freeze** n Tiefkühlung f; **~-fry** vt fritieren; **~ly** adv tief; **~-sea diving** n Tiefseetauchen nt; **~-seated** adj tiefsitzend

deer [dɪə*] n Reh nt; **~skin** n Hirsch-/Rehleder nt

deface [dɪ'feɪs] vt entstellen

defamation [defə'meɪʃən] n Verleumdung f

default [dɪ'fɔːlt] n Versäumnis nt; (*COMPUT*) Standardwert m ♦ vi versäumen; **by ~** durch Nichterscheinen

defeat [dɪ'fiːt] n Niederlage f ♦ vt schlagen; **~ist** adj defätistisch ♦ n Defätist m

defect [n 'diːfekt, vb dɪ'fekt] n Fehler m ♦ vi überlaufen; **~ive** [dɪ'fektɪv] adj fehlerhaft

defence [dɪ'fens] n Verteidigung f; **~less** adj wehrlos

defend [dɪ'fend] vt verteidigen; **~ant** n Angeklagte(r) m; **~er** n Verteidiger m

defense [dɪ'fens] (*US*) n = **defence**

defensive [dɪ'fensɪv] adj defensiv ♦ n: **on the ~** in der Defensive

defer [dɪ'fɜː*] vt verschieben

deference ['defərəns] n Rücksichtnahme f

defiance [dɪ'faɪəns] n Trotz m, Unnachgiebigkeit f; **in ~ of sth** einer Sache dat zum Trotz

defiant [dɪ'faɪənt] adj trotzig, unnachgiebig

deficiency [dɪ'fɪʃənsɪ] n (*lack*) Mangel m;

(*weakness*) Schwäche f

deficient [dɪ'fɪʃənt] adj mangelhaft

deficit ['defɪsɪt] n Defizit nt

defile [vb dɪ'faɪl, n 'diːfaɪl] vt beschmutzen ♦ n Hohlweg m

define [dɪ'faɪn] vt bestimmen; (*explain*) definieren

definite ['defɪnɪt] adj (*fixed*) definitiv; (*clear*) eindeutig; **~ly** adv bestimmt

definition [defɪ'nɪʃən] n Definition f; (*PHOT*) Schärfe f

deflate [diː'fleɪt] vt die Luft ablassen aus

deflect [dɪ'flekt] vt ablenken

deform [dɪ'fɔːm] vt deformieren; **~ity** n Mißbildung f

defraud [dɪ'frɔːd] vt betrügen

defray [dɪ'freɪ] vt (*costs*) übernehmen

defrost [diː'frɒst] vt (*fridge*) abtauen; (*food*) auftauen; **~er** (*US*) n (*demister*) Gebläse nt

deft [deft] adj geschickt

defunct [dɪ'fʌŋkt] adj verstorben

defuse [diː'fjuːz] vt entschärfen

defy [dɪ'faɪ] vt (*disobey*) sich widersetzen +dat; (*orders, death*) trotzen +dat; (*challenge*) herausfordern

degenerate [vb dɪ'dʒenəreɪt, adj dɪ'dʒenərɪt] vi degenerieren ♦ adj degeneriert

degrading [dɪ'greɪdɪŋ] adj erniedrigend

degree [dɪ'griː] n Grad m; (*UNIV*) Universitätsabschluß m; **by ~s** allmählich; **to some ~** zu einem gewissen Grad

dehydrated [diːhaɪ'dreɪtɪd] adj (*person*) ausgetrocknet; (*food*) Trocken-

de-ice [diː'aɪs] vt enteisen

deign [deɪn] vi sich herablassen

deity ['diːɪtɪ] n Gottheit f

dejected [dɪ'dʒektɪd] adj niedergeschlagen

delay [dɪ'leɪ] vt (*hold back*) aufschieben ♦ vi (*linger*) sich aufhalten ♦ n Aufschub m, Verzögerung f; (*of train etc*) Verspätung f; **to be ~ed** (*train*) Verspätung haben; **without ~** unverzüglich

delectable [dɪ'lektəbl] adj köstlich; (*fig*) reizend

delegate [*n* 'delɪgɪt, *vb* 'delɪgeɪt] *n* Delegierte(r) *mf* ♦ *vt* delegieren

delete [dɪ'liːt] *vt* (aus)streichen

deliberate [*adj* dɪ'lɪbərɪt, *vb* dɪ'lɪbəreɪt] *adj* (*intentional*) absichtlich; (*slow*) bedächtig ♦ *vi* (*consider*) überlegen; (*debate*) sich beraten; **~ly** *adv* absichtlich

delicacy ['delɪkəsɪ] *n* Zartheit *f*; (*weakness*) Anfälligkeit *f*; (*food*) Delikatesse *f*

delicate ['delɪkɪt] *adj* (*fine*) fein; (*fragile*) zart; (*situation*) heikel; (*MED*) empfindlich

delicatessen [delɪkə'tesn] *n* Feinkostgeschäft *nt*

delicious [dɪ'lɪʃəs] *adj* lecker

delight [dɪ'laɪt] *n* Wonne *f* ♦ *vt* entzücken; **to take ~ in sth** Freude an etw *dat* haben; **~ed** *adj*: **~ed (at** *or* **with sth)** entzückt (über +*acc* etw); **~ed to do sth** etw sehr gern tun; **~ful** *adj* entzückend, herrlich

delinquency [dɪ'lɪŋkwənsɪ] *n* Kriminalität *f*

delinquent [dɪ'lɪŋkwənt] *n* Straffällige(r) *mf* ♦ *adj* straffällig

delirious [dɪ'lɪrɪəs] *adj* im Fieberwahn

deliver [dɪ'lɪvə*] *vt* (*goods*) (ab)liefern; (*letter*) zustellen; (*speech*) halten; **~y** *n* (Ab)lieferung *f*; (*of letter*) Zustellung *f*; (*of speech*) Vortragsweise *f*; (*MED*) Entbindung *f*; **to take ~y of** in Empfang nehmen

delude [dɪ'luːd] *vt* täuschen

deluge ['deljuːdʒ] *n* Überschwemmung *f*; (*fig*) Flut *f* ♦ *vt* überfluten

delusion [dɪ'luːʒən] *n* (Selbst)täuschung *f*

de luxe [dɪ'lʌks] *adj* Luxus-

delve [delv] *vi*: **to ~ into** sich vertiefen in +*acc*

demand [dɪ'mɑːnd] *vt* verlangen ♦ *n* (*request*) Verlangen *nt*; (*COMM*) Nachfrage *f*; **in ~** gefragt; **on ~** auf Verlangen; **~ing** *adj* anspruchsvoll

demarcation [diːmɑː'keɪʃən] *n* Abgrenzung *f*

demean [dɪ'miːn] *vt*: **to ~ o.s.** sich erniedrigen

demeanour [dɪ'miːnə*] (*US* **demeanor**) *n* Benehmen *nt*

demented [dɪ'mentɪd] *adj* wahnsinnig

demise [dɪ'maɪz] *n* Ableben *nt*

demister [diː'mɪstə*] *n* (*AUT*) Gebläse *nt*

demo ['deməʊ] (*inf*) *n abbr* (= *demonstration*) Demo *f*

democracy [dɪ'mɒkrəsɪ] *n* Demokratie *f*

democrat ['deməkræt] *n* Demokrat *m*; **~ic** [demə'krætɪk] *adj* demokratisch

demolish [dɪ'mɒlɪʃ] *vt* abreißen; (*fig*) vernichten

demolition [demə'lɪʃən] *n* Abbruch *m*

demon ['diːmən] *n* Dämon *m*

demonstrate ['demənstreɪt] *vt*, *vi* demonstrieren

demonstration [demən'streɪʃən] *n* Demonstration *f*

demonstrator ['demənstreɪtə*] *n* (*POL*) Demonstrant(in) *m(f)*

demote [dɪ'məʊt] *vt* degradieren

demure [dɪ'mjʊə*] *adj* sittsam

den [den] *n* (*of animal*) Höhle *f*; (*study*) Bude *f*

denatured alcohol [diː'neɪtʃəd-] (*US*) *n* ungenießbar gemachte(r) Alkohol *m*

denial [dɪ'naɪəl] *n* Leugnung *f*; **official ~** Dementi *nt*

denim ['denɪm] *adj* Denim-; **~s** *npl* Denim-Jeans *pl*

Denmark ['denmɑːk] *n* Dänemark *nt*

denomination [dɪnɒmɪ'neɪʃən] *n* (*ECCL*) Bekenntnis *nt*; (*type*) Klasse *f*; (*FIN*) Wert *m*

denominator [dɪ'nɒmɪneɪtə*] *n* Nenner *m*

denote [dɪ'nəʊt] *vt* bedeuten

denounce [dɪ'naʊns] *vt* brandmarken

dense [dens] *adj* dicht; (*stupid*) schwer von Begriff; **~ly** *adv* dicht

density ['densɪtɪ] *n* Dichte *f*; **single-/double-density disk** Diskette *f* mit einfacher/doppelter Dichte

dent [dent] *n* Delle *f* ♦ *vt* (*also*: **make a ~ in**) einbeulen

dental ['dentl] *adj* Zahn-; **~ surgeon** *n* = **dentist**

dentist ['dentɪst] *n* Zahnarzt(ärztin) *m(f)*; **~ry** *n* Zahnmedizin *f*

dentures ['dentʃəz] *npl* Gebiß *nt*

deny [dɪ'naɪ] *vt* leugnen; (*officially*) dementieren; (*help*) abschlagen

deodorant [diː'əʊdərənt] n Deodorant nt
depart [dɪ'pɑːt] vi abfahren; **to ~ from**
(fig: differ from) abweichen von
department [dɪ'pɑːtmənt] n (COMM)
Abteilung f; (UNIV) Seminar nt; (POL)
Ministerium nt; **~ store** n Warenhaus nt
departure [dɪ'pɑːtʃə*] n (of person)
Abreise f; (of train) Abfahrt f; (of plane)
Abflug m; **new ~** Neuerung f; **~ lounge**
n (at airport) Abflughalle f
depend [dɪ'pend] vi: **to ~ on** abhängen
von; (rely on) angewiesen sein auf +acc; **it
~s** es kommt darauf an; **~ing on the
result ...** abhängend vom Resultat ...;
~able adj zuverlässig; **~ant** n
Angehörige(r) mf; **~ence** n Abhängigkeit
f, **~ent** adj abhängig ♦ n = **dependant**;
~ent on abhängig von
depict [dɪ'pɪkt] vt schildern
depleted [dɪ'pliːtɪd] adj aufgebraucht
deplorable [dɪ'plɔːrəbl] adj bedauerlich
deplore [dɪ'plɔː*] vt mißbilligen
deploy [dɪ'plɔɪ] vt einsetzen
depopulation ['diːpɒpjʊ'leɪʃən] n
Entvölkerung f
deport [dɪ'pɔːt] vt deportieren; **~ation**
[diːpɔː'teɪʃən] n Abschiebung f
deportment [dɪ'pɔːtmənt] n Betragen nt
depose [dɪ'pəʊz] vt absetzen
deposit [dɪ'pɒzɪt] n (in bank) Guthaben
nt; (down payment) Anzahlung f; (security)
Kaution f; (CHEM) Niederschlag m ♦ vt (in
bank) deponieren; (put down) niederlegen;
~ account n Sparkonto nt
depot ['depəʊ] n Depot nt
depraved [dɪ'preɪvd] adj verkommen
depreciate [dɪ'priːʃieɪt] vi im Wert
sinken; **depreciation** [dɪpriːʃi'eɪʃən] n
Wertminderung f
depress [dɪ'pres] vt (press down)
niederdrücken; (in mood) deprimieren;
~ed adj deprimiert; **~ing** adj
deprimierend; **~ion** [dɪ'preʃən] n (mood)
Depression f; (in trade) Wirtschaftskrise f;
(hollow) Vertiefung f; (MET)
Tief(druckgebiet) nt
deprivation [deprɪ'veɪʃən] n Not f
deprive [dɪ'praɪv] vt: **to ~ sb of sth** jdn
einer Sache gen berauben; **~d** adj (child)

sozial benachteiligt; (area)
unterentwickelt
depth [depθ] n Tiefe f; **in the ~s of
despair** in tiefster Verzweiflung
deputation [depjʊ'teɪʃən] n Abordnung f
deputize ['depjʊtaɪz] vi: **to ~ (for sb)**
(jdn) vertreten
deputy ['depjʊti] adj stellvertretend ♦ n
(Stell)vertreter m
derail [dɪ'reɪl] vt: **to be ~ed** entgleisen;
~ment n Entgleisung f
deranged [dɪ'reɪndʒd] adj verrückt
derby ['dɑːbɪ] (US) n (bowler hat) Melone f
derelict ['derɪlɪkt] adj verlassen
deride [dɪ'raɪd] vt auslachen
derisory [dɪ'raɪsərɪ] adj spöttisch
derivative [dɪ'rɪvətɪv] n Derivat nt ♦ adj
abgeleitet
derive [dɪ'raɪv] vt (get) gewinnen; (deduce)
ableiten ♦ vi (come from) abstammen
dermatitis [dɜːmə'taɪtɪs] n
Hautentzündung f
derogatory [dɪ'rɒgətərɪ] adj
geringschätzig
derrick ['derɪk] n Drehkran m
descend [dɪ'send] vt, vi hinuntersteigen;
to ~ from abstammen von; **~ant** n
Nachkomme m
descent [dɪ'sent] n (coming down)
Abstieg m; (origin) Abstammung f
describe [dɪs'kraɪb] vt beschreiben
description [dɪs'krɪpʃən] n Beschreibung
f; (sort) Art f
descriptive [dɪs'krɪptɪv] adj
beschreibend; (word) anschaulich
desecrate ['desɪkreɪt] vt schänden
desert [n 'dezət, vb dɪ'zɜːt] n Wüste f ♦ vt
verlassen; (temporarily) im Stich lassen
♦ vi (MIL) desertieren; **~s** npl (what one
deserves): **to get one's just ~s** seinen ge-
rechten Lohn bekommen; **~er** n
Deserteur m; **~ion** [dɪ'zɜːʃən] n (of wife)
Verlassen nt; (MIL) Fahnenflucht f; **~
island** n einsame Insel f
deserve [dɪ'zɜːv] vt verdienen
deserving [dɪ'zɜːvɪŋ] adj verdienstvoll
design [dɪ'zaɪn] n (plan) Entwurf m;
(planning) Design nt ♦ vt entwerfen
designate [vb 'dezɪgneɪt, adj 'dezɪgnɪt] vt

bestimmen ♦ *adj* designiert

designer [dɪ'zaɪnə*] *n* Designer(in) *m(f)*; (*TECH*) Konstrukteur(in) *m(f)*; (*fashion* ~) Modeschöpfer(in) *m(f)*

desirable [dɪ'zaɪərəbl] *adj* wünschenswert

desire [dɪ'zaɪə*] *n* Wunsch *m*, Verlangen *nt* ♦ *vt* (*lust*) begehren; (*ask for*) wollen

desk [desk] *n* Schreibtisch *m*; (*BRIT: in shop, restaurant*) Kasse *f*

desolate ['desəlɪt] *adj* öde; (*sad*) trostlos

desolation [desə'leɪʃən] *n* Trostlosigkeit *f*

despair [dɪs'pɛə*] *n* Verzweiflung *f* ♦ *vi*: to ~ (**of**) verzweifeln (an +*dat*)

despatch [dɪs'pætʃ] *n, vt* = **dispatch**

desperate ['despərɪt] *adj* verzweifelt; ~**ly** ['despərɪtlɪ] *adv* verzweifelt

desperation [despə'reɪʃən] *n* Verzweiflung *f*

despicable [dɪs'pɪkəbl] *adj* abscheulich

despise [dɪs'paɪz] *vt* verachten

despite [dɪs'paɪt] *prep* trotz +*gen*

despondent [dɪs'pɒndənt] *adj* mutlos

dessert [dɪ'zɜ:t] *n* Nachtisch *m*; ~**spoon** *n* Dessertlöffel *m*

destination [destɪ'neɪʃən] *n* (*of person*) (Reise)ziel *nt*; (*of goods*) Bestimmungsort *m*

destiny ['destɪnɪ] *n* Schicksal *nt*

destitute ['destɪtjuːt] *adj* notleidend

destroy [dɪs'trɔɪ] *vt* zerstören; ~**er** *n* (*NAUT*) Zerstörer *m*

destruction [dɪs'trʌkʃən] *n* Zerstörung *f*

destructive [dɪs'trʌktɪv] *adj* zerstörend

detach [dɪ'tætʃ] *vt* loslösen; ~**able** *adj* abtrennbar; ~**ed** *adj* (*attitude*) distanziert; (*house*) Einzel-; ~**ment** *n* (*MIL*) Sonderkommando *nt*; (*fig*) Abstand *m*

detail ['diːteɪl] *n* Einzelheit *f*, Detail *nt* ♦ *vt* (*relate*) ausführlich berichten; (*appoint*) abkommandieren; **in** ~ im Detail; ~**ed** *adj* detailliert

detain [dɪ'teɪn] *vt* aufhalten; (*imprison*) in Haft halten

detect [dɪ'tekt] *vt* entdecken; ~**ion** [dɪ'tekʃən] *n* Aufdeckung *f*; ~**ive** *n* Detektiv *m*; ~**ive story** *n* Kriminalgeschichte *f*, Krimi *m*; ~**or** *n*

Detektor *m*

détente [deɪ'tɑːnt] *n* Entspannung *f*

detention [dɪ'tenʃən] *n* Haft *f*; (*SCH*) Nachsitzen *nt*

deter [dɪ'tɜː*] *vt* abschrecken

detergent [dɪ'tɜːdʒənt] *n* Waschmittel *nt*

deteriorate [dɪ'tɪərɪəreɪt] *vi* sich verschlechtern; **deterioration** [dɪtɪərɪə'reɪʃən] *n* Verschlechterung *f*

determination [dɪtɜːmɪ'neɪʃən] *n* Entschlossenheit *f*

determine [dɪ'tɜːmɪn] *vt* bestimmen; ~**d** *adj* entschlossen

deterrent [dɪ'terənt] *n* Abschreckungs-mittel *nt*

detest [dɪ'test] *vt* verabscheuen

detonate ['detəneɪt] *vt* explodieren lassen ♦ *vi* detonieren

detour ['diːtuə*] *n* Umweg *m*; (*US: AUT: diversion*) Umleitung *f* ♦ *vt* (*US: AUT: traffic*) umleiten

detract [dɪ'trækt] *vi*: to ~ **from** schmälern

detriment ['detrɪmənt] *n*: **to the** ~ **of** zum Schaden +*gen*; ~**al** [detrɪ'mentl] *adj* schädlich

devaluation [dɪvæljʊ'eɪʃən] *n* Abwertung *f*

devastate ['devəsteɪt] *vt* verwüsten

devastating ['devəsteɪtɪŋ] *adj* verheerend

develop [dɪ'veləp] *vt* entwickeln; (*resources*) erschließen ♦ *vi* sich entwickeln; ~**ing country** *n* Entwicklungsland *nt*; ~**ment** *n* Entwicklung *f*

deviate ['diːvɪeɪt] *vi* abweichen; **deviation** [diːvɪ'eɪʃən] *n* Abweichung *f*

device [dɪ'vaɪs] *n* Gerät *nt*

devil ['devl] *n* Teufel *m*; ~**ish** *adj* teuflisch

devious ['diːvɪəs] *adj* (*means*) krumm; (*person*) verschlagen

devise [dɪ'vaɪz] *vt* entwickeln

devoid [dɪ'vɔɪd] *adj*: ~ **of** ohne

devolution [diːvə'luːʃən] *n* (*POL*) Dezentralisierung *f*

devote [dɪ'vəʊt] *vt*: to ~ **sth (to sth)** etw (einer Sache *dat*) widmen; ~**d** *adj* ergeben; **~e** [devəʊ'tiː] n Anhänger(in) m(f), Verehrer(in) m(f)

devotion [dɪ'vəʊʃən] n (piety) Andacht f; (loyalty) Ergebenheit f, Hingabe f

devour [dɪ'vaʊə*] vt verschlingen

devout [dɪ'vaʊt] adj andächtig

dew [djuː] n Tau m

dexterity [deks'terɪtɪ] n Geschicklichkeit f

diabetes [daɪə'biːtiːz] n Zuckerkrankheit f

diabetic [daɪə'betɪk] adj zuckerkrank; (food) Diabetiker- ♦ n Diabetiker m·

diabolical [daɪə'bɒlɪkl] (inf) adj (weather, behaviour) saumäßig

diagnose ['daɪəgnəʊz] vt diagnostizieren

diagnoses [daɪəg'nəʊsiːz] npl of **diagnosis**

diagnosis [daɪəg'nəʊsɪs] n Diagnose f

diagonal [daɪ'ægənl] adj diagonal ♦ n Diagonale f

diagram ['daɪəgræm] n Diagramm nt, Schaubild nt

dial ['daɪəl] n (TEL) Wählscheibe f; (of clock) Zifferblatt nt ♦ vt wählen

dialect ['daɪəlekt] n Dialekt m

dialling code ['daɪəlɪŋ-] n Vorwahl f

dialling tone ['daɪəlɪŋ-] n Amtszeichen nt

dialogue ['daɪəlɒg] n Dialog m

dial tone (US) n = **dialling tone**

diameter [daɪ'æmɪtə*] n Durchmesser m

diamond ['daɪəmənd] n Diamant m; **~s** npl (CARDS) Karo nt

diaper ['daɪəpə*] (US) n Windel f

diaphragm ['daɪəfræm] n Zwerchfell nt

diarrhoea [daɪə'riːə] (US **diarrhea**) n Durchfall m

diary ['daɪərɪ] n Taschenkalender m; (account) Tagebuch nt

dice [daɪs] n Würfel pl ♦ vt in Würfel schneiden

dichotomy [dɪ'kɒtəmɪ] n Kluft f

dictate [dɪk'teɪt] vt diktieren; **~s** ['dɪkteɪts] npl Gebote pl

dictation [dɪk'teɪʃən] n Diktat nt

dictator [dɪk'teɪtə*] n Diktator m; **~ship** [dɪk'teɪtəʃɪp] n Diktatur f

diction ['dɪkʃən] n Ausdrucksweise f

dictionary ['dɪkʃənrɪ] n Wörterbuch nt

did [dɪd] pt of **do**

didn't ['dɪdənt] = **did not**

die [daɪ] vi sterben; **to be dying for sth** etw unbedingt haben wollen; **to be dying to do sth** darauf brennen, etw zu tun; **~ away** vi schwächer werden; **~ down** vi nachlassen; **~ out** vi aussterben

diehard ['daɪhɑːd] n Dickkopf m; (POL) Reaktionär m

diesel ['diːzəl] n (car) Diesel m; **~ engine** n Dieselmotor m; **~ oil** n Dieselkraftstoff m

diet ['daɪət] n Nahrung f; (special food) Diät f; (slimming) Abmagerungskur f ♦ vi (also: be on a ~) eine Abmagerungskur machen

differ ['dɪfə*] vi sich unterscheiden; (disagree) anderer Meinung sein; **~ence** n Unterschied m; **~ent** adj anders; (two things) verschieden; **~ential** [dɪfə'renʃəl] n (in wages) Lohnstufe f; **~entiate** [dɪfə'renʃɪeɪt] vt, vi unterscheiden; **~ently** adv anders; (from one another) unterschiedlich

difficult ['dɪfɪkəlt] adj schwierig; **~y** n Schwierigkeit f

diffident ['dɪfɪdənt] adj schüchtern

diffuse [adj dɪ'fjuːs, vb dɪ'fjuːz] adj langatmig ♦ vt verbreiten

dig [dɪg] (pt, pp **dug**) vt graben ♦ n (prod) Stoß m; (remark) Spitze f; (archaeological) Ausgrabung f; **~ in** vi (MIL) sich eingraben; **~ into** vt fus (sb's past) wühlen in +dat; (savings) angreifen; **~ up** vt ausgraben; (fig) aufgabeln

digest [vb daɪ'dʒest, n 'daɪdʒest] vt verdauen ♦ n Auslese f; **~ion** [dɪ'dʒestʃən] n Verdauung f

digit ['dɪdʒɪt] n Ziffer f; (ANAT) Finger m; **~al** adj digital, Digital-

dignified ['dɪgnɪfaɪd] adj würdevoll

dignity ['dɪgnɪtɪ] n Würde f

digress [daɪ'gres] vi abschweifen

digs [dɪgz] (BRIT: inf) npl Bude f

dilapidated [dɪ'læpɪdeɪtɪd] adj baufällig

dilate [daɪ'leɪt] vt weiten ♦ vi sich weiten

dilemma [daɪ'lemə] n Dilemma nt

diligent ['dɪlɪdʒənt] adj fleißig

dilute [daɪ'lu:t] *vt* verdünnen

dim [dɪm] *adj* trübe; *(stupid)* schwer von Begriff ♦ *vt* verdunkeln; **to ~ one's headlights** *(esp US)* abblenden

dime [daɪm] *(US) n* Zehncentstück *nt*

dimension [dɪ'menʃən] *n* Dimension *f*

diminish [dɪ'mɪnɪʃ] *vt, vi* verringern

diminutive [dɪ'mɪnjutɪv] *adj* winzig ♦ *n* Verkleinerungsform *f*

dimmer ['dɪmə*] *(US) n (AUT)* Abblendschalter *m*; **~s** *npl* Abblendlicht *nt*; *(sidelights)* Begrenzungsleuchten *pl*

dimple ['dɪmpl] *n* Grübchen *nt*

din [dɪn] *n* Getöse *nt*

dine [daɪn] *vi* speisen; **~r** *n* Tischgast *m*; *(RAIL)* Speisewagen *m*

dinghy ['dɪŋgɪ] *n* Dinghy *nt*; **rubber ~** Schlauchboot *nt*

dingy ['dɪndʒɪ] *adj* armselig

dining car ['daɪnɪŋ-] *(BRIT) n* Speisewagen *m*

dining room ['daɪnɪŋ-] *n* Eßzimmer *nt*; *(in hotel)* Speisezimmer *nt*

dinner ['dɪnə*] *n (lunch)* Mittagessen *nt*; *(evening)* Abendessen *nt*; *(public)* Festessen *nt*; **~ jacket** *n* Smoking *m*; **~ party** *n* Tischgesellschaft *f*, **~ time** *n* Tischzeit *f*

dinosaur ['daɪnəsɔ:*] *n* Dinosaurier *m*

dint [dɪnt] *n*: **by ~ of** durch

diocese ['daɪəsɪs] *n* Diözese *f*

dip [dɪp] *n (hollow)* Senkung *f*; *(bathe)* kurze(s) Baden *nt* ♦ *vt* eintauchen; *(BRIT: AUT: lights)* abblenden ♦ *vi (slope)* sich senken, abfallen

diploma [dɪ'pləumə] *n* Diplom *nt*

diplomacy [dɪ'pləuməsɪ] *n* Diplomatie *f*

diplomat ['dɪpləmæt] *n* Diplomat(in) *m(f)*; **~ic** [dɪplə'mætɪk] *adj* diplomatisch

dip stick *n* Ölmeßstab *m*

dipswitch ['dɪpswɪtʃ] *(BRIT) n (AUT)* Abblendschalter *m*

dire [daɪə*] *adj* schrecklich

direct [daɪ'rekt] *adj* direkt ♦ *vt* leiten; *(film)* die Regie führen +*gen*; *(aim)* richten; *(order)* anweisen; **can you ~ me to ...?** können Sie mir sagen, wo ich zu ... komme?

direction [dɪ'rekʃən] *n* Richtung *f*; *(CINE)*

Regie *f*; Leitung *f*; **~s** *npl (for use)* Gebrauchsanleitung *f*; *(orders)* Anweisungen *pl*; **sense of ~** Orientierungssinn *m*

directly [dɪ'rektlɪ] *adv* direkt; *(at once)* sofort

director [dɪ'rektə*] *n* Direktor *m*; *(of film)* Regisseur *m*

directory [dɪ'rektərɪ] *n (TEL)* Telefonbuch *nt*

dirt [dɜ:t] *n* Schmutz *m*, Dreck *m*; **~-cheap** *adj* spottbillig; **~y** *adj* schmutzig ♦ *vt* beschmutzen; **~y trick** *n* gemeine(r) Trick *m*

disability [dɪsə'bɪlɪtɪ] *n* Körperbehinderung *f*

disabled [dɪs'eɪbld] *adj* körperbehindert

disadvantage [dɪsəd'vɑ:ntɪdʒ] *n* Nachteil *m*

disaffection [dɪsə'fekʃən] *n* Entfremdung *f*

disagree [dɪsə'gri:] *vi* nicht übereinstimmen; *(quarrel)* (sich) streiten; *(food)*: **to ~ with sb** jdm nicht bekommen; **~able** *adj* unangenehm; **~ment** *n (between persons)* Streit *m*; *(between things)* Widerspruch *m*

disallow [dɪsə'lau] *vt* nicht zulassen

disappear [dɪsə'pɪə*] *vi* verschwinden; **~ance** *n* Verschwinden *nt*

disappoint [dɪsə'pɔɪnt] *vt* enttäuschen; **~ed** *adj* enttäuscht; **~ing** *adj* enttäuschend; **~ment** *n* Enttäuschung *f*

disapproval [dɪsə'pru:vəl] *n* Mißbilligung *f*

disapprove [dɪsə'pru:v] *vi*: **to ~ of** mißbilligen

disarm [dɪs'ɑ:m] *vt* entwaffnen; *(POL)* abrüsten; **~ament** *n* Abrüstung *f*

disarray [dɪsə'reɪ] *n*: **to be in ~** *(army)* in Auflösung (begriffen) sein; *(clothes)* in unordentlichem Zustand sein

disaster [dɪ'zɑ:stə*] *n* Katastrophe *f*

disastrous [dɪ'zɑ:strəs] *adj* verhängnisvoll

disband [dɪs'bænd] *vt* auflösen ♦ *vi* auseinandergehen

disbelief ['dɪsbə'li:f] *n* Ungläubigkeit *f*

disc [dɪsk] *n* Scheibe *f*; *(record)*

(Schall)platte *f*; (*COMPUT*) = **disk**
discard ['dɪskɑːd] *vt* ablegen
discern [dɪ'sɜːn] *vt* erkennen; **~ing** *adj*
scharfsinnig
discharge [*vb* dɪs'tʃɑːdʒ, *n* 'dɪstʃɑːdʒ] *vt*
(*ship*) entladen; (*duties*) nachkommen
+*dat*; (*dismiss*) entlassen; (*gun*)
abschießen; (*JUR*) freisprechen ♦ *n* (*of
ship, ELEC*) Entladung *f*; (*dismissal*)
Entlassung *f*; (*MED*) Ausfluß *m*
disciple [dɪ'saɪpl] *n* Jünger *m*
discipline ['dɪsɪplɪn] *n* Disziplin *f* ♦ *vt*
(*train*) schulen; (*punish*) bestrafen
disc jockey *n* Diskjockey *m*
disclaim [dɪs'kleɪm] *vt* nicht anerkennen
disclose [dɪs'kləʊz] *vt* enthüllen
disclosure [dɪs'kləʊʒə*] *n* Enthüllung *f*
disco ['dɪskəʊ] *n abbr* = **discotheque**
discoloured [dɪs'kʌləd] (*US* **discolored**)
adj verfärbt
discomfort [dɪs'kʌmfət] *n* Unbehagen *nt*
disconcert [dɪskən'sɜːt] *vt* aus der
Fassung bringen
disconnect ['dɪskə'nekt] *vt* abtrennen
discontent [dɪskən'tent] *n*
Unzufriedenheit *f*; **~ed** *adj* unzufrieden
discontinue ['dɪskən'tɪnjuː] *vt* einstellen
discord ['dɪskɔːd] *n* Zwietracht *f*; (*noise*)
Dissonanz *f*; **~ant** [dɪs'kɔːdənt] *adj*
uneinig
discotheque ['dɪskəʊtek] *n* Diskothek *f*
discount [*n* 'dɪskaʊnt, *vb* dɪs'kaʊnt] *n*
Rabatt *m* ♦ *vt* außer acht lassen
discourage [dɪs'kʌrɪdʒ] *vt* entmutigen;
(*prevent*) abraten
discouraging [dɪs'kʌrɪdʒɪŋ] *adj*
entmutigend
discourteous [dɪs'kɜːtɪəs] *adj* unhöflich
discover [dɪs'kʌvə*] *vt* entdecken; **~y** *n*
Entdeckung *f*
discredit [dɪs'kredɪt] *vt* in Verruf
bringen
discreet [dɪs'kriːt] *adj* diskret
discrepancy [dɪs'krepənsɪ] *n* Diskrepanz
f
discriminate [dɪs'krɪmɪneɪt] *vi*
unterscheiden; **to ~ against**
diskriminieren
discriminating [dɪs'krɪmɪneɪtɪŋ] *adj*

anspruchsvoll
discrimination [dɪskrɪmɪ'neɪʃən] *n*
Urteilsvermögen *nt*; (*pej*) Diskriminierung
f
discuss [dɪs'kʌs] *vt* diskutieren,
besprechen; **~ion** [dɪs'kʌʃən] *n*
Diskussion *f*, Besprechung *f*
disdain [dɪs'deɪn] *vt* verachten ♦ *n*
Verachtung *f*
disease [dɪ'ziːz] *n* Krankheit *f*
disembark [dɪsɪm'bɑːk] *vt* aussteigen
lassen ♦ *vi* von Bord gehen
disenchanted ['dɪsɪn'tʃɑːntɪd] *adj*
desillusioniert
disengage [dɪsɪn'geɪdʒ] *vt* (*AUT*)
auskuppeln
disentangle ['dɪsɪn'tæŋgl] *vt* entwirren
disfigure [dɪs'fɪgə*] *vt* entstellen
disgrace [dɪs'greɪs] *n* Schande *f* ♦ *vt*
Schande bringen über +*acc*; **~ful** *adj*
unerhört
disgruntled [dɪs'grʌntld] *adj* verärgert
disguise [dɪs'gaɪz] *vt* verkleiden;
(*feelings*) verhehlen ♦ *n* Verkleidung *f*; **in
~** verkleidet, maskiert
disgust [dɪs'gʌst] *n* Abscheu *f* ♦ *vt*
anwidern; **~ing** *adj* widerlich
dish [dɪʃ] *n* Schüssel *f*; (*food*) Gericht *nt*;
to do *or* **wash the ~es** abwaschen; **~ up**
vt auftischen; **~ cloth** *n* Spüllappen *m*
dishearten [dɪs'hɑːtn] *vt* entmutigen
dishevelled [dɪ'ʃevəld] *adj* (*hair*)
zerzaust; (*clothing*) ungepflegt
dishonest [dɪs'ɒnɪst] *adj* unehrlich; **~y** *n*
Unehrlichkeit *f*
dishonour [dɪs'ɒnə*] (*US* **dishonor**) *n*
Unehre *f*; **~able** *adj* unehrenhaft
dishtowel ['dɪʃtaʊəl] *n* Geschirrtuch *nt*
dishwasher ['dɪʃwɒʃə*] *n*
Geschirrspülmaschine *f*
disillusion [dɪsɪ'luːʒən] *vt* enttäuschen,
desillusionieren
disincentive ['dɪsɪn'sentɪv] *n*
Entmutigung *f*
disinfect [dɪsɪn'fekt] *vt* desinfizieren;
~ant *n* Desinfektionsmittel *nt*
disintegrate [dɪs'ɪntɪgreɪt] *vi* sich
auflösen
disinterested [dɪs'ɪntrɪstɪd] *adj*

uneigennützig; *(inf)* uninteressiert
disjointed [dɪs'dʒɔɪntɪd] *adj*
unzusammenhängend
disk [dɪsk] *n (COMPUT)* Diskette *f*; **single-/
double-sided ~** einseitige/beidseitige
Diskette; **~ drive** *n* Diskettenlaufwerk *nt*;
~ette *(US) n* = **disk**
dislike [dɪs'laɪk] *n* Abneigung *f* ♦ *vt* nicht
leiden können
dislocate ['dɪsləʊkeɪt] *vt* auskugeln
dislodge [dɪs'lɒdʒ] *vt* verschieben; *(MIL)*
aus der Stellung werfen
disloyal [dɪs'lɔɪəl] *adj* treulos
dismal ['dɪzməl] *adj* trostlos, trübe
dismantle [dɪs'mæntl] *vt* demontieren
dismay [dɪs'meɪ] *n* Bestürzung *f* ♦ *vt*
bestürzen
dismiss [dɪs'mɪs] *vt (employee)* entlassen;
(idea) von sich weisen; *(send away)*
wegschicken; *(JUR)* abweisen; **~al** *n*
Entlassung *f*
dismount [dɪs'maʊnt] *vi* absteigen
disobedience [dɪsə'biːdɪəns] *n*
Ungehorsam *m*
disobedient [dɪsə'biːdɪənt] *adj*
ungehorsam
disobey ['dɪsə'beɪ] *vt* nicht gehorchen
+*dat*
disorder [dɪs'ɔːdə*] *n (confusion)*
Verwirrung *f*; *(commotion)* Aufruhr *m*;
(MED) Erkrankung *f*
disorderly [dɪs'ɔːdəlɪ] *adj (untidy)*
unordentlich; *(unruly)* ordnungswidrig
disorganized [dɪs'ɔːɡənaɪzd] *adj*
unordentlich
disorientated [dɪs'ɔːrɪenteɪtɪd] *adj*
(person: after journey, deep sleep) verwirrt
disown [dɪs'əʊn] *vt (child)* verstoßen
disparaging [dɪs'pærɪdʒɪŋ] *adj*
geringschätzig
disparity [dɪs'pærɪtɪ] *n* Verschiedenheit *f*
dispassionate [dɪs'pæʃnɪt] *adj* objektiv
dispatch [dɪs'pætʃ] *vt (goods)* abschicken,
abfertigen ♦ *n* Absendung *f*; *(esp MIL)*
Meldung *f*
dispel [dɪs'pel] *vt* zerstreuen
dispensary [dɪs'pensərɪ] *n* Apotheke *f*
dispense [dɪs'pens] *vt* verteilen,
austeilen; **~ with** *vt fus* verzichten auf

+*acc*; **~r** *n (container)* Spender *m*
dispensing [dɪs'pensɪŋ] *adj*: **~ chemist**
(BRIT) Apotheker *m*
dispersal [dɪs'pɜːsəl] *n* Zerstreuung *f*
disperse [dɪs'pɜːs] *vt* zerstreuen ♦ *vi* sich
verteilen
dispirited [dɪs'pɪrɪtɪd] *adj*
niedergeschlagen
displace [dɪs'pleɪs] *vt* verschieben; **~d
person** *n* Verschleppte(r) *mf*
display [dɪs'pleɪ] *n (of goods)* Auslage *f*;
(of feeling) Zurschaustellung *f* ♦ *vt* zeigen;
(ostentatiously) vorführen; *(goods)*
ausstellen
displease [dɪs'pliːz] *vt* mißfallen +*dat*
displeasure [dɪs'pleʒə*] *n* Mißfallen *nt*
disposable [dɪs'pəʊzəbl] *adj* Wegwerf-; **~
nappy** *n* Papierwindel *f*
disposal [dɪs'pəʊzəl] *n (of property)*
Verkauf *m*; *(throwing away)* Beseitigung
f; **to be at one's ~** einem zur Verfügung
stehen
dispose [dɪs'pəʊz] *vi*: **to ~ of** loswerden
disposed [dɪs'pəʊzd] *adj* geneigt
disposition [dɪspə'zɪʃən] *n* Wesen *nt*
disproportionate [dɪsprə'pɔːʃnɪt] *adj*
unverhältnismäßig
disprove [dɪs'pruːv] *vt* widerlegen
dispute [dɪs'pjuːt] *n* Streit *m*; *(also:
industrial ~)* Arbeitskampf *m* ♦ *vt*
bestreiten
disqualify [dɪs'kwɒlɪfaɪ] *vt*
disqualifizieren
disquiet [dɪs'kwaɪət] *n* Unruhe *f*
disregard [dɪsrɪ'ɡɑːd] *vt* nicht (be)achten
disrepair ['dɪsrɪ'peə*] *n*: **to fall into ~**
verfallen
disreputable [dɪs'repjʊtəbl] *adj* verrufen
disrespectful [dɪsrɪs'pektfʊl] *adj*
respektlos
disrupt [dɪs'rʌpt] *vt* stören; *(service)*
unterbrechen; **~ion** [dɪs'rʌpʃən] *n*
Störung *f*; Unterbrechung *f*
dissatisfaction ['dɪssætɪs'fækʃən] *n*
Unzufriedenheit *f*
dissatisfied ['dɪs'sætɪsfaɪd] *adj*
unzufrieden
dissect [dɪ'sekt] *vt* zerlegen, sezieren
disseminate [dɪ'semɪneɪt] *vt* verbreiten

dissent [dɪ'sent] *n* abweichende Meinung *f*

dissertation [dɪsə'teɪʃən] *n* wissenschaftliche Arbeit *f*; *(Ph.D.)* Doktorarbeit *f*

disservice [dɪs'sɜːvɪs] *n*: **to do sb a ~** jdm einen schlechten Dienst erweisen

dissident ['dɪsɪdənt] *adj* andersdenkend ♦ *n* Dissident *m*

dissimilar [dɪ'sɪmɪlə*] *adj*: **~ (to sb/sth)** (jdm/etw) unähnlich

dissipate ['dɪsɪpeɪt] *vt* *(waste)* verschwenden; *(scatter)* zerstreuen

dissociate [dɪ'səʊʃɪeɪt] *vt* trennen

dissolute ['dɪsəluːt] *adj* liederlich

dissolution [dɪsə'luːʃən] *n* Auflösung *f*

dissolve [dɪ'zɒlv] *vt* auflösen ♦ *vi* sich auflösen

dissuade [dɪ'sweɪd] *vt*: **to ~ sb from doing sth** jdn davon abbringen, etw zu tun

distance ['dɪstəns] *n* Entfernung *f*; **in the ~** in der Ferne

distant ['dɪstənt] *adj* entfernt, fern; *(with time)* fern; *(formal)* distanziert

distaste [dɪs'teɪst] *n* Abneigung *f*; **~ful** *adj* widerlich

distended [dɪs'tendɪd] *adj* *(stomach)* aufgebläht

distil [dɪs'tɪl] *vt* destillieren; **~lery** *f* Brennerei *f*

distinct [dɪs'tɪŋkt] *adj* *(separate)* getrennt; *(clear)* klar, deutlich; **as ~ from** im Unterschied zu; **~ion** [dɪs'tɪŋkʃən] *n* Unterscheidung *f*; *(eminence)* Auszeichnung *f*; **~ive** *adj* bezeichnend

distinguish [dɪs'tɪŋwɪʃ] *vt* unterscheiden; **~ed** *adj* *(eminent)* berühmt; **~ing** *adj* bezeichnend

distort [dɪs'tɔːt] *vt* verdrehen; *(misrepresent)* entstellen; **~ion** [dɪs'tɔːʃən] *n* Verzerrung *f*

distract [dɪs'trækt] *vt* ablenken; **~ing** *adj* verwirrend; **~ion** [dɪs'trækʃən] *n* *(distress)* Raserei *f*; *(diversion)* Zerstreuung *f*

distraught [dɪs'trɔːt] *adj* bestürzt

distress [dɪs'tres] *n* Not *f*; *(suffering)* Qual *f* ♦ *vt* quälen; **~ing** *adj*

erschütternd; **~ signal** *n* Notsignal *nt*

distribute [dɪs'trɪbjuːt] *vt* verteilen

distribution [dɪstrɪ'bjuːʃən] *n* Verteilung *f*

distributor [dɪs'trɪbjutə*] *n* Verteiler *m*

district ['dɪstrɪkt] *n* *(of country)* Kreis *m*; *(of town)* Bezirk *m*; **~ attorney** *(US)* *n* Oberstaatsanwalt *m*; **~ nurse** *n* Kreiskrankenschwester *f*

distrust [dɪs'trʌst] *n* Mißtrauen *nt* ♦ *vt* mißtrauen +*dat*

disturb [dɪs'tɜːb] *vt* stören; *(agitate)* erregen; **~ance** *n* Störung *f*; **~ed** *adj* beunruhigt; **emotionally ~ed** emotional gestört; **~ing** *adj* beunruhigend

disuse ['dɪs'juːs] *n*: **to fall into ~** außer Gebrauch kommen

disused ['dɪs'juːzd] *adj* außer Gebrauch; *(mine, railway line)* stillgelegt

ditch [dɪtʃ] *n* Graben *m* ♦ *vt* *(person)* loswerden; *(plan)* fallenlassen

dither ['dɪðə*] *vi* verdattert sein

ditto ['dɪtəʊ] *adv* dito, ebenfalls

divan [dɪ'væn] *n* Liegesofa *nt*

dive [daɪv] *n* *(into water)* Kopfsprung *m*; *(AVIAT)* Sturzflug *m* ♦ *vi* tauchen; **~r** *n* Taucher *m*

diverge [daɪ'vɜːdʒ] *vi* auseinandergehen

diverse [daɪ'vɜːs] *adj* verschieden

diversion [daɪ'vɜːʃən] *n* Ablenkung *f*; *(BRIT: AUT)* Umleitung *f*

diversity [daɪ'vɜːsɪtɪ] *n* Vielfalt *f*

divert [daɪ'vɜːt] *vt* ablenken; *(traffic)* umleiten

divide [dɪ'vaɪd] *vt* teilen ♦ *vi* sich teilen; **~d highway** *(US)* *n* Schnellstraße *f*

divine [dɪ'vaɪn] *adj* göttlich

diving ['daɪvɪŋ] *n* *(SPORT)* Turmspringen *nt*; *(underwater ~)* Tauchen *nt*; **~ board** *n* Sprungbrett *nt*

divinity [dɪ'vɪnɪtɪ] *n* Gottheit *f*; *(subject)* Religion *f*

division [dɪ'vɪʒən] *n* Teilung *f*; *(MIL)* Division *f*; *(part)* Abteilung *f*; *(in opinion)* Uneinigkeit *f*; *(BRIT: POL)* (Abstimmung *f* durch) Hammelsprung *m*

divorce [dɪ'vɔːs] *n* (Ehe)scheidung *f* ♦ *vt* scheiden; **~d** *adj* geschieden; **~e** [dɪvɔː'siː] *n* Geschiedene(r) *mf*

divulge [daɪ'vʌldʒ] *vt* preisgeben
D.I.Y. (*BRIT*) *n abbr* = **do-it-yourself**
dizzy ['dɪzɪ] *adj* schwindlig
DJ *n abbr* = **disc jockey**

KEYWORD
---

do [du:] (*pt* **did**, *pp* **done**) *n* (*inf: party etc*) Fete *f*
♦ *aux vb* **1** (*in negative constructions and questions*): **I don't understand** ich verstehe nicht; **didn't you know?** wußtest du das nicht?; **what do you think?** was meinen Sie?
2 (*for emphasis, in polite expressions*): **she does seem rather tired** sie scheint wirklich sehr müde zu sein; **do sit down/help yourself** setzen Sie sich doch hin/greifen Sie doch zu
3 (*used to avoid repeating vb*): **she swims better than I do** sie schwimmt besser als ich; **she lives in Glasgow — so do I** sie wohnt in Glasgow — ich auch
4 (*in question tags*): **you like him, don't you?** du magst ihn doch, oder?
♦ *vt* **1** (*carry out, perform etc*) tun, machen; **what are you doing tonight?** was machst du heute abend?; **I've got nothing to do** ich habe nichts zu tun; **to do one's hair/nails** sich die Haare/Nägel machen
2 (*AUT etc*) fahren
♦ *vi* **1** (*act, behave*): **do as I do** mach es wie ich
2 (*get on, fare*): **he's doing well/badly at school** er ist gut/schlecht in der Schule; **how do you do?** guten Tag
3 (*be suitable*) gehen; (*be sufficient*) reichen; **to make do (with)** auskommen mit
do away with *vt* (*kill*) umbringen; (*abolish: law etc*) abschaffen
do up *vt* (*laces, dress, buttons*) zumachen; (*renovate: room, house*) renovieren
do with *vt* (*need*) brauchen; (*be connected*) zu tun haben mit
do without *vt*, *vi* auskommen ohne

docile ['dəʊsaɪl] *adj* gefügig
dock [dɒk] *n* Dock *nt*; (*JUR*) Anklagebank

f ♦ *vi* ins Dock gehen; **~er** *n* Hafenarbeiter *m*; **~yard** *n* Werft *f*
doctor ['dɒktə*] *n* Arzt *m*, Ärztin *f*; (*UNIV*) Doktor *m* ♦ *vt* (*fig*) fälschen; (*drink etc*) etw beimischen +*dat*; **D~ of Philosophy** *n* Doktor *m* der Philosophie
document ['dɒkjʊmənt] *n* Dokument *nt*; **~ary** [dɒkjʊ'mentərɪ] *n* Dokumentarbericht *m*; (*film*) Dokumentarfilm *m* ♦ *adj* dokumentarisch; **~ation** [dɒkjʊmen'teɪʃən] *n* dokumentarische(r) Nachweis *m*
dodge [dɒdʒ] *n* Kniff *m* ♦ *vt* ausweichen +*dat*; **~ms** ['dɒdʒəmz] (*BRIT*) *npl* Autoskooter *m*
doe [dəʊ] *n* (*roe deer*) Ricke *f*; (*red deer*) Hirschkuh *f*; (*rabbit*) Weibchen *nt*
does [dʌz] *vb see* **do**; **~n't** = **does not**
dog [dɒg] *n* Hund *m*; **~ collar** *n* Hundehalsband *nt*; (*ECCL*) Kragen *m* des Geistlichen; **~-eared** *adj* mit Eselsohren
dogged ['dɒgɪd] *adj* hartnäckig
dogsbody ['dɒgzbɒdɪ] *n* Mädchen *nt* für alles
doings ['du:ɪŋz] *npl* (*activities*) Treiben *nt*
do-it-yourself ['du:ɪtjə'self] *n* Do-it-yourself *nt*
doldrums ['dɒldrəmz] *npl*: **to be in the ~** (*business*) Flaute haben; (*person*) deprimiert sein
dole [dəʊl] (*BRIT*) *n* Stempelgeld *nt*; **to be on the ~** stempeln gehen; **~ out** *vt* ausgeben, austeilen
doleful ['dəʊlful] *adj* traurig
doll [dɒl] *n* Puppe *f* ♦ *vt*: **to ~ o.s. up** sich aufdonnern
dollar ['dɒlə*] *n* Dollar *m*
dolphin ['dɒlfɪn] *n* Delphin *m*
dome [dəʊm] *n* Kuppel *f*
domestic [də'mestɪk] *adj* häuslich; (*within country*) Innen-, Binnen-; (*animal*) Haus-; **~ated** *adj* (*person*) häuslich; (*animal*) zahm
dominant ['dɒmɪnənt] *adj* vorherrschend
dominate ['dɒmɪneɪt] *vt* beherrschen
domineering [dɒmɪ'nɪərɪŋ] *adj* herrisch
dominion [də'mɪnɪən] *n* (*rule*) Regierungsgewalt *f*; (*land*) Staatsgebiet *nt* mit Selbstverwaltung

domino ['dɒmɪnəʊ] (*pl* **dominoes**) *n* Dominostein *m*; **~es** *n* (*game*) Domino(spiel) *nt*

don [dɒn] (*BRIT*) *n* akademische(r) Lehrer *m*

donate [dəʊ'neɪt] *vt* (*blood, little money*) spenden; (*lot of money*) stiften

donation [dəʊ'neɪʃən] *n* Spende *f*

done [dʌn] *pp of* **do**

donkey ['dɒŋkɪ] *n* Esel *m*

donor ['dəʊnə*] *n* Spender *m*

don't [dəʊnt] = **do not**

doodle ['du:dl] *vi* kritzeln

doom [du:m] *n* böse(s) Geschick *nt*; (*downfall*) Verderben *nt* ♦ *vt*: **to be ~ed** zum Untergang verurteilt sein; **~sday** *n* der Jüngste Tag

door [dɔ:*] *n* Tür *f*; **~bell** *n* Türklingel *f*; **~-handle** *n* Türklinke *f*; **~man** (*irreg*) *n* Türsteher *m*; **~mat** *n* Fußmatte *f*; **~step** *n* Türstufe *f*; **~way** *n* Türöffnung *f*

dope [dəʊp] *n* (*drug*) Aufputschmittel *nt* ♦ *vt* (*horse etc*) dopen

dopey ['dəʊpɪ] (*inf*) *adj* bekloppt

dormant ['dɔ:mənt] *adj* latent

dormitory ['dɔ:mɪtrɪ] *n* Schlafsaal *m*

dormouse ['dɔ:maʊs] (*pl* **-mice**) *n* Haselmaus *f*

DOS [dɒs] *n abbr* (= *disk operating system*) DOS *nt*

dosage ['dəʊsɪdʒ] *n* Dosierung *f*

dose [dəʊs] *n* Dosis *f*

doss house ['dɒs-] (*BRIT*) *n* Bleibe *f*

dot [dɒt] *n* Punkt *m*; **~ted with** übersät mit; **on the ~** pünktlich

dote [dəʊt] : **to ~ on** *vt fus* vernarrt sein in +*acc*

dot matrix printer *n* Matrixdrucker *m*

dotted line ['dɒtɪd-] *n* punktierte Linie *f*

double ['dʌbl] *adj, adv* doppelt ♦ *n* Doppelgänger *m* ♦ *vt* verdoppeln ♦ *vi* sich verdoppeln; **~s** *npl* (*TENNIS*) Doppel *nt*; *on or at the* **~** im Laufschritt; **~ bass** *n* Kontrabaß *m*; **~ bed** *n* Doppelbett *nt*; **~ bend** (*BRIT*) *n* S-Kurve *f*; **~-breasted** *adj* zweireihig; **~cross** *vt* hintergehen; **~decker** *n* Doppeldecker *m*; **~ glazing** (*BRIT*) *n* Doppelverglasung *f*; **~ room** *n* Doppelzimmer *nt*

doubly ['dʌblɪ] *adv* doppelt

doubt [daʊt] *n* Zweifel *m* ♦ *vt* bezweifeln; **~ful** *adj* zweifelhaft; **~less** *adv* ohne Zweifel

dough [dəʊ] *n* Teig *m*; **~nut** *n* Berliner *m*

douse [daʊz] *vt* (*drench*) mit Wasser begießen, durchtränken; (*extinguish*) ausmachen

dove [dʌv] *n* Taube *f*

Dover ['dəʊvə*] *n* (*GEOG*) Dover *nt*

dovetail ['dʌvteɪl] *vi* (*plans*) übereinstimmen

dowdy ['daʊdɪ] *adj* unmodern

down [daʊn] *n* (*fluff*) Flaum *m*; (*hill*) Hügel *m* ♦ *adv* unten; (*motion*) herunter; hinunter ♦ *prep*: **to go ~ the street** die Straße hinuntergehen ♦ *vt* niederschlagen; **~ with X!** nieder mit X!; **~-and-out** *n* Tramp *m*; **~-at-heel** *adj* schäbig; **~cast** *adj* niedergeschlagen; **~fall** *n* Sturz *m*; **~hearted** *adj* niedergeschlagen; **~hill** *adv* bergab; **~ payment** *n* Anzahlung *f*; **~pour** *n* Platzregen *m*; **~right** *adj* ausgesprochen

Down's syndrome [-'sɪndrəʊm] *n* (*MED*) Down-Syndrom *nt*

down: **~stairs** *adv* unten; (*motion*) nach unten; **~stream** *adv* flußabwärts; **~-to-earth** *adj* praktisch; **~town** *adv* in der Innenstadt; (*motion*) in die Innenstadt; **~ under** (*BRIT: inf*) *adv* in/nach Australien/Neuseeland; **~ward** *adj* Abwärts-, nach unten ♦ *adv* abwärts, nach unten; **~wards** *adv* abwärts, nach unten

doz. *abbr* (= *dozen*) Dtzd.

doze [dəʊz] *vi* dösen; **~ off** *vi* einnicken

dozen ['dʌzn] *n* Dutzend *nt*; **a ~ books** ein Dutzend Bücher; **~s of** Dutzende von

Dr. *abbr* = **doctor; drive**

drab [dræb] *adj* düster, eintönig

draft [drɑ:ft] *n* Entwurf *m*; (*FIN*) Wechsel *m*; (*US: MIL*) Einberufung *f* ♦ *vt* skizzieren; *see also* **draught**

draftsman ['drɑ:ftsmən] (*US: irreg*) *n* = **draughtsman**

drag [dræg] *vt* schleppen; (*river*) mit einem Schleppnetz absuchen ♦ *vi* sich (dahin)schleppen ♦ *n* (*bore*) etwas Blödes;

in ~ als Tunte; **a man in** ~ eine Tunte; ~
on *vi* sich in die Länge ziehen
dragon ['drægən] *n* Drache *m*; **~fly**
['drægənflaɪ] *n* Libelle *f*
drain [dreɪn] *n* Abfluß *m*; (*fig: burden*)
Belastung *f* ♦ *vt* ableiten; (*exhaust*)
erschöpfen ♦ *vi* (*of water*) abfließen; **~age**
n Kanalisation *f*; **~ing board** (*US*
~board) *n* Ablaufbrett *nt*; **~pipe** *n*
Abflußrohr *nt*
dram [dræm] *n* Schluck *m*
drama ['drɑːmə] *n* Drama *nt*; **~tic**
[drə'mætɪk] *adj* dramatisch; **~tist**
['dræmətɪst] *n* Dramatiker *m*; **~tize** *vt*
(*events*) dramatisieren; (*adapt: for TV,
cinema*) bearbeiten
drank [dræŋk] *pt of* **drink**
drape [dreɪp] *vt* drapieren; **~r** (*BRIT*) *n*
Tuchhändler *m*; **~s** (*US*) *npl* Vorhänge *pl*
drastic ['dræstɪk] *adj* drastisch
draught [drɑːft] (*US* **draft**) *n* (*of air*) Zug
m; (*NAUT*) Tiefgang *m*; **~s** *n* Damespiel *nt*;
on ~ (*beer*) vom Faß; **~board** (*BRIT*) *n*
Zeichenbrett *nt*
draughtsman ['drɑːftsmən] (*irreg*) *n*
technische(r) Zeichner *m*
draw [drɔː] (*pt* **drew**, *pp* **drawn**) *vt*
ziehen; (*crowd*) anlocken; (*picture*)
zeichnen; (*money*) abheben; (*water*)
schöpfen ♦ *vi* (*SPORT*) unentschieden
spielen ♦ *n* Unentschieden *nt*; (*lottery*)
Ziehung *f*; ~ **near** *vi* näherrücken; ~ **out**
vi (*train*) ausfahren; (*lengthen*) sich
hinziehen; ~ **up** *vi* (*stop*) halten ♦ *vt*
(*document*) aufsetzen; **~back** *n* Nachteil
m; **~bridge** *n* Zugbrücke *f*
drawer [drɔː*] *n* Schublade *f*
drawing ['drɔːɪŋ] *n* Zeichnung *f*;
Zeichnen *nt*; ~ **board** *n* Reißbrett *nt*; ~
pin (*BRIT*) *n* Reißzwecke *f*; ~ **room** *n*
Salon *m*
drawl [drɔːl] *n* schleppende Sprechweise *f*
drawn [drɔːn] *pp of* **draw**
dread [dred] *n* Furcht *f* ♦ *vt* fürchten;
~ful *adj* furchtbar
dream [driːm] (*pt, pp* **dreamed** *or*
dreamt) *n* Traum *m* ♦ *vt* träumen ♦ *vi*:
to ~ (**about**) träumen (von); **~er** *n*
Träumer *m*; **dreamt** [dremt] *pt, pp of*

dream; **~y** *adj* verträumt
dreary ['drɪərɪ] *adj* trostlos, öde
dredge [dredʒ] *vt* ausbaggern
dregs [dregz] *npl* Bodensatz *m*; (*fig*)
Abschaum *m*
drench [drentʃ] *vt* durchnässen
dress [dres] *n* Kleidung *f*; (*garment*) Kleid
nt ♦ *vt* anziehen; (*MED*) verbinden; **to get**
~ed sich anziehen; ~ **up** *vi* sich fein
machen; ~ **circle** (*BRIT*) *n* erste(r) Rang *m*;
~er *n* (*furniture*) Anrichte *f*; **~ing** *n* (*MED*)
Verband *m*; (*COOK*) Soße *f*; **~ing gown**
(*BRIT*) *n* Morgenrock *m*; **~ing room** *n*
(*THEAT*) Garderobe *f*; (*SPORT*)
Umkleideraum *m*; **~ing table** *n*
Toilettentisch *m*; **~maker** *n* Schneiderin
f; ~ **rehearsal** *n* Generalprobe *f*
drew [druː] *pt of* **draw**
dribble ['drɪbl] *vi* sabbern ♦ *vt* (*ball*)
dribbeln
dried [draɪd] *adj* getrocknet; (*fruit*) Dörr-,
gedörrte(r); ~ **milk** *n* Milchpulver *nt*
drier ['draɪə*] *n* = **dryer**
drift [drɪft] *n* Strömung *f*; (*snow~*)
Schneewehe *f*; (*fig*) Richtung *f* ♦ *vi* sich
treiben lassen; **~wood** *n* Treibholz *nt*
drill [drɪl] *n* Bohrer *m*; (*MIL*) Drill *m* ♦ *vt*
bohren; (*MIL*) ausbilden ♦ *vi*: **to** ~ (**for**)
bohren (nach)
drink [drɪŋk] (*pt* **drank**, *pp* **drunk**) *n*
Getränk *nt*; (*spirits*) Drink *m* ♦ *vt, vi*
trinken; **to have a** ~ etwas trinken; **~er**
n Trinker *m*; **~ing water** *n* Trinkwasser
nt
drip [drɪp] *n* Tropfen *m* ♦ *vi* tropfen; **~-**
dry *adj* bügelfrei; **~ping** *n* Bratenfett *nt*
drive [draɪv] (*pt* **drove**, *pp* **driven**) *n*
Fahrt *f*; (*road*) Einfahrt *f*; (*campaign*)
Aktion *f*; (*energy*) Schwung *m*; (*SPORT*)
Schlag *m*; (*also: disk ~*) Diskettenlaufwerk
nt ♦ *vt* (*car*) fahren; (*animals, people,
objects*) treiben; (*power*) antreiben ♦ *vi*
fahren; **left-/right-hand** ~ Links-/Rechts-
steuerung *f*; **to** ~ **sb mad** jdn verrückt
machen
drivel ['drɪvl] *n* Faselei *f*
driven ['drɪvn] *pp of* **drive**
driver ['draɪvə*] *n* Fahrer *m*; **~'s license**
(*US*) *n* Führerschein *m*

driveway ['draɪvweɪ] *n* Auffahrt *f*; (*longer*) Zufahrtsstraße *f*

driving ['draɪvɪŋ] *adj* (*rain*) stürmisch; ~ **instructor** *n* Fahrlehrer *m*; ~ **lesson** *n* Fahrstunde *f*; ~ **licence** (*BRIT*) *n* Führerschein *m*; ~ **school** *n* Fahrschule *f*; ~ **test** *n* Fahrprüfung *f*

drizzle ['drɪzl] *n* Nieselregen *m* ♦ *vi* nieseln

droll [drəʊl] *adj* drollig

drone [drəʊn] *n* (*sound*) Brummen *nt*; (*bee*) Drohne *f*

drool [druːl] *vi* sabbern

droop [druːp] *vi* (*schlaff*) herabhängen

drop [drɒp] *n* (*of liquid*) Tropfen *m*; (*fall*) Fall *m* ♦ *vt* fallen lassen; (*lower*) senken; (*abandon*) fallenlassen ♦ *vi* (*fall*) herunterfallen; ~**s** *npl* (*MED*) Tropfen *pl*; ~ **off** *vi* (*sleep*) einschlafen ♦ *vt* (*passenger*) absetzen; ~ **out** *vi* (*withdraw*) ausscheiden; ~**-out** *n* Aussteiger *m*; ~**per** *n* Pipette *f*; ~**pings** *npl* Kot *m*

drought [draʊt] *n* Dürre *f*

drove [drəʊv] *pt of* **drive**

drown [draʊn] *vt* ertränken; (*sound*) übertönen ♦ *vi* ertrinken

drowsy ['draʊzɪ] *adj* schläfrig

drudgery ['drʌdʒərɪ] *n* Plackerei *f*

drug [drʌg] *n* (*MED*) Arznei *f*; (*narcotic*) Rauschgift *nt* ♦ *vt* betäuben; ~ **addict** *n* Rauschgiftsüchtige(r) *mf*; ~**gist** (*US*) *n* Drogist(in) *m(f)*; ~**store** (*US*) *n* Drogerie *f*

drum [drʌm] *n* Trommel *f* ♦ *vi* trommeln; ~**s** *npl* (*MUS*) Schlagzeug *nt*; ~**mer** *n* Trommler *m*

drunk [drʌŋk] *pp of* **drink** ♦ *adj* betrunken ♦ *n* (*also*: ~**ard**) Trinker(in) *m(f)*; ~**en** *adj* betrunken

dry [draɪ] *adj* trocken ♦ *vt* (ab)trocknen ♦ *vi* trocknen; ~ **up** *vi* austrocknen ♦ *vt* (*dishes*) abtrocknen; ~ **cleaning** *n* chemische Reinigung *f*; ~**er** *n* Trockner *m*; (*US*: *spin-dryer*) (Wäsche)schleuder *f*; ~ **goods store** (*US*) *n* Kurzwarengeschäft *nt*; ~**ness** *n* Trockenheit *f*; ~ **rot** *n* Hausschwamm *m*

DSS *n abbr* (*BRIT*: = *Department of Social Security*) ≈ Sozialministerium *nt*

dual ['djʊəl] *adj* doppelt; ~ **carriageway** (*BRIT*) *n* zweispurige Fahrbahn *f*; ~ **nationality** *n* doppelte Staatsangehörigkeit *f*; ~**-purpose** *adj* Mehrzweck-

dubbed [dʌbd] *adj* (*film*) synchronisiert

dubious ['djuːbɪəs] *adj* zweifelhaft

duchess ['dʌtʃɪs] *n* Herzogin *f*

duck [dʌk] *n* Ente *f* ♦ *vi* sich ducken; ~**ling** *n* Entchen *nt*

duct [dʌkt] *n* Röhre *f*

dud [dʌd] *n* Niete *f* ♦ *adj* (*cheque*) ungedeckt

due [djuː] *adj* fällig; (*fitting*) angemessen ♦ *n* Gebühr *f*; (*right*) Recht *nt* ♦ *adv* (*south etc*) genau; ~**s** *npl* (*for club, union*) Beitrag *m*; (*in harbour*) Gebühren *pl*; ~ **to** wegen +*gen*

duel ['djʊəl] *n* Duell *nt*

duet [djuːˈet] *n* Duett *nt*

duffel ['dʌfl] *adj*: ~ **bag** Matchbeutel *m*, Matchsack *m*; ~ **coat** *n* Dufflecoat *m*

dug [dʌg] *pt, pp of* **dig**

duke [djuːk] *n* Herzog *m*

dull [dʌl] *adj* (*colour, weather*) trübe; (*stupid*) schwer von Begriff; (*boring*) langweilig ♦ *vt* abstumpfen

duly ['djuːlɪ] *adv* ordnungsgemäß

dumb [dʌm] *adj* stumm; (*inf*: *stupid*) doof, blöde; ~**founded** [dʌmˈfaʊndɪd] *adj* verblüfft

dummy ['dʌmɪ] *n* Schneiderpuppe *f*; (*substitute*) Attrappe *f*; (*BRIT*: *for baby*) Schnuller *m* ♦ *adj* Schein-

dump [dʌmp] *n* Abfallhaufen *m*; (*MIL*) Stapelplatz *m*; (*inf*: *place*) Nest *nt* ♦ *vt* abladen, auskippen; ~**ing** *n* (*COMM*) Schleuderexport *m*; (*of rubbish*) Schuttabladen *nt*

dumpling ['dʌmplɪŋ] *n* Kloß *m*, Knödel *m*

dumpy ['dʌmpɪ] *adj* pummelig

dunce [dʌns] *n* Dummkopf *m*

dune [djuːn] *n* Düne *f*

dung [dʌŋ] *n* Dünger *m*

dungarees [dʌŋgəˈriːz] *npl* Latzhose *f*

dungeon ['dʌndʒən] *n* Kerker *m*

dupe [djuːp] *n* Gefoppte(r) *m* ♦ *vt* hintergehen, anführen

duplex ['djuːpleks] (*US*) *n* zweistöckige Wohnung *f*

duplicate [*n* 'dju:plɪkɪt, *vb* 'dju:plɪkeɪt] *n* Duplikat *nt* ♦ *vt* verdoppeln; *(make copies)* kopieren; **in** ~ in doppelter Ausführung

duplicity [dju:'plɪsɪtɪ] *n* Doppelspiel *nt*

durable ['djʊərəbl] *adj* haltbar

duration [djʊə'reɪʃən] *n* Dauer *f*

duress [djʊə'res] *n*: **under** ~ unter Zwang

during ['djʊərɪŋ] *prep* während +*gen*

dusk [dʌsk] *n* Abenddämmerung *f*

dust [dʌst] *n* Staub *m* ♦ *vt* abstauben; *(sprinkle)* bestäuben; **~bin** (*BRIT*) *n* Mülleimer *m*; **~er** *n* Staubtuch *nt*; **~ jacket** *n* Schutzumschlag *m*; **~man** (*BRIT*; *irreg*) *n* Müllmann *m*; **~y** *adj* staubig

Dutch [dʌtʃ] *adj* holländisch, niederländisch ♦ *n* (*LING*) Holländisch *nt*, Niederländisch *nt*; **the** ~ *npl* (*people*) die Holländer *pl*, die Niederländer *pl*; **to go** ~ getrennte Kasse machen; **~man/woman** (*irreg*) *n* Holländer(in) *m(f)*, Niederländer(in) *m(f)*

dutiful ['dju:tɪfʊl] *adj* pflichtbewußt

duty ['dju:tɪ] *n* Pflicht *f*; (*job*) Aufgabe *f*; (*tax*) Einfuhrzoll *m*; **on** ~ im Dienst; **~-free** *adj* zollfrei

duvet ['du:veɪ] (*BRIT*) *n* Daunendecke *f*

dwarf [dwɔ:f] (*pl* **dwarves**) *n* Zwerg *m* ♦ *vt* überragen

dwell [dwel] (*pt, pp* **dwelt**) *vi* wohnen; ~ **on** *vt fus* verweilen bei; **~ing** *n* Wohnung *f*

dwelt [dwelt] *pt, pp of* **dwell**

dwindle ['dwɪndl] *vi* schwinden

dye [daɪ] *n* Farbstoff *m* ♦ *vt* färben

dying ['daɪɪŋ] *adj* (*person*) sterbend; (*moments*) letzt

dyke [daɪk] (*BRIT*) *n* (*channel*) Kanal *m*; (*barrier*) Deich *m*, Damm *m*

dynamic [daɪ'næmɪk] *adj* dynamisch

dynamite ['daɪnəmaɪt] *n* Dynamit *nt*

dynamo ['daɪnəməʊ] *n* Dynamo *m*

dyslexia [dɪs'leksɪə] *n* Legasthenie *f*

E e

E [i:] *n* (*MUS*) E *nt*

each [i:tʃ] *adj* jeder/jede/jedes ♦ *pron* (ein) jeder/(eine) jede/(ein) jedes; ~ **other** einander; **they have two books** ~ sie haben je 2 Bücher

eager ['i:gə*] *adj* eifrig

eagle ['i:gl] *n* Adler *m*

ear [ɪə*] *n* Ohr *nt*; (*of corn*) Ähre *f*; **~ache** *n* Ohrenschmerzen *pl*; **~drum** *n* Trommelfell *nt*

earl [ɜ:l] *n* Graf *m*

early ['ɜ:lɪ] *adj, adv* früh; ~ **retirement** *n* vorzeitige Pensionierung

earmark ['ɪəmɑ:k] *vt* vorsehen

earn [ɜ:n] *vt* verdienen

earnest ['ɜ:nɪst] *adj* ernst; **in** ~ im Ernst

earnings ['ɜ:nɪŋz] *npl* Verdienst *m*

earphones ['ɪəfəʊnz] *npl* Kopfhörer *pl*

earring ['ɪərɪŋ] *n* Ohrring *m*

earshot ['ɪəʃɒt] *n* Hörweite *f*

earth [ɜ:θ] *n* Erde *f*; (*BRIT*: *ELEC*) Erdung *f* ♦ *vt* erden; **~enware** *n* Steingut *nt*

earthquake ['ɜ:θkweɪk] *n* Erdbeben *nt*

earthy ['ɜ:θɪ] *adj* roh; (*sensual*) sinnlich

earwig ['ɪəwɪg] *n* Ohrwurm *m*

ease [i:z] *n* (*simplicity*) Leichtigkeit *f*; (*social*) Ungezwungenheit *f* ♦ *vt* (*pain*) lindern; (*burden*) erleichtern; **at** ~ ungezwungen; (*MIL*) rührt euch!; ~ **off** *or* **up** *vi* nachlassen

easel ['i:zl] *n* Staffelei *f*

easily ['i:zɪlɪ] *adv* leicht

east [i:st] *n* Osten *m* ♦ *adj* östlich ♦ *adv* nach Osten

Easter ['i:stə*] *n* Ostern *nt*; ~ **egg** *n* Osterei *nt*

easterly ['i:stəlɪ] *adj* östlich, Ost-

eastern ['i:stən] *adj* östlich

eastward(s) ['i:stwəd(z)] *adv* ostwärts

easy ['i:zɪ] *adj* (*task*) einfach; (*life*) bequem; (*manner*) ungezwungen, natürlich ♦ *adv* leicht; ~ **chair** *n* Sessel *m*; **~-going** *adj* gelassen; (*lax*) lässig

eat [i:t] (*pt* **ate**, *pp* **eaten**) *vt* essen; (*animals*) fressen; (*destroy*) (zer)fressen ♦ *vi* essen; fressen; ~ **away** *vt* zerfressen; ~ **into** *vt fus* zerfressen

eaten ['i:tn] *pp of* **eat**

eau de Cologne [əʊdəkə'ləʊn] *n* Kölnisch Wasser *nt*

eaves [i:vz] *npl* Dachrand *m*

eavesdrop ['iːvzdrɒp] *vi* lauschen; **to ~ on sb** jdn belauschen

ebb [eb] *n* Ebbe *f* ♦ *vi* (*fig: also:* ~ *away*) (ab)ebben

ebony ['ebənɪ] *n* Ebenholz *nt*

ebullient [ɪ'bʌlɪənt] *adj* sprudelnd, temperamentvoll

EC *n abbr* (= *European Community*) EG *f*

eccentric [ɪk'sentrɪk] *adj* exzentrisch ♦ *n* Exzentriker(in) *m(f)*

ecclesiastical [ɪkliːzɪ'æstɪkəl] *adj* kirchlich

echo ['ekəʊ] (*pl* ~**es**) *n* Echo *nt* ♦ *vt* zurückwerfen; (*fig*) nachbeten ♦ *vi* widerhallen

eclipse [ɪ'klɪps] *n* Finsternis *f* ♦ *vt* verfinstern

ecology [ɪ'kɒlədʒɪ] *n* Ökologie *f*

economic [iːkə'nɒmɪk] *adj* wirtschaftlich; ~**al** *adj* wirtschaftlich; (*person*) sparsam; ~**s** *n* Volkswirtschaft *f*

economist [ɪ'kɒnəmɪst] *n* Volkswirt(schaftler) *m*

economize [ɪ'kɒnəmaɪz] *vi* sparen

economy [ɪ'kɒnəmɪ] *n* (*thrift*) Sparsamkeit *f*; (*of country*) Wirtschaft *f*

ecstasy ['ekstəsɪ] *n* Ekstase *f*; (*drug*) Ecstasy *nt*

ecstatic [eks'tætɪk] *adj* hingerissen

ECU ['eɪkjuː] *n abbr* (= *European Currency Unit*) ECU *m*

ecumenical [iːkjʊ'menɪkəl] *adj* ökumenisch

eczema ['eksɪmə] *n* Ekzem *nt*

edge [edʒ] *n* Rand *m*; (*of knife*) Schneide *f* ♦ *vt* (*SEWING*) einfassen; **on ~** (*fig*) = **edgy**; **to ~ away from** langsam abrücken von; ~**ways** *adv*: **he couldn't get a word in ~ways** er kam überhaupt nicht zu Wort

edgy ['edʒɪ] *adj* nervös

edible ['edɪbl] *adj* eßbar

edict ['iːdɪkt] *n* Erlaß *m*

edifice ['edɪfɪs] *n* Gebäude *nt*

Edinburgh ['edɪnbərə] *n* (*GEO*) Edinburgh *nt*

edit ['edɪt] *vt* redigieren; ~**ion** [ɪ'dɪʃən] *n* Ausgabe *f*; ~**or** *n* (*of newspaper*) Redakteur *m*; (*of book*) Lektor *m*

editorial [edɪ'tɔːrɪəl] *adj* Redaktions- ♦ *n* Leitartikel *m*

educate ['edjʊkeɪt] *vt* erziehen, (aus)bilden

education [edjʊ'keɪʃən] *n* (*teaching*) Unterricht *m*; (*system*) Schulwesen *nt*; (*schooling*) Erziehung *f*; Bildung *f*; ~**al** *adj* pädagogisch

eel [iːl] *n* Aal *m*

eerie ['ɪərɪ] *adj* unheimlich

effect [ɪ'fekt] *n* Wirkung *f* ♦ *vt* bewirken; ~**s** *npl* (*sound, visual*) Effekte *pl*; **in ~** in der Tat; **to take ~** (*law*) in Kraft treten; (*drug*) wirken; ~**ive** *adj* wirksam, effektiv; ~**ively** *adv* wirksam, effektiv

effeminate [ɪ'femɪnɪt] *adj* weibisch

effervescent [efə'vesnt] *adj* (*also fig*) sprudelnd

efficacy ['efɪkəsɪ] *n* Wirksamkeit *f*

efficiency [ɪ'fɪʃənsɪ] *n* Leistungsfähigkeit *f*

efficient [ɪ'fɪʃənt] *adj* tüchtig; (*TECH*) leistungsfähig; (*method*) wirksam

effigy ['efɪdʒɪ] *n* Abbild *nt*

effort ['efət] *n* Anstrengung *f*; ~**less** *adj* mühelos

effrontery [ɪ'frʌntərɪ] *n* Unverfrorenheit *f*

effusive [ɪ'fjuːsɪv] *adj* überschwenglich

e.g. *adv abbr* (= *exempli gratia*) z.B.

egalitarian [ɪgælɪ'tɛərɪən] *adj* Gleichheits-, egalitär

egg [eg] *n* Ei *nt*; ~ **on** *vt* anstacheln; ~**cup** *n* Eierbecher *m*; ~**plant** *n* (*esp US*) Aubergine *f*; ~**shell** *n* Eierschale *f*

ego ['iːgəʊ] *n* Ich *nt*, Selbst *nt*

egotism ['egəʊtɪzəm] *n* Ichbezogenheit *f*

egotist ['egəʊtɪst] *n* Egozentriker *m*

Egypt ['iːdʒɪpt] *n* Ägypten *nt*; ~**ian** [ɪ'dʒɪpʃən] *adj* ägyptisch ♦ *n* Ägypter(in) *m(f)*

eiderdown ['aɪdədaʊn] *n* Daunendecke *f*

eight [eɪt] *num* acht; ~**een** *num* achtzehn; ~**h** [eɪtθ] *adj* achte(r, s) ♦ *n* Achtel *nt*; ~**y** *num* achtzig

Eire ['ɛərə] *n* Irland *nt*

either ['aɪðə*] *conj*: ~ ... **or** entweder ... oder ♦ *pron*: ~ **of the two** eine(r, s) von beiden ♦ *adj*: **on** ~ **side** auf beiden Seiten

♦ *adv*: **I don't ~** ich auch nicht; **I don't want ~** ich will keins von beiden
eject [ɪ'dʒekt] *vt* ausstoßen, vertreiben
eke [iːk] *vt*: **to ~ out** strecken
elaborate [*adj* ɪ'læbərɪt, *vb* ɪ'læbəreɪt] *adj* sorgfältig ausgearbeitet, ausführlich ♦ *vt* sorgfältig ausarbeiten ♦ *vi* ausführlich darstellen
elapse [ɪ'læps] *vi* vergehen
elastic [ɪ'læstɪk] *n* Gummiband *nt* ♦ *adj* elastisch; **~ band** (*BRIT*) *n* Gummiband *nt*
elated [ɪ'leɪtɪd] *adj* froh
elation [ɪ'leɪʃən] *n* gehobene Stimmung *f*
elbow ['elbəʊ] *n* Ellbogen *m*
elder ['eldə*] *adj* älter ♦ *n* Ältere(r) *mf*; **~ly** *adj* ältere(r, s) ♦ *npl*: **the ~ly** die Älteren *pl*
eldest ['eldɪst] *adj* älteste(r, s) ♦ *n* Älteste(r) *mf*
elect [ɪ'lekt] *vt* wählen ♦ *adj* zukünftig; **~ion** [ɪ'lekʃən] *n* Wahl *f*; **~ioneering** [ɪlekʃə'nɪərɪŋ] *n* Wahlpropaganda *f*; **~or** *n* Wähler *m*; **~oral** *adj* Wahl-; **~orate** *n* Wähler *pl*, Wählerschaft *f*
electric [ɪ'lektrɪk] *adj* elektrisch, Elektro-; **~al** *adj* elektrisch; **~ blanket** *n* Heizdecke *f*; **~ chair** *n* elektrische(r) Stuhl *m*; **~ fire** *n* elektrische(r) Heizofen *m*
electrician [ɪlek'trɪʃən] *n* Elektriker *m*
electricity [ɪlek'trɪsɪtɪ] *n* Elektrizität *f*
electrify [ɪ'lektrɪfaɪ] *vt* elektrifizieren; (*fig*) elektrisieren
electrocute [ɪ'lektrəʊkjuːt] *vt* durch elektrischen Strom töten
electronic [ɪlek'trɒnɪk] *adj* elektronisch, Elektronen-; **~ mail** *n* elektronische(r) Briefkasten *m*; **~s** *n* Elektronik *f*
elegance ['elɪgəns] *n* Eleganz *f*
elegant ['elɪgənt] *adj* elegant
element ['elɪmənt] *n* Element *nt*; **~ary** [elɪ'mentərɪ] *adj* einfach; (*primary*) Grund-
elephant ['elɪfənt] *n* Elefant *m*
elevate ['elɪveɪt] *vt* emporheben
elevation [elɪ'veɪʃən] *n* (*height*) Erhebung *f*; (*ARCHIT*) (Quer)schnitt *m*
elevator ['elɪveɪtə*] (*US*) *n* Fahrstuhl *m*, Aufzug *m*

eleven [ɪ'levn] *num* elf; **~ses** (*BRIT*) *npl* ≈ zweite(s) Frühstück *nt*; **~th** *adj* elfte(r, s)
elf [elf] (*pl* **elves**) *n* Elfe *f*
elicit [ɪ'lɪsɪt] *vt* herausbekommen
eligible ['elɪdʒəbl] *adj* wählbar; **to be ~ for a pension** pensionsberechtigt sein
eliminate [ɪ'lɪmɪneɪt] *vt* ausschalten
elimination [ɪlɪmɪ'neɪʃən] *n* Ausschaltung *f*
elite [eɪ'liːt] *n* Elite *f*
elm [elm] *n* Ulme *f*
elocution [elə'kjuːʃən] *n* Sprecherziehung *f*
elongated ['iːlɒŋgeɪtɪd] *adj* verlängert
elope [ɪ'ləʊp] *vi* entlaufen
eloquence ['eləkwəns] *n* Beredsamkeit *f*
eloquent ['eləkwənt] *adj* redegewandt
else [els] *adv* sonst; **who ~?** wer sonst?; **somebody ~** jemand anders; **or ~** sonst; **~where** *adv* anderswo, woanders
elucidate [ɪ'luːsɪdeɪt] *vt* erläutern
elude [ɪ'luːd] *vt* entgehen +*dat*
elusive [ɪ'luːsɪv] *adj* schwer faßbar
elves [elvz] *npl* of **elf**
emaciated [ɪ'meɪsɪeɪtɪd] *adj* abgezehrt
emanate ['eməneɪt] *vi*: **to ~ from** ausströmen aus
emancipate [ɪ'mænsɪpeɪt] *vt* emanzipieren; (*slave*) freilassen
emancipation [ɪmænsɪ'peɪʃən] *n* Emanzipation *f*; Freilassung *f*
embankment [ɪm'bæŋkmənt] *n* (*of river*) Uferböschung *f*; (*of road*) Straßendamm *m*
embargo [ɪm'bɑːgəʊ] (*pl* **~es**) *n* Embargo *nt*
embark [ɪm'bɑːk] *vi* sich einschiffen; **~ on** *vt fus* unternehmen; **~ation** [embɑː'keɪʃən] *n* Einschiffung *f*
embarrass [ɪm'bærəs] *vt* in Verlegenheit bringen; **~ed** *adj* verlegen; **~ing** *adj* peinlich; **~ment** *n* Verlegenheit *f*
embassy ['embəsɪ] *n* Botschaft *f*
embed [ɪm'bed] *vt* einbetten
embellish [ɪm'belɪʃ] *vt* verschönern
embers ['embəz] *npl* Glut(asche) *f*
embezzle [ɪm'bezl] *vt* unterschlagen; **~ment** *n* Unterschlagung *f*
embitter [ɪm'bɪtə*] *vt* verbittern

embody [ɪm'bɒdɪ] *vt* (*ideas*) verkörpern; (*new features*) (in sich) vereinigen

embossed [ɪm'bɒst] *adj* geprägt

embrace [ɪm'breɪs] *vt* umarmen; (*include*) einschließen ♦ *vi* sich umarmen ♦ *n* Umarmung *f*

embroider [ɪm'brɔɪdə*] *vt* (be)sticken; (*story*) ausschmücken; **~y** *n* Stickerei *f*

emerald ['emərəld] *n* Smaragd *m*

emerge [ɪ'mɜːdʒ] *vi* auftauchen; (*truth*) herauskommen

emergence [ɪ'mɜːdʒəns] *n* Erscheinen *nt*

emergency [ɪ'mɜːdʒənsɪ] *n* Notfall *m*; ~ **cord** (*US*) *n* Notbremse *f*; ~ **exit** *n* Notausgang *m*; ~ **landing** *n* Notlandung *f*; ~ **services** *npl* Notdienste *pl*

emery board ['emərɪ-] *n* Papiernagelfeile *f*

emetic [ɪ'metɪk] *n* Brechmittel *nt*

emigrant ['emɪgrənt] *n* Auswanderer *m*

emigrate ['emɪgreɪt] *vi* auswandern

emigration [emɪ'greɪʃən] *n* Auswanderung *f*

eminence ['emɪnəns] *n* hohe(r) Rang *m*

eminent ['emɪnənt] *adj* bedeutend

emission [ɪ'mɪʃən] *n* Ausströmen *nt*; ~**s** *npl* Emissionen *fpl*

emit [ɪ'mɪt] *vt* von sich *dat* geben

emotion [ɪ'məʊʃən] *n* Emotion *f*, Gefühl *nt*; ~**al** *adj* (*person*) emotional; (*scene*) ergreifend

emotive [ɪ'məʊtɪv] *adj* gefühlsbetont

emperor ['empərə*] *n* Kaiser *m*

emphases ['emfəsiːz] *npl of* **emphasis**

emphasis ['emfəsɪs] *n* (*LING*) Betonung *f*; (*fig*) Nachdruck *m*

emphasize ['emfəsaɪz] *vt* betonen

emphatic [ɪm'fætɪk] *adj* nachdrücklich; ~**ally** [ɪm'fætɪkəlɪ] *adv* nachdrücklich

empire ['empaɪə*] *n* Reich *nt*

empirical [em'pɪrɪkəl] *adj* empirisch

employ [ɪm'plɔɪ] *vt* (*hire*) anstellen; (*use*) verwenden; **~ee** [emplɔɪ'iː] *n* Angestellte(r) *mf*; **~er** *n* Arbeitgeber(in) *m(f)*; **~ment** *n* Beschäftigung *f*; **~ment agency** *n* Stellenvermittlung *f*

empower [ɪm'paʊə*] *vt*: **to ~ sb to do sth** jdn ermächtigen, etw zu tun

empress ['emprɪs] *n* Kaiserin *f*

emptiness ['emptɪnɪs] *n* Leere *f*

empty ['emptɪ] *adj* leer ♦ *n* (*bottle*) Leergut *nt* ♦ *vt* (*contents*) leeren; (*container*) ausleeren ♦ *vi* (*water*) abfließen; (*river*) münden; (*house*) sich leeren; **~-handed** *adj* mit leeren Händen

emulate ['emjʊleɪt] *vt* nacheifern +*dat*

emulsion [ɪ'mʌlʃən] *n* Emulsion *f*

enable [ɪ'neɪbl] *vt*: **to ~ sb to do sth** es jdm ermöglichen, etw zu tun

enact [ɪn'ækt] *vt* (*law*) erlassen; (*play*) aufführen; (*role*) spielen

enamel [ɪ'næməl] *n* Email *nt*; (*of teeth*) (Zahn)schmelz *m*

encased [ɪn'keɪst] *adj*: ~ **in** (*enclosed*) eingeschlossen in +*dat*; (*covered*) verkleidet mit

enchant [ɪn'tʃɑːnt] *vt* bezaubern; ~**ing** *adj* entzückend

encircle [ɪn'sɜːkl] *vt* umringen

encl. *abbr* (= *enclosed*) Anl.

enclose [ɪn'kləʊz] *vt* einschließen; **to ~ sth** (**in** *or* **with a letter**) etw (einem Brief) beilegen; **~d** (**in** *letter*) beiliegend, anbei

enclosure [ɪn'kləʊʒə*] *n* Einfriedung *f*; (*in letter*) Anlage *f*

encompass [ɪn'kʌmpəs] *vt* (*include*) umfassen

encore ['ɒŋkɔː*] *n* Zugabe *f*

encounter [ɪn'kaʊntə*] *n* Begegnung *f*; (*MIL*) Zusammenstoß *m* ♦ *vt* treffen; (*resistance*) stoßen auf +*acc*

encourage [ɪn'kʌrɪdʒ] *vt* ermutigen; ~**ment** *n* Ermutigung *f*, Förderung *f*

encouraging [ɪn'kʌrɪdʒɪŋ] *adj* ermutigend, vielversprechend

encroach [ɪn'krəʊtʃ] *vi*: **to ~ (up)on** eindringen in +*acc*; (*time*) in Anspruch nehmen

encrusted [ɪn'krʌstəd] *adj*: ~ **with** besetzt mit

encumber [ɪn'kʌmbə*] *vt*: **to be ~ed with** (*parcels*) beladen sein mit; (*debts*) belastet sein mit

encyclop(a)edia [ensaɪkləʊ'piːdɪə] *n* Konversationslexikon *nt*

end [end] *n* Ende *nt*, Schluß *m*; (*purpose*) Zweck *m* ♦ *vt* (*also*: **bring to an ~**, **put an**

~ *to*) beenden ♦ *vi* zu Ende gehen; **in the ~** zum Schluß; **on ~** (*object*) hochkant; **to stand on ~** (*hair*) zu Berge stehen; **for hours on ~** stundenlang; **~ up** *vi* landen
endanger [ɪn'deɪndʒə*] *vt* gefährden
endearing [ɪn'dɪərɪŋ] *adj* gewinnend
endeavour [ɪn'devə*] (*US* **endeavor**) *n* Bestrebung *f* ♦ *vi* sich bemühen
ending ['endɪŋ] *n* Ende *nt*
endive ['endaɪv] *n* Endivie *f*
endless ['endlɪs] *adj* endlos
endorse [ɪn'dɔːs] *vt* unterzeichnen; (*approve*) unterstützen; **~ment** *n* (*on licence*) Eintrag *m*
endow [ɪn'dau] *vt:* **to ~ sb with sth** jdm etw verleihen; (*with money*) jdm etw stiften
endurance [ɪn'djuərəns] *n* Ausdauer *f*
endure [ɪn'djuə*] *vt* ertragen ♦ *vi* (*last*) (fort)dauern
enemy ['enɪmɪ] *n* Feind *m* ♦ *adj* feindlich
energetic [enə'dʒetɪk] *adj* tatkräftig
energy ['enədʒɪ] *n* Energie *f*
enforce [ɪn'fɔːs] *vt* durchsetzen
engage [ɪn'geɪdʒ] *vt* (*employ*) einstellen; (*in conversation*) verwickeln; (*TECH*) einschalten ♦ *vi* ineinandergreifen; (*clutch*) fassen; **to ~ in** sich beteiligen an +*dat*; **~d** *adj* verlobt; (*BRIT: TEL, toilet*) besetzt; (*: busy*) beschäftigt; **to get ~d** sich verloben; **~d tone** (*BRIT*) *n* (*TEL*) Besetztzeichen *nt*; **~ment** *n* (*appointment*) Verabredung *f*; (*to marry*) Verlobung *f*; (*MIL*) Gefecht *nt*; **~ment ring** *n* Verlobungsring *m*
engaging [ɪn'geɪdʒɪŋ] *adj* gewinnend
engender [ɪn'dʒendə*] *vt* hervorrufen
engine ['endʒɪn] *n* (*AUT*) Motor *m*; (*RAIL*) Lokomotive *f*; **~ driver** *n* Lok(omotiv)führer(in) *m(f)*
engineer [endʒɪ'nɪə*] *n* Ingenieur *m*; (*US: RAIL*) Lok(omotiv)führer(in) *m(f)*; **~ing** [endʒɪ'nɪərɪŋ] *n* Technik *f*
England ['ɪŋglənd] *n* England *nt*
English ['ɪŋglɪʃ] *adj* englisch ♦ *n* (*LING*) Englisch *nt*; **the ~** *npl* (*people*) die Engländer *pl*; **the ~ Channel** *n* der Ärmelkanal *m*; **~man/woman** (*irreg*) *n* Engländer(in) *m(f)*

engraving [ɪn'greɪvɪŋ] *n* Stich *m*
engrossed [ɪn'grəust] *adj* vertieft
engulf [ɪn'gʌlf] *vt* verschlingen
enhance [ɪn'hɑːns] *vt* steigern, heben
enigma [ɪ'nɪgmə] *n* Rätsel *nt*; **~tic** [enɪg'mætɪk] *adj* rätselhaft
enjoy [ɪn'dʒɔɪ] *vt* genießen; (*privilege*) besitzen; **to ~ o.s.** sich amüsieren; **~able** *adj* erfreulich; **~ment** *n* Genuß *m*, Freude *f*
enlarge [ɪn'lɑːdʒ] *vt* erweitern; (*PHOT*) vergrößern ♦ *vi:* **to ~ on sth** etw weiter ausführen; **~ment** *n* Vergrößerung *f*
enlighten [ɪn'laɪtn] *vt* aufklären; **~ment** *n:* **the E~ment** (*HIST*) die Aufklärung
enlist [ɪn'lɪst] *vt* gewinnen ♦ *vi* (*MIL*) sich melden
enmity ['enmɪtɪ] *n* Feindschaft *f*
enormity [ɪ'nɔːmɪtɪ] *n* Ungeheuerlichkeit *f*
enormous [ɪ'nɔːməs] *adj* ungeheuer
enough [ɪ'nʌf] *adj, adv* genug; **funnily ~** komischerweise
enquire [ɪn'kwaɪə*] *vt, vi* = **inquire**
enrage [ɪn'reɪdʒ] *vt* wütend machen
enrich [ɪn'rɪtʃ] *vt* bereichern
enrol [ɪn'rəul] *vt* einschreiben ♦ *vi* (*register*) sich anmelden; **~ment** *n* (*for course*) Anmeldung *f*
en route [ɑːn'ruːt] *adv* unterwegs
ensign ['ensaɪn, 'ensən] *n* (*NAUT*) Flagge *f*; (*MIL*) Fähnrich *m*
enslave [ɪn'sleɪv] *vt* versklaven
ensue [ɪn'sjuː] *vi* folgen, sich ergeben
ensure [ɪn'ʃuə*] *vt* garantieren
entail [ɪn'teɪl] *vt* mit sich bringen
entangle [ɪn'tæŋgl] *vt* verwirren, verstricken; **~d** *adj:* **to become ~d (in)** (*in net, rope etc*) sich verfangen (in +*dat*)
enter ['entə*] *vt* eintreten in +*dat*, betreten; (*club*) beitreten +*dat*; (*in book*) eintragen ♦ *vi* hereinkommen, hineingehen; **~ for** *vt fus* sich beteiligen an +*dat*; **~ into** *vt fus* (*agreement*) eingehen; (*plans*) eine Rolle spielen bei; **~ (up)on** *vt fus* beginnen
enterprise ['entəpraɪz] *n* (*in person*) Initiative *f*; (*COMM*) Unternehmen *nt*
enterprising ['entəpraɪzɪŋ] *adj*

unternehmungslustig
entertain [entə'teɪn] vt (guest) bewirten; (amuse) unterhalten; **~er** n Unterhaltungskünstler(in) m(f); **~ing** adj unterhaltsam; **~ment** n Unterhaltung f
enthralled [ɪn'θrɔːld] adj gefesselt
enthusiasm [ɪn'θuːzɪæzəm] n Begeisterung f
enthusiast [ɪn'θuːzɪæst] n Enthusiast m; **~ic** [ɪnθuːzɪ'æstɪk] adj begeistert
entice [ɪn'taɪs] vt verleiten, locken
entire [ɪn'taɪə*] adj ganz; **~ly** adv ganz, völlig; **~ty** [ɪn'taɪərətɪ] n: **in its ~ty** in seiner Gesamtheit
entitle [ɪn'taɪtl] vt (allow) berechtigen; (name) betiteln; **~d** adj (book) mit dem Titel; **to be ~d to sth** das Recht auf etw acc haben; **to be ~d to do sth** das Recht haben, etw zu tun
entity ['entɪtɪ] n Ding nt, Wesen nt
entourage [ɒntuː'rɑːʒ] n Gefolge nt
entrails ['entreɪlz] npl Eingeweide pl
entrance [n 'entrəns, vb ɪn'trɑːns] n Eingang m; (entering) Eintritt m ♦ vt hinreißen; **~ examination** n Aufnahmeprüfung f; **~ fee** n Eintrittsgeld nt; **~ ramp** (US) n (AUT) Einfahrt f
entrant ['entrənt] n (for exam) Kandidat m; (in race) Teilnehmer m
entreat [ɪn'triːt] vt anflehen
entrenched [ɪn'trentʃt] adj (fig) verwurzelt
entrepreneur [ɒntrəprə'nɜː*] n Unternehmer(in) m(f)
entrust [ɪn'trʌst] vt: **to ~ sb with sth** or **sth to sb** jdm etw anvertrauen
entry ['entrɪ] n Eingang m; (THEAT) Auftritt m; (in account) Eintragung f; (in dictionary) Eintrag m; **"no ~"** „Eintritt verboten"; (for cars) „Einfahrt verboten"; **~ form** n Anmeldeformular nt; **~ phone** n Sprechanlage f
enumerate [ɪ'njuːməreɪt] vt aufzählen
enunciate [ɪ'nʌnsɪeɪt] vt aussprechen
envelop [ɪn'veləp] vt einhüllen
envelope ['envələʊp] n Umschlag m
enviable ['envɪəbl] adj beneidenswert
envious ['envɪəs] adj neidisch
environment [ɪn'vaɪərənmənt] n

Umgebung f; (ECOLOGY) Umwelt f; **~al** [ɪnvaɪərən'mentl] adj Umwelt-; **~-friendly** adj umweltfreundlich
envisage [ɪn'vɪzɪdʒ] vt sich dat vorstellen
envoy ['envɔɪ] n Gesandte(r) mf
envy ['envɪ] n Neid m ♦ vt: **to ~ sb sth** jdn um etw beneiden
enzyme ['enzaɪm] n Enzym nt
ephemeral [ɪ'femərəl] adj flüchtig
epic ['epɪk] n Epos nt ♦ adj episch
epidemic [epɪ'demɪk] n Epidemie f
epilepsy ['epɪlepsɪ] n Epilepsie f
epileptic [epɪ'leptɪk] adj epileptisch ♦ n Epileptiker(in) m(f)
episode ['epɪsəʊd] n (incident) Vorfall m; (story) Episode f
epitaph ['epɪtɑːf] n Grabinschrift f
epithet ['epɪθet] n Beiname m
epitome [ɪ'pɪtəmɪ] n Inbegriff m
epitomize [ɪ'pɪtəmaɪz] vt verkörpern
equable ['ekwəbl] adj ausgeglichen
equal ['iːkwl] adj gleich ♦ n Gleichgestellte(r) mf ♦ vt gleichkommen +dat; **~ to the task** der Aufgabe gewachsen; **~ity** [ɪ'kwɒlɪtɪ] n Gleichheit f; (~ rights) Gleichberechtigung f; **~ize** vt gleichmachen ♦ vi (SPORT) ausgleichen; **~izer** n (SPORT) Ausgleich(streffer) m; **~ly** adv gleich
equanimity [ekwə'nɪmɪtɪ] n Gleichmut m
equate [ɪ'kweɪt] vt gleichsetzen
equation [ɪ'kweɪʒən] n Gleichung f
equator [ɪ'kweɪtə*] n Äquator m
equestrian [ɪ'kwestrɪən] adj Reit-
equilibrium [iːkwɪ'lɪbrɪəm] n Gleichgewicht nt
equinox ['iːkwɪnɒks] n Tagundnachtgleiche f
equip [ɪ'kwɪp] vt ausrüsten; **~ment** n Ausrüstung f; (TECH) Gerät nt
equitable ['ekwɪtəbl] adj gerecht, billig
equities ['ekwɪtɪz] (BRIT) npl (FIN) Stammaktien pl
equivalent [ɪ'kwɪvələnt] adj gleichwertig, entsprechend ♦ n Äquivalent nt; (in money) Gegenwert m; **~ to** gleichwertig +dat, entsprechend +dat

equivocal [ɪ'kwɪvəkəl] *adj* zweideutig

era ['ɪərə] *n* Epoche *f*, Ära *f*

eradicate [ɪ'rædɪkeɪt] *vt* ausrotten

erase [ɪ'reɪz] *vt* ausradieren; *(tape)* löschen; **~r** *n* Radiergummi *m*

erect [ɪ'rekt] *adj* aufrecht ♦ *vt* errichten

erection [ɪ'rekʃən] *n* Errichtung *f*; *(ANAT)* Erektion *f*

ergonomics [ɜːgə'nɒmɪks] *n* Ergonomie *f*, Ergonomik *f*

ERM *n abbr* (= *Exchange Rate Mechanism*) Wechselkursmechanismus *m*

erode [ɪ'rəʊd] *vt* zerfressen; *(land)* auswaschen

erotic [ɪ'rɒtɪk] *adj* erotisch; **~ism** [ɪ'rɒtɪsɪzəm] *n* Erotik *f*

err [ɜː*] *vi* sich irren

errand ['erənd] *n* Besorgung *f*

erratic [ɪ'rætɪk] *adj* unberechenbar

erroneous [ɪ'rəʊnɪəs] *adj* irrig

error ['erə*] *n* Fehler *m*

erudite ['erʊdaɪt] *adj* gelehrt

erupt [ɪ'rʌpt] *vi* ausbrechen; **~ion** [ɪ'rʌpʃən] *n* Ausbruch *m*

escalate ['eskəleɪt] *vi* sich steigern

escalator ['eskəleɪtə*] *n* Rolltreppe *f*

escape [ɪs'keɪp] *n* Flucht *f*; *(of gas)* Entweichen *nt* ♦ *vi* entkommen; *(prisoners)* fliehen; *(leak)* entweichen ♦ *vt* entkommen +*dat*

escapism [ɪs'keɪpɪzəm] *n* Flucht *f* (vor der Wirklichkeit)

escort [*n* 'eskɔːt, *vb* ɪs'kɔːt] *n* (*person accompanying*) Begleiter *m*; *(guard)* Eskorte *f* ♦ *vt* (*lady*) begleiten; *(MIL)* eskortieren

especially [ɪs'peʃəlɪ] *adv* besonders

espionage ['espɪɑːnɑːʒ] *n* Spionage *f*

esplanade ['espləneɪd] *n* Promenade *f*

espouse [ɪ'spaʊz] *vt* Partei ergreifen für

Esquire [ɪs'kwaɪə*] *n*: **J. Brown ~** Herrn J. Brown

essay ['eseɪ] *n* Aufsatz *m*; *(LITER)* Essay *m*

essence ['esəns] *n* (*quality*) Wesen *nt*; *(extract)* Essenz *f*

essential [ɪ'senʃəl] *adj* (*necessary*) unentbehrlich; *(basic)* wesentlich ♦ *n* Allernötigste(s) *nt*; **~ly** *adv* eigentlich

establish [ɪs'tæblɪʃ] *vt* (*set up*) gründen;

(prove) nachweisen; **~ed** *adj* anerkannt; *(belief, laws etc)* herrschend; **~ment** *n* *(setting up)* Einrichtung *f*; **the E~ment** das Establishment

estate [ɪs'teɪt] *n* Gut *nt*; *(BRIT: housing ~)* Siedlung *f*; *(will)* Nachlaß *m*; **~ agent** *(BRIT)* *n* Grundstücksmakler *m*; **~ car** *(BRIT)* *n* Kombiwagen *m*

esteem [ɪs'tiːm] *n* Wertschätzung *f*

esthetic [ɪs'θetɪk] *(US)* *adj* = **aesthetic**

estimate [*n* 'estɪmət, *vb* 'estɪmeɪt] *n* Schätzung *f*; *(of price)* (Kosten)voranschlag *m* ♦ *vt* schätzen

estimation [estɪ'meɪʃən] *n* Einschätzung *f*; *(esteem)* Achtung *f*

estranged [ɪ'streɪndʒd] *adj* entfremdet

estuary ['estjʊərɪ] *n* Mündung *f*

etc *abbr* (= *et cetera*) usw

etching ['etʃɪŋ] *n* Kupferstich *m*

eternal [ɪ'tɜːnl] *adj* ewig

eternity [ɪ'tɜːnɪtɪ] *n* Ewigkeit *f*

ether ['iːθə*] *n* Äther *m*

ethical ['eθɪkəl] *adj* ethisch

ethics ['eθɪks] *n* Ethik *f* ♦ *npl* Moral *f*

Ethiopia [iːθɪ'əʊpɪə] *n* Äthiopien *nt*

ethnic ['eθnɪk] *adj* Volks-, ethnisch

ethos ['iːθɒs] *n* Gesinnung *f*

etiquette ['etɪket] *n* Etikette *f*

EU *abbr* (= *European Union*) EU *f*

euphemism ['juːfɪmɪzəm] *n* Euphemismus *m*

Eurocheque ['jʊərəʊ'tʃek] *n* Euroscheck *m*

Europe ['jʊərəp] *n* Europa *nt*; **~an** [jʊərə'piːən] *adj* europäisch ♦ *n* Europäer(in) *m(f)*

euro-sceptic ['jʊərəʊ'skeptɪk] *n* Kritiker(in) *m(f)* der Europäischen Gemeinschaft

evacuate [ɪ'vækjʊeɪt] *vt* (*place*) räumen; *(people)* evakuieren

evacuation [ɪvækjʊ'eɪʃən] *n* Räumung *f*; Evakuierung *f*

evade [ɪ'veɪd] *vt* (*escape*) entkommen +*dat*; *(avoid)* meiden; *(duty)* sich entziehen +*dat*

evaluate [ɪ'væljʊeɪt] *vt* bewerten; *(information)* auswerten

evaporate [ɪ'væpəreɪt] *vi* verdampfen ♦ *vt* verdampfen lassen; **~d milk** *n*

Kondensmilch f

evasion [ɪ'veɪʒən] n Umgehung f

evasive [ɪ'veɪzɪv] adj ausweichend

eve [iːv] n: on the ~ of am Vorabend +gen

even ['iːvən] adj eben; gleichmäßig; (score etc) unentschieden; (number) gerade ♦ adv: ~ you sogar du; to get ~ with sb jdm heimzahlen; ~ if selbst wenn; ~ so dennoch; ~ though obwohl; ~ more sogar noch mehr; ~ out vi sich ausgleichen

evening ['iːvnɪŋ] n Abend m; in the ~ abends, am Abend; ~ class n Abendschule f, ~ dress n (man's) Gesellschaftsanzug m; (woman's) Abendkleid nt

event [ɪ'vent] n (happening) Ereignis nt; (SPORT) Disziplin f; in the ~ of im Falle +gen; ~ful adj ereignisreich

eventual [ɪ'ventʃuəl] adj (final) schließlich; ~ity [ɪventʃu'ælɪtɪ] n Möglichkeit f; ~ly adv (at last) am Ende; (given time) schließlich

ever ['evə*] adv (always) immer; (at any time) je(mals) ♦ conj seit; ~ since seitdem; have you ~ seen it? haben Sie es je gesehen?; ~green n Immergrün nt; ~lasting adj immerwährend

every ['evrɪ] adj jede(r, s); ~ other/third day jeden zweiten/dritten Tag; ~ one of them alle; I have ~ confidence in him ich habe uneingeschränktes Vertrauen in ihn; we wish you ~ success wir wünschen Ihnen viel Erfolg; he's ~ bit as clever as his brother er ist genauso klug wie sein Bruder; ~ now and then ab und zu; ~body pron = everyone; ~day adj (daily) täglich; (commonplace) alltäglich, Alltags-; ~one pron jeder, alle pl; ~thing pron alles; ~where adv überall(hin); (wherever) wohin; ~where you go wohin du auch gehst

evict [ɪ'vɪkt] vt ausweisen; ~ion [ɪ'vɪkʃən] n Ausweisung f

evidence ['evɪdəns] n (sign) Spur f; (proof) Beweis m; (testimony) Aussage f

evident ['evɪdənt] adj augenscheinlich; ~ly adv offensichtlich

evil ['iːvl] adj böse ♦ n Böse nt

evocative [ɪ'vɒkətɪv] adj: to be ~ of sth an etw acc erinnern

evoke [ɪ'vəʊk] vt hervorrufen

evolution [iːvə'luːʃən] n Entwicklung f; (of life) Evolution f

evolve [ɪ'vɒlv] vt entwickeln ♦ vi sich entwickeln

ewe [juː] n Mutterschaf nt

ex- [eks] prefix Ex-, Alt-, ehemalig

exacerbate [ek'sæsəbeɪt] vt verschlimmern

exact [ɪg'zækt] adj genau ♦ vt (demand) verlangen; ~ing adj anspruchsvoll; ~ly adv genau

exaggerate [ɪg'zædʒəreɪt] vt, vi übertreiben

exaggeration [ɪgzædʒə'reɪʃən] n Übertreibung f

exalted [ɪg'zɔːltɪd] adj (position, style) hoch; (person) exaltiert

exam [ɪg'zæm] n abbr (SCH) = examination

examination [ɪgzæmɪ'neɪʃən] n Untersuchung f; (SCH) Prüfung f, Examen nt; (customs) Kontrolle f

examine [ɪg'zæmɪn] vt untersuchen; (SCH) prüfen; (consider) erwägen; ~r n Prüfer m

example [ɪg'zɑːmpl] n Beispiel nt; for ~ zum Beispiel

exasperate [ɪg'zɑːspəreɪt] vt zum Verzweifeln bringen

exasperating [ɪg'zɑːspəreɪtɪŋ] adj ärgerlich, zum Verzweifeln bringend

exasperation [ɪgzɑːspə'reɪʃən] n Verzweiflung f

excavate ['ekskəveɪt] vt ausgraben

excavation [ekskə'veɪʃən] n Ausgrabung f

exceed [ɪk'siːd] vt überschreiten; (hopes) übertreffen

exceedingly [ɪk'siːdɪŋlɪ] adv (enormously: stupid, rich, pleasant) äußerst

excel [ɪk'sel] vi sich auszeichnen

excellence ['eksələns] n Vortrefflichkeit f

excellency ['eksələnsɪ] n: His E~ Seine Exzellenz f

excellent ['eksələnt] adj ausgezeichnet

except [ɪk'sept] *prep* (*also*: ~ *for*, ~*ing*) außer +*dat* ♦ *vt* ausnehmen; ~**ion** [ɪk'sepʃən] *n* Ausnahme *f*; **to take ~ion to** Anstoß nehmen an +*dat*; ~**ional** [ɪk'sepʃənl] *adj* außergewöhnlich

excerpt ['eksɜːpt] *n* Auszug *m*

excess [ek'ses] *n* Übermaß *nt*; **an ~ of** ein Übermaß an +*dat*; ~ **baggage** *n* Mehrgepäck *nt*; ~ **fare** *n* Nachlösegebühr *f*; ~**ive** *adj* übermäßig

exchange [ɪks'tʃeɪndʒ] *n* Austausch *m*; (*also*: *telephone* ~) Zentrale *f* ♦ *vt* (*goods*) tauschen; (*greetings*) austauschen; (*money, blows*) wechseln; ~ **rate** *n* Wechselkurs *m*

Exchequer [ɪks'tʃekə*] (*BRIT*) *n*: **the ~** das Schatzamt

excise [*n* 'eksaɪz, *vb* ɪk'saɪz] *n* Verbrauchssteuer *f* ♦ *vt* (*MED*) herausschneiden

excite [ɪk'saɪt] *vt* erregen; **to get ~d** sich aufregen; ~**ment** *n* Aufregung *f*

exciting [ɪk'saɪtɪŋ] *adj* spannend

exclaim [ɪks'kleɪm] *vi* ausrufen

exclamation [eksklə'meɪʃən] *n* Ausruf *m*; ~ **mark** *n* Ausrufezeichen *nt*

exclude [ɪks'kluːd] *vt* ausschließen

exclusion [ɪks'kluːʒən] *n* Ausschluß *m*

exclusive [ɪks'kluːsɪv] *adj* (*select*) exklusiv; (*sole*) ausschließlich, Allein-; ~ **of** exklusive +*gen*; ~**ly** *adv* nur, ausschließlich

excommunicate [ekskə'mjuːnɪkeɪt] *vt* exkommunizieren

excrement ['ekskrɪmənt] *n* Kot *m*

excruciating [ɪks'kruːʃɪeɪtɪŋ] *adj* qualvoll

excursion [ɪks'kɜːʃən] *n* Ausflug *m*

excusable [ɪks'kjuːzəbl] *adj* entschuldbar

excuse [*n* ɪks'kjuːs, *vb* ɪks'kjuːz] *n* Entschuldigung *f* ♦ *vt* entschuldigen; ~ **me!** entschuldigen Sie!

ex-directory ['eksdɪ'rektərɪ] (*BRIT*) *adj*: **to be ~** nicht im Telefonbuch stehen

execute ['eksɪkjuːt] *vt* (*carry out*) ausführen; (*kill*) hinrichten

execution [eksɪ'kjuːʃən] *n* Ausführung *f*; (*killing*) Hinrichtung *f*; ~**er** *n* Scharfrichter *m*

executive [ɪg'zekjʊtɪv] *n* (*COMM*) Geschäftsführer *m*; (*POL*) Exekutive *f* ♦ *adj* Exekutiv-, ausführend

executor [ɪg'zekjʊtə*] *n* Testamentsvollstrecker *m*

exemplary [ɪg'zemplərɪ] *adj* musterhaft

exemplify [ɪg'zemplɪfaɪ] *vt* veranschaulichen

exempt [ɪg'zempt] *adj* befreit ♦ *vt* befreien; ~**ion** [ɪg'zempʃən] *n* Befreiung *f*

exercise ['eksəsaɪz] *n* Übung *f* ♦ *vt* (*power*) ausüben; (*muscle, patience*) üben; (*dog*) ausführen ♦ *vi* Sport treiben; ~ **bike** *n* Heimtrainer *m*; ~ **book** *n* (*School*)heft *nt*

exert [ɪg'zɜːt] *vt* (*influence*) ausüben; **to ~ o.s.** sich anstrengen; ~**ion** [ɪg'zɜːʃən] *n* Anstrengung *f*

exhale [eks'heɪl] *vt, vi* ausatmen

exhaust [ɪg'zɔːst] *n* (*fumes*) Abgase *pl*; (*pipe*) Auspuffrohr *nt* ♦ *vt* erschöpfen; ~**ed** *adj* erschöpft; ~**ion** [ɪg'zɔːstʃən] *n* Erschöpfung *f*; ~**ive** *adj* erschöpfend

exhibit [ɪg'zɪbɪt] *n* (*ART*) Ausstellungsstück *nt*; (*JUR*) Beweisstück *nt* ♦ *vt* ausstellen; ~**ion** [eksɪ'bɪʃən] *n* (*ART*) Ausstellung *f*; (*of temper etc*) Zurschaustellung *f*; ~**ionist** [eksɪ'bɪʃənɪst] *n* Exhibitionist *m*

exhilarating [ɪg'zɪləreɪtɪŋ] *adj* erhebend

exhort [ɪg'zɔːt] *vt* ermahnen

exile ['eksaɪl] *n* Exil *nt*; (*person*) Verbannte(r) *mf* ♦ *vt* verbannen

exist [ɪg'zɪst] *vi* existieren; ~**ence** *n* Existenz *f*; ~**ing** *adj* bestehend

exit ['eksɪt] *n* Ausgang *m*; (*THEAT*) Abgang *m* ♦ *vi* abtreten; (*COMPUT*) aus einem Programm herausgehen; ~ **poll** *n* bei Wahlen unmittelbar nach Verlassen der Wahllokal durchgeführte Umfrage; ~ **ramp** (*US*) *n* (*AUT*) Ausfahrt *f*

exodus ['eksədəs] *n* Auszug *m*

exonerate [ɪg'zɒnəreɪt] *vt* entlasten

exorbitant [ɪg'zɔːbɪtənt] *adj* übermäßig; (*price*) Phantasie-

exotic [ɪg'zɒtɪk] *adj* exotisch

expand [ɪks'pænd] *vt* ausdehnen ♦ *vi* sich ausdehnen

expanse [ɪks'pæns] *n* Fläche *f*

expansion [ɪks'pænʃən] *n* Erweiterung *f*

expatriate [eks'pætrɪɪt] *n* Ausländer(in) *m(f)*

expect [ɪks'pekt] *vt* erwarten; *(suppose)* annehmen ♦ *vi:* **to be ~ing** ein Kind erwarten; **~ancy** *n* Erwartung *f*; **~ant mother** *n* werdende Mutter *f*; **~ation** [ekspek'teɪʃən] *n* Hoffnung *f*

expedience [ɪks'piːdɪəns] *n* Zweckdienlichkeit *f*

expediency [ɪks'piːdɪənsɪ] *n* Zweckdienlichkeit *f*

expedient [ɪks'piːdɪənt] *adj* zweckdienlich ♦ *n* (Hilfs)mittel *nt*

expedition [ekspɪ'dɪʃən] *n* Expedition *f*

expel [ɪks'pel] *vt* ausweisen; *(student)* (ver)weisen

expend [ɪks'pend] *vt* *(effort)* aufwenden; **~iture** [ɪk'spendɪtʃə*] *n* Ausgaben *pl*

expense [ɪks'pens] *n* Kosten *pl*; **~s** *npl* *(COMM)* Spesen *pl*; **at the ~ of** auf Kosten von; **~ account** *n* Spesenkonto *nt*

expensive [ɪks'pensɪv] *adj* teuer

experience [ɪks'pɪərɪəns] *n* *(incident)* Erlebnis *nt*; *(practice)* Erfahrung *f* ♦ *vt* erleben; **~d** *adj* erfahren

experiment [*n* ɪks'perɪmənt, *vb* ɪks'perɪment] *n* Versuch *m*, Experiment *nt* ♦ *vi* experimentieren; **~al** [ɪksperɪ'mentl] *adj* experimentell

expert ['ekspɜːt] *n* Fachmann *m*; *(official)* Sachverständige(r) *m* ♦ *adj* erfahren; **~ise** [ekspə'tiːz] *n* Sachkenntnis *f*

expire [ɪks'paɪə*] *vi* *(end)* ablaufen; *(ticket)* verfallen; *(die)* sterben

expiry [ɪks'paɪərɪ] *n* Ablauf *m*

explain [ɪks'pleɪn] *vt* erklären

explanation [eksplə'neɪʃən] *n* Erklärung *f*

explanatory [ɪks'plænətərɪ] *adj* erklärend

explicit [ɪks'plɪsɪt] *adj* ausdrücklich

explode [ɪks'pləud] *vi* explodieren ♦ *vt* *(bomb)* sprengen; *(theory)* platzen lassen

exploit [*n* 'eksplɔɪt, *vb* ɪks'plɔɪt] *n* (Helden)tat *f* ♦ *vt* ausbeuten; **~ation** [eksplɔɪ'teɪʃən] *n* Ausbeutung *f*

exploration [eksplɔː'reɪʃən] *n*

Erforschung *f*

exploratory [eks'plɒrətərɪ] *adj* Probe-

explore [ɪks'plɔː*] *vt* *(travel)* erforschen; *(search)* untersuchen; **~r** *n* Erforscher(in) *m(f)*

explosion [ɪks'pləuʒən] *n* Explosion *f*; *(fig)* Ausbruch *m*

explosive [ɪks'pləuzɪv] *adj* explosiv, Spreng- ♦ *n* Sprengstoff *m*

exponent [eks'pəunənt] *n* Exponent *m*

export [*vb* eks'pɔːt, *n* 'ekspɔːt] *vt* exportieren ♦ *n* Export *m* ♦ *cpd* *(trade)* Export-; **~er** *n* Exporteur *m*

expose [ɪks'pəuz] *vt* *(to danger etc)* aussetzen; *(impostor)* entlarven; **to ~ sb to sth** jdn einer Sache *dat* aussetzen; **~d** [ɪks'pəuzd] *adj* *(position)* exponiert

exposure [ɪks'pəuʒə*] *n* *(MED)* Unterkühlung *f*; *(PHOT)* Belichtung *f*; **~ meter** *n* Belichtungsmesser *m*

expound [ɪks'paund] *vt* entwickeln

express [ɪks'pres] *adj* ausdrücklich; *(speedy)* Expreß-, Eil- ♦ *n* *(RAIL)* Schnellzug *m* ♦ *adv* *(send)* per Expreß ♦ *vt* ausdrücken; **to ~ o.s.** sich ausdrücken; **~ion** [ɪks'preʃən] *n* Ausdruck *m*; **~ive** *adj* ausdrucksvoll; **~ly** *adv* ausdrücklich; **~way** *(US)* *n* *(urban motorway)* Schnellstraße *f*

expulsion [ɪks'pʌlʃən] *n* Ausweisung *f*

expurgate ['ekspɜːgeɪt] *vt* zensieren

exquisite [eks'kwɪzɪt] *adj* erlesen

extend [ɪks'tend] *vt* *(visit etc)* verlängern; *(building)* ausbauen; *(hand)* ausstrecken; *(welcome)* bieten ♦ *vi* *(land)* sich erstrecken

extension [ɪks'tenʃən] *n* Erweiterung *f*; *(of building)* Anbau *m*; *(TEL)* Apparat *m*

extensive [ɪks'tensɪv] *adj* *(knowledge)* umfassend; *(use)* weitgehend

extent [ɪks'tent] *n* Ausdehnung *f*; *(fig)* Ausmaß *nt*; **to a certain ~** bis zu einem gewissen Grade; **to such an ~ that ...** dermaßen, daß ...; **to what ~?** inwieweit?

extenuating [eks'tenjueɪtɪŋ] *adj* mildernd

exterior [eks'tɪərɪə*] *adj* äußere(r, s), Außen- ♦ *n* Äußere(s) *nt*

exterminate [eks'tɜːmɪneɪt] *vt* ausrotten

external [eks'tɜ:nl] *adj* äußere(r, s), Außen‐

extinct [ɪks'tɪŋkt] *adj* ausgestorben; **~ion** [ɪks'tɪŋkʃən] *n* Aussterben *nt*

extinguish [ɪks'tɪŋgwɪʃ] *vt* (aus)löschen; **~er** *n* Löschgerät *nt*

extort [ɪks'tɔ:t] *vt* erpressen; **~ion** [ɪks'tɔ:ʃən] *n* Erpressung *f*; **~ionate** [ɪks'tɔ:ʃnɪt] *adj* überhöht, erpresserisch

extra ['ekstrə] *adj* zusätzlich ♦ *adv* besonders ♦ *n* (*for car etc*) Extra *nt*; (*charge*) Zuschlag *m*; (THEAT) Statist *m* ♦ *prefix* außer...

extract [*vb* ɪks'trækt, *n* 'ekstrækt] *vt* (heraus)ziehen ♦ *n* (*from book etc*) Auszug *m*; (COOK) Extrakt *m*

extracurricular ['ekstrəkə'rɪkjulə*] *adj* außerhalb des Stundenplans

extradite ['ekstrədaɪt] *vt* ausliefern

extramarital [ekstrə'mærɪtl] *adj* außerehelich

extramural [ekstrə'mjuərl] *adj* (*course*) Volkshochschul‐

extraordinary [ɪks'trɔ:dnrɪ] *adj* außerordentlich; (*amazing*) erstaunlich

extravagance [ɪks'trævəgəns] *n* Verschwendung *f*; (*lack of restraint*) Zügellosigkeit *f*; (*an ~*) Extravaganz *f*

extravagant [ɪks'trævəgənt] *adj* extravagant

extreme [ɪks'tri:m] *adj* (*edge*) äußerste(r, s), hinterste(r, s); (*cold*) äußerste(r, s); (*behaviour*) außergewöhnlich, übertrieben ♦ *n* Extrem *nt*; **~ly** *adv* äußerst, höchst

extremity [ɪks'tremɪtɪ] *n* (*end*) Spitze *f*, äußerste(s) Ende *nt*; (*hardship*) bitterste Not *f*; (ANAT) Hand *f*, Fuß *m*

extricate ['ekstrɪkeɪt] *vt* losmachen, befreien

extrovert ['ekstrəuvɜ:t] *n* extrovertierte(r) Mensch *m*

exuberant [ɪg'zu:bərənt] *adj* ausgelassen

exude [ɪg'zju:d] *vt* absondern

exult [ɪg'zʌlt] *vi* frohlocken

eye [aɪ] *n* Auge *nt*; (*of needle*) Öhr *nt* ♦ *vt* betrachten; (*up and down*) mustern; **to keep an ~ on** aufpassen auf +*acc*; **~ball** *n* Augapfel *m*; **~bath** *n* Augenbad *nt*; **~brow** *n* Augenbraue *f*; **~brow pencil** *n* Augenbrauenstift *m*; **~drops** *npl* Augentropfen *pl*; **~lash** *n* Augenwimper *f*; **~lid** *n* Augenlid *nt*; **~liner** *n* Eyeliner *nt*; **~opener** *n*: **that was an ~opener** das hat mir/ihm *etc* die Augen geöffnet; **~shadow** *n* Lidschatten *m*; **~sight** *n* Sehkraft *f*; **~sore** *n* Schandfleck *m*; **~ witness** *n* Augenzeuge *m*

F f

F [ef] *n* (MUS) F *nt*

F. *abbr* (= *Fahrenheit*) F

fable ['feɪbl] *n* Fabel *f*

fabric ['fæbrɪk] *n* Stoff *m*; (*fig*) Gefüge *nt*

fabrication [fæbrɪ'keɪʃən] *n* Erfindung *f*

fabulous ['fæbjuləs] *adj* sagenhaft

face [feɪs] *n* Gesicht *nt*; (*surface*) Oberfläche *f*; (*of clock*) Zifferblatt *nt* ♦ *vt* (*point towards*) liegen nach; (*situation, difficulty*) sich stellen +*dat*; **~ down** (*person*) mit dem Gesicht nach unten; (*card*) mit der Vorderseite nach unten; **to make** *or* **pull a ~** das Gesicht verziehen; **in the ~ of** angesichts +*gen*; **on the ~ of it** so, wie es aussieht; **~ to ~** Auge in Auge; **to ~ up to sth** einer Sache *dat* ins Auge sehen; **~ cloth** (BRIT) *n* Waschlappen *m*; **~ cream** *n* Gesichtscreme *f*; **~ lift** *n* Face-lifting *nt*; **~ powder** *n* (Gesichts)puder *m*

facet ['fæsɪt] *n* Aspekt *m*; (*of gem*) Facette *f*

facetious [fə'si:ʃəs] *adj* witzig

face value *n* Nennwert *m*; **to take sth at (its) ~** (*fig*) etw für bare Münze nehmen

facial ['feɪʃəl] *adj* Gesichts‐

facile ['fæsaɪl] *adj* oberflächlich; (US: *easy*) leicht

facilitate [fə'sɪlɪteɪt] *vt* erleichtern

facilities [fə'sɪlɪtɪz] *npl* Einrichtungen *pl*; **credit ~** Kreditmöglichkeiten *pl*

facing ['feɪsɪŋ] *adj* zugekehrt ♦ *prep* gegenüber

facsimile [fæk'sɪmɪlɪ] *n* Faksimile *nt*; (*machine*) Telekopierer *m*

fact [fækt] *n* Tatsache *f*; **in ~** in der Tat

faction ['fækʃən] *n* Splittergruppe *f*

factor ['fæktə*] *n* Faktor *m*

factory ['fæktərɪ] *n* Fabrik *f*

factual ['fæktjʊəl] *adj* sachlich

faculty ['fækəltɪ] *n* Fähigkeit *f*; (*UNIV*) Fakultät *f*; (*US: teaching staff*) Lehrpersonal *nt*

fad [fæd] *n* Tick *m*; (*fashion*) Masche *f*

fade [feɪd] *vi* (*lose colour*) verblassen; (*grow dim*) nachlassen; (*sound, memory*) schwächer werden; (*wither*) verwelken

fag [fæg] (*inf*) *n* (*cigarette*) Kippe *f*

fail [feɪl] *vt* (*exam*) nicht bestehen; (*student*) durchfallen lassen; (*courage*) verlassen; (*memory*) im Stich lassen ♦ *vi* (*supplies*) zu Ende gehen; (*student*) durchfallen; (*eyesight*) nachlassen; (*light*) schwächer werden; (*crop*) fehlschlagen; (*remedy*) nicht wirken; **to ~ to do sth** (*neglect*) es unterlassen, etw zu tun; (*be unable*) es nicht schaffen, etw zu tun; **without ~** unbedingt; **~ing** *n* Schwäche *f* ♦ *prep* mangels +*gen*; **~ure** ['feɪljə*] *n* (*person*) Versager *m*; (*act*) Versagen *nt*; (*TECH*) Defekt *m*

faint [feɪnt] *adj* schwach ♦ *n* Ohnmacht *f* ♦ *vi* ohnmächtig werden

fair [fɛə*] *adj* (*just*) gerecht, fair; (*hair*) blond; (*skin*) hell; (*weather*) schön; (*not very good*) mittelmäßig; (*sizeable*) ansehnlich ♦ *adv* (*play*) fair ♦ *n* (*COMM*) Messe *f*; (*BRIT: fun~*) Jahrmarkt *m*; **~ly** *adv* (*honestly*) gerecht, fair; (*rather*) ziemlich; **~ness** *n* Fairneß *f*

fairy ['fɛərɪ] *n* Fee *f*; **~ tale** *n* Märchen *nt*

faith [feɪθ] *n* Glaube *m*; (*trust*) Vertrauen *nt*; (*sect*) Bekenntnis *nt*; **~ful** *adj* treu; **~fully** *adv* treu; **yours ~fully** (*BRIT*) hochachtungsvoll

fake [feɪk] *n* (*thing*) Fälschung *f*; (*person*) Schwindler *m* ♦ *adj* vorgetäuscht ♦ *vt* fälschen

falcon ['fɔːlkən] *n* Falke *m*

fall [fɔːl] (*pt* **fell**, *pp* **fallen**) *n* Fall *m*, Sturz *m*; (*decrease*) Fallen *nt*; (*of snow*) (Schnee)fall *m*; (*US: autumn*) Herbst *m* ♦ *vi* (*also fig*) fallen; (*night*) hereinbrechen; **~s** *npl* (*waterfall*) Fälle *pl*; **to ~ flat** platt hinfallen; (*joke*) nicht

ankommen; **~ back** *vi* zurückweichen; **~ back on** *vt fus* zurückgreifen auf +*acc*; **~ behind** *vi* zurückbleiben; **~ down** *vi* (*person*) hinfallen; (*building*) einstürzen; **~ for** *vt fus* (*trick*) hereinfallen auf +*acc*; (*person*) sich verknallen in +*acc*; **~ in** *vi* (*roof*) einstürzen; **~ off** *vi* herunterfallen; (*diminish*) sich vermindern; **~ out** *vi* sich streiten; (*MIL*) wegtreten; **~ through** *vi* (*plan*) ins Wasser fallen

fallacy ['fæləsɪ] *n* Trugschluß *m*

fallen ['fɔːlən] *pp of* **fall**

fallible ['fæləbl] *adj* fehlbar

fallout ['fɔːlaʊt] *n* radioaktive(r) Niederschlag *m*; **~ shelter** *n* Atombunker *m*

fallow ['fæləʊ] *adj* brach(liegend)

false [fɔːls] *adj* falsch; (*artificial*) künstlich; **under ~ pretences** unter Vorspiegelung falscher Tatsachen; **~ alarm** *n* falscher *or* blinder Alarm *m*; **~ teeth** (*BRIT*) *npl* Gebiß *nt*

falter ['fɔːltə*] *vi* schwanken; (*in speech*) stocken

fame [feɪm] *n* Ruhm *m*

familiar [fə'mɪlɪə*] *adj* bekannt; (*intimate*) familiär; **to be ~ with** vertraut sein mit; **~ize** *vt* vertraut machen

family ['fæmɪlɪ] *n* Familie *f*; (*relations*) Verwandtschaft *f*; **~ business** *n* Familienunternehmen *nt*; **~ doctor** *n* Hausarzt *m*

famine ['fæmɪn] *n* Hungersnot *f*

famished ['fæmɪʃt] *adj* ausgehungert

famous ['feɪməs] *adj* berühmt; **~ly** *adv* (*get on*) prächtig

fan [fæn] *n* (*folding*) Fächer *m*; (*ELEC*) Ventilator *m*; (*admirer*) Fan *m* ♦ *vt* fächeln; **~ out** *vi* sich (fächerförmig) ausbreiten

fanatic [fə'nætɪk] *n* Fanatiker(in) *m(f)*

fan belt *n* Keilriemen *m*

fanciful ['fænsɪfʊl] *adj* (*odd*) seltsam; (*imaginative*) phantasievoll

fancy ['fænsɪ] *n* (*liking*) Neigung *f*; (*imagination*) Einbildung *f* ♦ *adj* schick ♦ *vt* (*like*) gern haben; wollen; (*imagine*) sich einbilden; **he fancies her** er mag sie; **~ dress** *n* Maskenkostüm *nt*; **~-**

dress ball *n* Maskenball *m*
fang [fæŋ] *n* Fangzahn *m*; (*of snake*) Giftzahn *m*
fantastic [fæn'tæstɪk] *adj* phantastisch
fantasy ['fæntəzɪ] *n* Phantasie *f*
far [fɑ:*] *adj* weit ♦ *adv* weit entfernt; (*very much*) weitaus; **by** ~ bei weitem; **so** ~ soweit; bis jetzt; **go as** ~ **as the farm** gehen Sie bis zum Bauernhof; **as** ~ **as I know** soweit *or* soviel ich weiß; **~away** *adj* weit entfernt
farce [fɑ:s] *n* Farce *f*
farcical ['fɑ:sɪkəl] *adj* lächerlich
fare [fɛə*] *n* Fahrpreis *m*; Fahrgeld *nt*; (*food*) Kost *f*; **half/full** ~ halber/voller Fahrpreis *m*
Far East *n*: **the** ~ der Ferne Osten
farewell [fɛə'wel] *n* Abschied(sgruß) *m* ♦ *excl* lebe wohl!
farm [fɑ:m] *n* Bauernhof *m*, Farm *f* ♦ *vt* bewirtschaften; **~er** *n* Bauer *m*, Landwirt *m*; **~hand** *n* Landarbeiter *m*; **~house** *n* Bauernhaus *nt*; **~ing** *n* Landwirtschaft *f*; **~land** *n* Ackerland *nt*; **~yard** *n* Hof *m*
far-reaching ['fɑ:'ri:tʃɪŋ] *adj* (*reform, effect*) weitreichend
fart [fɑ:t] (*inf!*) *n* Furz *m* ♦ *vi* furzen
farther ['fɑ:ðə*] *adv* weiter
farthest ['fɑ:ðɪst] *adj* fernste(r, s) ♦ *adv* am weitesten
fascinate ['fæsɪneɪt] *vt* faszinieren
fascination [fæsɪ'neɪʃən] *n* Faszination *f*
fascism ['fæʃɪzəm] *n* Faschismus *m*
fashion ['fæʃən] *n* (*of clothes*) Mode *f*; (*manner*) Art *f* (und Weise *f*) ♦ *vt* machen; **in** ~ in Mode; **out of** ~ unmodisch; **~able** *adj* (*clothes*) modisch; (*place*) elegant; ~ **show** *n* Mode(n)schau *f*
fast [fɑ:st] *adj* schnell; (*firm*) fest ♦ *adv* schnell; fest ♦ *n* Fasten *nt* ♦ *vi* fasten; **to be** ~ (*clock*) vorgehen
fasten ['fɑ:sn] *vt* (*attach*) befestigen; (*with rope*) zuschnüren; (*seat belt*) festmachen; (*coat*) zumachen ♦ *vi* sich schließen lassen; **~er** *n* Verschluß *m*; **~ing** *n* Verschluß *m*
fast food *n* Fast food *nt*
fastidious [fæs'tɪdɪəs] *adj* wählerisch
fat [fæt] *adj* dick ♦ *n* Fett *nt*

fatal ['feɪtl] *adj* tödlich; (*disastrous*) verhängnisvoll; **~ity** [fə'tælɪtɪ] *n* (*road death etc*) Todesopfer *nt*; **~ly** *adv* tödlich
fate [feɪt] *n* Schicksal *nt*; **~ful** *adj* (*prophetic*) schicksalsschwer; (*important*) schicksalhaft
father ['fɑ:ðə*] *n* Vater *m*; (*REL*) Pater *m*; **~-in-law** *n* Schwiegervater *m*; **~ly** *adj* väterlich
fathom ['fæðəm] *n* Klafter *m* ♦ *vt* ausloten; (*fig*) ergründen
fatigue [fə'ti:g] *n* Ermüdung *f*
fatten ['fætn] *vt* dick machen; (*animals*) mästen ♦ *vi* dick werden
fatty ['fætɪ] *adj* fettig ♦ *n* (*inf*) Dickerchen *nt*
fatuous ['fætjʊəs] *adj* albern, affig
faucet ['fɔ:sɪt] (*US*) *n* Wasserhahn *m*
fault [fɔ:lt] *n* (*defect*) Fehler *m*; (*ELEC*) Störung *f*; (*blame*) Schuld *f*; (*GEOG*) Verwerfung *f* ♦ *vt*: **it's your** ~ du bist daran schuld; **to find** ~ **with** (*sth/sb*) etwas auszusetzen haben an (etw/jdm); **at** ~ im Unrecht; **~less** *adj* tadellos; **~y** *adj* fehlerhaft, defekt
favour ['feɪvə*] (*US* **favor**) *n* (*approval*) Wohlwollen *nt*; (*kindness*) Gefallen *m* ♦ *vt* (*prefer*) vorziehen; **in** ~ **of** für; zugunsten +*gen*; **to find** ~ **with sb** bei jdm Anklang finden; **~able** *adj* günstig; **~ite** ['feɪvərɪt] *adj* Lieblings- ♦ *n* (*child*) Liebling *m*; (*SPORT*) Favorit *m*
fawn [fɔ:n] *adj* rehbraun ♦ *n* (*colour*) Rehbraun *nt*; (*animal*) (Reh)kitz *nt* ♦ *vi*: **to** ~ (**up**)**on** (*fig*) katzbuckeln vor +*dat*
fax [fæks] *n* (*document*) Fax *nt*; (*machine*) Telefax *nt* ♦ *vt*: **to** ~ **sth to sb** jdm etw faxen
FBI ['efbiː'aɪ] (*US*) *n abbr* (= *Federal Bureau of Investigation*) FBI *nt*
fear [fɪə*] *n* Furcht *f* ♦ *vt* fürchten; **~ful** *adj* (*timid*) furchtsam; (*terrible*) fürchterlich; **~less** *adj* furchtlos
feasible ['fiːzəbl] *adj* durchführbar
feast [fiːst] *n* Festmahl *nt*; (*REL*: *also*: ~ **day**) Feiertag *m* ♦ *vi*: **to** ~ (**on**) sich gütlich tun (an +*dat*)
feat [fiːt] *n* Leistung *f*
feather ['feðə*] *n* Feder *f*

feature ['fi:tʃə*] *n* (Gesichts)zug *m*; (*important part*) Grundzug *m*; (*CINE, PRESS*) Feature *nt* ♦ *vt* darstellen; (*advertising etc*) groß herausbringen ♦ *vi* vorkommen; **featuring X** mit X; **~ film** *n* Spielfilm *m*

February ['fɛbruərɪ] *n* Februar *m*

fed [fɛd] *pt, pp of* **feed**

federal ['fɛdərəl] *adj* Bundes-

federation [fɛdə'reɪʃən] *n* (*society*) Verband *m*; (*of states*) Staatenbund *m*

fed up *adj*: **to be ~ with sth** etw satt haben; **I'm ~** ich habe die Nase voll

fee [fi:] *n* Gebühr *f*

feeble ['fi:bl] *adj* (*person*) schwach; (*excuse*) lahm

feed [fi:d] (*pt, pp* **fed**) *n* (*for baby*) Essen *nt*; (*for animals*) Futter *m* ♦ *vt* füttern; (*support*) ernähren; (*data*) eingeben; **to ~ on** fressen; **~back** *n* (*information*) Feedback *nt*; **~ing bottle** (*BRIT*) *n* Flasche *f*

feel [fi:l] (*pt, pp* **felt**) *n*: **it has a soft ~** es fühlt sich weich an ♦ *vt* (*sense*) fühlen; (*touch*) anfassen; (*think*) meinen ♦ *vi* (*person*) sich fühlen; (*thing*) sich anfühlen; **to get the ~ of sth** sich an etw *acc* gewöhnen; **I ~ cold** mir ist kalt; **I ~ like a cup of tea** ich habe Lust auf eine Tasse Tee; **~ about** *or* **around** *vi* herumsuchen; **~er** *n* Fühler *m*; **~ing** *n* Gefühl *nt*; (*opinion*) Meinung *f*

feet [fi:t] *npl of* **foot**

feign [feɪn] *vt* vortäuschen

feline ['fi:laɪn] *adj* katzenartig

fell [fɛl] *pt of* **fall** ♦ *vt* (*tree*) fällen

fellow ['fɛləu] *n* (*man*) Kerl *m*; **~ citizen** *n* Mitbürger(in) *m(f)*; **~ countryman** (*irreg*) *n* Landsmann *m*; **~ men** *npl* Mitmenschen *pl*; **~ship** *n* (*group*) Körperschaft *f*; (*friendliness*) Kameradschaft *f*; (*scholarship*) Forschungsstipendium *nt*; **~ student** *n* Kommilitone *m*, Kommilitonin *f*

felony ['fɛlənɪ] *n* schwere(s) Verbrechen *nt*

felt [fɛlt] *pt, pp of* **feel** ♦ *n* Filz *m*; **~-tip pen** *n* Filzstift *m*

female ['fi:meɪl] *n* (*of animals*) Weibchen *nt* ♦ *adj* weiblich

feminine ['fɛmɪnɪn] *adj* (*LING*) weiblich; (*qualities*) fraulich

feminist ['fɛmɪnɪst] *n* Feminist(in) *m(f)*

fence [fɛns] *n* Zaun *m* ♦ *vt* (*also:* **~ in**) einzäunen ♦ *vi* fechten

fencing ['fɛnsɪŋ] *n* Zaun *m*; (*SPORT*) Fechten *nt*

fend [fɛnd] *vi*: **to ~ for o.s.** sich (allein) durchschlagen; **~ off** *vt* abwehren

fender ['fɛndə*] *n* Kaminvorsetzer *m*; (*US: AUT*) Kotflügel *m*

ferment [*vb* fə'mɛnt, *n* 'fɜːmɛnt] *vi* (*CHEM*) gären ♦ *n* (*excitement*) Unruhe *f*

fern [fɜːn] *n* Farn *m*

ferocious [fə'rəuʃəs] *adj* wild, grausam

ferret ['fɛrɪt] *n* Frettchen *nt* ♦ *vt*: **to ~ out** aufspüren

ferry ['fɛrɪ] *n* Fähre *f* ♦ *vt* übersetzen

fertile ['fɜːtaɪl] *adj* fruchtbar

fertilize ['fɜːtɪlaɪz] *vt* (*AGR*) düngen; (*BIOL*) befruchten; **~r** ['fɜːtɪlaɪzə*] *n* (Kunst)dünger *m*

fervent ['fɜːvənt] *adj* (*admirer*) glühend; (*hope*) innig

fervour ['fɜːvə*] (*US* **fervor**) *n* Leidenschaft *f*

fester ['fɛstə*] *vi* eitern

festival ['fɛstɪvəl] *n* (*REL etc*) Fest *nt*; (*ART, MUS*) Festspiele *pl*

festive ['fɛstɪv] *adj* festlich; **the ~ season** (*Christmas*) die Festzeit

festivities [fɛs'tɪvɪtɪz] *npl* Feierlichkeiten *pl*

festoon [fɛs'tu:n] *vt*: **to ~ with** schmücken mit

fetch [fɛtʃ] *vt* holen; (*in sale*) einbringen

fetching ['fɛtʃɪŋ] *adj* reizend

fête [feɪt] *n* Fest *nt*

fetus ['fi:təs] (*esp US*) *n* = **foetus**

feud [fju:d] *n* Fehde *f*

feudal ['fju:dl] *adj* Feudal-

fever ['fi:və*] *n* Fieber *nt*; **~ish** *adj* (*MED*) fiebrig; (*fig*) fieberhaft

few [fju:] *adj* wenig; **a ~** einige; **~er** *adj* weniger; **~est** *adj* wenigste(r,s)

fiancé [fɪ'ãːnseɪ] *n* Verlobte(r) *m*; **~e** *n* Verlobte *f*

fib [fɪb] *n* Flunkerei *f* ♦ *vi* flunkern

fibre ['faɪbə*] (*US* **fiber**) *n* Faser *f*; **~-**

glass n Glaswolle f
fickle ['fɪkl] adj unbeständig
fiction ['fɪkʃən] n (*novels*) Romanliteratur f; (*story*) Erdichtung f; **~al** adj erfunden
fictitious [fɪk'tɪʃəs] adj erfunden, fingiert
fiddle ['fɪdl] n Geige f; (*trick*) Schwindelei f ♦ vt (*BRIT: accounts*) frisieren; **~ with** vt fus herumfummeln an +dat
fidelity [fɪ'delɪtɪ] n Treue f
fidget ['fɪdʒɪt] vi zappeln
field [fiːld] n Feld nt; (*range*) Gebiet nt; **~ marshal** n Feldmarschall m; **~work** n Feldforschung f
fiend [fiːnd] n Teufel m
fierce [fɪəs] adj wild
fiery ['faɪərɪ] adj (*hot-tempered*) hitzig
fifteen [fɪf'tiːn] num fünfzehn
fifth [fɪfθ] adj fünfte(r, s) ♦ n Fünftel nt
fifty ['fɪftɪ] num fünfzig; **~-fifty** adj, adv halbe halbe, fifty fifty (*inf*)
fig [fɪg] n Feige f
fight [faɪt] (*pt, pp* **fought**) n Kampf m; (*brawl*) Schlägerei f; (*argument*) Streit m ♦ vt kämpfen gegen; sich schlagen mit; (*fig*) bekämpfen ♦ vi kämpfen; sich schlagen; streiten; **~er** n Kämpfer(in) m(f); (*plane*) Jagdflugzeug nt; **~ing** n Kämpfen nt; (*war*) Kampfhandlungen pl
figment ['fɪgmənt] n: **~ of the imagination** reine Einbildung f
figurative ['fɪgərətɪv] adj bildlich
figure ['fɪgə*] n (*of person*) Figur f; (*person*) Gestalt f; (*number*) Ziffer f ♦ vt (*US: imagine*) glauben ♦ vi (*appear*) erscheinen; **~ out** vt herausbekommen; **~head** n (*NAUT, fig*) Galionsfigur f; **~ of speech** n Redensart f
filament ['fɪləmənt] n Faden m; (*ELEC*) Glühfaden m
filch [fɪltʃ] (*inf*) vt filzen
file [faɪl] n (*tool*) Feile f; (*dossier*) Akte f; (*folder*) Aktenordner m; (*COMPUT*) Datei f; (*row*) Reihe f ♦ vt (*metal, nails*) feilen; (*papers*) abheften; (*claim*) einreichen ♦ vi: **to ~ in/out** hintereinander hereinkommen/hinausgehen; **to ~ past** vorbeimarschieren
filing ['faɪlɪŋ] n Ablage f; **~ cabinet** n Aktenschrank m

fill [fɪl] vt füllen; (*occupy*) ausfüllen; (*satisfy*) sättigen ♦ n: **to eat one's ~** sich richtig satt essen; **~ in** vt (*hole*) (auf)füllen; (*form*) ausfüllen; **~ up** vt (*container*) auffüllen; (*form*) ausfüllen ♦ vi (*AUT*) tanken
fillet ['fɪlɪt] n Filet nt; **~ steak** n Filetsteak nt
filling ['fɪlɪŋ] n (*COOK*) Füllung f; (*for tooth*) (Zahn)plombe f; **~ station** n Tankstelle f
film [fɪlm] n Film m ♦ vt (*scene*) filmen; **~ star** n Filmstar m; **~strip** n Filmstreifen m
filter ['fɪltə*] n Filter m ♦ vt filtern; **~ lane** n (*BRIT*) Abbiegespur f; **~-tipped** adj Filter-
filth [fɪlθ] n Dreck m; **~y** adj dreckig; (*weather*) scheußlich
fin [fɪn] n Flosse f
final ['faɪnl] adj letzte(r, s); End-; (*conclusive*) endgültig ♦ n (*FOOTBALL etc*) Endspiel nt; **~s** npl (*UNIV*) Abschlußexamen nt; (*SPORT*) Schlußrunde f; **~e** [fɪ'nɑːlɪ] n (*MUS*) Finale nt; **~ist** n (*SPORT*) Schlußrundenteilnehmer m; **~ize** vt endgültige Form geben +dat; abschließen; **~ly** adv (*lastly*) zuletzt; (*eventually*) endlich; (*irrevocably*) endgültig
finance [faɪ'næns] n Finanzwesen nt ♦ vt finanzieren; **~s** npl (*funds*) Finanzen pl
financial [faɪ'nænʃəl] adj Finanz-; finanziell
find [faɪnd] (*pt, pp* **found**) vt finden ♦ n Fund m; **to ~ sb guilty** jdn für schuldig erklären; **~ out** vt herausfinden; **~ings** npl (*JUR*) Ermittlungsergebnis nt; (*of report*) Befund m
fine [faɪn] adj fein; (*good*) gut; (*weather*) schön ♦ adv (*well*) gut; (*small*) klein ♦ n (*JUR*) Geldstrafe f ♦ vt mit einer Geldstrafe belegen; **~ arts** npl schöne(n) Künste pl
finery ['faɪnərɪ] n Putz m
finger ['fɪŋgə*] n Finger m ♦ vt befühlen; **~nail** n Fingernagel m; **~print** n Fingerabdruck m; **~tip** n Fingerspitze f
finicky ['fɪnɪkɪ] adj pingelig
finish ['fɪnɪʃ] n Ende nt; (*SPORT*) Ziel nt;

(*of object*) Verarbeitung *f*; (*of paint*) Oberflächenwirkung *f* ♦ *vt* beenden; (*book*) zu Ende lesen ♦ *vi* aufhören; (*SPORT*) ans Ziel kommen; **to be ~ed with sth** fertig sein mit etw; **to ~ doing sth** mit etw fertig werden; **~ off** *vt* (*complete*) fertigmachen; (*kill*) den Gnadenstoß geben +*dat*; (*knock out*) erledigen (*umg*); **~ up** *vt* (*food*) aufessen; (*drink*) austrinken ♦ *vi* (*end up*) enden; **~ing line** *n* Ziellinie *f*; **~ing school** *n* Mädchenpensionat *nt*

finite ['faɪnaɪt] *adj* endlich, begrenzt

Finland ['fɪnlənd] *n* Finnland *nt*

Finn [fɪn] *n* Finne *m*, Finnin *f*; **~ish** *adj* finnisch ♦ *n* (*LING*) Finnisch *nt*

fir [fɜ:*] *n* Tanne *f*

fire [faɪə*] *n* Feuer *nt*; (*in house etc*) Brand *m* ♦ *vt* (*gun*) abfeuern; (*imagination*) entzünden; (*dismiss*) hinauswerfen ♦ *vi* (*AUT*) zünden; **to be on ~** brennen; **~ alarm** *n* Feueralarm *m*; **~arm** *n* Schußwaffe *f*; **~ brigade** (*BRIT*) *n* Feuerwehr *f*; **~ department** (*US*) *n* Feuerwehr *f*; **~ engine** *n* Feuerwehrauto *nt*; **~ escape** *n* Feuerleiter *f*; **~ extinguisher** *n* Löschgerät *nt*; **~man** (*irreg*) *n* Feuerwehrmann *m*; **~place** *n* Kamin *m*; **~side** *n* Kamin *m*; **~ station** *n* Feuerwache *f*; **~works** *npl* Feuerwerk *nt*

firing ['faɪərɪŋ] *n* Schießen *nt*; **~ squad** *n* Exekutionskommando *nt*

firm [fɜ:m] *adj* fest ♦ *n* Firma *f*

firmly ['fɜ:mlɪ] *adv* (*grasp, speak*) fest; (*push, tug*) energisch; (*decide*) endgültig

first [fɜ:st] *adj* erste(r, s) ♦ *adv* zuerst; (*arrive*) als erste(r); (*happen*) zum erstenmal ♦ *n* (*person: in race*) Erste(r) *mf*; (*UNIV*) Eins *f*; (*AUT*) erste(r) Gang *m*; **at ~** zuerst; **~ of all** zu allererst; **~ aid** *n* Erste Hilfe *f*; **~-aid kit** *n* Verbandskasten *m*; **~-class** *adj* erstklassig; (*travel*) erster Klasse; **~-hand** *adj* aus erster Hand; **~ lady** (*US*) *n* First Lady *f*; **~ly** *adv* erstens; **~ name** *n* Vorname *m*; **~-rate** *adj* erstklassig

fiscal ['fɪskəl] *adj* Finanz-

fish [fɪʃ] *n inv* Fisch *m* ♦ *vi* fischen;

angeln; **to go ~ing** angeln gehen; (*in sea*) fischen gehen; **~erman** (*irreg*) *n* Fischer *m*; **~ farm** *n* Fischzucht *f*; **~ fingers** (*BRIT*) *npl* Fischstäbchen *pl*; **~ing boat** *n* Fischerboot *nt*; **~ing line** *n* Angelschnur *f*; **~ing rod** *n* Angel(rute) *f*; **~monger's (shop)** *n* Fischhändler *m*; **~ slice** *n* Fischvorleger *m*; **~ sticks** (*US*) *npl* = **fish fingers**; **~y** (*inf*) *adj* (*suspicious*) faul

fission ['fɪʃən] *n* Spaltung *f*

fissure ['fɪʃə*] *n* Riß *m*

fist [fɪst] *n* Faust *f*

fit [fɪt] *adj* (*MED*) gesund; (*SPORT*) in Form, fit; (*suitable*) geeignet ♦ *vt* passen +*dat*; (*insert, attach*) einsetzen ♦ *vi* passen; (*in space, gap*) hineinpassen ♦ *n* (*of clothes*) Sitz *m*; (*MED, of anger*) Anfall *m*; (*of laughter*) Krampf *m*; **by ~s and starts** (*move*) ruckweise; (*work*) unregelmäßig; **~ in** *vi* hineinpassen; (*fig: person*) passen; **~ out** *vt* (*also: ~ up*) ausstatten; **~ful** *adj* (*sleep*) unruhig; **~ment** *n* Einrichtungsgegenstand *m*; **~ness** *n* (*suitability*) Eignung *f*; (*MED*) Gesundheit *f*; (*SPORT*) Fitneß *f*; **~ted carpet** *n* Teppichboden *m*; **~ted kitchen** *n* Einbauküche *f*; **~ter** *n* (*TECH*) Monteur *m*; **~ting** *adj* passend ♦ *n* (*of dress*) Anprobe *f*; (*piece of equipment*) (Ersatz)teil *nt*; **~tings** *npl* (*equipment*) Zubehör *nt*; **~ting room** *n* Anproberaum *m*

five [faɪv] *num* fünf; **~r** (*inf*) *n* (*BRIT*) Fünf-Pfund-Note *f*; (*US*) Fünf-Dollar-Note *f*

fix [fɪks] *vt* befestigen; (*settle*) festsetzen; (*repair*) reparieren ♦ *n*: **in a ~** in der Klemme; **~ up** *vt* (*meeting*) arrangieren; **to ~ sb up with sth** jdm etw *acc* verschaffen; **~ation** [fɪks'eɪʃən] *n* Fixierung *f*; **~ed** [fɪkst] *adj* fest; **~ture** ['fɪkstʃə*] *n* Installationsteil *nt*; (*SPORT*) Spiel *nt*

fizzle ['fɪzl] *vi*: **to ~ out** verpuffen

fizzy ['fɪzɪ] *adj* Sprudel-, sprudelnd

flabbergasted ['flæbəgɑ:stɪd] (*inf*) *adj* platt

flabby ['flæbɪ] *adj* wabbelig

flag [flæg] *n* Fahne *f* ♦ *vi* (*strength*) nachlassen; (*spirit*) erlahmen; **~ down** *vt* anhalten

flagpole ['flægpəʊl] *n* Fahnenstange *f*

flagrant ['fleɪgrənt] *adj* kraß

flair [fleə*] *n* Talent *nt*

flak [flæk] *n* Flakfeuer *nt*

flake [fleɪk] *n* (*of snow*) Flocke *f*; (*of rust*) Schuppe *f* ♦ *vi* (*also:* ~ *off*) abblättern

flamboyant [flæm'bɔɪənt] *adj* extravagant

flame [fleɪm] *n* Flamme *f*

flamingo [flə'mɪŋgəʊ] *n* Flamingo *m*

flammable ['flæməbl] *adj* brennbar

flan [flæn] (*BRIT*) *n* Obsttorte *f*

flank [flæŋk] *n* Flanke *f* ♦ *vt* flankieren

flannel ['flænl] *n* Flanell *m*; (*BRIT: also:* *face* ~) Waschlappen *m*; (: *inf*) Geschwafel *nt*; ~**s** *npl* (*trousers*) Flanellhose *f*

flap [flæp] *n* Klappe *f*; (*inf: crisis*) (helle) Aufregung *f* ♦ *vt* (*wings*) schlagen mit ♦ *vi* flattern

flare [fleə*] *n* (*signal*) Leuchtsignal *nt*; (*in skirt etc*) Weite *f*; ~ **up** *vi* aufflammen; (*fig*) aufbrausen; (*revolt*) (plötzlich) ausbrechen

flash [flæʃ] *n* Blitz *m*; (*also: news* ~) Kurzmeldung *f*; (*PHOT*) Blitzlicht *nt* ♦ *vt* aufleuchten lassen ♦ *vi* aufleuchten; **in a** ~ im Nu; ~ **by** *or* **past** *vi* vorbeirasen; ~**back** *n* Rückblende *f*; ~**bulb** *n* Blitzlichtbirne *f*; ~ **cube** *n* Blitzwürfel *m*; ~**light** *n* Blitzlicht *nt*

flashy ['flæʃɪ] (*pej*) *adj* knallig

flask [flɑːsk] *n* (*CHEM*) Kolben *m*; (*also: vacuum* ~) Thermosflasche *f* ®

flat [flæt] *adj* flach; (*dull*) matt; (*MUS*) erniedrigt; (*beer*) schal; (*tyre*) platt ♦ *n* (*BRIT: rooms*) Wohnung *f*; (*MUS*) b *nt*; (*AUT*) Platte(r) *m*; **to work** ~ **out** auf Hochtouren arbeiten; ~**ly** *adv* glatt; ~**screen** *adj* (*TV*, *COMPUT*) mit flachem Bildschirm; ~**ten** *vt* (*also:* ~*ten out*) ebnen

flatter ['flætə*] *vt* schmeicheln +*dat*; ~**ing** *adj* schmeichelhaft; ~**y** *n* Schmeichelei *f*

flatulence ['flætjʊləns] *n* Blähungen *pl*

flaunt [flɔːnt] *vt* prunken mit

flavour ['fleɪvə*] (*US* **flavor**) *n* Geschmack *m* ♦ *vt* würzen; ~**ed** *adj*: **strawberry-~ed** mit Erdbeergeschmack; ~**ing** *n* Würze *f*

flaw [flɔː] *n* Fehler *m*; ~**less** *adj* einwandfrei

flax [flæks] *n* Flachs *m*; ~**en** *adj* flachsfarben

flea [fliː] *n* Floh *m*

fleck [flek] *n* (*mark*) Fleck *m*; (*pattern*) Tupfen *m*

fled [fled] *pt*, *pp* **of flee**

flee [fliː] (*pt*, *pp* **fled**) *vi* fliehen ♦ *vt* fliehen vor +*dat*; (*country*) fliehen aus

fleece [fliːs] *n* Vlies *nt* ♦ *vt* (*inf*) schröpfen

fleet [fliːt] *n* Flotte *f*

fleeting ['fliːtɪŋ] *adj* flüchtig

Flemish ['flemɪʃ] *adj* flämisch

flesh [fleʃ] *n* Fleisch *nt*; ~ **wound** *n* Fleischwunde *f*

flew [fluː] *pt* *of* **fly**

flex [fleks] *n* Kabel *nt* ♦ *vt* beugen; ~**ibility** [fleksɪ'bɪlɪtɪ] *n* Biegsamkeit *f*; (*fig*) Flexibilität *f*; ~**ible** *adj* biegsam; (*plans*) flexibel

flick [flɪk] *n* leichte(r) Schlag *m* ♦ *vt* leicht schlagen; ~ **through** *vt fus* durchblättern

flicker ['flɪkə*] *n* Flackern *nt* ♦ *vi* flackern

flier ['flaɪə*] *n* Flieger *m*

flight [flaɪt] *n* Flug *m*; (*fleeing*) Flucht *f*; (*also:* ~ *of steps*) Treppe *f*; **to take** ~ die Flucht ergreifen; ~ **attendant** (*US*) *n* Steward(eß) *m(f)*; ~ **deck** *n* Flugdeck *nt*

flimsy ['flɪmzɪ] *adj* (*thin*) hauchdünn; (*excuse*) fadenscheinig

flinch [flɪntʃ] *vi*: **to** ~ (**away from**) zurückschrecken (vor +*dat*)

fling [flɪŋ] (*pt*, *pp* **flung**) *vt* schleudern

flint [flɪnt] *n* Feuerstein *m*

flip [flɪp] *vt* werfen

flippant ['flɪpənt] *adj* schnippisch

flipper ['flɪpə*] *n* Flosse *f*

flirt [flɜːt] *vi* flirten ♦ *n*: **he/she is a** ~ er/sie flirtet gern; ~**ation** [flɜː'teɪʃən] *n* Flirt *m*

flit [flɪt] *vi* flitzen

float [fləʊt] *n* (*FISHING*) Schwimmer *m*; (*esp in procession*) Plattformwagen *m* ♦ *vi* schwimmen; (*in air*) schweben ♦ *vt* (*COMM*) gründen; (*currency*) floaten

flock [flɒk] *n* (*of sheep*, *REL*) Herde *f*; (*of*

birds) Schwarm *m*; (*of people*) Schar *f*

flog [flɒg] *vt* prügeln; (*inf: sell*) verkaufen

flood [flʌd] *n* Überschwemmung *f*; (*fig*) Flut *f* ♦ *vt* überschwemmen; **~ing** *n* Überschwemmung *f*; **~light** *n* Flutlicht *nt*

floor [flɔː*] *n* (Fuß)boden *m*; (*storey*) Stock *m* ♦ *vt* (*person*) zu Boden schlagen; **ground ~** (*BRIT*) Erdgeschoß *nt*; **first ~** erste(r) Stock *m*; (*US*) Erdgeschoß *nt*; **~board** *n* Diele *f*; **~ show** *n* Kabarettvorstellung *f*

flop [flɒp] *n* Plumps *m*; (*failure*) Reinfall *m* ♦ *vi* (*fail*) durchfallen

floppy ['flɒpɪ] *adj* hängend; **~ (disk)** *n* (*COMPUT*) Diskette *f*

flora ['flɔːrə] *n* Flora *f*; **~l** *adj* Blumen-

florid ['flɒrɪd] *adj* (*style*) blumig

florist ['flɒrɪst] *n* Blumenhändler(in) *m(f)*; **~'s (shop)** *n* Blumengeschäft *nt*

flotation [fləʊ'teɪʃən] *n* (*FINANCE*) Auflegung *f*

flounce [flaʊns] *n* Volant *m*

flounder ['flaʊndə*] *vi* (*fig*) ins Schleudern kommen ♦ *n* (*ZOOL*) Flunder *f*

flour ['flaʊə*] *n* Mehl *nt*

flourish ['flʌrɪʃ] *vi* blühen; gedeihen ♦ *n* (*waving*) Schwingen *nt*; (*of trumpets*) Tusch *m*, Fanfare *f*; **~ing** *adj* blühend

flout [flaʊt] *vt* mißachten

flow [fləʊ] *n* Fließen *nt*; (*of sea*) Flut *f* ♦ *vi* fließen; **~ chart** *n* Flußdiagramm *nt*

flower ['flaʊə*] *n* Blume *f* ♦ *vi* blühen; **~ bed** *n* Blumenbeet *nt*; **~pot** *n* Blumentopf *m*; **~y** *adj* (*style*) blumenreich

flown [fləʊn] *pp of* **fly**

flu [fluː] *n* Grippe *f*

fluctuate ['flʌktjʊeɪt] *vi* schwanken

fluctuation [flʌktjʊ'eɪʃən] *n* Schwankung *f*

fluency ['fluːənsɪ] *n* Flüssigkeit *f*

fluent ['fluːənt] *adj* fließend; **~ly** *adv* fließend

fluff [flʌf] *n* Fussel *f*; **~y** *adj* flaumig

fluid ['fluːɪd] *n* Flüssigkeit *f* ♦ *adj* flüssig; (*fig: plans*) veränderbar

fluke [fluːk] (*inf*) *n* Dusel *m*

flung [flʌŋ] *pt, pp of* **fling**

fluoride ['flʊəraɪd] *n* Fluorid *nt*; **~ toothpaste** *n* Fluorzahnpasta *f*

flurry ['flʌrɪ] *n* (*of snow*) Gestöber *nt*; (*of activity*) Aufregung *f*

flush [flʌʃ] *n* Erröten *nt*; (*of excitement*) Glühen *nt* ♦ *vt* (aus)spülen ♦ *vi* erröten ♦ *adj* glatt; **~ out** *vt* aufstöbern; **~ed** *adj* rot

flustered ['flʌstəd] *adj* verwirrt

flute [fluːt] *n* Querflöte *f*

flutter ['flʌtə*] *n* Flattern *nt* ♦ *vi* flattern

flux [flʌks] *n*: **in a state of ~** im Fluß

fly [flaɪ] (*pt* **flew**, *pp* **flown**) *n* (*insect*) Fliege *f*; (*on trousers: also:* **flies**) (Hosen)schlitz *m* ♦ *vt* fliegen ♦ *vi* fliegen; (*flee*) fliehen; (*flag*) wehen; **~ away** *or* **off** *vi* (*bird, insect*) wegfliegen; **~ing** *n* Fliegen *nt* ♦ *adj*: **with ~ing colours** mit fliegenden Fahnen; **~ing start** gute(r) Start *m*; **~ing visit** Stippvisite *f*; **~ing saucer** *n* fliegende Untertasse *f*; **~over** (*BRIT*) *n* Überführung *f*; **~past** *n* Luftparade *f*; **~sheet** *n* (*for tent*) Regendach *nt*

foal [fəʊl] *n* Fohlen *nt*

foam [fəʊm] *n* Schaum *m* ♦ *vi* schäumen; **~ rubber** *n* Schaumgummi *m*

fob [fɒb] *vt*: **to ~ sb off with sth** jdm mit etw andrehen; (*with promise*) jdm mit etw abspeisen

focal ['fəʊkəl] *adj* Brenn-; **~ point** *n* (*of room, activity*) Mittelpunkt *m*

focus ['fəʊkəs] (*pl* **~es**) *n* Brennpunkt *m* ♦ *vt* (*attention*) konzentrieren; (*camera*) scharf einstellen ♦ *vi*: **to ~ (on)** sich konzentrieren (auf +*acc*); **in ~** scharf eingestellt; **out of ~** unscharf

fodder ['fɒdə*] *n* Futter *nt*

foe [fəʊ] *n* Feind *m*

foetus ['fiːtəs] (*esp US* **fetus**) *n* Fötus *m*

fog [fɒg] *n* Nebel *m*; **~gy** *adj* neblig; **~ lamp** *n* (*AUT*) Nebellampe *f*

foil [fɔɪl] *vt* vereiteln ♦ *n* (*metal, also fig*) Folie *f*; (*FENCING*) Florett *nt*

fold [fəʊld] *n* (*bend, crease*) Falte *f*; (*AGR*) Pferch *m* ♦ *vt* falten; **~ up** *vt* (*map etc*) zusammenfalten ♦ *vi* (*business*) eingehen; **~er** *n* Schnellhefter *m*; **~ing** *adj* (*chair etc*) Klapp-

foliage ['fəʊlɪdʒ] *n* Laubwerk *nt*

folk [fəʊk] *npl* Leute *pl* ♦ *adj* Volks-; **~s**

npl (family) Leute *pl;* **~lore** ['fəʊklɔː*] *n (study)* Volkskunde *f; (tradition)* Folklore *f;* **~ song** *n* Volkslied *nt; (modern)* Folksong *m*

follow ['fɒləʊ] *vt* folgen +*dat; (fashion)* mitmachen ♦ *vi* folgen; **~ up** *vt* verfolgen; **~er** *n* Anhänger(in) *m(f);* **~ing** *adj* folgend ♦ *n (people)* Gefolgschaft *f*

folly ['fɒlɪ] *n* Torheit *f*

fond [fɒnd] *adj:* **to be ~ of** gern haben

fondle ['fɒndl] *vt* streicheln

font [fɒnt] *n* Taufbecken *nt*

food [fuːd] *n* Essen *nt; (for animals)* Futter *nt;* **~ mixer** *n* Küchenmixer *m;* **~ poisoning** *n* Lebensmittelvergiftung *f;* **~ processor** *n* Küchenmaschine *f;* **~stuffs** *npl* Lebensmittel *pl*

fool [fuːl] *n* Narr *m,* Närrin *f* ♦ *vt (deceive)* hereinlegen ♦ *vi (also: ~ around)* (herum)albern; **~hardy** *adj* tollkühn; **~ish** *adj* albern; **~proof** *adj* idiotensicher

foot [fʊt] *(pl feet) n* Fuß *m* ♦ *vt (bill)* bezahlen; **on ~** zu Fuß; **~age** ['fʊtɪdʒ] *n (CINE)* Filmmaterial *nt;* **~ball** *n* Fußball *m; (game: BRIT)* Fußball *m; (: US)* Football *m;* **~ball player** *n (BRIT: also: ~baller)* Fußballspieler *m,* Fußballer *m; (US)* Footballer *m;* **~brake** *n* Fußbremse *f;* **~bridge** *n* Fußgängerbrücke *f;* **~hills** *npl* Ausläufer *pl;* **~hold** *n* Halt *m;* **~ing** *n* Halt *m; (fig)* Verhältnis *nt;* **~lights** *npl* Rampenlicht *nt;* **~man** *(irreg) n* Bedienstete(r) *m;* **~note** *n* Fußnote *f;* **~path** *n* Fußweg *m;* **~print** *n* Fußabdruck *m;* **~sore** *adj* fußkrank; **~step** *n* Schritt *m;* **~wear** *n* Schuhzeug *nt*

---

for [fɔː*] *prep* **1** für; **is this for me?** ist das für mich?; **the train for London** der Zug nach London; **he went for the paper** er ging die Zeitung holen; **give it to me — what for?** gib es mir — warum?
2 *(because of)* wegen; **for this reason** aus diesem Grunde
3 *(referring to distance):* **there are roadworks for 5 km** die Baustelle ist 5 km lang; **we walked for miles** wir sind meilenweit gegangen

4 *(referring to time)* seit; *(: with future sense)* für; **he was away for 2 years** er war zwei Jahre lang weg
5 *(with infin clauses):* **it is not for me to decide** das kann ich nicht entscheiden; **for this to be possible ...** damit dies möglich wird/wurde ...
6 *(in spite of)* trotz +*gen or (inf) dat;* **for all his complaints** obwohl er sich ständig beschwert

♦ *conj* denn

---

forage ['fɒrɪdʒ] *n* (Vieh)futter *nt*

foray ['fɒreɪ] *n* Raubzug *m*

forbad(e) [fə'bæd] *pt of* **forbid**

forbid [fə'bɪd] *(pt* **forbad(e),** *pp* **forbidden)** *vt* verbieten; **~den** [fə'bɪdn] *pp of* **forbid;** **~ding** *adj* einschüchternd

force [fɔːs] *n* Kraft *f; (compulsion)* Zwang *m* ♦ *vt* zwingen; *(lock)* aufbrechen; **the F~s** *npl (BRIT)* die Streitkräfte; **in ~** *(rule)* gültig; *(group)* in großer Stärke; **~d** [fɔːst] *adj (smile)* gezwungen; *(landing)* Not-; **~-feed** *vt* zwangsernähren; **~ful** *adj (speech)* kraftvoll; *(personality)* resolut

forceps ['fɔːseps] *npl* Zange *f*

forcibly ['fɔːsəblɪ] *adv* zwangsweise

ford [fɔːd] *n* Furt *f* ♦ *vt* durchwaten

fore [fɔː*] *n:* **to the ~** in den Vordergrund

forearm ['fɔːrɑːm] *n* Unterarm *m*

foreboding [fɔː'bəʊdɪŋ] *n* Vorahnung *f*

forecast ['fɔːkɑːst] *(irreg: like* cast) *n* Vorhersage *f* ♦ *vt* voraussagen

forecourt ['fɔːkɔːt] *n (of garage)* Vorplatz *m*

forefathers ['fɔːfɑːðəz] *npl* Vorfahren *pl*

forefinger ['fɔːfɪŋgə*] *n* Zeigefinger *m*

forefront ['fɔːfrʌnt] *n* Spitze *f*

forego [fɔː'gəʊ] *(irreg: like* go) *vt* verzichten auf +*acc*

foregone ['fɔːgɒn] *adj:* **it's a ~ conclusion** es steht von vornherein fest

foreground ['fɔːgraʊnd] *n* Vordergrund *m*

forehead ['fɒrɪd] *n* Stirn *f*

foreign ['fɒrɪn] *adj* Auslands-; *(accent)* ausländisch; *(trade)* Außen-; *(body)* Fremd-; **~er** *n* Ausländer(in) *m(f);* **~**

exchange *n* Devisen *pl*; **F~ Office** (*BRIT*) *n* Außenministerium *nt*; **F~ Secretary** (*BRIT*) *n* Außenminister *m*

foreleg ['fɔːleg] *n* Vorderbein *nt*

foreman ['fɔːmən] (*irreg*) *n* Vorarbeiter *m*

foremost ['fɔːməust] *adj* erste(r, s) ♦ *adv*: **first and ~** vor allem

forensic [fəˈrensɪk] *adj* gerichtsmedizinisch

forerunner ['fɔːrʌnə*] *n* Vorläufer *m*

foresee [fɔːˈsiː] (*irreg*: *like* **see**) *vt* vorhersehen; **~able** *adj* absehbar

foreshadow [fɔːˈʃædəu] *vt* andeuten

foresight ['fɔːsaɪt] *n* Voraussicht *f*

forest ['fɒrɪst] *n* Wald *m*

forestall [fɔːˈstɔːl] *vt* zuvorkommen +*dat*

forestry ['fɒrɪstrɪ] *n* Forstwirtschaft *f*

foretaste ['fɔːteɪst] *n* Vorgeschmack *m*

foretell [fɔːˈtel] (*irreg*: *like* **tell**) *vt* vorhersagen

forever [fəˈrevə*] *adv* für immer

foreword ['fɔːwɜːd] *n* Vorwort *nt*

forfeit ['fɔːfɪt] *n* Einbuße *f* ♦ *vt* verwirken

forgave [fəˈgeɪv] *pt of* **forgive**

forge [fɔːdʒ] *n* Schmiede *f* ♦ *vt* fälschen; (*iron*) schmieden; **~ ahead** *vi* Fortschritte machen; **~r** *n* Fälscher *m*; **~ry** *n* Fälschung *f*

forget [fəˈget] (*pt* **forgot**, *pp* **forgotten**) *vt*, *vi* vergessen; **~ful** *adj* vergeßlich; **~-me-not** *n* Vergißmeinnicht *nt*

forgive [fəˈgɪv] (*pt* **forgave**, *pp* **forgiven**) *vt* verzeihen; **to ~ sb (for sth)** jdm (etw) verzeihen; **~n** *pp of* **forgive**; **~ness** *n* Verzeihung *f*

forgo [fɔːˈgəu] (*irreg*: *like* **go**) *vt* verzichten auf +*acc*

forgot [fəˈgɒt] *pt of* **forget**

forgotten [fəˈgɒtn] *pp of* **forget**

fork [fɔːk] *n* Gabel *f*; (*in road*) Gabelung *f* ♦ *vi* (*road*) sich gabeln; **~ out** (*inf*) *vt* (*pay*) blechen; **~-lift truck** *n* Gabelstapler *m*

forlorn [fəˈlɔːn] *adj* (*person*) verlassen; (*hope*) vergeblich

form [fɔːm] *n* Form *f*; (*type*) Art *f*; (*figure*) Gestalt *f*; (*SCH*) Klasse *f*; (*bench*)

(Schul)bank *f*; (*document*) Formular *nt* ♦ *vt* formen; (*be part of*) bilden

formal ['fɔːməl] *adj* formell; (*occasion*) offiziell; **~ly** *adv* (*ceremoniously*) formell; (*officially*) offiziell

format ['fɔːmæt] *n* Format *nt* ♦ *vt* (*COMPUT*) formatieren

formation [fɔːˈmeɪʃən] *n* Bildung *f*; (*AVIAT*) Formation *f*

formative ['fɔːmətɪv] *adj* (*years*) formend

former ['fɔːmə*] *adj* früher; (*opposite of latter*) erstere(r, s); **~ly** *adv* früher

formidable ['fɔːmɪdəbl] *adj* furchtbar

formula ['fɔːmjulə] (*pl* **~e** *or* **~s**) *n* Formel *f*; **formulae** ['fɔːmjuliː] *npl of* **formula**; **~te** ['fɔːmjuleɪt] *vt* formulieren

forsake [fəˈseɪk] (*pt* **forsook**, *pp* **forsaken**) *vt* verlassen

forsook [fəˈsuk] *pt of* **forsake**

fort [fɔːt] *n* Feste *f*, Fort *nt*

forte ['fɔːtɪ] *n* Stärke *f*, starke Seite *f*

forth [fɔːθ] *adv*: **and so ~** und so weiter; **~coming** *adj* kommend; (*character*) entgegenkommend; **~right** *adj* offen; **~with** *adv* umgehend

fortify ['fɔːtɪfaɪ] *vt* (ver)stärken; (*protect*) befestigen

fortitude ['fɔːtɪtjuːd] *n* Seelenstärke *f*

fortnight ['fɔːtnaɪt] (*BRIT*) *n* vierzehn Tage *pl*; **~ly** (*BRIT*) *adj* zweiwöchentlich ♦ *adv* alle vierzehn Tage

fortress ['fɔːtrɪs] *n* Festung *f*

fortuitous [fɔːˈtjuːɪtəs] *adj* zufällig

fortunate ['fɔːtʃənɪt] *adj* glücklich; **~ly** *adv* glücklicherweise, zum Glück

fortune ['fɔːtʃən] *n* Glück *nt*; (*money*) Vermögen *nt*; **~-teller** *n* Wahrsager(in) *m(f)*

forty ['fɔːtɪ] *num* vierzig

forum ['fɔːrəm] *n* Forum *nt*

forward ['fɔːwəd] *adj* vordere(r, s); (*movement*) Vorwärts-; (*person*) vorlaut; (*planning*) Voraus- ♦ *adv* vorwärts ♦ *n* (*SPORT*) Stürmer *m* ♦ *vt* (*send*) schicken; (*help*) fördern; **~s** *adv* vorwärts

forwent [fɔːˈwent] *pt of* **forgo**

fossil ['fɒsl] *n* Fossil *nt*, Versteinerung *f*

foster ['fɒstə*] *vt* (*talent*) fördern; **~ child** *n* Pflegekind *nt*; **~ mother** *n*

Pflegemutter f

fought [fɔːt] *pt, pp of* **fight**

foul [faʊl] *adj* schmutzig; *(language)* gemein; *(weather)* schlecht ♦ *n (SPORT)* Foul *nt* ♦ *vt (mechanism)* blockieren; *(SPORT)* foulen; **~ play** *n (SPORT)* Foulspiel *nt*; *(LAW)* Verbrechen *nt*

found [faʊnd] *pt, pp of* **find** ♦ *vt* gründen; **~ation** [faʊn'deɪʃən] *n (act)* Gründung f; *(fig)* Fundament *nt*; *(also: ~ation cream)* Grundierungscreme f; **~ations** *npl (of house)* Fundament *nt*

founder ['faʊndə*] *n* Gründer(in) *m(f)* ♦ *vi* sinken

foundry ['faʊndrɪ] *n* Gießerei f

fount [faʊnt] *n* Quelle f; **~ain** ['faʊntɪn] *n* (Spring)brunnen *m*; **~ain pen** *n* Füllfederhalter *m*

four [fɔː*] *num* vier; **on all ~s** auf allen vieren; **~-poster** *n* Himmelbett *nt*; **~some** *n* Quartett *nt*; **~teen** *num* vierzehn; **~teenth** *adj* vierzehnte(r, s); **~th** *adj* vierte(r, s)

fowl [faʊl] *n* Huhn *nt*; *(food)* Geflügel *nt*

fox [fɒks] *n* Fuchs *m* ♦ *vt* täuschen

foyer ['fɔɪeɪ] *n* Foyer *nt*, Vorhalle f

fraction ['frækʃən] *n (MATH)* Bruch *m*; *(part)* Bruchteil *m*

fracture ['fræktʃə*] *n (MED)* Bruch *m* ♦ *vt* brechen

fragile ['frædʒaɪl] *adj* zerbrechlich

fragment ['frægmənt] *n* Bruchstück *nt*; *(small part)* Splitter *m*

fragrance ['freɪgrəns] *n* Duft *m*

fragrant ['freɪgrənt] *adj* duftend

frail [freɪl] *adj* schwach, gebrechlich

frame [freɪm] *n* Rahmen *m*; *(of spectacles: also: ~s)* Gestell *nt*; *(body)* Gestalt f ♦ *vt* einrahmen; **to ~ sb** *(inf: incriminate)* jdm etwas anhängen; **~ of mind** Verfassung f; **~work** *n* Rahmen *m*; *(of society)* Gefüge *nt*

France [frɑːns] *n* Frankreich *nt*

franchise ['fræntʃaɪz] *n (POL)* (aktives) Wahlrecht *nt*; *(COMM)* Lizenz f

frank [fræŋk] *adj* offen ♦ *vt (letter)* frankieren; **~ly** *adv* offen gesagt; **~ness** *n* Offenheit f

frantic ['fræntɪk] *adj* verzweifelt

fraternal [frə'tɜːnl] *adj* brüderlich

fraternity [frə'tɜːnɪtɪ] *n (club)* Vereinigung f; *(spirit)* Brüderlichkeit f; *(US: SCH)* Studentenverbindung f

fraternize ['frætənaɪz] *vi* fraternisieren

fraud [frɔːd] *n (trickery)* Betrug *m*; *(person)* Schwindler(in) *m(f)*

fraudulent ['frɔːdjʊlənt] *adj* betrügerisch

fraught [frɔːt] *adj*: **~ with** voller +gen

fray [freɪ] *n* Rauferei f ♦ *vt, vi* ausfransen; **tempers were ~ed** die Gemüter waren erhitzt

freak [friːk] *n* Monstrosität f ♦ *cpd (storm etc)* anormal

freckle ['frekl] *n* Sommersprosse f

free [friː] *adj* frei; *(loose)* lose; *(liberal)* freigebig ♦ *vt (set free)* befreien; *(unblock)* freimachen; **~ (of charge)** gratis, umsonst; **for ~** gratis, umsonst; **~dom** ['friːdəm] *n* Freiheit f; **~-for-all** *n (fight)* allgemeine(s) Handgemenge *nt*; **~ gift** *n* Geschenk *nt*; **~hold property** *n* (freie(r)) Grundbesitz *m*; **~ kick** *n* Freistoß *m*; **~lance** *adj* frei; *(artist)* freischaffend; **~ly** *adv* frei; *(admit)* offen; **~mason** *n* Freimaurer *m*; **~post** *n* ≈ Gebühr zahlt Empfänger; **~-range** *adj (hen)* Farmhof-; *(eggs)* Land-; **~ trade** *n* Freihandel *m*; **~way** *(US)* *n* Autobahn f; **~wheel** *vi* im Freilauf fahren; **~ will** *n*: **of one's own ~ will** aus freien Stücken

freeze [friːz] *(pt froze, pp frozen)* *vi* gefrieren; *(feel cold)* frieren ♦ *vt (also fig)* einfrieren ♦ *n (fig, FIN)* Stopp *m*; **~r** *n* Tiefkühltruhe f; *(in fridge)* Gefrierfach *nt*

freezing ['friːzɪŋ] *adj* eisig; *(~ cold)* eiskalt; **~ point** *n* Gefrierpunkt *m*

freight [freɪt] *n* Fracht f; **~ train** *n* Güterzug *m*

French [frentʃ] *adj* französisch ♦ *n (LING)* Französisch *nt*; **the ~** *npl (people)* die Franzosen *pl*; **~ bean** *n* grüne Bohne f; **~ fried potatoes** *(BRIT)* *npl* Pommes frites *pl*; **~ fries** *(US)* *npl* Pommes frites *pl*; **~man/woman** *(irreg)* *n* Franzose *m*/Französin f; **~ window** *n* Verandatür f

frenzy ['frenzɪ] *n* Raserei f

frequency ['friːkwənsɪ] *n* Häufigkeit f; *(PHYS)* Frequenz f

frequent [*adj* 'fri:kwənt, *vb* fri:'kwent] *adj* häufig ♦ *vt* (regelmäßig) besuchen; **~ly** *adv* (*often*) häufig, oft

fresco ['freskəʊ] *n* Fresko *nt*

fresh [freʃ] *adj* frisch; **~en** *vi* (*also*: ~en up) (sich) auffrischen; (*person*) sich frisch machen; **~er** (*BRIT*: *inf*) *n* (*UNIV*) Erstsemester *nt*; **~ly** *adv* gerade; **~man** (*US*; *irreg*) *n* = **fresher**; **~ness** *n* Frische *f*; **~water** *adj* (*fish*) Süßwasser-

fret [fret] *vi* sich *dat* Sorgen machen

friar ['fraɪə*] *n* Klosterbruder *m*

friction ['frɪkʃən] *n* (*also fig*) Reibung *f*

Friday ['fraɪdeɪ] *n* Freitag *m*

fridge [frɪdʒ] (*BRIT*) *n* Kühlschrank *m*

fried [fraɪd] *adj* gebraten

friend [frend] *n* Freund(in) *m(f)*; **~ly** *adj* freundlich; (*relations*) freundschaftlich; **~ly fire** *n* Beschuß *m* durch die eigene Seite; **~ship** *n* Freundschaft *f*

frieze [fri:z] *n* Fries *m*

frigate ['frɪgɪt] *n* Fregatte *f*

fright [fraɪt] *n* Schrecken *m*; **to take ~** es mit der Angst zu tun bekommen; **~en** *vt* erschrecken; **to be ~ened** Angst haben; **~ening** *adj* schrecklich; **~ful** (*inf*) *adj* furchtbar; **~fully** (*inf*) *adv* furchtbar

frigid ['frɪdʒɪd] *adj* (*woman*) frigide

frill [frɪl] *n* Rüsche *f*

fringe [frɪndʒ] *n* Besatz *m*; (*BRIT*: *of hair*) Pony *m*; (*fig*) Peripherie *f*; **~ benefits** *npl* zusätzliche Leistungen *pl*

frisk [frɪsk] *vt* durchsuchen

frisky ['frɪskɪ] *adj* lebendig, ausgelassen

fritter ['frɪtə*] *vt*: **to ~ away** vergeuden

frivolous ['frɪvələs] *adj* frivol

frizzy ['frɪzɪ] *adj* kraus

fro [frəʊ] *adv see* **to**

frock [frɒk] *n* Kleid *nt*

frog [frɒg] *n* Frosch *m*; **~man** (*irreg*) *n* Froschmann *m*

frolic ['frɒlɪk] *vi* ausgelassen sein

KEYWORD
---

from [frɒm] *prep* **1** (*indicating starting place*) von; (*indicating origin etc*) aus +*dat*; **a letter/telephone call from my sister** ein Brief/Anruf von meiner Schwester; **where do you come from?**

woher kommen Sie?; **to drink from the bottle** aus der Flasche trinken

2 (*indicating time*) von ... an; (: *past*) seit; **from one o'clock to** *or* **until** *or* **till two** von ein Uhr bis zwei; **from January (on)** ab Januar

3 (*indicating distance*) von ... (entfernt)

4 (*indicating price, number etc*) ab +*dat*; **from £10** ab £10; **there were from 20 to 30 people there** es waren zwischen 20 und 30 Leute da

5 (*indicating difference*): **he can't tell red from green** er kann nicht zwischen rot und grün unterscheiden; **to be different from sb/sth** anders sein als jd/etw

6 (*because of, on the basis of*): **from what he says** aus dem, was er sagt; **weak from hunger** schwach vor Hunger

---

front [frʌnt] *n* Vorderseite *f*; (*of house*) Fassade *f*; (*promenade*: *also*: sea ~) Strandpromenade *f*; (*MIL, POL, MET*) Front *f*; (*fig*: *appearances*) Fassade *f* ♦ *adj* (*forward*) vordere(r, s), Vorder-; (*first*) vorderste(r, s); **in ~** vorne; **in ~ of** vor; **~age** ['frʌntɪdʒ] *n* Vorderfront *f*; **~al** *adj* frontal, Vorder-; **~ door** *n* Haustür *f*; **~ier** [frʌn'tɪə*] *n* Grenze *f*; **~ page** *n* Titelseite *f*; **~ room** (*BRIT*) *n* Wohnzimmer *nt*; **~-wheel drive** *n* Vorderradantrieb *m*

frost [frɒst] *n* Frost *m*; **~bite** *n* Erfrierung *f*; **~ed** *adj* (*glass*) Milch-; **~y** *adj* frostig

froth [frɒθ] *n* Schaum *m*

frown [fraʊn] *n* Stirnrunzeln *nt* ♦ *vi* die Stirn runzeln

froze [frəʊz] *pt of* **freeze**

frozen ['frəʊzn] *pp of* **freeze**

frugal ['fru:gəl] *adj* sparsam, bescheiden

fruit [fru:t] *n inv* (*as collective*) Obst *nt*; (*particular*) Frucht *f*; **~erer** *n* Obsthändler *m*; **~ful** *adj* fruchtbar; **~ion** [fru:'ɪʃən] *n*: **to come to ~ion** in Erfüllung gehen; **~ juice** *n* Fruchtsaft *m*; **~ machine** (*BRIT*) *n* Spielautomat *m*; **~ salad** *n* Obstsalat *m*

frustrate [frʌs'treɪt] *vt* vereiteln; **~d** *adj* gehemmt; (*PSYCH*) frustriert

fry [fraɪ] (*pt, pp* **fried**) *vt* braten ♦ *npl*:

small ~ kleine Fische *pl*; **~ing pan** *n* Bratpfanne *f*

ft. *abbr* = **foot**; **feet**

fuddy-duddy ['fʌdɪdʌdɪ] *n* altmodische(r) Kauz *m*

fudge [fʌdʒ] *n* Fondant *m*

fuel [fjʊəl] *n* Treibstoff *m*; (*for heating*) Brennstoff *m*; (*for lighter*) Benzin *nt*; **~ oil** *n* (*diesel fuel*) Heizöl *nt*; **~ tank** *n* Tank *m*

fugitive ['fjuːdʒɪtɪv] *n* Flüchtling *m*

fulfil [fʊl'fɪl] *vt* (*duty*) erfüllen; (*promise*) einhalten; **~ment** *n* Erfüllung *f*

full [fʊl] *adj* (*box, bottle, price*) voll; (*person: satisfied*) satt; (*member, power, employment, moon*) Voll-; (*complete*) vollständig, Voll-; (*speed*) höchste(r, s); (*skirt*) weit ♦ *adv*: **~ well** sehr wohl; **in ~** vollständig; **a ~ two hours** volle zwei Stunden; **~-length** *adj* (*lifesize*) lebensgroß; **a ~-length photograph** eine Ganzaufnahme; **~ moon** *n* Vollmond *m*; **~-scale** *adj* (*attack*) General-; (*drawing*) in Originalgröße; **~ stop** *n* Punkt *m*; **~-time** *adj* (*job*) Ganztags- ♦ *adv* (*work*) ganztags ♦ *n* (*SPORT*) Spielschluß *nt*; **~y** *adv* völlig; **~y-fledged** *adj* (*also fig*) flügge

fulsome ['fʊlsəm] *adj* übertrieben

fumble ['fʌmbl] *vi*: **to ~ (with)** herumfummeln (an +*dat*)

fume [fjuːm] *vi* qualmen; (*fig*) kochen (*inf*); **~s** *npl* (*of fuel, car*) Abgase *pl*

fumigate ['fjuːmɪgeɪt] *vt* ausräuchern

fun [fʌn] *n* Spaß *m*; **to make ~ of** sich lustig machen über +*acc*

function ['fʌŋkʃən] *n* Funktion *f*; (*occasion*) Veranstaltung *f* ♦ *vi* funktionieren; **~al** *adj* funktionell

fund [fʌnd] *n* (*money*) Geldmittel *pl*, Fonds *m*; (*store*) Vorrat *m*; **~s** *npl* (*resources*) Mittel *pl*

fundamental [fʌndə'mentl] *adj* fundamental, grundlegend

funeral ['fjuːnərəl] *n* Beerdigung *f*; **~ parlour** *n* Leichenhalle *f*; **~ service** *n* Trauergottesdienst *m*

funfair ['fʌnfeə*] (*BRIT*) *n* Jahrmarkt *m*

fungi ['fʌŋgaɪ] *npl of* **fungus**

fungus ['fʌŋgəs] *n* Pilz *m*

funnel ['fʌnl] *n* Trichter *m*; (*NAUT*) Schornstein *m*

funny ['fʌnɪ] *adj* komisch

fur [fɜː*] *n* Pelz *m*; **~ coat** *n* Pelzmantel *m*

furious ['fjʊərɪəs] *adj* wütend; (*attempt*) heftig

furlong ['fɜːlɒŋ] *n* = 201.17 m

furlough ['fɜːləʊ] *n* Urlaub *m*

furnace ['fɜːnɪs] *n* (Brenn)ofen *m*

furnish ['fɜːnɪʃ] *vt* einrichten; (*supply*) versehen; **~ings** *npl* Einrichtung *f*

furniture ['fɜːnɪtʃə*] *n* Möbel *pl*; **piece of ~** Möbelstück *nt*

furrow ['fʌrəʊ] *n* Furche *f*

furry ['fɜːrɪ] *adj* (*tongue*) pelzig; (*animal*) Pelz-

further ['fɜːðə*] *adj* weitere(r, s) ♦ *adv* weiter ♦ *vt* fördern; **~ education** *n* Weiterbildung *f*; Erwachsenenbildung *f*; **~more** *adv* ferner

furthest ['fɜːðɪst] *superl of* **far**

furtive ['fɜːtɪv] *adj* verstohlen

fury ['fjʊərɪ] *n* Wut *f*, Zorn *m*

fuse [fjuːz] (*US* **fuze**) *n* (*ELEC*) Sicherung *f*; (*of bomb*) Zünder *m* ♦ *vt* verschmelzen ♦ *vi* (*BRIT: ELEC*) durchbrennen; **~ box** *n* Sicherungskasten *m*

fuselage ['fjuːzəlɑːʒ] *n* Flugzeugrumpf *m*

fusion ['fjuːʒən] *n* Verschmelzung *f*

fuss [fʌs] *n* Theater *nt*; **~y** *adj* kleinlich

futile ['fjuːtaɪl] *adj* zwecklos, sinnlos

futility [fjuː'tɪlɪtɪ] *n* Zwecklosigkeit *f*

future ['fjuːtʃə*] *adj* zukünftig ♦ *n* Zukunft *f*; **in (the) ~** in Zukunft

fuze [fjuːz] (*US*) = **fuse**

fuzzy ['fʌzɪ] *adj* (*indistinct*) verschwommen; (*hair*) kraus

G g

G [dʒiː] *n* (*MUS*) G *nt*

G7 *n abbr* (= *Group of Seven*) G7 *f*

gabble ['gæbl] *vi* plappern

gable ['geɪbl] *n* Giebel *m*

gadget ['gædʒɪt] *n* Vorrichtung *f*

Gaelic ['geɪlɪk] *adj* gälisch ♦ *n* (*LING*)

Gälisch *nt*

gaffe [gæf] *n* Fauxpas *m*

gag [gæg] *n* Knebel *m*; (*THEAT*) Gag *m* ♦ *vt* knebeln

gaiety ['geɪətɪ] *n* Fröhlichkeit *f*

gaily ['geɪlɪ] *adv* lustig, fröhlich

gain [geɪn] *vt* (*obtain*) erhalten; (*win*) gewinnen ♦ *vi* (*clock*) vorgehen ♦ *n* Gewinn *m*; **to ~ in sth** an etw *dat* gewinnen; **~ on** *vt fus* einholen

gait [geɪt] *n* Gang *m*

gal. *abbr* = **gallon**

gala ['gɑːlə] *n* Fest *nt*

galaxy ['gæləksɪ] *n* Sternsystem *nt*

gale [geɪl] *n* Sturm *m*

gallant ['gælənt] *adj* tapfer; (*polite*) galant; **~ry** *n* Tapferkeit *f*, Galanterie *f*

gallbladder ['gɔːl-] *n* Gallenblase *f*

gallery ['gælərɪ] *n* (*also: art* ~) Galerie *f*

galley ['gælɪ] *n* (*ship's kitchen*) Kombüse *f*; (*ship*) Galeere *f*

gallon ['gælən] *n* Gallone *f*

gallop ['gæləp] *n* Galopp *m* ♦ *vi* galoppieren

gallows ['gæləʊz] *n* Galgen *m*

gallstone ['gɔːlstəʊn] *n* Gallenstein *m*

galore [gə'lɔː*] *adv* in Hülle und Fülle

galvanize ['gælvənaɪz] *vt* (*metal*) galvanisieren; (*fig*) elektrisieren

gambit ['gæmbɪt] *n* (*fig*): **opening ~** (einleitende(r)) Schachzug *m*

gamble ['gæmbl] *vi* (um Geld) spielen ♦ *vt* (*risk*) aufs Spiel setzen ♦ *n* Risiko *nt*; **~r** *n* Spieler(in) *m(f)*

gambling ['gæmblɪŋ] *n* Glücksspiel *nt*

game [geɪm] *n* Spiel *nt*; (*hunting*) Wild *nt* ♦ *adj*: **~ (for)** bereit (zu); **~keeper** *n* Wildhüter *m*; **~s console** *n* (*COMPUT*) Gameboy *m* ®, Konsole *f*

gammon ['gæmən] *n* geräucherte(r) Schinken *m*

gamut ['gæmət] *n* Tonskala *f*

gang [gæŋ] *n* (*of criminals, youths*) Bande *f*; (*of workmen*) Kolonne *f* ♦ *vi*: **to ~ up on sb** sich gegen jdn verschwören

gangrene ['gæŋɡriːn] *n* Brand *m*

gangster ['gæŋstə*] *n* Gangster *m*

gangway ['gæŋweɪ] *n* (*NAUT*) Laufplanke *f*; (*aisle*) Gang *m*

gaol [dʒeɪl] (*BRIT*) *n, vt* = **jail**

gap [gæp] *n* Lücke *f*

gape [geɪp] *vi* glotzen

gaping ['geɪpɪŋ] *adj* (*wound*) klaffend; (*hole*) gähnend

garage ['gærɑːʒ] *n* Garage *f*; (*for repair*) (Auto)reparaturwerkstatt *f*; (*for petrol*) Tankstelle *f*

garbage ['gɑːbɪdʒ] *n* Abfall *m*; **~ can** (*US*) *n* Mülltonne *f*

garbled ['gɑːbld] *adj* (*story*) verdreht

garden ['gɑːdn] *n* Garten *m*; **~er** *n* Gärtner(in) *m(f)*; **~ing** *n* Gärtnern *nt*

gargle ['gɑːɡl] *vi* gurgeln

gargoyle ['gɑːɡɔɪl] *n* Wasserspeier *m*

garish ['ɡeərɪʃ] *adj* grell

garland ['gɑːlənd] *n* Girlande *f*

garlic ['gɑːlɪk] *n* Knoblauch *m*

garment ['gɑːmənt] *n* Kleidungsstück *nt*

garnish ['gɑːnɪʃ] *vt* (*food*) garnieren

garrison ['gærɪsən] *n* Garnison *f*

garrulous ['gærʊləs] *adj* geschwätzig

garter ['gɑːtə*] *n* Strumpfband *nt*; (*US*) Strumpfhalter *m*

gas [gæs] *n* Gas *nt*; (*esp US: petrol*) Benzin *nt* ♦ *vt* vergasen; **~ cooker** (*BRIT*) *n* Gasherd *m*; **~ cylinder** *n* Gasflasche *f*, **~ fire** *n* Gasofen *m*

gash [gæʃ] *n* klaffende Wunde *f* ♦ *vt* tief verwunden

gasket ['gæskɪt] *n* Dichtungsring *m*

gas mask *n* Gasmaske *f*

gas meter *n* Gaszähler *m*

gasoline ['gæsəliːn] (*US*) *n* Benzin *nt*

gasp [gɑːsp] *vi* keuchen; (*in astonishment*) tief Luft holen ♦ *n* Keuchen *nt*

gas ring *n* Gasring *m*

gas tap *n* Gashahn *m*

gastric ['gæstrɪk] *adj* Magen-

gate [geɪt] *n* Tor *nt*; (*barrier*) Schranke *f*; **~crash** (*BRIT*) *vt* (*party*) platzen in +*acc*; **~way** *n* Toreingang *m*

gather ['gæðə*] *vt* (*people*) versammeln; (*things*) sammeln; (*understand*) annehmen ♦ *vi* (*assemble*) sich versammeln; **to ~ speed** schneller werden; **to ~ (from)** schließen (aus); **~ing** *n* Versammlung *f*

gauche [gəʊʃ] *adj* linkisch

gaudy ['gɔːdɪ] *adj* schreiend

gauge [geɪdʒ] *n* (*instrument*) Meßgerät *nt*; (*RAIL*) Spurweite *f*; (*dial*) Anzeiger *m*; (*measure*) Maß *nt* ♦ *vt* (ab)messen; (*fig*) abschätzen

gaunt [gɔːnt] *adj* hager

gauntlet ['gɔːntlɪt] *n* (*knight's*) (Fehde)handschuh *m*

gauze [gɔːz] *n* Gaze *f*

gave [geɪv] *pt of* **give**

gay [geɪ] *adj* (*homosexual*) schwul; (*lively*) lustig

gaze [geɪz] *n* Blick *m* ♦ *vi* starren; **to ~ at sth** etw *dat* anstarren

gazelle [gə'zel] *n* Gazelle *f*

gazette [gə'zet] *n* Zeitung *f*

gazetteer [gæzɪ'tɪə*] *n* geographische(s) Lexikon *nt*

gazumping [gə'zʌmpɪŋ] (*BRIT*) *n* Hausverkauf an Höherbietenden trotz Zusage an anderen

GB *n abbr* = **Great Britain**

GCE (*BRIT*) *n abbr* = **General Certificate of Education**

GCSE (*BRIT*) *n abbr* = **General Certificate of Secondary Education**

gear [gɪə*] *n* Getriebe *nt*; (*equipment*) Ausrüstung *f*; (*AUT*) Gang *m* ♦ *vt* (*fig: adapt*): **to be ~ed to** ausgerichtet sein auf +*acc*; **top ~** höchste(r) Gang *m*; **high ~** (*US*) höchste(r) Gang *m*; **low ~** niedrige(r) Gang *m*; **in ~** eingekuppelt; **~ box** *n* Getriebe(gehäuse) *nt*; **~ lever** *n* Schalthebel *m*; **~ shift** (*US*) *n* Schalthebel *m*

geese [giːs] *npl of* **goose**

gel [dʒel] *n* Gel *nt*

gelatin(e) ['dʒelətiːn] *n* Gelatine *f*

gelignite ['dʒelɪgnaɪt] *n* Plastiksprengstoff *m*

gem [dʒem] *n* Edelstein *m*; (*fig*) Juwel *nt*

Gemini ['dʒemɪniː] *n* Zwillinge *pl*

gender ['dʒendə*] *n* (*GRAM*) Geschlecht *nt*

gene [dʒiːn] *n* Gen *nt*

general ['dʒenərəl] *n* General *m* ♦ *adj* allgemein; **~ delivery** (*US*) *n* Ausgabe(schalter *m*) *f* postlagernder Sendungen; **~ election** *n* allgemeine Wahlen *pl*; **~ization** [dʒenərəlaɪ'zeɪʃən] *n* Verallgemeinerung *f*; **~ize** *vi*

verallgemeinern; **~ly** *adv* allgemein, im allgemeinen; **~ practitioner** *n* praktische(r) Arzt *m*, praktische Ärztin *f*

generate ['dʒenəreɪt] *vt* erzeugen

generation [dʒenə'reɪʃən] *n* Generation *f*; (*act*) Erzeugung *f*

generator ['dʒenəreɪtə*] *n* Generator *m*

generosity [dʒenə'rɒsɪtɪ] *n* Großzügigkeit *f*

generous ['dʒenərəs] *adj* großzügig

genetic [dʒɪ'netɪk]: **~ engineering** *n* Gentechnik *f*; **~ fingerprinting** *n* genetische Fingerabdrücke *pl*

genetics [dʒɪ'netɪks] *n* Genetik *f*

Geneva [dʒɪ'niːvə] *n* Genf *nt*

genial ['dʒiːnɪəl] *adj* freundlich, jovial

genitals ['dʒenɪtlz] *npl* Genitalien *pl*

genius ['dʒiːnɪəs] *n* Genie *nt*

genocide ['dʒenəʊsaɪd] *n* Völkermord *m*

gent [dʒent] *n abbr* = **gentleman**

genteel [dʒen'tiːl] *adj* (*polite*) wohlanständig; (*affected*) affektiert

gentle ['dʒentl] *adj* sanft, zart

gentleman ['dʒentlmən] *n* (*irreg*) Herr *m*; (*polite*) Gentleman *m*

gentleness ['dʒentlnɪs] *n* Zartheit *f*, Milde *f*

gently ['dʒentlɪ] *adv* zart, sanft

gentry ['dʒentrɪ] *n* Landadel *m*

gents [dʒents] *n*: **G~** (*lavatory*) Herren *pl*

genuine ['dʒenjuɪn] *adj* echt

geographic(al) [dʒɪə'græfɪk(əl)] *adj* geographisch

geography [dʒɪ'ɒgrəfɪ] *n* Geographie *f*

geological [dʒɪəʊ'lɒdʒɪkəl] *adj* geologisch

geologist [dʒɪ'ɒlədʒɪst] *n* Geologe *m*, Geologin *f*

geology [dʒɪ'ɒlədʒɪ] *n* Geologie *f*

geometric(al) [dʒɪə'metrɪk(l)] *adj* geometrisch

geometry [dʒɪ'ɒmɪtrɪ] *n* Geometrie *f*

geranium [dʒɪ'reɪnɪəm] *n* Geranie *f*

geriatric [dʒerɪ'ætrɪk] *adj* Alten- ♦ *n* Greis(in) *m(f)*

germ [dʒɜːm] *n* Keim *m*; (*MED*) Bazillus *m*

German ['dʒɜːmən] *adj* deutsch ♦ *n* Deutsche(r) *mf*; (*LING*) Deutsch *nt*; **~ measles** *n* Röteln *pl*

Germany ['dʒɜːmənɪ] *n* Deutschland *nt*

germination [dʒɜːmɪˈneɪʃən] n Keimen nt

gesticulate [dʒesˈtɪkjʊleɪt] vi gestikulieren

gesture [ˈdʒestʃə*] n Geste f

KEYWORD

get [get] (pt, pp **got**, pp **gotten** (US)) vi **1** (become, be) werden; **to get old/tired** alt/müde werden; **to get married** heiraten

2 (go) (an)kommen, gehen

3 (begin): **to get to know sb** jdn kennenlernen; **let's get going** or **started** fangen wir an!

4 (modal aux vb): **you've got to do it** du mußt es tun

♦ vt **1**: **to get sth done** (do) etw machen; (have done) etw machen lassen; **to get sth going** or **to go** etw in Gang bringen or bekommen; **to get sb to do sth** jdn dazu bringen, etw zu tun

2 (obtain: money, permission, results) erhalten; (find: job, flat) finden; (fetch: person, doctor, object) holen; **to get sth for sb** jdm etw besorgen; **get me Mr Jones, please** (TEL) verbinden Sie mich bitte mit Mr Jones

3 (receive: present, letter) bekommen, kriegen; (acquire: reputation etc) erwerben

4 (catch) bekommen, kriegen; (hit: target etc) treffen, erwischen; **get him!** (to dog) faß!

5 (take, move) bringen; **to get sth to sb** jdm etw bringen

6 (understand) verstehen; (hear) mitbekommen; **I've got it!** ich hab's!

7 (have, possess): **to have got sth** etw haben

get about vi herumkommen; (news) sich verbreiten

get along vi (people) (gut) zurechtkommen; (depart) sich acc auf den Weg machen

get at vt (facts) herausbekommen; **to get at sb** (nag) an jdm herumnörgeln

get away vi (leave) sich acc davonmachen; (escape): **to get away from sth** von etw dat entkommen; **to get away**

with sth mit etw davon kommen

get back vi (return) zurückkommen ♦ vt zurückbekommen

get by vi (pass) vorbeikommen; (manage) zurechtkommen

get down vi (her)untergehen ♦ vt (depress) fertigmachen; **to get down to** in Angriff nehmen; (find time to do) kommen zu

get in vi (train) ankommen; (arrive home) heimkommen

get into vt (enter) hinein-/hereinkommen in +acc; (: car, train•etc) einsteigen in +acc; (clothes) anziehen

get off vi (from train etc) aussteigen; (from horse) absteigen ♦ vt aussteigen aus; absteigen von

get on vi (progress) vorankommen; (be friends) auskommen; (age) alt werden; (onto train etc) einsteigen; (onto horse) aufsteigen ♦ vt einsteigen in +acc; **to get on sth** auf etw acc aufsteigen

get out vi (of house) herauskommen; (of vehicle) aussteigen ♦ vt (take out) herausholen

get out of vt (duty etc) herumkommen um

get over vt (illness) sich acc erholen von; (surprise) verkraften; (news) fassen; (loss) sich abfinden mit

get round vt herumkommen; (fig: person) herumkriegen

get through to vt (TEL) durchkommen zu

get together vi zusammenkommen

get up vi aufstehen ♦ vt hinaufbringen; (go up) hinaufgehen; (organize) auf die Beine stellen

get up to vt (reach) erreichen; (prank etc) anstellen

getaway [ˈgetəweɪ] n Flucht f

get-up [ˈgetʌp] (inf) n Aufzug m

geyser [ˈgiːzə*] n Geiser m; (heater) Durchlauferhitzer m

ghastly [ˈgɑːstlɪ] adj gräßlich

gherkin [ˈgɜːkɪn] n Gewürzgurke f

ghetto [ˈgetəʊ] n G(h)etto nt; ~ **blaster** n (groß(er)) Radiorekorder m

ghost [gəust] *n* Gespenst *nt*

giant ['dʒaɪənt] *n* Riese *m* ♦ *adj* riesig, Riesen-

gibberish ['dʒɪbərɪʃ] *n* dumme(s) Geschwätz *nt*

gibe [dʒaɪb] *n* spöttische Bemerkung *f*

giblets ['dʒɪblɪts] *npl* Geflügelinnereien *pl*

Gibraltar [dʒɪ'brɔːltə*] *n* Gibraltar *nt*

giddiness ['gɪdɪnəs] *n* Schwindelgefühl *nt*

giddy ['gɪdɪ] *adj* schwindlig

gift [gɪft] *n* Geschenk *nt*; *(ability)* Begabung *f*; **~ed** *adj* begabt; **~ token, ~ voucher** *n* Geschenkgutschein *m*

gigantic [dʒaɪ'gæntɪk] *adj* riesenhaft

giggle ['gɪgl] *vi* kichern ♦ *n* Gekicher *nt*

gild [gɪld] *vt* vergolden

gill [dʒɪl] *n* (1/4 pint) Viertelpinte *f*

gills [gɪlz] *npl (of fish)* Kiemen *pl*

gilt [gɪlt] *n* Vergoldung *f* ♦ *adj* vergoldet; **~-edged** *adj* mündelsicher

gimmick ['gɪmɪk] *n* Gag *m*

ginger ['dʒɪndʒə*] *n* Ingwer *m*; **~ ale** *n* Ingwerbier *nt*; **~ beer** *n* Ingwerbier *nt*; **~bread** *n* Pfefferkuchen *m*; **~-haired** *adj* rothaarig

gingerly ['dʒɪndʒəlɪ] *adv* behutsam

gipsy ['dʒɪpsɪ] *n* Zigeuner(in) *m(f)*

girder ['gɜːdə*] *n* Eisenträger *m*

girdle ['gɜːdl] *n* Hüftgürtel *m*

girl [gɜːl] *n* Mädchen *nt*; **an English ~** eine (junge) Engländerin; **~friend** *n* Freundin *f*; **~ish** *adj* mädchenhaft

giro ['dʒaɪrəu] *n (bank ~)* Giro *nt*; *(post office ~)* Postscheckverkehr *m*

girth [gɜːθ] *n (measure)* Umfang *m*; *(strap)* Sattelgurt *m*

gist [dʒɪst] *n* Wesentliche(s) *nt*

give [gɪv] *(pt* **gave***, pp* **given***) vt* geben ♦ *vi (break)* nachgeben; **~ away** *vt* verschenken; *(betray)* verraten; **~ back** *vt* zurückgeben; **~ in** *vi* nachgeben ♦ *vt (hand in)* abgeben; **~ off** *vt* abgeben; **~ out** *vt* verteilen; *(announce)* bekanntgeben; **~ up** *vt, vi* aufgeben; **to ~ o.s. up** sich stellen; *(after siege)* sich ergeben; **~ way** *vi (BRIT: traffic)* Vorfahrt lassen; *(to feelings)*: **to ~ way to**

nachgeben +*dat*; **~n** *pp of* **give**

glacier ['glæsɪə*] *n* Gletscher *m*

glad [glæd] *adj* froh

gladly ['glædlɪ] *adv* gern(e)

glamorous ['glæmərəs] *adj* reizvoll

glamour ['glæmə*] *n* Glanz *m*

glance [glɑːns] *n* Blick *m* ♦ *vi*: **to ~ (at)** (hin)blicken (auf +*acc*); **~ off** *vt fus (fly off)* abprallen von

glancing ['glɑːnsɪŋ] *adj (blow)* Streif-

gland [glænd] *n* Drüse *f*

glare [glɛə*] *n (light)* grelle(s) Licht *nt*; *(stare)* wilde(r) Blick *m* ♦ *vi* grell scheinen; *(angrily)*: **to ~ at** böse ansehen

glaring ['glɛərɪŋ] *adj (injustice)* schreiend; *(mistake)* kraß

glass [glɑːs] *n* Glas *nt*; *(mirror: also: looking ~)* Spiegel *m*; **~es** *npl (spectacles)* Brille *f*; **~house** *n* Gewächshaus *nt*; **~ware** *n* Glaswaren *pl*; **~y** *adj* glasig

glaze [gleɪz] *vt* verglasen; *(finish with a ~)* glasieren ♦ *n* Glasur *f*; **~d** *adj (eye)* glasig; *(pottery)* glasiert

glazier ['gleɪzɪə*] *n* Glaser *m*

gleam [gliːm] *n* Schimmer *m* ♦ *vi* schimmern; **~ing** *adj* schimmernd

glean [gliːn] *vt (fig)* ausfindig machen

glen [glen] *n* Bergtal *nt*

glib [glɪb] *adj* oberflächlich

glide [glaɪd] *vi* gleiten; **~r** *n (AVIAT)* Segelflugzeug *nt*

gliding ['glaɪdɪŋ] *n* Segelfliegen *nt*

glimmer ['glɪmə*] *n* Schimmer *m*

glimpse [glɪmps] *n* flüchtige(r) Blick *m* ♦ *vt* flüchtig erblicken

glint [glɪnt] *n* Glitzern *nt* ♦ *vi* glitzern

glisten ['glɪsn] *vi* glänzen

glitter ['glɪtə*] *vi* funkeln ♦ *n* Funkeln *nt*

gloat ['gləut] *vi*: **to ~ over** sich weiden an +*dat*

global ['gləubl] *adj*: **~ warming** globale(r) Temperaturanstieg *m*

globe [gləub] *n* Erdball *m*; *(sphere)* Globus *m*

gloom [gluːm] *n (darkness)* Dunkel *nt*; *(depression)* düstere Stimmung *f*; **~y** *adj* düster

glorify ['glɔːrɪfaɪ] *vt* verherrlichen

glorious ['glɔːrɪəs] *adj* glorreich

glory ['glɔ:rɪ] *n* Ruhm *m*

gloss [glɒs] *n* (*shine*) Glanz *m*; ~ **over** *vt fus* übertünchen

glossary ['glɒsərɪ] *n* Glossar *nt*

glossy ['glɒsɪ] *adj* (*surface*) glänzend

glove [glʌv] *n* Handschuh *m*; ~ **compartment** *n* (*AUT*) Handschuhfach *nt*

glow [gləʊ] *vi* glühen ♦ *n* Glühen *nt*

glower ['glaʊə*] *vi*: **to** ~ **at** finster anblicken

glucose ['glu:kəʊs] *n* Traubenzucker *m*

glue [glu:] *n* Klebstoff *m* ♦ *vt* kleben

glum [glʌm] *adj* bedrückt

glut [glʌt] *n* Überfluß *m*

glutton ['glʌtn] *n* Vielfraß *m*; **a** ~ **for work** ein Arbeitstier *nt*; ~**y** *n* Völlerei *f*

glycerin(e) ['glɪsəri:n] *n* Glyzerin *nt*

gnarled [nɑ:ld] *adj* knorrig

gnat [næt] *n* Stechmücke *f*

gnaw [nɔ:] *vt* nagen an +*dat*

gnome [nəʊm] *n* Gnom *m*

go [gəʊ] (*pt* **went**, *pp* **gone**; *pl* ~**es**) *vi* gehen; (*travel*) reisen, fahren; (*depart*: *train*) (ab)fahren; (*be sold*) verkauft werden; (*work*) gehen, funktionieren; (*fit, suit*) passen; (*become*) werden; (*break etc*) nachgeben ♦ *n* (*energy*) Schwung *m*; (*attempt*) Versuch *m*; **he's ~ing to do it** er wird es tun; **to ~ for a walk** spazieren gehen; **to ~ dancing** tanzen gehen; **how did it ~?** wie war's?; **to ~ with** (*be suitable*) passen zu; **to have a ~ at sth** etw versuchen; **to be on the ~** auf Trab sein; **whose ~ is it?** wer ist dran?; ~ **about** *vi* (*rumour*) umgehen ♦ *vt fus*: **how do I ~ about this?** wie packe ich das an?; ~ **ahead** *vi* (*proceed*) weitergehen; ~ **along** *vi* dahingehen, dahinfahren ♦ *vt* entlanggehen, entlangfahren; **to ~ along with** (*agree to support*) zustimmen +*dat*; ~ **away** *vi* (*depart*) weggehen; ~ **back** *vi* (*return*) zurückgehen; ~ **back on** *vt fus* (*promise*) nicht halten; ~ **by** *vi* (*years, time*) vergehen ♦ *vt fus* sich richten nach; ~ **down** *vi* (*sun*) untergehen ♦ *vt fus* hinuntergehen, hinunterfahren; ~ **for** *vt fus* (*fetch*) holen (gehen); (*like*) mögen; (*attack*) sich stürzen auf +*acc*; ~ **in** *vi*

hineingehen; ~ **in for** *vt fus* (*competition*) teilnehmen an; ~ **into** *vt fus* (*enter*) hineingehen in +*acc*; (*study*) sich befassen mit; ~ **off** *vi* (*depart*) weggehen; (*lights*) ausgehen; (*milk etc*) sauer werden; (*explode*) losgehen ♦ *vt fus* (*dislike*) nicht mehr mögen; ~ **on** *vi* (*continue*) weitergehen; (*inf*: *complain*) meckern; (*lights*) angehen; **to ~ on with sth** mit etw weitermachen; ~ **out** *vi* (*fire, light*) ausgehen; (*of house*) hinausgehen; ~ **over** *vi* (*ship*) kentern ♦ *vt fus* (*examine, check*) durchgehen; ~ **through** *vt fus* (*town etc*) durchgehen, durchfahren; ~ **up** *vi* (*price*) steigen; ~ **without** *vt fus* sich behelfen ohne; (*food*) entbehren

goad [gəʊd] *vt* anstacheln

go-ahead ['gəʊəhed] *adj* zielstrebig; (*progressive*) fortschrittlich ♦ *n* grüne(s) Licht *nt*

goal [gəʊl] *n* Ziel *nt*; (*SPORT*) Tor *nt*; ~**keeper** *n* Torwart *m*; ~-**post** *n* Torpfosten *m*

goat [gəʊt] *n* Ziege *f*

gobble ['gɒbl] *vt* (*also*: ~ **down**, ~ **up**) hinunterschlingen

go-between ['gəʊbɪtwi:n] *n* Mittelsmann *m*

goblet ['gɒblɪt] *n* Kelch(glas *nt*) *m*

god [gɒd] *n* Gott *m*; **G~** *n* Gott *m*; ~**child** *n* Patenkind *nt*; ~**daughter** *n* Patentochter *f*; ~**dess** *n* Göttin *f*; ~**father** *n* Pate *m*; ~-**forsaken** *adj* gottverlassen; ~**mother** *n* Patin *f*; ~**send** *n* Geschenk *nt* des Himmels; ~**son** *n* Patensohn *m*

goggles ['gɒglz] *npl* Schutzbrille *f*

going ['gəʊɪŋ] *n* (*HORSE-RACING*) Bahn *f* ♦ *adj* (*rate*) gängig; (*concern*) gutgehend; **it's hard** ~ es ist schwierig

gold [gəʊld] *n* Gold *nt* ♦ *adj* golden; ~**en** *adj* golden, Gold-; ~**fish** *n* Goldfisch *m*; ~ **mine** *n* Goldgrube *f*; ~-**plated** *adj* vergoldet; ~**smith** *n* Goldschmied(in) *m(f)*

golf [gɒlf] *n* Golf *nt*; ~**ball** *n* Golfball *m*; (*on typewriter*) Kugelkopf *m*; ~ **club** *n* (*society*) Golfklub *m*; (*stick*) Golfschläger *m*; ~ **course** *n* Golfplatz *m*; ~**er** *n* Golfspieler(in) *m(f)*

gondola ['gɒndələ] *n* Gondel *f*

gone [gɒn] *pp of* **go**
gong [gɒŋ] *n* Gong *m*
good [gʊd] *n* (*benefit*) Wohl *nt*; (*moral excellence*) Güte *f* ♦ *adj* gut; **~s** *npl* (*merchandise etc*) Waren *pl*, Güter *pl*; **a ~ deal (of)** ziemlich viel; **a ~ many** ziemlich viele; **~ morning!** guten Morgen!; **~ afternoon!** guten Tag!; **~ evening!** guten Abend!; **~ night!** gute Nacht!; **would you be ~ enough to ...?** könnten Sie bitte ...?; **~bye** *excl* auf Wiedersehen!; **G~ Friday** *n* Karfreitag *m*; **~-looking** *adj* gutaussehend; **~-natured** *adj* gutmütig; (*joke*) harmlos; **~ness** *n* Güte *f*; (*virtue*) Tugend *f*; **~s train** (*BRIT*) *n* Güterzug *m*; **~will** *n* (*favour*) Wohlwollen *nt*; (*COMM*) Firmenansehen *nt*
goose [guːs] (*pl* **geese**) *n* Gans *f*
gooseberry ['gʊzbərɪ] *n* Stachelbeere *f*
gooseflesh ['guːsfleʃ] *n* Gänsehaut *f*
goose pimples *npl* Gänsehaut *f*
gore [gɔː*] *vt* aufspießen ♦ *n* Blut *nt*
gorge [gɔːdʒ] *n* Schlucht *f* ♦ *vt*: **to ~ o.s.** (sich voll)fressen
gorgeous ['gɔːdʒəs] *adj* prächtig
gorilla [gə'rɪlə] *n* Gorilla *m*
gorse [gɔːs] *n* Stechginster *m*
gory ['gɔːrɪ] *adj* blutig
go-slow ['gəʊ'sləʊ] (*BRIT*) *n* Bummelstreik *m*
gospel ['gɒspəl] *n* Evangelium *nt*
gossip ['gɒsɪp] *n* Klatsch *m*; (*person*) Klatschbase *f* ♦ *vi* klatschen
got [gɒt] *pt, pp of* **get**
gotten ['gɒtən] (*US*) *pp of* **get**
gout [gaʊt] *n* Gicht *f*
govern ['gʌvən] *vt* regieren; verwalten
governess ['gʌvənɪs] *n* Gouvernante *f*
government ['gʌvnmənt] *n* Regierung *f*
governor ['gʌvənə*] *n* Gouverneur *m*
gown [gaʊn] *n* Gewand *nt*; (*UNIV*) Robe *f*
G.P. *n abbr* = **general practitioner**
grab [græb] *vt* packen
grace [greɪs] *n* Anmut *f*; (*blessing*) Gnade *f*; (*prayer*) Tischgebet *nt* ♦ *vt* (*adorn*) zieren; (*honour*) auszeichnen; **5 days' ~** 5 Tage Aufschub; **~ful** *adj* anmutig
gracious ['greɪʃəs] *adj* gnädig; (*kind*) freundlich

grade [greɪd] *n* Grad *m*; (*slope*) Gefälle *nt* ♦ *vt* (*classify*) einstufen; **~ crossing** (*US*) *n* Bahnübergang *m*; **~ school** (*US*) *n* Grundschule *f*
gradient ['greɪdɪənt] *n* Steigung *f*; Gefälle *nt*
gradual ['grædjʊəl] *adj* allmählich; **~ly** *adv* allmählich
graduate [*n* 'grædjʊɪt, *vb* 'grædjʊeɪt] *n*: **to be a ~** das Staatsexamen haben ♦ *vi* das Staatsexamen machen
graduation [grædjʊ'eɪʃən] *n* Abschlußfeier *f*
graffiti [grə'fiːtɪ] *npl* Graffiti *pl*
graft [grɑːft] *n* (*hard work*) Schufterei *f*; (*MED*) Verpflanzung *f* ♦ *vt* propfen; (*fig*) aufpfropfen; (*MED*) verpflanzen
grain [greɪn] *n* Korn *nt*; (*in wood*) Maserung *f*
gram [græm] *n* Gramm *nt*
grammar ['græmə*] *n* Grammatik *f*; **~ school** (*BRIT*) *n* Gymnasium *nt*
grammatical [grə'mætɪkl] *adj* grammat(ikal)isch
gramme [græm] *n* = **gram**
granary ['grænərɪ] *n* Kornspeicher *m*
grand [grænd] *adj* großartig; **~child** (*pl* **grandchildren**) *n* Enkelkind *nt*, Enkel(in) *m(f)*; **~dad** *n* Opa *m*; **~daughter** *n* Enkelin *f*; **~eur** ['grændjə*] *n* Erhabenheit *f*; **~father** *n* Großvater *m*; **~iose** ['grændɪəʊs] *adj* (*imposing*) großartig; (*pompous*) schwülstig; **~ma** *n* Oma *f*; **~mother** *n* Großmutter *f*; **~pa** *n* = **granddad**; **~parents** *npl* Großeltern *pl*; **~ piano** *n* Flügel *m*; **~son** *n* Enkel *m*; **~stand** *n* Haupttribüne *f*
granite ['grænɪt] *n* Granit *m*
granny ['grænɪ] *n* Oma *f*
grant [grɑːnt] *vt* gewähren ♦ *n* Unterstützung *f*; (*UNIV*) Stipendium *nt*; **to take sth for ~ed** etw als selbstverständlich (an)nehmen
granulated sugar ['grænjʊleɪtɪd-] *n* Zuckerraffinade *f*
granule ['grænjuːl] *n* Körnchen *nt*
grape [greɪp] *n* (Wein)traube *f*
grapefruit ['greɪpfruːt] *n* Pampelmuse *f*, Grapefruit *f*

graph [grɑːf] *n* Schaubild *nt*; **~ic**
['græfɪk] *adj* (*descriptive*) anschaulich;
(*drawing*) graphisch; **~ics** *npl* Grafik *f*

grapple ['græpl] *vi*: **to ~ with** kämpfen
mit

grasp [grɑːsp] *vt* ergreifen; (*understand*)
begreifen ♦ *n* Griff *m*; (*of subject*)
Beherrschung *f*; **~ing** *adj* habgierig

grass [grɑːs] *n* Gras *nt*; **~hopper** *n*
Heuschrecke *f*; **~land** *n* Weideland *nt*; **~-
roots** *adj* an der Basis; **~ snake** *n*
Ringelnatter *f*

grate [greɪt] *n* Kamin *m* ♦ *vi* (*sound*)
knirschen ♦ *vt* (*cheese etc*) reiben; **to ~ on
the nerves** auf die Nerven gehen

grateful ['greɪtful] *adj* dankbar

grater ['greɪtə*] *n* Reibe *f*

gratify ['grætɪfaɪ] *vt* befriedigen; **~ing**
['grætɪfaɪŋ] *adj* erfreulich

grating ['greɪtɪŋ] *n* (*iron bars*) Gitter *nt*
♦ *adj* (*noise*) knirschend

gratitude ['grætɪtjuːd] *n* Dankbarkeit *f*

gratuity [grə'tjuːɪtɪ] *n* Gratifikation *f*

grave [greɪv] *n* Grab *nt* ♦ *adj* (*serious*)
ernst

gravel ['grævəl] *n* Kies *m*

gravestone ['greɪvstəun] *n* Grabstein *m*

graveyard ['greɪvjɑːd] *n* Friedhof *m*

gravity ['grævɪtɪ] *n* Schwerkraft *f*;
(*seriousness*) Schwere *f*

gravy ['greɪvɪ] *n* (Braten)soße *f*

gray [greɪ] *adj* = **grey**

graze [greɪz] *vi* grasen ♦ *vt* (*touch*)
streifen; (*MED*) abschürfen ♦ *n*
Abschürfung *f*

grease [griːs] *n* (*fat*) Fett *nt*; (*lubricant*)
Schmiere *f* ♦ *vt* (ab)schmieren; **~proof**
(*BRIT*) *adj* (*paper*) Butterbrot-

greasy ['griːsɪ] *adj* fettig

great [greɪt] *adj* groß; (*inf: good*) prima;
G~ Britain *n* Großbritannien *nt*; **~-
grandfather** *n* Urgroßvater *m*; **~-
grandmother** *n* Urgroßmutter *f*; **~ly** *adv*
sehr; **~ness** *n* Größe *f*

Greece [griːs] *n* Griechenland *nt*

greed [griːd] *n* (*also*: **~iness**) Gier *f*;
(*meanness*) Geiz *m*; **~(iness) for** Gier
nach; **~y** *adj* gierig

Greek [griːk] *adj* griechisch ♦ *n* Grieche

m, Griechin *f*; (*LING*) Griechisch *nt*

green [griːn] *adj* grün ♦ *n* (*village* ~)
Dorfwiese *f*; **~ belt** *n* Grüngürtel *m*; **~
card** *n* (*AUT*) grüne Versicherungskarte *f*;
~ery *n* Grün *nt*; grüne(s) Laub *nt*; **~gage**
n Reineclaude *f*; **~grocer** (*BRIT*) *n* Obst-
und Gemüsehändler *m*; **~house** *n*
Gewächshaus *nt*; **~house effect** *n*
Treibhauseffekt *m*; **~house gas** *n*
Treibhausgas *nt*; **~ish** *adj* grünlich

Greenland ['griːnlənd] *n* Grönland *nt*

greet [griːt] *vt* grüßen; **~ing** *n* Gruß *m*;
~ing(s) card *n* Glückwunschkarte *f*

gregarious [grɪ'gɛərɪəs] *adj* gesellig

grenade [grɪ'neɪd] *n* Granate *f*

grew [gruː] *pt of* **grow**

grey [greɪ] *adj* grau; **~-haired** *adj*
grauhaarig; **~hound** *n* Windhund *m*;
~ish *adj* gräulich

grid [grɪd] *n* Gitter *nt*; (*ELEC*) Leitungsnetz
nt; (*on map*) Gitternetz *nt*

gridlock ['grɪdlɒk] *n* (*AUT: traffic jam*)
totale(r) Stau *m*

grief [griːf] *n* Gram *m*, Kummer *m*

grievance ['griːvəns] *n* Beschwerde *f*

grieve [griːv] *vi* sich grämen ♦ *vt*
betrüben

grievous ['griːvəs] *adj*: **~ bodily harm**
(*JUR*) schwere Körperverletzung *f*

grill [grɪl] *n* Grill *m* ♦ *vt* (*BRIT*) grillen;
(*question*) in die Mangel nehmen

grille [grɪl] *n* (*on car etc*) (Kühler)gitter *nt*

grim [grɪm] *adj* grimmig; (*situation*)
düster

grimace [grɪ'meɪs] *n* Grimasse *f* ♦ *vi*
Grimassen schneiden

grime [graɪm] *n* Schmutz *m*

grimy ['graɪmɪ] *adj* schmutzig

grin [grɪn] *n* Grinsen *nt* ♦ *vi* grinsen

grind [graɪnd] (*pt, pp* **ground**) *vt* mahlen;
(*US: meat*) durch den Fleischwolf drehen;
(*sharpen*) schleifen; (*teeth*) knirschen mit
♦ *n* (*bore*) Plackerei *f*

grip [grɪp] *n* Griff *m*; (*suitcase*)
Handkoffer *m* ♦ *vt* packen; **~ping** *adj*
(*exciting*) spannend

grisly ['grɪzlɪ] *adj* gräßlich

gristle ['grɪsl] *n* Knorpel *m*

grit [grɪt] *n* Splitt *m*; (*courage*) Mut *m*

♦ *vt* (*teeth*) zusammenbeißen; (*road*) (mit Splitt be)streuen

groan [grəʊn] *n* Stöhnen *nt* ♦ *vi* stöhnen

grocer ['grəʊsə*] *n* Lebensmittelhändler *m*; **~ies** *npl* Lebensmittel *pl*; **~'s (shop)** *n* Lebensmittelgeschäft *nt*

groggy ['grɒgɪ] *adj* benommen

groin [grɔɪn] *n* Leistengegend *f*

groom [gru:m] *n* (*also: bride~*) Bräutigam *m*; (*for horses*) Pferdeknecht *m* ♦ *vt* (*horse*) striegeln; **(well-)groomed** gepflegt

groove [gru:v] *n* Rille *f*, Furche *f*

grope [grəʊp] *vi* tasten; **~ for** *vt fus* suchen nach

gross [grəʊs] *adj* (*coarse*) dick, plump; (*bad*) grob, schwer; (*COMM*) brutto; **~ly** *adv* höchst

grotesque [grəʊ'tesk] *adj* grotesk

grotto ['grɒtəʊ] *n* Grotte *f*

ground [graʊnd] *pt, pp of* grind ♦ *n* Boden *m*; (*land*) Grundbesitz *m*; (*reason*) Grund *m*; (*US: also:* ~ *wire*) Erdleitung *f* ♦ *vi* (*run ashore*) stranden, auflaufen; **~s** *npl* (*dregs*) Bodensatz *m*; (*around house*) (Garten)anlagen *pl*; **on the ~** am Boden; **to the ~** zu Boden; **to gain/lose ~** Boden gewinnen/verlieren; **~ cloth** (*US*) *n* = **groundsheet**; **~ing** *n* (*instruction*) Anfangsunterricht *m*; **~less** *adj* grundlos; **~sheet** (*BRIT*) *n* Zeltboden *m*; **~ staff** *n* Bodenpersonal *nt*; **~ swell** *n* (*of sea*) Dünung *f*, (*fig*) Zunahme *f*; **~work** *n* Grundlage *f*

group [gru:p] *n* Gruppe *f* ♦ *vt* (*also:* ~ *together*) gruppieren ♦ *vi* sich gruppieren

grouse [graʊs] *n inv* (*bird*) schottische(s) Moorhuhn *nt* ♦ *vi* (*complain*) meckern

grove [grəʊv] *n* Gehölz *nt*, Hain *m*

grovel ['grɒvl] *vi* (*fig*) kriechen

grow [grəʊ] (*pt* grew, *pp* grown) *vi* wachsen; (*become*) werden ♦ *vt* (*raise*) anbauen; **~ up** *vi* aufwachsen; **~er** *n* Züchter *m*; **~ing** *adj* zunehmend

growl [graʊl] *vi* knurren

grown [grəʊn] *pp of* grow; **~-up** *n* Erwachsene(r) *mf*

growth [grəʊθ] *n* Wachstum *nt*; (*increase*) Zunahme *f*, (*of beard etc*) Wuchs *m*

grub [grʌb] *n* Made *f*, Larve *f*; (*inf: food*)

Futter *nt*; **~by** ['grʌbɪ] *adj* schmutzig

grudge [grʌdʒ] *n* Groll *m* ♦ *vt*: **to ~ sb sth** jdm etw mißgönnen; **to bear sb a ~** einen Groll gegen jdn hegen

gruelling ['grʊəlɪŋ] *adj* (*climb, race*) mörderisch

gruesome ['gru:səm] *adj* grauenhaft

gruff [grʌf] *adj* barsch

grumble ['grʌmbl] *vi* murren

grumpy ['grʌmpɪ] *adj* verdrießlich

grunt [grʌnt] *vi* grunzen ♦ *n* Grunzen *nt*

G-string ['dʒi:-] *n* Minislip *m*

guarantee [gærən'ti:] *n* Garantie *f* ♦ *vt* garantieren

guard [gɑ:d] *n* (*sentry*) Wache *f*; (*BRIT: RAIL*) Zugbegleiter *m* ♦ *vt* bewachen; **~ed** *adj* vorsichtig; **~ian** *n* Vormund *m*; (*keeper*) Hüter *m*; **~'s van** (*BRIT*) *n* (*RAIL*) Dienstwagen *m*

guerrilla [gə'rɪlə] *n* Guerilla(kämpfer) *m*; **~ warfare** *n* Guerillakrieg *m*

guess [ges] *vt, vi* (er)raten, schätzen ♦ *n* Vermutung *f*; **~work** *n* Raterei *f*

guest [gest] *n* Gast *m*; **~-house** *n* Pension *f*, **~ room** *n* Gastzimmer *nt*

guffaw [gʌ'fɔ:] *n* schallend lachen

guidance ['gaɪdəns] *n* (*control*) Leitung *f*; (*advice*) Beratung *f*

guide [gaɪd] *n* Führer *m*; (*also: girl ~*) Pfadfinderin *f* ♦ *vt* führen; **~book** *n* Reiseführer *m*; **~ dog** *n* Blindenhund *m*; **~lines** *npl* Richtlinien *pl*

guild [gɪld] *n* (*HIST*) Gilde *f*; **~hall** (*BRIT*) *n* Stadthalle *f*

guile [gaɪl] *n* Arglist *f*

guillotine ['gɪlə'ti:n] *n* Guillotine *f*

guilt [gɪlt] *n* Schuld *f*; **~y** *adj* schuldig

guinea pig ['gɪnɪ-] *n* Meerschweinchen *nt*; (*fig*) Versuchskaninchen *nt*

guise [gaɪz] *n*: **in the ~ of** in der Form +*gen*

guitar [gɪ'tɑ:*] *n* Gitarre *f*

gulf [gʌlf] *n* Golf *m*; (*fig*) Abgrund *m*

gull [gʌl] *n* Möwe *f*

gullet ['gʌlɪt] *n* Schlund *m*

gullible ['gʌlɪbl] *adj* leichtgläubig

gully ['gʌlɪ] *n* (Wasser)rinne *f*

gulp [gʌlp] *vt* (*also:* ~ *down*) hinunterschlucken ♦ *vi* (*gasp*) schlucken

gum [gʌm] n (around teeth) Zahnfleisch nt; (glue) Klebstoff m; (also: chewing-~) Kaugummi m ♦ vt gummieren; **~boots** (BRIT) npl Gummistiefel pl

gumption ['gʌmpʃən] (inf) n Mumm m

gun [gʌn] n Schußwaffe f; **~boat** n Kanonenboot nt; **~fire** n Geschützfeuer nt; **~man** (irreg) n bewaffnete(r) Verbrecher m; **~point** n: **at ~point** mit Waffengewalt; **~powder** n Schießpulver nt; **~shot** n Schuß m

gurgle ['gɜːgl] vi gluckern

guru ['guruː] n Guru m

gush [gʌʃ] vi (rush out) hervorströmen; (fig) schwärmen

gust [gʌst] n Windstoß m, Bö f

gusto ['gʌstəu] n Genuß m, Lust f

gut [gʌt] n (ANAT) Gedärme pl; (string) Darm m; **~s** npl (fig) Schneid m

gutter ['gʌtə*] n Dachrinne f; (in street) Gosse f

guttural ['gʌtərəl] adj guttural, Kehl-

guy [gaɪ] n (also: ~rope) Halteseil nt; (man) Typ m, Kerl m

guzzle ['gʌzl] vt, vi (drink) saufen; (eat) fressen

gym [dʒɪm] n (also: gymnasium) Turnhalle f; (: gymnastics) Turnen nt; **~nast** ['dʒɪmnæst] n Turner(in) m(f); **~nastics** [dʒɪm'næstɪks] n Turnen nt, Gymnastik f; **~ shoes** npl Turnschuhe pl; **~ slip** (BRIT) n Schulträgerrock m

gynaecologist [gaɪnɪ'kɒlədʒɪst] (US **gynecologist**) n Frauenarzt(ärztin) m(f)

gypsy ['dʒɪpsɪ] n = **gipsy**

gyrate [dʒaɪ'reɪt] vi kreisen

H h

haberdashery [hæbə'dæʃərɪ] (BRIT) n Kurzwaren pl

habit ['hæbɪt] n (An)gewohnheit f; (monk's) Habit nt or m

habitable ['hæbɪtəbl] adj bewohnbar

habitat ['hæbɪtæt] n Lebensraum m

habitual [hə'bɪtjuəl] adj gewohnheitsmäßig; **~ly** adv gewöhnlich

hack [hæk] vt hacken ♦ n Hieb m; (writer) Schreiberling m

hacker ['hækə*] n (COMPUT) Hacker m

hackneyed ['hæknɪd] adj abgedroschen

had [hæd] pt, pp of **have**

haddock ['hædək] (pl ~ or ~s) n Schellfisch m

hadn't ['hædnt] = **had not**

haemorrhage ['hemərɪdʒ] (US **hemorrhage**) n Blutung f

haemorrhoids ['hemərɔɪdz] (US **hemorrhoids**) npl Hämorrhoiden pl

haggard ['hægəd] adj abgekämpft

haggle ['hægl] vi feilschen

Hague [heɪg] n: **The ~** Den Haag nt

hail [heɪl] n Hagel m ♦ vt umjubeln ♦ vi hageln; **~stone** n Hagelkorn nt

hair [heə*] n Haar nt, Haare pl; (one ~) Haar nt; **~brush** n Haarbürste f; **~cut** n Haarschnitt m; **to get a ~cut** sich dat die Haare schneiden lassen; **~do** n Frisur f; **~dresser** n Friseur m, Friseuse f; **~dresser's** n Friseursalon m; **~ dryer** n Trockenhaube f, (hand-held) Fön m ®; **~grip** n Klemme f; **~net** n Haarnetz nt; **~pin** n Haarnadel f; **~pin bend** (US **~pin curve**) n Haarnadelkurve f; **~-raising** adj haarsträubend; **~ removing cream** n Enthaarungscreme nt; **~ spray** n Haarspray nt; **~style** n Frisur f; **~y** adj haarig

hake [heɪk] n Seehecht m

half [hɑːf] (pl **halves**) n Hälfte f ♦ adj halb ♦ adv halb, zur Hälfte; **~-an-hour** eine halbe Stunde; **two and a ~** zweieinhalb; **to cut sth in ~** etw halbieren; **~ a dozen** ein halbes Dutzend, sechs; **~-back** n Läufer m; **~ board** n Halbpension f; **~-caste** n Mischling m; **~-hearted** adj lustlos; **~-hour** n halbe Stunde f; **~penny** ['heɪpnɪ] (BRIT) n halbe(r) Penny m; **~-price** n: **(at) ~-price** zum halben Preis; **~ term** (BRIT) n (SCH) Ferien pl in der Mitte des Trimesters; **~-time** n Halbzeit f; **~way** adv halbwegs, auf halbem Wege

halibut ['hælɪbət] n inv Heilbutt m

hall [hɔːl] n Saal m; (entrance ~) Hausflur m; (building) Halle f; **~ of residence** (BRIT) Studentenwohnheim nt

hallmark ['hɔːlmɑːk] *n* Stempel *m*
hallo [həˈləʊ] *excl* = **hello**
Hallowe'en ['hæləʊˈiːn] *n* Tag *m* vor Allerheiligen
hallucination [həluːsɪˈneɪʃən] *n* Halluzination *f*
hallway ['hɔːlweɪ] *n* Korridor *m*
halo ['heɪləʊ] *n* Heiligenschein *m*
halt [hɔːlt] *n* Halt *m* ♦ *vt, vi* anhalten
halve [hɑːv] *vt* halbieren
halves [hɑːvz] *pl of* **half**
ham [hæm] *n* Schinken *m*
hamburger ['hæmbɜːgə*] *n* Hamburger *m*
hamlet ['hæmlɪt] *n* Weiler *m*
hammer ['hæmə*] *n* Hammer *m* ♦ *vt, vi* hämmern
hammock ['hæmək] *n* Hängematte *f*
hamper ['hæmpə*] *vt* (be)hindern ♦ *n* Picknickkorb *m*
hand [hænd] *n* Hand *f*; (*of clock*) (Uhr)zeiger *m*; (*worker*) Arbeiter *m* ♦ *vt* (*pass*) geben; **to give sb a ~** jdm helfen; **at ~** nahe; **to ~** zur Hand; **in ~** (*under control*) unter Kontrolle; (*being done*) im Gange; (*extra*) übrig; **on ~** zur Verfügung; **on the one ~ ..., on the other ~ ...** einerseits ..., andererseits ...; **~ in** *vt* abgeben; (*forms*) einreichen; **~ out** *vt* austeilen; **~ over** *vt* (*deliver*) übergeben; (*surrender*) abgeben; (: *prisoner*) ausliefern; **~bag** *n* Handtasche *f*; **~book** *n* Handbuch *nt*; **~brake** *n* Handbremse *f*; **~cuffs** *npl* Handschellen *pl*; **~ful** *n* Handvoll *f*; (*inf: person*) Plage *f*
handicap ['hændɪkæp] *n* Handikap *nt* ♦ *vt* benachteiligen; **mentally/physically ~ped** geistig/körperlich behindert
handicraft ['hændɪkrɑːft] *n* Kunsthandwerk *m*
handiwork ['hændɪwɜːk] *n* Arbeit *f*; (*fig*) Werk *nt*
handkerchief ['hæŋkətʃɪf] *n* Taschentuch *nt*
handle ['hændl] *n* (*of door etc*) Klinke *f*; (*of cup etc*) Henkel *m*; (*for winding*) Kurbel *f* ♦ *vt* (*touch*) anfassen; (*deal with: things*) sich befassen mit; (: *people*) umgehen mit; **~bar(s)** *n(pl)* Lenkstange *f*

hand: **~ luggage** *n* Handgepäck *nt*; **~made** *adj* handgefertigt; **~out** *n* (*distribution*) Verteilung *f*; (*charity*) Geldzuwendung *f*; (*leaflet*) Flugblatt *nt*; **~rail** *n* Geländer *nt*; (*on ship*) Reling *f*; **~shake** *n* Händedruck *m*
handsome ['hænsəm] *adj* gutaussehend
handwriting ['hændraɪtɪŋ] *n* Handschrift *f*
handy ['hændɪ] *adj* praktisch; (*shops*) leicht erreichbar; **~man** ['hændɪmæn] (*irreg*) *n* Bastler *m*
hang [hæŋ] (*pt, pp* **hung**) *vt* aufhängen; (*criminal: pt, pp* **hanged**) hängen ♦ *vi* hängen ♦ *n*: **to get the ~ of sth** (*inf*) den richtigen Dreh bei etw herauskriegen; **~ about** *vi* sich herumtreiben; **~ on** *vi* (*wait*) warten; **~ up** *vi* (*TEL*) auflegen
hangar ['hæŋə*] *n* Hangar *m*
hanger ['hæŋə*] *n* Kleiderbügel *m*
hanger-on ['hæŋərˈɒn] *n* Anhänger(in) *m(f)*
hang-gliding ['hæŋglaɪdɪŋ] *n* Drachenfliegen *nt*
hangover ['hæŋəʊvə*] *n* Kater *m*
hang-up ['hæŋʌp] *n* Komplex *m*
hanker ['hæŋkə*] *vi*: **to ~ for** *or* **after** sich sehnen nach
hankie ['hæŋkɪ] *n abbr* = **handkerchief**
hanky ['hæŋkɪ] *n abbr* = **handkerchief**
haphazard ['hæpˈhæzəd] *adj* zufällig
happen ['hæpən] *vi* sich ereignen, passieren; **as it ~s I'm going there today** zufällig(erweise) gehe ich heute (dort)hin; **~ing** *n* Ereignis *nt*
happily ['hæpɪlɪ] *adv* glücklich; (*fortunately*) glücklicherweise
happiness ['hæpɪnɪs] *n* Glück *nt*
happy ['hæpɪ] *adj* glücklich; **~ birthday!** alles Gute zum Geburtstag!; **~-go-lucky** *adj* sorglos
harass ['hærəs] *vt* plagen; **~ment** *n* Belästigung *f*
harbour ['hɑːbə*] (*US* **harbor**) *n* Hafen *m* ♦ *vt* (*hope etc*) hegen; (*criminal etc*) Unterschlupf gewähren
hard [hɑːd] *adj* (*firm*) hart; (*difficult*) schwer; (*harsh*) hart(herzig) ♦ *adv* (*work*) hart; (*try*) sehr; (*push, hit*) fest; **no ~**

feelings! ich nehme es dir nicht übel; ~ **of hearing** schwerhörig; **to be ~ done by** übel dran sein; **~back** n kartonierte Ausgabe f; **~ cash** n Bargeld nt; **~ disk** n (COMPUT) Festplatte f; **~en** vt erhärten; (fig) verhärten ♦ vi hart werden; (fig) sich verhärten; **~headed** adj nüchtern; **~ labour** n Zwangsarbeit f

hardly ['hɑːdlɪ] adv kaum

hard: ~ness n Härte f; (difficulty) Schwierigkeit f; **~ship** n Not f; **~-up** adj knapp bei Kasse; **~ware** n Eisenwaren pl; (COMPUT) Hardware f; **~ware shop** n Eisenwarenhandlung f; **~-wearing** adj strapazierfähig; **~-working** adj fleißig

hardy ['hɑːdɪ] adj widerstandsfähig

hare [hɛə*] n Hase m; **~-brained** adj schwachsinnig

harm [hɑːm] n Schaden m ♦ vt schaden +dat; **out of ~'s way** in Sicherheit; **~ful** adj schädlich; **~less** adj harmlos

harmonica [hɑːˈmɒnɪkə] n Mundharmonika f

harmonious [hɑːˈməʊnɪəs] adj harmonisch

harmonize ['hɑːmənaɪz] vt abstimmen ♦ vi harmonieren

harmony ['hɑːmənɪ] n Harmonie f

harness ['hɑːnɪs] n Geschirr nt ♦ vt (horse) anschirren; (fig) nutzbar machen

harp [hɑːp] n Harfe f ♦ vi: **to ~ on about sth** auf etw dat herumreiten

harpoon [hɑːˈpuːn] n Harpune f

harrowing ['hærəʊɪŋ] adj nervenaufreibend

harsh [hɑːʃ] adj (rough) rauh; (severe) streng; **~ness** n Härte f

harvest ['hɑːvɪst] n Ernte f ♦ vt, vi ernten; **~er** ['hɑːvɪstə*] n Mähbinder m

has [hæz] vb see **have**

hash [hæʃ] vt kleinhacken ♦ n (mess) Kuddelmuddel m; (meat) Haschee nt

hashish ['hæʃɪʃ] n Haschisch nt

hasn't ['hæznt] = **has not**

hassle ['hæsl] (inf) n Theater nt

haste [heɪst] n Eile f; **~n** ['heɪsn] vt beschleunigen ♦ vi eilen

hasty ['heɪstɪ] adj hastig; (rash) vorschnell

hat [hæt] n Hut m

hatch [hætʃ] n (NAUT: also: ~way) Luke f; (in house) Durchreiche f ♦ vi (young) ausschlüpfen ♦ vt (brood) ausbrüten; (plot) aushecken

hatchback ['hætʃbæk] n (AUT) (Auto nt mit) Heckklappe f

hatchet ['hætʃɪt] n Beil nt

hate [heɪt] vt hassen ♦ n Haß m; **~ful** adj verhaßt

hatred ['heɪtrɪd] n Haß m

haughty ['hɔːtɪ] adj hochnäsig, überheblich

haul [hɔːl] vt ziehen ♦ n (catch) Fang m; **~age** n Spedition f; **~ier** (US **~er**) n Spediteur m

haunch [hɔːntʃ] n Lende f

haunt [hɔːnt] vt (ghost) spuken in +dat; (memory) verfolgen; (pub) häufig besuchen ♦ n Lieblingsplatz m; **the castle is ~ed** in dem Schloß spukt es

---

KEYWORD

have [hæv] (pt, pp **had**) aux vb 1 haben; (esp with vbs of motion) sein; **to have arrived/slept** angekommen sein/ geschlafen haben; **to have been** gewesen sein; **having eaten** or **when he had eaten, he left** nachdem er gegessen hatte, ging er

2 (in tag questions): **you've done it, haven't you?** du hast es doch gemacht, oder nicht?

3 (in short answers and questions): **you've made a mistake — so I have/no I haven't** du hast einen Fehler gemacht — ja, stimmt/nein; **we haven't paid — yes we have!** wir haben nicht bezahlt — doch; **I've been there before, have you?** ich war schon einmal da, du auch?

♦ modal aux vb (be obliged): **to have (got) to do sth** etw tun müssen; **you haven't to tell her** du darfst es ihr nicht erzählen

♦ vt 1 (possess) haben; **he has (got) blue eyes** er hat blaue Augen; **I have (got) an idea** ich habe eine Idee

2 (referring to meals etc): **to have breakfast/a cigarette** frühstücken/eine

Zigarette rauchen
3 *(receive, obtain etc)* haben; **may I have your address?** kann ich Ihre Adresse haben?; **to have a baby** ein Kind bekommen
4 *(maintain, allow)*: **he will have it that he is right** er besteht darauf, daß er recht hat; **I won't have it** das lasse ich mir nicht bieten
5: **to have sth done** etw machen lassen; **to have sb do sth** jdn etw machen lassen; **he soon had them all laughing** er brachte sie alle zum Lachen
6 *(experience, suffer)*: **she had her bag stolen** man hat ihr die Tasche gestohlen; **he had his arm broken** er hat sich den Arm gebrochen
7 *(+noun: take, hold etc)*: **to have a walk/rest** spazierengehen/sich ausruhen; **to have a meeting/party** eine Besprechung/Party haben
have out *vt*: **to have it out with sb** *(settle a problem etc)* etw mit jdm bereden

haven ['heɪvn] *n* Zufluchtsort *m*
haven't ['hævnt] = **have not**
haversack ['hævəsæk] *n* Rucksack *m*
havoc ['hævək] *n* Verwüstung *f*
Hawaii [hə'waɪiː] *n* Hawaii *nt*
hawk [hɔːk] *n* Habicht *m*
hay [heɪ] *n* Heu *nt*; **~ fever** *n* Heuschnupfen *m*; **~stack** *n* Heuschober *m*
haywire ['heɪwaɪə*] *(inf) adj* durcheinander
hazard ['hæzəd] *n* Risiko *nt* ♦ *vt* aufs Spiel setzen; **~ous** *adj* gefährlich; **~ (warning) lights** *npl (AUT)* Warnblinklicht *nt*
haze [heɪz] *n* Dunst *m*
hazelnut ['heɪzlnʌt] *n* Haselnuß *f*
hazy ['heɪzɪ] *adj (misty)* dunstig; *(vague)* verschwommen
he [hiː] *pron er*
head [hed] *n* Kopf *m*; *(leader)* Leiter *m* ♦ *vt* (an)führen, leiten; *(ball)* köpfen; **~s (or tails)** Kopf (oder Zahl); **~ first** mit dem Kopf nach unten; **~ over heels** kopfüber; **~ for** *vt fus* zugehen auf +*acc*;

~ache *n* Kopfschmerzen *pl*; **~dress** *n* Kopfschmuck *m*; **~ing** *n* Überschrift *f*; **~lamp** *(BRIT) n* Scheinwerfer *m*; **~land** *n* Landspitze *f*; **~light** *n* Scheinwerfer *m*; **~line** *n* Schlagzeile *f*; **~long** *adv* kopfüber; **~master** *n (of primary school)* Rektor *m*; *(of secondary school)* Direktor *m*; **~mistress** *n* Rektorin *f*; Direktorin *f*; **~ office** *n* Zentrale *f*; **~-on** *adj* Frontal-; **~phones** *npl* Kopfhörer *pl*; **~quarters** *npl* Zentrale *f*; *(MIL)* Hauptquartier *nt*; **~rest** *n* Kopfstütze *f*; **~room** *n (of bridges etc)* lichte Höhe *f*; **~scarf** *n* Kopftuch *nt*; **~strong** *adj* eigenwillig; **~ waiter** *n* Oberkellner *m*; **~way** *n* Fortschritte *pl*; **~wind** *n* Gegenwind *m*; **~y** *adj* berauschend
heal [hiːl] *vt* heilen ♦ *vi* verheilen
health [helθ] *n* Gesundheit *f*; **~ food** *n* Reformkost *f*; **the H~ Service** *(BRIT) n* das Gesundheitswesen; **~y** *adj* gesund
heap [hiːp] *n* Haufen *m* ♦ *vt* häufen
hear [hɪə*] *(pt, pp heard) vt* hören; *(listen to)* anhören ♦ *vi* hören; **~d** [hɜːd] *pt, pp of* **hear**; **~ing** *n* Gehör *nt*; *(JUR)* Verhandlung *f*; **~ing aid** *n* Hörapparat *m*; **~say** *n* Hörensagen *nt*
hearse [hɜːs] *n* Leichenwagen *m*
heart [hɑːt] *n* Herz *nt*; **~s** *npl (CARDS)* Herz *nt*; **by ~** auswendig; **~ attack** *n* Herzanfall *m*; **~beat** *n* Herzschlag *m*; **~breaking** *adj* herzzerbrechend; **~broken** *adj* untröstlich; **~burn** *n* Sodbrennen *nt*; **~ failure** *n* Herzschlag *m*; **~felt** *adj* aufrichtig
hearth [hɑːθ] *n* Herd *m*
heartily ['hɑːtɪlɪ] *adv* herzlich; *(eat)* herzhaft
heartless ['hɑːtlɪs] *adj* herzlos
hearty ['hɑːtɪ] *adj* kräftig; *(friendly)* freundlich
heat [hiːt] *n* Hitze *f*; *(of food, water etc)* Wärme *f*; *(SPORT: also: qualifying ~)* Ausscheidungsrunde *f* ♦ *vt (house)* heizen; *(substance)* heiß machen, erhitzen; **~ up** *vi* warm werden ♦ *vt* aufwärmen; **~ed** *adj* erhitzt; *(fig)* hitzig; **~er** *n* (Heiz)ofen *m*
heath [hiːθ] *(BRIT) n* Heide *f*

heathen ['hiːðən] *n* Heide *m*/Heidin *f*
♦ *adj* heidnisch, Heiden-
heather ['heðə*] *n* Heidekraut *nt*
heating ['hiːtɪŋ] *n* Heizung *f*
heat-seeking ['hiːtsiːkɪŋ] *adj*
wärmesuchend
heatstroke ['hiːtstrəʊk] *n* Hitzschlag *m*
heat wave *n* Hitzewelle *f*
heave [hiːv] *vt* hochheben; (*sigh*)
ausstoßen ♦ *vi* wogen; (*breast*) sich heben
♦ *n* Heben *nt*
heaven ['hevn] *n* Himmel *m*; ~**ly** *adj*
himmlisch
heavily ['hevɪlɪ] *adv* schwer
heavy ['hevɪ] *adj* schwer; ~ **goods
vehicle** *n* Lastkraftwagen *m*; ~**weight** *n*
(*SPORT*) Schwergewicht *nt*
Hebrew ['hiːbruː] *adj* hebräisch ♦ *n*
(*LING*) Hebräisch *nt*
Hebrides ['hebrɪdiːz] *npl* Hebriden *pl*
heckle ['hekl] *vt* unterbrechen
hectic ['hektɪk] *adj* hektisch
he'd [hiːd] = **he had**; **he would**
hedge [hedʒ] *n* Hecke *f* ♦ *vt* einzäunen
♦ *vi* (*fig*) ausweichen; **to ~ one's bets**
sich absichern
hedgehog ['hedʒhɒg] *n* Igel *m*
heed [hiːd] *vt* (*also*: **take ~ of**) beachten
♦ *n* Beachtung *f*; ~**less** *adj* achtlos
heel [hiːl] *n* Ferse *f*; (*of shoe*) Absatz *m*
♦ *vt* (*shoes*) mit Absätzen versehen
hefty ['heftɪ] *adj* (*person*) stämmig;
(*portion*) reichlich
heifer ['hefə*] *n* Färse *f*
height [haɪt] *n* (*of person*) Größe *f*; (*of
object*) Höhe *f*; ~**en** *vt* erhöhen
heir [ɛə*] *n* Erbe *m*; ~**ess** ['ɛərɪs] *n* Erbin
f; ~**loom** *n* Erbstück *nt*
held [held] *pt, pp of* **hold**
helicopter ['helɪkɒptə*] *n* Hubschrauber
m
heliport ['helɪpɔːt] *n*
Hubschrauberlandeplatz *m*
hell [hel] *n* Hölle *f* ♦ *excl* verdammt!
he'll [hiːl] = **he will**; **he shall**
hellish ['helɪʃ] *adj* höllisch, verteufelt
hello [hə'ləʊ] *excl* hallo
helm [helm] *n* Ruder *nt*, Steuer *nt*
helmet ['helmɪt] *n* Helm *m*

help [help] *n* Hilfe *f* ♦ *vt* helfen +*dat*; **I
can't ~ it** ich kann nichts dafür; **~
yourself** bedienen Sie sich; ~**er** *n* Helfer
m; ~**ful** *adj* hilfreich; ~**ing** *n* Portion *f*;
~**less** *adj* hilflos
hem [hem] *n* Saum *m* ♦ *vt* säumen; ~ **in**
vt einengen
hemorrhage ['hemərɪdʒ] (*US*) *n*
= **haemorrhage**
hemorrhoids ['hemərɔɪdz] (*US*) *npl*
= **haemorrhoids**
hen [hen] *n* Henne *f*
hence [hens] *adv* von jetzt an; (*therefore*)
daher; ~**forth** *adv* von nun an; (*from then
on*) von da an
henchman ['hentʃmən] (*irreg*) *n*
Gefolgsmann *m*
her [həː*] *pron* (*acc*) sie; (*dat*) ihr ♦ *adj*
ihr; *see also* **me**; **my**
herald ['herəld] *n* (Vor)bote *m* ♦ *vt*
verkünden
heraldry ['herəldrɪ] *n* Wappenkunde *f*
herb [həːb] *n* Kraut *nt*
herd [həːd] *n* Herde *f*
here [hɪə*] *adv* hier; (*to this place*)
hierher; ~**after** *adv* hernach, künftig ♦ *n*
Jenseits *nt*; ~**by** *adv* hiermit
hereditary [hɪ'redɪtərɪ] *adj* erblich
heredity [hɪ'redɪtɪ] *n* Vererbung *f*
heresy ['herəsɪ] *n* Ketzerei *f*
heretic ['herətɪk] *n* Ketzer *m*
heritage ['herɪtɪdʒ] *n* Erbe *nt*
hermetically [həː'metɪkəlɪ] *adv*: ~
sealed hermetisch verschlossen
hermit ['həːmɪt] *n* Einsiedler *m*
hernia ['həːnɪə] *n* Bruch *m*
hero ['hɪərəʊ] (*pl* ~**es**) *n* Held *m*; ~**ic**
[hɪ'rəʊɪk] *adj* heroisch
heroin ['herəʊɪn] *n* Heroin *nt*
heroine ['herəʊɪn] *n* Heldin *f*
heroism ['herəʊɪzəm] *n* Heldentum *nt*
heron ['herən] *n* Reiher *m*
herring ['herɪŋ] *n* Hering *m*
hers [həːz] *pron* ihre(r, s); *see also* **mine**[2]
herself [həː'self] *pron* sich (selbst);
(*emphatic*) selbst; *see also* **oneself**
he's [hiːz] = **he is**; **he has**
hesitant ['hezɪtənt] *adj* zögernd
hesitate ['hezɪteɪt] *vi* zögern

hesitation [hezɪ'teɪʃən] *n* Zögern *nt*

hew [hjuː] (*pt* **hewed**, *pp* **hewn**) *vt* hauen, hacken

hexagon ['heksəgən] *n* Sechseck *nt*; **~al** [hek'sægənəl] *adj* sechseckig

heyday ['heɪdeɪ] *n* Blüte *f*, Höhepunkt *m*

HGV *n abbr* = **heavy goods vehicle**

hi [haɪ] *excl* he, hallo

hiatus [haɪ'eɪtəs] *n* (*gap*) Lücke *f*

hibernate ['haɪbəneɪt] *vi* Winterschlaf *m* halten

hibernation [haɪbə'neɪʃən] *n* Winterschlaf *m*

hiccough ['hɪkʌp] *vi* den Schluckauf haben; **~s** *npl* Schluckauf *m*

hiccup ['hɪkʌp] = **hiccough**

hid [hɪd] *pt of* **hide**; **~den** ['hɪdn] *pp of* **hide**

hide [haɪd] (*pt* **hid**, *pp* **hidden**) *n* (*skin*) Haut *f*, Fell *nt* ♦ *vt* verstecken ♦ *vi* sich verstecken; **~-and-seek** *n* Versteckspiel *nt*; **~away** *n* Versteck *nt*

hideous ['hɪdɪəs] *adj* abscheulich

hiding ['haɪdɪŋ] *n* (*beating*) Tracht *f* Prügel; **to be in ~** (*concealed*) sich versteckt halten; **~ place** *n* Versteck *nt*

hi-fi ['haɪfaɪ] *n* Hi-Fi *nt* ♦ *adj* Hi-Fi-

high [haɪ] *adj* hoch; (*wind*) stark ♦ *adv* hoch; **it is 20m ~** es ist 20 Meter hoch; **~brow** *adj* (betont) intellektuell; **~chair** *n* Hochstuhl *m*; **~er education** *n* Hochschulbildung *f*; **~-handed** *adj* eigenmächtig; **~-heeled** *adj* hochhackig; **~ jump** *n* (*SPORT*) Hochsprung *m*; **the H~lands** *npl* das schottische Hochland; **~light** *n* (*fig*) Höhepunkt *m* ♦ *vt* hervorheben; **~ly** *adv* höchst; **~ly strung** *adj* überempfindlich; **~ness** *n* Höhe *f*; **Her H~ness** Ihre Hoheit *f*; **~-pitched** *adj* hoch; **~-rise block** *n* Hochhaus *nt*; **~ school** (*US*) *n* Oberschule *f*; **~ season** (*BRIT*) *n* Hochsaison *f*; **~ street** (*BRIT*) *n* Hauptstraße *f*

highway ['haɪweɪ] *n* Landstraße *f*; **H~ Code** (*BRIT*) *n* Straßenverkehrsordnung *f*

hijack ['haɪdʒæk] *vt* entführen; **~er** *n* Entführer(in) *m(f)*

hike [haɪk] *vi* wandern ♦ *n* Wanderung *f*; **~r** *n* Wanderer *m*

hilarious [hɪ'lɛərɪəs] *adj* lustig

hill [hɪl] *n* Berg *m*; **~side** *n* (Berg)hang *m*; **~y** *adj* hügelig

hilt [hɪlt] *n* Heft *nt*; **(up) to the ~** ganz und gar

him [hɪm] *pron* (*acc*) ihn; (*dat*) ihm; *see also* **me**

himself [hɪm'self] *pron* sich (selbst); (*emphatic*) selbst; *see also* **oneself**

hind [haɪnd] *adj* hinter, Hinter-

hinder ['hɪndə*] *vt* (*stop*) hindern; (*delay*) behindern

hindrance ['hɪndrəns] *n* (*delay*) Behinderung *f*; (*obstacle*) Hindernis *nt*

hindsight ['haɪndsaɪt] *n*: **with ~** im nachhinein

Hindu ['hɪnduː] *n* Hindu *m*

hinge [hɪndʒ] *n* Scharnier *nt*; (*on door*) Türangel *f* ♦ *vi* (*fig*): **to ~ on** abhängen von

hint [hɪnt] *n* Tip *m*; (*trace*) Anflug *m* ♦ *vt*: **to ~ that** andeuten, daß ♦ *vi*: **to ~ at** andeuten

hip [hɪp] *n* Hüfte *f*

hippopotami [hɪpə'pɒtəmaɪ] *npl of* **hippopotamus**

hippopotamus [hɪpə'pɒtəməs] (*pl* **~es** *or* **hippopotami**) *n* Nilpferd *nt*

hire ['haɪə*] *vt* (*worker*) anstellen; (*BRIT*: *car*) mieten ♦ *n* Miete *f*; **for ~** (*taxi*) frei; **~ purchase** (*BRIT*) *n* Teilzahlungskauf *m*

his [hɪz] *adj* sein ♦ *pron* seine(r, s); *see also* **my; mine²**

hiss [hɪs] *vi* zischen ♦ *n* Zischen *nt*

historian [hɪs'tɔːrɪən] *n* Historiker *m*

historic [hɪs'tɒrɪk] *adj* historisch

historical [hɪs'tɒrɪkəl] *adj* historisch, geschichtlich

history ['hɪstərɪ] *n* Geschichte *f*

hit [hɪt] (*pt*, *pp* **hit**) *vt* schlagen; (*injure*) treffen ♦ *n* (*blow*) Schlag *m*; (*success*) Erfolg *m*; (*MUS*) Hit *m*; **to ~ it off with sb** prima mit jdm auskommen; **~-and-run driver** *n* jemand, der Fahrerflucht begeht

hitch [hɪtʃ] *vt* festbinden; (*also*: **~ up**) hochziehen ♦ *n* (*difficulty*) Haken *m*; **to ~ a lift** trampen

hitchhike ['hɪtʃhaɪk] *vi* trampen; **~r** *n* Tramper *m*

hi-tech ['haɪtek] *adj* Hi-tech- ♦ *n*
Spitzentechnologie *f*

hitherto ['hɪðə'tuː] *adv* bislang

HIV *n abbr*: **~-negative/-positive** HIV-
negativ/-positiv

hive [haɪv] *n* Bienenkorb *m*; **~ off** *vt*
ausgliedern

HMS *abbr* = **His (Her) Majesty's Ship**

hoard [hɔːd] *n* Schatz *m* ♦ *vt* horten,
hamstern

hoarding ['hɔːdɪŋ] *n* Bretterzaun *m*; (*BRIT*:
for advertising) Reklamewand *f*

hoarse [hɔːs] *adj* heiser, rauh

hoax [həʊks] *n* Streich *m*

hob [hɒb] *n* Kochmulde *f*

hobble ['hɒbl] *vi* humpeln

hobby ['hɒbɪ] *n* Hobby *nt*; **~-horse** *n*
(*fig*) Steckenpferd *nt*

hobo ['həʊbəʊ] (*US*) *n* Tippelbruder *m*

hock [hɒk] *n* (*wine*) weiße(r) Rheinwein
m

hockey ['hɒkɪ] *n* Hockey *nt*

hoe [həʊ] *n* Hacke *f* ♦ *vt* hacken

hog [hɒg] *n* Schlachtschwein *nt* ♦ *vt* mit
Beschlag belegen; **to go the whole ~** aufs
Ganze gehen

hoist [hɔɪst] *n* Winde *f* ♦ *vt* hochziehen

hold [həʊld] (*pt, pp* **held**) *vt* halten;
(*contain*) enthalten; (*be able to contain*)
fassen; (*breath*) anhalten; (*meeting*)
abhalten ♦ *vi* (*withstand pressure*)
aushalten ♦ *n* (*grasp*) Halt *m*; (*NAUT*)
Schiffsraum *m*; **~ the line!** (*TEL*) bleiben
Sie am Apparat!; **to ~ one's own** sich
behaupten; **~ back** *vt* zurückhalten; **~
down** *vt* niederhalten; (*job*) behalten; **~
off** *vt* (*enemy*) abwehren; **~ on** *vi* sich
festhalten; (*resist*) durchhalten; (*wait*)
warten; **~ on to** *vt fus* festhalten an
+*dat*; (*keep*) behalten; **~ out** *vt* hinhalten
♦ *vi* aushalten; **~ up** *vt* (*delay*) aufhalten;
(*rob*) überfallen; **~all** (*BRIT*) *n* Reisetasche
f; **~er** *n* Behälter *m*; **~ing** *n* (*share*)
(Aktien)anteil *m*; **~up** *n* (*BRIT*: *in traffic*)
Stockung *f*; (*robbery*) Überfall *m*; (*delay*)
Verzögerung *f*

hole [həʊl] *n* Loch *nt* ♦ *vt* durchlöchern

holiday ['hɒlədɪ] *n* (*day*) Feiertag *m*;
freie(r) Tag *m*; (*vacation*) Urlaub *m*; (*SCH*)

Ferien *pl*; **~ camp** *n* Ferienlager *nt*; **~-
maker** (*BRIT*) *n* Urlauber(in) *m(f)*; **~
resort** *n* Ferienort *m*

holiness ['həʊlɪnɪs] *n* Heiligkeit *f*

Holland ['hɒlənd] *n* Holland *nt*

hollow ['hɒləʊ] *adj* hohl; (*fig*) leer ♦ *n*
Vertiefung *f*; **~ out** *vt* aushöhlen

holly ['hɒlɪ] *n* Stechpalme *f*

holocaust ['hɒləkɔːst] *n* Inferno *nt*

holster ['həʊlstə*] *n* Pistolenhalfter *m*

holy ['həʊlɪ] *adj* heilig; **the H~ Ghost** *or*
Spirit *n* der Heilige Geist

homage ['hɒmɪdʒ] *n* Huldigung *f*; **to pay
~ to** huldigen +*dat*

home [həʊm] *n* Zuhause *nt*; (*institution*)
Heim *nt*, Anstalt *f* ♦ *adj* einheimisch;
(*POL*) inner ♦ *adv* heim, nach Hause; **at ~**
zu Hause; **~ address** *n* Heimatadresse *f*;
~coming *n* Heimkehr *f*; **~land** *n*
Heimat(land *nt*) *f*; **~less** *adj* obdachlos;
~ly *adj* häuslich; (*US*: *ugly*) unscheinbar;
~-made *adj* selbstgemacht; **H~ Office**
(*BRIT*) *n* Innenministerium *nt*; **~ rule** *n*
Selbstverwaltung *f*; **H~ Secretary** (*BRIT*)
n Innenminister(in) *m(f)*; **~sick** *adj*: **to be
~sick** Heimweh haben; **~ town** *n*
Heimatstadt *f*; **~ward** *adj* (*journey*)
Heim-; **~work** *n* Hausaufgaben *pl*

homicide ['hɒmɪsaɪd] (*US*) *n* Totschlag *m*

homoeopathy [həʊmɪ'ɒpəθɪ] *n*
Homöopathie *f*

homogeneous [hɒmə'dʒiːnɪəs] *adj*
homogen

homosexual ['hɒməʊ'seksjʊəl] *adj*
homosexuell ♦ *n* Homosexuelle(r) *mf*

honest ['ɒnɪst] *adj* ehrlich; **~ly** *adv*
ehrlich; **~y** *n* Ehrlichkeit *f*

honey ['hʌnɪ] *n* Honig *m*; **~comb** *n*
Honigwabe *f*; **~moon** *n* Flitterwochen *pl*,
Hochzeitsreise *f*; **~suckle** *n* Geißblatt *nt*

honk [hɒŋk] *vi* hupen

honor ['ɒnə*] *etc* (*US*) *vt, n* = **honour** *etc*

honorary ['ɒnərərɪ] *adj* Ehren-

honour ['ɒnə*] (*US* **honor**) *vt* ehren;
(*cheque*) einlösen ♦ *n* Ehre *f*; **~able** *adj*
ehrenwert; (*intention*) ehrenhaft; **~s
degree** *n* (*UNIV*) akademischer Grad mit
Prüfung im Spezialfach

hood [hʊd] *n* Kapuze *f*; (*BRIT*: *AUT*)

Verdeck nt; (US) Kühlerhaube f
hoodlum ['hu:dləm] n Rowdy m;
(member of gang) Gangster m
hoodwink ['hʊdwɪŋk] vt reinlegen
hoof [hu:f] (pl hooves) n Huf m
hook [hʊk] n Haken m ♦ vt einhaken
hooligan ['hu:lɪgən] n Rowdy m
hoop [hu:p] n Reifen m
hoot [hu:t] vi (AUT) hupen; **~er** n (NAUT)
Dampfpfeife f; (BRIT: AUT) (Auto)hupe f
Hoover ['hu:və*] (®; BRIT) n Staubsauger
m ♦ vt: **h~** staubsaugen
hooves [hu:vz] pl of **hoof**
hop [hɒp] vi hüpfen, hopsen ♦ n (jump)
Hopser m
hope [həʊp] vt, vi hoffen ♦ n Hoffnung f;
I ~ so/not hoffentlich/hoffentlich nicht;
~ful adj hoffnungsvoll; (promising)
vielversprechend; **~fully** adv hoffentlich;
~less adj hoffnungslos
hops [hɒps] npl Hopfen m
horizon [hə'raɪzn] n Horizont m; **~tal**
[hɒrɪ'zɒntl] adj horizontal
hormone ['hɔ:məʊn] n Hormon nt
horn [hɔ:n] n Horn nt; (AUT) Hupe f
hornet ['hɔ:nɪt] n Hornisse f
horny ['hɔ:nɪ] adj schwielig; (US: inf)
scharf
horoscope ['hɒrəskəʊp] n Horoskop nt
horrendous [hə'rendəs] adj (crime)
abscheulich; (error) schrecklich
horrible ['hɒrɪbl] adj fürchterlich
horrid ['hɒrɪd] adj scheußlich
horrify ['hɒrɪfaɪ] vt entsetzen
horror ['hɒrə*] n Schrecken m; **~ film** n
Horrorfilm m
hors d'oeuvre [ɔ:'dɜ:vr] n Vorspeise f
horse [hɔ:s] n Pferd nt; **~back** n: **on
~back** beritten; **~ chestnut** n
Roßkastanie f; **~man/woman** (irreg) n
Reiter(in) m(f); **~power** n Pferdestärke f;
~racing n Pferderennen nt; **~radish** n
Meerrettich m; **~shoe** n Hufeisen nt
horticulture ['hɔ:tɪkʌltʃə*] n Gartenbau
m
hose [həʊz] n (also: **~pipe**) Schlauch m
hosiery ['həʊzɪərɪ] n Strumpfwaren pl
hospitable [hɒs'pɪtəbl] adj
gastfreundlich

hospital ['hɒspɪtl] n Krankenhaus nt
hospitality [hɒspɪ'tælɪtɪ] n
Gastfreundschaft f
host [həʊst] n Gastgeber m; (innkeeper)
(Gast)wirt m; (large number) Heerschar f;
(ECCL) Hostie f
hostage ['hɒstɪdʒ] n Geisel f
hostel ['hɒstəl] n Herberge f; (also: youth
~) Jugendherberge f
hostess ['həʊstes] n Gastgeberin f
hostile ['hɒstaɪl] adj feindlich
hostility [hɒs'tɪlɪtɪ] n Feindschaft f;
hostilities npl (fighting) Feindseligkeiten
pl
hot [hɒt] adj heiß; (drink, food, water)
warm; (spiced) scharf; **I'm ~** mir ist heiß;
~bed n (fig) Nährboden m; **~ dog** n
heiße(s) Würstchen nt
hotel [həʊ'tel] n Hotel nt; **~ier** n Hotelier
m
hot: ~headed adj hitzig; **~house** n
Treibhaus nt; **~ line** n (POL) heiße(r)
Draht m; **~ly** adv (argue) hitzig; **~plate** n
Kochplatte f; **~-water bottle** n
Wärmflasche f
hound [haʊnd] n Jagdhund m ♦ vt hetzen
hour ['aʊə*] n Stunde f; (time of day)
(Tages)zeit f; **~ly** adj, adv stündlich
house [n haʊs, pl 'haʊzɪz, vb haʊz] n Haus
nt ♦ vt unterbringen; **on the ~** auf Kosten
des Hauses; **~ arrest** n (POL, MIL)
Hausarrest m; **~boat** n Hausboot nt;
~breaking n Einbruch m; **~-coat** n
Morgenmantel m; **~hold** n Haushalt m;
~keeper n Haushälterin f; **~keeping** n
Haushaltung f; **~-warming party** n
Einweihungsparty f; **~wife** (irreg) n
Hausfrau f; **~work** n Hausarbeit f
housing ['haʊzɪŋ] n (act) Unterbringung
f; (houses) Wohnungen pl; (POL)
Wohnungsbau m; (covering) Gehäuse nt; **~
estate** (US **~ development**) n
(Wohn)siedlung f
hovel ['hɒvəl] n elende Hütte f
hover ['hɒvə*] vi (bird) schweben;
(person) herumstehen; **~craft** n
Luftkissenfahrzeug nt
how [haʊ] adv wie; **~ are you?** wie geht
es Ihnen?; **~ much milk?** wieviel Milch?;

~ **many people?** wie viele Leute?
however [hau'evə*] *adv* (*but*) (je)doch,
aber; ~ **you phrase it** wie Sie es auch
ausdrücken
howl [haul] *n* Heulen *nt* ♦ *vi* heulen
H.P. *abbr* = **hire purchase**
h.p. *abbr* = **horsepower**
H.Q. *abbr* = **headquarters**
hub [hʌb] *n* Radnabe *f*
hubbub ['hʌbʌb] *n* Tumult *m*
hubcap ['hʌbkæp] *n* Radkappe *f*
huddle ['hʌdl] *vi*: **to ~ together** sich
zusammendrängen
hue [hjuː] *n* Färbung *f*; ~ **and cry** *n*
Zetergeschrei *nt*
huff [hʌf] *n*: **to go into a ~** einschnappen
hug [hʌg] *vt* umarmen ♦ *n* Umarmung *f*
huge [hjuːdʒ] *adj* groß, riesig
hulk [hʌlk] *n* (*ship*) abgetakelte(s) Schiff
nt; (*person*) Koloß *m*
hull [hʌl] *n* Schiffsrumpf *m*
hullo ['hʌ'ləu] *excl* = **hello**
hum [hʌm] *vt, vi* summen
human ['hjuːmən] *adj* menschlich ♦ *n*
(*also*: ~ **being**) Mensch *m*
humane [hjuːˈmeɪn] *adj* human
humanitarian [hjuːmænɪˈtɛərɪən] *adj*
humanitär
humanity [hjuːˈmænɪtɪ] *n* Menschheit *f*;
(*kindliness*) Menschlichkeit *f*
humble ['hʌmbl] *adj* demütig; (*modest*)
bescheiden ♦ *vt* demütigen
humbug ['hʌmbʌg] *n* Humbug *m*; (*BRIT*:
sweet) Pfefferminzbonbon *nt*
humdrum ['hʌmdrʌm] *adj* stumpfsinnig
humid ['hjuːmɪd] *adj* feucht; ~**ity** *n*
Feuchtigkeit *f*
humiliate [hjuːˈmɪlɪeɪt] *vt* demütigen
humiliation [hjuːmɪlɪˈeɪʃən] *n*
Demütigung *f*
humility [hjuːˈmɪlɪtɪ] *n* Demut *f*
humor ['hjuːmə*] *n*, *US vt* = **humour**
humorous ['hjuːmərəs] *adj* humorvoll
humour ['hjuːmə*] (*US* **humor**) *n* (*fun*)
Humor *m*; (*mood*) Stimmung *f* ♦ *vt* bei
Stimmung halten
hump [hʌmp] *n* Buckel *m*
hunch [hʌntʃ] *n* Buckel *m*; (*premonition*)
(Vor)ahnung *f*; ~**back** *n* Bucklige(r) *mf*;

~**ed** *adj* gekrümmt
hundred ['hʌndrɪd] *num* hundert;
~**weight** *n* Zentner *m* (*BRIT* = *50.8kg*; *US*
= *45.3kg*)
hung [hʌŋ] *pt, pp of* **hang**
Hungarian [hʌŋˈgɛərɪən] *adj* ungarisch
♦ *n* Ungar(in) *m(f)*; (*LING*) Ungarisch *nt*
Hungary ['hʌŋgərɪ] *n* Ungarn *nt*
hunger ['hʌŋgə*] *n* Hunger *m* ♦ *vi*
hungern
hungry ['hʌŋgrɪ] *adj* hungrig; **to be ~**
Hunger haben
hunk [hʌŋk] *n* (*of bread*) Stück *nt*
hunt [hʌnt] *vt, vi* jagen ♦ *n* Jagd *f*; **to ~**
for suchen; ~**er** *n* Jäger *m*; ~**ing** *n* Jagd *f*
hurdle ['hɜːdl] *n* (*also fig*) Hürde *f*
hurl [hɜːl] *vt* schleudern
hurrah [huˈrɑː] *n* Hurra *nt*
hurray [huˈreɪ] *n* Hurra *nt*
hurricane ['hʌrɪkən] *n* Orkan *m*
hurried ['hʌrɪd] *adj* eilig; (*hasty*) übereilt;
~**ly** *adv* übereilt, hastig
hurry ['hʌrɪ] *n* Eile *f* ♦ *vi* sich beeilen
♦ *vt* (an)treiben; (*job*) übereilen; **to be in**
a ~ es eilig haben; ~ **up** *vi* sich beeilen
♦ *vt* (*person*) zur Eile antreiben; (*work*)
vorantreiben
hurt [hɜːt] (*pt, pp* **hurt**) *vt* weh tun +*dat*;
(*injure, fig*) verletzen ♦ *vi* weh tun; ~**ful**
adj schädlich; (*remark*) verletzend
hurtle ['hɜːtl] *vi* sausen
husband ['hʌzbənd] *n* (Ehe)mann *m*
hush [hʌʃ] *n* Stille *f* ♦ *vt* zur Ruhe
bringen ♦ *excl* pst, still
husk [hʌsk] *n* Spelze *f*
husky ['hʌskɪ] *adj* (*voice*) rauh ♦ *n*
Eskimohund *m*
hustle ['hʌsl] *vt* (*push*) stoßen; (*hurry*)
antreiben ♦ *n*: ~ **and bustle**
Geschäftigkeit *f*
hut [hʌt] *n* Hütte *f*
hutch [hʌtʃ] *n* (Kaninchen)stall *m*
hyacinth ['haɪəsɪnθ] *n* Hyazinthe *f*
hybrid ['haɪbrɪd] *n* Kreuzung *f* ♦ *adj*
Misch-
hydrant ['haɪdrənt] *n* (*also*: *fire ~*)
Hydrant *m*
hydraulic [haɪˈdrɒlɪk] *adj* hydraulisch
hydroelectric [haɪdrəuˈlektrɪk] *adj*

(*energy*) durch Wasserkraft erzeugt; ~
power station *n* Wasserkraftwerk *nt*
hydrofoil ['haidrəʊfɔil] *n* Tragflügelboot
nt
hydrogen ['haidridʒən] *n* Wasserstoff *m*
hyena [hai'iːnə] *n* Hyäne *f*
hygiene ['haidʒiːn] *n* Hygiene *f*
hygienic [hai'dʒiːnik] *adj* hygienisch
hymn [him] *n* Kirchenlied *nt*
hype [haip] (*inf*) *n* Publicity *f*
hypermarket ['haipə'maːkit] (*BRIT*) *n*
Hypermarket *m*
hyphen ['haifən] *n* Bindestrich *m*
hypnosis [hip'nəʊsis] *n* Hypnose *f*
hypnotic [hip'nɒtik] *adj* hypnotisierend
hypnotize ['hipnətaiz] *vt* hypnotisieren
hypocrisy [hi'pɒkrisi] *n* Heuchelei *f*
hypocrite ['hipəkrit] *n* Heuchler *m*
hypocritical [hipə'kritikəl] *adj*
scheinheilig, heuchlerisch
hypothermia ['haipəʊ'θɜːmiə] *n*
Unterkühlung *f*
hypotheses [hai'pɒθisiːz] *npl of*
hypothesis
hypothesis [hai'pɒθisis] (*pl* **hypotheses**)
n Hypothese *f*
hypothetic(al) [haipəʊ'θetik(əl)] *adj*
hypothetisch
hysterical [his'terikəl] *adj* hysterisch
hysterics [his'teriks] *npl* hysterische(r)
Anfall *m*

I i

I [ai] *pron* ich
ice [ais] *n* Eis *nt* ♦ *vt* (*COOK*) mit
Zuckerguß überziehen ♦ *vi* (*also*: ~ *up*)
vereisen; ~ **axe** *n* Eispickel *m*; ~**berg** *n*
Eisberg *m*; ~**box** (*US*) *n* Kühlschrank *m*;
~ **cream** *n* Eis *nt*; ~ **cube** *n* Eiswürfel
m; ~ **hockey** *n* Eishockey *nt*
Iceland ['aislənd] *n* Island *nt*
ice: ~ **lolly** (*BRIT*) *n* Eis *nt* am Stiel; ~
rink *n* (Kunst)eisbahn *f*; ~ **skating** *n*
Schlittschuhlaufen *nt*
icicle ['aisikl] *n* Eiszapfen *m*
icing ['aisiŋ] *n* (*on cake*) Zuckerguß *m*;
(*on window*) Vereisung *f*; ~ **sugar** (*BRIT*) *n*

Puderzucker *m*
icon ['aikɒn] *n* Ikone *f*
icy ['aisi] *adj* (*slippery*) vereist; (*cold*) eisig
I'd [aid] = **I would; I had**
idea [ai'diə] *n* Idee *f*
ideal [ai'diəl] *n* Ideal *nt* ♦ *adj* ideal; ~**ist**
n Idealist *m*
identical [ai'dentikəl] *adj* identisch;
(*twins*) eineiig
identification [aidentifi'keiʃən] *n*
Identifizierung *f*; **means of** ~
Ausweispapiere *pl*
identify [ai'dentifai] *vt* identifizieren;
(*regard as the same*) gleichsetzen
Identikit picture [ai'dentikit-] *n*
Phantombild *nt*
identity [ai'dentiti] *n* Identität *f*; ~ **card**
n Personalausweis *m*
ideology [aidi'ɒlədʒi] *n* Ideologie *f*
idiom ['idiəm] *n* (*expression*)
Redewendung *f*; (*dialect*) Idiom *nt*; ~**atic**
[idiə'mætik] *adj* idiomatisch
idiosyncrasy [idiə'siŋkrəsi] *n* Eigenart *f*
idiot ['idiət] *n* Idiot(in) *m(f)*; ~**ic** [idi'ɒtik]
adj idiotisch
idle ['aidl] *adj* (*doing nothing*) untätig;
(*lazy*) faul; (*useless*) nutzlos; (*machine*)
still(stehend); (*threat, talk*) leer ♦ *vi*
(*machine*) leerlaufen ♦ *vt*: **to** ~ **away the
time** die Zeit vertrödeln; ~**ness** *n*
Müßiggang *m*; Faulheit *f*
idol ['aidl] *n* Idol *nt*; ~**ize** *vt* vergöttern
i.e. *abbr* (= *id est*) d.h.

KEYWORD

if [if] *conj* **1** *wenn*; (*in case also*) falls; **if I
were you** wenn ich Sie wäre
2 (*although*): (**even**) **if** (selbst *or* auch)
wenn
3 (*whether*) ob
4: if so/not wenn ja/nicht; **if only ...**
wenn ... doch nur ...; **if only I could**
wenn ich doch nur könnte; *see also* **as**

ignite [ig'nait] *vt* (an)zünden ♦ *vi* sich
entzünden
ignition [ig'niʃən] *n* Zündung *f*; **to
switch on/off the** ~ den Motor
anlassen/abstellen; ~ **key** *n* (*AUT*)

Zündschlüssel *m*

ignorance ['ɪgnərəns] *n* Unwissenheit *f*

ignorant ['ɪgnərənt] *adj* unwissend; **to be ~ of** nicht wissen

ignore [ɪg'nɔ:*] *vt* ignorieren

I'll [aɪl] = **I will; I shall**

ill [ɪl] *adj* krank ♦ *n* Übel *nt* ♦ *adv* schlecht; **~-advised** *adj* unklug; **~-at-ease** *adj* unbehaglich

illegal [ɪ'li:gəl] *adj* illegal

illegible [ɪ'ledʒəbl] *adj* unleserlich

illegitimate [ɪlɪ'dʒɪtɪmət] *adj* unehelich

ill-fated [ɪl'feɪtɪd] *adj* unselig

ill feeling *n* Verstimmung *f*

illicit [ɪ'lɪsɪt] *adj* verboten

illiterate [ɪ'lɪtərət] *adj* ungebildet

ill-mannered ['ɪl'mænəd] *adj* ungehobelt

illness ['ɪlnəs] *n* Krankheit *f*

illogical [ɪ'lɒdʒɪkəl] *adj* unlogisch

ill-treat ['ɪl'tri:t] *vt* mißhandeln

illuminate [ɪ'lu:mɪneɪt] *vt* beleuchten

illumination [ɪlu:mɪ'neɪʃən] *n* Beleuchtung *f*; **~s** *pl* (*decorative lights*) festliche Beleuchtung *f*

illusion [ɪ'lu:ʒən] *n* Illusion *f*; **to be under the ~ that ...** sich *dat* einbilden, daß ...

illusory [ɪ'lu:sərɪ] *adj* trügerisch

illustrate ['ɪləstreɪt] *vt* (*book*) illustrieren; (*explain*) veranschaulichen

illustration [ɪləs'treɪʃən] *n* Illustration *f*; (*explanation*) Veranschaulichung *f*

illustrious [ɪ'lʌstrɪəs] *adj* berühmt

ill will *n* Groll *m*

I'm [aɪm] = **I am**

image ['ɪmɪdʒ] *n* Bild *nt*; (*public ~*) Image *nt*; **~ry** *n* Symbolik *f*

imaginary [ɪ'mædʒɪnərɪ] *adj* eingebildet; (*world*) Phantasie-

imagination [ɪmædʒɪ'neɪʃən] *n* Einbildung *f*; (*creative*) Phantasie *f*

imaginative [ɪ'mædʒɪnətɪv] *adj* phantasiereich, einfallsreich

imagine [ɪ'mædʒɪn] *vt* sich vorstellen; (*wrongly*) sich einbilden

imbalance [ɪm'bæləns] *n* Unausgeglichenheit *f*

imbecile ['ɪmbəsi:l] *n* Schwachsinnige(r) *mf*

imbue [ɪm'bju:] *vt*: **to ~ sth with** etw erfüllen mit

imitate ['ɪmɪteɪt] *vt* imitieren

imitation [ɪmɪ'teɪʃən] *n* Imitation *f*

immaculate [ɪ'mækjʊlɪt] *adj* makellos; (*dress*) tadellos; (*ECCL*) unbefleckt

immaterial [ɪmə'tɪərɪəl] *adj* unwesentlich; **it is ~ whether ...** es ist unwichtig, ob ...

immature [ɪmə'tjʊə*] *adj* unreif

immediate [ɪ'mi:dɪət] *adj* (*instant*) sofortig; (*near*) unmittelbar; (*relatives*) nächste(r, s); (*needs*) dringlich; **~ly** *adv* sofort; **~ly next to** direkt neben

immense [ɪ'mens] *adj* unermeßlich

immerse [ɪ'mɜ:s] *vt* eintauchen; **to be ~d in** (*fig*) vertieft sein in +*acc*

immersion heater [ɪ'mɜ:ʃən-] (*BRIT*) *n* Boiler *m*

immigrant ['ɪmɪgrənt] *n* Einwanderer *m*

immigrate ['ɪmɪgreɪt] *vi* einwandern

immigration [ɪmɪ'greɪʃən] *n* Einwanderung *f*

imminent ['ɪmɪnənt] *adj* bevorstehend

immobile [ɪ'məʊbaɪl] *adj* unbeweglich

immobilize [ɪ'məʊbɪlaɪz] *vt* lähmen

immoral [ɪ'mɒrəl] *adj* unmoralisch; **~ity** [ɪmə'rælɪtɪ] *n* Unsittlichkeit *f*

immortal [ɪ'mɔ:tl] *adj* unsterblich

immune [ɪ'mju:n] *adj* (*secure*) sicher; (*MED*) immun; **~ from** sicher vor +*dat*

immunity [ɪ'mju:nɪtɪ] *n* (*MED, JUR*) Immunität *f*; (*fig*) Freiheit *f*

immunize ['ɪmjʊnaɪz] *vt* immunisieren

imp [ɪmp] *n* Kobold *m*

impact ['ɪmpækt] *n* Aufprall *m*; (*fig*) Wirkung *f*

impair [ɪm'pɛə*] *vt* beeinträchtigen

impale [ɪm'peɪl] *vt* aufspießen

impart [ɪm'pɑ:t] *vt* mitteilen; (*knowledge*) vermitteln; (*exude*) abgeben

impartial [ɪm'pɑ:ʃəl] *adj* unparteiisch

impassable [ɪm'pɑ:səbl] *adj* unpassierbar

impasse [æm'pɑ:s] *n* Sackgasse *f*

impassive [ɪm'pæsɪv] *adj* gelassen

impatience [ɪm'peɪʃəns] *n* Ungeduld *f*

impatient [ɪm'peɪʃənt] *adj* ungeduldig

impeccable [ɪm'pekəbl] *adj* tadellos

impede [ɪm'piːd] *vt* (be)hindern
impediment [ɪm'pedɪmənt] *n* Hindernis *nt*; (*in speech*) Sprachfehler *m*
impending [ɪm'pendɪŋ] *adj* bevorstehend
impenetrable [ɪm'penɪtrəbl] *adj* (*also fig*) undurchdringlich
imperative [ɪm'perətɪv] *adj* (*necessary*) unbedingt erforderlich ♦ *n* (*GRAM*) Imperativ *m*, Befehlsform *f*
imperceptible [ɪmpə'septəbl] *adj* nicht wahrnehmbar
imperfect [ɪm'pɜːfɪkt] *adj* (*faulty*) fehlerhaft; ~**ion** [ɪmpɜː'fekʃən] *n* Unvollkommenheit *f*; (*fault*) Fehler *m*
imperial [ɪm'pɪərɪəl] *adj* kaiserlich; ~**ism** *n* Imperialismus *m*
impersonal [ɪm'pɜːsnl] *adj* unpersönlich
impersonate [ɪm'pɜːsəneɪt] *vt* sich ausgeben als; (*for amusement*) imitieren
impertinent [ɪm'pɜːtɪnənt] *adj* unverschämt, frech
impervious [ɪm'pɜːvɪəs] *adj* (*fig*): ~ **(to)** unempfänglich (für)
impetuous [ɪm'petjʊəs] *adj* ungestüm
impetus ['ɪmpɪtəs] *n* Triebkraft *f*, (*fig*) Auftrieb *m*
impinge [ɪm'pɪndʒ] : ~ **on** *vt* beeinträchtigen
implacable [ɪm'plækəbl] *adj* unerbittlich
implement [*n* 'ɪmplɪmənt, *vb* 'ɪmplɪment] *n* Werkzeug *nt* ♦ *vt* ausführen
implicate ['ɪmplɪkeɪt] *vt* verwickeln
implication [ɪmplɪ'keɪʃən] *n* (*effect*) Auswirkung *f*; (*in crime*) Verwicklung *f*
implicit [ɪm'plɪsɪt] *adj* (*suggested*) unausgesprochen; (*utter*) vorbehaltlos
implore [ɪm'plɔː*] *vt* anflehen
imply [ɪm'plaɪ] *vt* (*hint*) andeuten; (*be evidence for*) schließen lassen auf +*acc*
impolite [ɪmpə'laɪt] *adj* unhöflich
import [*vb* ɪm'pɔːt, *n* 'ɪmpɔːt] *vt* einführen ♦ *n* Einfuhr *f*; (*meaning*) Bedeutung *f*
importance [ɪm'pɔːtəns] *n* Bedeutung *f*
important [ɪm'pɔːtənt] *adj* wichtig; **it's not** ~ es ist unwichtig
importer [ɪm'pɔːtə*] *n* Importeur *m*
impose [ɪm'pəʊz] *vt*, *vi*: **to** ~ **(on)** auferlegen (+*dat*); (*penalty, sanctions*) verhängen (gegen); **to** ~ **(o.s.) on sb** sich

jdm aufdrängen
imposing [ɪm'pəʊzɪŋ] *adj* eindrucksvoll
imposition [ɪmpə'zɪʃən] *n* (*of burden, fine*) Auferlegung *f*; (*SCH*) Strafarbeit *f*; **to be an** ~ (*on person*) eine Zumutung sein
impossible [ɪm'pɒsəbl] *adj* unmöglich
impostor [ɪm'pɒstə*] *n* Hochstapler *m*
impotent ['ɪmpətənt] *adj* machtlos; (*sexually*) impotent
impound [ɪm'paʊnd] *vt* beschlagnahmen
impoverished [ɪm'pɒvərɪʃt] *adj* verarmt
impracticable [ɪm'præktɪkəbl] *adj* undurchführbar
impractical [ɪm'præktɪkəl] *adj* unpraktisch
imprecise [ɪmprə'saɪs] *adj* ungenau
impregnable [ɪm'pregnəbl] *adj* (*castle*) uneinnehmbar
impregnate ['ɪmpregneɪt] *vt* (*saturate*) sättigen; (*fertilize*) befruchten
impress [ɪm'pres] *vt* (*influence*) beeindrucken; (*imprint*) (auf)drücken; **to** ~ **sth on sb** jdm etw einschärfen
impression [ɪm'preʃən] *n* Eindruck *m*; (*on wax, footprint*) Abdruck *m*; (*of book*) Auflage *f*; (*take-off*) Nachahmung *f*; **I was under the** ~ ich hatte den Eindruck; ~**able** *adj* leicht zu beeindrucken; ~**ist** *n* Impressionist *m*
impressive [ɪm'presɪv] *adj* eindrucksvoll
imprint ['ɪmprɪnt] *n* Abdruck *m*
imprison [ɪm'prɪzn] *vt* ins Gefängnis schicken; ~**ment** *n* Inhaftierung *f*
improbable [ɪm'prɒbəbl] *adj* unwahrscheinlich
impromptu [ɪm'prɒmptjuː] *adj*, *adv* aus dem Stegreif, improvisiert
improper [ɪm'prɒpə*] *adj* (*indecent*) unanständig; (*unsuitable*) unpassend
improve [ɪm'pruːv] *vt* verbessern ♦ *vi* besser werden; ~**ment** *n* (Ver)besserung *f*
improvise ['ɪmprəvaɪz] *vt*, *vi* improvisieren
imprudent [ɪm'pruːdənt] *adj* unklug
impudent ['ɪmpjʊdənt] *adj* unverschämt
impulse ['ɪmpʌls] *n* Impuls *m*; **to act on** ~ spontan handeln
impunity [ɪm'pjuːnɪtɪ] *n* Straflosigkeit *f*
impure [ɪm'pjʊə*] *adj* (*dirty*)

verunreinigt; (*bad*) unsauber
impurity [ɪmˈpjʊərɪtɪ] *n* Unreinheit *f*;
(*TECH*) Verunreinigung *f*

KEYWORD
---

in [ɪn] *prep* **1** (*indicating place, position*) in
+*dat*; (*with motion*) in +*acc*; **in here/
there** hier/dort; **in the USA** in den
Vereinigten Staaten
2 (*indicating time: during*) in +*dat*; **in
summer** im Sommer; **in 1988** (im Jahre)
1988; **in the afternoon** nachmittags, am
Nachmittag
3 (*indicating time: in the space of*)
innerhalb von; **I'll see you in 2 weeks**
or **in 2 weeks' time** ich sehe Sie in zwei
Wochen
4 (*indicating manner, circumstances, state
etc*) in +*dat*; **in the sun/rain** in der
Sonne/im Regen; **in English/French** auf
Englisch/Französisch; **in a loud/soft
voice** mit lauter/leiser Stimme
5 (*with ratios, numbers*): **1 in 10** jeder
zehnte; **20 pence in the pound** 20 Pence
pro Pfund; **they lined up in twos** sie
stellten sich in Zweierreihe auf
6 (*referring to people, works*): **the disease
is common in children** die Krankheit ist
bei Kindern häufig; **in Dickens** bei
Dickens; **we have a loyal friend in him**
er ist uns ein treuer Freund
7 (*indicating profession etc*): **to be in
teaching/the army** Lehrer(in)/beim
Militär sein; **to be in publishing** im
Verlagswesen arbeiten
8 (*with present participle*): **in saying this,
I ...** wenn ich das sage, ... ich; **in
accepting this view, he ...** weil er diese
Meinung akzeptierte, ... er
♦ *adv*: **to be in** (*person: at home, work*)
dasein; (*train, ship, plane*) angekommen
sein; (*in fashion*) in sein; **to ask sb in** jdn
hereinbitten; **to run/limp etc in**
hereingerannt/gehumpelt *etc* kommen
♦ *n*: **the ins and outs** (*of proposal,
situation etc*) die Feinheiten

in. *abbr* = **inch**
inability [ɪnəˈbɪlɪtɪ] *n* Unfähigkeit *f*

inaccessible [ɪnækˈsesəbl] *adj*
unzugänglich
inaccurate [ɪnˈækjʊrɪt] *adj* ungenau;
(*wrong*) unrichtig
inactivity [ɪnækˈtɪvɪtɪ] *n* Untätigkeit *f*
inadequate [ɪnˈædɪkwət] *adj*
unzulänglich
inadvertently [ɪnədˈvɜːtəntlɪ] *adv*
unabsichtlich
inadvisable [ɪnədˈvaɪzəbl] *adj* nicht
ratsam
inane [ɪˈneɪn] *adj* dumm, albern
inanimate [ɪnˈænɪmət] *adj* leblos
inappropriate [ɪnəˈprəʊprɪət] *adj*
(*clothing*) ungeeignet; (*remark*)
unangebracht
inarticulate [ɪnɑːˈtɪkjʊlət] *adj* unklar
inasmuch as [ɪnəzˈmʌtʃəz] *adv* da; (*in
so far as*) soweit
inaudible [ɪnˈɔːdəbl] *adj* unhörbar
inaugural [ɪˈnɔːgjʊrəl] *adj* Eröffnungs-
inaugurate [ɪˈnɔːgjʊreɪt] *vt* (*open*)
einweihen; (*admit to office*) (feierlich)
einführen
inauguration [ɪnɔːgjʊˈreɪʃən] *n*
Eröffnung *f*; (feierliche) Amtseinführung *f*
inborn [ˈɪnbɔːn] *adj* angeboren
inbred [ˈɪnbred] *adj* angeboren
Inc. *abbr* = **incorporated**
incalculable [ɪnˈkælkjʊləbl] *adj*
(*consequences*) unabsehbar
incapable [ɪnˈkeɪpəbl] *adj*: ~ **(of doing
sth)** unfähig(, etw zu tun)
incapacitate [ɪnkəˈpæsɪteɪt] *vt*
untauglich machen
incapacity [ɪnkəˈpæsɪtɪ] *n* Unfähigkeit *f*
incarcerate [ɪnˈkɑːsəreɪt] *vt* einkerkern
incarnation [ɪnkɑːˈneɪʃən] *n* (*ECCL*)
Menschwerdung *f*; (*fig*) Inbegriff *m*
incendiary [ɪnˈsendɪərɪ] *adj* Brand-
incense [*n* ˈɪnsens, *vb* ɪnˈsens] *n*
Weihrauch *m* ♦ *vt* erzürnen
incentive [ɪnˈsentɪv] *n* Anreiz *m*
incessant [ɪnˈsesnt] *adj* unaufhörlich;
~**ly** *adv* unaufhörlich
incest [ˈɪnsest] *n* Inzest *m*
inch [ɪntʃ] *n* Zoll *m* ♦ *vi*: **to ~ forward**
sich Stückchen für Stückchen vorwärts
bewegen; **to be within an ~ of** kurz

davor sein; **he didn't give an ~** er gab keinen Zentimeter nach

incidence ['ɪnsɪdəns] *n* Auftreten *nt*; *(of crime)* Quote *f*

incident ['ɪnsɪdənt] *n* Vorfall *m*; *(disturbance)* Zwischenfall *m*

incidental [ɪnsɪ'dentl] *adj (music)* Begleit-; *(unimportant)* nebensächlich; *(remark)* beiläufig; **~ly** *adv* übrigens

incinerator [ɪn'sɪnəreɪtə*] *n* Verbrennungsofen *m*

incipient [ɪn'sɪpɪənt] *adj* beginnend

incision [ɪn'sɪʒən] *n* Einschnitt *m*

incisive [ɪn'saɪsɪv] *adj (style)* treffend; *(person)* scharfsinnig

incite [ɪn'saɪt] *vt* anstacheln

inclination [ɪnklɪ'neɪʃən] *n* Neigung *f*

incline [*n* 'ɪnklaɪn, *vb* ɪn'klaɪn] *n* Abhang *m* ♦ *vt* neigen; *(fig)* veranlassen ♦ *vi* sich neigen; **to be ~d to do sth** dazu neigen, etw zu tun

include [ɪn'kluːd] *vt* einschließen; *(on list, in group)* aufnehmen

including [ɪn'kluːdɪŋ] *prep*: **~ X X** inbegriffen

inclusion [ɪn'kluːʒən] *n* Aufnahme *f*

inclusive [ɪn'kluːsɪv] *adj* einschließlich; *(COMM)* inklusive; **~ of** einschließlich +*gen*

incoherent [ɪnkəʊ'hɪərənt] *adj* zusammenhanglos

income ['ɪnkʌm] *n* Einkommen *nt*; *(from business)* Einkünfte *pl*; **~ tax** *n* Lohnsteuer *f*; *(of self-employed)* Einkommensteuer *f*

incoming ['ɪnkʌmɪŋ] *adj*: **~ flight** eintreffende Maschine *f*

incomparable [ɪn'kɒmpərəbl] *adj* unvergleichlich

incompatible [ɪnkəm'pætəbl] *adj* unvereinbar; *(people)* unverträglich

incompetence [ɪn'kɒmpɪtəns] *n* Unfähigkeit *f*

incompetent [ɪn'kɒmpɪtənt] *adj* unfähig

incomplete [ɪnkəm'pliːt] *adj* unvollständig

incomprehensible [ɪnkɒmprɪ'hensəbl] *adj* unverständlich

inconceivable [ɪnkən'siːvəbl] *adj* unvorstellbar

incongruous [ɪn'kɒŋgrʊəs] *adj* seltsam; *(remark)* unangebracht

inconsiderate [ɪnkən'sɪdərət] *adj* rücksichtslos

inconsistency [ɪnkən'sɪstənsɪ] *n* Widersprüchlichkeit *f*; *(state)* Unbeständigkeit *f*

inconsistent [ɪnkən'sɪstənt] *adj (action, speech)* widersprüchlich; *(person, work)* unbeständig; **~ with** nicht übereinstimmend mit

inconspicuous [ɪnkən'spɪkjʊəs] *adj* unauffällig

incontinent [ɪn'kɒntɪnənt] *adj (MED)* nicht fähig, Stuhl und Harn zurückzuhalten

inconvenience [ɪnkən'viːnɪəns] *n* Unbequemlichkeit *f*; *(trouble to others)* Unannehmlichkeiten *pl*

inconvenient [ɪnkən'viːnɪənt] *adj* ungelegen; *(journey)* unbequem

incorporate [ɪn'kɔːrpəreɪt] *vt (include)* aufnehmen; *(contain)* enthalten

incorporated [ɪn'kɔːpəreɪtɪd] *adj*: **~ company** *(US)* eingetragene Aktiengesellschaft *f*

incorrect [ɪnkə'rekt] *adj* unrichtig

incorrigible [ɪn'kɒrɪdʒəbl] *adj* unverbesserlich

incorruptible [ɪnkə'rʌptəbl] *adj* unzerstörbar; *(person)* unbestechlich

increase [*n* 'ɪnkriːs, *vb* ɪn'kriːs] *n* Zunahme *f*; *(pay ~)* Gehaltserhöhung *f*; *(in size)* Vergrößerung *f* ♦ *vt* erhöhen; *(wealth, rage)* vermehren; *(business)* erweitern ♦ *vi* zunehmen; *(prices)* steigen; *(in size)* größer werden; *(in number)* sich vermehren

increasing [ɪn'kriːsɪŋ] *adj (number)* steigend

increasingly [ɪn'kriːsɪŋlɪ] *adv* zunehmend

incredible [ɪn'kredəbl] *adj* unglaublich

incredulous [ɪn'kredjʊləs] *adj* ungläubig

increment ['ɪnkrɪmənt] *n* Zulage *f*

incriminate [ɪn'krɪmɪneɪt] *vt* belasten

incubation [ɪnkjʊ'beɪʃən] *n* Ausbrüten *nt*

incubator ['ɪnkjʊbeɪtə*] *n* Brutkasten *m*

incumbent [ɪn'kʌmbənt] *n* Amts-

inhaber(in) *m(f)* ♦ *adj*: **it is ~ on him to
... es obliegt ihm, ...**
incur [ɪn'kɜ:*] *vt* sich zuziehen; *(debts)*
machen
incurable [ɪn'kjʊərəbl] *adj* unheilbar;
(fig) unverbesserlich
incursion [ɪn'kɜ:ʃən] *n* Einfall *m*
indebted [ɪn'detɪd] *adj (obliged)*: **~ (to
sb)** (jdm) verpflichtet
indecent [ɪn'di:snt] *adj* unanständig; **~
assault** *(BRIT)* *n* Notzucht *f*; **~ exposure**
n Exhibitionismus *m*
indecisive [ɪndɪ'saɪsɪv] *adj (battle)* nicht
entscheidend; *(person)* unentschlossen
indeed [ɪn'di:d] *adv* tatsächlich, in der
Tat; **yes ~!** Allerdings!
indefinitely [ɪn'defɪnɪtlɪ] *adv* auf
unbestimmte Zeit; *(wait)* unbegrenzt
lange
indelible [ɪn'deləbl] *adj* unauslöschlich
independence [ɪndɪ'pendəns] *n*
Unabhängigkeit *f*; **independent** *adj*
unabhängig
indestructible [ˌɪndɪs'trʌktəbl] *adj*
unzerstörbar
indeterminate [ˌɪndɪ'tɜ:mɪnɪt] *adj*
unbestimmt
index ['ɪndeks] *(pl* **~es**) *n* Index *m*; **~
card** *n* Karteikarte *f*; **~ finger** *n*
Zeigefinger *m*; **~-linked** *(US* **~ed**) *adj*
(salaries) der Inflationsrate *dat*
angeglichen; *(pensions)* dynamisch
India ['ɪndɪə] *n* Indien *nt*; **~n** *adj* indisch
♦ *n* Inder(in) *m(f)*; **American ~n**
Indianer(in) *m(f)*; **the ~n Ocean** *n* der
Indische Ozean
indicate ['ɪndɪkeɪt] *vt* anzeigen; *(hint)*
andeuten
indication [ɪndɪ'keɪʃən] *n* Anzeichen *nt*;
(information) Angabe *f*
indicative [ɪn'dɪkətɪv] *adj*: **~ of**
bezeichnend für ♦ *n (GRAM)* Indikativ *m*
indicator ['ɪndɪkeɪtə*] *n (sign)*
(An)zeichen *nt*; *(AUT)* Richtungsanzeiger *m*
indices ['ɪndɪsi:z] *npl of* **index**
indictment [ɪn'daɪtmənt] *n* Anklage *f*
indifference [ɪn'dɪfrəns] *n*
Gleichgültigkeit *f*; Unwichtigkeit *f*
indifferent [ɪn'dɪfrənt] *adj* gleichgültig;

(mediocre) mäßig
indigenous [ɪn'dɪdʒɪnəs] *adj* einheimisch
indigestion [ɪndɪ'dʒestʃən] *n*
Verdauungsstörung *f*
indignant [ɪn'dɪgnənt] *adj*: **to be ~
about sth** über etw *acc* empört sein
indignation [ɪndɪg'neɪʃən] *n* Entrüstung
f
indignity [ɪn'dɪgnɪtɪ] *n* Demütigung *f*
indirect [ɪndɪ'rekt] *adj* indirekt; **~ly** *adv*
indirekt
indiscreet [ɪndɪs'kri:t] *adj (insensitive)*
taktlos; *(telling secrets)* indiskret
indiscretion [ɪndɪs'kreʃən] *n*
Taktlosigkeit *f*; Indiskretion *f*
indiscriminate [ɪndɪs'krɪmɪnət] *adj*
wahllos; kritiklos
indispensable [ɪndɪs'pensəbl] *adj*
unentbehrlich
indisposed [ɪndɪs'pəʊzd] *adj* unpäßlich
indisputable [ɪndɪs'pju:təbl] *adj*
unbestreitbar; *(evidence)* unanfechtbar
indistinct [ɪndɪs'tɪŋkt] *adj* undeutlich
individual [ɪndɪ'vɪdjʊəl] *n* Individuum *nt*
♦ *adj* individuell; *(case)* Einzel-; *(of, for
one person)* eigen, individuell;
(characteristic) eigentümlich; **~ly** *adv*
einzeln, individuell
indivisible [ɪndɪ'vɪzəbl] *adj* unteilbar
indoctrinate [ɪn'dɒktrɪneɪt] *vt*
indoktrinieren
indolent ['ɪndələnt] *adj* träge
Indonesia [ɪndəʊ'ni:zɪə] *n* Indonesien *nt*
indoor ['ɪndɔ:*] *adj* Haus-; Zimmer-;
Innen-; *(SPORT)* Hallen-; **~s** [ɪn'dɔ:z] *adv*
drinnen, im Haus
induce [ɪn'dju:s] *vt* dazu bewegen;
(reaction) herbeiführen; **~ment** *n*
Veranlassung *f*; *(incentive)* Anreiz *m*
induction course [ɪn'dʌkʃən-] *(BRIT)* *n*
Einführungskurs *m*
indulge [ɪn'dʌldʒ] *vt (give way)*
nachgeben +*dat*; *(gratify)* frönen +*dat*
♦ *vi*: **to ~ (in)** frönen (+*dat*); **~nce** *n*
Nachsicht *f*; *(enjoyment)* Genuß *m*; **~nt**
adj nachsichtig; *(pej)* nachgiebig
industrial [ɪn'dʌstrɪəl] *adj* Industrie-,
industriell; *(dispute, injury)* Arbeits-; **~
action** *n* Arbeitskampfmaßnahmen *pl*; **~**

estate *(BRIT)* n Industriegebiet nt; **~ist** n Industrielle(r) mf; **~ize** vt industrialisieren; **~ park** *(US)* n Industriegebiet nt

industrious [ɪnˈdʌstrɪəs] adj fleißig

industry [ˈɪndəstrɪ] n Industrie f; *(diligence)* Fleiß m

inebriated [ɪˈniːbrɪeɪtɪd] adj betrunken

inedible [ɪnˈedɪbl] adj ungenießbar

ineffective [ɪnɪˈfektɪv] adj unwirksam; *(person)* untauglich

ineffectual [ɪnɪˈfektjʊəl] adj = ineffective

inefficiency [ɪnɪˈfɪʃənsɪ] n Ineffizienz f

inefficient [ɪnɪˈfɪʃənt] adj ineffizient; *(ineffective)* unwirksam

inept [ɪˈnept] adj *(remark)* unpassend; *(person)* ungeeignet

inequality [ɪnɪˈkwɒlɪtɪ] n Ungleichheit f

inert [ɪˈnɜːt] adj träge; *(CHEM)* inaktiv; *(motionless)* unbeweglich

inertia [ɪˈnɜːʃə] n Trägheit f

inescapable [ɪnɪsˈkeɪpəbl] adj unvermeidbar

inevitable [ɪnˈevɪtəbl] adj unvermeidlich

inevitably [ɪnˈevɪtəblɪ] adv zwangsläufig

inexcusable [ɪnɪksˈkjuːzəbl] adj unverzeihlich

inexhaustible [ɪnɪɡˈzɔːstəbl] adj unerschöpflich

inexorable [ɪnˈeksərəbl] adj unerbittlich

inexpensive [ɪnɪksˈpensɪv] adj preiswert

inexperience [ɪnɪksˈpɪərɪəns] n Unerfahrenheit f; **~d** [ɪnɪksˈpɪərɪənst] adj unerfahren

inexplicable [ɪnɪksˈplɪkəbl] adj unerklärlich

inextricably [ɪnɪksˈtrɪkəblɪ] adv untrennbar

infallible [ɪnˈfæləbl] adj unfehlbar

infamous [ˈɪnfəməs] adj *(place)* verrufen; *(deed)* schändlich; *(person)* niederträchtig

infamy [ˈɪnfəmɪ] n Verrufenheit f; Niedertracht f; *(disgrace)* Schande f

infancy [ˈɪnfənsɪ] n frühe Kindheit f; *(fig)* Anfangsstadium nt

infant [ˈɪnfənt] n kleine(s) Kind nt, Säugling m; **~ile** adj kindisch, infantil; **~ school** *(BRIT)* n Vorschule f

infatuated [ɪnˈfætjʊeɪtɪd] adj vernarrt; **to become ~ with** sich vernarren in +acc

infatuation [ɪnfætjʊˈeɪʃən] n: **~ (with)** Vernarrtheit f (in +acc)

infect [ɪnˈfekt] vt anstecken *(also fig)*; **~ed with** *(illness)* infiziert mit; **~ion** [ɪnˈfekʃən] n Infektion f; **~ious** [ɪnˈfekʃəs] adj ansteckend

infer [ɪnˈfɜː*] vt schließen; **~ence** [ˈɪnfərəns] n Schlußfolgerung f

inferior [ɪnˈfɪərɪə*] adj *(rank)* untergeordnet; *(quality)* minderwertig ♦ n Untergebene(r) mf; **~ity** [ɪnfɪərɪˈɒrɪtɪ] n Minderwertigkeit f; *(in rank)* untergeordnete Stellung f; **~ity complex** n Minderwertigkeitskomplex m

infernal [ɪnˈfɜːnl] adj höllisch

infertile [ɪnˈfɜːtaɪl] adj unfruchtbar

infertility [ɪnfɜːˈtɪlɪtɪ] n Unfruchtbarkeit f

infested [ɪnˈfestɪd] adj: **to be ~ with** wimmeln von

infidelity [ɪnfɪˈdelɪtɪ] n Untreue f

infighting [ˈɪnfaɪtɪŋ] n Nahkampf m

infiltrate [ˈɪnfɪltreɪt] vt infiltrieren; *(spies)* einschleusen ♦ vi *(MIL. liquid)* einsickern; *(POL)*: **to ~ (into)** unterwandern (+acc)

infinite [ˈɪnfɪnɪt] adj unendlich

infinitive [ɪnˈfɪnɪtɪv] n Infinitiv m

infinity [ɪnˈfɪnɪtɪ] n Unendlichkeit f

infirm [ɪnˈfɜːm] adj gebrechlich

infirmary [ɪnˈfɜːmərɪ] n Krankenhaus nt

infirmity [ɪnˈfɜːmɪtɪ] n Schwäche f, Gebrechlichkeit f

inflamed [ɪnˈfleɪmd] adj entzündet

inflammable [ɪnˈflæməbl] *(BRIT)* adj feuergefährlich

inflammation [ɪnfləˈmeɪʃən] n Entzündung f

inflatable [ɪnˈfleɪtəbl] adj aufblasbar

inflate [ɪnˈfleɪt] vt aufblasen; *(tyre)* aufpumpen; *(prices)* hochtreiben

inflation [ɪnˈfleɪʃən] n Inflation f; **~ary** [ɪnˈfleɪʃnərɪ] adj *(increase)* inflationistisch; *(situation)* inflationär

inflexible [ɪnˈfleksəbl] adj *(person)* nicht flexibel; *(opinion)* starr; *(thing)* unbiegsam

inflict [ɪnˈflɪkt] vt: **to ~ sth on sb** jdm etw zufügen; *(wound)* jdm etw beibringen

influence ['ɪnfluəns] *n* Einfluß *m* ♦ *vt*
beeinflussen
influential [ɪnflu'enʃəl] *adj* einflußreich
influenza [ɪnflu'enzə] *n* Grippe *f*
influx ['ɪnflʌks] *n* (*of people*) Zustrom *m*;
(*of ideas*) Eindringen *nt*
inform [ɪn'fɔ:m] *vt* informieren ♦ *vi*: **to ~
on sb** jdn denunzieren; **to keep sb ~ed**
jdn auf dem laufenden halten
informal [ɪn'fɔ:məl] *adj* zwanglos; **~ity**
[ɪnfɔ:'mælɪtɪ] *n* Ungezwungenheit *f*
informant [ɪn'fɔ:mənt] *n* Informant(in)
m(f)
information [ɪnfə'meɪʃən] *n* Auskunft *f*,
Information *f*; **a piece of ~** eine
Auskunft, eine Information; **~ office** *n*
Informationsbüro *nt*
informative [ɪn'fɔ:mətɪv] *adj* informativ;
(*person*) mitteilsam
informer [ɪn'fɔ:mə*] *n* Denunziant(in)
m(f)
infra-red [ɪnfrə'red] *adj* infrarot
infrequent [ɪn'fri:kwənt] *adj* selten
infringe [ɪn'frɪndʒ] *vt* (*law*) verstoßen
gegen; **~ upon** *vt* verletzen; **~ment** *n*
Verstoß *m*, Verletzung *f*
infuriating [ɪn'fjʊərɪeɪtɪŋ] *adj* ärgerlich
infusion [ɪn'fju:ʒən] *n* (*tea etc*) Aufguß *m*
ingenious [ɪn'dʒi:nɪəs] *adj* genial
ingenuity [ɪndʒɪ'nju:ɪtɪ] *n* Genialität *f*
ingenuous [ɪn'dʒenjʊəs] *adj* aufrichtig;
(*naive*) naiv
ingot ['ɪŋgət] *n* Barren *m*
ingrained [ɪn'greɪnd] *adj* tiefsitzend
ingratiate [ɪn'greɪʃɪeɪt] *vt*: **to ~ o.s. with
sb** sich bei jdm einschmeicheln
ingratitude [ɪn'grætɪtju:d] *n*
Undankbarkeit *f*
ingredient [ɪn'gri:dɪənt] *n* Bestandteil *m*;
(*COOK*) Zutat *f*
inhabit [ɪn'hæbɪt] *vt* bewohnen; **~ant**
[ɪn'hæbɪtnt] *n* Bewohner(in) *m(f)*; (*of
island, town*) Einwohner(in) *m(f)*
inhale [ɪn'heɪl] *vt* einatmen; (*MED,
cigarettes*) inhalieren
inherent [ɪn'hɪərənt] *adj*: **~ (in)**
innewohnend (+*dat*)
inherit [ɪn'herɪt] *vt* erben; **~ance** *n* Erbe
nt, Erbschaft *f*

inhibit [ɪn'hɪbɪt] *vt* hemmen; **to ~ sb
from doing sth** jdn daran hindern, etw
zu tun; **~ion** [ɪnhɪ'bɪʃən] *n* Hemmung *f*
inhospitable [ɪnhɒs'pɪtəbl] *adj* (*person*)
ungastlich; (*country*) unwirtlich
inhuman [ɪn'hju:mən] *adj* unmenschlich
inimitable [ɪ'nɪmɪtəbl] *adj*
unnachahmlich
iniquity [ɪ'nɪkwɪtɪ] *n* Ungerechtigkeit *f*
initial [ɪ'nɪʃəl] *adj* anfänglich, Anfangs-
♦ *n* Initiale *f* ♦ *vt* abzeichnen; (*POL*)
paraphieren; **~ly** *adv* anfangs
initiate [ɪ'nɪʃɪeɪt] *vt* einführen;
(*negotiations*) einleiten; **to ~ sb into a
secret** jdn in ein Geheimnis einweihen;
to ~ proceedings against sb (*JUR*)
gerichtliche Schritte gegen jdn einleiten
initiation [ɪnɪʃɪ'eɪʃən] *n* Einführung *f*;
Einleitung *f*
initiative [ɪ'nɪʃətɪv] *n* Initiative *f*
inject [ɪn'dʒekt] *vt* einspritzen; (*fig*)
einflößen; **~ion** [ɪn'dʒekʃən] *n* Spritze *f*
injunction [ɪn'dʒʌŋkʃən] *n* Verfügung *f*
injure ['ɪndʒə*] *vt* verletzen; **~d** *adj*
(*person, arm*) verletzt
injury ['ɪndʒərɪ] *n* Verletzung *f*; **to play ~
time** (*SPORT*) nachspielen
injustice [ɪn'dʒʌstɪs] *n* Ungerechtigkeit *f*
ink [ɪŋk] *n* Tinte *f*
inkling ['ɪŋklɪŋ] *n* (dunkle) Ahnung *f*
inlaid ['ɪn'leɪd] *adj* eingelegt, Einlege-
inland [*adj* 'ɪnlənd, *adv* 'ɪnlænd] *adj*
Binnen-; (*domestic*) Inlands- ♦ *adv*
landeinwärts; **~ revenue** (*BRIT*) *n* Fiskus
m
in-laws ['ɪnlɔ:z] *npl* (*parents-in-law*)
Schwiegereltern *pl*; (*others*) angeheiratete
Verwandte *pl*
inlet ['ɪnlet] *n* Einlaß *m*; (*bay*) kleine
Bucht *f*
inmate ['ɪnmeɪt] *n* Insasse *m*
inn [ɪn] *n* Gasthaus *nt*, Wirtshaus *nt*
innate [ɪ'neɪt] *adj* angeboren
inner ['ɪnə*] *adj* inner, Innen-; (*fig*)
verborgen; **~ city** *n* Innenstadt *f*; **~ tube**
n (*of tyre*) Schlauch *m*
innings ['ɪnɪŋz] *n* (*CRICKET*) Innenrunde *f*
innocence ['ɪnəsns] *n* Unschuld *f*;
(*ignorance*) Unkenntnis *f*

innocent ['ɪnəsnt] *adj* unschuldig
innocuous [ɪ'nɒkjʊəs] *adj* harmlos
innovation [ɪnəʊ'veɪʃən] *n* Neuerung *f*
innuendo [ɪnjʊ'endəʊ] *n* (versteckte) Anspielung *f*
innumerable [ɪ'nju:mərəbl] *adj* unzählig
inoculation [ɪnɒkjʊ'leɪʃən] *n* Impfung *f*
inopportune [ɪn'ɒpətju:n] *adj* (*remark*) unangebracht; (*visit*) ungelegen
inordinately [ɪ'nɔ:dɪnɪtlɪ] *adv* unmäßig
inpatient ['ɪnpeɪʃənt] *n* stationäre(r) Patient *m*/stationäre Patientin *f*
input ['ɪnpʊt] *n* (*COMPUT*) Eingabe *f*; (*power ~*) Energiezufuhr *f*; (*of energy, work*) Aufwand *m*
inquest ['ɪnkwest] *n* gerichtliche Untersuchung *f*
inquire [ɪn'kwaɪə*] *vi* sich erkundigen ♦ *vt* (*price*) sich erkundigen nach; ~ **into** *vt* untersuchen
inquiry [ɪn'kwaɪərɪ] *n* (*question*) Erkundigung *f*; (*investigation*) Untersuchung *f*; ~ **office** (*BRIT*) *n* Auskunft(sbüro *nt*) *f*
inquisitive [ɪn'kwɪzɪtɪv] *adj* neugierig
inroad ['ɪnrəʊd] *n* (*MIL*) Einfall *m*; (*fig*) Eingriff *m*
ins. *abbr* = **inches**
insane [ɪn'seɪn] *adj* wahnsinnig; (*MED*) geisteskrank
insanity [ɪn'sænɪtɪ] *n* Wahnsinn *m*
insatiable [ɪn'seɪʃəbl] *adj* unersättlich
inscribe [ɪn'skraɪb] *vt* eingravieren
inscription [ɪn'skrɪpʃən] *n* (*on stone*) Inschrift *f*; (*in book*) Widmung *f*
inscrutable [ɪn'skru:təbl] *adj* unergründlich
insect ['ɪnsekt] *n* Insekt *nt*; ~**icide** [ɪn'sektɪsaɪd] *n* Insektenvertilgungsmittel *nt*
insecure [ɪnsɪ'kjʊə*] *adj* (*person*) unsicher; (*thing*) nicht fest *or* sicher
insecurity [ɪnsɪ'kjʊərɪtɪ] *n* Unsicherheit *f*
insemination [ɪnsemɪ'neɪʃən] *n*: **artificial ~** künstliche Befruchtung *f*
insensible [ɪn'sensəbl] *adj* (*unconscious*) bewußtlos
insensitive [ɪn'sensɪtɪv] *adj* (*to pain*) unempfindlich; (*without feelings*) gefühllos

inseparable [ɪn'sepərəbl] *adj* (*people*) unzertrennlich; (*word*) untrennbar
insert [*vb* ɪn'sɜ:t, *n* 'ɪnsɜ:t] *vt* einfügen; (*coin*) einwerfen; (*stick into*) hineinstecken; (*advertisement*) aufgeben ♦ *n* (*in book*) Einlage *f*; (*in magazine*) Beilage *f*; ~**ion** [ɪn'sɜ:ʃən] *n* Einfügung *f*; (*PRESS*) Inserat *nt*
in-service [ɪn'sɜ:vɪs] *adj* (*training*) berufsbegleitend
inshore ['ɪn'ʃɔ:*] *adj* Küsten- ♦ *adv* an der Küste
inside ['ɪn'saɪd] *n* Innenseite *f*, Innere(s) *nt* ♦ *adj* innere(r, s), Innen- ♦ *adv* (*place*) innen; (*direction*) nach innen, hinein ♦ *prep* (*place*) in +*dat*; (*direction*) in +*acc* ... hinein; (*time*) innerhalb +*gen*; ~**s** *npl* (*inf*) Eingeweide *nt*; ~ **10 minutes** unter 10 Minuten; ~ **lane** *n* (*AUT*: *in Britain*) linke Spur; ~ **out** *adv* linksherum; (*know*) in- und auswendig
insider dealing, insider trading [ɪn'saɪdə*] *n* (*STOCK EXCHANGE*) Insiderhandel *m*
insidious [ɪn'sɪdɪəs] *adj* heimtückisch
insight ['ɪnsaɪt] *n* Einsicht *f*; ~ **into** Einblick *m* in +*acc*
insignificant [ɪnsɪg'nɪfɪkənt] *adj* unbedeutend
insincere [ɪnsɪn'sɪə*] *adj* unaufrichtig
insinuate [ɪn'sɪnjʊeɪt] *vt* (*hint*) andeuten
insipid [ɪn'sɪpɪd] *adj* fad(e)
insist [ɪn'sɪst] *vi*: **to ~ (on)** bestehen (auf +*acc*); ~**ence** *n* Bestehen *nt*; ~**ent** *adj* hartnäckig; (*urgent*) dringend
insole ['ɪnsəʊl] *n* Einlegesohle *f*
insolence ['ɪnsələns] *n* Frechheit *f*
insolent ['ɪnsələnt] *adj* frech
insoluble [ɪn'sɒljʊbl] *adj* unlösbar; (*CHEM*) unlöslich
insolvent [ɪn'sɒlvənt] *adj* zahlungsunfähig
insomnia [ɪn'sɒmnɪə] *n* Schlaflosigkeit *f*
inspect [ɪn'spekt] *vt* prüfen; (*officially*) inspizieren; ~**ion** [ɪn'spekʃən] *n* Inspektion *f*; ~**or** *n* (*official*) Inspektor *m*; (*police*) Polizeikommissar *m*; (*BRIT*: *on buses, trains*) Kontrolleur *m*
inspiration [ɪnspɪ'reɪʃən] *n* Inspiration *f*

inspire [ɪn'spaɪə*] *vt (person)* inspirieren;
to ~ sth in sb *(respect)* jdm etw
einflößen; *(hope)* etw in jdm wecken
instability [ɪnstə'bɪlɪtɪ] *n*
Unbeständigkeit *f*, Labilität *f*
install [ɪn'stɔːl] *vt (put in)* installieren;
(telephone) anschließen; *(establish)*
einsetzen; **~ation** [ɪnstə'leɪʃən] *n (of
person)* (Amts)einsetzung *f*; *(of machinery)*
Installierung *f*; *(machines etc)* Anlage *f*
instalment [ɪn'stɔːlmənt] *(US
installment)* *n* Rate *f*; *(of story)*
Fortsetzung *f*; **to pay in ~s** auf Raten
zahlen
instance ['ɪnstəns] *n* Fall *m*; *(example)*
Beispiel *nt*; **for ~** zum Beispiel; **in the
first ~** zunächst
instant ['ɪnstənt] *n* Augenblick *m* ♦ *adj*
augenblicklich, sofortig
instantaneous [ɪnstən'teɪnɪəs] *adj*
unmittelbar
instant coffee *n* Instantkaffee *m*
instantly ['ɪnstəntlɪ] *adv* sofort
instead [ɪn'sted] *adv* statt dessen; **~ of**
prep anstatt +*gen*
instep ['ɪnstep] *n* Spann *m*; *(of shoe)* Blatt
nt
instil [ɪn'stɪl] *vt (fig)*: **to ~ sth in sb** jdm
etw beibringen
instinct ['ɪnstɪŋkt] *n* Instinkt *m*; **~ive**
[ɪn'stɪŋktɪv] *adj* instinktiv
institute ['ɪnstɪtjuːt] *n* Institut *nt* ♦ *vt*
einführen; *(search)* einleiten
institution [ɪnstɪ'tjuːʃən] *n* Institution *f*;
(home) Anstalt *f*
instruct [ɪn'strʌkt] *vt* anweisen;
(officially) instruieren; **~ion** [ɪn'strʌkʃən]
n Unterricht *m*; **~ions** *npl (orders)*
Anweisungen *pl*; *(for use)*
Gebrauchsanweisung *f*; **~ive** *adj*
lehrreich; **~or** *n* Lehrer *m*; *(MIL)*
Ausbilder *m*
instrument ['ɪnstrumənt] *n* Instrument
nt; **~al** [ɪnstru'mentl] *adj (MUS)*
Instrumental-; *(helpful)*: **~al (in)** behilflich
(bei); **~ panel** *n* Armaturenbrett *nt*
insubordinate [ɪnsə'bɔːdənət] *adj*
aufsässig, widersetzlich
insubordination [ɪnsəbɔːdɪ'neɪʃən] *n*

Gehorsamsverweigerung *f*
insufferable [ɪn'sʌfərəbl] *adj*
unerträglich
insufficient [ɪnsə'fɪʃənt] *adj* ungenügend
insular ['ɪnsjələ*] *adj (fig)* engstirnig
insulate ['ɪnsjuleɪt] *vt (ELEC)* isolieren;
(fig): **to ~ (from)** abschirmen (vor +*dat*)
insulating tape ['ɪnsjuleɪtɪŋ-] *n*
Isolierband *nt*
insulation [ɪnsju'leɪʃən] *n* Isolierung *f*
insulin ['ɪnsjulɪn] *n* Insulin *nt*
insult [*n* 'ɪnsʌlt, *vb* ɪn'sʌlt] *n* Beleidigung *f*
♦ *vt* beleidigen; **~ing** [ɪn'sʌltɪŋ] *adj*
beleidigend
insuperable [ɪn'suːpərəbl] *adj* unüber-
windlich
insurance [ɪn'ʃuərəns] *n* Versicherung *f*;
fire/life ~ Feuer-/Lebensversicherung; **~
agent** *n* Versicherungsvertreter *m*; **~
policy** *n* Versicherungspolice *f*
insure [ɪn'ʃuə*] *vt* versichern
insurrection [ɪnsə'rekʃən] *n* Aufstand *m*
intact [ɪn'tækt] *adj* unversehrt
intake ['ɪnteɪk] *n (place)* Einlaßöffnung *f*;
(act) Aufnahme *f*, *(BRIT: SCH)*: **an ~ of 200
a year** ein Neuzugang von 200 im Jahr
intangible [ɪn'tændʒəbl] *adj* nicht
greifbar
integral ['ɪntɪɡrəl] *adj (essential)*
wesentlich; *(complete)* vollständig; *(MATH)*
Integral-
integrate ['ɪntɪɡreɪt] *vt* integrieren ♦ *vi*
sich integrieren
integrity [ɪn'teɡrɪtɪ] *n (honesty)*
Redlichkeit *f*, Integrität *f*
intellect ['ɪntɪlekt] *n* Intellekt *m*; **~ual**
[ɪntɪ'lektjuəl] *adj* geistig, intellektuell ♦ *n*
Intellektuelle(r) *mf*
intelligence [ɪn'telɪdʒəns] *n*
(understanding) Intelligenz *f*; *(news)*
Information *f*; *(MIL)* Geheimdienst *m*
intelligent [ɪn'telɪdʒənt] *adj* intelligent;
~ly *adv* klug; *(write, speak)* verständlich
intelligentsia [ɪntelɪ'dʒentsɪə] *n*
Intelligenz *f*
intelligible [ɪn'telɪdʒəbl] *adj* verständlich
intend [ɪn'tend] *vt* beabsichtigen; **that
was ~ed for you** das war für dich
gedacht

intense [ɪn'tens] *adj* stark, intensiv; (*person*) ernsthaft; **~ly** *adv* äußerst; (*study*) intensiv

intensify [ɪn'tensɪfaɪ] *vt* verstärken, intensivieren

intensity [ɪn'tensɪtɪ] *n* Intensität *f*

intensive [ɪn'tensɪv] *adj* intensiv; **~ care unit** *n* Intensivstation *f*

intent [ɪn'tent] *n* Absicht *f* ♦ *adj*: **to be ~ on doing sth** fest entschlossen sein, etw zu tun; **to all ~s and purposes** praktisch

intention [ɪn'tenʃən] *n* Absicht *f*

intentional [ɪn'tenʃənl] *adj* absichtlich; **~ly** *adv* absichtlich

intently [ɪn'tentlɪ] *adv* konzentriert

interact [ɪntər'ækt] *vi* aufeinander einwirken; **~ion** *n* Wechselwirkung *f*

interactive [ɪntər'æktɪv] *adj* (*COMPUT*) interaktiv

intercede [ɪntə'siːd] *vi* sich verwenden

intercept [ɪntə'sept] *vt* abfangen

interchange [*n* 'ɪntətʃeɪndʒ, *vb* ɪntə'tʃeɪndʒ] *n* (*exchange*) Austausch *m*; (*on roads*) Verkehrskreuz *nt* ♦ *vt* austauschen; **~able** [ɪntə'tʃeɪndʒəbl] *adj* austauschbar

intercom ['ɪntəkɒm] *n* (Gegen)sprechanlage *f*

intercourse ['ɪntəkɔːs] *n* (*exchange*) Beziehungen *pl*; (*sexual*) Geschlechtsverkehr *m*

interest ['ɪntrest] *n* Interesse *nt*; (*FIN*) Zinsen *pl*; (*COMM: share*) Anteil *m*; (*group*) Interessengruppe *f* ♦ *vt* interessieren; **~ed** *adj* (*having claims*) beteiligt; (*attentive*) interessiert; **to be ~ed in** sich interessieren für; **~ing** *adj* interessant; **~ rate** *n* Zinssatz *m*

interface ['ɪntəfeɪs] *n* (*COMPUT*) Schnittstelle *f*, Interface *nt*

interfere [ɪntə'fɪə*] *vi*: **to ~ (with)** (*meddle*) sich einmischen (in +*acc*); (*disrupt*) stören +*acc*

interference [ɪntə'fɪərəns] *n* Einmischung *f*; (*TV*) Störung *f*

interim ['ɪntərɪm] *n*: **in the ~** inzwischen

interior [ɪn'tɪərɪə*] *n* Innere(s) *nt* ♦ *adj* innere(r, s), Innen-; **~ designer** *n* Innenarchitekt(in) *m(f)*

interjection [ɪntə'dʒekʃən] *n* Ausruf *m*

interlock [ɪntə'lɒk] *vi* ineinandergreifen

interlude ['ɪntəluːd] *n* Pause *f*

intermarry [ɪntə'mærɪ] *vi* untereinander heiraten

intermediary [ɪntə'miːdɪərɪ] *n* Vermittler *m*

intermediate [ɪntə'miːdɪət] *adj* Zwischen-, Mittel-

interminable [ɪn'tɜːmɪnəbl] *adj* endlos

intermission [ɪntə'mɪʃən] *n* Pause *f*

intermittent [ɪntə'mɪtənt] *adj* periodisch, stoßweise

intern [*vb* ɪn'tɜːn, *n* 'ɪntɜːn] *vt* internieren ♦ *n* (*US*) Assistenzarzt *m*/-ärztin *f*

internal [ɪn'tɜːnl] *adj* (*inside*) innere(r, s); (*domestic*) Inlands-; **~ly** *adv* innen; (*MED*) innerlich; "**not to be taken ~ly**" „nur zur äußerlichen Anwendung"; **I~ Revenue Service** (*US*) *n* Finanzamt *nt*

international [ɪntə'næʃnəl] *adj* international ♦ *n* (*SPORT*) Nationalspieler(in) *m(f)*; (: *match*) internationale(s) Spiel *nt*

interplay ['ɪntəpleɪ] *n* Wechselspiel *nt*

interpret [ɪn'tɜːprɪt] *vt* (*explain*) auslegen, interpretieren; (*translate*) dolmetschen; **~ation** [ɪntɜːprɪ'teɪʃən] *n* Interpretation *f*; **~er** *n* Dolmetscher(in) *m(f)*

interrelated [ɪntərɪ'leɪtɪd] *adj* untereinander zusammenhängend

interrogate [ɪn'terəgeɪt] *vt* verhören

interrogation [ɪntərə'geɪʃən] *n* Verhör *nt*

interrogative [ɪntə'rɒgətɪv] *adj* Frage-

interrupt [ɪntə'rʌpt] *vt* unterbrechen; **~ion** [ɪntə'rʌpʃən] *n* Unterbrechung *f*

intersect [ɪntə'sekt] *vt* (durch)schneiden ♦ *vi* sich schneiden; **~ion** [ɪntə'sekʃən] *n* (*of roads*) Kreuzung *f*; (*of lines*) Schnittpunkt *m*

intersperse [ɪntə'spɜːs] *vt*: **to ~ sth with sth** etw mit etw durchsetzen

intertwine [ɪntə'twaɪn] *vt* verflechten ♦ *vi* sich verflechten

interval ['ɪntəvəl] *n* Abstand *m*; (*BRIT: SCH, THEAT, SPORT*) Pause *f*; **at ~s** in Abständen

intervene [ɪntə'viːn] *vi* dazwischenliegen;

(*act*): **to ~ (in)** einschreiten (gegen)
intervention [ɪntə'venʃən] *n* Eingreifen
nt, Intervention *f*
interview ['ɪntəvju:] *n* (*PRESS etc*)
Interview *nt*; (*for job*)
Vorstellungsgespräch *nt* ♦ *vt* interviewen;
~er *n* Interviewer *m*
intestine [ɪn'testɪn] *n*: **large/small ~**
Dick-/Dünndarm *m*
intimacy ['ɪntɪməsɪ] *n* Intimität *f*
intimate [*adj* 'ɪntɪmət, *vb* 'ɪntɪmeɪt] *adj*
(*inmost*) innerste(r, s); (*knowledge*)
eingehend; (*familiar*) vertraut; (*friends*)
eng ♦ *vt* andeuten
intimidate [ɪn'tɪmɪdeɪt] *vt* einschüchtern
intimidation [ɪntɪmɪ'deɪʃən] *n*
Einschüchterung *f*
into ['ɪntu] *prep* (*motion*) in +*acc* ...
hinein; **5 ~ 25** 25 durch 5
intolerable [ɪn'tɒlərəbl] *adj* unerträglich
intolerance [ɪn'tɒlərns] *n* Unduldsamkeit
f
intolerant [ɪn'tɒlərənt] *adj*: **~ of**
unduldsam gegen(über)
intoxicate [ɪn'tɒksɪkeɪt] *vt* berauschen;
~d *adj* betrunken
intoxication [ɪntɒksɪ'keɪʃən] *n* Rausch *m*
intractable [ɪn'træktəbl] *adj* schwer zu
handhaben; (*problem*) schwer lösbar
intransigent [ɪn'trænsɪdʒənt] *adj*
unnachgiebig
intransitive [ɪn'trænsɪtɪv] *adj* intransitiv
intravenous [ɪntrə'vi:nəs] *adj* intravenös
in-tray ['ɪntreɪ] *n* Eingangskorb *m*
intrepid [ɪn'trepɪd] *adj* unerschrocken
intricate ['ɪntrɪkət] *adj* kompliziert
intrigue [ɪn'tri:g] *n* Intrige *f* ♦ *vt*
faszinieren ♦ *vi* intrigieren
intriguing [ɪn'tri:gɪŋ] *adj* faszinierend
intrinsic [ɪn'trɪnsɪk] *adj* innere(r, s);
(*difference*) wesentlich
introduce [ɪntrə'dju:s] *vt* (*person*)
vorstellen; (*sth new*) einführen; (*subject*)
anschneiden; **to ~ sb to sb** jdm jdn
vorstellen; **to ~ sb to sth** jdn in etw *acc*
einführen
introduction [ɪntrə'dʌkʃən] *n*
Einführung *f*; (*to book*) Einleitung *f*
introductory [ɪntrə'dʌktərɪ] *adj*

Einführungs-, Vor-
introspective [ɪntrəu'spektɪv] *adj* nach
innen gekehrt
introvert ['ɪntrəuvɜ:t] *n* Introvertierte(r)
mf ♦ *adj* introvertiert
intrude [ɪn'tru:d] *vi*: **to ~ (on sb/sth)**
(jdn/etw) stören; **~r** *n* Eindringling *m*
intrusion [ɪn'tru:ʒən] *n* Störung *f*
intrusive [ɪn'tru:sɪv] *adj* aufdringlich
intuition [ɪntju:'ɪʃən] *n* Intuition *f*
inundate ['ɪnʌndeɪt] *vt* (*also fig*)
überschwemmen
invade [ɪn'veɪd] *vt* einfallen in +*acc*; **~r** *n*
Eindringling *m*
invalid¹ ['ɪnvəlɪd] *n* (*disabled*) Invalide
m ♦ *adj* (*ill*) krank; (*disabled*) invalide
invalid² [ɪn'vælɪd] *adj* (*not valid*)
ungültig
invaluable [ɪn'væljuəbl] *adj* unschätzbar
invariable [ɪn'veərɪəbl] *adj*
unveränderlich
invariably [ɪn'veərɪəblɪ] *adv* ausnahmslos
invasion [ɪn'veɪʒən] *n* Invasion *f*
invent [ɪn'vent] *vt* erfinden; **~ion**
[ɪn'venʃən] *n* Erfindung *f*; **~ive** *adj*
erfinderisch; **~or** *n* Erfinder *m*
inventory ['ɪnvəntrɪ] *n* Inventar *nt*
inverse ['ɪnvɜ:s] *n* Umkehrung *f* ♦ *adj*
umgekehrt
invert [ɪn'vɜ:t] *vt* umdrehen; **~ed
commas** (*BRIT*) *npl* Anführungsstriche *pl*
invest [ɪn'vest] *vt* investieren
investigate [ɪn'vestɪgeɪt] *vt* untersuchen
investigation [ɪnvestɪ'geɪʃən] *n*
Untersuchung *f*
investigator [ɪn'vestɪgeɪtə*] *n*
Untersuchungsbeamte(r) *m*
investiture [ɪn'vestɪtʃə*] *n*
Amtseinsetzung *f*
investment [ɪn'vestmənt] *n* Investition *f*
investor [ɪn'vestə*] *n* (Geld)anleger *m*
inveterate [ɪn'vetərət] *adj*
unverbesserlich
invidious [ɪn'vɪdɪəs] *adj* unangenehm;
(*distinctions, remark*) ungerecht
invigilate [ɪn'vɪdʒɪleɪt] *vi* (*in exam*)
Aufsicht führen ♦ *vt* Aufsicht führen bei
invigorating [ɪn'vɪgəreɪtɪŋ] *adj* stärkend
invincible [ɪn'vɪnsəbl] *adj* unbesiegbar

invisible [ɪn'vɪzəbl] *adj* unsichtbar
invitation [ɪnvɪ'teɪʃən] *n* Einladung *f*
invite [ɪn'vaɪt] *vt* einladen
inviting [ɪn'vaɪtɪŋ] *adj* einladend
invoice ['ɪnvɔɪs] *n* Rechnung *f* ♦ *vt*
(*goods*): **to ~ sb for sth** jdm etw *acc* in
Rechnung stellen
invoke [ɪn'vəʊk] *vt* anrufen
involuntary [ɪn'vɒləntərɪ] *adj*
unabsichtlich
involve [ɪn'vɒlv] *vt* (*entangle*) verwickeln;
(*entail*) mit sich bringen; **~d** *adj*
verwickelt; **~ment** *n* Verwicklung *f*
inward ['ɪnwəd] *adj* innere(r, s); (*curve*)
Innen- ♦ *adv* nach innen; **~ly** *adv* im
Innern; **~s** *adv* nach innen
I/O *abbr* (COMPUT: = *input/output*) I/O
iodine ['aɪədiːn] *n* Jod *nt*
ioniser ['aɪənaɪzə*] *n* Ionisator *m*
iota [aɪ'əʊtə] *n* (*fig*) bißchen *nt*
IOU *n abbr* (= *I owe you*) Schuldschein *m*
IQ *n abbr* (= *intelligence quotient*) IQ *m*
IRA *n abbr* (= *Irish Republican Army*)
IRA *f*
Iran [ɪ'rɑːn] *n* Iran *m*; **~ian** [ɪ'reɪnɪən] *adj*
iranisch ♦ *n* Iraner(in) *m(f)*; (LING)
Iranisch *nt*
Iraq [ɪ'rɑːk] *n* Irak *m*; **~i** *adj* irakisch ♦ *n*
Iraker(in) *m(f)*
irascible [ɪ'ræsɪbl] *adj* reizbar
irate [aɪ'reɪt] *adj* zornig
Ireland ['aɪələnd] *n* Irland *nt*
iris ['aɪrɪs] (*pl* **~es**) *n* Iris *f*
Irish ['aɪrɪʃ] *adj* irisch ♦ *npl*: **the ~** die
Iren *pl*, die Irländer *pl*; **~man** (*irreg*) *n*
Ire *m*, Irländer *m*; **~ Sea** *n* (GEO): **the ~
Sea** die Irische See *f*; **~woman** (*irreg*) *n*
Irin *f*, Irländerin *f*
irksome ['ɜːksəm] *adj* lästig
iron ['aɪən] *n* Eisen *nt*; (*for ironing*)
Bügeleisen *nt* ♦ *adj* eisern ♦ *vt* bügeln; **~
out** *vt* (*also fig*) ausbügeln; **I~ Curtain** *n*
Eiserne(r) Vorhang *m*
ironic(al) [aɪ'rɒnɪk(l)] *adj* ironisch;
(*coincidence etc*) witzig
ironing ['aɪənɪŋ] *n* Bügeln *nt*; (*laundry*)
Bügelwäsche *f*; **~ board** *n* Bügelbrett *nt*
irony ['aɪərənɪ] *n* Ironie *f*
irrational [ɪ'ræʃənl] *adj* irrational

irreconcilable [ɪrekən'saɪləbl] *adj*
unvereinbar
irrefutable [ɪrɪ'fjuːtəbl] *adj*
unwiderlegbar
irregular [ɪ'regjʊlə*] *adj* unregelmäßig;
(*shape*) ungleich(mäßig); (*fig*) unüblich;
(: *behaviour*) ungehörig; **~ity**
[ɪregjʊ'lærɪtɪ] *n* Unregelmäßigkeit *f*;
Ungleichmäßigkeit *f*; (*fig*) Vergehen *nt*
irrelevant [ɪ'reləvənt] *adj* belanglos,
irrelevant
irreparable [ɪ'repərəbl] *adj* nicht
wiedergutzumachen
irreplaceable [ɪrɪ'pleɪsəbl] *adj*
unersetzlich
irresistible [ɪrɪ'zɪstəbl] *adj*
unwiderstehlich
irrespective [ɪrɪ'spektɪv]: **~ of** *prep*
ungeachtet +*gen*
irresponsible [ɪrɪ'spɒnsəbl] *adj*
verantwortungslos
irreverent [ɪ'revərənt] *adj* respektlos
irrevocable [ɪ'revəkəbl] *adj*
unwiderrufbar
irrigate ['ɪrɪgeɪt] *vt* bewässern
irrigation [ɪrɪ'geɪʃən] *n* Bewässerung *f*
irritable ['ɪrɪtəbl] *adj* reizbar
irritate ['ɪrɪteɪt] *vt* irritieren, reizen (*also*
MED)
irritation [ɪrɪ'teɪʃən] *n* (*anger*) Ärger *m*;
(MED) Reizung *f*
IRS *n abbr* = **Internal Revenue Service**
is [ɪz] *vb see* **be**
Islam ['ɪzlɑːm] *n* Islam *m*
island ['aɪlənd] *n* Insel *f*; **~er** *n*
Inselbewohner(in) *m(f)*
isle [aɪl] *n* (kleine) Insel *f*
isn't ['ɪznt] = **is not**
isolate ['aɪsəʊleɪt] *vt* isolieren; **~d** *adj*
isoliert; (*case*) Einzel-
isolation [aɪsəʊ'leɪʃən] *n* Isolierung *f*
Israel ['ɪzreɪəl] *n* Israel *nt*; **~i** [ɪz'reɪlɪ] *adj*
israelisch ♦ *n* Israeli *mf*
issue ['ɪʃuː] *n* (*matter*) Frage *f*; (*outcome*)
Ausgang *m*; (*of newspaper, shares*)
Ausgabe *f*; (*offspring*) Nachkommenschaft
f ♦ *vt* ausgeben; (*warrant*) erlassen;
(*documents*) ausstellen; (*orders*) erteilen;
(*books*) herausgeben; (*verdict*)

aussprechen; **to be at ~** zur Debatte
stehen; **to take ~ with sb over sth** jdm
in etw *dat* widersprechen
isthmus ['ɪsməs] *n* Landenge *f*

KEYWORD
---

it [ɪt] *pron* **1** (*specific: subject*) er/sie/es;
(*: direct object*) ihn/sie/es; (*: indirect
object*) ihm/ihr/ihm; **about/from/in/of
it** darüber/davon/darin/davon
2 (*impers*) es; **it's raining** es regnet; **it's
Friday tomorrow** morgen ist Freitag;
who is it? — it's me wer ist da? — ich
(bin's)

Italian [ɪ'tæljən] *adj* italienisch ♦ *n*
Italiener(in) *m(f)*; (*LING*) Italienisch *nt*
italic [ɪ'tælɪk] *adj* kursiv; **~s** *npl*
Kursivschrift *f*
Italy ['ɪtəlɪ] *n* Italien *nt*
itch [ɪtʃ] *n* Juckreiz *m*; (*fig*) Lust *f* ♦ *vi*
jucken; **to be ~ing to do sth** darauf
brennen, etw zu tun; **~y** *adj* juckend
it'd ['ɪtd] = **it would; it had**
item ['aɪtəm] *n* Gegenstand *m*; (*on list*)
Posten *m*; (*in programme*) Nummer *f*; (*in
agenda*) (Programm)punkt *m*; (*in
newspaper*) (Zeitungs)notiz *f*; **~ize** *vt*
verzeichnen
itinerant [ɪ'tɪnərənt] *adj* (*person*)
umherreisend
itinerary [aɪ'tɪnərərɪ] *n* Reiseroute *f*
it'll ['ɪtl] = **it will; it shall**
its [ɪts] *adj* (*masculine, neuter*) sein;
(*feminine*) ihr
it's [ɪts] = **it is; it has**
itself [ɪt'self] *pron* sich (selbst);
(*emphatic*) selbst
ITV (*BRIT*) *n abbr* = **Independent
Television**
I.U.D. *n abbr* (= *intra-uterine device*)
Pessar *nt*
I've [aɪv] = **I have**
ivory ['aɪvərɪ] *n* Elfenbein *nt*
ivy ['aɪvɪ] *n* Efeu *nt*

J j

jab [dʒæb] *vt* (hinein)stechen ♦ *n* Stich *m*,
Stoß *m*; (*inf*) Spritze *f*
jabber ['dʒæbə*] *vi* plappern
jack [dʒæk] *n* (*AUT*) (Wagen)heber *m*;
(*CARDS*) Bube *m*; **~ up** *vt* aufbocken
jackal ['dʒækəl] *n* (*ZOOL*) Schakal *m*
jackdaw ['dʒækdɔ:] *n* Dohle *f*
jacket ['dʒækɪt] *n* Jacke *f*; (*of book*)
Schutzumschlag *m*; (*TECH*) Ummantelung *f*
jackknife ['dʒæknaɪf] *vi* (*truck*) sich
zusammenschieben
jack plug *n* (*ELEC*) Buchsenstecker *m*
jackpot ['dʒækpɒt] *n* Haupttreffer *m*
jaded ['dʒeɪdɪd] *adj* ermattet
jagged ['dʒægɪd] *adj* zackig
jail [dʒeɪl] *n* Gefängnis *nt* ♦ *vt* einsperren;
~er *n* Gefängniswärter *m*
jam [dʒæm] *n* Marmelade *f*; (*also: traffic
~*) (Verkehrs)stau *m*; (*inf: trouble*)
Klemme *f* ♦ *vt* (*wedge*) einklemmen;
(*cram*) hineinzwängen; (*obstruct*)
blockieren ♦ *vi* sich verklemmen; **to ~
sth into sth** etw in etw *acc* hineinstopfen
Jamaica [dʒə'meɪkə] *n* Jamaika *nt*
jangle ['dʒæŋgl] *vt, vi* klimpern
janitor ['dʒænɪtə*] *n* Hausmeister *m*
January ['dʒænjuərɪ] *n* Januar *m*
Japan [dʒə'pæn] *n* Japan *nt*; **~ese**
[dʒæpə'ni:z] *adj* japanisch ♦ *n inv*
Japaner(in) *m(f)*; (*LING*) Japanisch *nt*
jar [dʒɑ:*] *n* Glas *nt* ♦ *vi* kreischen;
(*colours etc*) nicht harmonieren
jargon ['dʒɑ:gən] *n* Fachsprache *f*,
Jargon *m*
jaundice ['dʒɔ:ndɪs] *n* Gelbsucht *f*; **~d**
adj (*fig*) mißgünstig
jaunt [dʒɔ:nt] *n* Spritztour *f*; **~y** *adj*
(*lively*) munter; (*brisk*) flott
javelin ['dʒævlɪn] *n* Speer *m*
jaw [dʒɔ:] *n* Kiefer *m*
jay [dʒeɪ] *n* (*ZOOL*) Eichelhäher *m*
jaywalker ['dʒeɪwɔ:kə*] *n*
unvorsichtige(r) Fußgänger *m*
jazz [dʒæz] *n* Jazz *m*; **~ up** *vt* (*MUS*)
verjazzen; (*enliven*) aufpolieren; **~y** *adj*

(*colour*) schreiend, auffallend

jealous ['dʒeləs] *adj* (*envious*) mißgünstig; (*husband*) eifersüchtig; **~y** *n* Mißgunst *f*; Eifersucht *f*

jeans [dʒiːnz] *npl* Jeans *pl*

Jeep [dʒiːp] ® *n* Jeep *m* ®

jeer [dʒɪə*] *vi*: **to ~ (at sb)** (über jdn) höhnisch lachen, (jdn) verspotten

jelly ['dʒelɪ] *n* Gelee *nt*; (*dessert*) Grütze *f*; **~fish** *n* Qualle *f*

jeopardize ['dʒepədaɪz] *vt* gefährden

jeopardy ['dʒepədɪ] *n*: **to be in ~** in Gefahr sein

jerk [dʒɜːk] *n* Ruck *m*; (*inf: idiot*) Trottel *m* ♦ *vt* ruckartig bewegen ♦ *vi* sich ruckartig bewegen

jerkin ['dʒɜːkɪn] *n* Wams *nt*

jerky ['dʒɜːkɪ] *adj* (*movement*) ruckartig; (*ride*) rüttelnd

jersey ['dʒɜːzɪ] *n* Pullover *m*

jest [dʒest] *n* Scherz *m* ♦ *vi* spaßen; **in ~** im Spaß

Jesus ['dʒiːzəs] *n* Jesus *m*

jet [dʒet] *n* (*stream: of water etc*) Strahl *m*; (*spout*) Düse *f*, (*AVIAT*) Düsenflugzeug *nt*; **~-black** *adj* rabenschwarz; **~ engine** *n* Düsenmotor *m*; **~-lag** *n* Jet-lag *m*

jettison ['dʒetɪsn] *vt* über Bord werfen

jetty ['dʒetɪ] *n* Landesteg *m*, Mole *f*

Jew [dʒuː] *n* Jude *m*

jewel ['dʒuːəl] *n* (*also fig*) Juwel *nt*; **~ler** (*US* **jeweler**) *n* Juwelier *m*; **~ler's (shop)** *n* Juwelier *m*; **~lery** (*US* **jewelry**) *n* Schmuck *m*

Jewess ['dʒuːɪs] *n* Jüdin *f*

Jewish ['dʒuːɪʃ] *adj* jüdisch

jib [dʒɪb] *n* (*NAUT*) Klüver *m*

jibe [dʒaɪb] *n* spöttische Bemerkung *f*

jiffy ['dʒɪfɪ] (*inf*) *n*: **in a ~** sofort

jigsaw ['dʒɪgsɔː] *n* (*also:* **~ puzzle**) Puzzle(spiel) *nt*

jilt [dʒɪlt] *vt* den Laufpaß geben +*dat*

jingle ['dʒɪŋgl] *n* (*advertisement*) Werbesong *m* ♦ *vi* klimpern; (*bells*) bimmeln ♦ *vt* klimpern mit; bimmeln lassen

jinx [dʒɪŋks] *n*: **there's a ~ on it** es ist verhext

jitters ['dʒɪtəz] (*inf*) *npl*: **to get the ~**

einen Bammel kriegen

job [dʒɒb] *n* (*piece of work*) Arbeit *f*; (*position*) Stellung *f*; (*duty*) Aufgabe *f*; (*difficulty*) Mühe *f*; **it's a good ~ he ...** es ist ein Glück, daß er ...; **just the ~** genau das Richtige; **J~centre** (*BRIT*) *n* Arbeitsamt *nt*; **~less** *adj* arbeitslos

jockey ['dʒɒkɪ] *n* Jockei *m* ♦ *vi*: **to ~ for position** sich in eine gute Position drängeln

jocular ['dʒɒkjulə*] *adj* scherzhaft

jog [dʒɒg] *vt* (an)stoßen ♦ *vi* (*run*) joggen; **to ~ along** vor sich *acc* hinwursteln; (*work*) seinen Gang gehen; **~ging** *n* Jogging *nt*

join [dʒɔɪn] *vt* (*club*) beitreten +*dat*; (*person*) sich anschließen +*dat*; (*put together*): **to ~ (sth to sth)** (etw mit etw) verbinden ♦ *vi* (*unite*) sich vereinigen ♦ *n* Verbindungsstelle *f*, Naht *f*; **~ in** *vt*, *vi*: **to ~ in (sth)** (bei etw) mitmachen; **~ up** *vi* (*MIL*) zur Armee gehen

joiner ['dʒɔɪnə*] *n* Schreiner *m*; **~y** *n* Schreinerei *f*

joint [dʒɔɪnt] *n* (*TECH*) Fuge *f*; (*of bones*) Gelenk *nt*; (*of meat*) Braten *m*; (*inf: place*) Lokal *nt* ♦ *adj* gemeinsam; **~ account** *n* (*with bank etc*) gemeinsame(s) Konto *nt*; **~ly** *adv* gemeinsam

joke [dʒəuk] *n* Witz *m* ♦ *vi* Witze machen; **to play a ~ on sb** jdm einen Streich spielen; **~r** *n* Witzbold *m*; (*CARDS*) Joker *m*

jolly ['dʒɒlɪ] *adj* lustig ♦ *adv* (*inf*) ganz schön

jolt [dʒəult] *n* (*shock*) Schock *m*; (*jerk*) Stoß *m* ♦ *vt* (*push*) stoßen; (*shake*) durchschütteln; (*fig*) aufrütteln ♦ *vi* holpern

Jordan ['dʒɔːdən] *n* Jordanien *nt*; (*river*) Jordan *m*

jostle ['dʒɒsl] *vt* anrempeln

jot [dʒɒt] *n*: **not one ~** kein Jota *nt*; **~ down** *vt* notieren; **~ter** (*BRIT*) *n* Notizblock *m*

journal ['dʒɜːnl] *n* (*diary*) Tagebuch *nt*; (*magazine*) Zeitschrift *f*, **~ism** *n* Journalismus *m*; **~ist** *n* Journalist(in) *m(f)*

journey ['dʒɜːnɪ] *n* Reise *f*

jovial ['dʒəʊvɪəl] adj jovial

joy [dʒɔɪ] n Freude f; **~ful** adj freudig; **~ous** adj freudig; **~ ride** n Schwarzfahrt f; **~rider** n Autodieb m, der den Wagen nur für eine Spritztour stiehlt; **~stick** n Steuerknüppel m; (*COMPUT*) Joystick m

J.P. n abbr = **Justice of the Peace**

Jr abbr = **junior**

jubilant ['dʒuːbɪlənt] adj triumphierend

jubilee ['dʒuːbɪliː] n Jubiläum nt

judge [dʒʌdʒ] n Richter m; (*fig*) Kenner m ♦ vt (*JUR: person*) die Verhandlung führen über +acc; (*case*) verhandeln; (*assess*) beurteilen; (*estimate*) einschätzen; **~ment** n (*JUR*) Urteil nt; (*ECCL*) Gericht nt; (*ability*) Urteilsvermögen nt

judicial [dʒuːˈdɪʃəl] adj gerichtlich, Justiz-

judiciary [dʒuːˈdɪʃɪərɪ] n Gerichtsbehörden pl; (*judges*) Richterstand m

judicious [dʒuːˈdɪʃəs] adj weise

judo ['dʒuːdəʊ] n Judo nt

jug [dʒʌg] n Krug m

juggernaut ['dʒʌgənɔːt] (*BRIT*) n (*huge truck*) Schwertransporter m

juggle ['dʒʌgl] vt, vi jonglieren; **~r** n Jongleur m

Jugoslav ['juːgəʊˈslɑːv] etc = **Yugoslav** etc

juice [dʒuːs] n Saft m

juicy ['dʒuːsɪ] adj (*also fig*) saftig

jukebox ['dʒuːkbɒks] n Musikautomat m

July [dʒuːˈlaɪ] n Juli m

jumble ['dʒʌmbl] n Durcheinander nt ♦ vt (*also: ~ up*) durcheinanderwerfen; (*facts*) durcheinanderbringen; **~ sale** (*BRIT*) n Basar m, Flohmarkt m

jumbo (jet) ['dʒʌmbəʊ-] n Jumbo(-Jet) m

jump [dʒʌmp] vi springen; (*nervously*) zusammenzucken ♦ vt überspringen ♦ n Sprung m; **to ~ the queue** (*BRIT*) sich vordrängeln

jumper ['dʒʌmpə*] n (*BRIT: pullover*) Pullover m; (*US: dress*) Trägerkleid nt; **~ cables** (*US*) npl = **jump leads**

jump leads (*BRIT*) npl Starthilfekabel nt

jumpy ['dʒʌmpɪ] adj nervös

Jun. abbr = **junior**

junction ['dʒʌŋkʃən] n (*BRIT: of roads*) (Straßen)kreuzung f; (*RAIL*) Knotenpunkt m

juncture ['dʒʌŋktʃə*] n: **at this ~** in diesem Augenblick

June [dʒuːn] n Juni m

jungle ['dʒʌŋgl] n Dschungel m

junior ['dʒuːnɪə*] adj (*younger*) jünger; (*after name*) junior; (*SPORT*) Junioren-; (*lower position*) untergeordnet; (*for young people*) Junioren- ♦ n Jüngere(r) mf; **~ school** (*BRIT*) n Grundschule f

junk [dʒʌŋk] n (*rubbish*) Plunder m; (*ship*) Dschunke f; (*fig*) (*COMM*) niedrig eingestuftes Wertpapier mit hohen Ertragschancen bei erhöhtem Risiko; **~ food** n Plastikessen nt; **~ mail** n Reklame f die unangefordert in den Briefkasten gesteckt ist; **~shop** n Ramschladen m

Junr abbr = **junior**

jurisdiction [dʒʊərɪsˈdɪkʃən] n Gerichtsbarkeit f; (*range of authority*) Zuständigkeit(sbereich m) f

juror ['dʒʊərə*] n Geschworene(r) mf; (*in competition*) Preisrichter m

jury ['dʒʊərɪ] n (*court*) Geschworene pl; (*in competition*) Jury f

just [dʒʌst] adj gerecht ♦ adv (*recently, now*) gerade, eben; (*barely*) gerade noch; (*exactly*) genau, gerade; (*only*) nur, bloß; (*a small distance*) gleich; (*absolutely*) einfach; **~ as I arrived** gerade als ich ankam; **~ as nice** genauso nett; **~ as well** um so besser; **~ now** soeben, gerade; **~ try** versuch es mal; **she's ~ left** sie ist gerade or (so)eben gegangen; **he's ~ done it** er hat es gerade or (so)eben getan; **~ before** gerade or kurz bevor; **~ enough** gerade genug; **he ~ missed** er hat fast or beinahe getroffen

justice ['dʒʌstɪs] n (*fairness*) Gerechtigkeit f; **~ of the peace** n Friedensrichter m

justifiable ['dʒʌstɪfaɪəbl] adj berechtigt

justification [dʒʌstɪfɪˈkeɪʃən] n Rechtfertigung f

justify ['dʒʌstɪfaɪ] vt rechtfertigen; (*text*) justieren

justly ['dʒʌstlı] *adv* (*say*) mit Recht; (*condemn*) gerecht

jut [dʒʌt] *vi* (*also:* ~ *out*) herausragen, vorstehen

juvenile ['dʒuːvənaıl] *adj* (*young*) jugendlich; (*for the young*) Jugend- ♦ *n* Jugendliche(r) *mf*

juxtapose ['dʒʌkstəpəʊz] *vt* nebeneinanderstellen

K k

K *abbr* (= *one thousand*) Tsd.; (= *kilobyte*) K

kangaroo [kæŋgə'ruː] *n* Känguruh *nt*

karate [kə'rɑːtı] *n* Karate *nt*

kebab [kə'bæb] *n* Kebab *m*

keel [kiːl] *n* Kiel *m*; **on an even ~** (*fig*) im Lot

keen [kiːn] *adj* begeistert; (*intelligence, wind, blade*) scharf; (*sight, hearing*) gut; **to be ~ to do** *or* **on doing sth** etw unbedingt tun wollen; **to be ~ on sth/sb** scharf auf etw/jdn sein

keep [kiːp] (*pt, pp* **kept**) *vt* (*retain*) behalten; (*have*) haben; (*animals, one's word*) halten; (*support*) versorgen; (*maintain in state*) halten; (*preserve*) aufbewahren; (*restrain*) abhalten ♦ *vi* (*continue in direction*) sich halten; (*food*) sich halten; (*remain: quiet etc*) bleiben ♦ *n* Unterhalt *m*; (*tower*) Burgfried *m*; (*inf*): **for ~s** für immer; **to ~ sth to o.s.** etw für sich behalten; **it ~s happening** es passiert immer wieder; **~ back** *vt* fernhalten; (*secret*) verschweigen; **~ on** *vi*: **~ on doing sth** etw immer weiter tun; **~ out** *vt* nicht hereinlassen; **"~ out"** „Eintritt verboten!"; **~ up** *vi* Schritt halten ♦ *vt* aufrechterhalten; (*continue*) weitermachen; **to ~ up with** Schritt halten mit; **~er** *n* Wärter(in) *m(f)*; (*goalkeeper*) Torhüter(in) *m(f)*; **~-fit** *n* Keep-fit *nt*; **~ing** *n* (*care*) Obhut *f*; **in ~ing with** in Übereinstimmung mit; **~sake** *n* Andenken *nt*

keg [keg] *n* Faß *nt*

kennel ['kenl] *n* Hundehütte *f*; **~s** *npl* (*for*

boarding): **to put a dog in ~s** einen Hund in Pflege geben

Kenya ['kenjə] *n* Kenia *nt*; **~n** *adj* kenianisch ♦ *n* Kenianer(in) *m(f)*

kept [kept] *pt, pp* of **keep**

kerb ['kɜːb] (*BRIT*) *n* Bordstein *m*

kernel ['kɜːnl] *n* Kern *m*

kerosene ['kerəsiːn] *n* Kerosin *nt*

ketchup ['ketʃəp] *n* Ketchup *nt or m*

kettle ['ketl] *n* Kessel *m*; **~drum** *n* Pauke *f*

key [kiː] *n* Schlüssel *m*; (*of piano, typewriter*) Taste *f*; (*MUS*) Tonart *f* ♦ *vt* (*also:* ~ *in*) eingeben; **~board** *n* Tastatur *f*; **~ed up** *adj* (*person*) überdreht; **~hole** *n* Schlüsselloch *nt*; **~note** *n* Grundton *m*; **~ ring** *n* Schlüsselring *m*

khaki ['kɑːkı] *n* K(h)aki *nt* ♦ *adj* k(h)aki(farben)

kick [kık] *vt* einen Fußtritt geben +*dat*, treten ♦ *vi* treten; (*baby*) strampeln; (*horse*) ausschlagen ♦ *n* (Fuß)tritt *m*; (*thrill*) Spaß *m*; **he does it for ~s** er macht das aus Jux; **~ off** *vi* (*SPORT*) anstoßen; **~-off** *n* (*SPORT*) Anstoß *m*

kid [kıd] *n* (*inf: child*) Kind *nt*; (*goat*) Zicklein *nt*; (*leather*) Glacéleder *nt* ♦ *vi* (*inf*) Witze machen

kidnap ['kıdnæp] *vt* entführen; **~per** *n* Entführer *m*; **~ping** *n* Entführung *f*

kidney ['kıdnı] *n* Niere *f*

kill [kıl] *vt* töten, umbringen ♦ *vi* töten ♦ *n* Tötung *f*; (*hunting*) (Jagd)beute *f*; **~er** *n* Mörder(in) *m(f)*; **~ing** *n* Mord *m*; **~joy** *n* Spaßverderber(in) *m(f)*

kiln [kıln] *n* Brennofen *m*

kilo ['kiːləʊ] *n* Kilo *nt*; **~byte** *n* (*COMPUT*) Kilobyte *nt*; **~gram(me)** ['kıləʊgræm] *n* Kilogramm *nt*; **~metre** ['kıləmiːtə*] (*US* **~meter**) *n* Kilometer *m*; **~watt** *n* Kilowatt *nt*

kilt [kılt] *n* Schottenrock *m*

kind [kaınd] *adj* freundlich ♦ *n* Art *f*; **a ~ of** eine Art von; **(two) of a ~** (zwei) von der gleichen Art; **in ~** auf dieselbe Art; (*in goods*) in Naturalien

kindergarten ['kındəgɑːtn] *n* Kindergarten *m*

kind-hearted ['kaınd'hɑːtıd] *adj*

gutherzig

kindle ['kɪndl] *vt* (*set on fire*) anzünden; (*rouse*) reizen, (er)wecken

kindly ['kaɪndlɪ] *adj* freundlich ♦ *adv* liebenswürdig(erweise); **would you ~ ...?** wären Sie so freundlich und ...?

kindness ['kaɪndnəs] *n* Freundlichkeit *f*

kindred ['kɪndrɪd] *adj:* **~ spirit** Gleichgesinnte(r) *mf*

king [kɪŋ] *n* König *m*; **~dom** *n* Königreich *nt*; **~fisher** *n* Eisvogel *m*; **~-size** *adj* (*cigarette*) Kingsize

kinky ['kɪŋkɪ] (*inf*) *adj* (*person, ideas*) verrückt; (*sexual*) abartig

kiosk ['kiːɒsk] (*BRIT*) *n* (*TEL*) Telefonhäuschen *nt*

kipper ['kɪpə*] *n* Räucherhering *m*

kiss [kɪs] *n* Kuß *m* ♦ *vt* küssen ♦ *vi:* **they ~ed** sie küßten sich

kit [kɪt] *n* Ausrüstung *f*; (*tools*) Werkzeug *nt*

kitchen ['kɪtʃɪn] *n* Küche *f*; **~ sink** *n* Spülbecken *nt*

kite [kaɪt] *n* Drachen *m*

kith [kɪθ] *n:* **~ and kin** Blutsverwandte *pl*

kitten ['kɪtn] *n* Kätzchen *nt*

kitty ['kɪtɪ] *n* (*money*) Kasse *f*

km *abbr* (= *kilometre*) km

knack [næk] *n* Dreh *m*, Trick *m*

knapsack ['næpsæk] *n* Rucksack *m*; (*MIL*) Tornister *m*

knead [niːd] *vt* kneten

knee [niː] *n* Knie *nt*; **~cap** *n* Kniescheibe *f*

kneel [niːl] (*pt, pp* **knelt**) *vi* (*also:* **~ down**) knien

knell [nel] *n* Grabgeläute *nt*

knelt [nelt] *pt, pp of* **kneel**

knew [njuː] *pt of* **know**

knickers ['nɪkəz] (*BRIT*) *npl* Schlüpfer *m*

knife [naɪf] (*pl* **knives**) *n* Messer *nt* ♦ *vt* erstechen

knight [naɪt] *n* Ritter *m*; (*chess*) Springer *m*; **~hood** *n* (*title*): **to get a ~hood** zum Ritter geschlagen werden

knit [nɪt] *vt* stricken ♦ *vi* stricken; (*bones*) zusammenwachsen; **~ting** *n* (*occupation*) Stricken *nt*; (*work*) Strickzeug *nt*; **~ting needle** *n* Stricknadel *f*; **~wear** *n*

Strickwaren *pl*

knives [naɪvz] *pl of* **knife**

knob [nɒb] *n* Knauf *m*; (*on instrument*) Knopf *m*; (*BRIT: of butter etc*) kleine(s) Stück *nt*

knock [nɒk] *vt* schlagen; (*criticize*) heruntermachen ♦ *vi:* **to ~ at** *or* **on the door** an die Tür klopfen ♦ *n* Schlag *m*; (*on door*) Klopfen *nt*; **~ down** *vt* umwerfen; (*with car*) anfahren; **~ off** *vt* (*do quickly*) hinhauen; (*inf: steal*) klauen ♦ *vi* (*finish*) Feierabend machen; **~ out** *vt* ausschlagen; (*BOXING*) k.o. schlagen; **~ over** *vt* (*person, object*) umwerfen; (*with car*) anfahren; **~er** *n* (*on door*) Türklopfer *m*; **~-kneed** *adj* x-beinig; **~out** *n* K.O.-Schlag *m*; (*fig*) Sensation *f*

knot [nɒt] *n* Knoten *m* ♦ *vt* (ver)knoten

knotty ['nɒtɪ] *adj* (*fig*) kompliziert

know [nəʊ] (*pt* **knew**, *pp* **known**) *vt, vi* wissen; (*be able to*) können; (*be acquainted with*) kennen; (*recognize*) erkennen; **to ~ how to do sth** wissen, wie man etw macht, etw tun können; **to ~ about** *or* **of sth/sb** etw/jdn kennen; **~-all** *n* Alleswisser *m*; **~-how** *n* Kenntnis *f*, Know-how *nt*; **~ing** *adj* (*look, smile*) wissend; **~ingly** *adv* wissend; (*intentionally*) wissentlich

knowledge ['nɒlɪdʒ] *n* Wissen *nt*, Kenntnis *f*; **~able** *adj* informiert

known [nəʊn] *pp of* **know**

knuckle ['nʌkl] *n* Fingerknöchel *m*

K.O. *n abbr* = **knockout**

Koran [kɔː'rɑːn] *n* Koran *m*

Korea [kə'rɪə] *n* Korea *nt*

kosher ['kəʊʃə*] *adj* koscher

L *l*

l. *abbr* = **litre**

lab [læb] (*inf*) *n* Labor *nt*

label ['leɪbl] *n* Etikett *nt* ♦ *vt* etikettieren

labor *etc* ['leɪbə*] (*US*) = **labour** *etc*

laboratory [lə'bɒrətərɪ] *n* Laboratorium *nt*

laborious [lə'bɔːrɪəs] *adj* mühsam

labour ['leɪbə*] (*US* **labor**) *n* Arbeit *f*;

(*workmen*) Arbeitskräfte *pl*; (*MED*) Wehen *pl* ♦ *vi*: **to ~ (at)** sich abmühen (mit) ♦ *vt* breittreten (*inf*); **in ~** (*MED*) in den Wehen; **L~** (*BRIT: also:* **the L~ party**) die Labour Party; **~ed** *adj* (*movement*) gequält; (*style*) schwerfällig; **~er** *n* Arbeiter *m*; **farm ~er** (Land)arbeiter *m*

lace [leɪs] *n* (*fabric*) Spitze *f*; (*of shoe*) Schnürsenkel *m*; (*braid*) Litze *f* ♦ *vt* (*also:* **~ up**) (zu)schnüren

lack [læk] *n* Mangel *m* ♦ *vt* nicht haben; **sb ~s sth** jdm fehlt etw *nom*; **to be ~ing** fehlen; **sb is ~ing in sth** es fehlt jdm an etw *dat*; **through** *or* **for ~ of** aus Mangel an +*dat*

lacquer ['lækə*] *n* Lack *m*

lad [læd] *n* Junge *m*

ladder ['lædə*] *n* Leiter *f*; (*BRIT: in tights*) Laufmasche *f* ♦ *vt* (*BRIT*) Laufmaschen bekommen in +*dat*

laden ['leɪdn] *adj* beladen, voll

ladle ['leɪdl] *n* Schöpfkelle *f*

lady ['leɪdɪ] *n* Dame *f*; (*title*) Lady *f*; **young ~** junge Dame; **the ladies' (room)** die Damentoilette; **~bird** (*US* **~bug**) *n* Marienkäfer *m*; **~like** *adj* damenhaft, vornehm; **~ship** *n*: **Your L~ship** Ihre Ladyschaft

lag [læg] *vi* (*also:* **~ behind**) zurückbleiben ♦ *vt* (*pipes*) verkleiden

lager ['lɑ:gə*] *n* helle(s) Bier *nt*

lagging ['lægɪŋ] *n* Isolierung *f*

lagoon [lə'gu:n] *n* Lagune *f*

laid [leɪd] *pt, pp of* **lay**; **~ back** (*inf*) *adj* cool

lain [leɪn] *pp of* **lie**

lair [leə*] *n* Lager *nt*

laity ['leɪtɪ] *n* Laien *pl*

lake [leɪk] *n* See *m*

lamb [læm] *n* Lamm *nt*; (*meat*) Lammfleisch *nt*; **~ chop** *n* Lammkotelett *nt*; **~swool** *n* Lammwolle *f*

lame [leɪm] *adj* lahm; (*excuse*) faul

lament [lə'ment] *n* Klage *f* ♦ *vt* beklagen

laminated ['læmɪneɪtɪd] *adj* beschichtet

lamp [læmp] *n* Lampe *f*; (*in street*) Straßenlaterne *f*

lamppost ['læmppəʊst] *n* Laternenpfahl *m*

lampshade ['læmpʃeɪd] *n* Lampenschirm *m*

lance [lɑ:ns] *n* Lanze *f* ♦ *vt* (*MED*) aufschneiden; **~ corporal** (*BRIT*) *n* Obergefreite(r) *m*

land [lænd] *n* Land *nt* ♦ *vi* (*from ship*) an Land gehen; (*AVIAT, end up*) landen ♦ *vt* (*obtain*) kriegen; (*passengers*) absetzen; (*goods*) abladen; (*troops, space probe*) landen; **~fill site** ['lændfɪl-] *n* Mülldeponie *f*; **~ing** *n* Landung *f*; (*on stairs*) (Treppen)absatz *m*; **~ing gear** *n* Fahrgestell *nt*; **~ing stage** (*BRIT*) *n* Landesteg *m*; **~ing strip** *n* Landebahn *f*; **~lady** *n* (Haus)wirtin *f*; **~locked** *adj* landumschlossen, Binnen-; **~lord** *n* (*of house*) Hauswirt *m*, Besitzer *m*; (*of pub*) Gastwirt *m*; (*of land*) Grundbesitzer *m*; **~mark** *n* Wahrzeichen *nt*; (*fig*) Meilenstein *m*; **~owner** *n* Grundbesitzer *m*

landscape ['lændskeɪp] *n* Landschaft *f*

landslide ['lændslaɪd] *n* (*GEOG*) Erdrutsch *m*; (*POL*) überwältigende(r) Sieg *m*

lane [leɪn] *n* (*in town*) Gasse *f*; (*in country*) Weg *m*; (*of motorway*) Fahrbahn *f*, Spur *f*; (*SPORT*) Bahn *f*

language ['læŋgwɪdʒ] *n* Sprache *f*; **bad ~** unanständige Ausdrücke *pl*; **~ laboratory** *n* Sprachlabor *nt*

languid ['læŋgwɪd] *adj* schlaff, matt

languish ['læŋgwɪʃ] *vi* schmachten

lank [læŋk] *adj* dürr

lanky ['læŋkɪ] *adj* schlaksig

lantern ['læntən] *n* Laterne *f*

lap [læp] *n* Schoß *m*; (*SPORT*) Runde *f* ♦ *vt* (*also:* **~ up**) auflecken ♦ *vi* (*water*) plätschern

lapel [lə'pel] *n* Revers *nt or m*

Lapland ['læplænd] *n* Lappland *nt*

lapse [læps] *n* (*moral*) Fehltritt *m* ♦ *vi* (*decline*) nachlassen; (*expire*) ablaufen; (*claims*) erlöschen; **to ~ into bad habits** sich schlechte Gewohnheiten angewöhnen

laptop (computer) ['læptɒp] *n* Laptop (-Computer) *m*

larceny ['lɑ:sənɪ] *n* Diebstahl *m*

lard [lɑ:d] *n* Schweineschmalz *nt*

larder ['lɑ:də*] *n* Speisekammer *f*

large [lɑːdʒ] adj groß; **at ~** auf freiem Fuß; **~ly** adv zum größten Teil; **~-scale** adj groß angelegt, Groß-

largesse [lɑːˈʒes] n Freigebigkeit f

lark [lɑːk] n (*bird*) Lerche f; (*joke*) Jux m; **~ about** (*inf*) vi herumalbern

laryngitis [lærɪnˈdʒaɪtɪs] n Kehlkopfentzündung f

larynx [ˈlærɪŋks] n Kehlkopf m

laser [ˈleɪzə*] n Laser m; **~ printer** n Laserdrucker m

lash [læʃ] n Peitschenhieb m; (*eye~*) Wimper f ♦ vt (*rain*) schlagen gegen; (*whip*) peitschen; (*bind*) festbinden; **~ out** vi (*with fists*) um sich schlagen; (*spend money*) sich in Unkosten stürzen ♦ vt (*money etc*) springen lassen

lass [læs] n Mädchen nt

lasso [læˈsuː] n Lasso nt

last [lɑːst] adj letzte(r, s) ♦ adv zuletzt; (*last time*) das letztemal ♦ vi (*continue*) dauern; (*remain good*) sich halten; (*money*) ausreichen; **at ~** endlich; **~ night** gestern abend; **~ week** letzte Woche; **~ but one** vorletzte(r, s); **~-ditch** adj (*attempt*) in letzter Minute; **~ing** adj dauerhaft; (*shame etc*) andauernd; **~ly** adv schließlich; **~-minute** adj in letzter Minute

latch [lætʃ] n Riegel m

late [leɪt] adj spät; (*dead*) verstorben ♦ adv spät; (*after proper time*) zu spät; **to be ~** zu spät kommen; **of ~** in letzter Zeit; **in ~ May** Ende Mai; **~comer** n Nachzügler(in) m(f); **~ly** adv in letzter Zeit

later [ˈleɪtə*] adj (*date etc*) später; (*version etc*) neuer ♦ adv später

lateral [ˈlætərəl] adj seitlich

latest [ˈleɪtɪst] adj (*fashion*) neueste(r, s) ♦ n (*news*) Neu(e)ste(s) nt; **at the ~** spätestens

lathe [leɪð] n Drehbank f

lather [ˈlɑːðə*] n (Seifen)schaum m ♦ vt einschäumen ♦ vi schäumen

Latin [ˈlætɪn] n Latein nt ♦ adj lateinisch; (*Roman*) römisch; **~ America** n Lateinamerika nt; **~-American** adj lateinamerikanisch

latitude [ˈlætɪtjuːd] n (GEOG) Breite f; (*freedom*) Spielraum m

latter [ˈlætə*] adj (*second of two*) letztere; (*coming at end*) letzte(r, s), später ♦ n: **the ~** der/die/das letztere, die letzteren; **~ly** adv in letzter Zeit

lattice [ˈlætɪs] n Gitter nt

laudable [ˈlɔːdəbl] adj löblich

laugh [lɑːf] n Lachen nt ♦ vi lachen; **~ at** vt lachen über +acc; **~ off** vt lachend abtun; **~able** adj lachhaft; **~ing stock** n Zielscheibe f des Spottes; **~ter** n Gelächter nt

launch [lɔːntʃ] n (*of ship*) Stapellauf m; (*of rocket*) Abschuß m; (*boat*) Barkasse f; (*of product*) Einführung f ♦ vt (*set afloat*) vom Stapel lassen; (*rocket*) (ab)schießen; (*product*) auf den Markt bringen; **~(ing) pad** n Abschußrampe f

launder [ˈlɔːndə*] vt waschen

Launderette [lɔːnˈdret] (®: BRIT) n Waschsalon m

Laundromat [ˈlɔːndrəmæt] (®: US) n Waschsalon m

laundry [ˈlɔːndrɪ] n (*place*) Wäscherei f; (*clothes*) Wäsche f; **to do the ~** waschen

laureate [ˈlɔːrɪət] adj see **poet**

laurel [ˈlɒrəl] n Lorbeer m

lava [ˈlɑːvə] n Lava f

lavatory [ˈlævətrɪ] n Toilette f

lavender [ˈlævɪndə*] n Lavendel m

lavish [ˈlævɪʃ] adj (*extravagant*) verschwenderisch; (*generous*) großzügig ♦ vt (*money*): **to ~ sth on sth** etw auf etw acc verschwenden; (*attention, gifts*): **to ~ sth on sb** jdn mit etw überschütten

law [lɔː] n Gesetz nt; (*system*) Recht nt; (*as studies*) Jura no art; **~-abiding** adj gesetzestreu; **~ and order** n Recht nt und Ordnung f; **~ court** n Gerichtshof m; **~ful** adj gesetzlich; **~less** adj gesetzlos

lawn [lɔːn] n Rasen m; **~mower** n Rasenmäher m; **~ tennis** n Rasentennis m

law school n Rechtsakademie f

lawsuit [ˈlɔːsuːt] n Prozeß m

lawyer [ˈlɔːjə*] n Rechtsanwalt m, Rechtsanwältin f

lax [læks] adj (*behaviour*) nachlässig;

(standards) lax

laxative ['læksətɪv] *n* Abführmittel *nt*

lay [leɪ] *(pt, pp* **laid)** *pt of* **lie** ♦ *adj* Laien- ♦ *vt (place)* legen; *(table)* decken; *(egg)* legen; *(trap)* stellen; *(money)* wetten; ~ **aside** *vt* zurücklegen; ~ **by** *vt (set aside)* beiseite legen; ~ **down** *vt* hinlegen; *(rules)* vorschreiben; *(arms)* strecken; **to** ~ **down the law** Vorschriften machen; ~ **off** *vt (workers)* (vorübergehend) entlassen; ~ **on** *vt (water, gas)* anschließen; *(concert etc)* veranstalten; ~ **out** *vt* (her)auslegen; *(money)* ausgeben; *(corpse)* aufbahren; ~ **up** *vt (subj: illness)* ans Bett fesseln; *(supplies)* anlegen; **~about** *n* Faulenzer *m*; **~-by** *(BRIT) n* Parkbucht *f*; *(bigger)* Rastplatz *m*

layer ['leɪə*] *n* Schicht *f*

layette [leɪ'et] *n* Babyausstattung *f*

layman ['leɪmən] *n* Laie *m*

layout ['leɪaʊt] *n* Anlage *f*; *(ART)* Layout *nt*

laze [leɪz] *vi* faulenzen

laziness ['leɪzɪnəs] *n* Faulheit *f*

lazy ['leɪzɪ] *adj* faul; *(slow-moving)* träge

lb. *abbr* = **pound** *(weight)*

lead¹ [led] *n (chemical)* Blei *nt*; *(of pencil)* (Bleistift)mine *f* ♦ *adj* bleiern, Blei-

lead² [li:d] *(pt, pp* **led)** *n (front position)* Führung *f*; *(distance, time ahead)* Vorsprung *m*; *(example)* Vorbild *nt*; *(clue)* Tip *m*; *(of police)* Spur *f*; *(THEAT)* Hauptrolle *f*; *(dog's)* Leine *f* ♦ *vt (guide)* führen; *(group etc)* leiten ♦ *vi (be first)* führen; **in the** ~ *(SPORT, fig)* in Führung; ~ **astray** *vt* irreführen; ~ **away** *vt* wegführen; *(prisoner)* abführen; ~ **back** *vi* zurückführen; ~ **on** *vt* anführen; ~ **on to** *vt (induce)* dazu bringen; ~ **to** *vt (street)* (hin)führen nach; *(result in)* führen zu; ~ **up to** *vt (drive)* führen zu; *(speaker etc)* hinführen auf *+acc*

leaden ['ledn] *adj (sky, sea)* bleiern; *(heavy: footsteps)* bleischwer

leader ['li:də*] *n* Führer *m*, Leiter *m*; *(of party)* Vorsitzende(r) *m*; *(PRESS)* Leitartikel *m*; **~ship** *n (office)* Leitung *f*; *(quality)* Führerschaft *f*

lead-free ['ledfri:] *adj (petrol)* bleifrei

leading ['li:dɪŋ] *adj* führend; ~ **lady** *n* *(THEAT)* Hauptdarstellerin *f*; ~ **light** *n* *(person)* führende(r) Geist *m*

leaf [li:f] *(pl* **leaves)** *n* Blatt *nt* ♦ *vi:* **to** ~ **through** durchblättern; **to turn over a new** ~ einen neuen Anfang machen

leaflet ['li:flɪt] *n (advertisement)* Prospekt *m*; *(pamphlet)* Flugblatt *nt*; *(for information)* Merkblatt *nt*

league [li:g] *n (union)* Bund *m*; *(SPORT)* Liga *f*; **to be in** ~ **with** unter einer Decke stecken mit

leak [li:k] *n* undichte Stelle *f*; *(in ship)* Leck *nt* ♦ *vt (liquid etc)* durchlassen ♦ *vi (pipe etc)* undicht sein; *(liquid etc)* auslaufen; **the information was ~ed to the enemy** die Information wurde dem Feind zugespielt; ~ **out** *vi (liquid etc)* auslaufen; *(information)* durchsickern

leaky ['li:kɪ] *adj* undicht

lean [li:n] *(pt, pp* **leaned** *or* **leant)** *adj* mager ♦ *vi* sich neigen ♦ *vt* (an)lehnen; **to** ~ **against sth** an etw *dat* angelehnt sein; sich an etw *acc* anlehnen; ~ **back** *vi* sich zurücklehnen; ~ **forward** *vi* sich vorbeugen; ~ **on** *vt fus* sich stützen auf *+acc*; ~ **out** *vi* sich hinauslehnen; ~ **over** *vi* sich hinüberbeugen; **~ing** *n* Neigung *f* ♦ *adj* schief; **leant** [lent] *pt, pp of* **lean**; **~-to** *n* Anbau *m*

leap [li:p] *(pt, pp* **leaped** *or* **leapt)** *n* Sprung *m* ♦ *vi* springen; **~frog** *n* Bockspringen *nt*; **leapt** [lept] *pt, pp of* **leap**; ~ **year** *n* Schaltjahr *nt*

learn [lɜ:n] *(pt, pp* **learned** *or* **learnt)** *vt, vi* lernen; *(find out)* erfahren; **to** ~ **how to do sth** etw (er)lernen; **~ed** ['lɜ:nɪd] *adj* gelehrt; **~er** *n* Anfänger(in) *m(f)*; *(AUT: BRIT: also* **~er driver)** Fahrschüler(in) *m(f)*; **~ing** *n* Gelehrsamkeit *f*; **~t** [lɜ:nt] *pt, pp of* **learn**

lease [li:s] *n (of property)* Mietvertrag *m* ♦ *vt* pachten

leash [li:ʃ] *n* Leine *f*

least [li:st] *adj* geringste(r, s) ♦ *adv* am wenigsten ♦ *n* Mindeste(s) *nt*; **the** ~ **possible effort** möglichst geringer Aufwand; **at** ~ zumindest; **not in the** ~! durchaus nicht!

leather ['leðə*] *n* Leder *nt*
leave [li:v] (*pt, pp* left) *vt* verlassen; (~ *behind*) zurücklassen; (*forget*) vergessen; (*allow to remain*) lassen; (*after death*) hinterlassen; (*entrust*) ~ **sth to sb** jdm etw überlassen ♦ *vi* weggehen, wegfahren; (*for journey*) abreisen; (*bus, train*) abfahren ♦ *n* Erlaubnis *f*; (*MIL*) Urlaub *m*; **to be left** (*remain*) übrigbleiben; **there's some milk left over** es ist noch etwas Milch übrig; **on** ~ auf Urlaub; **~ behind** *vt* (*person, object*) dalassen; (: *forget*) liegenlassen, stehenlassen; **~ out** *vt* auslassen; **~ of absence** *n* Urlaub *m*
leaves [li:vz] *pl of* leaf
Lebanon ['lebənən] *n* Libanon *m*
lecherous ['letʃərəs] *adj* lüstern
lecture ['lektʃə*] *n* Vortrag *m*; (*UNIV*) Vorlesung *f* ♦ *vi* einen Vortrag halten; (*UNIV*) lesen ♦ *vt* (*scold*) abkanzeln; **to give a** ~ **on sth** einen Vortrag über etwas halten; **~r** ['lektʃərə*] *n* Vortragende(r) *mf*; (*BRIT: UNIV*) Dozent(in) *m(f)*
led [led] *pt, pp of* lead[2]
ledge [ledʒ] *n* Leiste *f*; (*window* ~) Sims *m or nt*; (*of mountain*) (Fels)vorsprung *m*
ledger ['ledʒə*] *n* Hauptbuch *nt*
leech [li:tʃ] *n* Blutegel *m*
leek [li:k] *n* Lauch *m*
leer [liə*] *vi*: **to** ~ (**at sb**) (nach jdm) schielen
leeway ['li:weɪ] *n* (*fig*): **to have some** ~ etwas Spielraum haben
left [left] *pt, pp of* leave ♦ *adj* linke(r, s) ♦ *n* (*side*) linke Seite *f* ♦ *adv* links; **on the** ~ links; **to the** ~ nach links; **the L~** (*POL*) die Linke *f*; **~-handed** *adj* linkshändig; **~-hand side** *n* linke Seite *f*; **~-luggage (office)** (*BRIT*) *n* Gepäckaufbewahrung *f*; **~-overs** *npl* Reste *pl*; **~-wing** *adj* linke(r, s)
leg [leg] *n* Bein *nt*; (*of meat*) Keule *f*; (*stage*) Etappe *f*; **1st/2nd** ~ (*SPORT*) 1./2. Etappe
legacy ['legəsɪ] *n* Erbe *nt*, Erbschaft *f*
legal ['li:gəl] *adj* gesetzlich; (*allowed*) legal; ~ **holiday** (*US*) *n* gesetzliche(r) Feiertag *m*; **~ize** *vt* legalisieren; **~ly** *adv* gesetzlich; legal; ~ **tender** *n*

gesetzliche(s) Zahlungsmittel *nt*
legend ['ledʒənd] *n* Legende *f*; **~ary** *adj* legendär
legible ['ledʒəbl] *adj* leserlich
legislation [ledʒɪs'leɪʃən] *n* Gesetzgebung *f*
legislative ['ledʒɪslətɪv] *adj* gesetzgebend
legislature ['ledʒɪslətʃə*] *n* Legislative *f*
legitimate [lɪ'dʒɪtɪmət] *adj* rechtmäßig, legitim; (*child*) ehelich
legroom ['legrum] *n* Platz *m* für die Beine
leisure ['leʒə*] *n* Freizeit *f*; **to be at** ~ Zeit haben; ~ **centre** *n* Freizeitzentrum *nt*; **~ly** *adj* gemächlich
lemon ['lemən] *n* Zitrone *f*; (*colour*) Zitronengelb *nt*; **~ade** [lemə'neɪd] *n* Limonade *f*; ~ **tea** *n* Zitronentee *m*
lend [lend] (*pt, pp* lent) *vt* leihen; **to** ~ **sb sth** jdm etw leihen; **~ing library** *n* Leihbibliothek *f*
length [leŋθ] *n* Länge *f*; (*section of road, pipe etc*) Strecke *f*; (*of material*) Stück *nt*; **at** ~ (*lengthily*) ausführlich; (*at last*) schließlich; **~en** *vt* verlängern ♦ *vi* länger werden; **~ways** *adv* längs; **~y** *adj* sehr lang, langatmig
lenient ['li:nɪənt] *adj* nachsichtig
lens [lenz] *n* Linse *f*; (*PHOT*) Objektiv *nt*
Lent [lent] *n* Fastenzeit *f*
lent [lent] *pt, pp of* lend
lentil ['lentl] *n* Linse *f*
Leo ['li:əʊ] *n* Löwe *m*
leotard ['li:ətɑ:d] *n* Trikot *nt*, Gymnastikanzug *m*
leper ['lepə*] *n* Leprakranke(r) *f(m)*
leprosy ['leprəsɪ] *n* Lepra *f*
lesbian ['lezbɪən] *adj* lesbisch ♦ *n* Lesbierin *f*
less [les] *adj, adv* weniger ♦ *n* weniger ♦ *pron* weniger; ~ **than half** weniger als die Hälfte; ~ **than ever** weniger denn je; ~ **and** ~ immer weniger; **the** ~ **he works** je weniger er arbeitet
lessen ['lesn] *vi* abnehmen ♦ *vt* verringern, verkleinern
lesser ['lesə*] *adj* kleiner, geringer; **to a** ~ **extent** in geringerem Maße
lesson ['lesn] *n* (*SCH*) Stunde *f*; (*unit of*

study) Lektion *f*; (*fig*) Lehre *f*; (*ECCL*) Lesung *f*; **a maths ~** eine Mathestunde

lest [lest] *conj*: **~ it happen** damit es nicht passiert

let [let] (*pt, pp* let) *vt* lassen; (*BRIT: lease*) vermieten; **to ~ sb do sth** jdn etw tun lassen; **to ~ sb know sth** jdn etw wissen lassen; **~'s go!** gehen wir!; **~ him come** soll er doch kommen; **~ down** *vt* hinunterlassen; (*disappoint*) enttäuschen; **~ go** *vi* loslassen ♦ *vt* (*things*) loslassen; (*person*) gehen lassen; **~ in** *vt* hereinlassen; (*water*) durchlassen; **~ off** *vt* (*gun*) abfeuern; (*steam*) ablassen; (*forgive*) laufen lassen; **~ on** *vi* durchblicken lassen; (*pretend*) vorgeben; **~ out** *vt* herauslassen; (*scream*) fahren lassen; **~ up** *vi* nachlassen; (*stop*) aufhören

lethal ['liːθəl] *adj* tödlich

lethargic [le'θɑːdʒɪk] *adj* lethargisch

letter ['letə*] *n* (*of alphabet*) Buchstabe *m*; (*message*) Brief *m*; **~ bomb** *n* Briefbombe *f*; **~box** (*BRIT*) *n* Briefkasten *m*; **~ing** *n* Beschriftung *f*; **~ of credit** *n* Akkreditiv *m*

lettuce ['letɪs] *n* (Kopf)salat *m*

let-up ['letʌp] (*inf*) *n* Nachlassen *nt*

leukaemia [luː'kiːmɪə] (*US* **leukemia**) *n* Leukämie *f*

level ['levl] *adj* (*ground*) eben; (*at same height*) auf gleicher Höhe; (*equal*) gleich gut; (*head*) kühl ♦ *adv* auf gleicher Höhe ♦ *n* (*instrument*) Wasserwaage *f*; (*altitude*) Höhe *f*; (*flat place*) ebene Fläche *f*; (*position on scale*) Niveau *nt*; (*amount, degree*) Grad *m* ♦ *vt* (*ground*) einebnen; **to draw ~ with** gleichziehen mit; **to be ~ with** auf einer Höhe sein mit; **A ~s** (*BRIT*) ≈ Abitur *nt*; **O ~s** ≈ mittlere Reife *f*; **on the ~** (*fig: honest*) ehrlich; **to ~ sth at sb** (*blow*) jdm etw versetzen; (*remark*) etw gegen jdn richten; **~ off** *or* **out** *vi* flach *or* eben werden; (*fig*) sich ausgleichen; (*plane*) horizontal fliegen ♦ *vt* (*ground*) planieren; (*differences*) ausgleichen; **~ crossing** (*BRIT*) *n* Bahnübergang *m*; **~-headed** *adj* vernünftig

lever ['liːvə*] *n* Hebel *m*; (*fig*) Druckmittel

nt ♦ *vt* (hoch)stemmen; **~age** *n* Hebelkraft *f*; (*fig*) Einfluß *m*

levity ['levɪtɪ] *n* Leichtfertigkeit *f*

levy ['levɪ] *n* (*of taxes*) Erhebung *f*; (*tax*) Abgaben *pl*; (*MIL*) Aushebung *f* ♦ *vt* erheben; (*MIL*) ausheben

lewd [luːd] *adj* unzüchtig, unanständig

liability [laɪə'bɪlɪtɪ] *n* (*burden*) Belastung *f*; (*duty*) Pflicht *f*; (*debt*) Verpflichtung *f*; (*proneness*) Anfälligkeit *f*; (*responsibility*) Haftung *f*

liable ['laɪəbl] *adj* (*responsible*) haftbar; (*prone*) anfällig; **to be ~ for sth** etw *dat* unterliegen; **it's ~ to happen** es kann leicht vorkommen

liaise [liː'eɪz] *vi*: **to ~ (with sb)** (mit jdm) zusammenarbeiten

liaison [liː'eɪzɒn] *n* Verbindung *f*

liar ['laɪə*] *n* Lügner *m*

libel ['laɪbl] *n* Verleumdung *f* ♦ *vt* verleumden

liberal ['lɪbərəl] *adj* (*generous*) großzügig; (*open-minded*) aufgeschlossen; (*POL*) liberal

liberate ['lɪbəreɪt] *vt* befreien

liberation [lɪbə'reɪʃən] *n* Befreiung *f*

liberty ['lɪbətɪ] *n* Freiheit *f*; (*permission*) Erlaubnis *f*; **to be at ~ to do sth** etw tun dürfen; **to take the ~ of doing sth** sich *dat* erlauben, etw zu tun

Libra ['liːbrə] *n* Waage *f*

librarian [laɪ'breərɪən] *n* Bibliothekar(in) *m(f)*

library ['laɪbrərɪ] *n* Bibliothek *f*; (*lending ~*) Bücherei *f*

Libya ['lɪbɪə] *n* Libyen *nt*; **~n** *adj* libysch ♦ *n* Libyer(in) *m(f)*

lice [laɪs] *npl of* **louse**

licence ['laɪsəns] (*US* **license**) *n* (*permit*) Erlaubnis *f*; (*also: driving ~*, (*US*) *driver's ~*) Führerschein *m*; (*excess*) Zügellosigkeit *f*

license ['laɪsəns] *n* (*US*) = **licence** ♦ *vt* genehmigen, konzessionieren; **~d** *adj* (*for alcohol*) konzessioniert (*für den Alkoholausschank*)

license plate (*US*) *n* (*AUT*) Nummernschild *nt*

licentious [laɪ'senʃəs] *adj* ausschweifend

lichen ['laɪkən] *n* Flechte *f*

lick [lɪk] *vt* lecken ♦ *n* Lecken *nt*; **a ~ of**

paint ein bißchen Farbe
licorice ['lɪkərɪs] (*US*) *n* = **liquorice**
lid [lɪd] *n* Deckel *m*; (*eye*~) Lid *nt*
lie [laɪ] (*pt* **lay**, *pp* **lain**) *vi* (*rest, be
situated*) liegen; (*put o.s. in position*) sich
legen; (*pt, pp* **lied**: *tell lies*) lügen ♦ *n* Lüge
f; **to** ~ **low** (*fig*) untertauchen; ~ **about**
vi (*things*) herumliegen; (*people*)
faulenzen; ~**down** (*BRIT*) *n*: **to have a** ~-
down ein Nickerchen machen; ~**in** (*BRIT*)
n: **to have a** ~-**in** sich ausschlafen
lieu [luː] *n*: **in** ~ **of** anstatt +*gen*
lieutenant [lef'tenənt, (*US*) luː'tenənt] *n*
Leutnant *m*
life [laɪf] (*pl* **lives**) *n* Leben *nt*; ~
assurance (*BRIT*) *n* = **life insurance**;
~**belt** (*BRIT*) *n* Rettungsring *m*; ~**boat** *n*
Rettungsboot *nt*; ~**guard** *n*
Rettungsschwimmer *m*; ~ **insurance** *n*
Lebensversicherung *f*; ~ **jacket** *n*
Schwimmweste *f*; ~**less** *adj* (*dead*) leblos;
(*dull*) langweilig; ~**like** *adj* lebenswahr,
naturgetreu; ~**line** *n* Rettungsleine *f*; (*fig*)
Rettungsanker *m*; ~**long** *adj* lebenslang;
~ **preserver** (*US*) *n* = **lifebelt**; ~**saver** *n*
Lebensretter(in) *m(f)*; ~ **sentence** *n*
lebenslängliche Freiheitsstrafe *f*; ~**sized**
adj in Lebensgröße; ~ **span** *n*
Lebensspanne *f*; ~**style** *n* Lebensstil *m*; ~
support system *n* (*MED*)
Lebenserhaltungssystem *nt*; ~**time** *n*: **in
his** ~**time** während er lebte; **once in a**
~**time** einmal im Leben
lift [lɪft] *vt* hochheben ♦ *vi* sich heben ♦ *n*
(*BRIT: elevator*) Aufzug *m*, Lift *m*; **to give
sb a** ~ jdn mitnehmen; ~**off** *n* Abheben
nt (vom Boden)
ligament ['lɪɡəmənt] *n* Band *nt*
light [laɪt] (*pt, pp* **lighted** *or* **lit**) *n* Licht
nt; (*for cigarette etc*): **have you got a** ~?
haben Sie Feuer? ♦ *vt* beleuchten; (*lamp*)
anmachen; (*fire, cigarette*) anzünden ♦ *adj*
(*bright*) hell; (*pale*) hell-; (*not heavy, easy*)
leicht; (*punishment*) milde; (*touch*) leicht;
~**s** *npl* (*AUT*) Beleuchtung *f*; ~ **up** *vi*
(*lamp*) angehen; (*face*) aufleuchten ♦ *vt*
(*illuminate*) beleuchten; (*lights*)
anmachen; ~ **bulb** *n* Glühbirne *f*; ~**en** *vi*
(*brighten*) hell werden; (*lightning*) blitzen

♦ *vt* (*give light to*) erhellen; (*hair*)
aufhellen; (*gloom*) aufheitern; (*make less
heavy*) leichter machen; (*fig*) erleichtern;
~**er** *n* Feuerzeug *nt*; ~**headed** *adj*
(*thoughtless*) leichtsinnig; (*giddy*)
schwindlig; ~**hearted** *adj* leichtherzig,
fröhlich; ~**house** *n* Leuchtturm *m*; ~**ing**
n Beleuchtung *f*; ~**ly** *adv* leicht;
(*irresponsibly*) leichtfertig; **to get off** ~**ly**
mit einem blauen Auge davonkommen;
~**ness** *n* (*of weight*) Leichtigkeit *f*; (*of
colour*) Helle *f*
lightning ['laɪtnɪŋ] *n* Blitz *m*; ~
conductor (*US* ~ **rod**) *n* Blitzableiter *m*
light: ~ **pen** *n* Lichtstift *m*; ~**weight** *adj*
(*suit*) leicht; ~**weight boxer** *n*
Leichtgewichtler *m*; ~ **year** *n* Lichtjahr
nt
like [laɪk] *vt* mögen, gernhaben ♦ *prep* wie
♦ *adj* (*similar*) ähnlich; (*equal*) gleich ♦ *n*:
the ~ dergleichen; **I would** *or* **I'd** ~ ich
möchte gern; **would you** ~ **a coffee**?
möchten Sie einen Kaffee?; **to be** *or* **look
~ **sb/sth jdm/etw ähneln; **that's just** ~
him das ist typisch für ihn; **do it** ~ **this**
mach es so; **it is nothing** ~ ... es ist
nicht zu vergleichen mit ...; **what does it
look** ~? wie sieht es aus?; **what does it
sound** ~? wie hört es sich an?; **what
does it taste** ~? wie schmeckt es?; **his** ~**s
and dislikes** was er mag und was er
nicht mag; ~**able** *adj* sympathisch
likelihood ['laɪklɪhʊd] *n*
Wahrscheinlichkeit *f*
likely ['laɪklɪ] *adj* wahrscheinlich; **he's** ~
to leave er geht möglicherweise; **not** ~!
wohl kaum!
likeness ['laɪknɪs] *n* Ähnlichkeit *f*;
(*portrait*) Bild *nt*
likewise ['laɪkwaɪz] *adv* ebenso
liking ['laɪkɪŋ] *n* Zuneigung *f*; (*taste*)
Vorliebe *f*
lilac ['laɪlək] *n* Flieder *m* ♦ *adj* (*colour*)
fliederfarben
lily ['lɪlɪ] *n* Lilie *f*; ~ **of the valley** *n*
Maiglöckchen *nt*
limb [lɪm] *n* Glied *nt*
limber up ['lɪmbər-] *vi* sich auflockern;
(*fig*) sich vorbereiten

limbo ['lɪmbəʊ] *n*: **to be in ~** (*fig*) in der Schwebe sein

lime [laɪm] *n* (*tree*) Linde *f*; (*fruit*) Limone *f*; (*substance*) Kalk *m*

limelight ['laɪmlaɪt] *n*: **to be in the ~** (*fig*) im Rampenlicht stehen

limestone ['laɪmstəʊn] *n* Kalkstein *m*

limit ['lɪmɪt] *n* Grenze *f*; (*inf*) Höhe *f* ♦ *vt* begrenzen, einschränken; **~ation** [lɪmɪ'teɪʃən] *n* Einschränkung *f*; **~ed** *adj* beschränkt; **to be ~ed to** sich beschränken auf +*acc*; **~ed** (**liability**) **company** (*BRIT*) *n* Gesellschaft *f* mit beschränkter Haftung

limp [lɪmp] *n* Hinken *nt* ♦ *vi* hinken ♦ *adj* schlaff

limpet ['lɪmpɪt] *n* (*fig*) Klette *f*

line [laɪn] *n* Linie *f*; (*rope*) Leine *f*; (*on face*) Falte *f*; (*row*) Reihe *f*; (*of hills*) Kette *f*; (*US: queue*) Schlange *f*; (*company*) Linie *f*, Gesellschaft *f*; (*RAIL*) Strecke *f*; (*TEL*) Leitung *f*; (*written*) Zeile *f*; (*direction*) Richtung *f*; (*fig: business*) Branche *f*; (*range of items*) Kollektion *f* ♦ *vt* (*coat*) füttern; (*border*) säumen; **~s** *npl* (*RAIL*) Gleise *pl*; **in ~ with** in Übereinstimmung mit; **~ up** *vi* sich aufstellen ♦ *vt* aufstellen; (*prepare*) sorgen für; (*support*) mobilisieren; (*surprise*) planen

linear ['lɪnɪə*] *adj* gerade; (*measure*) Längen-

lined [laɪnd] *adj* (*face*) faltig; (*paper*) liniert

linen ['lɪnɪn] *n* Leinen *nt*; (*sheets etc*) Wäsche *f*

liner ['laɪnə*] *n* Überseedampfer *m*

linesman ['laɪnzmən] (*irreg*) *n* (*SPORT*) Linienrichter *m*

line-up ['laɪnʌp] *n* Aufstellung *f*

linger ['lɪŋgə*] *vi* (*remain long*) verweilen; (*taste*) (zurück)bleiben; (*delay*) zögern, verharren

lingerie ['lænʒəriː] *n* Damenunterwäsche *f*

lingering ['lɪŋgərɪŋ] *adj* (*doubt*) zurückbleibend; (*disease*) langwierig; (*taste*) nachhaltend; (*look*) lang

lingo ['lɪŋgəʊ] (*pl* ~**es**; *inf*) *n* Sprache *f*

linguist ['lɪŋgwɪst] *n* Sprachkundige(r)

mf; (*UNIV*) Sprachwissenschaftler(in) *m(f)*

linguistic [lɪŋ'gwɪstɪk] *adj* sprachlich; sprachwissenschaftlich; **~s** [lɪŋ'gwɪstɪks] *n* Sprachwissenschaft *f*, Linguistik *f*

lining ['laɪnɪŋ] *n* Futter *nt*

link [lɪŋk] *n* Glied *nt*; (*connection*) Verbindung *f* ♦ *vt* verbinden; **~s** *npl* (*GOLF*) Golfplatz *m*; **~ up** *vt* verbinden ♦ *vi* zusammenkommen; (*companies*) sich zusammenschließen; **~-up** *n* (*TEL*) Verbindung *f*; (*of spaceships*) Kopplung *f*

lino ['laɪnəʊ] *n* = **linoleum**

linoleum [lɪ'nəʊliəm] *n* Linoleum *nt*

linseed oil ['lɪnsiːd-] *n* Leinöl *nt*

lion ['laɪən] *n* Löwe *m*; **~ess** *n* Löwin *f*

lip [lɪp] *n* Lippe *f*; (*of jug*) Schnabel *m*; **to pay ~ service (to)** ein Lippenbekenntnis ablegen (zu)

liposuction ['lɪpəʊsʌkʃən] *n* Fettabsaugen *nt*

lip: **~-read** (*irreg*) *vi* von den Lippen ablesen; **~ salve** *n* Lippenbalsam *m*; **~stick** *n* Lippenstift *m*

liqueur [lɪ'kjʊə*] *n* Likör *m*

liquid ['lɪkwɪd] *n* Flüßigkeit *f* ♦ *adj* flüssig

liquidate ['lɪkwɪdeɪt] *vt* liquidieren

liquidation [lɪkwɪ'deɪʃən] *n* Liquidation *f*

liquidize ['lɪkwɪdaɪz] *vt* (*COOK*) (im Mixer) pürieren; **~r** ['lɪkwɪdaɪzə*] *n* Mixgerät *nt*

liquor ['lɪkə*] *n* Alkohol *m*

liquorice ['lɪkərɪs] (*BRIT*) *n* Lakritze *f*

liquor store (*US*) *n* Spirituosengeschäft *f*

Lisbon ['lɪzbən] *n* Lissabon *nt*

lisp [lɪsp] *n* Lispeln *nt* ♦ *vt, vi* lispeln

list [lɪst] *n* Liste *f*, Verzeichnis *nt*; (*of ship*) Schlagseite *f* ♦ *vt* (*write down*) eine Liste machen von; (*verbally*) aufzählen ♦ *vi* (*ship*) Schlagseite haben

listen ['lɪsn] *vi* hören; **~ to** *vt* zuhören +*dat*; **~er** *n* (Zu)hörer(in) *m(f)*

listless ['lɪstləs] *adj* lustlos

lit [lɪt] *pt, pp of* **light**

liter ['liːtə*] (*US*) *n* = **litre**

literacy ['lɪtərəsɪ] *n* Fähigkeit *f* zu lesen und zu schreiben

literal ['lɪtərəl] *adj* buchstäblich;

(translation) wortwörtlich; ~ly *adv*
wörtlich; buchstäblich

literary ['lɪtərərɪ] *adj* literarisch

literate ['lɪtərət] *adj* des Lesens und
Schreibens kundig

literature ['lɪtrətʃə*] *n* Literatur *f*

lithe [laɪð] *adj* geschmeidig

litigation [lɪtɪ'geɪʃən] *n* Prozeß *m*

litre ['li:tə*] *(US* liter) *n* Liter *m*

litter ['lɪtə*] *n (rubbish)* Abfall *m; (of
animals)* Wurf *m* ♦ *vt* in Unordnung
bringen; **to be ~ed with** übersät sein mit;
~ bin *(BRIT)* Abfalleimer *m*

little ['lɪtl] *adj* klein ♦ *adv*, *n* wenig; **a ~**
ein bißchen; **~ by ~** nach und nach

live¹ [laɪv] *adj* lebendig; *(MIL)* scharf;
(ELEC) geladen; *(broadcast)* live

live² [lɪv] *vi* leben; *(dwell)* wohnen ♦ *vt
(life)* führen; **~ down** *vt*: **I'll never ~ it
down** das wird man mir nie vergessen; **~
on** *vi* weiterleben ♦ *vt fus*: **to ~ on sth**
von etw leben; **~ together** *vi* zusam-
menleben; *(share a flat)* zusammen-
wohnen; **~ up to** *vt (standards)*
gerecht werden +*dat*; *(principles)*
anstreben; *(hopes)* entsprechen
+*dat*

livelihood ['laɪvlɪhʊd] *n* Lebensunterhalt
m

lively ['laɪvlɪ] *adj* lebhaft, lebendig

liven up ['laɪvn-] *vt* beleben

liver ['lɪvə*] *n (ANAT)* Leber *f*

lives [laɪvz] *pl of* **life**

livestock ['laɪvstɒk] *n* Vieh *nt*

livid ['lɪvɪd] *adj* bläulich; *(furious)*
fuchsteufelswild

living ['lɪvɪŋ] *n* (Lebens)unterhalt *m* ♦ *adj*
lebendig; *(language etc)* lebend; **to earn
or make a ~** sich *dat* seinen
Lebensunterhalt verdienen; **~ conditions**
npl Wohnverhältnisse *pl*; **~ room** *n*
Wohnzimmer *nt*; **~ standards** *npl*
Lebensstandard *m*; **~ wage** *n*
ausreichender Lohn *m*

lizard ['lɪzəd] *n* Eidechse *f*

load [ləʊd] *n (burden)* Last *f; (amount)*
Ladung *f* ♦ *vt (also: ~ up)* (be)laden;
(COMPUT) laden; *(camera)* Film einlegen in
+*acc; (gun)* laden; **a ~ of, ~s of** *(fig)* jede

Menge; **~ed** *adj* beladen; *(dice)*
präpariert; *(question)* Fang-; *(inf: rich)*
steinreich; **~ing bay** *n* Ladeplatz *m*

loaf [ləʊf] *(pl* **loaves**) *n* Brot *nt* ♦ *vi (also:
~ about, ~ around)* herumlungern,
faulenzen

loan [ləʊn] *n* Leihgabe *f; (FIN)* Darlehen *nt*
♦ *vt* leihen; **on ~** geliehen

loath [ləʊθ] *adj*: **to be ~ to do sth** etw
ungern tun

loathe [ləʊð] *vt* verabscheuen

loathing ['ləʊðɪŋ] *n* Abscheu *f*

loaves [ləʊvz] *pl of* **loaf**

lobby ['lɒbɪ] *n* Vorhalle *f; (POL)* Lobby *f*
♦ *vt* politisch beeinflussen (wollen)

lobe [ləʊb] *n* Ohrläppchen *nt*

lobster ['lɒbstə*] *n* Hummer *m*

local ['ləʊkəl] *adj* ortsansässig, Orts- ♦ *n
(pub)* Stammwirtschaft *f*; **the ~s** *npl
(people)* die Ortsansässigen *pl*; **~
anaesthetic** *n (MED)* örtliche Betäubung
f; **~ authority** *n* städtische Behörden *pl*;
~ call *n (TEL)* Ortsgespräch *nt*; **~
government** *n* Gemeinde-/
Kreisverwaltung *f*; **~ity** [ləʊ'kælɪtɪ] *n* Ort
m; **~ly** *adv* örtlich, am Ort

locate [ləʊ'keɪt] *vt* ausfindig machen;
(establish) errichten

location [ləʊ'keɪʃən] *n* Platz *m*, Lage *f*;
on ~ *(CINE)* auf Außenaufnahme

loch [lɒx] *(SCOTTISH)* *n* See *m*

lock [lɒk] *n* Schloß *nt; (NAUT)* Schleuse *f;
(of hair)* Locke *f* ♦ *vt (fasten)*
(ver)schließen ♦ *vi (door etc)* sich
schließen (lassen); *(wheels)* blockieren; **~
up** *vt (criminal, mental patient)*
einsperren; *(house)* abschließen

locker ['lɒkə*] *n* Spind *m*

locket ['lɒkɪt] *n* Medaillon *nt*

lock-out ['lɒkaʊt] *n* Aussperrung *f*

locksmith ['lɒksmɪθ] *n* Schlosser(in) *m(f)*

lockup ['lɒkʌp] *n (jail)* Gefängnis *nt;
(garage)* Garage *f*

locomotive [ləʊkə'məʊtɪv] *n* Lokomotive
f

locum ['ləʊkəm] *n (MED)* Vertreter(in)
m(f)

locust ['ləʊkəst] *n* Heuschrecke *f*

lodge [lɒdʒ] *n (gatehouse)* Pförtnerhaus

nt; *(freemasons')* Loge *f* ♦ *vi* (*get stuck*) stecken(bleiben); (*in Untermiete*): **to ~ (with)** wohnen (bei) ♦ *vt* (*protest*) einreichen; **~r** *n* (Unter)mieter *m*

lodgings ['lɒdʒɪŋz] *n* (Miet)wohnung *f*

loft [lɒft] *n* (Dach)boden *m*

lofty ['lɒftɪ] *adj* hoch(ragend); (*proud*) hochmütig

log [lɒg] *n* Klotz *m*; (*book*) = **logbook**

logbook ['lɒgbʊk] *n* Bordbuch *nt*; (*for lorry*) Fahrtenschreiber *m*; (*AUT*) Kraftfahrzeugbrief *m*

loggerheads ['lɒgəhedz] *npl*: **to be at ~** sich in den Haaren liegen

logic ['lɒdʒɪk] *n* Logik *f*; **~al** *adj* logisch

logistics [lɒ'dʒɪstɪks] *npl* Logistik *f*

logo ['ləʊgəʊ] *n* Firmenzeichen *nt*

loin [lɔɪn] *n* Lende *f*

loiter ['lɔɪtə*] *vi* herumstehen

loll [lɒl] *vi* (*also:* **~ about**) sich rekeln

lollipop ['lɒlɪpɒp] *n* (Dauer)lutscher *m*; **~ man/lady** (*BRIT*) *n* ≈ Schülerlotse *m*

London ['lʌndən] *n* London *nt*; **~er** *n* Londoner(in) *m(f)*

lone [ləʊn] *adj* einsam

loneliness ['ləʊnlɪnəs] *n* Einsamkeit *f*

lonely ['ləʊnlɪ] *adj* einsam

loner ['ləʊnə*] *n* Einzelgänger(in) *m(f)*

long [lɒŋ] *adj* lang; (*distance*) weit ♦ *adv* lange ♦ *vi*: **to ~ for** sich sehnen nach; **before ~** bald; **as ~ as** solange; **in the ~ run** auf die Dauer; **don't be ~!** beeil dich!; **how ~ is the street?** wie lang ist die Straße?; **how ~ is the lesson?** wie lange dauert die Stunde?; **6 metres ~** 6 Meter lang; **6 months ~** 6 Monate lang; **all night ~** die ganze Nacht; **he no ~er comes** er kommt nicht mehr; **~ ago** vor langer Zeit; **~ before** lange vorher; **at ~ last** endlich; **~-distance** *adj* Fern-

longevity [lɒn'dʒevɪtɪ] *n* Langlebigkeit *f*

long: **~-haired** *adj* langhaarig; **~hand** *n* Langschrift *f*; **~ing** *n* Sehnsucht *f* ♦ *adj* sehnsüchtig

longitude ['lɒŋgɪtjuːd] *n* Längengrad *m*

long: **~ jump** *n* Weitsprung *m*; **~-lost** *adj* längst verloren geglaubt; **~-playing record** *n* Langspielplatte *f*; **~-range** *adj* Langstrecken-, Fern-; **~-sighted** *adj*

weitsichtig; **~-standing** *adj* alt, seit langer Zeit bestehend; **~-suffering** *adj* schwer geprüft; **~-term** *adj* langfristig; **~ wave** *n* Langwelle *f*; **~-winded** *adj* langatmig

loo [luː] (*BRIT: inf*) *n* Klo *nt*

look [lʊk] *vi* schauen; (*seem*) aussehen; (*building etc*): **to ~ on to the sea** aufs Meer gehen ♦ *n* Blick *m*; **~s** *npl* (*appearance*) Aussehen *nt*; **~ after** *vt* (*care for*) sorgen für; (*watch*) aufpassen auf +*acc*; **~ at** *vt* ansehen; (*consider*) sich überlegen; **~ back** *vi* sich umsehen; (*fig*) zurückblicken; **~ down on** *vt* (*fig*) herabsehen auf +*acc*; **~ for** *vt* (*seek*) suchen; **~ forward** *vi* sich freuen auf +*acc*; (*in letters*): **we ~ forward to hearing from you** wir hoffen, bald von Ihnen zu hören; **~ into** *vt* untersuchen; **~ on** *vi* zusehen; **~ out** *vi* hinaussehen; (*take care*) aufpassen; **~ out for** *vt* Ausschau halten nach; (*be careful*) achtgeben auf +*acc*; **~ round** *vi* sich umsehen; **~ to** *vt* (*take care of*) achtgeben auf +*acc*; (*rely on*) sich verlassen auf +*acc*; **~ up** *vi* aufblicken; (*improve*) sich bessern ♦ *vt* (*word*) nachschlagen; (*person*) besuchen; **~ up to** *vt* aufsehen zu; **~-out** *n* (*watch*) Ausschau *f*; (*person*) Wachposten *m*; (*place*) Ausguck *m*; (*prospect*) Aussichten *pl*; **to be on the ~-out for sth** nach etw Ausschau halten

loom [luːm] *n* Webstuhl *m* ♦ *vi* sich abzeichnen

loony ['luːnɪ] (*inf*) *n* Verrückte(r) *mf*

loop [luːp] *n* Schlaufe *f*; **~hole** *n* (*fig*) Hintertürchen *nt*

loose [luːs] *adj* lose, locker; (*free*) frei; (*inexact*) unpräzise ♦ *vt* lösen, losbinden; **~ change** *n* Kleingeld *nt*; **~ chippings** *npl* (*on road*) Rollsplit *m*; **~ end** *n*: **to be at a ~ end** (*BRIT*) *or* **at ~-ends** (*US*) nicht wissen, was man tun soll; **~ly** *adv* locker, lose; **~n** *vt* lockern, losmachen

loot [luːt] *n* Beute *f* ♦ *vt* plündern

lop off [lɒp-] *vt* abhacken

lopsided ['lɒp'saɪdɪd] *adj* schief

lord [lɔːd] *n* (*ruler*) Herr *m*; (*BRIT: title*) Lord *m*; **the L~** (*Gott*) der Herr; **the**

(House of) L~s das Oberhaus; **~ship** *n*: **Your L~ship** Eure Lordschaft

lore [lɔː*] *n* Überlieferung *f*

lorry ['lɒrɪ] (BRIT) *n* Lastwagen *m*; **~ driver** (BRIT) *n* Lastwagenfahrer(in) *m(f)*

lose [luːz] (*pt, pp* **lost**) *vt* verlieren; (*chance*) verpassen ♦ *vi* verlieren; **to ~ (time)** (*clock*) nachgehen; **~r** *n* Verlierer *m*

loss [lɒs] *n* Verlust *m*; **at a ~** (COMM) mit Verlust; (*unable*) außerstande

lost [lɒst] *pt, pp of* **lose** ♦ *adj* verloren; **~ property** (US **~ and found**) *n* Fundsachen *pl*

lot [lɒt] *n* (*quantity*) Menge *f*; (*fate, at auction*) Los *nt*; (*inf: people, things*) Haufen *m*; **the ~** alles; (*people*) alle; **a ~ of** (*with sg*) viel; (*with pl*) viele; **~s of** massenhaft, viel(e); **I read a ~** ich lese viel; **to draw ~s for sth** etw verlosen

lotion ['ləʊʃən] *n* Lotion *f*

lottery ['lɒtərɪ] *n* Lotterie *f*

loud [laʊd] *adj* laut; (*showy*) schreiend ♦ *adv* laut; **~hailer** (BRIT) *n* Megaphon *nt*; **~ly** *adv* laut; **~speaker** *n* Lautsprecher *m*

lounge [laʊndʒ] *n* (*in hotel*) Gesellschaftsraum *m*; (*in house*) Wohnzimmer *nt* ♦ *vi* sich herumlümmeln; **~ suit** (BRIT) *n* Straßenanzug *m*

louse [laʊs] (*pl* **lice**) *n* Laus *f*

lousy ['laʊzɪ] *adj* (*fig*) miserabel

lout [laʊt] *n* Lümmel *m*

louvre ['luːvə*] (US **louver**) *adj* (*door, window*) Jalousie-

lovable ['lʌvəbl] *adj* liebenswert

love [lʌv] *n* Liebe *f*; (*person*) Liebling *m*; (SPORT) null ♦ *vt* (*person*) lieben; (*activity*) gerne mögen; **to be in ~ with sb** in jdn verliebt sein; **to make ~** sich lieben; **for the ~ of** aus Liebe zu; **"15 ~"** (TENNIS) „15 null"; **to ~ to do sth** etw (sehr) gerne tun; **~ affair** *n* (Liebes)verhältnis *nt*; **~ letter** *n* Liebesbrief *m*; **~ life** *n* Liebesleben *nt*

lovely ['lʌvlɪ] *adj* schön

lover ['lʌvə*] *n* Liebhaber(in) *m(f)*

loving ['lʌvɪŋ] *adj* liebend, liebevoll

low [ləʊ] *adj* niedrig; (*rank*) niedere(r, s); (*level, note, neckline*) tief; (*intelligence, density*) gering; (*vulgar*) ordinär; (*not loud*) leise; (*depressed*) gedrückt ♦ *adv* (*not high*) niedrig; (*not loudly*) leise ♦ *n* (*low point*) Tiefstand *m*; (MET) Tief *nt*; **to feel ~** sich mies fühlen; **to turn (down) ~** leiser stellen; **~-cut** *adj* (*dress*) tiefausgeschnitten

lower ['ləʊə*] *vt* herunterlassen; (*eyes, gun*) senken; (*reduce*) herabsetzen, senken ♦ *vr*: **to ~ o.s. to** (*fig*) sich herablassen zu

low: **~-fat** *adj* fettarm, Mager-; **~lands** *npl* (GEOG) Flachland *nt*; **~ly** *adj* bescheiden; **~-lying** *adj* tiefgelegen

loyal ['lɔɪəl] *adj* treu; **~ty** *n* Treue *f*

lozenge ['lɒzɪndʒ] *n* Pastille *f*

L.P. *n abbr* = **long-playing record**

L-plates ['elpleɪts] (BRIT) *npl* L-Schild *nt* (*für Fahrschüler*)

Ltd *abbr* (= *limited company*) GmbH.

lubricant ['luːbrɪkənt] *n* Schmiermittel *nt*

lubricate ['luːbrɪkeɪt] *vt* schmieren

lucid ['luːsɪd] *adj* klar; (*sane*) bei klarem Verstand; (*moment*) licht

luck [lʌk] *n* Glück *nt*; **bad** *or* **hard** *or* **tough ~!** (so ein) Pech!; **good ~!** viel Glück!; **~ily** *adv* glücklicherweise, zum Glück; **~y** *adj* Glücks-; **to be ~y** Glück haben

lucrative ['luːkrətɪv] *adj* einträglich

ludicrous ['luːdɪkrəs] *adj* grotesk

lug [lʌg] *vt* schleppen

luggage ['lʌgɪdʒ] *n* Gepäck *nt*; **~ rack** *n* Gepäcknetz *nt*

lukewarm ['luːkwɔːm] *adj* lauwarm; (*indifferent*) lau

lull [lʌl] *n* Flaute *f* ♦ *vt* einlullen; (*calm*) beruhigen

lullaby ['lʌləbaɪ] *n* Schlaflied *nt*

lumbago [lʌm'beɪgəʊ] *n* Hexenschuß *m*

lumber ['lʌmbə*] *n* Plunder *m*; (*wood*) Holz *nt*; **~jack** *n* Holzfäller *m*

luminous ['luːmɪnəs] *adj* Leucht-

lump [lʌmp] *n* Klumpen *m*; (MED) Schwellung *f*; (*in breast*) Knoten *m*; (*of sugar*) Stück *nt* ♦ *vt* (*also:* **~ together**) zusammentun; (*judge together*) in einen Topf werfen; **~ sum** *n* Pauschalsumme *f*; **~y** *adj* klumpig

lunacy ['lu:nəsɪ] *n* Irrsinn *m*
lunar ['lu:nə*] *adj* Mond-
lunatic ['lu:nətɪk] *n* Wahnsinnige(r) *mf*
♦ *adj* wahnsinnig, irr
lunch [lʌntʃ] *n* Mittagessen *nt*
luncheon ['lʌntʃən] *n* Mittagessen *nt*; ~
meat *n* Frühstücksfleisch *nt*; ~ **voucher**
(*BRIT*) *n* Essensmarke *f*
lunchtime ['lʌntʃtaɪm] *n* Mittagszeit *f*
lung [lʌŋ] *n* Lunge *f*
lunge [lʌndʒ] *vi* (*also:* ~ *forward*)
(los)stürzen; **to ~ at** sich stürzen auf +*acc*
lurch [lɜ:tʃ] *vi* taumeln; (*NAUT*) schlingern
♦ *n* Ruck *m*; (*NAUT*) Schlingern *nt*; **to**
leave sb in the ~ jdn im Stich lassen
lure [ljʊə*] *n* Köder *m*; (*fig*) Lockung *f*
♦ *vt* (ver)locken
lurid ['ljʊərɪd] *adj* (*shocking*) grausig,
widerlich; (*colour*) grell
lurk [lɜ:k] *vi* lauern
luscious ['lʌʃəs] *adj* köstlich
lush [lʌʃ] *adj* satt; (*vegetation*) üppig
lust [lʌst] *n* (*sensation*) Wollust *f*; (*greed*)
Gier *f* ♦ *vi*: **to ~ after** gieren nach
lustre ['lʌstə*] (*US* **luster**) *n* Glanz *m*
lusty ['lʌstɪ] *adj* gesund und munter
Luxembourg ['lʌksəmbɜ:g] *n*
Luxemburg *nt*
luxuriant [lʌg'zjʊərɪənt] *adj* üppig
luxurious [lʌg'zjʊərɪəs] *adj* luxuriös,
Luxus-
luxury ['lʌkʃərɪ] *n* Luxus *m* ♦ *cpd* Luxus-
lying ['laɪɪŋ] *n* Lügen *nt* ♦ *adj* verlogen
lynx [lɪŋks] *n* Luchs *m*
lyric ['lɪrɪk] *n* Lyrik *f* ♦ *adj* lyrisch; ~**s** *pl*
(*words for song*) (Lied)text *m*; ~**al** *adj*
lyrisch, gefühlvoll

M m

m *abbr* = **metre**; **mile**; **million**
M.A. *n abbr* = **Master of Arts**
mac [mæk] (*BRIT*: *inf*) *n* Regenmantel *m*
macaroni [mækə'rəʊnɪ] *n* Makkaroni *pl*
machine [mə'ʃi:n] *n* Maschine *f* ♦ *vt*
(*dress etc*) mit der Maschine nähen; ~
gun *n* Maschinengewehr *nt*; ~ **language**
n (*COMPUT*) Maschinensprache *f*; ~**ry**

[mə'ʃi:nərɪ] *n* Maschinerie *f*
macho ['mætʃəʊ] *adj* macho
mackerel ['mækrəl] *n* Makrele *f*
mackintosh ['mækɪntɒʃ] (*BRIT*) *n*
Regenmantel *m*
mad [mæd] *adj* verrückt; (*dog*) tollwütig;
(*angry*) wütend; ~ **about** (*fond of*)
verrückt nach, versessen auf +*acc*
madam ['mædəm] *n* gnädige Frau *f*
madden ['mædn] *vt* verrückt machen;
(*make angry*) ärgern
made [meɪd] *pt, pp of* **make**
Madeira [mə'dɪərə] *n* (*GEOG*) Madeira *nt*;
(*wine*) Madeira *m*
made-to-measure ['meɪdtə'meʒə*]
(*BRIT*) *adj* Maß-
madly ['mædlɪ] *adv* wahnsinnig
madman ['mædmən] (*irreg*) *n*
Verrückte(r) *m*, Irre(r) *m*
madness ['mædnəs] *n* Wahnsinn *m*
Madrid [mə'drɪd] *n* Madrid *nt*
magazine ['mægəzi:n] *n* Zeitschrift *f*; (*in*
gun) Magazin *nt*
maggot ['mægət] *n* Made *f*
magic ['mædʒɪk] *n* Zauberei *f*, Magie *f*;
(*fig*) Zauber *m* ♦ *adj* magisch, Zauber-;
~**al** *adj* magisch; ~**ian** [mə'dʒɪʃən] *n*
Zauberer *m*
magistrate ['mædʒɪstreɪt] *n*
(Friedens)richter *m*
magnanimous [mæg'nænɪməs] *adj*
großmütig
magnesium [mæg'ni:zɪəm] *n* Magnesium
nt
magnet ['mægnɪt] *n* Magnet *m*; ~**ic**
[mæg'netɪk] *adj* magnetisch; ~**ic tape** *n*
Magnetband *nt*; ~**ism** *n* Magnetismus *m*;
(*fig*) Ausstrahlungskraft *f*
magnificent [mæg'nɪfɪsənt] *adj*
großartig
magnify ['mægnɪfaɪ] *vt* vergrößern; ~**ing**
glass *n* Lupe *f*
magnitude ['mægnɪtju:d] *n* (*size*) Größe
f; (*importance*) Ausmaß *nt*
magpie ['mægpaɪ] *n* Elster *f*
mahogany [mə'hɒgənɪ] *n* Mahagoni *nt*
♦ *cpd* Mahagoni-
maid [meɪd] *n* Dienstmädchen *nt*; **old ~**
alte Jungfer *f*

maiden ['meɪdn] n Maid f ♦ adj (flight, speech) Jungfern-

mail [meɪl] n Post f ♦ vt aufgeben; ~ box (US) n Briefkasten m; ~ing list n Anschreibeliste f; ~ order n Bestellung f durch die Post; ~ order firm n Versandhaus nt

maim [meɪm] vt verstümmeln

main [meɪn] adj hauptsächlich, Haupt- ♦ n (pipe) Hauptleitung f; the ~s npl (ELEC) das Stromnetz; **in the** ~ im großen und ganzen; ~frame n (COMPUT) Großrechner m; ~land n Festland nt; ~ly adv hauptsächlich; ~ road n Hauptstraße f, ~stay n (fig) Hauptstütze f; ~stream n Hauptrichtung f

maintain [meɪn'teɪn] vt (machine, roads) instand halten; (support) unterhalten; (keep up) aufrechterhalten; (claim) behaupten; (innocence) beteuern

maintenance ['meɪntənəns] n (TECH) Wartung f, (of family) Unterhalt m

maize [meɪz] n Mais m

majestic [mə'dʒestɪk] adj majestätisch

majesty ['mædʒɪstɪ] n Majestät f

major ['meɪdʒə*] n Major m ♦ adj (MUS) Dur; (more important) Haupt-; (bigger) größer

Majorca [mə'jɔːkə] n Mallorca nt

majority [mə'dʒɒrɪtɪ] n Mehrheit f; (JUR) Volljährigkeit f

make [meɪk] (pt, pp **made**) vt machen; (appoint) ernennen (zu); (cause to do sth) veranlassen; (reach) erreichen; (in time) schaffen; (earn) verdienen ♦ n Marke f; **to** ~ **sth happen** etw geschehen lassen; **to** ~ **it** es schaffen; **what time do you** ~ **it?** wie spät hast du es?; **to** ~ **do with** auskommen mit; ~ **for** vi gehen/fahren nach; ~ **out** vt (write out) ausstellen; (understand) verstehen; (write: cheque) ausstellen; ~ **up** vt machen; (face) schminken; (quarrel) beilegen; (story etc) erfinden ♦ vi sich versöhnen; ~ **up for** vt wiedergutmachen; (COMM) vergüten; ~**believe** n Phantasie f, ~**r** n (COMM) Hersteller m; ~**shift** adj behelfsmäßig, Not-; ~**-up** n Schminke f, Make-up nt; ~**-up remover** n Make-up-Entferner m

making ['meɪkɪŋ] n: **in the** ~ im Entstehen; **to have the** ~**s of** das Zeug haben zu

malaise [mæ'leɪz] n Unbehagen nt

malaria [mə'lɛərɪə] n Malaria f

Malaysia [mə'leɪzɪə] n Malaysia nt

male [meɪl] n (animal) Männchen nt ♦ adj männlich

malevolent [mə'levələnt] adj übelwollend

malfunction [mæl'fʌŋkʃən] n (MED) Funktionsstörung f, (of machine) Defekt m

malice ['mælɪs] n Bosheit f

malicious [mə'lɪʃəs] adj böswillig, gehässig

malign [mə'laɪn] vt verleumden ♦ adj böse

malignant [mə'lɪgnənt] adj bösartig

mall [mɔːl] n (also: shopping ~) Einkaufszentrum nt

malleable ['mælɪəbl] adj formbar

mallet ['mælɪt] n Holzhammer m

malnutrition ['mælnju'trɪʃən] n Unterernährung f

malpractice ['mæl'præktɪs] n Amtsvergehen nt

malt [mɔːlt] n Malz nt

Malta ['mɔːltə] n Malta nt; **Maltese** [mɔːl'tiːz] adj inv maltesisch ♦ n inv Malteser(in) m(f)

maltreat [mæl'triːt] vt mißhandeln

mammal ['mæməl] n Säugetier nt

mammoth ['mæməθ] n Mammut nt ♦ adj Mammut-

man [mæn] (pl **men**) n Mann m; (human race) der Mensch, die Menschen pl ♦ vt bemannen; **an old** ~ ein alter Mann, ein Greis m; ~ **and wife** Mann und Frau

manage ['mænɪdʒ] vi zurechtkommen ♦ vt (control) führen, leiten; (cope with) fertigwerden mit; ~**able** adj (person, animal) fügsam; (object) handlich; ~**ment** n (control) Führung f, Leitung f; (directors) Management nt; ~**r** n Geschäftsführer m; ~**ress** [mænɪdʒə'res] n Geschäftsführerin f, ~**rial** [mænə'dʒɪərɪəl] adj (post) leitend; (problem etc) Management-

managing ['mænɪdʒɪŋ] adj: ~ **director**

Betriebsleiter *m*

mandarin ['mændərin] *n (fruit)*
Mandarine *f*

mandatory ['mændətəri] *adj*
obligatorisch

mane [mein] *n* Mähne *f*

maneuver [mə'nu:və*] *(US)*
= **manoeuvre**

manfully ['mænfuli] *adv* mannhaft

mangle ['mæŋgl] *vt* verstümmeln ♦ *n*
Mangel *f*

mango ['mæŋgəu] *(pl ~es) n*
Mango(pflaume) *f*

mangy ['meindʒi] *adj (dog)* räudig

manhandle ['mænhændl] *vt* grob
behandeln

manhole ['mænhəul] *n* (Straßen)schacht
m

manhood ['mænhud] *n* Mannesalter *nt*;
(manliness) Männlichkeit *f*

man-hour ['mæn'auə*] *n* Arbeitsstunde *f*

manhunt ['mænhʌnt] *n* Fahndung *f*

mania ['meiniə] *n* Manie *f*; **~c** ['meiniæk]
n Wahnsinnige(r) *mf*

manic ['mænik] *adj (behaviour, activity)*
hektisch

manicure ['mænikjuə*] *n* Maniküre *f*; **~
set** *n* Necessaire *nt*

manifest ['mænifest] *vt* offenbaren ♦ *adj*
offenkundig; **~ation** [mænife'steiʃən] *n*
(sign) Anzeichen *nt*

manifesto [mæni'festəu] *n* Manifest *nt*

manipulate [mə'nipjuleit] *vt* handhaben;
(fig) manipulieren

mankind [mæn'kaind] *n* Menschheit *f*

manly ['mænli] *adj* männlich; mannhaft

man-made ['mæn'meid] *adj (fibre)*
künstlich

manner ['mænə*] *n* Art *f*, Weise *f*; **~s** *npl*
(behaviour) Manieren *pl*; **in a ~ of
speaking** sozusagen; **~ism** *n (of person)*
Angewohnheit *f*; *(of style)* Maniertheit *f*

manoeuvre [mə'nu:və*] *(US* **maneuver)**
vt, vi manövrieren ♦ *n (MIL)* Feldzug *m*;
(general) Manöver *nt*, Schachzug *m*

manor ['mænə*] *n* Landgut *nt*; **~ house**
n Herrenhaus *nt*

manpower ['mænpauə*] *n* Arbeitskräfte
pl

mansion ['mænʃən] *n* Villa *f*

manslaughter ['mænslɔ:tə*] *n* Totschlag
m

mantelpiece ['mæntlpi:s] *n* Kaminsims
m

manual ['mænjuəl] *adj* manuell, Hand-
♦ *n* Handbuch *nt*

manufacture [mænju'fæktʃə*] *vt*
herstellen ♦ *n* Herstellung *f*; **~r** *n*
Hersteller *m*

manure [mə'njuə*] *n* Dünger *m*

manuscript ['mænjuskript] *n*
Manuskript *nt*

Manx [mæŋks] *adj* der Insel Man

many ['meni] *adj, pron* viele; **a great ~**
sehr viele; **~ a time** oft

map [mæp] *n* (Land)karte *f*, *(of town)*
Stadtplan *m* ♦ *vt* eine Karte machen von;
~ out *vt (fig)* ausarbeiten

maple ['meipl] *n* Ahorn *m*

mar [ma:*] *vt* verderben

marathon ['mærəθən] *n (SPORT)*
Marathonlauf *m*; *(fig)* Marathon *m*

marauder [mə'rɔ:də*] *n* Plünderer *m*

marble ['ma:bl] *n* Marmor *m*; *(for game)*
Murmel *f*

March [ma:tʃ] *n* März *m*

march [ma:tʃ] *vi* marschieren ♦ *n*
Marsch *m*

mare [meə*] *n* Stute *f*

margarine [ma:dʒə'ri:n] *n* Margarine *f*

margin ['ma:dʒin] *n* Rand *m*; *(extra
amount)* Spielraum *m*; *(COMM)* Spanne *f*;
~al *adj (note)* Rand-; *(difference etc)*
geringfügig; **~al (seat)** *n (POL)* Wahlkreis,
*der nur mit knapper Mehrheit gehalten
wird*

marigold ['mærigəuld] *n* Ringelblume *f*

marijuana [mæri'wa:nə] *n* Marihuana *nt*

marina [mə'ri:nə] *n* Yachthafen *m*

marinate ['mærineit] *vt* marinieren

marine [mə'ri:n] *adj* Meeres-, See- ♦ *n*
(MIL) Marineinfanterist *m*

marital ['mæritl] *adj* ehelich, Ehe-; **~
status** *n* Familienstand *m*

maritime ['mæritaim] *adj* See-

mark [ma:k] *n (coin)* Mark *f*; *(spot)* Fleck
m; *(scar)* Kratzer *m*; *(sign)* Zeichen *nt*;
(target) Ziel *nt*; *(SCH)* Note *f* ♦ *vt (make ~*

on) Flecken/Kratzer machen auf +acc; (*indicate*) markieren; (*exam*) korrigieren; **to ~ time** (*also fig*) auf der Stelle treten; **~ out** vt bestimmen; (*area*) abstecken; **~ed** adj deutlich; **~er** n (*in book*) (Lese)zeichen nt; (*on road*) Schild nt

market ['mɑ:kɪt] n Markt m; (*stock ~*) Börse f ♦ vt (COMM: *new product*) auf den Markt bringen; (*sell*) vertreiben; **~ garden** (BRIT) n Handelsgärtnerei f; **~ing** n Marketing nt; **~ research** n Marktforschung f; **~ value** n Marktwert m

marksman ['mɑ:ksmən] (*irreg*) n Scharfschütze m

marmalade ['mɑ:məleɪd] n Orangenmarmelade f

maroon [mə'ru:n] vt aussetzen ♦ adj (*colour*) dunkelrot

marquee [mɑ:'ki:] n große(s) Zelt nt

marriage ['mærɪdʒ] n Ehe f; (*wedding*) Heirat f; **~ bureau** n Heiratsinstitut nt; **~ certificate** n Heiratsurkunde f

married ['mærɪd] adj (*person*) verheiratet; (*couple, life*) Ehe-

marrow ['mærəu] n (Knochen)mark nt; (*vegetable*) Kürbis m

marry ['mærɪ] vt (*join*) trauen; (*take as husband, wife*) heiraten ♦ vi (*also: get married*) heiraten

Mars [mɑ:z] n (*planet*) Mars m

marsh [mɑ:ʃ] n Sumpf m

marshal ['mɑ:ʃəl] n (US) Bezirkspolizeichef m ♦ vt (an)ordnen, arrangieren

marshy ['mɑ:ʃɪ] adj sumpfig

martial ['mɑ:ʃəl] adj kriegerisch; **~ law** n Kriegsrecht nt

martyr ['mɑ:tə*] n (*also fig*) Märtyrer(in) m(f) ♦ vt zum Märtyrer machen; **~dom** n Martyrium nt

marvel ['mɑ:vəl] n Wunder nt ♦ vi: **to ~ (at)** sich wundern (über +acc); **~lous** (US **~ous**) adj wunderbar

Marxist ['mɑ:ksɪst] n Marxist(in) m(f)

marzipan ['mɑ:zɪpæn] n Marzipan nt

mascara [mæs'kɑ:rə] n Wimperntusche f

mascot ['mæskət] n Maskottchen nt

masculine ['mæskjulɪn] adj männlich

mash [mæʃ] n Brei m; **~ed potatoes**

npl Kartoffelbrei m or -püree nt

mask [mɑ:sk] n (*also fig*) Maske f ♦ vt maskieren, verdecken

mason ['meɪsn] n (*stone~*) Steinmetz m; (*free~*) Freimaurer m; **~ic** [mə'sɒnɪk] adj Freimaurer-; **~ry** n Mauerwerk nt

masquerade [mæskə'reɪd] n Maskerade f ♦ vi: **to ~ as** sich ausgeben als

mass [mæs] n Masse f; (*greater part*) Mehrheit f; (REL) Messe f ♦ vi sich sammeln; **the ~es** npl (*people*) die Masse(n) f(pl)

massacre ['mæsəkə*] n Blutbad nt ♦ vt niedermetzeln, massakrieren

massage ['mæsɑ:ʒ] n Massage f ♦ vt massieren

massive ['mæsɪv] adj gewaltig, massiv

mass media npl Massenmedien pl

mass production n Massenproduktion f

mast [mɑ:st] n Mast m

master ['mɑ:stə*] n Herr m; (NAUT) Kapitän m; (*teacher*) Lehrer m; (*artist*) Meister m ♦ vt meistern; (*language etc*) beherrschen; **~ly** adj meisterhaft; **~mind** n Kapazität f ♦ vt geschickt lenken; **M~ of Arts** n Magister m der philosophischen; **M~ of Science** n Magister m der naturwissenschaftlichen Fakultät; **~piece** n Meisterwerk nt; **~ plan** n kluge(r) Plan m; **~y** n Können nt

masturbate ['mæstəbeɪt] vi masturbieren, onanieren

mat [mæt] n Matte f; (*for table*) Untersetzer m ♦ adj = **matt(t)**

match [mætʃ] n Streichholz nt; (*sth corresponding*) Pendant nt; (SPORT) Wettkampf m; (*ball games*) Spiel nt ♦ vt (*be like, suit*) passen zu; (*equal*) gleichkommen +dat ♦ vi zusammenpassen; **it's a good ~ (for)** es paßt gut (zu); **~box** n Streichholzschachtel f; **~ing** adj passend

mate [meɪt] n (*companion*) Kamerad m; (*spouse*) Lebensgefährte m; (*of animal*) Weibchen nt/Männchen nt; (NAUT) Schiffsoffizier m ♦ vi (*animals*) sich paaren ♦ vt paaren

material [mə'tɪərɪəl] n Material nt; (*for*

book, cloth) Stoff m ♦ adj (*important*)
wesentlich; (*damage*) Sach-; (*comforts etc*)
materiell; ~s npl (*for building etc*)
Materialien pl; ~istic [-'lıstık] adj
materialistisch; ~ize vi sich
verwirklichen, zustande kommen
maternal [mə'tɜ:nl] adj mütterlich,
Mutter-
maternity [mə'tɜ:nıtı] adj (*dress*)
Umstands-; (*benefit*) Wochen-; ~ **hospital**
n Entbindungsheim nt
math [mæθ] (*US*) n = **maths**
mathematical [mæθə'mætıkl] adj
mathematisch
mathematics [mæθə'mætıks] n
Mathematik f
maths [mæθs] (*US* **math**) n Mathe f
matinée ['mætıneı] n Matinee f
mating call ['meıtıŋ-] n Lockruf m
matrices ['meıtrısi:z] npl of **matrix**
matriculation [mətrıkju'leıʃən] n
Immatrikulation f
matrimonial [mætrı'məunıəl] adj
ehelich, Ehe-
matrimony ['mætrımənı] n Ehestand m
matrix ['meıtrıks] (*pl* **matrices**) n
Matrize f; (*GEOL etc*) Matrix f
matron ['meıtrən] n (*MED*) Oberin f; (*SCH*)
Hausmutter f; ~**ly** adj matronenhaft
mat(t) [mæt] adj (*paint*) matt
matted ['mætıd] adj verfilzt
matter ['mætə*] n (*substance*) Materie f;
(*affair*) Angelegenheit f ♦ vi darauf
ankommen; **no** ~ **how/what** egal wie/
was; **what is the** ~? was ist los?; **as a** ~
of course selbstverständlich; **as a** ~ **of
fact** eigentlich; **it doesn't** ~ es macht
nichts; ~**-of-fact** adj sachlich, nüchtern
mattress ['mætrəs] n Matratze f
mature [mə'tjuə*] adj reif ♦ vi reif
werden
maturity [mə'tjuərıtı] n Reife f
maudlin ['mɔ:dlın] adj gefühlsduselig
maul [mɔ:l] vt übel zurichten
maxima ['mæksımə] npl of **maximum**
maximum ['mæksıməm] (*pl* **maxima**)
adj Höchst-, Maximal- ♦ n Maximum nt
May [meı] n Mai m
may [meı] (*conditional* **might**) vi (*be*

possible) können; (*have permission*)
dürfen; **he** ~ **come** er kommt vielleicht
maybe ['meıbi:] adv vielleicht
May Day n der 1. Mai
mayhem ['meıhem] n Chaos nt; (*US*)
Körperverletzung f
mayonnaise [meıə'neız] n Mayonnaise f
mayor [mɛə*] n Bürgermeister m; ~**ess**
n (*wife*) (die) Frau f Bürgermeister; (*lady*
~) Bürgermeisterin f
maypole ['meıpəul] n Maibaum m
maze [meız] n Irrgarten m; (*fig*)
Wirrwarr nt
M.D. abbr = **Doctor of Medicine**

<hr>

KEYWORD

<hr>

me [mi:] pron **1** (*direct*) mich; **it's me** ich
bin's
2 (*indirect*) mir; **give them to me** gib sie
mir
3 (*after prep:* +*acc*) mich; (: +*dat*) mir;
with/without me mit mir/ohne mich

<hr>

meadow ['medəu] n Wiese f
meagre ['mi:gə*] (*US* **meager**) adj
dürftig, spärlich
meal [mi:l] n Essen nt, Mahlzeit f; (*grain*)
Schrotmehl nt; **to have a** ~ essen (gehen);
~**time** n Essenszeit f
mean [mi:n] (*pt, pp* **meant**) adj (*stingy*)
geizig; (*spiteful*) gemein; (*average*)
durchschnittlich, Durchschnitts- ♦ vt
(*signify*) bedeuten; (*intend*) vorhaben,
beabsichtigen ♦ n (*average*) Durchschnitt
m; ~**s** npl (*wherewithal*) Mittel pl; (*wealth*)
Vermögen nt; **do you** ~ **me?** meinst du
mich?; **do you** ~ **it?** meinst du das ernst?;
what do you ~? was willst du damit
sagen?; **to be** ~**t for sb/sth** für jdn/etw
bestimmt sein; **by** ~**s of** durch; **by all** ~**s**
selbstverständlich; **by no** ~**s** keineswegs
meander [mı'ændə*] vi sich schlängeln
meaning ['mi:nıŋ] n Bedeutung f; (*of life*)
Sinn m; ~**ful** adj bedeutungsvoll; (*life*)
sinnvoll; ~**less** adj sinnlos
meanness ['mi:nnəs] n (*stinginess*) Geiz
m; (*spitefulness*) Gemeinheit f
meant [ment] pt, pp of **mean**
meantime ['mi:n'taım] adv inzwischen

meanwhile ['miːnwaıl] *adv* inzwischen

measles ['miːzlz] *n* Masern *pl*

measly ['miːzlı] (*inf*) *adj* poplig

measure ['meʒə*] *vt, vi* messen ♦ *n* Maß *nt*; (*step*) Maßnahme *f*; **~d** *adj* (*slow*) gemessen; **~ments** *npl* Maße *pl*

meat [miːt] *n* Fleisch *nt*; **cold ~** Aufschnitt *m*; **~ ball** *n* Fleischkloß *m*; **~ pie** *n* Fleischpastete *f*; **~y** *adj* fleischig; (*fig*) gehaltvoll

Mecca ['mekə] *n* Mekka *nt* (*also fig*)

mechanic [mı'kænık] *n* Mechaniker *m*; **~al** *adj* mechanisch; **~s** *n* Mechanik *f* ♦ *npl* Technik *f*

mechanism ['mekənızəm] *n* Mechanismus *m*

mechanize ['mekənaız] *vt* mechanisieren

medal ['medl] *n* Medaille *f*; (*decoration*) Orden *m*; **~list** (*US* **~ist**) *n* Medaillengewinner(in) *m(f)*

meddle ['medl] *vi*: **to ~ (in)** sich einmischen (in +*acc*); **to ~ with sth** sich an etw *dat* zu schaffen machen

media ['miːdıə] *npl* Medien *pl*

mediaeval [medı'iːvəl] *adj* = **medieval**

median ['miːdıən] (*US*) *n* (*also*: **~ strip**) Mittelstreifen *m*

mediate ['miːdıeıt] *vi* vermitteln

mediator ['miːdıeıtə*] *n* Vermittler *m*

Medicaid ['medıkeıd] (®: *US*) *n* *medizinisches Versorgungsprogramm für Sozialschwache*

medical ['medıkəl] *adj* medizinisch; Medizin-; ärztlich ♦ *n* (ärztliche) Untersuchung *f*

Medicare ['medıkɛə*] (*US*) *n* *staatliche Krankenversicherung besonders für Ältere*

medicated ['medıkeıtıd] *adj* medizinisch

medication [medı'keıʃən] *n* (*drugs etc*) Medikamente *pl*

medicinal [me'dısınl] *adj* medizinisch, Heil-

medicine ['medsın] *n* Medizin *f*; (*drugs*) Arznei *f*

medieval [medı'iːvəl] *adj* mittelalterlich

mediocre [miːdı'əʊkə*] *adj* mittelmäßig

mediocrity [miːdı'ɒkrıtı] *n* Mittelmäßigkeit *f*

meditate ['medıteıt] *vi* meditieren; **to ~ (on sth)** (über etw *acc*) nachdenken

meditation [medı'teıʃən] *n* Nachsinnen *nt*; Meditation *f*

Mediterranean [medıtə'reınıən] *adj* Mittelmeer-; (*person*) südländisch; **the ~ (Sea)** das Mittelmeer

medium ['miːdıəm] *adj* mittlere(r, s) Mittel-, mittel- ♦ *n* Mitte *f*; (*means*) Mittel *nt*; (*person*) Medium *nt*; **happy ~** goldener Mittelweg; **~ wave** *n* Mittelwelle *f*

medley ['medlı] *n* Gemisch *nt*

meek [miːk] *adj* sanft(mütig); (*pej*) duckmäuserisch

meet [miːt] (*pt, pp* **met**) *vt* (*encounter*) treffen, begegnen +*dat*; (*by arrangement*) sich treffen mit; (*difficulties*) stoßen auf +*acc*; (*become acquainted with*) kennenlernen; (*fetch*) abholen; (*join*) zusammentreffen mit; (*satisfy*) entsprechen +*dat* ♦ *vi* sich treffen; (*become acquainted*) sich kennenlernen; **~ with** *vt* (*problems*) stoßen auf +*acc*; (*US*: *people*) zusammentreffen mit; **~ing** *n* Treffen *nt*; (*business meeting*) Besprechung *f*; (*of committee*) Sitzung *f*; (*assembly*) Versammlung *f*

megabyte ['megəbaıt] *n* (*COMPUT*) Megabyte *nt*

megaphone ['megəfəʊn] *n* Megaphon *nt*

melancholy ['melənkəlı] *adj* (*person*) melancholisch; (*sight, event*) traurig

mellow ['meləʊ] *adj* mild, weich; (*fruit*) reif; (*fig*) gesetzt ♦ *vi* reif werden

melodious [mı'ləʊdıəs] *adj* wohlklingend

melody ['melədı] *n* Melodie *f*

melon ['melən] *n* Melone *f*

melt [melt] *vi* schmelzen; (*anger*) verfliegen ♦ *vt* schmelzen; **~ away** *vi* dahinschmelzen; **~ down** *vt* einschmelzen; **~down** *n* (*in nuclear reactor*) Kernschmelze *f*; **~ing point** *n* Schmelzpunkt *m*; **~ing pot** *n* (*fig*) Schmelztiegel *m*

member ['membə*] *n* Mitglied *nt*; (*of tribe, species*) Angehörige(r) *m*; (*ANAT*) Glied *nt*; **M~ of Parliament** (*BRIT*) *n* Parlamentsmitglied *nt*; **M~ of the European Parliament** (*BRIT*) *n* Mitglied *nt* des Europäischen Parlaments; **~ship** *n*

Mitgliedschaft *f*; **to seek ~ship of** einen
Antrag auf Mitgliedschaft stellen; **~ship
card** *n* Mitgliedskarte *f*
memento [mə'mentəu] *n* Andenken *nt*
memo ['meməu] *n* Mitteilung *f*
memoirs ['memwɑ:z] *npl* Memoiren *pl*
memorable ['memərəbl] *adj* denkwürdig
memoranda [memə'rændə] *npl of*
memorandum
memorandum [memə'rændəm] (*pl*
memoranda) *n* Mitteilung *f*
memorial [mɪ'mɔ:rɪəl] *n* Denkmal *nt*
♦ *adj* Gedenk-
memorize ['meməraɪz] *vt* sich einprägen
memory ['memərɪ] *n* Gedächtnis *nt*; (*of
computer*) Speicher *m*; (*sth recalled*)
Erinnerung *f*
men [men] *pl of* **man** ♦ *n* (*human race*)
die Menschen *pl*
menace ['menɪs] *n* Drohung *f*; Gefahr *f*
♦ *vt* bedrohen
menacing ['menɪsɪŋ] *adj* drohend
menagerie [mɪ'nædʒərɪ] *n* Tierschau *f*
mend [mend] *vt* reparieren, flicken ♦ *vi*
(ver)heilen ♦ *n* ausgebesserte Stelle *f*; **on
the ~** auf dem Wege der Besserung; **~ing**
n (*articles*) Flickarbeit *f*
menial ['mi:nɪəl] *adj* niedrig
meningitis [menɪn'dʒaɪtɪs] *n*
Hirnhautentzündung *f*, Meningitis *f*
menopause ['menəupɔ:z] *n*
Wechseljahre *pl*, Menopause *f*
menstruation [menstru'eɪʃən] *n*
Menstruation *f*
mental ['mentl] *adj* geistig, Geistes-;
(*arithmetic*) Kopf-; (*hospital*) Nerven-;
(*cruelty*) seelisch; (*inf: abnormal*)
verrückt; **~ity** [men'tælɪtɪ] *n* Mentalität *f*
menthol ['menθɒl] *n* Menthol *nt*
mention ['menʃən] *n* Erwähnung *f* ♦ *vt*
erwähnen; **don't ~ it!** bitte (sehr), gern
geschehen
mentor ['mentɔ:*] *n* Mentor *m*
menu ['menju:] *n* Speisekarte *f*
MEP *n abbr* = **Member of the
European Parliament**
mercenary ['mɜ:sɪnərɪ] *adj* (*person*)
geldgierig; (*MIL*) Söldner- ♦ *n* Söldner *m*
merchandise ['mɜ:tʃəndaɪz] *n*

(Handels)ware *f*
merchant ['mɜ:tʃənt] *n* Kaufmann *m*; **~
navy** (*US* ~ **marine**) *n* Handelsmarine *f*
merciful ['mɜ:sɪful] *adj* gnädig
merciless ['mɜ:sɪləs] *adj* erbarmungslos
mercury ['mɜ:kjʊrɪ] *n* Quecksilber *nt*
mercy ['mɜ:sɪ] *n* Erbarmen *nt*; Gnade *f*;
at the ~ of ausgeliefert +*dat*
mere [mɪə*] *adj* bloß
merely *adv* bloß
merge [mɜ:dʒ] *vt* verbinden; (*COMM*)
fusionieren ♦ *vi* verschmelzen; (*roads*)
zusammenlaufen; (*COMM*) fusionieren; **~r**
n (*COMM*) Fusion *f*
meringue [mə'ræŋ] *n* Baiser *nt*
merit ['merɪt] *n* Verdienst *nt*; (*advantage*)
Vorzug *m* ♦ *vt* verdienen
mermaid ['mɜ:meɪd] *n* Wassernixe *f*
merry ['merɪ] *adj* fröhlich; **~-go-round** *n*
Karussell *nt*
mesh [meʃ] *n* Masche *f* ♦ *vi* (*gears*)
ineinandergreifen
mesmerize ['mezməraɪz] *vt*
hypnotisieren; (*fig*) faszinieren
mess [mes] *n* Unordnung *f*; (*dirt*)
Schmutz *m*; (*trouble*) Schwierigkeiten *pl*;
(*MIL*) Messe *f*; **~ about or around** *vi*
(*play the fool*) herumalbern; (*do nothing
in particular*) herumgammeln; **~ about
or around with** *vt fus* (*tinker with*)
herummurksen an +*dat*; **~ up** *vt*
verpfuschen; (*make untidy*) in Unordnung
bringen
message ['mesɪdʒ] *n* Mitteilung *f*; **to get
the ~** kapieren
messenger ['mesɪndʒə*] *n* Bote *m*
Messrs ['mesəz] *abbr* (*on letters*) die
Herren
messy ['mesɪ] *adj* schmutzig; (*untidy*)
unordentlich
met [met] *pt, pp of* **meet**
metabolism [me'tæbəlɪzəm] *n*
Stoffwechsel *m*
metal ['metl] *n* Metall *nt*
metaphor ['metəfɔ:*] *n* Metapher *f*
mete [mi:t] : **to ~ out** *vt* austeilen
meteorology [mi:tɪə'rɒlədʒɪ] *n*
Meteorologie *f*
meter ['mi:tə*] *n* Zähler *m*; (*US*) = **metre**

method ['meθəd] n Methode f; **~ical**
[mɪ'θɒdɪkəl] adj methodisch; **M~ist**
['meθədɪst] adj methodistisch ♦ n
Methodist(in) m(f); **~ology** [meθə'dɒlədʒɪ]
n Methodik f

meths [meθs] (BRIT) n = **methylated
spirit(s)**

methylated spirit(s) ['meθɪleɪtɪd
'spɪrɪt(s)] (BRIT) n(pl) (Brenn)spiritus m

meticulous [mɪ'tɪkjʊləs] adj (über)genau

metre ['miːtə*] (US **meter**) n Meter m or
nt

metric ['metrɪk] adj (also: ~al) metrisch

metropolitan [metrə'pɒlɪtən] adj der
Großstadt; **the M~ Police** (BRIT) n die
Londoner Polizei

mettle ['metl] n Mut m

mew [mjuː] vi (cat) miauen

mews [mjuːz] n: ~ **cottage** (BRIT) n
ehemaliges Kutscherhäuschen

Mexican ['meksɪkən] adj mexikanisch
♦ n Mexikaner(in) m(f)

Mexico ['meksɪkəʊ] n Mexiko nt; ~ **City**
n Mexiko City f

miaow [miː'aʊ] vi miauen

mice [maɪs] pl of **mouse**

micro ['maɪkrəʊ] n (also: ~computer)
Mikrocomputer m

microchip ['maɪkrəʊtʃɪp] n Mikrochip m

microcosm ['maɪkrəʊkɒzəm] n
Mikrokosmos m

microfilm ['maɪkrəʊfɪlm] n Mikrofilm m
♦ vt auf Mikrofilm aufnehmen

microphone ['maɪkrəfəʊn] n Mikrophon
nt

microprocessor ['maɪkrəʊ'prəʊsesə*] n
Mikroprozessor m

microscope ['maɪkrəskəʊp] n Mikroskop
nt

microwave ['maɪkrəʊweɪv] n (also: ~
oven) Mikrowelle(nherd nt) f

mid [mɪd] adj: **in ~ afternoon** am
Nachmittag; **in ~ air** in der Luft; **in ~
May** Mitte Mai

midday ['mɪd'deɪ] n Mittag m

middle ['mɪdl] n Mitte f; (waist) Taille f
♦ adj mittlere(r, s), Mittel-; **in the ~ of**
mitten in +dat; **~-aged** adj mittleren
Alters; **the M~ Ages** npl das Mittelalter;

~-class adj Mittelstands-; **the M~ East**
n der Nahe Osten; **~man** (irreg) n (COMM)
Zwischenhändler m; ~ **name** n zweiter
Vorname m; ~ **weight** n (BOXING)
Mittelgewicht nt

middling ['mɪdlɪŋ] adj mittelmäßig

midge [mɪdʒ] n Mücke f

midget ['mɪdʒɪt] n Liliputaner(in) m(f)

Midlands ['mɪdləndz] npl Midlands pl

midnight ['mɪdnaɪt] n Mitternacht f

midriff ['mɪdrɪf] n Taille f

midst [mɪdst] n: **in the ~ of** (persons)
mitten unter +dat; (things) mitten in +dat

midsummer ['mɪd'sʌmə*] n
Hochsommer m

midway ['mɪd'weɪ] adv auf halbem Wege
♦ adj Mittel-

midweek ['mɪd'wiːk] adv in der Mitte
der Woche

midwife ['mɪdwaɪf] (irreg) n Hebamme f;
~ry [mɪd'wɪfərɪ] n Geburtshilfe f

midwinter ['mɪd'wɪntə*] n tiefste(r)
Winter m

might [maɪt] vi see **may** ♦ n Macht f,
Kraft f; **I ~ come** ich komme vielleicht;
~y adj, adv mächtig

migraine ['miːgreɪn] n Migräne f

migrant ['maɪgrənt] adj Wander-; (bird)
Zug-

migrate [maɪ'greɪt] vi (ab)wandern;
(birds) (fort)ziehen

migration [maɪ'greɪʃən] n Wanderung f,
Zug m

mike [maɪk] n = **microphone**

Milan [mɪ'læn] n Mailand nt

mild [maɪld] adj mild; (medicine, interest)
leicht; (person) sanft

mildew ['mɪldjuː] n (on plants) Mehltau
m; (on food) Schimmel m

mildly ['maɪldlɪ] adv leicht; **to put it ~**
gelinde gesagt

mile [maɪl] n Meile f; **~age** n Meilenzahl
f

mileometer n = **milometer**

milestone n (also fig) Meilenstein m

military ['mɪlɪtərɪ] adj militärisch,
Militär-, Wehr-

militate ['mɪlɪteɪt] vi: **to ~ against**
entgegenwirken +dat

militia [mɪˈlɪʃə] *n* Miliz *f*

milk [mɪlk] *n* Milch *f* ♦ *vt* (*also fig*) melken; ~ **chocolate** *n* Milchschokolade *f*; **~man** (*irreg*) *n* Milchmann *m*; ~ **shake** *n* Milchmixgetränk *nt*; **~y** *adj* milchig; **M~y Way** *n* Milchstraße *f*

mill [mɪl] *n* Mühle *f*; (*factory*) Fabrik *f* ♦ *vt* mahlen ♦ *vi* (*move around*) umherlaufen

millennia [mɪˈlenɪə] *npl of* **millennium**

millennium [mɪˈlenɪəm] (*pl* **~s** *or* **millennia**) *n* Jahrtausend *nt*

miller [ˈmɪlə*] *n* Müller *m*

millet [ˈmɪlɪt] *n* Hirse *f*

milligram(me) [ˈmɪlɪgræm] *n* Milligramm *nt*

millimetre [ˈmɪlimiːtə*] (*US* **millimeter**) *n* Millimeter *m*

million [ˈmɪljən] *n* Million *f*; **a ~ times** tausendmal; **~aire** [mɪljəˈnɛə*] *n* Millionär(in) *m(f)*

millstone [ˈmɪlstəun] *n* Mühlstein *m*

milometer [maɪˈlɒmɪtə*] *n* ≈ Kilometerzähler *m*

mime [maɪm] *n* Pantomime *f* ♦ *vt, vi* mimen

mimic [ˈmɪmɪk] *n* Mimiker *m* ♦ *vt, vi* nachahmen; **~ry** [ˈmɪmɪkrɪ] *n* Nachahmung *f*; (*BIOL*) Mimikry *f*

min. *abbr* = **minutes; minimum**

minaret [mɪnəˈret] *n* Minarett *nt*

mince [mɪns] *vt* (zer)hacken ♦ *vi* (*walk*) trippeln ♦ *n* (*meat*) Hackfleisch *nt*; **~meat** *n* süße Pastetenfüllung *f*; ~ **pie** *n* gefüllte (süße) Pastete *f*; **~r** *n* Fleischwolf *m*

mind [maɪnd] *n* Verstand *m*, Geist *m*; (*opinion*) Meinung *f* ♦ *vt* aufpassen auf +*acc*; (*object to*) etwas haben gegen; **on my ~** auf dem Herzen; **to my ~** meiner Meinung nach; **to be out of one's ~** wahnsinnig sein; **to bear** *or* **keep in ~** bedenken; **to change one's ~** es sich *dat* anders überlegen; **to make up one's ~** sich entschließen; **I don't ~** das macht mir nichts aus; **~ you, ...** allerdings ...; **never ~!** macht nichts!; **"~ the step"** „Vorsicht Stufe"; ~ **your own business** kümmern Sie sich um Ihre eigenen

Angelegenheiten; **~er** *n* Aufpasser(in) *m(f)*; **~ful** *adj*: **~ful of** achtsam auf +*acc*; **~less** *adj* sinnlos

mine[1] [maɪn] *n* (*coal~*) Bergwerk *nt*; (*MIL*) Mine *f* ♦ *vt* abbauen; (*MIL*) verminen

mine[2] [maɪn] *pron* meine(r, s); **that book is ~** das Buch gehört mir; **a friend of ~** ein Freund von mir

minefield [ˈmaɪnfiːld] *n* Minenfeld *nt*

miner [ˈmaɪnə*] *n* Bergarbeiter *m*

mineral [ˈmɪnərəl] *adj* mineralisch, Mineral- ♦ *n* Mineral *nt*; **~s** *npl* (*BRIT: soft drinks*) alkoholfreie Getränke *pl*; ~ **water** *n* Mineralwasser *nt*

minesweeper [ˈmaɪnswiːpə*] *n* Minensuchboot *nt*

mingle [ˈmɪŋgl] *vi*: **to ~ (with)** sich mischen (unter +*acc*)

miniature [ˈmɪnɪtʃə*] *adj* Miniatur- ♦ *n* Miniatur *f*

minibus [ˈmɪnɪbʌs] *n* Kleinbus *m*

minim [ˈmɪnɪm] *n* halbe Note *f*

minimal [ˈmɪnɪməl] *adj* minimal

minimize [ˈmɪnɪmaɪz] *vt* auf das Mindestmaß beschränken

minimum [ˈmɪnɪməm] (*pl* **minima**) *n* Minimum *nt* ♦ *adj* Mindest-

mining [ˈmaɪnɪŋ] *n* Bergbau *m* ♦ *adj* Bergbau-, Berg-

miniskirt [ˈmɪnɪskɜːt] *n* Minirock *m*

minister [ˈmɪnɪstə*] *n* (*BRIT: POL*) Minister *m*; (*ECCL*) Pfarrer *m* ♦ *vi*: **to ~ to sb/sb's needs** sich um jdn kümmern; **~ial** [mɪnɪsˈtɪərɪəl] *adj* ministeriell, Minister-

ministry [ˈmɪnɪstrɪ] *n* (*BRIT: POL*) Ministerium *nt*; (*ECCL: office*) geistliche(s) Amt *nt*

mink [mɪŋk] *n* Nerz *m*

minnow [ˈmɪnəu] *n* Elritze *f*

minor [ˈmaɪnə*] *adj* kleiner; (*operation*) leicht; (*problem, poet*) unbedeutend; (*MUS*) Moll ♦ *n* (*BRIT: under 18*) Minderjährige(r) *mf*

minority [maɪˈnɒrɪtɪ] *n* Minderheit *f*

mint [mɪnt] *n* Minze *f*; (*sweet*) Pfefferminzbonbon *nt* ♦ *vt* (*coins*) prägen; **the (Royal** (*BRIT*) *or* **US** (*US*)) **M~** die Münzanstalt; **in ~ condition** in tadellosem Zustand

minus ['maɪnəs] *n* Minuszeichen *nt*; (*amount*) Minusbetrag *m* ♦ *prep* minus, weniger

minuscule ['mɪnəskjuːl] *adj* winzig

minute¹ [maɪ'njuːt] *adj* winzig; (*detailed*) minuziös

minute² ['mɪnɪt] *n* Minute *f*; (*moment*) Augenblick *m*; ~s *npl* (*of meeting etc*) Protokoll *nt*

miracle ['mɪrəkl] *n* Wunder *nt*

miraculous [mɪ'rækjʊləs] *adj* wunderbar

mirage ['mɪrɑːʒ] *n* Fata Morgana *f*

mire ['maɪə*] *n* Morast *m*

mirror ['mɪrə*] *n* Spiegel *m* ♦ *vt* (wider)spiegeln

mirth [mɜːθ] *n* Heiterkeit *f*

misadventure [mɪsəd'ventʃə*] *n* Mißgeschick *nt*, Unfall *m*

misanthropist [mɪ'zænθrəpɪst] *n* Menschenfeind *m*

misapprehension ['mɪsæprɪ'henʃən] *n* Mißverständnis *nt*

misbehave ['mɪsbɪ'heɪv] *vi* sich schlecht benehmen

miscalculate ['mɪs'kælkjʊleɪt] *vt* falsch berechnen

miscarriage ['mɪskærɪdʒ] *n* (*MED*) Fehlgeburt *f*; ~ **of justice** Fehlurteil *nt*

miscellaneous [mɪsɪ'leɪnɪəs] *adj* verschieden

mischance [mɪs'tʃɑːns] *n* Mißgeschick *nt*

mischief ['mɪstʃɪf] *n* Unfug *m*

mischievous ['mɪstʃɪvəs] *adj* (*person*) durchtrieben; (*glance*) verschmitzt; (*rumour*) bösartig

misconception ['mɪskən'sepʃən] *n* fälschliche Annahme *f*

misconduct [mɪs'kɒndʌkt] *n* Vergehen *nt*; **professional** ~ Berufsvergehen *nt*

misconstrue ['mɪskən'struː] *vt* mißverstehen

misdeed [mɪs'diːd] *n* Untat *f*

misdemeanour [mɪsdɪ'miːnə*] *n* (*US* **misdemeanor**) *n* Vergehen *nt*

miser ['maɪzə*] *n* Geizhals *m*

miserable ['mɪzərəbl] *adj* (*unhappy*) unglücklich; (*headache, weather*) fürchterlich; (*poor*) elend; (*contemptible*) erbärmlich

miserly ['maɪzəlɪ] *adj* geizig

misery ['mɪzərɪ] *n* Elend *nt*, Qual *f*

misfire ['mɪs'faɪə*] *vi* (*gun*) versagen; (*engine*) fehlzünden; (*plan*) fehlgehen

misfit ['mɪsfɪt] *n* Außenseiter *m*

misfortune [mɪs'fɔːtʃən] *n* Unglück *nt*

misgiving(s) [mɪs'gɪvɪŋ(z)] *n(pl)* Bedenken *pl*

misguided ['mɪs'gaɪdɪd] *adj* fehlgeleitet; (*opinions*) irrig

mishandle ['mɪs'hændl] *vt* falsch handhaben

mishap ['mɪshæp] *n* Mißgeschick *nt*

misinform ['mɪsɪn'fɔːm] *vt* falsch unterrichten

misinterpret ['mɪsɪn'tɜːprɪt] *vt* falsch auffassen

misjudge ['mɪs'dʒʌdʒ] *vt* falsch beurteilen

mislay [mɪs'leɪ] (*irreg: like* lay) *vt* verlegen

mislead [mɪs'liːd] (*irreg: like* lead) *vt* (*deceive*) irreführen; ~**ing** *adj* irreführend

mismanage ['mɪs'mænɪdʒ] *vt* schlecht verwalten

misnomer ['mɪs'nəʊmə*] *n* falsche Bezeichnung *f*

misogynist [mɪ'sɒdʒɪnɪst] *n* Weiberfeind *m*

misplace ['mɪs'pleɪs] *vt* verlegen

misprint ['mɪsprɪnt] *n* Druckfehler *m*

Miss [mɪs] *n* Fräulein *nt*

miss [mɪs] *vt* (*fail to hit, catch*) verfehlen; (*not notice*) verpassen; (*be too late*) versäumen, verpassen; (*omit*) auslassen; (*regret the absence of*) vermissen ♦ *vi* fehlen ♦ *n* (*shot*) Fehlschuß *m*; (*failure*) Fehlschlag *m*; **I** ~ **you** du fehlst mir; ~ **out** *vt* auslassen

missal ['mɪsəl] *n* Meßbuch *nt*

misshapen [mɪs'ʃeɪpən] *adj* mißgestaltet

missile ['mɪsaɪl] *n* Rakete *f*

missing ['mɪsɪŋ] *adj* (*person*) vermißt; (*thing*) fehlend; **to be** ~ fehlen

mission ['mɪʃən] *n* (*work*) Auftrag *m*; (*people*) Delegation *f*; (*REL*) Mission *f*; ~**ary** *n* Missionar(in) *m(f)*

misspell ['mɪs'spel] (*irreg: like* spell) *vt* falsch schreiben

misspent ['mɪs'spent] *adj* (*youth*)
vergeudet

mist [mɪst] *n* Dunst *m*, Nebel *m* ♦ *vi*
(*also:* ~ *over*, ~ *up*) sich trüben; (*BRIT:
windows*) sich beschlagen

mistake [mɪs'teɪk] (*irreg: like take*) *n*
Fehler *m* ♦ *vt* (*misunderstand*)
mißverstehen; (*mix up*): **to** ~ (**sth for
sth**) (etw mit etw) verwechseln; **to make
a ~** einen Fehler machen; **by** ~ aus
Versehen; **to** ~ **A for B** A mit B
verwechseln; **mistaken** *pp of* **mistake**
♦ *adj* (*idea*) falsch; **to be ~n** sich irren

mister ['mɪstə*] *n* (*inf*) Herr *m*; *see* **Mr**

mistletoe ['mɪsltəʊ] *n* Mistel *f*

mistook [mɪs'tʊk] *pt of* **mistake**

mistress ['mɪstrɪs] *n* (*teacher*) Lehrerin *f*;
(*in house*) Herrin *f*; (*lover*) Geliebte *f*; *see*
Mrs

mistrust ['mɪs'trʌst] *vt* mißtrauen +*dat*

misty ['mɪstɪ] *adj* neblig

misunderstand ['mɪsʌndə'stænd] (*irreg:
like* **understand**) *vt, vi* mißverstehen,
falsch verstehen; **~ing** *n* Mißverständnis
nt; (*disagreement*)
Meinungsverschiedenheit *f*

misuse [*n* 'mɪs'juːs, *vb* 'mɪs'juːz] *n*
falsche(r) Gebrauch *m* ♦ *vt* falsch
gebrauchen

mitigate ['mɪtɪgeɪt] *vt* mildern

mitt(en) ['mɪt(n)] *n* Fausthandschuh *m*

mix [mɪks] *vt* (*blend*) (ver)mischen ♦ *vi*
(*liquids*) sich (ver)mischen lassen; (*people:
get on*) sich vertragen; (: *associate*) Kontakt haben ♦ *n* (*mixture*) Mischung *f*; ~
up *vt* zusammenmischen; (*confuse*) verwechseln; **~ed** *adj* gemischt; **~ed-up** *adj*
durcheinander; **~er** *n* (*for food*) Mixer *m*;
~ture *n* Mischung *f*; **~-up** *n*
Durcheinander *nt*

mm *abbr* (= *millimetre(s)*) mm

moan [məʊn] *n* Stöhnen *nt*; (*complaint*)
Klage *f* ♦ *vi* stöhnen; (*complain*) maulen

moat [məʊt] *n* (Burg)graben *m*

mob [mɒb] *n* Mob *m*; (*the masses*) Pöbel
m ♦ *vt* (*star*) herfallen über +*acc*

mobile ['məʊbaɪl] *adj* beweglich; (*library
etc*) fahrbar ♦ *n* (*decoration*) Mobile *nt*; ~
home *n* Wohnwagen *m*; ~ **phone** *n* (*TEL*)

Mobiltelefon *nt*

mobility [məʊ'bɪlɪtɪ] *n* Beweglichkeit *f*

mobilize ['məʊbɪlaɪz] *vt* mobilisieren

moccasin ['mɒkəsɪn] *n* Mokassin *m*

mock [mɒk] *vt* verspotten; (*defy*) trotzen
+*dat* ♦ *adj* Schein-; **~ery** *n* Spott *m*;
(*person*) Gespött *nt*

mod [mɒd] *adj see* **convenience**

mode [məʊd] *n* (Art *f* und) Weise *f*

model ['mɒdl] *n* Modell *nt*; (*example*)
Vorbild *nt*; (*in fashion*) Mannequin *nt*
♦ *adj* (*railway*) Modell-; (*perfect*) Muster-;
vorbildlich ♦ *vt* (*make*) bilden; (*clothes*)
vorführen ♦ *vi* als Mannequin arbeiten

modem ['məʊdem] *n* (*COMPUT*) Modem *nt*

moderate [*adj, n* 'mɒdərət, *vb* 'mɒdəreɪt]
adj gemäßigt ♦ *n* (*POL*) Gemäßigte(r) *mf*
♦ *vi* sich mäßigen ♦ *vt* mäßigen

moderation [mɒdə'reɪʃən] *n* Mäßigung *f*;
in ~ mit Maßen

modern ['mɒdən] *adj* modern; (*history,
languages*) neuere(r, s); (*Greek etc*) Neu-;
~ize *vt* modernisieren

modest ['mɒdɪst] *adj* bescheiden; **~y** *n*
Bescheidenheit *f*

modicum ['mɒdɪkəm] *n* bißchen *nt*

modification [mɒdɪfɪ'keɪʃən] *n* (Ab)ände-
rung *f*

modify ['mɒdɪfaɪ] *vt* abändern

module ['mɒdjuːl] *n* (*component*)
(Bau)element *nt*; (*SPACE*) (Raum)kapsel *f*

mogul ['məʊgəl] *n* (*fig*) Mogul *m*

mohair ['məʊheə*] *n* Mohair *m*

moist [mɔɪst] *adj* feucht; **~en** ['mɔɪsn] *vt*
befeuchten; **~ure** ['mɔɪstʃə*] *n*
Feuchtigkeit *f*; **~urizer** ['mɔɪstʃəraɪzə*] *n*
Feuchtigkeitscreme *f*

molar ['məʊlə*] *n* Backenzahn *m*

molasses [mə'læsɪz] *n* Melasse *f*

mold [məʊld] (*US*) = **mould**

mole [məʊl] *n* (*spot*) Leberfleck *m*;
(*animal*) Maulwurf *m*; (*pier*) Mole *f*

molest [məʊ'lest] *vt* belästigen

mollycoddle ['mɒlɪkɒdl] *vt* verhätscheln

molt [məʊlt] (*US*) *vi* = **moult**

molten ['məʊltən] *adj* geschmolzen

mom [mɒm] (*US*) *n* = **mum**

moment ['məʊmənt] *n* Moment *m*,
Augenblick *m*; (*importance*) Tragweite *f*;

at the ~ im Augenblick; **~ary** *adj* kurz;
~ous [məʊˈmentəs] *adj* folgenschwer
momentum [məʊˈmentəm] *n* Schwung
m; **to gather ~** in Fahrt kommen
mommy [ˈmɒmɪ] (*US*) *n* = **mummy**
Monaco [ˈmɒnəkəʊ] *n* Monaco *nt*
monarch [ˈmɒnək] *n* Herrscher(in) *m(f)*;
~y *n* Monarchie *f*
monastery [ˈmɒnəstrɪ] *n* Kloster *nt*
monastic [məˈnæstɪk] *adj* klösterlich,
Kloster-
Monday [ˈmʌndeɪ] *n* Montag *m*
monetary [ˈmʌnɪtərɪ] *adj* Geld-; (*of
currency*) Währungs-
money [ˈmʌnɪ] *n* Geld *nt*; **to make ~**
Geld verdienen; **~lender** *n* Geldverleiher
m; **~ order** *n* Postanweisung *f*; **~
spinner** (*inf*) *n* Verkaufsschlager *m* (*inf*)
mongol [ˈmɒŋgəl] *n* (*MED*) mongoloide(s)
Kind *nt* ♦ *adj* mongolisch; (*MED*)
mongoloid
mongrel [ˈmʌŋgrəl] *n*
Promenadenmischung *f*
monitor [ˈmɒnɪtə*] *n* (*SCH*) Klassenordner
m; (*television* ~) Monitor *m* ♦ *vt*
(*broadcasts*) abhören; (*control*)
überwachen
monk [mʌŋk] *n* Mönch *m*
monkey [ˈmʌŋkɪ] *n* Affe *m*; **~ nut** (*BRIT*)
n Erdnuß *f*; **~ wrench** *n* (*TECH*)
Engländer *m*, Franzose *m*
monochrome [ˈmɒnəkrəʊm] *adj*
schwarz-weiß
monopolize [məˈnɒpəlaɪz] *vt*
beherrschen
monopoly [məˈnɒpəlɪ] *n* Monopol *nt*
monosyllable [ˈmɒnəsɪləbl] *n*
einsilbige(s) Wort *nt*
monotone [ˈmɒnətəʊn] *n*
gleichbleibende(r) Ton(fall) *m*; **to speak
in a ~** monoton sprechen
monotonous [məˈnɒtənəs] *adj* eintönig
monotony [məˈnɒtənɪ] *n* Eintönigkeit *f*,
Monotonie *f*
monsoon [mɒnˈsuːn] *n* Monsun *m*
monster [ˈmɒnstə*] *n* Ungeheuer *nt*;
(*person*) Scheusal *nt*
monstrosity [mɒnsˈtrɒsɪtɪ] *n*
Ungeheuerlichkeit *f*; (*thing*) Monstrosität

f
monstrous [ˈmɒnstrəs] *adj* (*shocking*)
gräßlich, ungeheuerlich; (*huge*) riesig
month [mʌnθ] *n* Monat *m*; **~ly** *adj*
monatlich, Monats- ♦ *adv* einmal im
Monat ♦ *n* (*magazine*) Monatsschrift *f*
monument [ˈmɒnjʊmənt] *n* Denkmal *nt*;
~al [mɒnjʊˈmentl] *adj* (*huge*) gewaltig;
(*ignorance*) ungeheuer
moo [muː] *vi* muhen
mood [muːd] *n* Stimmung *f*, Laune *f*; **to
be in a good/bad ~** gute/schlechte
Laune haben; **~y** *adj* launisch
moon [muːn] *n* Mond *m*; **~light** *n*
Mondlicht *nt*; **~lighting** *n* Schwarzarbeit
f; **~lit** *adj* mondhell
moor [mʊə*] *n* Heide *f*, Hochmoor *nt* ♦ *vt*
(*ship*) festmachen, verankern ♦ *vi*
anlegen; **~ings** *npl* Liegeplatz *m*
moorland [ˈmʊələnd] *n* Heidemoor *nt*
moose [muːs] *n* Elch *m*
mop [mɒp] *n* Mop *m* ♦ *vt* (auf)wischen; **~
up** *vt* aufwischen
mope [məʊp] *vi* Trübsal blasen
moped [ˈməʊped] *n* Moped *nt*
moral [ˈmɒrəl] *adj* moralisch; (*values*)
sittlich; (*virtuous*) tugendhaft ♦ *n* Moral *f*;
~s *npl* (*ethics*) Moral *f*; **~e** [mɒˈrɑːl] *n*
Moral *f*; **~ity** [məˈrælɪtɪ] *n* Sittlichkeit *f*
morass [məˈræs] *n* Sumpf *m*
morbid [ˈmɔːbɪd] *adj* krankhaft; (*jokes*)
makaber

KEYWORD

more [mɔː*] *adj* (*greater in number etc*)
mehr; (*additional*) noch mehr; **do you
want (some) more tea?** möchten Sie
noch etwas Tee?; **I have no** *or* **I don't
have any more money** ich habe kein
Geld mehr

♦ *pron* (*greater amount*) mehr; (*further or
additional amount*) noch mehr; **is there
any more?** gibt es noch mehr?; (*left
over*) ist noch etwas da?; **there's no more** es
ist nichts mehr da

♦ *adv* mehr; **more dangerous/easily** *etc*
(**than**) gefährlicher/einfacher *etc* (als);
more and more immer mehr; **more and
more excited** immer aufgeregter; **more**

or less mehr oder weniger; **more than ever** mehr denn je; **more beautiful than ever** schöner denn je

moreover [mɔː'rəʊvə*] *adv* überdies
morgue [mɔːg] *n* Leichenschauhaus *nt*
moribund ['mɒrɪbʌnd] *adj* aussterbend
Mormon ['mɔːmən] *n* Mormone *m*, Mormonin *f*
morning ['mɔːnɪŋ] *n* Morgen *m*; **in the ~** am Morgen; **7 o'clock in the ~** 7 Uhr morgens
Morocco [mə'rɒkəʊ] *n* Marokko *nt*
moron ['mɔːrɒn] *n* Schwachsinnige(r) *mf*
morose [mə'rəʊs] *adj* mürrisch
morphine ['mɔːfiːn] *n* Morphium *nt*
Morse [mɔːs] *n* (*also*: **~ code**) Morsealphabet *nt*
morsel ['mɔːsl] *n* Bissen *m*
mortal ['mɔːtl] *adj* sterblich; (*deadly*) tödlich; (*very great*) Todes- ♦ *n* (*human being*) Sterbliche(r) *mf*; **~ity** [mɔː'tælɪtɪ] *n* Sterblichkeit *f*; (*death rate*) Sterblichkeitsziffer *f*
mortar ['mɔːtə*] *n* (*for building*) Mörtel *m*; (*bowl*) Mörser *m*; (MIL) Granatwerfer *m*
mortgage ['mɔːgɪdʒ] *n* Hypothek *f* ♦ *vt* hypothekarisch belasten; **~ company** *n* ≈ Bausparkasse *f*
mortify ['mɔːtɪfaɪ] *vt* beschämen
mortuary ['mɔːtjʊərɪ] *n* Leichenhalle *f*
mosaic [məʊ'zeɪɪk] *n* Mosaik *nt*
Moscow ['mɒskəʊ] *n* Moskau *nt*
Moslem ['mɒzləm] = **Muslim**
mosque [mɒsk] *n* Moschee *f*
mosquito [mɒs'kiːtəʊ] (*pl* **~es**) *n* Moskito *m*
moss [mɒs] *n* Moos *nt*
most [məʊst] *adj* meiste(r, s) ♦ *adv* am meisten; (*very*) höchst ♦ *n* das meiste, der größte Teil; (*people*) die meisten; **~ men** die meisten Männer; **at the (very) ~** allerhöchstens; **to make the ~ of** das Beste machen aus; **a ~ interesting book** ein höchst interessantes Buch; **~ly** *adv* größtenteils
MOT (BRIT) *n abbr* (= *Ministry of Transport*): **the ~ (test)** ≈ der TÜV
motel [məʊ'tel] *n* Motel *nt*

moth [mɒθ] *n* Nachtfalter *m*; (*wool-eating*) Motte *f*; **~ball** *n* Mottenkugel *f*
mother ['mʌðə*] *n* Mutter *f* ♦ *vt* bemuttern; **~hood** *n* Mutterschaft *f*; **~-in-law** *n* Schwiegermutter *f*; **~ly** *adj* mütterlich; **~-to-be** *n* werdende Mutter *f*; **~ tongue** *n* Muttersprache *f*
motif [məʊ'tiːf] *n* Motiv *nt*
motion ['məʊʃən] *n* Bewegung *f*; (*in meeting*) Antrag *m* ♦ *vt*, *vi*: **to ~ (to) sb** jdm winken, jdm zu verstehen geben; **~less** *adj* regungslos; **~ picture** *n* Film *m*
motivated ['məʊtɪveɪtɪd] *adj* motiviert
motivation [məʊtɪ'veɪʃən] *n* Motivierung *f*
motive ['məʊtɪv] *n* Motiv *nt*, Beweggrund *m* ♦ *adj* treibend
motley ['mɒtlɪ] *adj* bunt
motor ['məʊtə*] *n* Motor *m*; (BRIT: *inf*: *vehicle*) Auto *nt* ♦ *adj* Motor-; **~bike** *n* Motorrad *nt*; **~boat** *n* Motorboot *nt*; **~car** (BRIT) *n* Auto *nt*; **~cycle** *n* Motorrad *nt*; **~cyclist** *n* Motorradfahrer(in) *m(f)*; **~ing** (BRIT) *n* Autofahren *nt* ♦ *adj* Auto-; **~ist** ['məʊtərɪst] *n* Autofahrer(in) *m(f)*; **~ racing** (BRIT) *n* Autorennen *nt*; **~ vehicle** *n* Kraftfahrzeug *nt*; **~way** (BRIT) *n* Autobahn *f*
mottled ['mɒtld] *adj* gesprenkelt
motto ['mɒtəʊ] (*pl* **~es**) *n* Motto *nt*
mould [məʊld] (US **mold**) *n* Form *f*; (*mildew*) Schimmel *m* ♦ *vt* (*also fig*) formen; **~er** *vi* (*decay*) vermodern; **~y** *adj* schimmelig
moult [məʊlt] (US **molt**) *vi* sich mausern
mound [maʊnd] *n* (Erd)hügel *m*
mount [maʊnt] *n* (liter: *hill*) Berg *m*; (*horse*) Pferd *nt*; (*for jewel etc*) Fassung *f* ♦ *vt* (*horse*) steigen auf +*acc*; (*put in setting*) fassen; (*exhibition*) veranstalten; (*attack*) unternehmen ♦ *vi* (*also*: **~ up**) sich häufen; (*on horse*) aufsitzen
mountain ['maʊntɪn] *n* Berg *m* ♦ *cpd* Berg-; **~ bike** *n* Mountain-Bike *nt*; **~eer** [maʊntɪ'nɪə*] *n* Bergsteiger(in) *m(f)*; **~eering** *n* Bergsteigen *nt*; **~ous** *adj* bergig; **~ rescue team** *n* Bergwacht *f*; **~side** *n* Berg(ab)hang *m*

mourn [mɔːn] *vt* betrauen, beklagen ♦ *vi*: **to ~ (for sb)** (um jdn) trauern; **~er** *n* Trauernde(r) *mf*; **~ful** *adj* traurig; **~ing** *n* (*grief*) Trauer *f* ♦ *cpd* (*dress*) Trauer-; **in ~ing** (*period etc*) in Trauer; (*dress*) in Trauerkleidung *f*

mouse [maʊs] (*pl* **mice**) *n* Maus *f*; **~trap** *n* Mausefalle *f*

mousse [muːs] *n* (*COOK*) Creme *f*; (*cosmetic*) Schaumfestiger *m*

moustache [məs'tɑːʃ] *n* Schnurrbart *m*

mousy ['maʊsɪ] *adj* (*colour*) mausgrau; (*person*) schüchtern

mouth [maʊθ, *pl* maʊðz] *n* Mund *m*; (*opening*) Öffnung *f*; (*of river*) Mündung *f*; **~ful** *n* Mundvoll *m*; **~ organ** *n* Mundharmonika *f*; **~piece** *n* Mundstück *nt*; (*fig*) Sprachrohr *nt*; **~wash** *n* Mundwasser *nt*; **~watering** *adj* lecker, appetitlich

movable ['muːvəbl] *adj* beweglich

move [muːv] *n* (*movement*) Bewegung *f*; (*in game*) Zug *m*; (*step*) Schritt *m*; (*of house*) Umzug *m* ♦ *vt* bewegen; (*people*) transportieren; (*in job*) versetzen; (*emotionally*) bewegen ♦ *vi* sich bewegen; (*vehicle, ship*) fahren; (*go to another house*) umziehen; **to get a ~ on** sich beeilen; **to ~ sb to do sth** jdn veranlassen, etw zu tun; **~ about** *or* **around** *vi* sich hin- und herbewegen; (*travel*) unterwegs sein; **~ along** *vi* weitergehen; (*cars*) weiterfahren; **~ away** *vi* weggehen; **~ back** *vi* zurückgehen; (*to the rear*) zurückweichen; **~ forward** *vi* vorwärtsgehen, sich vorwärtsbewegen ♦ *vt* vorschieben; (*time*) vorverlegen; **~ in** *vi* (*to house*) einziehen; (*troops*) einrücken; **~ on** *vi* weitergehen ♦ *vt* weitergehen lassen; (*troops*) abziehen; **~ over** *vi* zur Seite rücken; **~ up** *vi* aufsteigen; (*in job*) befördert werden ♦ *vt* nach oben bewegen; (*in job*) befördern

movement ['muːvmənt] *n* Bewegung *f*

movie ['muːvɪ] *n* Film *m*; **to go to the ~s** ins Kino gehen; **~ camera** *n* Filmkamera *f*

moving ['muːvɪŋ] *adj* beweglich; (*touching*) ergreifend

mow [məʊ] (*pt* **mowed**, *pp* **mowed** *or* **mown**) *vt* mähen; **~ down** *vt* (*fig*) niedermähen; **~er** *n* (*machine*) Mähmaschine *f*; (*lawn~er*) Rasenmäher *m*

mown [məʊn] *pp of* **mow**

MP *n abbr* = **Member of Parliament**

m.p.h. *abbr* = **miles per hour**

Mr ['mɪstə*] (*US* **Mr.**) *n* Herr *m*

Mrs ['mɪsɪz] (*US* **Mrs.**) *n* Frau *f*

Ms [mɪz] (*US* **Ms.**) *n* (= *Miss or Mrs*) Frau *f*

M.Sc. *n abbr* = **Master of Science**

much [mʌtʃ] *adj* viel ♦ *adv* sehr; viel ♦ *n* viel, eine Menge; **how ~ is it?** wieviel kostet das?; **too ~** zuviel; **it's not ~** es ist nicht viel; **as ~ as** sosehr, soviel; **however ~ he tries** sosehr er es auch versucht

muck [mʌk] *n* Mist *m*; (*fig*) Schmutz *m*; **~ about** *or* **around** (*inf*) *vi*: **to ~ about** *or* **around (with sth)** (an etw *dat*) herumalbern; **~ up** *vt* (*inf*: *ruin*) vermasseln; (*dirty*) dreckig machen; **~y** *adj* (*dirty*) dreckig

mucus ['mjuːkəs] *n* Schleim *m*

mud [mʌd] *n* Schlamm *m*

muddle ['mʌdl] *n* Durcheinander *nt* ♦ *vt* (*also:* **~ up**) durcheinanderbringen; **~ through** *vi* sich durchwursteln

muddy ['mʌdɪ] *adj* schlammig

mudguard ['mʌdgɑːd] *n* Schutzblech *nt*

mud-slinging ['mʌdslɪŋɪŋ] (*inf*) *n* Verleumdung *f*

muff [mʌf] *n* Muff *m* ♦ *vt* (*chance*) verpassen; (*lines*) verpatzen (*inf*)

muffin ['mʌfɪn] *n* süße(s) Teilchen *nt*

muffle ['mʌfl] *vt* (*sound*) dämpfen; (*wrap up*) einhüllen; **~d** *adj* gedämpft

muffler ['mʌflə*] (*US*) *n* (*AUT*) Schalldämpfer *m*

mug [mʌg] *n* (*cup*) Becher *m*; (*inf*: *face*) Visage *f*; (*: fool*) Trottel *m* ♦ *vt* überfallen und ausrauben; **~ging** *n* Überfall *m*

muggy ['mʌgɪ] *adj* (*weather*) schwül

mule [mjuːl] *n* Maulesel *m*

mull [mʌl] : **~ over** *vt* nachdenken über +*acc*

mulled [mʌld] *adj* (*wine*) Glüh-

multi- ['mʌltɪ] *prefix* Multi-, multi-
multicoloured ['mʌltɪ'kʌləd] (*US* **multicolored**) *adj* mehrfarbig
multi-level ['mʌltɪlevl] (*US*) *adj* = **multistorey**
multiple ['mʌltɪpl] *n* Vielfache(s) *nt* ♦ *adj* mehrfach; (*many*) mehrere; **~ sclerosis** *n* multiple Sklerose *f*
multiply ['mʌltɪplaɪ] *vt*: **to ~ (by)** multiplizieren (mit) ♦ *vi* (*BIOL*) sich vermehren
multistorey ['mʌltɪ'stɔːrɪ] (*BRIT*) *adj* (*building, car park*) mehrstöckig
multitude ['mʌltɪtjuːd] *n* Menge *f*
mum [mʌm] *n* (*BRIT: inf*) Mutti *f* ♦ *adj*: **to keep ~ (about)** den Mund halten (über +*acc*)
mumble ['mʌmbl] *vt, vi* murmeln ♦ *n* Gemurmel *nt*
mummy ['mʌmɪ] *n* (*dead body*) Mumie *f*; (*BRIT: inf*) Mami *f*
mumps [mʌmps] *n* Mumps *m*
munch [mʌntʃ] *vt, vi* mampfen
mundane ['mʌn'deɪn] *adj* banal
municipal [mjuː'nɪsɪpəl] *adj* städtisch, Stadt-; **~ity** [mjuː'nɪsɪ'pælɪtɪ] *n* Stadt *f* mit Selbstverwaltung
mural ['mjʊərəl] *n* Wandgemälde *nt*
murder ['mɜːdə*] *n* Mord *m* ♦ *vt* ermorden; **~er** *n* Mörder *m*; **~ous** *adj* Mord-; (*fig*) mörderisch
murky ['mɜːkɪ] *adj* finster
murmur ['mɜːmə*] *n* Murmeln *nt*; (*of water, wind*) Rauschen *nt* ♦ *vt, vi* murmeln
muscle ['mʌsl] *n* Muskel *m*; **~ in** *vi* mitmischen
muscular ['mʌskjʊlə*] *adj* Muskel-; (*strong*) muskulös
muse [mjuːz] *vi* (nach)sinnen
museum [mjuː'zɪəm] *n* Museum *nt*
mushroom ['mʌʃruːm] *n* Champignon *m*; Pilz *m* ♦ *vi* (*fig*) emporschießen
music ['mjuːzɪk] *n* Musik *f*; (*printed*) Noten *pl*; **~al** *adj* (*sound*) melodisch; (*person*) musikalisch ♦ *n* (*show*) Musical *nt*; **~al instrument** *n* Musikinstrument *nt*; **~ hall** (*BRIT*) *n* Varieté *nt*; **~ian** [mjuː'zɪʃən] *n* Musiker(in) *m(f)*

musk [mʌsk] *n* Moschus *m*
Muslim ['mʌzlɪm] *adj* moslemisch ♦ *n* Moslem *m*
muslin ['mʌzlɪn] *n* Musselin *m*
mussel ['mʌsl] *n* Miesmuschel *f*
must [mʌst] *vb aux* müssen; (*in negation*) dürfen ♦ *n* Muß *nt*; **the film is a ~** den Film muß man einfach gesehen haben
mustard ['mʌstəd] *n* Senf *m*
muster ['mʌstə*] *vt* (*MIL*) antreten lassen; (*courage*) zusammennehmen
mustn't ['mʌsnt] = **must not**
musty ['mʌstɪ] *adj* muffig
mute [mjuːt] *adj* stumm ♦ *n* (*person*) Stumme(r) *mf*; (*MUS*) Dämpfer *m*
muted ['mjuːtɪd] *adj* gedämpft
mutilate ['mjuːtɪleɪt] *vt* verstümmeln
mutiny ['mjuːtɪnɪ] *n* Meuterei *f* ♦ *vi* meutern
mutter ['mʌtə*] *vt, vi* murmeln
mutton ['mʌtn] *n* Hammelfleisch *nt*
mutual ['mjuːtjʊəl] *adj* gegenseitig; beiderseitig; **~ly** *adv* gegenseitig; für beide Seiten
muzzle ['mʌzl] *n* (*of animal*) Schnauze *f*; (*for animal*) Maulkorb *m*; (*of gun*) Mündung *f* ♦ *vt* einen Maulkorb anlegen +*dat*
my [maɪ] *adj* mein; **this is ~ car** das ist mein Auto; **I've washed ~ hair** ich habe mir die Haare gewaschen
myopic [maɪ'ɒpɪk] *adj* kurzsichtig
myriad ['mɪrɪəd] *n*: **a ~ of** (*people, things*) unzählige
myself [maɪ'self] *pron* mich *acc*; mir *dat*; (*emphatic*) selbst; *see also* **oneself**
mysterious [mɪs'tɪərɪəs] *adj* geheimnisvoll
mystery ['mɪstərɪ] *n* (*secret*) Geheimnis *nt*; (*sth difficult*) Rätsel *nt*
mystify ['mɪstɪfaɪ] *vt* ein Rätsel sein +*dat*; verblüffen
mystique [mɪs'tiːk] *n* geheimnisvolle Natur *f*
myth [mɪθ] *n* Mythos *m*; (*fig*) Erfindung *f*; **~ology** [mɪ'θɒlədʒɪ] *n* Mythologie *f*

N n

n/a *abbr* (= *not applicable*) nicht zutreffend

nab [næb] (*inf*) *vt* schnappen

nag [næg] *n* (*horse*) Gaul *m*; (*person*) Nörgler(in) *m(f)* ♦ *vt*, *vi*: **to ~ (at)** sb an jdm herumnörgeln; **~ging** *adj* (*doubt*) nagend ♦ *n* Nörgelei *f*

nail [neɪl] *n* Nagel *m* ♦ *vt* nageln; **to ~ sb down to doing sth** jdn darauf festnageln, etw zu tun; **~brush** *n* Nagelbürste *f*; **~file** *n* Nagelfeile *f*; **~ polish** *n* Nagellack *m*; **~ polish remover** *n* Nagellackentferner *m*; **~ scissors** *npl* Nagelschere *f*; **~ varnish** (*BRIT*) *n* = **nail polish**

naïve [naɪˈiːv] *adj* naiv

naked [ˈneɪkɪd] *adj* nackt

name [neɪm] *n* Name *m*; (*reputation*) Ruf *m* ♦ *vt* nennen; (*sth new*) benennen; (*appoint*) ernennen; **by ~** mit Namen; **I know him only by ~** ich kenne ihn nur dem Namen nach; **what's your ~?** wie heißen Sie?; **in the ~ of** im Namen +*gen*; (*for the sake of*) um +*gen* ...willen; **~less** *adj* namenlos; **~ly** *adv* nämlich; **~sake** *n* Namensvetter *m*

nanny [ˈnænɪ] *n* Kindermädchen *nt*

nap [næp] *n* (*sleep*) Nickerchen *nt*; (*on cloth*) Strich *m* ♦ *vi*: **to be caught ~ping** (*fig*) überrumpelt werden

nape [neɪp] *n* Nacken *m*

napkin [ˈnæpkɪn] *n* (*at table*) Serviette *f*; (*BRIT: for baby*) Windel *f*

nappy [ˈnæpɪ] (*BRIT*) *n* (*for baby*) Windel *f*; **~ liner** *n* Windeleinlage *f*; **~ rash** *n* wunde Stellen *pl*

narcissi [nɑːˈsɪsaɪ] *npl of* **narcissus**

narcissus [nɑːˈsɪsəs] *n* (*BOT*) Narzisse *f*

narcotic [nɑːˈkɒtɪk] *adj* betäubend ♦ *n* Betäubungsmittel *nt*

narrative [ˈnærətɪv] *n* Erzählung *f* ♦ *adj* erzählend

narrator [nəˈreɪtə*] *n* Erzähler(in) *m(f)*

narrow [ˈnærəʊ] *adj* eng, schmal; (*limited*) beschränkt ♦ *vi* sich verengen; **to have a ~ escape** mit knapper Not

davonkommen; **to ~ sth down to sth** etw auf etw *acc* einschränken; **~ly** *adv* (*miss*) knapp; (*escape*) mit knapper Not; **~-minded** *adj* engstirnig

nasty [ˈnɑːstɪ] *adj* ekelhaft, fies; (*business, wound*) schlimm

nation [ˈneɪʃən] *n* Nation *f*, Volk *nt*; **~al** [ˈnæʃənl] *adj* national, National-, Landes- ♦ *n* Staatsangehörige(r) *mf*; **~al dress** *n* Tracht *f*; **N~al Health Service** (*BRIT*) *n* Insurance (*BRIT*) *n* Sozialversicherung *f*; **~alism** [ˈnæʃnəlɪzəm] *n* Nationalismus *m*; **~alist** [ˈnæʃnəlɪst] *n* Nationalist(in) *m(f)* ♦ *adj* nationalistisch; **~ality** [næʃəˈnælɪtɪ] *n* Staatsangehörigkeit *f*; **~alize** [ˈnæʃnəlaɪz] *vt* verstaatlichen; **~ally** [ˈnæʃnəlɪ] *adv* national, auf Staatsebene; **~-wide** [ˈneɪʃənwaɪd] *adj*, *adv* allgemein, landesweit

native [ˈneɪtɪv] *n* (*born in*) Einheimische(r) *mf*; (*original inhabitant*) Eingeborene(r) *mf* ♦ *adj* (*coming from a certain place*) einheimisch; (*of the original inhabitants*) Eingeborenen-; (*belonging by birth*) heimatlich, Heimat-; (*inborn*) angeboren, natürlich; **a ~ of Germany** ein gebürtiger Deutscher; **a ~ speaker of French** ein französischer Muttersprachler; **N~ American** *n* Indianer(in) *m(f)*, Ureinwohner(in) Americas *m(f)*; **~ language** *n* Muttersprache *f*

Nativity [nəˈtɪvɪtɪ] *n*: **the ~** Christi Geburt *no art*

NATO [ˈneɪtəʊ] *n abbr* (= *North Atlantic Treaty Organization*) NATO *f*

natter [ˈnætə*] (*BRIT*; *inf*) *vi* quatschen ♦ *n* Gequatsche *nt*

natural [ˈnætʃrəl] *adj* natürlich; Natur-; (*inborn*) (an)geboren; **~ gas** *n* Erdgas *nt*; **~ist** *n* Naturkundler(in) *m(f)*; **~ize** *vt* (*foreigner*) einbürgern; (*plant etc*) einführen; **~ly** *adv* natürlich

nature [ˈneɪtʃə*] *n* Natur *f*; **by ~** von Natur (aus)

naught [nɔːt] *n* = **nought**

naughty [ˈnɔːtɪ] *adj* (*child*) unartig, ungezogen; (*action*) ungehörig

nausea ['nɔːsɪə] *n* (*sickness*) Übelkeit *f*; (*disgust*) Ekel *m*; **~te** ['nɔːsɪeɪt] *vt* anekeln

nautical ['nɔːtɪkəl] *adj* nautisch; See-; (*expression*) seemännisch

naval ['neɪvəl] *adj* Marine-, Flotten-; **~ officer** *n* Marineoffizier *m*

nave [neɪv] *n* Kirchen(haupt)schiff *nt*

navel ['neɪvəl] *n* Nabel *m*

navigate ['nævɪɡeɪt] *vi* navigieren

navigation [nævɪ'ɡeɪʃən] *n* Navigation *f*

navigator ['nævɪɡeɪtə*] *n* Steuermann *m*; (*AVIAT*) Navigator *m*; (*AUT*) Beifahrer(in) *m(f)*

navvy ['nævɪ] (*BRIT*) *n* Straßenarbeiter *m*

navy ['neɪvɪ] *n* (Kriegs)marine *f* ♦ *adj* marineblau

Nazi ['nɑːtsɪ] *n* Nazi *m*

NB *abbr* (= *nota bene*) NB

near [nɪə*] *adj* nah ♦ *adv* in der Nähe ♦ *prep* (*also*: **~ to**: *space*) in der Nähe +*gen*; (: *time*) um +*acc* ... herum ♦ *vt* sich nähern +*dat*; **a ~ miss** knapp daneben; **~by** *adj* nahe (gelegen) ♦ *adv* in der Nähe; **~ly** *adv* fast; **I ~ly fell** ich wäre fast gefallen; **~side** *n* (*AUT*) Beifahrerseite *f* ♦ *adj* auf der Beifahrerseite

near-sighted *adj* kurzsichtig

neat ['niːt] *adj* (*tidy*) ordentlich; (*solution*) sauber; (*pure*) pur; **~ly** *adv* (*tidily*) ordentlich

nebulous ['nebjʊləs] *adj* nebulös

necessarily ['nesɪsərɪlɪ] *adv* unbedingt

necessary ['nesɪsərɪ] *adj* notwendig, nötig; **he did all that was ~** er erledigte alles, was nötig war; **it is ~ to/that ...** man muß ...

necessitate [nɪ'sesɪteɪt] *vt* erforderlich machen

necessity [nɪ'sesɪtɪ] *n* (*need*) Not *f*; (*compulsion*) Notwendigkeit *f*; **necessities** *npl* (*things needed*) das Notwendigste

neck [nek] *n* Hals *m* ♦ *vi* (*inf*) knutschen; **~ and ~** Kopf an Kopf

necklace ['neklɪs] *n* Halskette *f*

neckline ['neklaɪn] *n* Ausschnitt *m*

necktie ['nektaɪ] (*US*) *n* Krawatte *f*

née [neɪ] *adj* geborene

need [niːd] *n* Bedürfnis *nt*; (*lack*) Mangel *m*; (*necessity*) Notwendigkeit *f*; (*poverty*) Not *f* ♦ *vt* brauchen; **I ~ to do it** ich muß es tun; **you don't ~ to go** du brauchst nicht zu gehen

needle ['niːdl] *n* Nadel *f* ♦ *vt* (*fig: inf*) ärgern

needless ['niːdlɪs] *adj* unnötig; **~ to say** natürlich

needlework ['niːdlwɜːk] *n* Handarbeit *f*

needn't ['niːdnt] = **need not**

needy ['niːdɪ] *adj* bedürftig

negation [nɪ'ɡeɪʃən] *n* Verneinung *f*

negative ['neɡətɪv] *n* (*PHOT*) Negativ *nt* ♦ *adj* negativ; (*answer*) abschlägig

neglect [nɪ'ɡlekt] *vt* vernachlässigen ♦ *n* Vernachlässigung *f*

negligee ['neɡlɪʒeɪ] *n* Negligé *nt*

negligence ['neɡlɪdʒəns] *n* Nachlässigkeit *f*

negligible ['neɡlɪdʒəbl] *adj* unbedeutend, geringfügig

negotiable [nɪ'ɡəʊʃɪəbl] *adj* (*cheque*) übertragbar, einlösbar

negotiate [nɪ'ɡəʊʃɪeɪt] *vi* verhandeln ♦ *vt* (*treaty*) abschließen; (*difficulty*) überwinden; (*corner*) nehmen; **negotiation** [nɪɡəʊʃɪ'eɪʃən] *n* Verhandlung *f*; **negotiator** *n* Unterhändler *m*

Negress ['niːɡres] *n* Negerin *f*

Negro ['niːɡrəʊ] *n* Neger *m* ♦ *adj* Neger-

neigh [neɪ] *vi* wiehern

neighbour ['neɪbə*] (*US* **neighbor**) *n* Nachbar(in) *m(f)*; **~hood** *n* Nachbarschaft *f*; Umgebung *f*; **~ing** *adj* benachbart, angrenzend; **~ly** *adj* (*person*, *attitude*) nachbarlich

neither ['naɪðə*] *adj*, *pron* keine(r, s) (von beiden) ♦ *conj*: **he can't do it, and ~ can I** er kann es nicht und ich auch nicht ♦ *adv*: **~ good nor bad** weder gut noch schlecht; **~ story is true** keine der beiden Geschichten stimmt

neon ['niːɔn] *n* Neon *nt*

nephew ['nefjuː] *n* Neffe *m*

nerve [nɜːv] *n* Nerv *m*; (*courage*) Mut *m*; (*impudence*) Frechheit *f*; **to have a fit of ~s** in Panik geraten; **~-racking** *adj* nervenaufreibend

nervous ['nɜːvəs] *adj* (*of the nerves*)
Nerven-; (*timid*) nervös, ängstlich; ~
breakdown *n* Nervenzusammenbruch
m; ~**ness** *n* Nervosität *f*
nest [nest] *n* Nest *nt* ♦ *vi* nisten; ~ **egg** *n*
(*fig*) Notgroschen *m*
nestle ['nesl] *vi* sich kuscheln
net [net] *n* Netz *nt* ♦ *adj* netto, Netto- ♦ *vt*
netto einnehmen; ~**ball** *n* Netzball *m*; ~
curtain *n* Store *m*
Netherlands ['neðələndz] *npl*: **the** ~ die
Niederlande *pl*
nett [net] *adj* = **net**
netting ['netɪŋ] *n* Netz(werk) *nt*
nettle ['netl] *n* Nessel *f*
network ['netwɜːk] *n* Netz *nt*
neurotic [njuə'rɒtɪk] *adj* neurotisch ♦ *n*
Neurotiker(in) *m(f)*
neuter ['njuːtə*] *adj* (*BIOL*) geschlechtslos;
(*GRAM*) sächlich ♦ *vt* kastrieren
neutral ['njuːtrəl] *adj* neutral ♦ *n* (*AUT*)
Leerlauf *m*; ~**ity** [njuː'trælɪtɪ] *n*
Neutralität *f*; ~**ize** *vt* (*fig*) ausgleichen
never ['nevə*] *adv* nie(mals); **I** ~ **went**
ich bin gar nicht gegangen; ~ **in my life**
nie im Leben; ~**-ending** *adj* endlos;
~**theless** [nevəðə'les] *adv* trotzdem,
dennoch
new [njuː] *adj* neu; **N~ Age** *adj* New-
Age-; ~**born** *adj* neugeboren; ~**comer**
['njuːkʌmə*] *n* Neuankömmling *m*; ~-
fangled (*pej*) *adj* neumodisch; ~**found**
adj neuentdeckt; ~**ly** *adv* frisch, neu;
~**ly-weds** *npl* Frischvermählte *pl*; ~
moon *n* Neumond *m*
news [njuːz] *n* Nachricht *f*; (*RAD, TV*)
Nachrichten *pl*; **a piece of** ~ eine
Nachricht; ~ **agency** *n*
Nachrichtenagentur *f*; ~**agent** (*BRIT*)
Zeitungshändler *m*; ~**caster** *n*
Nachrichtensprecher(in) *m(f)*; ~ **dealer**
(*US*) *n* = **newsagent**; ~ **flash** *n*
Kurzmeldung *f*; ~**letter** *n* Rundschreiben
nt; ~**paper** *n* Zeitung *f*; ~**print** *n*
Zeitungspapier *nt*; ~**reader** *n*
= **newscaster**; ~**reel** *n* Wochenschau *f*; ~
stand *n* Zeitungsstand *m*
newt [njuːt] *n* Wassermolch *m*
New Year *n* Neujahr *nt*; ~'**s Day** *n*

Neujahrstag *m*; ~'**s Eve** *n*
Silvester(abend *m*) *nt*
New York [-'jɔːk] *n* New York *nt*
New Zealand [-'ziːlənd] *n* Neuseeland
nt; ~**er** *n* Neuseeländer(in) *m(f)*
next [nekst] *adj* nächste(r, s) ♦ *adv* (*after*)
dann, darauf; (~ *time*) das nächstemal;
the ~ **day** am nächsten *or* folgenden Tag;
~ **time** das nächste Mal; ~ **year** nächstes
Jahr; ~ **door** *adv* nebenan ♦ *adj*
(*neighbour, flat*) von nebenan; ~ **of kin** *n*
nächste(r) Verwandte(r) *mf*; ~ **to** *prep*
neben; ~ **to nothing** so gut wie nichts
NHS *n abbr* = **National Health Service**
nib [nɪb] *n* Spitze *f*
nibble ['nɪbl] *vt* knabbern an +*dat*
nice [naɪs] *adj* (*person*) nett; (*thing*)
schön; (*subtle*) fein; ~**-looking** *adj*
gutaussehend; ~**ly** *adv* gut, nett; ~**ties**
['naɪsɪtɪz] *npl* Feinheiten *pl*
nick [nɪk] *n* Einkerbung *f* ♦ *vt* (*inf: steal*)
klauen; **in the** ~ **of time** gerade
rechtzeitig
nickel ['nɪkl] *n* Nickel *nt*; (*US*) Nickel *m* (*5*
cents)
nickname ['nɪkneɪm] *n* Spitzname *m* ♦ *vt*
taufen
niece [niːs] *n* Nichte *f*
Nigeria [naɪ'dʒɪərɪə] *n* Nigeria *nt*
niggling ['nɪglɪŋ] *adj* pedantisch; (*doubt,*
worry) quälend; (*detail*) kleinlich
night [naɪt] *n* Nacht *f*; (*evening*) Abend *m*;
the ~ **before last** vorletzte Nacht; **at** *or*
by ~ (*after midnight*) nachts; (*before*
midnight) abends; ~**cap** *n* (*drink*)
Schlummertrunk *m*; ~**club** *n* Nachtlokal
nt; ~**dress** *n* Nachthemd *nt*; ~**fall** *n*
Einbruch *m* der Nacht; ~ **gown** *n*
= **nightdress**; ~**ie** ['naɪtɪ] (*inf*) *n*
Nachthemd *nt*
nightingale ['naɪtɪŋgeɪl] *n* Nachtigall *f*
nightlife ['naɪtlaɪf] *n* Nachtleben *nt*
nightly ['naɪtlɪ] *adj, adv* jeden Abend;
jede Nacht
nightmare ['naɪtmeə*] *n* Alptraum *m*
night: ~ **porter** *n* Nachtportier *m*; ~
school *n* Abendschule *f*; ~ **shift** *n*
Nachtschicht *f*; ~**time** *n* Nacht *f*
nil [nɪl] *n* Null *f*

Nile [naɪl] *n*: **the ~** der Nil
nimble ['nɪmbl] *adj* beweglich
nine [naɪn] *num* neun; **~teen** *num* neunzehn; **~ty** *num* neunzig
ninth [naɪnθ] *adj* neunte(r, s)
nip [nɪp] *vt* kneifen ♦ *n* Kneifen *nt*
nipple ['nɪpl] *n* Brustwarze *f*
nippy ['nɪpɪ] (*inf*) *adj* (*person*) flink; (*BRIT*: *car*) flott; (: *cold*) frisch
nitrogen ['naɪtrədʒən] *n* Stickstoff *m*

KEYWORD

no [nəʊ] (*pl* **~es**) *adv* (*opposite of yes*) nein; **to answer no** (*to question*) mit Nein antworten; (*to request*) nein sagen; **no thank you** nein, danke
♦ *adj* (*not any*) kein(e); **I have no money/time** ich habe kein Geld/keine Zeit; **no smoking** Rauchen verboten
♦ *n* Nein *nt*; (*no vote*) Neinstimme *f*

nobility [nəʊ'bɪlɪtɪ] *n* Adel *m*
noble ['nəʊbl] *adj* (*rank*) adlig; (*splendid*) nobel, edel
nobody ['nəʊbədɪ] *pron* niemand, keiner
nocturnal [nɒk'tɜːnl] *adj* (*tour, visit*) nächtlich; (*animal*) Nacht-
nod [nɒd] *vi* nicken ♦ *vt* nicken mit ♦ *n* Nicken *nt*; **~ off** *vi* einnicken
noise [nɔɪz] *n* (*sound*) Geräusch *nt*; (*unpleasant, loud*) Lärm *m*
noisy ['nɔɪzɪ] *adj* laut; (*crowd*) lärmend
nominal ['nɒmɪnl] *adj* nominell
nominate ['nɒmɪneɪt] *vt* (*suggest*) vorschlagen; (*in election*) aufstellen; (*appoint*) ernennen
nomination [nɒmɪ'neɪʃən] *n* (*election*) Nominierung *f*; (*appointment*) Ernennung *f*
nominee [nɒmɪ'niː] *n* Kandidat(in) *m(f)*
non- [nɒn] *prefix* Nicht-, un-; **~-alcoholic** *adj* alkoholfrei; **~-aligned** *adj* bündnisfrei
nonchalant ['nɒnʃələnt] *adj* lässig
non-committal ['nɒnkə'mɪtl] *adj* (*reserved*) zurückhaltend; (*uncommitted*) unverbindlich
nondescript ['nɒndɪskrɪpt] *adj* mittelmäßig

none [nʌn] *adj, pron* kein(e, er, es) ♦ *adv*: **he's ~ the worse for it** es hat ihm nicht geschadet; **~ of you** keiner von euch; **I've ~ left** ich habe keinen mehr
nonentity [nɒ'nentɪtɪ] *n* Null *f* (*inf*)
nonetheless ['nʌnðə'les] *adv* nichtsdestoweniger
non-existent [nɒnɪg'zɪstənt] *adj* nicht vorhanden
non-fiction ['nɒn'fɪkʃən] *n* Sachbücher *pl*
nonplussed ['nɒn'plʌst] *adj* verdutzt
nonsense ['nɒnsəns] *n* Unsinn *m*
non: **~-smoker** *n* Nichtraucher(in) *m(f)*; **~-stick** *adj* (*pan, surface*) Teflon- ®; **~-stop** *adj* Nonstop-
noodles ['nuːdlz] *npl* Nudeln *pl*
nook [nʊk] *n* Winkel *m*; **~s and crannies** Ecken und Winkel
noon [nuːn] *n* (12 Uhr) Mittag *m*
no one ['nəʊwʌn] *pron* = **nobody**
noose [nuːs] *n* Schlinge *f*
nor [nɔː*] *conj* = **neither** ♦ *adv see* **neither**
norm [nɔːm] *n* (*convention*) Norm *f*; (*rule, requirement*) Vorschrift *f*
normal ['nɔːməl] *adj* normal; **~ly** *adv* normal; (*usually*) normalerweise
north [nɔːθ] *n* Norden *m* ♦ *adj* nördlich, Nord- ♦ *adv* nördlich, nach *or* im Norden; **N~ Africa** *n* Nordafrika *nt*; **~-east** *n* Nordosten *m*; **~erly** ['nɔːðəlɪ] *adj* nördlich; **~ern** ['nɔːðən] *adj* nördlich, Nord-; **N~ern Ireland** *n* Nordirland *nt*; **N~ Pole** *n* Nordpol *m*; **N~ Sea** *n* Nordsee *f*; **~ward(s)** ['nɔːθwəd(z)] *adv* nach Norden; **~-west** *n* Nordwesten *m*
Norway ['nɔːweɪ] *n* Norwegen *nt*
Norwegian [nɔː'wiːdʒən] *adj* norwegisch ♦ *n* Norweger(in) *m(f)*; (*LING*) Norwegisch *nt*
nose [nəʊz] *n* Nase *f* ♦ *vi*: **to ~ about** herumschnüffeln; **~bleed** *n* Nasenbluten *nt*; **~-dive** *n* Sturzflug *m*; **~y** *adj* = **nosy**
nostalgia [nɒs'tældʒɪə] *n* Nostalgie *f*; **nostalgic** *adj* nostalgisch
nostril ['nɒstrɪl] *n* Nasenloch *nt*
nosy ['nəʊzɪ] (*inf*) *adj* neugierig
not [nɒt] *adv* nicht; **he is ~** *or* **isn't here**

er ist nicht hier; **it's too late, isn't it?** es ist zu spät, oder *or* nicht wahr?; **~ yet/ now** noch nicht/nicht jetzt; *see also* **all; only**

notably ['nəʊtəblɪ] *adv* (*especially*) besonders; (*noticeably*) bemerkenswert

notary ['nəʊtərɪ] *n* Notar(in) *m(f)*

notch [nɒtʃ] *n* Kerbe *f*, Einschnitt *m*

note [nəʊt] *n* (*MUS*) Note *f*, Ton *m*; (*short letter*) Nachricht *f*; (*POL*) Note *f*; (*comment, attention*) Notiz *f*; (*of lecture etc*) Aufzeichnung *f*; (*bank~*) Schein *m*; (*fame*) Ruf *m* ♦ *vt* (*observe*) bemerken; (*write down*) notieren; **~book** *n* Notizbuch *nt*; **~d** ['nəʊtɪd] *adj* bekannt; **~pad** *n* Notizblock *m*; **~paper** *n* Briefpapier *nt*

nothing ['nʌθɪŋ] *n* nichts; **~ new/much** nichts Neues/nicht viel; **for ~** umsonst

notice ['nəʊtɪs] *n* (*announcement*) Bekanntmachung *f*; (*warning*) Ankündigung *f*; (*dismissal*) Kündigung *f* ♦ *vt* bemerken; **to take ~ of** beachten; **at short ~** kurzfristig; **until further ~** bis auf weiteres; **to hand in one's ~** kündigen; **~able** *adj* merklich; **~ board** *n* Anschlagtafel *f*

notify ['nəʊtɪfaɪ] *vt* benachrichtigen

notion ['nəʊʃən] *n* Idee *f*

notorious [nəʊ'tɔːrɪəs] *adj* berüchtigt

notwithstanding [nɒtwɪθ'stændɪŋ] *adv* trotzdem; **~ this** ungeachtet dessen

nought [nɔːt] *n* Null *f*

noun [naʊn] *n* Substantiv *nt*

nourish ['nʌrɪʃ] *vt* nähren; **~ing** *adj* nahrhaft; **~ment** *n* Nahrung *f*

novel ['nɒvəl] *n* Roman *m* ♦ *adj* neu(artig); **~ist** *n* Schriftsteller(in) *m(f)*; **~ty** *n* Neuheit *f*

November [nəʊ'vembə*] *n* November *m*

novice ['nɒvɪs] *n* Neuling *m*; (*ECCL*) Novize *m*

now [naʊ] *adv* jetzt; **right ~** jetzt, gerade; **by ~** inzwischen; **just ~** gerade; **~ and then, ~ and again** ab und zu, manchmal; **from ~ on** von jetzt an; **~adays** ['naʊədeɪz] *adv* heutzutage

nowhere ['nəʊwɛə*] *adv* nirgends

nozzle ['nɒzl] *n* Düse *f*

nubile ['njuːbaɪl] *adj* (*woman*) gut entwickelt

nuclear ['njuːklɪə*] *adj* (*energy etc*) Atom-, Kern-

nuclei ['njuːklɪaɪ] *npl of* **nucleus**

nucleus ['njuːklɪəs] *n* Kern *m*

nude [njuːd] *adj* nackt ♦ *n* (*ART*) Akt *m*; **in the ~** nackt

nudge [nʌdʒ] *vt* leicht anstoßen

nudist ['njuːdɪst] *n* Nudist(in) *m(f)*

nudity ['njuːdɪtɪ] *n* Nacktheit *f*

nuisance ['njuːsns] *n* Ärgernis *nt*; **what a ~!** wie ärgerlich!

nuke [njuːk] (*inf*) *n* Kernkraftwerk *nt* ♦ *vt* atomar vernichten

null [nʌl] *adj*: **~ and void** null und nichtig

numb [nʌm] *adj* taub, gefühllos ♦ *vt* betäuben

number ['nʌmbə*] *n* Nummer *f*; (*numeral also*) Zahl *f*; (*quantity*) (An)zahl *f* ♦ *vt* (*give a ~ to*) numerieren; (*amount to*) sein; **to be ~ed among** gezählt werden zu; **a ~ of** (*several*) einige; **they were ten in ~** sie waren zehn an der Zahl; **~ plate** (*BRIT*) *n* (*AUT*) Nummernschild *nt*

numeral ['njuːmərəl] *n* Ziffer *f*

numerate ['njuːmərɪt] *adj* rechenkundig

numerical [njuː'merɪkəl] *adj* (*order*) zahlenmäßig

numerous ['njuːmərəs] *adj* zahlreich

nun [nʌn] *n* Nonne *f*

nurse [nɜːs] *n* Krankenschwester *f*; (*for children*) Kindermädchen *nt* ♦ *vt* (*patient*) pflegen; (*doubt etc*) hegen

nursery ['nɜːsərɪ] *n* (*for children*) Kinderzimmer *nt*; (*for plants*) Gärtnerei *f*; (*for trees*) Baumschule *f*; **~ rhyme** *n* Kinderreim *m*; **~ school** *n* Kindergarten *m*; **~ slope** (*BRIT*) *n* (*SKI*) Idiotenhügel *m* (*inf*), Anfängerhügel *m*

nursing ['nɜːsɪŋ] *n* (*profession*) Krankenpflege *f*; **~ home** *n* Privatklinik *f*

nurture ['nɜːtʃə*] *vt* aufziehen

nut [nʌt] *n* Nuß *f*; (*screw*) Schraubenmutter *f*; (*inf*) Verrückte(r) *mf*; **he's ~s** er ist verrückt

nutcrackers ['nʌtkrækəz] *npl* Nußknacker *m*

nutmeg ['nʌtmeg] *n* Muskat(nuß *f*) *m*
nutrient ['nju:trɪənt] *n* Nährstoff *m*
nutrition [nju:'trɪʃən] *n* Nahrung *f*
nutritious [nju:'trɪʃəs] *adj* nahrhaft
nylon ['naɪlɒn] *n* Nylon *nt* ♦ *adj* Nylon-

O o

oak [əʊk] *n* Eiche *f* ♦ *adj* Eichen(holz)-
O.A.P. *abbr* = **old-age pensioner**
oar [ɔ:*] *n* Ruder *nt*
oases [əʊ'eɪsi:z] *npl of* **oasis**
oasis [əʊ'eɪsɪs] *n* Oase *f*
oath [əʊθ] *n* (*statement*) Eid *m*, Schwur *m*; (*swearword*) Fluch *m*
oatmeal ['əʊtmi:l] *n* Haferschrot *m*
oats [əʊts] *npl* Hafer *m*
obedience [ə'bi:dɪəns] *n* Gehorsam *m*
obedient [ə'bi:dɪənt] *adj* gehorsam
obesity [əʊ'bi:sɪtɪ] *n* Fettleibigkeit *f*
obey [ə'beɪ] *vt, vi:* **to ~ (sb)** (jdm) gehorchen
obituary [ə'bɪtjʊərɪ] *n* Nachruf *m*
object [*n* 'ɒbdʒɪkt, *vb* əb'dʒekt] *n* (*thing*) Gegenstand *m*, Objekt *nt*; (*purpose*) Ziel *nt* ♦ *vi* dagegen sein; **expense is no ~** Ausgaben spielen keine Rolle; **I ~!** ich protestiere!; **to ~ to sth** Einwände gegen etw haben; (*morally*) Anstoß an etw *acc* nehmen; **to ~ that** einwenden, daß; **~ion** [əb'dʒekʃən] *n* (*reason against*) Einwand *m*, Einspruch *m*; (*dislike*) Abneigung *f*; **I have no ~ion to ...** ich habe nichts gegen ... einzuwenden; **~ionable** [əb'dʒekʃnəbl] *adj* nicht einwandfrei; (*language*) anstößig; **~ive** [əb'dʒektɪv] *n* Ziel *nt* ♦ *adj* objektiv
obligation [ɒblɪ'geɪʃən] *n* Verpflichtung *f*; **without ~** unverbindlich
obligatory [ə'blɪgətərɪ] *adj* obligatorisch
oblige [ə'blaɪdʒ] *vt* (*compel*) zwingen; (*do a favour*) einen Gefallen tun +*dat*; **to be ~d to sb for sth** jdm für etw verbunden sein
obliging [ə'blaɪdʒɪŋ] *adj* entgegenkommend
oblique [ə'bli:k] *adj* schräg, schief ♦ *n* Schrägstrich *m*

obliterate [ə'blɪtəreɪt] *vt* auslöschen
oblivion [ə'blɪvɪən] *n* Vergessenheit *f*
oblivious [ə'blɪvɪəs] *adj* nicht bewußt
oblong ['ɒblɒŋ] *n* Rechteck *nt* ♦ *adj* länglich
obnoxious [əb'nɒkʃəs] *adj* widerlich
obscene [əb'si:n] *adj* obszön
obscenity [əb'senɪtɪ] *n* Obszönität *f*; **obscenities** *npl* (*swearwords*) Zoten *pl*
obscure [əb'skjʊə*] *adj* unklar; (*indistinct*) undeutlich; (*unknown*) unbekannt, obskur; (*dark*) düster ♦ *vt* verdunkeln; (*view*) verbergen; (*confuse*) verwirren
obscurity [əb'skjʊərɪtɪ] *n* Unklarheit *f*; (*darkness*) Dunkelheit *f*
obsequious [əb'si:kwɪəs] *adj* servil
observance [əb'zɜ:vəns] *n* Befolgung *f*
observant [əb'zɜ:vənt] *adj* aufmerksam
observation [ɒbzə'veɪʃən] *n* (*noticing*) Beobachtung *f*; (*surveillance*) Überwachung *f*; (*remark*) Bemerkung *f*
observatory [əb'zɜ:vətrɪ] *n* Sternwarte *f*, Observatorium *nt*
observe [əb'zɜ:v] *vt* (*notice*) bemerken; (*watch*) beobachten; (*customs*) einhalten; **~r** *n* Beobachter(in) *m(f)*
obsess [əb'ses] *vt* verfolgen, quälen; **~ion** [əb'seʃən] *n* Besessenheit *f*, Wahn *m*; **~ive** *adj* krankhaft
obsolescence [ɒbsə'lesns] *n* Veralten *nt*
obsolete ['ɒbsəli:t] *adj* überholt, veraltet
obstacle ['ɒbstəkl] *n* Hindernis *nt*; **~ race** *n* Hindernisrennen *nt*
obstetrics [ɒb'stetrɪks] *n* Geburtshilfe *f*
obstinate ['ɒbstɪnət] *adj* hartnäckig, stur
obstruct [əb'strʌkt] *vt* versperren; (*pipe*) verstopfen; (*hinder*) hemmen; **~ion** [əb'strʌkʃən] *n* Versperrung *f*; Verstopfung *f*; (*obstacle*) Hindernis *nt*
obtain [əb'teɪn] *vt* erhalten, bekommen; (*result*) erzielen
obtrusive [əb'tru:sɪv] *adj* aufdringlich
obvious ['ɒbvɪəs] *adj* offenbar, offensichtlich; **~ly** *adv* offensichtlich
occasion [ə'keɪʒən] *n* Gelegenheit *f*; (*special event*) Ereignis *nt*; (*reason*) Anlaß *m* ♦ *vt* veranlassen; **~al** *adj* gelegentlich; **~ally** *adv* gelegentlich

occupant ['ɒkjʊpənt] *n* Inhaber(in) *m(f)*; (*of house etc*) Bewohner(in) *m(f)*

occupation [ɒkjʊ'peɪʃən] *n* (*employment*) Tätigkeit *f*, Beruf *m*; (*pastime*) Beschäftigung *f*; (*of country*) Besetzung *f*, Okkupation *f*; **~al hazard** *n* Berufsrisiko *nt*

occupier ['ɒkjʊpaɪə*] *n* Bewohner(in) *m(f)*

occupy ['ɒkjʊpaɪ] *vt* (*take possession of*) besetzen; (*seat*) belegen; (*live in*) bewohnen; (*position, office*) bekleiden; (*position in sb's life*) einnehmen; (*time*) beanspruchen; **to ~ o.s. with sth** sich mit etw beschäftigen; **to ~ o.s. by doing sth** sich damit beschäftigen, etw zu tun

occur [ə'kɜ:*] *vi* vorkommen; **to ~ to sb** jdm einfallen; **~rence** *n* (*event*) Ereignis *nt*; (*appearing*) Auftreten *nt*

ocean ['əʊʃən] *n* Ozean *m*, Meer *nt*; **~ going** *adj* Hochsee-

o'clock [ə'klɒk] *adv*: **it is 5 ~** es ist 5 Uhr

OCR *n abbr* = **optical character reader**

octagonal [ɒk'tægənl] *adj* achteckig

October [ɒk'təʊbə*] *n* Oktober *m*

octopus ['ɒktəpəs] *n* Krake *f*; (*small*) Tintenfisch *m*

odd [ɒd] *adj* (*strange*) sonderbar; (*not even*) ungerade; (*the other part missing*) einzeln; (*surplus*) übrig; **60-~** so um die 60; **at ~ times** ab und zu; **to be the ~ one out** (*person*) das fünfte Rad am Wagen sein; (*thing*) nicht dazugehören; **~ity** *n* (*strangeness*) Merkwürdigkeit *f*; (*queer person*) seltsame(r) Kauz *m*; (*thing*) Kuriosität *f*; **~-job man** (*irreg*) *n* Mädchen *nt* für alles; **~ jobs** *npl* gelegentlich anfallende Arbeiten; **~ly** *adv* seltsam; **~ments** *npl* Reste *pl*; **~s** *npl* Chancen *pl*; (*betting*) Gewinnchancen *pl*; **it makes no ~s** es spielt keine Rolle; **at ~s** uneinig; **~s and ends** *npl* Krimskrams *m*

odious ['əʊdɪəs] *adj* verhaßt; (*action*) abscheulich

odometer [əʊ'dɒmətə*] (*esp US*) *n* Tacho(meter) *m*

odour ['əʊdə*] (*US* **odor**) *n* Geruch *m*

of [ɒv, əv] *prep* **1** von +*dat, use of gen*; **the history of Germany** die Geschichte Deutschlands; **a friend of ours** ein Freund von uns; **a boy of 10** ein 10-jähriger Junge; **that was kind of you** das war sehr freundlich von Ihnen

2 (*expressing quantity, amount, dates etc*): **a kilo of flour** ein Kilo Mehl; **how much of this do you need?** wieviel brauchen Sie (davon)?; **there were 3 of them** (*people*) sie waren zu dritt; (*objects*) es gab 3 (davon); **a cup of tea/vase of flowers** eine Tasse Tee/Vase mit Blumen; **the 5th of July** der 5 Juli

3 (*from, out of*) aus; **a bridge made of wood** eine Holzbrücke, eine Brücke aus Holz

off [ɒf] *adj, adv* (*absent*) weg, fort; (*switch*) aus(geschaltet), ab(geschaltet); (*BRIT: food: bad*) schlecht; (*cancelled*) abgesagt ♦ *prep* von +*dat*; **to be ~** (*to leave*) gehen; **to be ~ sick** krank sein; **a day ~** ein freier Tag; **to have an ~ day** einen schlechten Tag haben; **he had his coat ~** er hatte seinen Mantel aus; **10% ~** (*COMM*) 10% Rabatt; **5 km ~ (the road)** 5 km (von der Straße) entfernt; **~ the coast** vor der Küste; **I'm ~ meat** (*no longer eat it*) ich esse kein Fleisch mehr; (*no longer like it*) ich mag kein Fleisch mehr; **on the ~ chance** auf gut Glück

offal ['ɒfəl] *n* Innereien *pl*

offbeat ['ɒfbiːt] *adj* unkonventionell

off-colour ['ɒf'kʌlə*] *adj* nicht wohl

offence [ə'fens] (*US* **offense**) *n* (*crime*) Vergehen *nt*, Straftat *f*; (*insult*) Beleidigung *f*; **to take ~ at** gekränkt sein wegen

offend [ə'fend] *vt* beleidigen; **~er** *n* Gesetzesübertreter *m*

offense [ə'fens] (*US*) *n* = **offence**

offensive [ə'fensɪv] *adj* (*unpleasant*) übel, abstoßend; (*weapon*) Kampf-; (*remark*) verletzend ♦ *n* Angriff *m*

offer ['ɒfə*] *n* Angebot *f* ♦ *vt* anbieten; (*opinion*) äußern; (*resistance*) leisten; **on ~**

zum Verkauf angeboten; **~ing** *n* Gabe *f*

offhand ['ɒf'hænd] *adj* lässig ♦ *adv* ohne weiteres

office ['ɒfɪs] *n* Büro *nt*; (*position*) Amt *nt*; **doctor's ~** (*US*) Praxis *f*; **to take ~** sein Amt antreten; (*POL*) die Regierung übernehmen; **~ automation** *n* Büroautomatisierung *f*; **~ block** (*US ~ building*) *n* Büro(hoch)haus *nt*; **~ hours** *npl* Dienstzeit *f*; (*US: MED*) Sprechstunde *f*

officer ['ɒfɪsə*] *n* (*MIL*) Offizier *m*; (*public ~*) Beamte(r) *m*

official [ə'fɪʃəl] *adj* offiziell, amtlich ♦ *n* Beamte(r) *m*; **~dom** *n* Beamtentum *nt*

officiate [ə'fɪʃɪeɪt] *vi* amtieren

officious [ə'fɪʃəs] *adj* aufdringlich

offing ['ɒfɪŋ] *n*: **in the ~** in (Aus)sicht

off: **~-licence** (*BRIT*) *n* (*shop*) Wein- und Spirituosenhandlung *f*; **~-line** *adj* (*COMPUT*) Off-line- ♦ *adv* (*COMPUT*) off line; **~-peak** *adj* (*charges*) verbilligt; **~-putting** (*BRIT*) *adj* (*person, remark etc*) abstoßend; **~-season** *adj* außer Saison

offset ['ɒfset] (*irreg: like* set) *vt* ausgleichen ♦ *n* (*also: ~ printing*) Offset(druck) *m*

offshoot ['ɒfʃuːt] *n* (*fig: of organization*) Zweig *m*; (: *of discussion etc*) Randergebnis *nt*

offshore ['ɒf'ʃɔː*] *adv* in einiger Entfernung von der Küste ♦ *adj* küstennah, Küsten-

offside ['ɒf'saɪd] *adj* (*SPORT*) im Abseits ♦ *adv* abseits ♦ *n* (*AUT*) Fahrerseite *f*

offspring ['ɒfsprɪŋ] *n* Nachkommenschaft *f*; (*one*) Sprößling *m*

off: **~stage** *adv* hinter den Kulissen; **~-the-cuff** *adj* unvorbereitet, aus dem Stegreif; **~-the-peg** (*US ~-the-rack*) *adv* von der Stange; **~-white** *adj* naturweiß

often ['ɒfən] *adv* oft

ogle ['əʊgl] *vt* liebäugeln mit

oh [əʊ] *excl* oh, ach

oil [ɔɪl] *n* Öl *nt* ♦ *vt* ölen; **~can** *n* Ölkännchen *nt*; **~field** *n* Ölfeld *nt*; **~ filter** *n* (*AUT*) Ölfilter *m*; **~-fired** *adj* Öl-; **~ painting** *n* Ölgemälde *nt*; **~-rig** *n* Ölplattform *f*; **~skins** *npl* Ölzeug *nt*; **~ tanker** *n* (Öl)tanker *m*; **~ well** *n*

Ölquelle *f*; **~y** *adj* ölig; (*dirty*) ölbeschmiert

ointment ['ɔɪntmənt] *n* Salbe *f*

O.K. ['əʊ'keɪ] *excl* in Ordnung, O.K. ♦ *adj* in Ordnung ♦ *vt* genehmigen

okay ['əʊ'keɪ] = **O.K.**

old [əʊld] *adj* alt; **how ~ are you?** wie alt bist du?; **he's 10 years ~** er ist 10 Jahre alt; **~er brother** ältere(r) Bruder *m*; **~ age** *n* Alter *nt*; **~-age pensioner** (*BRIT*) *n* Rentner(in) *m(f)*; **~-fashioned** *adj* altmodisch

olive ['ɒlɪv] *n* (*fruit*) Olive *f*; (*colour*) Olive *nt* ♦ *adj* Oliven-; (*coloured*) olivenfarbig; **~ oil** *n* Olivenöl *nt*

Olympic [əʊ'lɪmpɪk] *adj* olympisch; **the ~ Games, the ~s** die Olympischen Spiele

omelet(te) ['ɒmlət] *n* Omelett *nt*

omen ['əʊmən] *n* Omen *nt*

ominous ['ɒmɪnəs] *adj* bedrohlich

omission [əʊ'mɪʃən] *n* Auslassung *f*; (*neglect*) Versäumnis *nt*

omit [əʊ'mɪt] *vt* auslassen; (*fail to do*) versäumen

KEYWORD

---

on [ɒn] *prep* **1** (*indicating position*) auf +*dat*; (*with vb of motion*) auf +*acc*; (*on vertical surface, part of body*) an +*dat/acc*; **it's on the table** es ist auf dem Tisch; **she put the book on the table** sie legte das Buch auf den Tisch; **on the left** links

2 (*indicating means, method, condition etc*): **on foot** (*go, be*) zu Fuß; **on the train/plane** (*go*) mit dem Zug/Flugzeug; (*be*) im Zug/Flugzeug; **on the telephone/television** am Telefon/im Fernsehen; **to be on drugs** Drogen nehmen; **to be on holiday/business** im Urlaub/auf Geschäftsreise sein

3 (*referring to time*): **on Friday** (am) Freitag; **on Fridays** freitags; **on June 20th** am 20. Juni; **a week on Friday** Freitag in einer Woche; **on arrival he ...** als er ankam, ... er ...

4 (*about, concerning*) über +*acc*

♦ *adv* **1** (*referring to dress*) an; **she put her boots/hat on** sie zog ihre Stiefel an/ setzte ihren Hut auf

2 (*further, continuously*) weiter; **to walk on** weitergehen
♦ adj 1 (*functioning, in operation: machine, TV, light*) an; (: *tap*) aufgedreht; (: *brakes*) angezogen; **is the meeting still on?** findet die Versammlung noch statt?; **there's a good film on** es läuft ein guter Film
2: **that's not on!** (*inf: of behaviour*) das liegt nicht drin!

once [wʌns] *adv* einmal ♦ *conj* wenn ... einmal; ~ **he had left/it was done** nachdem er gegangen war/es fertig war; **at** ~ sofort; (*at the same time*) gleichzeitig; ~ **a week** einmal in der Woche; ~ **more** noch einmal; ~ **and for all** ein für allemal; ~ **upon a time** es war einmal
oncoming ['ɒnkʌmɪŋ] *adj* (*traffic*) Gegen-, entgegenkommend

---

KEYWORD

one [wʌn] *num* eins; (*with noun, referring back to noun*) ein/eine/ein; **it is one (o'clock)** es ist eins, es ist ein Uhr; **one hundred and fifty** einhundertfünfzig
♦ *adj* 1 (*sole*) einzige(r, s); **the one book which** das einzige Buch, welches
2 (*same*) derselbe/dieselbe/dasselbe; **they came in the one car** sie kamen alle in dem einen Auto
3 (*indef*): **one day I discovered ...** eines Tages bemerkte ich ...
♦ *pron* 1 eine(r, s); **do you have a red one?** haben Sie einen roten/eine rote/ein rotes?; **this one** diese(r, s); **that one** der/die/das; **which one?** welche(r, s)?; **one by one** einzeln
2: **one another** einander; **do you two ever see one another?** seht ihr beide euch manchmal?
3 (*impers*): man; **one never knows** man kann nie wissen; **to cut one's finger** sich in den Finger schneiden

---

one: ~-**armed bandit** *n* einarmiger Bandit *m*; ~-**day excursion** (*US*) *n* (*day return*) Tagesrückfahrkarte *f*; ~-**man** *adj* Einmann-; ~-**man band** *n* Einmann-

kapelle *f*; (*fig*) Einmannbetrieb *m*; ~-**off** (*BRIT: inf*) *n* Einzelfall *m*
oneself [wʌn'self] *pron* (*reflexive: after prep*) sich; (~ *personally*) sich selbst *or* selber; (*emphatic*) (sich) selbst; **to hurt** ~ sich verletzen
one: ~-**sided** *adj* (*argument*) einseitig; ~-**to-one** *adj* (*relationship*) eins-zu-eins; ~-**upmanship** *n* die Kunst, anderen um eine Nasenlänge voraus zu sein; ~-**way** *adj* (*street*) Einbahn-
ongoing ['ɒngəʊɪŋ] *adj* momentan; (*progressing*) sich entwickelnd
onion ['ʌnjən] *n* Zwiebel *f*
on-line ['ɒn'laɪn] *adj* (*COMPUT*) On-line-
onlooker ['ɒnlʊkə*] *n* Zuschauer(in) *m(f)*
only ['əʊnlɪ] *adv* nur, bloß ♦ *adj* einzige(r, s) ♦ *conj* nur, bloß; **an** ~ **child** ein Einzelkind; **not** ~ ... **but also** ... nicht nur ... sondern auch ...
onset ['ɒnset] *n* (*beginning*) Beginn *m*
onshore ['ɒnʃɔː*] *adj* (*wind*) See-
onslaught ['ɒnslɔːt] *n* Angriff *m*
onto ['ɒntʊ] *prep* = **on to**
onus ['əʊnəs] *n* Last *f*, Pflicht *f*
onward(s) ['ɒnwəd(z)] *adv* (*place*) voran, vorwärts; **from that day onwards** von dem Tag an; **from today onwards** ab heute
ooze [uːz] *vi* sickern
opaque [əʊ'peɪk] *adj* undurchsichtig
OPEC ['əʊpek] *n abbr* (= *Organization of Petroleum-Exporting Countries*) OPEC *f*
open ['əʊpən] *adj* offen; (*public*) öffentlich; (*mind*) aufgeschlossen ♦ *vt* öffnen, aufmachen; (*trial, motorway, account*) eröffnen ♦ *vi* (*begin*) anfangen; (*shop*) aufmachen; (*door, flower*) aufgehen; (*play*) Premiere haben; **in the** ~ (**air**) im Freien; ~ **on to** *vt fus* sich öffnen auf +*acc*; ~ **up** *vt* (*route*) erschließen; (*shop, prospects*) eröffnen ♦ *vi* öffnen; ~**ing** *n* (*hole*) Öffnung *f*; (*beginning*) Anfang *m*; (*good chance*) Gelegenheit *f*; ~ **learning centre** *n* Weiterbildungseinrichtung auf Teilzeitbasis; ~**ly** *adv* offen; (*publicly*) öffentlich; ~-**minded** *adj* aufgeschlossen; ~-**necked** *adj* offen; ~-**plan** *adj* (*office*) Großraum-; (*flat etc*) offen angelegt

opera ['ɒpərə] *n* Oper *f*; ~ **house** *n* Opernhaus *nt*

operate ['ɒpəreɪt] *vt* (*machine*) bedienen; (*brakes, light*) betätigen ♦ *vi* (*machine*) laufen, in Betrieb sein; (*person*) arbeiten; (*MED*): **to ~ on** operieren

operatic [ɒpə'rætɪk] *adj* Opern-

operating ['ɒpəreɪtɪŋ] *adj*: ~ **table/ theatre** Operationstisch *m*/-saal *m*

operation [ɒpə'reɪʃən] *n* (*working*) Betrieb *m*; (*MED*) Operation *f*; (*undertaking*) Unternehmen *nt*; (*MIL*) Einsatz *m*; **to be in ~** (*JUR*) in Kraft sein; (*machine*) in Betrieb sein; **to have an ~** (*MED*) operiert werden; ~**al** *adj* einsatzbereit

operative ['ɒpərətɪv] *adj* wirksam; (*MED*) operativ

operator ['ɒpəreɪtə*] *n* (*of machine*) Arbeiter *m*; (*TEL*) Telefonist(in) *m(f)*

ophthalmic [ɒf'θælmɪk] *adj* Augen-

opinion [ə'pɪnjən] *n* Meinung *f*; **in my ~** meiner Meinung nach; ~**ated** *adj* starrsinnig; ~ **poll** *n* Meinungsumfrage *f*

opponent [ə'pəʊnənt] *n* Gegner *m*

opportunity [ɒpə'tjuːnɪtɪ] *n* Gelegenheit *f*, Möglichkeit *f*; **to take the ~ of doing sth** die Gelegenheit ergreifen, etw zu tun

oppose [ə'pəʊz] *vt* entgegentreten +*dat*; (*argument, idea*) ablehnen; (*plan*) bekämpfen; **to be ~d to sth** gegen etw sein; **as ~d to** im Gegensatz zu

opposing [ə'pəʊzɪŋ] *adj* gegnerisch; (*points of view*) entgegengesetzt

opposite ['ɒpəzɪt] *adj* (*house*) gegenüberliegend; (*direction*) entgegengesetzt ♦ *adv* gegenüber ♦ *prep* gegenüber ♦ *n* Gegenteil *nt*

opposition [ɒpə'zɪʃən] *n* (*resistance*) Widerstand *m*; (*POL*) Opposition *f*; (*contrast*) Gegensatz *m*

oppress [ə'pres] *vt* unterdrücken; (*heat etc*) bedrücken; ~**ion** [ə'preʃən] *n* Unterdrückung *f*; ~**ive** *adj* (*authority, law*) repressiv; (*burden, thought*) bedrückend; (*heat*) drückend

opt [ɒpt] *vi*: **to ~ for** sich entscheiden für; **to ~ to do sth** sich entscheiden, etw zu tun; **to ~ out of** sich drücken vor

`+dat`; (*of society*) ausflippen aus

optical ['ɒptɪkəl] *adj* optisch; ~ **character reader** *n* optische(s) Lesegerät *nt*

optician [ɒp'tɪʃən] *n* Optiker *m*

optimist ['ɒptɪmɪst] *n* Optimist *m*; ~**ic** ['ɒptɪˈmɪstɪk] *adj* optimistisch

optimum ['ɒptɪməm] *adj* optimal

option ['ɒpʃən] *n* Wahl *f*; (*COMM*) Option *f*; **to keep one's ~s open** sich alle Möglichkeiten offenhalten; ~**al** *adj* freiwillig; (*subject*) wahlfrei; ~**al extras** *npl* Extras auf Wunsch

opulent ['ɒpjʊlənt] *adj* sehr reich

or [ɔː*] *conj* oder; **he could not read ~ write** er konnte weder lesen noch schreiben; ~ **else** sonst

oral ['ɔːrəl] *adj* mündlich ♦ *n* (*exam*) mündliche Prüfung *f*

orange ['ɒrɪndʒ] *n* (*fruit*) Apfelsine *f*, Orange *f*; (*colour*) Orange *nt* ♦ *adj* orange

orator ['ɒrətə*] *n* Redner(in) *m(f)*

orbit ['ɔːbɪt] *n* Umlaufbahn *f*

orchard ['ɔːtʃəd] *n* Obstgarten *m*

orchestra ['ɔːkɪstrə] *n* Orchester *nt*; (*US: seating*) Parkett *nt*; ~**l** [ɔː'kestrəl] *adj* Orchester-, orchestral

orchid ['ɔːkɪd] *n* Orchidee *f*

ordain [ɔː'deɪn] *vt* (*ECCL*) weihen; (*decide*) verfügen

ordeal [ɔː'diːl] *n* Qual *f*

order ['ɔːdə*] *n* (*sequence*) Reihenfolge *f*; (*good arrangement*) Ordnung *f*; (*command*) Befehl *m*; (*JUR*) Anordnung *f*; (*peace*) Ordnung *f*; (*condition*) Zustand *m*; (*rank*) Klasse *f*; (*COMM*) Bestellung *f*; (*ECCL, honour*) Orden *m* ♦ *vt* (*also: put in ~*) ordnen; (*command*) befehlen; (*COMM*) bestellen; **in ~** in der Reihenfolge; **in (working)** ~ in gutem Zustand; **in ~ to do sth** um etw zu tun; **on ~** (*COMM*) auf Bestellung; **to ~ sb to do sth** jdm befehlen, etw zu tun; **to ~ sth** (*command*) etw *acc* befehlen; (*COMM*) etw in Bestellung geben; ~ **form** *n* Bestellschein *m*; ~**ly** *n* (*MIL*) Sanitäter *m*; (*MED*) Pfleger *m* ♦ *adj* (*tidy*) ordentlich; (*well-behaved*) ruhig

ordinary ['ɔːdnrɪ] *adj* gewöhnlich ♦ *n*: **out of the ~** außergewöhnlich

ordnance ['ɔːdnəns] *n* Artillerie *f*; **O~ Survey** (*BRIT*) *n* amtliche(r) Kartographiedienst *m*

ore [ɔː*] *n* Erz *nt*

organ ['ɔːgən] *n* (*MUS*) Orgel *f*; (*BIOL, fig*) Organ *nt*

organic [ɔː'gænɪk] *adj* (*food, farming etc*) biodynamisch

organization [ɔːgənaɪ'zeɪʃən] *n* Organisation *f*; (*make-up*) Struktur *f*

organize ['ɔːgənaɪz] *vt* organisieren; **~r** *n* Organisator *m*, Veranstalter *m*

orgasm ['ɔːgæzəm] *n* Orgasmus *m*

orgy ['ɔːdʒɪ] *n* Orgie *f*

Orient ['ɔːrɪənt] *n* Orient *m*

oriental [ɔːrɪ'entl] *adj* orientalisch

origin ['ɒrɪdʒɪn] *n* Ursprung *m*; (*of the world*) Anfang *m*, Entstehung *f*

original [ə'rɪdʒɪnl] *adj* (*first*) ursprünglich; (*painting*) original; (*idea*) originell ♦ *n* Original *nt*; **~ly** *adv* ursprünglich; originell

originate [ə'rɪdʒɪneɪt] *vi* entstehen ♦ *vt* ins Leben rufen; **to ~ from** stammen aus

Orkneys ['ɔːknɪz] *npl* (*also*: **the Orkney Islands**) die Orkneyinseln *pl*

ornament ['ɔːnəmənt] *n* Schmuck *m*; (*on mantelpiece*) Nippesfigur *f*; **~al** [ɔːnə'mentl] *adj* Zier-

ornate [ɔː'neɪt] *adj* reich verziert

orphan ['ɔːfən] *n* Waise *f*, Waisenkind *nt* ♦ *vt*: **to be ~ed** Waise werden; **~age** *n* Waisenhaus *nt*

orthodox ['ɔːθədɒks] *adj* orthodox; **~y** *n* Orthodoxie *f*; (*fig*) Konventionalität *f*

orthopaedic [ɔːθəʊ'piːdɪk] (*US* **orthopedic**) *adj* orthopädisch

ostensibly [ɒs'tensəblɪ] *adv* vorgeblich, angeblich

ostentatious [ɒsten'teɪʃəs] *adj* großtuerisch, protzig

ostracize ['ɒstrəsaɪz] *vt* ausstoßen

ostrich ['ɒstrɪtʃ] *n* Strauß *m*

other ['ʌðə*] *adj* andere(r, s) ♦ *pron* andere(r, s) ♦ *adv*: **~ than** anders als; **the ~ (one)** der/die/das andere; **the ~ day** neulich; **~s** (*~ people*) andere; **~wise** *adv* (*in a different way*) anders; (*or else*) sonst

ouch [aʊtʃ] *excl* aua

ought [ɔːt] *vb aux* sollen; **I ~ to do it** ich sollte es tun; **this ~ to have been corrected** das hätte korrigiert werden sollen

ounce [aʊns] *n* Unze *f*

our [aʊə*] *adj* unser; *see also* **my**; **~s** *pron* unsere(r, s); *see also* **mine²**; **~selves** *pron* uns (selbst); (*emphatic*) (wir) selbst; *see also* **oneself**

oust [aʊst] *vt* verdrängen

out [aʊt] *adv* hinaus/heraus; (*not indoors*) draußen; (*not alight*) aus; (*unconscious*) bewußtlos; (*results*) bekanntgegeben; **to eat/go ~** auswärts essen/ausgehen; **~ there** da draußen; **he is ~** (*absent*) er ist nicht da; **he was ~ in his calculations** seine Berechnungen waren nicht richtig; **~ loud** laut; **~ of** aus; (*away from*) außerhalb +*gen*; **to be ~ of milk** *etc* keine Milch *etc* mehr haben; **~ of order** außer Betrieb; **~-and-out** *adj* (*liar, thief etc*) ausgemacht

outback ['aʊtbæk] *n* Hinterland *nt*

outboard (motor) ['aʊtbɔːd-] *n* Außenbordmotor *m*

outbreak ['aʊtbreɪk] *n* Ausbruch *m*

outburst ['aʊtbɜːst] *n* Ausbruch *m*

outcast ['aʊtkɑːst] *n* Ausgestoßene(r) *mf*

outcome ['aʊtkʌm] *n* Ergebnis *nt*

outcrop ['aʊtkrɒp] *n* (*of rock*) Felsnase *f*

outcry ['aʊtkraɪ] *n* Protest *m*

outdated [aʊt'deɪtɪd] *adj* überholt

outdo [aʊt'duː] (*irreg: like* **do**) *vt* übertrumpfen

outdoor ['aʊtdɔː*] *adj* Außen-; (*SPORT*) im Freien; **~s** [aʊt'dɔːz] *adv* im Freien

outer ['aʊtə*] *adj* äußere(r, s); **~ space** *n* Weltraum *m*

outfit ['aʊtfɪt] *n* Kleidung *f*, **~ters** (*BRIT*) *n* (*for men's clothes*) Herrenausstatter *m*

outgoing ['aʊtgəʊɪŋ] *adj* (*character*) aufgeschlossen; **~s** (*BRIT*) *npl* Ausgaben *pl*

outgrow [aʊt'grəʊ] (*irreg: like* **grow**) *vt* (*clothes*) herauswachsen aus; (*habit*) ablegen

outhouse ['aʊthaʊs] *n* Nebengebäude *nt*

outing ['aʊtɪŋ] *n* Ausflug *m*

outlandish [aʊt'lændɪʃ] *adj* eigenartig

outlaw ['aʊtlɔː] *n* Geächtete(r) *m* ♦ *vt*

ächten; (*thing*) verbieten
outlay ['aʊtleɪ] *n* Auslage *f*
outlet ['aʊtlet] *n* Auslaß *m*, Abfluß *m*;
(*also: retail ~*) Absatzmarkt *m*; (*US: ELEC*)
Steckdose *f*; (*for emotions*) Ventil *nt*
outline ['aʊtlaɪn] *n* Umriß *m*
outlive [aʊt'lɪv] *vt* überleben
outlook ['aʊtlʊk] *n* (*also fig*) Aussicht *f*;
(*attitude*) Einstellung *f*
outlying ['aʊtlaɪɪŋ] *adj* entlegen; (*district*)
Außen-
outmoded [aʊt'məʊdɪd] *adj* veraltet
outnumber [aʊt'nʌmbə*] *vt* zahlenmäßig
überlegen sein +*dat*
out-of-date [aʊtəv'deɪt] *adj* (*passport*)
abgelaufen; (*clothes etc*) altmodisch; (*ideas
etc*) überholt
out-of-the-way [aʊtəvðə'weɪ] *adj*
abgelegen
outpatient ['aʊtpeɪʃənt] *n* ambulante(r)
Patient *m*/ambulante Patientin *f*
outpost ['aʊtpəʊst] *n* (*MIL, fig*) Vorposten
m
output ['aʊtpʊt] *n* Leistung *f*, Produktion
f; (*COMPUT*) Ausgabe *f*
outrage ['aʊtreɪdʒ] *n* (*cruel deed*)
Ausschreitung *f*; (*indecency*) Skandal *m*
♦ *vt* (*morals*) verstoßen gegen; (*person*)
empören; **~ous** [aʊt'reɪdʒəs] *adj* unerhört
outright [*adv* aʊt'raɪt, *adj* 'aʊtraɪt] *adv* (*at
once*) sofort; (*openly*) ohne Umschweife
♦ *adj* (*denial*) völlig; (*sale*) Total-;
(*winner*) unbestritten
outset ['aʊtset] *n* Beginn *m*
outside ['aʊt'saɪd] *n* Außenseite *f* ♦ *adj*
äußere(r, s), Außen-; (*chance*) gering
♦ *adv* außen ♦ *prep* außerhalb +*gen*; **at**
the ~ (*fig*) maximal; (*time*) spätestens; **to**
go ~ nach draußen gehen; **~ lane** *n* (*AUT*)
äußere Spur *f*; **~ line** *n* (*TEL*)
Amtsanschluß *m*; **~r** *n* Außenseiter(in)
m(f)
outsize ['aʊtsaɪz] *adj* übergroß
outskirts ['aʊtskɜːts] *npl* Stadtrand *m*
outspoken [aʊt'spəʊkən] *adj* freimütig
outstanding [aʊt'stændɪŋ] *adj*
hervorragend; (*debts etc*) ausstehend
outstay [aʊt'steɪ] *vt*: **to ~ one's welcome**
länger bleiben als erwünscht

outstretched ['aʊtstretʃt] *adj*
ausgestreckt
outstrip [aʊt'strɪp] *vt* übertreffen
out-tray ['aʊttreɪ] *n* Ausgangskorb *m*
outward ['aʊtwəd] *adj* äußere(r, s);
(*journey*) Hin-; (*freight*) ausgehend ♦ *adv*
nach außen; **~ly** *adv* äußerlich
outweigh [aʊt'weɪ] *vt* (*fig*) überwiegen
outwit [aʊt'wɪt] *vt* überlisten
oval ['əʊvəl] *adj* oval ♦ *n* Oval *nt*
ovary ['əʊvərɪ] *n* Eierstock *m*
ovation [əʊ'veɪʃən] *n* Beifallssturm *m*
oven ['ʌvn] *n* Backofen *m*; **~proof** *adj*
feuerfest
over ['əʊvə*] *adv* (*across*) hinüber/
herüber; (*finished*) vorbei; (*left*) übrig;
(*again*) wieder, noch einmal ♦ *prep* über
♦ *prefix* (*excessively*) übermäßig; **~ here**
hier(hin); **~ there** dort(hin); **all ~**
(*everywhere*) überall; (*finished*) vorbei; **~**
and ~ immer wieder; **~ and above**
darüber hinaus; **to ask sb ~** jdn einladen;
to bend ~ sich bücken
overall [*adj, n* 'əʊvərɔːl, *adv* əʊvə'rɔːl] *adj*
(*situation*) allgemein; (*length*) Gesamt- ♦ *n*
(*BRIT*) Kittel *m* ♦ *adv* insgesamt; **~s** *npl*
(*for man*) Overall *m*
overawe [əʊvər'ɔː] *vt* (*frighten*)
einschüchtern; (*make impression*)
überwältigen
overbalance [əʊvə'bæləns] *vi*
Übergewicht bekommen
overbearing [əʊvə'bɛərɪŋ] *adj*
aufdringlich
overboard ['əʊvəbɔːd] *adv* über Bord
overbook [əʊvə'bʊk] *vi* überbuchen
overcast ['əʊvəkɑːst] *adj* bedeckt
overcharge ['əʊvə'tʃɑːdʒ] *vt*: **to ~ sb**
von jdm zuviel verlangen
overcoat ['əʊvəkəʊt] *n* Mantel *m*
overcome [əʊvə'kʌm] (*irreg: like* come)
vt überwinden
overcrowded [əʊvə'kraʊdɪd] *adj*
überfüllt
overcrowding [əʊvə'kraʊdɪŋ] *n* Über-
füllung *f*
overdo [əʊvə'duː] (*irreg: like* do) *vt* (*cook
too much*) verkochen; (*exaggerate*)
übertreiben

overdose ['əʊvədəʊs] *n* Überdosis *f*

overdraft ['əʊvədrɑːft] *n* (Konto)überziehung *f*

overdrawn ['əʊvə'drɔːn] *adj* (*account*) überzogen

overdue ['əʊvə'djuː] *adj* überfällig

overestimate ['əʊvər'estimeit] *vt* überschätzen

overexcited ['əʊvərɪk'saitid] *adj* überreizt; (*children*) aufgeregt

overflow [*vb* əʊvə'fləʊ, *n* 'əʊvəfləʊ] *vi* überfließen ♦ *n* (*excess*) Überschuß *m*; (*also*: ~ *pipe*) Überlaufrohr *nt*

overgrown ['əʊvə'grəʊn] *adj* (*garden*) verwildert

overhaul [*vb* əʊvə'hɔːl, *n* 'əʊvəhɔːl] *vt* (*car*) überholen; (*plans*) überprüfen ♦ *n* Überholung *f*

overhead [*adv* əʊvə'hed, *adj, n* 'əʊvəhed] *adv* oben ♦ *adj* Hoch-; (*wire*) oberirdisch; (*lighting*) Decken- ♦ *n* (*US*) = ~s; ~s *npl* (*costs*) allgemeine Unkosten *pl*

overhear [əʊvə'hiə*] (*irreg: like* **hear**) *vt* (mit an)hören

overheat [əʊvə'hiːt] *vi* (*engine*) heiß laufen

overjoyed [əʊvə'dʒɔid] *adj* überglücklich

overkill ['əʊvəkil] *n* (*fig*) Rundumschlag *m*

overland [*adj* 'əʊvəlænd, *adv* əʊvə'lænd] *adj* Überland- ♦ *adv* (*travel*) über Land

overlap [*vb* əʊvə'læp, *n* 'əʊvəlæp] *vi* sich überschneiden; (*objects*) sich teilweise decken ♦ *n* Überschneidung *f*

overleaf [əʊvə'liːf] *adv* umseitig

overload ['əʊvə'ləʊd] *vt* überladen

overlook [əʊvə'luk] *vt* (*view from above*) überblicken; (*not notice*) übersehen; (*pardon*) hinwegsehen über +*acc*

overnight [*adv* 'əʊvə'nait, *adj* 'əʊvənait] *adv* über Nacht ♦ *adj* (*journey*) Nacht-; ~ **stay** Übernachtung *f*; **to stay** ~ übernachten

overpass ['əʊvəpɑːs] *n* Überführung *f*

overpower [əʊvə'paʊə*] *vt* überwältigen; ~**ing** *adj* überwältigend

overrate ['əʊvə'reit] *vt* überschätzen

override [əʊvə'raid] (*irreg: like* **ride**) *vt* (*order, decision*) aufheben; (*objection*)

übergehen

overriding [əʊvə'raidiŋ] *adj* vorherrschend

overrule [əʊvə'ruːl] *vt* verwerfen

overrun [əʊvə'rʌn] (*irreg: like* **run**) *vt* (*country*) einfallen in; (*time limit*) überziehen

overseas [əʊvə'siːz] *adv* nach/in Übersee ♦ *adj* überseeisch, Übersee-

overseer ['əʊvəsiə*] *n* Aufseher *m*

overshadow [əʊvə'ʃædəʊ] *vt* überschatten

overshoot ['əʊvə'ʃuːt] (*irreg: like* **shoot**) *vt* (*runway*) hinausschießen über +*acc*

oversight ['əʊvəsait] *n* (*mistake*) Versehen *nt*

oversleep ['əʊvə'sliːp] (*irreg: like* **sleep**) *vi* verschlafen

overspill ['əʊvəspil] *n* (Bevölkerungs)überschuß *m*

overstate ['əʊvə'steit] *vt* übertreiben

overstep [əʊvə'step] *vt*: **to ~ the mark** zu weit gehen

overt [əʊ'vɜːt] *adj* offen(kundig)

overtake [əʊvə'teik] (*irreg: like* **take**) *vt, vi* überholen

overthrow [əʊvə'θrəʊ] (*irreg: like* **throw**) *vt* (*POL*) stürzen

overtime ['əʊvətaim] *n* Überstunden *pl*

overtone ['əʊvətəʊn] *n* (*fig*) Note *f*

overture ['əʊvətʃʊə*] *n* Ouvertüre *f*

overturn [əʊvə'tɜːn] *vt, vi* umkippen

overweight ['əʊvə'weit] *adj* zu dick

overwhelm [əʊvə'welm] *vt* überwältigen; ~**ing** *adj* überwältigend

overwork ['əʊvə'wɜːk] *n* Überarbeitung *f* ♦ *vt* überlasten ♦ *vi* sich überarbeiten

overwrought ['əʊvə'rɔːt] *adj* überreizt

owe [əʊ] *vt* schulden; **to ~ sth to sb** (*money*) jdm etw schulden; (*favour etc*) jdm etw verdanken

owing to ['əʊiŋ-] *prep* wegen +*gen*

owl [aʊl] *n* Eule *f*

own [əʊn] *vt* besitzen ♦ *adj* eigen; **a room of my** ~ mein eigenes Zimmer; **to get one's** ~ **back** sich rächen; **on one's** ~ allein; ~ **up** *vi*: **to** ~ **up (to sth)** (etw) zugeben; ~**er** *n* Besitzer(in) *m(f)*; ~**ership** *n* Besitz *m*

ox [ɒks] (*pl* **oxen**) *n* Ochse *m*
oxen ['ɒksn] *npl of* **ox**
oxtail ['ɒksteɪl] *n*: ~ **soup**
Ochsenschwanzsuppe *f*
oxygen ['ɒksɪdʒən] *n* Sauerstoff *m*; ~
mask *n* Sauerstoffmaske *f*; ~ **tent** *n*
Sauerstoffzelt *nt*
oyster ['ɔɪstə*] *n* Auster *f*
oz. *abbr* = **ounce(s)**
ozone ['əʊzəʊn] *n* Ozon *nt*; ~**-friendly**
adj (*aerosol*) ohne Treibgas; (*fridge*)
FCKW-frei; ~ **hole** *n* Ozonloch *nt*; ~
layer *n* Ozonschicht *f*

P p

p [piː] *abbr* = **penny; pence**
pa [pɑː] (*inf*) *n* Papa *m*
P.A. *n abbr* = **personal assistant; public
address system**
p.a. *abbr* = **per annum**
pace [peɪs] *n* Schritt *m*; (*speed*) Tempo *nt*
♦ *vi* schreiten; **to keep ~ with** Schritt
halten mit; ~**-maker** *n* Schrittmacher *m*
pacific [pə'sɪfɪk] *adj* pazifisch ♦ *n*: **the P~
(Ocean)** der Pazifik
pacifist ['pæsɪfɪst] *n* Pazifist *m*
pacify ['pæsɪfaɪ] *vt* befrieden; (*calm*)
beruhigen
pack [pæk] *n* (*of goods*) Packung *f*; (*of
hounds*) Meute *f*; (*of cards*) Spiel *nt*;
(*gang*) Bande *f* ♦ *vt* (*case*) packen;
(*clothes*) einpacken ♦ *vi* packen; **to ~ sb
off to ...** jdn nach ... schicken; ~ **it in!**
laß es gut sein!
package ['pækɪdʒ] *n* Paket *nt*; ~ **tour** *n*
Pauschalreise *f*
packed lunch ['pækt-] *n* Lunchpaket *nt*
packet ['pækɪt] *n* Päckchen *nt*
packing ['pækɪŋ] *n* (*action*) Packen *nt*;
(*material*) Verpackung *f*; ~ **case** *n*
(Pack)kiste *f*
pact [pækt] *n* Pakt *m*, Vertrag *m*
pad [pæd] *n* (*of paper*) (Schreib)block *m*;
(*stuffing*) Polster *nt* ♦ *vt* polstern; ~**ding**
n Polsterung *f*
paddle ['pædl] *n* Paddel *nt*; (*US: for table
tennis*) Schläger *m* ♦ *vt* (*boat*) paddeln

♦ *vi* (*in sea*) planschen; ~ **steamer** *n*
Raddampfer *m*
paddling pool ['pædlɪŋ-] (*BRIT*) *n*
Planschbecken *nt*
paddock ['pædək] *n* Koppel *f*
paddy field ['pædɪ-] *n* Reisfeld *nt*
padlock ['pædlɒk] *n* Vorhängeschloß *nt*
♦ *vt* verschließen
paediatrics [piːdɪ'ætrɪks] (*US* **pediatrics**)
n Kinderheilkunde *f*
pagan ['peɪgən] *adj* heidnisch ♦ *n* Heide
m, Heidin *f*
page [peɪdʒ] *n* Seite *f*; (*person*) Page *m*
♦ *vt* (*in hotel etc*) ausrufen lassen
pageant ['pædʒənt] *n* Festzug *m*; ~**ry** *n*
Gepränge *nt*
pager ['peɪdʒə*] *n* (*TEL*)
Funkrufempfänger *m*, Piepser *m* (*inf*)
paging device ['peɪdʒɪŋ-] *n* (*TEL*)
= **pager**
paid [peɪd] *pt, pp of* **pay** ♦ *adj* bezahlt; **to
put ~ to** (*BRIT*) zunichte machen
pail [peɪl] *n* Eimer *m*
pain [peɪn] *n* Schmerz *m*; **to be in ~**
Schmerzen haben; **on ~ of death** bei
Todesstrafe; **to take ~s to do sth** sich
dat Mühe geben, etw zu tun; ~**ed** *adj*
(*expression*) gequält; ~**ful** *adj* (*physically*)
schmerzhaft; (*embarrassing*) peinlich;
(*difficult*) mühsam; ~**fully** *adv* (*fig: very*)
schrecklich; ~**killer** *n* Schmerzmittel *nt*;
~**less** *adj* schmerzlos; ~**staking**
['peɪnzteɪkɪŋ] *adj* gewissenhaft
paint [peɪnt] *n* Farbe *f* ♦ *vt* anstreichen;
(*picture*) malen; **to ~ the door blue** die
Tür blau streichen; ~**brush** *n* Pinsel *m*;
~**er** *n* Maler *m*; ~**ing** *n* Malerei *f*;
(*picture*) Gemälde *nt*; ~**work** *n* Anstrich
m; (*of car*) Lack *m*
pair [peə*] *n* Paar *nt*; ~ **of scissors**
Schere *f*; ~ **of trousers** Hose *f*
pajamas [pə'dʒɑːməz] (*US*) *npl*
Schlafanzug *m*
Pakistan [pɑːkɪ'stɑːn] *n* Pakistan *nt*; ~**i**
adj pakistanisch ♦ *n* Pakistani *mf*
pal [pæl] (*inf*) *n* Kumpel *m*
palace ['pæləs] *n* Palast *m*, Schloß *nt*
palatable ['pælətəbl] *adj* schmackhaft
palate ['pælɪt] *n* Gaumen *m*

palatial [pə'leɪʃəl] *adj* palastartig
pale [peɪl] *adj* blaß, bleich ♦ *n*: **to be beyond the ~** die Grenzen überschreiten
Palestine ['pælɪstaɪn] *n* Palästina *nt*
Palestinian [pælɪs'tɪnɪən] *adj* palästinensisch ♦ *n* Palästinenser(in) *m(f)*
palette ['pælɪt] *n* Palette *f*
paling ['peɪlɪŋ] *n* (*stake*) Zaunpfahl *m*; (*fence*) Lattenzaun *m*
pall [pɔːl] *n* (*of smoke*) (Rauch)wolke *f* ♦ *vi* jeden Reiz verlieren, verblassen
pallet ['pælɪt] *n* (*for goods*) Palette *f*
pallid ['pælɪd] *adj* blaß, bleich
pallor ['pælə*] *n* Blässe *f*
palm [pɑːm] *n* (*of hand*) Handfläche *f*; (*also: ~ tree*) Palme *f* ♦ *vt*: **to ~ sth off on sb** jdm etw andrehen; **P~ Sunday** *n* Palmsonntag *m*
palpable ['pælpəbl] *adj* (*also fig*) greifbar
palpitation [pælpɪ'teɪʃən] *n* Herzklopfen *nt*
paltry ['pɔːltrɪ] *adj* armselig
pamper ['pæmpə*] *vt* verhätscheln
pamphlet ['pæmflət] *n* Broschüre *f*
pan [pæn] *n* Pfanne *f* ♦ *vi* (*CINE*) schwenken
panacea [pænə'sɪə] *n* (*fig*) Allheilmittel *nt*
panache [pə'næʃ] *n* Schwung *m*
pancake ['pænkeɪk] *n* Pfannkuchen *m*
pancreas ['pæŋkrɪəs] *n* Bauchspeicheldrüse *f*
panda ['pændə] *n* Panda *m*; **~ car** (*BRIT*) *n* (Funk)streifenwagen *m*
pandemonium [pændɪ'məʊnɪəm] *n* Hölle *f*; (*noise*) Höllenlärm *m*
pander ['pændə*] *vi*: **to ~ to** sich richten nach
pane [peɪn] *n* (*Fenster*)scheibe *f*
panel ['pænl] *n* (*of wood*) Tafel *f*; (*TV*) Diskussionsrunde *f*; **~ling** (*US* **~ing**) *n* Täfelung *f*
pang [pæŋ] *n*: **~s of hunger** quälende(r) Hunger *m*; **~s of conscience** Gewissensbisse *pl*
panic ['pænɪk] *n* Panik *f* ♦ *vi* in Panik geraten; **don't ~** (nur) keine Panik!; **~ky** *adj* (*person*) überängstlich; **~-stricken** *adj* von panischem Schrecken erfaßt;

(*look*) panisch
pansy ['pænzɪ] *n* (*flower*) Stiefmütterchen *nt*; (*inf*) Schwule(r) *m*
pant [pænt] *vi* keuchen; (*dog*) hecheln
panther ['pænθə*] *n* Panther *m*
panties ['pæntɪz] *npl* (Damen)slip *m*
pantihose ['pæntɪhəʊz] (*US*) *n* Strumpfhose *f*
pantomime ['pæntəmaɪm] (*BRIT*) *n* Märchenkomödie *f* um Weihnachten
pantry ['pæntrɪ] *n* Vorratskammer *f*
pants [pænts] *npl* (*BRIT*: *woman's*) Schlüpfer *m*; (: *man's*) Unterhose *f*; (*US*: *trousers*) Hose *f*
papal ['peɪpəl] *adj* päpstlich
paper ['peɪpə*] *n* Papier *nt*; (*news~*) Zeitung *f*; (*essay*) Referat *nt* ♦ *adj* Papier-, aus Papier ♦ *vt* (*wall*) tapezieren; **~s** *npl* (*identity ~s*) Ausweis(papiere *pl*) *m*; **~back** *n* Taschenbuch *nt*; **~ bag** *n* Tüte *f*; **~ clip** *n* Büroklammer *f*; **~ hankie** *n* Tempotaschentuch *nt* ®; **~weight** *n* Briefbeschwerer *m*; **~work** *n* Schreibarbeit *f*
par [pɑː*] *n* (*COMM*) Nennwert *m*; (*GOLF*) Par *nt*; **on a ~ with** ebenbürtig +*dat*
parable ['pærəbl] *n* (*REL*) Gleichnis *nt*
parachute ['pærəʃuːt] *n* Fallschirm *m* ♦ *vi* (mit dem Fallschirm) abspringen
parade [pə'reɪd] *n* Parade *f* ♦ *vt* aufmarschieren lassen; (*fig*) zur Schau stellen ♦ *vi* paradieren, vorbeimarschieren
paradise ['pærədaɪs] *n* Paradies *nt*
paradox ['pærədɒks] *n* Paradox *nt*; **~ically** [pærə'dɒksɪkəlɪ] *adv* paradoxerweise
paraffin ['pærəfɪn] (*BRIT*) *n* Paraffin *nt*
paragon ['pærəgən] *n* Muster *nt*
paragraph ['pærəgrɑːf] *n* Absatz *m*
parallel ['pærəlel] *adj* parallel ♦ *n* Parallele *f*
paralyse ['pærəlaɪz] (*US* **paralyze**) *vt* (*MED*) lähmen, paralysieren; (*fig*: *organization, production etc*) lahmlegen
paralysis [pə'rælɪsɪs] *n* Lähmung *f*
paralyze ['pærəlaɪz] *vt* = **paralyse**
parameter [pə'ræmɪtə*] *n* Parameter *m*; **~s** *npl* (*framework, limits*) Rahmen *m*

paramount ['pærəmaʊnt] *adj* höchste(r, s), oberste(r, s)

paranoid ['pærənɔɪd] *adj* (*person*) paranoid, an Verfolgungswahn leidend; (*feeling*) krankhaft

parapet ['pærəpɪt] *n* Brüstung *f*

paraphernalia [pærəfə'neɪlɪə] *n* Zubehör *nt*, Utensilien *pl*

paraphrase ['pærəfreɪz] *vt* umschreiben

paraplegic [pærə'pli:dʒɪk] *n* Querschnittsgelähmte(r) *mf*

parasite ['pærəsaɪt] *n* (*also fig*) Schmarotzer *m*, Parasit *m*

parasol ['pærəsɒl] *n* Sonnenschirm *m*

paratrooper ['pærətru:pə*] *n* Fallschirmjäger *m*

parcel ['pɑ:sl] *n* Paket *nt* ♦ *vt* (*also*: ~ *up*) einpacken

parch [pɑ:tʃ] *vt* (aus)dörren; **~ed** *adj* ausgetrocknet; (*person*) am Verdursten

parchment ['pɑ:tʃmənt] *n* Pergament *nt*

pardon ['pɑ:dn] *n* Verzeihung *f* ♦ *vt* (*JUR*) begnadigen; ~ **me!, I beg your ~!** verzeihen Sie bitte!; ~ **me?** (*US*) wie bitte?; **(I beg your) ~?** wie bitte?

parent ['pɛərənt] *n* Elternteil *m*; **~s** *npl* (*mother and father*) Eltern *pl*; **~al** [pə'rɛntl] *adj* elterlich, Eltern-

parentheses [pə'renθɪsi:z] *npl of* **parenthesis**

parenthesis [pə'renθɪsɪs] *n* Klammer *f*; (*sentence*) Parenthese *f*

Paris ['pærɪs] *n* Paris *nt*

parish ['pærɪʃ] *n* Gemeinde *f*

parity ['pærɪtɪ] *n* (*FIN*) Umrechnungskurs *m*, Parität *f*

park [pɑ:k] *n* Park *m* ♦ *vt, vi* parken

parking ['pɑ:kɪŋ] *n* Parken *nt*; "**no ~**" „Parken verboten"; **~ lot** (*US*) *n* Parkplatz *m*; **~ meter** *n* Parkuhr *f*; **~ ticket** *n* Strafzettel *m*

parlance ['pɑ:ləns] *n* Sprachgebrauch *m*

parliament ['pɑ:ləmənt] *n* Parlament *nt*; **~ary** [pɑ:lə'mentərɪ] *adj* parlamentarisch, Parlaments-

parlour ['pɑ:lə*] (*US* **parlor**) *n* Salon *m*

parochial [pə'rəʊkɪəl] *adj* Gemeinde-; (*narrow-minded*) eng(stirnig)

parole [pə'rəʊl] *n*: **on ~** (*prisoner*) auf Bewährung

paroxysm ['pærəksɪzəm] *n* Anfall *m*

parrot ['pærət] *n* Papagei *m*

parry ['pærɪ] *vt* parieren, abwehren

parsimonious [pɑ:sɪ'məʊnɪəs] *adj* knauserig

parsley ['pɑ:slɪ] *n* Petersilie *m*

parsnip ['pɑ:snɪp] *n* Pastinake *f*

parson ['pɑ:sn] *n* Pfarrer *m*

part [pɑ:t] *n* (*piece*) Teil *m*; (*THEAT*) Rolle *f*; (*of machine*) Teil *n* ♦ *adv* = **partly** ♦ *vt* trennen; (*hair*) scheiteln ♦ *vi* (*people*) sich trennen; **to take ~ in** teilnehmen an +*dat*; **to take sth in good ~** etw nicht übelnehmen; **to take sb's ~** sich auf jds Seite *acc* stellen; **for my ~** ich für meinen Teil; **for the most ~** meistens, größtenteils; **in ~ exchange** (*BRIT*) in Zahlung; **~ with** *vt fus* hergeben; (*renounce*) aufgeben; **~ial** ['pɑ:ʃəl] *adj* (*incomplete*) teilweise; (*biased*) parteiisch; **to be ~ial to** eine (besondere) Vorliebe haben für

participant [pɑ:'tɪsɪpənt] *n* Teilnehmer(in) *m(f)*

participate [pɑ:'tɪsɪpeɪt] *vi*: **to ~ (in)** teilnehmen (an +*dat*) .

participation [pɑ:tɪsɪ'peɪʃən] *n* Teilnahme *f*; (*sharing*) Beteiligung *f*

participle ['pɑ:tɪsɪpl] *n* Partizip *nt*

particle ['pɑ:tɪkl] *n* Teilchen *nt*; (*GRAM*) Partikel *m*

particular [pə'tɪkjʊlə*] *adj* bestimmt; (*exact*) genau; (*fussy*) eigen; **in ~** besonders; **~ly** *adv* besonders; **~s** *npl* (*details*) Einzelheiten *pl*; (*of person*) Personalien *pl*

parting ['pɑ:tɪŋ] *n* (*separation*) Abschied *m*; (*BRIT*: *of hair*) Scheitel *m* ♦ *adj* Abschieds-

partition [pɑ:'tɪʃən] *n* (*wall*) Trennwand *f*; (*division*) Teilung *f* ♦ *vt* aufteilen

partly ['pɑ:tlɪ] *adv* zum Teil, teilweise

partner ['pɑ:tnə*] *n* Partner *m* ♦ *vt* der Partner sein von; **~ship** *n* Partnerschaft *f*, (*COMM*) Teilhaberschaft *f*

partridge ['pɑ:trɪdʒ] *n* Rebhuhn *nt*

part-time ['pɑ:t'taɪm] *adj* Teilzeit- ♦ *adv* stundenweise

party ['pɑːtɪ] n (POL, JUR) Partei f; (group) Gesellschaft f; (celebration) Party f ♦ adj (dress) Party-; (politics) Partei-; ~ **line** n (TEL) Gemeinschaftsanschluß m

pass [pɑːs] vt (on foot) vorbeigehen an +dat; (driving) vorbeifahren an +dat; (surpass) übersteigen; (hand on) weitergeben; (approve) genehmigen; (time) verbringen; (exam) bestehen ♦ vi (go by) vorbeigehen; vorbeifahren; (years) vergehen; (be successful) bestehen ♦ n (in mountains, SPORT) Paß m; (permission) Passierschein m; (in exam): to **get a ~** bestehen; to **~ sth through sth** etw durch etw führen; to **make a ~ at sb** (inf) bei jdm Annäherungsversuche machen; **~ away** vi (euph) verscheiden; **~ by** vi vorbeigehen; vorbeifahren; (years) vergehen; **~ for** vt fus gehalten werden für; **~ on** vt weitergeben; **~ out** vi (faint) ohnmächtig werden; **~ up** vt vorbeigehen lassen; **~able** adj (road) passierbar; (fairly good) passabel

passage ['pæsɪdʒ] n (corridor) Gang m; (in book) (Text)stelle f; (voyage) Überfahrt f; **~way** n Durchgang m

passbook ['pɑːsbʊk] n Sparbuch nt

passenger ['pæsɪndʒə*] n Passagier m; (on bus) Fahrgast m

passer-by ['pɑːsə'baɪ] n Passant(in) m(f)

passing ['pɑːsɪŋ] adj (car) vorbeifahrend; (thought, affair) momentan ♦ n: **in ~** en passant; **~ place** n (AUT) Ausweichstelle f

passion ['pæʃən] n Leidenschaft f; **~ate** adj leidenschaftlich

passive ['pæsɪv] adj passiv; (LING) passivisch; **~ smoking** n Passivrauchen nt

Passover ['pɑːsəʊvə*] n Passahfest nt

passport ['pɑːspɔːt] n (Reise)paß m; **~ control** n Paßkontrolle f

password ['pɑːswɜːd] n Parole f, Kennwort nt, Losung f

past [pɑːst] prep (motion) an +dat ... vorbei; (position) hinter +dat; (later than) nach ♦ adj (years) vergangen; (president etc) ehemalig ♦ n Vergangenheit f; **he's ~ forty** er ist über vierzig; **for the ~ few/3 days** in den letzten paar/3 Tagen; to **run**

~ vorbeilaufen; ten/quarter ~ eight zehn/viertel nach acht

pasta ['pæstə] n Teigwaren pl

paste [peɪst] n (fish ~ etc) Paste f; (glue) Kleister m ♦ vt kleben; (put ~ on) mit Kleister bestreichen

pasteurized ['pæstʃəraɪzd] adj pasteurisiert

pastime ['pɑːstaɪm] n Zeitvertreib m

pastor ['pɑːstə*] n Pfarrer m

pastry ['peɪstrɪ] n Blätterteig m; **pastries** npl (tarts etc) Stückchen pl

pasture ['pɑːstʃə*] n Weide f

pasty [n 'pæstɪ, adj 'peɪstɪ] n (Fleisch)pastete f ♦ adj bläßlich, käsig

pat [pæt] n leichte(r) Schlag m, Klaps m ♦ vt tätscheln

patch [pætʃ] n Fleck m ♦ vt flicken; **(to go through) a bad ~** eine Pechsträhne (haben); **~ up** vt flicken; (quarrel) beilegen; **~y** adj (irregular) ungleichmäßig

pâté ['pæteɪ] n Pastete f

patent ['peɪtənt] n Patent nt ♦ vt patentieren lassen; (by authorities) patentieren ♦ adj offenkundig; **~ leather** n Lackleder nt

paternal [pə'tɜːnl] adj väterlich

paternity [pə'tɜːnɪtɪ] n Vaterschaft f

path [pɑːθ] n Pfad m; Weg m; (of the sun) Bahn f

pathetic [pə'θetɪk] adj (very bad) kläglich

pathological [pæθə'lɒdʒɪkl] adj pathologisch

pathology [pə'θɒlədʒɪ] n Pathologie f

pathos ['peɪθɒs] n Rührseligkeit f

pathway ['pɑːθweɪ] n Weg m

patience ['peɪʃəns] n Geduld f; (BRIT: CARDS) Patience f

patient ['peɪʃənt] n Patient(in) m(f), Kranke(r) mf ♦ adj geduldig

patio ['pætɪəʊ] n Terrasse f

patriotic [pætrɪ'ɒtɪk] adj patriotisch

patrol [pə'trəʊl] n Patrouille f; (police) Streife f ♦ vt patrouillieren in +dat ♦ vi (police) die Runde machen; (MIL) patrouillieren; **~ car** n Streifenwagen m; **~man** (US: irreg) n (Streifen)polizist m

patron ['peɪtrən] n (in shop)

(Stamm)kunde *m*; (*in hotel*) (Stamm)gast *m*; (*supporter*) Förderer *m*; ~ **of the arts** Mäzen *m*; **~age** ['pætrənɪdʒ] *n* Schirmherrschaft *f*; **~ize** ['pætrənaɪz] *vt* (*support*) unterstützen; (*shop*) besuchen; (*treat condescendingly*) von oben herab behandeln; ~ **saint** *n* Schutzpatron(in) *m(f)*

patter ['pætə*] *n* (*sound: of feet*) Trappeln *nt*; (: *of rain*) Prasseln *nt*; (*sales talk*) Gerede *nt* ♦ *vi* (*feet*) trappeln; (*rain*) prasseln

pattern ['pætən] *n* Muster *nt*; (*SEWING*) Schnittmuster *nt*; (*KNITTING*) Strickanleitung *f*

paunch [pɔ:ntʃ] *n* Wanst *m*

pauper ['pɔ:pə*] *n* Arme(r) *mf*

pause [pɔ:z] *n* Pause *f* ♦ *vi* innehalten

pave [peɪv] *vt* pflastern; **to ~ the way for** den Weg bahnen für

pavement ['peɪvmənt] (*BRIT*) *n* Bürgersteig *m*

pavilion [pə'vɪlɪən] *n* Pavillon *m*; (*SPORT*) Klubhaus *nt*

paving ['peɪvɪŋ] *n* Straßenpflaster *nt*; ~ **stone** *n* Pflasterstein *m*

paw [pɔ:] *n* Pfote *f*; (*of big cats*) Tatze *f*, Pranke *f* ♦ *vt* (*scrape*) scharren; (*handle*) betatschen

pawn [pɔ:n] *n* Pfand *nt*; (*chess*) Bauer *m* ♦ *vt* verpfänden; **~broker** *n* Pfandleiher *m*; **~shop** *n* Pfandhaus *nt*

pay [peɪ] (*pt, pp* **paid**) *n* Bezahlung *f*, Lohn *m* ♦ *vt* bezahlen ♦ *vi* zahlen; (*be profitable*) sich bezahlt machen; **to ~ attention (to)** achtgeben (auf +*acc*); **to ~ sb a visit** jdn besuchen; ~ **back** *vt* zurückzahlen; ~ **for** *vt fus* bezahlen; ~ **in** *vt* einzahlen; ~ **off** *vt* abzahlen ♦ *vi* (*scheme, decision*) sich bezahlt machen; ~ **up** *vi* bezahlen; **~able** *adj* zahlbar, fällig; **~ee** [peɪ'i:] *n* Zahlungsempfänger *m*; ~ **envelope** (*US*) *n* Lohntüte *f*; **~ment** *n* Bezahlung *f*; **~advance ~ment** Vorauszahlung *f*; **monthly ~ment** monatliche Rate *f*; ~ **packet** (*BRIT*) *n* Lohntüte *f*; ~ **phone** *n* Münzfernsprecher *m*; **~roll** *n* Lohnliste *f*; ~ **slip** *n* Lohn-/Gehaltsstreifen *m*; ~ **television** *n* Münzfernsehen *nt*

PC *n abbr* = **personal computer**

p.c. *abbr* = **per cent**

pea [pi:] *n* Erbse *f*

peace [pi:s] *n* Friede(n) *m*; **~able** *adj* friedlich; **~ful** *adj* friedlich, ruhig; **~keeping** *adj* Friedens-

peach [pi:tʃ] *n* Pfirsich *m*

peacock ['pi:kɔk] *n* Pfau *m*

peak [pi:k] *n* Spitze *f*; (*of mountain*) Gipfel *m*; (*fig*) Höhepunkt *m*; ~ **hours** *npl* (*traffic*) Hauptverkehrszeit *f*; (*telephone, electricity*) Hauptbelastungszeit *f*; ~ **period** *n* Stoßzeit *f*, Hauptzeit *f*

peal [pi:l] *n* (*Glocken*)läuten *nt*; **~s of laughter** schallende(s) Gelächter *nt*

peanut ['pi:nʌt] *n* Erdnuß *f*; ~ **butter** *n* Erdnußbutter *f*

pear [pɛə*] *n* Birne *f*

pearl [pɜ:l] *n* Perle *f*

peasant ['pezənt] *n* Bauer *m*

peat [pi:t] *n* Torf *m*

pebble ['pebl] *n* Kiesel *m*

peck [pek] *vt, vi* picken ♦ *n* (*with beak*) Schnabelhieb *m*; (*kiss*) flüchtige(r) Kuß *m*; **~ing order** *n* Hackordnung *f*; **~ish** (*BRIT: inf*) *adj* ein bißchen hungrig

peculiar [pɪ'kju:lɪə*] *adj* (*odd*) seltsam; ~ **to** charakteristisch für; **~ity** [pɪkju:lɪ'ærɪtɪ] *n* (*singular quality*) Besonderheit *f*; (*strangeness*) Eigenartigkeit *f*

pedal ['pedl] *n* Pedal *nt* ♦ *vt, vi* (*cycle*) fahren, radfahren

pedantic [pɪ'dæntɪk] *adj* pedantisch

peddler ['pedlə*] *n* Hausierer(in) *m(f)*; (*of drugs*) Drogenhändler(in) *m(f)*

pedestal ['pedɪstl] *n* Sockel *m*

pedestrian [pɪ'destrɪən] *n* Fußgänger *m* ♦ *adj* Fußgänger-; (*humdrum*) langweilig; ~ **crossing** (*BRIT*) *n* Fußgängerüberweg *m*

pediatrics [pi:dɪ'ætrɪks] (*US*) *n* = **paediatrics**

pedigree ['pedɪgri:] *n* Stammbaum *m* ♦ *cpd* (*animal*) reinrassig, Zucht-

pedlar ['pedlə*] *n* = **peddler**

pee [pi:] (*inf*) *vi* pissen, pinkeln

peek [pi:k] *vi* gucken

peel [pi:l] *n* Schale *f* ♦ *vt* schälen ♦ *vi*

(*paint etc*) abblättern; (*skin*) sich schälen

peep [piːp] *n* (*BRIT: look*) kurze(r) Blick *m*; (*sound*) Piepsen *nt* ♦ *vi* (*BRIT: look*) gucken; **~ out** *vi* herausgucken; **~hole** *n* Guckloch *nt*

peer [pɪə*] *vi* starren; (*peep*) gucken ♦ *n* (*nobleman*) Peer *m*; (*equal*) Ebenbürtige(r) *m*; **~age** *n* Peerswürde *f*

peeved [piːvd] *adj* ärgerlich; (*person*) sauer

peevish ['piːvɪʃ] *adj* verdrießlich

peg [peg] *n* (*stake*) Pflock *m*; (*BRIT: also: clothes ~*) Wäscheklammer *f*

Peking [piːˈkɪŋ] *n* Peking *nt*

pelican ['pelɪkən] *n* Pelikan *m*; **~ crossing** (*BRIT*) *n* (*AUT*) Ampelüberweg *m*

pellet ['pelɪt] *n* Kügelchen *nt*

pelmet ['pelmɪt] *n* Blende *f*

pelt [pelt] *vt* bewerfen ♦ *vi* (*rain*) schütten ♦ *n* Pelz *m*, Fell *nt*

pelvis ['pelvɪs] *n* Becken *nt*

pen [pen] *n* (*fountain ~*) Federhalter *m*; (*ball-point ~*) Kuli *m*; (*for sheep*) Pferch *m*

penal ['piːnl] *adj* Straf-; **~ize** *vt* (*punish*) bestrafen; (*disadvantage*) benachteiligen; **~ty** ['penltɪ] *n* Strafe *f*; (*FOOTBALL*) Elfmeter *m*; **~ty (kick)** *n* Elfmeter *m*

penance ['penəns] *n* Buße *f*

pence [pens] (*BRIT*) *npl of* **penny**

pencil ['pensl] *n* Bleistift *m*; **~ case** *n* Federmäppchen *nt*; **~ sharpener** *n* Bleistiftspitzer *m*

pendant ['pendənt] *n* Anhänger *m*

pending ['pendɪŋ] *prep* bis (zu) ♦ *adj* unentschieden, noch offen

pendulum ['pendjʊləm] *n* Pendel *nt*

penetrate ['penɪtreɪt] *vt* durchdringen; (*enter into*) eindringen in +*acc*

penetration [penɪˈtreɪʃən] *n* Durchdringen *nt*; Eindringen *nt*

penfriend ['penfrend] (*BRIT*) *n* Brieffreund(in) *m(f)*

penguin ['peŋgwɪn] *n* Pinguin *m*

penicillin [penɪˈsɪlɪn] *n* Penizillin *nt*

peninsula [pɪˈnɪnsjʊlə] *n* Halbinsel *f*

penis ['piːnɪs] *n* Penis *m*

penitence ['penɪtəns] *n* Reue *f*

penitent ['penɪtənt] *adj* reuig

penitentiary [penɪˈtenʃərɪ] (*US*) *n* Zucht-

haus *nt*

penknife ['pennaɪf] *n* Federmesser *nt*

pen name *n* Pseudonym *nt*

penniless ['penɪləs] *adj* mittellos

penny ['penɪ] (*pl* **pennies** *or* (*BRIT*) **pence**) *n* Penny *m*; (*US*) Centstück *nt*

penpal ['penpæl] (*inf*) *n* Brieffreund(in) *m(f)*

pension ['penʃən] *n* Rente *f*; **~er** (*BRIT*) *n* Rentner(in) *m(f)*; **~ fund** *n* Rentenfonds *m*

pensive ['pensɪv] *adj* nachdenklich

Pentecost ['pentɪkɒst] *n* Pfingsten *pl or nt*

penthouse ['penthaʊs] *n* Dachterrassenwohnung *f*

pent-up ['pentʌp] *adj* (*feelings*) angestaut

penultimate [pɪˈnʌltɪmət] *adj* vorletzte(r, s)

people ['piːpl] *n* (*nation*) Volk *nt* ♦ *npl* (*persons*) Leute *pl*; (*inhabitants*) Bevölkerung *f* ♦ *vt* besiedeln; **several ~ came** mehrere Leute kamen; **~ say that ...** man sagt, daß ...

pep [pep] (*inf*) *n* Schwung *m*, Schmiß *m*; **~ up** *vt* aufmöbeln

pepper ['pepə*] *n* Pfeffer *m*; (*vegetable*) Paprika *m* ♦ *vt* (*pelt*) bombardieren; **~mint** *n* (*plant*) Pfefferminze *f*; (*sweet*) Pfefferminz *nt*

peptalk ['peptɔːk] (*inf*) *n* Anstachelung *f*

per [pɜː*] *prep* pro; **~ day/person** pro Tag/Person; **~ annum** *adv* pro Jahr; **~ capita** *adj* (*income*) Pro-Kopf- ♦ *adv* pro Kopf

perceive [pəˈsiːv] *vt* (*realize*) wahrnehmen; (*understand*) verstehen

per cent [pəˈsent] *n* Prozent *nt*

percentage [pəˈsentɪdʒ] *n* Prozentsatz *m*

perception [pəˈsepʃən] *n* Wahrnehmung *f*; (*insight*) Einsicht *f*

perceptive [pəˈseptɪv] *adj* (*person*) aufmerksam; (*analysis*) tiefgehend

perch [pɜːtʃ] *n* Stange *f*; (*fish*) Flußbarsch *m* ♦ *vi* sitzen, hocken

percolator ['pɜːkəleɪtə*] *n* Kaffeemaschine *f*

percussion [pəˈkʌʃən] *n* (*MUS*) Schlagzeug *nt*

peremptory [pəˈremptərɪ] *adj* schroff

perennial [pə'renɪəl] *adj* wiederkehrend; (*everlasting*) unvergänglich

perfect [*adj, n* 'pɜːfɪkt, *vb* pə'fekt] *adj* vollkommen; (*crime, solution*) perfekt ♦ *n* (*GRAM*) Perfekt *nt* ♦ *vt* vervollkommnen; **~ion** [pə'fekʃən] *n* Vollkommenheit *f*; **~ionist** [pə'fekʃənɪst] *n* Perfektionist *m*; **~ly** *adv* vollkommen, perfekt; (*quite*) ganz, einfach

perforate ['pɜːfəreɪt] *vt* durchlöchern

perforation [pɜːfə'reɪʃən] *n* Perforieren *nt*; (*line of holes*) Perforation *f*

perform [pə'fɔːm] *vt* (*carry out*) durch- *or* ausführen; (*task*) verrichten; (*THEAT*) spielen, geben ♦ *vi* auftreten; **~ance** *n* Durchführung *f*; (*efficiency*) Leistung *f*; (*show*) Vorstellung *f*; **~er** *n* Künstler(in) *m(f)*; **~ing** *adj* (*animal*) dressiert

perfume ['pɜːfjuːm] *n* Duft *m*; (*lady's*) Parfüm *nt*

perfunctory [pə'fʌŋktərɪ] *adj* oberflächlich, mechanisch

perhaps [pə'hæps] *adv* vielleicht

peril ['perɪl] *n* Gefahr *f*

perimeter [pə'rɪmɪtə*] *n* Peripherie *f*; (*of circle etc*) Umfang *m*

period ['pɪərɪəd] *n* Periode *f*; (*GRAM*) Punkt *m*; (*MED*) Periode *f* ♦ *adj* (*costume*) historisch; **~ic** [pɪərɪ'ɒdɪk] *adj* periodisch; **~ical** [pɪərɪ'ɒdɪkəl] *n* Zeitschrift *f*; **~ically** [pɪərɪ'ɒdɪkəlɪ] *adv* periodisch

peripheral [pə'rɪfərəl] *adj* Rand-, peripher ♦ *n* (*COMPUT*) Peripheriegerät *nt*

perish ['perɪʃ] *vi* umkommen; (*fruit*) verderben; **~able** *adj* leicht verderblich

perjury ['pɜːdʒərɪ] *n* Meineid *m*

perk [pɜːk] (*inf*) *n* (*fringe benefit*) Vergünstigung *f*; **~ up** *vi* munter werden; **~y** *adj* (*cheerful*) keck

perm [pɜːm] *n* Dauerwelle *f*

permanent ['pɜːmənənt] *adj* dauernd, ständig

permeate ['pɜːmɪeɪt] *vt, vi* durchdringen

permissible [pə'mɪsəbl] *adj* zulässig

permission [pə'mɪʃən] *n* Erlaubnis *f*

permissive [pə'mɪsɪv] *adj* nachgiebig; **the ~ society** die permissive Gesellschaft

permit [*n* 'pɜːmɪt, *vb* pə'mɪt] *n* Zulassung *f* ♦ *vt* erlauben, zulassen

pernicious [pɜː'nɪʃəs] *adj* schädlich

perpendicular [pɜːpən'dɪkjʊlə*] *adj* senkrecht

perpetrate ['pɜːpɪtreɪt] *vt* begehen

perpetual [pə'petjʊəl] *adj* dauernd, ständig

perpetuate [pə'petjʊeɪt] *vt* verewigen, bewahren

perplex [pə'pleks] *vt* verblüffen

persecute ['pɜːsɪkjuːt] *vt* verfolgen

persecution [pɜːsɪ'kjuːʃən] *n* Verfolgung *f*

perseverance [pɜːsɪ'vɪərəns] *n* Ausdauer *f*

persevere [pɜːsɪ'vɪə*] *vi* durchhalten

Persian ['pɜːʃən] *adj* persisch ♦ *n* Perser(in) *m(f)*; **the (~) Gulf** der Persische Golf

persist [pə'sɪst] *vi* (*in belief etc*) bleiben; (*rain, smell*) andauern; (*continue*) nicht aufhören; **to ~ in** bleiben bei; **~ence** *n* Beharrlichkeit *f*; **~ent** *adj* beharrlich; (*unending*) ständig

person ['pɜːsn] *n* Person *f*; **in ~** persönlich; **~able** *adj* gut aussehend; **~al** *adj* persönlich; (*private*) privat; (*of body*) körperlich, Körper-; **~al assistant** *n* Assistent(in) *m(f)*; **~al computer** *n* Personalcomputer *m*; **~ality** [pɜːsə'nælɪtɪ] *n* Persönlichkeit *f*; **~ally** *adv* persönlich; **~al organizer** *n* Terminplaner *m*, Zeitplaner *m*; (*electronic*) elektronisches Notizbuch *nt*; **~al stereo** *n* Walkman *m* ®; **~ify** [pɜː'sɒnɪfaɪ] *vt* verkörpern

personnel [pɜːsə'nel] *n* Personal *nt*

perspective [pə'spektɪv] *n* Perspektive *f*

Perspex ['pɜːspeks] ® *n* Acrylglas *nt*

perspiration [pɜːspə'reɪʃən] *n* Transpiration *f*

perspire [pəs'paɪə*] *vi* transpirieren

persuade [pə'sweɪd] *vt* überreden; (*convince*) überzeugen

persuasion [pə'sweɪʒən] *n* Überredung *f*; Überzeugung *f*

persuasive [pə'sweɪsɪv] *adj* überzeugend

pert [pɜːt] *adj* keck

pertaining [pɜː'teɪnɪŋ]: **~ to** *prep* betreffend +*acc*

pertinent ['pɜːtɪnənt] *adj* relevant

perturb [pə'tɜːb] *vt* beunruhigen

peruse [pə'ruːz] *vt* lesen

pervade [pə'veɪd] *vt* erfüllen

perverse [pə'vɜːs] *adj* pervers; *(obstinate)* eigensinnig

pervert [*n* 'pɜːvɜːt, *vb* pə'vɜːt] *n* perverse(r) Mensch *m* ♦ *vt* verdrehen; *(morally)* verderben

pessimist ['pesɪmɪst] *n* Pessimist *m*; **~ic** [pesɪ'mɪstɪk] *adj* pessimistisch

pest [pest] *n* (insect) Schädling *m*; (fig: person) Nervensäge *f*; (: thing) Plage *f*

pester ['pestə*] *vt* plagen

pesticide ['pestɪsaɪd] *n* Insektenvertilgungsmittel *nt*

pet [pet] *n* (animal) Haustier *nt* ♦ *vt* liebkosen, streicheln ♦ *vi* (inf) Petting machen

petal ['petl] *n* Blütenblatt *nt*

peter out ['piːtə-] *vi* allmählich zu Ende gehen

petite [pə'tiːt] *adj* zierlich

petition [pə'tɪʃən] *n* Bittschrift *f*

petrified ['petrɪfaɪd] *adj* versteinert; (person) starr (vor Schreck)

petrify ['petrɪfaɪ] *vt* versteinern; (person) erstarren lassen

petrol ['petrəl] (BRIT) *n* Benzin *nt*, Kraftstoff *m*; **two-/four-star ~** ≈ Normal-/Superbenzin *nt*; **~ can** *n* Benzinkanister *m*

petroleum [pɪ'trəʊlɪəm] *n* Petroleum *nt*

petrol: **~ pump** (BRIT) *n* (in car) Benzinpumpe *f*; (at garage) Zapfsäule *f*; **~ station** (BRIT) *n* Tankstelle *f*; **~ tank** (BRIT) *n* Benzintank *m*

petticoat ['petɪkəʊt] *n* Unterrock *m*

petty ['petɪ] *adj* (unimportant) unbedeutend; (mean) kleinlich; **~ cash** *n* Portokasse *f*; **~ officer** *n* Maat *m*

petulant ['petjʊlənt] *adj* leicht reizbar

pew [pjuː] *n* Kirchenbank *f*

pewter ['pjuːtə*] *n* Zinn *nt*

pharmacist ['fɑːməsɪst] *n* Pharmazeut *m*; (druggist) Apotheker *m*

pharmacy ['fɑːməsɪ] *n* Pharmazie *f*; (shop) Apotheke *f*

phase [feɪz] *n* Phase *f* ♦ *vt*: **to ~ sth in** etw allmählich einführen; **to ~ sth out**

etw auslaufen lassen

Ph.D. *n abbr* = **Doctor of Philosophy**

pheasant ['feznt] *n* Fasan *m*

phenomena [fɪ'nɒmɪnə] *npl of* **phenomenon**

phenomenon [fɪ'nɒmɪnən] *n* Phänomen *nt*

philanthropist [fɪ'lænθrəpɪst] *n* Philanthrop *m*, Menschenfreund *m*

Philippines ['fɪlɪpiːnz] *npl*: **the ~** die Philippinen *pl*

philosopher [fɪ'lɒsəfə*] *n* Philosoph *m*

philosophical [fɪlə'sɒfɪkl] *adj* philosophisch

philosophy [fɪ'lɒsəfɪ] *n* Philosophie *f*

phlegm [flem] *n* (MED) Schleim *m*; (calmness) Gelassenheit *f*; **~atic** [fleg'mætɪk] *adj* gelassen

phobia ['fəʊbjə] *n* (irrational fear: of insects, flying, water etc) Phobie *f*

phone [fəʊn] *n* Telefon *nt* ♦ *vt, vi* telefonieren, anrufen; **to be on the ~** telefonieren; **~ back** *vt, vi* zurückrufen; **~ up** *vt, vi* anrufen; **~ book** *n* Telefonbuch *nt*; **~ booth** *n* Telefonzelle *f*; **~ box** *n* Telefonzelle *f*; **~ call** *n* Telefonanruf *m*; **~ card** *n* (TEL) Telefonkarte *f*; **~-in** *n* (RADIO, TV) Phone-in *nt*

phonetics [fə'netɪks] *n* Phonetik *f*

phoney ['fəʊnɪ] (inf) *adj* unecht ♦ *n* (person) Schwindler *m*; (thing) Fälschung *f*; (banknote) Blüte *f*

phony ['fəʊnɪ] *adj, n* = **phoney**

photo ['fəʊtəʊ] *n* Foto *nt*

photocopier ['fəʊtəʊ'kɒpɪə*] *n* Kopiergerät *nt*

photocopy ['fəʊtəʊkɒpɪ] *n* Fotokopie *f* ♦ *vt* fotokopieren

photogenic [fəʊtəʊ'dʒenɪk] *adj* fotogen

photograph ['fəʊtəʊgrɑːf] *n* Fotografie *f*, Aufnahme *f* ♦ *vt* fotografieren; **~er** [fə'tɒgrəfə*] *n* Fotograf *m*; **~ic** [fəʊtə'græfɪk] *adj* fotografisch; **~y** [fə'tɒgrəfɪ] *n* Fotografie *f*

phrase [freɪz] *n* Satz *m*; (expression) Ausdruck *m* ♦ *vt* ausdrücken, formulieren; **~ book** *n* Sprachführer *m*

physical ['fɪzɪkəl] *adj* physikalisch; (bodily) körperlich, physisch; **~**

education n Turnen nt; **~ly** adv physikalisch
physician [fɪˈzɪʃən] n Arzt m
physicist [ˈfɪzɪsɪst] n Physiker(in) m(f)
physics [ˈfɪzɪks] n Physik f
physiotherapy [fɪzɪəˈθerəpɪ] n Heilgymnastik f, Physiotherapie f
physique [fɪˈziːk] n Körperbau m
pianist [ˈpɪənɪst] n Pianist(in) m(f)
piano [pɪˈænəʊ] n Klavier nt
pick [pɪk] n (tool) Pickel m; (choice) Auswahl f ♦ vt (fruit) pflücken; (choose) aussuchen; **take your ~** such dir etwas aus; **to ~ sb's pocket** jdn bestehlen; **~ off** vt (kill) abschießen; **~ on** vt fus (person) herumhacken auf +dat; **~ out** vt auswählen; **~ up** vi (improve) sich erholen ♦ vt (lift up) aufheben; (learn) (schnell) mitbekommen; (collect) abholen; (girl) (sich dat) anlachen; (AUT: passenger) mitnehmen; (speed) gewinnen an +dat; **to ~ o.s. up** aufstehen
picket [ˈpɪkɪt] n (striker) Streikposten m ♦ vt (factory) (Streik)posten aufstellen vor +dat ♦ vi (Streik)posten stehen
pickle [ˈpɪkl] n (salty mixture) Pökel m; (inf) Klemme f ♦ vt (in Essig) einlegen; einpökeln
pickpocket [ˈpɪkpɒkɪt] n Taschendieb m
pick-up [ˈpɪkʌp] n (BRIT: on record player) Tonabnehmer m; (small truck) Lieferwagen m
picnic [ˈpɪknɪk] n Picknick nt ♦ vi picknicken
pictorial [pɪkˈtɔːrɪəl] adj in Bildern
picture [ˈpɪktʃə*] n Bild nt ♦ vt (visualize) sich dat vorstellen; **the ~s** npl (BRIT) das Kino; **~ book** n Bilderbuch nt
picturesque [pɪktʃəˈresk] adj malerisch
pie [paɪ] n (meat) Pastete f, (fruit) Torte f
piece [piːs] n Stück nt ♦ vt: **to ~ together** zusammenstückeln; (fig) sich dat zusammenreimen; **to take to ~s** in Einzelteile zerlegen; **~meal** adv stückweise, Stück für Stück; **~work** n Akkordarbeit f
pie chart n Kreisdiagramm nt
pier [pɪə*] n Pier m, Mole f
pierce [pɪəs] vt durchstechen,

durchbohren (also look); **piercing** [ˈpɪəsɪŋ] adj (cry) durchdringend
piety [ˈpaɪətɪ] n Frömmigkeit f
pig [pɪg] n Schwein nt
pigeon [ˈpɪdʒən] n Taube f; **~hole** n (compartment) Ablegefach nt
piggy bank [ˈpɪgɪ-] n Sparschwein nt
pigheaded [ˈpɪgˈhedɪd] adj dickköpfig
piglet [ˈpɪglət] n Ferkel nt
pigskin [ˈpɪgskɪn] n Schweinsleder nt
pigsty [ˈpɪgstaɪ] n (also fig) Schweinestall m
pigtail [ˈpɪgteɪl] n Zopf m
pike [paɪk] n Pike f; (fish) Hecht m
pilchard [ˈpɪltʃəd] n Sardine f
pile [paɪl] n Haufen m; (of books, wood) Stapel m; (in ground) Pfahl m; (on carpet) Flausch m ♦ vt (also: ~ up) anhäufen ♦ vi (also: ~ up) sich anhäufen
piles [paɪlz] npl Hämorrhoiden pl
pile-up [ˈpaɪlʌp] n (AUT) Massenzusammenstoß m
pilfering [ˈpɪlfərɪŋ] n Diebstahl m
pilgrim [ˈpɪlgrɪm] n Pilger(in) m(f); **~age** n Wallfahrt f
pill [pɪl] n Tablette f, Pille f; **the ~** die (Antibaby)pille
pillage [ˈpɪlɪdʒ] vt plündern
pillar [ˈpɪlə*] n Pfeiler m, Säule f (also fig); **~ box** (BRIT) n Briefkasten m
pillion [ˈpɪljən] n Soziussitz m
pillory [ˈpɪlərɪ] vt (fig) anprangern
pillow [ˈpɪləʊ] n Kissen nt; **~case** n Kissenbezug m
pilot [ˈpaɪlət] n Pilot m; (NAUT) Lotse m ♦ adj (scheme etc) Versuchs- ♦ vt führen; (ship) lotsen; **~ light** n Zündflamme f
pimp [pɪmp] n Zuhälter m
pimple [ˈpɪmpl] n Pickel m
pimply [ˈpɪmplɪ] adj pick(e)lig
pin [pɪn] n Nadel f; (for sewing) Stecknadel f; (TECH) Stift m, Bolzen m ♦ vt stecken; (keep in one position) pressen, drücken; **to ~ sth to sth** etw an etw acc heften; **to ~ sth on sb** (fig) jdm etw anhängen; **~s and needles** Kribbeln nt; **~ down** vt (fig: person): **to ~ sb down (to sth)** jdn (auf etw acc) festnageln
pinafore [ˈpɪnəfɔː*] n Schürze f; **~ dress**

n Kleiderrock *m*

pinball ['pɪnbɔːl] *n* Flipper *m*

pincers ['pɪnsəz] *npl* Kneif- *or* Beißzange *f*; (MED) Pinzette *f*

pinch [pɪntʃ] *n* Zwicken *nt*, Kneifen *nt*; (*of salt*) Prise *f* ♦ *vt* zwicken, kneifen; (*inf: steal*) klauen; (: *arrest*) schnappen ♦ *vi* (*shoe*) drücken; **at a ~** notfalls, zur Not

pincushion ['pɪnkʊʃən] *n* Nadelkissen *nt*

pine [paɪn] *n* (*also: ~ tree*) Kiefer *f* ♦ *vi*: **to ~ for** sich sehnen nach; **~ away** *vi* sich zu Tode sehnen

pineapple ['paɪnæpl] *n* Ananas *f*

ping [pɪŋ] *n* Klingeln *nt*; **~-pong** ® *n* Pingpong *nt*

pink [pɪŋk] *adj* rosa *inv* ♦ *n* Rosa *nt*; (BOT) Nelke *f*

pinnacle ['pɪnəkl] *n* Spitze *f*

PIN (number) *n* Geheimnummer *f*

pinpoint ['pɪnpɔɪnt] *vt* festlegen

pinstripe ['pɪnstraɪp] *n* Nadelstreifen *m*

pint [paɪnt] *n* Pint *nt*; (BRIT: *inf: of beer*) große(s) Bier *nt*

pioneer [paɪə'nɪə*] *n* Pionier *m*; (*fig also*) Bahnbrecher *m*

pious ['paɪəs] *adj* fromm

pip [pɪp] *n* Kern *m*; **the ~s** *npl* (BRIT: *time signal on radio*) das Zeitzeichen

pipe [paɪp] *n* (*smoking*) Pfeife *f*; (*tube*) Rohr *nt*; (*in house*) (Rohr)leitung *f* ♦ *vt* (*durch Rohre*) leiten; (MUS) blasen; **~s** *npl* (*also: bagpipes*) Dudelsack *m*; **~ down** *vi* (*be quiet*) die Luft anhalten; **~ cleaner** *n* Pfeifenreiniger *m*; **~-dream** *n* Luftschloß *nt*; **~line** *n* (*for oil*) Pipeline *f*; **~r** *n* Pfeifer *m*; (*bagpipes*) Dudelsackbläser *m*

piping ['paɪpɪŋ] *adv*: **~ hot** siedend heiß

pique [piːk] *n* gekränkte(r) Stolz *m*

pirate ['paɪərɪt] *n* Pirat *m*, Seeräuber *m*; **~ radio** (BRIT) *n* Piratensender *m*

Pisces ['paɪsiːz] *n* Fische *pl*

piss [pɪs] (*inf*) *vi* pissen; **~ed** (*inf*) *adj* (*drunk*) voll

pistol ['pɪstl] *n* Pistole *f*

piston ['pɪstən] *n* Kolben *m*

pit [pɪt] *n* Grube *f*; (THEAT) Parterre *nt*; (*orchestra ~*) Orchestergraben *m* ♦ *vt* (*mark with scars*) zerfressen; (*compare*):

to ~ sb against sb jdn an jdm messen; **the ~s** *npl* (MOTOR RACING) die Boxen

pitch [pɪtʃ] *n* Wurf *m*; (*of trader*) Stand *m*; (SPORT) (Spiel)feld *nt*; (MUS) Tonlage *f*; (*substance*) Pech *nt* ♦ *vt* werfen; (*set up*) aufschlagen ♦ *vi* (NAUT) rollen; **to ~ a tent** ein Zelt aufbauen; **~-black** *adj* pechschwarz; **~ed battle** *n* offene Schlacht *f*

pitcher ['pɪtʃə*] *n* Krug *m*

piteous ['pɪtɪəs] *adj* kläglich, erbärmlich

pitfall ['pɪtfɔːl] *n* (*fig*) Falle *f*

pith [pɪθ] *n* Mark *nt*

pithy ['pɪθɪ] *adj* prägnant

pitiful ['pɪtɪfʊl] *adj* (*deserving pity*) bedauernswert; (*contemptible*) jämmerlich

pitiless ['pɪtɪləs] *adj* erbarmungslos

pittance ['pɪtəns] *n* Hungerlohn *m*

pity ['pɪtɪ] *n* (*sympathy*) Mitleid *nt* ♦ *vt* Mitleid haben mit; **what a ~!** wie schade!

pivot ['pɪvət] *n* Drehpunkt *m* ♦ *vi*: **to ~ (on)** sich drehen (um)

pixie ['pɪksɪ] *n* Elf *m*, Elfe *f*

pizza ['piːtsə] *n* Pizza *f*

placard ['plækɑːd] *n* Plakat *nt*, Anschlag *m*

placate [plə'keɪt] *vt* beschwichtigen

place [pleɪs] *n* Platz *m*; (*spot*) Stelle *f*; (*town etc*) Ort *m* ♦ *vt* setzen, stellen, legen; (*order*) aufgeben; (SPORT) plazieren; (*identify*) unterbringen; **to take ~** stattfinden; **out of ~** nicht am rechten Platz; (*fig: remark*) unangebracht; **in the first ~** erstens; **to change ~s with sb** mit jdm den Platz tauschen; **to be ~d third** (*in race, exam*) auf dem dritten Platz liegen

placid ['plæsɪd] *adj* gelassen, ruhig

plagiarism ['pleɪdʒɪərɪzəm] *n* Plagiat *nt*

plague [pleɪg] *n* Pest *f*; (*fig*) Plage *f* ♦ *vt* plagen

plaice [pleɪs] *n* Scholle *f*

plain [pleɪn] *adj* (*clear*) klar, deutlich; (*simple*) einfach, schlicht; (*not beautiful*) alltäglich ♦ *n* Ebene *f*; **in ~ clothes** (*police*) in Zivil(kleidung); **~ chocolate** *n* Bitterschokolade *f*

plaintiff ['pleɪntɪf] *n* Kläger *m*

plaintive ['pleɪntɪv] *adj* wehleidig

plait [plæt] *n* Zopf *m* ♦ *vt* flechten

plan [plæn] *n* Plan *m* ♦ *vt*, *vi* planen; **according to ~** planmäßig; **to ~ to do sth** vorhaben, etw zu tun

plane [pleɪn] *n* Ebene *f*; (*AVIAT*) Flugzeug *nt*; (*tool*) Hobel *m*; (*tree*) Platane *f*

planet ['plænɪt] *n* Planet *m*

plank [plæŋk] *n* Brett *nt*

planning ['plænɪŋ] *n* Planung *f*; **family ~** Familienplanung *f*; **~ permission** *n* Baugenehmigung *f*

plant [plɑ:nt] *n* Pflanze *f*; (*TECH*) (Maschinen)anlage *f*; (*factory*) Fabrik *f*, Werk *nt* ♦ *vt* pflanzen; (*set firmly*) stellen

plantation [plæn'teɪʃən] *n* Plantage *f*

plaque [plæk] *n* Gedenktafel *f*; (*on teeth*) (Zahn)belag *m*

plaster ['plɑ:stə*] *n* Gips *m*; (*in house*) Verputz *m*; (*BRIT: also: sticking ~*) Pflaster *nt*; (*for fracture: ~ of Paris*) Gipsverband *m* ♦ *vt* gipsen; (*hole*) zugipsen; (*ceiling*) verputzen; (*fig: with pictures etc*) bekleben, verkleben; **~ed** (*inf*) *adj* besoffen; **~er** *n* Gipser *m*

plastic ['plæstɪk] *n* Plastik *nt or* *f* ♦ *adj* (*made of ~*) Plastik-; (*ART*) plastisch, bildend; **~ bag** *n* Plastiktüte *f*

plasticine ['plæstɪsi:n] ® *n* Plastilin *nt*

plastic surgery *n* plastische Chirurgie *f*

plate [pleɪt] *n* Teller *m*; (*gold/silver ~*) vergoldete(s)/versilberte(s) Tafelgeschirr *nt*; (*flat sheet*) Platte *f*; (*in book*) (Bild)tafel *f*

plateau ['plætəʊ] (*pl ~s or ~x*) *n* (*GEOG*) Plateau *nt*, Hochebene *f*

plateaux ['plætəʊz] *npl of* **plateau**

plate glass *n* Tafelglas *nt*

platform ['plætfɔ:m] *n* (*at meeting*) Plattform *f*, Podium *nt*; (*RAIL*) Bahnsteig *m*; (*POL*) Parteiprogramm *nt*; **~ ticket** *n* Bahnsteigkarte *f*

platinum ['plætɪnəm] *n* Platin *nt*

platoon [plə'tu:n] *n* (*MIL*) Zug *m*

platter ['plætə*] *n* Platte *f*

plausible ['plɔ:zəbl] *adj* (*theory, excuse, statement*) plausibel; (*person*) überzeugend

play [pleɪ] *n* (*also TECH*) Spiel *nt*; (*THEAT*) (Theater)stück *nt* ♦ *vt* spielen; (*another team*) spielen gegen ♦ *vi* spielen; **to ~**

safe auf Nummer sicher gehen; **~ down** *vt* herunterspielen; **~ up** *vi* (*cause trouble*) frech werden; (*bad leg etc*) weh tun ♦ *vt* (*person*) plagen; **to ~ up to sb** jdm flattieren; **~-acting** *n* Schauspielerei *f*; **~boy** *n* Playboy *m*; **~er** *n* Spieler(in) *m(f)*; **~ful** *adj* spielerisch; **~ground** *n* Spielplatz *m*; **~group** *n* Kindergarten *m*; **~ing card** *n* Spielkarte *f*; **~ing field** *n* Sportplatz *m*; **~mate** *n* Spielkamerad *m*; **~-off** *n* (*SPORT*) Entscheidungsspiel *nt*; **~pen** *n* Laufstall *m*; **~school** *n* = **playgroup**; **~thing** *n* Spielzeug *nt*; **~wright** *n* Theaterschriftsteller *m*

plc *abbr* (= *public limited company*) AG

plea [pli:] *n* Bitte *f*; (*general appeal*) Appell *m*; (*JUR*) Plädoyer *nt*; **~ bargaining** *n* (*LAW*) Aushandeln der Strafe zwischen Staatsanwaltschaft und Verteidigung

plead [pli:d] *vt* (*poverty*) zur Entschuldigung anführen; (*JUR: sb's case*) vertreten ♦ *vi* (*beg*) dringend bitten; (*JUR*) plädieren; **to ~ with sb** jdn dringend bitten

pleasant ['plezənt] *adj* angenehm; **~ness** *n* Angenehme(s) *nt*; (*of person*) Freundlichkeit *f*; **~ries** *npl* (*polite remarks*) Nettigkeiten *pl*

please [pli:z] *vt*, *vi* (*be agreeable to*) gefallen +*dat*; **~!** bitte!; **~ yourself!** wie du willst!; **~d** *adj* zufrieden; (*glad*): **~d (about sth)** erfreut (über etw *acc*); **~d to meet you** angenehm

pleasing ['pli:zɪŋ] *adj* erfreulich

pleasure ['pleʒə*] *n* Freude *f*; (*old: will*) Wünsche *pl* ♦ *cpd* Vergnügungs-; **"it's a ~"** „gern geschehen"

pleat [pli:t] *n* Falte *f*

plectrum ['plektrəm] *n* Plektron *nt*

pledge [pledʒ] *n* Pfand *nt*; (*promise*) Versprechen *nt* ♦ *vt* verpfänden; (*promise*) geloben, versprechen

plentiful ['plentɪfʊl] *adj* reichlich

plenty ['plentɪ] *n* Fülle *f*, Überfluß *m*; **~ of** eine Menge, viel

pleurisy ['plʊərɪsɪ] *n* Rippenfellentzündung *f*

pliable ['plaɪəbl] *adj* biegsam; (*person*)

beeinflußbar

pliers ['plaɪəz] *npl* (Kneif)zange *f*

plight [plaɪt] *n* (Not)lage *f*

plimsolls ['plɪmsəlz] (*BRIT*) *npl* Turnschuhe *pl*

plinth [plɪnθ] *n* Sockel *m*

plod [plɒd] *vi* (*work*) sich abplagen; (*walk*) trotten; **~der** *n* Arbeitstier *nt*

plonk [plɒŋk] *n* (*BRIT: inf: wine*) billige(r) Wein ♦ *vt*: **to ~ sth down** etw hinknallen

plot [plɒt] *n* Komplott *nt*; (*story*) Handlung *f*; (*of land*) Grundstück *nt* ♦ *vt* markieren; (*curve*) zeichnen; (*movements*) nachzeichnen ♦ *vi* (*plan secretly*) sich verschwören; **~ter** *n* (*instrument*) Plotter *m*

plough [plaʊ] (*US* **plow**) *n* Pflug *m* ♦ *vt* pflügen; **~ back** *vt* (*COMM*) wieder in das Geschäft stecken; **~ through** *vt fus* (*water*) durchpflügen; (*book*) sich kämpfen durch

plow [plaʊ] (*US*) = **plough**

ploy [plɔɪ] *n* Masche *f*

pluck [plʌk] *vt* (*fruit*) pflücken; (*guitar*) zupfen; (*goose etc*) rupfen ♦ *n* Mut *m*; **to ~ up courage** all seinen Mut zusammennehmen; **~y** *adj* beherzt

plug [plʌg] *n* Stöpsel *m*; (*ELEC*) Stecker *m*; (*inf: publicity*) Schleichwerbung *f*; (*AUT*) Zündkerze *f* ♦ *vt* (zu)stopfen; (*inf: advertise*) Reklame machen für; **~ in** *vt* (*ELEC*) anschließen

plum [plʌm] *n* Pflaume *f*, Zwetsch(g)e *f* ♦ *adj* (*job etc*) Bomben-

plumage ['pluːmɪdʒ] *n* Gefieder *nt*

plumb [plʌm] *adj* senkrecht ♦ *n* Lot *nt* ♦ *adv* (*exactly*) genau ♦ *vt* ausloten; (*fig*) sondieren

plumber ['plʌmə*] *n* Klempner *m*, Installateur *m*

plumbing ['plʌmɪŋ] *n* (*craft*) Installieren *nt*; (*fittings*) Leitungen *pl*

plume [pluːm] *n* Feder *f*; (*of smoke etc*) Fahne *f*

plummet ['plʌmɪt] *vi* (ab)stürzen

plump [plʌmp] *adj* rundlich, füllig ♦ *vt* plumpsen lassen; **to ~ for** (*inf: choose*) sich entscheiden für

plunder ['plʌndə*] *n* Plünderung *f*; (*loot*) Beute *f* ♦ *vt* plündern

plunge [plʌndʒ] *n* Sturz *m* ♦ *vt* stoßen ♦ *vi* (sich) stürzen; **to take the ~** den Sprung wagen

plunging ['plʌndʒɪŋ] *adj* (*neckline*) offenherzig

pluperfect ['pluː'pɜːfɪkt] *n* Plusquamperfekt *nt*

plural ['plʊərəl] *n* Plural *m*, Mehrzahl *f*

plus [plʌs] *n* (*also*: **~ sign**) Plus(zeichen) *nt* ♦ *prep* plus, und; **ten/twenty ~** mehr als zehn/zwanzig

plush [plʌʃ] *adj* (*also* **~y**: *inf: luxurious*) feudal

ply [plaɪ] *vt* (*trade*) (be)treiben; (*with questions*) zusetzen +*dat*; (*ship, taxi*) befahren ♦ *vi* verkehren ♦ *n*: **three-~** (*wool*) Dreifach-; **to ~ sb with drink** jdn zum Trinken animieren; **~wood** *n* Sperrholz *nt*

P.M. *n abbr* = **Prime Minister**

p.m. *adv abbr* (= *post meridiem*) nachmittags

pneumatic [njuː'mætɪk] *adj* pneumatisch; (*TECH*) Luft-; **~ drill** *n* Preßlufthammer *m*

pneumonia [njuː'məʊnɪə] *n* Lungenentzündung *f*

poach [pəʊtʃ] *vt* (*COOK*) pochieren; (*game*) stehlen ♦ *vi* (*steal*) wildern; **~ed** *adj* (*egg*) verloren; **~er** *n* Wilddieb *m*

P.O. Box *n abbr* = **Post Office Box**

pocket ['pɒkɪt] *n* Tasche *f*; (*of resistance*) (Widerstands)nest *nt* ♦ *vt* einstecken; **to be out of ~** (*BRIT*) draufzahlen; **~book** *n* Taschenbuch *nt*; **~ knife** *n* Taschenmesser *nt*; **~ money** *n* Taschengeld *nt*

pod [pɒd] *n* Hülse *f*; (*of peas also*) Schote *f*

podgy ['pɒdʒɪ] *adj* pummelig

podiatrist [pɒ'daɪətrɪst] (*US*) *n* Fußpfleger(in) *m(f)*

poem ['pəʊɪm] *n* Gedicht *nt*

poet ['pəʊɪt] *n* Dichter *m*, Poet *m*; **~ic** [pəʊ'etɪk] *adj* poetisch, dichterisch; **~ laureate** *n* Hofdichter *m*; **~ry** *n* Poesie *f*; (*poems*) Gedichte *pl*

poignant ['pɔɪnjənt] *adj* (*touching*)
ergreifend

point [pɔɪnt] *n* (*also in discussion,
scoring*) Punkt *m*; (*spot*) Punkt *m*, Stelle *f*;
(*sharpened tip*) Spitze *f*; (*moment*)
(Zeit)punkt *m*; (*purpose*) Zweck *m*; (*idea*)
Argument *nt*; (*decimal*) Dezimalstelle *f*;
(*personal characteristic*) Seite *f* ♦ *vt* zeigen
mit; (*gun*) richten ♦ *vi* zeigen; **~s** *npl*
(*RAIL*) Weichen *pl*; **to be on the ~ of
doing sth** drauf und dran sein, etw zu
tun; **to make a ~ of** Wert darauf legen;
to get the ~ verstehen, worum es geht;
to come to the ~ zur Sache kommen;
there's no ~ (in doing sth) es hat
keinen Sinn(, etw zu tun); **~ out** *vt*
hinweisen auf +*acc*; **~ to** *vt fus* zeigen
auf +*acc*; **~-blank** *adv* (*at close range*) aus
nächster Entfernung; (*bluntly*)
unverblümt; **~ed** *adj* (*also fig*) spitz,
scharf; **~edly** *adv* (*fig*) spitz; **~er** *n*
Zeigestock *m*; (*on dial*) Zeiger *m*; **~less**
adj sinnlos; **~ of view** *n* Stand- *or*
Gesichtspunkt *m*

poise [pɔɪz] *n* Haltung *f*; (*fig*)
Gelassenheit *f*

poison ['pɔɪzn] *n* (*also fig*) Gift *nt* ♦ *vt*
vergiften; **~ing** *n* Vergiftung *f*; **~ous** *adj*
giftig, Gift-

poke [pəʊk] *vt* stoßen; (*put*) stecken; (*fire*)
schüren; (*hole*) bohren; **~ about** *vi*
herumstochern; (*nose around*)
herumwühlen

poker ['pəʊkə*] *n* Schürhaken *m*; (*CARDS*)
Poker *nt*; **~-faced** *adj* undurchdringlich

poky ['pəʊkɪ] *adj* eng

Poland ['pəʊlənd] *n* Polen *nt*

polar ['pəʊlə*] *adj* Polar-, polar; **~ bear** *n*
Eisbär *m*; **~ize** *vt* polarisieren

Pole [pəʊl] *n* Pole *m*, Polin *f*

pole [pəʊl] *n* Stange *f*, Pfosten *m*; (*flag~,
telegraph ~*) Stange *f*, Mast *m*; (*ELEC, GEOG*)
Pol *m*; (*SPORT: vaulting ~*) Stab *m*; (*ski ~*)
Stock *m*; **~ bean** (*US*) *n* (*runner bean*)
Stangenbohne *f*; **~ vault** *n* Stabhoch-
sprung *m*

police [pə'liːs] *n* Polizei *f* ♦ *vt*
kontrollieren; **~ car** *n* Polizeiwagen *m*;
~man (*irreg*) *n* Polizist *m*; **~ state** *n*

Polizeistaat *m*; **~ station** *n*
(Polizei)revier *nt*, Wache *f*; **~woman**
(*irreg*) *n* Polizistin *f*

policy ['pɒlɪsɪ] *n* Politik *f*; (*insurance*)
(Versicherungs)police *f*

polio ['pəʊlɪəʊ] *n* (*spinale*)
Kinderlähmung *f*, Polio *f*

Polish ['pəʊlɪʃ] *adj* polnisch ♦ *n* (*LING*)
Polnisch *nt*

polish ['pɒlɪʃ] *n* Politur *f*; (*for floor*)
Wachs *nt*; (*for shoes*) Creme *f*; (*for nails*)
Lack *m*; (*shine*) Glanz *m*; (*of furniture*)
Politur *f*; (*fig*) Schliff *m* ♦ *vt* polieren;
(*shoes*) putzen; (*fig*) den letzten Schliff
geben +*dat*; **~ off** *vt* (*inf: work*) erledigen;
(: *food*) wegputzen; (: *drink*)
hinunterschütten; **~ed** *adj* (*also fig*)
glänzend; (*manners*) verfeinert

polite [pə'laɪt] *adj* höflich; **~ness** *n*
Höflichkeit *f*

politic ['pɒlɪtɪk] *adj* (*prudent*)
diplomatisch; **~al** [pə'lɪtɪkəl] *adj* politisch;
~ally *adv* politisch; **~ian** [pɒlɪ'tɪʃən] *n*
Politiker *m*; **~s** *npl* Politik *f*

polka dot ['pɒlkə-] *n* Tupfen *m*

poll [pəʊl] *n* Abstimmung *f*; (*in election*)
Wahl *f*; (*votes cast*) Wahlbeteiligung *f*;
(*opinion ~*) Umfrage *f* ♦ *vt* (*votes*)
erhalten

pollen ['pɒlən] *n* (*BOT*) Blütenstaub *m*,
Pollen *m*

pollination [pɒlɪ'neɪʃən] *n* Befruchtung *f*

polling ['pəʊlɪŋ]: **~ booth** (*BRIT*) *n*
Wahlkabine *f*; **~ day** (*BRIT*) *n* Wahltag *m*;
~ station (*BRIT*) *n* Wahllokal *nt*

pollute [pə'luːt] *vt* verschmutzen,
verunreinigen; **pollution** [pə'luːʃən] *n*
Verschmutzung *f*

polo ['pəʊləʊ] *n* Polo *nt*; **~-neck** *n*
Rollkragen *m*; Rollkragenpullover *m*; **~
shirt** *n* Polohemd *nt*

polystyrene [pɒlɪ'staɪriːn] *n* Styropor *nt*

polytechnic [pɒlɪ'teknɪk] *n* technische
Hochschule *f*

polythene ['pɒlɪθiːn] *n* Plastik *nt*

pomegranate ['pɒməgrænɪt] *n*
Granatapfel *m*

pommel ['pʌml] *vt* mit den Fäusten
bearbeiten ♦ *n* Sattelknopf *m*

pompom ['pɒmpɒm] n Troddel f, Pompon m

pompous ['pɒmpəs] adj aufgeblasen; (language) geschwollen

pond [pɒnd] n Teich m, Weiher m

ponder ['pɒndə*] vt nachdenken über +acc; **~ous** adj schwerfällig

pong [pɒŋ] (BRIT: inf) n Mief m

pontiff ['pɒntɪf] n Pontifex m

pontificate [pɒn'tɪfɪkeɪt] vi (fig) geschwollen reden

pontoon [pɒn'tuːn] n Ponton m; (CARDS) 17-und-4 nt

pony ['pəʊnɪ] n Pony nt; **~tail** n Pferdeschwanz m; **~ trekking** (BRIT) n Ponyreiten nt

poodle ['puːdl] n Pudel m

pool [puːl] n (swimming ~) Schwimmbad nt; (: private) Swimmingpool m; (of spilt liquid, blood) Lache f; (fund) (gemeinsame) Kasse f; (billiards) Poolspiel nt ♦ vt (money etc) zusammenlegen; **typing ~** Schreibzentrale f; (football) **~s** Toto nt

poor [pʊə*] adj arm; (not good) schlecht ♦ npl: **the ~** die Armen pl; **~ in** (resources etc) arm an +dat; **~ly** adv schlecht; (dressed) ärmlich ♦ adj schlecht

pop [pɒp] n Knall m; (music) Popmusik f; (drink) Limo(nade) f; (US: inf) Pa m ♦ vt (put) stecken; (balloon) platzen lassen ♦ vi knallen; **~ in** vi kurz vorbeigehen or vorbeikommen; **~ out** vi (person) kurz rausgehen; (thing) herausspringen; **~ up** vi auftauchen; **~corn** n Puffmais m

pope [pəʊp] n Papst m

poplar ['pɒplə*] n Pappel f

poppy ['pɒpɪ] n Mohn m

Popsicle ['pɒpsɪkl] ((R); US) n (ice lolly) Eis nt am Stiel

populace ['pɒpjʊlɪs] n Volk nt

popular ['pɒpjʊlə*] adj beliebt, populär; (of the people) volkstümlich; (widespread) allgemein; **~ity** [pɒpjʊ'lærɪtɪ] n Beliebtheit f, Popularität f; **~ize** ['pɒpjʊləraɪz] vt popularisieren; **~ly** adv allgemein, überall

population [pɒpjʊ'leɪʃən] n Bevölkerung f; (of town) Einwohner pl

populous ['pɒpjʊləs] adj dicht besiedelt

porcelain ['pɔːslɪn] n Porzellan nt

porch [pɔːtʃ] n Vorbau m, Veranda f

porcupine ['pɔːkjʊpaɪn] n Stachelschwein nt

pore [pɔː*] n Pore f ♦ vi: **to ~ over** brüten über +dat

pork [pɔːk] n Schweinefleisch nt

pornography [pɔː'nɒgrəfɪ] n Pornographie f

porous ['pɔːrəs] adj porös; (skin) porig

porpoise ['pɔːpəs] n Tümmler m

porridge ['pɒrɪdʒ] n Haferbrei m

port [pɔːt] n Hafen m; (town) Hafenstadt f; (NAUT: left side) Backbord nt; (wine) Portwein m; **~ of call** Anlaufhafen m

portable ['pɔːtəbl] adj tragbar

portent ['pɔːtent] n schlimme(s) Vorzeichen nt

porter ['pɔːtə*] n Pförtner(in) m(f); (for luggage) (Gepäck)träger m

portfolio [pɔːt'fəʊlɪəʊ] n (case) Mappe f; (POL) Geschäftsbereich m; (FIN) Portefeuille nt; (of artist) Kollektion f

porthole ['pɔːthəʊl] n Bullauge nt

portion ['pɔːʃən] n Teil m, Stück nt; (of food) Portion f

portly ['pɔːtlɪ] adj korpulent, beleibt

portrait ['pɔːtrɪt] n Porträt nt

portray [pɔː'treɪ] vt darstellen; **~al** n Darstellung f

Portugal ['pɔːtjʊgəl] n Portugal nt

Portuguese [pɔːtjʊ'giːz] adj portugiesisch ♦ n inv Portugiese m, Portugiesin f; (LING) Portugiesisch nt

pose [pəʊz] n Stellung f, Pose f; (affectation) Pose f ♦ vi posieren ♦ vt stellen

posh [pɒʃ] (inf) adj (piek)fein

position [pə'zɪʃən] n Stellung f; (place) Lage f; (job) Stelle f; (attitude) Standpunkt m ♦ vt aufstellen

positive ['pɒzɪtɪv] adj positiv; (convinced) sicher; (definite) eindeutig

posse ['pɒsɪ] (US) n Aufgebot nt

possess [pə'zes] vt besitzen; **~ion** [pə'zeʃən] n Besitz m; **~ive** adj besitzergreifend, eigensüchtig

possibility [pɒsə'bɪlɪtɪ] n Möglichkeit f

possible ['pɒsəbl] adj möglich; **as big as ~** so groß wie möglich, möglichst groß

possibly ['pɒsəblɪ] *adv* möglicherweise, vielleicht; **I cannot ~ come** ich kann unmöglich kommen

post [pəʊst] *n* (*BRIT: letters, delivery*) Post *f*; (*pole*) Pfosten *m*, Pfahl *m*; (*place of duty*) Posten *m*; (*job*) Stelle *f* ♦ *vt* (*notice*) anschlagen; (*BRIT: letters*) aufgeben; (*: appoint*) versetzen; (*soldiers*) aufstellen; **~age** *n* Postgebühr *f*, Porto *nt*; **~al** *adj* Post-; **~al order** *n* Postanweisung *f*; **~box** (*BRIT*) *n* Briefkasten *m*; **~card** *n* Postkarte *f*; **~code** (*BRIT*) *n* Postleitzahl *f*

postdate [pəʊst'deɪt] *vt* (*cheque*) nachdatieren

poster ['pəʊstə*] *n* Plakat *nt*, Poster *nt*

poste restante ['pəʊstres'tɑ̃:nt] *n* Aufbewahrungsstelle *f* für postlagernde Sendungen

posterior [pɒs'tɪərɪə*] (*inf*) *n* Hintern *m*

posterity [pɒs'terɪtɪ] *n* Nachwelt *f*

postgraduate ['pəʊst'grædjʊɪt] *n* Weiterstudierende(r) *mf*

posthumous ['pɒstjʊməs] *adj* post(h)um

postman ['pəʊstmən] (*irreg*) *n* Briefträger *m*

postmark ['pəʊstmɑ:k] *n* Poststempel *m*

post-mortem ['pəʊst'mɔ:təm] *n* Autopsie *f*

post office *n* Postamt *nt*, Post *f*; (*organization*) Post *f*; **P~ O~ Box** *n* Postfach *nt*

postpone [pə'spəʊn] *vt* verschieben

postscript ['pəʊsskrɪpt] *n* Postskript *nt*; (*to affair*) Nachspiel *nt*

postulate ['pɒstjʊleɪt] *vt* voraussetzen; (*maintain*) behaupten

posture ['pɒstʃə*] *n* Haltung *f* ♦ *vi* posieren

postwar ['pəʊst'wɔ:*] *adj* Nachkriegs-

posy ['pəʊzɪ] *n* Blumenstrauß *m*

pot [pɒt] *n* Topf *m*; (*tea~*) Kanne *f*; (*inf: marijuana*) Hasch *m* ♦ *vt* (*plant*) eintopfen; **to go to ~** (*inf: work, performance*) auf den Hund kommen

potato [pə'teɪtəʊ] (*pl* **~es**) *n* Kartoffel *f*; **~ peeler** *n* Kartoffelschäler *m*

potent ['pəʊtənt] *adj* stark; (*argument*) zwingend

potential [pə'tenʃəl] *adj* potentiell ♦ *n*

Potential *nt*; **~ly** *adv* potentiell

pothole ['pɒthəʊl] *n* (*in road*) Schlagloch *nt*; (*BRIT: underground*) Höhle *f*

potholing ['pɒthəʊlɪŋ] (*BRIT*) *n*: **to go ~** Höhlen erforschen

potion ['pəʊʃən] *n* Trank *m*

potluck ['pɒt'lʌk] *n*: **to take ~ with sth** etw auf gut Glück nehmen

potshot ['pɒtʃɒt] *n*: **to take a ~ at sth** auf etw *acc* ballern

potted ['pɒtɪd] *adj* (*food*) eingelegt, eingemacht; (*plant*) Topf-; (*fig: book, version*) konzentriert

potter ['pɒtə*] *n* Töpfer *m* ♦ *vi* herumhantieren; **~y** *n* Töpferwaren *pl*; (*place*) Töpferei *f*

potty ['pɒtɪ] *adj* (*inf: mad*) verrückt ♦ *n* Töpfchen *nt*

pouch [paʊtʃ] *n* Beutel *m*

pouf(fe) [pu:f] *n* Sitzkissen *nt*

poultry ['pəʊltrɪ] *n* Geflügel *nt*

pounce [paʊns] *vi* sich stürzen ♦ *n* Sprung *m*, Satz *m*; **to ~ on** sich stürzen auf +*acc*

pound [paʊnd] *n* (*FIN, weight*) Pfund *nt*; (*for cars, animals*) Auslösestelle *f* ♦ *vt* (zer)stampfen ♦ *vi* klopfen, hämmern; **~ sterling** *n* Pfund Sterling *nt*

pour [pɔ:*] *vt* gießen, schütten ♦ *vi* gießen; (*crowds etc*) strömen; **~ away** *vt* abgießen; **~ in** *vi* (*people*) hereinströmen; **~ off** *vt* abgießen; **~ out** *vi* (*people*) herausströmen ♦ *vt* (*drink*) einschenken; **~ing** *adj*: **~ing rain** strömende(r) Regen *m*

pout [paʊt] *vi* schmollen

poverty ['pɒvətɪ] *n* Armut *f*; **~-stricken** *adj* verarmt, sehr arm

powder ['paʊdə*] *n* Pulver *nt*; (*cosmetic*) Puder *m* ♦ *vt* pulverisieren; **to ~ one's nose** sich *dat* die Nase pudern; **~ compact** *n* Puderdose *f*; **~ed milk** *n* Milchpulver *nt*; **~ room** *n* Damentoilette *f*; **~y** *adj* pulverig

power ['paʊə*] *n* (*also POL*) Macht *f*; (*ability*) Fähigkeit *f*; (*strength*) Stärke *f*; (*MATH*) Potenz *f*; (*ELEC*) Strom *m* ♦ *vt* betreiben, antreiben; **to be in ~** (*POL etc*) an der Macht sein; **~ cut** *n* Stromausfall m; **~ed** adj: **~ed by** betrieben mit; **~ failure** (US) n Stromausfall m; **~ful** adj (person) mächtig; (engine, government) stark; **~less** adj machtlos; **~ point** (BRIT) n elektrische(r) Anschluß m; **~ station** n Elektrizitätswerk nt

p.p. abbr (= per procurationem): **~ J. Smith** i.A. J. Smith

PR n abbr = **public relations**

practicable ['præktɪkəbl] adj durchführbar

practical ['præktɪkəl] adj praktisch; **~ity** [præktɪ'kælɪtɪ] n (of person) praktische Veranlagung f; (of situation etc) Durchführbarkeit f; **~ joke** n Streich m; **~ly** adv praktisch

practice ['præktɪs] n Übung f; (reality, also of doctor, lawyer) Praxis f; (custom) Brauch m; (in business) Usus m ♦ vt, vi (US) = **practise**; **in ~** (in reality) in der Praxis; **out of ~** außer Übung

practicing ['præktɪsɪŋ] (US) adj = **practising**

practise ['præktɪs] (US **practice**) vt üben; (profession) ausüben ♦ vi (sich) üben; (doctor, lawyer) praktizieren

practising ['præktɪsɪŋ] (US **practicing**) adj praktizierend; (Christian etc) aktiv

practitioner [præk'tɪʃənə*] n praktische(r) Arzt m, praktische Ärztin f

pragmatic [præg'mætɪk] adj pragmatisch

prairie ['prɛərɪ] n Prärie f, Steppe f

praise [preɪz] n Lob nt ♦ vt loben; **~worthy** adj lobenswert

pram [præm] (BRIT) n Kinderwagen m

prance [prɑːns] vi (horse) tänzeln; (person) stolzieren; (: gaily) herumhüpfen

prank [præŋk] n Streich m

prattle ['prætl] vi schwatzen, plappern

prawn [prɔːn] n Garnele f; Krabbe f

pray [preɪ] vi beten; **~er** [prɛə*] n Gebet nt

preach [priːtʃ] vi predigen; **~er** n Prediger m

preamble [priː'æmbl] n Einleitung f

precarious [prɪ'kɛərɪəs] adj prekär, unsicher

precaution [prɪ'kɔːʃən] n (Vorsichts)maßnahme f

precede [prɪ'siːd] vi vorausgehen ♦ vt vorausgehen +dat; **~nce** ['presɪdəns] n Vorrang m; **~nt** ['presɪdənt] n Präzedenzfall m

preceding [prɪ'siːdɪŋ] adj vorhergehend

precept ['priːsept] n Gebot nt, Regel f

precinct ['priːsɪŋkt] n (US: district) Bezirk m; **~s** npl (round building) Gelände nt; (area, environs) Umgebung f; **pedestrian ~** Fußgängerzone f; **shopping ~** Geschäftsviertel nt

precious ['preʃəs] adj kostbar, wertvoll; (affected) preziös, geziert

precipice ['presɪpɪs] n Abgrund m

precipitate [adj prɪ'sɪpɪtɪt, vb prɪ'sɪpɪteɪt] adj überstürzt, übereilt ♦ vt hinunterstürzen; (events) heraufbeschwören

precise [prɪ'saɪs] adj genau, präzis; **~ly** adv genau, präzis

precision [prɪ'sɪʒən] n Präzision f

preclude [prɪ'kluːd] vt ausschließen

precocious [prɪ'kəʊʃəs] adj frühreif

preconceived ['priːkən'siːvd] adj (idea) vorgefaßt

precondition ['priːkən'dɪʃən] n Vorbedingung f, Voraussetzung f

precursor [priː'kɜːsə*] n Vorläufer m

predator ['predətə*] n Raubtier nt

predecessor ['priːdɪsesə*] n Vorgänger m

predestination [priːdestɪ'neɪʃən] n Vorherbestimmung f

predicament [prɪ'dɪkəmənt] n mißliche Lage f

predict [prɪ'dɪkt] vt voraussagen; **~able** adj vorhersagbar; **~ion** [prɪ'dɪkʃən] n Voraussage f

predominantly [prɪ'dɒmɪnəntlɪ] adv überwiegend, hauptsächlich

predominate [prɪ'dɒmɪneɪt] vi vorherrschen; (fig) vorherrschen, überwiegen

pre-eminent [priː'emɪnənt] adj hervorragend, herausragend

pre-empt [priː'empt] vt (action, decision) vorwegnehmen

preen [priːn] vt putzen; **to ~ o.s.** (person) sich brüsten

prefab ['pri:fæb] *n* Fertighaus *nt*
prefabricated [pri:'fæbrikeɪtɪd] *adj* vorgefertigt, Fertig-
preface ['prefɪs] *n* Vorwort *nt*
prefect ['pri:fekt] *n* Präfekt *m*; (*SCH*) Aufsichtsschüler(in) *m(f)*
prefer [prɪ'fɜ:*] *vt* vorziehen, lieber mögen; **to ~ to do sth** etw lieber tun; **~ably** ['prefrəblɪ] *adv* vorzugsweise, am liebsten; **~ence** ['prefərəns] *n* Präferenz *f*, Vorzug *m*; **~ential** [prefə'renʃəl] *adj* bevorzugt, Vorzugs-
prefix ['pri:fɪks] *n* Vorsilbe *f*, Präfix *nt*
pregnancy ['pregnənsɪ] *n* Schwangerschaft *f*
pregnant ['pregnənt] *adj* schwanger
prehistoric [pri:hɪs'tɒrɪk] *adj* prähistorisch, vorgeschichtlich
prejudice ['predʒudɪs] *n* (*opinion*) Vorurteil *nt*; (*bias*) Voreingenommenheit *f*; (*harm*) Schaden *m* ♦ *vt* beeinträchtigen; **~d** *adj* (*person*) voreingenommen
preliminary [prɪ'lɪmɪnərɪ] *adj* einleitend, Vor-
prelude ['prelju:d] *n* Vorspiel *nt*; (*fig*) Auftakt *m*
premarital ['pri:'mærɪtl] *adj* vorehelich
premature ['premətʃuə*] *adj* vorzeitig, verfrüht; (*birth*) Früh-
premeditated [pri:'medɪteɪtɪd] *adj* geplant; (*murder*) vorsätzlich
premier ['premɪə*] *adj* erste(r, s) ♦ *n* Premier *m*
première [premɪ'ɛə*] *n* Premiere *f*; Uraufführung *f*
premise ['premɪs] *n* Voraussetzung *f*, Prämisse *f*; **~s** *npl* (*shop*) Räumlichkeiten *pl*; (*grounds*) Gelände *nt*; **on the ~s** im Hause
premium ['pri:mɪəm] *n* Prämie *f*; **to be at a ~** über pari stehen; **~ bond** (*BRIT*) *n* Prämienanleihe *f*
premonition [premə'nɪʃən] *n* Vorahnung *f*
preoccupation [pri:ɒkjʊ'peɪʃən] *n* Sorge *f*
preoccupied [pri:'ɒkjʊpaɪd] *adj* (*look*) geistesabwesend
prep [prep] *n* (*SCH*: *study*) Hausaufgabe *f*

prepaid ['pri:'peɪd] *adj* vorausbezahlt; (*letter*) frankiert
preparation [prepə'reɪʃən] *n* Vorbereitung *f*
preparatory [prɪ'pærətərɪ] *adj* Vor(bereitungs)-; **~ school** *n* (*BRIT*) *private Vorbereitungsschule für die Public School*; (*US*) *private Vorbereitungsschule für die Hochschule*
prepare [prɪ'pɛə*] *vt* vorbereiten ♦ *vi* sich vorbereiten; **to ~ for/~ sth for** sich/etw vorbereiten auf +*acc*; **to be ~d to ...** bereit sein zu ...
preponderance [prɪ'pɒndərəns] *n* Übergewicht *nt*
preposition [prepə'zɪʃən] *n* Präposition *f*, Verhältniswort *nt*
preposterous [prɪ'pɒstərəs] *adj* absurd
prep school *n* = **preparatory school**
prerequisite ['pri:'rekwɪzɪt] *n* (unerläßliche) Voraussetzung *f*
prerogative [prɪ'rɒgətɪv] *n* Vorrecht *nt*
Presbyterian [prezbɪ'tɪərɪən] *adj* presbyterianisch ♦ *n* Presbyterier(in) *m(f)*
preschool ['pri:sku:l] *adj* Vorschul-
prescribe [prɪ'skraɪb] *vt* vorschreiben; (*MED*) verschreiben
prescription [prɪs'krɪpʃən] *n* (*MED*) Rezept *nt*
presence ['prezns] *n* Gegenwart *f*; **~ of mind** Geistesgegenwart *f*
present [*adj, n* 'preznt, *vb* prɪ'zent] *adj* (*here*) anwesend; (*current*) gegenwärtig ♦ *n* Gegenwart *f*; (*gift*) Geschenk *nt* ♦ *vt* vorlegen; (*introduce*) vorstellen; (*show*) zeigen; (*give*): **to ~ sb with sth** jdm etw überreichen; **at ~** im Augenblick; **to give sb a ~** jdm ein Geschenk machen; **~able** [prɪ'zentəbl] *adj* präsentabel; **~ation** [prezən'teɪʃən] *adj* Überreichung *f*; **~-day** *adj* heutig; **~er** [prɪ'zentə*] *n* (*RADIO, TV*) Moderator(in) *m(f)*; **~ly** *adv* bald; (*at present*) im Augenblick
preservation [prezə'veɪʃən] *n* Erhaltung *f*
preservative [prɪ'zɜ:vətɪv] *n* Konservierungsmittel *nt*
preserve [prɪ'zɜ:v] *vt* erhalten; (*food*) einmachen ♦ *n* (*jam*) Eingemachte(s) *nt*;

(*hunting*) Schutzgebiet *nt*
preside [prɪ'zaɪd] *vi* den Vorsitz haben
presidency ['prezɪdənsɪ] *n* (*POL*)
Präsidentschaft *f*
president ['prezɪdənt] *n* Präsident *m*;
~ial [prezɪ'denʃəl] *adj* Präsidenten-;
(*election*) Präsidentschafts-; (*system*)
Präsidial-
press [pres] *n* Presse *f*; (*printing house*)
Druckerei *f* ♦ *vt* drücken; (*iron*) bügeln;
(*urge*) (be)drängen ♦ *vi* (*push*) drücken; **to
be ~ed for time** unter Zeitdruck stehen;
to ~ for sth drängen auf etw *acc*; **~ on** *vi*
vorwärtsdrängen; **~ agency** *n*
Presseagentur *f*; **~ conference** *n*
Pressekonferenz *f*; **~ing** *adj* dringend; **~-
stud** (*BRIT*) *n* Druckknopf *m*; **~-up** (*BRIT*)
n Liegestütz *m*
pressure ['preʃə*] *n* Druck *m*; **~ cooker**
n Schnellkochtopf *m*; **~ gauge** *n*
Druckmesser *m*
pressurized ['preʃəraɪzd] *adj* Druck-
prestige [pres'tiːʒ] *n* Prestige *nt*
prestigious [pres'tɪdʒəs] *adj* Prestige-
presumably [prɪ'zjuːməblɪ] *adv*
vermutlich
presume [prɪ'zjuːm] *vt*, *vi* annehmen; **to
~ to do sth** sich erlauben, etw zu tun
presumption [prɪ'zʌmpʃən] *n* Annahme
f
presumptuous [prɪ'zʌmptjuəs] *adj*
anmaßend
presuppose [priːsə'pəuz] *vt* voraussetzen
pretence [prɪ'tens] (*US* **pretense**) *n*
Vorgabe *f*, Vortäuschung *f*; (*false claim*)
Vorwand *m*
pretend [prɪ'tend] *vt* vorgeben, so tun als
ob ... ♦ *vi* so tun; **to ~ to sth** Anspruch
erheben auf etw *acc*
pretense [prɪ'tens] (*US*) *n* = **pretence**
pretension [prɪ'tenʃən] *n* Anspruch *m*;
(*impudent claim*) Anmaßung *f*
pretentious [prɪ'tenʃəs] *adj* angeberisch
pretext ['priːtekst] *n* Vorwand *m*
pretty ['prɪtɪ] *adj* hübsch ♦ *adv* (*inf*) ganz
schön
prevail [prɪ'veɪl] *vi* siegen; (*custom*)
vorherrschen; **to ~ against** *or* **over**
siegen über +*acc*; **to ~ (up)on sb to do**

sth jdn dazu bewegen, etw zu tun; **~ing**
adj vorherrschend
prevalent ['prevələnt] *adj* vorherrschend
prevent [prɪ'vent] *vt* (*stop*) verhindern,
verhüten; **to ~ sb from doing sth** jdn
(daran) hindern, etw zu tun; **~ative** *n*
Vorbeugungsmittel *nt*; **~ion** [prɪ'venʃən]
n Verhütung *f*; **~ive** *adj* vorbeugend,
Schutz-
preview ['priːvjuː] *n* private
Voraufführung *f*; (*trailer*) Vorschau *f*
previous ['priːvɪəs] *adj* früher, vorherig;
~ly *adv* früher
prewar ['priː'wɔː*] *adj* Vorkriegs-
prey [preɪ] *n* Beute *f*; **~ on** *vt fus* Jagd
machen auf +*acc*; **it was ~ing on his
mind** es quälte sein Gewissen
price [praɪs] *n* Preis *m*; (*value*) Wert *m*
♦ *vt* (*label*) auszeichnen; **~less** *adj* (*also
fig*) unbezahlbar; **~ list** *n* Preisliste *f*
prick [prɪk] *n* Stich *m* ♦ *vt*, *vi* stechen; **to
~ up one's ears** die Ohren spitzen
prickle ['prɪkl] *n* Stachel *m*, Dorn *m*
prickly ['prɪklɪ] *adj* stachelig; (*fig: person*)
reizbar; **~ heat** *n* Hitzebläschen *pl*
pride [praɪd] *n* Stolz *m*; (*arrogance*)
Hochmut *m* ♦ *vt*: **to ~ o.s. on sth** auf etw
acc stolz sein
priest [priːst] *n* Priester *m*; **~ess** *n*
Priesterin *f*; **~hood** *n* Priesteramt *nt*
prig [prɪg] *n* Selbstgefällige(r) *mf*
prim [prɪm] *adj* prüde
primarily ['praɪmərɪlɪ] *adv* vorwiegend
primary ['praɪmərɪ] *adj* (*main*) Haupt-;
(*SCH*) Grund-; **~ school** (*BRIT*) *n*
Grundschule *f*
prime [praɪm] *adj* erste(r, s); (*excellent*)
erstklassig ♦ *vt* vorbereiten; (*gun*) laden;
in the ~ of life in der Blüte der Jahre;
P~ Minister *n* Premierminister *m*,
Ministerpräsident *m*; **~r** ['praɪmə*] *n*
Fibel *f*
primeval [praɪ'miːvəl] *adj* vorzeitlich;
(*forests*) Ur-
primitive ['prɪmɪtɪv] *adj* primitiv
primrose ['prɪmrəuz] *n* (gelbe) Primel *f*
primus (stove) ['praɪməs-] (®; *BRIT*) *n*
Primuskocher *m*
prince [prɪns] *n* Prinz *m*; (*ruler*) Fürst *m*

princess [prɪn'ses] n Prinzessin f;
Fürstin f
principal ['prɪnsɪpəl] adj Haupt- ♦ n (SCH)
(Schul)direktor m, Rektor m; (money)
(Grund)kapital nt
principle ['prɪnsəpl] n Grundsatz m,
Prinzip nt; **in ~** im Prinzip; **on ~** aus
Prinzip, prinzipiell
print [prɪnt] n Druck m; (made by feet,
fingers) Abdruck m; (PHOT) Abzug m ♦ vt
drucken; (name) in Druckbuchstaben
schreiben; (PHOT) abziehen; **out of ~**
vergriffen; **~ed matter** n Drucksache f;
~er n Drucker m; **~ing** n Drucken nt; (of
photos) Abziehen nt; **~out** n (COMPUT)
Ausdruck m
prior ['praɪə*] adj früher ♦ n Prior m; **~
to sth** vor etw dat; **~ to going abroad,
she had ...** bevor sie ins Ausland ging,
hatte sie ...
priority [praɪ'ɒrɪtɪ] n Vorrang m;
Priorität f
prise [praɪz] vt: **to ~ open** aufbrechen
prison ['prɪzn] n Gefängnis nt ♦ adj
Gefängnis-; (system etc) Strafvollzugs-; **~er**
n Gefangene(r) m/f
pristine ['prɪstiːn] adj makellos
privacy ['prɪvəsɪ] n Ungestörtheit f, Ruhe
f; Privatleben nt
private ['praɪvɪt] adj privat, Privat-;
(secret) vertraulich, geheim ♦ n
einfache(r) Soldat m; **"~"** (on envelope)
„persönlich"; (on door) „Privat"; **in ~**
privat, unter vier Augen; **~ enterprise** n
Privatunternehmen nt; **~ eye** n Pri-
vatdetektiv m; **~ly** adv privat; vertraulich, geheim; **~ property** n Pri-
vatbesitz m; **~ school** n Privatschule f;
privatize vt privatisieren
privet ['prɪvɪt] n Liguster m
privilege ['prɪvɪlɪdʒ] n Privileg nt; **~d**
adj bevorzugt, privilegiert
privy ['prɪvɪ] adj geheim, privat; **P~
Council** n Geheime(r) Staatsrat m
prize [praɪz] n Preis m ♦ adj (example)
erstklassig; (idiot) Voll- ♦ vt (hoch)-
schätzen; **~-giving** n Preisverteilung
f; **~winner** n Preisträger(in) m(f)
pro [prəʊ] n (professional) Profi m; **the ~s**

and cons (for and against) das Für und
Wider
probability [prɒbə'bɪlɪtɪ] n
Wahrscheinlichkeit f
probable ['prɒbəbl] adj wahrscheinlich
probably ['prɒbəblɪ] adv wahrscheinlich
probation [prə'beɪʃən] n Probe(zeit) f;
(JUR) Bewährung f; **on ~** auf Probe; auf
Bewährung
probe [prəʊb] n Sonde f; (enquiry)
Untersuchung f ♦ vt, vi erforschen
problem ['prɒbləm] n Problem nt; **~atic**
[prɒblɪ'mætɪk] adj problematisch
procedure [prə'siːdʒə*] n Verfahren nt
proceed [prə'siːd] vi (advance)
vorrücken; (start) anfangen; (carry on)
fortfahren; (set about) vorgehen; **~ings**
npl Verfahren nt; **~s** ['prəʊsiːdz] npl
Erlös m
process ['prəʊses] n Prozeß m; (method)
Verfahren nt ♦ vt bearbeiten; (food)
verarbeiten; (film) entwickeln; **~ing** n
(PHOT) Entwickeln nt
procession [prə'seʃən] n Prozession f,
Umzug m; **funeral ~** Trauerprozession
f
pro-choice adj (movement) Pro-
Abtreibungs-; **~ campaigner**
Abtreibungsbefürworter(in) m(f)
proclaim [prə'kleɪm] vt verkünden
proclamation [prɒklə'meɪʃən] n
Verkündung f
procrastinate [prəʊ'kræstɪneɪt] vi
zaudern
procreation [prəʊkrɪ'eɪʃən] n
(Er)zeugung f
procure [prə'kjʊə*] vt beschaffen
prod [prɒd] vt stoßen ♦ n Stoß m
prodigal ['prɒdɪgəl] adj: **~ (with or of)**
verschwenderisch (mit)
prodigious [prə'dɪdʒəs] adj gewaltig;
(wonderful) wunderbar
prodigy ['prɒdɪdʒɪ] n Wunder nt
produce [n 'prɒdjuːs, vb prə'djuːs] n (AGR)
(Boden)produkte pl, (Natur)erzeugnis nt
♦ vt herstellen, produzieren; (cause)
hervorrufen; (farmer) erzeugen; (yield)
liefern, bringen; (play) inszenieren; **~r** n
Hersteller m, Produzent m (also CINE);

Erzeuger *m*

product ['prɒdʌkt] *n* Produkt *nt*, Erzeugnis *nt*

production [prə'dʌkʃən] *n* Produktion *f*, Herstellung *f*; (*thing*) Erzeugnis *nt*, Produkt *nt*; (*THEAT*) Inszenierung *f*; ~ **line** *n* Fließband *nt*

productive [prə'dʌktɪv] *adj* produktiv; (*fertile*) ertragreich, fruchtbar

productivity [prɒdʌk'tɪvɪtɪ] *n* Produktivität *f*

profane [prə'feɪn] *adj* (*secular, lay*) weltlich, profan; (*language etc*) gotteslästerlich

profess [prə'fes] *vt* bekennen; (*show*) zeigen; (*claim to be*) vorgeben

profession [prə'feʃən] *n* Beruf *m*; (*declaration*) Bekenntnis *nt*; **~al** *n* Fachmann *m*; (*SPORT*) Berufsspieler(in) *m(f)* ♦ *adj* Berufs-; (*expert*) fachlich; (*player*) professionell

professor [prə'fesə*] *n* Professor *m*

proficiency [prə'fɪʃənsɪ] *n* Können *nt*

proficient [prə'fɪʃənt] *adj* fähig

profile ['prəʊfaɪl] *n* Profil *nt*; (*fig: report*) Kurzbiographie *f*

profit ['prɒfɪt] *n* Gewinn *m* ♦ *vi*: **to ~ (by** *or* **from)** profitieren (von); **~ability** [prɒfɪtə'bɪlɪtɪ] *n* Rentabilität *f*; **~able** *adj* einträglich, rentabel

profiteering [prɒfɪ'tɪərɪŋ] *n* Profitmacherei *f*

profound [prə'faʊnd] *adj* tief

profuse [prə'fjuːs] *adj* überreich; **~ly** [prə'fjuːslɪ] *adv* überschwenglich; (*sweat*) reichlich

profusion [prə'fjuːʒən] *n*: ~ (**of**) Überfülle *f* (von), Überfluß *m* (an +*dat*)

progeny ['prɒdʒɪnɪ] *n* Nachkommenschaft *f*

programme ['prəʊgræm] (*US* **program**) *n* Programm *nt* ♦ *vt* planen; (*computer*) programmieren

programmer ['prəʊgræmə*] (*US* **programer**) *n* Programmierer(in) *m(f)*

programming ['prəʊgræmɪŋ] (*US* **programing**) *n* Programmieren *nt*

progress [*n* 'prəʊgres, *vb* prə'gres] *n* Fortschritt *m* ♦ *vi* fortschreiten,

weitergehen; **in ~** im Gang; **~ion** [prə'greʃən] *n* Folge *f*; **~ive** [prə'gresɪv] *adj* fortschrittlich, progressiv

prohibit [prə'hɪbɪt] *vt* verbieten; **to ~ sb from doing sth** jdm untersagen, etw zu tun; **~ion** [prəʊɪ'bɪʃən] *n* Verbot *nt*; (*US*) Alkoholverbot *nt*, Prohibition *f*; **~ive** *adj* (*price etc*) unerschwinglich

project [*n* 'prɒdʒekt, *vb* prə'dʒekt] *n* Projekt *nt* ♦ *vt* vorausplanen; (*film etc*) projizieren; (*personality, voice*) zum Tragen bringen ♦ *vi* (*stick out*) hervorragen, (her)vorstehen

projectile [prə'dʒektaɪl] *n* Geschoß *nt*

projection [prə'dʒekʃən] *n* Projektion *f*; (*sth prominent*) Vorsprung *m*

projector [prə'dʒektə*] *n* Projektor *m*

proletariat [prəʊlə'tɛərɪət] *n* Proletariat *nt*

pro-life *adj* (*movement*) Anti-Abtreibungs-; ~ **campaigner** Abtreibungsgegner(in) *m(f)*

proliferate [prə'lɪfəreɪt] *vi* sich vermehren

prolific [prə'lɪfɪk] *adj* fruchtbar; (*author etc*) produktiv

prologue ['prəʊlɒg] *n* Prolog *m*; (*event*) Vorspiel *nt*

prolong [prə'lɒŋ] *vt* verlängern

prom [prɒm] *n abbr* = **promenade; promenade concert** ♦ *n* (*US: college ball*) Studentenball *m*

promenade [prɒmɪ'nɑːd] *n* Promenade *f*; ~ **concert** *n* Promenadenkonzert *nt*

prominence ['prɒmɪnəns] *n* (große) Bedeutung *f*

prominent ['prɒmɪnənt] *adj* bedeutend; (*politician*) prominent; (*easily seen*) herausragend, auffallend

promiscuous [prə'mɪskjʊəs] *adj* lose

promise ['prɒmɪs] *n* Versprechen *nt*; (*hope*): **promise of sth** Aussicht *f* auf etw *acc* ♦ *vt, vi* versprechen

promising ['prɒmɪsɪŋ] *adj* vielversprechend

promontory ['prɒməntrɪ] *n* Vorsprung *m*

promote [prə'məʊt] *vt* befördern; (*help on*) fördern, unterstützen; **~r** *n* (*in sport, entertainment*) Veranstalter *m*; (*for charity* *etc*) Organisator *m*

promotion [prə'məʊʃən] *n* (*in rank*) Beförderung *f*; (*furtherance*) Förderung *f*; (*COMM*): ~ (**of**) Werbung *f* (für)

prompt [prɒmpt] *adj* prompt, schnell ♦ *adv* (*punctually*) genau ♦ *n* (*COMPUT*) Meldung *f* ♦ *vt* veranlassen; (*THEAT*) soufflieren +*dat*; **to ~ sb to do sth** jdn dazu veranlassen, etw zu tun; **~ly** *adv* sofort

prone [prəʊn] *adj* hingestreckt; **to be ~ to sth** zu etw neigen

prong [prɒŋ] *n* Zinke *f*

pronoun ['prəʊnaʊn] *n* Fürwort *nt*

pronounce [prə'naʊns] *vt* aussprechen; (*JUR*) verkünden ♦ *vi* (*give an opinion*): **to ~ (on)** sich äußern (zu); **~d** *adj* ausgesprochen; **~ment** *n* Erklärung *f*

pronunciation [prənʌnsi'eɪʃən] *n* Aussprache *f*

proof [pruːf] *n* Beweis *m*; (*PRINT*) Korrekturfahne *f*; (*of alcohol*) Alkoholgehalt *m* ♦ *adj* sicher

prop [prɒp] *n* (*also fig*) Stütze *f*; (*THEAT*) Requisit *nt* ♦ *vt* (*also:* ~ **up**) (ab)stützen

propaganda [prɒpə'gændə] *n* Propaganda *f*

propagate ['prɒpəgeɪt] *vt* fortpflanzen; (*news*) propagieren, verbreiten

propel [prə'pel] *vt* (an)treiben; **~ler** *n* Propeller *m*; **~ling pencil** (*BRIT*) *n* Drehbleistift *m*

propensity [prə'pensɪtɪ] *n* Tendenz *f*

proper ['prɒpə*] *adj* richtig; (*seemly*) schicklich; **~ly** *adv* richtig; **~ noun** *n* Eigenname *m*

property ['prɒpətɪ] *n* Eigentum *nt*; (*quality*) Eigenschaft *f*; (*land*) Grundbesitz *m*; **~ owner** *n* Grundbesitzer *m*

prophecy ['prɒfɪsɪ] *n* Prophezeiung *f*

prophesy ['prɒfɪsaɪ] *vt* prophezeien

prophet ['prɒfɪt] *n* Prophet *m*

proportion [prə'pɔːʃən] *n* Verhältnis *nt*; (*share*) Teil *m* ♦ *vt*: **to ~ (to)** abstimmen (auf +*acc*); **~al** *adj* proportional; **~ate** *adj* verhältnismäßig

proposal [prə'pəʊzl] *n* Vorschlag *m*; (*of marriage*) Heiratsantrag *m*

propose [prə'pəʊz] *vt* vorschlagen; (*toast*)

ausbringen ♦ *vi* (*offer marriage*) einen Heiratsantrag machen; **to ~ to do sth** beabsichtigen, etw zu tun

proposition [prɒpə'zɪʃən] *n* Angebot *nt*; (*statement*) Satz *m*

proprietor [prə'praɪətə*] *n* Besitzer *m*, Eigentümer *m*

propriety [prə'praɪətɪ] *n* Anstand *m*

pro rata [prəʊ'rɑːtə] *adv* anteilmäßig

prose [prəʊz] *n* Prosa *f*

prosecute ['prɒsɪkjuːt] *vt* (strafrechtlich) verfolgen

prosecution [prɒsɪ'kjuːʃən] *n* (*JUR*) strafrechtliche Verfolgung *f*; (*party*) Anklage *f*

prosecutor ['prɒsɪkjuːtə*] *n* Vertreter *m* der Anklage; **Public P~** Staatsanwalt *m*

prospect [*n* 'prɒspekt, *vb* prə'spekt] *n* Aussicht *f* ♦ *vt* auf Bodenschätze hin untersuchen ♦ *vi*: **to ~ (for)** suchen (nach); **~ing** [prə'spektɪŋ] *n* (*for minerals*) Suche *f*; **~or** *n* (Gold)sucher *m*; **~us** [prə'spektəs] *n* (Werbe)prospekt *m*

prosper ['prɒspə*] *vi* blühen, gedeihen; (*person*) erfolgreich sein; **~ity** [prɒ'sperɪtɪ] *n* Wohlstand *m*; **~ous** *adj* wohlhabend, reich

prostitute ['prɒstɪtjuːt] *n* Prostituierte *f*

prostrate ['prɒstreɪt] *adj* ausgestreckt (liegend); ~ **with grief/exhaustion** von Schmerz/Erschöpfung übermannt

protagonist [prəʊ'tægənɪst] *n* Hauptperson *f*, Held *m*

protect [prə'tekt] *vt* (be)schützen; **~ion** *n* Schutz *m*; **~ive** *adj* Schutz-, (be)schützend

protégé ['prɒtɪʒeɪ] *n* Schützling *m*

protein ['prəʊtiːn] *n* Protein *nt*, Eiweiß *nt*

protest [*n* 'prəʊtest, *vb* prə'test] *n* Protest *m* ♦ *vi* protestieren ♦ *vt* (*affirm*) beteuern

Protestant ['prɒtɪstənt] *adj* protestantisch ♦ *n* Protestant(in) *m(f)*

protester [prə'testə*] *n* (*demonstrator*) Demonstrant(in) *m(f)*

protracted [prə'træktɪd] *adj* sich hinziehend

protrude [prə'truːd] *vi* (her)vorstehen

proud [praʊd] *adj*: ~ (**of**) stolz (auf +*acc*)

prove [pruːv] *vt* beweisen ♦ *vi*: **to ~ (to be) correct** sich als richtig erweisen; **to**

~ **o.s.** sich bewähren

proverb ['provɜːb] *n* Sprichwort *nt*; **~ial**
[prə'vɜːbɪəl] *adj* sprichwörtlich

provide [prə'vaɪd] *vt* versehen; (*supply*)
besorgen; **to ~ sb with sth** jdn mit etw
versorgen; **~ for** *vt fus* sorgen für;
(*emergency*) Vorkehrungen treffen für; **~d**
(that) *conj* vorausgesetzt(, daß)

Providence ['prɒvɪdəns] *n* die Vorsehung

providing [prə'vaɪdɪŋ] *conj*
vorausgesetzt(, daß)

province ['prɒvɪns] *n* Provinz *f*; (*division
of work*) Bereich *m*

provincial [prə'vɪnʃəl] *adj* provinziell,
Provinz-

provision [prə'vɪʒən] *n* Vorkehrung *f*;
(*condition*) Bestimmung *f*; **~s** *npl* (*food*)
Vorräte *pl*, Proviant *m*; **~al** *adj*
provisorisch

proviso [prə'vaɪzəʊ] *n* Bedingung *f*

provocative [prə'vɒkətɪv] *adj*
provozierend

provoke [prə'vəʊk] *vt* provozieren;
(*cause*) hervorrufen

prow [praʊ] *n* Bug *m*

prowess ['praʊes] *n* überragende(s)
Können *nt*

prowl [praʊl] *vi* herumstreichen; (*animal*)
schleichen ♦ *n*: **on the ~** umherstreifend;
~er *n* Herumtreiber(in) *m(f)*

proximity [prɒk'sɪmɪtɪ] *n* Nähe *f*

proxy ['prɒksɪ] *n* (Stell)vertreter *m*;
(*authority, document*) Vollmacht *f*; **by ~**
durch einen Stellvertreter

prudence ['pruːdəns] *n* Umsicht *f*

prudent ['pruːdənt] *adj* klug, umsichtig

prudish ['pruːdɪʃ] *adj* prüde

prune [pruːn] *n* Backpflaume *f* ♦ *vt*
ausputzen; (*fig*) zurechtstutzen

pry [praɪ] *vi*: **to ~ (into)** seine Nase
stecken (in +*acc*)

PS *n abbr* (= *postscript*) PS

pseudo- ['sjuːdəʊ] *prefix* Pseudo-; **~nym**
['sjuːdənɪm] *n* Pseudonym *nt*, Deckname
m

psychiatric [saɪkɪ'ætrɪk] *adj*
psychiatrisch

psychiatrist [saɪ'kaɪətrɪst] *n* Psychiater
m

psychic ['saɪkɪk] *adj* (*also*: **~al**)
übersinnlich; (*person*) paranormal begabt

psychoanalyse [saɪkəʊ'ænəlaɪz] (*US*
psychoanalyze) *vt* psychoanalytisch behandeln

psychoanalyst [saɪkəʊ'ænəlɪst] *n*
Psychoanalytiker(in) *m(f)*

psychological [saɪkə'lɒdʒɪkəl] *adj*
psychologisch

psychologist [saɪ'kɒlədʒɪst] *n*
Psychologe *m*, Psychologin *f*

psychology [saɪ'kɒlədʒɪ] *n* Psychologie *f*

PTO *abbr* = **please turn over**

pub [pʌb] *n abbr* (= *public house*) Kneipe
f

pubic ['pjuːbɪk] *adj* Scham-

public ['pʌblɪk] *adj* öffentlich ♦ *n* (*also*:
general ~) Öffentlichkeit *f*; **in ~** in der
Öffentlichkeit; **~ address system** *n*
Lautsprecheranlage *f*

publican ['pʌblɪkən] *n* Wirt *m*

publication [pʌblɪ'keɪʃən] *n*
Veröffentlichung *f*

public: **~ company** *n* Aktiengesellschaft
f; **~ convenience** (*BRIT*) *n* öffentliche
Toiletten *pl*; **~ holiday** *n* gesetzliche(r)
Feiertag *m*; **~ house** (*BRIT*) *n* Lokal *nt*,
Kneipe *f*

publicity [pʌb'lɪsɪtɪ] *n* Publicity *f*,
Werbung *f*

publicize ['pʌblɪsaɪz] *vt* bekannt machen;
(*advertise*) Publicity machen für

publicly ['pʌblɪklɪ] *adv* öffentlich

public: **~ opinion** *n* öffentliche Meinung
f; **~ relations** *npl* Public Relations *pl*; **~
school** *n* (*BRIT*) Privatschule *f*; (*US*)
staatliche Schule *f*; **~-spirited** *adj* mit
Gemeinschaftssinn; **~ transport** *n*
öffentliche Verkehrsmittel *pl*

publish ['pʌblɪʃ] *vt* veröffentlichen;
(*event*) bekanntgeben; **~er** *n* Verleger *m*;
~ing *n* (*business*) Verlagswesen *nt*

pucker ['pʌkə*] *vt* (*face*) verziehen; (*lips*)
kräuseln

pudding ['pʊdɪŋ] *n* (*BRIT*: *course*)
Nachtisch *m*; Pudding *m*; **black ~**
≈ Blutwurst *f*

puddle ['pʌdl] *n* Pfütze *f*

puff [pʌf] *n* (*of wind etc*) Stoß *m*;

(*cosmetic*) Puderquaste *f* ♦ *vt* blasen, pusten; (*pipe*) paffen ♦ *vi* keuchen, schnaufen; (*smoke*) paffen; **to ~ out smoke** Rauch ausstoßen; **~ed** (*inf*) *adj* (*out of breath*) außer Puste; **~ pastry** (*US* ~ **paste**) *n* Blätterteig *m*; **~y** *adj* aufgedunsen

pull [pʊl] *n* Ruck *m*; (*influence*) Beziehung *f* ♦ *vt* ziehen; (*trigger*) abdrücken ♦ *vi* ziehen; **to ~ sb's leg** jdn auf den Arm nehmen; **to ~ to pieces** in Stücke reißen; (*fig*) verreißen; **to ~ one's punches** sich zurückhalten; **to ~ one's weight** sich in die Riemen legen; **to ~ o.s. together** sich zusammenreißen; **~ apart** *vt* (*break*) zerreißen; (*dismantle*) auseinandernehmen; (*fighters*) trennen; **~ down** *vt* (*house*) abreißen; **~ in** *vi* hineinfahren; (*stop*) anhalten; (*RAIL*) einfahren; **~ off** *vt* (*deal etc*) abschließen; **~ out** *vi* (*car*) herausfahren; (*fig: partner*) aussteigen ♦ *vt* herausziehen; **~ over** *vi* (*AUT*) an die Seite fahren; **~ round** *vi* durchkommen; **~ through** *vi* durchkommen; **~ up** *vi* anhalten ♦ *vt* (*uproot*) herausreißen; (*stop*) anhalten

pulley ['pʊlɪ] *n* Rolle *f*, Flaschenzug *m*
pullover ['pʊləʊvə*] *n* Pullover *m*
pulp [pʌlp] *n* Brei *m*; (*of fruit*) Fruchtfleisch *nt*
pulpit ['pʊlpɪt] *n* Kanzel *f*
pulsate [pʌl'seɪt] *vi* pulsieren
pulse [pʌls] *n* Puls *m*
pummel ['pʌml] *vt* mit den Fäusten bearbeiten
pump [pʌmp] *n* Pumpe *f*; (*shoe*) leichter (Tanz)schuh *m* ♦ *vt* pumpen; **~ up** *vt* (*tyre*) aufpumpen
pumpkin ['pʌmpkɪn] *n* Kürbis *m*
pun [pʌn] *n* Wortspiel *nt*
punch [pʌntʃ] *n* (*tool*) Locher *m*; (*blow*) (Faust)schlag *m*; (*drink*) Punsch *m*, Bowle *f* ♦ *vt* lochen; (*strike*) schlagen, boxen; **~line** *n* Pointe *f*; **~-up** (*BRIT: inf*) *n* Keilerei *f*
punctual ['pʌŋktjʊəl] *adj* pünktlich
punctuate ['pʌŋktjʊeɪt] *vt* mit Satzzeichen versehen; (*fig*) unterbrechen
punctuation [pʌŋktjʊ'eɪʃən] *n* Zeichensetzung *f*, Interpunktion *f*
puncture ['pʌŋktʃə*] *n* Loch *nt*; (*AUT*) Reifenpanne *f* ♦ *vt* durchbohren
pundit ['pʌndɪt] *n* Gelehrte(r) *m*
pungent ['pʌndʒənt] *adj* scharf
punish ['pʌnɪʃ] *vt* bestrafen; (*in boxing etc*) übel zurichten; **~ment** *n* Strafe *f*; (*action*) Bestrafung *f*
punk [pʌŋk] *n* (*also*: ~ **rocker**) Punker(in) *m(f)*; (: ~ **rock**) Punk *m*; (*US: inf: hoodlum*) Ganove *m*
punt [pʌnt] *n* Stechkahn *m*
punter ['pʌntə*] (*BRIT*) *n* (*better*) Wetter *m*
puny ['pjuːnɪ] *adj* kümmerlich
pup [pʌp] *n* = **puppy**
pupil ['pjuːpl] *n* Schüler(in) *m(f)*; (*in eye*) Pupille *f*
puppet ['pʌpɪt] *n* Puppe *f*; Marionette *f*
puppy ['pʌpɪ] *n* (*also POL*) junge(r) Hund *m*
purchase ['pɜːtʃɪs] *n* Kauf *m*; (*grip*) Halt *m* ♦ *vt* kaufen, erwerben; **~r** *n* Käufer(in) *m(f)*
pure [pjʊə*] *adj* (*also fig*) rein; **~ly** ['pjʊəlɪ] *adv* rein
purgatory ['pɜːgətərɪ] *n* Fegefeuer *nt*
purge [pɜːdʒ] *n* (*also POL*) Säuberung *f*; (*medicine*) Abführmittel *nt* ♦ *vt* reinigen; (*body*) entschlacken
purify ['pjʊərɪfaɪ] *vt* reinigen
purity ['pjʊərɪtɪ] *n* Reinheit *f*
purl [pɜːl] *n* linke Masche *f*
purple ['pɜːpl] *adj* violett; (*face*) dunkelrot
purport [pɜː'pɔːt] *vi* vorgeben
purpose ['pɜːpəs] *n* Zweck *m*, Ziel *nt*; (*of person*) Absicht *f*; **on ~** absichtlich; **~ful** *adj* zielbewußt, entschlossen
purr [pɜː*] *n* Schnurren *nt* ♦ *vi* schnurren
purse [pɜːs] *n* Portemonnaie *nt*, Geldbeutel *m* ♦ *vt* (*lips*) zusammenpressen, schürzen
purser ['pɜːsə*] *n* Zahlmeister *m*
pursue [pə'sjuː] *vt* verfolgen; (*study*) nachgehen +*dat*; **~r** *n* Verfolger *m*
pursuit [pə'sjuːt] *n* Verfolgung *f*; (*occupation*) Beschäftigung *f*
purveyor [pɜː'veɪə*] *n* Lieferant *m*
pus [pʌs] *n* Eiter *m*
push [pʊʃ] *n* Stoß *m*, Schub *m*; (*MIL*)

Vorstoß *m* ♦ *vt* stoßen, schieben; *(button)* drücken; *(idea)* durchsetzen ♦ *vi* stoßen, schieben; **~ aside** *vt* beiseiteschieben; **~ off** *(inf)* *vi* abschieben; **~ on** *vi* weitermachen; **~ through** *vt* durchdrücken; *(policy)* durchsetzen; **~ up** *vt* *(total)* erhöhen; *(prices)* hochtreiben; **~chair** *(BRIT)* n (Kinder)sportwagen *m*; **~over** *(inf)* n Kinderspiel *nt*; **~-up** *(US)* n *(press-up)* Liegestütz *m*; **~y** *(inf)* adj aufdringlich

puss [pʊs] *n* Mieze(katze) *f*; **~y(-cat)** ['pʊsɪ(kæt)] *n* Mieze(katze) *f*

put [pʊt] *(pt, pp put)* *vt* setzen, stellen, legen; *(express)* ausdrücken, sagen; *(write)* schreiben; **~ about** *vi* *(turn back)* wenden ♦ *vt* *(spread)* verbreiten; **~ across** *vt* *(explain)* erklären; **~ away** *vt* weglegen; *(store)* beiseite legen; **~ back** *vt* zurückstellen *or* -legen; **~ by** *vt* zurücklegen, sparen; **~ down** *vt* hinstellen *or* -legen; *(rebellion)* niederschlagen; *(animal)* einschläfern; *(in writing)* niederschreiben; **~ forward** *vt* *(idea)* vorbringen; *(clock)* vorstellen; **~ in** *vt* *(application, complaint)* einreichen; **~ off** *vt* verschieben; *(discourage)*: **to ~ sb off sth** jdn von etw abbringen; **~ on** *vt* *(clothes etc)* anziehen; *(light etc)* anschalten, anmachen; *(play etc)* aufführen; *(brake)* anziehen; **~ out** *vt* *(hand etc)* (her)ausstrecken; *(news, rumour)* verbreiten; *(light etc)* ausschalten, ausmachen; **~ through** *vt* *(TEL: person)* verbinden; *(: call)* durchstellen; **~ up** *vt* *(tent)* aufstellen; *(building)* errichten; *(price)* erhöhen; *(person)* unterbringen; **~ up with** *vt fus* sich abfinden mit

putrid ['pjuːtrɪd] *adj* faul

putt [pʌt] *vt* *(golf)* putten ♦ *n* Putten *nt*; **~ing green** *n* kleine(r) Golfplatz *m* nur zum Putten

putty ['pʌtɪ] *n* Kitt *m*; *(fig)* Wachs *nt*

put-up ['pʊtʌp] *adj*: **~ job** abgekartete(s) Spiel *nt*

puzzle ['pʌzl] *n* Rätsel *nt*; *(toy)* Geduldspiel *nt* ♦ *vt* verwirren ♦ *vi* sich den Kopf zerbrechen

puzzling ['pʌzlɪŋ] *adj* rätselhaft, verwirrend

pyjamas [pɪ'dʒɑːməz] *(BRIT)* npl Schlafanzug *m*, Pyjama *m*

pylon ['paɪlən] *n* Mast *m*

pyramid ['pɪrəmɪd] *n* Pyramide *f*

Q q

quack [kwæk] *n* Quaken *nt*; *(doctor)* Quacksalber *m* ♦ *vi* quaken

quad [kwɒd] *n abbr* = **quadrangle; quadruplet**

quadrangle ['kwɒdræŋgl] *n* *(court)* Hof *m*; *(MATH)* Viereck *nt*

quadruple [kwɒ'druːpl] *adj* vierfach ♦ *vi* sich vervierfachen ♦ *vt* vervierfachen

quadruplets [kwɒ'druːpləts] *npl* Vierlinge *pl*

quagmire ['kwægmaɪə*] *n* Morast *m*

quail [kweɪl] *n* *(bird)* Wachtel *f* ♦ *vi* (vor Angst) zittern

quaint [kweɪnt] *adj* kurios; malerisch

quake [kweɪk] *vi* beben, zittern ♦ *n abbr* = **earthquake**

qualification [kwɒlɪfɪ'keɪʃən] *n* Qualifikation *f*; *(sth which limits)* Einschränkung *f*

qualified ['kwɒlɪfaɪd] *adj* *(competent)* qualifiziert; *(limited)* bedingt

qualify ['kwɒlɪfaɪ] *vt* *(prepare)* befähigen; *(limit)* einschränken ♦ *vi* sich qualifizieren; **to ~ as a lawyer/doctor** sein juristisches/medizinisches Staatsexamen machen

quality ['kwɒlɪtɪ] *n* Qualität *f*; *(characteristic)* Eigenschaft *f*

qualm [kwɑːm] *n* Bedenken *nt*

quandary ['kwɒndərɪ] *n*: **to be in a ~** in Verlegenheit sein

quantity ['kwɒntɪtɪ] *n* Menge *f*; **~ surveyor** *n* Baukostenkalkulator *m*

quarantine ['kwɒrəntiːn] *n* Quarantäne *f*

quarrel ['kwɒrəl] *n* Streit *m* ♦ *vi* sich streiten; **~some** *adj* streitsüchtig

quarry ['kwɒrɪ] *n* Steinbruch *m*; *(animal)* Wild *nt*; *(fig)* Opfer *nt*

quart [kwɔːt] *n* Quart *nt*

quarter ['kwɔːtə*] *n* Viertel *nt*; *(of year)*

Quartal *nt* ♦ *vt* (*divide*) vierteln; (*MIL*)
einquartieren; **~s** *npl* (*esp MIL*) Quartier
nt; **~ of an hour** Viertelstunde *f*; **~ final**
n Viertelfinale *nt*; **~ly** *adj* vierteljährlich

quartet(te) [kwɔː'tet] *n* Quartett *nt*

quartz [kwɔːts] *n* Quarz *m*

quash [kwɒʃ] *vt* (*verdict*) aufheben

quasi- ['kwɑːzɪ] *prefix* Quasi-

quaver ['kweɪvə*] *n* (*BRIT: MUS*)
Achtelnote *f* ♦ *vi* (*tremble*) zittern

quay [kiː] *n* Kai *m*

queasy ['kwiːzɪ] *adj* übel

queen [kwiːn] *n* Königin *f*; **~ mother** *n*
Königinmutter *f*

queer [kwɪə*] *adj* seltsam ♦ *n* (*inf*:
homosexual) Schwule(r) *m*

quell [kwel] *vt* unterdrücken

quench [kwentʃ] *vt* (*thirst*) löschen

querulous ['kwerʊləs] *adj* nörglerisch

query ['kwɪərɪ] *n* (*question*) (An)frage *f*;
(*question mark*) Fragezeichen *nt* ♦ *vt* in
Zweifel ziehen, in Frage stellen

quest [kwest] *n* Suche *f*

question ['kwestʃən] *n* Frage *f* ♦ *vt* (*ask*)
(be)fragen; (*suspect*) verhören; (*doubt*) in
Frage stellen, bezweifeln; **beyond ~** ohne
Frage; **out of the ~** ausgeschlossen;
~able *adj* zweifelhaft; **~ mark** *n*
Fragezeichen *nt*

questionnaire [kwestʃə'nɛə*] *n*
Fragebogen *m*

queue [kjuː] (*BRIT*) *n* Schlange *f* ♦ *vi* (*also*:
~ up) Schlange stehen

quibble ['kwɪbl] *vi* kleinlich sein

quick [kwɪk] *adj* schnell ♦ *n* (*of nail*)
Nagelhaut *f*; **be ~!** mach schnell!; **cut to
the ~** (*fig*) tief getroffen; **~en** *vt* (*hasten*)
beschleunigen ♦ *vi* sich beschleunigen;
~ly *adv* schnell; **~sand** *n* Treibsand *m*;
~-witted *adj* schlagfertig

quid [kwɪd] (*BRIT: inf*) *n* (*£1*) Pfund *nt*

quiet ['kwaɪət] *adj* (*without noise*) leise;
(*peaceful, calm*) still, ruhig ♦ *n* Stille *f*,
Ruhe *f* ♦ *vt, vi* (*US* = **quieten**); **keep ~!**
sei still!; **~en** *vi* (*also*: **~en down**) ruhig
werden ♦ *vt* beruhigen; **~ly** *adv* leise,
ruhig; **~ness** *n* Ruhe *f*, Stille *f*

quilt [kwɪlt] *n* (*continental ~*) Steppdecke *f*

quin [kwɪn] *n abbr* = **quintuplet**

quinine [kwɪ'niːn] *n* Chinin *nt*

quintuplets [kwɪn'tjuːpləts] *npl*
Fünflinge *pl*

quip [kwɪp] *n* witzige Bemerkung *f*

quirk [kwɜːk] *n* (*oddity*) Eigenart *f*

quit [kwɪt] (*pt, pp* **quit** *or* **quitted**) *vt*
verlassen ♦ *vi* aufhören

quite [kwaɪt] *adv* (*completely*) ganz, völlig;
(*fairly*) ziemlich; **~ a few of them**
ziemlich viele von ihnen; **~ (so)!** richtig!

quits [kwɪts] *adj* quitt; **let's call it ~**
lassen wir's gut sein

quiver ['kwɪvə*] *vi* zittern ♦ *n* (*for
arrows*) Köcher *m*

quiz [kwɪz] *n* (*competition*) Quiz *nt* ♦ *vt*
prüfen; **~zical** *adj* fragend

quorum ['kwɔːrəm] *n* beschlußfähige
Anzahl *f*

quota ['kwəʊtə] *n* Anteil *m*; (*COMM*) Quote
f

quotation [kwəʊ'teɪʃən] *n* Zitat *nt*;
(*price*) Kostenvoranschlag *m*; **~ marks**
npl Anführungszeichen *pl*

quote [kwəʊt] *n* = **quotation** ♦ *vi* (*from
book*) zitieren ♦ *vt* zitieren; (*price*)
angeben

R r

rabbi ['ræbaɪ] *n* Rabbiner *m*; (*title*) Rabbi
m

rabbit ['ræbɪt] *n* Kaninchen *nt*; **~ hole** *n*
Kaninchenbau *m*; **~ hutch** *n*
Kaninchenstall *m*

rabble ['ræbl] *n* Pöbel *m*

rabies ['reɪbiːz] *n* Tollwut *f*

RAC (*BRIT*) *n abbr* = **Royal Automobile
Club**

raccoon [rə'kuːn] *n* Waschbär *m*

race [reɪs] *n* (*species*) Rasse *f*;
(*competition*) Rennen *nt*; (*on foot*) Rennen
nt, Wettlauf *m*; (*rush*) Hetze *f* ♦ *vt* um die
Wette laufen mit; (*horses*) laufen lassen
♦ *vi* (*run*) rennen; (*in contest*) am Rennen
teilnehmen; **~ car** (*US*) *n* = **racing car**; **~
car driver** (*US*) *n* = **racing driver**;
~course *n* (*for horses*) Rennbahn *f*;
~horse *n* Rennpferd *nt*; **~track** *n* (*for*

cars etc) Rennstrecke *f*

racial ['reɪʃəl] *adj* Rassen-; **~ist** *adj* rassistisch ♦ *n* Rassist *m*

racing ['reɪsɪŋ] *n* Rennen *nt*; **~ car** (*BRIT*) *n* Rennwagen *m*; **~ driver** (*BRIT*) *n* Rennfahrer *m*

racism ['reɪsɪzəm] *n* Rassismus *m*

racist ['reɪsɪst] *n* Rassist *m* ♦ *adj* rassistisch

rack [ræk] *n* Ständer *m*, Gestell *nt* ♦ *vt* plagen; **to go to ~ and ruin** verfallen; **to ~ one's brains** sich *dat* den Kopf zerbrechen

racket ['rækɪt] *n* (*din*) Krach *m*; (*scheme*) (Schwindel)geschäft *nt*; (*TENNIS: also* *racquet*) (Tennis)schläger *m*

racoon [rə'ku:n] *n* = **raccoon**

racquet ['rækɪt] *n* (Tennis)schläger *m*

racy ['reɪsɪ] *adj* gewagt; (*style*) spritzig

radar ['reɪdɑː*] *n* Radar *nt or m*

radial ['reɪdɪəl] *adj* (*also: US: ~-ply*) radial

radiance ['reɪdɪəns] *n* strahlende(r) Glanz *m*

radiant ['reɪdɪənt] *adj* strahlend; (*giving out rays*) Strahlungs-

radiate ['reɪdɪeɪt] *vi* ausstrahlen; (*roads, lines*) strahlenförmig wegführen ♦ *vt* ausstrahlen

radiation [reɪdɪ'eɪʃən] *n* (Aus)strahlung *f*

radiator ['reɪdɪeɪtə*] *n* (*for heating*) Heizkörper *m*; (*AUT*) Kühler *m*

radical ['rædɪkəl] *adj* radikal

radii ['reɪdɪaɪ] *npl of* **radius**

radio ['reɪdɪəu] *n* Rundfunk *m*, Radio *nt*; (*set*) Radio *nt*, Radioapparat *m*; **on the ~** im Radio; **~active** [reɪdɪəu'æktɪv] *adj* radioaktiv; **~logy** [reɪdɪ'ɒlədʒɪ] *n* Strahlenkunde *f*; **~ station** *n* Rundfunkstation *f*; **~therapy** *n* Röntgentherapie *f*

radish ['rædɪʃ] *n* (*big*) Rettich *m*; (*small*) Radieschen *nt*

radius ['reɪdɪəs] (*pl* **radii**) *n* Radius *m*; (*area*) Umkreis *m*

RAF *n abbr* = **Royal Air Force**

raffle ['ræfl] *n* Verlosung *f*, Tombola *f* ♦ *vt* verlosen

raft [rɑːft] *n* Floß *nt*

rafter ['rɑːftə*] *n* Dachsparren *m*

rag [ræg] *n* (*cloth*) Lumpen *m*, Lappen *m*; (*inf: newspaper*) Käseblatt *nt*; (*UNIV: for charity*) studentische Sammelaktion *f* ♦ *vt* (*BRIT*) auf den Arm nehmen; **~s** *npl* (*cloth*) Lumpen *pl*; **~-and-bone man** (*irreg; BRIT*) *n* = **ragman**; **~ doll** *n* Flickenpuppe *f*

rage [reɪdʒ] *n* Wut *f*; (*fashion*) große Mode *f* ♦ *vi* wüten, toben

ragged ['rægɪd] *adj* (*edge*) gezackt; (*clothes*) zerlumpt

ragman ['rægmæn] (*irreg*) *n* Lumpensammler *m*

raid [reɪd] *n* Überfall *m*; (*MIL*) Angriff *m*; (*by police*) Razzia *f* ♦ *vt* überfallen

rail [reɪl] *n* (*also RAIL*) Schiene *f*; (*on stair*) Geländer *nt*; (*of ship*) Reling *f*; **~s** *npl* (*RAIL*) Geleise *pl*; **by ~** per Bahn; **~ing(s)** *n(pl)* Geländer *nt*; **~road** (*US*) *n* Eisenbahn *f*; **~way** (*BRIT*) *n* Eisenbahn *f*; **~way line** (*BRIT*) *n* (Eisen)bahnlinie *f*; (*track*) Gleis *nt*; **~wayman** (*irreg; BRIT*) *n* Eisenbahner *m*; **~way station** (*BRIT*) *n* Bahnhof *m*

rain [reɪn] *n* Regen *m* ♦ *vt, vi* regnen; **in the ~** im Regen; **it's ~ing** es regnet; **~bow** *n* Regenbogen *m*; **~coat** *n* Regenmantel *m*; **~drop** *n* Regentropfen *m*; **~fall** *n* Niederschlag *m*; **~forest** *n* Regenwald *m*; **~y** *adj* (*region, season*) Regen-; (*day*) regnerisch, verregnet

raise [reɪz] *n* (*esp US: increase*) (Gehalts)erhöhung *f* ♦ *vt* (*lift*) (hoch)heben; (*increase*) erhöhen; (*question*) aufwerfen; (*doubts*) äußern; (*funds*) beschaffen; (*family*) großziehen; (*livestock*) züchten; **to ~ one's voice** die Stimme erheben

raisin ['reɪzən] *n* Rosine *f*

rake [reɪk] *n* Rechen *m*, Harke *f*; (*person*) Wüstling *m* ♦ *vt* rechen, harken; (*with gun*) (mit Feuer) bestreichen; (*search*) (durch)suchen

rakish ['reɪkɪʃ] *adj* verwegen

rally ['rælɪ] *n* (*POL etc*) Kundgebung *f*; (*AUT*) Rallye *f* ♦ *vt* (*MIL*) sammeln ♦ *vi* Kräfte sammeln; **~ round** *vt fus* (sich) scharen um; (*help*) zu Hilfe kommen +*dat* ♦ *vi* zu Hilfe kommen

RAM [ræm] *n abbr* (= *random access memory*) RAM *m*

ram [ræm] *n* Widder *m*; (*instrument*) Ramme *f* ♦ *vt* (*strike*) rammen; (*stuff*) (hinein)stopfen

ramble ['ræmbl] *n* Wanderung *f* ♦ *vi* (*talk*) schwafeln; ~**r** *n* Wanderer *m*

rambling ['ræmblɪŋ] *adj* (*speech*) weitschweifig; (*town*) ausgedehnt

ramp [ræmp] *n* Rampe *f*; **on/off** ~ (*US: AUT*) Ein-/Ausfahrt *f*

rampage [ræm'peɪdʒ] *n*: **to be on the** ~ randalieren ♦ *vi* randalieren

rampant ['ræmpənt] *adj* wild wuchernd

rampart ['ræmpɑːt] *n* (Schutz)wall *m*

ram raid *n* Raubüberfall, bei dem eine Geschäftsfront mit einem Fahrzeug gerammt wird

ramshackle ['ræmʃækl] *adj* baufällig

ran [ræn] *pt of* **run**

ranch [rɑːntʃ] *n* Ranch *f*

rancid ['rænsɪd] *adj* ranzig

rancour ['ræŋkə*] (*US* **rancor**) *n* Verbitterung *f*, Groll *m*

random ['rændəm] *adj* ziellos, wahllos ♦ *n*: **at** ~ aufs Geratewohl; ~ **access** *n* (*COMPUT*) wahlfreie(r) Zugriff *m*

randy ['rændɪ] (*BRIT: inf*) *adj* geil, scharf

rang [ræŋ] *pt of* **ring**

range [reɪndʒ] *n* Reihe *f*; (*of mountains*) Kette *f*; (*COMM*) Sortiment *nt*; (*reach*) (Reich)weite *f*; (*of gun*) Schußweite *f*; (*for shooting practice*) Schießplatz *m*; (*stove*) (großer) Herd *m* ♦ *vt* (*set in row*) anordnen, aufstellen; (*roam*) durchstreifen ♦ *vi*: **to** ~ **over** (*wander*) umherstreifen in +*dat*; (*extend*) sich erstrecken auf +*acc*; **a** ~ **of** (*selection*) eine (große) Auswahl an +*dat*; **prices ranging from £5 to £10** Preise, die sich zwischen £5 und £10 bewegen; ~**r** ['reɪndʒə*] *n* Förster *m*

rank [ræŋk] *n* (*row*) Reihe *f*; (*BRIT: also*: **taxi** ~) (Taxi)stand *m*; (*MIL*) Rang *m*; (*social position*) Stand *m* ♦ *vi* (*have* ~): **to** ~ **among** gehören zu ♦ *adj* (*strong-smelling*) stinkend; (*extreme*) krass; **the** ~ **and file** (*fig*) die breite Masse

rankle ['ræŋkl] *vi* nagen

ransack ['rænsæk] *vt* (*plunder*) plündern; (*search*) durchwühlen

ransom ['rænsəm] *n* Lösegeld *nt*; **to hold sb to** ~ jdn gegen Lösegeld festhalten

rant [rænt] *vi* hochtrabend reden

rap [ræp] *n* Schlag *m*; (*music*) Rap *m* ♦ *vt* klopfen

rape [reɪp] *n* Vergewaltigung *f*; (*BOT*) Raps *m* ♦ *vt* vergewaltigen; ~**(seed) oil** *n* Rapsöl *nt*

rapid ['ræpɪd] *adj* rasch, schnell; ~**ity** [rə'pɪdɪtɪ] *n* Schnelligkeit *f*; ~**ly** *adv* schnell; ~**s** *npl* Stromschnellen *pl*

rapist ['reɪpɪst] *n* Vergewaltiger *m*

rapport [ræ'pɔː*] *n* gute(s) Verhältnis *nt*

rapture ['ræptʃə*] *n* Entzücken *nt*

rapturous ['ræptʃərəs] *adj* (*applause*) stürmisch; (*expression*) verzückt

rare [rɛə*] *adj* selten, rar; (*underdone*) nicht durchgebraten

rarely ['rɛəlɪ] *adv* selten

raring ['rɛərɪŋ] *adj*: **to be** ~ **to go** (*inf*) es kaum erwarten können, bis es losgeht

rarity ['rɛərɪtɪ] *n* Seltenheit *f*

rascal ['rɑːskəl] *n* Schuft *m*

rash [ræʃ] *adj* übereilt; (*reckless*) unbesonnen ♦ *n* (*Haut*)ausschlag *m*

rasher ['ræʃə*] *n* Speckscheibe *f*

raspberry ['rɑːzbərɪ] *n* Himbeere *f*

rasping ['rɑːspɪŋ] *adj* (*noise*) kratzend; (*voice*) krächzend

rat [ræt] *n* (*animal*) Ratte *f*; (*person*) Halunke *m*

rate [reɪt] *n* (*proportion*) Rate *f*; (*price*) Tarif *m*; (*speed*) Tempo *nt* ♦ *vt* (ein)schätzen; ~**s** *npl* (*BRIT: tax*) Grundsteuer *f*; **to** ~ **as** für etw halten; ~**able value** (*BRIT*) *n* Einheitswert *m* (*als Bemessungsgrundlage*); ~**payer** (*BRIT*) *n* Steuerzahler(in) *m(f)*

rather ['rɑːðə*] *adv* (*in preference*) lieber, eher; (*to some extent*) ziemlich; **I would** *or* **I'd** ~ **go** ich würde lieber gehen; **it's** ~ **expensive** (*quite*) es ist ziemlich teuer; (*too*) es ist etwas zu teuer; **there's** ~ **a lot** es ist ziemlich viel

ratify ['rætɪfaɪ] *vt* bestätigen; (*POL*) ratifizieren

rating ['reɪtɪŋ] *n* Klasse *f*; (*BRIT: sailor*)

Matrose m

ratio ['reɪʃɪəʊ] n Verhältnis nt; **in the ~ of 100 to 1** im Verhältnis 100 zu 1

ration ['ræʃən] n (usu pl) Ration f ♦ vt rationieren

rational ['ræʃənl] adj rational; **~e** [ræʃə'nɑːl] n Grundprinzip nt; **~ize** ['ræʃnəlaɪz] vt rationalisieren; **~ly** adv rational

rat race n Konkurrenzkampf m

rattle ['rætl] n (sound) Rasseln nt; (toy) Rassel f ♦ vi ratteln, klappern ♦ vt rasseln mit; **~snake** n Klapperschlange f

raucous ['rɔːkəs] adj heiser, rauh

ravage ['rævɪdʒ] vt verheeren; **~s** npl verheerende Wirkungen pl

rave [reɪv] vi (talk wildly) phantasieren; (rage) toben

raven ['reɪvn] n Rabe m

ravenous ['rævənəs] adj heißhungrig

ravine [rə'viːn] n Schlucht f

raving ['reɪvɪŋ] adj: **~ lunatic** völlig Wahnsinnige(r) mf

ravishing ['rævɪʃɪŋ] adj atemberaubend

raw [rɔː] adj roh; (tender) wund(gerieben); (inexperienced) unerfahren; **to get a ~ deal** (inf) schlecht wegkommen; **~ material** n Rohmaterial nt

ray [reɪ] n (of light) Strahl m; **~ of hope** Hoffnungsschimmer m

raze [reɪz] vt (also: **raze to the ground**) dem Erdboden gleichmachen

razor ['reɪzə*] n Rasierapparat m; **~ blade** n Rasierklinge f

Rd abbr = **road**

re [riː] prep (COMM) betreffs +gen

reach [riːtʃ] n Reichweite f; (of river) Strecke f ♦ vt (arrive at) erreichen; (give) reichen ♦ vi (stretch) sich erstrecken; **within ~** (shops etc) in erreichbarer Weite or Entfernung; **out of ~** außer Reichweite; **to ~ for** (try to get) langen nach; **~ out** vi die Hand ausstrecken; **to ~ out for sth** nach etw greifen

react [riː'ækt] vi reagieren; **~ion** [riː'ækʃən] n Reaktion f

reactor [riː'æktə*] n Reaktor m

read¹ [red] pt, pp of **read²**

read² [riːd] (pt, pp **read**) vt, vi lesen; (aloud) vorlesen; **~ out** vt vorlesen; **~able** adj leserlich; (worth reading) lesenswert; **~er** n (person) Leser(in) m(f); (book) Lesebuch nt; **~ership** n Leserschaft f

readily ['redɪlɪ] adv (willingly) bereitwillig; (easily) prompt

readiness ['redɪnəs] n (willingness) Bereitwilligkeit f; (being ready) Bereitschaft f; **in ~** (prepared) bereit

reading ['riːdɪŋ] n Lesen nt

readjust ['riːə'dʒʌst] vt neu einstellen ♦ vi (person): **to ~** sich wieder anpassen an +acc

ready ['redɪ] adj (prepared, willing) bereit ♦ adv: **~-cooked** vorgekocht ♦ n: **at the ~** bereit; **~-made** adj gebrauchsfertig, Fertig-; (clothes) Konfektions-; **~ money** n Bargeld nt; **~ reckoner** n Rechentabelle f; **~-to-wear** adj Konfektions-

real [rɪəl] adj wirklich; (actual) eigentlich; (not fake) echt; **in ~ terms** effektiv; **~ estate** n Grundbesitz m; **~istic** [rɪə'lɪstɪk] adj realistisch

reality [riː'ælɪtɪ] n Wirklichkeit f, Realität f; **in ~** in Wirklichkeit

realization [rɪəlaɪ'zeɪʃən] n (understanding) Erkenntnis f; (fulfilment) Verwirklichung f

realize ['rɪəlaɪz] vt (understand) begreifen; (make real) verwirklichen; (money) einbringen; **I didn't ~ ...** ich wußte nicht, ...

really ['rɪəlɪ] adv wirklich; **~?** (indicating interest) tatsächlich?; (expressing surprise) wirklich?

realm [relm] n Reich nt

realtor ['rɪəltɔː*] (®; US) n Grundstücksmakler(in) m(f)

reap [riːp] vt ernten

reappear ['riːə'pɪə*] vi wieder erscheinen

rear [rɪə*] adj hintere(r, s), Rück- ♦ n Rückseite f; (last part) Schluß m ♦ vt (bring up) aufziehen ♦ vi (horse) sich aufbäumen; **~guard** n Nachhut f

rearmament ['riːˈɑːməmənt] n Wiederaufrüstung f

rearrange ['riːə'reɪndʒ] vt umordnen

rear-view mirror ['rɪəvjuː-] *n*
Rückspiegel *m*

reason ['riːzn] *n* (*cause*) Grund *m*; (*ability
to think*) Verstand *m*; (*sensible thoughts*)
Vernunft *f* ♦ *vi* (*think*) denken; (*use
arguments*) argumentieren; **it stands to ~
that** es ist logisch, daß; **to ~ with sb** mit
jdm diskutieren; **~able** *adj* vernünftig;
~ably *adv* vernünftig; (*fairly*) ziemlich;
~ed *adj* (*argument*) durchdacht; **~ing** *n*
Urteilen *nt*; (*argumentation*)
Beweisführung *f*

reassurance ['riːə'ʃʊərəns] *n* Beruhigung
f; (*confirmation*) Bestätigung *f*

reassure ['riːə'ʃʊə*] *vt* beruhigen; **to ~
sb of sth** jdm etw versichern

reassuring ['riːə'ʃʊərɪŋ] *adj* beruhigend

rebate ['riːbeɪt] *n* Rückzahlung *f*

rebel [*n* 'rebl, *vb* rɪ'bel] *n* Rebell *m* ♦ *vi*
rebellieren; **~lion** [rɪ'belɪən] *n* Rebellion *f*,
Aufstand *m*; **~lious** *adj* (*subject, child,
behaviour*) rebellisch

rebirth ['riː'bɜːθ] *n* Wiedergeburt *f*

rebound [*vb* rɪ'baʊnd, *n* 'riːbaʊnd] *vi*
zurückprallen ♦ *n* Rückprall *m*

rebuff [rɪ'bʌf] *n* Abfuhr *f* ♦ *vt* abblitzen
lassen

rebuild ['riː'bɪld] (*irreg*) *vt*
wiederaufbauen; (*fig*) wiederherstellen

rebuke [rɪ'bjuːk] *n* Tadel *m* ♦ *vt* tadeln,
rügen

rebut [rɪ'bʌt] *vt* widerlegen

recalcitrant [rɪ'kælsɪtrənt] *adj*
widerspenstig

recall [*vb* rɪ'kɔːl, *n* 'riːkɔːl] *vt* (*call back*)
zurückrufen; (*remember*) sich erinnern an
+*acc* ♦ *n* Rückruf *m*

recant [rɪ'kænt] *vi* widerrufen

recap ['riːkæp] *vt, vi* wiederholen

recapitulate [riːkə'pɪtjʊleɪt] *vt, vi*
= **recap**

rec'd *abbr* (= *received*) Eing.

recede [rɪ'siːd] *vi* zurückweichen

receding [rɪ'siːdɪŋ] *adj*: **~ hairline**
Stirnglatze *f*

receipt [rɪ'siːt] *n* (*document*) Quittung *f*;
(*receiving*) Empfang *m*; **~s** *npl* (*ECON*)
Einnahmen *pl*

receive [rɪ'siːv] *vt* erhalten; (*visitors etc*)

empfangen; **~r** [rɪ'siːvə*] *n* (*TEL*) Hörer *m*

recent ['riːsnt] *adj* vor kurzem
(geschehen), neuerlich; (*modern*) neu; **~ly**
adv kürzlich, neulich

receptacle [rɪ'septəkl] *n* Behälter *m*

reception [rɪ'sepʃən] *n* Empfang *m*; **~
desk** *n* Empfang *m*; (*in hotel*) Rezeption *f*;
~ist *n* (*in hotel*) Empfangschef *m*, Emp-
fangsdame *f*; (*MED*) Sprechstundenhilfe
f

receptive [rɪ'septɪv] *adj* aufnahmebereit

recess ['riːses] *n* (*break*) Ferien *pl*;
(*hollow*) Nische *f*, **~ion** [rɪ'seʃən] *n*
Rezession *f*

recharge ['riː'tʃɑːdʒ] *vt* (*battery*) aufladen

recipe ['resɪpɪ] *n* Rezept *nt*

recipient [rɪ'sɪpɪənt] *n* Empfänger *m*

reciprocal [rɪ'sɪprəkəl] *adj* gegenseitig;
(*mutual*) wechselseitig

recital [rɪ'saɪtl] *n* Vortrag *m*

recite [rɪ'saɪt] *vt* vortragen, aufsagen

reckless ['rekləs] *adj* leichtsinnig;
(*driving*) fahrlässig

reckon ['rekən] *vt* (*count*) rechnen,
berechnen, errechnen; (*estimate*) schätzen;
(*think*): **I ~ that ...** ich nehme an, daß ...;
~ on *vt fus* rechnen mit; **~ing** *n*
(*calculation*) Rechnen *nt*

reclaim [rɪ'kleɪm] *vt* (*expenses*)
zurückverlangen; (*land*): **to ~ (from sth)**
(etw *dat*) gewinnen

reclamation [reklə'meɪʃən] *n* (*of land*)
Gewinnung *f*

recline [rɪ'klaɪn] *vi* sich zurücklehnen

reclining [rɪ'klaɪnɪŋ] *adj* Liege-

recluse [rɪ'kluːs] *n* Einsiedler *m*

recognition [rekəg'nɪʃən] *n* (*recognizing*)
Erkennen *nt*; (*acknowledgement*)
Anerkennung *f*; **transformed beyond ~**
völlig verändert

recognizable ['rekəgnaɪzəbl] *adj*
erkennbar

recognize ['rekəgnaɪz] *vt* erkennen; (*POL,
approve*) anerkennen; **to ~ as** anerkennen
als; **to ~ by** erkennen an +*dat*

recoil [rɪ'kɔɪl] *vi* (*in horror*)
zurückschrecken; (*rebound*)
zurückprallen; (*person*): **to ~ from doing
sth** davor zurückschrecken, etw zu tun

recollect [rekə'lekt] *vt* sich erinnern an
+*acc*; **~ion** [rekə'lekʃən] *n* Erinnerung *f*

recommend [rekə'mend] *vt* empfehlen;
~ation [-'deıʃən] *n* Empfehlung *f*

recompense ['rekəmpens] *n*
(*compensation*) Entschädigung *f*; (*reward*)
Belohnung *f* ♦ *vt* entschädigen; belohnen

reconcile ['rekənsaıl] *vt* (*facts*)
vereinbaren; (*people*) versöhnen; **to ~ o.s.
to sth** sich mit etw abfinden

reconciliation [rekənsılı'eıʃən] *n*
Versöhnung *f*

recondition ['riːkən'dıʃən] *vt* (*machine*)
generalüberholen

reconnaissance [rı'kɔnısəns] *n*
Aufklärung *f*

reconnoitre [rekə'nɔıtə*] (*US*
reconnoiter) *vt* erkunden ♦ *vi* aufklären

reconsider ['riːkən'sıdə*] *vt* von neuem
erwägen, noch einmal überdenken ♦ *vi* es
noch einmal überdenken

reconstruct ['riːkən'strʌkt] *vt*
wiederaufbauen; (*crime*) rekonstruieren;
~ion ['riːkən'strʌkʃən] *n* Rekonstruktion *f*

record [*n* 'rekɔːd, *vb* rı'kɔːd] *n*
Aufzeichnung *f*; (*MUS*) Schallplatte *f*; (*best
performance*) Rekord *m* ♦ *vt* aufzeichnen;
(*music etc*) aufnehmen; **off the ~**
vertraulich ♦ *adv* im Vertrauen; **in ~
time** in Rekordzeit; **~ card** *n* (*in file*)
Karteikarte *f*; **~ed delivery** (*BRIT*) *n* (*POST*)
Einschreiben *nt*; **~er** *n* (*TECH*)
Registriergerät *nt*; (*MUS*) Blockflöte *f*; **~
holder** *n* (*SPORT*) Rekordinhaber *m*; **~ing**
n (*MUS*) Aufnahme *f*; **~ player** *n*
Plattenspieler *m*

recount [rı'kaunt] *vt* (*tell*) berichten

re-count ['riːkaunt] *n* Nachzählung *f* ♦ *vt*
nachzählen

recoup [rı'kuːp] *vt*: **to ~ one's losses**
seinen Verlust wiedergutmachen

recourse [rı'kɔːs] *n*: **to have ~ to**
Zuflucht nehmen zu *or* bei

recover [rı'kʌvə*] *vt* (*get back*)
zurückerhalten ♦ *vi* sich erholen

re-cover ['riː'kʌvə*] *vt* (*quilt etc*) neu
überziehen

recovery [rı'kʌvərı] *n* Wiedererlangung *f*;
(*of health*) Erholung *f*

recreate ['riːkrı'eıt] *vt* wiederherstellen

recreation [rekrı'eıʃən] *n* Erholung *f*; **~al**
adj Erholungs-; **~al drug** *n* Freizeitdroge
f

recrimination [rıkrımı'neıʃən] *n*
Gegenbeschuldigung *f*

recruit [rı'kruːt] *n* Rekrut *m* ♦ *vt*
rekrutieren; **~ment** *n* Rekrutierung *f*

rectangle ['rektæŋgl] *n* Rechteck *nt*

rectangular [rek'tæŋgjʊlə*] *adj*
rechteckig, rechtwinklig

rectify ['rektıfaı] *vt* berichtigen

rector ['rektə*] *n* (*REL*) Pfarrer *m*; (*SCH*)
Direktor(in) *m(f)*; **~y** ['rektərı] *n*
Pfarrhaus *nt*

recuperate [rı'kuːpəreıt] *vi* sich erholen

recur [rı'kɜː*] *vi* sich wiederholen;
~rence *n* Wiederholung *f*; **~rent** *adj*
wiederkehrend

recycle [riː'saıkl] *vt* wiederverwerten,
wiederaufbereiten

red [red] *n* Rot *nt*; (*POL*) Rote(r) *m* ♦ *adj*
rot; **in the ~** in den roten Zahlen; **~
carpet treatment** *n* Sonderbehandlung
f, große(r) Bahnhof *m*; **R~ Cross** *n*
Rote(s) Kreuz *nt*; **~currant** *n* rote
Johannisbeere *f*; **~den** *vi* sich röten;
(*blush*) erröten ♦ *vt* röten; **~dish** *adj*
rötlich

redeem [rı'diːm] *vt* (*COMM*) einlösen;
(*save*) retten

redeeming [rı'diːmıŋ] *adj*: **~ feature**
versöhnende(s) Moment *nt*

redeploy ['riːdı'plɔı] *vt* (*resources*)
umverteilen

red-haired ['red'hɛəd] *adj* rothaarig

red-handed ['red'hændıd] *adv*: **to be
caught ~** auf frischer Tat ertappt werden

redhead ['redhed] *n* Rothaarige(r) *mf*

red herring *n* Ablenkungsmanöver *nt*

red-hot ['red'hɔt] *adj* rotglühend

redirect ['riːdaı'rekt] *vt* umleiten

red light *n*: **to go through a ~** (*AUT*) bei
Rot über die Ampel fahren; **red-light
district** *n* Strichviertel *nt*

redo ['riː'duː] (*irreg: like* do) *vt* nochmals
machen

redolent ['redəʊlənt] *adj*: **~ of** riechend
nach; (*fig*) erinnernd an +*acc*

redouble [riːˈdʌbl] *vt*: **to ~ one's efforts** seine Anstrengungen verdoppeln

redress [rɪˈdres] *n* Entschädigung *f* ♦ *vt* wiedergutmachen

Red Sea *n*: **the ~** das Rote Meer

redskin [ˈredskɪn] *n* Rothaut *f*

red tape *n* Bürokratismus *m*

reduce [rɪˈdjuːs] *vt* (*speed, temperature*) vermindern; (*photo*) verkleinern; **"~ speed now"** (*AUT*) ≈ „langsam"; **to ~ the price (to)** den Preis herabsetzen (auf +*acc*); **at a ~d price** zum ermäßigten Preis

reduction [rɪˈdʌkʃən] *n* Verminderung *f*; Verkleinerung *f*; Herabsetzung *f*; (*amount of money*) Nachlaß *m*

redundancy [rɪˈdʌndənsɪ] *n* Überflüssigkeit *f*; (*of workers*) Entlassung *f*

redundant [rɪˈdʌndənt] *adj* überflüssig; (*workers*) ohne Arbeitsplatz; **to be made ~** arbeitslos werden

reed [riːd] *n* Schilf *nt*; (*MUS*) Rohrblatt *nt*

reef [riːf] *n* Riff *nt*

reek [riːk] *vi*: **to ~ (of)** stinken (nach)

reel [riːl] *n* Spule *f*, Rolle *f* ♦ *vt* (*also: ~ in*) wickeln, spulen ♦ *vi* (*stagger*) taumeln

ref [ref] (*inf*) *n abbr* (= *referee*) Schiri *m*

refectory [rɪˈfektərɪ] *n* (*UNIV*) Mensa *f*; (*SCH*) Speisesaal *m*; (*ECCL*) Refektorium *nt*

refer [rɪˈfɜː*] *vt*: **to ~ sb to sb/sth** jdn an jdn/etw verweisen ♦ *vi*: **to ~ to** (*to book*) nachschlagen in +*dat*; (*mention*) sich beziehen auf +*acc*

referee [refəˈriː] *n* Schiedsrichter *m*; (*BRIT: for job*) Referenz *f* ♦ *vt* schiedsrichtern

reference [ˈrefrəns] *n* (*for job*) Referenz *f*; (*in book*) Verweis *m*; (*number, code*) Aktenzeichen *nt*; (*allusion*): **~ (to)** Anspielung (auf +*acc*); **with ~ to** in bezug auf +*acc*; **~ book** *n* Nachschlagewerk *nt*; **~ number** *n* Aktenzeichen *nt*

referenda [refəˈrendə] *npl of* **referendum**

referendum [refəˈrendəm] (*pl* -da) *n* Volksabstimmung *f*

refill [*vb* ˈriːˈfɪl, *n* ˈriːfɪl] *vt* nachfüllen ♦ *n* (*for pen*) Ersatzmine *f*

refine [rɪˈfaɪn] *vt* (*purify*) raffinieren; **~d** *adj* kultiviert; **~ment** *n* Kultiviertheit *f*

reflect [rɪˈflekt] *vt* (*light*) reflektieren; (*fig*) (wider)spiegeln ♦ *vi* (*meditate*): **to ~ (on)** nachdenken (über +*acc*); **it ~s badly/well on him** das stellt ihn in ein schlechtes/gutes Licht; **~ion** [rɪˈflekʃən] *n* Reflexion *f*; (*image*) Spiegelbild *nt*; (*thought*) Überlegung *f*; **on ~ion** wenn man sich *dat* das recht überlegt

reflex [ˈriːfleks] *adj* Reflex- ♦ *n* Reflex *m*; **~ive** [rɪˈfleksɪv] *adj* reflexiv

reform [rɪˈfɔːm] *n* Reform *f* ♦ *vt* (*person*) bessern; **the R~ation** [refəˈmeɪʃən] *n* die Reformation; **~atory** (*US*) *n* Besserungsanstalt *f*

refrain [rɪˈfreɪn] *vi*: **to ~ from** unterlassen ♦ *n* Refrain *m*

refresh [rɪˈfreʃ] *vt* erfrischen; **~er course** (*BRIT*) *n* Wiederholungskurs *m*; **~ing** *adj* erfrischend; **~ments** *npl* Erfrischungen *pl*

refrigeration [rɪfrɪdʒəˈreɪʃən] *n* Kühlung *f*

refrigerator [rɪˈfrɪdʒəreɪtə*] *n* Kühlschrank *m*

refuel [ˈriːˈfjʊəl] *vt, vi* auftanken

refuge [ˈrefjuːdʒ] *n* Zuflucht *f*; **to take ~ in** sich flüchten in +*acc*

refugee [refjuˈdʒiː] *n* Flüchtling *m*

refund [*n* ˈriːfʌnd, *vb* rɪˈfʌnd] *n* Rückvergütung *f* ♦ *vt* zurückerstatten

refurbish [ˈriːˈfɜːbɪʃ] *vt* aufpolieren

refusal [rɪˈfjuːzəl] *n* (Ver)weigerung *f*; **first ~** *n* Vorkaufsrecht *nt*

refuse¹ [rɪˈfjuːz] *vt* abschlagen ♦ *vi* sich weigern

refuse² [ˈrefjuːs] *n* Abfall *m*, Müll *m*; **~ collection** *n* Müllabfuhr *f*

refute [rɪˈfjuːt] *vt* widerlegen

regain [rɪˈgeɪn] *vt* wiedergewinnen; (*consciousness*) wiedererlangen

regal [ˈriːgəl] *adj* königlich

regalia [rɪˈgeɪlɪə] *npl* Insignien *pl*

regard [rɪˈgɑːd] *n* Achtung *f* ♦ *vt* ansehen; **to send one's ~s to sb** jdn grüßen lassen; **"with kindest ~s"** „mit freundlichen Grüßen"; **~ing** *or* **as ~s** *or* **with ~ to** bezüglich +*gen*, in bezug auf

+acc; ~less adj: ~less of ohne Rücksicht auf +acc ♦ adv trotzdem

regenerate [rɪ'dʒenəreɪt] vt erneuern

régime [reɪ'ʒiːm] n Regime nt

regiment [n 'redʒɪmənt, vb 'redʒɪment] n Regiment nt ♦ vt (fig) reglementieren; ~al [redʒɪ'mentl] adj Regiments-

region ['riːdʒən] n Region f; in the ~ of (fig) so um; ~al adj örtlich, regional

register ['redʒɪstə*] n Register nt ♦ vt (list) registrieren; (emotion) zeigen; (write down) eintragen ♦ vi (at hotel) sich eintragen; (with police) sich melden; (make impression) wirken, ankommen; to ~ with the police sich bei der Polizei melden, sich polizeilich melden; ~ed (BRIT) adj (letter) Einschreibe-, eingeschrieben; ~ed trademark n eingetragene(s) Warenzeichen nt

registrar [redʒɪs'trɑː*] n Standesbeamte(r) m

registration [redʒɪs'treɪʃən] n (act) Registrierung f; (AUT: also: ~ number) polizeiliche(s) Kennzeichen nt

registry ['redʒɪstrɪ] n Sekretariat nt; ~ office (BRIT) n Standesamt nt; to get married in a ~ office standesamtlich heiraten

regret [rɪ'gret] n Bedauern nt ♦ vt bedauern; ~fully adv mit Bedauern, ungern; ~table adj bedauerlich

regroup [riː'gruːp] vt umgruppieren ♦ vi sich umgruppieren

regular ['regjʊlə*] adj regelmäßig; (usual) üblich; (inf) regelrecht ♦ n (client etc) Stammkunde m; ~ity [regjʊ'lærɪtɪ] n Regelmäßigkeit f; ~ly adv regelmäßig

regulate ['regjʊleɪt] vt regeln, regulieren

regulation [regjʊ'leɪʃən] n (rule) Vorschrift f; (control) Regulierung f

rehabilitation ['riːhəbɪlɪ'teɪʃən] n (of criminal) Resozialisierung f

rehearsal [rɪ'hɜːsəl] n Probe f

rehearse [rɪ'hɜːs] vt proben

reign [reɪn] n Herrschaft f ♦ vi herrschen

reimburse [riːɪm'bɜːs] vt: to ~ sb for sth jdn für etw entschädigen, jdm etw zurückzahlen

rein [reɪn] n Zügel m

reincarnation ['riːɪnkɑː'neɪʃən] n Wiedergeburt f

reindeer ['reɪndɪə*] n Ren nt

reinforce [riːɪn'fɔːs] vt verstärken; ~d concrete n Stahlbeton m; ~ment n Verstärkung f; ~ments npl (MIL) Verstärkungstruppen pl

reinstate [riːɪn'steɪt] vt wiedereinsetzen

reissue ['riː'ɪʃuː] vt neu herausgeben

reiterate [riː'ɪtəreɪt] vt wiederholen

reject [n 'riːdʒekt, vb rɪ'dʒekt] n (COMM) Ausschuß(artikel) m ♦ vt ablehnen; ~ion [rɪ'dʒekʃən] n Zurückweisung f

rejoice [rɪ'dʒɔɪs] vi: to ~ at or over sich freuen über +acc

rejuvenate [rɪ'dʒuːvɪneɪt] vt verjüngen

rekindle ['riː'kɪndl] vt wieder anfachen

relapse [rɪ'læps] n Rückfall m

relate [rɪ'leɪt] vt (tell) erzählen; (connect) verbinden ♦ vi: to ~ to zusammenhängen mit; (form relationship) eine Beziehung aufbauen zu; ~d adj: ~d (to) verwandt (mit); relating prep: relating to bezüglich +gen

relation [rɪ'leɪʃən] n Verwandte(r) mf; (connection) Beziehung f; ~ship n Verhältnis nt, Beziehung f

relative ['relətɪv] n Verwandte(r) mf ♦ adj relativ; ~ly adv verhältnismäßig

relax [rɪ'læks] vi (slacken) sich lockern; (muscles, person) sich entspannen ♦ vt (ease) lockern, entspannen; ~ation [riːlæk'seɪʃən] n Entspannung f; ~ed adj entspannt, locker; ~ing adj entspannend

relay ['riːleɪ] n (SPORT) Staffel f ♦ vt (message) weiterleiten; (RADIO, TV) übertragen

release [rɪ'liːs] n (freedom) Entlassung f; (TECH) Auslöser m ♦ vt befreien; (prisoner) entlassen; (report, news) verlautbaren, bekanntgeben

relegate ['reləgeɪt] vt (SPORT): to be ~d absteigen

relent [rɪ'lent] vi nachgeben; ~less adj unnachgiebig; ~lessly adv unnachgiebig

relevant ['reləvənt] adj wichtig, relevant; ~ to relevant für

reliability [rɪlaɪə'bɪlɪtɪ] n Zuverlässigkeit f

reliable [rɪ'laɪəbl] *adj* zuverlässig;
reliably *adv* zuverlässig; **to be reliably
informed that ...** aus zuverlässiger
Quelle wissen, daß ...

reliance [rɪ'laɪəns] *n*: ~ **(on)** Abhängigkeit *f* (von)

relic ['relɪk] *n (from past)* Überbleibsel *nt*;
(REL) Reliquie *f*

relief [rɪ'liːf] *n* Erleichterung *f*; *(help)*
Hilfe *f*; *(person)* Ablösung *f*

relieve [rɪ'liːv] *vt (ease)* erleichtern;
(bring help) entlasten; *(person)* ablösen; **to
~ sb of sth** jdm etw abnehmen; **to ~ o.s.**
(euph) sich erleichtern *(euph)*

religion [rɪ'lɪdʒən] *n* Religion *f*

religious [rɪ'lɪdʒəs] *adj* religiös

relinquish [rɪ'lɪŋkwɪʃ] *vt* aufgeben

relish ['relɪʃ] *n* Würze *f* ♦ *vt* genießen; **to
~ doing** gern tun

relocate ['riːləʊ'keɪt] *vt* verlegen ♦ *vi*
umziehen

reluctance [rɪ'lʌktəns] *n* Widerstreben
nt, Abneigung *f*

reluctant [rɪ'lʌktənt] *adj* widerwillig; **~ly**
adv ungern

rely [rɪ'laɪ] : **to ~ on** *vt fus* sich verlassen
auf +*acc*

remain [rɪ'meɪn] *vi (be left)* übrigbleiben;
(stay) bleiben; **~der** *n* Rest *m*; **~ing** *adj*
übrig(geblieben); **~s** *npl* Überreste *pl*

remand [rɪ'mɑːnd] *n*: **on ~** in
Untersuchungshaft ♦ *vt*: **to ~ in custody**
in Untersuchungshaft schicken; **~ home**
(BRIT) *n* Untersuchungsgefängnis *nt* für
Jugendliche

remark [rɪ'mɑːk] *n* Bemerkung *f* ♦ *vt*
bemerken; **~able** *adj* bemerkenswert

remarry ['riː'mærɪ] *vi* sich wieder
verheiraten

remedial [rɪ'miːdɪəl] *adj* Heil-; *(teaching)*
Hilfsschul-

remedy ['remədɪ] *n* Mittel *nt* ♦ *vt (pain)*
abhelfen +*dat*; *(trouble)* in Ordnung
bringen

remember [rɪ'membə*] *vt* sich erinnern
an +*acc*

remembrance [rɪ'membrəns] *n*
Erinnerung *f*; *(official)* Gedenken *nt*

remind [rɪ'maɪnd] *vt*: **to ~ sb to do sth**
jdn daran erinnern, etw zu tun; **to ~ sb
of sth** jdn an etw *acc* erinnern; **she ~s
me of her mother** sie erinnert mich an
ihre Mutter; **~er** *n* Mahnung *f*

reminisce [remɪ'nɪs] *vi* in Erinnerungen
schwelgen

reminiscent [remɪ'nɪsnt] *adj*: **to be ~ of
sth** an etw *acc* erinnern

remiss [rɪ'mɪs] *adj* nachlässig

remission [rɪ'mɪʃən] *n* Nachlaß *m*; *(of
debt, sentence)* Erlaß *m*

remit [rɪ'mɪt] *vt (money)*: **to ~ (to)**
überweisen (an +*acc*); **~tance** *n*
Geldanweisung *f*

remnant ['remnənt] *n* Rest *m*; **~s** *npl*
(COMM) Einzelstücke *pl*

remorse [rɪ'mɔːs] *n* Gewissensbisse *pl*;
~ful *adj* reumütig; **~less** *adj*
unbarmherzig; **~lessly** *adv* unbarmherzig

remote [rɪ'məʊt] *adj* abgelegen; *(slight)*
gering; **~ control** *n* Fernsteuerung *f*; **~ly**
adv entfernt

remould ['riːməʊld] *(BRIT)* *n*
runderneuerte(r) Reifen *m*

removable [rɪ'muːvəbl] *adj* entfernbar

removal [rɪ'muːvəl] *n* Beseitigung *f*; *(of
furniture)* Umzug *m*; *(from office)*
Entlassung *f*; **~ van** *(BRIT)* *n* Möbelwagen
m

remove [rɪ'muːv] *vt* beseitigen,
entfernen; **removers** *npl* Möbelspedition
f

remuneration [rɪmjuːnə'reɪʃən] *n*
Vergütung *f*, Honorar *nt*

render ['rendə*] *vt* machen; *(translate)*
übersetzen; **~ing** *n* *(MUS)* Wiedergabe *f*

rendezvous ['rɒndɪvuː] *n* *(meeting)*
Rendezvous *nt*; *(place)* Treffpunkt *m* ♦ *vi*
sich treffen

renew [rɪ'njuː] *vt* erneuern; *(contract,
licence)* verlängern; *(replace)* ersetzen;
~able *adj* regenerierbar; **~al** *n*
Erneuerung *f*; Verlängerung *f*

renounce [rɪ'naʊns] *vt (give up)*
verzichten auf +*acc*; *(disown)* verstoßen

renovate ['renəveɪt] *vt* renovieren;
(building) restaurieren

renown [rɪ'naʊn] *n* Ruf *m*; **~ed** *adj*
namhaft

rent [rent] *n* Miete *f*; *(for land)* Pacht *f*
♦ *vt (hold as tenant)* pachten; *(let)*
vermieten; verpachten; *(car etc)* mieten;
(firm) vermieten; **~al** *n* Miete *f*

renunciation [rɪnʌnsɪ'eɪʃən] *n*: **~ (of)**
Verzicht *m* (auf +*acc*)

reorganize ['riː'ɔːgənaɪz] *vt* umgestalten,
reorganisieren

rep [rep] *n abbr (COMM)*
= **representative**; *(THEAT)* = **repertory**

repair [rɪ'peə*] *n* Reparatur *f* ♦ *vt*
reparieren; *(damage)* wiedergutmachen;
in good/bad ~ in gutem/schlechtem
Zustand; **~ kit** *n* Werkzeugkasten *m*

repartee [repɑː'tiː] *n* Witzeleien *pl*

repatriate [riː'pætrɪeɪt] *vt* in die Heimat
zurückschicken

repay [riː'peɪ] *(irreg) vt* zurückzahlen;
(reward) vergelten; **~ment** *n*
Rückzahlung *f*; *(fig)* Vergeltung *f*

repeal [rɪ'piːl] *n* Aufhebung *f* ♦ *vt*
aufheben

repeat [rɪ'piːt] *n (RADIO, TV)*
Wiederholung(ssendung) *f* ♦ *vt*
wiederholen; **~edly** *adv* wiederholt

repel [rɪ'pel] *vt (drive back)*
zurückschlagen; *(disgust)* abstoßen; **~lent**
adj abstoßend ♦ *n*: **insect ~lent**
Insektenmittel *nt*

repent [rɪ'pent] *vt, vi*: **to ~ (of)** bereuen;
~ance *n* Reue *f*

repercussion [riːpə'kʌʃən] *n*
Auswirkung *f*; **to have ~s** ein Nachspiel
haben

repertory ['repətərɪ] *n* Repertoire *nt*

repetition [repə'tɪʃən] *n* Wiederholung *f*

repetitive [rɪ'petɪtɪv] *adj* sich
wiederholend

replace [rɪ'pleɪs] *vt* ersetzen; *(put back)*
zurückstellen; **~ment** *n* Ersatz *m*

replay ['riː'pleɪ] *n (of match)*
Wiederholungsspiel *nt*; *(of tape, film)*
Wiederholung *f*

replenish [rɪ'plenɪʃ] *vt* ergänzen

replete [rɪ'pliːt] *adj* (zum Platzen) voll

replica ['replɪkə] *n* Kopie *f*

reply [rɪ'plaɪ] *n* Antwort *f* ♦ *vi* antworten;
~ coupon *n* Antwortschein *m*

report [rɪ'pɔːt] *n* Bericht *m*; *(BRIT: SCH)*

Zeugnis *nt* ♦ *vt (tell)* berichten; *(give
information against)* melden; *(to police)*
anzeigen ♦ *vi (make report)* Bericht
erstatten; *(present o.s.)*: **to ~ (to sb)** sich
(bei jdm) melden; **~ card** *n (US, SCOTTISH) n*
Zeugnis *nt*; **~edly** *adv* wie verlautet; **~er**
n Reporter *m*

repose [rɪ'pəuz] *n*: **in ~** *(face, body)*
entspannt; *(mind)* gelassen

reprehensible [reprɪ'hensəbl] *adj*
tadelnswert

represent [reprɪ'zent] *vt* darstellen;
(speak for) vertreten; **~ation**
[reprɪzen'teɪʃən] *n* Darstellung *f*; *(being
represented)* Vertretung *f*; **~ations** *npl*
(protest) Vorhaltungen *pl*; **~ative** *n*
(person) Vertreter *m*; *(US: POL)*
Abgeordnete(r) *mf* ♦ *adj* repräsentativ

repress [rɪ'pres] *vt* unterdrücken; **~ion**
[rɪ'preʃən] *n* Unterdrückung *f*

reprieve [rɪ'priːv] *n (JUR)* Begnadigung *f*;
(fig) Gnadenfrist *f* ♦ *vt (JUR)* begnadigen

reprimand ['reprɪmɑːnd] *n* Verweis *m*
♦ *vt* einen Verweis erteilen +*dat*

reprint [*n* 'riːprɪnt, *vb* 'riː'prɪnt] *n*
Neudruck *m* ♦ *vt* wieder abdrucken

reprisal [rɪ'praɪzəl] *n* Vergeltung *f*

reproach [rɪ'prəutʃ] *n* Vorwurf *m* ♦ *vt*
Vorwürfe machen +*dat*; **to ~ sb with sth**
jdm etw vorwerfen; **~ful** *adj* vorwurfsvoll

reproduce [riːprə'djuːs] *vt* reproduzieren
♦ *vi (have offspring)* sich vermehren

reproduction [riːprə'dʌkʃən] *n (ART,
PHOT)* Reproduktion *f*; *(breeding)*
Fortpflanzung *f*

reproductive [riːprə'dʌktɪv] *adj*
reproduktiv; *(breeding)* Fortpflanzungs-

reproof [rɪ'pruːf] *n* Tadel *m*

reprove [rɪ'pruːv] *vt* tadeln

reptile ['reptaɪl] *n* Reptil *nt*

republic [rɪ'pʌblɪk] *n* Republik *f*

repudiate [rɪ'pjuːdɪeɪt] *vt* zurückweisen

repugnant [rɪ'pʌgnənt] *adj* widerlich

repulse [rɪ'pʌls] *vt (drive back)*
zurückschlagen; *(reject)* abweisen

repulsive [rɪ'pʌlsɪv] *adj* abstoßend

reputable ['repjutəbl] *adj* angesehen

reputation [repju'teɪʃən] *n* Ruf *m*

repute [rɪ'pjuːt] *n* hohe(s) Ansehen *nt*;

~**d** *adj* angeblich; ~**dly** *adv* angeblich

request [rɪ'kwest] *n* Bitte *f* ♦ *vt* (*thing*) erbitten; **to ~ sth of** *or* **from sb** jdn um etw bitten; (*formally*) jdn um etw ersuchen; ~ **stop** (*BRIT*) *n* Bedarfshaltestelle *f*

require [rɪ'kwaɪə*] *vt* (*need*) brauchen; (*demand*) erfordern; ~**ment** *n* (*condition*) Anforderung *f*, (*need*) Bedarf *m*

requisite ['rekwɪzɪt] *n* Erfordernis *nt* ♦ *adj* erforderlich

requisition [rekwɪ'zɪʃən] *n* Anforderung *f* ♦ *vt* beschlagnahmen

resale ['riːseɪl] *n* Weiterverkauf *m*

rescind [rɪ'sɪnd] *vt* aufheben

rescue ['reskjuː] *n* Rettung *f* ♦ *vt* retten; ~ **party** *n* Rettungsmannschaft *f*; ~**r** *n* Retter *m*

research [rɪ'sɜːtʃ] *n* Forschung *f* ♦ *vi* forschen ♦ *vt* erforschen; ~**er** *n* Forscher *m*

resemblance [rɪ'zembləns] *n* Ähnlichkeit *f*

resemble [rɪ'zembl] *vt* ähneln +*dat*

resent [rɪ'zent] *vt* übelnehmen; ~**ful** *adj* nachtragend, empfindlich; ~**ment** *n* Verstimmung *f*, Unwille *m*

reservation [rezə'veɪʃən] *n* (*booking*) Reservierung *f*; (*THEAT*) Vorbestellung *f*; (*doubt*) Vorbehalt *m*; (*land*) Reservat *nt*

reserve [rɪ'zɜːv] *n* (*store*) Vorrat *m*, Reserve *f*; (*manner*) Zurückhaltung *f*; (*game* ~) Naturschutzgebiet *nt*; (*SPORT*) Ersatzspieler(in) *m(f)* ♦ *vt* reservieren; (*judgement*) sich *dat* vorbehalten; ~**s** *npl* (*MIL*) Reserve *f*; **in** ~ in Reserve; ~**d** *adj* reserviert

reshape ['riː'ʃeɪp] *vt* umformen

reshuffle ['riː'ʃʌfl] *n* (*POL*): **cabinet** ~ Kabinettsumbildung *f* ♦ *vt* (*POL*) umbilden

reside [rɪ'zaɪd] *vi* wohnen, ansässig sein

residence ['rezɪdəns] *n* (*house*) Wohnsitz *m*; (*living*) Aufenthalt *m*

resident ['rezɪdənt] *n* (*in house*) Bewohner *m*; (*in area*) Einwohner *m* ♦ *adj* wohnhaft, ansässig; ~**ial** [rezɪ'denʃəl] *adj* Wohn-

residue ['rezɪdjuː] *n* Rest *m*; (*CHEM*) Rückstand *m*; (*fig*) Bodensatz *m*

resign [rɪ'zaɪn] *vt* (*office*) aufgeben, zurücktreten von ♦ *vi* (*from office*) zurücktreten; (*employee*) kündigen; **to be ~ed to sth, to ~ o.s. to sth** sich mit etw abfinden; ~**ation** [rezɪg'neɪʃən] *n* (*from job*) Kündigung *f*, (*POL*) Rücktritt *m*; (*submission*) Resignation *f*; ~**ed** *adj* resigniert

resilience [rɪ'zɪlɪəns] *n* Spannkraft *f*; (*of person*) Unverwüstlichkeit *f*

resilient [rɪ'zɪlɪənt] *adj* unverwüstlich

resin ['rezɪn] *n* Harz *nt*

resist [rɪ'zɪst] *vt* widerstehen +*dat*; ~**ance** *n* Widerstand *m*

resolute ['rezəluːt] *adj* entschlossen, resolut

resolution [rezə'luːʃən] *n* (*firmness*) Entschlossenheit *f*; (*intention*) Vorsatz *m*; (*decision*) Beschluß *m*

resolve [rɪ'zɒlv] *n* Entschlossenheit *f* ♦ *vt* (*decide*) beschließen ♦ *vi* sich lösen; ~**d** *adj* (*fest*) entschlossen

resonant ['rezənənt] *adj* voll

resort [rɪ'zɔːt] *n* (*holiday place*) Erholungsort *m*; (*help*) Zuflucht *f* ♦ *vi*: **to ~ to** Zuflucht nehmen zu; **as a last** ~ als letzter Ausweg

resound [rɪ'zaʊnd] *vi*: **to ~ (with)** widerhallen (von); ~**ing** [rɪ'zaʊndɪŋ] *adj* nachhallend; (*success*) groß

resource [rɪ'sɔːs] *n* Findigkeit *f*; ~**s** *npl* (*financial*) Geldmittel *pl*; (*natural*) Bodenschätze *pl*; ~**ful** *adj* findig

respect [rɪs'pekt] *n* Respekt *m* ♦ *vt* achten, respektieren; ~**s** *npl* (*regards*) Grüße *pl*; **with** ~ **to** in bezug auf +*acc*, hinsichtlich +*gen*; **in this** ~ in dieser Hinsicht; ~**ability** [rɪspektə'bɪlɪtɪ] *n* Anständigkeit *f*; ~**able** *adj* (*decent*) anständig; (*fairly good*) leidlich; ~**ful** *adj* höflich

respective [rɪs'pektɪv] *adj* jeweilig; ~**ly** *adv* beziehungsweise

respiration [respɪ'reɪʃən] *n* Atmung *f*

respite ['respaɪt] *n* Ruhepause *f*

resplendent [rɪs'plendənt] *adj* strahlend

respond [rɪs'pɒnd] *vi* antworten; (*react*): **to ~ (to)** reagieren (auf +*acc*)

response [rɪs'pɒns] *n* Antwort *f*;

Reaktion *f*; (*to advertisement etc*)
Resonanz *f*
responsibility [rɪspɒnsə'bɪlɪtɪ] *n*
Verantwortung *f*
responsible [rɪs'pɒnsəbl] *adj*
verantwortlich; (*reliable*)
verantwortungsvoll
responsive [rɪs'pɒnsɪv] *adj* empfänglich
rest [rest] *n* Ruhe *f*; (*break*) Pause *f*;
(*remainder*) Rest *m* ♦ *vi* sich ausruhen;
(*be supported*) (auf)liegen ♦ *vt* (*lean*): **to ~
sth on/against sth** etw gegen etw *acc*
lehnen; **the ~ of them** die übrigen; **it ~s
with him to ...** es liegt bei ihm, zu ...
restaurant ['restərɒŋ] *n* Restaurant *nt*; ~
car (*BRIT*) *n* Speisewagen *m*
restful ['restful] *adj* erholsam, ruhig
rest home *n* Erholungsheim *nt*
restive ['restɪv] *adj* unruhig
restless ['restləs] *adj* unruhig
restoration [restə'reɪʃən] *n* Rückgabe *f*;
(*of building etc*) Rückerstattung *f*
restore [rɪ'stɔː*] *vt* (*order*)
wiederherstellen; (*customs*) wieder
einführen; (*person to position*)
wiedereinsetzen; (*give back*) zurückgeben;
(*paintings, buildings*) restaurieren
restrain [rɪs'treɪn] *vt* zurückhalten;
(*curiosity etc*) beherrschen; (*person*): **to ~
sb from doing sth** jdn davon abhalten,
etw zu tun; ~**ed** *adj* (*style etc*) gedämpft,
verhalten; ~**t** *n* (*self-control*)
Zurückhaltung *f*
restrict [rɪs'trɪkt] *vt* einschränken; ~**ion**
[rɪs'trɪkʃən] *n* Einschränkung *f*; ~**ive** *adj*
einschränkend
rest room (*US*) *n* Toilette *f*
restructure ['riː'strʌktʃə*] *vt*
umstrukturieren
result [rɪ'zʌlt] *n* Resultat *nt*, Folge *f*; (*of
exam, game*) Ergebnis *nt* ♦ *vi*: **to ~ in sth**
etw zur Folge haben; **as a ~ of** als Folge
+*gen*
resume [rɪ'zjuːm] *vt* fortsetzen; (*occupy
again*) wieder einnehmen ♦ *vi* (*work etc*)
wieder beginnen
résumé ['reɪzjuːmeɪ] *n* Zusammenfassung
f
resumption [rɪ'zʌmpʃən] *n*

Wiederaufnahme *f*
resurgence [rɪ'sɜːdʒəns] *n* Wiedererwachen *nt*
resurrection [rezə'rekʃən] *n*
Auferstehung *f*
resuscitate [rɪ'sʌsɪteɪt] *vt* wiederbeleben
resuscitation [rɪsʌsɪ'teɪʃən] *n*
Wiederbelebung *f*
retail [*n, adj* 'riːteɪl, *vb* 'riːteɪl] *n*
Einzelhandel *m* ♦ *adj* Einzelhandels- ♦ *vt*
im kleinen verkaufen ♦ *vi* im
Einzelhandel kosten; ~**er** ['riːteɪlə*] *n*
Einzelhändler *m*, Kleinhändler *m*; ~
price *n* Ladenpreis *m*
retain [rɪ'teɪn] *vt* (*keep*) (zurück)behalten;
~**er** *n* (*servant*) Gefolgsmann *m*; (*fee*)
(Honorar)vorschuß *m*
retaliate [rɪ'tælɪeɪt] *vi* zum
Vergeltungsschlag ausholen
retaliation [rɪtælɪ'eɪʃən] *n* Vergeltung *f*
retarded [rɪ'tɑːdɪd] *adj* zurückgeblieben
retch [retʃ] *vi* würgen
retentive [rɪ'tentɪv] *adj* (*memory*) gut
reticent ['retɪsənt] *adj* schweigsam
retina ['retɪnə] *n* Netzhaut *f*
retinue ['retɪnjuː] *n* Gefolge *nt*
retire [rɪ'taɪə*] *vi* (*from work*) in den
Ruhestand treten; (*withdraw*) sich
zurückziehen; (*go to bed*) schlafen gehen;
~**d** *adj* (*person*) pensioniert, im
Ruhestand; ~**ment** *n* Ruhestand *m*
retiring [rɪ'taɪərɪŋ] *adj* zurückhaltend
retort [rɪ'tɔːt] *n* (*reply*) Erwiderung *f*;
(*SCI*) Retorte *f* ♦ *vi* (*scharf*) erwidern
retrace [rɪ'treɪs] *vt* zurückverfolgen; **to ~
one's steps** denselben Weg zurückgehen
retract [rɪ'trækt] *vt* (*statement*)
zurücknehmen; (*claws*) einziehen ♦ *vi*
einen Rückzieher machen; ~**able** *adj*
(*aerial*) ausziehbar
retrain ['riː'treɪn] *vt* umschulen; ~**ing** *n*
Umschulung *f*
retread ['riːtred] *n* (*tyre*) Reifen *m* mit
erneuerter Lauffläche
retreat [rɪ'triːt] *n* Rückzug *m*; (*place*)
Zufluchtsort *m* ♦ *vi* sich zurückziehen
retribution [retrɪ'bjuːʃən] *n* Strafe *f*
retrieval [rɪ'triːvəl] *n* Wiedergewinnung *f*
retrieve [rɪ'triːv] *vt* wiederbekommen;

(*rescue*) retten; **~r** n Apportierhund m
retrograde ['retrəʊgreɪd] adj (*step*)
Rück-; (*policy*) rückschrittlich
retrospect ['retrəʊspekt] n: **in ~** im
Rückblick, rückblickend; **~ive**
[retrəʊ'spektɪv] adj (*action*) rückwirkend;
(*look*) rückblickend
return [rɪ'tɜːn] n Rückkehr f; (*profits*)
Ertrag m; (*BRIT: rail ticket etc*)
Rückfahrkarte f; (: *plane ticket*)
Rückflugkarte f ♦ adj (*journey, match*)
Rück- ♦ vi zurückkehren, zurückkommen
♦ vt zurückgeben, zurücksenden; (*pay
back*) zurückzahlen; (*elect*) wählen;
(*verdict*) aussprechen; **~s** npl (*COMM*)
Gewinn m; (*receipts*) Einkünfte pl; **in ~**
dafür; **by ~ of post** postwendend; **many
happy ~s (of the day)!** herzlichen
Glückwunsch zum Geburtstag!
reunion [riː'juːnjən] n Wiedervereinigung
f; (*SCH etc*) Treffen nt
reunite ['riːjuː'naɪt] vt wiedervereinigen
rev [rev] n abbr (*AUT: = revolution*)
Drehzahl f ♦ vt (*also: ~ up: engine*) auf
Touren bringen ♦ vi (*also: ~ up*) den
Motor auf Touren bringen
revamp ['riː'væmp] vt aufpolieren
reveal [rɪ'viːl] vt enthüllen; **~ing** adj
aufschlußreich
reveille [rɪ'vælɪ] n Wecken nt
revel ['revl] vi: **to ~ in sth/in doing sth**
seine Freude an etw dat haben/daran
haben, etw zu tun
revelation [revə'leɪʃən] n Offenbarung f
revelry ['revlrɪ] n Rummel m
revenge [rɪ'vendʒ] n Rache f; **to take ~
on** sich rächen an +dat
revenue ['revənjuː] n Einnahmen pl
reverberate [rɪ'vɜːbəreɪt] vi widerhallen
revere [rɪ'vɪə*] vt (ver)ehren; **~nce**
['revərəns] n Ehrfurcht f
Reverend ['revərənd] adj: **the ~ Robert
Martin** ≈ Pfarrer Robert Martin
reverent ['revərənt] adj ehrfurchtsvoll
reversal [rɪ'vɜːsəl] n Umkehrung f
reverse [rɪ'vɜːs] n Rückseite f; (*AUT: gear*)
Rückwärtsgang m ♦ adj (*order, direction*)
entgegengesetzt ♦ vt umkehren ♦ vi (*BRIT:
AUT*) rückwärts fahren; **~-charge call**

(*BRIT*) n R-Gespräch nt; **reversing
lights** npl (*AUT*) Rückfahrscheinwerfer pl
revert [rɪ'vɜːt] vi: **to ~ to** zurückkehren
zu; (*to bad state*) zurückfallen in +acc
review [rɪ'vjuː] n (*MIL*) Truppenschau f;
(*of book*) Rezension f; (*magazine*)
Zeitschrift f ♦ vt Rückschau halten auf
+acc; (*MIL*) mustern; (*book*) rezensieren;
(*reexamine*) von neuem untersuchen; **~er**
n (*critic*) Rezensent m
revile [rɪ'vaɪl] vt verunglimpfen
revise [rɪ'vaɪz] vt (*book*) überarbeiten;
(*reconsider*) ändern, revidieren
revision [rɪ'vɪʒən] n Prüfung f; (*COMM*)
Revision f; (*SCH*) Wiederholung f
revitalize ['riː'vaɪtəlaɪz] vt neu beleben
revival [rɪ'vaɪvəl] n Wiederbelebung f;
(*REL*) Erweckung f; (*THEAT*)
Wiederaufnahme f
revive [rɪ'vaɪv] vt wiederbeleben; (*fig*)
wieder auffrischen ♦ vi wiedererwachen;
(*fig*) wieder aufleben
revoke [rɪ'vəʊk] vt aufheben
revolt [rɪ'vəʊlt] n Aufstand m, Revolte f
♦ vi sich auflehnen ♦ vt entsetzen; **~ing**
adj widerlich
revolution [revə'luːʃən] n (*turn*)
Umdrehung f; (*POL*) Revolution f; **~ary**
adj revolutionär ♦ n Revolutionär m;
~ize vt revolutionieren
revolve [rɪ'vɒlv] vi kreisen; (*on own axis*)
sich drehen
revolver [rɪ'vɒlvə*] n Revolver m
revolving door [rɪ'vɒlvɪŋ-] n Drehtür f
revulsion [rɪ'vʌlʃən] n Ekel m
reward [rɪ'wɔːd] n Belohnung f ♦ vt
belohnen; **~ing** adj lohnend
rewire ['riː'waɪə*] vt (*house*) neu
verkabeln
reword ['riː'wɜːd] vt anders formulieren
rewrite ['riː'raɪt] (*irreg: like* **write**) vt
umarbeiten, neu schreiben
rheumatism ['ruːmətɪzəm] n
Rheumatismus m, Rheuma nt
Rhine [raɪn] n: **the ~** der Rhein
rhinoceros [raɪ'nɒsərəs] n Nashorn nt
Rhone [rəʊn] n: **the ~** die Rhone
rhubarb ['ruːbɑːb] n Rhabarber m
rhyme [raɪm] n Reim m

rhythm ['rɪðəm] *n* Rhythmus *m*

rib [rɪb] *n* Rippe *f* ♦ *vt* (*mock*) hänseln, aufziehen

ribald ['rɪbəld] *adj* saftig

ribbon ['rɪbən] *n* Band *nt*; **in ~s** (*torn*) in Fetzen

rice [raɪs] *n* Reis *m*; **~ pudding** *n* Milchreis *m*

rich [rɪtʃ] *adj* reich; (*food*) reichhaltig ♦ *npl*: **the ~** die Reichen *pl*; **~es** *npl* Reichtum *m*; **~ly** *adv* reich; (*deserve*) völlig

rickets ['rɪkɪts] *n* Rachitis *f*

rickety ['rɪkɪtɪ] *adj* wack(e)lig

rickshaw ['rɪkʃɔː] *n* Rickscha *f*

ricochet ['rɪkəʃeɪ] *n* Abprallen *nt*; (*shot*) Querschläger *m* ♦ *vi* abprallen

rid [rɪd] (*pt, pp* rid) *vt* befreien; **to get ~ of** loswerden

riddle ['rɪdl] *n* Rätsel *nt* ♦ *vt*: **to be ~d with** völlig durchlöchert sein von

ride [raɪd] (*pt* rode, *pp* ridden) *n* (*in vehicle*) Fahrt *f*; (*on horse*) Ritt *m* ♦ *vt* (*horse*) reiten; (*bicycle*) fahren ♦ *vi* fahren, reiten; **to take sb for a ~** mit jdm eine Fahrt *etc* machen; (*fig*) jdn aufs Glatteis führen; **~r** *n* Reiter *m*; (*addition*) Zusatz *m*

ridge [rɪdʒ] *n* Kamm *m*; (*of roof*) First *m*

ridicule ['rɪdɪkjuːl] *n* Spott *m* ♦ *vt* lächerlich machen

ridiculous [rɪ'dɪkjʊləs] *adj* lächerlich; **~ly** *adv* lächerlich

riding ['raɪdɪŋ] *n* Reiten *nt*; **~ school** *n* Reitschule *f*

rife [raɪf] *adj* weit verbreitet; **to be ~** grassieren; **to be ~ with** voll sein von

riffraff ['rɪfræf] *n* Pöbel *m*

rifle ['raɪfl] *n* Gewehr *nt* ♦ *vt* berauben; **~ range** *n* Schießstand *m*

rift [rɪft] *n* Spalte *f*; (*fig*) Bruch *m*

rig [rɪg] *n* (*outfit*) Takelung *f*; (*fig*) Aufmachung *f*; (*oil ~*) Bohrinsel *f* ♦ *vt* (*election etc*) manipulieren; **~ out** (*BRIT*) *vt* ausstatten; **~ up** *vt* zusammenbasteln; **~ging** *n* Takelage *f*

right [raɪt] *adj* (*correct, just*) richtig, recht; (*~ side*) rechte(r, s) ♦ *n* Recht *nt*; (*not left, POL*) Rechte *f* ♦ *adv* (*on the ~*)

rechts; (*to the ~*) nach rechts; (*look, work*) richtig, recht; (*directly*) gerade; (*exactly*) genau ♦ *vt* in Ordnung bringen, korrigieren ♦ *excl* gut; **on the ~** rechts; **to be in the ~** im Recht sein; **by ~s** von Rechts wegen; **to be ~** recht haben; **~ away** sofort; **~ now** in diesem Augenblick, eben; **~ in the middle** genau in der Mitte; **~ angle** *n* rechte(r) Winkel *m*; **~eous** ['raɪtʃəs] *adj* rechtschaffen; **~ful** *adj* rechtmäßig; **~-handed** *adj* rechtshändig; **~-hand man** (*irreg*) *n* rechte Hand *f*; **~-hand side** *n* rechte Seite *f*; **~ly** *adv* mit Recht; **~ of way** *n* Vorfahrt *f*; **~-wing** *adj* rechtsorientiert

rigid ['rɪdʒɪd] *adj* (*stiff*) starr, steif; (*strict*) streng; **~ity** [rɪ'dʒɪdɪtɪ] *n* Starrheit *f*, Strenge *f*

rigmarole ['rɪgmərəʊl] *n* Gewäsch *nt*

rigor ['rɪgə*] (*US*) *n* = **rigour**

rigorous ['rɪgərəs] *adj* streng

rigour ['rɪgə*] (*US* rigor) *n* Strenge *f*, Härte *f*

rile [raɪl] *vt* ärgern

rim [rɪm] *n* (*edge*) Rand *m*; (*of wheel*) Felge *f*

rind [raɪnd] *n* Rinde *f*

ring [rɪŋ] (*pt* rang, *pp* rung) *n* Ring *m*; (*of people*) Kreis *m*; (*arena*) Manege *f*; (*of telephone*) Klingeln *nt* ♦ *vt, vi* (*bell*) läuten; (*BRIT*) anrufen; **~ back** (*BRIT*) *vt, vi* zurückrufen; **~ off** (*BRIT*) *vi* aufhängen; **~ up** (*BRIT*) *vt* anrufen; **~ing** *n* Klingeln *nt*; (*of large bell*) Läuten *nt*; (*in ears*) Klingen *nt*; **~ing tone** *n* (*TEL*) Rufzeichen *nt*

ringleader ['rɪŋliːdə*] *n* Anführer *m*, Rädelsführer *m*

ringlets ['rɪŋlɪts] *npl* Ringellocken *pl*

ring road (*BRIT*) *n* Umgehungsstraße *f*

rink [rɪŋk] *n* (*ice ~*) Eisbahn *f*

rinse [rɪns] *n* Spülen *nt* ♦ *vt* spülen

riot ['raɪət] *n* Aufruhr *m* ♦ *vi* randalieren; **to run ~** (*people*) randalieren; (*vegetation*) wuchern; **~er** *n* Aufrührer *m*; **~ous** *adj* aufrührerisch; (*noisy*) lärmend; **~ously** *adv* aufrührerisch

rip [rɪp] *n* Schlitz *m*, Riß *m* ♦ *vt, vi* (zer)reißen; **~cord** ['rɪpkɔːd] *n* Reißleine *f*

ripe [raɪp] *adj* reif; **~n** *vi* reifen ♦ *vt*

reifen lassen
rip-off ['rɪpɒf] (*inf*) *n*: **it's a ~!** das ist Wucher!
ripple ['rɪpl] *n* kleine Welle *f* ♦ *vt* kräuseln ♦ *vi* sich kräuseln
rise [raɪz] (*pt* **rose**, *pp* **risen**) *n* (*slope*) Steigung *f*; (*esp in wages*: *BRIT*) Erhöhung *f*; (*growth*) Aufstieg *m* ♦ *vi* (*sun*) aufgehen; (*smoke*) aufsteigen; (*mountain*) sich erheben; (*ground*) ansteigen; (*prices*) steigen; (*in revolt*) sich erheben; **to give ~ to** Anlaß geben zu; **to ~ to the occasion** sich der Lage gewachsen zeigen; **risen** ['rɪzn] *pp* of **rise**
rising ['raɪzɪŋ] *adj* (*increasing*: *tide, numbers, prices*) steigend; (*sun, moon*) aufgehend ♦ *n* (*uprising*) Aufstand *m*
risk [rɪsk] *n* Gefahr *f*, Risiko *nt* ♦ *vt* (*venture*) wagen; (*chance loss of*) riskieren, aufs Spiel setzen; **to take** *or* **run the ~ of doing** das Risiko eingehen, zu tun; **at ~** in Gefahr; **at one's own ~** auf eigene Gefahr; **~y** *adj* riskant
risqué ['ri:skeɪ] *adj* gewagt
rissole ['rɪsəʊl] *n* Fleischklößchen *nt*
rite [raɪt] *n* Ritus *m*; **last ~s** Letzte Ölung *f*
ritual ['rɪtjʊəl] *n* Ritual *nt* ♦ *adj* ritual, Ritual-; (*fig*) rituell
rival ['raɪvəl] *n* Rivale *m*, Konkurrent *m* ♦ *adj* rivalisierend ♦ *vt* rivalisieren mit; (*COMM*) konkurrieren mit; **~ry** *n* Rivalität *f*; Konkurrenz *f*
river ['rɪvə*] *n* Fluß *m*, Strom *m* ♦ *cpd* (*port, traffic*) Fluß-; **up/down ~** flußaufwärts/-abwärts; **~bank** *n* Flußufer *nt*; **~bed** *n* Flußbett *nt*
rivet ['rɪvɪt] *n* Niete *f* ♦ *vt* (*fasten*) (ver)nieten
Riviera [rɪvɪ'eərə] *n*: **the ~** die Riviera
road [rəʊd] *n* Straße *f* ♦ *cpd* Straßen-; **major/minor ~** Haupt-/Nebenstraße *f*; **~block** *n* Straßensperre *f*; **~hog** *n* Verkehrsrowdy *m*; **~map** *n* Straßenkarte *f*; **~ safety** *n* Verkehrssicherheit *f*; **~side** *n* Straßenrand *m* ♦ *adj* an der Landstraße (gelegen); **~ sign** *n* Straßenschild *nt*; **~ user** *n* Verkehrsteilnehmer *m*; **~way** *n* Fahrbahn *f*; **~ works** *npl*

Straßenbauarbeiten *pl*; **~worthy** *adj* verkehrssicher
roam [rəʊm] *vi* (umher)streifen ♦ *vt* durchstreifen
roar [rɔ:*] *n* Brüllen *nt*, Gebrüll *nt* ♦ *vi* brüllen; **to ~ with laughter** vor Lachen brüllen; **to do a ~ing trade** ein Riesengeschäft machen
roast [rəʊst] *n* Braten *m* ♦ *vt* braten, schmoren; **~ beef** *n* Roastbeef *nt*
rob [rɒb] *vt* bestehlen, berauben; (*bank*) ausrauben; **to ~ sb of sth** jdm etw rauben; **~ber** *n* Räuber *m*; **~bery** *n* Raub *m*
robe [rəʊb] *n* (*dress*) Gewand *nt*; (*US*) Hauskleid *nt*; (*judge's*) Robe *f*
robin ['rɒbɪn] *n* Rotkehlchen *nt*
robot ['rəʊbɒt] *n* Roboter *m*
robust [rəʊ'bʌst] *adj* (*person*) robust; (*appetite, economy*) gesund
rock [rɒk] *n* Felsen *m*; (*BRIT*: *sweet*) Zuckerstange *f* ♦ *vt* wiegen, schaukeln ♦ *vi* schaukeln; **on the ~s** (*drink*) mit Eis(würfeln); (*marriage*) gescheitert; (*ship*) aufgelaufen; **~ and roll** *n* Rock and Roll *m*; **~-bottom** *n* (*fig*) Tiefpunkt *m*; **~ery** *n* Steingarten *m*
rocket ['rɒkɪt] *n* Rakete *f*
rocking chair ['rɒkɪŋ-] *n* Schaukelstuhl *m*
rocking horse ['rɒkɪŋ-] *n* Schaukelpferd *nt*
rocky ['rɒkɪ] *adj* felsig
rod [rɒd] *n* (*bar*) Stange *f*; (*stick*) Rute *f*
rode [rəʊd] *pt* of **ride**
rodent ['rəʊdənt] *n* Nagetier *nt*
roe [rəʊ] *n* (*deer*) Reh *nt*; (*of fish*: *also*: *hard ~*) Rogen *m*; **soft ~** Milch *f*
rogue [rəʊg] *n* Schurke *m*
role [rəʊl] *n* Rolle *f*
roll [rəʊl] *n* Rolle *f*; (*bread*) Brötchen *nt*; (*list*) (Namens)liste *f*; (*of drum*) Wirbel *m* ♦ *vt* (*turn*) rollen, (herum)wälzen; (*grass etc*) walzen ♦ *vi* (*swing*) schlingern; (*sound*) rollen, grollen; **~ about** *or* **around** *vi* herumkugeln; (*ship*) schlingern; (*dog etc*) sich wälzen; **~ by** *vi* (*time*) verfließen; **~ in** *vi* (*mail*) hereinkommen; **~ over** *vi* sich

(herum)drehen; **~ up** *vi* (*arrive*) kommen, auftauchen ♦ *vt* (*carpet*) aufrollen; **~ call** *n* Namensaufruf *m*; **~er** *n* Rolle *f*, Walze *f*; (*road roller*) Straßenwalze *f*; **~er coaster** *n* Achterbahn *f*; **~er skates** *npl* Rollschuhe *pl*

rolling ['rəʊlɪŋ] *adj* (*landscape*) wellig; **~ pin** *n* Nudel- *or* Wellholz *nt*; **~ stock** *n* Wagenmaterial *nt*

ROM [rɒm] *n abbr* (= *read only memory*) ROM *m*

Roman ['rəʊmən] *adj* römisch ♦ *n* Römer(in) *m(f)*; **~ Catholic** *adj* römisch-katholisch ♦ *n* Katholik(in) *m(f)*

romance [rəʊ'mæns] *n* Romanze *f*; (*story*) (Liebes)roman *m*

Romania [rəʊ'meɪnɪə] *n* = **Rumania**

Roman numeral *n* römische Ziffer

romantic [rəʊ'mæntɪk] *adj* romantisch; **~ism** [rəʊ'mæntɪsɪzəm] *n* Romantik *f*

Rome [rəʊm] *n* Rom *nt*

romp [rɒmp] *n* Tollen *nt* ♦ *vi* (*also: ~ about*) herumtollen

rompers ['rɒmpəz] *npl* Spielanzug *m*

roof [ru:f] (*pl* **roofs**) *n* Dach *nt*; (*of mouth*) Gaumen *m* ♦ *vt* überdachen, überdecken; **~ing** *n* Deckmaterial *nt*; **~ rack** *n* (*AUT*) Dachgepäckträger *m*

rook [rʊk] *n* (*bird*) Saatkrähe *f*; (*chess*) Turm *m*

room [rʊm] *n* Zimmer *nt*, Raum *m*; (*space*) Platz *m*; (*fig*) Spielraum *m*; **~s** *npl* (*accommodation*) Wohnung *f*; "**~s to let** (*BRIT*) *or* **for rent** (*US*)" „Zimmer zu vermieten"; **single/double ~** Einzel-/Doppelzimmer *nt*; **~ing house** (*US*) *n* Mietshaus *nt* (*mit möblierten Wohnungen*); **~mate** *n* Mitbewohner(in) *m(f)*; **~ service** *n* Zimmerbedienung *f*; **~y** *adj* geräumig

roost [ru:st] *n* Hühnerstange *f* ♦ *vi* auf der Stange hocken

rooster ['ru:stə*] *n* Hahn *m*

root [ru:t] *n* (*also fig*) Wurzel *f* ♦ *vi* wurzeln; **~ about** *vi* (*fig*) herumwühlen; **~ for** *vt fus* Stimmung machen für; **~ out** *vt* ausjäten; (*fig*) ausrotten

rope [rəʊp] *n* Seil *nt* ♦ *vt* (*tie*) festschnüren; **to know the ~s** sich

auskennen; **to ~ sb in** jdn gewinnen; **~ off** *vt* absperren; **~ ladder** *n* Strickleiter *f*

rosary ['rəʊzərɪ] *n* Rosenkranz *m*

rose [rəʊz] *pt of* **rise** ♦ *n* Rose *f* ♦ *adj* Rosen-, rosenrot

rosé ['rəʊzeɪ] *n* Rosé *m*

rosebud ['rəʊzbʌd] *n* Rosenknospe *f*

rosebush ['rəʊzbʊʃ] *n* Rosenstock *m*

rosemary ['rəʊzmərɪ] *n* Rosmarin *m*

rosette [rəʊ'zet] *n* Rosette *f*

roster ['rɒstə*] *n* Dienstplan *m*

rostrum ['rɒstrəm] *n* Rednerbühne *f*

rosy ['rəʊzɪ] *adj* rosig

rot [rɒt] *n* Fäulnis *f*; (*nonsense*) Quatsch *m* ♦ *vi* verfaulen ♦ *vt* verfaulen lassen

rota ['rəʊtə] *n* Dienstliste *f*

rotary ['rəʊtərɪ] *adj* rotierend

rotate [rəʊ'teɪt] *vt* rotieren lassen; (*two or more things in order*) turnusmäßig wechseln ♦ *vi* rotieren

rotating [rəʊ'teɪtɪŋ] *adj* rotierend

rotation [rəʊ'teɪʃən] *n* Umdrehung *f*

rote [rəʊt] *n*: **by ~** auswendig

rotten ['rɒtn] *adj* faul; (*fig*) schlecht, gemein; **to feel ~** (*ill*) sich elend fühlen

rotund [rəʊ'tʌnd] *adj* rundlich

rouble ['ru:bl] (*US* **ruble**) *n* Rubel *m*

rough [rʌf] *adj* (*not smooth*) rauh; (*path*) uneben; (*violent*) roh, grob; (*crossing*) stürmisch; (*without comforts*) hart, unbequem; (*unfinished, makeshift*) grob; (*approximate*) ungefähr ♦ *n* (*BRIT: person*) Rowdy *m*, Rohling *m*; (*GOLF*): **in the ~** im Rauh ♦ *vt*: **to ~ it** primitiv leben; **to sleep ~** im Freien schlafen; **~age** *n* Ballaststoffe *pl*; **~-and-ready** *adj* provisorisch; (*work*) zusammengehauen; **~ copy** *n* Entwurf *m*; **~ draft** *n* Entwurf *m*; **~en** *vt* aufrauhen; **~ly** *adv* grob; (*about*) ungefähr; **~ness** *n* Rauheit *f*; (*of manner*) Ungeschliffenheit *f*

roulette [ru:'let] *n* Roulett(e) *nt*

Roumania [ru:'meɪnɪə] *n* = **Rumania**

round [raʊnd] *adj* rund; (*figures*) aufgerundet ♦ *adv* (*in a circle*) rundherum ♦ *prep* um ... herum ♦ *n* Runde *f*; (*of ammunition*) Magazin *nt* ♦ *vt* (*corner*) biegen um; **all ~** überall; **the**

long way ~ der Umweg; **all the year** ~ das ganze Jahr über; **it's just** ~ **the corner** (*fig*) es ist gerade um die Ecke; ~ **the clock** rund um die Uhr; **to go** ~ **to sb's (house)** jdn besuchen; **to go** ~ **the back** hinterherum gehen; **to go** ~ **a house** um ein Haus herumgehen; **enough to go** ~ genug für alle; **to go the** ~**s** (*story*) die Runde machen; **a** ~ **of applause** ein Beifall *m*; **a** ~ **of drinks** eine Runde Drinks; **a** ~ **of sandwiches** ein Sandwich *nt or m*, ein belegtes Brot; ~ **off** *vt* abrunden; ~ **up** *vt* (*end*) abschließen; (*figures*) aufrunden; (*criminals*) hochnehmen; ~**about** *n* (*BRIT: traffic*) Kreisverkehr *m*; (: *merry-go-round*) Karussell *nt* ♦ *adj* auf Umwegen; ~**ers** *npl* (*game*) ≈ Schlagball *m*; ~**ly** *adv* (*fig*) gründlich; ~**-shouldered** *adj* mit abfallenden Schultern; ~ **trip** *n* Rundreise *f*; ~**up** *n* Zusammentreiben *nt*, Sammeln *nt*

rouse [raʊz] *vt* (*waken*) (auf)wecken; (*stir up*) erregen

rousing ['raʊzɪŋ] *adj* (*welcome*) stürmisch; (*speech*) zündend

route [ruːt] *n* Weg *m*, Route *f*; ~ **map** (*BRIT*) *n* (*for journey*) Streckenkarte *f*

routine [ruːˈtiːn] *n* Routine *f* ♦ *adj* Routine-

row¹ [raʊ] *n* (*noise*) Lärm *m*; (*dispute*) Streit *m* ♦ *vi* sich streiten

row² [rəʊ] *n* (*line*) Reihe *f* ♦ *vt, vi* (*boat*) rudern; **in a** ~ (*fig*) hintereinander

rowboat ['rəʊbəʊt] (*US*) *n* Ruderboot *nt*

rowdy ['raʊdɪ] *adj* rüpelhaft ♦ *n* (*person*) Rowdy *m*

rowing ['rəʊɪŋ] *n* Rudern *nt*; (*SPORT*) Rudersport *m*; ~ **boat** (*BRIT*) *n* Ruderboot *nt*

royal ['rɔɪəl] *adj* königlich, Königs-; **R~ Air Force** *n* Königliche Luftwaffe *f*

royalty ['rɔɪəltɪ] *n* (*family*) königliche Familie *f*; (*for book*) Tantieme *f*

rpm *abbr* (= *revs per minute*) U/min

R.S.V.P. *abbr* (= *répondez s'il vous plaît*) u.A.w.g.

Rt. Hon. (*BRIT*) *abbr* (= *Right Honourable*) Abgeordnete(r) *mf*

rub [rʌb] *n* (*with cloth*) Polieren *nt*; (*on person*) Reiben *nt* ♦ *vt* reiben; **to** ~ **sb up** (*BRIT*) or **to** ~ **sb** (*US*) **the wrong way** jdn aufreizen; ~ **off** *vi* (*also fig*): **to** ~ **off (on)** abfärben (auf +*acc*); ~ **out** *vt* herausreiben; (*with eraser*) ausradieren

rubber ['rʌbə*] *n* Gummi *m*; (*BRIT*) Radiergummi *m*; ~ **band** *n* Gummiband *nt*; ~ **plant** *n* Gummibaum *m*; ~**y** *adj* gummiartig

rubbish ['rʌbɪʃ] *n* (*waste*) Abfall *m*; (*nonsense*) Blödsinn *m*, Quatsch *m*; ~ **bin** (*BRIT*) *n* Mülleimer *m*; ~ **dump** *n* Müllabladeplatz *m*

rubble ['rʌbl] *n* (*Stein*)schutt *m*

ruby ['ruːbɪ] *n* Rubin *m* ♦ *adj* rubinrot

rucksack ['rʌksæk] *n* Rucksack *m*

ructions ['rʌkʃənz] *npl* Krach *m*

rudder ['rʌdə*] *n* Steuerruder *nt*

ruddy ['rʌdɪ] *adj* (*colour*) rötlich; (*inf: bloody*) verdammt

rude [ruːd] *adj* unverschämt; (*shock*) hart; (*awakening*) unsanft; (*unrefined, rough*) grob; ~**ness** *n* Unverschämtheit *f*; Grobheit *f*

rudiment ['ruːdɪmənt] *n* Grundlage *f*

rueful ['ruːfʊl] *adj* reuevoll; (*situation*) beklagenswert

ruffian ['rʌfɪən] *n* Rohling *m*

ruffle ['rʌfl] *vt* kräuseln

rug [rʌg] *n* Brücke *f*; (*in bedroom*) Bettvorleger *m*; (*BRIT: for knees*) (Reise)decke *f*

rugby ['rʌgbɪ] *n* (*also:* ~ *football*) Rugby *nt*

rugged ['rʌgɪd] *adj* (*coastline*) zerklüftet; (*features*) markig

rugger ['rʌgə*] (*BRIT: inf*) *n* Rugby *nt*

ruin ['ruːɪn] *n* Ruine *f*; (*downfall*) Ruin *m* ♦ *vt* ruinieren; ~**s** *npl* (*fig*) Trümmer *pl*; ~**ous** *adj* ruinierend

rule [ruːl] *n* Regel *f*; (*government*) Regierung *f*; (*for measuring*) Lineal *nt* ♦ *vt* (*govern*) herrschen über +*acc*, regieren; (*decide*) anordnen, entscheiden; (*make lines on*) linieren ♦ *vi* herrschen, regieren; entscheiden; **as a** ~ in der Regel; ~ **out** *vt* ausschließen; ~**d** *adj* (*paper*) liniert; ~**r** *n* Lineal *nt*; Herrscher *m*

ruling ['ru:lɪŋ] *adj (party)* Regierungs-; *(class)* herrschend ♦ *n (JUR)* Entscheid *m*

rum [rʌm] *n* Rum *m*

Rumania [ru:'meɪnɪə] *n* Rumänien *nt*; **~n** *adj* rumänisch ♦ *n* Rumäne *m*, Rumänin *f*; *(LING)* Rumänisch *nt*

rumble ['rʌmbl] *n* Rumpeln *nt*; *(of thunder)* Grollen *nt* ♦ *vi* rumpeln; grollen

rummage ['rʌmɪdʒ] *vi* durchstöbern

rumour ['ru:mə*] *(US* **rumor**) *n* Gerücht *nt* ♦ *vt*: **it is ~ed that** man sagt *or* man munkelt, daß

rump [rʌmp] *n* Hinterteil *nt*; **~ steak** *n* Rumpsteak *nt*

rumpus ['rʌmpəs] *n* Spektakel *m*

run [rʌn] *(pt* ran, *pp* run) *n* Lauf *m*; *(in car)* (Spazier)fahrt *f*; *(series)* Serie *f*, Reihe *f*; *(ski ~)* (Ski)abfahrt *f*; *(in stocking)* Laufmasche *f* ♦ *vt (cause to ~)* laufen lassen; *(car, train, bus)* fahren; *(race, distance)* laufen, rennen; *(manage)* leiten; *(COMPUT)* laufen lassen; *(pass: hand, eye)* gleiten lassen ♦ *vi* laufen; *(move quickly)* laufen, rennen; *(bus, train)* fahren; *(flow)* fließen, laufen; *(colours)* (ab)färben; **there was a ~ on** *(meat, tickets)* es gab einen Ansturm auf +*acc*; **on the ~** auf der Flucht; **in the long ~** auf die Dauer; **I'll ~ you to the station** ich fahre dich zum Bahnhof; **to ~ a risk** ein Risiko eingehen; **~ about** *or* **around** *vi (children)* umherspringen; **~ across** *vt fus (find)* stoßen auf +*acc*; **~ away** *vi* weglaufen; **~ down** *vi (clock)* ablaufen ♦ *vt (production, factory)* allmählich auflösen; *(with car)* überfahren; *(talk against)* heruntermachen; **to be ~ down** erschöpft *or* abgespannt sein; **~ in** *(BRIT) vt (car)* einfahren; **~ into** *vt fus (meet: person)* zufällig treffen; *(: trouble)* bekommen; *(collide with)* rennen gegen; fahren gegen; **~ off** *vi* fortlaufen; **~ out** *vi (person)* hinausrennen; *(liquid)* auslaufen; *(lease)* ablaufen; *(money)* ausgehen; **he ran out of money/petrol** ihm ging das Geld/Benzin aus; **~ over** *vt (in accident)* überfahren; **~ through** *vt (instructions)* durchgehen; **~ up** *vt (debt, bill)* machen;

~ up against *vt fus (difficulties)* stoßen auf +*acc*; **~away** *adj (horse)* ausgebrochen; *(person)* flüchtig

rung [rʌŋ] *pp of* **ring** ♦ *n* Sprosse *f*

runner ['rʌnə*] *n* Läufer(in) *m(f)*; *(for sleigh)* Kufe *f*; **~ bean** *n (BRIT)* Stangenbohne *f*; **~-up** *n* Zweite(r) *mf*

running ['rʌnɪŋ] *n (of business)* Leitung *f*; *(of machine)* Betrieb *m* ♦ *adj (water)* fließend; *(commentary)* laufend; **to be in/out of the ~ for sth** im/aus dem Rennen für etw sein; **3 days ~** 3 Tage lang *or* hintereinander

runny ['rʌnɪ] *adj* dünn; *(nose)* laufend

run-of-the-mill ['rʌnəvðə'mɪl] *adj* gewöhnlich, alltäglich

runt ['rʌnt] *n (animal)* Kümmerer *m*; *(pej: person)* Wicht *m*

run-up ['rʌnʌp] *n*: **the ~ to** *(election etc)* die Endphase vor +*dat*

runway ['rʌnweɪ] *n* Startbahn *f*

rupee [ru:'pi:] *n* Rupie *f*

rupture ['rʌptʃə*] *n (MED)* Bruch *m*

rural ['ruərəl] *adj* ländlich, Land-

ruse [ru:z] *n* Kniff *m*, List *f*

rush [rʌʃ] *n* Eile *f*, Hetze *f*; *(FIN)* starke Nachfrage *f* ♦ *vt (carry along)* auf dem schnellsten Wege schaffen *or* transportieren; *(attack)* losstürmen auf +*acc* ♦ *vi (hurry)* eilen, stürzen; **don't ~ me** dräng mich nicht; **~ hour** *n* Hauptverkehrszeit *f*

rusk [rʌsk] *n* Zwieback *m*

Russia ['rʌʃə] *n* Rußland *nt*; **~n** *adj* russisch ♦ *n* Russe *m*, Russin *f*; *(LING)* Russisch *nt*

rust [rʌst] *n* Rost *m* ♦ *vi* rosten

rustic ['rʌstɪk] *adj* bäuerlich, ländlich

rustle ['rʌsl] *vi* rauschen, rascheln ♦ *vt* rascheln lassen; *(cattle)* stehlen

rustproof ['rʌstpru:f] *adj* rostfrei

rusty ['rʌstɪ] *adj* rostig

rut [rʌt] *n (in track)* Radspur *f*; **to be in a ~** im Trott stecken

ruthless ['ru:θləs] *adj* rücksichtslos

rye [raɪ] *n* Roggen *m*; **~ bread** *n* Roggenbrot *nt*

S s

sabbath ['sæbəθ] *n* Sabbat *m*

sabotage ['sæbətɑːʒ] *n* Sabotage *f* ♦ *vt* sabotieren

saccharin ['sækərın] *n* Saccharin *nt*

sachet ['sæʃeɪ] *n* (*of shampoo etc*) Briefchen *nt*, Kissen *nt*

sack [sæk] *n* Sack *m* ♦ *vt* (*inf*) hinauswerfen; (*pillage*) plündern; **to get the ~ rausfliegen;** **~ing** *n* (*material*) Sackleinen *nt*; (*inf*) Rausschmiß *m*

sacrament ['sækrəmənt] *n* Sakrament *nt*

sacred ['seɪkrɪd] *adj* heilig

sacrifice ['sækrɪfaɪs] *n* Opfer *nt* ♦ *vt* (*also fig*) opfern

sacrilege ['sækrɪlɪdʒ] *n* Schändung *f*

sad [sæd] *adj* traurig; **~den** *vt* traurig machen, betrüben

saddle ['sædl] *n* Sattel *m* ♦ *vt* (*burden*): **to ~ sb with sth** jdm etw aufhalsen; **~bag** *n* Sätteltasche *f*

sadistic [sə'dɪstɪk] *adj* sadistisch

sadly ['sædlɪ] *adv* traurig; (*unfortunately*) leider

sadness ['sædnəs] *n* Traurigkeit *f*

sae *abbr* (= *stamped addressed envelope*) adressierte(r) Rückumschlag *m*

safe [seɪf] *adj* (*free from danger*) sicher; (*careful*) vorsichtig ♦ *n* Safe *m*; **~ and sound** gesund und wohl; **(just) to be on the ~ side** um ganz sicher zu gehen; **~ from** (*attack*) sicher vor +*dat*; **~-conduct** *n* freie(s) Geleit *nt*; **~-deposit** *n* (*vault*) Tresorraum *m*; (*box*) Banksafe *m*; **~guard** *n* Sicherung *f* ♦ *vt* sichern, schützen; **~keeping** *n* sichere Verwahrung *f*; **~ly** *adv* sicher; (*arrive*) wohlbehalten; **~ sex** *n* (*MED*) geschützter Sex *m*

safety ['seɪftɪ] *n* Sicherheit *f*; **~ belt** *n* Sicherheitsgurt *m*; **~ pin** *n* Sicherheitsnadel *f*; **~ valve** *n* Sicherheitsventil *nt*

sag [sæg] *vi* (*durch*)sacken

sage [seɪdʒ] *n* (*herb*) Salbei *m*; (*person*) Weise(r) *mf*

Sagittarius [sædʒɪ'tɛərɪəs] *n* Schütze *m*

Sahara [sə'hɑːrə] *n*: **the ~ (Desert)** die (Wüste) Sahara

said [sed] *pt, pp of* **say**

sail [seɪl] *n* Segel *nt*; (*trip*) Fahrt *f* ♦ *vt* segeln ♦ *vi* segeln; (*begin voyage: person*) abfahren; (*: ship*) auslaufen; (*fig: cloud etc*) dahinsegeln; **to go for a ~** segeln gehen; **they ~ed into Copenhagen** sie liefen in Kopenhagen ein; **~ through** *vt fus, vi* (*fig*) (es) spielend schaffen; **~boat** (*US*) *n* Segelboot *nt*; **~ing** *n* Segeln *nt*; **~ing ship** *n* Segelschiff *nt*; **~or** *n* Matrose *m*, Seemann *m*

saint [seɪnt] *n* Heilige(r) *mf*; **~ly** *adj* heilig, fromm

sake [seɪk] *n*: **for the ~ of** um +*gen* willen

salad ['sæləd] *n* Salat *m*; **~ bowl** *n* Salatschüssel *f*; **~ cream** (*BRIT*) *n* gewürzte Mayonnaise *f*; **~ dressing** *n* Salatsoße *f*

salami [sə'lɑːmɪ] *n* Salami *f*

salary ['sælərɪ] *n* Gehalt *nt*

sale [seɪl] *n* Verkauf *m*; (*reduced prices*) Schlußverkauf *m*; **"for ~"** „zu verkaufen"; **on ~** zu verkaufen; **~room** *n* Verkaufsraum *m*; **~s assistant** *n* Verkäufer(in) *m(f)*; **~s clerk** (*US*) *n* Verkäufer(in) *m(f)*; **~sman** (*irreg*) *n* Verkäufer *m*; (*representative*) Vertreter *m*; **~swoman** (*irreg*) *n* Verkäuferin *f*

salient ['seɪlɪənt] *adj* bemerkenswert

saliva [sə'laɪvə] *n* Speichel *m*

sallow ['sæləʊ] *adj* fahl; (*face*) bleich

salmon ['sæmən] *n* Lachs *m*

saloon [sə'luːn] *n* (*BRIT: AUT*) Limousine *f*; (*ship's lounge*) Salon *m*

salt [sɔːlt] *n* Salz *nt* ♦ *vt* (*cure*) einsalzen; (*flavour*) salzen; **~ away** (*inf*) *vt* (*money*) auf die hohe Kante legen; **~cellar** *n* Salzfaß *nt*; **~-water** *adj* Salzwasser-; **~y** *adj* salzig

salutary ['sæljʊtərɪ] *adj* nützlich

salute [sə'luːt] *n* (*MIL*) Gruß *m*; (*with guns*) Salutschüsse *pl* ♦ *vt* (*MIL*) salutieren

salvage ['sælvɪdʒ] *n* (*from ship*) Bergung *f*; (*property*) Rettung *f* ♦ *vt* bergen; retten

salvation [sæl'veɪʃən] *n* Rettung *f*; **S~ Army** *n* Heilsarmee *f*

same [seɪm] *adj, pron* (*similar*) gleiche(r, s); (*identical*) derselbe/dieselbe/dasselbe; **the ~ book as** das gleiche Buch wie; **at the ~ time** zur gleichen Zeit, gleichzeitig; (*however*) zugleich, andererseits; **all** *or* **just the ~** trotzdem; **the ~ to you!** gleichfalls!; **to do the ~ (as sb)** das gleiche tun (wie jd)

sample ['sɑ:mpl] *n* Probe *f* ♦ *vt* probieren

sanctify ['sæŋktɪfaɪ] *vt* weihen

sanctimonious [sæŋktɪ'məʊnɪəs] *adj* scheinheilig

sanction ['sæŋkʃən] *n* Sanktion *f*

sanctity ['sæŋktɪtɪ] *n* Heiligkeit *f*; (*fig*) Unverletzlichkeit *f*

sanctuary ['sæŋktjʊərɪ] *n* (*for fugitive*) Asyl *nt*; (*refuge*) Zufluchtsort *m*; (*for animals*) Schutzgebiet *nt*

sand [sænd] *n* Sand *m* ♦ *vt* (*furniture*) schmirgeln

sandal ['sændl] *n* Sandale *f*

sand: **~box** (*US*) *n* = **sandpit**; **~castle** *n* Sandburg *f*; **~ dune** *n* (Sand)düne *f*; **~paper** *n* Sandpapier *nt*; **~pit** *n* Sandkasten *m*; **~stone** *n* Sandstein *m*

sandwich ['sænwɪdʒ] *n* Sandwich *m or nt* ♦ *vt* (*also:* **~ in**) einklemmen; **cheese/ ham** ~ Käse-/Schinkenbrot; **~ed between** eingeklemmt zwischen; **~ board** *n* Reklametafel *f*; **~ course** (*BRIT*) *n* theorie- und praxisabwechselnde(r) Ausbildungsgang

sandy ['sændɪ] *adj* sandig; (*hair*) rotblond

sane [seɪn] *adj* geistig gesund *or* normal; (*sensible*) vernünftig, gescheit

sang [sæŋ] *pt of* **sing**

sanitary ['sænɪtərɪ] *adj* hygienisch; **~ napkin** (*US*) *n* (Monats)binde *f*; **~ towel** *n* (Monats)binde *f*

sanitation [sænɪ'teɪʃən] *n* sanitäre Einrichtungen *pl*; **~ department** (*US*) *n* Stadtreinigung *f*

sanity ['sænɪtɪ] *n* geistige Gesundheit *f*; (*good sense*) Vernunft *f*

sank [sæŋk] *pt of* **sink**

Santa Claus [sæntə'klɔ:z] *n* Nikolaus *m*, Weihnachtsmann *m*

sap [sæp] *n* (*of plants*) Saft *m* ♦ *vt*

(*strength*) schwächen

sapling ['sæplɪŋ] *n* junge(r) Baum *m*

sapphire ['sæfaɪə*] *n* Saphir *m*

sarcasm ['sɑ:kæzəm] *n* Sarkasmus *m*

sarcastic [sɑ:'kæstɪk] *adj* sarkastisch

sardine [sɑ:'di:n] *n* Sardine *f*

Sardinia [sɑ:'dɪnɪə] *n* Sardinien *nt*

sardonic [sɑ:'dɒnɪk] *adj* zynisch

sash [sæʃ] *n* Schärpe *f*

sat [sæt] *pt, pp of* **sit**

Satan ['seɪtn] *n* Satan *m*

satchel ['sætʃəl] *n* (*for school*) Schulmappe *f*

sated ['seɪtɪd] *adj* (*appetite, person*) gesättigt

satellite dish *n* (*TECH*) Parabolantenne *f*

satellite television *n* Satellitenfernsehen *nt*

satisfaction [sætɪs'fækʃən] *n* Befriedigung *f*, Genugtuung *f*

satisfactory [sætɪs'fæktərɪ] *adj* zufriedenstellend, befriedigend

satisfy ['sætɪsfaɪ] *vt* befriedigen, zufriedenstellen; (*convince*) überzeugen; (*conditions*) erfüllen; **~ing** *adj* befriedigend; (*meal*) sättigend

saturate ['sætʃəreɪt] *vt* (durch)tränken

saturation [sætʃə'reɪʃən] *n* Durchtränkung *f*, (*CHEM, fig*) Sättigung *f*

Saturday ['sætədeɪ] *n* Samstag *m*, Sonnabend *m*

sauce [sɔ:s] *n* Soße *f*, Sauce *f*; **~pan** *n* Kasserolle *f*

saucer ['sɔ:sə*] *n* Untertasse *f*

saucy ['sɔ:sɪ] *adj* frech, keck

Saudi ['saʊdɪ] *n*: **~ Arabia** *n* Saudi-Arabien *nt*; **~ (Arabian)** *adj* saudiarabisch ♦ *n* Saudiaraber(in) *m(f)*

sauna ['sɔ:nə] *n* Sauna *f*

saunter ['sɔ:ntə*] *vi* schlendern

sausage ['sɒsɪdʒ] *n* Wurst *f*; **~ roll** *n* Wurst *f* im Schlafrock, Wurstpastete *f*

sauté ['səʊteɪ] *adj* Röst-

savage ['sævɪdʒ] *adj* wild ♦ *n* Wilde(r) *mf* ♦ *vt* (*animals*) zerfleischen; **~ry** *n* Roheit *f*, Grausamkeit *f*

save [seɪv] *vt* retten; (*money, electricity etc*) sparen; (*strength etc*) aufsparen; (*COMPUT*) speichern ♦ *vi* (*also:* **~ up**) sparen ♦ *n* (*SPORT*) (Ball)abwehr *f* ♦ *prep*, *conj* außer, ausgenommen

saving ['seɪvɪŋ] *adj*: **the ~ grace of** das Versöhnende an +*dat* ♦ *n* Sparen *nt*, Ersparnis *f*; **~s** *npl* (*money*) Ersparnisse *pl*; **~s account** *n* Sparkonto *nt*; **~s bank** *n* Sparkasse *f*

saviour ['seɪvjə*] (*US* **savior**) *n* (*REL*) Erlöser *m*

savour ['seɪvə*] (*US* **savor**) *vt* (*taste*) schmecken; (*fig*) genießen; **~y** *adj* pikant, würzig

saw [sɔː] (*pt* **sawed**, *pp* **sawed** *or* **sawn**) *pt of* **see** ♦ *n* (*tool*) Säge *f* ♦ *vt*, *vi* sägen; **~dust** *n* Sägemehl *nt*; **~mill** *n* Sägewerk *nt*; **sawn** [sɔːn] *pp of* **saw**; **~n-off shotgun** *n* Gewehr *nt* mit abgesägtem Lauf

say [seɪ] (*pt*, *pp* **said**) *n*: **to have a/no ~ in sth** Mitspracherecht/kein Mitspracherecht bei etw haben ♦ *vt*, *vi* sagen; **let him have his ~** laß ihn doch reden; **to ~ yes/no** ja/nein sagen; **that goes without ~ing** das versteht sich von selbst; **that is to ~** das heißt; **~ing** *n* Sprichwort *nt*

scab [skæb] *n* Schorf *m*; (*pej*) Streikbrecher *m*

scaffold ['skæfəuld] *n* (*for execution*) Schafott *nt*; **~ing** *n* (Bau)gerüst *nt*

scald [skɔːld] *n* Verbrühung *f* ♦ *vt* (*burn*) verbrühen; (*clean*) (ab)brühen

scale [skeɪl] *n* (*of fish*) Schuppe *f*; (*MUS*) Tonleiter *f*; (*on map, size*) Maßstab *m*; (*gradation*) Skala *f* ♦ *vt* (*climb*) erklimmen; **~s** *npl* (*balance*) Waage *f*; **on a large ~** (*fig*) im großen, in großem Umfang; **~ of charges** Gebührenordnung *f*; **~ down** *vt* verkleinern; **~ model** *n* maßstabgetreue(s) Modell *nt*

scallop ['skɒləp] *n* Kammuschel *f*

scalp [skælp] *n* Kopfhaut *f*

scamper ['skæmpə*] *vi*: **to ~ away** *or* **off** sich davonmachen

scampi ['skæmpɪ] *npl* Scampi *pl*

scan [skæn] *vt* (*examine*) genau prüfen; (*quickly*) überfliegen; (*horizon*) absuchen; (*poetry*) skandieren

scandal ['skændl] *n* Skandal *m*; (*piece of gossip*) Skandalgeschichte *f*

Scandinavia [skændɪ'neɪvɪə] *n* Skandinavien *nt*; **~n** *adj* skandinavisch ♦ *n* Skandinavier(in) *m(f)*

scant [skænt] *adj* knapp; **~ily** *adv* knapp, dürftig; **~y** *adj* knapp, unzureichend

scapegoat ['skeɪpgəut] *n* Sündenbock *m*

scar [skɑ:*] *n* Narbe *f* ♦ *vt* durch Narben entstellen

scarce ['skeəs] *adj* selten, rar; (*goods*) knapp; **~ly** *adv* kaum

scarcity ['skeəsɪtɪ] *n* Mangel *m*

scare ['skeə*] *n* Schrecken *m* ♦ *vt* erschrecken; **bomb ~** Bombendrohung *f*; **to ~ sb stiff** jdn zu Tode erschrecken; **to be ~d** Angst haben; **~crow** *n* Vogelscheuche *f*

scarf [skɑ:f] (*pl* **scarves**) *n* Schal *m*; (*head~*) Kopftuch *nt*

scarlet ['skɑ:lɪt] *adj* scharlachrot ♦ *n* Scharlachrot *nt*; **~ fever** *n* Scharlach *m*

scarves [skɑ:vz] *npl of* **scarf**

scary ['skeərɪ] (*inf*) *adj* schaurig

scathing ['skeɪðɪŋ] *adj* scharf, vernichtend

scatter ['skætə*] *vt* (*sprinkle*) (ver)streuen; (*disperse*) zerstreuen ♦ *vi* sich zerstreuen; **~brained** *adj* flatterhaft, schusselig

scavenger ['skævɪndʒə*] *n* (*animal*) Aasfresser *m*

scenario [sɪ'nɑ:rɪəu] *n* (*THEAT, CINE*) Szenarium *nt*; (*fig*) Szenario *nt*

scene [si:n] *n* (*of happening*) Ort *m*; (*of play, incident*) Szene *f*; (*view*) Anblick *m*; (*argument*) Szene *f*, Auftritt *m*; **~ry** ['si:nərɪ] *n* (*THEAT*) Bühnenbild *nt*; (*landscape*) Landschaft *f*

scenic ['si:nɪk] *adj* landschaftlich

scent [sent] *n* Parfüm *nt*; (*smell*) Duft *m* ♦ *vt* parfümieren

sceptical ['skeptɪkəl] (*US* **skeptical**) *adj* skeptisch

schedule ['ʃedju:l, (*US*) 'skedju:l] *n* (*list*) Liste *f*; (*plan*) Programm *nt*; (*of work*) Zeitplan *m* ♦ *vt* planen; **on ~** pünktlich; **to be ahead of/behind ~** dem Zeitplan voraus/im Rückstand sein; **~d flight** *n* (*not charter*) Linienflug *m*

scheme [ski:m] *n* Schema *nt*; (*dishonest*) Intrige *f*; (*plan of action*) Plan *m* ♦ *vi* intrigieren ♦ *vt* planen

scheming ['ski:mɪŋ] *adj* intrigierend

scholar ['skɒlə*] *n* Gelehrte(r) *m*; (*holding ~ship*) Stipendiat *m*; ~**ly** *adj* gelehrt; ~**ship** *n* Gelehrsamkeit *f*; (*grant*) Stipendium *nt*

school [sku:l] *n* Schule *f*; (*UNIV*) Fakultät *f* ♦ *vt* schulen; (*dog*) trainieren; ~ **age** *n* schulpflichtige(s) Alter *nt*; ~**book** *n* Schulbuch *nt*; ~**boy** *n* Schüler *m*; ~**children** *npl* Schüler *pl*, Schulkinder *pl*; ~**days** *npl* (alte) Schulzeit *f*; ~**girl** *n* Schülerin *f*; ~**ing** *n* Schulung *f*, Ausbildung *f*; ~**master** *n* Lehrer *m*; ~**mistress** *n* Lehrerin *f*; ~**teacher** *n* Lehrer(in) *m(f)*

sciatica [saɪ'ætɪkə] *n* Ischias *m or nt*

science ['saɪəns] *n* Wissenschaft *f*; (*natural ~*) Naturwissenschaft *f*

scientific [saɪən'tɪfɪk] *adj* wissenschaftlich; (*natural sciences*) naturwissenschaftlich

scientist ['saɪəntɪst] *n* Wissenschaftler(in) *m(f)*

scintillating ['sɪntɪleɪtɪŋ] *adj* sprühend

scissors ['sɪzəz] *npl* Schere *f*; **a pair of ~** eine Schere

scoff [skɒf] *vt* (*BRIT: inf: eat*) fressen ♦ *vi* (*mock*): **to ~ (at)** spotten (über +*acc*)

scold [skəʊld] *vt* schimpfen

scone [skɒn] *n* weiche(s) Teegebäck *nt*

scoop [sku:p] *n* Schaufel *f*; (*news*) sensationelle Erstmeldung *f*; ~ **out** *vt* herausschaufeln; (*liquid*) herausschöpfen; ~ **up** *vt* aufschaufeln; (*liquid*) aufschöpfen

scooter ['sku:tə*] *n* Motorroller *m*; (*child's*) Roller *m*

scope [skəʊp] *n* Ausmaß *nt*; (*opportunity*) (Spiel)raum *m*

scorch [skɔ:tʃ] *n* Brandstelle *f* ♦ *vt* versengen; ~**ing** *adj* brennend

score [skɔ:*] *n* (*in game*) Punktzahl *f*; (*final ~*) (Spiel)ergebnis *nt*; (*MUS*) Partitur *f*; (*line*) Kratzer *m*; (*twenty*) zwanzig, zwanzig Stück ♦ *vt* (*goal*) schießen; (*points*) machen; (*mark*) einritzen ♦ *vi* (*keep record*) Punkte zählen; **on that ~** in

dieser Hinsicht; **what's the ~?** wie steht's?; **to ~ 6 out of 10** 6 von 10 Punkten erzielen; ~ **out** *vt* ausstreichen; ~**board** *n* Anschreibetafel *f*; ~**r** *n* Torschütze *m*; (*recorder*) (Auf)schreiber *m*

scorn ['skɔ:n] *n* Verachtung *f* ♦ *vt* verhöhnen; ~**ful** *adj* verächtlich

Scorpio ['skɔ:pɪəʊ] *n* Skorpion *m*

Scot [skɒt] *n* Schotte *m*, Schottin *f*

Scotch [skɒtʃ] *n* Scotch *m*

scotch *vt* (*end*) unterbinden

scot-free ['skɒt'fri:] *adv*: **to get off ~** (*unpunished*) ungeschoren davonkommen

Scotland ['skɒtlənd] *n* Schottland *nt*

Scots [skɒts] *adj* schottisch; ~**man/ woman** (*irreg*) *n* Schotte *m*/Schottin *f*

Scottish ['skɒtɪʃ] *adj* schottisch

scoundrel ['skaʊndrəl] *n* Schuft *m*

scour ['skaʊə*] *vt* (*search*) absuchen; (*clean*) schrubben

scourge [skɜ:dʒ] *n* (*whip*) Geißel *f*; (*plague*) Qual *f*

scout [skaʊt] *n* (*MIL*) Späher *m*; (*also: boy ~*) Pfadfinder *m*; ~ **around** *vi*: **to ~ around (for)** sich umsehen (nach)

scowl [skaʊl] *n* finstere(r) Blick *m* ♦ *vi* finster blicken

scrabble ['skræbl] (*also: ~ around: search*) (herum)tasten ♦ *vi* (*claw*): **to ~ (at)** kratzen (an +*dat*) ♦ *n*: **S~** ® Scrabble *nt* ®

scraggy ['skrægɪ] *adj* dürr, hager

scram [skræm] (*inf*) *vi* abhauen

scramble ['skræmbl] *n* (*climb*) Kletterei *f*; (*struggle*) Kampf *m* ♦ *vi* klettern; (*fight*) sich schlagen; **to ~ out/through** krabbeln aus/durch; **to ~ for sth** sich um etw raufen; ~**d eggs** *npl* Rührei *nt*

scrap [skræp] *n* (*bit*) Stückchen *nt*; (*fight*) Keilerei *f*; (*also: ~ iron*) Schrott *m* ♦ *vt* verwerfen ♦ *vi* (*fight*) streiten, sich prügeln; ~**s** *npl* (*leftovers*) Reste *pl*; (*waste*) Abfall *m*; ~**book** *n* Einklebealbum *nt*; ~ **dealer** *n* Schrotthändler(in) *m(f)*

scrape [skreɪp] *n* Kratzen *nt*; (*trouble*) Klemme *f* ♦ *vt* kratzen; (*car*) zerkratzen; (*clean*) abkratzen ♦ *vi* (*make harsh noise*) kratzen; **to ~ through** gerade noch durchkommen; **~r** *n* Kratzer *m*

scrap: **~ heap** *n* Schrotthaufen *m*; **on the ~ heap** *(fig)* beim alten Eisen; **~ iron** *n* Schrott *m*; **~ merchant** *(BRIT)* *n* Altwarenhändler(in) *m(f)*

scrappy ['skræpɪ] *adj* zusammengestoppelt

scratch [skrætʃ] *n* *(wound)* Kratzer *m*, Schramme *f* ♦ *adj:* **~ team** zusammengewürfelte Mannschaft ♦ *vt* kratzen; *(car)* zerkratzen ♦ *vi* (sich) kratzen; **to start from ~** ganz von vorne anfangen; **to be up to ~** den Anforderungen entsprechen

scrawl [skrɔːl] *n* Gekritzel *nt* ♦ *vt, vi* kritzeln

scrawny ['skrɔːnɪ] *adj* *(person, neck)* dürr

scream [skriːm] *n* Schrei *m* ♦ *vi* schreien

scree [skriː] *n* Geröll(halde *f*) *nt*

screech [skriːtʃ] *n* Schrei *m* ♦ *vi* kreischen

screen [skriːn] *n* *(protective)* Schutzschirm *m*; *(CINE)* Leinwand *f*; *(TV)* Bildschirm *m* ♦ *vt* *(shelter)* (be)schirmen; *(film)* zeigen, vorführen; **~ing** *n* *(MED)* Untersuchung *f*; **~play** *n* Drehbuch *nt*

screw [skruː] *n* Schraube *f* ♦ *vt* *(fasten)* schrauben; *(vulgar)* bumsen; **~ up** *vt* *(paper etc)* zerknüllen; *(inf: ruin)* vermasseln *(inf)*; **~driver** *n* Schraubenzieher *m*

scribble ['skrɪbl] *n* Gekritzel *nt* ♦ *vt* kritzeln

script [skrɪpt] *n* *(handwriting)* Handschrift *f*; *(for film)* Drehbuch *nt*; *(THEAT)* Manuskript *nt*, Text *m*

Scripture ['skrɪptʃə*] *n* Heilige Schrift *f*

scroll [skrəʊl] *n* Schriftrolle *f*

scrounge [skraʊndʒ] *(inf)* *vt:* **to ~ sth off** *or* **from sb** etw bei jdm abstauben ♦ *n:* **on the ~** beim Schnorren

scrub [skrʌb] *n* *(clean)* Schrubben *nt*; *(in countryside)* Gestrüpp *nt* ♦ *vt* *(clean)* schrubben; *(reject)* fallenlassen

scruff [skrʌf] *n:* **by the ~ of the neck** am Genick

scruffy ['skrʌfɪ] *adj* unordentlich, vergammelt

scrum(mage) ['skrʌm(ɪdʒ)] *n* Getümmel

nt

scruple ['skruːpl] *n* Skrupel *m*, Bedenken *nt*

scrupulous ['skruːpjʊləs] *adj* peinlich genau, gewissenhaft

scrutinize ['skruːtɪnaɪz] *vt* genau prüfen

scrutiny ['skruːtɪnɪ] *n* genaue Untersuchung *f*

scuff [skʌf] *vt* *(shoes)* abstoßen

scuffle ['skʌfl] *n* Handgemenge *nt*

scullery ['skʌlərɪ] *n* Spülküche *f*

sculptor ['skʌlptə*] *n* Bildhauer(in) *m(f)*

sculpture ['skʌlptʃə*] *n* *(ART)* Bildhauerei *f*; *(statue)* Skulptur *f*

scum [skʌm] *n* *(also fig)* Abschaum *m*

scupper ['skʌpə*] *vt* *(NAUT)* versenken; *(fig)* zerstören

scurrilous ['skʌrɪləs] *adj* unflätig

scurry ['skʌrɪ] *vi* huschen

scuttle ['skʌtl] *n* *(also: coal ~)* Kohleneimer *m* ♦ *vt* *(ship)* versenken ♦ *vi* *(scamper):* **to ~ away** *or* **off** sich davonmachen

scythe [saɪð] *n* Sense *f*

SDP *(BRIT)* *n abbr* = **Social Democratic Party**

sea [siː] *n* Meer *nt*, See *f*; *(fig)* Meer *nt* ♦ *adj* Meeres-, See-; **by ~** *(travel)* auf dem Seeweg; **on the ~** *(boat)* auf dem Meer; *(town)* am Meer; **out to ~** aufs Meer hinaus; **out at ~** aufs Meer; **to be all at ~** *(fig)* nicht durchblicken; **~ coast** *n* Küste *f*; **~food** *n* Meeresfrüchte *pl*; **~ front** *n* Strandpromenade *f*; **~going** *adj* seetüchtig, Hochsee-; **~gull** *n* Möwe *f*

seal [siːl] *n* *(animal)* Robbe *f*, Seehund *m*; *(stamp, impression)* Siegel *nt* ♦ *vt* versiegeln

sea level *n* Meeresspiegel *m*

sea lion *n* Seelöwe *m*

seam [siːm] *n* Saum *m*; *(edges joining)* Naht *f*; *(of coal)* Flöz *nt*

seaman ['siːmən] *(irreg)* *n* Seemann *m*

seamy ['siːmɪ] *adj* *(people, café)* zwielichtig; *(life)* anrüchig

seaplane ['siːpleɪn] *n* Wasserflugzeug *nt*

seaport ['siːpɔːt] *n* Seehafen *m*

search [sɜːtʃ] *n* *(for person, thing)* Suche *f*; *(of drawer, pockets, house)*

Durchsuchung f ♦ vi suchen ♦ vt
durchsuchen; **in** ~ **of** auf der Suche nach;
to ~ **for** suchen nach; ~ **through** vt
durchsuchen; ~**ing** adj (look) forschend;
~**light** n Scheinwerfer m; ~ **party** n
Suchmannschaft f; ~ **warrant** n
Durchsuchungsbefehl m

seashore ['siːʃɔː*] n Meeresküste f

seasick ['siːsɪk] adj seekrank; ~**ness** n
Seekrankheit f

seaside ['siːsaɪd] n Küste f; ~ **resort** n
Badeort m

season ['siːzn] n Jahreszeit f; (Christmas
etc) Zeit f, Saison f ♦ vt (flavour) würzen;
~**al** adj Saison-; ~**ed** adj (fig) erfahren;
~**ing** n Gewürz nt, Würze f; ~ **ticket** n
(RAIL) Zeitkarte f; (THEAT) Abonnement nt

seat [siːt] n Sitz m, Platz m; (in
Parliament) Sitz m; (part of body) Gesäß
nt; (of trousers) Hosenboden m ♦ vt (place)
setzen; (have space for) Sitzplätze bieten
für; **to be** ~**ed** sitzen; ~ **belt** n
Sicherheitsgurt m

sea water n Meerwasser nt

seaweed ['siːwiːd] n (See)tang m

seaworthy ['siːwɜːðɪ] adj seetüchtig

sec. abbr (= second(s)) Sek.

secluded [sɪ'kluːdɪd] adj abgelegen

seclusion [sɪ'kluːʒən] n
Zurückgezogenheit f

second ['sekənd] adj zweite(r,s) ♦ adv (in
~ position) an zweiter Stelle ♦ n Sekunde
f; (person) Zweite(r) mf; (COMM: imperfect)
zweite Wahl f; (SPORT) Sekundant m; (AUT:
also: ~ gear) zweite(r) Gang m; (BRIT: UNIV:
degree) mittlere Note bei Abschluß-
prüfungen ♦ vt (support) unterstützen;
~**ary** adj zweitrangig; ~**ary school** n
höhere Schule f, Mittelschule f; ~**class**
adj zweiter Klasse; ~**hand** adj aus
zweiter Hand; (car etc) gebraucht; ~
hand n (on clock) Sekundenzeiger m; ~**ly**
adv zweitens; ~**ment** [sɪ'kɒndmənt] (BRIT)
n Abordnung f; ~**rate** adj mittelmäßig; ~
thoughts npl: **to have** ~ **thoughts** es
sich dat anders überlegen; **on** ~ **thoughts**
(BRIT) or **thought** (US) oder lieber
(nicht)

secrecy ['siːkrəsɪ] n Geheimhaltung f

secret ['siːkrət] n Geheimnis nt ♦ adj
geheim, Geheim-; **in** ~ geheim

secretarial [sekrə'tɛərɪəl] adj
Sekretärinnen-

secretary ['sekrətrɪ] n Sekretär(in) m(f)

Secretary of State (BRIT) n (POL): ~
(for) Minister(in) m(f) (für)

secretion [sɪ'kriːʃən] n Absonderung f

secretive ['siːkrətɪv] adj geheimtuerisch

secretly adv geheim

sectarian [sek'tɛərɪən] adj (riots etc)
Konfessions-, zwischen den Konfessionen

section ['sekʃən] n Teil m; (department)
Abteilung f; (of document) Abschnitt m

sector ['sektə*] n Sektor m

secular ['sekjulə*] adj weltlich, profan

secure [sɪ'kjuə*] adj (safe) sicher; (firmly
fixed) fest ♦ vt (make firm) befestigen,
sichern; (obtain) sichern

security [sɪ'kjuərɪtɪ] n Sicherheit f;
(pledge) Pfand nt; (document) Wertpapier
nt; (national ~) Staatssicherheit f

sedan [sɪ'dæn] (US) n (AUT) Limousine f

sedate [sɪ'deɪt] adj gesetzt ♦ vt (MED) ein
Beruhigungsmittel geben +dat

sedation [sɪ'deɪʃən] n (MED) Einfluß m
von Beruhigungsmitteln

sedative ['sedətɪv] n Beruhigungsmittel
nt ♦ adj beruhigend, einschläfernd

sedentary ['sedntərɪ] adj (job) sitzend

sediment ['sedɪmənt] n (Boden)satz m

sedition [sə'dɪʃən] n Aufwiegelung f

seduce [sɪ'djuːs] vt verführen

seduction [sɪ'dʌkʃən] n Verführung f

seductive [sɪ'dʌktɪv] adj verführerisch

see [siː] (pt saw, pp seen) vt sehen;
(understand) (ein)sehen, erkennen; (visit)
besuchen ♦ vi (be aware) sehen; (find out)
nachsehen ♦ n (ECCL: R.C.) Bistum nt
(: Protestant) Kirchenkreis m; **to** ~ **sb to
the door** jdn hinausbegleiten; **to** ~ **that**
(ensure) dafür sorgen, daß; **you soon!**
bis bald!; ~ **about** vt fus sich kümmern
um; ~ **off** vt: **to** ~ **sb off** jdn zum Zug etc
begleiten; ~ **through** vt: **to** ~ **sth
through** etw durchfechten; **to** ~ **through**
sb/sth jdn/etw durchschauen; ~ **to** vt
fus: **to** ~ **to it** dafür sorgen

seed [siːd] n Samen m ♦ vt (TENNIS)

plazieren; **to go to ~** (*plant*) schießen; (*fig*) herunterkommen; **~ling** *n* Setzling *m*; **~y** *adj* (*café*) übel; (*person*) zweifelhaft

seeing ['si:ɪŋ] *conj*: **~ (that)** da

seek [si:k] (*pt, pp* **sought**) *vt* suchen

seem [si:m] *vi* scheinen; **it ~s that ...** es scheint, daß ...; **~ingly** *adv* anscheinend

seen [si:n] *pp of* **see**

seep [si:p] *vi* sickern

seesaw ['si:sɔ:] *n* Wippe *f*

seethe [si:ð] *vi*: **to ~ with anger** vor Wut kochen

see-through ['si:θru:] *adj* (*dress etc*) durchsichtig

segment ['segmənt] *n* Teil *m*; (*of circle*) Ausschnitt *m*

segregate ['segrɪgeɪt] *vt* trennen

seize [si:z] *vt* (*grasp*) (er)greifen, packen; (*power*) ergreifen; (*take legally*) beschlagnahmen; **~ (up)on** *vt fus* sich stürzen auf +*acc*; **~ up** *vi* (*TECH*) sich festfressen

seizure ['si:ʒə*] *n* (*illness*) Anfall *m*

seldom ['seldəm] *adv* selten

select [sɪ'lekt] *adj* ausgewählt ♦ *vt* auswählen; **~ion** [sɪ'lekʃən] *n* Auswahl *f*; **~ive** *adj* (*person*) wählerisch

self [self] (*pl* **selves**) *pron* selbst ♦ *n* Selbst *nt*, Ich *nt*; **the ~** das Ich; **~-assured** *adj* selbstbewußt; **~-catering** (*BRIT*) *adj* für Selbstversorger; **~-centred** (*US* **~-centered**) *adj* egozentrisch; **~-coloured** (*US* **~-colored**) *adj* (*of one colour*) einfarbig, uni; **~-confidence** *n* Selbstvertrauen *nt*, Selbstbewußtsein *nt*; **~-conscious** *adj* gehemmt, befangen; **~-contained** *adj* (*complete*) (in sich) geschlossen; (*person*) verschlossen; (*BRIT*: *flat*) separat; **~-control** *n* Selbstbeherrschung *f*; **~-defence** (*US* **~-defense**) *n* Selbstverteidigung *f*; (*JUR*) Notwehr *f*; **~-discipline** *n* Selbstdisziplin *f*; **~-employed** *adj* frei(schaffend) *n*; **~-evident** *adj* offensichtlich; **~-governing** *adj* selbstverwaltet; **~-indulgent** *adj* zügellos; **~-interest** *n* Eigennutz *m*; **~-ish** *adj* egoistisch, selbstsüchtig; **~ishness** *n* Egoismus *m*, Selbstsucht *f*; **~lessly** *adv* selbstlos; **~-made** *adj*: **~-made man**

Selfmademan *m*; **~-pity** *n* Selbstmitleid *nt*; **~-portrait** *n* Selbstbildnis *nt*; **~-possessed** *adj* selbstbeherrscht; **~-preservation** *n* Selbsterhaltung *f*; **~-reliant** *adj* unabhängig; **~-respect** *n* Selbstachtung *f*; **~-righteous** *adj* selbstgerecht; **~-sacrifice** *n* Selbstaufopferung *f*; **~-satisfied** *adj* selbstzufrieden; **~-service** *adj* Selbstbedienungs-; **~-sufficient** *adj* selbstgenügsam; **~-taught** *adj* selbsterlernt; **~-taught person** Autodidakt *m*

sell [sel] (*pt, pp* **sold**) *vt* verkaufen ♦ *vi* verkaufen; (*goods*) sich verkaufen; **to ~ at** *or* **for £10** für £10 verkaufen; **~ off** *vt* verkaufen; **~ out** *vi* alles verkaufen; **~-by date** *n* Verfalldatum *nt*; **~er** *n* Verkäufer *m*; **~ing price** *n* Verkaufspreis *m*

Sellotape ['seləuteɪp] (®; *BRIT*) *n* Tesafilm *m* ®

sellout ['selaut] *n* (*of tickets*): **it was a ~** es war ausverkauft

selves [selvz] *npl of* **self**

semaphore ['seməfɔ:*] *n* Winkzeichen *pl*

semblance ['sembləns] *n* Anschein *m*

semen ['si:mən] *n* Sperma *nt*

semester [sɪ'mestə*] (*US*) *n* Semester *nt*

semi ['semɪ] *n* = **semidetached house**; **~circle** *n* Halbkreis *m*; **~colon** *n* Semikolon *nt*; **~conductor** *n* Halbleiter *m*; **~detached house** (*BRIT*) *n* halbe(s) Doppelhaus *nt*; **~final** *n* Halbfinale *nt*

seminary ['semɪnərɪ] *n* (*REL*) Priesterseminar *nt*

semiskilled ['semɪ'skɪld] *adj* angelernt

senate ['senɪt] *n* Senat *m*; **senator** *n* Senator *m*

send [send] (*pt, pp* **sent**) *vt* senden, schicken; (*inf*: *inspire*) hinreißen; **~ away** *vt* wegschicken; **~ away for** *vt fus* anfordern; **~ back** *vt* zurückschicken; **~ for** *vt fus* holen lassen; **~ off** *vt* (*goods*) abschicken; (*BRIT*: *SPORT*: *player*) vom Feld schicken; **~ out** *vt* (*invitation*) aussenden; **~ up** *vt* hinaufsenden; (*BRIT*: *parody*) verulken; **~er** *n* Absender *m*; **~-off** *n*: **to give sb a good ~-off** jdn (ganz) groß

verabschieden
senior ['si:niə*] adj (older) älter; (higher
rank) Ober- ♦ n (older person) Ältere(r)
mf; (higher ranking) Rangälteste(r) mf; ~
citizen n ältere(r) Mitbürger(in) m(f);
~ity [si:nɪ'ɒrɪtɪ] n (of age) höhere(s) Alter
nt; (in rank) höhere(r) Dienstgrad m
sensation [sen'seɪʃən] n Gefühl nt;
(excitement) Sensation f, Aufsehen nt
sense [sens] n Sinn m; (understanding)
Verstand m, Vernunft f; (feeling) Gefühl
nt ♦ vt fühlen, spüren; ~ **of humour**
Humor m; **to make ~** Sinn ergeben;
~less adj sinnlos; (unconscious)
besinnungslos
sensibility [sensɪ'bɪlɪtɪ] n
Empfindsamkeit f; (feeling hurt)
Empfindlichkeit f; **sensibilities** npl
(feelings) Zartgefühl nt
sensible ['sensəbl] adj vernünftig
sensitive ['sensɪtɪv] adj: ~ **(to)**
empfindlich (gegen)
sensitivity [sensɪ'tɪvɪtɪ] n
Empfindlichkeit f; (artistic) Feingefühl nt;
(tact) Feinfühligkeit f
sensual ['sensjʊəl] adj sinnlich
sensuous ['sensjʊəs] adj sinnlich
sent [sent] pt, pp of **send**
sentence ['sentəns] n Satz m; (JUR) Strafe
f; Urteil nt ♦ vt: **to ~ sb to death/to 5
years** jdn zum Tode/zu 5 Jahren
verurteilen
sentiment ['sentɪmənt] n Gefühl nt;
(thought) Gedanke m; **~al** [sentɪ'mentl]
adj sentimental; (of feelings rather than
reason) gefühlsmäßig
sentry ['sentrɪ] n (Schild)wache f
separate [adj 'seprət, vb 'sepəreɪt] adj
getrennt, separat ♦ vt trennen ♦ vi sich
trennen; **~ly** adv getrennt; **~s** npl
(clothes) Röcke, Pullover etc
separation [sepə'reɪʃən] n Trennung f
September [sep'tembə*] n September m
septic ['septɪk] adj vereitert, septisch; ~
tank n Klärbehälter m
sequel ['si:kwəl] n Folge f
sequence ['si:kwəns] n (Reihen)folge f
sequin ['si:kwɪn] n Paillette f
Serbia ['sɜːbɪə] n Serbien nt

serene [sə'ri:n] adj heiter
serenity [sɪ'renɪtɪ] n Heiterkeit f
sergeant ['sɑːdʒənt] n Feldwebel m;
(POLICE) (Polizei)wachtmeister m
serial ['sɪərɪəl] n Fortsetzungsroman m;
(TV) Fernsehserie f ♦ adj (number)
(fort)laufend; **~ize** vt in Fortsetzungen
veröffentlichen; in Fortsetzungen senden
series ['sɪərɪz] n inv Serie f, Reihe f
serious ['sɪərɪəs] adj ernst; (injury)
schwer; **~ly** adv ernst(haft); (hurt)
schwer; **~ness** n Ernst m, Ernsthaftigkeit
f
sermon ['sɜːmən] n Predigt f
serrated [se'reɪtɪd] adj gezackt
servant ['sɜːvənt] n Diener(in) m(f)
serve [sɜːv] vt dienen +dat; (guest,
customer) bedienen; (food) servieren ♦ vi
dienen, nützen; (at table) servieren;
(TENNIS) geben, aufschlagen; **it ~s him
right** das geschieht ihm recht; **that'll ~
as a table** das geht als Tisch; **to ~ a
summons (on sb)** (jdn) vor Gericht
laden; ~ **out** or **up** vt (food) auftragen,
servieren
service ['sɜːvɪs] n (help) Dienst m; (trains
etc) Verbindung f; (hotel) Service m,
Bedienung f; (set of dishes) Service nt;
(REL) Gottesdienst m; (car) Inspektion f;
(for TVs etc) Kundendienst m; (TENNIS)
Aufschlag m ♦ vt (AUT, TECH) warten,
überholen; **the S~s** npl (armed forces) die
Streitkräfte pl; **to be of ~ to sb** jdm
einen großen Dienst erweisen; **~able** adj
brauchbar; ~ **area** n (on motorway)
Raststätte f; ~ **charge** (BRIT) n Bedienung
f; **~man** (irreg) n (soldier etc) Soldat m; ~
station n (Groß)tankstelle f
serviette [sɜːvɪ'et] n Serviette f
servile ['sɜːvaɪl] adj unterwürfig
session ['seʃən] n Sitzung f; (POL)
Sitzungsperiode f; **to be in** ~ tagen
set [set] (pt, pp set) n (collection of things)
Satz m, Set nt; (RADIO, TV) Apparat m;
(TENNIS) Satz m; (group of people) Kreis m;
(CINE) Szene f; (THEAT) Bühnenbild nt ♦ adj
festgelegt; (ready) bereit ♦ vt (place)
setzen, stellen, legen; (arrange)
(an)ordnen; (table) decken; (time, price)

festsetzen; (*alarm, watch, task*) stellen; (*jewels*) (ein)fassen; (*exam*) ausarbeiten ♦ *vi* (*sun*) untergehen; (*become hard*) fest werden; (*bone*) zusammenwachsen; **to be ~ on doing sth** etw unbedingt tun wollen; **to ~ to music** vertonen; **to ~ on fire** anstecken; **to ~ free** freilassen; **to ~ sth going** etw in Gang bringen; **to ~ sail** losfahren; **~ about** *vi fus* (*task*) anpacken; **~ aside** *vt* beiseitelegen; **~ back** *vt*: **to ~ back (by)** zurückwerfen (um); **~ off** *vi* aufbrechen ♦ *vt* (*explode*) sprengen; (*alarm*) losgehen lassen; (*show up well*) hervorheben; **~ out** *vi*: **to ~ out to do sth** vorhaben, etw zu tun (*arrange*) anlegen, arrangieren; (*state*) darlegen; **~ up** *vt* (*organization*) aufziehen; (*record*) aufstellen; (*monument*) erstellen; **~back** *n* Rückschlag *m*; **~ menu** *n* Tageskarte *f*

settee [se'tiː] *n* Sofa *nt*

setting ['setɪŋ] *n* Hintergrund *m*

settle ['setl] *vt* beruhigen; (*pay*) begleichen, bezahlen; (*agree*) regeln ♦ *vi* sich einleben; (*come to rest*) sich niederlassen; (*sink*) sich setzen; (*calm down*) sich beruhigen; **to ~ for sth** sich mit etw zufriedengeben; **to ~ on sth** sich für etw entscheiden; **to ~ up with sb** mit jdm abrechnen; **~ down** *vi* (*feel at home*) sich einleben; (*calm down*) sich beruhigen; **~ in** *vi* sich eingewöhnen; **~ment** *n* Regelung *f*; (*payment*) Begleichung *f*; (*colony*) Siedlung *f*; **~r** *n* Siedler *m*

setup ['setʌp] *n* (*situation*) Lage *f*

seven ['sevn] *num* sieben; **~teen** *num* siebzehn; **~th** *adj* siebte(r, s) ♦ *n* Siebtel *nt*; **~ty** *num* siebzig

sever ['sevə*] *vt* abtrennen

several ['sevrəl] *adj* mehrere, verschiedene ♦ *pron* mehrere; **~ of us** einige von uns

severance ['sevərəns] *n*: **~ pay** Abfindung *f*

severe [sɪ'vɪə*] *adj* (*strict*) streng; (*serious*) schwer; (*climate*) rauh

severity [sɪ'verɪtɪ] *n* Strenge *f*; Schwere *f*; Rauheit *f*

sew [səʊ] (*pt* **sewed**, *pp* **sewn**) *vt, vi*

nähen; **~ up** *vt* zunähen

sewage ['sjuːɪdʒ] *n* Abwässer *pl*

sewer ['sjʊə*] *n* (Abwasser)kanal *m*

sewing ['səʊɪŋ] *n* Näharbeit *f*; **~ machine** *n* Nähmaschine *f*

sewn [səʊn] *pp of* **sew**

sex [seks] *n* Sex *m*; (*gender*) Geschlecht *nt*; **to have ~ with sb** mit jdm Geschlechtsverkehr haben; **~ist** *adj* sexistisch ♦ *n* Sexist(in) *m(f)*

sexual ['seksjʊəl] *adj* sexuell, geschlechtlich, Geschlechts-

sexy ['seksɪ] *adj* sexy

shabby ['ʃæbɪ] *adj* (*also fig*) schäbig

shack [ʃæk] *n* Hütte *f*

shackles ['ʃæklz] *npl* (*also fig*) Fesseln *pl*, Ketten *pl*

shade [ʃeɪd] *n* Schatten *m*; (*for lamp*) Lampenschirm *m*; (*colour*) Farbton *m* ♦ *vt* abschirmen; **in the ~** im Schatten; **a ~ smaller** ein bißchen kleiner

shadow ['ʃædəʊ] *n* Schatten *m* ♦ *vt* (*follow*) beschatten ♦ *adj*: **~ cabinet** (*BRIT: POL*) Schattenkabinett *nt*; **~y** *adj* schattig

shady ['ʃeɪdɪ] *adj* schattig; (*fig*) zwielichtig

shaft [ʃɑːft] *n* (*of spear etc*) Schaft *m*; (*in mine*) Schacht *m*; (*TECH*) Welle *f*; (*of light*) Strahl *m*

shaggy ['ʃægɪ] *adj* struppig

shake [ʃeɪk] (*pt* **shook**, *pp* **shaken**) *vt* schütteln, rütteln; (*shock*) erschüttern ♦ *vi* (*move*) schwanken; (*tremble*) zittern, beben ♦ *n* (*jerk*) Schütteln *nt*, Rütteln *nt*; **to ~ hands with** die Hand geben +*dat*; **to ~ one's head** den Kopf schütteln; **~ off** *vt* abschütteln; **~ up** *vt* aufschütteln; (*fig*) aufrütteln; **shaken** ['ʃeɪkn] *pp of* **shake**

shaky ['ʃeɪkɪ] *adj* zittrig; (*weak*) unsicher

shall [ʃæl] *vb aux*: **I ~ go** ich werde gehen; **~ I open the door?** soll ich die Tür öffnen?; **I'll buy some cake, ~ I?** soll ich Kuchen kaufen?, ich kaufe Kuchen, oder?

shallow ['ʃæləʊ] *adj* seicht

sham [ʃæm] *n* Schein *m* ♦ *adj* unecht, falsch

shambles ['ʃæmblz] *n* Durcheinander *nt*

shame [ʃeɪm] *n* Scham *f*; (*disgrace, pity*)

Schande *f* ♦ *vt* beschämen; **it is a ~ that** es ist schade, daß; **it is a ~ to do ...** es ist eine Schande, ... zu tun; **what a ~!** wie schade!; **~faced** *adj* beschämt; **~ful** *adj* schändlich; **~less** *adj* schamlos

shampoo [ʃæm'puː] *n* Shampoo(n) *nt* ♦ *vt* (*hair*) waschen; **~ and set** *n* Waschen *nt* und Legen

shamrock ['ʃæmrɒk] *n* Kleeblatt *nt*

shandy ['ʃændɪ] *n* Bier *nt* mit Limonade

shan't [ʃɑːnt] = **shall not**

shantytown ['ʃæntɪtaʊn] *n* Bidonville *f*

shape [ʃeɪp] *n* Form *f* ♦ *vt* formen, gestalten ♦ *vi* (*also:* **~ up**) sich entwickeln; **to take ~** Gestalt annehmen; **-shaped** *suffix*: **heart-shaped** herzförmig; **~less** *adj* formlos; **~ly** *adj* wohlproportioniert

share [ʃɛə*] *n* (An)teil *m*; (*FIN*) Aktie *f* ♦ *vt* teilen; **to ~ out (among/between)** verteilen (unter/zwischen); **~holder** *n* Aktionär(in) *m(f)*

shark [ʃɑːk] *n* Hai(fisch) *m*; (*swindler*) Gauner *m*

sharp [ʃɑːp] *adj* scharf; (*pin*) spitz; (*person*) clever; (*MUS*) erhöht ♦ *n* Kreuz *nt* ♦ *adv* zu hoch; **nine o'clock ~** Punkt neun; **~en** *vt* schärfen; (*pencil*) spitzen; **~ener** *n* (*also: pencil ~ener*) Anspitzer *m*; **~-eyed** *adj* scharfsichtig; **~ly** *adv* (*turn, stop*) plötzlich; (*stand out, contrast*) deutlich; (*criticize, retort*) scharf

shatter ['ʃætə*] *vt* zerschmettern; (*fig*) zerstören ♦ *vi* zerspringen

shave [ʃeɪv] *n* Rasur *f* ♦ *vt* rasieren ♦ *vi* sich rasieren; **to have a ~** sich rasieren (lassen); **~r** *n* (*also: electric ~r*) Rasierapparat *m*

shaving ['ʃeɪvɪŋ] *n* (*action*) Rasieren *nt*; **~s** *npl* (*of wood etc*) Späne *pl*; **~ brush** *n* Rasierpinsel *m*; **~ cream** *n* Rasierkrem *f*; **~ foam** *n* Rasierschaum *m*

shawl [ʃɔːl] *n* Schal *m*, Umhang *m*

she [ʃiː] *pron* sie ♦ *adj* weiblich; **~-bear** Bärenweibchen *nt*

sheaf [ʃiːf] (*pl* **sheaves**) *n* Garbe *f*

shear [ʃɪə*] (*pt* **~ed**, *pp* **~ed** *or* **shorn**) *vt* scheren; **~ off** *vi* abbrechen; **~s** *npl* Heckenschere *f*

sheath [ʃiːθ] *n* Scheide *f*; (*condom*) Kondom *m or nt*

sheaves [ʃiːvz] *npl of* **sheaf**

shed [ʃed] (*pt, pp* **shed**) *n* Schuppen *m*; (*for animals*) Stall *m* ♦ *vt* verlieren; (*leaves etc*) verlieren; (*tears*) vergießen

she'd [ʃiːd] = **she had; she would**

sheen [ʃiːn] *n* Glanz *m*

sheep [ʃiːp] *n inv* Schaf *nt*; **~dog** *n* Schäferhund *m*; **~ish** *adj* verlegen; **~skin** *n* Schaffell *nt*

sheer [ʃɪə*] *adj* bloß, rein; (*steep*) steil; (*transparent*) (hauch)dünn ♦ *adv* (*directly*) direkt

sheet [ʃiːt] *n* Bettuch *nt*, Bettlaken *nt*; (*of paper*) Blatt *nt*; (*of metal etc*) Platte *f*; (*of ice*) Fläche *f*

sheik(h) [ʃeɪk] *n* Scheich *m*

shelf [ʃelf] (*pl* **shelves**) *n* Bord *nt*, Regal *nt*

shell [ʃel] *n* Schale *f*; (*sea~*) Muschel *f*; (*explosive*) Granate *f* ♦ *vt* (*peas*) schälen; (*fire on*) beschießen

she'll [ʃiːl] = **she will; she shall**

shellfish ['ʃelfɪʃ] *n* Schalentier *nt*; (*as food*) Meeresfrüchte *pl*

shell suit *n* Ballonseidenanzug *m*

shelter ['ʃeltə*] *n* Schutz *m*; (*air-raid ~*) Bunker *m* ♦ *vt* schützen, bedecken; (*refugees*) aufnehmen ♦ *vi* sich unterstellen; **~ed** *adj* (*life*) behütet; (*spot*) geschützt

shelve [ʃelv] *vt* aufschieben ♦ *vi* abfallen

shelves [ʃelvz] *npl of* **shelf**

shepherd ['ʃepəd] *n* Schäfer *m* ♦ *vt* treiben, führen; **~'s pie** *n* Auflauf *m* aus Hackfleisch und Kartoffelbrei

sheriff ['ʃerɪf] *n* Sheriff *m*; (*SCOTTISH*) Friedensrichter *m*

sherry ['ʃerɪ] *n* Sherry *m*

she's [ʃiːz] = **she is; she has**

Shetland ['ʃetlənd] *n* (*also: the ~s, the ~ Isles*) die Shetlandinseln *pl*

shield [ʃiːld] *n* Schild *m*; (*fig*) Schirm *m* ♦ *vt* (be)schirmen; (*TECH*) abschirmen

shift [ʃɪft] *n* Verschiebung *f*; (*work*) Schicht *f* ♦ *vt* (ver)rücken, verschieben; (*arm*) wegnehmen ♦ *vi* sich verschieben; **~less** *adj* (*person*) träge; **~ work** *n*

Schichtarbeit f; **~y** adj verschlagen

shilly-shally ['ʃɪlɪʃælɪ] vi zögern

shin [ʃɪn] n Schienbein nt

shine [ʃaɪn] (pt, pp **shone**) n Glanz m, Schein m ♦ vt polieren ♦ vi scheinen; (fig) glänzen; **to ~ a torch on sb** jdn (mit einer Lampe) anleuchten

shingle ['ʃɪŋgl] n Strandkies m; **~s** npl (MED) Gürtelrose f

shiny ['ʃaɪnɪ] adj glänzend

ship [ʃɪp] n Schiff nt ♦ vt verschiffen; **~building** n Schiffbau m; **~ment** n Schiffsladung f; **~per** n Verschiffer m; **~ping** n (act) Verschiffung f; (ships) Schiffahrt f; **~wreck** n Schiffbruch m; (destroyed ship) Wrack nt ♦ vt: **to be ~wrecked** Schiffbruch erleiden; **~yard** n Werft f

shire ['ʃaɪə*] (BRIT) n Grafschaft f

shirk [ʃɜːk] vt ausweichen +dat

shirt [ʃɜːt] n (Ober)hemd nt; **in ~ sleeves** in Hemdsärmeln; **~y** (inf) adj mürrisch

shit [ʃɪt] (inf!) excl Scheiße (!)

shiver ['ʃɪvə*] n Schauer m ♦ vi frösteln, zittern

shoal [ʃəʊl] n (Fisch)schwarm m

shock [ʃɒk] n Erschütterung f; (mental) Schock m; (ELEC) Schlag m ♦ vt erschüttern; (offend) schockieren; **~ absorber** n Stoßdämpfer m; **~ing** adj unerhört

shod [ʃɒd] pt, pp of **shoe** ♦ adj beschuht

shoddy ['ʃɒdɪ] adj schäbig

shoe [ʃuː] (pt, pp **shod**) n Schuh m; (of horse) Hufeisen nt ♦ vt (horse) beschlagen; **~brush** n Schuhbürste f; **~horn** n Schuhlöffel m; **~lace** n Schnürsenkel m; **~ polish** n Schuhcreme f; **~ shop** n Schuhgeschäft nt; **~string** n (fig): **on a ~string** mit sehr wenig Geld

shone [ʃɒn] pt, pp of **shine**

shoo [ʃuː] excl sch; (to dog etc) pfui

shook [ʃʊk] pt of **shake**

shoot [ʃuːt] (pt, pp **shot**) n (branch) Schößling m ♦ vt (gun) abfeuern; (goal, arrow) schießen; (person) anschießen; (kill) erschießen; (film) drehen ♦ vi (gun, move quickly) schießen; **to ~ (at)** schießen (auf +acc); **~ down** vt abschießen; **~ in** vi hineinschießen; **~ out** vi hinausschießen; **~ up** vi (fig) aus dem Boden schießen; **~ing** n Schießerei f; **~ing star** n Sternschnuppe f

shop [ʃɒp] n (esp BRIT) Geschäft nt, Laden m; (work~) Werkstatt f ♦ vi (also: **go ~ping**) einkaufen gehen; **~ assistant** (BRIT) n Verkäufer(in) m(f); **~ floor** (BRIT) n Werkstatt f; **~keeper** n Geschäftsinhaber m; **~lifting** n Ladendiebstahl m; **~per** n Käufer(in) m(f); **~ping** n Einkaufen nt, Einkauf m; **~ping bag** n Einkaufstasche f; **~ping centre** (US **~ping center**) n Einkaufszentrum nt; **~-soiled** adj angeschmutzt; **~ steward** (BRIT) n (INDUSTRY) Betriebsrat m; **~ window** n Schaufenster nt

shore [ʃɔː*] n Ufer nt; (of sea) Strand m ♦ vt: **to ~ up** abstützen

shorn [ʃɔːn] pp of **shear**

short [ʃɔːt] adj kurz; (person) klein; (curt) kurz angebunden; (measure) zu knapp ♦ n (also: **~ film**) Kurzfilm m ♦ adv (suddenly) plötzlich ♦ vi (ELEC) einen Kurzschluß haben; **~s** npl (clothes) Shorts pl; **to be ~ of sth** nicht genug von etw haben; **in ~** kurz gesagt; **~ of doing sth** ohne so weit zu gehen, etw zu tun; **everything ~ of ...** alles außer ...; **it is ~ for** das ist die Kurzform von; **to cut ~** abkürzen; **to fall ~ of sth** etw nicht erreichen; **to stop ~** plötzlich anhalten; **to stop ~ of** haltmachen vor; **~age** n Knappheit f, Mangel m; **~bread** n Mürbegebäck nt; **~change** vt: **to ~-change sb** jdm zuwenig herausgeben; **~-circuit** n Kurzschluß m ♦ vi einen Kurzschluß haben ♦ vt kurzschließen; **~coming** n Mangel m; **~(crust) pastry** (BRIT) n Mürbeteig m; **~ cut** n Abkürzung f; **~en** vt (ab)kürzen; (clothes) kürzer machen; **~fall** n Defizit nt; **~hand** (BRIT) n Stenographie f; **~hand typist** (BRIT) n Stenotypistin f; **~list** (BRIT) n (for job) engere Wahl f; **~-lived** adj kurzlebig; **~ly** adv bald; **~-sighted** (BRIT) adj (also fig) kurzsichtig; **~-staffed** adj: **to be ~-staffed** zu wenig Personal haben; **~ story** n Kurzgeschichte f; **~-tempered**

adj leicht aufbrausend; **~-term** *adj*
(*effect*) kurzfristig; **~ wave** *n* (*RADIO*)
Kurzwelle *f*

shot [ʃɒt] *pt, pp of* **shoot ♦** *n* (*from gun*)
Schuß *m*; (*person*) Schütze *m*; (*try*)
Versuch *m*; (*injection*) Spritze *f*; (*PHOT*)
Aufnahme *f*; **like a ~** wie der Blitz; **~gun**
n Schrotflinte *f*

should [ʃʊd] *vb aux*: **I ~ go now** ich
sollte jetzt gehen; **he ~ be there now** er
sollte eigentlich schon da sein; **I ~ go if I
were you** ich würde gehen, wenn ich du
wäre; **I ~ like to** ich möchte gerne

shoulder ['ʃəʊldə*] *n* Schulter *f*; (*BRIT: of
road*): **hard ~** Seitenstreifen *m* ♦ *vt* (*rifle*)
schultern; (*fig*) auf sich nehmen; **~ bag** *n*
Umhängetasche *f*; **~ blade** *n*
Schulterblatt *nt*; **~ strap** *n* (*MIL*)
Schulterklappe *f*; (*of dress etc*) Träger *m*

shouldn't ['ʃʊdnt] = **should not**

shout [ʃaʊt] *n* Schrei *m*; (*call*) Ruf *m* ♦ *vt*
rufen ♦ *vi* schreien; **~ down** *vt*
niederbrüllen; **~ing** *n* Geschrei *nt*

shove [ʃʌv] *n* Schubs *m*, Stoß *m* ♦ *vt*
schieben, stoßen, schubsen; (*inf: put*): **to
~ sth in(to) sth** etw in etw *acc*
hineinschieben; **~ off** *vi* (*NAUT*) abstoßen;
(*fig: inf*) abhauen

shovel ['ʃʌvl] *n* Schaufel *f* ♦ *vt* schaufeln

show [ʃəʊ] (*pt* **showed**, *pp* **shown**) *n*
(*display*) Schau *f*; (*exhibition*) Ausstellung
f; (*CINE, THEAT*) Vorstellung *f*, Show *f* ♦ *vt*
zeigen; (*kindness*) erweisen ♦ *vi* zu sehen
sein; **to be on ~** (*exhibits etc*) ausgestellt
sein; **to ~ sb in** jdn hereinführen; **to ~ sb
out** jdn hinausbegleiten; **~ off** *vi* (*pej*)
angeben ♦ *vt* (*display*) ausstellen; **~ up** *vi*
(*stand out*) sich abheben; (*arrive*)
erscheinen ♦ *vt* aufzeigen; (*unmask*)
bloßstellen; **~ business** *n* Showbusineß
nt; **~down** *n* Kraftprobe *f*

shower ['ʃaʊə*] *n* Schauer *m*; (*of stones*)
(Stein)hagel *m*; (*~ bath*) Dusche *f* ♦ *vi*
duschen ♦ *vt*: **to ~ sb with sth** jdn mit
etw überschütten; **~proof** *adj*
wasserabstoßend

showing ['ʃəʊɪŋ] *n* Vorführung *f*

show jumping *n* Turnierreiten *nt*

shown [ʃəʊn] *pp of* **show**

show: **~-off** ['ʃəʊɒf] *n* Angeber(in) *m(f)*;
~piece ['ʃəʊpiːs] *n* Paradestück *nt*;
~room ['ʃəʊrʊm] *n* Ausstellungsraum *m*

shrank [ʃræŋk] *pt of* **shrink**

shred [ʃred] *n* Fetzen *m* ♦ *vt* zerfetzen;
(*COOK*) raspeln; **~der** *n* (*for vegetables*)
Gemüseschneider *m*; (*for documents*)
Reißwolf *m*

shrewd [ʃruːd] *adj* clever

shriek [ʃriːk] *n* Schrei *m* ♦ *vt, vi*
kreischen, schreien

shrimp [ʃrɪmp] *n* Krabbe *f*, Garnele *f*

shrink [ʃrɪŋk] (*pt* **shrank**, *pp* **shrunk**) *vi*
schrumpfen, eingehen ♦ *vt* einschrumpfen
lassen; **to ~ from doing sth** davor
zurückschrecken, etw zu tun; **~age** *n*
Schrumpfung *f*; **~wrap** *vt* einschweißen

shrivel ['ʃrɪvl] *vt, vi* (*also: ~ up*)
schrumpfen, schrumpeln

shroud [ʃraʊd] *n* Leichentuch *nt* ♦ *vt*:
~ed in mystery mit einem Geheimnis
umgeben

Shrove Tuesday ['ʃrəʊv-] *n*
Fastnachtsdienstag *m*

shrub [ʃrʌb] *n* Busch *m*, Strauch *m*;
~bery *n* Gebüsch *nt*

shrug [ʃrʌg] *n* Achselzucken *nt* ♦ *vt, vi*:
to ~ (one's shoulders) die Achseln
zucken; **~ off** *vt* auf die leichte Schulter
nehmen

shrunk [ʃrʌŋk] *pp of* **shrink**

shudder ['ʃʌdə*] *n* Schauder *m* ♦ *vi*
schaudern

shuffle ['ʃʌfl] *n* (*CARDS*) (Karten)mischen
nt ♦ *vt* (*cards*) mischen; **to ~ (one's feet)**
schlurfen

shun [ʃʌn] *vt* scheuen, (ver)meiden

shunt [ʃʌnt] *vt* rangieren

shut [ʃʌt] (*pt, pp* **shut**) *vt* schließen,
zumachen ♦ *vi* sich schließen (lassen); **~
down** *vt, vi* schließen; **~ off** *vt* (*supply*)
abdrehen; **~ up** *vi* (*keep quiet*) den Mund
halten ♦ *vt* (*close*) zuschließen; **~ter** *n*
Fensterladen *m*; (*PHOT*) Verschluß *m*

shuttle ['ʃʌtl] *n* (*plane, train etc*)
Pendelflugzeug *nt/*-zug *m* *etc*; (*space ~*)
Raumtransporter *m*; (*also: ~ service*)
Pendelverkehr *m*

shuttlecock ['ʃʌtlkɒk] *n* Federball *m*

shy [ʃaɪ] *adj* schüchtern; **~ness** *n* Schüchternheit *f*

Siamese [saɪə'miːz] *adj*: ~ **cat** Siamkatze *f*

Siberia [saɪ'bɪərɪə] *n* Sibirien *nt*

sibling ['sɪblɪŋ] *n* Geschwister *nt*

Sicily ['sɪsɪlɪ] *n* Sizilien *nt*

sick [sɪk] *adj* krank; (*joke*) makaber; **I feel ~** mir ist schlecht; **I was ~** ich habe gebrochen; **to be ~ of sb/sth** jdn/etw satt haben; **~ bay** *n* (Schiffs)lazarett *nt*; **~en** *vt* (*disgust*) krankmachen ♦ *vi* krank werden; **~ening** *adj* (*sight*) widerlich; (*annoying*) zum Weinen

sickle ['sɪkl] *n* Sichel *f*

sick: ~ **leave** *n*: **to be on ~ leave** krank geschrieben sein; **~ly** *adj* kränklich, blaß; (*causing nausea*) widerlich; **~ness** *n* Krankheit *f*; (*vomiting*) Übelkeit *f*, Erbrechen *nt*; ~ **pay** *n* Krankengeld *nt*

side [saɪd] *n* Seite *f* ♦ *adj* (*door, entrance*) Seiten-, Neben- ♦ *vi*: **to ~ with sb** jds Partei ergreifen; **by the ~ of** neben; ~ **by ~** nebeneinander; **on all ~s** von allen Seiten; **to take ~s (with)** Partei nehmen (für); **from all ~s** von allen Seiten; **~boards** (*BRIT*) *npl* Koteletten *pl*; **~burns** *npl* Koteletten *pl*; **~car** *n* Beiwagen *m*; ~ **drum** *n* (*MUS*) kleine Trommel; **~ effect** *n* Nebenwirkung *f*; **~light** *n* (*AUT*) Parkleuchte *f*; **~line** *n* (*SPORT*) Seitenlinie *f*; (*fig: hobby*) Nebenbeschäftigung *f*; **~long** *adj* Seiten-; **~saddle** *adv* im Damensattel; ~ **show** *n* Nebenausstellung *f*; **~step** *vt* (*fig*) ausweichen; ~ **street** *n* Seitenstraße *f*; **~track** *vt* (*fig*) ablenken; **~walk** (*US*) *n* Bürgersteig *m*; **~ways** *adv* seitwärts

siding ['saɪdɪŋ] *n* Nebengleis *nt*

sidle ['saɪdl] *vi*: **to ~ up (to)** sich heranmachen (an +*acc*)

siege [siːdʒ] *n* Belagerung *f*

sieve [sɪv] *n* Sieb *nt* ♦ *vt* sieben

sift [sɪft] *vt* sieben; (*fig*) sichten

sigh [saɪ] *n* Seufzer *m* ♦ *vi* seufzen

sight [saɪt] *n* (*power of seeing*) Sehvermögen *nt*; (*look*) Blick *m*; (*fact of seeing*) Anblick *m*; (*of gun*) Visier *nt* ♦ *vt* sichten; **in ~** in Sicht; **out of ~** außer

Sicht; **~seeing** *n* Besuch *m* von Sehenswürdigkeiten; **to go ~seeing** Sehenswürdigkeiten besichtigen

sign [saɪn] *n* Zeichen *nt*; (*notice, road ~ etc*) Schild *nt* ♦ *vt* unterschreiben; **to ~ sth over to sb** jdm etw überschreiben; ~ **on** *vi* (*MIL*) sich verpflichten; (*as unemployed*) sich (arbeitslos) melden ♦ *vt* (*MIL*) unterschreiben; (*employee*) anstellen; ~ **up** *vi* (*MIL*) sich verpflichten ♦ *vt* verpflichten

signal ['sɪgnl] *n* Signal *nt* ♦ *vt* ein Zeichen geben +*dat*; **~man** (*irreg*) *n* (*RAIL*) Stellwerkswärter *m*

signature ['sɪgnətʃə*] *n* Unterschrift *f*; ~ **tune** *n* Erkennungsmelodie *f*

signet ring ['sɪgnət-] *n* Siegelring *m*

significance [sɪg'nɪfɪkəns] *n* Bedeutung *f*

significant [sɪg'nɪfɪkənt] *adj* (*meaning sth*) bedeutsam; (*important*) bedeutend

signify ['sɪgnɪfaɪ] *vt* bedeuten; (*show*) andeuten, zu verstehen geben

sign language *n* Zeichensprache *f*, Fingersprache *f*

signpost ['saɪnpəʊst] *n* Wegweiser *m*

silence ['saɪləns] *n* Stille *f*; (*of person*) Schweigen *nt* ♦ *vt* zum Schweigen bringen; **~r** *n* (*on gun*) Schalldämpfer *m*; (*BRIT: AUT*) Auspufftopf *m*

silent ['saɪlənt] *adj* still; (*person*) schweigsam; **to remain ~** schweigen; ~ **partner** *n* (*COMM*) stille(r) Teilhaber *m*

silicon chip ['sɪlɪkən-] *n* Siliciumchip *nt*

silk [sɪlk] *n* Seide *f* ♦ *adj* seiden, Seiden-; **~y** *adj* seidig

silly ['sɪlɪ] *adj* dumm, albern

silt [sɪlt] *n* Schlamm *m*, Schlick *m*

silver ['sɪlvə*] *n* Silber *nt* ♦ *adj* silbern, Silber-; ~ **paper** (*BRIT*) *n* Silberpapier *nt*; **~-plated** *adj* versilbert; **~smith** *n* Silberschmied *m*; **~ware** *n* Silber *nt*; **~y** *adj* silbern

similar ['sɪmɪlə*] *adj*: ~ **(to)** ähnlich (+*dat*); **~ity** [sɪmɪ'lærɪtɪ] *n* Ähnlichkeit *f*; **~ly** *adv* in ähnlicher Weise

simile ['sɪmɪlɪ] *n* Vergleich *m*

simmer ['sɪmə*] *vi* sieden ♦ *vt* sieden lassen

simpering ['sɪmpərɪŋ] *adj* albern

simple ['sɪmpl] *adj* einfach; **~(-minded)** *adj* einfältig; **~ton** *n* Einfaltspinsel *m*
simplicity [sɪm'plɪsɪtɪ] *n* Einfachheit *f*; *(of person)* Einfältigkeit *f*
simplify ['sɪmplɪfaɪ] *vt* vereinfachen
simply ['sɪmplɪ] *adv* einfach
simulate ['sɪmjuleɪt] *vt* simulieren
simultaneous [sɪməl'teɪnɪəs] *adj* gleichzeitig
sin [sɪn] *n* Sünde *f* ♦ *vi* sündigen
since [sɪns] *adv* seither ♦ *prep* seit, seitdem ♦ *conj (time)* seit; *(because)* da, weil; **~ then** seitdem
sincere [sɪn'sɪə*] *adj* aufrichtig; **~ly** *adv*: **yours ~ly** mit freundlichen Grüßen
sincerity [sɪn'serɪtɪ] *n* Aufrichtigkeit *f*
sinew ['sɪnjuː] *n* Sehne *f*
sinful ['sɪnful] *adj* sündig, sündhaft
sing [sɪŋ] *(pt* **sang,** *pp* **sung)** *vt, vi* singen
Singapore [sɪŋə'pɔː*] *n* Singapur *nt*
singe [sɪndʒ] *vt* versengen
singer ['sɪŋə*] *n* Sänger(in) *m(f)*
single ['sɪŋgl] *adj (one only)* einzig; *(bed, room)* Einzel-, einzeln; *(unmarried)* ledig; *(BRIT: ticket)* einfach; *(having one part only)* einfache Fahrkarte *f*; **in ~ file** hintereinander; **~ out** *vt* aussuchen, auswählen; **~ bed** *n* Einzelbett *nt*; **~-breasted** *adj* einreihig; **~-handed** *adj* allein; **~-minded** *adj* zielstrebig; **~ room** *n* Einzelzimmer *nt*; **~s** *n (TENNIS)* Einzel *nt*
singlet ['sɪŋglət] *n* Unterhemd *nt*
singly ['sɪŋglɪ] *adv* einzeln, allein
singular ['sɪŋgjulə*] *adj (GRAM)* Singular-; *(odd)* merkwürdig, seltsam ♦ *n (GRAM)* Einzahl *f*, Singular *m*
sinister ['sɪnɪstə*] *adj (evil)* böse; *(ghostly)* unheimlich
sink [sɪŋk] *(pt* **sank,** *pp* **sunk)** *n* Spülbecken *nt* ♦ *vt (ship)* versenken ♦ *vi* sinken; **to ~ sth into** *(teeth, claws)* etw schlagen in *+acc*; **~ in** *vi (news etc)* eingehen
sinner ['sɪnə*] *n* Sünder(in) *m(f)*
sinus ['saɪnəs] *n (ANAT)* Sinus *m*
sip [sɪp] *n* Schlückchen *nt* ♦ *vt* nippen an *+dat*
siphon ['saɪfən] *n* Siphon(flasche *f*) *m*; **~**

off *vt* absaugen; *(fig)* abschöpfen
sir [sɜː*] *n (respect)* Herr *m*; *(knight)* Sir *m*; **S~ John Smith** Sir John Smith; **yes ~** ja(wohl, mein Herr)
siren ['saɪərən] *n* Sirene *f*
sirloin ['sɜːlɔɪn] *n* Lendenstück *nt*
sissy ['sɪsɪ] *(inf)* *n* Waschlappen *m*
sister ['sɪstə*] *n* Schwester *f*; *(BRIT: nurse)* Oberschwester *f*; *(nun)* Ordensschwester *f*; **~-in-law** *n* Schwägerin *f*
sit [sɪt] *(pt, pp* **sat)** *vi* sitzen; *(hold session)* tagen ♦ *vt (exam)* machen; **~ down** *vi* sich hinsetzen; **~ in on** *vt fus* dabeisein bei; **~ up** *vi (after lying)* sich aufsetzen; *(straight)* sich gerade setzen; *(at night)* aufbleiben
sitcom ['sɪtkɒm] *n abbr (= situation comedy)* Situationskomödie *f*
site [saɪt] *n* Platz *m*; *(also: building ~)* Baustelle *f* ♦ *vt* legen
sitting ['sɪtɪŋ] *n (meeting)* Sitzung *f*; **~ room** *n* Wohnzimmer *nt*
situated ['sɪtjueɪtɪd] *adj*: **to be ~** liegen
situation [sɪtjʊ'eɪʃən] *n* Situation *f*, Lage *f*; *(place)* Lage *f*; *(employment)* Stelle *f*; **"~s vacant"** *(BRIT)* „Stellenangebote" *pl*
six [sɪks] *num* sechs; **~teen** *num* sechzehn; **~th** *adj* sechste(r, s) ♦ *n* Sechstel *nt*; **~ty** *num* sechzig
size [saɪz] *n* Größe *f*; *(of project)* Umfang *m*; **~ up** *vt (assess)* abschätzen, einschätzen; **~able** *adj* ziemlich groß, ansehnlich
sizzle ['sɪzl] *vi* zischen; *(COOK)* brutzeln
skate [skeɪt] *n* Schlittschuh *m*; *(fish: pl inv)* Rochen *m* ♦ *vi* Schlittschuh laufen; **~r** *n* Schlittschuhläufer(in) *m(f)*
skating ['skeɪtɪŋ] *n* Eislauf *m*; **to go ~** Eislaufen gehen; **~ rink** *n* Eisbahn *f*
skeleton ['skelɪtn] *n* Skelett *nt*; *(fig)* Gerüst *nt*; **~ key** *n* Dietrich *m*; **~ staff** *n* Notbesetzung *f*
skeptical ['skeptɪkl] *(US) adj* = **sceptical**
sketch [sketʃ] *n* Skizze *f*; *(THEAT)* Sketch *m* ♦ *vt* skizzieren; **~book** *n* Skizzenbuch *nt*; **~y** *adj* skizzenhaft
skewer ['skjuə*] *n* Fleischspieß *m*
ski [skiː] *n* Ski *m*, Schi *m* ♦ *vi* Ski *or* Schi laufen; **~ boot** *n* Skistiefel *m*

skid [skɪd] *n* (AUT) Schleudern *nt* ♦ *vi* rutschen; (AUT) schleudern

skier ['skiːə*] *n* Skiläufer(in) *m(f)*

skiing ['skiːɪŋ] *n*: **to go ~** Skilaufen gehen

ski-jump *n* Sprungschanze *f* ♦ *vi* Ski springen

skilful ['skɪlful] *adj* geschickt

ski-lift *n* Skilift *m*

skill [skɪl] *n* Können *nt*; **~ed** *adj* geschickt; (*worker*) Fach-, gelernt

skim [skɪm] *vt* (*liquid*) abschöpfen; (*glide over*) gleiten über +*acc* ♦ *vi*: **~ through** (*book*) überfliegen; **~med milk** *n* Magermilch *f*

skimp [skɪmp] *vt* (*do carelessly*) oberflächlich tun; **~y** *adj* (*work*) schlecht gemacht; (*dress*) knapp

skin [skɪn] *n* Haut *f*; (*peel*) Schale *f* ♦ *vt* abhäuten; schälen; **~ cancer** *n* Hautkrebs *m*; **~-deep** *adj* oberflächlich; **~ diving** *n* Schwimmtauchen *nt*; **~ny** *adj* dünn; **~tight** *adj* (*dress etc*) hauteng

skip [skɪp] *n* Sprung *m* ♦ *vi* hüpfen; (*with rope*) Seil springen ♦ *vt* (*pass over*) übergehen

ski pants *npl* Skihosen *pl*

ski pole *n* Skistock *m*

skipper ['skɪpə*] *n* Kapitän *m* ♦ *vt* führen

skipping rope ['skɪpɪŋ-] (BRIT) *n* Hüpfseil *nt*

skirmish ['skɜːmɪʃ] *n* Scharmützel *nt*

skirt [skɜːt] *n* Rock *m* ♦ *vt* herumgehen um; (*fig*) umgehen; **~ing board** (BRIT) *n* Fußleiste *f*

ski suit *n* Skianzug *m*

skit [skɪt] *n* Parodie *f*

skittle ['skɪtl] *n* Kegel *m*; **~s** *n* (*game*) Kegeln *nt*

skive [skaɪv] (BRIT: *inf*) *vi* schwänzen

skulk [skʌlk] *vi* sich herumdrücken

skull [skʌl] *n* Schädel *m*

skunk [skʌŋk] *n* Stinktier *nt*

sky [skaɪ] *n* Himmel *m*; **~light** *n* Oberlicht *nt*; **~scraper** *n* Wolkenkratzer *m*

slab [slæb] *n* (*of stone*) Platte *f*

slack [slæk] *adj* (*loose*) locker; (*business*) flau; (*careless*) nachlässig, lasch ♦ *vi*

nachlässig sein ♦ *n*: **to take up the ~** straffziehen; **~s** *npl* (*trousers*) Hose(n *pl*) *f*; **~en** *vi* (*also*: *~en off*) locker werden; (: *become slower*) nachlassen, stocken ♦ *vt* (: *loosen*) lockern

slag [slæg] *n* Schlacke *f*; **~ heap** *n* Halde *f*

slain [sleɪn] *pp* of **slay**

slam [slæm] *n* Knall *m* ♦ *vt* (*door*) zuschlagen; (*throw down*) knallen ♦ *vi* zuschlagen

slander ['slɑːndə*] *n* Verleumdung *f* ♦ *vt* verleumden

slant [slɑːnt] *n* Schräge *f*; (*fig*) Tendenz *f* ♦ *vt* schräg legen ♦ *vi* schräg liegen; **~ed** *adj* schräg; **~ing** *adj* schräg

slap [slæp] *n* Klaps *m* ♦ *vt* einen Klaps geben +*dat* ♦ *adv* (*directly*) geradewegs; **~dash** *adj* salopp; **~stick** *n* (*comedy*) Klamauk *m*; **~-up** (BRIT) *adj* (*meal*) erstklassig, prima

slash [slæʃ] *n* Schnittwunde *f* ♦ *vt* (auf)schlitzen; (*expenditure*) radikal kürzen

slat [slæt] *n* (*of wood, plastic*) Leiste *f*

slate [sleɪt] *n* (*stone*) Schiefer *m*; (*roofing*) Dachziegel *m* ♦ *vt* (*criticize*) verreißen

slaughter ['slɔːtə*] *n* (*of animals*) Schlachten *nt*; (*of people*) Gemetzel *nt* ♦ *vt* schlachten; (*people*) niedermetzeln; **~house** *n* Schlachthof *m*

Slav [slɑːv] *adj* slawisch

slave [sleɪv] *n* Sklave *m*, Sklavin *f* ♦ *vi* schuften, sich schinden; **~ry** *n* Sklaverei *f*; (*work*) Schinderei *f*

slay [sleɪ] (*pt* **slew**, *pp* **slain**) *vt* ermorden

sleazy ['sliːzɪ] *adj* (*place*) schmierig

sledge [sledʒ] *n* Schlitten *m*; **~hammer** *n* Schmiedehammer *m*

sleek [sliːk] *adj* glatt; (*shape*) rassig

sleep [sliːp] (*pt, pp* **slept**) *n* Schlaf *m* ♦ *vi* schlafen; **to go to ~** einschlafen; **~ in** *vi* ausschlafen; (*oversleep*) verschlafen; **~er** *n* (*person*) Schläfer *m*; (BRIT: RAIL) Schlafwagen *m*; (: *beam*) Schwelle *f*; **~ing bag** *n* Schlafsack *m*; **~ing car** *n* Schlafwagen *m*; **~ing pill** *n* Schlaftablette *f*; **~less** *adj* (*night*) schlaflos; **~walker** *n* Schlafwandler(in) *m(f)*; **~y** *adj* schläfrig

sleet [sliːt] n Schneeregen m
sleeve [sliːv] n Ärmel m; (of record)
Umschlag m; **~less** adj ärmellos
sleigh [sleɪ] n Pferdeschlitten m
sleight [slaɪt] n: **~ of hand**
Fingerfertigkeit f
slender ['slendə*] adj schlank; (fig)
gering
slept [slept] pt, pp of **sleep**
slew [sluː] vi (veer) (herum)schwenken
♦ pt of **slay**
slice [slaɪs] n Scheibe f ♦ vt in Scheiben
schneiden
slick [slɪk] adj (clever) raffiniert, aalglatt
♦ n Ölteppich m
slid [slɪd] pt, pp of **slide**
slide [slaɪd] (pt, pp **slid**) n Rutschbahn f;
(PHOT) Dia(positiv) nt; (BRIT: for hair)
(Haar)spange f ♦ vt schieben ♦ vi (slip)
gleiten, rutschen
sliding ['slaɪdɪŋ] adj (door) Schiebe-; **~
scale** n gleitende Skala f
slight [slaɪt] adj zierlich; (trivial)
geringfügig; (small) gering ♦ n Kränkung
f ♦ vt (offend) kränken; **not in the ~est**
nicht im geringsten; **~ly** adv etwas, ein
bißchen
slim [slɪm] adj schlank; (book) dünn;
(chance) gering ♦ vi eine Schlankheitskur
machen
slime [slaɪm] n Schleim m
slimming ['slɪmɪŋ] n Schlankheitskur f
slimy ['slaɪmɪ] adj glitschig; (dirty)
schlammig; (person) schmierig
sling [slɪŋ] (pt, pp **slung**) n Schlinge f;
(weapon) Schleuder f ♦ vt schleudern
slip [slɪp] n (mistake) Flüchtigkeitsfehler
m; (petticoat) Unterrock m; (of paper)
Zettel m ♦ vt (put) stecken, schieben ♦ vi
(lose balance) ausrutschen; (move) gleiten,
rutschen; (decline) nachlassen; (move
smoothly): **to ~ in/out** (person) hinein-/
hinausschlüpfen; **to give sb the ~** jdm
entwischen; **~ of the tongue** Versprecher
m; **it ~ped my mind** das ist mir
entfallen; **to ~ sth on/off** etw über-/
abstreifen; **~ away** vi sich wegstehlen; **~
by** vi (time) verstreichen; **~ in** vt
hineingleiten lassen ♦ vi (errors) sich

einschleichen; **~ped disc** n
Bandscheibenschaden m
slipper ['slɪpə*] n Hausschuh m
slippery ['slɪpərɪ] adj glatt
slip: **~-road** (BRIT) n Auffahrt f/Ausfahrt
f; **~shod** ['slɪpʃɒd] adj schlampig; **~-up**
['slɪpʌp] n Panne f; **~way** ['slɪpweɪ] n
Auslaufbahn f
slit [slɪt] (pt, pp **slit**) n Schlitz m ♦ vt
aufschlitzen
slither ['slɪðə*] vi schlittern; (snake) sich
schlängeln
sliver ['slɪvə*] n (of glass, wood) Splitter
m; (of cheese etc) Scheibchen nt
slob [slɒb] (inf) n Klotz m
slog [slɒg] vi (work hard) schuften ♦ n: **it
was a ~** es war eine Plackerei
slogan ['sləʊgən] n Schlagwort nt; (COMM)
Werbespruch m
slop [slɒp] vi (also: ~ over)
überschwappen ♦ vt verschütten
slope [sləʊp] n Neigung f; (of mountains)
(Ab)hang m ♦ vi: **to ~ down** sich senken;
to ~ up ansteigen
sloping ['sləʊpɪŋ] adj schräg
sloppy ['slɒpɪ] adj schlampig
slot [slɒt] n Schlitz m ♦ vt: **to ~ sth in**
etw einlegen
sloth [sləʊθ] n (laziness) Faulheit f
slot machine n (BRIT: vending machine)
Automat m; (for gambling) Spielautomat
m
slouch [slaʊtʃ] vi: **to ~ about** (laze)
herumhängen (inf)
slovenly ['slʌvnlɪ] adj schlampig; (speech)
salopp
slow [sləʊ] adj langsam ♦ adv langsam;
to be ~ (clock) nachgehen; (stupid)
begriffsstutzig sein; **"~"** (road sign)
„Langsam"; **in ~ motion** in Zeitlupe; **~
down** vi langsamer werden ♦ vt
verlangsamen; **~ up** vi sich
verlangsamen, sich verzögern ♦ vt
aufhalten, langsamer machen; **~ly** adv
langsam
sludge [slʌdʒ] n Schlamm m
slug [slʌg] n Nacktschnecke f; (inf: bullet)
Kugel f; **~gish** adj träge; (COMM)
schleppend

sluice [sluːs] *n* Schleuse *f*

slum [slʌm] *n (house)* Elendsquartier *nt*

slumber ['slʌmbə*] *n* Schlummer *m*

slump [slʌmp] *n* Rückgang *m* ♦ *vi* fallen, stürzen

slung [slʌŋ] *pt, pp of* **sling**

slur [slɜː*] *n* Undeutlichkeit *f*; *(insult)* Verleumdung *f*; ~**red** [slɜːd] *adj (pronunciation)* undeutlich

slush [slʌʃ] *n (snow)* Schneematsch *m*; ~ **fund** *n* Schmiergeldfonds *m*

slut [slʌt] *n* Schlampe *f*

sly [slaɪ] *adj* schlau

smack [smæk] *n* Klaps *m* ♦ *vt* einen Klaps geben +*dat* ♦ *vi*: **to ~ of** riechen nach; **to ~ one's lips** schmatzen, sich *dat* die Lippen lecken

small [smɔːl] *adj* klein; **in the ~ hours** in den frühen Morgenstunden; ~ **ads** *(BRIT) npl* Kleinanzeigen *pl*; ~ **change** *n* Kleingeld *nt*; ~ **holder** *(BRIT) n* Kleinbauer *m*; ~**pox** *n* Pocken *pl*; ~ **talk** *n* Geplauder *nt*

smart [smɑːt] *adj (fashionable)* elegant, schick; *(neat)* adrett; *(clever)* clever; *(quick)* scharf ♦ *vi* brennen, schmerzen; ~**en up** *vi* sich in Schale werfen ♦ *vt* herausputzen

smash [smæʃ] *n* Zusammenstoß *m*; *(TENNIS)* Schmetterball *m* ♦ *vt (break)* zerschmettern; *(destroy)* vernichten ♦ *vi (break)* zersplittern, zerspringen; ~**ing** *(inf) adj* toll

smattering ['smætərɪŋ] *n* oberflächliche Kenntnis *f*

smear [smɪə*] *n* Fleck *m* ♦ *vt* beschmieren

smell [smel] *(pt, pp* **smelt** *or* **smelled)** *n* Geruch *m*; *(sense)* Geruchssinn *m* ♦ *vt* riechen ♦ *vi*: **to ~ (of)** riechen (nach); *(fragrantly)* duften (nach); ~**y** *adj* übelriechend

smile [smaɪl] *n* Lächeln *nt* ♦ *vi* lächeln

smiling ['smaɪlɪŋ] *adj* lächelnd

smirk [smɜːk] *n* blöde(s) Grinsen *nt*

smith [smɪθ] *n* Schmied *m*; ~**y** ['smɪðɪ] *n* Schmiede *f*

smock [smɒk] *n* Kittel *m*

smoke [sməʊk] *n* Rauch *m* ♦ *vt* rauchen;

(food) räuchern ♦ *vi* rauchen; ~**d** *adj (bacon)* geräuchert; *(glass)* Rauch-; ~**r** *n* Raucher(in) *m(f)*; *(RAIL)* Raucherabteil *nt*; ~ **screen** *n* Rauchwand *f*

smoking ['sməʊkɪŋ] *n*: **"no ~"** „Rauchen verboten"

smoky ['sməʊkɪ] *adj* rauchig; *(room)* verraucht; *(taste)* geräuchert

smolder ['sməʊldə*] *(US) vi* = **smoulder**

smooth [smuːð] *adj* glatt ♦ *vt (also: ~ out)* glätten, glattstreichen

smother ['smʌðə*] *vt* ersticken

smoulder ['sməʊldə*] *(US* **smolder)** *vi* schwelen

smudge [smʌdʒ] *n* Schmutzfleck *m* ♦ *vt* beschmieren

smug [smʌg] *adj* selbstgefällig

smuggle ['smʌgl] *vt* schmuggeln; ~**r** *n* Schmuggler *m*

smuggling ['smʌglɪŋ] *n* Schmuggel *m*

smutty ['smʌtɪ] *adj* schmutzig

snack [snæk] *n* Imbiß *m*; ~ **bar** *n* Imbißstube *f*

snag [snæg] *n* Haken *m*

snail [sneɪl] *n* Schnecke *f*

snake [sneɪk] *n* Schlange *f*

snap [snæp] *n* Schnappen *nt*; *(photograph)* Schnappschuß *m* ♦ *adj (decision)* schnell ♦ *vt (break)* zerbrechen; *(PHOT)* knipsen ♦ *vi (break)* brechen; *(speak)* anfauchen; **to ~ shut** zuschnappen; ~ **at** *vt fus* schnappen nach; ~ **off** *vt (break)* abbrechen; ~ **up** *vt* aufschnappen; ~**py** *adj* flott; ~**shot** *n* Schnappschuß *m*

snare [snɛə*] *n* Schlinge *f* ♦ *vt* mit einer Schlinge fangen

snarl [snɑːl] *n* Zähnefletschen *nt* ♦ *vi (dog)* knurren

snatch [snætʃ] *n (small amount)* Bruchteil *m* ♦ *vt* schnappen, packen

sneak [sniːk] *vi* schleichen ♦ *n (inf)* Petze(r) *mf*

sneakers ['sniːkəz] *(US) npl* Freizeitschuhe *pl*

sneaky ['sniːkɪ] *adj* raffiniert

sneer [snɪə*] *n* Hohnlächeln *nt* ♦ *vi* spötteln

sneeze [sniːz] *n* Niesen *nt* ♦ *vi* niesen

sniff [snɪf] *n* Schnüffeln *nt* ♦ *vi* schnieben; (*smell*) schnüffeln ♦ *vt* schnuppern

snigger ['snɪgə*] *n* Kichern *nt* ♦ *vi* hämisch kichern

snip [snɪp] *n* Schnippel *m*, Schnipsel *m* ♦ *vt* schnippeln

sniper ['snaɪpə*] *n* Heckenschütze *m*

snippet ['snɪpɪt] *n* Schnipsel *m*; (*of conversation*) Fetzen *m*

snivelling ['snɪvlɪŋ] *adj* weinerlich

snooker ['snuːkə*] *n* Snooker *nt*

snoop [snuːp] *vi*: **to ~ about** herumschnüffeln

snooty ['snuːtɪ] (*inf*) *adj* hochnäsig

snooze [snuːz] *n* Nickerchen *nt* ♦ *vi* ein Nickerchen machen, dösen

snore [snɔː*] *vi* schnarchen ♦ *n* Schnarchen *nt*

snorkel ['snɔːkl] *n* Schnorchel *m*

snort [snɔːt] *n* Schnauben *nt* ♦ *vi* schnauben

snout [snaut] *n* Schnauze *f*

snow [snəu] *n* Schnee *m* ♦ *vi* schneien; **~ball** *n* Schneeball *m* ♦ *vi* eskalieren; **~bound** *adj* eingeschneit; **~drift** *n* Schneewehe *f*; **~drop** *n* Schneeglöckchen *nt*; **~fall** *n* Schneefall *m*; **~flake** *n* Schneeflocke *f*; **~man** (*irreg*) *n* Schneemann *m*; **~plough** (*US* **~plow**) *n* Schneepflug *m*; **~ shoe** *n* Schneeschuh *m*; **~storm** *n* Schneesturm *m*

snub [snʌb] *vt* schroff abfertigen ♦ *n* Verweis *m*; **~-nosed** *adj* stupsnasig

snuff [snʌf] *n* Schnupftabak *m*

snug [snʌg] *adj* gemütlich, behaglich

snuggle ['snʌgl] *vi*: **to ~ up to sb** sich an jdn kuscheln

---
KEYWORD
---

so [səu] *adv* **1** (*thus*) so; (*likewise*) auch; **so saying he walked away** indem er das sagte, ging er; **if so** wenn ja; **I didn't do it — you did so!** ich hab das nicht gemacht — hast du wohl!; **so do I, so am I** *etc* ich auch; **so it is!** tatsächlich!; **I hope/think so** hoffentlich/ich glaube schon; **so far** bis jetzt

2 (*in comparisons etc: to such a degree*) so; **so quickly/big (that)** so schnell/groß, daß; **I'm so glad to see you** ich freue mich so, dich zu sehen

3 so many so viele; **so much work** so viel Arbeit; **I love you so much** ich liebe dich so sehr

4 (*phrases*): **10 or so** etwa 10; **so long!** (*inf: goodbye*) tschüs!

♦ *conj* **1** (*expressing purpose*): **so as to** um ... zu; **so (that)** damit

2 (*expressing result*) also; **so I was right after all** ich hatte also doch recht; **so you see ...** wie du siehst ...

---

soak [səuk] *vt* durchnässen; (*leave in liquid*) einweichen ♦ *vi* (ein)weichen; **~ in** *vi* einsickern; **~ up** *vt* aufsaugen

so-and-so ['səuənsəu] *n* (*somebody*) Soundso *m*

soap [səup] *n* Seife *f*; **~flakes** *npl* Seifenflocken *pl*; **~ opera** *n* Familienserie *f* (*im Fernsehen, Radio*); **~ powder** *n* Waschpulver *nt*; **~y** *adj* seifig, Seifen-

soar [sɔː*] *vi* aufsteigen; (*prices*) in die Höhe schnellen

sob [sɒb] *n* Schluchzen *nt* ♦ *vi* schluchzen

sober ['səubə*] *adj* (*also fig*) nüchtern; **~ up** *vi* nüchtern werden

so-called ['səu'kɔːld] *adj* sogenannt

soccer ['sɒkə*] *n* Fußball *m*

sociable ['səuʃəbl] *adj* gesellig

social ['səuʃəl] *adj* sozial; (*friendly, living with others*) gesellig ♦ *n* gesellige(r) Abend *m*; **~ club** *n* Verein *m* (*für Freizeitgestaltung*); **~ism** *n* Sozialismus *m*; **~ist** *n* Sozialist(in) *m(f)* ♦ *adj* sozialistisch; **~ize** *vi*: **to ~ize (with)** gesellschaftlich verkehren (mit); **~ly** *adv* gesellschaftlich, privat; **~ security** *n* Sozialversicherung *f*; **~ work** *n* Sozialarbeit *f*; **~ worker** *n* Sozialarbeiter(in) *m(f)*

society [sə'saɪətɪ] *n* Gesellschaft *f*; (*fashionable world*) die große Welt

sociology [səusɪ'ɒlədʒɪ] *n* Soziologie *f*

sock [sɒk] *n* Socke *f*

socket ['sɒkɪt] *n* (*ELEC*) Steckdose *f*; (*of eye*) Augenhöhle *f*; (*TECH*) Rohransatz *m*

sod [sɒd] n Rasenstück nt; (inf!) Saukerl m (!)

soda ['səʊdə] n Soda f; (also: ~ water) Soda(wasser) nt; (US: also: ~ pop) Limonade f

sodden ['sɒdn] adj durchweicht

sodium ['səʊdɪəm] n Natrium nt

sofa ['səʊfə] n Sofa nt

soft [sɒft] adj weich; (not loud) leise; (weak) nachgiebig; ~ **drink** n alkoholfreie(s) Getränk nt; **~en** ['sɒfn] vt weich machen; (bread) aufgeweicht machen; (blow) abschwächen, mildern ♦ vi weich werden; **~ly** adv sanft; leise; **~ness** n Weichheit f; (fig) Sanftheit f

software ['sɒftweə*] n (COMPUT) Software f

soggy ['sɒgɪ] adj (ground) sumpfig; (bread) aufgeweicht

soil [sɔɪl] n Erde f ♦ vt beschmutzen; **~ed** adj beschmutzt

solace ['sɒləs] n Trost m

solar ['səʊlə*] adj Sonnen-; ~ **cell** n Solarzelle f; ~ **energy** n Sonnenenergie f; ~ **panel** n Sonnenkollektor m; ~ **power** n Sonnenenergie f

sold [səʊld] pt, pp of **sell**; ~ **out** (COMM) ausverkauft

solder ['səʊldə*] vt löten ♦ n Lötmetall nt

soldier ['səʊldʒə*] n Soldat m

sole [səʊl] n Sohle f; (fish) Seezunge f ♦ adj alleinig, Allein-; **~ly** adv ausschließlich

solemn ['sɒləm] adj feierlich

sole trader n (COMM) Einzelunternehmen nt

solicit [sə'lɪsɪt] vt (request) bitten um ♦ vi (prostitute) Kunden anwerben

solicitor [sə'lɪsɪtə*] n Rechtsanwalt m/ -anwältin f

solid ['sɒlɪd] adj (hard) fest; (of same material, not hollow) massiv; (without break) voll, ganz; (reliable, sensible) solide ♦ n Festkörper m

solidarity [sɒlɪ'dærɪtɪ] n Solidarität f

solidify [sə'lɪdɪfaɪ] vi fest werden

solitary ['sɒlɪtərɪ] adj einsam, einzeln; ~ **confinement** n Einzelhaft f

solitude ['sɒlɪtjuːd] n Einsamkeit f

solo ['səʊləʊ] n Solo nt

soloist ['səʊləʊɪst] n Solist(in) m(f)

soluble ['sɒljʊbl] adj (substance) löslich; (problem) (auf)lösbar

solution [sə'luːʃən] n (also fig) Lösung f; (of mystery) Erklärung f

solve [sɒlv] vt (auf)lösen

solvent ['sɒlvənt] adj (FIN) zahlungsfähig ♦ n (CHEM) Lösungsmittel nt

sombre ['sɒmbə*] (US **somber**) adj düster

KEYWORD

some [sʌm] adj **1** (a certain amount or number of) einige; (a few) ein paar; (with singular nouns) etwas; **some tea/biscuits** etwas Tee/ein paar Plätzchen; **I've got some money, but not much** ich habe ein bißchen Geld, aber nicht viel

2 (certain: in contrasts) manche(r, s); **some people say that ...** manche Leute sagen, daß ...

3 (unspecified) irgendein(e); **some woman was asking for you** da hat eine Frau nach Ihnen gefragt; **some day** eines Tages; **some day next week** irgendwann nächste Woche

♦ pron **1** (a certain number) einige; **have you got some?** haben Sie welche?

2 (a certain amount) etwas; **I've read some of the book** ich habe das Buch teilweise gelesen

♦ adv: **some 10 people** etwa 10 Leute

somebody ['sʌmbədɪ] pron = **someone**

somehow ['sʌmhaʊ] adv (in some way, for some reason) irgendwie

someone ['sʌmwʌn] pron jemand; (direct obj) jemand(en); (indirect obj) jemandem

someplace ['sʌmpleɪs] (US) adv = **somewhere**

somersault ['sʌməsɔːlt] n Salto m ♦ vi einen Salto machen

something ['sʌmθɪŋ] pron etwas

sometime ['sʌmtaɪm] adv (irgend)einmal

sometimes ['sʌmtaɪmz] adv manchmal

somewhat ['sʌmwɒt] adv etwas

somewhere ['sʌmweə*] adv irgendwo; (to a place) irgendwohin; ~ **else** irgendwo anders

son [sʌn] *n* Sohn *m*
sonar ['səunɑ:*] *n* Echolot *nt*
song [sɒŋ] *n* Lied *nt*
sonic boom *n* Überschallknall *m*
son-in-law ['sʌnɪnlɔ:] *n* Schwiegersohn *m*
sonny ['sʌnɪ] (*inf*) *n* Kleine(r) *m*
soon [su:n] *adv* bald; ~ **afterwards** kurz danach; ~**er** *adv* (*time*) früher; (*for preference*) lieber; ~**er or later** früher oder später
soot [sut] *n* Ruß *m*
soothe [su:ð] *vt* (*person*) beruhigen; (*pain*) lindern
sophisticated [sə'fɪstɪkeɪtɪd] *adj* (*person*) kultiviert; (*machinery*) hochentwickelt
sophomore ['sɒfəmɔ:*] (*US*) *n* College-Student *m* im 2. Jahr
soporific [sɒpə'rɪfɪk] *adj* einschläfernd
sopping ['sɒpɪŋ] *adj* patschnaß
soppy ['sɒpɪ] (*inf*) *adj* schmalzig
soprano [sə'prɑ:nəu] *n* Sopran *m*
sorcerer ['sɔ:sərə*] *n* Hexenmeister *m*
sordid ['sɔ:dɪd] *adj* erbärmlich
sore [sɔ:*] *adj* schmerzend; (*point*) wund ♦ *n* Wunde *f*; ~**ly** *adv* (*tempted*) stark, sehr
sorrow ['sɒrəu] *n* Kummer *m*, Leid *nt*; ~**ful** *adj* sorgenvoll
sorry ['sɒrɪ] *adj* traurig, erbärmlich; ~! Entschuldigung!; **to feel** ~ **for sb** jdn bemitleiden; **I feel** ~ **for him** er tut mir leid; ~? (*pardon*) wie bitte?
sort [sɔ:t] *n* Art *f*, Sorte *f* ♦ *vt* (*also*: ~ *out: papers*) sortieren; (: *problems*) sichten, in Ordnung bringen; ~**ing office** *n* Sortierstelle *f*
SOS *n* SOS *nt*
so-so ['səu'səu] *adv* so(-so) la-la
sought [sɔ:t] *pt, pp of* **seek**
soul [səul] *n* Seele *f*; (*music*) Soul *m*; ~-**destroying** *adj* trostlos; ~**ful** *adj* seelenvoll
sound [saund] *adj* (*healthy*) gesund; (*safe*) sicher; (*sensible*) vernünftig; (*theory*) stichhaltig; (*thorough*) tüchtig, gehörig ♦ *adv*: **to be** ~ **asleep** fest schlafen ♦ *n* (*noise*) Geräusch *nt*, Laut *m*; (*GEOG*) Sund

m ♦ *vt* erschallen lassen; (*alarm*) (Alarm) schlagen; (*MED*) abhorchen ♦ *vi* (*make a* ~) schallen, tönen; (*seem*) klingen; **to** ~ **like** sich anhören wie; ~ **out** *vt* (*opinion*) erforschen; (*person*) auf den Zahn fühlen +*dat*; ~ **barrier** *n* Schallmauer *f*; ~ **bite** *n* (*RAD, TV*) prägnante(s) Zitat *nt*; ~ **effects** *npl* Toneffekte *pl*; ~**ing** *n* (*NAUT etc*) Lotung *f*; ~**ly** *adv* (*sleep*) fest; (*beat*) tüchtig; ~**proof** *adj* (*room*) schalldicht; ~**track** *n* Tonstreifen *m*; (*music*) Filmmusik *f*
soup [su:p] *n* Suppe *f*; **in the** ~ (*inf*) in der Tinte; ~ **plate** *n* Suppenteller *m*; ~**spoon** *n* Suppenlöffel *m*
sour ['sauə*] *adj* (*also fig*) sauer; **it's** ~ **grapes** (*fig*) die Trauben hängen zu hoch
source [sɔ:s] *n* (*also fig*) Quelle *f*
south [sauθ] *n* Süden *m* ♦ *adj* Süd-, südlich ♦ *adv* nach Süden, südwärts; **S~ Africa** *n* Südafrika *nt*; **S~ African** *adj* südafrikanisch ♦ *n* Südafrikaner(in) *m(f)*; **S~ America** *n* Südamerika *nt*; **S~ American** *adj* südamerikanisch ♦ *n* Südamerikaner(in) *m(f)*; ~-**east** *n* Südosten *m*; ~**erly** ['sʌðəlɪ] *adj* südlich; ~**ern** ['sʌðən] *adj* südlich, Süd-; **S~ Pole** *n* Südpol *m*; ~**ward(s)** *adv* südwärts, nach Süden; ~-**west** *n* Südwesten *m*
souvenir [su:və'nɪə*] *n* Souvenir *nt*
sovereign ['sɒvrɪn] *n* (*ruler*) Herrscher(in) *m(f)* ♦ *adj* (*independent*) souverän
soviet ['səuvɪət] *adj* sowjetisch; **the S~ Union** die Sowjetunion
sow[1] [sau] *n* Sau *f*
sow[2] [səu] (*pt* **sowed**, *pp* **sown**) *vt* (*also fig*) säen
soya ['sɔɪə] (*US* **soy**) *n*: ~ **bean** Sojabohne *f*; ~ **sauce** Sojasauce *f*
spa [spɑ:] *n* (*place*) Kurort *m*
space [speɪs] *n* Platz *m*, Raum *m*; (*universe*) Weltraum *m*, All *nt*; (*length of time*) Abstand *m* ♦ *vt* (*also*: ~ *out*) verteilen; ~**craft** *n* Raumschiff *nt*; ~**man** (*irreg*) *n* Raumfahrer *m*; ~ **ship** *n* Raumschiff *nt*
spacing *n* Abstand *m*; (*also*: ~ *out*) Verteilung *f*

spacious ['speɪʃəs] *adj* geräumig, weit
spade [speɪd] *n* Spaten *m*; **~s** *npl* (CARDS)
Pik *nt*
Spain [speɪn] *n* Spanien *nt*
span [spæn] *n* Spanne *f*; (*of bridge etc*)
Spannweite *f* ♦ *vt* überspannen
Spaniard ['spænjəd] *n* Spanier(in) *m(f)*
Spanish ['spænɪʃ] *adj* spanisch ♦ *n* (LING)
Spanisch *nt*; **the ~** *npl* (*people*) die
Spanier *pl*
spank [spæŋk] *vt* verhauen, versohlen
spanner ['spænə*] (BRIT) *n*
Schraubenschlüssel *m*
spar [spɑ:*] *n* (NAUT) Sparren *m* ♦ *vi*
(BOXING) einen Sparring machen
spare [speə*] *adj* Ersatz- ♦ *n* = **spare
part** ♦ *vt* (*lives, feelings*) verschonen;
(*trouble*) ersparen; **to ~** (*surplus*) übrig; **~
part** *n* Ersatzteil *nt*; **~ time** *n* Freizeit *f*;
~ wheel *n* (AUT) Reservereifen *m*
sparing ['speərɪŋ] *adj*: **to be ~ with**
geizen mit; **~ly** *adv* sparsam; (*eat, spend
etc*) in Maßen
spark [spɑ:k] *n* Funken *m*; **~(ing) plug** *n*
Zündkerze *f*
sparkle ['spɑ:kl] *n* Funkeln *nt*; (*gaiety*)
Schwung *m* ♦ *vi* funkeln
sparkling ['spɑ:klɪŋ] *adj* funkelnd; (*wine*)
Schaum-; (*mineral water*) mit
Kohlensäure; (*conversation*) spritzig,
geistreich
sparrow ['spærəʊ] *n* Spatz *m*
sparse [spɑ:s] *adj* spärlich
spasm ['spæzəm] *n* (MED) Krampf *m*; (*fig*)
Anfall *m*; **~odic** [spæz'mɒdɪk] *adj* (*fig*)
sprunghaft
spat [spæt] *pt, pp of* **spit**
spate [speɪt] *n* (*fig*) Flut *f*, Schwall *m*; **in
~** (*river*) angeschwollen
spatter ['spætə*] *vt* bespritzen,
verspritzen
spatula ['spætjʊlə] *n* Spatel *m*
spawn [spɔ:n] *vi* laichen ♦ *n* Laich *m*
speak [spi:k] (*pt* **spoke**, *pp* **spoken**) *vt*
sprechen, reden; (*truth*) sagen; (*language*)
sprechen ♦ *vi*: **to ~ (to)** sprechen (mit *or*
zu); **to ~ to sb of** *or* **about sth** mit jdm
über etw *acc* sprechen; **~ up!** sprich
lauter!; **~er** *n* Sprecher(in) *m(f)*,

Redner(in) *m(f)*; (*loudspeaker*)
Lautsprecher *m*; (POL): **the S~er** der
Vorsitzende des Parlaments (BRIT) *or* des
Kongresses (US)
spear [spɪə*] *n* Speer *m* ♦ *vt* aufspießen;
~head *vt* (*attack etc*) anführen
spec [spek] (*inf*) *n*: **on ~** auf gut Glück
special ['speʃəl] *adj* besondere(r, s); **~ist**
n (TECH) Fachmann *m*; (MED) Facharzt *m*/
Fachärztin *f*; **~ity** [speʃɪ'ælɪtɪ] *n*
Spezialität *f*; (*study*) Spezialgebiet *nt*; **~ize**
vi: **to ~ize (in)** sich spezialisieren (auf
+*acc*); **~ly** *adv* besonders; (*explicitly*) extra
species ['spi:ʃi:z] *n* Art *f*
specific [spə'sɪfɪk] *adj* spezifisch; **~ally**
adv spezifisch
specification [spesɪfɪ'keɪʃən] *n* Angabe *f*;
(*stipulation*) Bedingung *f*; **~s** *npl* (TECH)
technische Daten *pl*
specify ['spesɪfaɪ] *vt* genau angeben
specimen ['spesɪmɪn] *n* Probe *f*
speck [spek] *n* Fleckchen *nt*
speckled ['spekld] *adj* gesprenkelt
specs [speks] (*inf*) *npl* Brille *f*
spectacle ['spektəkl] *n* Schauspiel *nt*; **~s**
npl (*glasses*) Brille *f*
spectacular [spek'tækjʊlə*] *adj*
sensationell; (*success etc*) spektakulär
spectator [spek'teɪtə*] *n* Zuschauer(in)
m(f)
spectre ['spektə*] (US **specter**) *n* Geist *m*,
Gespenst *nt*
speculate ['spekjʊleɪt] *vi* spekulieren
speech [spi:tʃ] *n* Sprache *f*; (*address*)
Rede *f*; (*manner of speaking*) Sprechweise
f; **~less** *adj* sprachlos
speed [spi:d] *n* Geschwindigkeit *f*; (*gear*)
Gang *m* ♦ *vi* (JUR) (zu) schnell fahren; **at
full** *or* **top ~** mit Höchstgeschwindigkeit;
~ up *vt* beschleunigen ♦ *vi* schneller
werden; schneller fahren; **~boat** *n*
Schnellboot *nt*; **~ily** *adv* schleunigst; **~ing**
n Geschwindigkeitsüberschreitung *f*; **~
limit** *n* Geschwindigkeitsbegrenzung *f*;
~ometer [spɪ'dɒmɪtə*] *n* Tachometer *m*;
~way *n* (*bike racing*)
Motorradrennstrecke *f*; **~y** *adj* schnell
spell [spel] (*pt, pp* **spelt** (BRIT) *or* **~ed**) *n*
(*magic*) Bann *m*; (*period of time*) Zeitlang

f ♦ *vt* buchstabieren; (*imply*) bedeuten; **to cast a ~ on sb** jdn verzaubern; **~bound** *adj* (wie) gebannt; **~ing** *n* Rechtschreibung *f*

spelt [spelt] (*BRIT*) *pt, pp of* **spell**

spend [spend] (*pt, pp* **spent**) *vt* (*money*) ausgeben; (*time*) verbringen; **~thrift** *n* Verschwender(in) *m(f)*

spent [spent] *pt, pp of* **spend**

sperm [spɜːm] *n* (*BIOL*) Samenflüssigkeit *f*

spew [spjuː] *vt* (er)brechen

sphere [sfɪə*] *n* (*globe*) Kugel *f*; (*fig*) Sphäre *f*, Gebiet *nt*

spherical ['sferɪkəl] *adj* kugelförmig

spice [spaɪs] *n* Gewürz *nt* ♦ *vt* würzen

spick-and-span ['spɪkən'spæn] *adj* blitzblank

spicy ['spaɪsɪ] *adj* (*food*) stark gewürzt; (*fig*) pikant

spider ['spaɪdə*] *n* Spinne *f*

spike [spaɪk] *n* Dorn *m*, Spitze *f*

spill [spɪl] (*pt, pp* **spilt** *or* **~ed**) *vt* verschütten ♦ *vi* sich ergießen; **~ over** *vi* überlaufen; (*fig*) sich ausbreiten

spilt [spɪlt] *pt, pp of* **spill**

spin [spɪn] (*pt, pp* **spun**) *n* (*trip in car*) Spazierfahrt *f*; (*AVIAT*) (Ab)trudeln *nt*; (*on ball*) Drall *m* ♦ *vt* (*thread*) spinnen; (*like top*) (herum)wirbeln ♦ *vi* sich drehen; **~ out** *vt* in die Länge ziehen

spinach ['spɪnɪtʃ] *n* Spinat *m*

spinal ['spaɪnl] *adj* Rückgrat-; **~ cord** *n* Rückenmark *nt*

spindly ['spɪndlɪ] *adj* spindeldürr

spin doctor *n* PR-Fachmann *m*, PR-Frau *f*

spin-dryer ['spɪn'draɪə*] (*BRIT*) *n* Wäscheschleuder *f*

spine [spaɪn] *n* Rückgrat *nt*; (*thorn*) Stachel *m*; **~less** *adj* (*also fig*) rückgratlos

spinning ['spɪnɪŋ] *n* Spinnen *nt*; **~ top** *n* Kreisel *m*; **~ wheel** *n* Spinnrad *nt*

spin-off ['spɪnɒf] *n* Nebenprodukt *nt*

spinster ['spɪnstə*] *n* unverheiratete Frau *f*; (*pej*) alte Jungfer *f*

spiral ['spaɪərl] *n* Spirale *f* ♦ *adj* spiralförmig; (*movement etc*) in Spiralen ♦ *vi* sich (hoch)winden; **~ staircase** *n* Wendeltreppe *f*

spire ['spaɪə*] *n* Turm *m*

spirit ['spɪrɪt] *n* Geist *m*; (*humour, mood*) Stimmung *f*; (*courage*) Mut *m*; (*verve*) Elan *m*; (*alcohol*) Alkohol *m*; **~s** *npl* (*drink*) Spirituosen *pl*; **in good ~s** gut aufgelegt; **~ed** *adj* beherzt; **~ level** *n* Wasserwaage *f*

spiritual ['spɪrɪtjʊəl] *adj* geistig, seelisch; (*REL*) geistlich ♦ *n* Spiritual *nt*

spit [spɪt] (*pt, pp* **spat**) *n* (*for roasting*) (Brat)spieß *m*; (*saliva*) Spucke *f* ♦ *vi* spucken; (*rain*) sprühen; (*make a sound*) zischen; (*cat*) fauchen

spite [spaɪt] *n* Gehässigkeit *f* ♦ *vt* kränken; **in ~ of** trotz; **~ful** *adj* gehässig

spittle ['spɪtl] *n* Speichel *m*, Spucke *f*

splash [splæʃ] *n* Spritzer *m*; (*of colour*) (Farb)fleck *m* ♦ *vt* bespritzen ♦ *vi* spritzen

spleen [spliːn] *n* (*ANAT*) Milz *f*

splendid ['splendɪd] *adj* glänzend

splendour ['splendə*] (*US* **splendor**) *n* Pracht *f*

splint [splɪnt] *n* Schiene *f*

splinter ['splɪntə*] *n* Splitter *m* ♦ *vi* (zer)splittern

split [splɪt] (*pt, pp* **split**) *n* Spalte *f*; (*fig*) Spaltung *f*; (*division*) Trennung *f* ♦ *vt* spalten ♦ *vi* (*divide*) reißen; **~ up** *vi* sich trennen

splutter ['splʌtə*] *vi* stottern

spoil [spɔɪl] (*pt, pp* **spoilt** *or* **~ed**) *vt* (*ruin*) verderben; (*child*) verwöhnen; **~s** *npl* Beute *f*; **~sport** *n* Spielverderber *m*; **~t** [spɔɪlt] *pt, pp of* **spoil**

spoke [spəʊk] *pt of* **speak** ♦ *n* Speiche *f*

spoken ['spəʊkn] *pp of* **speak**

spokesman ['spəʊksmən] (*irreg*) *n* Sprecher *m*

spokeswoman ['spəʊkswʊmən] (*irreg*) *n* Sprecherin *f*

sponge [spʌndʒ] *n* Schwamm *m* ♦ *vt* abwaschen ♦ *vi*: **to ~ on** auf Kosten leben +*gen*; **~ bag** (*BRIT*) *n* Kulturbeutel *m*; **~ cake** *n* Rührkuchen *m*

sponsor ['spɒnsə*] *n* Sponsor *m* ♦ *vt* fördern; **~ship** *n* Finanzierung *f*; (*public*) Schirmherrschaft *f*

spontaneous [spɒn'teɪnɪəs] *adj* spontan

spooky ['spu:kɪ] (*inf*) *adj* gespenstisch
spool [spu:l] *n* Spule *f*, Rolle *f*
spoon [spu:n] *n* Löffel *m*; **~-feed** (*irreg*) *vt* mit dem Löffel füttern; (*fig*) hochpäppeln; **~ful** *n* Löffel(voll) *m*
sport [spɔ:t] *n* Sport *m*; (*person*) feine(r) Kerl *m*; **~ing** *adj* (*fair*) sportlich, fair; **to give sb a ~ing chance** jdm eine faire Chance geben; **~ jacket** (*US*) *n* = **sports jacket**; **~s car** *n* Sportwagen *m*; **~s jacket** *n* Sportjackett *nt*; **~sman** (*irreg*) *n* Sportler *m*; **~smanship** *n* Sportlichkeit *f*; **~swear** *n* Sportkleidung *f*; **~swoman** (*irreg*) *n* Sportlerin *f*; **~y** *adj* sportlich
spot [spɒt] *n* Punkt *m*; (*dirty*) Fleck(en) *m*; (*place*) Stelle *f*; (*MED*) Pickel *m* ♦ *vt* erspähen; (*mistake*) bemerken; **on the ~** an Ort und Stelle; (*at once*) auf der Stelle; **~ check** *n* Stichprobe *f*; **~less** *adj* fleckenlos; **~light** *n* Scheinwerferlicht *nt*; (*lamp*) Scheinwerfer *m*; **~ted** *adj* gefleckt; **~ty** *adj* (*face*) pickelig
spouse [spaʊs] *n* Gatte *m*/Gattin *f*
spout [spaʊt] *n* (*of pot*) Tülle *f*; (*jet*) Wasserstrahl *m* ♦ *vi* speien
sprain [spreɪn] *n* Verrenkung *f* ♦ *vt* verrenken
sprang [spræŋ] *pt of* **spring**
sprawl [sprɔ:l] *vi* sich strecken
spray [spreɪ] *n* Spray *nt*; (*off sea*) Gischt *f*; (*of flowers*) Zweig *m* ♦ *vt* besprühen, sprayen
spread [spred] (*pt, pp* **spread**) *n* (*extent*) Verbreitung *f*; (*inf: meal*) Schmaus *m*; (*for bread*) Aufstrich *m* ♦ *vt* ausbreiten; (*scatter*) verbreiten; (*butter*) streichen ♦ *vi* sich ausbreiten; **~-eagled** ['spredi:gld] *adj*: **to be ~-eagled** alle viere von sich strecken
spree [spri:] *n* (*shopping*) Einkaufsbummel *m*; **to go on a ~** einen draufmachen
sprightly ['spraɪtlɪ] *adj* munter, lebhaft
spring [sprɪŋ] (*pt* **sprang**, *pp* **sprung**) *n* (*leap*) Sprung *m*; (*metal*) Feder *f*; (*season*) Frühling *m*; (*water*) Quelle *f* ♦ *vi* (*leap*) springen; **~ up** *vi* (*problem*) auftauchen; **~board** *n* Sprungbrett *nt*; **~-clean** *n* (*also*: **~-cleaning**) Frühjahrsputz *m*; **~time** *n*

Frühling *m*; **~y** *adj* federnd, elastisch
sprinkle ['sprɪŋkl] *vt* (*salt*) streuen; (*liquid*) sprenkeln; **to ~ water on, to ~ with water** mit Wasser besprengen
sprinkler ['sprɪŋklə*] *n* (*for lawn*) Sprenger *m*; (*for fire fighting*) Sprinkler *m*
sprint [sprɪnt] *n* (*race*) Sprint *m* ♦ *vi* (*gen: run fast*) rennen; (*SPORT*) sprinten
sprite [spraɪt] *n* Elfe *f*; Kobold *m*
sprout [spraʊt] *vi* sprießen; **~s** *npl* (*also*: *Brussels* **~s**) Rosenkohl *m*
spruce [spru:s] *n* Fichte *f* ♦ *adj* schmuck, adrett
sprung [sprʌŋ] *pp of* **spring**
spry [spraɪ] *adj* flink, rege
spun [spʌn] *pt, pp of* **spin**
spur [spɜ:*] *n* Sporn *m*; (*fig*) Ansporn *m* ♦ *vt* (*also*: **~ on**: *fig*) anspornen; **on the ~ of the moment** spontan
spurious ['spjʊərɪəs] *adj* falsch
spurn [spɜ:n] *vt* verschmähen
spurt [spɜ:t] *n* (*jet*) Strahl *m*; (*acceleration*) Spurt *m* ♦ *vi* (*liquid*) schießen
spy [spaɪ] *n* Spion(in) *m(f)* ♦ *vi* spionieren ♦ *vt* erspähen; **~ing** *n* Spionage *f*
sq. *abbr* = **square**
squabble ['skwɒbl] *n* Zank *m* ♦ *vi* sich zanken
squad [skwɒd] *n* (*MIL*) Abteilung *f*; (*POLICE*) Kommando *nt*
squadron ['skwɒdrən] *n* (*cavalry*) Schwadron *f*; (*NAUT*) Geschwader *nt*; (*air force*) Staffel *f*
squalid ['skwɒlɪd] *adj* verkommen
squall [skwɔ:l] *n* Bö *f*, Windstoß *m*
squalor ['skwɒlə*] *n* Verwahrlosung *f*
squander ['skwɒndə*] *vt* verschwenden
square [skwɛə*] *n* Quadrat *nt*; (*open space*) Platz *m*; (*instrument*) Winkel *m*; (*inf: person*) Spießer *m* ♦ *adj* viereckig; (*inf: ideas, tastes*) spießig ♦ *vt* (*arrange*) ausmachen; (*MATH*) ins Quadrat erheben ♦ *vi* (*agree*) übereinstimmen; **all ~** quitt; **a ~ meal** eine ordentliche Mahlzeit; **2 metres ~** 2 Meter im Quadrat; **1 ~ metre** 1 Quadratmeter; **~ly** *adv* fest, gerade
squash [skwɒʃ] *n* (*BRIT: drink*) Saft *m*; (*game*) Squash *nt* ♦ *vt* zerquetschen

squat [skwɒt] *adj* untersetzt ♦ *vi* hocken; **~ter** *n* Hausbesetzer *m*

squawk [skwɔ:k] *vi* kreischen

squeak [skwi:k] *vi* quiek(s)en; (*spring, door etc*) quietschen

squeal [skwi:l] *vi* schrill schreien

squeamish ['skwi:mɪʃ] *adj* empfindlich

squeeze [skwi:z] *n* (*POL*) Geldknappheit *f* ♦ *vt* pressen, drücken; (*orange*) auspressen; **~ out** *vt* ausquetschen

squelch [skwɛltʃ] *vi* platschen

squib [skwɪb] *n* Knallfrosch *m*

squid [skwɪd] *n* Tintenfisch *m*

squiggle ['skwɪgl] *n* Schnörkel *m*

squint [skwɪnt] *vi* schielen ♦ *n*: **to have a ~** schielen; **to ~ at sb/sth** nach jdm/ etw schielen

squire ['skwaɪə*] (*BRIT*) *n* Gutsherr *m*

squirm [skwɜ:m] *vi* sich winden

squirrel ['skwɪrəl] *n* Eichhörnchen *nt*

squirt [skwɜ:t] *vt, vi* spritzen

Sr *abbr* (= *senior*) sen.

St *abbr* (= *saint*) hl., St.; (= *street*) Str.

stab [stæb] *n* (*blow*) Stich *m*; (*inf: try*) Versuch *m* ♦ *vt* erstechen

stabilize ['steɪbəlaɪz] *vt* stabilisieren ♦ *vi* sich stabilisieren

stable ['steɪbl] *adj* stabil ♦ *n* Stall *m*

stack [stæk] *n* Stapel *m* ♦ *vt* stapeln

stadium ['steɪdɪəm] *n* Stadion *nt*

staff [stɑ:f] *n* (*stick, MIL*) Stab *m*; (*personnel*) Personal *nt*; (*BRIT: SCH*) Lehrkräfte *pl* ♦ *vt* (*with people*) besetzen

stag [stæg] *n* Hirsch *m*

stage [steɪdʒ] *n* Bühne *f*; (*of journey*) Etappe *f*; (*degree*) Stufe *f*; (*point*) Stadium *nt* ♦ *vt* (*put on*) aufführen; (*simulate*) inszenieren; (*demonstration*) veranstalten; **in ~s** etappenweise; **~coach** *n* Postkutsche *f*; **~ door** *n* Bühneneingang *m*; **~ manager** *n* Intendant *m*

stagger ['stægə*] *vi* wanken, taumeln ♦ *vt* (*amaze*) verblüffen; (*hours*) staffeln; **~ing** *adj* unglaublich

stagnant ['stægnənt] *adj* stagnierend; (*water*) stehend

stagnate [stæg'neɪt] *vi* stagnieren

stag party *n* Männerabend *m* (vom Bräutigam vor der Hochzeit gegeben)

staid [steɪd] *adj* gesetzt

stain [steɪn] *n* Fleck *m* ♦ *vt* beflecken; **~ed glass window** buntes Glasfenster *nt*; **~less** *adj* (*steel*) rostfrei; **~ remover** *n* Fleckentferner *m*

stair [steə*] *n* (*Treppen*)stufe *f*; **~s** *npl* (*flight of steps*) Treppe *f*; **~case** *n* Treppenhaus *nt*, Treppe *f*; **~way** *n* Treppenaufgang *m*

stake [steɪk] *n* (*post*) Pfahl *m*; (*money*) Einsatz *m* ♦ *vt* (*bet: money*) setzen; **to be at ~** auf dem Spiel stehen

stale [steɪl] *adj* alt; (*bread*) altbacken

stalemate ['steɪlmeɪt] *n* (*CHESS*) Patt *nt*; (*fig*) Stillstand *m*

stalk [stɔ:k] *n* Stengel *m*, Stiel *m* ♦ *vt* (*game*) jagen; **~ off** *vi* abstolzieren

stall [stɔ:l] *n* (*in stable*) Stand *m*, Box *f*; (*in market*) (Verkaufs)stand *m* ♦ *vt* (*AUT*) abwürgen ♦ *vi* stehenbleiben; (*fig*) Ausflüchte machen; **~s** *npl* (*BRIT: THEAT*) Parkett *nt*

stallion ['stælɪən] *n* Zuchthengst *m*

stalwart ['stɔ:lwət] *n* treue(r) Anhänger *m*

stamina ['stæmɪnə] *n* Durchhaltevermögen *nt*, Zähigkeit *f*

stammer ['stæmə*] *n* Stottern *nt* ♦ *vt, vi* stottern, stammeln

stamp [stæmp] *n* Briefmarke *f*; (*for document*) Stempel *m* ♦ *vi* stampfen ♦ *vt* (*mark*) stempeln; (*mail*) frankieren; (*foot*) stampfen mit; **~ album** *n* Briefmarkenalbum *nt*; **~ collecting** *n* Briefmarkensammeln *nt*

stampede [stæm'pi:d] *n* panische Flucht *f*

stance [stæns] *n* Haltung *f*

stand [stænd] (*pt, pp stood*) *n* (*for objects*) Gestell *nt*; (*seats*) Tribüne *f* ♦ *vi* stehen; (*rise*) aufstehen; (*decision*) feststehen ♦ *vt* setzen, stellen; (*endure*) aushalten; (*person*) ausstehen; (*nonsense*) dulden; **to make a ~** Widerstand leisten; **to ~ for parliament** (*BRIT*) für das Parlament kandidieren; **~ by** *vi* (*be ready*) bereitstehen ♦ *vt fus* (*opinion*) treu bleiben +*dat*; **~ down** *vi* (*withdraw*) zurücktreten; **~ for** *vt fus* (*signify*) stehen

für; (*permit, tolerate*) hinnehmen; **~ in
for** *vt fus* einspringen für; **~ out** *vi* (*be
prominent*) hervorstechen; **~ up** *vi* (*rise*)
aufstehen; **~ up for** *vt fus* sich einsetzen
für; **~ up to** *vt fus:* **to ~ up to sth** einer
Sache *dat* gewachsen sein; **to ~ up to sb**
sich jdm gegenüber behaupten
standard ['stændəd] *n* (*measure*) Norm *f*;
(*flag*) Fahne *f* ♦ *adj* (*size etc*) Normal-; **~s**
npl (*morals*) Maßstäbe *pl*; **~ize** *vt*
vereinheitlichen; **~ lamp** (*BRIT*) *n*
Stehlampe *f*; **~ of living** *n*
Lebensstandard *m*
stand-by ['stændbaɪ] *n* Reserve *f*; **to be
on ~** in Bereitschaft sein; **~ ticket** *n*
(*AVIAT*) Standby-Ticket *nt*
stand-in ['stændɪn] *n* Ersatz *m*
standing ['stændɪŋ] *adj* (*erect*) stehend;
(*permanent*) ständig; (*invitation*) offen ♦ *n*
(*duration*) Dauer *f*; (*reputation*) Ansehen
nt; **of many years' ~** langjährig; **~ order**
(*BRIT*) *n* (*at bank*) Dauerauftrag *m*; **~
orders** *npl* (*MIL*) Vorschrift *f*; **~ room** *n*
Stehplatz *m*
stand-offish ['stænd'ɒfɪʃ] *adj*
zurückhaltend, sehr reserviert
standpoint ['stændpɔɪnt] *n* Standpunkt
m
standstill ['stændstɪl] *n*: **to be at a ~**
stillstehen; **to come to a ~** zum Stillstand
kommen
stank [stæŋk] *pt of* **stink**
staple ['steɪpl] *n* (*in paper*) Heftklammer *f*;
(*article*) Haupterzeugnis *nt* ♦ *adj* Grund-,
Haupt- ♦ *vt* (fest)klammern; **~r** *n*
Heftmaschine *f*
star [stɑ:*] *n* Stern *m*; (*person*) Star *m*
♦ *vi* die Hauptrolle spielen ♦ *vt*: **~ring ...**
in der Hauptrolle/den Hauptrollen ...
starboard ['stɑ:bəd] *n* Steuerbord *nt*
starch [stɑ:tʃ] *n* Stärke *f*
stardom ['stɑ:dəm] *n* Berühmtheit *f*
stare [steə*] *n* starre(r) Blick *m* ♦ *vi*: **to
~ at** starren auf +*acc*, anstarren
starfish ['stɑ:fɪʃ] *n* Seestern *m*
stark [stɑ:k] *adj* öde ♦ *adv*: **~ naked**
splitternackt
starling ['stɑ:lɪŋ] *n* Star *m*
starry ['stɑ:rɪ] *adj* Sternen-; **~-eyed** *adj*

(*innocent*) blauäugig
start [stɑ:t] *n* Anfang *m*; (*SPORT*) Start *m*;
(*lead*) Vorsprung *m* ♦ *vt* in Gang setzen;
(*car*) anlassen ♦ *vi* anfangen; (*car*)
anspringen; (*on journey*) aufbrechen;
(*SPORT*) starten; (*with fright*)
zusammenfahren; **to ~ doing** *or* **to do
sth** anfangen, etw zu tun; **~ off** *vi*
anfangen; (*begin moving*) losgehen;
losfahren; **~ up** *vi* anfangen; (*startled*)
auffahren ♦ *vt* beginnen; (*car*) anlassen;
(*engine*) starten; **~er** *n* (*AUT*) Anlasser *m*;
(*for race*) Starter *m*; (*BRIT: COOK*) Vorspeise
f; **~ing point** *n* Ausgangspunkt *m*
startle ['stɑ:tl] *vt* erschrecken
startling ['stɑ:tlɪŋ] *adj* erschreckend
starvation [stɑ:'veɪʃən] *n* Verhungern *nt*
starve [stɑ:v] *vi* verhungern ♦ *vt*
verhungern lassen; **I'm starving** ich
sterbe vor Hunger
state [steɪt] *n* (*condition*) Zustand *m*; (*POL*)
Staat *m* ♦ *vt* erklären; (*facts*) angeben;
the S~s (*USA*) die Staaten; **to be in a ~**
durchdrehen; **~ly** *adj* würdevoll; **~ment**
n Aussage *f*; (*POL*) Erklärung *f*; **~sman**
(*irreg*) *n* Staatsmann *m*
static ['stætɪk] *n* (*also:* **~ electricity**)
Reibungselektrizität *f*
station ['steɪʃən] *n* (*RAIL etc*) Bahnhof *m*;
(*police etc*) Wache *f*; (*in society*) Stand *m*
♦ *vt* stationieren
stationary ['steɪʃənərɪ] *adj* stillstehend;
(*car*) parkend
stationer ['steɪʃənə*] *n*
Schreibwarenhändler *m*; **~'s** *n* (*shop*)
Schreibwarengeschäft *nt*; **~y** *n*
Schreibwaren *pl*
station master *n* Bahnhofsvorsteher *m*
station wagon *n* Kombiwagen *m*
statistics [stə'tɪstɪks] *n* Statistik *f*
statue ['stætju:] *n* Statue *f*
stature ['stætʃə*] *n* Größe *f*
status ['steɪtəs] *n* Status *m*
statute ['stætju:t] *n* Gesetz *nt*
statutory ['stætjutərɪ] *adj* gesetzlich
staunch [stɔ:ntʃ] *adj* standhaft
stave [steɪv] *n* (*MUS*) Notenlinien *pl* ♦ *vt*:
to ~ off (*threat*) abwenden; (*attack*)
abwehren

stay [steɪ] *n* Aufenthalt *m* ♦ *vi* bleiben; *(reside)* wohnen; **to ~ put** an Ort und Stelle bleiben; **to ~ the night** übernachten; **~ behind** *vi* zurückbleiben; **~ in** *vi (at home)* zu Hause bleiben; **~ on** *vi (continue)* länger bleiben; **~ out** *vi (of house)* wegbleiben; **~ up** *vi (at night)* aufbleiben; **~ing power** *n* Durchhaltevermögen *nt*

stead [sted] *n*: **in sb's ~** an jds Stelle *dat*; **to stand sb in good ~** jdm zugute kommen

steadfast ['stedfəst] *adj* standhaft, treu

steadily ['stedɪlɪ] *adv* stetig, regelmäßig

steady ['stedɪ] *adj (firm)* fest, stabil; *(regular)* gleichmäßig; *(reliable)* beständig; *(hand)* ruhig; *(job, boyfriend)* fest ♦ *vt* festigen; **to ~ o.s. on/against sth** sich stützen auf/gegen etw *acc*

steak [steɪk] *n* Steak *nt*; *(fish)* Filet *nt*

steal [stiːl] *(pt* **stole**, *pp* **stolen)** *vt* stehlen ♦ *vi* stehlen; *(go stealthily)* sich stehlen

stealth [stelθ] *n* Heimlichkeit *f*; **~y** ['stelθɪ] *adj* verstohlen, heimlich

steam [stiːm] *n* Dampf *m* ♦ *vt (COOK)* im Dampfbad erhitzen ♦ *vi* dampfen; **~ engine** *n* Dampfmaschine *f*; **~er** *n* Dampfer *m*; **~roller** *n* Dampfwalze *f*; **~ship** *n* = **steamer**; **~y** *adj* dampfig

steel [stiːl] *n* Stahl *m* ♦ *adj* Stahl-; *(fig)* stählern; **~works** *n* Stahlwerke *pl*

steep [stiːp] *adj* steil; *(price)* gepfeffert ♦ *vt* einweichen

steeple ['stiːpl] *n* Kirchturm *m*; **~chase** *n* Hindernisrennen *nt*

steer [stɪə*] *vt, vi* steuern; *(car etc)* lenken; **~ing** *n (AUT)* Steuerung *f*; **~ing wheel** *n* Steuer- *or* Lenkrad *nt*

stellar ['stelə*] *adj* Stern(en)-

stem [stem] *n* Stiel *m* ♦ *vt* aufhalten; **~ from** *vt fus* abstammen von

stench [stentʃ] *n* Gestank *m*

stencil ['stensl] *n* Schablone *f* ♦ *vt* (auf)drucken

stenographer [ste'nɒɡrəfə*] *(US) n* Stenograph(in) *m(f)*

step [step] *n* Schritt *m*; *(stair)* Stufe *f* ♦ *vi* treten, schreiten; **~s** *npl (BRIT)* = **stepladder**; **to take ~s** Schritte

unternehmen; **in/out of ~ (with)** im/ nicht im Gleichklang (mit); **~ down** *vi (fig)* abtreten; **~ off** *vt fus* aussteigen aus; **~ up** *vt* steigern; **~brother** *n* Stiefbruder *m*; **~daughter** *n* Stieftochter *f*; **~father** *n* Stiefvater *m*; **~ladder** *n* Trittleiter *f*; **~mother** *n* Stiefmutter *f*; **~ping stone** *n* Stein *m*; *(fig)* Sprungbrett *nt*; **~sister** *n* Stiefschwester *f*; **~son** *n* Stiefsohn *m*

stereo ['steriəʊ] *n* Stereoanlage *f* ♦ *adj (also*: **~phonic)** stereophonisch

stereotype ['stɪərɪətaɪp] *n* Prototyp *m*; *(fig)* Klischee *nt* ♦ *vt* stereotypieren; *(fig)* stereotyp machen

sterile ['steraɪl] *adj* steril; *(person)* unfruchtbar

sterling ['stɜːlɪŋ] *adj (FIN)* Sterling-; *(character)* gediegen ♦ *n (ECON)* das Pfund Sterling; **a pound ~** ein Pfund Sterling

stern [stɜːn] *adj* streng ♦ *n* Heck *nt*, Achterschiff *nt*

stew [stjuː] *n* Eintopf *m* ♦ *vt, vi* schmoren

steward ['stjuːəd] *n* Steward *m*; **~ess** *n* Stewardess *f*

stick [stɪk] *(pt, pp* **stuck)** *n* Stock *m*; *(of chalk etc)* Stück *nt* ♦ *vt (stab)* stechen; *(fix)* stecken; *(put)* stellen; *(gum)* (an)kleben; *(inf: tolerate)* vertragen ♦ *vi (stop)* steckenbleiben; *(get stuck)* klemmen; *(hold fast)* kleben, haften; **~ out** *vi (project)* hervorstehen; **~ up** *vi (project)* in die Höhe stehen; **~ up for** *vt fus (defend)* eintreten für; **~er** *n* Aufkleber *m*; **~ing plaster** *n* Heftpflaster *nt*

stickler ['stɪklə*] *n*: **~ (for)** Pedant *m* (in +*acc*)

stick-up ['stɪkʌp] *(inf) n* (Raub)überfall *m*

sticky ['stɪkɪ] *adj* klebrig; *(atmosphere)* stickig

stiff [stɪf] *adj* steif; *(difficult)* hart; *(paste)* dick; *(drink)* stark; **~en** *vt* versteifen, (ver)stärken ♦ *vi* sich versteifen

stifle ['staɪfl] *vt* unterdrücken

stifling ['staɪflɪŋ] *adj* drückend

stigma ['stɪɡmə] *(pl BOT, MED, REL* **~ta**; *fig* **~s)** *n* Stigma *nt*

stigmata ['stɪɡmətə] *npl of* **stigma**

stile [staɪl] *n* Steige *f*

stiletto [stɪ'letəʊ] (*BRIT*) *n* (*also:* ~ *heel*) Pfennigabsatz *m*

still [stɪl] *adj* still ♦ *adv* (immer) noch; (*anyhow*) immerhin; **~born** *adj* totgeboren; **~ life** *n* Stilleben *nt*

stilt [stɪlt] *n* Stelze *f*

stilted ['stɪltɪd] *adj* gestelzt

stimulate ['stɪmjʊleɪt] *vt* anregen, stimulieren

stimuli ['stɪmjʊlaɪ] *npl of* **stimulus**

stimulus ['stɪmjʊləs] (*pl* **-li**) *n* Anregung *f*, Reiz *m*

sting [stɪŋ] (*pt, pp* **stung**) *n* Stich *m*; (*organ*) Stachel *m* ♦ *vi* stechen; (*on skin*) brennen ♦ *vt* stechen

stingy ['stɪndʒɪ] *adj* geizig, knauserig

stink [stɪŋk] (*pt* **stank**, *pp* **stunk**) *n* Gestank *m* ♦ *vi* stinken; **~ing** *adj* (*fig*) widerlich

stint [stɪnt] *n* Pensum *nt*; (*period*) Betätigung *f* ♦ *vi* knausern; **to do one's ~** seine Arbeit tun; (*share*) seinen Teil beitragen

stipulate ['stɪpjʊleɪt] *vt* festsetzen

stir [stɜ:*] *n* Bewegung *f*; (*COOK*) Rühren *nt*; (*sensation*) Aufsehen *nt* ♦ *vt* (um)rühren ♦ *vi* sich rühren; **~ up** *vt* (*mob*) aufhetzen; (*mixture*) umrühren; (*dust*) aufwirbeln

stirrup ['stɪrəp] *n* Steigbügel *m*

stitch [stɪtʃ] *n* (*with needle*) Stich *m*; (*MED*) Faden *m*; (*of knitting*) Masche *f*; (*pain*) Stich *m* ♦ *vt* nähen

stoat [stəʊt] *n* Wiesel *nt*

stock [stɒk] *n* Vorrat *m*; (*COMM*) (Waren)lager *nt*; (*live~*) Vieh *nt*; (*COOK*) Brühe *f*; (*FIN*) Grundkapital *nt* ♦ *adj* stets vorrätig; (*standard*) Normal- ♦ *vt* (*in shop*) führen; **~s** *npl* (*FIN*) Aktien *pl*; **in/out of ~** vorrätig/nicht vorrätig; **to take ~ of** Inventur machen von; (*fig*) Bilanz ziehen aus; **~s and shares** Effekten *pl*; **~ up** *vi*: **to ~ up (with)** Reserven anlegen (von)

stockbroker ['stɒkbrəʊkə*] *n* Börsenmakler *m*

stock cube *n* Brühwürfel *m*

stock exchange *n* Börse *f*

stocking ['stɒkɪŋ] *n* Strumpf *m*

stockist ['stɒkɪst] *n* Händler *m*

stock: **~ market** *n* Börse *f*; **~ phrase** *n* Standardsatz *m*; **~pile** *n* Vorrat *m* ♦ *vt* aufstapeln; **~taking** (*BRIT*) *n* (*COMM*) Inventur *f*, Bestandsaufnahme *f*

stocky ['stɒkɪ] *adj* untersetzt

stodgy ['stɒdʒɪ] *adj* pampig; (*fig*) trocken

stoke [stəʊk] *vt* schüren

stole [stəʊl] *pt of* **steal** ♦ *n* Stola *f*

stolen ['stəʊlən] *pp of* **steal**

stolid ['stɒlɪd] *adj* stur

stomach ['stʌmək] *n* Bauch *m*, Magen *m* ♦ *vt* vertragen; **~-ache** *n* Magen- *or* Bauchschmerzen *pl*

stone [stəʊn] *n* Stein *m*; (*BRIT: weight*) *Gewichtseinheit* = 6.35 kg ♦ *vt* (*olive*) entkernen; (*kill*) steinigen; **~-cold** *adj* eiskalt; **~-deaf** *adj* stocktaub; **~work** *n* Mauerwerk *nt*

stony ['stəʊnɪ] *adj* steinig

stood [stʊd] *pt, pp of* **stand**

stool [stu:l] *n* Hocker *m*

stoop [stu:p] *vi* sich bücken

stop [stɒp] *n* Halt *m*; (*bus* ~) Haltestelle *f*; (*punctuation*) Punkt *m* ♦ *vt* anhalten; (*bring to an end*) aufhören (mit), sein lassen ♦ *vi* aufhören; (*clock*) stehenbleiben; (*remain*) bleiben; **to ~ doing sth** aufhören, etw zu tun; **to ~ dead** innehalten; **~ off** *vi* kurz haltmachen; **~ up** *vt* (*hole*) zustopfen, verstopfen; **~gap** *n* Notlösung *f*; **~lights** *npl* (*AUT*) Bremslichter *pl*; **~over** *n* (*on journey*) Zwischenaufenthalt *m*

stoppage ['stɒpɪdʒ] *n* (An)halten *nt*; (*traffic*) Verkehrsstockung *f*; (*strike*) Arbeitseinstellung *f*

stopper ['stɒpə*] *n* Propfen *m*, Stöpsel *m*

stop press *n* letzte Meldung *f*

stopwatch ['stɒpwɒtʃ] *n* Stoppuhr *f*

storage ['stɔ:rɪdʒ] *n* Lagerung *f*; **~ heater** *n* (Nachtstrom)speicherofen *m*

store [stɔ:*] *n* Vorrat *m*; (*place*) Lager *nt*, Warenhaus *nt*; (*BRIT: large shop*) Kaufhaus *nt*; (*US*) Laden *m* ♦ *vt* lagern; **~s** *npl* (*supplies*) Vorräte *pl*; **~ up** *vt* sich eindecken mit; **~room** *n* Lagerraum *m*, Vorratsraum *m*

storey ['stɔːrɪ] (*US* **story**) *n* Stock *m*

stork [stɔːk] *n* Storch *m*

storm [stɔːm] *n* (*also fig*) Sturm *m* ♦ *vt, vi* stürmen; **~y** *adj* stürmisch

story ['stɔːrɪ] *n* Geschichte *f*; (*lie*) Märchen *nt*; (*US*) = **storey**; **~book** *n* Geschichtenbuch *nt*; **~teller** *n* Geschichtenerzähler *m*

stout [staut] *adj* (*bold*) tapfer; (*fat*) beleibt ♦ *n* Starkbier *nt*; (*also: sweet ~*) ≈ Malzbier *nt*

stove [stəuv] *n* (Koch)herd *m*; (*for heating*) Ofen *m*

stow [stəu] *vt* verstauen; **~away** *n* blinde(r) Passagier *m*

straddle ['strædl] *vt* (*horse, fence*) rittlings sitzen auf +*dat*; (*fig*) überbrücken

straggle ['strægl] *vi* (*branches etc*) wuchern; (*people*) nachhinken; **~r** *n* Nachzügler *m*; **straggly** *adj* (*hair*) zottig

straight [streɪt] *adj* gerade; (*honest*) offen, ehrlich; (*drink*) pur ♦ *adv* (*direct*) direkt, geradewegs; **to put** *or* **get sth ~** etw in Ordnung bringen; **~ away** sofort; **~ off** sofort; **~en** *vt* (*also: ~ out*) gerade machen; (*fig*) klarstellen; **~-faced** *adv* ohne die Miene zu verziehen ♦ *adj*: **to be ~-faced** keine Miene verziehen; **~forward** *adj* einfach, unkompliziert

strain [streɪn] *n* Belastung *f*; (*streak, trace*) Zug *m*; (*of music*) Fetzen *m* ♦ *vt* überanstrengen; (*stretch*) anspannen; (*muscle*) zerren; (*filter*) (durch)seihen ♦ *vi* sich anstrengen; **~ed** *adj* (*laugh*) gezwungen; (*relations*) gespannt; **~er** *n* Sieb *nt*

strait [streɪt] *n* Straße *f*, Meerenge *f*; **~jacket** *n* Zwangsjacke *f*; **~-laced** *adj* engherzig, streng

strand [strænd] *n* (*of hair*) Strähne *f*; (*also fig*) Faden *m*; **~ed** *adj* (*also fig*) gestrandet

strange [streɪndʒ] *adj* fremd; (*unusual*) seltsam; **~r** *n* Fremde(r) *mf*

strangle ['stræŋgl] *vt* erwürgen; **~hold** *n* (*fig*) Umklammerung *f*

strap [stræp] *n* Riemen *m*; (*on clothes*) Träger *m* ♦ *vt* (*fasten*) festschnallen

strapping ['stræpɪŋ] *adj* stramm

strata ['strɑːtə] *npl of* **stratum**

stratagem ['strætədʒəm] *n* (Kriegs)list *f*

strategic [strə'tiːdʒɪk] *adj* strategisch

strategy ['strætədʒɪ] *n* (*fig*) Strategie *f*

stratum ['strɑːtəm] (*pl* **-ta**) *n* Schicht *f*

straw [strɔː] *n* Stroh *nt*; (*single stalk, drinking ~*) Strohhalm *m*; **that's the last ~!** das ist der Gipfel!

strawberry ['strɔːbərɪ] *n* Erdbeere *f*

stray [streɪ] *adj* (*animal*) verirrt; (*thought*) zufällig ♦ *vi* herumstreunen

streak ['striːk] *n* Streifen *m*; (*in character*) Einschlag *m*; (*in hair*) Strähne *f* ♦ *vt* streifen ♦ *vi* zucken; (*move quickly*) flitzen; **~ of bad luck** Pechsträhne *f*; **~y** *adj* gestreift; (*bacon*) durchwachsen

stream [striːm] *n* (*brook*) Bach *m*; (*fig*) Strom *m* ♦ *vt* (*SCH*) in (Leistungs)gruppen einteilen ♦ *vi* strömen; **to ~ in/out** (*people*) hinein-/hinausströmen

streamer ['striːmə*] *n* (*flag*) Wimpel *m*; (*of paper*) Luftschlange *f*

streamlined ['striːmlaɪnd] *adj* stromlinienförmig; (*effective*) rationell

street [striːt] *n* Straße *f* ♦ *adj* Straßen-; **~car** (*US*) *n* Straßenbahn *f*; **~ lamp** *n* Straßenlaterne *f*; **~ plan** *n* Stadtplan *m*; **~wise** (*inf*) *adj*: **to be ~wise** wissen, wo es lang geht

strength [streŋθ] *n* (*also fig*) Stärke *f*; Kraft *f*; **~en** *vt* (ver)stärken

strenuous ['strenjuəs] *adj* anstrengend

stress [stres] *n* Druck *m*; (*mental*) Streß *m*; (*GRAM*) Betonung *f* ♦ *vt* betonen

stretch [stretʃ] *n* Strecke *f* ♦ *vt* ausdehnen, strecken ♦ *vi* sich erstrecken; (*person*) sich strecken; **~ out** *vi* sich ausstrecken ♦ *vt* ausstrecken

stretcher ['stretʃə*] *n* Tragbahre *f*

strewn [struːn] *adj*: **~ with** übersät mit

stricken ['strɪkən] *adj* (*person*) ergriffen; (*city, country*) heimgesucht; **~ with** (*arthritis, disease*) leidend unter +*dat*

strict [strɪkt] *adj* (*exact*) genau; (*severe*) streng; **~ly** *adv* streng, genau

stridden ['strɪdn] *pp of* **stride**

stride [straɪd] (*pt* **strode**, *pp* **stridden**) *n* lange(r) Schritt *m* ♦ *vi* schreiten

strident ['straɪdənt] *adj* schneidend, durchdringend

strife [straɪf] *n* Streit *m*

strike [straɪk] (*pt, pp* **struck**) *n* Streik *m*; (*attack*) Schlag *m* ♦ *vt* (*hit*) schlagen; (*collide*) stoßen gegen; (*come to mind*) einfallen +*dat*; (*stand out*) auffallen +*dat*; (*find*) finden ♦ *vi* (*stop work*) streiken; (*attack*) zuschlagen; (*clock*) schlagen; **on ~** (*workers*) im Streik; **to ~ a match** ein Streichholz anzünden; **~ down** *vt* (*lay low*) niederschlagen; **~ out** *vt* (*cross out*) ausstreichen; **~ up** *vt* (*music*) anstimmen; (*friendship*) schließen; **~r** *n* Streikende(r) *mf*

striking ['straɪkɪŋ] *adj* auffallend

string [strɪŋ] (*pt, pp* **strung**) *n* Schnur *f*; (*row*) Reihe *f*; (*MUS*) Saite *f* ♦ *vt*: **to ~ together** aneinanderreihen ♦ *vi*: **to ~ out** (sich) verteilen; **the ~s** *npl* (*MUS*) die Streichinstrumente *pl*; **to pull ~s** (*fig*) Fäden ziehen; **~ bean** *n* grüne Bohne *f*; **~(ed) instrument** *n* (*MUS*) Saiteninstrument *nt*

stringent ['strɪndʒənt] *adj* streng

strip [strɪp] *n* Streifen *m* ♦ *vt* (*uncover*) abstreifen, abziehen; (*clothes*) ausziehen; (*TECH*) auseinandernehmen ♦ *vi* (*undress*) sich ausziehen; **~ cartoon** *n* Bildserie *f*

stripe [straɪp] *n* Streifen *m*; **~d** *adj* gestreift

strip lighting *n* Neonlicht *nt*

stripper ['strɪpə*] *n* Stripteasetänzerin *f*

strive [straɪv] (*pt* **strove**, *pp* **striven**) *vi*: **to ~ (for)** streben (nach)

strode [strəʊd] *pt of* **stride**

stroke [strəʊk] *n* Schlag *m*; (*SWIMMING, ROWING*) Stoß *m*; (*TECH*) Hub *m*; (*MED*) Schlaganfall *m*; (*caress*) Streicheln *nt* ♦ *vt* streicheln; **at a ~** mit einem Schlag

stroll [strəʊl] *n* Spaziergang *m* ♦ *vi* schlendern; **~er** (*US*) *n* (*pushchair*) Sportwagen *m*

strong [strɒŋ] *adj* stark; (*firm*) fest; **they are 50 ~** sie sind 50 Mann stark; **~box** *n* Kassette *f*; **~hold** *n* Hochburg *f*; **~ly** *adv* stark; **~room** *n* Tresor *m*

strove [strəʊv] *pt of* **strive**

struck [strʌk] *pt, pp of* **strike**

structure ['strʌktʃə*] *n* Struktur *f*, Aufbau *m*; (*building*) Bau *m*

struggle ['strʌgl] *n* Kampf *m* ♦ *vi* (*fight*) kämpfen

strum [strʌm] *vt* (*guitar*) klimpern auf +*dat*

strung [strʌŋ] *pt, pp of* **string**

strut [strʌt] *n* Strebe *f*, Stütze *f* ♦ *vi* stolzieren

stub [stʌb] *n* Stummel *m*; (*of cigarette*) Kippe *f* ♦ *vt*: **to ~ one's toe** sich *dat* den Zeh anstoßen; **~ out** *vt* ausdrücken

stubble ['stʌbl] *n* Stoppel *f*

stubborn ['stʌbən] *adj* hartnäckig

stucco ['stʌkəʊ] *n* Stuck *m*

stuck [stʌk] *pt, pp of* **stick** ♦ *adj* (*jammed*) klemmend; **~-up** *adj* hochnäsig

stud [stʌd] *n* (*button*) Kragenknopf *m*; (*place*) Gestüt *nt* ♦ *vt* (*fig*): **~ded with** übersät mit

student ['stjuːdənt] *n* Student(in) *m(f)*; (*US*) Student(in) *m(f)*, Schüler(in) *m(f)* ♦ *adj* Studenten-; **~ driver** (*US*) *n* Fahrschüler(in) *m(f)*

studio ['stjuːdɪəʊ] *n* Studio *nt*; (*for artist*) Atelier *nt*; **~ apartment** (*US*) *n* Appartement *nt*; **~ flat** *n* Appartement *nt*

studious ['stjuːdɪəs] *adj* lernbegierig

study ['stʌdɪ] *n* Studium *nt*; (*investigation*) Studium *nt*, Untersuchung *f*; (*room*) Arbeitszimmer *nt*; (*essay etc*) Studie *f* ♦ *vt* studieren; (*face*) erforschen; (*evidence*) prüfen ♦ *vi* studieren

stuff [stʌf] *n* Stoff *m*; (*inf*) Zeug *nt* ♦ *vt* stopfen, füllen; (*animal*) ausstopfen; **~ing** *n* Füllung *f*; **~y** *adj* (*room*) schwül; (*person*) spießig

stumble ['stʌmbl] *vi* stolpern; **to ~ across** (*fig*) zufällig stoßen auf +*acc*

stumbling block ['stʌmblɪŋ-] *n* Hindernis *nt*

stump [stʌmp] *n* Stumpf *m* ♦ *vt* umwerfen

stun [stʌn] *vt* betäuben; (*shock*) niederschmettern

stung [stʌŋ] *pt, pp of* **sting**

stunk [stʌŋk] *pp of* **stink**

stunning ['stʌnɪŋ] *adj* betäubend; (*news*) überwältigend, umwerfend

stunt [stʌnt] *n* Kunststück *nt*, Trick *m*;
~ed *adj* verkümmert; ~man (*irreg*) *n*
Stuntman *m*
stupefy ['stju:pɪfaɪ] *vt* betäuben; (*by
news*) bestürzen
stupendous [stjʊ'pendəs] *adj*
erstaunlich, enorm
stupid ['stju:pɪd] *adj* dumm; ~ity
[stju:'pɪdɪtɪ] *n* Dummheit *f*
stupor ['stju:pə*] *n* Betäubung *f*
sturdy ['stɜ:dɪ] *adj* kräftig, robust
stutter ['stʌtə*] *n* Stottern *nt* ♦ *vi*
stottern
sty [staɪ] *n* Schweinestall *m*
stye [staɪ] *n* Gerstenkorn *nt*
style [staɪl] *n* Stil *m*; (*fashion*) Mode *f*
stylish ['staɪlɪʃ] *adj* modisch
stylist ['staɪlɪst] *n* (*hair* ~) Friseur *m*,
Friseuse *f*
stylus ['staɪləs] *n* (Grammophon)nadel *f*
suave [swɑːv] *adj* zuvorkommend
sub... *prefix* Unter...; ~**conscious** *adj*
unterbewußt ♦ *n*: **the ~conscious** das
Unterbewußte; ~**contract** *vt* (vertraglich)
untervermitteln; ~**divide** *vt* unterteilen
subdue [səb'dju:] *vt* unterwerfen; ~d *adj*
(*lighting*) gedämpft; (*person*) still
subject [*n, adj* 'sʌbdʒɪkt, *vb* səb'dʒekt] *n*
(*of kingdom*) Untertan *m*; (*citizen*)
Staatsangehörige(r) *mf*; (*topic*) Thema *nt*;
(*SCH*) Fach *nt*; (*GRAM*) Subjekt *nt* ♦ *adj*: **to
be ~ to** unterworfen sein +*dat*; (*exposed*)
ausgesetzt sein +*dat* ♦ *vt* (*subdue*)
unterwerfen; (*expose*) aussetzen; ~**ive**
[səb'dʒektɪv] *adj* subjektiv; ~ **matter** *n*
Thema *nt*
subjugate ['sʌbdʒʊgeɪt] *vt* unterjochen
subjunctive [səb'dʒʌŋktɪv] *adj*
Konjunktiv- ♦ *n* Konjunktiv *m*
sublet ['sʌb'let] (*irreg: like* let) *vt*
untervermieten
sublime [sə'blaɪm] *adj* erhaben
submachine gun ['sʌbmə'ʃiːn-] *n*
Maschinenpistole *f*
submarine [sʌbmə'riːn] *n* Unterseeboot
nt, U-Boot *nt*
submerge [səb'mɜːdʒ] *vt* untertauchen;
(*flood*) überschwemmen ♦ *vi* untertauchen
submission [səb'mɪʃən] *n* (*obedience*)

Gehorsam *m*; (*claim*) Behauptung *f*; (*of
plan*) Unterbreitung *f*
submissive [səb'mɪsɪv] *adj* demütig,
unterwürfig (*pej*)
submit [səb'mɪt] *vt* behaupten; (*plan*)
unterbreiten ♦ *vi* (*give in*) sich ergeben
subnormal ['sʌb'nɔːməl] *adj*
minderbegabt
subordinate [sə'bɔːdɪnət] *adj*
untergeordnet ♦ *n* Untergebene(r) *mf*
subpoena [sə'piːnə] *n* Vorladung *f* ♦ *vt*
vorladen
subscribe [səb'skraɪb] *vi*: **to ~ to** (*view
etc*) unterstützen; (*newspaper*) abonnieren;
~**r** *n* (*to periodical*) Abonnent *m*; (*TEL*)
Telefonteilnehmer *m*
subscription [səb'skrɪpʃən] *n*
Abonnement *nt*; (*money subscribed*)
(Mitglieds)beitrag *m*
subsequent ['sʌbsɪkwənt] *adj* folgend,
später; ~**ly** *adv* später
subside [səb'saɪd] *vi* sich senken; ~**nce**
[sʌb'saɪdəns] *n* Senkung *f*
subsidiarity [səbsɪdɪ'ærɪtɪ] *n* (*POL*)
Subsidiarität *f*
subsidiary [səb'sɪdɪərɪ] *adj* Neben- ♦ *n*
(*company*) Tochtergesellschaft *f*
subsidize ['sʌbsɪdaɪz] *vt* subventionieren
subsidy ['sʌbsɪdɪ] *n* Subvention *f*
subsistence [səb'sɪstəns] *n* Unterhalt *m*
substance ['sʌbstəns] *n* Substanz *f*
substantial [səb'stænʃəl] *adj* (*strong*)
fest, kräftig; (*important*) wesentlich; ~**ly**
adv erheblich
substantiate [səb'stænʃɪeɪt] *vt*
begründen, belegen
substitute ['sʌbstɪtjuːt] *n* Ersatz *m* ♦ *vt*
ersetzen
substitution [sʌbstɪ'tjuːʃən] *n* Ersetzung
f
subterfuge ['sʌbtəfjuːdʒ] *n* Vorwand *m*;
(*trick*) Trick *m*
subterranean [sʌbtə'reɪnɪən] *adj*
unterirdisch
subtitle ['sʌbtaɪtl] *n* Untertitel *m*
subtle ['sʌtl] *adj* fein; ~**ty** *n* Feinheit *f*
subtotal [sʌb'təʊtl] *n* Zwischensumme *f*
subtract [səb'trækt] *vt* abziehen; ~**ion**
[səb'trækʃən] *n* Abziehen *nt*, Subtraktion

f

suburb ['sʌbɜ:b] *n* Vorort *m*; **the ~s** die Außenbezirke *pl*; **~an** [sə'bɜ:bən] *adj* Vorort(s)-, Stadtrand-; **~ia** [sə'bɜ:bɪə] *n* Vorstadt *f*

subversive [səb'vɜ:sɪv] *adj* subversiv

subway ['sʌbweɪ] *n* (*US*) U-Bahn *f*; (*BRIT*) Unterführung *f*

succeed [sək'si:d] *vi* (*person*) erfolgreich sein, Erfolg haben; (*plan etc also*) gelingen ♦ *vt* (nach)folgen +*dat*; **he ~ed in doing it** es gelang ihm, es zu tun; **~ing** *adj* (nach)folgend

success [sək'ses] *n* Erfolg *m*; **to be ~ful (in doing sth)** Erfolg haben (bei etw); **~ful** *adj* erfolgreich; **~fully** *adv* erfolgreich

succession [sək'seʃən] *n* (Aufeinander)folge *f*; (*to throne*) Nachfolge *f*

successive [sək'sesɪv] *adj* aufeinanderfolgend

successor [sək'sesə*] *n* Nachfolger(in) *m(f)*

succinct [sək'sɪŋkt] *adj* knapp

succulent ['sʌkjʊlənt] *adj* saftig

succumb [sə'kʌm] *vi*: **to ~ (to)** erliegen (+*dat*); (*yield*) nachgeben (+*dat*)

such [sʌtʃ] *adj* solche(r, s); **~ a book** so ein Buch; **~ books** solche Bücher; **~ courage** so ein Mut; **~ a long trip** so eine lange Reise; **~ a lot of** so viel(e); **~ as** wie; **a noise ~ as** so ein derartiger Lärm, daß; **as ~** an sich; **~-and-~ a time/town** die und die Zeit/Stadt

suck [sʌk] *vt* saugen; (*ice cream etc*) lutschen; **~er** (*inf*) *n* Idiot *m*

suction ['sʌkʃən] *n* Saugkraft *f*

sudden ['sʌdn] *adj* plötzlich; **all of a ~** auf einmal; **~ly** *adv* plötzlich

suds [sʌdz] *npl* Seifenlauge *f*; (*lather*) Seifenschaum *m*

sue [su:] *vt* verklagen

suede [sweɪd] *n* Wildleder *nt*

suet ['su:ɪt] *n* Nierenfett *nt*

Suez [su:ɪz] *n*: **the ~ Canal** der Suezkanal

suffer ['sʌfə*] *vt* (er)leiden ♦ *vi* leiden; **~er** *n* Leidende(r) *mf*; **~ing** *n* Leiden *nt*

suffice [sə'faɪs] *vi* genügen

sufficient [sə'fɪʃənt] *adj* ausreichend; **~ly** *adv* ausreichend

suffix ['sʌfɪks] *n* Nachsilbe *f*

suffocate ['sʌfəkeɪt] *vt*, *vi* ersticken

suffrage ['sʌfrɪdʒ] *n* Wahlrecht *nt*

suffused [sə'fju:zd] *adj*: **to be ~ with sth** von etw erfüllt sein

sugar ['ʃʊgə*] *n* Zucker *m* ♦ *vt* zuckern; **~ beet** *n* Zuckerrübe *f*; **~ cane** *n* Zuckerrohr *nt*; **~y** *adj* süß

suggest [sə'dʒest] *vt* vorschlagen; (*show*) schließen lassen auf +*acc*; **~ion** [sə'dʒestʃən] *n* Vorschlag *m*; **~ive** *adj* anregend; (*indecent*) zweideutig

suicide ['sʊɪsaɪd] *n* Selbstmord *m*; **to commit ~** Selbstmord begehen

suit [su:t] *n* Anzug *m*; (*CARDS*) Farbe *f* ♦ *vt* passen +*dat*; (*clothes*) stehen +*dat*; **well ~ed** (*well matched: couple*) gut zusammenpassend; **~able** *adj* geeignet, passend; **~ably** *adv* passend, angemessen

suitcase ['su:tkeɪs] *n* (Hand)koffer *m*

suite [swi:t] *n* (*of rooms*) Zimmerflucht *f*; (*of furniture*) Einrichtung *f*; (*MUS*) Suite *f*

suitor ['su:tə*] *n* (*JUR*) Kläger(in) *m(f)*

sulfur ['sʌlfə*] (*US*) *n* = **sulphur**

sulk [sʌlk] *vi* schmollen; **~y** *adj* schmollend

sullen ['sʌlən] *adj* mürrisch

sulphur ['sʌlfə*] (*US* **sulfur**) *n* Schwefel *m*

sultana [sʌl'tɑ:nə] *n* (*fruit*) Sultanine *f*

sultry ['sʌltrɪ] *adj* schwül

sum [sʌm] *n* Summe *f*; (*money*) Betrag *m*, Summe *f*; (*arithmetic*) Rechenaufgabe *f*; **~ up** *vt*, *vi* zusammenfassen

summarize ['sʌməraɪz] *vt* kurz zusammenfassen

summary ['sʌmərɪ] *n* Zusammenfassung *f* ♦ *adj* (*justice*) kurzerhand erteilt

summer ['sʌmə*] *n* Sommer *m* ♦ *adj* Sommer-; **~house** *n* (*in garden*) Gartenhaus *nt*; **~time** *n* Sommerzeit *f*

summit ['sʌmɪt] *n* Gipfel *m*; **~ (conference)** *n* Gipfelkonferenz *f*

summon ['sʌmən] *vt* herbeirufen; (*JUR*) vorladen; (*gather up*) aufbringen; **~s** (*JUR*) *n* Vorladung *f* ♦ *vt* vorladen

sump [sʌmp] (*BRIT*) *n* (*AUT*) Ölwanne *f*

sumptuous ['sʌmptjʊəs] *adj* prächtig

sun [sʌn] *n* Sonne *f*; ~**bathe** *vi* sich sonnen; ~**burn** *n* Sonnenbrand *m*

Sunday ['sʌndeɪ] *n* Sonntag *m*; ~ **school** *n* Sonntagsschule *f*

sundial ['sʌndaɪəl] *n* Sonnenuhr *f*

sundown ['sʌndaʊn] *n* Sonnenuntergang *m*

sundry ['sʌndrɪ] *adj* verschieden; **all and** ~ alle; **sundries** *npl* (*miscellaneous items*) Verschiedene(s) *nt*

sunflower ['sʌnflaʊə*] *n* Sonnenblume *f*

sung [sʌŋ] *pp of* **sing**

sunglasses ['sʌnglɑːsɪz] *npl* Sonnenbrille *f*

sunk [sʌŋk] *pp of* **sink**

sun: ~**light** ['sʌnlaɪt] *n* Sonnenlicht *nt*; ~**lit** ['sʌnlɪt] *adj* sonnenbeschienen; ~**ny** ['sʌnɪ] *adj* sonnig; ~**rise** ['sʌnraɪz] *n* Sonnenaufgang *m*; ~**set** ['sʌnset] *n* Sonnenuntergang *m*; ~**shade** ['sʌnʃeɪd] *n* Sonnenschirm *m*; ~**shine** ['sʌnʃaɪn] *n* Sonnenschein *m*; ~**stroke** ['sʌnstrəʊk] *n* Hitzschlag *m*; ~**tan** ['sʌntæn] *n* (Sonnen)bräune *f*; ~**tan oil** *n* Sonnenöl *nt*

super ['suːpə*] (*inf*) *adj* prima, klasse

superannuation ['suːpərænjʊ'eɪʃən] *n* Pension *f*

superb [suː'pɜːb] *adj* ausgezeichnet, hervorragend

supercilious [suːpə'sɪlɪəs] *adj* herablassend

superficial [suːpə'fɪʃəl] *adj* oberflächlich

superfluous [sʊ'pɜːflʊəs] *adj* überflüssig

superhuman [suːpə'hjuːmən] *adj* (*effort*) übermenschlich

superimpose ['suːpərɪm'pəʊz] *vt* übereinanderlegen

superintendent [suːpərɪn'tendənt] *n* Polizeichef *m*

superior [sʊ'pɪərɪə*] *adj* überlegen; (*better*) besser ♦ *n* Vorgesetzte(r) *mf*; ~**ity** [sʊpɪərɪ'ɒrɪtɪ] *n* Überlegenheit *f*

superlative [suː'pɜːlətɪv] *adj* überragend

superman ['suːpəmæn] (*irreg*) *n* Übermensch *m*

supermarket ['suːpəmɑːkɪt] *n* Supermarkt *m*

supernatural [suːpə'nætʃərəl] *adj* übernatürlich

superpower ['suːpəpaʊə*] *n* Weltmacht *f*

supersede [suːpə'siːd] *vt* ersetzen

supersonic ['suːpə'sɒnɪk] *adj* Überschall-

superstition [suːpə'stɪʃən] *n* Aberglaube *m*

superstitious [suːpə'stɪʃəs] *adj* abergläubisch

supervise ['suːpəvaɪz] *vt* beaufsichtigen, kontrollieren

supervision [suːpə'vɪʒən] *n* Aufsicht *f*

supervisor [suːpəvaɪzə*] *n* Aufsichtsperson *f*; ~**y** *adj* Aufsichts-

supine ['suːpaɪn] *adj* auf dem Rücken liegend

supper ['sʌpə*] *n* Abendessen *nt*

supplant [sə'plɑːnt] *vt* (*person, thing*) ersetzen

supple ['sʌpl] *adj* geschmeidig

supplement [*n* 'sʌplɪmənt, *vb* 'sʌplɪment] *n* Ergänzung *f*; (*in book*) Nachtrag *m* ♦ *vt* ergänzen; ~**ary** [sʌplɪ'mentərɪ] *adj* ergänzend

supplier [sə'plaɪə*] *n* Lieferant *m*

supplies [sə'plaɪz] *npl* (*food*) Vorräte *pl*; (*MIL*) Nachschub *m*

supply [sə'plaɪ] *vt* liefern ♦ *n* Vorrat *m*; (*supplying*) Lieferung *f* ♦ *adj* (*teacher etc*) Aushilfs-; *see also* **supplies**

support [sə'pɔːt] *n* Unterstützung *f*; (*TECH*) Stütze *f* ♦ *vt* (*hold up*) stützen, tragen; (*provide for*) ernähren; (*be in favour of*) unterstützen; ~**er** *n* Anhänger(in) *m(f)*

suppose [sə'pəʊz] *vt, vi* annehmen; **to be** ~**d to do sth** etw tun sollen; ~**dly** [sə'pəʊzɪdlɪ] *adv* angeblich

supposing [sə'pəʊzɪŋ] *conj* angenommen

supposition [sʌpə'zɪʃən] *n* Voraussetzung *f*

suppress [sə'pres] *vt* unterdrücken; ~**ion** [sə'preʃən] *n* Unterdrückung *f*

supremacy [sʊ'preməsɪ] *n* Vorherrschaft *f*, Oberhoheit *f*

supreme [sʊ'priːm] *adj* oberste(r, s), höchste(r, s)

surcharge ['sɜːtʃɑːdʒ] *n* Zuschlag *m*

sure [ʃʊə*] *adj* sicher, gewiß; ~! (*of*

course) klar!; **to make ~ of sth/that** sich einer Sache *gen* vergewissern/vergewissern, daß; **~ enough** (*with past*) tatsächlich; (*with future*) ganz bestimmt; **~-footed** *adj* sicher (auf den Füßen); **~ly** *adv* (*certainly*) sicherlich, gewiß; **~ly it's wrong** das ist doch wohl falsch

surety ['ʃʊərətɪ] *n* Sicherheit *f*, (*person*) Bürge *m*

surf [sɜːf] *n* Brandung *f*

surface ['sɜːfɪs] *n* Oberfläche *f* ♦ *vt* (*roadway*) teeren ♦ *vi* auftauchen; **~ mail** *n* gewöhnliche Post *f*

surfboard ['sɜːfbɔːd] *n* Wellenreiterbrett *nt*

surfeit ['sɜːfɪt] *n* Übermaß *nt*

surfing ['sɜːfɪŋ] *n* Wellenreiten *nt*

surge [sɜːdʒ] *n* Woge *f* ♦ *vi* wogen

surgeon ['sɜːdʒən] *n* Chirurg(in) *m(f)*

surgery ['sɜːdʒərɪ] *n* (*BRIT: place*) Praxis *f*; (: *time*) Sprechstunde *f*; (*treatment*) Operation *f*; **to undergo ~** operiert werden; **~ hours** *npl* (*BRIT*) Sprechstunden *pl*

surgical ['sɜːdʒɪkəl] *adj* chirurgisch; **~ spirit** (*BRIT*) *n* Wundbenzin *nt*

surly ['sɜːlɪ] *adj* verdrießlich, grob

surmount [sɜːˈmaʊnt] *vt* überwinden

surname ['sɜːneɪm] *n* Zuname *m*

surpass [sɜːˈpɑːs] *vt* übertreffen

surplus ['sɜːpləs] *n* Überschuß *m* ♦ *adj* überschüssig, Über(schuß)-

surprise [səˈpraɪz] *n* Überraschung *f* ♦ *vt* überraschen

surprising [səˈpraɪzɪŋ] *adj* überraschend; **~ly** *adv* überraschend(erweise)

surrender [səˈrendə*] *n* Kapitulation *f* ♦ *vi* sich ergeben

surreptitious [sʌrəpˈtɪʃəs] *adj* heimlich; (*look also*) verstohlen

surrogate ['sʌrəgɪt] *n* Ersatz *m*; **~ mother** *n* Leihmutter *f*

surround [səˈraʊnd] *vt* umgeben; **~ing** *adj* (*countryside*) umliegend; **~ings** *npl* Umgebung *f*; (*environment*) Umwelt *f*

surveillance [sɜːˈveɪləns] *n* Überwachung *f*

survey [*n* 'sɜːveɪ, *vb* sɜːˈveɪ] *n* Übersicht *f* ♦ *vt* überblicken; (*land*) vermessen; **~or**

[səˈveɪə*] *n* Land(ver)messer(in) *m(f)*

survival [səˈvaɪvəl] *n* Überleben *nt*

survive [səˈvaɪv] *vt, vi* überleben

survivor [səˈvaɪvə*] *n* Überlebende(r) *mf*

susceptible [səˈseptəbl] *adj:* **~ (to)** empfindlich (gegen); (*charms etc*) empfänglich (für)

suspect [*n, adj* 'sʌspekt, *vb* səsˈpekt] *n* Verdächtige(r) *mf* ♦ *adj* verdächtig ♦ *vt* verdächtigen; (*think*) vermuten

suspend [səsˈpend] *vt* verschieben; (*from work*) suspendieren; (*hang up*) aufhängen; (*SPORT*) sperren; **~ed sentence** *n* (*JUR*) zur Bewährung ausgesetzte Strafe; **~er belt** *n* Strumpf(halter)gürtel *m*; **~ers** *npl* (*BRIT*) Strumpfhalter *m*; (: *men's*) Sockenhalter *m*; (*US*) Hosenträger *m*

suspense [səsˈpens] *n* Spannung *f*

suspension [səsˈpenʃən] *n* (*from work*) Suspendierung *f*, (*SPORT*) Sperrung *f*; (*AUT*) Federung *f*; **~ bridge** *n* Hängebrücke *f*

suspicion [səsˈpɪʃən] *n* Mißtrauen *nt*; Verdacht *m*

suspicious [səsˈpɪʃəs] *adj* mißtrauisch; (*causing suspicion*) verdächtig

sustain [səsˈteɪn] *vt* (*maintain*) aufrechterhalten; (*confirm*) bestätigen; (*JUR*) anerkennen; (*injury*) davontragen; **~able** *adj* (*development, growth etc*) aufrechtzuerhalten; **~ed** *adj* (*effort*) anhaltend

sustenance ['sʌstɪnəns] *n* Nahrung *f*

swab [swɒb] *n* (*MED*) Tupfer *m*

swagger ['swægə*] *vi* stolzieren

swallow ['swɒləʊ] *n* (*bird*) Schwalbe *f*; (*of food etc*) Schluck *m* ♦ *vt* (ver)schlucken; **~ up** *vt* verschlingen

swam [swæm] *pt of* **swim**

swamp [swɒmp] *n* Sumpf *m* ♦ *vt* überschwemmen

swan [swɒn] *n* Schwan *m*

swap [swɒp] *n* Tausch *m* ♦ *vt:* **to ~ sth (for sth)** etw (gegen etw) tauschen *or* eintauschen

swarm [swɔːm] *n* Schwarm *m* ♦ *vi:* **to ~** *or* **be ~ing with** wimmeln von

swarthy ['swɔːðɪ] *adj* dunkel, braun

swastika ['swɒstɪkə] *n* Hakenkreuz *nt*

swat [swɒt] *vt* totschlagen

sway [sweɪ] *vi* schwanken; (*branches*) schaukeln, sich wiegen ♦ *vt* schwenken; (*influence*) beeinflussen

swear [swɛə*] (*pt* swore, *pp* sworn) *vi* (*promise*) schwören; (*curse*) fluchen; **to ~ to sth** schwören auf etw *acc*; **~word** *n* Fluch *m*

sweat [swet] *n* Schweiß *m* ♦ *vi* schwitzen

sweater ['swetə*] *n* Pullover *m*

sweatshirt ['swetʃɜːt] *n* Sweatshirt *nt*

sweaty ['swetɪ] *adj* verschwitzt

Swede [swiːd] *n* Schwede *m*, Schwedin *f*

swede [swiːd] (*BRIT*) *n* Steckrübe *f*

Sweden ['swiːdn] *n* Schweden *nt*

Swedish ['swiːdɪʃ] *adj* schwedisch ♦ *n* (*LING*) Schwedisch *nt*

sweep [swiːp] (*pt, pp* swept) *n* (*chimney ~*) Schornsteinfeger *m* ♦ *vt* fegen, kehren ♦ *vi* (*go quickly*) rauschen; **~ away** *vt* wegfegen; **~ past** *vt* vorbeisausen; **~ up** *vt* zusammenkehren; **~ing** *adj* (*gesture*) schwungvoll; (*statement*) verallgemeinernd

sweet [swiːt] *n* (*course*) Nachtisch *m*; (*candy*) Bonbon *nt* ♦ *adj* süß; **~corn** *n* Zuckermais *m*; **~en** *vt* süßen; (*fig*) versüßen; **~heart** *n* Liebste(r) *mf*; **~ness** *n* Süße *f*; **~ pea** *n* Gartenwicke *f*

swell [swel] (*pt* ~ed, *pp* swollen *or* ~ed) *n* Seegang *m* ♦ *adj* (*inf*) todschick ♦ *vt* (*numbers*) vermehren ♦ *vi* (*also:* ~ up) (an)schwellen; **~ing** *n* Schwellung *f*

sweltering ['sweltərɪŋ] *adj* drückend

swept [swept] *pt, pp of* sweep

swerve [swɜːv] *vt, vi* ausscheren

swift [swɪft] *n* Mauersegler *m* ♦ *adj* geschwind, schnell, rasch; **~ly** *adv* geschwind, schnell, rasch

swig [swɪɡ] *n* Zug *m*

swill [swɪl] *n* (*for pigs*) Schweinefutter *nt* ♦ *vt* spülen

swim [swɪm] (*pt* swam, *pp* swum) *n*: **to go for a ~** schwimmen gehen ♦ *vi* schwimmen ♦ *vt* (*cross*) (durch)schwimmen; **~mer** *n* Schwimmer(in) *m(f)*; **~ming** *n* Schwimmen *nt*; **~ming cap** *n* Badehaube *f*, Badekappe *f*; **~ming costume** (*BRIT*) *n* Badeanzug *m*; **~ming pool** *n* Schwimmbecken *nt*; (*private*) Swimmingpool *m*; **~suit** *n* Badeanzug *m*

swindle ['swɪndl] *n* Schwindel *m*, Betrug *m* ♦ *vt* betrügen

swine [swaɪn] *n* (*also fig*) Schwein *nt*

swing [swɪŋ] (*pt, pp* swung) *n* (*child's*) Schaukel *f*; (*movement*) Schwung *m*; (*MUS*) Swing *m* ♦ *vt* schwingen ♦ *vi* schwingen, schaukeln; (*turn quickly*) schwenken; **in full ~** in vollem Gange; **~ bridge** *n* Drehbrücke *f*; **~ door** (*BRIT*) *n* Schwingtür *f*

swingeing ['swɪndʒɪŋ] (*BRIT*) *adj* hart; (*taxation, cuts*) extrem

swinging door ['swɪŋɪŋ-] (*US*) *n* Schwingtür *f*

swipe [swaɪp] *n* Hieb *m* ♦ *vt* (*inf: hit*) hart schlagen; (: *steal*) klauen

swirl [swɜːl] *vi* wirbeln

swish [swɪʃ] *adj* (*inf: smart*) schick ♦ *vi* zischen; (*grass, skirts*) rascheln

Swiss [swɪs] *adj* Schweizer, schweizerisch ♦ *n* Schweizer(in) *m(f)*; **the ~** *npl* (*people*) die Schweizer *pl*

switch [swɪtʃ] *n* (*ELEC*) Schalter *m*; (*change*) Wechsel *m* ♦ *vt* (*ELEC*) schalten; (*change*) wechseln ♦ *vi* wechseln; **~ off** *vt* ab- *or* ausschalten; **~ on** *vt* an- *or* einschalten; **~board** *n* Zentrale *f*; (*board*) Schaltbrett *nt*

Switzerland ['swɪtsələnd] *n* die Schweiz

swivel ['swɪvl] *vt* (*also:* ~ round) drehen ♦ *vi* sich drehen

swollen ['swəʊlən] *pp of* swell

swoon [swuːn] *vi* (*old*) in Ohnmacht fallen

swoop [swuːp] *n* Sturzflug *m*; (*esp by police*) Razzia *f* ♦ *vi* (*also:* ~ down) stürzen

swop [swɒp] = swap

sword [sɔːd] *n* Schwert *nt*; **~fish** *n* Schwertfisch *m*

swore [swɔː*] *pt of* swear

sworn [swɔːn] *pp of* swear

swot [swɒt] *vt, vi* pauken

swum [swʌm] *pp of* swim

swung [swʌŋ] *pt, pp of* swing

sycamore ['sɪkəmɔː*] *n* (*US*) Platane *f*; (*BRIT*) Bergahorn *m*

syllable ['sɪləbl] *n* Silbe *f*

syllabus ['sıləbəs] *n* Lehrplan *m*

symbol ['sımbəl] *n* Symbol *nt*; **~ic(al)** [sım'bɒlık(əl)] *adj* symbolisch

symmetry ['sımıtrı] *n* Symmetrie *f*

sympathetic [sımpə'θetık] *adj* mitfühlend

sympathize ['sımpəθaız] *vi* mitfühlen; **~r** *n* Mitfühlende(r) *mf*; *(POL)* Sympathisant(in) *m(f)*

sympathy ['sımpəθı] *n* Mitleid *nt*, Mitgefühl *nt*; *(condolence)* Beileid *nt*; **with our deepest ~** mit tiefempfundenem Beileid

symphony ['sımfənı] *n* Sinfonie *f*

symposium [sım'pəʊzıəm] *n* Tagung *f*

symptom ['sımptəm] *n* Symptom *nt*; **~atic** [sımptə'mætık] *adj* (*fig*): **~atic of** bezeichnend für

synagogue ['sınəgɒg] *n* Synagoge *f*

synchronize ['sıŋkrənaız] *vt* synchronisieren ♦ *vi* gleichzeitig sein *or* ablaufen

syncopated ['sınkəpeıtıd] *adj* synkopiert

syndicate ['sındıkət] *n* Konsortium *nt*

synonym ['sınənım] *n* Synonym *nt*

synonymous [sı'nɒnıməs] *adj* gleichbedeutend

synopsis [sı'nɒpsıs] *n* Zusammenfassung *f*

syphon ['saıfən] = siphon

Syria ['sırıə] *n* Syrien *nt*

syringe [sı'rındʒ] *n* Spritze *f*

syrup ['sırəp] *n* Sirup *m*; *(of sugar)* Melasse *f*

system ['sıstəm] *n* System *nt*; **~atic** [sıstə'mætık] *adj* systematisch; **~ disk** *n* (*COMPUT*) Systemdiskette *f*; **~s analyst** *n* Systemanalytiker(in) *m(f)*

T t

ta [tɑ:] (*BRIT: inf*) *excl* danke!

tab [tæb] *n* Aufhänger *m*; *(name ~)* Schild *nt*; **to keep ~s on** (*fig*) genau im Auge behalten

tabby ['tæbı] *n* (*also: ~ cat*) getigerte Katze *f*

table ['teıbl] *n* Tisch *m*; *(list)* Tabelle *f* ♦ *vt* (*PARL: propose*) vorlegen, einbringen; **to lay** *or* **set the ~** den Tisch decken; **~cloth** ['teıblklɒθ] *n* Tischtuch *nt*; **~ of contents** *n* Inhaltsverzeichnis *nt*; **~ d'hôte** ['tɑ:bl'dəʊt] *n* Tagesmenü *nt*; **~ lamp** *n* Tischlampe *f*; **~mat** *n* Untersatz *m*; **~spoon** *n* Eßlöffel *m*; **~spoonful** *n* Eßlöffel(voll) *m*

tablet ['tæblət] *n* (*MED*) Tablette *f*; *(for writing)* Täfelchen *nt*

table tennis ['teıbltenıs] *n* Tischtennis *nt*

table wine ['teıblwaın] *n* Tafelwein *m*

tabloid ['tæblɔıd] *n* Zeitung *f* in kleinem Format; *(pej)* Boulevardzeitung *f*

tabulate ['tæbjʊleıt] *vt* tabellarisch ordnen

tacit ['tæsıt] *adj* stillschweigend

taciturn ['tæsıtɜ:n] *adj* wortkarg

tack [tæk] *n* (*small nail*) Stift *m*; (*US: thumb~*) Reißzwecke *f*; *(stitch)* Heftstich *m*; *(NAUT)* Lavieren *nt*; *(course)* Kurs *m* ♦ *vt* (*nail*) nageln; *(stitch)* heften ♦ *vi* aufkreuzen

tackle ['tækl] *n* (*for lifting*) Flaschenzug *m*; *(NAUT)* Takelage *f*; *(SPORT)* Tackling *nt* ♦ *vt* (*deal with*) anpacken, in Angriff nehmen; *(person)* festhalten; *(player)* angehen

tacky ['tækı] *adj* klebrig

tact [tækt] *n* Takt *m*; **~ful** *adj* taktvoll

tactical ['tæktıkəl] *adj* taktisch

tactics ['tæktıks] *npl* Taktik *f*

tactless ['tæktləs] *adj* taktlos

tadpole ['tædpəʊl] *n* Kaulquappe *f*

taffy ['tæfı] (*US*) *n* Sahnebonbon *nt*

tag [tæg] *n* (*label*) Schild *nt*, Anhänger *m*; *(maker's name)* Etikett *nt*; *(phrase)* Floskel *f*; **~ along** *vi* mitkommen

tail [teıl] *n* Schwanz *m*; *(of list)* Schluß *m* ♦ *vt* folgen +*dat*; **~ away** *or* **off** *vi* abfallen, schwinden; **~back** (*BRIT*) *n* (*AUT*) (Rück)stau *m*; **~ coat** *n* Frack *m*; **~ end** *n* Schluß *m*, Ende *nt*; **~gate** *n* (*AUT*) Heckklappe *f*

tailor ['teılə*] *n* Schneider *m*; **~ing** *n* Schneidern *nt*; **~-made** *adj* maßgeschneidert; (*fig*): **~-made for sb** jdm wie auf den Leib geschnitten

tailwind ['teɪlwɪnd] *n* Rückenwind *m*

tainted ['teɪntɪd] *adj* verdorben

take [teɪk] (*pt* **took**, *pp* **taken**) *vt* nehmen; (*trip, exam, PHOT*) machen; (*capture: person*) fassen; (*: town; also COMM, FIN*) einnehmen; (*carry to a place*) bringen; (*get for o.s.*) sich *dat* nehmen; (*gain, obtain*) bekommen; (*put up with*) hinnehmen; (*respond to*) aufnehmen; (*interpret*) auffassen; (*assume*) annehmen; (*contain*) Platz haben für; (*GRAM*) stehen mit; **to ~ sth from sb** jdm etw wegnehmen; **to ~ sth from sth** (*MATH: subtract*) etw von etw abziehen; (*extract, quotation*) etw entnehmen; **~ after** *vt fus* ähnlich sein +*dat*; **~ apart** *vt* auseinandernehmen; **~ away** *vt* (*remove*) wegnehmen; (*carry off*) wegbringen; **~ back** *vt* (*return*) zurückbringen; (*retract*) zurücknehmen; **~ down** *vt* (*pull down*) abreißen; (*write down*) aufschreiben; **~ in** *vt* (*deceive*) hereinlegen; (*understand*) begreifen; (*include*) einschließen; **~ off** *vi* (*plane*) starten ♦ *vt* (*remove*) wegnehmen; (*clothing*) ausziehen; (*imitate*) nachmachen; **~ on** *vt* (*undertake*) übernehmen; (*engage*) einstellen; (*opponent*) antreten gegen; **~ out** *vt* (*girl, dog*) ausführen; (*extract*) herausnehmen; (*insurance*) abschließen; (*licence*) sich *dat* geben lassen; (*book*) ausleihen; (*remove*) entfernen; **to ~ sth out of sth** (*drawer, pocket etc*) etw aus etw herausnehmen; **~ over** *vt* übernehmen ♦ *vi*: **to ~ over from sb** jdn ablösen; **~ to** *vt fus* (*like*) mögen; (*adopt as practice*) sich *dat* angewöhnen; **~ up** *vt* (*raise*) aufnehmen; (*dress etc*) kürzer machen; (*occupy*) in Anspruch nehmen; (*engage in*) sich befassen mit; **~away** *adj* zum Mitnehmen; **~home pay** *n* Nettolohn *m*; **taken** ['teɪkn] *pp* of **take**; **~off** *n* (*AVIAT*) Start *m*; (*imitation*) Nachahmung *f*; **~out** (*US*) *adj* = **takeaway**; **~over** *n* (*COMM*) Übernahme *f*

takings ['teɪkɪŋz] *npl* (*COMM*) Einnahmen *pl*

talc [tælk] *n* (*also*: **talcum powder**)

Talkumpuder *m*

tale [teɪl] *n* Geschichte *f*, Erzählung *f*; **to tell ~s** (*fig: lie*) Geschichten erfinden

talent ['tælənt] *n* Talent *nt*; **~ed** *adj* begabt

talk [tɔːk] *n* (*conversation*) Gespräch *nt*; (*rumour*) Gerede *nt*; (*speech*) Vortrag *m* ♦ *vi* sprechen, reden; **~s** *npl* (*POL etc*) Gespräche *pl*; **to ~ about** sprechen von +*dat or* über +*acc*; **to ~ sb into doing sth** jdn überreden, etw zu tun; **to ~ sb out of doing sth** jdm ausreden, etw zu tun; **to ~ shop** fachsimpeln; **~ over** *vt* besprechen; **~ative** *adj* gesprächig

tall [tɔːl] *adj* groß; (*building*) hoch; **to be 1 m 80 ~** 1,80 m groß sein; **~boy** (*BRIT*) *n* Kommode *f*; **~ story** *n* übertriebene Geschichte *f*

tally ['tælɪ] *n* Abrechnung *f* ♦ *vi* übereinstimmen

talon ['tælən] *n* Kralle *f*

tame [teɪm] *adj* zahm; (*fig*) fade

tamper ['tæmpə*] *vi*: **to ~ with** herumpfuschen an +*dat*

tampon ['tæmpɒn] *n* Tampon *m*

tan [tæn] *n* (*on skin*) (Sonnen)bräune *f*; (*colour*) Gelbbraun *nt* ♦ *adj* (gelb)braun ♦ *vt* bräunen; (*skins*) gerben ♦ *vi* braun werden

tang [tæŋ] *n* Schärfe *f*

tangent ['tændʒənt] *n* Tangente *f*; **to go off at a ~** (*fig*) vom Thema abkommen

tangerine [tændʒə'riːn] *n* Mandarine *f*

tangible ['tændʒəbl] *adj* greifbar

tangle ['tæŋgl] *n* Durcheinander *nt*; (*trouble*) Schwierigkeiten *pl*; **to get in(to) a ~** sich verheddern

tank [tæŋk] *n* (*container*) Tank *m*, Behälter *m*; (*MIL*) Panzer *m*

tanker ['tæŋkə*] *n* (*ship*) Tanker *m*; (*vehicle*) Tankwagen *m*

tanned [tænd] *adj* (*skin*) gebräunt

tantalizing ['tæntəlaɪzɪŋ] *adj* verlockend; (*annoying*) quälend

tantamount ['tæntəmaʊnt] *adj*: **~ to** gleichbedeutend mit

tantrum ['tæntrəm] *n* Wutanfall *m*

tap [tæp] *n* Hahn *m*; (*gentle blow*) Klopfen *nt* ♦ *vt* (*strike*) klopfen; (*supply*) anzapfen;

(*telephone*) abhören; **on ~** (*fig: resources*) zur Hand; **~-dancing** ['tæpdɑ:nsɪŋ] *n* Steppen *nt*

tape [teɪp] *n* Band *nt*; (*magnetic*) (Ton)band *nt*; (*adhesive*) Klebstreifen *m* ♦ *vt* (*record*) aufnehmen; **~ measure** *n* Maßband *nt*

taper ['teɪpə*] *n* (dünne) Wachskerze *f* ♦ *vi* spitz zulaufen

tape recorder *n* Tonbandgerät *nt*

tapestry ['tæpɪstrɪ] *n* Wandteppich *m*

tar [tɑ:*] *n* Teer *m*

target ['tɑ:gɪt] *n* Ziel *nt*; (*board*) Zielscheibe *f*

tariff ['tærɪf] *n* (*duty paid*) Zoll *m*; (*list*) Tarif *m*

tarmac ['tɑ:mæk] *n* (AVIAT) Rollfeld *nt*

tarnish ['tɑ:nɪʃ] *vt* matt machen; (*fig*) beflecken

tarpaulin [tɑ:'pɔ:lɪn] *n* Plane *f*

tarragon ['tærəgən] *n* Estragon *m*

tart [tɑ:t] *n* (Obst)torte *f*; (*inf*) Nutte *f* ♦ *adj* scharf; **~ up** (*inf*) *vt* aufmachen (*inf*); (*person*) auftakeln (*inf*)

tartan ['tɑ:tən] *n* Schottenkaro *nt* ♦ *adj* mit Schottenkaro

tartar ['tɑ:tə*] *n* Zahnstein *m*; **~(e) sauce** *n* Remouladensoße *f*

task [tɑ:sk] *n* Aufgabe *f*; **to take sb to ~** sich *dat* jdn vornehmen; **~ force** *n* Sondertrupp *m*

tassel ['tæsəl] *n* Quaste *f*

taste [teɪst] *n* Geschmack *m*; (*sense*) Geschmackssinn *m*; (*small quantity*) Kostprobe *f*; (*liking*) Vorliebe *f* ♦ *vt* schmecken; (*try*) probieren ♦ *vi* schmecken; **can I have a ~ of this wine?** kann ich diesen Wein probieren?; **to have a ~ for sth** etw mögen; **in good/ bad ~** geschmackvoll/geschmacklos; **you can ~ the garlic (in it)** man kann den Knoblauch herausschmecken; **~ful** *adj* geschmackvoll; **~less** *adj* (*insipid*) fade; (*in bad ~*) geschmacklos

tasty ['teɪstɪ] *adj* schmackhaft

tattered ['tætəd] *adj* = **in tatters**

tatters ['tætəz] *npl*: **in ~** in Fetzen

tattoo [tə'tu:] *n* (MIL) Zapfenstreich *m*;

(*on skin*) Tätowierung *f* ♦ *vt* tätowieren

tatty ['tætɪ] (*BRIT: inf*) *adj* schäbig

taught [tɔ:t] *pt, pp of* **teach**

taunt [tɔ:nt] *n* höhnische Bemerkung *f* ♦ *vt* verhöhnen

Taurus ['tɔ:rəs] *n* Stier *m*

taut [tɔ:t] *adj* straff

tawdry ['tɔ:drɪ] *adj* (bunt und) billig

tawny ['tɔ:nɪ] *adj* gelbbraun

tax [tæks] *n* Steuer *f* ♦ *vt* besteuern; (*strain*) strapazieren; (*strength*) angreifen; **~able** *adj* (*income*) steuerpflichtig; **~ation** [tæk'seɪʃən] *n* Besteuerung *f*; **~ avoidance** *n* Steuerumgehung *f*; **~ disc** (*BRIT*) *n* (AUT) Kraftfahrzeugsteuerplakette *f*; **~ evasion** *n* Steuerhinterziehung *f*; **~- free** *adj* steuerfrei

taxi ['tæksɪ] *n* Taxi *nt* ♦ *vi* (*plane*) rollen; **~ driver** *n* Taxifahrer *m*; **~ rank** (*BRIT*) *n* Taxistand *m*; **~ stand** *n* Taxistand *m*

tax: ~payer ['tækspeɪə*] *n* Steuerzahler *m*; **~ relief** *n* Steuerermäßigung *f*; **~ return** *n* Steuererklärung *f*

TB *n abbr* (= *tuberculosis*) Tb *f*, Tbc *f*

tea [ti:] *n* Tee *m*; (*meal*) (frühes) Abendessen *nt*; **high ~** (*BRIT*) Abendessen *nt*; **~ bag** *n* Teebeutel *m*; **~ break** (*BRIT*) *n* Teepause *f*

teach [ti:tʃ] (*pt, pp* **taught**) *vt* lehren; (*SCH*) lehren, unterrichten; (*show*): **to ~ sb sth** jdm etw beibringen ♦ *vi* lehren, unterrichten; **~er** *n* Lehrer(in) *m(f)*; **~ing** *n* (*~er's work*) Unterricht *m*; (*doctrine*) Lehre *f*

tea: ~cosy *n* Teewärmer *m*; **~cup** *n* Teetasse *f*; **~ leaves** *npl* Teeblätter *pl*

team [ti:m] *n* (*workers*) Team *nt*; (*SPORT*) Mannschaft *f*; (*animals*) Gespann *nt*

teamwork *n* Gemeinschaftsarbeit *f*, Teamarbeit *f*

teapot ['ti:pɒt] *n* Teekanne *f*

tear[1] [tɛə*] (*pt* **tore**, *pp* **torn**) *n* Riß *m* ♦ *vt* zerreißen; (*muscle*) zerren ♦ *vi* (zer)reißen; (*rush*) rasen; **~ along** *vi* (*rush*) entlangrasen; **~ up** *vt* (*sheet of paper etc*) zerreißen

tear[2] [tɪə*] *n* Träne *f*

tearful ['tɪəful] *adj* weinend; (*voice*) weinerlich

tear gas ['tɪəgæs] n Tränengas nt
tearoom ['tiːrum] n Teestube f
tease [tiːz] n Hänsler m ♦ vt necken
tea set n Teeservice nt
teaspoon ['tiːspuːn] n Teelöffel m
teat [tiːt] n (of woman) Brustwarze f; (of animal) Zitze f; (of bottle) Sauger m
tea time n (in the afternoon) Teestunde f; (mealtime) Abendessen nt
tea towel n Geschirrtuch nt
technical ['teknɪkəl] adj technisch; (knowledge, terms) Fach-; ~**ity** [teknɪ'kælɪtɪ] n technische Einzelheit f; (JUR) Formsache f; ~**ly** adv technisch; (speak) spezialisiert; (fig) genau genommen
technician [tek'nɪʃən] n Techniker m
technique [tek'niːk] n Technik f
technological [teknə'lɒdʒɪkəl] adj technologisch
technology [tek'nɒlədʒɪ] n Technologie f
teddy (bear) ['tedɪ(bɛə*)] n Teddybär m
tedious ['tiːdɪəs] adj langweilig, ermüdend
tee [tiː] n (GOLF) Abschlagstelle f; (object) Tee m
teem [tiːm] vi (swarm): to ~ (with) wimmeln (von); it is ~**ing (with rain)** es gießt in Strömen
teenage ['tiːneɪdʒ] adj (fashions etc) Teenager-, jugendlich; ~**r** n Teenager m, Jugendliche(r) mf
teens [tiːnz] npl Teenageralter nt
tee-shirt ['tiːʃɜːt] n T-Shirt nt
teeter ['tiːtə*] vi schwanken
teeth [tiːθ] npl of **tooth**
teethe [tiːð] vi zahnen
teething ring ['tiːðɪŋ-] n Beißring m
teething troubles ['tiːðɪŋ-] npl (fig) Kinderkrankheiten pl
teetotal ['tiː'təʊtl] adj abstinent
telecommunications ['telɪkəmjuːnɪ'keɪʃənz] npl Fernmeldewesen nt
telegram ['telɪgræm] n Telegramm nt
telegraph ['telɪgrɑːf] n Telegraph m
telephone ['telɪfəʊn] n Telefon nt, Fernsprecher m ♦ vt anrufen; (message) telefonisch mitteilen; **to be on the ~** (talking) telefonieren; (possessing phone) Telefon haben; ~ **booth** n Telefonzelle f;

~ **box** (BRIT) n Telefonzelle f; ~ **call** n Telefongespräch nt, Anruf m; ~ **directory** n Telefonbuch nt; ~ **number** n Telefonnummer f
telephonist [tə'lefənɪst] (BRIT) n Telefonist(in) m(f)
telephoto lens ['telɪfəʊtəʊ'lenz] n Teleobjektiv nt
telescope ['telɪskəʊp] n Teleskop nt, Fernrohr nt ♦ vt ineinanderschieben
televise ['telɪvaɪz] vt durch das Fernsehen übertragen
television ['telɪvɪʒən] n Fernsehen nt; **on ~** im Fernsehen; ~ **(set)** n Fernsehapparat m, Fernseher m
telex ['teleks] n Telex nt ♦ vt per Telex schicken
tell [tel] (pt, pp told) vt (story) erzählen; (secret) ausplaudern; (say, make known) sagen; (distinguish) erkennen; (be sure) wissen ♦ vi (talk) sprechen; (be sure) wissen; (divulge) es verraten; (have effect) sich auswirken; **to ~ sb to do sth** jdm sagen, daß er etw tun soll; **to ~ sb sth** or **sth to sb** jdm etw sagen; **to ~ sb by sth** jdn an etw dat erkennen; **to ~ sth from** etw unterscheiden von; **to ~ of sth** von etw sprechen; ~ **off** vt: **to ~ sb off** jdn ausschimpfen; ~**er** n Kassenbeamte(r) mf; ~**ing** adj verräterisch; (blow) hart; ~**tale** adj verräterisch
telly ['telɪ] (BRIT: inf) n abbr (= television) TV nt
temerity [tɪ'merɪtɪ] n (Toll)kühnheit f
temp [temp] n abbr (= temporary) Aushilfssekretärin f ♦ vi als Aushilfskraft arbeiten
temper ['tempə*] n (disposition) Temperament nt; (anger) Zorn m ♦ vt (tone down) mildern; (metal) härten; **to be in a (bad) ~** wütend sein; **to lose one's ~** die Beherrschung verlieren
temperament ['tempərəmənt] n Temperament nt; ~**al** [tempərə'mentl] adj (moody) launisch
temperance ['tempərəns] n Mäßigung f; (abstinence) Enthaltsamkeit f
temperate ['tempərət] adj gemäßigt
temperature ['temprɪtʃə*] n Temperatur

f; (*MED*: **high ~**) Fieber *nt*; **to have** or **run a ~** Fieber haben

template ['templət] *n* Schablone *f*

temple ['templ] *n* Tempel *m*; (*ANAT*) Schläfe *f*

temporal ['tempərəl] *adj* (*of time*) zeitlich; (*worldly*) irdisch, weltlich

temporarily ['tempərərɪlɪ] *adv* zeitweilig, vorübergehend

temporary ['tempərərɪ] *adj* vorläufig; (*road, building*) provisorisch

tempt [tempt] *vt* (*persuade*) verleiten; (*attract*) reizen, (ver)locken; **to ~ sb into doing sth** jdn dazu verleiten, etw zu tun; **~ation** [temp'teɪʃən] *n* Versuchung *f*; **~ing** *adj* (*person*) verführerisch; (*object, situation*) verlockend

ten [ten] *num* zehn

tenable ['tenəbl] *adj* haltbar

tenacious [tə'neɪʃəs] *adj* zäh, hartnäckig

tenacity [tə'næsɪtɪ] *n* Zähigkeit *f*, Hartnäckigkeit *f*

tenancy ['tenənsɪ] *n* Mietverhältnis *nt*

tenant ['tenənt] *n* Mieter *m*; (*of larger property*) Pächter *m*

tend [tend] *vt* (*look after*) sich kümmern um ♦ *vi*: **to ~ to do sth** etw gewöhnlich tun

tendency ['tendənsɪ] *n* Tendenz *f*; (*of person*) Tendenz *f*, Neigung *f*

tender ['tendə*] *adj* zart; (*loving*) zärtlich ♦ *n* (*COMM*: *offer*) Kostenanschlag *m* ♦ *vt* (an)bieten; (*resignation*) einreichen; **~ness** *n* Zartheit *f*; (*being loving*) Zärtlichkeit *f*

tendon ['tendən] *n* Sehne *f*

tenement ['tenəmənt] *n* Mietshaus *nt*

tenet ['tenət] *n* Lehre *f*

tennis ['tenɪs] *n* Tennis *nt*; **~ ball** *n* Tennisball *m*; **~ court** *n* Tennisplatz *m*; **~ player** *n* Tennisspieler(in) *m(f)*; **~ racket** *n* Tennisschläger *m*; **~ shoes** *npl* Tennisschuhe *pl*

tenor ['tenə*] *n* Tenor *m*

tenpin bowling ['tenpɪn-] *n* Bowling *nt*

tense [tens] *adj* angespannt ♦ *n* Zeitform *f*

tension ['tenʃən] *n* Spannung *f*

tent [tent] *n* Zelt *nt*

tentacle ['tentəkl] *n* Fühler *m*; (*of sea animals*) Fangarm *m*

tentative ['tentətɪv] *adj* (*movement*) unsicher; (*offer*) Probe-; (*arrangement*) vorläufig; (*suggestion*) unverbindlich; **~ly** *adv* versuchsweise; (*try, move*) vorsichtig

tenterhooks ['tentəhʊks] *npl*: **to be on ~** auf die Folter gespannt sein

tenth [tenθ] *adj* zehnte(r, s)

tent peg *n* Hering *m*

tent pole *n* Zeltstange *f*

tenuous ['tenjʊəs] *adj* schwach

tenure ['tenjʊə*] *n* (*of land*) Besitz *m*; (*of office*) Amtszeit *f*

tepid ['tepɪd] *adj* lauwarm

term [tɜːm] *n* (*period of time*) Zeit(raum *m*) *f*; (*limit*) Frist *f*; (*SCH*) Quartal *nt*; (*UNIV*) Trimester *nt*; (*expression*) Ausdruck *m* ♦ *vt* (be)nennen; **~s** *npl* (*conditions*) Bedingungen *pl*; **in the short/long ~** auf kurze/lange Sicht; **to be on good ~s with sb** gut mit jdm auskommen; **to come to ~s with** (*person*) sich einigen mit; (*problem*) sich abfinden mit

terminal ['tɜːmɪnl] *n* (*BRIT*: *also*: **coach ~**) Endstation *f*; (*AVIAT*) Terminal *m*; (*COMPUT*) Terminal *m* or *nt* ♦ *adj* Schluß-; (*MED*) unheilbar

terminate ['tɜːmɪneɪt] *vt* beenden ♦ *vi* enden, aufhören

termini ['tɜːmɪnaɪ] *npl of* **terminus**

terminus ['tɜːmɪnəs] (*pl* **termini**) *n* Endstation *f*

terrace ['terəs] *n* (*BRIT*: *row of houses*) Häuserreihe *f*; (*in garden etc*) Terrasse *f*; **the ~s** *npl* (*BRIT*: *SPORT*) die Ränge; **~d** *adj* (*garden*) terrassenförmig angelegt; (*house*) Reihen-

terrain [te'reɪn] *n* Terrain *nt*, Gelände *nt*

terrible ['terəbl] *adj* schrecklich, entsetzlich, fürchterlich

terribly ['terəblɪ] *adv* fürchterlich

terrific [tə'rɪfɪk] *adj* unwahrscheinlich; **~!** klasse!

terrify ['terɪfaɪ] *vt* erschrecken

territorial [terɪ'tɔːrɪəl] *adj* Gebiets-, territorial

territory ['terɪtərɪ] *n* Gebiet *nt*

terror ['terə*] *n* Schrecken *m*; (*POL*)

Terror m; **~ist** n Terrorist(in) m(f); **~ize** vt terrorisieren

terse [tɜːs] adj knapp, kurz, bündig

test [test] n Probe f; (*examination*) Prüfung f; (*PSYCH, TECH*) Test m ♦ vt prüfen; (*PSYCH*) testen

testicle ['testɪkl] n (*ANAT*) Hoden m

testify ['testɪfaɪ] vi aussagen; **to ~ to sth** etw bezeugen

testimony ['testɪmənɪ] n (*JUR*) Zeugenaussage f; (*fig*) Zeugnis nt

test match n (*SPORT*) Länderkampf m

test tube n Reagenzglas nt

testy ['testɪ] adj gereizt; reizbar

tetanus ['tetənəs] n Wundstarrkrampf m, Tetanus m

tetchy ['tetʃɪ] adj empfindlich

tether ['teðə*] vt anbinden ♦ n: **at the end of one's ~** völlig am Ende

text [tekst] n Text m; (*of document*) Wortlaut m; **~book** n Lehrbuch nt

textiles ['tekstaɪlz] npl Textilien pl

texture ['tekstʃə*] n Beschaffenheit f

Thai [taɪ] adj thailändisch ♦ n Thailänder(in) m(f); (*LING*) Thailändisch nt; **~land** n Thailand nt

Thames [temz] n: **the ~** die Themse

than [ðæn, ðən] prep (*in comparisons*) als

thank [θæŋk] vt danken +dat; **you've him to ~ for your success** Sie haben Ihren Erfolg ihm zu verdanken; **~ you (very much)** danke (vielmals), danke schön; **~ful** adj dankbar; **~less** adj undankbar; **~s** npl Dank m ♦ excl danke!; **~s to** dank +gen; **T~sgiving (Day)** (*US*) n Thanksgiving Day m

that [ðæt, ðət] adj (*demonstrative: pl those*) der/die/das; jene(r, s); **that one** das da

♦ pron 1 (*demonstrative: pl those*) das; **who's/what's that?** wer ist da/was ist das?; **is that you?** bist du das?; **that's what he said** genau das hat er gesagt; **what happened after that?** was passierte danach?; **that is** das heißt

2 (*relative: subj*) der/die/das, die; (: *direct obj*) den/die/das, die; (: *indirect obj*)

dem/der/dem, denen; **all (that) I have** alles, was ich habe

3 (*relative: of time*): **the day (that)** an dem Tag, als; **the winter (that) he came** in dem Winter, in dem er kam

♦ conj daß; **he thought that I was ill** er dachte, daß ich krank sei, er dachte, ich sei krank

♦ adv (*demonstrative*) so; **I can't work that much** ich kann nicht soviel arbeiten

thatched [θætʃt] adj strohgedeckt; (*cottage*) mit Strohdach

thaw [θɔː] n Tauwetter nt ♦ vi tauen; (*frozen foods, fig: people*) auftauen ♦ vt (auf)tauen lassen

the [ðiː, ðə] def art 1 der/die/das; **to play the piano/violin** Klavier/Geige spielen; **I'm going to the butcher's/the cinema** ich gehe zum Fleischer/ins Kino; **Elizabeth the First** Elisabeth die Erste

2 (+adj to form noun) das, die; **the rich and the poor** die Reichen und die Armen

3 (*in comparisons*): **the more he works the more he earns** je mehr er arbeitet, desto mehr verdient er

theatre ['θɪətə*] (*US* **theater**) n Theater nt; (*for lectures etc*) Saal m; (*MED*) Operationssaal m; **~goer** n Theaterbesucher(in) m(f)

theatrical [θɪ'ætrɪkəl] adj Theater-; (*career*) Schauspieler-; (*showy*) theatralisch

theft [θeft] n Diebstahl m

their [ðeə*] adj ihr; see also **my**; **~s** pron ihre(r, s); see also **mine²**

them [ðem, ðəm] pron (*acc*) sie; (*dat*) ihnen; see also **me**

theme [θiːm] n Thema nt; (*MUS*) Motiv nt; **~ park** n (thematisch gestalteter) Freizeitpark m; **~ song** n Titelmusik f

themselves [ðəm'selvz] pl pron (*reflexive*) sich (selbst); (*emphatic*) selbst; see also **oneself**

then [ðen] adv (*at that time*) damals; (*next*) dann ♦ conj also, folglich;

(furthermore) ferner ♦ *adj* damalig; **from ~ on** von da an; **by ~** bis dahin; **the ~ president** der damalige Präsident

theology [θɪˈɒlədʒɪ] *n* Theologie *f*

theoretical [θɪəˈretɪkəl] *adj* theoretisch; **~ly** *adv* theoretisch

theory [ˈθɪərɪ] *n* Theorie *f*

therapist [ˈθerəpɪst] *n* Therapeut(in) *m(f)*

therapy [ˈθerəpɪ] *n* Therapie *f*

[KEYWORD]

there [ðɛə*] *adv* **1: there is, there are** es or da ist/sind; *(there exists/exist also)* es gibt; **there are 3 of them** *(people, things)* es gibt 3 davon; **there has been an accident** da war ein Unfall
2 *(referring to place)* da, dort; *(with vb of movement)* dahin, dorthin; **put it in/on there** leg es dahinein/dorthinauf
3: there, there *(esp to child)* na, na

thereabouts [ðɛərəˈbaʊts] *adv (place)* dort in der Nähe, dort irgendwo; *(amount)*: **20 or ~** ungefähr 20

thereafter [ðɛərˈɑːftə*] *adv* danach

thereby [ðɛəˈbaɪ] *adv* dadurch, damit

therefore [ˈðɛəfɔː*] *adv* deshalb, daher

there's [ˈðɛəz] = **there is; there has**

thermometer [θəˈmɒmɪtə*] *n* Thermometer *nt*

Thermos [ˈθɜːməs] ® *n* Thermosflasche *f*

thesaurus [θɪˈsɔːrəs] *n* Synonymwörterbuch *nt*

these [ðiːz] *pron, adj (pl)* diese

theses [ˈθiːsiːz] *npl of* **thesis**

thesis [ˈθiːsɪs] *(pl* **theses***) n (for discussion)* These *f*; *(UNIV)* Dissertation *f*, Doktorarbeit *f*

they [ðeɪ] *pl pron* sie; *(people in general)* man; **~ say that ...** *(it is said that)* es wird gesagt, daß ...; **they'd** = **they had; they would; they'll** = **they shall; they will; they're** = **they are; they've** = **they have**

thick [θɪk] *adj* dick; *(forest)* dicht; *(liquid)* dickflüssig; *(slow, stupid)* dumm, schwer von Begriff ♦ *n*: **in the ~ of** mitten in +*dat*; **it's 20 cm ~** es ist 20 cm dick or

stark; **~en** *vi (fog)* dichter werden ♦ *vt (sauce etc)* verdicken; **~ness** *n* Dicke *f*; Dichte *f*; Dickflüssigkeit *f*; **~set** *adj* untersetzt; **~skinned** *adj* dickhäutig

thief [θiːf] *(pl* **thieves***) n* Dieb(in) *m(f)*

thieving [ˈθiːvɪŋ] *n* Stehlen *nt* ♦ *adj* diebisch

thigh [θaɪ] *n* Oberschenkel *m*

thimble [ˈθɪmbl] *n* Fingerhut *m*

thin [θɪn] *adj* dünn; *(person)* dünn, mager; *(excuse)* schwach ♦ *vt*: **to ~ (down)** *(sauce, paint)* verdünnen

thing [θɪŋ] *n* Ding *nt*; *(affair)* Sache *f*; **my ~s** meine Sachen *pl*; **the best ~ would be to ...** das Beste wäre, ...; **how are ~s?** wie geht's?

think [θɪŋk] *(pt, pp* **thought***) vt, vi* denken; **what did you ~ of them?** was halten Sie von ihnen?; **to ~ about sth/sb** nachdenken über etw/jdn; **I'll ~ about it** ich überlege es mir; **to ~ of doing sth** vorhaben *or* beabsichtigen, etw zu tun; **I ~ so/not** ich glaube (schon)/glaube nicht; **to ~ well of sb** viel von jdm halten; **~ over** *vt* überdenken; **~ up** *vt* sich *dat* ausdenken; **~ tank** *n* Expertengruppe *f*

thinly [ˈθɪnlɪ] *adv* dünn; *(disguised)* kaum

third [θɜːd] *adj* dritte(r, s) ♦ *n (person)* Dritte(r) *mf*; *(part)* Drittel *nt*; **~ly** *adv* drittens; **~ party insurance** *(BRIT) n* Haftpflichtversicherung *f*; **~-rate** *adj* minderwertig; **the T~ World** *n* die Dritte Welt *f*

thirst [θɜːst] *n (also fig)* Durst *m*; **~y** *adj (person)* durstig; *(work)* durstig machend; **to be ~y** Durst haben

thirteen [ˈθɜːˈtiːn] *num* dreizehn

thirty [ˈθɜːtɪ] *num* dreißig

[KEYWORD]

this [ðɪs] *adj (demonstrative: pl* **these***)* diese(r, s); **this evening** heute abend; **this one** diese(r, s) (da)
♦ *pron (demonstrative: pl* **these***)* dies, das; **who/what is this?** wer/was ist das?; **this is where I live** hier wohne ich; **this is what he said** das hat er gesagt; **this is Mr Brown** *(in introductions/photo)* dies ist Mr Brown; *(on telephone)* hier ist Mr

Brown
♦ *adv* (*demonstrative*): **this high/long** *etc*
so groß/lang *etc*

thistle ['θɪsl] *n* Distel *f*

thorn [θɔːn] *n* Dorn *m*; **~y** *adj* dornig;
(*problem*) schwierig

thorough ['θʌrə] *adj* gründlich; **~bred** *n*
Vollblut *nt* ♦ *adj* reinrassig, Vollblut-;
~fare *n* Straße *f*; **"no ~fare"** „Durchfahrt
verboten"; **~ly** *adv* gründlich; (*extremely*)
äußerst

those [ðəʊz] *pl pron* die (da), jene ♦ *adj*
die, jene

though [ðəʊ] *conj* obwohl ♦ *adv* trotzdem

thought [θɔːt] *pt, pp of* **think** ♦ *n* (*idea*)
Gedanke *m*; (*thinking*) Denken *nt*,
Denkvermögen *nt*; **~ful** *adj* (*thinking*)
gedankenvoll, nachdenklich; (*kind*)
rücksichtsvoll, aufmerksam; **~less** *adj*
gedankenlos, unbesonnen; (*unkind*)
rücksichtslos

thousand ['θaʊzənd] *num* tausend; **two
~** zweitausend; **~s of** Tausende (von); **~th**
adj tausendste(r, s)

thrash [θræʃ] *vt* verdreschen; (*fig*)
(vernichtend) schlagen; **~ about** *vi* um
sich schlagen; **~ out** *vt* ausdiskutieren

thread [θred] *n* Faden *m*, Garn *nt*; (*on
screw*) Gewinde *nt*; (*in story*) Faden *m*
♦ *vt* (*needle*) einfädeln; **~bare** *adj* (*also
fig*) fadenscheinig

threat [θret] *n* Drohung *f*; (*danger*)
Gefahr *f*; **~en** *vt* bedrohen ♦ *vi* drohen; **to
~en sb with sth** jdm etw androhen

three [θriː] *num* drei; **~-dimensional** *adj*
dreidimensional; **~-piece suit** *n*
dreiteilige(r) Anzug *m*; **~-piece suite** *n*
dreiteilige Polstergarnitur *f*; **~-wheeler** *n*
Dreiradwagen *m*

thresh [θreʃ] *vt, vi* dreschen

threshold ['θreʃhəʊld] *n* Schwelle *f*

threw [θruː] *pt of* **throw**

thrift [θrɪft] *n* Sparsamkeit *f*; **~y** *adj*
sparsam

thrill [θrɪl] *n* Reiz *m*, Erregung *f* ♦ *vt*
begeistern, packen; **to be ~ed with** (*gift
etc*) sich unheimlich freuen über +*acc*;
~er *n* Krimi *m*; **~ing** *adj* spannend;

(*news*) aufregend

thrive [θraɪv] (*pt* **~d**, **throve**, *pp* **~d**,
thriven) *vi*: **to ~ (on)** gedeihen (bei);
thriven ['θrɪvn] *pp of* **thrive**

thriving ['θraɪvɪŋ] *adj* blühend

throat [θrəʊt] *n* Hals *m*, Kehle *f*; **to have
a sore ~** Halsschmerzen haben

throb [θrɒb] *n* Pochen *nt* ♦ *vi* klopfen,
pochen

throes [θrəʊz] *npl*: **in the ~ of** mitten in
+*dat*

throng [θrɒŋ] *n* (*Menschen*)schar *f* ♦ *vt*
sich drängen in +*dat*

throttle ['θrɒtl] *n* Gashebel *m* ♦ *vt*
erdrosseln

through [θruː] *prep* durch; (*time*)
während +*gen*; (*because of*) aus, durch
♦ *adv* durch ♦ *adj* (*ticket, train*)
durchgehend; (*finished*) fertig; **to put sb ~
(to)** jdn verbinden (mit); **to be ~** (*TEL*)
eine Verbindung haben; (*have finished*)
fertig sein; **no ~ way** (*BRIT*) Sackgasse *f*;
~out [θruː'aʊt] *prep* (*place*) überall in
+*dat*; (*time*) während +*gen* ♦ *adv* überall;
die ganze Zeit

throve [θrəʊv] *pt of* **thrive**

throw [θrəʊ] (*pt* **threw**, *pp* **thrown**) *n*
Wurf *m* ♦ *vt* werfen; **to ~ a party** eine
Party geben; **~ away** *vt* wegwerfen;
(*money*) verschwenden; **~ off** *vt* abwerfen;
(*pursuer*) abschütteln; **~ out** *vt*
hinauswerfen; (*rubbish*) wegwerfen;
(*plan*) verwerfen; **~ up** *vt, vi* (*vomit*)
speien; **~away** *adj* Wegwerf-; **~-in** *n*
Einwurf *m*; **thrown** [θrəʊn] *pp of* **throw**

thru [θruː] (*US*) = **through**

thrush [θrʌʃ] *n* Drossel *f*

thrust [θrʌst] (*pt, pp* **thrust**) *n* (*TECH*)
Schubkraft *f* ♦ *vt, vi* (*push*) stoßen

thud [θʌd] *n* dumpfe(r) (Auf)schlag *m*

thug [θʌg] *n* Schlägertyp *m*

thumb [θʌm] *n* Daumen *m* ♦ *vt* (*book*)
durchblättern; **to ~ a lift** per Anhalter
fahren (wollen); **~tack** (*US*) *n* Reißwecke
f

thump [θʌmp] *n* (*blow*) Schlag *m*; (*noise*)
Bums *m* ♦ *vi* hämmern, pochen ♦ *vt*
schlagen auf +*acc*

thunder ['θʌndə*] n Donner m ♦ vi donnern; (*train etc*): **to ~ past** vorbeidonnern ♦ vt brüllen; **~ bolt** n Blitz nt; **~clap** n Donnerschlag m; **~storm** n Gewitter nt, Unwetter nt; **~y** adj gewitterschwül

Thursday ['θɜːzdeɪ] n Donnerstag m

thus [ðʌs] adv (*in this way*) so; (*therefore*) somit, also, folglich

thwart [θwɔːt] vt vereiteln, durchkreuzen; (*person*) hindern

thyme [taɪm] n Thymian m

thyroid ['θaɪrɔɪd] n Schilddrüse f

tiara [tɪ'ɑːrə] n Diadem nt; (*of pope*) Tiara nt

tic [tɪk] n Tick m

tick [tɪk] n (*sound*) Ticken nt; (*mark*) Häkchen nt ♦ vi ticken ♦ vt abhaken; **in a ~** (*BRIT: inf*) sofort; **~ off** vt abhaken; (*person*) ausschimpfen; **~ over** vi (*engine*) im Leerlauf laufen; (*fig*) auf Sparflamme laufen

ticket ['tɪkɪt] n (*for travel*) Fahrkarte f; (*for entrance*) (Eintritts)karte f; (*price ~*) Preisschild nt; (*luggage ~*) (Gepäck)schein m; (*raffle ~*) Los nt; (*parking ~*) Strafzettel m; (*in car park*) Parkschein m; **~ collector** n Fahrkartenkontrolleur m; **~ office** n (*RAIL etc*) Fahrkartenschalter m; (*THEAT etc*) Kasse f

tickle ['tɪkl] n Kitzeln nt ♦ vt kitzeln; (*amuse*) amüsieren

ticklish ['tɪklɪʃ] adj (*also fig*) kitzlig

tidal ['taɪdl] adj Flut-, Tide-; **~ wave** n Flutwelle f

tidbit ['tɪdbɪt] (*US*) n Leckerbissen m

tiddlywinks ['tɪdlɪwɪŋks] n Floh(hüpf)spiel nt

tide [taɪd] n Gezeiten pl; **high/low ~** Flut f/Ebbe f

tidy ['taɪdɪ] adj ordentlich ♦ vt aufräumen, in Ordnung bringen

tie [taɪ] n (*BRIT: neck*) Krawatte f, Schlips m; (*sth connecting*) Band nt; (*SPORT*) Unentschieden nt ♦ vt (*fasten, restrict*) binden ♦ vi (*SPORT*) unentschieden spielen; (*in competition*) punktgleich sein; **to ~ in a bow** zur Schleife binden; **to ~ a knot in sth** einen Knoten in etw acc machen;

~ down vt festbinden; **to ~ sb down to** jdn binden an +acc; **~ up** vt (*dog*) anbinden; (*parcel*) verschnüren; (*boat*) festmachen; (*person*) fesseln; **to be ~d up** (*busy*) beschäftigt sein

tier [tɪə*] n Rang m; (*of cake*) Etage f

tiff [tɪf] n Krach m

tiger ['taɪgə*] n Tiger m

tight [taɪt] adj (*close*) eng, knapp; (*schedule*) gedrängt; (*firm*) fest; (*control*) streng; (*stretched*) stramm, (an)gespannt; (*inf: drunk*) blau, stramm ♦ adv (*squeeze*) fest; **~en** vt anziehen, anspannen; (*restrictions*) verschärfen ♦ vi sich spannen; **~-fisted** adj knauserig; **~ly** adv eng; fest; (*stretched*) straff; **~rope** n Seil nt; **~s** npl (*esp BRIT*) Strumpfhose f

tile [taɪl] n (*on roof*) Dachziegel m; (*on wall or floor*) Fliese f; **~d** adj (*roof*) gedeckt, Ziegel-; (*floor, wall*) mit Fliesen belegt

till [tɪl] n Kasse f ♦ vt bestellen ♦ prep, conj = **until**

tiller ['tɪlə*] n Ruderpinne f

tilt [tɪlt] vt kippen, neigen ♦ vi sich neigen

timber ['tɪmbə*] n Holz nt; (*trees*) Baumbestand m

time [taɪm] n Zeit f; (*occasion*) Mal nt; (*rhythm*) Takt m ♦ vt zur rechten Zeit tun, zeitlich einrichten; (*SPORT*) stoppen; **in 2 weeks' ~** in 2 Wochen; **a long ~** lange; **for the ~ being** vorläufig; **4 at a ~** zu jeweils 4; **from ~ to ~** gelegentlich; **to have a good ~** sich amüsieren; **in ~** (*soon enough*) rechtzeitig; (*after some ~*) mit der Zeit; (*MUS*) im Takt; **in no ~** im Handumdrehen; **any ~** jederzeit; **on ~** pünktlich, rechtzeitig; **five ~s 5** fünfmal 5; **what ~ is it?** wieviel Uhr ist es?, wie spät ist es?; **at ~s** manchmal; **~ bomb** n Zeitbombe f; **~less** adj (*beauty*) zeitlos; **~ limit** n Frist f; **~ly** adj rechtzeitig; günstig; **~ off** n freie Zeit f; **~r** n (*~r switch*) Schaltuhr f; (*in kitchen*) Schaltuhr f; **~ scale** n Zeitspanne f; **~-share** adj Time-sharing-; **~ switch** (*BRIT*) n Zeitschalter m; **~table** n Fahrplan m; (*SCH*) Stundenplan m; **~ zone** n Zeitzone f

timid ['tɪmɪd] *adj* ängstlich, schüchtern

timing ['taɪmɪŋ] *n* Wahl *f* des richtigen Zeitpunkts, Timing *nt*; (*AUT*) Einstellung *f*

timpani ['tɪmpənɪ] *npl* Kesselpauken *pl*

tin [tɪn] *n* (*metal*) Blech *nt*; (*BRIT: can*) Büchse *f*, Dose *f*; **~foil** *n* Staniolpapier *nt*

tinge [tɪndʒ] *n* (*colour*) Färbung *f*; (*fig*) Anflug *m* ♦ *vt* färben; **~d with** mit einer Spur von

tingle ['tɪŋgl] *n* Prickeln *nt* ♦ *vi* prickeln

tinker ['tɪŋkə*] *n* Kesselflicker *m*; **~ with** *vt fus* herumpfuschen an +*dat*

tinkle ['tɪŋkl] *vi* klingeln

tinned [tɪnd] (*BRIT*) *adj* (*food*) Dosen-, Büchsen-

tin opener ['-əupnə*] (*BRIT*) *n* Dosen- *or* Büchsenöffner *m*

tinsel ['tɪnsəl] *n* Rauschgold *nt*

tint [tɪnt] *n* Farbton *m*; (*slight colour*) Anflug *m*; (*hair*) Tönung *f*; **~ed** *adj* getönt

tiny ['taɪnɪ] *adj* winzig

tip [tɪp] *n* (*pointed end*) Spitze *f*; (*money*) Trinkgeld *nt*; (*hint*) Wink *m*, Tip *m* ♦ *vt* (*slant*) kippen; (*hat*) antippen; (**~ over**) umkippen; (*waiter*) ein Trinkgeld geben +*dat*; **~-off** *n* Hinweis *m*, Tip *m*; **~ped** (*BRIT*) *adj* (*cigarette*) Filter-

tipsy ['tɪpsɪ] *adj* beschwipst

tiptoe ['tɪptəu] *n*: **on ~** auf Zehenspitzen

tiptop ['tɪp'tɒp] *adj*: **in ~ condition** tipptopp, erstklassig

tire ['taɪə*] *n* (*US*) = **tyre** ♦ *vt*, *vi* ermüden, müde machen/werden; **~d** *adj* müde; **to be ~d of sth** etw satt haben; **~less** *adj* unermüdlich; **~lessly** *adv* unermüdlich; **~some** *adj* lästig

tiring ['taɪərɪŋ] *adj* ermüdend

tissue ['tɪʃuː] *n* Gewebe *nt*; (*paper handkerchief*) Papiertaschentuch *nt*; **~ paper** *n* Seidenpapier *nt*

tit [tɪt] *n* (*bird*) Meise *f*; **~ for tat** wie du mir, so ich dir

titbit ['tɪtbɪt] (*US* **tidbit**) *n* Leckerbissen *m*

titillate ['tɪtɪleɪt] *vt* kitzeln

titivate ['tɪtɪveɪt] *vt* schniegeln

title ['taɪtl] *n* Titel *m*; **~ deed** *n* Eigentumsurkunde *f*; **~ role** *n* Hauptrolle *f*

titter ['tɪtə*] *vi* kichern

titular ['tɪtjulə*] *adj* (*in name only*) nominell

TM *abbr* (= *trademark*) Wz

to [tuː, tə] *prep* **1** (*direction*) zu, nach; **I go to France/school** ich gehe nach Frankreich/zur Schule; **to the left** nach links

2 (*as far as*) bis

3 (*with expressions of time*) vor; **a quarter to 5** Viertel vor 5

4 (*for, of*) für; **secretary to the director** Sekretärin des Direktors

5 (*expressing indirect object*): **to give sth to sb** jdm etw geben; **to talk to sb** mit jdm sprechen; **I sold it to a friend** ich habe es einem Freund verkauft

6 (*in relation to*) zu; **30 miles to the gallon** 30 Meilen pro Gallone

7 (*purpose, result*) zu; **to my surprise** zu meiner Überraschung

♦ *with vb* **1** (*infin*): **to go/eat** gehen/essen; **to want to do sth** etw tun wollen; **to try/start to do sth** versuchen/anfangen, etw zu tun; **he has a lot to lose** er hat viel zu verlieren

2 (*with vb omitted*): **I don't want to** ich will (es) nicht

3 (*purpose, result*) um; **I did it to help you** ich tat es, um dir zu helfen

4 (*after adj etc*): **ready to use** gebrauchsfertig; **too old/young to ...** zu alt/jung, um ... zu ...

♦ *adv*: **push/pull the door to** die Tür zuschieben/zuziehen

toad [təud] *n* Kröte *f*; **~stool** *n* Giftpilz *m*

toast [təust] *n* (*bread*) Toast *m*; (*drinking*) Trinkspruch *m* ♦ *vt* trinken auf +*acc*; (*bread*) toasten; (*warm*) wärmen; **~er** *n* Toaster *m*

tobacco [tə'bækəu] *n* Tabak *m*; **~nist** [tə'bækənɪst] *n* Tabakhändler *m*; **~nist's (shop)** *n* Tabakladen *m*

toboggan [tə'bɒgən] *n* (Rodel)schlitten *m*

today [tə'deɪ] *adv* heute; (*at the present*

time) heutzutage
toddler ['tɒdlə*] *n* Kleinkind *nt*
toddy ['tɒdɪ] *n* (Whisky)grog *m*
to-do [tə'du:] *n* Theater *nt*
toe [təu] *n* Zehe *f*; *(of sock, shoe)* Spitze *f*
♦ *vt:* **to ~ the line** *(fig)* sich einfügen;
~nail *n* Zehennagel *m*
toffee ['tɒfɪ] *n* Sahnebonbon *nt*; **~ apple**
(*BRIT*) *n* kandierte(r) Apfel *m*
together [tə'geðə*] *adv* zusammen; *(at
the same time)* gleichzeitig; **~ with**
zusammen mit; gleichzeitig mit; **~ness** *n*
(*company*) Beisammensein *nt*
toil [tɔɪl] *n* harte Arbeit *f*, Plackerei *f* ♦ *vi*
sich abmühen, sich plagen
toilet ['tɔɪlət] *n* Toilette *f* ♦ *cpd*
Toiletten-; **~ bag** *n* Waschbeutel *m*; **~
paper** *n* Toilettenpapier *nt*; **~ries**
['tɔɪlətrɪz] *npl* Toilettenartikel *pl*; **~ roll** *n*
Rolle *f* Toilettenpapier; **~ water** *n*
Toilettenwasser *nt*
token ['təukən] *n* Zeichen *nt*; *(gift ~)*
Gutschein *m*; **book/record ~** (*BRIT*)
Bücher-/Plattengutschein *m*
Tokyo ['təukjəu] *n* Tokio *nt*
told [təuld] *pt, pp of* **tell**
tolerable ['tɒlərəbl] *adj (bearable)*
erträglich; *(fairly good)* leidlich
tolerant ['tɒlərnt] *adj:* **be ~ (of)**
vertragen +*acc*
tolerate ['tɒləreɪt] *vt* dulden; *(noise)*
ertragen
toll [təul] *n* Gebühr *f* ♦ *vi (bell)* läuten
tomato [tə'mɑ:təu] *n (pl* **~es**) Tomate *f*
tomb [tu:m] *n* Grab(mal) *nt*
tomboy ['tɒmbɔɪ] *n* Wildfang *m*
tombstone ['tu:mstəun] *n* Grabstein *m*
tomcat ['tɒmkæt] *n* Kater *m*
tomorrow [tə'mɒrəu] *n* Morgen *nt* ♦ *adv*
morgen; **the day after ~** übermorgen; **~
morning** morgen früh; **a week ~** morgen
in einer Woche
ton [tʌn] *n* Tonne *f* (*BRIT* = 1016kg; *US
= 907kg*); *(NAUT: also: register ~)*
Registertonne *f*; **~s of** *(inf)* eine Unmenge
von
tone [təun] *n* Ton *m*; **~ down** *vt*
(criticism, demands) mäßigen; *(colours)*
abtonen; **~ up** *vt* in Form bringen; **~-**

deaf *adj* ohne musikalisches Gehör
tongs [tɒŋz] *npl* Zange *f*; *(curling ~)*
Lockenstab *m*
tongue [tʌŋ] *n* Zunge *f*; *(language)*
Sprache *f*; **with ~ in cheek** scherzhaft;
~-tied *adj* stumm, sprachlos; **~-twister**
n Zungenbrecher *m*
tonic ['tɒnɪk] *n (MED)* Stärkungsmittel *nt*;
(drink) Tonic *nt*
tonight [tə'naɪt] *adv* heute abend
tonsil ['tɒnsl] *n* Mandel *f*; **~litis**
[tɒnsɪ'laɪtɪs] *n* Mandelentzündung *f*
too [tu:] *adv* zu; *(also)* auch; **~ bad!**
Pech!; **~ many** zu viele
took [tuk] *pt of* **take**
tool [tu:l] *n (also fig)* Werkzeug *nt*; **~box**
n Werkzeugkasten *m*
toot [tu:t] *n* Hupen *nt* ♦ *vi* tuten; *(AUT)*
hupen
tooth [tu:θ] *(pl* **teeth**) *n* Zahn *m*; **~ache**
n Zahnschmerzen *pl*, Zahnweh *nt*;
~brush *n* Zahnbürste *f*; **~paste** *n*
Zahnpasta *f*; **~pick** *n* Zahnstocher *m*
top [tɒp] *n* Spitze *f*; *(of mountain)* Gipfel
m; *(of tree)* Wipfel *m*; *(toy)* Kreisel *m*; *(~
gear)* vierte(r)/fünfte(r) Gang *m* ♦ *adj*
oberste(r, s) ♦ *vt (list)* an erster Stelle
stehen auf +*dat*; **on ~ of** oben auf +*dat*;
from ~ to bottom von oben bis unten; **~
off** (*US*) *vt* auffüllen; **~ up** *vt* auffüllen; **~
floor** *n* oberste(s) Stockwerk *nt*; **~ hat** *n*
Zylinder *m*; **~-heavy** *adj* kopflastig
topic ['tɒpɪk] *n* Thema *nt*,
Gesprächsgegenstand *m*; **~al** *adj* aktuell
topless ['tɒpləs] *adj (bather etc)* oben
ohne
top-level ['tɒp'levl] *adj* auf höchster
Ebene
topmost ['tɒpməust] *adj* oberste(r, s)
topple ['tɒpl] *vt, vi* stürzen, kippen
top-secret ['tɒp'si:krət] *adj* streng
geheim
topsy-turvy ['tɒpsɪ'tɜ:vɪ] *adv*
durcheinander ♦ *adj* auf den Kopf gestellt
torch [tɔ:tʃ] *n (BRIT: ELEC)* Taschenlampe
f; *(with flame)* Fackel *f*
tore [tɔ:*] *pt of* **tear**[1]
torment [*n* 'tɔ:ment, *vb* tɔ:'ment] *n* Qual *f*
♦ *vt (distress)* quälen

torn [tɔːn] *pp of* **tear**[1] ♦ *adj* hin- und hergerissen

torrent ['tɒrənt] *n* Sturzbach *m*; **~ial** [təˈrenʃəl] *adj* wolkenbruchartig

torrid ['tɒrɪd] *adj* heiß

tortoise ['tɔːtəs] *n* Schildkröte *f*; **~shell** ['tɔːtəʃel] *n* Schildpatt *m*

tortuous ['tɔːtjʊəs] *adj* gewunden

torture ['tɔːtʃə*] *n* Folter *f* ♦ *vt* foltern

Tory ['tɔːrɪ] (*BRIT*) *n* (*POL*) Tory *m* ♦ *adj* Tory-, konservativ

toss [tɒs] *vt* schleudern; **to ~ a coin** *or* **to ~ up for sth** etw mit einer Münze entscheiden; **to ~ and turn** (*in bed*) sich hin und her werfen

tot [tɒt] *n* (*small quantity*) bißchen *nt*; (*small child*) Knirps *m*

total ['təʊtl] *n* Gesamtheit *f*; (*money*) Endsumme *f* ♦ *adj* Gesamt-, total ♦ *vt* (*add up*) zusammenzählen; (*amount to*) sich belaufen auf

totalitarian [təʊtælɪˈtɛərɪən] *adj* totalitär

totally ['təʊtəlɪ] *adv* total

totter ['tɒtə*] *vi* wanken, schwanken

touch [tʌtʃ] *n* Berührung *f*; (*sense of feeling*) Tastsinn *m* ♦ *vt* (*feel*) berühren; (*come against*) leicht anstoßen; (*emotionally*) rühren; **a ~ of** (*fig*) eine Spur von; **to get in ~ with sb** sich mit jdm in Verbindung setzen; **to lose ~** (*friends*) Kontakt verlieren; **~ on** *vt fus* (*topic*) berühren, erwähnen; **~ up** *vt* (*paint*) auffrischen; **~-and-go** *adj* riskant, knapp; **~down** *n* Landen *nt*, Niedergehen *nt*; **~ed** *adj* (*moved*) gerührt; **~ing** *adj* rührend; **~line** *n* Seitenlinie *f*; **~-sensitive screen** *n* (*COMPUT*) berührungsempfindlicher Bildschirm *m*; **~y** *adj* empfindlich, reizbar

tough [tʌf] *adj* zäh; (*difficult*) schwierig ♦ *n* Schläger(typ) *m*; **~en** *vt* zäh machen; (*make strong*) abhärten

toupee ['tuːpeɪ] *n* Toupet *nt*

tour ['tʊə*] *n* Tour *f* ♦ *vi* umherreisen; (*THEAT*) auf Tour sein; auf Tour gehen; **~ing** *n* Umherreisen *nt*; (*THEAT*) Tournee *f*

tourism ['tʊərɪzm] *n* Fremdenverkehr *m*, Tourismus *m*

tourist ['tʊərɪst] *n* Tourist(in) *m(f)* ♦ *cpd* (*class*) Touristen-; **~ office** *n* Verkehrsamt *nt*

tournament ['tʊənəmənt] *n* Turnier *nt*

tousled ['taʊzld] *adj* zerzaust

tout [taʊt] *vi*: **to ~ for** auf Kundenfang gehen für ♦ *n*: **ticket ~** Kundenschlepper(in) *m(f)*

tow [təʊ] *vt* (ab)schleppen; **on** (*BRIT*) *or* **in** (*US*) ~ (*AUT*) im Schlepp

toward(s) [təˈwɔːd(z)] *prep* (*with time*) gegen; (*in direction of*) nach

towel ['taʊəl] *n* Handtuch *nt*; **~ling** *n* (*fabric*) Frottee *nt or m*; **~ rack** (*US*) *n* Handtuchstange *f*; **~ rail** *n* Handtuchstange *f*

tower ['taʊə*] *n* Turm *m*; **~ block** (*BRIT*) *n* Hochhaus *nt*; **~ing** *adj* hochragend

town [taʊn] *n* Stadt *f*; **to go to ~** (*fig*) sich ins Zeug legen; **~ centre** *n* Stadtzentrum *nt*; **~ clerk** *n* Stadtdirektor *m*; **~ council** *n* Stadtrat *m*; **~ hall** *n* Rathaus *nt*; **~ plan** *n* Stadtplan *m*; **~ planning** *n* Stadtplanung *f*

towrope ['təʊrəʊp] *n* Abschlepptau *nt*

tow truck (*US*) *n* (*breakdown lorry*) Abschleppwagen *m*

toxic ['tɒksɪk] *adj* giftig, Gift-

toy [tɔɪ] *n* Spielzeug *nt*; **~ with** *vt fus* spielen mit; **~shop** *n* Spielwarengeschäft *nt*

trace [treɪs] *n* Spur *f* ♦ *vt* (*follow a course*) nachspüren +*dat*; (*find out*) aufspüren; (*copy*) durchpausen; **tracing paper** *n* Pauspapier *nt*

track [træk] *n* (*mark*) Spur *f*; (*path*) Weg *m*; (*race~*) Rennbahn *f*; (*RAIL*) Gleis *nt* ♦ *vt* verfolgen; **to keep ~ of sb** jdn im Auge behalten; **~ down** *vt* aufspüren; **~suit** *n* Trainingsanzug *m*

tract [trækt] *n* (*of land*) Gebiet *nt*; (*booklet*) Traktat *nt*

traction ['trækʃən] *n* (*power*) Zugkraft *f*; (*AUT: grip*) Bodenhaftung *f*; (*MED*): **in ~** im Streckverband

trade [treɪd] *n* (*commerce*) Handel *m*; (*business*) Geschäft *nt*, Gewerbe *nt*; (*people*) Geschäftsleute *pl*; (*skilled manual work*) Handwerk *nt* ♦ *vi*: **to ~ (in)** handeln (mit) ♦ *vt* tauschen; **~ in** *vt* in

Zahlung geben; **~ fair** n Messe nt; **~-in price** n Preis m, zu dem etw in Zahlung genommen wird; **~mark** n Warenzeichen nt; **~ name** n Handelsbezeichnung f; **~r** n Händler m; **~sman** (irreg) n (shopkeeper) Geschäftsmann m; (workman) Handwerker m; (delivery man) Lieferant m; **~ union** n Gewerkschaft f; **~ unionist** n Gewerkschaftler(in) m(f)

trading ['treɪdɪŋ] n Handel m; **~ estate** n (BRIT) n Industriegelände nt

tradition [trə'dɪʃən] n Tradition f; **~al** adj traditionell, herkömmlich

traffic ['træfɪk] n Verkehr m; (esp in drugs): **~ (in)** Handel m (mit) ♦ vi: **to ~ in** (esp drugs) handeln mit; **~ circle** (US) n Kreisverkehr m; **~ jam** n Verkehrsstauung f; **~ lights** npl Verkehrsampel f; **~ warden** n ≈ Verkehrspolizist m (ohne amtliche Befugnisse), Politesse f (ohne amtliche Befugnisse)

tragedy ['trædʒədɪ] n Tragödie f

tragic ['trædʒɪk] adj tragisch

trail [treɪl] n (track) Spur f; (of smoke) Rauchfahne f; (of dust) Staubwolke f; (road) Pfad m, Weg m ♦ vt (animal) verfolgen; (person) folgen +dat; (drag) schleppen ♦ vi (hang loosely) schleifen; (plants) sich ranken; (be behind) hinterherhinken; (SPORT) weit zurückliegen; (walk) zuckeln; **~ behind** vi zurückbleiben; **~er** n Anhänger m; (US: caravan) Wohnwagen m; (for film) Vorschau f; **~er truck** (US) n Sattelschlepper m

train [treɪn] n Zug m; (of dress) Schleppe f; (series) Folge f ♦ vt (teach: person) ausbilden; (: animal) abrichten; (: mind) schulen; (SPORT) trainieren; (aim) richten ♦ vi (exercise) trainieren; (study) ausgebildet werden; **~ of thought** Gedankengang m; **to ~ sth on** (aim) etw richten auf +acc; **~ed** adj (eye) geschult; (person, voice) ausgebildet; **~ee** [treɪ'niː] n Lehrling m; Praktikant(in) m(f); **~er** n (SPORT) Trainer m; Ausbilder m; **~ing** n (for occupation) Ausbildung f; (SPORT) Training nt; **in ~ing** im Training; **~ing**

college n Pädagogische Hochschule f, Lehrerseminar nt; **~ing shoes** npl Turnschuhe pl

traipse [treɪps] vi latschen

trait [treɪ(t)] n Zug m, Merkmal nt

traitor ['treɪtə*] n Verräter m

trajectory [trə'dʒektərɪ] n Flugbahn f

tram [træm] (BRIT) n (also: ~car) Straßenbahn f

tramp [træmp] n Landstreicher m ♦ vi (walk heavily) stampfen, stapfen; (travel on foot) wandern

trample ['træmpl] vt (nieder)trampeln ♦ vi (herum)trampeln; **to ~ (underfoot)** herumtrampeln auf +dat

tranquil ['træŋkwɪl] adj ruhig, friedlich; **~lity** (US **~ity**) n Ruhe f; **~lizer** (US **~izer**) n Beruhigungsmittel nt

transact [træn'zækt] vt abwickeln; **~ion** [træn'zækʃən] n Abwicklung f; (piece of business) Geschäft nt, Transaktion f

transcend [træn'send] vt übersteigen

transcript ['trænskrɪpt] n Abschrift f, Kopie f; (JUR) Protokoll nt; **~ion** [træn'skrɪpʃən] n Transkription f; (product) Abschrift f

transfer [n 'trænsfə*, vt træns'fɜː*] n (~ring) Übertragung f; (of business) Umzug m; (being ~red) Versetzung f; (design) Abziehbild nt; (SPORT) Transfer m ♦ vt (business) verlegen; (person) versetzen; (prisoner) überführen; (drawing) übertragen; (money) überweisen; **to ~ the charges** (BRIT: TEL) ein R-Gespräch führen

transform [træns'fɔːm] vt umwandeln; **~ation** [trænsfə'meɪʃən] n Umwandlung f, Verwandlung f; **~er** n (ELEC) Transformator m

transfusion [træns'fjuːʒən] n Blutübertragung f, Transfusion f

transient ['trænzɪənt] adj kurz(lebig)

transistor [træn'zɪstə*] n (ELEC) Transistor m; (radio) Transistorradio nt

transit ['trænzɪt] n: **in ~** unterwegs

transition [træn'zɪʃən] n Übergang m; **~al** adj Übergangs-

transit lounge n (at airport etc) Warteraum m

transitory ['trænzɪtərɪ] *adj*
vorübergehend

translate [trænz'leɪt] *vt, vi* übersetzen

translation [trænz'leɪʃən] *n* Übersetzung *f*

translator [trænz'leɪtə*] *n* Übersetzer(in) *m(f)*

transmission [trænz'mɪʃən] *n* (*of information*) Übermittlung *f*; (*ELEC, MED, TV*) Übertragung *f*; (*AUT*) Getriebe *nt*

transmit [trænz'mɪt] *vt* (*message*) übermitteln; (*ELEC, MED, TV*) übertragen; **~ter** *n* Sender *m*

transparency [træns'pɛərənsɪ] *n* Durchsichtigkeit *f*; (*BRIT: PHOT*) Dia(positiv) *nt*

transparent [træns'pærənt] *adj* durchsichtig; (*fig*) offenkundig

transpire [træns'paɪə*] *vi* (*turn out*) sich herausstellen; (*happen*) passieren

transplant [*vb* træns'plɑːnt, *n* 'trænsplɑːnt] *vt* umpflanzen; (*MED, also fig: person*) verpflanzen ♦ *n* (*MED*) Transplantation *f*; (*organ*) Transplantat *nt*

transport [*n* 'trænspɔːt, *vb* træns'pɔːt] *n* Transport *m*, Beförderung *f* ♦ *vt* befördern; transportieren; **means of ~** Transportmittel *nt*; **~ation** [trænspɔː'teɪʃən] *n* Transport *m*, Beförderung *f*; (*means*) Beförderungsmittel *nt*; (*cost*) Transportkosten *pl*; **~ café** (*BRIT*) Fernfahrerlokal *nt*

transverse ['trænzvɜːs] *adj* Quer-; (*position*) horizontal; (*engine*) querliegend

trap [træp] *n* Falle *f*; (*carriage*) zweirädrige(r) Einspänner *m*; (*inf: mouth*) Klappe *f* ♦ *vt* fangen; (*person*) in eine Falle locken; **~door** *n* Falltür *f*

trappings ['træpɪŋz] *npl* Aufmachung *f*

trash [træʃ] *n* (*rubbish*) Plunder *m*; (*nonsense*) Mist *m*; **~ can** (*US*) *n* Mülleimer *m*

traumatic [trɔː'mætɪk] *adj* traumatisch

travel ['trævl] *n* Reisen *nt* ♦ *vi* reisen ♦ *vt* (*distance*) zurücklegen; (*country*) bereisen; **~s** *npl* (*journeys*) Reisen *pl*; **~ agency** *n* Reisebüro *nt*; **~ agent** *n* Reisebürokaufmann(frau) *m(f)*; **~ler** (*US* **~er**) *n* Reisende(r) *mf*; (*salesman*)

Handlungsreisende(r) *m*; **~ler's cheque** (*US* **~er's check**) *n* Reisescheck *m*; **~ling** (*US* **~ing**) *n* Reisen *nt*; **~ sickness** *n* Reisekrankheit *f*

trawler ['trɔːlə*] *n* (*NAUT, FISHING*) Fischdampfer *m*, Trawler *m*

tray [treɪ] *n* (*tea ~*) Tablett *nt*; (*receptacle*) Schale *f*; (*for mail*) Ablage *f*

treacherous ['tretʃərəs] *adj* verräterisch; (*road*) tückisch

treachery ['tretʃərɪ] *n* Verrat *m*

treacle ['triːkl] *n* Sirup *m*, Melasse *f*

tread [tred] (*pt* trod, *pp* **trodden**) *n* Schritt *m*, Tritt *m*; (*of stair*) Stufe *f*; (*on tyre*) Profil *nt* ♦ *vi* treten; **~ on** *vt fus* treten auf +*acc*

treason ['triːzn] *n* Verrat *m*

treasure ['treʒə*] *n* Schatz *m* ♦ *vt* schätzen

treasurer ['treʒərə*] *n* Kassenverwalter *m*, Schatzmeister *m*

treasury ['treʒərɪ] *n* (*POL*) Finanzministerium *nt*

treat [triːt] *n* besondere Freude *f* ♦ *vt* (*deal with*) behandeln; **to ~ sb to sth** jdm etw spendieren

treatise ['triːtɪz] *n* Abhandlung *f*

treatment ['triːtmənt] *n* Behandlung *f*

treaty ['triːtɪ] *n* Vertrag *m*

treble ['trebl] *adj* dreifach ♦ *vt* verdreifachen; **~ clef** *n* Violinschlüssel *m*

tree [triː] *n* Baum *m*; **~ trunk** *n* Baumstamm *m*

trek [trek] *n* Treck *m*, Zug *m*; (*inf*) anstrengende(r) Weg *m* ♦ *vi* trecken

trellis ['trelɪs] *n* Gitter *nt*; (*for gardening*) Spalier *m*

tremble ['trembl] *vi* zittern; (*ground*) beben

trembling ['tremblɪŋ] *n* Zittern *nt* ♦ *adj* zitternd

tremendous [trə'mendəs] *adj* gewaltig, kolossal; (*inf: very good*) prima

tremor ['tremə*] *n* Zittern *nt*; (*of earth*) Beben *nt*

trench [trentʃ] *n* Graben *m*; (*MIL*) Schützengraben *m*

trend [trend] *n* Tendenz *f*; **~y** (*inf*) *adj* modisch

trepidation [trepɪˈdeɪʃən] *n* Beklommenheit *f*

trespass [ˈtrespəs] *vi*: **to ~ on** widerrechtlich betreten; **"no ~ing"** „Betreten verboten"

tress [tres] *n* Locke *f*

trestle [ˈtresl] *n* Bock *m*; **~ table** *n* Klapptisch *m*

trial [ˈtraɪəl] *n* (*JUR*) Prozeß *m*; (*test*) Versuch *m*, Probe *f*; (*hardship*) Prüfung *f*; **by ~ and error** durch Ausprobieren

triangle [ˈtraɪæŋgl] *n* Dreieck *nt*; (*MUS*) Triangel *f*

triangular [traɪˈæŋgjʊlə*] *adj* dreieckig

tribal [ˈtraɪbəl] *adj* Stammes-

tribe [traɪb] *n* Stamm *m*; **~sman** (*irreg*) *n* Stammesangehörige(r) *m*

tribulation [trɪbjʊˈleɪʃən] *n* Not *f*, Mühsal *f*

tribunal [traɪˈbjuːnl] *n* Gericht *nt*; (*inquiry*) Untersuchungsausschuß *m*

tributary [ˈtrɪbjʊtərɪ] *n* Nebenfluß *m*

tribute [ˈtrɪbjuːt] *n* (*admiration*) Zeichen *nt* der Hochachtung; **to pay ~ to sb/sth** jdm/einer Sache Tribut zollen

trick [trɪk] *n* Trick *m*; (*CARDS*) Stich *m* ♦ *vt* überlisten, beschwindeln; **to play a ~ on sb** jdm einen Streich spielen; **that should do the ~** daß müßte eigentlich klappen; **~ery** *n* Tricks *pl*

trickle [ˈtrɪkl] *n* Tröpfeln *nt*; (*small river*) Rinnsal *nt* ♦ *vi* tröpfeln; (*seep*) sickern

tricky [ˈtrɪkɪ] *adj* (*problem*) schwierig; (*situation*) kitzlig

tricycle [ˈtraɪsɪkl] *n* Dreirad *nt*

trifle [ˈtraɪfl] *n* Kleinigkeit *f*; (*COOK*) Trifle *m* ♦ *adv*: **a ~ ...** ein bißchen ...

trifling [ˈtraɪflɪŋ] *adj* geringfügig

trigger [ˈtrɪgə*] *n* Drücker *m*; **~ off** *vt* auslösen

trim [trɪm] *adj* gepflegt; (*figure*) schlank ♦ *n* (gute) Verfassung *f*; (*embellishment, on car*) Verzierung *f* ♦ *vt* (*clip*) schneiden; (*trees*) stutzen; (*decorate*) besetzen; (*sails*) trimmen; **~mings** *npl* (*decorations*) Verzierung *f*, Verzierungen *pl*; (*extras*) Zubehör *nt*

Trinity [ˈtrɪnɪtɪ] *n*: **the ~** die Dreieinigkeit *f*

trinket [ˈtrɪŋkɪt] *n* kleine(s) Schmuckstück *nt*

trip [trɪp] *n* (kurze) Reise *f*; (*outing*) Ausflug *m*; (*stumble*) Stolpern *nt* ♦ *vi* (*walk quickly*) trippeln; (*stumble*) stolpern; **on a ~** auf Reisen; **~ up** *vi* stolpern; (*fig*) stolpern, einen Fehler machen ♦ *vt* zu Fall bringen; (*fig*) hereinlegen

tripe [traɪp] *n* (*food*) Kutteln *pl*; (*rubbish*) Mist *m*

triple [ˈtrɪpl] *adj* dreifach

triplets [ˈtrɪplɪts] *npl* Drillinge *pl*

triplicate [ˈtrɪplɪkət] *n*: **in ~** in dreifacher Ausfertigung

tripod [ˈtraɪpɒd] *n* (*PHOT*) Stativ *nt*

trite [traɪt] *adj* banal

triumph [ˈtraɪʌmf] *n* Triumph *m* ♦ *vi*: **to ~ (over)** triumphieren (über +*acc*); **~ant** [traɪˈʌmfənt] *adj* triumphierend

trivia [ˈtrɪvɪə] *npl* Trivialitäten *pl*

trivial [ˈtrɪvɪəl] *adj* gering(fügig), trivial

trod [trɒd] *pt of* **tread**; **~den** [ˈtrɒdn] *pp of* **tread**

trolley [ˈtrɒlɪ] *n* Handwagen *m*; (*in shop*) Einkaufswagen *m*; (*for luggage*) Kofferkuli *m*; (*table*) Teewagen *m*; **~ bus** *n* Oberleitungsbus *m*, Obus *m*

trombone [trɒmˈbəʊn] *n* Posaune *f*

troop [truːp] *n* Schar *f*; (*MIL*) Trupp *m*; **~s** *npl* Truppen *pl*; **~ in/out** *vi* hinein-/hinausströmen; **~ing the colour** *n* (*ceremony*) Fahnenparade *f*

trophy [ˈtrəʊfɪ] *n* Trophäe *f*

tropic [ˈtrɒpɪk] *n* Wendekreis *m*; **~al** *adj* tropisch

trot [trɒt] *n* Trott *m* ♦ *vi* trotten; **on the ~** (*BRIT*: *fig*: *inf*) in einer Tour

trouble [ˈtrʌbl] *n* (*problems*) Ärger *m*; (*worry*) Sorge *f*; (*in country, industry*) Unruhen *pl*; (*effort*) Mühe *f*; (*MED*): **stomach ~** Magenbeschwerden *pl* ♦ *vt* (*disturb*) stören; **~s** *npl* (*POL etc*) Unruhen *pl*; **to ~ to do sth** sich bemühen, etw zu tun; **to be in ~** Probleme *or* Ärger haben; **to go to the ~ of doing sth** sich die Mühe machen, etw zu tun; **what's the ~?** was ist los?; (*to sick person*) wo fehlt's?; **~d** *adj* (*person*) beunruhigt; (*country*) geplagt; **~-free** *adj* sorglos; **~maker** *n*

Unruhestifter *m*; **~shooter** *n* Vermittler
m; **~some** *adj* lästig, unangenehm;
(*child*) schwierig

trough [trɒf] *n* (*vessel*) Trog *m*; (*channel*)
Rinne *f*, Kanal *m*; (*MET*) Tief *nt*

trounce [traʊns] *vt* (*esp SPORT*)
vernichtend schlagen

trousers ['traʊzəz] *npl* Hose *f*

trout [traʊt] *n* Forelle *f*

trowel ['traʊəl] *n* Kelle *f*

truant ['truːənt] *n*: **to play ~** (*BRIT*) (die
Schule) schwänzen

truce [truːs] *n* Waffenstillstand *m*

truck [trʌk] *n* Lastwagen *m*; (*RAIL*)
offene(r) Güterwagen *m*; **~ driver** *n*
Lastwagenfahrer *m*; **~ farm** (*US*) *n*
Gemüsegärtnerei *f*

truculent ['trʌkjʊlənt] *adj* trotzig

trudge [trʌdʒ] *vi* sich (mühselig)
dahinschleppen

true [truː] *adj* (*exact*) wahr; (*genuine*)
echt; (*friend*) treu

truffle ['trʌfl] *n* Trüffel *f or m*

truly ['truːlɪ] *adv* wirklich; **yours ~** Ihr
sehr ergebener

trump [trʌmp] *n* (*CARDS*) Trumpf *m*; **~ed-
up** *adj* erfunden

trumpet ['trʌmpɪt] *n* Trompete *f*

truncheon ['trʌntʃən] *n* Gummiknüppel
m

trundle ['trʌndl] *vt* schieben ♦ *vi*: **to ~
along** entlangrollen

trunk [trʌŋk] *n* (*of tree*) (Baum)stamm *m*;
(*ANAT*) Rumpf *m*; (*box*) Truhe *f*,
Überseekoffer *m*; (*of elephant*) Rüssel *m*;
(*US: AUT*) Kofferraum *m*; **~s** *npl* (*also:
swimming ~s*) Badehose *f*

truss [trʌs] *n* (*MED*) Bruchband *nt* ♦ *vt*
(*also: ~ up*) fesseln

trust [trʌst] *n* (*confidence*) Vertrauen *nt*;
(*for property etc*) Treuhandvermögen *nt*
♦ *vt* (*rely on*) vertrauen +*dat*, sich
verlassen auf +*acc*; (*hope*) hoffen;
(*entrust*): **to ~ sth to sb** jdm etw
anvertrauen; **~ed** *adj* treu; **~ee** [trʌs'tiː]
n Vermögensverwalter *m*; **~ful** *adj*
vertrauensvoll; **~ing** *adj* vertrauensvoll;
~worthy *adj* vertrauenswürdig; (*account*)
glaubwürdig

truth [truːθ, *pl* truːðz] *n* Wahrheit *f*; **~ful**
adj ehrlich

try [traɪ] *n* Versuch *m* ♦ *vt* (*attempt*)
versuchen; (*test*) (aus)probieren; (*JUR:
person*) unter Anklage stellen; (: *case*)
verhandeln; (*courage, patience*) auf die
Probe stellen ♦ *vi* (*make effort*)
versuchen, sich bemühen; **to have a ~** es
versuchen; **to ~ to do sth** versuchen, etw
zu tun; **~ on** *vt* (*dress*) anprobieren; (*hat*)
aufprobieren; **~ out** *vt* ausprobieren;
~ing *adj* schwierig

T-shirt ['tiːʃɜːt] *n* T-shirt *nt*

T-square ['tiːskweə*] *n* Reißschiene *f*

tub [tʌb] *n* Wanne *f*, Kübel *m*; (*for
margarine etc*) Becher *m*

tubby ['tʌbɪ] *adj* rundlich

tube [tjuːb] *n* (*pipe*) Röhre *f*, Rohr *nt*; (*for
toothpaste etc*) Tube *f*; (*in London*) U-Bahn
f; (*AUT: for tyre*) Schlauch *m*; **~ station** *n*
(*in London*) U-Bahnstation *f*

tubing ['tjuːbɪŋ] *n* Schlauch *m*

tubular ['tjuːbjʊlə*] *adj* röhrenförmig

TUC (*BRIT*) *n abbr* = **Trades Union
Congress**

tuck [tʌk] *n* (*fold*) Falte *f*, Einschlag *m*
♦ *vt* (*put*) stecken; (*gather*) fälteln,
einschlagen; **~ away** *vt* wegstecken; **~ in**
vt hineinstecken; (*blanket etc*) feststecken;
(*person*) zudecken ♦ *vi* (*eat*) hineinhauen,
zulangen; **~ up** *vt* (*child*) warm zudecken;
~ shop *n* Süßwarenladen *m*

Tuesday ['tjuːzdeɪ] *n* Dienstag *m*

tuft [tʌft] *n* Büschel *m*

tug [tʌg] *n* (*jerk*) Zerren *nt*, Ruck *m*;
(*NAUT*) Schleppdampfer *m* ♦ *vt*, *vi* zerren,
ziehen; (*boat*) schleppen; **~-of-war** *n*
Tauziehen *nt*

tuition [tjuː'ɪʃən] *n* (*BRIT*) Unterricht *m*;
(: *private ~*) Privatunterricht *m*; (*US:
school fees*) Schulgeld *nt*

tulip ['tjuːlɪp] *n* Tulpe *f*

tumble ['tʌmbl] *n* (*fall*) Sturz *m* ♦ *vi*
fallen, stürzen; **~ to** *vt fus* kapieren;
~down *adj* baufällig; **~ dryer** (*BRIT*) *n*
Trockner *m*; **~r** ['tʌmblə*] *n* (*glass*)
Trinkglas *nt*

tummy ['tʌmɪ] (*inf*) *n* Bauch *m*

tumour ['tjuːmə*] (*US* **tumor**) *n*

Geschwulst *f*, Tumor *m*

tumultuous [tjuːˈmʌltjuəs] *adj* (*welcome, applause etc*) stürmisch

tuna [ˈtjuːnə] *n* Thunfisch *m*

tune [tjuːn] *n* Melodie *f* ♦ *vt* (*MUS*) stimmen; (*AUT*) richtig einstellen; **to sing in ~/out of ~** richtig/falsch singen; **to be out of ~ with** nicht harmonieren mit; **~ in** *vi* einschalten; **~ up** *vi* (*MUS*) stimmen; **~ful** *adj* melodisch; **~r** *n* (*person*) (Instrumenten)stimmer *m*; (*part of radio*) Tuner *m*; **piano ~r** Klavierstimmer(in) *m(f)*

tunic [ˈtjuːnɪk] *n* Waffenrock *m*; (*loose garment*) lange Bluse *f*

tuning [ˈtjuːnɪŋ] *n* (*RAD, AUT*) Einstellen *nt*; (*MUS*) Stimmen *nt*; **~ fork** *n* Stimmgabel *f*

Tunisia [tjuːˈnɪzɪə] *n* Tunesien *nt*

tunnel [ˈtʌnl] *n* Tunnel *m*, Unterführung *f* ♦ *vi* einen Tunnel anlegen

turbulent [ˈtɜːbjʊlənt] *adj* stürmisch

tureen [tjʊˈriːn] *n* Terrine *f*

turf [tɜːf] *n* Rasen *m*; (*piece*) Sode *f* ♦ *vt* mit Grassoden belegen; **~ out** (*inf*) *vt* rauswerfen

turgid [ˈtɜːdʒɪd] *adj* geschwollen

Turk [tɜːk] *n* Türke *m*, Türkin *f*

Turkey [ˈtɜːkɪ] *n* Türkei *f*

turkey [ˈtɜːkɪ] *n* Puter *m*, Truthahn *m*

Turkish [ˈtɜːkɪʃ] *adj* türkisch ♦ *n* (*LING*) Türkisch *nt*

turmoil [ˈtɜːmɔɪl] *n* Aufruhr *m*, Tumult *m*

turn [tɜːn] *n* (*rotation*) (Um)drehung *f*; (*performance*) (Programm)nummer *f*; (*MED*) Schock *m* ♦ *vt* (*rotate*) drehen; (*change position of*) umdrehen, wenden; (*page*) umblättern; (*transform*): **to ~ sth into sth** etw in etw *acc* verwandeln; (*direct*) zuwenden ♦ *vi* (*rotate*) sich drehen; (*change direction: in car*) abbiegen; (*: wind*) drehen; (*~ round*) umdrehen, wenden; (*become*) werden; (*leaves*) sich verfärben; (*milk*) sauer werden; (*weather*) umschlagen; **to do sb a good ~** jdm etwas Gutes tun; **it's your ~** du bist dran *or* an der Reihe; **in ~, by ~s** abwechselnd; **to take ~s** sich abwechseln;

it gave me quite a ~ das hat mich schön erschreckt; **"no left ~"** (*AUT*) „Linksabbiegen verboten"; **~ away** *vi* sich abwenden; **~ back** *vt* umdrehen; (*person*) zurückschicken; (*clock*) zurückstellen ♦ *vi* umkehren; **~ down** *vt* (*refuse*) ablehnen; (*fold down*) umschlagen; **~ in** *vi* (*go to bed*) ins Bett gehen ♦ *vt* (*fold inwards*) einwärts biegen; **~ off** *vi* abbiegen ♦ *vt* ausschalten; (*tap*) zudrehen; (*machine, electricity*) abstellen; **~ on** *vt* (*light*) anschalten, einschalten; (*tap*) aufdrehen; (*machine*) anstellen; **~ out** *vi* (*prove to be*) sich erweisen; (*people*) sich entwickeln ♦ *vt* (*light*) ausschalten; (*gas*) abstellen; (*produce*) produzieren; **how did the cake ~ out?** wie ist der Kuchen geworden?; **~ round** *vi* (*person, vehicle*) sich herumdrehen; (*rotate*) sich drehen; **~ up** *vi* auftauchen; (*happen*) passieren, sich ereignen ♦ *vt* (*collar*) hochklappen, hochstellen; (*nose*) rümpfen; (*increase: radio*) lauter stellen; (*: heat*) höher drehen; **~ing** *n* (*in road*) Abzweigung *f*; **~ing point** *n* Wendepunkt *m*

turnip [ˈtɜːnɪp] *n* Steckrübe *f*

turnout [ˈtɜːnaʊt] *n* (Besucher)zahl *f*; (*COMM*) Produktion *f*

turnover [ˈtɜːnəʊvə*] *n* Umsatz *m*; (*of staff*) Wechsel *m*

turnpike [ˈtɜːnpaɪk] (*US*) *n* gebührenpflichtige Straße *f*

turnstile [ˈtɜːnstaɪl] *n* Drehkreuz *nt*

turntable [ˈtɜːnteɪbl] *n* (*of record player*) Plattenteller *m*; (*RAIL*) Drehscheibe *f*

turn-up [ˈtɜːnʌp] (*BRIT*) *n* (*on trousers*) Aufschlag *m*

turpentine [ˈtɜːpəntaɪn] *n* Terpentin *nt*

turquoise [ˈtɜːkwɔɪz] *n* (*gem*) Türkis *m*; (*colour*) Türkis *nt* ♦ *adj* türkisfarben

turret [ˈtʌrɪt] *n* Turm *m*

turtle [ˈtɜːtl] *n* Schildkröte *f*; **~ neck (sweater)** *n* Pullover *m* mit Schildkrötkragen

tusk [tʌsk] *n* Stoßzahn *m*

tussle [ˈtʌsl] *n* Balgerei *f*

tutor [ˈtjuːtə*] *n* (*teacher*) Privatlehrer *m*; (*college instructor*) Tutor *m*; **~ial**

underclothes ['ʌndəkləʊðz] *npl*
Unterwäsche *f*
undercoat ['ʌndəkəʊt] *n* (*paint*)
Grundierung *f*
undercover ['ʌndəkʌvə*] *adj* Geheim-
undercurrent ['ʌndəkʌrənt] *n*
Unterströmung *f*
undercut ['ʌndəkʌt] (*irreg: like* cut) *vt*
unterbieten
underdeveloped ['ʌndədɪ'veləpt] *adj*
Entwicklungs-, unterentwickelt
underdog ['ʌndədɒg] *n* Unterlegene(r)
mf
underdone ['ʌndə'dʌn] *adj* (*COOK*) nicht
gar, nicht durchgebraten
underestimate ['ʌndər'estɪmeɪt] *vt*
unterschätzen
underexposed ['ʌndərɪks'pəʊzd] *adj*
unterbelichtet
underfed ['ʌndə'fed] *adj* unterernährt
underfoot ['ʌndə'fʊt] *adv* am Boden
undergo ['ʌndə'gəʊ] (*irreg: like* go) *vt*
(*experience*) durchmachen; (*operation, test*)
sich unterziehen +*dat*
undergraduate ['ʌndə'grædjʊət] *n*
Student(in) *m(f)*
underground ['ʌndəgraʊnd] *n* U-Bahn *f*
♦ *adj* Untergrund-
undergrowth ['ʌndəgrəʊθ] *n* Gestrüpp
nt, Unterholz *nt*
underhand(ed) ['ʌndə'hænd(ɪd)] *adj*
hinterhältig
underlie [ʌndə'laɪ] (*irreg: like* lie) *vt*
(*form the basis of*) zugrundeliegen +*dat*
underline [ʌndə'laɪn] *vt* unterstreichen;
(*emphasize*) betonen
underling ['ʌndəlɪŋ] *n* Handlanger *m*
undermine [ʌndə'maɪn] *vt* untergraben
underneath [ʌndə'niːθ] *adv* darunter
♦ *prep* unter
underpaid [ʌndə'peɪd] *adj* unterbezahlt
underpants ['ʌndəpænts] *npl* Unterhose
f
underpass ['ʌndəpɑːs] (*BRIT*) *n*
Unterführung *f*
underprivileged [ʌndə'prɪvɪlɪdʒd] *adj*
benachteiligt, unterprivilegiert
underrate [ʌndə'reɪt] *vt* unterschätzen
undershirt ['ʌndəʃɜːt] (*US*) *n* Unterhemd

nt
undershorts ['ʌndəʃɔːts] (*US*) *npl*
Unterhose *f*
underside ['ʌndəsaɪd] *n* Unterseite *f*
underskirt ['ʌndəskɜːt] (*BRIT*) *n*
Unterrock *m*
understand [ʌndə'stænd] (*irreg: like*
stand) *vt, vi* verstehen; **I ~ that ...** ich
habe gehört, daß ...; **am I to ~ that ...?**
soll das (etwa) heißen, daß ...?; **what do
you ~ by that?** was verstehen Sie
darunter?; **it is understood that ...** es
wurde vereinbart, daß ...; **to make o.s.
understood** sich verständlich machen; **is
that understood?** ist das klar?; **~able**
adj verständlich; **~ing** *n* Verständnis *nt*
♦ *adj* verständnisvoll
understatement ['ʌndəsteɪtmənt] *n*
(*quality*) Untertreibung *f*; **that's an ~!** das
ist untertrieben!
understood [ʌndə'stʊd] *pt, pp of*
understand ♦ *adj* klar; (*implied*)
angenommen
understudy ['ʌndəstʌdɪ] *n*
Ersatz(schau)spieler(in) *m(f)*
undertake [ʌndə'teɪk] (*irreg: like* take)
vt unternehmen ♦ *vi*: **to ~ to do sth** sich
verpflichten, etw zu tun
undertaker ['ʌndəteɪkə*] *n*
Leichenbestatter *m*
undertaking [ʌndə'teɪkɪŋ] *n* (*enterprise*)
Unternehmen *nt*; (*promise*) Verpflichtung
f
undertone ['ʌndətəʊn] *n*: **in an ~** mit
gedämpfter Stimme
underwater ['ʌndə'wɔːtə*] *adv* unter
Wasser ♦ *adj* Unterwasser-
underwear ['ʌndəwɛə*] *n* Unterwäsche *f*
underworld ['ʌndəwɜːld] *n* (*of crime*)
Unterwelt *f*
underwriter ['ʌndəraɪtə*] *n* Assekurant
m
undesirable [ʌndɪ'zaɪərəbl] *adj*
unerwünscht
undies ['ʌndɪz] (*inf*) *npl* (Damen)unterwä-
sche *f*
undisputed ['ʌndɪs'pjuːtɪd] *adj*
unbestritten
undo ['ʌn'duː] (*irreg: like* do) *vt*

(*unfasten*) öffnen, aufmachen; (*work*) zunichte machen; **~ing** *n* Verderben *nt*

undoubted [ʌnˈdautɪd] *adj* unbezweifelt; **~ly** *adv* zweifellos, ohne Zweifel

undress [ʌnˈdres] *vt* ausziehen ♦ *vi* sich ausziehen

undue [ʌnˈdjuː] *adj* übermäßig

undulating [ˈʌndjʊleɪtɪŋ] *adj* wellenförmig; (*country*) wellig

unduly [ʌnˈdjuːlɪ] *adv* übermäßig

unearth [ʌnˈɜːθ] *vt* (*dig up*) ausgraben; (*discover*) ans Licht bringen

unearthly [ʌnˈɜːθlɪ] *adj* (*hour*) nachtschlafen

uneasy [ʌnˈiːzɪ] *adj* (*worried*) unruhig; (*feeling*) ungut

uneconomic(al) [ˈʌniːkəˈnɒmɪk(əl)] *adj* unwirtschaftlich

uneducated [ˈʌnˈedjʊkeɪtɪd] *adj* ungebildet

unemployed [ˈʌnɪmˈplɔɪd] *adj* arbeitslos ♦ *npl*: **the ~** die Arbeitslosen *pl*

unemployment [ˈʌnɪmˈplɔɪmənt] *n* Arbeitslosigkeit *f*

unending [ʌnˈendɪŋ] *adj* endlos

unerring [ʌnˈɜːrɪŋ] *adj* unfehlbar

uneven [ʌnˈiːvən] *adj* (*surface*) uneben; (*quality*) ungleichmäßig

unexpected [ˈʌnɪkˈspektɪd] *adj* unerwartet; **~ly** *adv* unerwartet

unfailing [ʌnˈfeɪlɪŋ] *adj* nie versagend

unfair [ʌnˈfeə*] *adj* ungerecht, unfair

unfaithful [ʌnˈfeɪθfʊl] *adj* untreu

unfamiliar [ʌnfəˈmɪlɪə*] *adj* ungewohnt; (*person, subject*) unbekannt; **to be ~ with** nicht kennen +*acc*, nicht vertraut sein mit

unfashionable [ʌnˈfæʃnəbl] *adj* unmodern; (*area, hotel etc*) nicht in Mode

unfasten [ʌnˈfɑːsn] *vt* öffnen, aufmachen

unfavourable [ʌnˈfeɪvərəbl] (*US* **unfavorable**) *adj* ungünstig

unfeeling [ʌnˈfiːlɪŋ] *adj* gefühllos, kalt

unfinished [ʌnˈfɪnɪʃt] *adj* unvollendet

unfit [ˈʌnˈfɪt] *adj* ungeeignet; (*in bad health*) nicht fit; **~ for sth** zu *or* für etw ungeeignet

unfold [ʌnˈfəʊld] *vt* entfalten; (*paper*) auseinanderfalten ♦ *vi* (*develop*) sich entfalten

unforeseen [ˈʌnfɔːˈsiːn] *adj* unvorhergesehen

unforgettable [ʌnfəˈɡetəbl] *adj* unvergeßlich

unforgivable [ˈʌnfəˈɡɪvəbl] *adj* unverzeihlich

unfortunate [ʌnˈfɔːtʃnət] *adj* unglücklich, bedauerlich; **~ly** *adv* leider

unfounded [ˈʌnˈfaʊndɪd] *adj* unbegründet

unfriendly [ʌnˈfrendlɪ] *adj* unfreundlich

ungainly [ʌnˈɡeɪnlɪ] *adj* linkisch

ungodly [ʌnˈɡɒdlɪ] *adj* (*hour*) nachtschlafend; (*row*) heillos

ungrateful [ʌnˈɡreɪtfʊl] *adj* undankbar

unhappiness [ʌnˈhæpɪnəs] *n* Unglück *nt*, Unglückseligkeit *f*

unhappy [ʌnˈhæpɪ] *adj* unglücklich; **~ with** (*arrangements etc*) unzufrieden mit

unharmed [ʌnˈhɑːmd] *adj* wohlbehalten, unversehrt

unhealthy [ʌnˈhelθɪ] *adj* ungesund

unheard-of [ʌnˈhɜːdɒv] *adj* unerhört

unhurt [ʌnˈhɜːt] *adj* unverletzt

unidentified [ˈʌnaɪˈdentɪfaɪd] *adj* unbekannt, nicht identifiziert

uniform [ˈjuːnɪfɔːm] *n* Uniform *f* ♦ *adj* einheitlich; **~ity** [juːnɪˈfɔːmɪtɪ] *n* Einheitlichkeit *f*

unify [ˈjuːnɪfaɪ] *vt* vereinigen

unilateral [ˈjuːnɪˈlætərəl] *adj* einseitig

uninhabited [ʌnɪnˈhæbɪtɪd] *adj* unbewohnt

unintentional [ˈʌnɪnˈtenʃənl] *adj* unabsichtlich

union [ˈjuːnjən] *n* (*uniting*) Vereinigung *f*; (*alliance*) Bund *m*, Union *f*; (*trade ~*) Gewerkschaft *f*; **U~ Jack** *n* Union Jack *m*

unique [juːˈniːk] *adj* einzig(artig)

unison [ˈjuːnɪzn] *n* Einstimmigkeit *f*; **in ~** einstimmig

unit [ˈjuːnɪt] *n* Einheit *f*; **kitchen ~** Küchenelement *nt*

unite [juːˈnaɪt] *vt* vereinigen ♦ *vi* sich vereinigen; **~d** *adj* vereinigt; (*together*) vereint; **U~d Kingdom** *n* Vereinigte(s) Königreich *nt*; **U~d Nations**

(Organization) n Vereinte Nationen pl;
U~d States (of America) n Vereinigte
Staaten pl (von Amerika)
unit trust (BRIT) n Treuhandgesellschaft f
unity ['juːnɪtɪ] n Einheit f; (agreement)
Einigkeit f
universal [juːnɪ'vɜːsəl] adj allgemein
universe ['juːnɪvɜːs] n (Welt)all nt
university [juːnɪ'vɜːsɪtɪ] n Universität f
unjust ['ʌn'dʒʌst] adj ungerecht
unkempt ['ʌn'kempt] adj ungepflegt
unkind [ʌn'kaɪnd] adj unfreundlich
unknown ['ʌn'nəʊn] adj: ~ **(to sb)** (jdm)
unbekannt
unlawful [ʌn'lɔːfʊl] adj illegal
unleaded [ʌn'ledɪd] adj (petrol) bleifrei,
unverbleit; **I use** ~ ich fahre bleifrei
unleash ['ʌn'liːʃ] vt entfesseln
unless [ən'les] conj wenn nicht, es sei
denn; ~ **he comes** es sei denn, er kommt;
~ **otherwise stated** sofern nicht anders
angegeben
unlike ['ʌn'laɪk] adj unähnlich ♦ prep im
Gegensatz zu
unlikely [ʌn'laɪklɪ] adj (not likely)
unwahrscheinlich; (unexpected:
combination etc) merkwürdig
unlimited [ʌn'lɪmɪtɪd] adj unbegrenzt
unlisted [ʌn'lɪstɪd] (US) adj nicht im
Telefonbuch stehend
unload ['ʌn'ləʊd] vt entladen
unlock ['ʌn'lɒk] vt aufschließen
unlucky [ʌn'lʌkɪ] adj unglücklich;
(person) unglückselig; **to be** ~ Pech haben
unmarried ['ʌn'mærɪd] adj
unverheiratet, ledig
unmask ['ʌn'mɑːsk] vt entlarven
unmistakable ['ʌnmɪs'teɪkəbl] adj
unverkennbar
unmitigated [ʌn'mɪtɪgeɪtɪd] adj
ungemildert, ganz
unnatural [ʌn'nætʃrəl] adj unnatürlich
unnecessary [ʌn'nesəsərɪ] adj unnötig
unnoticed [ʌn'nəʊtɪst] adj: **to go** ~
unbemerkt bleiben
UNO ['juːnəʊ] n abbr = **United Nations
Organization**
unobtainable ['ʌnəb'teɪnəbl] adj: **this
number is** ~ kein Anschluß unter dieser

Nummer
unobtrusive [ʌnəb'truːsɪv] adj
unauffällig
unofficial [ʌnə'fɪʃl] adj inoffiziell
unpack ['ʌn'pæk] vt, vi auspacken
unpalatable [ʌn'pælətəbl] adj (truth)
bitter
unparalleled [ʌn'pærəleld] adj
beispiellos
unpleasant [ʌn'pleznt] adj unangenehm
unplug ['ʌn'plʌg] vt den Stecker
herausziehen von
unpopular [ʌn'pɒpjʊlə*] adj (person)
unbeliebt; (decision etc) unpopulär
unprecedented [ʌn'presɪdəntɪd] adj
beispiellos
unpredictable [ʌnprɪ'dɪktəbl] adj
unvorhersehbar; (weather, person)
unberechenbar
unprofessional [ʌnprə'feʃənl] adj
unprofessionell
unqualified ['ʌn'kwɒlɪfaɪd] adj (success)
uneingeschränkt, voll; (person)
unqualifiziert
unquestionably [ʌn'kwestʃənəblɪ] adv
fraglos
unravel [ʌn'rævəl] vt (disentangle)
ausfasern, entwirren; (solve) lösen
unreal ['ʌn'rɪəl] adj unwirklich
unrealistic [ʌnrɪə'lɪstɪk] adj unrealistisch
unreasonable [ʌn'riːznəbl] adj
unvernünftig; (demand) übertrieben
unrelated [ʌnrɪ'leɪtɪd] adj ohne
Beziehung; (family) nicht verwandt
unrelenting [ʌnrɪ'lentɪŋ] adj
unerbittlich
unreliable [ʌnrɪ'laɪəbl] adj unzuverlässig
unremitting [ʌnrɪ'mɪtɪŋ] adj (efforts,
attempts) unermüdlich
unreservedly [ʌnrɪ'zɜːvɪdlɪ] adv offen;
(believe, trust) uneingeschränkt; (cry)
rückhaltlos
unrest [ʌn'rest] n (discontent) Unruhe f;
(fighting) Unruhen pl
unroll ['ʌn'rəʊl] vt aufrollen
unruly [ʌn'ruːlɪ] adj (child)
undiszipliniert; schwer lenkbar
unsafe ['ʌn'seɪf] adj nicht sicher
unsaid ['ʌn'sed] adj: **to leave sth** ~ etw

ungesagt lassen

unsatisfactory [ˈʌnsætɪsˈfæktərɪ] *adj* unbefriedigend; unzulänglich

unsavoury [ˈʌnˈseɪvərɪ] (*US* **unsavory**) *adj* (*fig*) widerwärtig

unscathed [ʌnˈskeɪðd] *adj* unversehrt

unscrew [ˈʌnˈskruː] *vt* aufschrauben

unscrupulous [ʌnˈskruːpjʊləs] *adj* skrupellos

unsettled [ˈʌnˈsetld] *adj* (*person*) rastlos; (*weather*) wechselhaft

unshaven [ˈʌnˈʃeɪvn] *adj* unrasiert

unsightly [ʌnˈsaɪtlɪ] *adj* unansehnlich

unskilled [ˈʌnˈskɪld] *adj* ungelernt

unspeakable [ʌnˈspiːkəbl] *adj* (*joy*) unsagbar; (*crime*) scheußlich

unstable [ʌnˈsteɪbl] *adj* instabil; (*mentally*) labil

unsteady [ʌnˈstedɪ] *adj* unsicher; (*growth*) unregelmäßig

unstuck [ˈʌnˈstʌk] *adj*: **to come ~** sich lösen; (*fig*) ins Wasser fallen

unsuccessful [ˈʌnsəkˈsesfʊl] *adj* erfolglos

unsuitable [ˈʌnˈsuːtəbl] *adj* unpassend

unsure [ʌnˈʃʊəʳ] *adj* (*uncertain*) unsicher; **to be ~ of o.s.** unsicher sein

unsuspecting [ˈʌnsəsˈpektɪŋ] *adj* nichtsahnend

unsympathetic [ˈʌnsɪmpəˈθetɪk] *adj* gefühllos; (*response*) abweisend; (*unlikeable*) unsympathisch

untapped [ˈʌnˈtæpt] *adj* (*resources*) ungenützt

unthinkable [ʌnˈθɪŋkəbl] *adj* unvorstellbar

untidy [ʌnˈtaɪdɪ] *adj* unordentlich

untie [ˈʌnˈtaɪ] *vt* aufschnüren

until [ənˈtɪl] *prep, conj* bis; **~ he comes** bis er kommt; **~ then** bis dann; **~ now** bis jetzt

untimely [ʌnˈtaɪmlɪ] *adj* (*death*) vorzeitig

untold [ˈʌnˈtəʊld] *adj* unermeßlich

untoward [ʌntəˈwɔːd] *adj* widrig

untranslatable [ʌntrænzˈleɪtəbl] *adj* unübersetzbar

unused [ˈʌnˈjuːzd] *adj* unbenutzt

unusual [ʌnˈjuːʒʊəl] *adj* ungewöhnlich

unveil [ʌnˈveɪl] *vt* enthüllen

unwavering [ʌnˈweɪvərɪŋ] *adj* standhaft, unerschütterlich

unwelcome [ʌnˈwelkəm] *adj* (*at a bad time*) unwillkommen; (*unpleasant*) unerfreulich

unwell [ʌnˈwel] *adj*: **to feel** *or* **be ~** sich nicht wohl fühlen

unwieldy [ʌnˈwiːldɪ] *adj* sperrig

unwilling [ˈʌnˈwɪlɪŋ] *adj*: **to be ~ to do sth** nicht bereit sein, etw zu tun; **~ly** *adv* widerwillig

unwind [ˈʌnˈwaɪnd] (*irreg: like* **wind²**) *vt* abwickeln ♦ *vi* (*relax*) sich entspannen

unwise [ʌnˈwaɪz] *adj* unklug

unwitting [ʌnˈwɪtɪŋ] *adj* unwissentlich

unworkable [ʌnˈwɜːkəbl] *adj* (*plan*) undurchführbar

unworthy [ʌnˈwɜːðə] *adj* (*person*): **~ (of sth)** (einer Sache *gen*) nicht wert

unwrap [ˈʌnˈræp] *vt* auspacken

unwritten [ˈʌnˈrɪtn] *adj* ungeschrieben

KEYWORD

---

up [ʌp] *prep*: **to be up sth** oben auf etw *dat* sein; **to go up sth** (auf) etw *acc* hinauf gehen; **go up that road** gehen Sie die Straße hinauf

♦ *adv* **1** (*upwards, higher*) oben; **put it up a bit higher** stell es etwas weiter nach oben; **up there** da oben, dort oben; **up above** hoch oben

2: **to be up** (*out of bed*) auf sein; (*prices, level*) gestiegen sein; (*building, tent*) stehen

3: **up to** (*as far as*) bis; **up to now** bis jetzt

4: **to be up to** (*depending on*): **it's up to you** das hängt von dir ab; (*equal to*): **he's not up to it** (*job, task etc*) er ist dem nicht gewachsen; (*inf: be doing: showing disapproval, suspicion*): **what is he up to?** was führt er im Schilde?; **it's not up to me to decide** die Entscheidung liegt nicht bei mir; **his work is not up to the required standard** seine Arbeit entspricht nicht dem geforderten Niveau

♦ *n*: **ups and downs** (*in life, career*) Höhen und Tiefen *pl*

up-and-coming [ʌpənd'kʌmɪŋ] *adj* aufstrebend

upbringing ['ʌpbrɪŋɪŋ] *n* Erziehung *f*

update [ʌp'deɪt] *vt* auf den neuesten Stand bringen

upgrade [ʌp'greɪd] *vt* höher einstufen

upheaval [ʌp'hi:vəl] *n* Umbruch *m*

uphill ['ʌp'hɪl] *adj* ansteigend; *(fig)* mühsam ♦ *adv:* **to go ~** bergauf gehen/ fahren

uphold [ʌp'həʊld] *(irreg: like hold) vt* unterstützen

upholstery [ʌp'həʊlstərɪ] *n* Polster *nt*; Polsterung *f*

upkeep ['ʌpki:p] *n* Instandhaltung *f*

upon [ə'pɒn] *prep* auf

upper ['ʌpə*] *n* (on shoe)* Oberleder *nt* ♦ *adj* obere(r, s), höhere(r, s); **to have the ~ hand** die Oberhand haben; **~-class** *adj* vornehm; **~most** *adj* oberste(r, s), höchste(r, s); **what was ~most in my mind** was mich in erster Linie beschäftigte

upright ['ʌpraɪt] *adj* aufrecht

uprising ['ʌpraɪzɪŋ] *n* Aufstand *m*

uproar ['ʌprɔ:*] *n* Aufruhr *m*

uproot [ʌp'ru:t] *vt* ausreißen

upset [*n* 'ʌpset, *vb, adj* ʌp'set] *(irreg: like set) n* Aufregung *f* ♦ *vt (overturn)* umwerfen; *(disturb)* aufregen, bestürzen; *(plans)* durcheinanderbringen ♦ *adj (person)* aufgeregt; *(stomach)* verdorben

upshot ['ʌpʃɒt] *n* (End)ergebnis *nt*

upside-down ['ʌpsaɪd'daʊn] *adv* verkehrt herum; *(fig)* drunter und drüber

upstairs ['ʌp'steəz] *adv* oben; *(go)* nach oben ♦ *adj (room)* obere(r, s), Ober- ♦ *n* obere(s) Stockwerk *nt*

upstart ['ʌpstɑ:t] *n* Emporkömmling *m*

upstream ['ʌp'stri:m] *adv* stromaufwärts

uptake ['ʌpteɪk] *n:* **to be quick on the ~** schnell begreifen; **to be slow on the ~** schwer von Begriff sein

uptight ['ʌp'taɪt] *(inf) adj (nervous)* nervös; *(inhibited)* verklemmt

up-to-date ['ʌptə'deɪt] *adj (clothes)* modisch, modern; *(information)* neueste(r, s)

upturn ['ʌptɜ:n] *n* Aufschwung *m*

upward ['ʌpwəd] *adj* nach oben gerichtet; **~(s)** *adv* aufwärts

uranium [juə'reɪnɪəm] *n* Uran *nt*

urban ['ɜ:bən] *adj* städtisch, Stadt-

urbane [ɜ:'beɪn] *adj* höflich

urchin ['ɜ:tʃɪn] *n (boy)* Schlingel *m*; *(sea ~)* Seeigel *m*

urge [ɜ:dʒ] *n* Drang *m* ♦ *vt:* **to ~ sb to do sth** jdn (dazu) drängen, etw zu tun

urgency ['ɜ:dʒənsɪ] *n* Dringlichkeit *f*

urgent ['ɜ:dʒənt] *adj* dringend

urinal ['juərɪnl] *n (MED)* Urinflasche *f*; *(public)* Pissoir *nt*

urinate ['juərɪneɪt] *vi* urinieren

urine ['juərɪn] *n* Urin *m*, Harn *m*

urn [ɜ:n] *n* Urne *f*; *(tea ~)* Teemaschine *f*

us [ʌs] *pron* uns; *see also* **me**

US *n abbr* = **United States**

USA *n abbr* = **United States of America**

usage ['ju:zɪdʒ] *n* Gebrauch *m*; *(esp LING)* Sprachgebrauch *m*

use [*n* ju:s, *vb* ju:z] *n (employment)* Gebrauch *m*; *(point)* Zweck *m* ♦ *vt* gebrauchen; **in ~** in Gebrauch; **out of ~** außer Gebrauch; **to be of ~** nützlich sein; **it's no ~** es hat keinen Zweck; **what's the ~?** was soll's?; **~d to** *(accustomed to)* gewöhnt an *+acc*; **she ~d to live here** *(formerly)* sie hat früher mal hier gewohnt; **~ up** *vt* aufbrauchen, verbrauchen; **~d** *adj (car)* Gebraucht-; **~ful** *adj* nützlich; **~fulness** *n* Nützlichkeit *f*, **~less** *adj* nutzlos, unnütz; **~r** *n* Benutzer *m*; **~r-friendly** *adj (computer)* benutzerfreundlich

usher ['ʌʃə*] *n* Platzanweiser *m*

usherette [ʌʃə'ret] *n* Platzanweiserin *f*

usual ['ju:ʒʊəl] *adj* gewöhnlich, üblich; **as ~** wie üblich; **~ly** *adv* gewöhnlich

usurp [ju:'zɜ:p] *vt* an sich reißen

utensil [ju:'tensl] *n* Gerät *nt*; **kitchen ~s** Küchengeräte *pl*

uterus ['ju:tərəs] *n* Gebärmutter *f*

utilitarian [ju:tɪlɪ'teərɪən] *adj* Nützlich-keits-

utility [ju:'tɪlɪtɪ] *n (usefulness)* Nütz-lichkeit *f*; *(also: public ~)* öffentliche(r) Versorgungsbetrieb *m*; **~ room** *n*

Hauswirtschaftsraum *m*
utilize ['juːtɪlaɪz] *vt* benützen
utmost ['ʌtməʊst] *adj* äußerste(r, s) ♦ *n*:
to do one's ~ sein möglichstes tun
utter ['ʌtə*] *adj* äußerste(r, s), höchste(r,
s), völlig ♦ *vt* äußern, aussprechen;
~ance *n* Äußerung *f*; **~ly** *adv* äußerst,
absolut, völlig
U-turn ['juːtɜːn] *n* (AUT) Kehrtwendung *f*

V v

v. *abbr* = **verse**; **versus**; **volt**; (= *vide*)
siehe
vacancy ['veɪkənsɪ] *n* (BRIT: *job*) offene
Stelle *f*; (*room*) freie(s) Zimmer *nt*
vacant ['veɪkənt] *adj* leer; (*unoccupied*)
frei; (*house*) leerstehend, unbewohnt;
(*stupid*) (gedanken)leer; **~ lot** (US) *n*
unbebaute(s) Grundstück *nt*
vacate [və'keɪt] *vt* (*seat*) frei machen;
(*room*) räumen
vacation [və'keɪʃən] *n* Ferien *pl*, Urlaub
m; **~ist** (US) *n* Ferienreisende(r) *mf*
vaccinate ['væksɪneɪt] *vt* impfen
vaccine ['væksiːn] *n* Impfstoff *m*
vacuum ['vækjʊm] *n* Vakuum *nt*; **~
bottle** (US) *n* Thermosflasche *f*; **~
cleaner** *n* Staubsauger *m*; **~ flask** (BRIT)
n Thermosflasche *f*; **~-packed** *adj*
vakuumversiegelt
vagina [və'dʒaɪnə] *n* Scheide *f*
vagrant ['veɪɡrənt] *n* Landstreicher *m*
vague [veɪɡ] *adj* vag(e); (*absent-minded*)
geistesabwesend; **~ly** *adv* unbestimmt,
vag(e)
vain [veɪn] *adj* eitel; (*attempt*) vergeblich;
in ~ vergebens, umsonst
valentine ['væləntaɪn] *n* (*also:* **~ card**)
Valentinsgruß *m*
valet ['væleɪ] *n* Kammerdiener *m*
valiant ['væljənt] *adj* tapfer
valid ['vælɪd] *adj* gültig; (*argument*)
stichhaltig; (*objection*) berechtigt; **~ity**
[və'lɪdɪtɪ] *n* Gültigkeit *f*
valley ['vælɪ] *n* Tal *nt*
valour ['vælə*] (US **valor**) *n* Tapferkeit *f*
valuable ['væljʊəbl] *adj* wertvoll; (*time*)

kostbar; **~s** *npl* Wertsachen *pl*
valuation [væljʊ'eɪʃən] *n* (FIN) Schätzung
f; Beurteilung *f*
value ['væljuː] *n* Wert *m*; (*usefulness*)
Nutzen *m* ♦ *vt* (*prize*) (hoch)schätzen,
werthalten; (*estimate*) schätzen; **~ added
tax** (BRIT) *n* Mehrwertsteuer *f*; **~d** *adj*
(hoch)geschätzt
valve [vælv] *n* Ventil *nt*; (BIOL) Klappe *f*;
(RAD) Röhre *f*
van [væn] *n* Lieferwagen *m*; (BRIT: RAIL)
Waggon *m*
vandal ['vændl] *n* Rowdy *m*
vandalism ['vændəlɪzəm] *n* mutwillige
Beschädigung *f*
vandalize ['vændəlaɪz] *vt* mutwillig
beschädigen
vanguard ['væŋɡɑːd] *n* (*fig*) Spitze *f*
vanilla [və'nɪlə] *n* Vanille *f*; **~ ice cream**
n Vanilleeis *nt*
vanish ['vænɪʃ] *vi* verschwinden
vanity ['vænɪtɪ] *n* Eitelkeit *f*; **~ case** *n*
Schminkkoffer *m*
vantage ['vɑːntɪdʒ] *n*: **~ point** gute(r)
Aussichtspunkt *m*
vapour ['veɪpə*] (US **vapor**) *n* (*mist*)
Dunst *m*; (*gas*) Dampf *m*
variable ['vɛərɪəbl] *adj* wechselhaft,
veränderlich; (*speed, height*) regulierbar
variance ['vɛərɪəns] *n*: **to be at ~ (with)**
nicht übereinstimmen (mit)
variation [vɛərɪ'eɪʃən] *n* Variation *f*; (*of
temperature, prices*) Schwankung *f*
varicose ['værɪkəʊs] *adj*: **~ veins**
Krampfadern *pl*
varied ['vɛərɪd] *adj* unterschiedlich; (*life*)
abwechslungsreich
variety [və'raɪətɪ] *n* (*difference*)
Abwechslung *f*; (*varied collection*) Vielfalt
f; (COMM) Auswahl *f*; (*sort*) Sorte *f*, Art *f*; **~
show** *n* Varieté *nt*
various ['vɛərɪəs] *adj* verschieden;
(*several*) mehrere
varnish ['vɑːnɪʃ] *n* Lack *m*; (*on pottery*)
Glasur *f* ♦ *vt* lackieren
vary ['vɛərɪ] *vt* (*alter*) verändern; (*give
variety to*) abwechslungsreicher gestalten
♦ *vi* sich (ver)ändern; (*prices*) schwanken;
(*weather*) unterschiedlich sein

vase [vɑːz] *n* Vase *f*

Vaseline ['væsɪliːn] ® *n* Vaseline *f*

vast [vɑːst] *adj* weit, groß, riesig

VAT [væt] *n abbr* (= *value added tax*) MwSt *f*

vat [væt] *n* große(s) Faß *nt*

vault [vɔːlt] *n* (*of roof*) Gewölbe *nt*; (*tomb*) Gruft *f*; (*in bank*) Tresorraum *m*; (*leap*) Sprung *m* ♦ *vt* (*also*: ~ *over*) überspringen

vaunted ['vɔːntɪd] *adj*: **much-~** vielgerühmt

VCR *n abbr* = **video cassette recorder**

VD *n abbr* = **venereal disease**

VDU *n abbr* = **visual display unit**

veal [viːl] *n* Kalbfleisch *nt*

veer [vɪə*] *vi* sich drehen; (*of car*) ausscheren

vegeburger ['vedʒɪbɜːgə*] *n* vegetarische Frikadelle *f*

vegetable ['vedʒətəbl] *n* Gemüse *nt* ♦ *adj* Gemüse-; **~s** *npl* (*CULIN*) Gemüse *nt*

vegetarian [vedʒɪ'tɛərɪən] *n* Vegetarier(in) *m(f)* ♦ *adj* vegetarisch

vegetate ['vedʒɪteɪt] *vi* (dahin)vegetieren

veggieburger *n* = **vegeburger**

vehemence ['viːɪməns] *n* Heftigkeit *f*

vehement ['viːɪmənt] *adj* heftig

vehicle ['viːɪkl] *n* Fahrzeug *nt*; (*fig*) Mittel *nt*

veil [veɪl] *n* (*also fig*) Schleier *m* ♦ *vt* verschleiern

vein [veɪn] *n* Ader *f*; (*mood*) Stimmung *f*

velocity [vɪ'lɒsɪtɪ] *n* Geschwindigkeit *f*

velvet ['velvɪt] *n* Samt *m* ♦ *adj* Samt-

vendetta [ven'detə] *n* Fehde *f*; (*in family*) Blutrache *f*

vending machine ['vendɪŋ-] *n* Automat *m*

vendor ['vendɔː*] *n* Verkäufer *m*

veneer [və'nɪə*] *n* Furnier(holz) *nt*; (*fig*) äußere(r) Anstrich *m*

venereal disease [vɪ'nɪərɪəl-] *n* Geschlechtskrankheit *f*

Venetian blind [vɪ'niːʃən-] *n* Jalousie *f*

vengeance ['vendʒəns] *n* Rache *f*; **with a ~** gewaltig

venison ['venɪsn] *n* Reh(fleisch) *nt*

venom ['venəm] *n* Gift *nt*

vent [vent] *n* Öffnung *f*; (*in coat*) Schlitz

m; (*fig*) Ventil *nt* ♦ *vt* (*emotion*) abreagieren

ventilate ['ventɪleɪt] *vt* belüften

ventilator ['ventɪleɪtə*] *n* Ventilator *m*

ventriloquist [ven'trɪləkwɪst] *n* Bauchredner *m*

venture ['ventʃə*] *n* Unternehmung *f*, Projekt *nt* ♦ *vt* wagen; (*life*) aufs Spiel setzen ♦ *vi* sich wagen

venue ['venjuː] *n* Schauplatz *m*

verb [vɜːb] *n* Zeitwort *nt*, Verb *nt*; **~al** *adj* (*spoken*) mündlich; (*translation*) wörtlich; **~ally** *adv* mündlich

verbatim [vɜː'beɪtɪm] *adv* Wort für Wort ♦ *adj* wortwörtlich

verbose [vɜː'bəus] *adj* wortreich

verdict ['vɜːdɪkt] *n* Urteil *nt*

verge [vɜːdʒ] *n* (*BRIT*) Rand *m* ♦ *vi*: **to ~ on** grenzen an +*acc*; **"soft ~s"** (*BRIT*: *AUT*) „Seitenstreifen nicht befahrbar"; **on the ~ of doing sth** im Begriff, etw zu tun

verify ['verɪfaɪ] *vt* (über)prüfen; (*confirm*) bestätigen; (*theory*) beweisen

veritable ['verɪtəbl] *adj* wirklich, echt

vermin ['vɜːmɪn] *npl* Ungeziefer *nt*

vermouth ['vɜːməθ] *n* Wermut *m*

vernacular [və'nækjulə*] *n* Landessprache *f*

versatile ['vɜːsətaɪl] *adj* vielseitig

versatility [vɜːsə'tɪlɪtɪ] *n* Vielseitigkeit *f*

verse [vɜːs] *n* (*poetry*) Poesie *f*; (*stanza*) Strophe *f*; (*of Bible*) Vers *m*; **in ~** in Versform

versed [vɜːst] *adj*: **(well-)~ in** bewandert in +*dat*, beschlagen in +*dat*

version ['vɜːʃən] *n* Version *f*; (*of car*) Modell *nt*

versus ['vɜːsəs] *prep* gegen

vertebrate ['vɜːtɪbrət] *adj* (*animal*) Wirbel-

vertical ['vɜːtɪkəl] *adj* senkrecht

vertigo ['vɜːtɪɡəu] *n* Schwindel *m*

verve [vɜːv] *n* Schwung *m*

very ['verɪ] *adv* sehr ♦ *adj* (*extreme*) äußerste(r, s); **the ~ book** which genau das Buch, welches; **the ~ last** der/die/das allerletzte; **at the ~ least** allerwenigstens; **~ much** sehr

vessel ['vesl] *n* (*ship*) Schiff *nt*;

(container) Gefäß *nt*

vest [vest] *n (BRIT)* Unterhemd *nt; (US: waistcoat)* Weste *f;* ~**ed interests** *npl* finanzielle Beteiligung *f; (people)* finanzielle Beteiligte *pl; (fig)* persönliche(s) Interesse *nt*

vestige ['vestɪdʒ] *n* Spur *f*

vestry ['vestrɪ] *n* Sakristei *f*

vet [vet] *n abbr (= veterinary surgeon)* Tierarzt *m/*-ärztin *f* ♦ *vt* genau prüfen

veteran ['vetərn] *n* Veteran(in) *m(f)*

veterinarian [vetrə'neərɪən] *(US) n* Tierarzt *m/*-ärztin *f*

veterinary ['vetrɪnərɪ] *adj* Veterinär-; ~ **surgeon** *n* Tierarzt *m/*-ärztin *f*

veto ['viːtəʊ] *(pl ~es) n* Veto *nt* ♦ *vt* sein Veto einlegen gegen

vex [veks] *vt* ärgern; ~**ed** *adj* verärgert; ~**ed question** umstrittene Frage *f*

VHF *abbr (= very high frequency)* UKW *f*

via ['vaɪə] *prep* über *+acc*

viable ['vaɪəbl] *adj (plan)* durchführbar; *(company)* rentabel

vibrant ['vaɪbrənt] *adj (lively)* lebhaft; *(bright)* leuchtend; *(full of emotion: voice)* bebend

vibrate [vaɪ'breɪt] *vi* zittern, beben; *(machine, string)* vibrieren

vibration [vaɪ'breɪʃən] *n* Schwingung *f; (of machine)* Vibrieren *nt*

vicar ['vɪkə*] *n* Pfarrer *m;* ~**age** *n* Pfarrhaus *nt*

vicarious [vɪ'keərɪəs] *adj* nachempfunden

vice [vaɪs] *n (evil)* Laster *nt; (TECH)* Schraubstock *m*

vice-chairman *n* stellvertretende(r) Vorsitzende(r) *m*

vice-president *n* Vizepräsident *m*

vice squad *n* ≈ Sittenpolizei *f*

vice versa ['vaɪsɪ'vɜːsə] *adv* umgekehrt

vicinity [vɪ'sɪnɪtɪ] *n* Umgebung *f; (closeness)* Nähe *f*

vicious ['vɪʃəs] *adj* gemein, böse; ~ **circle** *n* Teufelskreis *m*

victim ['vɪktɪm] *n* Opfer *nt;* ~**ize** *vt* benachteiligen

victor ['vɪktə*] *n* Sieger *m*

Victorian [vɪk'tɔːrɪən] *adj* viktorianisch; *(fig)* (sitten)streng

victorious [vɪk'tɔːrɪəs] *adj* siegreich

victory ['vɪktərɪ] *n* Sieg *m*

video ['vɪdɪəʊ] *adj* Fernseh-, Bild- ♦ *n (~ film)* Video *nt; (also:* ~ *cassette)* Videokassette *f; (:* ~ *cassette recorder)* Videorekorder *m;* ~ **tape** *n* Videoband *nt*

vie [vaɪ] *vi* wetteifern

Vienna [vɪ'enə] *n* Wien *nt*

view [vjuː] *n (sight)* Sicht *f,* Blick *m; (scene)* Aussicht *f; (opinion)* Ansicht *f; (intention)* Absicht *f* ♦ *vt (situation)* betrachten; *(house)* besichtigen; **to have sth in** ~ etw beabsichtigen; **on** ~ ausgestellt; **in** ~ **of** wegen *+gen,* angesichts *+gen;* ~**er** *n (~finder)* Sucher *m; (PHOT: small projector)* Gucki *m; (TV)* Fernsehzuschauer(in) *m(f);* ~**finder** *n* Sucher *m;* ~**point** *n* Standpunkt *m*

vigil ['vɪdʒɪl] *n* (Nacht)wache *f;* ~**ance** *n* Wachsamkeit *f;* ~**ant** *adj* wachsam

vigorous ['vɪgərəs] *adj* kräftig; *(protest)* energisch, heftig; ~**ly** *adv* kräftig; energisch, heftig

vile [vaɪl] *adj (mean)* gemein; *(foul)* abscheulich

vilify ['vɪlɪfaɪ] *vt* verleumden

villa ['vɪlə] *n* Villa *f*

village ['vɪlɪdʒ] *n* Dorf *nt;* ~**r** *n* Dorfbewohner(in) *m(f)*

villain ['vɪlən] *n* Schurke *m*

vindicate ['vɪndɪkeɪt] *vt* rechtfertigen

vindictive [vɪn'dɪktɪv] *adj* nachtragend, rachsüchtig

vine [vaɪn] *n* Rebstock *m,* Rebe *f*

vinegar ['vɪnɪgə*] *n* Essig *m*

vineyard ['vɪnjəd] *n* Weinberg *m*

vintage ['vɪntɪdʒ] *n (of wine)* Jahrgang *m;* ~ **wine** *n* edle(r) Wein *m*

viola [vɪ'əʊlə] *n* Bratsche *f*

violate ['vaɪəleɪt] *vt (law)* übertreten; *(rights, rule, neutrality)* verletzen; *(sanctity, woman)* schänden

violation [vaɪə'leɪʃən] *n* Verletzung *f,* Übertretung *f*

violence ['vaɪələns] *n (force)* Heftigkeit *f; (brutality)* Gewalttätigkeit *f*

violent ['vaɪələnt] *adj (strong)* heftig; *(brutal)* gewalttätig, brutal; *(contrast)* kraß; *(death)* gewaltsam

violet ['vaɪələt] n Veilchen nt ♦ adj
veilchenblau, violett
violin [vaɪə'lɪn] n Geige f, Violine f; **~ist**
n Geiger(in) m(f)
VIP n abbr (= *very important person*) VIP
m
virgin ['vɜːdʒɪn] n Jungfrau f ♦ adj
jungfräulich, unberührt; **~ity** [vɜː'dʒɪnɪtɪ]
n Unschuld f
Virgo ['vɜːgəʊ] n Jungfrau f
virile ['vɪraɪl] adj männlich
virility [vɪ'rɪlɪtɪ] n Männlichkeit f
virtually ['vɜːtjʊəlɪ] adv praktisch, fast
virtual reality ['vɜːtjʊəl-] n (*COMPUT*)
virtuelle Realität f
virtue ['vɜːtjuː] n (*moral goodness*)
Tugend f; (*good quality*) Vorteil m,
Vorzug m; **by ~ of** aufgrund +*gen*
virtuous ['vɜːtjʊəs] adj tugendhaft
virulent ['vɪrjʊlənt] adj (*poisonous*)
bösartig; (*bitter*) scharf, geharnischt
virus ['vaɪərəs] n (*also COMPUT*) Virus m
visa ['viːzə] n Visum nt
vis-à-vis ['viːzəviː] prep gegenüber
viscous ['vɪskəs] adj zähflüssig
visibility [vɪzɪ'bɪlɪtɪ] n (*MET*) Sicht(weite) f
visible ['vɪzəbl] adj sichtbar
visibly ['vɪzəblɪ] adv sichtlich
vision ['vɪʒən] n (*ability*) Sehvermögen
nt; (*foresight*) Weitblick m; (*in dream*,
image) Vision f
visit ['vɪzɪt] n Besuch m ♦ vt besuchen;
(*town, country*) fahren nach; **~ing** adj
(*professor*) Gast-; **~ing hours** npl (*in
hospital etc*) Besuchszeiten pl; **~or** n (*in
house*) Besucher(in) m(f); (*in hotel*) Gast m
visor ['vaɪzə*] n Visier nt; (*on cap*)
Schirm m; (*AUT*) Blende f
vista ['vɪstə] n Aussicht f
visual ['vɪzjʊəl] adj Seh-, visuell; **~ aid** n
Anschauungsmaterial nt; **~ display unit**
n Bildschirm(gerät nt) m; **~ize**
['vɪzjʊəlaɪz] vt sich +*dat* vorstellen
vital ['vaɪtl] adj (*important*) unerläßlich;
(*necessary for life*) Lebens-, lebenswichtig;
(*lively*) vital; **~ity** [vaɪ'tælɪtɪ] n Vitalität f;
~ly adv: **~ly important** äußerst wichtig;
~ statistics npl (*fig*) Maße pl
vitamin ['vɪtəmɪn] n Vitamin nt

vivacious [vɪ'veɪʃəs] adj lebhaft
vivid ['vɪvɪd] adj (*graphic*) lebendig;
(*memory*) lebhaft; (*bright*) leuchtend; **~ly**
adv lebendig; lebhaft; leuchtend
V-neck ['viːnek] n V-Ausschnitt m
vocabulary [vəʊ'kæbjʊlərɪ] n Wortschatz
m, Vokabular nt
vocal ['vəʊkəl] adj Vokal-, Gesang-; (*fig*)
lautstark; **~ cords** npl Stimmbänder pl
vocation [vəʊ'keɪʃən] n (*calling*)
Berufung f; **~al** adj Berufs-
vociferous [vəʊ'sɪfərəs] adj lautstark
vodka ['vɒdkə] n Wodka m
vogue [vəʊg] n Mode f
voice [vɔɪs] n Stimme f; (*fig*)
Mitspracherecht nt ♦ vt äußern
void [vɔɪd] n Leere f ♦ adj (*invalid*)
nichtig, ungültig; (*empty*): **~ of** ohne, bar
+*gen*; see **null**
volatile ['vɒlətaɪl] adj (*gas*) flüchtig;
(*person*) impulsiv; (*situation*) brisant
volcano [vɒl'keɪnəʊ] n Vulkan m
volition [və'lɪʃən] n Wille m; **of one's
own ~** aus freiem Willen
volley ['vɒlɪ] n (*of guns*) Salve f; (*of
stones*) Hagel m; (*of words*) Schwall m;
(*tennis*) Flugball m; **~ball** n Volleyball m
volt [vəʊlt] n Volt nt; **~age** n
(Volt)spannung f
voluble ['vɒljʊbl] adj redselig
volume ['vɒljuːm] n (*book*) Band m; (*size*)
Umfang m; (*space*) Rauminhalt m; (*of
sound*) Lautstärke f
voluminous [və'luːmɪnəs] adj üppig;
(*clothes*) wallend; (*correspondence, notes*)
umfangreich
voluntarily ['vɒləntrəlɪ] adv freiwillig
voluntary ['vɒləntərɪ] adj freiwillig
volunteer [vɒlən'tɪə*] n Freiwillige(r) mf
♦ vi sich freiwillig melden; **to ~ to do
sth** sich anbieten, etw zu tun
voluptuous [və'lʌptjʊəs] adj sinnlich
vomit ['vɒmɪt] n Erbrochene(s) nt ♦ vt
spucken ♦ vi sich übergeben
vote [vəʊt] n Stimme f; (*ballot*)
Abstimmung f; (*result*)
Abstimmungsergebnis nt; (*franchise*)
Wahlrecht nt ♦ vt, vi wählen; **~ of
thanks** n Dankesworte pl; **~r** n

Wähler(in) *m(f)*
voting ['vəʊtɪŋ] *n* Wahl *f*
voucher ['vaʊtʃə*] *n* Gutschein *m*
vouch for [vaʊtʃ-] *vt* bürgen für
vow [vaʊ] *n* Versprechen *nt*; (*REL*)
Gelübde *nt* ♦ *vt* geloben
vowel ['vaʊəl] *n* Vokal *m*
voyage ['vɔɪdʒ] *n* Reise *f*
vulgar ['vʌlɡə*] *adj* (*rude*) vulgär; (*of
common people*) allgemein, Volks-; **~ity**
[vʌl'ɡærɪtɪ] *n* Vulgarität *f*
vulnerable ['vʌlnərəbl] *adj* (*easily
injured*) verwundbar; (*sensitive*)
verletzlich
vulture ['vʌltʃə*] *n* Geier *m*

W w

wad [wɒd] *n* (*bundle*) Bündel *nt*; (*of
paper*) Stoß *m*; (*of money*) Packen *m*
waddle ['wɒdl] *vi* watscheln
wade [weɪd] *vi*: **to ~ through** waten
durch
wafer ['weɪfə*] *n* Waffel *f*; (*REL*) Hostie *f*;
(*COMPUT*) Wafer *f*
waffle ['wɒfl] *n* Waffel *f*; (*inf: empty talk*)
Geschwafel *nt* ♦ *vi* schwafeln
waft [wɑːft] *vt, vi* wehen
wag [wæɡ] *vt* (*tail*) wedeln mit ♦ *vi*
wedeln
wage [weɪdʒ] *n* (*also:* ~s) (Arbeits)lohn *m*
♦ *vt*: **to ~ war** Krieg führen; **~ earner** *n*
Lohnempfänger(in) *m(f)*; **~ packet** *n*
Lohntüte *f*
wager ['weɪdʒə*] *n* Wette *f* ♦ *vt, vi*
wetten
waggle ['wæɡl] *vt* (*tail*) wedeln mit ♦ *vi*
wedeln
wag(g)on ['wæɡən] *n* (*horse-drawn*)
Fuhrwerk *nt*; (*US: AUT*) Wagen *m*; (*BRIT:
RAIL*) Waggon *m*
wail [weɪl] *n* Wehgeschrei *nt* ♦ *vi*
wehklagen, jammern
waist [weɪst] *n* Taille *f*; **~coat** (*BRIT*) *n*
Weste *f*; **~line** *n* Taille *f*
wait [weɪt] *n* Wartezeit *f* ♦ *vi* warten; **to
lie in ~ for sb** jdm auflauern; **I can't ~
to see him** ich kann's kaum erwarten,

ihn zu sehen; **"no ~ing"** (*BRIT: AUT*)
„Halteverbot"; ~ **behind** *vi*
zurückbleiben; ~ **for** *vt fus* warten auf
+*acc*; ~ **on** *vt fus* bedienen; **~er** *n* Kellner
m; **~ing list** *n* Warteliste *f*; **~ing room**
n (*MED*) Wartezimmer *nt*; (*RAIL*) Wartesaal
m; **~ress** *n* Kellnerin *f*
waive [weɪv] *vt* verzichten auf +*acc*
wake [weɪk] (*pt* **woke**, **~d**, *pp* **woken**) *vt*
wecken ♦ *vi* (*also:* ~ **up**) aufwachen ♦ *n*
(*NAUT*) Kielwasser *nt*; (*for dead*)
Totenwache *f*; **to ~ up to** (*fig*) sich
bewußt werden +*gen*
waken ['weɪkən] *vt* aufwecken
Wales [weɪlz] *n* Wales *nt*
walk [wɔːk] *n* Spaziergang *m*; (*gait*) Gang
m; (*route*) Weg *m* ♦ *vi* gehen; (*stroll*)
spazierengehen; (*longer*) wandern; **~s of
life** Sphären *pl*; **a 10-minute ~** 10
Minuten zu Fuß; **to ~ out on sb** (*inf*) jdn
sitzenlassen; **~er** *n* Spaziergänger *m*;
(*hiker*) Wanderer *m*; **~ie-talkie**
['wɔːkɪ'tɔːkɪ] *n* tragbare(s)
Sprechfunkgerät *nt*; **~ing** *n* Gehen *nt*;
(*hiking*) Wandern *nt* ♦ *adj* Wander-;
~ing shoes *npl* Wanderschuhe *pl*; **~ing
stick** *n* Spazierstock *m*; **~out** *n* Streik *m*;
~over (*inf*) *n* leichte(r) Sieg *m*; **~way** *n*
Fußweg *m*
wall [wɔːl] *n* (*inside*) Wand *f*; (*outside*)
Mauer *f*; **~ed** *adj* von Mauern umgeben
wallet ['wɒlɪt] *n* Brieftasche *f*
wallflower ['wɔːlflaʊə*] *n* Goldlack *m*;
to be a ~ (*fig*) ein Mauerblümchen sein
wallop ['wɒləp] (*inf*) *vt* schlagen,
verprügeln
wallow ['wɒləʊ] *vi* sich wälzen
wallpaper ['wɔːlpeɪpə*] *n* Tapete *f*
wally ['wɒlɪ] (*inf*) *n* Idiot *m*
walnut ['wɔːlnʌt] *n* Walnuß *f*
walrus ['wɔːlrəs] *n* Walroß *nt*
waltz [wɔːlts] *n* Walzer *m* ♦ *vi* Walzer
tanzen
wan [wɒn] *adj* bleich
wand [wɒnd] *n* (*also: magic* ~)
Zauberstab *m*
wander ['wɒndə*] *vi* (*roam*)
(herum)wandern; (*fig*) abschweifen
wane [weɪn] *vi* abnehmen; (*fig*)

schwinden

wangle ['wæŋgl] (*BRIT: inf*) *vt*: **to ~ sth** etw richtig hindrehen

want [wɒnt] *n* (*lack*) Mangel *m* ♦ *vt* (*need*) brauchen; (*desire*) wollen; (*lack*) nicht haben; **~s** *npl* (*needs*) Bedürfnisse *pl*; **for ~ of** aus Mangel an +*dat*; mangels +*gen*; **to ~ to do sth** etw tun wollen; **to ~ sb to do sth** wollen, daß jd etw tut; **~ed** *adj* (*criminal etc*) gesucht; **"cook ~ed"** (*in advertisements*) „Koch/Köchin gesucht"; **~ing** *adj*: **to be found ~ing** sich als unzulänglich erweisen

wanton ['wɒntən] *adj* mutwillig, zügellos

war [wɔː*] *n* Krieg *m*; **to make ~** Krieg führen

ward [wɔːd] *n* (*in hospital*) Station *f*; (*of city*) Bezirk *m*; (*child*) Mündel *nt*; **~ off** *vt* abwenden, abwehren

warden ['wɔːdən] *n* (*guard*) Wächter *m*, Aufseher *m*; (*BRIT: in youth hostel*) Herbergsvater *m*; (*UNIV*) Heimleiter *m*; (*BRIT: also: traffic ~*) ≈ Verkehrspolizist *m*, ≈ Politesse *f*

warder ['wɔːdə*] (*BRIT*) *n* Gefängniswärter *m*

wardrobe ['wɔːdrəʊb] *n* Kleiderschrank *m*; (*clothes*) Garderobe *f*

warehouse ['wɛəhaʊs] *n* Lagerhaus *nt*

wares [wɛəz] *npl* Ware *f*

warfare ['wɔːfɛə*] *n* Krieg *m*; Kriegsführung *f*

warhead ['wɔːhed] *n* Sprengkopf *m*

warily ['wɛərɪlɪ] *adv* vorsichtig

warlike ['wɔːlaɪk] *adj* kriegerisch

warm [wɔːm] *adj* warm; (*welcome*) herzlich ♦ *vt, vi* wärmen; **I'm ~** mir ist warm; **it's ~** es ist warm; **~ up** *vt* aufwärmen ♦ *vi* warm werden; **~-hearted** *adj* warmherzig; **~ly** *adv* warm; herzlich; **~th** *n* Wärme *f*; Herzlichkeit *f*

warn [wɔːn] *vt*: **to ~ (of or against)** warnen (vor +*dat*); **~ing** *n* Warnung *f*; **without ~ing** unerwartet; **~ing light** *n* Warnlicht *nt*; **~ing triangle** *n* (*AUT*) Warndreieck *nt*

warp [wɔːp] *vt* verziehen; **~ed** *adj* wellig; (*fig*) pervers

warrant ['wɒrənt] *n* (*for arrest*) Haftbefehl *m*

warranty ['wɒrəntɪ] *n* Garantie *f*

warren ['wɒrən] *n* Labyrinth *nt*

warrior ['wɒrɪə*] *n* Krieger *m*

Warsaw ['wɔːsɔː] *n* Warschau *nt*

warship ['wɔːʃɪp] *n* Kriegsschiff *nt*

wart [wɔːt] *n* Warze *f*

wartime ['wɔːtaɪm] *n* Krieg *m*

wary ['wɛərɪ] *adj* mißtrauisch

was [wɒz, wəz] *pt of* **be**

wash [wɒʃ] *n* Wäsche *f* ♦ *vt* waschen; (*dishes*) abwaschen ♦ *vi* sich waschen; (*do ~ing*) waschen; **to have a ~** sich waschen; **~ away** *vt* abwaschen, wegspülen; **~ off** *vt* abwaschen; **~ up** *vi* (*BRIT*) spülen; (*US*) sich waschen; **~able** *adj* waschbar; **~basin** *n* Waschbecken *nt*; **~ bowl** (*US*) *n* Waschbecken *nt*; **~ cloth** (*US*) *n* (*face cloth*) Waschlappen *m*; **~er** *n* (*TECH*) Dichtungsring *m*; (*machine*) Waschmaschine *f*; **~ing** *n* Wäsche *f*; **~ing machine** *n* Waschmaschine *f*; **~ing powder** (*BRIT*) *n* Waschpulver *nt*

Washington ['wɒʃɪŋtən] *n* Washington *nt*

wash: **~ing-up** *n* Abwasch *m*; **~ing-up liquid** *n* Spülmittel *nt*; **~-out** (*inf*) *n* (*event*) Reinfall *m*; (*person*) Niete *f*; **~-room** *n* Waschraum *m*

wasn't ['wɒznt] = **was not**

wasp [wɒsp] *n* Wespe *f*

wastage ['weɪstɪdʒ] *n* Verlust *m*; **natural ~** Verschleiß *m*

waste [weɪst] *n* (*wasting*) Verschwendung *f*; (*what is wasted*) Abfall *m* ♦ *adj* (*useless*) überschüssig; Abfall- ♦ *vt* (*object*) verschwenden; (*time, life*) vergeuden ♦ *vi*: **to ~ away** verfallen; **~s** *npl* (*land*) Einöde *f*; **~ disposal unit** (*BRIT*) *n* Müllschlucker *m*; **~ful** *adj* verschwenderisch; (*process*) aufwendig; **~ ground** (*BRIT*) *n* unbebaute(s) Grundstück *nt*; **~land** *n* Ödland *nt*; **~paper basket** *n* Papierkorb *m*; **~ pipe** *n* Abflußrohr *nt*

watch [wɒtʃ] *n* Wache *f*; (*for time*) Uhr *f* ♦ *vt* ansehen; (*observe*) beobachten; (*be careful of*) aufpassen auf +*acc*; (*guard*) bewachen ♦ *vi* zusehen; **to be on the ~ (for sth)** (auf etw *acc*) aufpassen; **to ~ TV**

fernsehen; **to ~ sb doing sth** jdm bei etw zuschauen; **~ out** *vi* Ausschau halten; *(be careful)* aufpassen; **~ out!** paß auf!; **~dog** *n* Wachthund *m*; *(fig)* Wächter *m*; **~ful** *adj* wachsam; **~maker** *n* Uhrmacher *m*; **~man** *(irreg)* *n* *(also: night ~man)* (Nacht)wächter *m*; **~ strap** *n* Uhrarmband *nt*

water ['wɔ:tə*] *n* Wasser *nt* ♦ *vt* (be)gießen; *(river)* bewässern; *(horses)* tränken ♦ *vi* *(eye)* tränen; **~s** *npl* *(of sea, river etc)* Gewässer *nt*; **~ down** *vt* verwässern; **~ closet** *(BRIT)* *n* (Wasser)klosett *nt*; **~colour** *(US* **~color**) *n* *(painting)* Aquarell *nt*; *(paint)* Wasserfarbe *f*; **~cress** *n* (Brunnen)kresse *f*; **~fall** *n* Wasserfall *m*; **~ heater** *n* Heißwassergerät *nt*; **~ing can** *n* Gießkanne *f*; **~ level** *n* Wasserstand *m*; **~lily** *n* Seerose *f*; **~line** *n* Wasserlinie *f*; **~logged** *adj* *(ground)* voll Wasser; *(wood)* mit Wasser vollgesogen; **~ main** *n* Haupt(wasser)leitung *f*; **~mark** *n* Wasserzeichen *nt*; *(on wall)* Wasserstandsmarke *f*; **~melon** *n* Wassermelone *f*; **~ polo** *n* Wasserball(spiel) *nt*; **~proof** *adj* wasserdicht; **~shed** *n* Wasserscheide *f*; **~-skiing** *n* Wasserschilaufen *nt*; **~ tank** *n* Wassertank *m*; **~tight** *adj* wasserdicht; **~way** *n* Wasserweg *m*; **~works** *npl* Wasserwerk *nt*; **~y** *adj* wäss(e)rig

watt [wɒt] *n* Watt *nt*

wave [weɪv] *n* Welle *f*; *(with hand)* Winken *nt* ♦ *vt* *(move to and fro)* schwenken; *(hand, flag)* winken mit; *(hair)* wellen ♦ *vi* *(person)* winken; *(flag)* wehen; **~length** *n* *(also fig)* Wellenlänge *f*

waver ['weɪvə*] *vi* schwanken

wavy ['weɪvɪ] *adj* wellig

wax [wæks] *n* Wachs *nt*; *(sealing ~)* Siegellack *m*; *(in ear)* Ohrenschmalz *nt* ♦ *vt* *(floor)* (ein)wachsen ♦ *vi* *(moon)* zunehmen; **~works** *npl* Wachsfigurenkabinett *nt*

way [weɪ] *n* Weg *m*; *(method)* Art und Weise *f*; *(direction)* Richtung *f*; *(habit)* Gewohnheit *f*; *(distance)* Entfernung *f*; *(condition)* Zustand *m*; **which ~? - this ~** welche Richtung? - hier entlang; **on the ~** *(en route)* unterwegs; **to be in the ~** im Weg sein; **to go out of one's ~ to do sth** sich besonders anstrengen, um etw zu tun; **to lose one's ~** sich verirren; **"give ~"** *(BRIT: AUT)* "Vorfahrt achten!"; **in a ~** in gewisser Weise; **by the ~** übrigens; **in some ~s** in gewisser Hinsicht; **"~ in"** *(BRIT)* "Eingang"; **"~ out"** "Ausgang"

waylay [weɪ'leɪ] *(irreg: like* lay*)* *vt* auflauern +*dat*

wayward ['weɪwəd] *adj* eigensinnig

W.C. *(BRIT)* *n* WC *nt*

we [wi:] *pl pron* wir

weak [wi:k] *adj* schwach; **~en** *vt* schwächen ♦ *vi* schwächer werden; **~ling** *n* Schwächling *m*; **~ness** *n* Schwäche *f*

wealth [welθ] *n* Reichtum *m*; *(abundance)* Fülle *f*; **~y** *adj* reich

wean [wi:n] *vt* entwöhnen

weapon ['wepən] *n* Waffe *f*

wear [wɛə*] *(pt* wore, *pp* worn*)* *n* *(clothing)*: **sports/baby ~** Sport-/Babykleidung *f*; *(use)* Verschleiß *m* ♦ *vt* *(have on)* tragen; *(smile etc)* haben; *(use)* abnutzen ♦ *vi* *(last)* halten; *(become old)* (sich) verschleißen; **evening ~** Abendkleidung *f*; **~ and tear** Verschleiß *m*; **~ away** *vt* verbrauchen ♦ *vi* schwinden; **~ down** *vt* *(people)* zermürben; **~ off** *vi* sich verlieren; **~ out** *vt* verschleißen; *(person)* erschöpfen

weary ['wɪərɪ] *adj* müde ♦ *vt* ermüden ♦ *vi* überdrüssig werden

weasel ['wi:zl] *n* Wiesel *nt*

weather ['weðə*] *n* Wetter *nt* ♦ *vt* verwittern lassen; *(resist)* überstehen; **under the ~** *(fig: ill)* angeschlagen *(inf)*; **~-beaten** *adj* verwittert; **~cock** *n* Wetterhahn *m*; **~ forecast** *n* Wettervorhersage *f*; **~ vane** *n* Wetterfahne *f*

weave [wi:v] *(pt* wove, *pp* woven*)* *vt* weben; **~r** *n* Weber(in) *m(f)*; **weaving** *n* *(craft)* Webkunst *f*

web [web] *n* Netz *nt*; *(membrane)* Schwimmhaut *f*

wed [wed] *(pt, pp* wedded*)* *vt* heiraten ♦ *n*: **the newly-weds** *npl* die

Frischvermählten pl

we'd [wi:d] = **we had; we would**

wedding ['wedɪŋ] n Hochzeit f; **silver/ golden ~ anniversary** Silberhochzeit f/ Goldene Hochzeit f; **~ day** n Hochzeitstag m; **~ dress** n Hochzeitskleid nt; **~ present** n Hochzeitsgeschenk nt; **~ ring** n Trauring m, Ehering m

wedge [wedʒ] n Keil m; (of cheese etc) Stück nt ♦ vt (fasten) festklemmen; (pack tightly) einkeilen

wedlock ['wedlɒk] n Ehe f

Wednesday ['wenzdeɪ] n Mittwoch m

wee [wi:] (SCOTTISH) adj klein, winzig

weed [wi:d] n Unkraut nt ♦ vt jäten; **~-killer** n Unkrautvertilgungsmittel nt; **~y** adj (person) schmächtig

week [wi:k] n Woche f; **a ~ today/on Friday** heute/Freitag in einer Woche; **~day** n Wochentag m; **~end** n Wochenende nt; **~ly** adj wöchentlich; (wages, magazine) Wochen- ♦ adv wöchentlich

weep [wi:p] (pt, pp **wept**) vi weinen; **~ing willow** n Trauerweide f

weigh [weɪ] vt, vi wiegen; **to ~ anchor** den Anker lichten; **~ down** vt niederdrücken; **~ up** vt abschätzen

weight [weɪt] n Gewicht nt; **to lose/put on ~** abnehmen/zunehmen; **~ing** n (allowance) Zulage f; **~-lifter** n Gewichtheber m; **~y** adj (heavy) gewichtig; (important) schwerwiegend

weir [wɪə*] n (Stau)wehr nt

weird [wɪəd] adj seltsam

welcome ['welkəm] n Willkommen nt, Empfang m ♦ vt begrüßen; **thank you - you're ~!** danke - nichts zu danken

welder ['weldə*] n (person) Schweißer(in) m(f)

welding ['weldɪŋ] n Schweißen nt

welfare ['welfeə*] n Wohl nt; (social) Fürsorge f; **~ state** n Wohlfahrtsstaat m; **~ work** n Fürsorge f

well [wel] n Brunnen m; (oil ~) Quelle f ♦ adj (in good health) gesund ♦ adv gut ♦ excl nun!, na schön!; **I'm ~** es geht mir gut; **get ~ soon!** gute Besserung!; **as ~** auch; **as ~ as** sowohl als auch; **~ done!**

gut gemacht!; **to do ~** (person) gut zurechtkommen; (business) gut gehen; **~ up** vi emporsteigen; (fig) aufsteigen

we'll [wi:l] = **we will; we shall**

well: ~-behaved ['welbɪ'heɪvd] adj wohlerzogen; **~-being** ['welbi:ɪŋ] n Wohl nt; **~-built** ['wel'bɪlt] adj kräftig gebaut; **~-deserved** ['weldɪ'zɜ:vd] adj wohlverdient; **~-dressed** ['wel'drest] adj gut gekleidet; **~-heeled** ['wel'hi:ld] (inf) adj (wealthy) gut gepolstert

wellingtons ['welɪŋtənz] npl (also: wellington boots) Gummistiefel pl

well: ~-known ['wel'nəʊn] adj bekannt; **~-mannered** ['wel'mænəd] adj wohlerzogen; **~-meaning** ['wel'mi:nɪŋ] adj (person) wohlmeinend; (action) gutgemeint; **~-off** ['wel'ɒf] adj gut situiert; **~-read** ['wel'red] adj (sehr) belesen; **~-to-do** ['weltə'du:] adj wohlhabend; **~-wisher** ['welwɪʃə*] n Gönner m

Welsh [welʃ] adj walisisch ♦ n (LING) Walisisch nt; **the ~** npl (people) die Waliser pl; **~man/woman** (irreg) n Waliser(in) m(f); **~ rarebit** n überbackene Käseschnitte pl

went [went] pt of go

wept [wept] pt, pp of weep

were [wɜ:*] pt pl of be

we're [wɪə*] = **we are**

weren't [wɜ:nt] = **were not**

west [west] n Westen m ♦ adj West-, westlich ♦ adv westwärts, nach Westen; **the W~** der Westen; **the W~ Country** (BRIT) n der Südwesten Englands; **~erly** adj westlich; **~ern** adj westlich, West- ♦ n (CINE) Western m; **W~ Indian** adj westindisch ♦ n Westindier(in) m(f); **W~ Indies** npl Westindische Inseln pl; **~ward(s)** adv westwärts

wet [wet] adj naß; **to get ~** naß werden; **"~ paint"** „frisch gestrichen"; **~ blanket** n (fig) Triefel pl; **~ suit** n Taucheranzug m

we've [wi:v] = **we have**

whack [wæk] n Schlag m ♦ vt schlagen

whale [weɪl] n Wal m

wharf [wɔ:f] n Kai m

wharves [wɔːvz] *npl of* **wharf**

what [wɒt] *adj* 1 (*in direct/indirect questions*) welche(r, s), was für ein(e); **what size is it?** welche Größe ist das? 2 (*in exclamations*) was für ein(e); **what a mess!** was für ein Durcheinander!
♦ *pron* (*interrogative/relative*) was; **what are you doing?** was machst du gerade?; **what are you talking about?** wovon reden Sie?; **what is it called?** wie heißt das?; **what about ...?** wie wär's mit ...?; I **saw what you did** ich habe gesehen, was du gemacht hast
♦ *excl* (*disbelieving*) wie, was; **what, no coffee!** wie, kein Kaffee?; **I've crashed the car - what!** ich hatte einen Autounfall - was!

whatever [wɒt'evə*] *adj*: ~ **book** welches Buch auch immer ♦ *pron*: **do ~ is necessary** tu, was (immer auch) nötig ist; ~ **happens** egal, was passiert; **nothing ~** überhaupt *or* absolut gar nichts; **do ~ you want** tu, was (immer) du (auch) möchtest; **no reason ~** *or* **whatsoever** überhaupt *or* absolut kein Grund

whatsoever ['wɒtsəʋevə*] *adj see* **whatever**

wheat [wiːt] *n* Weizen *m*; ~ **germ** *n* Weizenkeim *m*

wheedle ['wiːdl] *vt*: **to ~ sb into doing sth** jdn dazu überreden, etw zu tun; **to ~ sth out of sb** jdm etw abluchsen

wheel [wiːl] *n* Rad *nt*; (*steering ~*) Lenkrad *nt*; (*disc*) Scheibe *f* ♦ *vt* schieben; ~**barrow** *n* Schubkarren *m*; ~**chair** *n* Rollstuhl *m*; ~ **clamp** (*AUT*) Parkkralle *f*

wheeze [wiːz] *vi* keuchen

when [wen] *adv* wann
♦ *conj* 1 (*at, during, after the time that*) wenn; (*with past reference*) als; **she was reading when I came in** sie las, als ich hereinkam; **be careful when you cross the road** seien Sie vorsichtig, wenn Sie

über die Straße gehen
2 (*on, at which*) als; **on the day when I met him** an dem Tag, an dem ich ihn traf
3 (*whereas*) wo ... doch

whenever [wen'evə*] *adv* wann (auch) immer ♦ *conj* (*any time*) wenn ♦ *adv* (*every time that*) jedesmal wenn

where [weə*] *adv* (*place*) wo; (*direction*) wohin; ~ **from** woher; **this is ~ ...** hier ...; ~**abouts** ['weərə'bauts] *adv* wo ♦ *n* Aufenthaltsort *m*; **nobody knows his ~abouts** niemand weiß, wo er ist; ~**as** [weər'æz] *conj* während, wo ... doch; ~**by** *pron* woran, wodurch, womit, wovon; ~**upon** *conj* worauf, wonach; (*at beginning of sentence*) daraufhin

wherever [weər'evə*] *adv* wo (immer)

wherewithal ['weəwɪðɔːl] *n* nötige (Geld)mittel *pl*

whet [wet] *vt* (*appetite*) anregen

whether ['weðə*] *conj* ob; **I don't know ~ to accept or not** ich weiß nicht, ob ich es annehmen soll oder nicht; ~ **you go or not** ob du gehst oder nicht; **it's doubtful/unclear ~ ...** est ist zweifelhaft/nicht klar ob ...

which [wɪtʃ] *adj* 1 (*interrogative: direct, indirect*) welche(r, s); **which one?** welche(r, s)?
2: **in which case** in diesem Fall; **by which time** zu dieser Zeit
♦ *pron* 1 (*interrogative*) welche(r, s); (*of people also*) wer
2 (*relative*) der/die/das; (*referring to people*) was; **the apple which you ate/ which is on the table** der Apfel, den du gegessen hast/der auf dem Tisch liegt; **he said he saw her, which is true** er sagte, er habe sie gesehen, was auch stimmt

whichever [wɪtʃ'evə*] *adj* welche(r, s) auch immer; (*no matter which*) ganz gleich welche(r, s); ~ **book you take** welches Buch du auch nimmst; ~ **car you prefer** egal, welches Auto du vorziehst

whiff [wɪf] *n* Hauch *m*

while [waɪl] *n* Weile *f* ♦ *conj* während;
for a ~ eine Zeitlang; **~ away** *vt* (*time*)
sich *dat* vertreiben

whim [wɪm] *n* Laune *f*

whimper ['wɪmpə*] *n* Wimmern *nt* ♦ *vi*
wimmern

whimsical ['wɪmzɪkəl] *adj* launisch

whine [waɪn] *n* Gewinsel *nt*, Gejammer
nt ♦ *vi* heulen, winseln

whip [wɪp] *n* Peitsche *f*; (*POL*)
Fraktionsführer *m* ♦ *vt* (*beat*) peitschen;
(*snatch*) reißen; **~ped cream** *n*
Schlagsahne *f*; **~-round** (*BRIT: inf*) *n*
Geldsammlung *f*

whirl [wɜːl] *n* Wirbel *m* ♦ *vt*, *vi*
(herum)wirbeln; **~pool** *n* Wirbel *m*;
~wind *n* Wirbelwind *m*

whirr [wɜː*] *vi* schwirren, surren

whisk [wɪsk] *n* Schneebesen *m* ♦ *vt*
(*cream etc*) schlagen; **to ~ sb away** *or* **off**
mit jdm davon sausen

whisker ['wɪskə*] *n*: **~s** (*of animal*)
Barthaare *pl*; (*of man*) Backenbart *m*

whisky ['wɪskɪ] (*US, IRISH* **whiskey**) *n*
Whisky *m*

whisper ['wɪspə*] *n* Flüstern *nt* ♦ *vt*, *vi*
flüstern

whistle ['wɪsl] *n* Pfiff *m*; (*instrument*)
Pfeife *f* ♦ *vt*, *vi* pfeifen

white [waɪt] *n* Weiß *nt*; (*of egg*) Eiweiß *nt*
♦ *adj* weiß; **~ coffee** (*BRIT*) *n* Kaffee *m*
mit Milch; **~-collar worker** *n*
Angestellte(r) *m*; **~ elephant** *n* (*fig*)
Fehlinvestition *f*; **~ lie** *n* Notlüge *f*; **~
paper** *n* (*POL*) Weißbuch *nt*; **~wash** *n*
(*paint*) Tünche *f*; (*fig*) Ehrenrettung *f* ♦ *vt*
weißen, tünchen; (*fig*) reinwaschen

whiting ['waɪtɪŋ] *n* Weißfisch *m*

Whitsun ['wɪtsn] *n* Pfingsten *nt*

whittle ['wɪtl] *vt*: **to ~ away** *or* **down**
stutzen, verringern

whizz [wɪz] *vi*: **to ~ past** *or* **by**
vorbeizischen, vorbeischwirren; **~ kid**
(*inf*) *n* Kanone *f*

who [huː] *pron* **1** (*interrogative*) wer; (*acc*)

wen; (*dat*) wem; **who is it?, who's there?**
wer ist da?

2 (*relative*) der/die/das; **the man/woman
who spoke to me** der Mann/die Frau,
der/die mit mir sprach

whodu(n)nit [huːˈdʌnɪt] (*inf*) *n* Krimi *m*

whoever [huːˈevə*] *pron* wer/wen/wem
auch immer; (*no matter who*) ganz gleich
wer/wen/wem

whole [həʊl] *adj* ganz ♦ *n* Ganze(s) *nt*;
the ~ of the town die ganze Stadt; **on
the ~** im großen und ganzen; **as a ~** im
großen und ganzen; **~hearted** *adj*
rückhaltlos; **~heartedly** *adv* von ganzem
Herzen; **~meal** *adj* (*bread, flour*)
Vollkorn-; **~sale** *n* Großhandel *m* ♦ *adj*
(*trade*) Großhandels-; (*destruction*)
Massen-; **~saler** *n* Großhändler *m*;
~some *adj* bekömmlich, gesund;
~wheat *adj* = **wholemeal**

wholly ['həʊlɪ] *adv* ganz, völlig

whom [huːm] *pron* **1** (*interrogative*: *acc*)
wen; (: *dat*) wem; **whom did you see?**
wen haben Sie gesehen?; **to whom did
you give it?** wem haben Sie es gegeben?

2 (*relative*: *acc*) den/die/das; (: *dat*) dem/
der/dem; **the man whom I saw/to
whom I spoke** der Mann, den ich sah/
mit dem ich sprach

whooping cough ['huːpɪŋ-] *n*
Keuchhusten *m*

whore ['hɔː*] *n* Hure *f*

whose [huːz] *adj* (*possessive*:
interrogative) wessen; (: *relative*) dessen;
(*after f and pl*) deren ♦ *pron* wessen; **~
book is this?, ~ is this book?** wessen
Buch ist dies?; **~ is this?** wem gehört
das?

why [waɪ] *adv* warum, weshalb
♦ *conj* warum, weshalb; **that's not why
I'm here** ich bin nicht deswegen hier;
that's the reason why deshalb
♦ *excl* (*expressing surprise, shock,*

annoyance) na so was; (*explaining*) also dann; **why, it's you!** na so was, du bist es!

---

wick [wɪk] *n* Docht *m*

wicked ['wɪkɪd] *adj* böse

wicker ['wɪkə*] *n* (*also:* ~**work**) Korbgeflecht *nt*

wicket ['wɪkɪt] *n* Tor *nt*, Dreistab *m*

wide [waɪd] *adj* breit; (*plain*) weit; (*in firing*) daneben ♦ *adv*: **to open** ~ weit öffnen; **to shoot** ~ daneben schießen; ~**angle lens** *n* Weitwinkelobjektiv *nt*; ~**awake** *adj* hellwach; ~**ly** *adv* weit; (*known*) allgemein; ~**n** *vt* erweitern; ~ **open** *adj* weit geöffnet; ~**spread** *adj* weitverbreitet

widow ['wɪdəʊ] *n* Witwe *f*; ~**ed** *adj* verwitwet; ~**er** *n* Witwer *m*

width [wɪdθ] *n* Breite *f*, Weite *f*

wield [wiːld] *vt* schwingen, handhaben

wife [waɪf] (*pl* **wives**) *n* (Ehe)frau *f*, Gattin *f*

wig [wɪg] *n* Perücke *f*

wiggle ['wɪgl] *n* Wackeln *nt* ♦ *vt* wackeln mit ♦ *vi* wackeln

wild [waɪld] *adj* wild; (*violent*) heftig; (*plan, idea*) verrückt; ~**erness** ['wɪldənəs] *n* Wildnis *f*, Wüste *f*; ~**goose chase** *n* (*fig*) fruchtlose(s) Unternehmen *nt*; ~**life** *n* Tierwelt *f*; ~**ly** *adv* wild, ungestüm; (*exaggerated*) irrsinnig; ~**s** *npl*: **the** ~**s** die Wildnis *f*

wilful ['wɪlfʊl] (*US* **willful**) *adj* (*intended*) vorsätzlich; (*obstinate*) eigensinnig

---
KEYWORD
---

will [wɪl] *aux vb* **1** (*forming future tense*) werden; **I will finish it tomorrow** ich mache es morgen zu Ende

2 (*in conjectures, predictions*): **he will** *or* **he'll be there by now** er dürfte jetzt da sein; **that will be the postman** das wird der Postbote sein

3 (*in commands, requests, offers*): **will you be quiet!** sei endlich still!; **will you help me?** hilfst du mir?; **will you have a cup of tea?** trinken Sie eine Tasse Tee?; **I won't put up with it!** das lasse ich mir

nicht gefallen!

♦ *vt* wollen

♦ *n* Wille *m*; (*JUR*) Testament *nt*

---

willing ['wɪlɪŋ] *adj* gewillt, bereit; ~**ly** *adv* bereitwillig, gern; ~**ness** *n* (Bereit)willigkeit *f*

willow ['wɪləʊ] *n* Weide *f*

willpower ['wɪlpaʊə*] *n* Willenskraft *f*

willy-nilly ['wɪlɪ'nɪlɪ] *adv* einfach so

wilt [wɪlt] *vi* (ver)welken

wily ['waɪlɪ] *adj* gerissen

win [wɪn] (*pt, pp* **won**) *n* Sieg *m* ♦ *vt, vi* gewinnen; **to** ~ **sb over** *or* **round** jdn gewinnen, jdn dazu bringen

wince [wɪns] *n* Zusammenzucken *nt* ♦ *vi* zusammenzucken

winch¹ [wɪntʃ] *n* Winde *f*

wind¹ [wɪnd] *n* Wind *m*; (*MED*) Blähungen *pl*

wind² [waɪnd] (*pt, pp* **wound**) *vt* (*rope*) winden; (*bandage*) wickeln ♦ *vi* (*turn*) sich winden; ~ **up** *vt* (*clock*) aufziehen; (*debate*) (ab)schließen

windfall ['wɪndfɔːl] *n* unverhoffte(r) Glücksfall *m*

winding ['waɪndɪŋ] *adj* (*road*) gewunden

wind instrument ['wɪndɪnstrəmənt] *n* Blasinstrument *nt*

windmill ['wɪndmɪl] *n* Windmühle *f*

window ['wɪndəʊ] *n* Fenster *nt*; ~ **box** *n* Blumenkasten *m*; ~ **cleaner** *n* Fensterputzer *m*; ~ **envelope** *n* Fensterbriefumschlag *m*; ~ **ledge** *n* Fenstersims *m*; ~ **pane** *n* Fensterscheibe *f*; ~**sill** *n* Fensterbank *f*

windpipe ['wɪndpaɪp] *n* Luftröhre *f*

wind power [wɪnd-] *n* Windenergie *f*

windscreen ['wɪndskriːn] (*BRIT*) *n* Windschutzscheibe *f*; ~ **washer** *n* Scheibenwaschanlage *f*; ~ **wiper** *n* Scheibenwischer *m*

windshield ['wɪndʃiːld] (*US*) *n* = **windscreen**

windswept ['wɪndswept] *adj* vom Wind gepeitscht; (*person*) zerzaust

windy ['wɪndɪ] *adj* windig

wine [waɪn] *n* Wein *m*; ~ **cellar** *n* Weinkeller *m*; ~**glass** *n* Weinglas *nt*; ~

list *n* Weinkarte *f*; ~ **merchant** *n* Weinhändler *m*; ~ **tasting** *n* Weinprobe *f*; ~ **waiter** *n* Weinkellner *m*

wing [wɪŋ] *n* Flügel *m*; (*MIL*) Gruppe *f*; ~**s** *npl* (*THEAT*) Seitenkulisse *f*; ~**er** *n* (*SPORT*) Flügelstürmer *m*

wink [wɪŋk] *n* Zwinkern *nt* ♦ *vi* zwinkern, blinzeln

winner ['wɪnə*] *n* Gewinner *m*; (*SPORT*) Sieger *m*

winning ['wɪnɪŋ] *adj* (*team*) siegreich, Sieger-; (*goal*) entscheidend; ~ **post** *n* Ziel *nt*; ~**s** *npl* Gewinn *m*

winter ['wɪntə*] *n* Winter *m* ♦ *adj* (*clothes*) Winter-; ♦ *vi* überwintern; ~ **sports** *npl* Wintersport *m*

wintry ['wɪntrɪ] *adj* Winter-, winterlich

wipe [waɪp] *n*: **to give sth a** ~ etw (ab)wischen ♦ *vt* wischen; ~ **off** *vt* abwischen; ~ **out** *vt* (*debt*) löschen; (*destroy*) auslöschen; ~ **up** *vt* aufwischen

wire ['waɪə*] *n* Draht *m*; (*telegram*) Telegramm *nt* ♦ *vt* telegrafieren; **to** ~ **sb** jdm telegrafieren

wireless ['waɪəlɪs] (*BRIT*) *n* Radio(apparat *m*) *nt*

wiring ['waɪərɪŋ] *n* elektrische Leitungen *pl*

wiry ['waɪərɪ] *adj* drahtig

wisdom ['wɪzdəm] *n* Weisheit *f*; (*of decision*) Klugheit *f*; ~ **tooth** *n* Weisheitszahn *m*

wise [waɪz] *adj* klug, weise ♦ *suffix*: **timewise** zeitlich gesehen

wisecrack ['waɪzkræk] *n* Witzelei *f*

wish [wɪʃ] *n* Wunsch *m* ♦ *vt* wünschen; **best ~es** (*on birthday etc*) alles Gute; **with best ~es** herzliche Grüße; **to ~ sb goodbye** jdn verabschieden; **he ~ed me well** er wünschte mir Glück; **to ~ to do sth** etw tun wollen; ~ **for** *vt fus* sich *dat* wünschen; ~**ful thinking** *n* Wunschdenken *nt*

wishy-washy ['wɪʃɪ'wɒʃɪ] (*inf*) *adj* (*colour*) verwaschen; (*ideas, argument*) verschwommen

wisp [wɪsp] *n* (Haar)strähne *f*; (*of smoke*) Wölkchen *nt*

wistful ['wɪstfʊl] *adj* sehnsüchtig

wit [wɪt] *n* (*also*: ~**s**) Verstand *m no pl*; (*amusing ideas*) Witz *m*; (*person*) Witzbold *m*

witch [wɪtʃ] *n* Hexe *f*; ~**craft** *n* Hexerei *f*

KEYWORD

with [wɪð, wɪθ] *prep* **1** (*accompanying, in the company of*) mit; **we stayed with friends** wir übernachteten bei Freunden; **I'll be with you in a minute** einen Augenblick, ich bin sofort da; **I'm not with you** (*I don't understand*) das verstehe ich nicht; **to be with it** (*inf: up-to-date*) auf dem laufenden sein; (: *alert*) (voll) da sein (*inf*)

2 (*descriptive, indicating manner etc*) mit; **the man with the grey hat** der Mann mit dem grauen Hut; **red with anger** rot vor Wut

---

withdraw [wɪθ'drɔ:] (*irreg: like* **draw**) *vt* zurückziehen; (*money*) abheben; (*remark*) zurücknehmen ♦ *vi* sich zurückziehen; ~**al** *n* Zurückziehung *f*; Abheben *nt*; Zurücknahme *f*; ~**n** *adj* (*person*) verschlossen

wither ['wɪðə*] *vi* (ver)welken

withhold [wɪθ'həʊld] (*irreg: like* **hold**) *vt*: **to** ~ **sth (from sb)** (jdm) etw vorenthalten

within [wɪð'ɪn] *prep* innerhalb +*gen* ♦ *adv* innen; ~ **sight of** in Sichtweite von; ~ **the week** innerhalb dieser Woche; ~ **a mile of** weniger als eine Meile von

without [wɪð'aʊt] *prep* ohne; ~ **speaking/ sleeping** *etc* ohne zu sprechen/schlafen *etc*

withstand [wɪθ'stænd] (*irreg: like* **stand**) *vt* widerstehen +*dat*

witness ['wɪtnəs] *n* Zeuge *m*, Zeugin *f* ♦ *vt* (*see*) sehen, miterleben; (*document*) beglaubigen; ~ **box** *n* Zeugenstand *m*; ~ **stand** (*US*) *n* Zeugenstand *m*

witticism ['wɪtɪsɪzəm] *n* witzige Bemerkung *f*

witty ['wɪtɪ] *adj* witzig, geistreich

wives [waɪvz] *pl of* **wife**

wizard ['wɪzəd] *n* Zauberer *m*

wk *abbr* = **week**

wobble ['wɒbl] *vi* wackeln
woe [wəʊ] *n* Kummer *m*
woke [wəʊk] *pt of* wake
woken ['wəʊkən] *pp of* wake
woman ['wʊmən] (*pl* women) *n* Frau *f*;
~ **doctor** *n* Ärztin *f*; ~**ly** *adj* weiblich
womb [wu:m] *n* Gebärmutter *f*
women ['wɪmɪn] *npl of* woman; ~'**s lib**
(*inf*) *n* Frauenrechtsbewegung *f*
won [wʌn] *pt, pp of* win
wonder ['wʌndə*] *n* (*marvel*) Wunder *nt*;
(*surprise*) Staunen *nt*, Verwunderung *f*
♦ *vi* sich wundern ♦ *vt*: **I** ~ **whether ...**
ich frage mich, ob ...; **it's no** ~ **that** es ist
kein Wunder, daß; **to** ~ **at** sich wundern
über +*acc*; **to** ~ **about** sich Gedanken
machen über +*acc*; ~**ful** *adj* wunderbar,
herrlich; ~**fully** *adv* wunderbar
won't [wəʊnt] = **will not**
woo [wu:] *vt* (*woman*) den Hof machen
+*dat*, umwerben; (*audience etc*) umwerben
wood [wʊd] *n* Holz *nt*; (*forest*) Wald *m*; ~
carving *n* Holzschnitzerei *f*; ~**ed** *adj*
bewaldet; ~**en** *adj* (*also fig*) hölzern;
~**pecker** *n* Specht *m*; ~**wind** *n* Blasin-
strumente *pl*; ~**work** *n* Holzwerk *nt*;
(*craft*) Holzarbeiten *pl*; ~**worm** *n*
Holzwurm *m*
wool [wʊl] *n* Wolle *f*; **to pull the** ~ **over**
sb's eyes (*fig*) jdm Sand in die Augen
streuen; ~**len** (*US* ~**en**) *adj* Woll-; ~**lens**
npl Wollsachen *pl*; ~**ly** (*US* ~**y**) *adj* wollig;
(*fig*) schwammig
word [wɜ:d] *n* Wort *nt*; (*news*) Bescheid
m ♦ *vt* formulieren; **in other** ~s anders
gesagt; **to break/keep one's** ~ sein Wort
brechen/halten; ~**ing** *n* Wortlaut *m*; ~
processing *n* Textverarbeitung *f*; ~
processor *n* Textverarbeitungsgerät *nt*
wore [wɔ:*] *pt of* wear
work [wɜ:k] *n* Arbeit *f*; (*ART, LITER*) Werk
nt ♦ *vi* arbeiten; (*machine*) funktionieren;
(*medicine*) wirken; (*succeed*) klappen; ~**s** *n*
sg (*BRIT: factory*) Fabrik *f*, Werk *nt* ♦ *npl*
(*of watch*) Werk *nt*; **to be out of** ~
arbeitslos sein; **in** ~**ing order** in
betriebsfähigem Zustand; ~ **loose** *vi* sich
lockern; ~ **on** *vi* weiterarbeiten ♦ *vt fus*
(*be engaged in*) arbeiten an +*dat*;

(*influence*) bearbeiten; ~ **out** *vi* (*sum*)
aufgehen; (*plan*) klappen ♦ *vt* (*problem*)
lösen; (*plan*) ausarbeiten; **it** ~s **out at**
£100 das gibt *or* macht £100; ~ **up** *vt*: **to**
get ~**ed up** sich aufregen; ~**able** *adj*
(*soil*) bearbeitbar; (*plan*) ausführbar;
~**aholic** [wɜ:kə'hɒlɪk] *n*
Arbeitssüchtige(r) *mf*; ~**er** *n* Arbeiter(in)
m(f); ~**force** *n* Arbeiterschaft *f*; ~**ing**
class *n* Arbeiterklasse *f*; ~**ing-class** *adj*
Arbeiter-; ~**man** (*irreg*) *n* Arbeiter *m*;
~**manship** *n* Arbeit *f*, Ausführung *f*;
~**sheet** *n* Arbeitsblatt *nt*; ~**shop** *n*
Werkstatt *f*; ~ **station** *n* Arbeitsplatz *m*;
~**-to-rule** (*BRIT*) *n* Dienst *m* nach
Vorschrift
world [wɜ:ld] *n* Welt *f*; **to think the** ~ **of**
sb große Stücke auf jdn halten; ~**ly** *adj*
weltlich, irdisch; ~**-wide** *adj* weltweit
worm [wɜ:m] *n* Wurm *m*
worn [wɔ:n] *pp of* wear ♦ *adj* (*clothes*)
abgetragen; ~**out** *adj* (*object*) abgenutzt;
(*person*) völlig erschöpft
worried ['wʌrɪd] *adj* besorgt, beunruhigt
worry ['wʌrɪ] *n* Sorge *f* ♦ *vt* beunruhigen
♦ *vi* (*feel uneasy*) sich sorgen, sich *dat*
Gedanken machen; ~**ing** *adj*
beunruhigend
worse [wɜ:s] *adj* schlechter, schlimmer
♦ *adv* schlimmer, ärger ♦ *n*
Schlimmere(s) *nt*, Schlechtere(s) *nt*; **a**
change for the ~ eine Verschlechterung;
~**n** *vt* verschlimmern ♦ *vi* sich
verschlechtern; ~ **off** *adj* (*fig*) schlechter
dran
worship ['wɜ:ʃɪp] *n* Verehrung *f* ♦ *vt*
anbeten; **Your W**~ (*BRIT: to mayor*) Herr/
Frau Bürgermeister (: *to judge*) Euer
Ehren
worst [wɜ:st] *adj* schlimmste(r, s),
schlechteste(r, s) ♦ *adv* am schlimmsten,
am ärgsten ♦ *n* Schlimmste(s) *nt*,
Ärgste(s) *nt*; **at** ~ schlimmstenfalls
worsted ['wʊstɪd] *n* Kammgarn *nt*
worth [wɜ:θ] *n* Wert *m* ♦ *adj* wert; **it's** ~
it es lohnt sich; **to be** ~ **one's while (to**
do sth) die Mühe wert sein(, etw zu
tun); ~**less** *adj* wertlos; (*person*)
nichtsnutzig; ~**while** *adj* lohnend, der

Mühe wert
worthy ['wɜːðɪ] *adj* wert, würdig

---KEYWORD---

would [wʊd] *aux vb* **1** (*conditional tense*):
if you asked him he would do it wenn
du ihn fragtest, würde er es tun; **if you
had asked him he would have done it**
wenn du ihn gefragt hättest, hätte er es
getan
2 (*in offers, invitations, requests*): **would
you like a biscuit?** möchten Sie ein
Plätzchen?; **would you ask him to come
in?** würden Sie ihn bitte hineinbitten?
3 (*in indirect speech*): **I said I would do
it** ich sagte, ich würde es tun
4 (*emphatic*): **it WOULD have to snow
today!** es mußte ja ausgerechnet heute
schneien!
5 (*insistence*): **she wouldn't behave** sie
wollte sich partout nicht anständig
benehmen
6 (*conjecture*): **it would have been
midnight** es mag ungefähr Mitternacht
gewesen sein; **it would seem so** es sieht
wohl so aus
7 (*indicating habit*): **he would go there
on Mondays** er ging jeden Montag
dorthin

---

would-be ['wʊdbiː] (*pej*) *adj* Möchtegern-
wouldn't ['wʊdnt] = **would not**
wound¹ [wuːnd] *n* (*also fig*) Wunde *f*
♦ *vt* verwunden, verletzen (*also fig*)
wound² [waʊnd] *pt, pp of* **wind²**
wove [wəʊv] *pt of* **weave**; **~n** ['wəʊvn]
pp of **weave**
wrangle ['ræŋgl] *n* Streit *m* ♦ *vi* sich
zanken
wrap [ræp] *n* (*stole*) Schal *m* ♦ *vt*
einwickeln; **~ up** *vt* einwickeln; (*deal*) abschließen; **~per** *n* Umschlag *m*, Schutz-
hülle *f*; **~ping paper** *n* Einwickelpapier
nt
wrath [rɒθ] *n* Zorn *m*
wreak [riːk] *vt* (*havoc*) anrichten;
(*vengeance*) üben
wreath [riːθ, *pl* riːðz] *n* Kranz *m*
wreck [rek] *n* (*ship*) Wrack *nt*; (*sth*
ruined) Ruine *f* ♦ *vt* zerstören; **~age** *n*
Trümmer *pl*
wren [ren] *n* Zaunkönig *m*
wrench [rentʃ] *n* (*spanner*)
Schraubenschlüssel *m*; (*twist*) Ruck *m*
♦ *vt* reißen, zerren; **to ~ sth from sb** jdm
etw entreißen *or* entwinden
wrestle ['resl] *vi*: **to ~ (with sb)** (mit
jdm) ringen; **~r** *n* Ringer(in) *m(f)*;
wrestling *n* Ringen *nt*
wretched ['retʃɪd] *adj* (*hovel*) elend; (*inf*)
verflixt; **I feel ~** mir ist elend
wriggle ['rɪgl] *n* Schlängeln *nt* ♦ *vi* sich
winden
wring [rɪŋ] (*pt, pp* **wrung**) *vt* wringen
wrinkle ['rɪŋkl] *n* Falte *f*, Runzel *f* ♦ *vt*
runzeln ♦ *vi* sich runzeln; (*material*)
knittern
wrist [rɪst] *n* Handgelenk *nt*; **~watch** *n*
Armbanduhr *f*
writ [rɪt] *n* gerichtliche(r) Befehl *m*
write [raɪt] (*pt* **wrote**, *pp* **written**) *vt, vi*
schreiben; **~ down** *vt* aufschreiben; **~
off** *vt* (*dismiss*) abschreiben; **~ out** *vt*
(*essay*) abschreiben; (*cheque*) ausstellen; **~
up** *vt* schreiben; **~-off** *n*: **it is a ~-off** das
kann man abschreiben; **~r** *n*
Schriftsteller *m*
writhe [raɪð] *vi* sich winden
writing ['raɪtɪŋ] *n* (*act*) Schreiben *nt*;
(*hand~*) (Hand)schrift *f*; **in ~** schriftlich;
~ paper *n* Schreibpapier *nt*
written ['rɪtn] *pp of* **write**
wrong [rɒŋ] *adj* (*incorrect*) falsch;
(*morally*) unrecht ♦ *n* Unrecht *nt* ♦ *vt*
Unrecht tun +*dat*; **he was ~ in doing
that** es war nicht recht von ihm, das zu
tun; **you are ~ about that, you've got it
~** da hast du unrecht; **to be in the ~** im
Unrecht sein; **what's ~ with your leg?**
was ist mit deinem Bein los?; **to go ~**
(*plan*) schiefgehen; (*person*) einen Fehler
machen; **~ful** *adj* unrechtmäßig; **~ly** *adv*
falsch; (*accuse*) zu Unrecht
wrote [rəʊt] *pt of* **write**
wrought [rɔːt] *adj*: **~ iron** Schmiedeei-
sen *nt*
wrung [rʌŋ] *pt, pp of* **wring**
wry [raɪ] *adj* ironisch

wt. *abbr* = **weight**

X x

Xmas ['eksməs] *n abbr* = **Christmas**
X-ray ['eksreɪ] *n* Röntgenaufnahme *f* ♦ *vt* röntgen; **~s** *npl* Röntgenstrahlen *pl*
xylophone ['zaɪləfəʊn] *n* Xylophon *nt*

Y y

yacht [jɒt] *n* Jacht *f*; **~ing** *n* (Sport)segeln *nt*; **~sman** *n* Sportsegler *m*
Yank [jæŋk] (*inf*) *n* Ami *m*
yap [jæp] *vi* (*dog*) kläffen
yard [jɑːd] *n* Hof *m*; (*measure*) (englische) Elle *f*, Yard *nt* (*0,91 m*); **~stick** *n* (*fig*) Maßstab *m*
yarn [jɑːn] *n* (*thread*) Garn *nt*; (*story*) (Seemanns)garn *nt*
yawn [jɔːn] *n* Gähnen *nt* ♦ *vi* gähnen; **~ing** *adj* (*gap*) gähnend
yd. *abbr* = **yard(s)**
yeah [jeə] (*inf*) *adv* ja
year [jɪə*] *n* Jahr *nt*; **to be 8 ~s old** acht Jahre alt sein; **an eight-~-old child** ein achtjähriges Kind; **~ly** *adj, adv* jährlich
yearn [jɜːn] *vi*: **to ~ (for)** sich sehnen (nach); **~ing** *n* Verlangen *nt*, Sehnsucht *f*
yeast [jiːst] *n* Hefe *f*
yell [jel] *n* gellende(r) Schrei *m* ♦ *vi* laut schreien
yellow ['jeləʊ] *adj* gelb ♦ *n* Gelb *nt*
yelp [jelp] *n* Gekläff *nt* ♦ *vi* kläffen
yeoman ['jəʊmən] (*irreg*) *n*: **Y~ of the Guard** Leibgardist *m*
yes [jes] *adv* ja ♦ *n* Ja *nt*, Jawort *nt*; **to say ~** ja sagen; **to answer ~** mit Ja antworten
yesterday ['jestədeɪ] *adv* gestern ♦ *n* Gestern *nt*; **~ morning/evening** gestern morgen/abend; **all day ~** gestern den ganzen Tag; **the day before ~** vorgestern
yet [jet] *adv* noch; (*in question*) schon; (*up to now*) bis jetzt ♦ *conj* doch, dennoch; **it is not finished ~** es ist noch nicht fertig; **the best ~** das bisher beste;

as ~ bis jetzt; (*in past*) bis dahin
yew [juː] *n* Eibe *f*
yield [jiːld] *n* Ertrag *m* ♦ *vt* (*result, crop*) hervorbringen; (*interest, profit*) abwerfen; (*concede*) abtreten ♦ *vi* nachgeben; (*MIL*) sich ergeben; **"~"** (*US: AUT*) „Vorfahrt gewähren"
YMCA *n abbr* (= *Young Men's Christian Association*) CVJM *m*
yoga ['jəʊgə] *n* Joga *m*
yoghourt ['jɒgət] *n* Joghurt *m*
yog(h)urt ['jɒgət] *n* = **yoghourt**
yoke [jəʊk] *n* (*also fig*) Joch *nt*
yolk [jəʊk] *n* Eidotter *m*, Eigelb *nt*
yonder ['jɒndə*] *adv* dort drüben, da drüben ♦ *adj* jene(r, s) dort

<hr>

KEYWORD

you [juː] *pron* **1** (*subj, in comparisons: German familiar form: sg*) du; (: *pl*) ihr; (*in letters also*) Du, Ihr; (: *German polite form*) Sie; **you Germans** ihr Deutschen; **she's younger than you** sie ist jünger als du/Sie

2 (*direct object, after prep +acc: German familiar form: sg*) dich; (: *pl*) euch; (*in letters also*) Dich, Euch; (: *German polite form*) Sie; **I know you** ich kenne dich/euch/Sie

3 (*indirect object, after prep +dat: German familiar form: sg*) dir; (: *pl*) euch; (*in letters also*) Dir, Euch; (: *German polite form*) Ihnen; **I gave it to you** ich gab es dir/euch/Ihnen

4 (*impers: one: subj*) man; (: *direct object*) einen; (: *indirect object*) einem; **fresh air does you good** frische Luft tut gut

<hr>

you'd [juːd] = **you had**; **you would**
you'll [juːl] = **you will**; **you shall**
young [jʌŋ] *adj* jung ♦ *npl*: **the ~** die Jungen *pl*; **~ish** *adj* ziemlich jung; **~ster** *n* Junge *m*, junge(r) Bursche *m*, junge(s) Mädchen *nt*
your ['jɔː*] *adj* (*familiar: sg*) dein; (: *pl*) euer, eure *pl*; (*polite*) Ihr; *see also* **my**
you're ['jʊə*] = **you are**
yours [jɔːz] *pron* (*familiar: sg*) deine(r, s); (: *pl*) eure(r, s); (*polite*) Ihre(r, s); *see also*

mine²

yourself [jɔː'self] *pron (emphatic)* selbst; *(familiar: sg: acc)* dich (selbst); (: *dat)* dir (selbst); (: *pl)* euch (selbst); *(polite)* sich (selbst); *see also* **oneself**

youth [juːθ, *pl* juːðz] *n* Jugend *f*; *(young man)* junge(r) Mann *m*; **~s** *npl (young people)* Jugendliche *pl*; **~ club** *n* Jugendzentrum *nt*; **~ful** *adj* jugendlich; **~ hostel** *n* Jugendherberge *f*

you've [juːv] = **you have**

YTS *(BRIT) n abbr* (= *Youth Training Scheme) staatliches Förderprogramm für arbeitslose Jugendliche*

Yugoslav ['juːɡəʊ'slɑːv] *adj* jugoslawisch ♦ *n* Jugoslawe *m*, Jugoslawin *f*

Yugoslavia ['juːɡəʊ'slɑːvɪə] *n* Jugoslawien *nt*

yuppie ['jʌpɪ] *(inf) n* Yuppie *m* ♦ *adj* yuppiehaft, Yuppie-

YWCA *n abbr* (= *Young Women's Christian Association)* CVJF *m*

Z z

zany ['zeɪnɪ] *adj (ideas, sense of humour)* verrückt

zap [zæp] *vt (COMPUT)* löschen

zeal [ziːl] *n* Eifer *m*; **~ous** ['zeləs] *adj* eifrig

zebra ['ziːbrə] *n* Zebra *nt*; **~ crossing** *(BRIT) n* Zebrastreifen *m*

zero ['zɪərəʊ] *n* Null *f*; *(on scale)* Nullpunkt *m*

zest [zest] *n* Begeisterung *f*

zigzag ['zɪɡzæɡ] *n* Zickzack *m*

zip [zɪp] *n* Reißverschluß *m* ♦ *vt (also:*

~ up) den Reißverschluß zumachen +*gen*; **~ code** *(US) n* Postleitzahl *f*; **~ fastener** *n* Reißverschluß *m*; **~per** *(esp US) n* Reißverschluß *m*

zodiac ['zəʊdɪæk] *n* Tierkreis *m*

zombie ['zɒmbɪ] *n*: **like a ~** *(fig)* wie im Tran

zoo [zuː] *n* Zoo *m*

zoology [zəʊ'ɒlədʒɪ] *n* Zoologie *f*

zoom [zuːm] *vi*: **to ~ past** vorbeisausen; **~ lens** *n* Zoomobjektiv *nt*

zucchini [zuː'kiːnɪ] *(US) npl* Zucchini *pl*

GERMAN IRREGULAR VERBS

*with 'sein'

infinitive	present indicative (2nd, 3rd sg)	imperfect	past participle
aufschrecken*	schrickst auf, schrickt auf	schrak *or* schreckte auf	aufgeschreckt
ausbedingen	bedingst aus, bedingt aus	bedang *or* bedingte aus	ausbedungen
backen	bäckst, bäckt	backte *or* buk	gebacken
befehlen	befiehlst, befiehlt	befahl	befohlen
beginnen	beginnst, beginnt	begann	begonnen
beißen	beißt, beißt	biß	gebissen
bergen	birgst, birgt	barg	geborgen
bersten*	birst, birst	barst	geborsten
bescheißen*	bescheißt, bescheißt	beschiß	beschissen
bewegen	bewegst, bewegt	bewog	bewogen
biegen	biegst, biegt	bog	gebogen
bieten	bietest, bietet	bot	geboten
binden	bindest, bindet	band	gebunden
bitten	bittest, bittet	bat	gebeten
blasen	bläst, bläst	blies	geblasen
bleiben*	bleibst, bleibt	blieb	geblieben
braten	brätst, brät	briet	gebraten
brechen*	brichst, bricht	brach	gebrochen
brennen	brennst, brennt	brannte	gebrannt
bringen	bringst, bringt	brachte	gebracht
denken	denkst, denkt	dachte	gedacht
dreschen	drisch(e)st, drischt	drosch	gedroschen
dringen*	dringst, dringt	drang	gedrungen
dürfen	darfst, darf	durfte	gedurft
empfehlen	empfiehlst, empfiehlt	empfahl	empfohlen
erbleichen*	erbleichst, erbleicht	erbleichte	erblichen
erlöschen*	erlischt, erlischt	erlosch	erloschen
erschrecken*	erschrickst, erschrickt	erschrak	erschrocken
essen	ißt, ißt	aß	gegessen
fahren*	fährst, fährt	fuhr	gefahren
fallen*	fällst, fällt	fiel	gefallen
fangen	fängst, fängt	fing	gefangen
fechten	fichtst, ficht	focht	gefochten

614

infinitive	present indicative (2nd, 3rd sg)	imperfect	past participle
finden	findest, findet	fand	gefunden
flechten	flichtst, flicht	flocht	geflochten
fliegen*	fliegst, fliegt	flog	geflogen
fliehen*	fliehst, flieht	floh	geflohen
fließen*	fließt, fließt	floß	geflossen
fressen	frißt, frißt	fraß	gefressen
frieren	frierst, friert	fror	gefroren
gären*	gärst, gärt	gor	gegoren
gebären	gebierst, gebiert	gebar	geboren
geben	gibst, gibt	gab	gegeben
gedeihen*	gedeihst, gedeiht	gedieh	gediehen
gehen*	gehst, geht	ging	gegangen
gelingen*	——, gelingt	gelang	gelungen
gelten	giltst, gilt	galt	gegolten
genesen*	gene(se)st, genest	genas	genesen
genießen	genießt, genießt	genoß	genossen
geraten*	gerätst, gerät	geriet	geraten
geschehen*	——, geschieht	geschah	geschehen
gewinnen	gewinnst, gewinnt	gewann	gewonnen
gießen	gießt, gießt	goß	gegossen
gleichen	gleichst, gleicht	glich	geglichen
gleiten*	gleitest, gleitet	glitt	geglitten
glimmen	glimmst, glimmt	glomm	geglommen
graben	gräbst, gräbt	grub	gegraben
greifen	greifst, greift	griff	gegriffen
haben	hast, hat	hatte	gehabt
halten	hältst, hält	hielt	gehalten
hängen	hängst, hängt	hing	gehangen
hauen	haust, haut	haute	gehauen
heben	hebst, hebt	hob	gehoben
heißen	heißt, heißt	hieß	geheißen
helfen	hilfst, hilft	half	geholfen
kennen	kennst, kennt	kannte	gekannt
klimmen*	klimmst, klimmt	klomm	geklommen
klingen	klingst, klingt	klang	geklungen
kneifen	kneifst, kneift	kniff	gekniffen
kommen*	kommst, kommt	kam	gekommen
können	kannst, kann	konnte	gekonnt
kriechen*	kriechst, kriecht	kroch	gekrochen
laden	lädst, lädt	lud	geladen
lassen	läßt, läßt	ließ	gelassen
laufen*	läufst, läuft	lief	gelaufen
leiden	leidest, leidet	litt	gelitten
leihen	leihst, leiht	lieh	geliehen
lesen	liest, liest	las	gelesen

infinitive	present indicative (2nd, 3rd sg)	imperfect	past participle
liegen*	liegst, liegt	lag	gelegen
lügen	lügst, lügt	log	gelogen
mahlen	mahlst, mahlt	mahlte	gemahlen
meiden	meidest, meidet	mied	gemieden
melken	melkst, melkt	melkte	gemolken
messen	mißt, mißt	maß	gemessen
mißlingen*	——, mißlingt	mißlang	mißlungen
mögen	magst, mag	mochte	gemocht
müssen	mußt, muß	mußte	gemußt
nehmen	nimmst, nimmt	nahm	genommen
nennen	nennst, nennt	nannte	genannt
pfeifen	pfeifst, pfeift	pfiff	gepfiffen
preisen	preist, preist	pries	gepriesen
quellen*	quillst, quillt	quoll	gequollen
raten	rätst, rät	riet	geraten
reiben	reibst, reibt	rieb	gerieben
reißen*	reißt, reißt	riß	gerissen
reiten*	reitest, reitet	ritt	geritten
rennen*	rennst, rennt	rannte	gerannt
riechen	riechst, riecht	roch	gerochen
ringen	ringst, ringt	rang	gerungen
rinnen*	rinnst, rinnt	rann	geronnen
rufen	rufst, ruft	rief	gerufen
salzen	salzt, salzt	salzte	gesalzen
saufen	säufst, säuft	soff	gesoffen
saugen	saugst, saugt	sog	gesogen
schaffen	schaffst, schafft	schuf	geschaffen
scheiden	scheidest, scheidet	schied	geschieden
scheinen	scheinst, scheint	schien	geschienen
schelten	schiltst, schilt	schalt	gescholten
scheren	scherst, schert	schor	geschoren
schieben	schiebst, schiebt	schob	geschoben
schießen	schießt, schießt	schoß	geschossen
schinden	schindest, schindet	schindete	geschunden
schlafen	schläfst, schläft	schlief	geschlafen
schlagen	schlägst, schlägt	schlug	geschlagen
schleichen*	schleichst, schleicht	schlich	geschlichen
schleifen	schleifst, schleift	schliff	geschliffen
schließen	schließt, schließt	schloß	geschlossen
schlingen	schlingst, schlingt	schlang	geschlungen
schmeißen	schmeißt, schmeißt	schmiß	geschmissen
schmelzen*	schmilzt, schmilzt	schmolz	geschmolzen

infinitive	present indicative (2nd, 3rd sg)	imperfect	past participle
schneiden	schneidest, schneidet	schnitt	geschnitten
schreiben	schreibst, schreibt	schrieb	geschrieben
schreien	schreist, schreit	schrie	geschrie(e)n
schreiten	schreitest, schreitet	schritt	geschritten
schweigen	schweigst, schweigt	schwieg	geschwiegen
schwellen*	schwillst, schwillt	schwoll	geschwollen
schwimmen*	schwimmst, schwimmt	schwamm	geschwommen
schwinden*	schwindest, schwindet	schwand	geschwunden
schwingen	schwingst, schwingt	schwang	geschwungen
schwören	schwörst, schwört	schwor	geschworen
sehen	siehst, sieht	sah	gesehen
sein*	bist, ist	war	gewesen
senden	sendest, sendet	sandte	gesandt
singen	singst, singt	sang	gesungen
sinken*	sinkst, sinkt	sank	gesunken
sinnen	sinnst, sinnt	sann	gesonnen
sitzen*	sitzt, sitzt	saß	gesessen
sollen	sollst, soll	sollte	gesollt
speien	speist, speit	spie	gespie(e)n
spinnen	spinnst, spinnt	spann	gesponnen
sprechen	sprichst, spricht	sprach	gesprochen
sprießen*	sprießt, sprießt	sproß	gesprossen
springen*	springst, springt	sprang	gesprungen
stechen	stichst, sticht	stach	gestochen
stecken	steckst, steckt	steckte or stak	gesteckt
stehen	stehst, steht	stand	gestanden
stehlen	stiehlst, stiehlt	stahl	gestohlen
steigen*	steigst, steigt	stieg	gestiegen
sterben*	stirbst, stirbt	starb	gestorben
stinken	stinkst, stinkt	stank	gestunken
stoßen	stößt, stößt	stieß	gestoßen
streichen	streichst, streicht	strich	gestrichen
streiten*	streitest, streitet	stritt	gestritten
tragen	trägst, trägt	trug	getragen
treffen	triffst, trifft	traf	getroffen
treiben*	treibst, treibt	trieb	getrieben
treten*	trittst, tritt	trat	getreten
trinken	trinkst, trinkt	trank	getrunken
trügen	trügst, trügt	trog	getrogen

infinitive	present indicative (2nd, 3rd sg)	imperfect	past participle
tun	tust, tut	tat	getan
verderben	verdirbst, verdirbt	verdarb	verdorben
verdrießen	verdrießt, verdrießt	verdroß	verdrossen
vergessen	vergißt, vergißt	vergaß	vergessen
verlieren	verlierst, verliert	verlor	verloren
verschleißen	verschleißt, verschleißt	verschliß	verschlissen
wachsen*	wächst, wächst	wuchs	gewachsen
weben	webst, webt	webte or wob	gewoben
wägen	wägst, wägt	wog	gewogen
waschen	wäschst, wäscht	wusch	gewaschen
weichen*	weichst, weicht	wich	gewichen
weisen	weist, weist	wies	gewiesen
wenden	wendest, wendet	wandte	gewandt
werben	wirbst, wirbt	warb	geworben
werden*	wirst, wird	wurde	geworden
werfen	wirfst, wirft	warf	geworfen
wiegen	wiegst, wiegt	wog	gewogen
winden	windest, windet	wand	gewunden
wissen	weißt, weiß	wußte	gewußt
wollen	willst, will	wollte	gewollt
wringen	wringst, wringt	wrang	gewrungen
zeihen	zeihst, zeiht	zieh	geziehen
ziehen*	ziehst, zieht	zog	gezogen
zwingen	zwingst, zwingt	zwang	gezwungen

GERMAN SPELLING CHANGES

In July 1996, all German-speaking countries signed a declaration concerning the reform of German spelling, with the result that the new spelling rules can now be taught in all schools. To ensure that you have the most up-to-date information at your fingertips, the following list contains the old and new spellings of all German headwords in this dictionary which are affected by the reform.

ALT/OLD	NEU/NEW	ALT/OLD	NEU/NEW
abend	Abend	Ausschluß	Ausschluss
Abfluß	Abfluss	Ausschluß	Ausschuss
Abflußrohr	Abflussrohr	aussein	aus sein
Abriß	Abriss	Baß	Bass
Abschluß	Abschluss	Baßstimme	Bassstimme
Abschlußfeier	Abschlussfeier		or Bass-Stimme
Abschlußprüfung	Abschlussprüfung	bekanntgeben	bekannt geben
Abschuß	Abschuss	bekanntmachen	bekannt machen
Abszeß	Abszess	Beschluß	Beschluss
Adreßbuch	Adressbuch	Beschuß	Beschuss
Alleinerziehende(r)	Alleinerziehende(r)	bewußt	bewusst
	or allein Erziehende(r)	bewußtlos	bewusstlos
alleinstehend	allein stehend	Bewußtlosigkeit	Bewusstlosigkeit
allgemeingültig	allgemein gültig	Bewußtsein	Bewusstsein
allzuviel	allzu viel	Bibliographie	Bibliographie
Alptraum	Alptraum		or Bibliografie
	or Albtraum	Biographie	Biographie
Amboß	Amboss		or Biografie
aneinandergeraten	aneinander geraten	Biß	Biss
Anlaß	Anlass	bißchen	bisschen
anläßlich	anlässlich	blaß	blass
Anschluß	Anschluss	bleibenlassen	bleiben lassen
As	Ass	Bluterguß	Bluterguss
aufeinanderfolgen	aufeinander folgen	braungebrannt	braun gebrannt
aufeinanderfolgend	aufeinander folgend	breitmachen	breit machen
aufeinanderlegen	aufeinander legen	Brenn(n)essel	Brennnessel
aufeinanderprallen	aufeinander prallen		or Brenn-Nessel
Aufschluß	Aufschluss	Büroschluß	Büroschluss
aufschlußreich	aufschlussreich	Chicorée	Chicorée
aufsehenerregend	Aufsehen erregend		or Schikoree
aufsein	auf sein	Choreograph	Choreograph
aufwendig	aufwendig		or Choreograf
	or aufwändig	Coupé	Coupé
auseinanderbringen	auseinander bringen		or Kupee
auseinanderfallen	auseinander fallen	dabeisein	dabei sein
auseinandergehen	auseinander gehen	dafürkönnen	dafür können
auseinanderhalten	auseinander halten	dahinterkommen	dahinter kommen
auseinandernehmen	auseinander nehmen	darauffolgend	darauf folgend
auseinandersetzen	auseinander setzen	dasein	da sein
Ausfluß	Ausfluss	daß	dass
Ausguß	Ausguss	Dekolleté	Dekolleté

ALT/OLD	NEU/NEW	ALT/OLD	NEU/NEW
	or Dekolletee	floß	floss
Delphin	Delphin	Fluß	Fluss
	or Delfin	flüssigmachen	flüssig machen
dessenungeachtet	dessen ungeachtet	Fön ®	Föhn
dichtbevölkert	dicht bevölkert		or Fön ®
diensthabend	Dienst habend	fönen	föhnen
Differentialrechnung	Differentialrechnung	Fönfrisur	Föhnfrisur
	or Differenzialrechnung	Friedensschluß	Friedensschluss
Diktaphon	Diktaphon	frühzeitig	früh zeitig
	or Diktafon	Gebiß	Gebiss
dreiviertel	drei Viertel	Gebührenerlaß	Gebührenerlass
durcheinanderbringen	durcheinander bringen	gefangenhalten	gefangen halten
durcheinanderreden	durcheinander reden	gefangennehmen	gefangen nehmen
durchnumerieren	durchnummerieren	gefaßt	gefasst
Einfluß	Einfluss	geheimhalten	geheim halten
Einflußbereich	Einflussbereich	gehenlassen	gehen lassen
Einlaß	Einlass	Gemse	Gämse
ekelerregend	Ekel erregend	gemußt	gemusst
Elsaß	Elsass	genaugenommen	genau genommen
Engpaß	Engpass	Genuß	Genuss
Entschluß	Entschluss	genüßlich	genüsslich
entschlußfreudig	entschlussfreudig	Genußmittel	Genussmittel
Entschlußkraft	Entschlusskraft	Geograph	Geograph
epochemachend	Epoche machend		or Geograf
Erdgeschoß	Erdgeschoss	Geographie	Geographie
Erdnuß	Erdnuss		or Geografie
erfolgversprechend	Erfolg versprechend	geographisch	geographisch
Erguß	Erguss		or geografisch
Erlaß	Erlass	geringachten	gering achten
ernstgemeint	ernst gemeint	Geschäftsschluß	Geschäftsschluss
erstemal	erste Mal	Geschoß	Geschoss
eßbar	essbar	gewinnbringend	Gewinn bringend
Eßbesteck	Essbesteck	gewiß	gewiss
Eßecke	Essecke	Gewißheit	Gewissheit
Eßgeschirr	Essgeschirr	gewußt	gewusst
Eßkastanie	Esskastanie	gleichbleibend	gleich bleibend
Eßlöffel	Esslöffel	gleichgesinnt	gleich gesinnt
Eßtisch	Esstisch	Glimmstengel	Glimmstängel
Eßwaren	Esswaren	Grammophon	Grammophon
Eßzimmer	Esszimmer		or Grammofon
Expreßgut	Expressgut	graphisch	graphisch
Expreßzug	Expresszug		or grafisch
Exzeß	Exzess	gräßlich	grässlich
fallenlassen	fallen lassen	Greuel	Gräuel
Faß	Fass	greulich	gräulich
fernhalten	fern halten	Grundriß	Grundriss
fertigbringen	fertig bringen	Guß	Guss
fertigmachen	fertig machen	Gußeisen	Gusseisen
fertigstellen	fertig stellen	gutgehen	gut gehen
festangestellt	fest angestellt	gutgemeint	gut gemeint
Fitneß	Fitness	guttun	gut tun

ALT/OLD	NEU/NEW	ALT/OLD	NEU/NEW
haftenbleiben	haften bleiben	Kompaß	Kompass
halboffen	halb offen	Kompromiß	Kompromiss
haltmachen	Halt machen	kompromißbereit	kompromissbereit
Hämorrhoiden	Hämorrhoiden	Kompromißlösung	Kompromisslösung
	or Hämorriden	Kongreß	Kongress
hängenbleiben	hängen bleiben	Kontrabaß	Kontrabass
hängenlassen	hängen lassen	kraß	krass
hartgekocht	hart gekocht	Kreppapier	Krepppapier
Haselnuß	Haselnuss		or Krepp-Papier
Haß	Hass	krummnehmen	krumm nehmen
häßlich	hässlich	kurzhalten	kurz halten
Häßlichkeit	Hässlichkeit	Kurzschluß	Kurzschluss
haushalten	haushalten	Kuß	Kuss
	or Haus halten	Ladenschluß	Ladenschluss
heiligsprechen	heilig sprechen	Laufpaß	Laufpass
Hexenschuß	Hexenschuss	leerstehend	leer stehend
hierbehalten	hier behalten	leichtfallen	leicht fallen
hierbleiben	hier bleiben	leichtmachen	leicht machen
hierlassen	hier lassen	liebgewinnen	lieb gewinnen
hierzulande	hier zu Lande	liebhaben	lieb haben
hochachten	hoch achten	liegenbleiben	liegen bleiben
hochbegabt	hoch begabt	liegenlassen	liegen lassen
hochdotiert	hoch dotiert	Litfaßsäule	Litfasssäule
Imbiß	Imbiss		or Litfass-Säule
Imbißhalle	Imbisshalle	Lithographie	Lithographie
Imbißstube	Imbissstube		or Lithografie
	or Imbiss-Stube	maschineschreiben	Maschine schreiben
imstande	imstande	maßhalten	Maß halten
	or im Stande	Megaphon	Megaphon
Jahresabschluß	Jahresabschluss		or Megafon
Joghurt	Joghurt	meßbar	messbar
	or Jogurt	Meßbecher	Messbecher
kahlgeschoren	kahl geschoren	Meßgerät	Messgerät
kaltbleiben	kalt bleiben	Mikrophon	Mikrophon
Känguruh	Känguru		or Mikrofon
Karamel	Karamell	Mißbehagen	Missbehagen
Katarrh	Katarrh	Mißbildung	Missbildung
	or Katarr	mißbilligen	missbilligen
keß	kess	Mißbilligung	Missbilligung
klarsehen	klar sehen	Mißbrauch	Missbrauch
klarwerden	klar werden	mißbrauchen	missbrauchen
Klassenbewußtsein	Klassenbewusstsein	Mißerfolg	Misserfolg
klatschnaß	klatschnass	mißfallen	missfallen
kleinhacken	klein hacken	Mißfallen	Missfallen
kleinschneiden	klein schneiden	Mißgeburt	Missgeburt
knapphalten	knapp halten	Mißgeschick	Missgeschick
Kokosnuß	Kokosnuss	mißglücken	missglücken
Koloß	Koloss	Mißgriff	Missgriff
Kombinationsschloß	Kombinationsschloss	Mißgunst	Missgunst
Kommuniqué	Kommuniqué	mißgünstig	missgünstig
	or Kommunikee	mißhandeln	misshandeln

ALT/OLD	NEU/NEW	ALT/OLD	NEU/NEW
Mißhandlung	Misshandlung	**offenlassen**	offen lassen
Mißklang	Missklang	**offenstehen**	offen stehen
Mißkredit	Misskredit	**Ölmeßstab**	Ölmessstab
mißlingen	misslingen		or Ölmess–Stab
Mißmut	Missmut	**Orthographie**	Orthographie
mißmutig	missmutig		or Orthografie
mißraten	missraten	**orthographisch**	orthographisch
Mißstand	Missstand		or orthografisch
	or Miss–Stand	**Panther**	Panther
Mißstimmung	Missstimmung		or Panter
	or Miss–Stimmung	**Pappmaché**	Pappmaché
mißtrauen	misstrauen		or Pappmaschee
Mißtrauen	Misstrauen	**Paragraph**	Paragraph
Mißtrauensantrag	Misstrauensantrag		or Paragraf
Mißtrauensvotum	Misstrauensvotum	**Paranuß**	Paranuss
mißtrauisch	misstrauisch	**Parlamentsbeschluß**	Parlamentsbeschluss
Mißverhältnis	Missverhältnis	**Paß**	Pass
Mißverständnis	Missverständnis	**Paßamt**	Passamt
mißverstehen	missverstehen	**Paßbild**	Passbild
Mißwirtschaft	Misswirtschaft	**Paßkontrolle**	Passkontrolle
mittag	Mittag	**Paßstelle**	Passstelle
Muß	Muss		or Pass–Stelle
Nachlaß	Nachlass	**Paßstraße**	Passstraße
nahegehen	nahe gehen		or Pass–Straße
nahekommen	nahe kommen	**patschnaß**	patschnass
nahelegen	nahe legen	**pflichtbewußt**	pflichtbewusst
naheliegen	nahe liegen	**Phantasie**	Phantasie
naheliegend	nahe liegend		or Fantasie
näherkommen	näher kommen	**phantasielos**	phantasielos
nahestehen	nahe stehen		or fantasielos
naß	nass	**phantasieren**	phantasieren
naßkalt	nasskalt		or fantasieren
Naßrasur	Nassrasur	**phantasievoll**	phantasievoll
Nebenanschluß	Nebenanschluss		or fantasievoll
nebeneinanderlegen	nebeneinander legen	**phantastisch**	phantastisch
Nebenfluß	Nebenfluss		or fantastisch
Necessaire	Necessaire	**platschnaß**	platschnass
	or Nessessär	**plazieren**	platzieren
Netzanschluß	Netzanschluss	**Pornographie**	Pornographie
nichtrostend	nicht rostend		or Pornografie
nichtssagend	nichts sagend	**pornographisch**	pornographisch
notleidend	Not leidend		or pornografisch
numerieren	nummerieren	**Portemonnaie**	Portemonnaie
numerisch	nummerisch		or Portmonee
Nuß	Nuss	**Potential**	Potential
Nußbaum	Nussbaum		or Potenzial
Nußknacker	Nussknacker	**potentiell**	potentiell
obenerwähnt	oben erwähnt		or potenziell
Obergeschoß	Obergeschoss	**Preßluft**	Pressluft
offenbleiben	offen bleiben	**Preßluftbohrer**	Pressluftbohrer
offenhalten	offen halten	**preisbewußt**	preisbewusst

ALT/OLD	NEU/NEW		ALT/OLD	NEU/NEW
rozeß	Prozess		selbständig	selbständig
rüfungsausschuß	Prüfungsausschuss			or selbstständig
adfahren	Rad fahren		Selbständigkeit	Selbständigkeit
assenhaß	Rassenhass			or Selbstständigkeit
auh	rau		selbstbewußt	selbstbewusst
auhreif	Raureif		Selbstbewußtsein	Selbstbewusstsein
eisepaß	Reisepass		selbstgemacht	selbst gemacht
iß	Riss		selbstverständlich	selbst verständlich
oll(l)aden	Rollladen		seßhaft	sesshaft
	or Roll–Laden		Sicherheitsschloß	Sicherheitsschloss
oß	Ross		sitzenbleiben	sitzen bleiben
oßkastanie	Rosskastanie		sitzenlassen	sitzen lassen
ückschluß	Rückschluss		sogenannt	so genannt
ußland	Russland		soviel	so viel
auberhalten	sauber halten		soweit	so weit
axophon	Saxophon		sowenig	so wenig
	or Saxofon		Sommerschlußverkauf	Sommerschlussverkauf
chattenriß	Schattenriss		sonstjemand	sonst jemand
chiefgehen	schief gehen		sonstwo	sonst wo
chlangenbiß	Schlangenbiss		sonstwohin	sonst wohin
chlechtgehen	schlecht gehen		spazierenfahren	spazieren fahren
chlechtmachen	schlecht machen		spazierengehen	spazieren gehen
chlegel	Schlägel		Sprößling	Sprössling
chloß	Schloss		steckenbleiben	stecken bleiben
chluß	Schluss		steckenlassen	stecken lassen
chlußlicht	Schlusslicht		stehenbleiben	stehen bleiben
chlußstrich	Schlussstrich		stehenlassen	stehen lassen
	or Schluss–Strich		Stengel	Stängel
chlußverkauf	Schlussverkauf		Stenographie	Stenographie
chmiß	Schmiss			or Stenografie
chnappschloß	Schnappschloss		stenographieren	stenographieren
chnappschuß	Schnappschuss			or stenografieren
chnellimbiß	Schnellimbiss		Stewardeß	Stewardess
chneuzen	schnäuzen		stillhalten	still halten
chritt(t)empo	Schritttempo		Strafstoß	Strafstoss
	or Schritt–Tempo		Streifschuß	Streifschuss
chuld	Schuld		strenggenommen	streng genommen
chuß	Schuss		strenggläubig	streng gläubig
chußbereich	Schussbereich		Streß	Stress
chußlinie	Schusslinie		Thunfisch	Thunfisch
chußverletzung	Schussverletzung			or Tunfisch
chußwaffe	Schusswaffe		tiefgekühlt	tief gekühlt
chwererziehbar	schwer erziehbar		tiefgreifend	tief greifend
chwerfallen	schwer fallen		tiefschürfend	tief schürfend
chwermachen	schwer machen		tiefsinnig	tief sinnig
hwernehmen	schwer nehmen		Tip	Tipp
wertun	schwer tun		topographisch	topographisch
erverdaulich	schwer verdaulich			or topografisch
rverletzt	schwer verletzt		totenblaß	totenblass
raph	Seismograph		totgeboren	tot geboren
	or Seismograf		trockenlegen	trocken legen

ALT/OLD	NEU/NEW	ALT/OLD	NEU/NEW
Trugschluß	Trugschluss	vorwärtskommen	vorwärts kommen
tschüs	tschüs	Waggon	Waggon
	or tschüss		or Wagon
übelgelaunt	übel gelaunt	Walnuß	Walnuss
übelnehmen	übel nehmen	Walroß	Walross
Überdruß	Überdruss	wäßrig	wässrig
Überfluß	Überfluss	weitreichend	weit reichend
Überschuß	Überschuss	weitverbreitet	weit verbreitet
überschwenglich	überschwänglich	wiederaufnehmen	wieder aufnehmen
übrigbleiben	übrig bleiben	wiedererkennen	wieder erkennen
übriglassen	übrig lassen	wiedergutmachen	wieder gutmachen
Umriß	Umriss	wiederherstellen	wieder herstellen
unbewußt	unbewusst	wiedersehen	wieder sehen
unerläßlich	unerlässlich	wiedervereinigen	wieder vereinigen
unermeßlich	unermesslich	wiederverwerten	wieder verwerten
unfaßbar	unfassbar	wieviel	wie viel
ungewiß	ungewiss	Wißbegier(de)	Wissbegier(de)
Ungewißheit	Ungewissheit	wißbegierig	wissbegierig
unmißverständlich	unmissverständlich	wohltun	wohl tun
unpäßlich	unpässlich	wußte	wusste
unselbständig	unselbständig	Xylophon	Xylophon
	or unselbstständig		or Xylofon
Unterbewußtsein	Unterbewusstsein	Zahlenschloß	Zahlenschloss
Untergeschoß	Untergeschoss	zielbewußt	zielbewusst
Untersuchungsausschuß		Zuckerguß	Zuckerguss
	Untersuchungsausschuss	zufriedengeben	zufrieden geben
unvergeßlich	unvergesslich	zufriedenstellen	zufrieden stellen
verantwortungsbewußt		zugrunde	zugrunde
	verantwortungsbewusst		or zu Grunde
Verdruß	Verdruss	zugunsten	zugunsten
vergeßlich	vergesslich		or zu Gunsten
Vergeßlichkeit	Vergesslichkeit	zuleide	zuleide
Vergißmeinnicht	Vergissmeinnicht		or zu Leide
verhaßt	verhasst	zumute	zumute
Verlaß	Verlass		or zu Mute
verläßlich	verlässlich	zunutze	zunutze
verlorengehen	verloren gehen		or zu Nutze
Verschluß	Verschluss	Zusammenschluß	Zusammenschluss
vertrauenerweckend	Vertrauen erweckend	zuschulden	zuschulden
vielsagend	viel sagend		or zu Schulden
vielversprechend	viel versprechend	Zuschuß	Zuschuss
vollbringen	voll bringen	zustande	zustande
vollenden	voll enden		or zu Stande
volltanken	voll tanken	zutage	zutage
vorgefaßt	vorgefasst		or zu Tage
Vorhängeschloß	Vorhängeschloss	zuviel	zu viel
vorhinein	Vorhinein	zuwege	zuwege
vorliebnehmen	vorlieb nehmen		or zu Wege
Vorschuß	Vorschuss	zuwenig	zu wenig
vorwärtsgehen	vorwärts gehen		